Rick Steves'

BEST OF
EUROPE

2010

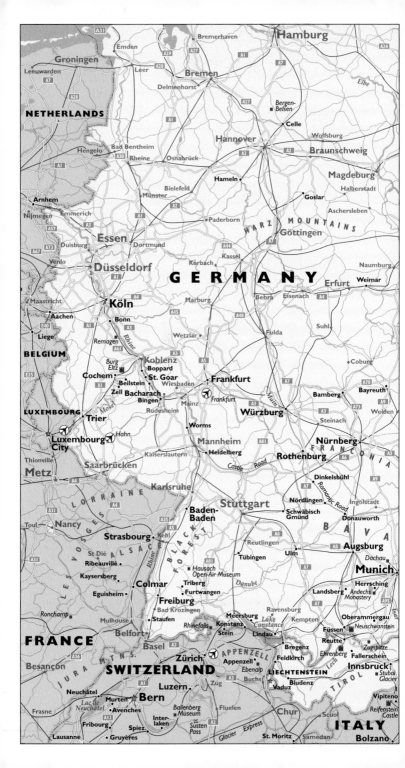

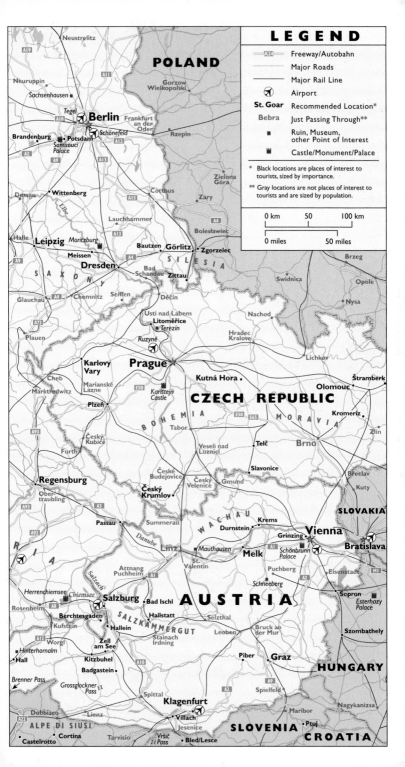

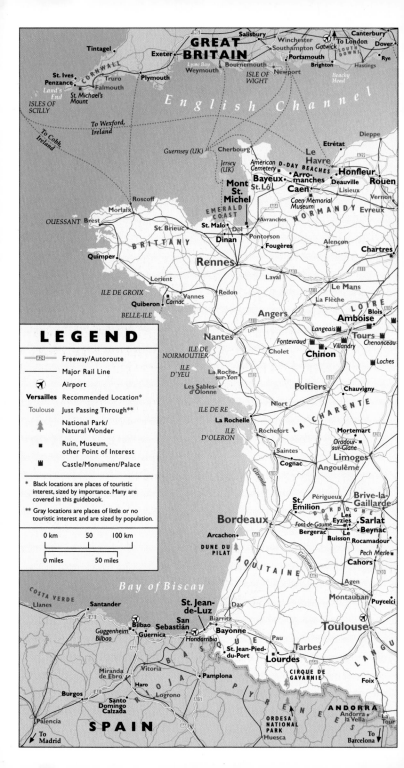

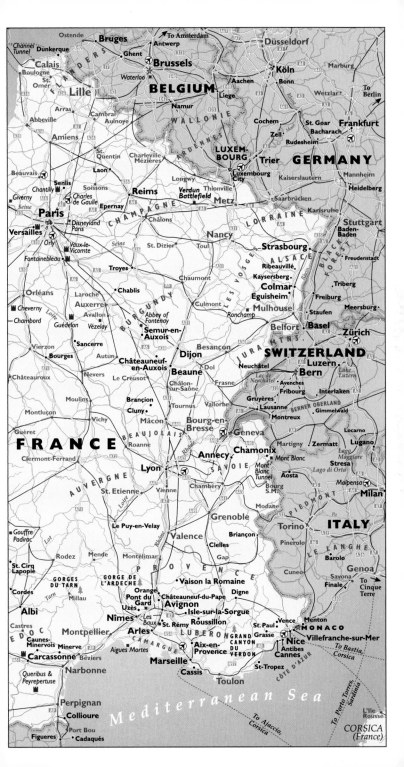

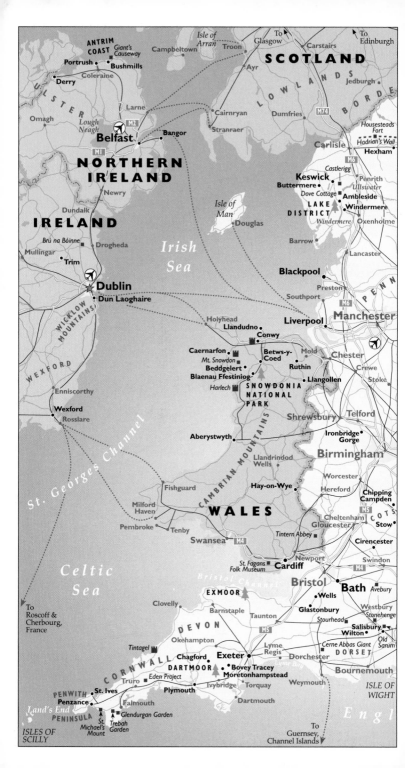

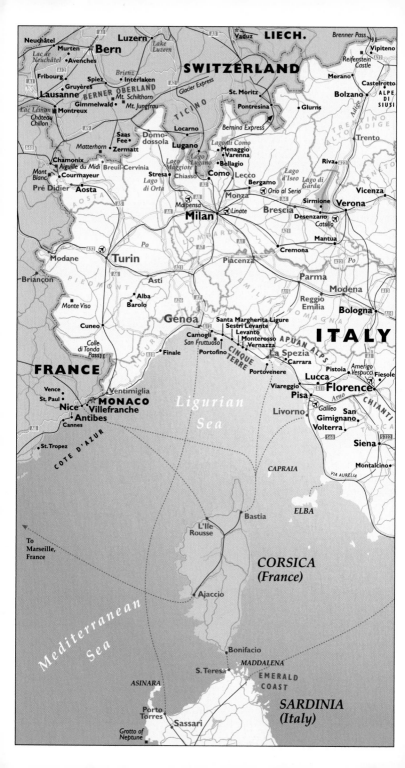

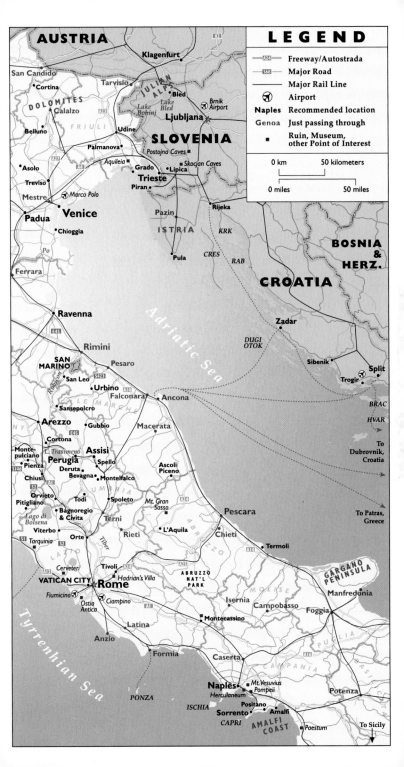

LEGEND

A24	Freeway/Autostrada
S68	Major Road
	Major Rail Line
✈	Airport
Naples	Recommended location
Genoa	Just passing through
■	Ruin, Museum, other Point of Interest

0 km — 50 kilometers
0 miles — 50 miles

AUSTRIA

San Candido
• Cortina
Tarvisio
Klagenfurt
DOLOMITES
Calalzo
JULIAN ALPS
Bled
• Belluno
FRIULI
Udine
Brnik Airport
Lake Bohinj
Lake Bled
Ljubljana ✈
Palmanova
SLOVENIA
• Asolo
Aquileia
Postojna Caves
Treviso
Grado
Lipica
Škocjan Caves
Mestre
Marco Polo ✈
Trieste
Piran
Padua
Venice
Chioggia
Pazin
Rijeka
Po
ISTRIA
KRK
Ferrara
Pula
CRES
RAB

BOSNIA & HERZ.

CROATIA

Adriatic Sea

Ravenna
Rimini
Pesaro
Zadar
SAN MARINO
DUGI OTOK
San Leo
Urbino
Falconara
Ancona
Šibenik
Split
LE MARCHE
Trogir
Sansepolcro
BRAC
Arezzo
• Gubbio
Macerata
HVAR
Cortona
Montepulciano
L. Trasimeno
Assisi
Spello
Perugia
Deruta
Bevagna
Montefalco
UMBRIA
Ascoli Piceno
To Dubrovnik, Croatia
• Pienza
Chiusi
Orvieto
Todi
Spoleto
Mt. Gran Sasso
Pitigliano
Bagnoregio & Civita
Terni
Lago di Bolsena
Viterbo
Orte
Rieti
• L'Aquila
Pescara
To Patras, Greece
Tarquinia
Tiber
LAZIO
ABRUZZO
Chieti
• Termoli
Cerveteri
Tivoli
Hadrian's Villa
ABRUZZO NAT'L PARK
GARGANO PENINSULA
VATICAN CITY
Rome
MOLISE
Manfredonia
Fiumicino ✈
Ostia Antica
Ciampino ✈
Isernia
Campobasso
Foggia
Montecassino
Tyrrhenian Sea
Latina
Caserta
PUGLIA
CAMPANIA
Anzio
Formia
Potenza
PONZA
Naples
Mt. Vesuvius
Pompeii
Herculaneum
ISCHIA
Positano
Amalfi
Sorrento
CAPRI
AMALFI COAST
Paestum
To Sicily

Atlantic Ocean

Ferrol
A Coruña
San Martín
Ribadeo
Canero
La Espina
Avilés
Gijón
COSTA VERDE
Santander
Santillana del Mar
Altamira Caves
Comillas

Santiago de Compostela
Lugo
Oviedo
Cangas
PICOS DE EUROPA
Potes
Fuente Dé
Cillervelo

Cabo Finisterre
GALICIA
ASTURIAS
Piedrafita
O Cebreiro
CANTABRIA

Pontevedra
Ourense
Ponferrada
León
Aguilar
Burgos

Vigo
Redondela
EL BIERZO
Astorga
S. Maria
Becilla
Benevente
Palencia
Lerma

RÍAS BAIXAS
Gullarei
Valença
Bragança
Mirandela
Zamora
Valladolid
Aranda

Viana do Castelo
Braga
DOURO VALLEY
S P A
Medina del Campo

Porto
Amarante
Vila Real
Pinhão
Mesão Frio
Peso da Régua
Pocinho
CASTILE-LEÓN
AVE High
Segovia
La Granja

Vila Nova de Gaia
Douro
PORTUGAL
Aveiro
Viseu
Salamanca
Peñaranda
Valley of the Fallen
Ávila
El Escorial
Barajas

Figueira da Foz
Coimbra
Conímbriga
Mondego
Guarda
Vilar
Ciudad Rodrigo
Piedranita
Madrid

Batalha
Leiria
Tomar
Castelo Branco
Plasencia
Talavera de la Reina
Toledo
Aranjuez

Nazaré
Valado
Alcobaça
Fátima
Tajo
Valencia de Alcántara
Cáceres
La Nava
Trujillo
Almoncid
Consuegra
CASTILE
LA

Óbidos
Cabo da Roca
Sintra
Estoril
Cascais
Lisbon
Entroncamento
Santarém
Tejo
Portalegre
Elvas
Badajoz
Mérida
Zorita
Puerto Lapice
Tomelloso
Manzanares
Valdepeñas

Cromleque dos Almendres
Évora
Anta do Zambujeiro
Escoural
La Albuera
Don Benito
Ciudad Real

Casa Branca
Setúbal
Cabo Espichel
ALENTEJO
Beja
EXTREMADURA
Llerena
Alcarecejos
Puertollano
Linares

Sines
Cercal
Funcheira
Galaroza
AVE High-Speed Rail
Úbeda

Odemira
Vila do Bispo
Sagres
Salema
Lagos
Tunes
Loulé
Albufeira
Faro
Vila Real
Cacela Velha
Tavira
ALGARVE
Ayamonte
Italica
Carmona
Écija
Córdoba
Jaén

Huelva
Sevilla
Utrera
ANDALUCÍA

COSTA DE LA LUZ
Guadalquivir
WHITE HILL TOWN
Bobadilla
Alhambra
Granada

Atlantic Ocean
Sanlúcar
Rota
Jerez
Cádiz
Arcos
Benaoján
Medina-Sidonia
Zahara
Grazalema
Ronda
Pileta Caves
Antequera
Málaga
Frigiliana
Nerja
SIERRA NEVADA
Nerja Caves
Motril

Marbella
San Pedro
Torremolinos
Fuengirola
COSTA DEL SOL
Salobreña

Vejer
Cabo Trafalgar
Algeciras
La Línea
Tarifa
Strait of Gibraltar
GIBRALTAR (UK)
CEUTA (Spain)

Tangier
MOROCCO
Tetouan

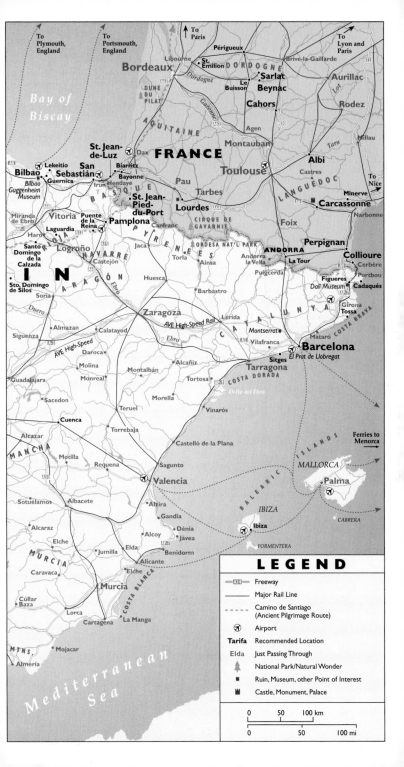

LEGEND

A7	Freeway
———	Major Rail Line
·············	Ferry Lines
✈	Airport
Haarlem	Recommended Location*
Nijmegen	Just Passing Through**
■	Ruin, Museum, Other Point of Interest

* Black locations are places of interest to tourists, sized by importance. Many are covered in this guidebook.

** Gray locations are places of little or no interest to tourists and are sized by population.

0 km   50 km   100 km

0 mi   50 mi

North

Sea

Wadden Islands

Emden

Groningen

Leeuwarden   A7   A28

Den
Helder Afsluitdijk • Hindeloopen

NETHERLANDS   A31

Medemblik •   ■ Zuiderzee Museum

Alkmaar   A7   ■ Enkhuizen ■ Schokland

Zaanse Schans   Hoorn   • Lelystad

IJmuiden   Edam *Flevoland*   Bad
Haarlem →   • Marken   Bentheim

Zandvoort   ☆ **Amsterdam**   Hengelo   A30

Keukenhof   ✈ Schiphol   A1

Aalsmeer   HOGUE VELUWE
NATIONAL PARK

Scheveningen •   Leiden   Utrecht

The Hague   A2   A12   Open-Air

• **Delft**   ■ Museum

To Harwich,
England   Hoek van
Holland   Arnhem   Emmerich

Rotterdam   A15   *Waal*   Nijmegen   A3

A16 A27   *Maas*

Middelburg •   A2   A57   *Rhine*   **Essen**

A58   ✈ Eindhoven   A73 Duisburg •

Zeebrugge   A67   Venlo   ✈

Ostende • • **Bruges**   **Düsseldorf**

FLANDERS   • **Antwerp**   A1

*Flanders Fields
Museum*   E313   **GERMANY**

■• Ieper   E17   • **Ghent**   **Brussels**   Hasselt   • Maastricht   **Köln** •

Waterloo ■   Leuven   • Aachen

Tournai •   E40

Lille •   **BELGIUM**   Liège   Remagen
A26   E42   Namur *Meuse*   A1   A61

Mons   E25

Arras • Cambrai •   Dinant •   *WALLONIE*   Cochem

Aulnoye   La
Roche   A1   Zell

FRANCE   Bastogne   *ARDENNES*   Vianden •   *Mosel*

St. Quentin •   **LUXEMBOURG**

Charleville-   • **Trier**
Mézières

Laon •   ✈

Soissons •   A26   Longwy   **Luxembourg
City**

• **Senlis**   Thionville •   Saarbrücken

✈ *Charles de Gaulle* A4   A4   *Verdun
Battlefield*

↙ **To Paris**   • **Reims**   A4

To Newcastle
England

To Harwich,
England

Rick Steves' ®

BEST OF
EUROPE

2010

AVALON
TRAVEL

CONTENTS

INTRODUCTION

Big Ben, the Eiffel Tower, and the Roman Colosseum. Yodeling in the Alps, biking down cobblestone paths, and taking a canal ride under the stars. Michelangelo's *David* and "Mad" King Ludwig's castles. Sunny Riviera beaches, medieval German towns, and Spanish streets that teem with people at night. Pasta and bratwurst, strudel and scones, Parisian crêpes and Tuscan grapes....

Europe offers a rich smorgasbord of cultures. To wrestle it down to a manageable size, this book breaks Europe into its top destinations. It then gives you all the information and opinions necessary to wring the maximum value out of your limited time and money in each location. If you plan to stay for two months or less in Europe, this book is all you need for a blitz trip.

Experiencing Europe's culture, people, and natural wonders economically and hassle-free has been my goal for more than 30 years of traveling, tour guiding, and travel writing. With this book, I pass on to you the lessons I've learned, updated for 2010.

Rick Steves' Best of Europe is the crème de la crème of places featured in my country guidebooks. It's balanced to include a comfortable mix of exciting cities and cozy towns: from Paris, London, and Rome to traffic-free Italian Riviera ports, alpine villages, and mom-and-pop châteaux. It covers the predictable biggies and mixes in a healthy dose of Back Door intimacy. Along with Leonardo in the Louvre, you'll enjoy Caterina in her cantina. I've been selective. For example, rather than listing countless medieval towns, I recommend only the best.

The best is, of course, only my opinion. But after three decades of travel research, I've developed a sixth sense for what travelers enjoy.

About This Book

This book is organized by destinations. I cover each destination as a mini-vacation on its own, filled with exciting sights and homey, affordable places to stay. In each chapter, you'll find:

Planning Your Time contains a suggested schedule, with thoughts on how to best use your limited time.

Orientation includes tourist information, specifics on public transportation, local tour options, helpful hints, and easy-to-read maps designed to make the text clear and your arrival smooth.

Sights are rated as follows:

▲▲▲—Don't miss.

▲▲—Try hard to see.

▲—Worthwhile if you can make it.

No rating—Worth knowing about.

Sleeping and Eating includes descriptions, addresses, and phone numbers of my favorite good-value hotels and restaurants.

Connections covers how to reach nearby destinations by train or bus.

The **appendix** has a calling chart, climate chart, a hotel reservation form, and information on US embassies for the countries in this book.

Browse through this book, choose your favorite destinations, and create your own itinerary. Then have a great trip! You'll travel like a temporary local, getting the most out of every mile, minute, and dollar.

Planning

Trip Costs

Five components make up your trip cost: airfare, surface transportation, room and board, sightseeing and entertainment, and shopping and miscellany.

Airfare: A basic round-trip US-to-Europe flight costs around $800–1,600 (cheaper in winter), depending on where you fly from and when. Consider saving time and money in Europe by flying "open jaw" (flying into one city and out of another, such as flying into London and out of Rome).

Surface Transportation: Your best mode of travel depends on the time you have and the scope of your trip. For many, the best option is a Eurailpass. Note that train passes are generally only available outside of Europe. You may save money by simply buying tickets as you go (for more information, see "Traveling by Train," later in this chapter).

Drivers can figure $300 per person per week (based on two people splitting the cost of the car, tolls, gas, and insurance). For trips over three weeks, leasing is cheaper. Car rental is cheapest to

European Almanac

Population: The European Union (EU) has 491 million (the US has 304 million, and all of Europe, including the non-EU countries, numbers 730 million).

Area: The EU countries measure 1.7 million square miles (roughly half of the continental US).

Languages: Three main groups: Romance (Italian, Spanish, French), Slavic (Eastern Europe and Russia), and Germanic (German, Dutch, Scandinavian...and English). Most popular second languages are English and French.

Climate: Moderate, warmed by prevailing westerly sea winds. Average of about 65°F in summer, 40°F in winter.

Vegetation: In the north, a mix of conifers (pine and fir) and deciduous trees (oak, elm, and maple). Along the Mediterranean, there are olives, figs, and grapes.

Major Rivers: Danube, Rhine, Rhône, Po, and Seine.

Life Expectancy: About 77 years, among the highest in the world.

Religion: Largely Protestant in the North, Catholic in the South. Many Europeans claim no church affiliation.

Government: The EU is a federation of independent nations. Formed as an economic trade bloc, it is increasingly a political body with elected representatives.

Gross Domestic Product: The EU's nominal GDP is $18.9 trillion (a little more than the US).

arrange from the US; for trips over three weeks, look into leasing.

Room and Board: You can easily manage in Europe in 2010 on an overall average of $120 a day per person for room and board (more for cities, less for towns). A $120-a-day budget allows $15 for lunch, $5 for a snack, $25 for dinner, and $75 for lodging (based on two people splitting the cost of a $150 double room that includes breakfast). That's doable. Students and tightwads can do it on $60 ($30 per hostel bed, $30 for groceries).

Sightseeing and Entertainment: In big cities, figure $15–20 per major sight, $8 for minor ones, and $30 for splurge experiences (e.g., tours, concerts, gelato binges). An overall average of $30 a day works for most. Don't skimp here. After all, this category is the driving force behind your trip—you came to sightsee, enjoy, and experience Europe.

Shopping and Miscellany: Figure $2 per postcard, $3 per coffee and ice-cream cone, and $6 per beer. Shopping can vary in cost from nearly nothing to a small fortune. Good budget travelers find that this category has little to do with assembling a trip full of lifelong and wonderful memories.

When to Go

May, June, September, and October are the best travel months. Peak season, July and August, offers the sunniest weather and the most exciting slate of activities—but the worst crowds. During this busy time, it's best to reserve rooms well in advance, particularly in big cities.

During the off-season, October through April, expect generally shorter hours at attractions, more closures for lunchtime (especially at smaller sights), fewer activities, and fewer—if any—guided tours in English. Especially off-season, be sure to confirm opening hours for sights at local tourist information offices.

As a general rule any time of year, the climate north of the Alps is mild (like Seattle), while south of the Alps it's like Arizona. For specifics, see the Climate Chart in the appendix. If you wilt in the heat, avoid the Mediterranean in summer. If you want blue skies in the Alps, Britain, and Scandinavia, travel during the height of summer.

Plan your itinerary to meet your needs. To beat the heat, start in the south in the spring and work your way north. To moderate culture shock, start in Britain and travel south and east. You can minimize exposure to crowds by remembering that touristy places in the core of Europe—Germany, the Alps, France, and Italy—are the most crowded.

Sightseeing Priorities

Only have a week to "see" Europe? You can't, of course, but if you're organized and energetic, you can see the two art-filled cultural capitals of London and Paris plus Europe's most magnificent landscape—the Swiss Alps.

Whether you have a week or longer, here are my recommended priorities. These itineraries are fast-paced, but doable by car or train, and each allows about two nights in each spot (I've taken geographical proximity into account). Most work best if you fly "open jaw."

If you have...

If you have...	
5 days:	Paris, Swiss Alps
7 days, add:	London
10 days, add:	Rome
14 days, add:	Rhine, Amsterdam, Haarlem
18 days, add:	Venice, Florence
24 days, add:	Cinque Terre, Rothenburg, Bavaria
31 days, add:	Bath, Salzburg, Hallstatt, Nice
37 days, add:	Provence, Barcelona, Madrid
43 days, add:	Vienna, Prague, Berlin
45 days, add:	Bruges

Best of Europe Itinerary

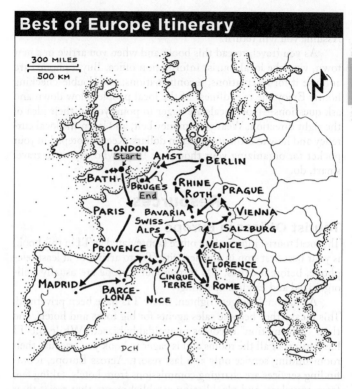

300 MILES
500 KM

LONDON
Start
AMST
BERLIN
BATH
BRUGES
End
RHINE
ROTH
PRAGUE
PARIS
BAVARIA
VIENNA
Swiss
Alps
SALZBURG
PROVENCE
VENICE
FLORENCE
CINQUE
TERRE
ROME
MADRID
BARCE-
LONA
NICE

DCH

Travel Smart

Your trip to Europe is like a complex play—easier to follow and really appreciate on a second viewing. While no one does the same trip twice to gain that advantage, reading this book's chapters on your intended destinations before your trip accomplishes much the same thing.

As you read this book, note the days of markets and festivals and when sights are closed. When setting up your itinerary, anticipate problem days. On Mondays, many sights are closed in Florence; Tuesdays are bad in Paris. Museums and sights, especially large ones, usually stop admitting people 30–60 minutes before closing time.

Sundays have the same pros and cons as they do for travelers in the US. Sightseeing attractions are generally open, shops and banks are closed, and city traffic is light. Rowdy evenings are rare on Sundays. Saturdays in Europe are virtually weekdays with earlier closing hours. Hotels in tourist areas are most crowded on Fridays and Saturdays.

Be sure to mix intense and relaxed periods in your itinerary. Every trip (and every traveler) needs at least a few slack days.

Plan ahead for laundry, picnics, and Internet stops. Pace yourself. Assume you will return.

As you travel, reread this book, and when you arrive in a new town, visit the local tourist information office. Buy a phone card and use it for reservations, reconfirmations, and double-checking hours. Enjoy the friendliness of the local people. Slow down and ask questions—most locals are eager to point you in their idea of the right direction. Wear your money belt, and learn the local currency and how to estimate prices in dollars. Keep a notepad in your pocket for organizing your thoughts. Those who expect to travel smart, do.

Resources

Tourist Offices in Europe
The local tourist information office (abbreviated as **TI** in this book) is your best first stop in any new city. Try to arrive, or at least telephone, before it closes. TIs throughout Europe are usually well-organized and English-speaking.

As national budgets tighten, many TIs have been privatized. This means they become sales agents for big tours and hotels, and their "information" becomes unavoidably biased. While the TI has listings of all the rooms and is eager to book you one, use their room-finding service only as a last resort. Across Europe, room-finding services are charging commissions from hotels, taking fees from travelers, and blacklisting establishments that resist their rules. They are also not allowed to give opinions on the relative value of one place over another. By using the listings in this book, you can avoid that kind of "help."

More Resources from Rick Steves
Guidebooks and Online Updates
This book is updated every year—but once you pin Europe down, it wiggles. For the latest, visit www.ricksteves.com/update (then select the country rather than this book's title). Also at my website, you'll find a valuable list of reports and experiences—good and bad—from fellow travelers (www.ricksteves.com/feedback).

This book is only one of a series of 30+ books on European travel that includes country guidebooks, city guidebooks (Paris, London, etc.), and my budget-travel skills handbook, *Rick Steves' Europe Through the Back Door;* most are annually updated. My phrase books—for Italian, French, German, Spanish, and Portuguese—are practical and budget-oriented. My other books are *Europe 101* (a crash course on art and history), *European Christmas* (on traditional and modern-day celebrations), *Postcards from Europe* (a fun memoir of my travels over 25 years), and *Travel*

Know Before You Go

Your trip is more likely to go smoothly if you plan ahead. Check this list of things to arrange while you're still at home.

Be sure that your **passport** is valid at least six months after your ticketed date of return to the US. If you need to get or renew a passport, it can take up to one month (for more on passports, see www.travel.state.gov).

Book your rooms in advance if you'll be traveling during any major **holidays.** It's smart to reserve rooms in peak season if you'd like to stay in my lead listings—and definitely reserve for your first night. See "Making Reservations," later in this chapter.

Call your **debit- and credit-card companies** to let them know the countries you'll be visiting, so that they'll accept (and not deny) your international charges. Confirm your daily withdrawal limit; consider asking to have it raised so you can take out more cash at each ATM stop. Ask about international transaction fees.

If you'll be planning **renting a car** in Europe, you'll need your driver's license, and it's recommended that you carry an International Driving Permit (IDP), available at your local AAA office ($15 plus the cost of two passport photos, www.aaa .com). Confirm pick-up hours—many car-rental offices close Saturday afternoon and all day Sunday.

Since **airline carry-on restrictions** are always changing, visit the Transportation Security Administration's website (www.tsa.gov/travelers) for an up-to-date list of what you can bring on the plane with you...and what you have to check. Remember to arrive with plenty of time to get through security.

as a Political Act (on the life-changing value of travel to broaden our perspectives, and help us become better citizens and stewards of the planet). For a complete list of my books, see the inside of the last page of this book.

Rick Steves on TV, Radio, and Podcast

My public-television series, *Rick Steves' Europe,* covers my favorite continent in 100 episodes, with 80 of these shows also available on DVD. We're working on new shows every year. I've also done several TV specials, including *Rick Steves' European Christmas* and *Rick Steves' Iran,* a one-hour special on my visit to that proud if perplexing nation of 70 million people.

My weekly hour-long radio show, *Travel with Rick Steves,* is carried by more than 125 public radio stations across the US. I've interviewed the top experts on world travel. Guests have included European royalty, Irish politicians, and even authors Salman

INTRODUCTION

Begin Your Trip at www.ricksteves.com

At our travel website, you'll find a wealth of free information on European destinations, including fresh monthly news and helpful tips from thousands of fellow travelers.

Our **online Travel Store** offers travel bags and accessories specially designed by Rick Steves to help you travel smarter and lighter. These include Rick's popular carry-on bags (wheeled and rucksack versions), money belts, totes, toiletries kits, adapters, other accessories, and a wide selection of guidebooks, planning maps, and DVDs.

Choosing the right railpass for your trip—amidst hundreds of options—can drive you nutty. We'll help you choose the best pass for your needs, plus give you a bunch of free extras.

Travel agents will tell you about mainstream tours of Europe, but they won't tell you about **Rick Steves' tours.** Rick Steves' Europe Through the Back Door travel company offers more than 35 itineraries and about 300 departures reaching the best destinations in this book...and beyond. You'll enjoy great guides, a fun bunch of travel partners (with small groups of generally around 26), and plenty of room to spread out in a big, comfy bus. You'll find European adventures to fit every vacation length. To get our Tour Catalog and a free Rick Steves Tour Experience DVD (filmed on location during an actual tour), visit www.ricksteves.com.

Rushdie and David Sedaris—and I also take questions from Road Scholars like you. All of the radio shows are organized by topic and can be downloaded for free from the radio archive at www .ricksteves.com.

At most major European museums, you can rent audioguides that offer a dry headphone commentary on the great works of art. If you prefer your art-history information in a light, easy-to-digest style, consider my free audio tours—a recorded version of what I'd tell you if I were your tour guide. These guided walking tours are available at www.ricksteves.com/audiotours. Download the tours to your iPod (or other MP3 player) before you go, then take them with you to Europe. In Paris, I lead you through the Louvre, Orsay, Versailles, and the historic core of the city. In Italy, 12 different audio tours cover the top sights of Venice, Florence, and Rome. Look for London audio tours in 2010.

Other Guidebooks

You may want additional information, especially if you'll be traveling beyond my recommended destinations. When you consider the improvements they'll make in your $5,000 vacation, $30 or $40 for extra maps and books is money well-spent. The weight and expense are negligible, especially for several people traveling by car.

The following series of guidebooks are not updated annually; be sure to check the publication date before you buy. The Lonely Planet guides to various European countries are thorough, well-researched, and packed with good maps and hotel recommendations for low- to moderate-budget travelers. The hip, insightful Rough Guide series (by British researchers) and the highly opinionated Let's Go series (by Harvard students) are great for students and vagabonds. The skinny, green Michelin guides (covering several regions of France and most countries of Europe) are excellent, especially if you're driving. They're known for their city and sightseeing maps, dry but concise and helpful information on all major sights, and good cultural and historical background. You can buy English editions at tourist shops and gas stations.

Maps

The black-and-white maps in this book, designed by my well-traveled staff, are concise and simple. The maps are intended to help you locate recommended places and get to the tourist offices, where you can pick up a more in-depth map (usually free) of the city or region. More detailed maps are also sold at newsstands and bookstores—look before you buy to be sure the map has the level of detail you want. For drivers, I'd recommend a 1:200,000- or 1:300,000-scale map for each country.

Money

Cash from ATMs

Throughout Europe, cash machines (ATMs) are the standard way for travelers to get local currency. As an emergency backup, bring several hundred US dollars in hard cash. Avoid using currency exchange booths (lousy rates and/or outrageous fees); if you have currency to exchange, take it to a bank. Also avoid traveler's checks, which are a waste of time (long waits at banks) and a waste of money (in fees).

To use an ATM to withdraw money from your account, you'll need a debit card (ideally with a Visa or MasterCard logo for maximum usability), plus a PIN code. Know your PIN code in numbers; there are only numbers—no letters—on European keypads. It's smart to bring two cards, in case one gets demagnetized or eaten by a temperamental machine.

Before you go, verify with your bank that your cards will work overseas, and alert them that you'll be making withdrawals in Europe; otherwise, the bank may not approve transactions if it perceives unusual spending patterns. Also ask about international

INTRODUCTION

Exchange Rates

1 euro (€) = about $1.40. To roughly convert prices in euros to dollars, add 40 percent: €20 is about $28.

1 British pound (£1) = about $1.60. To easily convert prices in pounds to dollars, add 60 percent.

1 Swiss franc (SF) = about $0.90. The Swiss franc is approximately equivalent to the dollar.

25 Czech crowns (koruna, Kč) = about $1. To estimate prices in dollars, multiply by four and drop the last two digits (e.g., 1,000 Kč = about $40).

---

fees; see "Credit and Debit Cards," below.

When using an ATM, try to take out large sums of money to reduce your per-transaction bank fees. If the machine refuses your request, try again and select a smaller amount (some cash machines limit the amount you can withdraw—don't take it personally). If that doesn't work, try a different machine.

Keep your cash safe. Use a money belt—a pouch with a strap that you buckle around your waist like a belt, and wear under your clothes. Thieves target tourists. A money belt provides peace of mind, allowing you to carry lots of cash safely. Don't waste time every few days tracking down a cash machine—withdraw a week's worth of money, stuff it in your money belt, and travel!

Credit and Debit Cards

For purchases, Visa and MasterCard are more commonly accepted than American Express. Just like at home, credit or debit cards work easily at larger hotels, restaurants, and shops, but smaller businesses prefer payment in local currency (in small bills—break large bills at a bank or larger store). If receipts show your credit-card number, don't toss these thoughtlessly.

Credit and debit cards—whether used for purchases or ATM withdrawals—often come with additional, tacked-on "international transaction" fees of up to 3 percent plus up to $5 per transaction. To avoid unpleasant surprises, call your bank or credit-card company before your trip to ask about these fees.

If merchants offer to convert your purchase price into dollars (called dynamic currency conversion), refuse this "service." You'll pay even more in fees for the expensive convenience of seeing your charge in dollars.

Recently in northern Europe and Great Britain, merchants have begun using debit cards with embedded "smart chips." You may see signs or keypads referring to this technology, called "Chip and PIN." European cardholders must enter a PIN in order to use these chip-embedded cards in retail stores. In most cases, you can still use your credit or debit card at the cashier and sign the receipt the old-fashioned way. However, a few merchants might insist on the PIN. For this reason, it's smart to know the PIN for your credit card (ask your credit-card company); in a pinch, use your debit card and PIN instead. Another problem is that US credit or debit cards often don't work at automated machines (such as ticket machines in a train or a subway station, or a pay-at-the-pump gas station). But in most of these situations, there's a cashier nearby who can take your credit or debit card and make it work.

Damage Control for Lost Cards

If you lose your credit, debit, or ATM card, you can stop people from using it by reporting the loss immediately to the respective global customer-assistance centers. Call these 24-hour US numbers collect: Visa (410/581-9994), MasterCard (636/722-7111), and American Express (623/492-8427).

At a minimum, you'll need to know the name of the financial institution that issued you the card, along with the type of card (classic, platinum, or whatever). Providing the following information will allow for a quicker cancellation of your missing card: full card number, whether you are the primary or secondary cardholder, the cardholder's name exactly as printed on the card, billing address, home phone number, circumstances of the loss or theft, and identification verification (your birth date, your mother's maiden name, or your Social Security number—memorize this, don't carry a copy). If you are the secondary cardholder, you'll also need to provide the primary cardholder's identification-verification details. You can generally receive a temporary card within two or three business days in Europe.

If you promptly report your card lost or stolen, you typically won't be responsible for any unauthorized transactions on your account, although many banks charge a liability fee of $50.

Sleeping

For hassle-free efficiency, I favor accommodations that are handy to your sightseeing activities. Rather than list hotels, B&Bs, and hostels scattered throughout a city, I describe two or three favorite neighborhoods and recommend the best accommodations values in each, from cheap hostels to plush splurges. A major feature of this book is its extensive listing of good-value accommodations. I look for places that are clean, small, central, quiet at night, comfortable (firm beds), traditional, inexpensive, friendly, and not listed in other guidebooks.

Hotels

Double rooms in hotels listed in this book will range from about $50 (very simple, toilet and shower down the hall) to $450 (maximum plumbing and more), with most clustering at about $150 (with private bathrooms). Prices are higher in big cities and heavily touristed cities, and lower off the beaten path. Three or four people economize by requesting larger rooms.

Prices at nearly any hotel can get soft if you book direct (without using a pricey middleman like the TI or a Web booking service), travel off-season, and/or pay cash (cash payment gets you an additional 5–10 percent discount at many hotels—ask when you check in). Assume that breakfast is included in the prices I've listed, unless otherwise noted. If breakfast costs extra and is optional, you may want to skip it. While convenient, it's often a poor value.

Bed-and-Breakfasts and Pensions

Between hotels and hostels in price and style is a special class of accommodations: bed-and-breakfasts (B&Bs) and pensions. These are small, warm, and family-run, and offer a personal touch at a budget price—about $40–60 per person. Each country has these friendly accommodations in varying degrees of abundance, facilities, and service. Some include breakfast; some don't. They have different names from country to country—they're called *Privatzimmer* in Germany, *chambre d'hôte* in France, *affitta camere* in Italy, and *casa particulare* in Spain—but all have one thing in common: They satisfy the need for a place to stay that gives you the privacy of a hotel and the comforts of home at an affordable price.

Making Reservations

Given the quality of the B&Bs and hotels I've found for this book, I'd recommend that you reserve your rooms in advance, particularly if you'll be traveling during peak season. Book several weeks ahead, or as soon as you've pinned down your travel dates. Note that some national holidays jam things up and merit your making reservations far in advance (see www.ricksteves.com/festivals, and tourist board websites per country—listed at www.towd.com).

To make a reservation in advance, contact hotels directly by email, phone, or fax. Email is the clearest and most economical way to make a reservation. In addition, many hotel websites now have online reservation forms. Most hotels listed are accustomed to English-only travelers. To ensure that you have all the information you need for your reservation, use the form at the back of this book or at www.ricksteves.com/reservation. If you don't get a response within a few days, call to follow up.

When you request a room in writing for a certain time period, use the European style for writing dates: day/month/year. Hoteliers need to know your arrival and departure dates. For example, a two-night stay in July would be "2 nights, 16/07/10 to 18/07/10." Consider in advance how long you'll stay; don't just assume you can extend your reservation for extra days once you arrive. Mention any discounts offered (for Rick Steves readers or otherwise) when you make the reservation.

If you don't get a reply to your email or fax, it usually means the hotel is already fully booked. If the response from the hotel gives its room availability and rates, it's not a confirmation. You must tell them that you want that room at the given rate.

For more spontaneity, you can make reservations as you travel, calling hotels or B&Bs a few days to a week before your visit. If traveling without any reservations, you'll have greater success snaring rooms if you arrive at your destination early in the day.

The hotelier will sometimes request your credit-card number for a one-night deposit. While you can email your credit-card information (I do), it's safer to share that personal info via phone call, fax, or secure online reservation form (if the hotel has one on its website).

If you must cancel your reservation, it's courteous to do so with as much advance notice as possible (simply make a quick phone call or send an email). Family-run hotels and B&Bs lose money if they turn away customers while holding a room for someone who doesn't show up. Understandably, some hotels bill no-shows for one night. Ask about cancellation policies before you book.

Always reconfirm your room reservation a few days in advance from the road. If you'll be arriving after 17:00, let them know. On the small chance that a hotel loses track of your reservation, bring along a hard copy of their emailed or faxed confirmation.

Hostels

You'll pay about $25–30 per bed to stay at a hostel. Travelers of any age are welcome if they don't mind dorm-style accommodations or meeting other travelers. Cheap meals are sometimes available, and kitchen facilities are usually provided. Expect youth groups in spring, crowds in the summer, snoring, and great variability in quality from one hostel to the next. Family and private rooms are sometimes available on request, but it's basically boys' dorms and girls' dorms. You usually can't check in before 17:00 and must be out by 10:00. There is often a late-night curfew.

Transportation

By Car or Train?

Each has pros and cons. Cars are an expensive headache in big cities, but let you delve deep into the countryside. Groups of three

INTRODUCTION

Point-to-Point Rail Tickets: Cost & Time

This chart shows the cost of second-class train tickets. Connect the dots of your itinerary, add up the cost, compare it with a railpass, and see what is better for your trip.

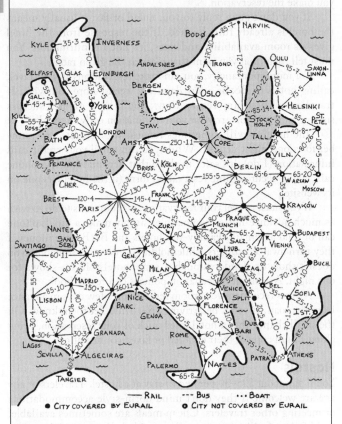

——— Rail --- Bus ···Boat
● City covered by Eurail ○ City not covered by Eurail

First number between cities = Approximate cost in US dollars for a one-way, second class ticket. **Second number** = Number of hours the trip takes.

Important: These fares and times are based on European web sources. Actual prices may vary due to currency fluctuations and local promotions. Local competition can cut the actual price of some boat crossings (from Italy to Greece, for example) by 50 percent or more. For approximate first-class rail prices, add 50 percent. Travel times and fares are for express trains where applicable.

or more travel cheaper by car, and if you're packing heavy (with kids), go by car. Trains are best for city-to-city travel and give you the convenience of doing long stretches overnight. By train, I arrive relaxed and well rested—not so by car. Many countries offer a "Rail & Drive" pass that allows you to mix train and car travel. When thoughtfully used, this pass economically gives you the best of both transportation worlds.

Traveling by Train

A major mistake Americans make is relating public transportation in Europe to the pathetic public transportation they're used to at home. By rail, you'll have Europe by the tail. While many people simply buy tickets as they go ("point to point"), the various train passes give you the simplicity of ticket-free, unlimited travel, and depending on how many trips you do, often offer a savings over regular point-to-point tickets. Fast, long-distance, international, or overnight trains are more likely to require reservations at some point before boarding; you can make your more critical reservations from home.

For a summary of railpass deals and point-to-point ticket options (available in the US and in Europe), check out our free, annually updated *Guide to Eurail Passes* at www.ricksteves.com /rail. If you decide to get a railpass, this guide will help you know you're getting the right one for your trip. To study train schedules in advance on the Web, look up http://bahn.hafas.de/bin/query .exe/en (Germany's excellent all-Europe timetable).

Eurail Global Pass and Eurail Selectpass

The granddaddy of European railpasses, the Eurail Global pass, gives you unlimited first-class travel on all public railways in 21 European countries. That's 100,000 miles of track through most of Europe (but excluding Great Britain and some of Eastern Europe). The pass includes many bonuses, such as several international ferries and free boat rides on the Rhine, Mosel, and lakes of Switzerland.

The Eurail Selectpass gives you a selected number of "flexi" travel days in your choice of three, four, or five adjoining Eurail countries connected by rail or ferry (e.g., a three-country Selectpass could cover France, Italy, and Switzerland). Selectpasses are fine for a focused trip, but to see the Best of Europe, you'd do best with a Global Eurailpass. Either pass gives a 15 percent Saverpass discount to two or more companions traveling together.

Eurail Analysis

For an at-a-glance break-even point, remember that a one-month Eurail Global pass is a good value if, for example, your route is

Amsterdam–Rome–Madrid–Paris. A one-month Eurail Youthpass saves you money if you're traveling from Amsterdam to Rome to Madrid and back to Amsterdam. Passes pay for themselves quicker in the north, where the cost per mile is higher. Check the "Europe by Rail: Dollars and Hours" map earlier in this chapter to see if your planned travels merit purchasing a train pass. If it's about even, go with the pass for the convenience of not having to wait in line to buy tickets (on trains that don't require paid reservations) and for the fun and freedom to travel "free." Even if second-class tickets work out a bit cheaper than a first-class pass for travelers over 26, consider the added value of a first-class pass: On a crowded train, your chances of getting a seat are much better if your pass allows you to sit anywhere on the train.

Rail-and-drive passes are popular varieties of many of these passes. Along with a railpass (Eurailpass, Eurail Selectpass, or individual country), you get vouchers for a few Hertz or Avis car-rental days. These allow travelers to do long trips by train and enjoy a car where they need the freedom to explore. Great areas for a day of joyriding include the Germany's Rhine or Bavaria, France's Provence, and the Alps (for "car hiking"). When comparing prices, remember that each day of car rental comes with about $30 of extra expenses (CDW insurance, gas, parking), which you can divide among the people in your party.

Renting a Car

Your American or Canadian driver's license is all you need in most European countries, but it can help to also carry an International Driving Permit (IDP), which provides a translation of your license—making it easier for the cop to write out the ticket. You can get one at your local American Automobile Association or Canadian Automobile Association office ($15 plus the cost of two passport-type photos, www.aaa.com or www.caa.ca).

I use the freeways whenever possible. They're free in the Netherlands and Germany; you'll pay about $4–6 per hour in Italy, France, and Spain; $34 for the toll sticker as you enter Switzerland; and $10 each for toll stickers in Austria and the Czech Republic. It costs about $20 a day to park safely in big cities, and there's a $13 "congestion charge" to drive in downtown London.

Be warned that driving is restricted in many Italian city centers. If you drive in an area marked *Zona Traffico Limitato*, your license plate can be photographed and a hefty (€100-plus) fine mailed to your home, without your ever being stopped by a cop.

As Europe's internal borders fade, your car comes with the paperwork you need to drive wherever you like in Western and most of Eastern Europe. But if you're heading to a country that

STOP AND LEARN THESE ROAD SIGNS

Speed Limit (km/hr)
Yield
No Passing
End of No Passing Zone

One Way
Intersection
Main Road
Freeway

Danger
No Entry
No Entry for cars
All Vehicles Prohibited

Parking
No Parking
Customs
Peace

still has closed borders (for example, deep in far-eastern or southeastern Europe), state your travel plans up front to the rental company when making your reservation. Some companies have limits on eastward excursions (for example, you can only take cheaper cars, and you may have to pay extra insurance fees). When you cross these borders, you may be asked to show proof of insurance (called a "green card"). Ask your car-rental company if you need any other documentation for crossing the borders on your itinerary.

When you rent a car, you are liable for a very high deductible, sometimes equal to the entire value of the car. There are various ways you can limit your financial risk in case of an accident. You have three main options: buy Collision Damage Waiver insurance from the car-rental company; get coverage through your credit card if your card automatically includes zero-deductible coverage; or buy protection from Travel Guard, which sells collision insurance at very affordable rates (tel. 800-826-4919, www.travelguard.com; valid everywhere in Europe but the Republic of Ireland, and some Italian car-rental companies refuse to honor it). Buying CDW insurance is the easiest but priciest option. Using the coverage that comes with your credit card is cheaper, but can involve more hassle. If you're taking a short trip (but not in Ireland), the cheapest solution is to buy Travel Guard's CDW insurance (though oddly, it's not sold in Washington State). For more information, see www.ricksteves.com/cdw. For trips of at least three weeks, leasing—which includes taxes and insurance—is the best way to go.

Note that if you'll be driving in Italy, you are required to have theft insurance, and most car-rental companies' rates automatically include CDW coverage (which you sometimes can't decline). It's not unusual to decline CDW when you reserve your Italian car, only to find when you show up at the counter that you must buy it after all.

Cheap Flights

Connecting your itinerary by air is cheaper than you might think. Thanks to Europe's budget airlines, you can get between many European cities for about $100 one-way. Some amazing promotional deals can even bring fares down into the single digits. The best deals are from major hub cities.

New budget airlines are continually being launched, but a handful of them are more established, including easyJet (www.easyjet.com) and Ryanair (www.ryanair.com). Some good websites you can use to search routes on multiple cheap airlines include www.skyscanner.net (this is the best one), www.wegolo.com, www.mobissimo.com, and www.kayak.com.

Europe by Air is another good budget resource (www.europebyair.com, tel. 888-321-4737). They work with 20 different European airlines, offering flights between 170 European cities in 30 countries. Using their "flight pass" system, each coupon for a nonstop flight costs $99 plus tax (which can range from $50–90). Note that if you make a connection through one of Europe by Air's many hubs, you pay double—$99 for each flight to and from the hub.

Be warned that these no-frills airlines can come with tradeoffs: minimal customer service, non-refundable tickets, and stringent restrictions on the amount of baggage you're allowed to check without paying extra. Often you can only book these flights online. Also note that you'll sometimes fly out of less convenient, secondary airports. For example, Ryanair's England hub is Stansted Airport, the farthest of London's airports from the city center.

Traveling As a Temporary Local

We travel all the way to Europe to enjoy differences—to become temporary locals. You'll experience frustrations. Certain truths that we find "God-given" or "self-evident," like cold beer, ice in drinks, bottomless cups of coffee, hot showers, and bigger being better, are suddenly not so true. One of the benefits of travel is the eye-opening realization that there are logical, civil, and even better alternatives.

If there is a negative aspect to the European image of Americans, we can appear aggressive, impolite, rich, loud, superficially friendly, and a bit naive. Americans tend to be noisy in public places, such as restaurants and trains. Our raised voices can demolish Europe's reserved ambience. Talk softly. While Europeans look bemusedly at some of our Yankee excesses—and worriedly at others—they nearly always afford us individual travelers all the warmth we deserve.

While updating this book, I heard over and over again that my readers are considerate and fun to have as guests. Thank you for traveling as temporary locals who are sensitive to the culture. It's fun to follow you in my travels.

Judging from all the positive comments I receive from travelers who have used this book, it's safe to assume you'll enjoy a great, affordable vacation—with the finesse of an experienced, independent traveler. Thanks, and happy travels!

Back Door Travel Philosophy
From *Rick Steves' Europe Through the Back Door*

Travel is intensified living—maximum thrills per minute and one of the last great sources of legal adventure. Travel is freedom. It's recess, and we need it.

Experiencing the real Europe requires catching it by surprise, going casual..."Through the Back Door."

Affording travel is a matter of priorities. (Make do with the old car.) You can eat and sleep—simply, safely, and enjoyably—anywhere in Europe for $120 a day plus transportation costs. In many ways, spending more money only builds a thicker wall between you and what you traveled so far to see. Europe is a cultural carnival, and time after time, you'll find that its best acts are free and the best seats are the cheap ones.

A tight budget forces you to travel close to the ground, meeting and communicating with the people. Never sacrifice sleep, nutrition, safety, or cleanliness to save money. Simply enjoy the local-style alternatives to expensive hotels and restaurants.

Connecting with people carbonates your experience. Extroverts have more fun. If your trip is low on magic moments, kick yourself and make things happen. If you don't enjoy a place, maybe you don't know enough about it. Seek the truth. Recognize tourist traps. Give a culture the benefit of your open mind. See things as different, but not better or worse. Any culture has plenty to share.

Of course, travel, like the world, is a series of hills and valleys. Be fanatically positive and militantly optimistic. If something's not to your liking, change your liking.

Travel can make you a happier American, as well as a citizen of the world. Our Earth is home to six and a half billion equally precious people. It's humbling to travel and find that other people don't have the "American Dream"—they have their own dreams. Europeans like us, but with all due respect, they wouldn't trade passports.

Thoughtful travel engages us with the world. In tough economic times, it reminds us what is truly important. By broadening perspectives, travel teaches new ways to measure quality of life.

Globetrotting destroys ethnocentricity, helping us understand and appreciate other cultures. Rather than fear the diversity on this planet, celebrate it. Among your most prized souvenirs will be the strands of different cultures you choose to knit into your own character. The world is a cultural yarn shop, and Back Door travelers are weaving the ultimate tapestry. Join in!

AUSTRIA

VIENNA

Vienna is the capital of Austria, the cradle of classical music, the home of the rich Habsburg heritage, and one of Europe's most livable cities. The city center is skyscraper-free, pedestrian-friendly, dotted with quiet parks, and traversed by quaint electric trams. Many buildings still reflect 18th- and 19th-century elegance, when the city was at the forefront of the arts and sciences. Compared with most modern European urban centers, the pace of life is slow.

Vienna was also the capital of the enormous, once-grand Habsburg Empire—for 640 years. Vienna is now a head without a body, but culturally, historically, and from a sightseeing point of view, this city is the sum of its illustrious past.

The city reached its peak in the 19th century. After Napoleon's defeat and the Congress of Vienna in 1815 (which shaped 19th-century Europe), Vienna enjoyed its violin-filled belle époque, giving us our romantic image of the city: fine wine, chocolates, cafés, waltzes, and the good life. In 1900, Vienna's 2.2 million inhabitants made it the world's fifth-largest city—after New York, London, Paris, and Berlin. Vienna sat on the cusp between stuffy Old World monarchy and subversive modern trends.

However, after starting and losing World War I, the Habsburgs lost their far-flung holdings. Then came World War II: While Vienna's old walls had long held out would-be invaders—Germanic barbarians (in Roman times), Mongol hordes (13th century), Ottoman Turks (the sieges of 1529 and 1683)—they were no match for WWII bombs, which destroyed nearly a quarter of the city's buildings.

After the turmoil of the two world wars, Vienna has settled

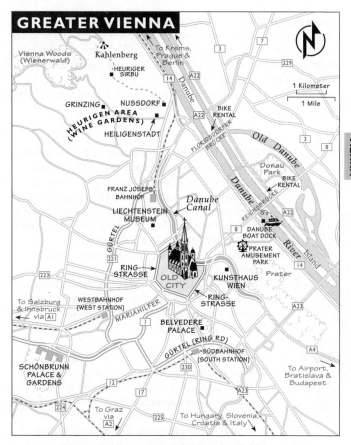

down into a somewhat sleepy, pleasant place where culture is still king. Classical music is everywhere. People nurse a pastry and coffee over the daily paper at small cafés. It's a city of world-class museums, big and small. Anyone with an interest in painting, music, architecture, beautiful objects, or Sacher torte with whipped cream will feel right at home.

Planning Your Time

For a big city, Vienna is pleasant and laid-back. Packed with sights, it's worth two days and two nights on the speediest trip. To be grand-tour efficient, you could sleep in and sleep out on the train—Berlin, Venice, Rome, the Swiss Alps (via Zürich), Paris, the Rhine Valley, and Kraków are each handy night trains away.

The Hofburg and Schönbrunn are both world-class palaces, but seeing both is redundant—with limited time or money, I'd choose just one. The Hofburg comes with the popular Sisi Museum and is right in the town center, making for an easy visit. With more time, a visit to Schönbrunn—set outside town amid a grand and regal garden—is also a great experience. (For efficient sightseeing, drivers should note that Schönbrunn Palace is conveniently on the way out of town toward Salzburg.)

If you have two days for Vienna, here's a good way to spend them:

Day 1

9:00 Drop by the TI for any planning and ticket needs, then see the sights in Vienna's old center (taking the Vienna City Walk, in this chapter); consider breaking en route to take in St. Stephen's Cathedral (nave closed 11:30–13:30) and climb its south tower.

12:00 Lunch of finger sandwiches at Buffet Trzesniewski.

13:00 Tour the Hofburg Palace and Treasury.

16:00 Hit one more museum, or shop, browse, and people-watch.

19:30 Choose classical music (concert or opera), Haus der Musik, a *Heuriger* wine garden, or visit a museum—many of Vienna's sights are open late at least one night a week.

Day 2

Morning Choose between Schönbrunn Palace (which could be redundant if you've seen the Hofburg Palace yesterday) or the Lipizzaner stallions. If you choose Schönbrunn Palace, arrive by 9:00 and return to central Vienna by noon. The Spanish Riding School's Lipizzaner stallions begin their practice at 10:00 (about March–June and mid-Aug–Dec Tue–Sat 10:00–12:00, no practice Sun–Mon or July–mid-Aug).

12:00 Have lunch at the Naschmarkt, and consider ducking into one or two sights (such as the Secession) on nearby Karlsplatz.

13:00 Tour the Opera (check red sign on door for today's schedule).

14:00 Visit the Kunsthistorisches Museum.

16:00 Choose from the many sights left to see in Vienna.

Evening See Day 1 evening options. In summer, hit the City Hall food circus for dinner or a drink (on Rathausplatz).

Orientation

(area code: 01)

Vienna sits between the Vienna Woods (Wienerwald) and the Danube (Donau). To the southeast is industrial sprawl. The Alps, which arc across Europe from Marseille, end at Vienna's wooded hills, providing a popular playground for walking and sipping new wine. This greenery's momentum carries on into the city. More than half of Vienna is parkland, filled with ponds, gardens, trees, and statue-maker memories of Austria's glory days.

Think of the city map as a target with concentric sections: The bull's-eye is St. Stephen's Cathedral, the towering cathedral south of the Danube. Surrounding that is the old town, bound tightly by the circular road known as the Ringstrasse, marking what used to be the city wall. The Gürtel, a broader ring road, contains the rest of downtown. Outside the Gürtel lies the (uninteresting) sprawl of modern Vienna.

Addresses start with the district, or *Bezirk,* followed by the street and building number. The Ringstrasse (a.k.a. the Ring) circles the first *Bezirk.* Any address higher than the ninth *Bezirk* is beyond the Gürtel, far from the center. The middle two digits of Vienna's postal codes show the *Bezirk.* The address "7, Linden-gasse 4" is in the seventh district, #4 on Linden street. Its postal code would be 1070.

Nearly all your sightseeing will be in the old town, located inside (and along) the Ringstrasse. To walk across this circular district takes about 30 minutes. St. Stephen's Cathedral sits in the center, at the intersection of the two main (pedestrian-only) streets: Kärntner Strasse runs north–south and Graben runs east–west. Within a few blocks of the cathedral is the Hofburg, a sprawling complex of palaces and museums.

Several sights lie on or just outside the Ringstrasse. A branch of the Danube River (*Donau* in German, DOH-now) borders the Ring to the north. On the south edge are the Opera, Karlsplatz, and the Kunsthistorisches and Natural History museums.

As a tourist, concern yourself only with this compact old center. When you do, sprawling Vienna suddenly becomes manageable.

Arrival in Vienna

For a comprehensive rundown on Vienna's two main train stations and nearby airports, see "Connections," at the end of this chapter.

Tourist Information

Vienna's one real TI is a block behind the Opera at Albertinaplatz (daily 9:00–19:00, tel. 01/24555, press 2 for English info, www.vienna.info).

Confirm your sightseeing plans at the TI, and pick up the free and essential city map with a list of museums and hours (also available at most hotels), the monthly program of concerts (called *Wien-Programm*—details below), the *Vienna from A to Z* booklet (details below), and the biannual city guide *(Vienna Journal)*. The TI also books rooms for a €2.90 fee. While hotel and ticket-booking agencies at the train station and airport can answer questions and give out maps and brochures, I'd rely on the official TI if possible.

Wien-Programm: This monthly entertainment guide is particularly important, listing all of the events, including music, walks, expositions, and evening museum hours (*E* means "in English"). Note the key for abbreviations on the inside cover, which helps make this dense booklet useful even for non-German speakers.

Vienna from A to Z: Consider this handy booklet, sold by TIs for €3.60. Every major building in Vienna sports a numbered flag banner that keys into this booklet and into the TI's city map. If you get lost, find one of the "famous-building flags" and match its number to your map. If you're at a famous building, check the map to see what other key numbers are nearby, then check the *A to Z* book description to see if you want to go in. This system is especially helpful for those just wandering aimlessly among Vienna's historic charms.

Vienna Card: The much-promoted €18.50 Vienna Card is not worth the mental overhead for most travelers. It gives you a 72-hour transit pass (worth €13.60) and discounts of 10–40 percent at the city's museums. It might save the busy sightseer a few euros (though seniors and students will do better with their own discounts).

Helpful Hints

Internet Access: The TI has a list of Internet cafés. **BigNet** is the dominant outfit (www.bignet.at), with lots of computers at Hoher Markt 8–9 (daily 9:00–23:00). **Surfland Internet Café** is near the Opera (daily 10:00–23:00, Krugerstrasse 10, tel. 01/512-7701), and **Netcafe** is close to many of my recommended hotels (Mon–Fri 9:00–22:00, Sat 10:00–22:00, Sun 12:00–22:00, Mariahilfer Strasse 103, tel. 01/595-5558).

Post Offices: The main post office is near Schwedenplatz at Fleischmarkt 19 (Mon–Fri 7:00–22:00, Sat–Sun 9:00–22:00). Branch offices are at the Westbahnhof (Mon–Fri 7:00–22:00, Sat–Sun 9:00–20:00), near the Opera (Mon–Fri 7:00–19:00, closed Sat–Sun, Krugerstrasse 13), and scattered throughout town.

English Bookstore: Stop by the woody and cool **Shakespeare**

& Co. (Mon–Sat 9:00–19:00 and sometimes later, generally closed Sun, north of Hoher Markt at Sterngasse 2, tel. 01/535-5053).

Keeping Up with the News: Don't buy newspapers. Read them for free in Vienna's marvelous coffee houses. It's much classier.

Travel Agency: Intropa is convenient, with good service for flights and train tickets. They'll waive the service charge for my readers (Mon–Fri 9:00–18:00, Sat 10:00–13:00, closed Sun, Spiegelgasse 15, tel. 01/513-4000).

Getting Around Vienna

By Public Transportation: Take full advantage of Vienna's simple, cheap, and super-efficient transit system, which includes trams (a.k.a streetcars), buses, U-Bahn (subway), and S-Bahn (faster suburban trains). The smooth, modern trams are Porsche-designed, with "backpack technology" that locates the engines and mechanical hardware on the roofs for a lower ride and easier entry. I generally stick to the tram to zip around the Ring and take the U-Bahn to outlying sights or hotels. Trams #1, #2, and #D all travel partway around the Ring.

The free Vienna map, available at TIs and hotels, includes a smaller schematic map of the major public transit lines, making the too-big €2.50 transit map unnecessary. (Transit maps are also posted conveniently on U-Bahn station walls.) As you study the map, note that tram lines are marked with numbers (such as #38). Buses have numbers followed by an *A* (such as #38A). U-Bahn lines begin with U (e.g., U-1), and the directions are designated by the end-of-the-line stops. Blue lines are the speedier S-Bahns (transit info tel. 01/790-9100).

Trams, buses, the U-Bahn, and the S-Bahn all use the same tickets. Buy your tickets from *Tabak-Trafik* shops, station machines, marked *Vorverkauf* offices in the station, or—for trams only—on board (tickets only, more expensive). You have lots of choices:

- Single tickets (€1.70, €2.20 if bought on tram, good for one journey with necessary transfers);
- 24-hour transit pass (€5.70);
- 72-hour transit pass (€13.60);
- 7-day transit pass (*Wochenkarte*, €14, pass always starts on Mon); or
- 8-day card *(Acht Tage Karte)*, covering eight full days of free transportation for €27.20 (can be shared—for example, 4 people for 2 days each). With a per-person cost of €3.50/day (compared to €5.70/day for a 24-hour pass), this can be a real saver for groups.

Kids under 15 travel free on Sundays and holidays; kids under 6 always travel free.

Stamp a time on your ticket as you enter the Metro system, tram, or bus (stamp it only the first time for a multiple-use pass). Cheaters pay a stiff €70 fine, plus the cost of the ticket. Rookies miss stops because they fail to open the door. Push buttons, pull latches—do whatever it takes. Before you exit a U-Bahn station, study the wall-mounted street map. Choosing the right exit— signposted from the moment you step off the train—saves lots of walking.

Cute little electric buses wind through the tangled old center. Bus #1A is best for a joy ride—hop on and see where it takes you.

By Taxi: Vienna's comfortable, civilized, and easy-to-flag-down taxis start at €2.50. You'll pay about €10 to go from the Opera to the Westbahnhof. Pay only what's on the meter—any surcharges (other than the €2 fee added to fares when you telephone them, or €10 for the airport) are just crude cabbie rip-offs.

By Car with Driver: Consider the luxury of having your own car and driver. Johann (a.k.a. John) Lichtl is a kind, honest, English-speaking cabbie who can take up to four passengers in his car (€27/1 hr, €22/hr for 2 or more hours, €27 to or from airport, mobile 0676-670-6750). Consider hiring gentle Johann to drive you to Salzburg with Danube Valley sightseeing en route (€330, up to 14 hours; other trips can be arranged). These special prices are valid with this book in 2010.

By Bike: Vienna is a great city for biking, though cheap bike-rental options are scarce in the city center (see recommendations below and get a list at the TI). The bike path along the Ring is wonderfully entertaining. Your best biking is likely up and down the traffic-free and people-filled Donauinsel (Danube Island).

Weather permitting from March through October, you can rent a bike all day (about 9:30 until dusk) from one of two shops near these bridges: **Floridsdorferbrücke** (€3.60/hr, €18/day, near tram #31 stop, tel. 01/278-8698) and **Reichsbrücke** (€5.40/hr, €27/day, tel. 01/263-5242).

American Rick Watts runs **Pedal Power,** and will deliver your bike to your hotel and pick it up when you're done (€32/day including delivery, Ausstellungsstrasse 3, tel. 01/729-7234, www.pedalpower.at). Rick also operates guided city tours on Segway scooters (2/day, see website for details) and by bike (see "Bike Tours," next page).

Crazy Chicken bike rental, a short tram ride from the Westbahnhof, is less convenient, but a lot cheaper (€3/hr, €12/day, daily 8:30–19:00, near recommended Pension Fünfhaus at Grangasse 8—see pension listing on page 87 for directions, tel. 01/892-2134, mobile 0664-421-4789).

Citybikewien, which has bikes parked in public racks all over town, is a clever program that works fine for locals, but can be headachy for tourists to figure out. The bikes lock in their stalls (50 of which are scattered through the city center) and are released when you insert a Citybike Tourist Card, sold for €2 at Pedal Power (listed on previous page) and at Royal Tours (Herrengasse 1–3). Bikes cost €2 per hour (first hour free, fliers explain the process in English, www.citybikewien.at).

Tours

Walking Tours—The TI's *Walks in Vienna* brochure describes Vienna's many guided walks. The basic 90-minute "Vienna at First Glance" introductory walk is offered daily throughout the summer (€13, leaves at 14:00 from near the Opera, in English and German, tel. 01/876-7111, mobile 0664-260-4388, www.wienguide.at). Various specialized tours go once a week and are listed on their website.

Bike Tours—Several companies offer city tours. **Pedal Power** runs two different three-hour tours daily from May to September (€23 per tour includes bike, €40 for both tours, departs at 9:45 and 14:15 in front of Opera at corner of Operngasse and the Kärntner Ring, also rents bikes, tel. 01/729-7234, www.pedalpower.at). **Wolfgang Höfler** leads bike tours as well as walking tours (€135/2 hrs, office@vienna-aktivtours.com, listed on the next page under "Private Guides").

Hop-On, Hop-Off Bus Tour—Vienna Sightseeing operates hop-on, hop-off bus tours (departures from the Opera 2–3/hr April–Oct 10:00–18:00, at top of each hour Nov–March 10:00–17:00, recorded commentary). The schedule is posted curbside (three different routes, €13 for one hour, €16 for two). You could pay much more to get 24 hours of hop-on and hop-off privileges, but given the city's excellent public transportation and this outfit's meager frequency, I'd take this not to hop on and off, but only to get the narrated orientation drive through town.

Ring Tram Tour—The **Vienna Ring Tram,** a made-for-tourists streetcar, runs along the entire Ringstrasse (€6 for one loop, €9 for 24-hour hop-on, hop-off privileges, runs twice hourly 10:00–18:00, July–Aug until 19:00, recorded narration).

City Bus Tour—Vienna Sightseeing offers a basic three-hour city tour, including a tour of Schönbrunn Palace (€36, 3/day April–Oct, 2/day Nov–March, call 01/7124-6830 or go to www.viennasight seeingtours.com, which also lists their many other tours).

Horse and Buggy Tour—These traditional horse-and-buggies, called *Fiakers,* take rich romantics on clip-clop tours lasting 20 minutes (€40–old town), 40 minutes (€65–old town and the Ring), or one hour (€95–all of the above, but more thorough). You can share the ride and cost with up to five people. Because it's a kind of guided tour, talk to a few drivers before choosing a carriage, and pick a driver who's fun and speaks English (tel. 01/401-060).

Private Guides—The tourist board's website (www.vienna.info) has a long list of local guides with their specialties and contact information. **Lisa Zeiler** is an excellent English-speaking guide (two-hour walks for €130—if she's booked up, she can set you up with another guide, tel. 01/402-3688, lisa.zeiler@gmx.at). **Ursula Klaus**—an art scholar specializing in turn-of-the-20th-century Vienna, music, art, and architecture—also offers two-hour tours for €130 (mobile 0676-421-4884, ursula.klaus@aon.at). Lisa and Ursula are both top-notch, bring art museums to life masterfully, and can tailor tours to your interests. **Wolfgang Höfler** focuses on Vienna's 20th-century history (€135/2 hrs, also leads bike tours—see previous page, www.vienna-aktivtours.com, office@vienna-aktivtours.com).

Self-Guided Walk

▲▲Vienna City Walk

This walk connects the top three sights in Vienna's old center: the Opera, St. Stephen's Cathedral, and the Hofburg Palace. Along the way, you'll see sights covered elsewhere in the book, and get an overview of Vienna's past and present. Allow one hour, and more time if you plan to stop into any of the major sights along the way.

• *Begin at the square outside Vienna's landmark Opera House. (The Opera's entrance faces the Ringstrasse; we're starting at the busy pedestrian square that's to the right of the entrance as you're facing it.)*

Opera

If Vienna is the world capital of classical music, this building is its throne room, one of the planet's premier houses of music. It's typical of Vienna's 19th-century buildings in that it features a revival style—"Neo"-Renaissance—with arched windows, half-columns, and the sloping copper roof typical of French Renaissance châteaux.

Since it was built in 1869, almost all of opera's luminaries have passed through here. Its former musical directors include Gustav Mahler, Herbert von Karajan, and Richard Strauss. Luciano Pavarotti, Maria Callas, Placido Domingo, and many other greats have sung from its stage.

In the pavement along the side of the Opera (and all along Kärntner Strasse, the bustling shopping street we'll visit shortly), you'll find star plaques forming a Hollywood-style walk of fame. These are the stars of classical music—famous composers, singers, musicians, and conductors.

If you're a fan, take a guided tour of the Opera (see page 44).

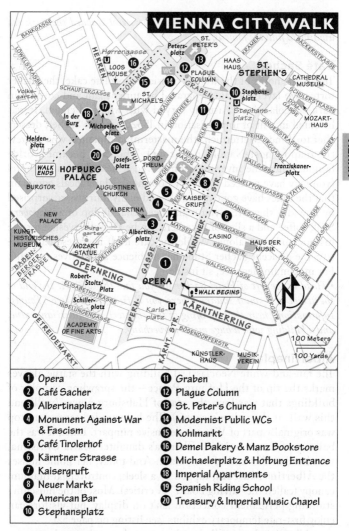

VIENNA CITY WALK

1. Opera
2. Café Sacher
3. Albertinaplatz
4. Monument Against War & Fascism
5. Café Tirolerhof
6. Kärntner Strasse
7. Kaisergruft
8. Neuer Markt
9. American Bar
10. Stephansplatz
11. Graben
12. Plague Column
13. St. Peter's Church
14. Modernist Public WCs
15. Kohlmarkt
16. Demel Bakery & Manz Bookstore
17. Michaelerplatz & Hofburg Entrance
18. Imperial Apartments
19. Spanish Riding School
20. Treasury & Imperial Music Chapel

Even if you're not, consider springing for an evening performance (standing-room tickets are surprisingly cheap; see "Experiences—Live Music" on page 70). Check the Wien Ticket kiosk in the booth on this square for information on this and other entertainment options during your visit.

The Opera marks a busy intersection in Vienna, where Kärntner Strasse meets the Ring. The Karlsplatz U-Bahn station in front of the Opera is actually a huge underground shopping mall with fast food, newsstands, lots of pickpockets, and even a Vienna Opera Toilet experience (€0.60, *mit Musik*).

• *Walk behind the Opera and across the street toward the dark red awning to find the famous...*

Café Sacher

This is the home of the world's classiest chocolate cake, the Sacher torte: two layers of cake separated by apricot jam and covered in dark-chocolate icing, usually served with whipped cream. It was invented in a fit of improvisation in 1832 by Franz Sacher, dessert chef to Prince Metternich (the mastermind diplomat who redrew the map of post-Napoleon Europe). The cake became world-famous when the inventor's son served it next door at his hotel (you may have noticed the fancy doormen). Many locals complain that the cakes have gone downhill, and many tourists are surprised by how dry they are—you really need that dollop of *Schlagobers*. Still, coffee and a slice of cake here can be €8 well invested for the historic ambience alone. While the café itself is grotesquely touristy, the adjacent Sacher Stube has ambience and natives to spare. For maximum elegance, sit inside.

• *Head to the left of Hotel Sacher (as you face the café). At the end of the street is a small square where you'll find the **TI** (see "Tourist Information," near the beginning of this chapter), an equestrian statue, and a building with a huge modern overhang.*

Albertinaplatz

The tan-and-white Neoclassical building with the statue alcoves marks the tip of the Hofburg Palace—the sprawling complex of buildings that was long the seat of Habsburg power (we'll end this walk at the palace's center). The balustraded terrace up top was originally part of Vienna's defensive rampart. Later, it was the balcony of Empress Maria Theresa's daughter Maria Christina, who lived at this end of the palace. And today, her home houses the **Albertina Museum,** topped by a sleek, controversial titanium canopy (called the "diving board" by critics). Most of the museum's stunning permanent collection isn't on display, but visitors can enjoy first-rate temporary exhibits (see listing on page 52).

Albertinaplatz is filled with statues that make up the powerful, thought-provoking **Monument Against War and Fascism,** which remembers the dark years when Austria came under Nazi rule (1938–1945).

The statue group has four parts. The split white monument, *The Gates of Violence,* remembers victims of all wars and violence. Standing directly in front of it, you're at the gates of a concentration camp. Step into a montage of wartime images: clubs and WWI gas masks, a dying woman birthing a future soldier, and chained slave laborers sitting on a pedestal of granite cut from the infamous quarry at Mauthausen Concentration Camp in the

Danube Valley. The hunched-over figure on the ground behind is a Jew forced to scrub anti-Nazi graffiti off a street with a toothbrush. The statue with its head buried in the stone is Orpheus entering the underworld, meant to remind Austrians (and the rest of us) of the victims of Nazism...and the consequences of not keeping our governments on track. Behind that, the 1945 declaration that established Austria's second republic—and enshrined human rights—is cut into the stone.

The experience gains emotional impact when you realize this monument stands on the spot where several hundred people were buried alive when the cellar they were hiding in was demolished during a WWII bombing attack (see photo to right of park, English description of memorial on the left).

Austria was led into World War II by Germany, which annexed the country in 1938, saying Austrians were wannabe Germans anyway. But Austrians are not Germans—never were, never will be. They're quick to tell you that while Austria was founded in the 10th century, Germany wasn't born until 1870. For seven years just before and during World War II (1938–1945), there was no Austria. In 1955, after 10 years of joint occupation by the victorious Allies, Austria regained total independence on the condition that it would be forever neutral (and never join NATO or the Warsaw Pact). To this day, Austria is outside of NATO (and Germany).

Behind the monument is **Café Tirolerhof,** a classic Viennese cafe full of things that time has passed by: chandeliers, marble tables, upholstered booths, waiters in tuxes, and newspapers. For more on Vienna's cafés, see "Vienna's Cafés," under "Experiences," later in this chapter.

• *From the café, turn right on Führichsgasse, passing the cafeteria-style Rosenberger Markt Restaurant (listed under "Eating," later in this chapter). Walk one block until you hit...*

Kärntner Strasse

This grand, mall-like street (traffic-free since 1974) is the people-watching delight of this in-love-with-life city. Today's Kärntner Strasse (KAYRNT-ner SHTRAH-seh) is mostly a crass commercial pedestrian mall—its famed elegant shops long gone. But locals know it's the same road Crusaders marched down as they headed off from St. Stephen's Cathedral for the Holy Land in the 12th century. Its name indicates that it leads south, toward the region of Kärnten (Carinthia, a province divided between Austria and Slovenia). Today it's full of shoppers and street musicians.

Where Führichsgasse meets Kärntner Strasse, note the city **Casino** (across the street and a half-block to your right, at #41)—once venerable, now tacky, it exemplifies the worst of the street's evolution. Turn left to head up Kärntner Strasse, going away from the Opera. As you walk along, be sure to look up, above the modern storefronts, for glimpses of the street's former glory. On the left at #26, **J & L Lobmeyr Crystal** ("Founded in 1823") still has its impressive brown storefront with gold trim, statues, and the Habsburg double-eagle. Inside, breathe in the classic Old World ambience as you climb up to the glass museum. In the market for some $400 napkin rings? Lobmeyr's your place.

• *At the end of the block, turn left on Marco d'Aviano Gasse to make a short detour to the square called Neuer Markt. Straight ahead is an orange-ish church with a triangular roof and cross, the Capuchin Church. In its basement is the...*

Kaisergruft

Under the church sits the Imperial Crypt, filled with what's left of Austria's emperors, empresses, and other Habsburg royalty. For centuries, Vienna was the heart of a vast empire ruled by the Habsburg family, and here is where they lie buried in their fancy coffins. You'll find all the Habsburg greats, including Maria Theresa, her son Josef II (Mozart's patron), Franz Josef, and "Sisi." Before moving on, consider paying your respects here (see listing on page 53).

Neuer Markt

In the center of Neuer Markt square is the **four rivers fountain** showing Lady Providence surrounded by figures symbolizing the rivers that flow into the Danube. The statues, originally nude, were replaced with more modest versions by Maria Teresa. The buildings all around you were rebuilt after World War II. Half of the city's inner center was intentionally destroyed by Churchill to demoralize the Viennese, who were disconcertingly enthusiastic about the Nazis.

• *Lady Providence's one bare breast points back to Kärntner Strasse (50 yards away). Before you head back to the busy shopping street, you could stop for a sweet treat at the heavenly Kurkonditorei Oberlaa (look for the vertical sign at the far corner of the square; see page 94). Leave the square by returning to Kärntner Strasse and turn left. Two blocks along, on the left, is the...*

American Bar

Over the door, the jutting American-flag sign (in red, white, and blue glass) is one of the few ornaments on this minimalist building. This is the first of several structures along this walk designed by the architect Adolf Loos (Vienna's answer to Frank Lloyd Wright). Inside it's dark, plush, and small, with great €8 cocktails (note that gawkers are discouraged in this still-hip bar).

• *Continue down Kärntner Strasse to the main square. As you approach the cathedral, you're likely to first see it as a reflection in the round-glass windows of the modern Haas Haus (described below). Pass the U-Bahn station (which has WCs), where the street spills into...*

Stephansplatz

The cathedral's massive spire looms overhead, worshippers and tourists pour inside the church, and shoppers and top-notch street entertainers buzz around the outside. You're at the center of Vienna.

The Gothic church (c. 1300–1450) is known for its 450-foot south tower, its colorful roof, and its place in Viennese history. When it was built, it was a huge church for what was then a tiny town, and it helped put the fledgling city on the map.

At this point, you may want to take a break from the walk to tour the church (see page 39). Even if you don't go inside, you can check out some of the exterior sights: the south tower, remnants of earlier churches (underground in the U-Bahn station, follow *Virgilkapelle* signs), the old facade, and World War II-era photos that show the destruction during the war (to the right of the church). If the weather's clear, consider heading up the cathedral's spire for the view over Vienna's rooftops (see "Climbing the South Tower," page 44).

Surrounding the church are buildings featuring centuries of architectural styles. Start at the cathedral and pan the square clockwise. To the right of the Gothic cathedral, the upper floors of the **International Building/Bank of Austria** have decorative Art Nouveau elements. Where Kärntner Strasse hits Stephansplatz (at #3), the **Equitable Building** (filled with lawyers, bankers, and insurance brokers) is a fine example of Neoclassicism from the turn of the 20th century. Look up and imagine how slick Vienna must have felt in 1900.

Facing St. Stephen's is the sleek concrete-and-glass **Haas Haus,** a postmodern building by noted Austrian architect Hans Hollein (finished in 1990). The curved facade is supposed to echo the Roman fortress of Vindobona (its ruins were found near here). The Viennese initially protested having this stark modern tower right next to their beloved cathedral, but since then, it's become a fixture of Vienna's main square. Notice how the smooth, rounded glass reflects St. Stephen's pointy architecture, providing a great photo opportunity. The café and pricey restaurant inside offer a nice perch, complete with a view of Stephansplatz below.

At the north end of the square is the (somewhat run-down) Modernist **J. F. Kennedy Haus,** named for the popular American president who came to Vienna for a summit hoping (but failing) to halt the construction of the Berlin Wall.

To the left of the church, the **Manner** store is known for its wafer cookies with the church logo. For a quick detour, turn right at the Manner store and walk past the touristy horse carts to the doorway at #6. This leads to a picturesque **lane** lined with shops and restaurants. Behind the church, a block away (but not worth the detour) is **Mozarthaus,** where the composer lived while writing the opera *The Marriage of Figaro.*

• *Exit the square with your back to the cathedral entrance. Walk past the Haas Haus, down the street called...*

Graben

This was once a *Graben,* or ditch—originally the moat for the Roman military camp. Back during Vienna's 19th-century heyday, there were nearly 200,000 people packed into the city's inner center (inside Ringstrasse), walking through dirt streets. Today this area houses 20,000. Graben was a busy street with three lanes of traffic until the 1970s, when it was turned into one of Europe's first pedestrian-only zones.

As you walk down Graben, you'll reach Dorotheergasse (two blocks on your left after leaving Stephansplatz), which leads to the **Dorotheum** auction house (consider poking your nose in here later for some fancy window-shopping—see page 55).

In the middle of this pedestrian zone is the extravagantly blobby **Holy Trinity plague column** *(Pestsäule).* The 70-foot pillar of clouds sprouts angels and cherubs, with the wonderfully gilded Father, Son, and Holy Ghost at the top.

In 1679, Vienna was hit by a massive epidemic of bubonic plague. Around 75,000 Viennese died—about a third of the city. Emperor Leopold I dropped to his knees (something emperors never did in public) and begged God to save the city. (Find Leopold about a quarter of the way up the monument. Hint: The typical inbreeding of royal families left him with a gaping underbite.) His prayer was heard by Lady Faith (the statue below Leopold, carrying a cross). With the help of a heartless little cupid, she tosses an old naked woman—symbolizing the plague—into the abyss and saves the city. In gratitude, Leopold vowed to erect this monument, which became a model for other cities ravaged by the same plague.

• *Just past the plague monument, look down the short street to the right, which frames a Baroque church with a stately green dome.*

St. Peter's Church

Leopold I also ordered this church to be built as a thank-you for surviving the 1679 plague. The church stands on the site of a much older church that may have been Vienna's first (or second) Christian church. Inside, St. Peter's shows Vienna at its Baroque best (see page 56).

• *Continue west on Graben, where you'll immediately find some stairs leading underground to two...*

Public WCs

In about 1900, a local chemical-maker needed a publicity stunt to prove that his chemicals really got things clean. He purchased two wine cellars under Graben and had Adolf Loos turn them into classy WCs in the Modernist style, complete with chandeliers and finely crafted mahogany (that's right—they're Loos' loos). The restrooms remain clean to this day—in fact, they're so inviting that they're used for poetry readings. Locals and tourists happily pay €0.50 for a quick visit.

• *Graben dead-ends at the aristocratic supermarket Julius Meinl am Graben (see page 94). From here, turn left. In the distance is the big green and gold dome of the Hofburg, where we'll end this walk. The street leading up to the Hofburg is...*

Kohlmarkt

This is Vienna's most elegant and unaffordable shopping street— Tiffany, Cartier, Giorgio Armani—with the emperor's palace at the end. Strolling Kohlmarkt, daydream about the edible window displays at **Demel** (#14, daily 10:00–19:00). Demel is the ultimate Viennese chocolate shop. The room is filled with Art Nouveau boxes of Empress Sisi's choco-dreams come true: *Kandierte Veilchen* (candied violet petals), *Katzenzungen* (cats' tongues), and so on. The cakes here are moist (compared to the dry Sacher tortes). The enticing window displays change monthly, reflecting current happenings in Vienna. Inside, an impressive cancan of cakes is displayed to tempt visitors into springing for the €10 cake-and-coffee deal (point to the cake you want). You can sit inside, with a view of the cake-making, or outside, with the street action. (Upstairs is less crowded.) Shops like this boast "K.u.K."—good enough for the *König und Kaiser* (king and emperor—same guy).

Next to Demel, the **Manz Bookstore** has a Loos-designed facade. Just beyond Demel and across the street, at #1152, you can pop in to a charming little Baroque **carriage courtyard,** with the surviving original carriage garages.

• *Kohlmarkt ends at the square called...*

Michaelerplatz

This square is dominated by the impressive facade of the Hofburg Palace. Opposite the facade, notice the modern **Loos House** (now a bank) built at about the same time as the palace's grandiose facade. In the center of this square, a scant bit of Roman Vienna lies exposed just beneath street level. On the left is the fancy Loden Plankl shop, with traditional Austrian formal wear. Next door (at #6), pop through the passageway to find a quiet courtyard with a big wooden carving of Jesus praying in Gethsemane. Across Augustinerstrasse, to the left of the Hofburg entrance, is the wing of the palace that houses the Spanish Riding School and its famous white Lipizzaner stallions (see page 54). Farther down this street lies Josefsplatz, with its Augustinian Church (see page 54), and at the end of the street, Albertinaplatz and the Opera (where we started this walk).

• *We'll finish up our tour where Austria's glorious history began—at the...*

Hofburg

This is the complex of palaces where the Habsburg emperors lived (except in summer, when they lived out at Schönbrunn Palace). Study the grand entry facade to the Hofburg Palace—it's Neo-Baroque from about 1900. The four heroic giants illustrate Hercules wrestling with his great challenges (much like the late-empire Habsburgs, I'm sure).

Enter the Hofburg through the gate, where you immediately find yourself beneath a big rotunda (the netting is there to keep birds from perching). The doorway on the right is the entrance to the **Imperial Apartments,** where the Habsburg emperors once lived in chandeliered elegance. Today you can tour its lavish rooms, as well as a museum on Empress Sisi, and a porcelain and silver collection (see page 45). To the left is the ticket office for the **Spanish Riding School** (see page 54).

Continuing on, you emerge from the rotunda into the main courtyard of the Hofburg, called **In der Burg.** The Caesar-like statue is of Habsburg Emperor Franz II (1768–1835), grandson of Maria Theresa, grandfather of Franz Josef, and father-in-law of Napoleon. Behind him is a tower with three kinds of clocks (the yellow disk shows the phase of the moon tonight). To the right of Franz are the Imperial Apartments, and to the left are the offices of Austria's mostly ceremonial president (the more powerful chancellor lives in a building just behind this courtyard).

Franz faces the oldest part of the palace. The colorful red, black, and gold gateway (behind you), which used to have a drawbridge, leads to the 13th-century Swiss Court (Schweizerhof), named for the Swiss mercenary guards once stationed there. Here you'll find the **Treasury** (Schatzkammer) and the **Imperial Music Chapel** (Hofmusikkapelle, see "Experiences—Live Music," later in this chapter) where the Boys' Choir sings the Mass.

Back at In der Burg, face Franz and turn left, passing through the **tunnel,** with a few tourist shops and restaurants (see page 45).

The tunnel spills out into spacious **Heldenplatz** (Heroes'

Square). On the left is the impressive curved facade of the **New Palace** (Neue Burg). This vast wing was built in the early 1900s to be the new Habsburg living quarters (and was meant to have a matching building facing it). But in 1914, the heir-to-the-throne Archduke Franz Ferdinand—while waiting politely for his long-lived uncle, Emperor Franz Josef, to die—was assassinated in Sarajevo. The archduke's death sparked World War I and the eventual end of eight centuries of Habsburg rule.

This impressive building saw even sadder days a few decades later, when Adolf Hitler addressed adoring throngs from the New Palace balcony in 1938, after Austria was annexed.

Inside the building nowadays are the **New Palace Museums,** an eclectic collection of weaponry, suits of armor, musical instruments, and ancient Greek statues (listed on page 52). The two equestrian statues are Prince Eugene of Savoy (1663–1736), who battled the Ottoman Turks, and Archduke Charles (1771–1847), who battled Napoleon. Eugene gazes to the far distance at the prickly Neo-Gothic spires of Vienna's City Hall.

The Hofburg's **Burggarten** (with the much-photographed Mozart statue) is not visible from here, but it's just behind the New Palace. If you were to continue on through the Greek-columned passageway (the Äussere Burgtor), you'd reach the Ringstrasse, the Kunsthistorisches Museum (see page 57), and the MuseumsQuartier (see page 60).

Walk Over
You're in the heart of Viennese sightseeing. The Hofburg contains some of Vienna's best sights and museums. From the Opera to the Hofburg, from chocolate to churches, from St. Stephen's to Sacher torte—Vienna waits for you.

Sights

The sights listed below are arranged by neighborhood for handy sightseeing.

Inside the Ring
▲▲▲**St. Stephen's Cathedral (Stephansdom)**—This massive church is the Gothic needle around which Vienna spins. According to the medieval vision of its creators, it stands like a giant jeweled reliquary, offering praise to God from the center of the city. The church and its towers, especially the 450-foot south tower, give the city its most iconic image. (Check your pockets for 10-cent euro coins; ones minted in Austria feature the south tower on the back.) The cathedral has survived Vienna's many wars and today symbolizes the city's freedom.

VIENNA

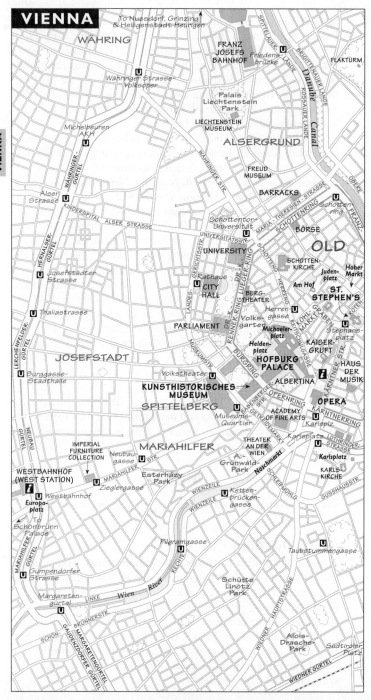

VIENNA

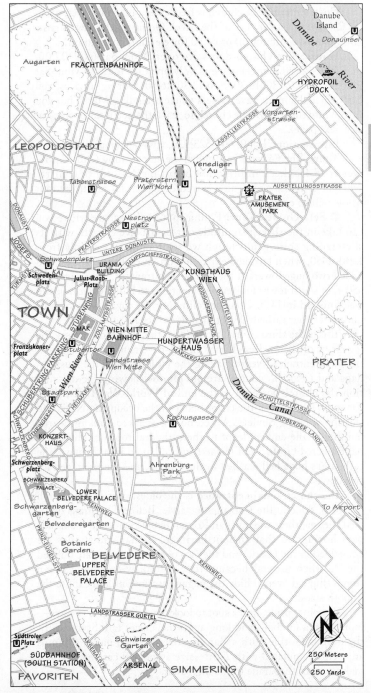

Danube Island

Danube River

Donauinsel

Augarten

FRACHTENBAHNHOF

HYDROFOIL DOCK

LEOPOLDSTADT

LASSALLESTRASSE

Vorgarten-strasse

Taborstrasse

Praterstern Wien Nord

Venediger Au

AUSSTELLUNGSSTRASSE

PRATER AMUSEMENT PARK

PRATERSTRASSE

Nestroy-platz

UNTERE DONAUSTR.

DONAUSTR.

JOSEFS-

Schwedenplatz

URANIA BUILDING

KAI

Schweden-platz

Julius-Raab-Platz

DAMPFSCHIFFSTRASSE

KUNSTHAUS WIEN

WEISSGERBERLÄNDE

SCHÜTTELSTR.

TURIST.

TOWN

STUBENRING

MAK

WIEN MITTE BAHNHOF

HUNDERTWASSER HAUS

Franziskaner-platz

SCHUBERTRING PARKRING

V. ZOLLAMTSSTRASSE

Stubentor

Landstrasse Wien Mitte

MARXERGASSE

PRATER

Wien River

Stadtpark

AM HEUMARKT

Danube Canal

SCHÜTTELSTRASSE

ERDBERGER LÄNDE

SCHWARZENBERG-PLATZ

LOTHRINGERSTR.

Rochusgasse

KONZERT-HAUS

Schwarzenberg-platz

Ahrenburg-Park

SCHWARZENBERG PALACE

LOWER BELVEDERE PALACE

RENNWEG

Schwarzenberg-garten

Belvederegarten

To Airport

Botanic Garden

PRINZ-EUGEN-STR.

BELVEDERE

UPPER BELVEDERE PALACE

RENNWEG

LANDSTRASSER GÜRTEL

Südtiroler Platz

Schweizer Garten

ARSENALSTR.

SÜDBAHNHOF (SOUTH STATION)

ARSENAL

SIMMERING

FAVORITEN

N

250 Meters

250 Yards

Cost: Entering the church is free (except July–mid-Oct, when it's €3 to get past the rear of the nave). Going up the towers costs €3 (by stairs, south tower) or €4.50 (by elevator, north tower).

Hours: The church doors are open Mon–Sat 6:00–22:00, Sun 7:00–22:00, but the nave is only open for tourists Mon–Sat 9:00–11:30 & 13:30–16:30, Sun 13:30–16:30. During services, you can't enter the main nave (unless you're attending Mass), but you can go into the back of the church to reach the north tower elevator (see next page).

Information: Tel. 01/515-523-526, www.stephanskirche.at.

Tours: The €4 tours in English are entertaining (daily April–Oct at 15:45, check information board inside entry to confirm schedule). The €2 audioguide is well done, but for most, the tour below will be enough.

❍ Self-Guided Tour: Find a spot in the square where you can take in the sheer magnitude of this massive church, with its skyscraping spire. The church we see today dates mainly from 1300–1450, when builders expanded on an earlier structure and added two huge towers at the end of each transept. The impressive 450-foot south tower took two generations to build (65 years), and was finished in 1433. Consider climbing the tower now, or wait until after your cathedral visit (details at the end of this tour).

This is the third church to stand on this spot. You can see the footprint of the **earlier church** in the pavement, to the right of the main entrance. Nearby (along the building with the Austrian flags and *Churhaus* plaque) are **old photos** showing the destruction the church suffered at the end of World War II. In 1945, Vienna was caught in the chaos between the occupying Nazis and the approaching Soviets. Allied bombs sparked fires in nearby buildings. The embers leapt to the cathedral rooftop. The original timbered Gothic roof burned and collapsed into the nave, the cathedral's huge bell crashed to the ground, and the fire raged for two days.

The church's **main entrance** is the oldest part of the church (c. 1240), done in the Romanesque style. Before Christians occupied Vienna, there was a pagan Roman temple here, and the facade pays homage to that ancient heritage. Roman-era statues are embedded in the facade, and the two octagonal towers are dubbed the "heathen towers" because they're built with a few Roman stones (flipped over to hide the pagan inscriptions and expose the smooth sides).

Stepping inside, find a spot to look down the immense **nave**—more than a football field long and nine stories tall. Stylistically, the nave is Gothic with a Baroque overlay. The nave's columns are richly populated with 77 life-size stone and ceramic statues, making a saintly parade to the high altar.

Start down the nave toward the altar. At the second pillar on the left is the Gothic sandstone **pulpit** (c. 1515), a masterpiece carved from three separate blocks (see if you can find the seams). The pulpit is as crammed with religious meaning as it is with beautifully realistic carvings. The top of the stairway's railing swarms with lizards as animals of light, and toads as animals of darkness. The "Dog of the Lord" stands at the top, making sure none of those toads pollutes the sermon. Below the toads, wheels with three parts (the Trinity) roll up, while wheels with four spokes (the four seasons, symbolizing mortal life) roll down.

Find the guy peeking out from under the stairs. This may be a self-portrait of the artist. In medieval times, art was done for the glory of God, and artists worked anonymously. But this pulpit was carved as humanist Renaissance ideals were creeping in from Italy—and individual artists were becoming famous. So the artist included what may be a rare self-portrait bust in his work. He leans out from a window, sculptor's compass in hand, to observe the world and his work.

During World War II, many of the city's top art treasures were hidden safely in cellars and salt mines—hidden by both the Nazi occupiers (to protect against war damage) and by citizens (to protect against Nazi looters). The **stained-glass windows** behind the high altar were meticulously dismantled and packed away. The pulpit was encased in a shell of brick. As the war was drawing to a close, it appeared St. Stephen's would escape major damage. But as the Nazis were fleeing, the bitter Nazi commander in charge of the city ordered that the church be destroyed. Fortunately, his underlings disobeyed. Unfortunately, the church accidentally caught fire during Allied bombing shortly thereafter, and the roof collapsed. Among the other losses, the nave's precious stained-glass windows were blown out in the big fire, and had to be replaced with lesser-quality, Tupperware-colored glass. Before the fire, the entire church was lit with windows like the richly colored ones behind the altar.

Ascending the North Tower: This tower, reached from inside the church (look for the *Aufzug zur Pummerin* sign), holds the famous "Pummerin" bell and is easier to ascend than the south tower (see next page), but it's much shorter and not as exciting, with lesser views (no stairs, elevator-€4.50, daily July–Aug 8:30–18:00, April–June and Sept–Oct 8:30–17:30, Nov–March 8:30–17:00, last elevator ascends 20 min before closing, entrance on the left side of the nave). The Pummerin is supposedly the second biggest bell in the world that rings by swinging. A physical symbol of victory over the Ottoman Turks in 1683, it was cast from cannons (and cannon balls) captured from the Ottomans when Vienna was liberated from the siege. During the WWII fire that damaged the church, the Pummerin fell to the ground and cracked. It had to be melted down and recast. These days, locals know the Pummerin as the bell that rings in the Austrian New Year.

Climbing the South Tower: The iconic south tower offers a far better view than the north one, but you'll earn it by climbing 343 tightly wound steps up the spiral staircase (€3, daily 9:00–17:30, this hike burns about one Sacher torte of calories). To reach the entrance, exit the church and make a U-turn to the left. Note: If the top is still surrounded by scaffolding on your visit, views may be obscured. This tower, once key to the city's defense as a lookout point, is still dear to Viennese hearts. (It's long been affectionately nicknamed "Steffl," Viennese for "Stevie.") No church spire in (what was) the Austro-Hungarian Empire is taller—by Habsburg decree. From the top, use your city map to locate the famous sights.

▲▲▲Opera (Staatsoper)—The Opera, facing the Ring and near the TI, is a central point for any visitor. Vienna remains one of the world's great cities for classical music, and this building still belts out some of the finest opera, both classic and cutting-edge. While the critical reception of the building 130 years ago led the architect to commit suicide, and though it's been rebuilt since its destruction by WWII bombs, it's still a sumptuous place. The interior has a chandeliered lobby and carpeted staircases perfect for making the scene. The theater itself features five wrap-around balconies, gold and red decor, and a bracelet-like chandelier.

Depending on your level of tolerance for opera, you can: simply admire the Neo-Renaissance building from the outside; take a guided tour of the lavish interior; visit the Opera Museum; or attend a performance.

Tours: Unless you're attending a performance, you can enter the Opera only with a guided 50-minute tour, offered nearly daily in English (€6.50; generally July–Aug at 11:00, 13:00, 14:00, 15:00, and often at 10:00 and 16:00; Sept–June fewer tours, afternoons only; tel. 01/514-442-624). Tour times are often changed or cancelled due to rehearsals and performances. The opera posts a monthly schedule (blue, on the wall), but the more accurate schedule is the daily listing (red, posted on the door on the Operngasse side of building, farthest from St. Stephen's Cathedral). Tour tickets include the tiny and disappointing Opera Museum (across the street toward the Hofburg), except on Monday, when the museum is closed.

Opera Museum: New and included in your opera tour ticket (whether you like it or not), the Opera Museum is a let-down, with descriptions only in German and rotating six-month-long special exhibits (€3, or included in the €6.50 tour ticket, Tue–Sun 10:00–18:00, closed Mon, a block away from the Opera, near Albertina Museum, tel. 01/514-442-100).

For information on attending a performance, see "Experiences—Live Music," later in this chapter.

Habsburg Sights in and near the Hofburg Palace

The complex, confusing, and imposing Imperial Palace, with 640 years of architecture, demands your attention. This first Habsburg residence grew with the family empire from the 13th century until 1913, when the last "new wing" opened. The winter residence of the Habsburg rulers until 1918, it's still the home of the Spanish Riding School, the Vienna Boys' Choir, the Austrian president's office, 5,000 government workers, and several important museums. For an overview of the palace layout, see the next page. Don't get confused by the Hofburg's myriad courtyards and many museums. Focus on three sights: the Imperial Apartments, Treasury, and the museums at the New Palace (Neue Burg).

The section below also covers Habsburg sights located near—but not actually inside—the Hofburg (including the Albertina Museum, Kaisergruft, and Augustinian Church).

Eating at the Hofburg: Down the tunnel to Heroes' Square is a tiny but handy sandwich bar called **Hofburg Stüberl** (same €2.50 sandwich price whether you sit or go, Mon–Fri 7:00–18:00, Sat–Sun 10:00–16:00). For a cheap, quick meal, duck into **Restaurant zum Alten Hofkeller** in a cellar under the palace (€5 plates, Mon–Fri 7:30–14:30, closed Sat–Sun and in Aug, cafeteria-style, mod and efficient, Schauflergasse 7).

▲▲▲**Imperial Apartments (Kaiserappartements)**—These lavish, Versailles-type, "wish-I-were-God" royal rooms are the downtown version of the grander Schönbrunn Palace. If you're rushed and have time for only one palace, do this. Palace visits are a one-way romp through three sections: the luxurious Imperial Apartments themselves, the Sisi Museum dedicated to the troubled Empress, and a porcelain and silver collection.

The Imperial Apartments are a mix of Old World luxury and modern 19th-century convenience. See the lavish, Versailles-like rooms that were home to the hardworking Emperor Franz Josef I and his reclusive, eccentric Empress, known as "Sisi." From here, the emperor struggled to control his vast empire, seemingly oblivious to how the world was changing around them. Franz Josef was (for all intents and purposes) the last of the Habsburg monarchs, and these apartments straddle the transition from old to new. You'll see chandeliered luxury alongside office furniture and electric lights.

Cost, Hours, Location: €10, includes well-done audioguide, daily July–Aug 9:00–18:00, Sept–June 9:00–17:00, last entry 30 min before closing, enter from courtyard through St. Michael's Gate—just off Michaelerplatz, tel. 01/533-7570, www.hofburg -wien.at.

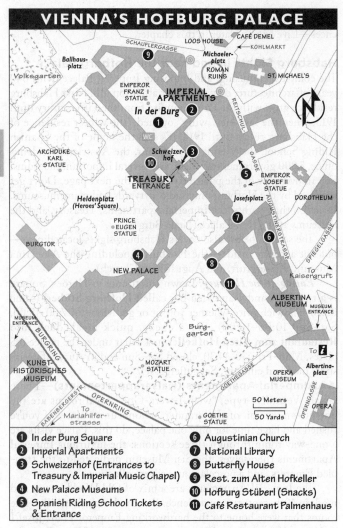

VIENNA'S HOFBURG PALACE

1. In der Burg Square
2. Imperial Apartments
3. Schweizerhof (Entrances to Treasury & Imperial Music Chapel)
4. New Palace Museums
5. Spanish Riding School Tickets & Entrance
6. Augustinian Church
7. National Library
8. Butterfly House
9. Rest. zum Alten Hofkeller
10. Hofburg Stüberl (Snacks)
11. Café Restaurant Palmenhaus

◆ Self-Guided Tour: Your visit (and the excellent audio-guide) starts on the ground floor, with the Habsburg court's vast tableware collection, which the audioguide actually manages to make fairly interesting. Browse the collection to gawk at the opulence and to take in some colorful Habsburg trivia (who'd have thunk that the court had an official way to fold a napkin—and that the technique remains a closely guarded secret?).

Once you're through all those rooms of dishes, climb the stairs—the same staircase used by the emperors and empresses who lived here. At the top is a timeline of Sisi's life. Pass through the turnstile, consider the WC, and enter the room with the **model of the Hofburg.** Circle to the far side to find where you're standing right now, near the smallest of the Hofburg's three domes.

The Hofburg was the epicenter of one of Europe's great political powers. Six hundred years of Habsburgs lived here in the winter and at Schönbrunn Palace in the heat of summer. The Hofburg started as a 13th-century medieval castle (near where you are right now) and expanded over the centuries to today's 240,000-square-meter (60-acre) complex, now owned by the state.

To the left of the dome (as you face the facade) is the steeple of the Augustiner church. It was there, in 1854, that Franz Josef married 16-year-old Elisabeth of Bavaria, and their story began.

Sisi Museum: Empress Elisabeth, known as "Sisi" (SEE-see) since childhood, became an instant celebrity upon her marriage to Franz Josef. She was the 19th-century equivalent of Princess Diana—her beauty, fabulous but unhappy life, and tragic death helped create her larger-than-life legacy. However, her importance is often inflated by melodramatic accounts of her life; this museum seeks to tell a more accurate story. The exhibit starts where her life ended and her legend began (see her death mask, and pictures of her funeral procession). You'll read bits of her poetic writing, see exact copies of her now-lost jewelry, and learn about her escapes, dieting mania, and chocolate bills. Admire Sisi's hard-earned thin waist (20 inches at age 16, 21 inches at age 50...after giving birth to four children). The black statue in the dark room represents the empress after the suicide of her son—aloof, thin, in black, with her back to the world. At the end, ponder the crude knife that killed Sisi. In 1898, while visiting Geneva, Switzerland, she was murdered by an Italian anarchist.

Imperial Apartments—Emperor's Rooms: After the Sisi Museum, a one-way route takes you through a series of royal rooms. The first room—as if to make clear that there was more to the Habsburgs than Sisi—shows a family tree tracing the Habsburgs from 1273 to their messy WWI demise. From here, you enter the private apartments of the royal family (Franz Josef's first, then Sisi's). These were the private apartments and public meeting rooms for the emperor and empress. Franz Josef I lived here from 1857 until his death in 1916. (He had hoped to move to new digs in the New Palace, but that was not finished until after his death.)

Franz Josef was the last great Habsburg ruler. In these rooms, he presided over defeats and liberal inroads, as the world was changing and the monarchy became obsolete. Here he met with advisors and welcomed foreign dignitaries, hosted lavish, white-gloved balls and stuffy formal dinners, and raised three children. He slept (alone) on his austere bed while his beloved wife Sisi retreated to her own rooms. He suffered through the assassination of his brother, the suicide of his son and heir, the murder of his wife, and the assassination of his nephew, Archduke Ferdinand, which sparked World War I and spelled the end of the Habsburg monarchy.

In the **waiting room for the Audience Room,** mannequins from the many corners of the Habsburg realm illustrate the multi-ethnic nature of the vast empire. (Also see the map of the empire, by the window.) Every citizen had the right to meet privately with the emperor, and people traveled fairly far to do so. While they waited nervously, they had these three huge paintings to stare at—propaganda showing crowds of commoners enthusiastic about their Habsburg rulers.

The **Audience Room** is where Franz Josef received commoners from around the empire. They came from far and wide to show gratitude or to make a request. Imagine you've traveled for days to have your say before the emperor. You're wearing your new fancy suit—Franz Josef required that men coming before him wear a tailcoat, women a black gown with a train. You've rehearsed what you want to say. You hope your hair looks good.

Suddenly, you're face-to-face with the emp himself. (The portrait on the easel shows Franz Josef in 1915, when he was more than 80 years old.) Despite your efforts, you probably weren't in this room long. He'd stand at the high table (far left) as the visiting commoners had their say. (Standing kept things moving.) You'd hear a brief response from him (quite likely the same he'd given all day), and then you'd back out of the room while bowing (also required). On the table, you can read a partial list of 56 appointments he had on January 3, 1910 (three columns: family name, meeting topic, and *Anmerkung*—the emperor's "action log").

In the **conference room,** the emperor presided over the equivalent of cabinet meetings. An ongoing topic was what to do with unruly Hungary. After 1867, Franz Josef granted Hungary a measure of independence (thus creating the "Austro-Hungarian Empire"). Hungarian diplomats attended meetings here, watched over by paintings on the wall showing Austria's army suppressing the popular Hungarian uprising...subtle.

Next, Franz Josef's **study** evokes how seriously the emperor took his responsibilities as the top official of a vast empire. The walls between the rooms are wide enough to hide servants' corridors (the hidden door to his valet's room is in the back left corner).

Moving on to the emperor's **bedroom,** note his famously no-frills iron bed. He typically rose at 3:30, and started his day in prayer, kneeling at the prayer stool against the far wall. While he had a typical emperor's share of mistresses, his dresser was always well-stocked with photos of Sisi.

The **Large Salon** was for royal family gatherings, and went unused after Sisi's death. The **Small Salon,** used as a smoking room (no women allowed), is dedicated to the memory of Franz Josef's brother (see the bearded portrait), the Emperor Maximilian of Mexico, who was assassinated in 1867. After the birth of their last child in 1868, Franz Josef and his wife Sisi began to drift farther apart. Left of the door is a small button the emperor had to buzz before entering his estranged wife's quarters. You, however, can go right in.

Imperial Apartments—Empress' Rooms: Sisi's **bedroom/ drawing room** was refurbished in the Neo-Rococo style in 1854. There's the red carpet, covered with oriental rugs. Sisi kept this room filled with fresh flowers. She not only slept here, but also lived here—the bed was rolled in and out daily—until her death in 1898.

Next comes Sisi's **dressing/exercise room.** Servants worked three hours a day on Sisi's famous hair, while she passed the time reading. She'd exercise on the wooden structure and on the rings suspended from the doorway to the left. Afterward, she'd get a massage on the red-covered bed.

Detour into the behind-the-scenes palace. In the narrow passageway, you'll walk by Sisi's hand-painted porcelain, dolphin-head WC (on the right). In the main **bathroom,** you'll see her huge copper tub (with the original wall coverings behind it) where servants washed her hair—an all-day affair. Sisi was the first Habsburg to have running water in her bathroom (notice the hot and cold faucets).

Next, enter the **servants' quarters,** with hand-painted tropical scenes. Take time to enjoy the playful details. As you leave these rooms and re-enter the imperial world, look back to the room on the left.

The empress' **Great Salon** is painted with Mediterranean escapes, the 19th-century equivalent of travel posters. A print shows how Franz Josef and Sisi would—on their good days—share breakfast in this room.

The portrait in the **Small Salon** is of Crown Prince Rudolf, Franz Josef and Sisi's only son. On the morning of January 30, 1889, 30-year-old Rudolf and a beautiful baroness were found shot dead in his hunting lodge in Mayerling. An investigation never came up with a complete explanation, but Rudolf had obviously been cheating on his wife, and the affair ended in an apparent murder-suicide. The scandal shocked the empire and tainted the Habsburgs, Sisi retreated further into her fantasy world, and Franz Josef carried on stoically with a broken heart.

Alexander Apartments: Leaving Sisi's wing, turn the corner into the white-and-gold rooms, used for formal occasions and public functions. In the **Red Salon,** the Gobelin wall hangings were a 1776 gift from Marie-Antoinette and Louis XVI in Paris to their Viennese counterparts.

The tour ends in the **dining room.** It's dinnertime, and Franz Josef has called his extended family together. The settings are modest...just silver. Gold was saved for formal state dinners. Next to each name card was a menu naming the chef responsible for each dish. (Talk about pressure.) While the Hofburg had tableware for 4,000, feeding 3,000 was a typical day. The cellar was stocked with 60,000 bottles of wine. The kitchen was huge—50 birds could be roasted on the hand-driven spits at once.

The emperor sat in the center of the long table. "Ladies and gentlemen" alternated in the seating. Franz Josef enforced strict protocol at mealtime: No one could speak without being spoken to by the emperor, and no one could eat after he was done. While the rest of Europe was growing democracy and expanding personal freedoms, the Habsburgs preserved their ossified worldview to the bitter end.

In 1918, World War I ended, Austria was created as a modern nation-state, the Habsburgs were tossed out...and the Hofburg Palace was destined to become a museum.

▲▲▲**Hofburg Treasury (Weltliche und Geistliche Schatz-kammer)**—This "Secular and Religious Treasure Room" contains the best jewels on the Continent. Slip through the vault doors and reflect on the glitter of 21 rooms filled with scepters, swords, crowns, orbs, weighty robes, double-headed eagles, gowns, gem-studded bangles, and a unicorn horn. Not only are the objects beautiful, they're also historic—some crowns and scepters date back to the time of Charlemagne.

Cost, Hours, Information: €10, €18 combo-ticket with Kunsthistorisches Museum, Wed–Mon 10:00–18:00, closed Tue; from the Hofburg's central courtyard, follow *Schatzkammer* signs to the Schweizerhof; tel. 01/525-240, www.khm.at. While no English descriptions are provided within the Treasury, the well-produced, €3 audioguide provides a wealth of information and is worth renting.

❍ Self-Guided Tour: Here's a rundown of the highlights (the audioguide is much more complete).

Room 2: The personal crown of Rudolf II has survived since 1602—it was considered too well-crafted to cannibalize for other crowns. It's a big deal because it's the adopted crown of the Austrian Empire, established in 1806 after Napoleon dissolved the Holy Roman Empire (an alliance of Germanic kingdoms so named because it wanted to be considered the continuation of the Roman Empire). Pressured by Napoleon, the Austrian Francis II—who had been Holy Roman Emperor—became Francis I, Emperor of

Austria (the stern guy on the wall, near where you entered). Look at the crown. Its design symbolically merges the typical medieval king's crown and a bishop's miter.

Rooms 3 and 4: These rooms contain some of the coronation vestments and regalia needed for the new Austrian (not Holy Roman) emperor. There was a different one for each of the emperor's subsidiary titles, e.g., King of Hungary or King of Lombardy. So many crowns and kingdoms in the Habsburg's vast empire!

Room 5: Ponder the Cradle of the King of Rome, once occupied by Napoleon's son, who was born in 1811 and made King of Rome. While pledging allegiance to democracy, Napoleon in fact crowned himself Emperor of France and hobnobbed with Europe's royalty. When his wife Josephine could not bear him a male heir, Napoleon divorced her and married into the Habsburg family. With the birth of the baby King of Rome, Napoleon and Marie Louise (Franz I/II's daughter) were poised to start a new dynasty of European rulers...but then Napoleon met his Waterloo, and the Habsburgs remained in power.

Room 7: These jewels are the true "treasures," a cabinet of wonders used by Habsburgs to impress their relatives (or to hock when funds got low).

Room 8: The eight-foot-tall, 500-year-old "unicorn horn" (a narwhal tusk), was considered to have magical healing powers bestowed from on high. This one was owned by the Holy Roman Emperor—clearly a divine monarch.

Room 10: The next few rooms contain some of the oldest and most venerated objects in the Treasury—the robes, crowns, and sacred objects of the Holy Roman Emperor.

Room 11: The collection's highlight is the 10th-century **crown of the Holy Roman Emperor.** It was probably made for the first king to call himself Holy Roman Emperor, Otto I (c. 960). The Imperial Crown swirls with symbolism "proving" that the emperor was both holy and Roman: The cross on top says the HRE ruled as Christ's representative on earth, and the jeweled arch over the top is reminiscent of the parade helmet of ancient Romans. The crown's eight sides represent the celestial city of Jerusalem's eight gates. The jewels on the front panel symbolize the 12 apostles. Imagine the impression this priceless, glittering crown must have made on the emperor's medieval subjects.

The nearby 11th-century **Imperial Cross** preceded the emperor in ceremonies. Encrusted with jewels, it had a hollow compartment (its core is wood) that carried substantial chunks thought to be from *the* **cross** and *the* **Holy Lance** used to pierce the side of Jesus when he was crucified (both pieces are displayed in the same glass case). Holy Roman Emperors actually carried the lance into battle in the 10th century. Look behind the cross to see how it was a box that could be clipped open and shut, used for holding holy relics. You can see bits of the "true cross" anywhere, but this is a prime piece—with the actual nail hole.

Another glass case contains objects that may have belonged to Charlemagne (a.k.a. Karl der Grosse). On the wall nearby, the **tall painting** depicts Charlemagne modeling the Imperial Crown—although the crown was actually made a hundred years after he died.

Room 12: Now picture all this regalia used together. The painting shows the coronation of Maria Theresa's son Josef II as Holy Roman Emperor in 1764. Set in a church in Frankfurt (filled with the bigwigs—literally—of the day), Josef is wearing the same crown and royal garb that you've just seen.

Room 16: This last room contains the **royal vestments** (15th century), which display perhaps the most exquisite workmanship in the entire Treasury. Look closely—they're "painted" with gold and silver threads. But after seeing so much bling, by the time you view these vestments, they can seem downright understated—just another example of the pomp and circumstance of the majestic Habsburgs.

▲▲**Hofburg New Palace Museums: Armor, Music, and Ancient Greek Statues**—The New Palace (Neue Burg) houses three separate collections, all included in a single ticket price—an armory (with a killer collection of medieval weapons), historical musical instruments, and classical statuary from ancient Ephesus (in modern-day Turkey). The included audioguide brings the exhibits to life and lets you actually hear the collection's fascinating old instruments being played. An added bonus is the chance to wander alone among the royal Habsburg halls, stairways, and painted ceilings (€8, Wed–Mon 10:00–18:00, closed Tue, last entry 30 min before closing, almost no tourists, tel. 01/525-240, www.khm.at).

▲▲**Albertina Museum**—This building, at the southern tip of the Hofburg complex (near the Opera), was the residence of Maria Teresa's favorite daughter: Maria Christina, who was the only one allowed to marry for love rather than political strategy. Her many sisters were jealous. (Marie-Antoinette had to marry the French king...and lost her head over it.) Maria Christina's husband, Albert of Saxony, was a great collector of original drawings, and amassed an enormous assortment of works by Dürer, Rembrandt, Rubens, Schiele, and others. Today, reproductions of some of these works hang in the Albertina's elegant French Classicist–style state rooms *(Prunkräume)*. Head here first—this offers a great opportunity to wander freely under the chandeliers of a Habsburg palace, unconstrained by velvet ropes. Then browse the modern galleries, which hold a rotating exhibit from the museum's Batliner collection of modern art (with minor works by major artists—Monet, Picasso,

Chagall, Matisse), along with temporary exhibits. Though the entry fee is a bit steep, the Albertina's temporary exhibits are often top-notch—if you're unsure whether it's worth the admission fee, check flyers and posters around town to see what's on.

Cost, Hours, Location: €9.50, price can vary based on special exhibits, audioguide-€4, daily 10:00–18:00, Wed until 21:00, over-looking Albertinaplatz across from the TI and Opera, tel. 01/534-830, www.albertina.at.

▲▲**Kaisergruft, the Remains of the Habsburgs**—Visiting the imperial remains is not as easy as you might imagine. These original organ donors left their bodies—about 150 in all—in the unassuming Kaisergruft (the Imperial Crypt at the Capuchin Church), their hearts in the Augustinian Church (described next page; church open long hours daily), and their entrails in the crypt below St. Stephen's Cathedral. Don't tripe.

Cost, Hours, Location: €4, daily 10:00–18:00, last entry at 17:40, behind the Opera on Neuer Markt, tel. 01/512-6853. As you enter, be sure to buy the €0.50 map with a Habsburg family tree and a chart locating each coffin.

Highlights: The double coffin of **Maria Theresa** (1717–1780) and her husband, **Franz I** (1708–1765), is worth a close look for its artwork. Maria Theresa outlived her husband by 15 years—which she spent in mourning. Old and fat, she installed a special lift enabling her to get down into the crypt to be with her dear, departed Franz (even though he had been far from faithful). The couple recline—Etruscan-style—atop their fancy lead coffin. At each corner are the crowns of the Habsburgs—the Holy Roman Empire, Hungary, Bohemia, and Jerusalem. Notice the contrast between the Rococo splendor of Maria Theresa's tomb and the simple box holding her more modest son, **Josef II** (at his parents' feet).

Franz Josef (1830–1916) is nearby, in an appropriately austere military tomb. Flanking Franz Josef are the tombs of his son, the archduke **Rudolf,** and Empress Elisabeth. Rudolf and his teen-age mistress supposedly committed suicide together in 1889 at Mayerling hunting lodge and—since the Church figured he forced her and was therefore a murderer—it took considerable legal hair-splitting to win Rudolf this spot (after examining his brain, it was determined that he was mentally disabled and therefore incapable of knowingly killing himself and his girl). *Kaiserin* Elisabeth (1837–1898), a.k.a. **Sisi,** always gets the "Most Flowers" award.

In front of those three are the two most recent Habsburg tombs. **Empress Zita** was laid to rest here in 1989, followed by her son, **Karl Ludwig,** in 2007. The funeral procession for Ludwig, the fourth son of the last Austrian emperor, was probably the last such Old Regime event in European history. The monarchy died hard in Austria. Today there are about 700 living Habsburg royals, mostly living in exile. When they die, they get buried in their countries of exile.

Body parts and ornate tombs aside, the real legacy of the Habsburgs is the magnificence of this city. Step outside. Pan up. Watch the clouds glide by the ornate gables of Vienna.

▲Spanish Riding School and Lipizzaner Stallions—While the famous court horses of the Habsburg emperors were originally from Spain, by the 16th century they were moved closer to Vienna (to the Slovenian town of Lipica, then part of the Habsburg Empire). For four centuries, the "Lipizzaner stallions" have been bred, raised, and trained in Lipica. They actually have "surnames" that can be traced to the original six 16th-century stallions that made the trip from Spain.

The dressage movements of the stallions originated as battle moves, and include the *pirouette* (quick turns for surviving in the thick of battle), *levade* (rearing on hind legs, to make a living shield for the knight), and the *capriole* (a strong back-kick that could floor any enemy). After tanks replaced horses on the battlefield, these equestrian military moves morphed to court entertainment. Lipizzaner fans have a warm spot in their hearts for US General George Patton. At the end of World War II—knowing that the Soviets were about to take control of Vienna—he ordered a raid on the stables to save the horses and ensure the survival of their fine old bloodlines.

Seats for performances book up months in advance, but standing room is sometimes available the same day (tickets-€35–165, standing room-€20–28, March–June and Sept–Dec Sun at 11:00 and either Sat at 11:00 or Fri at 19:00, no shows July–Aug, fewer Feb, none in Jan, tel. 01/533-9031, www.srs.at). Luckily for the masses, training sessions with music in a chandeliered Baroque hall are open to the public (€12 at the door, roughly March–June and mid-Aug–Dec Tue–Sat 10:00–12:00—but only when the horses are in town).

Tourists line up early at Josefsplatz (the large courtyard between Michaelerplatz and Albertinaplatz), at the door marked *Spanische Hofreitschule*. If you want to hang out with tour groups, get there early and wait for the doors to open at 10:00. Better yet, simply show up late. Almost no one stays for the full two hours—except for the horses. As people leave, new tickets are printed continuously, so you can just prance in with no wait at all. Don't have high expectations, as the horses often do little more than trot and warm up.

▲Augustinian Church (Augustinerkirche)—This is the Gothic and Neo-Gothic church where the Habsburgs latched, then buried, their hearts (weddings took place here, and the royal hearts are in the vault). Don't miss the exquisite, tomb-like Canova memorial (Neoclassical, 1805) to Maria Theresa's favorite daughter, Maria Christina, with its incredibly sad white-marble procession. The church's 11:00 Sunday Mass is a hit with music-lovers—both a Mass and a concert, often with an orchestra accompanying the choir. To pay, contribute to the offering plate and buy a CD afterwards. Programs are posted by the entry (church open long hours daily, Augustinerstrasse 3).

The church faces Josefsplatz, with its statue of the great reform emperor Josef II. Next to the Augustinian Church, the **National Library** and its State Hall are impressive (€7, Tue–Sun 10:00–18:00, Thu until 21:00, closed Mon).

Burggarten (Palace Garden)—This greenbelt, once the backyard of the Hofburg and now a people's park, welcomes people to loiter on the grass. On nice days, it's lively with office workers enjoying a break. The statue of Mozart facing the Ringstrasse is popular. The iron-and-glass pavilion now houses the recommended Café Restaurant Palmenhaus (see "Eating," later in this chapter) and a small but fluttery butterfly exhibit (€5.50; April–Oct Mon–Fri 10:00–16:45, Sat–Sun 10:00–18:15; Nov–March daily 10:00–15:45). The butterfly zone is delightfully muggy on a brisk off-season day, but trippy any time of year. If you tour it, notice the butterflies hanging out on the trays with rotting slices of banana. They lick the fermented banana juice as it beads, and then just hang out there in a stupor...or fly giddy loop-de-loops.

More Sights Inside the Ring

▲▲Haus der Musik—Vienna's "House of Music" has a small first-floor exhibit on the Vienna Philharmonic, and upstairs you'll enjoy fine audiovisual exhibits on each of the famous hometown boys (Haydn, Mozart, Beethoven, Strauss, and Mahler). But the museum is unique for its effective use of interactive touch-screen computers and headphones to actually explore the physics of sound. You can twist, dissect, and bend sounds to make your own musical language, merging your voice with a duck's quack or a city's traffic roar. Wander through the "sonosphere" and marvel at the amazing acoustics—I could actually hear what I thought only a piano tuner could hear. Pick up a virtual baton to conduct the Vienna Philharmonic Orchestra (each time you screw up, the musicians put their instruments down and ridicule you). Really experiencing the place takes time. It's open late and makes a good evening activity (€10, €15 combo-ticket with Mozarthaus, daily 10:00–22:00, last entry one hour before closing, 2 blocks from the Opera at Seilerstätte 30, tel. 01/51648, www.hdm.at).

▲Vienna's Auction House, the Dorotheum—For an aristocrat's flea market, drop by Austria's answer to Sotheby's, the Dorotheum. Its five floors of antique furniture and fancy knickknacks have been put up either for immediate sale or auction, often by people who inherited old things they don't have room for. Wandering through here, you feel like you're touring a museum with exhibits you can buy (Mon–Fri 10:00–18:00, Sat 9:00–17:00, closed Sun, classy little café on second floor, between the Graben pedestrian street and Hofburg at Dorotheergasse 17, tel. 01/51560, www.dorotheum.com). The info desk at the ground floor has a building map and schedule of upcoming auctions. Labels on each item predict the auction value. Continue your hunt for the perfect curio on the streets around the Dorotheum, lined with many fine antique shops.

St. Peter's Church (Peterskirche)—Baroque Vienna is at its best in this gem, tucked away a few steps from the Graben. Admire the rose-and-gold, oval-shaped Baroque interior, topped with a ceiling fresco of Mary kneeling to be crowned by Jesus and the Father, while the dove of the Holy Spirit floats way up in the lantern. Taken together, the church's elements—especially the organ, altar painting, pulpit, and coat of arms (in the base of the dome) of church founder Leopold I—make St. Peter's one of the city's most beautiful and ornate churches.

To the right of the altar, a dramatic golden statue shows the martyrdom of St. John Nepomuk (c. 1340–1393). The Czech saint defied the heretical King Wenceslaus, so he was tossed to his death off the Charles Bridge in Prague. In true Baroque style, we see the dramatic peak of his fall, when John has just passed the point of no return. The Virgin Mary floats overhead in a silver cloud.

The present church (from 1733) stands atop earlier churches dating back 1,600 years. On either side of the nave are glass cases containing skeletons of Christian martyrs from Roman times. Above the relic on the left is a painting of the modern saint Josemaria Escriva, founder of the conservative Catholic organization Opus Dei, of *Da Vinci Code* notoriety (free, church open Mon–Fri 7:00–19:00, Sat–Sun 9:00–19:00; organ concert Mon–Fri at 15:00, Sat–Sun at 20:00; just off the Graben between the Plague Monument and Kohlmarkt, tel. 01/533-6433).

Mozarthaus—Opened in 2006 to commemorate Wolfgang's 250th birthday, this museum is easy to get excited about, but it disappoints. Exhibits fill the only surviving Mozart residence in Vienna, where he lived from 1784 to 1787, when he had lots of money. You'll learn his life story, with an emphasis on his most creative years...when he lived here. Included is a rundown on the Vienna music scene during the Mozart years, a quirky look at his gambling habits and his interest in crudely erotic peep shows, and a four-minute montage of his most famous arias in a mini-theater. Unfortunately, visiting the museum is like reading a book standing up—rather than turning pages, you climb stairs. There are almost no real artifacts. Wolfie would have found the audioguide dreadful. While the museum might be worth the time and money for Mozart enthusiasts, both Mozart sights in Salzburg (the Birthplace and the Residence—see Salzburg chapter) are more gratifying. In Vienna, I enjoy the Haus der Musik (described previously) much more (€9, €15 combo-ticket with Haus der Musik, daily 10:00–19:00, a block behind the cathedral, go through arcade at #5 and walk 50 yards to Domgasse 5, tel. 01/512-1791, www.mozarthausvienna.at).

Judenplatz Memorial and Museum—The classy square called Judenplatz marks the location of Vienna's 15th-century Jewish community, one of Europe's largest at the time. The square, once filled with a long-gone synagogue, is now dominated by a blocky memorial to the 65,000 Austrian Jews killed by the Nazis. The memorial—a library turned inside out—symbolizes Jews as "people of the book" and causes viewers to ponder the huge loss of culture, knowledge, and humanity that took place between 1938 and 1945.

The Judenplatz Museum, while sparse, has displays on medieval Jewish life and a well-done video recreating the ghetto as it looked five centuries ago. (If you're skipping the museum, at least pop into its entry hall to check the model of Vienna as it was in the 1500s.) Wander the scant remains of the medieval synagogue below street level—discovered during the construction of the Holocaust memorial. This was the scene of a medieval massacre. Since Christians weren't allowed to lend money, Jews were Europe's moneylenders. As so often happened in Europe, when Viennese Christians fell too deeply into debt, they found a convenient excuse to wipe out the local ghetto—and their debts at the same time. In 1421, 200 of Vienna's Jews were burned at the stake. Others who refused a forced conversion committed mass suicide in the synagogue (€4, Sun–Thu 10:00–18:00, Fri 10:00–14:00, closed Sat, Judenplatz 8, tel. 01/535-0431, www.jmw.at).

Kunsthistorisches Museum and Nearby

▲▲▲**Kunsthistorisches Museum**—This exciting museum, across the Ring from the Hofburg Palace, showcases the grandeur and opulence of the Habsburgs' collected artwork in a grand building (built as a museum in 1888). There are European masterpieces galore, all well-hung on one glorious floor, plus a fine display of Egyptian, classical, and applied arts.

The Kunsthistorwhateveritis Museum—let's just say "Koonst"—houses some of the most beautiful, sexy, and fun art from two centuries (c. 1450–1650). The collection reflects the *joie de vivre* of Austria's luxury-loving Habsburg rulers. At their peak of power in the 1500s, the Habsburgs ruled Austria, Germany, northern Italy, the Netherlands, and Spain—and you'll see a wide variety of art from all these places and beyond.

KUNSTHISTORISCHES MUSEUM

If you're short on time, focus on the Painting Gallery *(Gemäldegalerie)* on the first floor. Climb the main staircase, featuring Antonio Canova's statue of *Theseus Clubbing the Centaur.* Italian Art is in the right half of the building (as you face Theseus), and Northern Art to the left. Notice that the museum labels the largest rooms with Roman numerals (Saal I, II, III), and the smaller rooms around the perimeter with Arabic (Rooms 1, 2, 3).

Saals I–III cover the Venetian renaissance. The first spans the long career of **Titian,** who painted portraits, Christian Madonnas, and sexy Venuses with equal ease. Next comes Paolo **Vernese,** whose colorful works reflect the wealth of Venice, the funnel where luxury goods from the exotic East flowed into northern Europe. And **Tintoretto**'s many portraits give us a peek at the movers and shakers of the Venetian Empire.

Rooms 1-4 hold some of the museum's most important works: **Mantegna**'s *St. Sebastian,* **Correggio**'s *Jupiter and Io,* and **Raphael**'s *Madonna of the Meadow (Die Madonna im Grünen),* a geometrically perfect masterpiece of the High Renaissance, painted when Raphael was just 22.

Farther along, through the small rooms along the far end of this wing, find the cleverly deceptive portraits by Giuseppe **Arcimboldo.** His *Summer*—a.k.a "Fruit Face"—is one of four paintings the Habsburg court painter did showing the seasons (and elements) as people. With a pickle nose, pear chin, and corn-husk ears, this guy literally is what he eats.

Caravaggio (in Saal V) shocked the art world with brutally honest reality. Compared with Raphael's super-sweet *Madonna of the Meadow*, Caravaggio's *Madonna of the Rosary* (*Die Rosenkranzmadonna*, the biggest canvas in the room) looks perfectly ordinary, and the saints kneeling around her have dirty feet. In *David with the Head of Goliath (David mit dem Haupt des Goliath)* Caravaggio turns a third-degree-interrogation light on a familiar Bible story. David shoves the dripping head of the slain giant—the artist's self portrait—right in our noses.

When the Habsburgs ruled both Austria and Spain, cousins kept in touch through portraits of themselves and their kids. Diego **Velázquez** (in Room 10) was the greatest of Spain's "photojournalist" painters: heavily influenced by Caravaggio's realism, capturing his subjects without passing judgment, flattering, or glorifying them.

The half of this floor features works of the "Northern Renaissance," which was more secular and Protestant than Catholic-funded Italian art (that means fewer Madonnas, saints, and Greek gods and more peasants, landscapes, and food). Paintings are smaller and darker, full of down-to-earth objects. Northern artists sweated the details, encouraging the patient viewer to appreciate the beauty in everyday things.

Don't miss the slice-of-village-life scenes by Pieter **Breugel** the Elder (the Normal Rockwell of the 16th century), **Rubens'** large, lush canvases; **Vermeer's** *The Art of Painting (Die Malkunst)*; and **Rembrandt's** frank, defiant self-portraits.

Cost, Hours, Location: €10, €18 combo-ticket with the Hofburg Treasury, audioguide-€3, Tue–Sun 10:00–18:00, Thu until 21:00, closed Mon, on the Ringstrasse at Maria-Theresien-Platz, U-2 or U-3: Volkstheater/Museumsplatz, tel. 01/525-240, www.khm.at.

▲**Natural History Museum**—In the twin building facing the Kunsthistorisches Museum, you'll find moon rocks, dinosaur stuff, and the fist-sized *Venus of Willendorf*—at 25,000 years old, the world's oldest sex symbol, found in the Danube Valley. Even though the museum is not glitzy or high-tech, it's a hit with children and scientifically curious grown-ups.

For a quick visit, head first to the *Venus of Willendorf*—she's on the mezzanine level, in Room 11 (from the entrance lobby, climb the stairs, head for the back, and turn left). The 4-inch-tall, chubby stone statuette is a generic female (no face or feet) resting her hands on her ample breasts. The statue's purpose is unknown, but she may have been a symbol of fertility for our mammoth-hunting ancestors. In Room 10 nearby are big dinosaur skeletons.

For a more chronological visit, start upstairs on the first floor (in Room 21), and follow hundreds of millions of years of evolution—from single cells to sea creatures, reptiles, birds, mammals, and primates. Finish with the hairless primate—man—downstairs in Rooms 11–14.

The collection of rocks (mezzanine, Rooms 1–5, to the right of the entrance lobby) is also impressive, and includes one of the largest collections of meteorites in the world. Of the museum's 20 million objects, you're sure to find something interesting.

Cost, Hours, Information: €8, Wed–Mon 9:00–18:30, Wed until 21:00, closed Tue, on the Ringstrasse at Maria-Theresien-Platz, U-2 or U-3: Volkstheater/Museumsplatz, tel. 01/521-770, www.nhm-wien.ac.at.

MuseumsQuartier—The vast grounds of the former imperial stables now corral several impressive, cutting-edge museums. Walk into the complex from the Hofburg side, where the main entrance (with visitors center) leads to a big courtyard with cafés, fountains, and ever-changing "installation lounge furniture," all surrounded by the quarter's various museums (behind Kunsthistorisches Museum, U-2 or U-3: Volkstheater/Museumsplatz). Various combo-tickets are available for those interested in more than just the Leopold and Modern Art museums (visit www.mqw.at).

The **Leopold Museum** features several temporary exhibits of modern Austrian art, and a top floor that holds the largest collection of works by Egon Schiele (1890–1918; these works make some people uncomfortable—Schiele's nudes are *really* nude) and a few paintings by Gustav Klimt, Kolo Moser, and Oskar Kokoschka (€10, €3 audioguide—worth it only for enthusiasts, daily 10:00–18:00, Thu until 21:00, tel. 01/525-700, www.leopoldmuseum.org). Note that for these artists, you'll do better in the Belvedere Palace (described on page 64).

The **Museum of Modern Art** (Museum Moderner Kunst Stiftung Ludwig, a.k.a. "MUMOK") is Austria's leading modern-art gallery. It's the striking lava-paneled building—three stories tall and four stories deep, offering seven floors of far-out art that's hard for most visitors to appreciate. This huge, state-of-the-art museum displays revolving exhibits showing off art of the last generation—including Paul Klee, Pablo Picasso, and Pop artists (€9, €2 audioguide has more than you probably want to hear, daily 10:00–18:00, Thu until 21:00, tel. 01/52500, www.mumok.at).

Rounding out the sprawling MuseumsQuartier are an architecture museum, Transeuropa, Electronic Avenue, children's museum, and the Kunsthalle Wien—an exhibition center for contemporary art (€7.50, daily 10:00–19:00, Thu until 22:00, tel. 01/521-8933, www.kunsthallewien.at).

Karlsplatz and Nearby

These sights cluster around Karlsplatz, just southeast of the Ringstrasse (U-1, U-2, or U-4: Karlsplatz). From the U-Bahn station's passageway, it's a 30-minute walk around the sights on Karlsplatz: the Karlskirche, Secession, and Naschmarkt (allow more time to actually visit these sights).

Karlsplatz—This picnic-friendly square, with its Henry Moore sculpture in the pond, is ringed with sights. The massive, domed Karlskirche and its twin spiral columns dominate the square. The small green, white, and gold pavilions near the church are from the late 19th-century municipal train system *(Stadtbahn)*. One of Europe's first subway systems, this precursor to today's U-Bahn was built with a military purpose in mind: to move troops quickly in time of civil unrest—specifically, out to Schönbrunn Palace. With curvy iron frames, decorative marble slabs, and painted gold trim, these are pioneering works in the *Jugendstil* style, designed by Otto Wagner, who influenced Klimt and the Secessionists. One of the pavilions is open as an exhibit on Otto Wagner (€2, April–Oct Tue–Sun 9:00–18:00, closed Mon and Nov–March, near the Ringstrasse).

▲**Karlskirche (St. Charles' Church)**—Charles Borromeo, a 16th-century bishop from Milan, was an inspiration during plague times. This "votive church" was dedicated to him in 1713, when an epidemic spared Vienna. The church offers the best Baroque in Vienna, with a unique combination of columns (showing scenes from the life of Charles Borromeo, à la Trajan's Column in Rome), a classic pediment, and an elliptical dome. But this church is especially worthwhile for the chance (probably through 2010) to see restoration work in progress.

Inside, the fresco in the dome shows Signor Borromeo (in red and white bishops' robes) gazing up into heaven, spreading his arms wide and pleading with Christ to spare Vienna from the plague. The colorful 13,500-square-foot fresco was painted in the 1730s by Johann Michael Rottmayr.

To get a closer look, ride the industrial lift to a platform at the base of the 235-foot dome. (Consider that the church was built and decorated with a scaffolding system essentially the same as this one.) Once up there, you'll climb stairs to the steamy lantern at the extreme top of the church. At that dizzying height, you're in the clouds with cupids and angels.

Many details that appear smooth and beautiful from ground level—such as gold leaf, paintings, and fake marble—look rough and sloppy up close. It's surreal to observe the 3-D figures from an unintended angle—check out Christ's leg, which looks dwarf-sized up close. Faith, Hope, and Charity triumph and inspire. Borromeo lobbies heaven for plague relief. Meanwhile, a Protestant's Lutheran Bible is put to the torch by angels. At the very top, you'll see the tiny dove representing the Holy Ghost, surrounded by a cheering squad of nipple-lipped cupids.

Cost and Hours: €6, includes audioguide, visit to renovation site, and skippable one-room museum; Mon–Sat 9:00–18:00, Sun 13:00–18:00, last entry 30 min before closing. The entry fee may seem steep, but remember that it funds the restoration.

Wien Museum Karlsplatz—This underappreciated museum walks you through the history of Vienna with fine historic artifacts. You'll work your way up, chronologically: The ground floor exhibits Roman artifacts and original statues from St. Stephen's Cathedral (c. 1350), with various Habsburgs showing off the slinky hip-hugging fashion of the day. The first floor features old city maps, booty from an Ottoman siege, and an 1850 city model showing the town just before the wall was replaced by the Ring. Finally, the second floor displays a city model from 1898 (with the new Ringstrasse), sentimental Biedermeier paintings and objets d'art, and early 20th-century paintings (including some by Gustav Klimt). The museum is worth the €6 admission (free Sun, open Tue–Sun 9:00–18:00, closed Mon, www.wienmuseum.at).

▲Academy of Fine Arts (Akademie der Bildenden Künste)—This small but exciting collection includes works by Bosch, Botticelli, and Rubens (quick, sketchy cartoons used to create his giant canvases); a Venice series by Guardi; and a self-portrait by a 15-year-old van Dyck. It's all magnificently lit and well-described by the €2.50 audioguide, and comes with comfy chairs.

The fact that this is a working art academy gives it a certain realness. As you wander the halls of the academy, ponder how history might have been different if Hitler—who applied to study architecture here but was rejected—had been accepted as a student. Before leaving, peek into the ground floor's central hall—textbook Historicism, the Ringstrasse style of the late 1800s.

Cost, Hours, Location: €7; Tue–Sun 10:00–18:00, closed Mon, closed Aug 2009–Feb 2010, 3 blocks from the Opera at Schillerplatz 3, tel. 01/588-162-222, www.akademiegalerie.at.

▲The Secession—This little building, behind the Academy of Fine Arts, was created by the Vienna Secession movement, a group of nonconformist artists led by Gustav Klimt, Otto Wagner, and friends.

The young trees carved into the walls and its bushy "golden cabbage" rooftop are symbolic of a renewal cycle. The Secessionist motto, under the cabbage, reads: "To each age its art, and to art its liberty." Today, the Secession continues to showcase cutting-edge art, as well as one of Gustav Klimt's most famous works.

While the staff hopes you take a look at the temporary exhibits (and the ticket includes this price whether you like it or not), most tourists head directly for the basement, home to a small exhibit about the history of the building and the museum's highlight: Klimt's classic *Beethoven Frieze* (a.k.a. the "Searching Souls"). The piece features floating female figures yearning for happiness, who drift and weave and search—like we all do—through internal and external temptations and forces, falling victim to base and ungodly temptations, and losing their faith. Then, they become inspired by poetry, music, and art to carry on, and they finally reach true happiness, represented by Mr. Poetry. At the climax of the frieze, a naked couple embraces in ecstasy as a heavenly choir sings the "Ode to Joy" from the Ninth Symphony: "Joy, you beautiful spark of the gods...under thy gentle wings, all men shall become brothers."

Glass cases show sketches Klimt did in preparation for this work. Klimt embellished the painting with painted-on gold (his brother and colleague was a goldsmith), and by gluing on reflecting glass and mother-of-pearl for the ladies' dresses and jewelry. The adjacent room tells the history of this masterpiece (transferred from screens to the Secession walls), and how the building was damaged in World War II.

Cost, Hours, Location: €3.50, but temporary exhibits often boost the price to €6, Tue–Sun 10:00–18:00, Thu until 20:00, closed Mon, Friedrichstrasse 12, tel. 01/587-5307, www.secession.at.

▲**Naschmarkt**—In 1898, the city decided to cover up its Vienna River. The long, wide square they created was filled with a lively produce market that still bustles most days (closed Sun). It's long been known as *the* place to get exotic faraway foods. In fact, locals say, "From here start the Balkans."

From near the Opera, the Naschmarkt (roughly, "Munchies Market") stretches along Wienzeile street. This "Belly of Vienna" comes with two parallel lanes—one lined with fun and reasonable eateries, and the other featuring the town's top-end produce and gourmet goodies. This is where top chefs like to get their ingredients. At the gourmet vinegar stall, you sample the vinegar like perfume—with a drop on your wrist. Farther from the center, the Naschmarkt becomes likeably seedy and surrounded by sausage stands, Turkish *Döner Kebab* stalls, cafés, and theaters. At the market's far end is a line of buildings with fine Art Nouveau facades. Each Saturday, the Naschmarkt is infested by a huge flea market where, in olden days, locals would come to hire a monkey to pick little critters out of their hair (Mon–Fri 6:00–18:30, Sat 6:00–17:00, closed Sun, closes earlier in winter; U-1, U-2, or U-4: Karlsplatz). For a picnic in the park, pick up your grub here and walk over to Karlsplatz (described previously).

Museum of Applied Art

The Österreichisches Museum für Angewandte Kunst, or MAK, is Vienna's answer to London's Victoria and Albert Museum. It shows off the fancies of local aristocratic society, including a fine *Jugendstil* collection.

The MAK is more than just another grand building on the Ringstrasse. It was built to provide models of historic design for Ringstrasse architects, and is a delightful space in itself (many locals stop in to enjoy a coffee on the plush couches in the main lobby). Each wing is dedicated to a different era. Exhibits, well-described in English, come with a playful modern flair—notable modern designers were assigned various spaces.

Cost, Hours, Location: €8, €10 includes a hefty English guidebook, free on Sat, open Tue–Sun 10:00–18:00, Tue until 24:00, closed Mon, Stubenring 5, tel. 01/711-360, www.mak.at.

The associated **Restaurant Österreicher im MAK** is named for a chef renowned for his classic and modern Viennese cuisine. Classy and mod, it's trendy for locals (open daily, reserve for evening, €10–15 plates).

Beyond the Ring

The following museums are located outside the Ringstrasse but inside the Gürtel, or outer ring road.

▲▲**Belvedere Palace**—This is the elegant palace of Prince Eugène of Savoy (1663–1736), the still-much-appreciated conqueror of the Ottomans. Eugène, a Frenchman considered too short and too ugly to be in the service of Louis XIV, offered his services to the Habsburgs. While he was indeed short and ugly, he became the greatest military genius of his age and the toast of Viennese society. When you conquer cities, as Eugène did, you get really rich. He had no heirs, so the state got his property and Emperor Josef II established the Belvedere as Austria's first great public art gallery.

You can tour the lavish palace, see sweeping views of the gardens and the Vienna skyline, and enjoy world-class art starring Gustav Klimt, French Impressionism, and a grab-bag of other 19th- and early-20th-century artists.

The Belvedere Palace is actually two grand buildings—the Upper Palace and Lower Palace—separated by a fine garden. For our purposes, the Upper Palace is what matters. The Lower Palace exhibits a less-interesting collection of Austrian Baroque and medieval art. *Belvedere* means "beautiful view." From the Upper Palace's **Marble Hall,** look over the Baroque gardens, the Lower Palace, and the city.

The Upper Palace's eclectic collection, arranged chronologically, is tailor-made for browsing. Skip the second floor, and focus

instead on the first floor, where you'll find Historicism, Romanticism, Impressionism, Realism, tired tourism, Expressionism, Art
Nouveau, and early Modernism. Each room tries to pair Austrian
works from that period with much better-known European works.

In the two rooms full of sumptuous paintings by Klimt you
can get caught up in his fascination with the beauty and danger
he saw in women. To Klimt, all art was erotic art. Be sure to see
his famous *Judith I* (holding the head of her biblical victim, she's
the modern femme fatale) and his glowingly radiant masterpiece,
The Kiss.

Cost, Hours, Information: €9.50 for Upper Belvedere Palace
only, €12.50 for Upper and Lower palaces—not worth it, audio-
guide-€3, daily 10:00–18:00, no photos allowed inside, entrance at
Prinz-Eugen-Strasse 27, tel. 01/7955-7134, www.belvedere.at.

Location: The palace is a 15-minute walk south of the Ring.
To get there from the center, catch tram #D at the Opera (direction Südbahnhof; it stops at the palace gate).

▲**Imperial Furniture Collection (Kaiserliches Hofmobiliendepot)**—Bizarre, sensuous, eccentric, or precious, this collection
is your peek at the Habsburgs' furniture—from grandma's wheel-
chair to the emperor's spittoon—all thoughtfully described in
English. The Habsburgs had many palaces, but only the Hofburg
was permanently furnished. The rest were furnished on the fly—
set up and taken down by a gang of royal roadies called the "Depot
of Court Movables" (Hofmobiliendepot). When the monarchy
was dissolved in 1918, the state of Austria took possession of the
Hofmobiliendepot's inventory—165,000 items. Now this royal
storehouse is open to the public in a fine and sprawling museum.
Don't go here for the *Jugendstil* furnishings. The older Baroque,
Rococo, and Biedermeier pieces are the most impressive and tied
most intimately to the royals. Combine a visit to this museum with
a stroll down the lively shopping boulevard, Mariahilfer Strasse.

Cost, Hours, Location: €7, Tue–Sun 10:00–18:00, closed
Mon, Mariahilfer Strasse 88, U-3: Zieglergasse, tel. 01/5243-3570.

▲**Liechtenstein Museum**—The noble Liechtenstein family (who
own only a tiny country, but whose friendship with the Habsburgs
goes back generations) amassed an incredible private art collection.
Their palace was long a treasure for Vienna art lovers. Then, in
1938—knowing Hitler was intent on plundering artwork to create an immense "Führer Museum"—the family fled to their tiny
homeland with their best art. Attendance has been disappointing
since the museum reopened in 2004, but the problem is its location
(and perhaps its steep price)...not its worthiness.

The Liechtensteins' "world of Baroque pleasures" includes the
family's rare "Golden Carriage" which was used for their grand
entry into Paris in 1738. It was carted to the edge of town and

assembled there. It's a rare example of the French Rococo style, as nearly all such carriages were destroyed in the French Revolution. The museum also has a plush Baroque library, an inviting English Garden, and an impressive collection of paintings, including a complete cycle of early Rubens.

Cost, Hours, Location: €10, audioguide-€1, Fri–Tue 10:00–17:00, last entry 30 min before closing, closed Wed–Thu, tram #D to Bauernfeldplatz, Fürstengasse 1, tel. 01/319-5767-252, www.liechtensteinmuseum.at. The gardens are free and open until 20:30 (but aren't worth the trip on their own).

▲**KunstHausWien: Hundertwasser Museum**—This "make yourself at home" museum and nearby apartment complex are a hit with lovers of modern art, mixing the work and philosophy of local painter/environmentalist Friedensreich Hundertwasser (1928–2000). Stand in front of the colorful checkerboard building and consider Hundertwasser's style. He was against "window racism": Neighboring houses allow only one kind of window, but $100H_2O$'s windows are each different—and he encouraged residents in the Hundertwasserhaus (a 5–10 minute walk away, see below) to personalize them. He recognized "tree tenants" as well as human tenants. His buildings are spritzed with a forest and topped with dirt and grassy little parks—close to nature and good for the soul.

Floors and sidewalks are irregular—to "stimulate the brain" (although current residents complain it just causes wobbly furniture and sprained ankles). Thus $100H_2O$ waged a one-man fight—during the 1950s and 1960s, when concrete and glass ruled—to save the human soul from the city. (Hundertwasser claimed that "straight lines are godless.")

Inside the museum, start with his interesting biography. His fun paintings are half psychedelic *Jugendstil* and half just kids' stuff. Notice the photographs from his 1950s days as part of Vienna's bohemian scene. Throughout the museum, keep an eye out for the fun philosophical quotes from an artist who believed, "If man is creative, he comes nearer to his creator."

Cost, Hours, Location: €9 for Hundertwasser Museum, €12 combo-ticket includes special exhibitions, half-price on Mon, open daily 10:00–19:00, extremely fragrant and colorful garden café, Untere Weissgerberstrasse 13, tram #1: Hetzgasse or U-3: Landstrasse—but the tram stop is much closer than the U-Bahn stop, tel. 01/712-0491, www.kunsthauswien.com.

Hundertwasserhaus: The KunstHausWien provides by far the best look at Hundertwasser, but for an actual lived-in apartment complex by the green master, walk five minutes to the one-with-nature Hundertwasserhaus (at Löwengasse and Kegelgasse). This complex of 50 apartments, subsidized by the government to provide affordable housing, was built in the 1980s as a breath of architectural fresh air in a city of boring, blocky apartment complexes. While not open to visitors, it's worth visiting for its fun and colorful patchwork exterior and the Hundertwasser festival of shops across the street. Don't miss the view from Kegelgasse to see the "tree tenants" and the internal winter garden that residents enjoy.

Hundertwasser detractors—of which there are many—remind visitors that $100H_2O$ was a painter, not an architect. They describe the Hundertwasserhaus as a "1950s house built in the 1980s," and colorfully painted with no real concern about the environment, communal living, or even practical comfort. Almost all of the original inhabitants got fed up with the novelty and moved out.

Sigmund Freud Museum—Freud enthusiasts enjoy seeing the humble apartment and workplace of the man who fundamentally changed our understanding of the human psyche. Dr. Sigmund Freud (1856-1939), a graduate of Vienna University, established his practice here in 1891. For the next 47 years, he received troubled patients who hoped to find peace by telling him their dreams, life traumas, and secret urges. It was here that he wrote his influential works, including the landmark *Interpretation of Dreams* (€7, audioguide-€2, daily July–Sept 9:00–18:00, Oct–June 9:00–17:00, cool shop, half a block downhill from the Schlickgasse tram #D stop, Berggasse 19, tel. 01/319-1596, www.freud-museum.at).

Schönbrunn Palace (Schloss Schönbrunn)

Among Europe's palaces, only Schönbrunn rivals Versailles. This former summer residence of the Habsburgs is big, with 1,441 rooms. But don't worry—only 40 rooms are shown to the public. Of the plethora of sights at the palace, the highlight is a tour of the Royal Apartments—the chandeliered rooms where the Habsburg nobles lived. You can also stroll the gardens, tour the coach museum, and visit a handful of lesser sights nearby.

Getting There: Take U-4 to Schönbrunn and walk 400 yards (just follow the crowds). The main entrance is in the left side of the palace as you face it.

▲▲▲**Royal Apartments**—While the exterior is Baroque, the interior was finished under Maria Theresa in let-them-eat-cake Rococo. The chandeliers are either of Bohemian crystal or of hand-carved wood with gold-leaf gilding. Thick walls hid the servants as they ran around stoking the ceramic stoves from the back, and attending to other behind-the-scenes matters. When WWII bombs rained on the city and the palace grounds, the palace itself took only one direct hit. Thankfully, that bomb, which crashed through three floors—including the sumptuous central ballroom—was a dud. Most of the public rooms are decorated in

Neo-Baroque, as they were under Franz Josef (r. 1848–1916). The rest of the palace has been converted to simple apartments and rented to the families of 260 civil servants, who enjoy rent control and governmental protections so they can't be evicted.

Cost: The admission price is based on which route you select (each one includes an audioguide): the 22-room **Imperial Tour** (€9.50, 45 min, Grand Palace rooms plus apartments of Franz Josef and Elisabeth—mostly 19th-century and therefore least interesting) or the 40-room **Grand Tour** (€13, 60 min, includes Imperial tour plus Maria Theresa's apartments—18th-century Rococo). A combo-ticket called the **Schönbrunn Pass Classic** includes the Grand Tour, as well as other sights on the grounds: the Gloriette viewing terrace, maze, privy garden, and court bakery—complete with *Apfelstrudel* demo and tasting (€16, available April–Oct only). I'd go for the Grand Tour.

Hours: Daily July–Aug 8:30–18:00, April–June and Sept–Oct 8:30–17:00, Nov–March 8:30–16:30. Information: www.schoen brunn.at.

Crowd-Beating Tips: Schönbrunn suffers from crowds. It can be a jam-packed sauna in the summer. It's busiest from 9:30 to 11:30, especially on weekends and in July and August; it's least crowded from after 14:00, when there are no groups. To avoid the long delays in summer, make a reservation by telephone a few days in advance (tel. 01/8111-3239, answered daily 8:00–17:00, wait through the long message for the operator). You'll get an appointment time and a ticket number. Check in at least 30 minutes early. Upon arrival, go to the "Group and Reservations" desk (immediately inside the gate on the left at the gate house—long before the actual palace), give your number, pick up your ticket, and jump in ahead of the masses. If you show up in peak season without calling first, you deserve the frustration. (In this case, you'll have to wait in line, buy your ticket, and wait until the listed time to enter—which could be tomorrow.) If you have any time to kill, spend it exploring the gardens or Coach Museum.

Palace Gardens—Unlike the gardens of Versailles, meant to shut out the real world, Schönbrunn's park was opened to the public in 1779 while the monarchy was in full swing. It was part of Maria Theresa's reform policy, making the garden a celebration of the evolution of civilization from autocracy into real democracy.

Most of the park itself is free, as it has been since the 1700s (open daily sunrise to dusk, entrance on either side of the palace). The small side gardens are the most elaborate. The Kammergarten on the left was a fancy private garden for the Habsburgs (now restored and with a fee). The so-called Sisi Gardens on the right are free. Inside are several other sights, including a **palm house** (€4, daily May–Sept 9:30–18:00, Oct–April 9:30–17:00, last entry

30 min before closing); Europe's oldest **zoo,** or *Tiergarten,* built by Maria Theresa's husband for the entertainment and education of the court in 1752 (€12, April–Sept daily 9:00–18:30, closes earlier off-season, tel. 01/877-9294); and—at the end of the gardens—the **Gloriette,** a purely decorative monument celebrating an obscure Austrian military victory and offering a fine city view (viewing terrace-€2, included in €16 Schönbrunn Pass Classic, daily April–Sept 9:00–18:00, July–Aug until 19:00, Oct 9:00–17:00, closed Nov–March). A touristy choo-choo train makes the rounds all day, connecting Schönbrunn's many attractions.

Wagenburg Coach Museum—The Schönbrunn coach museum is a 19th-century traffic jam of 50 impressive royal carriages and sleighs. Highlights include silly sedan chairs, the death-black hearse carriage (used for Franz Josef in 1916, and most recently for Empress Zita in 1989), and an extravagantly gilded imperial carriage pulled by eight Cinderella horses. This was rarely used other than for the coronation of Holy Roman Emperors, when it was disassembled and taken to Frankfurt for the big event (€4.50; daily April–Oct 9:00–18:00; Nov–March 10:00–16:00; last entry 30 min before closing, 200 yards from palace, walk through right arch as you face palace, tel. 01/525-24-3470).

Activities

People-Watching and Strolling

These activities allow you to take it easy and enjoy the Viennese good life.

▲**Stadtpark (City Park)**—Vienna's major park is a waltzing world of gardens, memorials to local musicians, ponds, peacocks, music in bandstands, and Viennese escaping the city. Notice the *Jugendstil* entrance at the Stadtpark U-Bahn station. The Kursalon, where Strauss was the violin-toting master of waltzing ceremonies, hosts daily touristy concerts in three-quarter time.

▲**Prater**—Since the 1780s, when the reformist Emperor Josef II gave his hunting grounds to the people of Vienna as a public park, this place has been Vienna's playground. While tired and a bit rundown these days, Vienna's sprawling amusement park still tempts visitors with its huge 220-foot-tall, famous, and lazy Ferris wheel *(Riesenrad),* roller coaster, bumper cars, Lilliputian railroad, and endless eateries. Especially if you're traveling with kids, this is a fun, goofy place to share the evening with thousands of Viennese (rides run May–Sept 9:00–24:00—but quiet after 22:00, March–April and Oct 10:00–22:00, Nov–Dec 10:00–20:00, grounds always open, U-1: Praterstern). For a local-style family dinner, eat at Schweizerhaus (good food, great Czech Budvar—the original "Budweiser"—beer, classic conviviality).

Donauinsel (Danube Island)—In the 1970s, the city dug a canal parallel to the mighty Danube River, creating both a flood barrier and a much-loved island escape from the city (easy U-Bahn access on U-1 to Donauinsel). This skinny, 12-mile long island provides a natural wonderland. All along the traffic-free, grassy park you'll find locals—both Viennese, and especially immigrants and those who can't afford their own cabin or fancy vacation—at play. The swimming comes tough, though, with rocky entries rather than sand. The best activity here is a bike ride (see "Getting Around Vienna—By Bike," near the beginning of this chapter). Note that if you venture far from the crowds, you're likely to encounter nudists on Rollerblades.

Experiences

Vienna—the birthplace of what we call classical music—still thrives as a music capital. On any given evening, you'll have your choice of opera, Strauss waltzes, Mozart chamber concerts, the famous Boys' Choir, and lighthearted musicals.

Live Music

As far back as the 12th century, Vienna was a mecca for musicians—both sacred and secular (troubadours). The Habsburg emperors of the 17th and 18th centuries were not only generous supporters of music, but fine musicians and composers themselves. (Maria Theresa played a mean double bass.) Composers such as Haydn, Mozart, Beethoven, Schubert, Brahms, and Mahler gravitated to this music-friendly environment. They taught each other, jammed together, and spent a lot of time in Habsburg palaces. Beethoven was a famous figure, walking—lost in musical thought—through Vienna's woods. In the city's 19th-century belle époque, "Waltz King" Johann Strauss and his brothers kept Vienna's 300 ballrooms spinning.

This musical tradition continues into modern times, leaving some prestigious Viennese institutions for today's tourists to enjoy: the Opera (described later in this section), the Boys' Choir (see next page), and the great Baroque halls and churches, all busy with classical and waltz concerts. As you poke into churches and palaces, you may hear groups practicing. You're welcome to sit and listen.

Vienna is Europe's music capital. It's music *con brio* (with brilliance) from October through June, reaching a symphonic climax during the Vienna Festival each May and June. Sadly, in July and August, the Boys' Choir, the Opera, and many more music companies are—like you—on vacation. But Vienna hums year-round with live classical music. Except for the Boys' Choir, the musical events listed below are offered in summer.

The best-known entertainment venues are the Staatsoper (for straight-up opera), the Volksoper (for musicals and "operettas"), the Wiener Musikverein (home of the Vienna Philharmonic Orchestra), and the Wiener Konzerthaus (various events).

Vienna Boys' Choir—The boys sing (from a high balcony, where they are heard but not seen) at the 9:15 Sunday Mass from September through June in the Hofburg's Imperial Music Chapel (Hofmusikkapelle). The entrance is at Schweizerhof; you can get there from In der Burg square or go through the tunnel from Josefsplatz.

Reserved seats must be booked two months in advance (€5–29; reserve by fax, email, or mail: fax from the US 011-431-533-992-775, whmk@chello.at, or write Hofmusikkapelle, Hofburg-Schweizerhof, 1010 Wien; call 01/533-9927 for information only—they can't book tickets at this number).

Much easier, standing room inside is free and open to the first 60 who line up. Even better, rather than line up early, you can simply swing by and stand in the narthex just outside, where you can hear the boys and see the Mass on a TV monitor.

Boys' Choir concerts are also given Fridays at 16:00 in late April, May, June, September, and October on stage at the Musikverein, near the Opera and Karlskirche (€36–56, around 30 standing-room tickets go on sale at 15:30 for €15, Karlsplatz 6; U-1, U-2, or U-4: Karlsplatz; tel. 01/5880-4173).

They're talented kids, but, for my taste, not worth all the commotion. Remember, many churches have great music during Sunday Mass. Just 200 yards from the Boys' Choir chapel, Augustinian Church has a glorious 11:00 service each Sunday (see page 54).

Touristy Mozart and Strauss Concerts—If the music comes to you, it's touristy—designed for flash-in-the-pan Mozart fans. Powdered-wig orchestra performances are given almost nightly in grand traditional settings (€25–50). Pesky wigged-and-powdered Mozarts peddle tickets in the streets. They rave about the quality of the musicians, but you'll get second-rate chamber orchestras, clad in historic costumes, performing the greatest hits of Mozart and Strauss. These are casual, easygoing concerts with lots of tour groups. While there's not a Viennese person in the audience, the tourists generally enjoy the evening.

To sort through all your options, check with the ticket office in the TI (same price as on the street, but with all venues to choose from). Savvy locals suggest getting the cheapest tickets, as no one seems to care if cheapskates move up to fill unsold pricier seats. Critics explain that the musicians are actually very good (often Hungarians, Poles, and Russians working a season here to fund an entire year of music studies back home), but that they haven't performed much together so aren't "tight."

Of the many fine venues, the Mozarthaus might be my favorite—a small room richly decorated in Venetian Renaissance style with intimate chamber-music concerts (€35–42, Thu–Fri at 19:30, Sat at 18:00, near St. Stephen's Cathedral at Singerstrasse 7, tel. 01/911-9077).

Strauss Concerts in the Kursalon—For years, Strauss concerts have been held in the Kursalon, where the "Waltz King" himself directed wildly popular concerts 100 years ago (€39–56, concerts nightly generally at 20:15, just east of the Ringstrasse in the Stadtpark, tel. 01/512-5790 to reserve). Shows last 1.75 hours and are a mix of ballet, waltzes, and a 15-piece orchestra. It's touristy—tour guides holding up banners with group numbers wait out front after the show. Even so, the performance is playful, visually fun, fine quality for most, and with a tried-and-tested, crowd-pleasing format. The conductor welcomes the crowd in German (with a wink) and English; after that...it's English only.

Serious Concerts—These events, including the Opera, are listed in the monthly *Wien-Programm* (available at TI). Most tickets run €40–55 (plus a stiff booking fee when booked in advance or through a box office like the one at the TI). A few venues charge as little as €25; look around if you're not set on any particular concert. While it's easy to book tickets online long in advance, spontaneity is also workable, as there are invariably people selling their extra tickets at face value or less outside the door before concert time. If you call a concert hall directly, they can advise you on the availability of (cheaper) tickets at the door. Vienna takes care of its starving artists (and tourists) by offering cheap standing-room tickets to top-notch music and opera (generally an hour before each performance).

The Opera—The Vienna State Opera (Staatsoper)—with musicians provided by the Vienna Philharmonic Orchestra in the pit—is one of the world's top opera houses. They put on 300 performances a year, but in July and August the singers rest their voices (or go on tour). Since there are different operas nearly nightly, you'll see big trucks out back and constant action backstage—all the sets need to be switched each day. Even though the expensive seats normally sell out long in advance, the opera is perpetually in the red and subsidized by the state.

Opera Tickets: To buy tickets in advance, call 01/514-440 or 01/513-1513 (phone answered daily 10:00–21:00, www.wiener -staatsoper.at). The theater's box office is open from 9:00 until two hours before each performance. Unless Placido Domingo is in town, it's easy to get one of 567 **standing-room tickets** (*Stehplätze*, €3 up top or €4 downstairs). While the front doors open one hour before the show starts, a side door (middle of building, on the Operngasse side) opens 80 minutes before curtain time, giving those in the know an early grab at standing-room tickets (tickets sold until 20 min after curtain time). Just walk straight in, then head right until you see the ticket booth marked *Stehplätze* (tel. 01/514-447-880). If fewer than 567 people are in line, there's no need to line up early. If you're one of the first 160 in line, try for the "Parterre" section and you'll end up dead-center at stage level, directly under the Emperor's Box (otherwise, you can choose between the third floor—*Balkon*, or the fourth floor—*Galerie*). Dress is casual (but do your best) at the standing-room bar. Locals save their spot along the rail by tying a scarf to it.

The excellent "electronic libretto" translation screens help make the experience worthwhile for opera newbies. (Press the button to turn yours on; press again for English.)

Rick's Crude Tips: For me, three hours is a lot of opera. But just to see and hear the Opera in action for half an hour is a treat. You can buy a standing-room spot and just drop in for part of the show. Ending time is posted in the lobby—you could stop by for just the finale. If you go at the start or finish, you'll see Vienna dressed up. Of the 567 people with cheap standing-room tickets, invariably many will not stand through the entire performance. If you drop by after show-time, you can wait for tourists to leave and bum their tickets off them—be sure to ask them for clear directions to your spot. (While it's perfectly legal to swap standing-room spots, be discreet if finding your spot mid-performance—try to look like you know where you're going.) Even those with standing-room tickets are considered "ticket-holders," and are welcome to explore the building. As you leave, wander around the first floor (fun if leaving early, when halls are empty) to enjoy the sumptuous halls (with prints of famous stage sets and performers) and the grand entry staircase. The last resort (and worst option) is to drop into the Café Oper Vienna inside the Opera, and watch the opera live on TV screens (reasonable menu and drinks).

Vienna Volksoper: For less-serious operettas and musicals, try Vienna's other opera house, located along the Gürtel, west of the city center (see *Wien-Programm* brochure or ask at TI for schedule, Währinger Strasse 78, tel. 01/5144-4360, www.volksoper.at).

Theater an der Wien—Considered the oldest theater in Vienna, this venue was designed in 1801 for Mozart operas—intimate, with just a thousand seats. Reopened in 2006 for Mozart's 250th birthday, it treats Vienna's music lovers to a different opera every month—generally Mozart with a contemporary setting and modern interpretation—with the excellent Vienna Radio Orchestra in the pit. With the reopening of Theater an der Wien, Vienna now supports three opera companies. This one is the only company playing through the summer (facing the Naschmarkt at Linke Wienzeile 6, tel. 01/5883-0660 for information, tickets available at www.theater-wien.at).

Musicals—The Wien Ticket pavilion sells tickets to contemporary American and British musicals performed in the German language (€10–100, €5 standing-room tickets available 2 hours before curtain time), and offers these tickets at half-price from 14:00 until 17:00 the day of the show. Or you can reserve (full-price) tickets for the musicals by phone (call Wien Ticket at tel. 01/58885).

Dance Evening—If you'd like to actually dance (waltz and ballroom), or watch people who are really good at it, consider the Dance Evening at the Tanz Café in the Volksgarten (€5–6, May–Sept, Sat from 19:00 and Sun from 18:00, www.volksgarten.at).

Films of Concerts—To see free films of great concerts in a lively, outdoor setting near City Hall, see "Nightlife," later in this chapter.

Classical Music to Go—To bring home Beethoven, Strauss, or the Wiener Philharmonic on a top-quality CD, shop at Gramola on the Graben or EMI on Kärntner Strasse.

Vienna's Cafés

In Vienna, the living room is down the street at the neighborhood coffee house. This tradition is just another example of Viennese expertise in good living. Each of Vienna's many long-established (and sometimes even legendary) coffee houses has its individual character (and characters). These classic cafés are a bit tired, with a shabby patina and famously grumpy waiters who treat you like an uninvited guest invading their living room. Still, it's a welcoming place. They offer newspapers, pastries, sofas, quick and light workers' lunches, elegant ambience, and "take all the time you want" charm for the price of a cup of coffee. Order it *melange* (like a cappuccino), *brauner* (strong coffee with a little milk), or *schwarzer* (black). Americans who ask for a latte are mistaken for Italians and given a cup of hot milk. Rather than buy the *International Herald Tribune* ahead of time, spend the money on a cup of coffee and read the paper for free, Vienna-style, in a café.

These are my favorites:

Café Hawelka has a dark, "brooding Trotsky" atmosphere, paintings by struggling artists who couldn't pay for coffee, a saloon-wood flavor, chalkboard menu, smoked velvet couches, an international selection of newspapers, and a phone that rings for regulars. Mrs. Hawelka died just a couple weeks after Pope John Paul II. Locals suspect the pontiff wanted her much-loved *Buchteln* (marmalade-filled doughnuts) in heaven. Mr. Hawelka, now alone and understandably a bit forlorn, still oversees the action (Wed–Mon 8:00–2:00 in the morning, Sun from 10:00, closed Tue, just off the Graben, Dorotheergasse 6).

Café Sperl dates from 1880, and is still furnished identically to the day it opened—from the coat tree to the chairs (Mon–Sat 7:00–23:00, Sun 11:00–20:00 except closed Sun July–Aug, just off Naschmarkt near Mariahilfer Strasse, Gumpendorfer 11, tel. 01/586-4158).

Café Bräunerhof, between the Hofburg and the Graben, offers a classic ambience with no tourists and live music on weekends (light classics, no cover, Sat–Sun 15:00–18:00), and a practical menu with daily specials (open long hours daily, Stallburgasse 2).

Other Classics in the Old Center: All of these places are open long hours daily: **Café Pruckel** (at Dr.-Karl-Lueger-Platz, across from Stadtpark at Stubenring 24); **Café Tirolerhof** (2 blocks from the Opera, behind the TI on Tegetthoffstrasse, at Führichgasse 8); and **Café Landtmann** (directly across from the City Hall on the Ringstrasse at Dr.-Karl-Lueger-Ring 4). The Landtmann is unique, as it's the only grand café built along the Ring with all the other grand buildings.

Wein in Wien: Vienna's Wine Gardens *(Heurigen)*

The *Heuriger* (HOY-rih-gur) is a uniquely Viennese institution. When the Habsburgs let Vienna's vintners sell their own new wine (called *Sturm*) tax-free, several hundred families opened *Heurigen* (HOY-rih-gehn)—wine-garden restaurants clustered around the edge of town). A tradition was born. Today, they do their best to maintain the old-village atmosphere, serving the homemade new wine (the last vintage, until November 11, when a new vintage year begins) with small meals and strolling musicians. Most *Heurigen* are decorated with enormous antique presses from their vineyards. Wine gardens might be closed on any given day; call ahead to confirm if you have your heart set on a particular place. (For a near-*Heuriger* experience in downtown Vienna, drop by Gigerl Stadtheuriger, listed at the top of "Eating," later in this chapter.)

At any *Heuriger,* fill your plate at a self-serve cold cut buffet (€6–9 for dinner). Food is sold by the *"10 dag"* unit. (A *dag* is a decigram, so *10 dag* is 100 grams—about a quarter-pound.) Waitresses will then take your wine order (€2.50 per quarter-liter, about 8 oz). Many locals claim it takes several years of practice to distinguish between the *Sturm* wine and vinegar.

Dishes to look for...or look out for: *Stelze* (grilled knuckle of pork), *Fleischlaberln* (fried ground-meat patties), *Schinkenfleckerln* (pasta with cheese and ham), *Schmalz* (a spread made with pig fat), *Blunzen* (black pudding...sausage made from blood), *Presskopf* (jellied brains and innards), *Liptauer* (spicy cheese spread), *Kornspitz* (whole-meal bread roll), and *Kummelbraten* (crispy roast pork with caraway).

For a *Heuriger* evening, rather than go to a particular place, take a tram to the wine-garden district of your choice and wander around, choosing the place with the best ambience. I've listed three good *Heuriger* neighborhoods, plus one rural *Heuriger*, on the outskirts of Vienna (see map on page 23). To reach the neighborhoods from downtown Vienna, it's best to use public transportation (cheap, 30 min, runs late in the evening, directions given per listing below), or you can take a 15-minute taxi ride from the Ring.

Nussdorf—An untouristy district, characteristic and popular with the Viennese, Nussdorf has plenty of *Heuriger* ambience. Right at the last stop on tram #D's route (Beethovengang), you'll find three long and skinny places side by side. Of these, **Schübel-Auer Heuriger** is my favorite (Tue–Sat 16:00–24:00, closed Sun–Mon, Kahlenberger Strasse 22, tel. 01/370-2222). Also consider **Heuriger Kierlinger** (daily 15:30–24:00, Kahlenberger Strasse 20, tel. 01/370-2264) and **Steinschaden** (daily 15:00–24:00, Kahlenberger Strasse 18, tel. 01/370-1375). Walk through any of these and you pop out on Kahlenberger Strasse, where a walk 20 yards uphill takes you to some more eating and drinking fun: **Bamkraxler** ("Tree Jumper"), the only *Biergarten* amid all these vineyards. It's a fun-loving, youthful place with fine keg beer and a regular menu—traditional, ribs, veggie, kids' menu—rather than the *Heuriger* cafeteria line (€8–12 meals, kids' playground, Tue–Sat 16:00–24:00, Sun 11:00–24:00, closed Mon, Kahlenberger Strasse 17, tel. 01/318-8800).

Getting to the Nussdorf **Heurigen:** Take tram #D from the Ringstrasse (stops include the Opera, Hofburg/Kunsthistorisches Museum, and City Hall) to its endpoint (the stop labeled *Nussdorf* isn't the end—stay on for one more stop to Beethovengang). If you're not starting from somewhere near tram #D's route, take the U-4 to Heiligenstadt, then catch tram #D from in front of the U-Bahn station. Tram #D runs every 5–10 minutes (fewer trams after 23:00, last tram around 24:30).

Grinzing—Of the many *Heuriger* suburbs, Grinzing is the most famous, lively...and touristy. If you're looking to avoid tour groups, head elsewhere.

Getting to the Grinzing **Heurigen:** From the Heiligenstadt U-4 station, take bus #38A and get off at Himmelstrasse, just past the green onion-top dome (runs every 10–20 minutes, 2/hr after 21:00, last bus around 22:30).

Don't confuse bus #38A with tram #38—which also goes to Grinzing, but starts at the Ring (at Schottentor). From the Grinzing tram stop, follow Himmelgasse uphill toward the green onion-top dome. You'll pass plenty of wine gardens—and tour buses—on your way up. Just past the dome, you'll find the heart of the *Heurigen.*

Heiligenstadt (Pfarrplatz)—Between Nussdorf and Grinzing, this neighborhood features several decent spots, including the famous and touristy **Mayer am Pfarrplatz** (a.k.a Beethovenhaus, Mon–Sat 16:00–24:00, Sun 11:00–23:00, Pfarrplatz 2, tel. 01/370-1287). This place has a charming inner courtyard with an accordion player and a sprawling backyard with a big children's play zone. Beethoven lived—and began work on his Ninth Symphony—here in 1817; he'd previously written his Sixth Symphony *(Pastorale)* while staying in this then-rural district. He hoped the local spa would cure his worsening deafness. **Weingut and Heuriger Werner Welser,** a block uphill from Beethoven's place, is lots of fun, with music nightly from 19:00 (open daily 15:30–24:00, Probusgasse 12, tel. 01/318-9797).

> *Getting to the Heiligenstadt* **Heurigen:** From the Heiligenstadt U-4 station, take bus #38A (runs every 10–20 min, 2/hr after 21:00, last bus around 22:30). Get off at Fernsprechamt/Heiligenstadt, walk uphill, and take the first right onto Nestelbachgasse, which leads to Pfarrplatz and the Beethovenhaus.

Heuriger Sirbu—This option is actually in the vineyards, high above Vienna with great city and countryside views, a top-notch buffet, a glass veranda, and a traditional interior for cool weather. It's a bit touristy, and dinner reservations are often required, since it's more upmarket and famous as "the ultimate setting" (May–mid-Oct from 15:00, closed Sun, big play zone for kids, Kahlenberger Strasse 210, tel. 01/320-5928). It's high above regular transit service, but fun to incorporate with a little walking. Ideally, ride bus #38A to Kahlenberg, and walk behind the buildings to find Kahlenberger Strasse—then follow it downhill for 15 minutes. (If you're starting with Nussdorf, then going on to Sirbu, follow directions to Bamkraxler—see Nussdorf listing, above—then follow Kahlenberger Strasse uphill for 35 min).

Nightlife

If old music and new wine aren't your thing, Vienna has plenty of alternatives. For an up-to-date rundown on fun after dark, check www.viennahype.at.

City Hall Open-Air Classical-Music Cinema and Food Circus—A thriving people scene erupts each evening in summer (July–early Sept) at the park in front of City Hall (Rathaus, on the Ringstrasse). Thousands of people keep a food circus of 24 simple stalls busy. There's not a plastic cup anywhere, just real plates and glasses—Vienna wants the quality of eating to be as high as the music that's about to begin. About 3,000 folding chairs face a 60-foot-wide screen up against the City Hall's Neo-Gothic facade. When darkness falls, an announcer explains the program, and then the music starts. The program is different every night—mostly movies of opera and classical concerts, with some films. The TI has the schedule (programs generally last about two hours, starting when it's dark—between 21:30 in July and 20:30 in Aug and early Sept).

Since 1991, the city has paid for 60 of these summer event nights each year. Why? To promote culture. Officials know that the City Hall Music Festival is mostly a "meat market" where young people come to hook up. But they believe many of these people will develop a little appreciation of classical music and high culture on the side.

English Cinema—Two great theaters offer three or four screens of English movies nightly (€6–9): **English Cinema Haydn,** near my recommended hotels on Mariahilfer Strasse (Mariahilfer Strasse 57, tel. 01/587-2262, www.haydnkino.at); and **Artis International Cinema,** right in the town center a few minutes from the cathedral (Schultergasse 5, tel. 01/535-6570).

The Third Man at Burg Kino—This movie, voted the best British film ever by the British Film Institute, takes place in 1949 Vienna—when it was divided, like Berlin, between the four victorious Allies. With a dramatic Vienna cemetery scene, coffee-house culture surviving amid the rubble, and Orson Welles being chased through the sewers, the tale of a divided city about to fall under Soviet rule and rife with smuggling is an enjoyable two-hour experience while in Vienna (€8, in English with German subtitles; three or four showings weekly: Fri at 22:45, Tue and Sun afternoons depending on other film times; Opernring 19, tel. 01/587-8406, www.burgkino.at).

Sleeping

As you move out from the center, hotel prices drop. My listings are in the old center (figure at least €100 for a decent double), along the likeable Mariahilfer Strasse (about €90), and near the Westbahnhof (about €70).

Book ahead for Vienna if you can, particularly for holidays. Business hotels have their highest rates in September and October, when it's peak convention time. Prices are also high right around New Year's Eve.

While few accommodations in Vienna are air-conditioned, you can generally get fans on request. Places with elevators often have a few stairs to climb, too.

These hotels lose big and you pay more if you find a room

Sleep Code

(€1 = about $1.40, country code: 43, area code: 01)
S = Single, **D** = Double/Twin, **T** = Triple, **Q** = Quad, **b** = bathroom, **s** = shower only. English is spoken at each place. Unless otherwise noted, credit cards are accepted, rooms have no air conditioning, and breakfast is included.

To help you sort easily through these listings, I've divided the rooms into three categories, based on the price for a standard double room with bath:

$$$ Higher Priced—Most rooms €120 or more.
  $$ Moderately Priced—Most rooms between €75–120.
    $ Lower Priced—Most rooms €75 or less.

VIENNA

through Internet booking sites. Book direct by phone, fax, or email and save. For tips on reaching these hotels upon arrival in Vienna, see "Connections," at the end of this chapter.

Within the Ring, in the Old City Center

You'll pay extra to sleep in the atmospheric old center, but if you can afford it, staying here gives you the best classy Vienna experience.

$$$ Hotel am Stephansplatz is a four-star business hotel with 56 rooms. It's plush but not over-the-top, and reasonably priced for its incredible location—literally facing the cathedral—and sleek comfort. Every detail is modern and quality; breakfast is superb, with a view of the city waking up around the cathedral; and the staff is always ready with a friendly welcome (Sb-€160–180, Db-€210–250, prices vary with season and room size, prices shoot up during conventions—most often in Sept–Oct, €20 less July–Aug and in winter, €15 less Fri–Sun, extra bed-€50, children free or very cheap, air-con, free Internet access, Wi-Fi in lobby, sauna, elevator, Stephansplatz 9, U-1 or U-3: Stephansplatz, tel. 01/534-050, fax 01/5340-5710, www.hotelamstephansplatz.at, office@hotelamstephansplatz.at).

$$$ Hotel Pertschy, circling an old courtyard, is big and hotelesque. Its 56 huge rooms are elegantly creaky, with chandeliers and Baroque touches. Those on the courtyard are quietest (Sb-€95–114, Db-€139–169 depending on room size, €20–30 cheaper off-season, extra bed-€36, non-smoking rooms, free Internet terminal in lobby, free Wi-Fi, elevator, Habsburgergasse 5, U-1 or U-3: Stephansplatz, tel. 01/534-490, fax 01/534-4949, www.pertschy.com/cms/index.html, pertschy@pertschy.com).

$$$ Pension Aviano is another peaceful place, with 17 comfortable rooms on the fourth floor above lots of old-center action

VIENNA

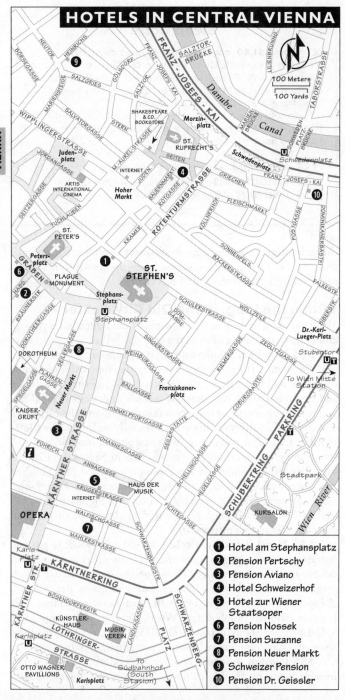

HOTELS IN CENTRAL VIENNA

100 Meters
100 Yards

1 Hotel am Stephansplatz
2 Pension Pertschy
3 Pension Aviano
4 Hotel Schweizerhof
5 Hotel zur Wiener Staatsoper
6 Pension Nossek
7 Pension Suzanne
8 Pension Neuer Markt
9 Schweizer Pension
10 Pension Dr. Geissler

(Sb-€104, Db-€148–169 depending on size, roughly €20 cheaper per room in July–Aug and Nov–March, extra bed-€33, non-smoking rooms, fans, elevator, between Neuer Markt and Kärntner Strasse at Marco d'Avianogasse 1, tel. 01/512-8330, fax 01/5128-3306, www.secrethomes.at, aviano@secrethomes.at).

$$$ Hotel Schweizerhof is classy, with 55 big rooms, all the comforts, shiny public spaces, and a formal ambience. It's centrally located midway between St. Stephen's Cathedral and the Danube Canal (Sb-€85–95, Db-€115–145, extra bed-€35, low prices are for July–Aug and slow times, with cash and this book get your best price and then claim a 10 percent discount, free Wi-Fi, elevator, Bauernmarkt 22, U-1 or U-3: Stephansplatz, tel. 01/533-1931, fax 01/533-0214, www.schweizerhof.at, office@schweizerhof.at). Since this is in a busy nightclub area, it can be noisy on weekends (Thu–Sat). If you'll be here then, ask for a quiet room when you reserve.

$$$ Hotel zur Wiener Staatsoper, the Schweizerhof's sister hotel, is quiet, with a more traditional elegance. Its 22 tidy rooms come with high ceilings, chandeliers, and fancy carpets on parquet floors (tiny Sb-€80–90, Db-€115–145, Tb-€135–155, extra bed-€25, cheaper prices are for July–Aug and Dec–March, fans on request, elevator, a block from the Opera at Krugerstrasse 11; U-1, U-2, or U-4: Karlsplatz; tel. 01/513-1274, fax 01/513-127-415, www.zurwienerstaatsoper.at, office@zurwienerstaatsoper.at, manager Claudia).

$$ At Pension Nossek, an elevator takes you above any street noise into Frau Bernad's and Frau Gundolf's world, where the children seem to be placed among the lace and flowers by an interior designer. With 30 rooms right on the wonderful Graben, this is a particularly good value (S-€52–60, Ss-€62, Sb-€76–80, Db-€120, €30 extra for sprawling suites, extra bed-€35, cash only, elevator, Graben 17, U-1 or U-3: Stephansplatz, tel. 01/5337-0410, fax 01/535-3646, www.pension-nossek.at, reservation@pension-nossek.at).

$$ Pension Suzanne, as Baroque and doily as you'll find in this price range, is wonderfully located a few yards from the Opera. It's small, but run with the class of a bigger hotel. The 25 rooms are packed with properly Viennese antique furnishings and paintings (Sb-€81, Db-€103–124 depending on size, 4 percent discount with this book and cash, extra bed-€25, spacious apartment for up to 6 also available, discounts in winter, fans on request, elevator, free Internet access, free Wi-Fi, Walfischgasse 4; U-1, U-2, or U-4: Karlsplatz and follow signs for Opera exit; tel. 01/513-2507, fax 01/513-2500, www.pension-suzanne.at, info@pension-suzanne.at, manager Michael).

$$ Pension Neuer Markt is family-run, with 37 quiet, comfy rooms in a perfectly central locale. Its hallways have the ambience of a cheap cruise ship (Ss-€60–77, Sb-€90–130, smaller Ds-€80–96, Db-€110–135, prices vary with season and room size, extra bed-€20, request a quiet room when you reserve, fans, fee to use lobby Internet terminal, elevator, Seilergasse 9, tel. 01/512-2316, fax 01/513-9105, www.hotelpension.at/neuermarkt, neuermarkt @hotelpension.at).

$$ Schweizer Pension has been family-owned for three generations. Anita and Gerhard run an extremely tight ship, offering 11 homey rooms for a great price, with parquet floors and lots of tourist info (S-€42–51, big Sb-€65–78, D-€60–75, Db-€82–93, Tb-€105–119, prices depend on season and room size, cash only, entirely non-smoking, elevator, laundry-€18/load, Heinrichsgasse 2, U-2 or U-4: Schottenring, tel. 01/533-8156, fax 01/535-6469, www.schweizerpension.com, schweizer.pension@chello.at). They also rent a quad with bath (€125–132—too small for 4 adults but great for combos of 2 adults/2 kids or 3 adults/1 kid).

$$ Pension Dr. Geissler has 23 plain-but-comfortable rooms in a modern, nondescript apartment building about 10 blocks northeast of St. Stephen's, near the canal (S-€48, Ss-€68, Sb-€76, D-€65, Ds-€77, Db-€95, 20 percent less in winter, elevator, Postgasse 14, U-1 or U-4: Schwedenplatz—Postgasse is to the left as you face Hotel Capricorno, tel. 01/533-2803, fax 01/533-2635, www.hotelpension.at/dr-geissler, dr.geissler@hotelpension.at).

Hotels and Pensions on and near Mariahilfer Strasse

Lively Mariahilfer Strasse connects the Westbahnhof (West Station) and the city center. The U-3 line, starting at the Westbahnhof, goes down Mariahilfer Strasse to the cathedral. This tourist-friendly, vibrant area is filled with shopping malls, simpler storefronts, and cafés. Its smaller hotels and private rooms are generally run by people from the non-German-speaking part of the former Habsburg Empire (i.e., Eastern Europe). Most hotels are within a few steps of a U-Bahn stop, just one or two stops from the Westbahnhof (direction from the station: Simmering). The nearest place to do laundry is **Schnell & Sauber Waschcenter** (wash-€4.50 for small load or €9 for large load, plus a few euros to dry, daily 6:00–23:00, a few blocks north of Westbahnhof on the east side of Urban-Loritz-Platz).

$$$ NH Hotels, a Spanish chain, runs two stern, stylish-but-passionless business hotels a few blocks apart on Mariahilfer Strasse. Both rent ideal-for-families suites, each with a living room, two TVs, bathroom, desk, and kitchenette (rack rate: Db suite-€118–237, going rate usually closer to €130, plus €16 per person for optional breakfast, apartments for 2–3 adults, 1 kid under 12 free, non-smoking rooms, elevator, free Internet access, fee for Wi-Fi).

The 78-room **NH Atterseehaus** is at Mariahilfer Strasse 78 (U-3: Zieglergasse, tel. 01/524-5600, fax 01/524-560-015, nhattersee haus@nh-hotels.com), and the slightly pricier **NH Wien** has 106 rooms at Mariahilfer Strasse 32 (usually around Db-€145, U-3: Neubaugasse—follow *Stiftgasse* signs to exit and turn left from top of escalator; from Mariahilferstrasse, enter through shop passage-way between Nordsee and Edusco—or from Lindengasse 9, tel. 01/521-720, fax 01/521-7215, nhwien@nh-hotels.com). The website for both is www.nh-hotels.com.

$$ Hotel Pension Corvinus is bright, modern, and proudly and warmly run by a Hungarian family: Miklós, Judit, Anthony, and Zoltan. Its 12 comfortable rooms are spacious, and some are downright sumptuous (Sb-€59–69, Db-€95–105, Tb-€109–119, get these special Rick Steves prices with this book, extra bed-€26, also has apartments with kitchens, most rooms non-smoking, air-con, elevator, free Internet access and Wi-Fi, parking garage-€15/day with this book, on the third floor at Mariahilfer Strasse 57–59, U-3: Neubaugasse, tel. 01/587-7239, fax 01/587-723-920, www.corvinus.at, hotel@corvinus.at).

$$ Hotel Pension Mariahilf's 12 rooms are clean, well-priced, and good-sized (if outmoded), with a slight Art Deco flair. Book direct and ask for a Rick Steves discount (Sb-€60–75, twin Db-€78–98, Db-€88–115, Tb-€110–138, 5- to 6-person apartment with kitchen-€115–160, lower prices are for off-season or longer stays, elevator, free Wi-Fi, parking-€15, Mariahilfer Strasse 49, U-3: Neubaugasse, tel. 01/586-1781, fax 01/586-178-122, www.mariahilf-hotel.at, office@mariahilf-hotel.at).

$$ K&T Boardinghouse rents spacious, comfortable, good-value rooms at both of its two locations. The first has three bright and airy rooms three flights above lively Mariahilfer Strasse (no elevator). The second location, just across the street, has five newly-furnished units on the first floor (Db-€79, Tb-€99, Qb-€119, 2-night minimum, no breakfast, air-con-€10/day, cash only but reserve with credit card, non-smoking, free Internet access and Wi-Fi, coffee in rooms, first location: Mariahilfer Strasse 72, second location: Chwallagasse 2; for either, get off at U-3: Neubaugasse; tel. 01/523-2989, mobile 0676-553-6063, fax 01/522-0345, www.ktboardinghouse.at, k.t@chello.at, Tina). To reach the Chwallagasse location from Mariahilfer Strasse, turn left at Café Ritter and walk down Schadekgasse one short block; tiny Chwallagasse is the first right.

$$ Haydn Hotel is big and formal, with masculine pub-lic spaces and 50 spacious rooms (Sb-€80–90, Db-€110–120, suites and family apartments, extra bed-€30, ask for 10 percent Rick Steves discount, all rooms non-smoking, air-con, elevator, free Internet access, fee for Wi-Fi, parking-€15/day, Mariahilfer

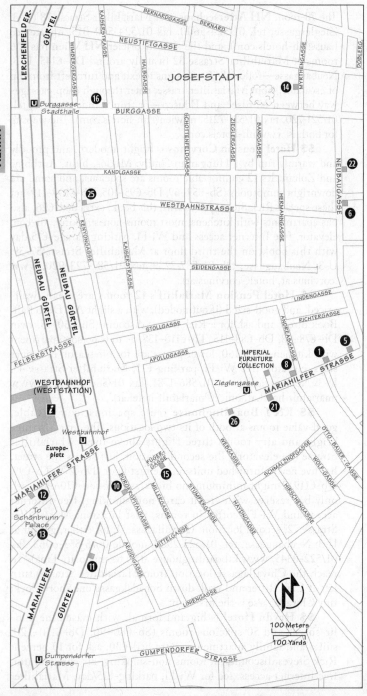

VIENNA

VIENNA

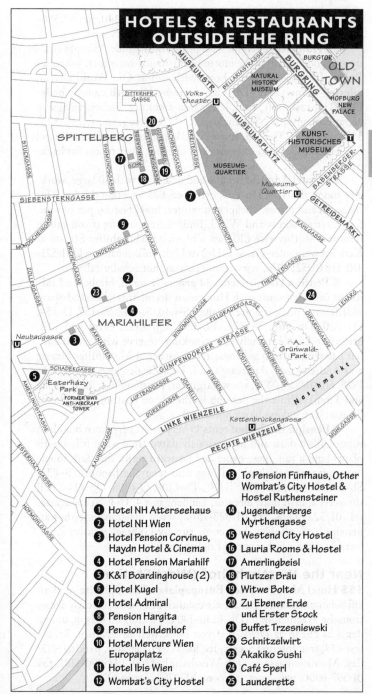

HOTELS & RESTAURANTS
OUTSIDE THE RING

1 Hotel NH Atterseehaus
2 Hotel NH Wien
3 Hotel Pension Corvinus,
   Haydn Hotel & Cinema
4 Hotel Pension Mariahilf
5 K&T Boardinghouse (2)
6 Hotel Kugel
7 Hotel Admiral
8 Pension Hargita
9 Pension Lindenhof
10 Hotel Mercure Wien
   Europaplatz
11 Hotel Ibis Wien
12 Wombat's City Hostel

13 To Pension Fünfhaus, Other
   Wombat's City Hostel &
   Hostel Ruthensteiner
14 Jugendherberge
   Myrthengasse
15 Westend City Hostel
16 Lauria Rooms & Hostel
17 Amerlingbeisl
18 Plutzer Bräu
19 Witwe Bolte
20 Zu Ebener Erde
   und Erster Stock
21 Buffet Trzesniewski
22 Schnitzelwirt
23 Akakiko Sushi
24 Café Sperl
25 Launderette

Strasse 57–59, U-3: Neubaugasse, tel. 01/5874-4140, fax 01/586-1950, www.haydn-hotel.at, info@haydn-hotel.at, Nouri).

$$ Hotel Kugel is run with pride and attitude. "Simple quality and good value" is the motto of the hands-on owner, Johannes Roller. It's a big 34-room hotel with simple Old World charm, offering a fine value (Db-€85, supreme Db with canopy beds-€105–115, cash only, completely non-smoking, Siebensterngasse 43, at corner with Neubaugasse, U-3: Neubaugasse, tel. 01/523-3355, fax 01/5233-3555, www.hotelkugel.at, office@hotelkugel.at). Herr Roller also offers several cheaper basic rooms for backpackers.

$$ Hotel Admiral is huge and practical, with 80 large, workable rooms (Sb-€70, Db-€94, extra bed-€25, mention this book for these special prices, cheaper in winter, breakfast-€6 per person, free Internet access and Wi-Fi, limited free parking if you call to reserve it—otherwise €10/day, a block off Mariahilfer Strasse at Karl-Schweighofer-Gasse 7, U-2 or U-3: Volkstheater, tel. 01/521-410, fax 01/521-4116, www.admiral.co.at, hotel@admiral.co.at).

$ Pension Hargita rents 24 generally small, bright, and tidy rooms (mostly twins) with Hungarian decor. This spick-and-span, well-located place is a great value (S-€40, Ss-€47, Sb-€57, D-€54, Ds-€60, Db-€68, Ts-€75, Tb-€82, Qb-€112, extra bed-€12, breakfast-€5, completely non-smoking, reserve with credit card but pay with cash to get these rates, corner of Mariahilfer Strasse and Andreasgasse, Andreasgasse 1, U-3: Zieglergasse, tel. 01/526-1928, fax 01/526-0492, www.hargita.at, pension@hargita.at, Erika and Tibor). While the pension is directly on bustling Mariahilfer Strasse, its windows block noise well.

$ Pension Lindenhof rents 19 very basic, very worn but clean rooms. It's a dark and mysteriously dated time warp filled with plants (and a fun guest-generated postcard wall); the stark rooms have outrageously high ceilings and teeny bathrooms (S-€32, Sb-€40, D-€54, Db-€72, T-€81, Tb-€108, Q-€108, Qb-€144, hall shower-€2, cash only, elevator, Lindengasse 4, U-3: Neubaugasse, tel. 01/523-0498, fax 01/523-7362, www.pensionlindenhof.at, pensionlindenhof@yahoo.com, run by Gebrael family; Zara, Keram, and his father speak English).

Near the Westbahnhof (West Station)

$$$ Hotel Mercure Wien Europaplatz offers high-rise modern efficiency and comfort in 211 air-conditioned rooms, directly across from the Westbahnhof (Db-€130–170 depending on season, online deals as cheap as Db-€70 if you book well in advance, breakfast-€14, free Internet access, fee for Wi-Fi, elevator, parking-€15/day, Matrosengasse 6, U-3: Westbahnhof, tel. 01/5990-1181, fax 01/597-6900, www.mercure.com, h1707@accor.com).

$$ Hotel Ibis Wien, a modern high-rise hotel with American charm, is ideal for anyone tired of quaint old Europe. Its 340 cookie-cutter rooms are bright, comfortable, and modern, with all the conveniences (Sb-€72, Db-€89, Tb-€106, breakfast-€9.50, air-con, elevator, free Internet access and Wi-Fi in lobby, parking garage-€11/day; exit Westbahnhof to the right and walk 400 yards, Mariahilfer Gürtel 22–24, U-3: Westbahnhof; tel. 01/59998, fax 01/597-9090, www.ibishotel.com, h0796@accor.com).

$ Pension Fünfhaus is big, plain, clean, and bare bones—almost institutional. The neighborhood is rundown (with a few ladies loitering late at night) and the floors are tile, but this 47-room pension offers the best doubles you'll find for about €50 (S-€37, Sb-€45, D-€50–53, Db-€60–63, T-€73–79, Tb-€88–94, 4-person apartment-€100–110, cash only, closed mid-Nov–Feb, Sperrgasse 12, U-3: Westbahnhof, tel. 01/892-3545 or 01/892-0286, fax 01/892-0460, www.pension5haus.at, pension5haus @tiscali.at, Frau Susi Tersch). Half the rooms are in the main building and half are in the annex, which has good rooms but is near the train tracks and a bit scary on the street at night. From the station, ride tram #52 or #58 two stops down Mariahilfer Strasse away from center, and ask for Sperrgasse. Crazy Chicken bike rental, listed under "Getting Around Vienna," near the beginning of this chapter, is just a block farther down Sperrgasse.

Cheap Dorms and Hostels near Mariahilfer Strasse

$ Jugendherberge Myrthengasse is your classic huge and well-run youth hostel, with 260 beds (€17–21 per person in 2- to 6-bed rooms, includes sheets and breakfast, non-members pay €3.50 extra, fee for Internet access, free Wi-Fi, always open, no curfew, lockers and lots of facilities, Myrthengasse 7, tel. 01/523-6316, fax 01/523-5849, hostel@chello.at).

$ Westend City Hostel, just a block from the Westbahnhof and Mariahilfer Strasse, is well-run and well-located, with 180 beds in 4- to 12-bed dorms (€21–25 per person, depending on how many in the room, D-€62–68, €4 cheaper Nov–mid-March—except around New Year's, includes sheets, breakfast, and locker; cash only, fee for Internet access, free Wi-Fi, laundry-€7, Fügergasse 3, tel. 01/597-6729, fax 01/597-672-927, www.westendhostel.at, info @westendhostel.at).

$ Lauria Rooms and Hostel is a creative little place run by friendly Gosha, with two 10-bed coed dorms with lockers for travelers ages 17 to 30 (€16/bed), plus several other rooms sleeping two to four each (any age, €22–25/bed, Ds-€62, Ts-€78, Qs-€96; Kaiserstrasse 77, tram #5 or a 10-min walk from Westbahnhof, tel. 01/522-2555, www.lauria-vienna.at, lauria_vienna@hotmail.com).

$ *More Hostels:* Other hostels with €17–19 beds and €50 doubles near Mariahilfer Strasse are **Wombat's City Hostel** (2 locations: one near tracks behind the station at Grangasse 6, another even closer to station at Mariahilfer Strasse 137, tel. 01/897-2336, www.wombats-hostels.com, office@wombats-vienna.at) and **Hostel Ruthensteiner** (smoke-free; leave the Westbahnhof to the right and follow Mariahilfer Strasse behind the station, then left on Haidmannsgasse for a block, then turn right and find Robert-Hamerling-Gasse 24; tel. 01/893-4202, www.hostelruthensteiner .com, info@hostelruthensteiner.com).

Eating

The Viennese appreciate the fine points of life, and right up there with waltzing is eating. The city has many atmospheric restaurants. As you ponder the Eastern European specialties on menus, remember that Vienna's diverse empire may be no more, but its flavor lingers.

While cuisines are routinely named for countries, Vienna claims to be the only *city* with a cuisine of its own: Vienna soups come with fillings (semolina dumpling, liver dumpling, or pancake slices). *Gulasch* is a beef ragout of Hungarian origin (spiced with onion and paprika). Of course, Wiener schnitzel is traditionally a breaded and fried veal cutlet (though pork is more common these days). Another meat specialty is boiled beef *(Tafelspitz).* While you're sure to have *Apfelstrudel,* try the sweet cheese strudel, too (*Topfenstrudel*—wafer-thin strudel pastry filled with sweet cheese and raisins).

On nearly every corner, you can find a colorful *Beisl* (BYE-zul). These uniquely Viennese taverns are a characteristic cross between an English pub and a French brasserie—filled with poetry teachers and their students, couples loving without touching, housewives on their way home from cello lessons, and waiters who enjoy serving hearty food and drinks at an affordable price. Ask at your hotel for a good *Beisl.*

Two other don't-miss Viennese institutions, its cafés and wine gardens, are covered under "Experiences," earlier in this chapter.

For hardcore Viennese cuisine on a budget, drop by a *Würstel-stand.* The local hot-dog stand is a fixture on city squares throughout the old center, serving a variety of hot dogs and pickled side dishes with a warm corner-meeting-place atmosphere. Be adventurous: Generally, the darker the weenie, the spicier it is. Key words: *Weisswurst*—boiled white sausage; *Bosna*—with onions and curry; *Käsekrainer*—with melted cheese inside; *Debreziner*—spicy Hungarian; *Frankfurter*—our weenie; *frische*—fresh; *Kren*—horseradish; and *Senf*—mustard (ask for *süss*—sweet; or *scharf*—

sharp). Note: Only a tourist puts the sausage in a bun like a hot dog. Munch alternately between the meat and the bread ("that's why you have two hands"), and you'll look like a native.

Near St. Stephen's Cathedral

Each of these eateries is within about a five-minute walk of the cathedral.

Gigerl Stadtheuriger offers a friendly near-*Heuriger* wine cellar experience (à la Grinzing—see "*Wein* in Wien," page 75), often with accordion or live music, without leaving the city center. Just point to what looks good. Food is sold by the weight; 100 grams *(10 dag)* is about a quarter-pound (cheese and cold meats cost about €3 per 100 grams, salads are about €2 per 100 grams; price sheet is posted on the wall to right of buffet line). The *Karree* pork with herbs is particularly tasty and tender. They also have menu entrées, spinach strudel, quiche, *Apfelstrudel,* and, of course, casks of new and local wines (sold by the *Achtel*—eighth-liter glass). Meals run €7–12 (daily 15:00–24:00, indoor/outdoor seating, behind cathedral, a block off Kärntner Strasse, a few cobbles off Rauhensteingasse on Blumenstock, tel. 01/513-4431).

Zu den Drei Hacken, another fun and typical wine cellar, is famous for its local specialties (€10 plates, Mon–Sat 11:00–23:00, closed Sun, indoor/outdoor seating, Singerstrasse 28, tel. 01/512-5895). A third recommended *Stadtheuriger,* the Melker Stiftskeller, sits between Am Hof square and the Ring (listed later in this section).

Buffet Trzesniewski is an institution—justly famous for its elegant and cheap finger sandwiches and small beers (€1 each). Three different sandwiches and a *kleines Bier (Pfiff)* make a fun, light lunch. Point to whichever delights look tasty (or grab the English translation sheet and take time to study your 22 sandwich options). The classic favorites are *Geflügelleber* (chicken liver), *Matjes mit Zwiebel* (herring with onions), and *Speck mit Ei* (bacon and eggs). Pay for your sandwiches and a drink. Take your drink tokens to the lady on the right. Sit on the bench and scoot over to a tiny table when a spot opens up. Trzesniewski has been a Vienna favorite for a century...and many of its regulars seem to have been here for the grand opening (Mon–Fri 8:30–19:30, Sat 9:00–17:00, closed Sun; 50 yards off the Graben, nearly across from brooding Café Hawelka, Dorotheergasse 2; tel. 01/512-3291). In the fall, this is a good opportunity to try the fancy grape juices—*Most* or *Traubenmost.* Their other location, at Mariahilfer Strasse 95, serves the same sandwiches with the same menu in the same ambience, and is near many recommended hotels (Mon–Fri 8:30–19:00, Sat 9:00–18:00, closed Sun).

VIENNA

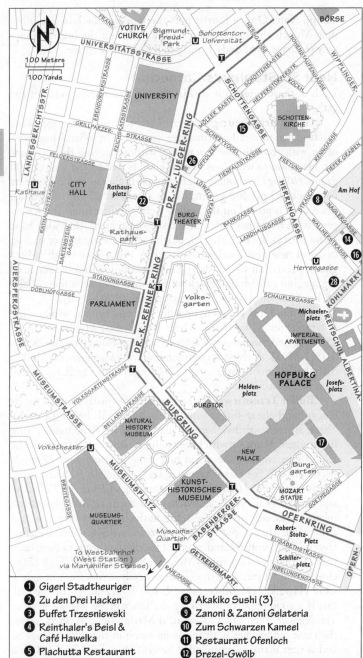

N

100 Meters
100 Yards

FRANK

VOTIVE
CHURCH

Sigmund-
Freud-
Park

Schottentor-
Universität

BÖRSE

UNIVERSITÄTSSTRASSE

WIPPLINGER-

LANDESGERICHTSSTR.

EBENDORFERSTRASSE

REICHSRATSSTRASSE

UNIVERSITY

SCHOTTENGASSE

SCHOTTENBASTEI

HELFERSTORFERSTR.

HOHENSTAUFENGASSE

ROCKH

SCHOTTEN-
KIRCHE

GRILLPARZER-
STRASSE

DR.-K.-LUEGER-RING

MÖLKER BASTEI

SCHREYVOGEL

15

FREYUNG

REINGASSE

TIEFER GRABEN

FELDERSTRASSE

OPOLZER

TIEFENFALTSTRASSE

26

LÖWELSTRASSE

STRAUCH

Am Hof

8

NAGLERGASSE

Rathaus

U

CITY
HALL

Rathaus-
platz

22

Rathaus-
park

BURG-
THEATER

BANKGASSE

LANDHAUSGASSE

HERRENGASSE

WALLNERSTRASSE

14

16

KATHHAUSSTRASSE

BARTENSTEIN-
GASSE

STADIONGASSE

Herrengasse

28

KOHLMARKT

SCHAUFLERGASSE

AUERSPERGSTRASSE

DOBLHOFGASSE

PARLIAMENT

Volks-
garten

Michaeler-
platz

IMPERIAL
APARTMENTS

BREITSCHLI-ALBERTINA-

MUSEUMSTRASSE

VOLKSGARTENSTRASSE

T

BELLARIASTRASSE

NATURAL
HISTORY
MUSEUM

BURGRING

BURGTOR

Helden-
platz

HOFBURG
PALACE

Josefs-
platz

Volkstheater

U

NEW
PALACE

17

Burg-
garten

BREITEGASSE

MUSEUMSPLATZ

KUNST-
HISTORISCHES
MUSEUM

BABENBERGER-
STRASSE

MOZART
STATUE

GOETHEGASSE

OPERNRING

MUSEUMS-
QUARTIER

Museums-
Quartier

U

Robert-
Stoltz-
Platz

ELISABETHSTRASSE

OPERN-

To Westbahnhof
(West Station)
via Mariahilfer Strasse

GETREIDEMARKT

RAHLGASSE

Schiller-
platz

NIBELUNGENGASSE

① Gigerl Stadtheuriger
② Zu den Drei Hacken
③ Buffet Trzesniewski
④ Reinthaler's Beisl &
   Café Hawelka
⑤ Plachutta Restaurant
⑥ Cantinetta La Norma
⑦ Gyros

⑧ Akakiko Sushi (3)
⑨ Zanoni & Zanoni Gelateria
⑩ Zum Schwarzen Kameel
⑪ Restaurant Ofenloch
⑫ Brezel-Gwölb
⑬ Beisl zum Scherer
⑭ Esterhazykeller

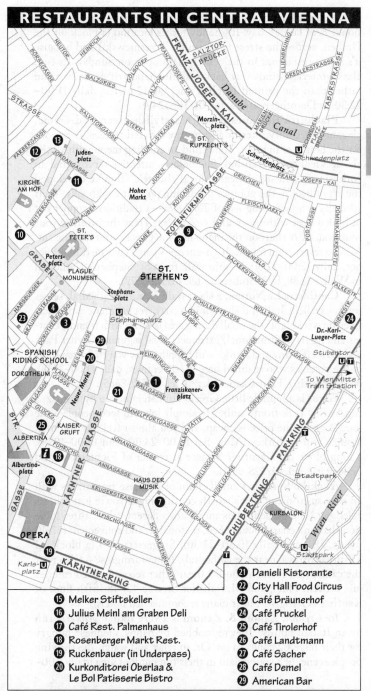

RESTAURANTS IN CENTRAL VIENNA

15 Melker Stiftskeller
16 Julius Meinl am Graben Deli
17 Café Rest. Palmenhaus
18 Rosenberger Markt Rest.
19 Ruckenbauer (in Underpass)
20 Kurkonditorei Oberlaa &
   Le Bol Patisserie Bistro

21 Danieli Ristorante
22 City Hall Food Circus
23 Café Bräunerhof
24 Café Pruckel
25 Café Tirolerhof
26 Café Landtmann
27 Café Sacher
28 Café Demel
29 American Bar

Reinthaler's Beisl is a time warp that serves simple, traditional *Beisl* fare all day. It's handy for its location (a block off the
Graben, across the street from Buffet Trzesniewski) and because
it's a rare restaurant in the center that's open on Sunday. Its fun,
classic interior winds way back (use the handwritten daily menu
rather than the printed English one, €6–12 plates, daily 11:00–
22:30, at Dorotheergasse 4, tel. 01/513-1249).

Plachutta Restaurant, with a stylish green-and-crème,
elegant-but-comfy interior and breezy covered terrace, is famous
for the best beef in town. You'll find an enticing menu with all the
classic Viennese beef dishes, fine deserts, attentive service, and an
enthusiastic and sophisticated local clientele. They've developed
the art of beef to the point of producing popular cookbooks. Their
specialty is a page-long list of *Tafelspitz*—a traditional copper pot
of boiled beef with broth and vegetables. Treat the broth as your
soup course. A chart on the menu lets you choose your favorite cut.
Make a reservation for this high-energy Vienna favorite (€16–21 per
pot, daily 12:00–22:30, 10-min walk from St. Stephen's Cathedral
to Wollzeile 38, U-3: Stubentor, tel. 01/512-1577).

Cantinetta La Norma, a short walk from the cathedral, serves
fresh, excellent Italian dishes amid a cozy, yet energetic ambience.
Even on weeknights the small dining area is abuzz with friendly chat-
ter among its multinational, extremely loyal regulars. Owner Paco
and his staff Hany and Novka will happily show you their snapshots
of the notables who've dined here (€7–18 entrées, daily 11:00–24:00,
outdoor seating, Franziskaner Platz 3, tel. 01/512-8665).

Gyros is a humble little Greek/Turkish joint run by Yilmaz, a
fun-loving Turk from Izmir. He simply loves to feed people—the
food is great, the price is cheap, and you almost feel like you took
a quick trip to Turkey (Mon–Sat 10:00–24:00, Sun 10:00–18:00,
a long block off Kärntner Strasse at corner of Fichtegasse and
Seilerstätte, tel. 01/228-9551).

Akakiko Sushi is a small chain of Japanese restaurants with
an easy sushi menu that's worth considering if you're just schnit-
zeled out. The €9 bento box meals are a decent value. Three locations have no charm but are fast, reasonable, and convenient (€7–10
meals, all open daily 10:30–23:30): Singerstrasse 4 (a block off
Kärntner Strasse near the cathedral), Rotenturmgasse 6 (also near
the cathedral), Heidenschuss 3 (near other recommended eateries
just off Am Hof), and Mariahilfer Strasse 42–48 (fifth floor of
Kaufhaus Gerngross, near many recommended hotels).

Ice Cream!: **Zanoni & Zanoni** is a very Italian *gelateria* run
by an Italian family. They're mobbed by happy Viennese hungry
for their huge €2 cones to go. Or, to relax and watch the thriving
people scene, lick your gelato in their fun outdoor area (daily 7:00–

24:00, 2 blocks up Rotenturmstrasse from cathedral at Lugeck 7, tel. 01/512-7979).

Near Am Hof Square

The square called Am Hof (U-3: Herrengasse) is surrounded by a maze of atmospheric medieval lanes; the following eateries are all within a block of the square.

Zum Schwarzen Kameel ("The Black Camel") is popular for its two classy but very different scenes: a tiny, elegant restaurant and a trendy wine bar. The small, dark-wood, 12-table, Art Nouveau restaurant serves fine gourmet Viennese cuisine (three-course dinner-€60–75 plus pricey wine). The wine bar is filled with a professional local crowd enjoying small plates from the same kitchen at a better price. This is *the* place for horseradish and thin-sliced ham (*Beinschinken mit Kren*, €7 a plate, *Achtung*—the horseradish is *hot*). I'd order the *Vorspeisenteller* (a great antipasti dish that comes with ham and horseradish) and their *Tafelspitz* (€16). Stand, grab a stool, or sit anywhere you can—it's customary to share tables in the wine-bar section. Fine Austrian wines are listed on the board; Aussie bartender Karl can help you choose. They also have a buffet of tiny €1–2 sandwiches (daily 8:30–24:00, Bognergasse 5, tel. 01/533-8125).

Restaurant Ofenloch serves good, old-fashioned Viennese cuisine with friendly service, both indoors and out. This 300-year-old eatery, with great traditional ambience, is dressy (with white tablecloths) but intimate and woodsy. It's central but not overrun with tourists (€13–19 main dishes, Mon–Sat 11:00–22:30, closed Sun, Kurrentgasse 8, tel. 01/533-8844).

Brezel-Gwölb, a Tolkienesque wine cellar with outdoor dining on a quiet square, serves delicious light meals, fine *Krautsuppe* (cabbage soup), and old-fashioned Viennese dishes. It's ideal for a romantic late-night glass of wine (daily 11:30–23:30; leave Am Hof on Drahtgasse, then take first left to Ledererhof 9; tel. 01/533-8811).

Beisl zum Scherer, around the corner, is untouristy and serves traditional plates for €10–15. Sitting outside, you'll face a stern Holocaust memorial. Inside comes with a soothing woody atmosphere and intriguing decor (Mon–Sat 11:30–22:00, closed Sun, Judenplatz 7, tel. 01/533-5164).

Esterhazykeller, both ancient and popular, has traditional fare deep underground. For a cheap and sloppy buffet, climb down to the lowest cellar. For table service on a pleasant square, sit outside (Mon–Sat 11:00–23:00, Sun 16:00–23:00, may close for lunch in Aug–Sept and/or in bad weather, just below Am Hof at Haarhof 1, tel. 01/533-3482).

VIENNA

VIENNA

Melker Stiftskeller is an untouristy *Stadtheuriger* in a deep and rustic circa-1626 cellar with hearty, inexpensive meals and new wine (Tue–Sat 17:00–24:00, closed Sun–Mon and mid-July–mid-Aug, between Am Hof and Schottentor U-Bahn stop at Schottengasse 3, tel. 01/533-5530).

Julius Meinl am Graben, a posh supermarket right on the Graben, has been famous since 1862 as a top-end delicatessen with all the gourmet fancies. Along with the picnic fixings on the shelves, there's a café with light meals and great outdoor seating, a stuffy and pricey restaurant upstairs, and a take-away counter (shop open Mon–Fri 8:00–19:30, Sat 9:00–18:00, closed Sun; restaurant open Mon–Sat until 24:00, closed Sun; Am Graben 19, tel. 01/532-3334).

Near the Opera

Café Restaurant Palmenhaus overlooks the Burggarten (Palace Garden—see page 55). Tucked away in a green and peaceful corner two blocks behind the Opera in the Hofburg's back yard, this is a world apart. If you want to eat modern Austrian cuisine surrounded by palm trees rather than tourists, this is it. And, since it's at the edge of a huge park, it's great for families. Their fresh fish with generous vegetables specials are on the board (€8.50 two-course lunches available Mon–Fri, €15–18 entrées, open daily 10:00–24:00, serious vegetarian dishes, fish, extensive wine list, indoors in greenhouse or outdoors, tel. 01/533-1033).

Rosenberger Markt Restaurant is mobbed with tour groups. Still, if you don't mind a freeway-cafeteria ambience in the center of the German-speaking world's classiest city, this self-service eatery is fast and easy. It's just a block toward the cathedral from the Opera. The best cheap meal here is a small salad or veggie plate stacked high (daily 10:30–23:00, lots of fruits, veggies, fresh-squeezed juices, addictive banana milk, ride the glass elevator downstairs, Maysedergasse 2, tel. 01/512-3458).

Ruckenbauer, a favorite for a quick bite, is a fast-food kiosk in a transit underpass under the street in front of the Opera, between the entryways marked *U2/U4* and *U1* (Mon–Fri 6:00–20:00, Sat–Sun 9:00–20:00). Their €1.60 *Tramezzini* sandwiches and fine pastries make a classy, quick picnic lunch or dinner before the Opera, just 100 yards away.

Kurkonditorei Oberlaa may not have the royal and plush fame of Demel (see page 37), but this is where Viennese connoisseurs serious about the quality of their pastries go to get fat. With outdoor seating on Neuer Markt, it's particularly nice on a hot summer day (€10 daily three-course lunches, great selection of cakes, daily 8:00–20:00, Neuer Markt 16, other locations about town, including the Naschmarkt, tel. 01/5132-9360). Next door, **Le Bol Patisserie Bistro** satisfies your need for something French. The staff speaks to you in French, serving fine €8 salads, baguette sandwiches, and fresh croissants (Mon–Sat 8:00–22:00, Sun 10:00–20:00, Neuer Markt 14).

Danieli Ristorante is your best classy Italian bet in the old center. White-tablecloth dressy, but not stuffy, it has reasonable prices (€10–18 pizza and pastas, fresh fish, open daily, 30 yards off Kärntner Strasse opposite Neuer Markt at Himmelpfortgasse 3, tel. 01/513-7913).

City Hall (Rathausplatz) Food Circus

During the summer, scores of outdoor food stands and hundreds of picnic tables are set up in the park in front of the City Hall. Local mobs enjoy mostly ethnic meals for decent-but-not-cheap prices, and classical entertainment on a big screen (see page 77). The fun thing here is the energy of the crowd, and a feeling that you're truly eating as the Viennese do...not schnitzel and quaint traditions, but trendy "world food" with young people out having fun in a fine Vienna park setting (July–mid-Sept daily from 11:00 until late, in front of City Hall on the Ringstrasse).

Spittelberg Quarter

A charming cobbled grid of traffic-free lanes and Biedermeier apartments has become a favorite neighborhood for Viennese wanting a little dining charm between the MuseumsQuartier and Mariahilfer Strasse (handy to many recommended hotels; take Stiftgasse from Mariahilfer Strasse, or wander over here after you close down the Kunsthistorisches Museum). Tables tumble down sidewalks and into breezy courtyards filled with appreciative natives enjoying dinner or a relaxing drink. It's only worth the trip on a balmy summer evening, as it's dead in bad weather. Stroll Spittelberggasse, Schrankgasse, and Gutenberggasse and pick your favorite. Don't miss the vine-strewn wine garden at Schrankgasse 1. To locate these restaurants, see the map on pages 84–85.

Amerlingbeisl, with a casual atmosphere both on the cobbled street and in its vine-covered courtyard, is a great value (€7 plates, €6–8 daily specials, salads, veggie dishes, traditional specialties, daily 9:00–2:00 in the morning, Stiftgasse 8, tel. 01/526-1660).

Plutzer Bräu, next door, is also good (ribs, burgers, traditional dishes, Tirolean beer from the keg, daily 11:00–2:00 in the morning, food until 24:00, Schrankgasse 4, tel. 01/526-1215).

Witwe Bolte is classier and a good choice for uninspired Viennese cuisine with tablecloths. Its tiny square has wonderful leafy ambience (daily 11:30–23:30 except closed 15:00–17:30

mid-Jan–mid-March, Gutenberggasse 13, tel. 01/523-1450).

Zu Ebener Erde und Erster Stock is a charming little restaurant with a near-gourmet menu. The upstairs is Biedermeier-style, with violet tablecloths and seating for about 20. The downstairs is more casual and woody. Reservations are smart (traditional three-course fixed-price meal-€30, Mon–Fri 7:00–20:30, closed Sat–Sun, Burggasse 13, tel. 01/523-6254).

Near Mariahilfer Strasse

Mariahilfer Strasse (see map on pages 84–85) is filled with reasonable cafés serving all types of cuisine. For a quick yet traditional bite, consider the venerable **Buffet Trzesniewski** sandwich bar at Mariahilfer Strasse 95 (see page 89).

Schnitzelwirt is an old classic with a 1950s patina and a clientele to match. In this once-smoky, still-working-class place, no one finishes their schnitzel ("to-go" for the dog is wrapped in newspaper, "to-go" for you is wrapped in foil). You'll find no tourists, just cheap €6 schnitzel meals (Mon–Sat 10:00–23:00, closed Sun, Neubaugasse 52, tel. 01/523-3771).

Naschmarkt (described on page 63) is Vienna's best Old World market, with plenty of fresh produce, cheap local-style eateries, cafés, *Döner Kebab* and sausage stands, and the best-value sushi in town (Mon–Fri 6:00–18:30, Sat 6:00–17:00, closed Sun, closes earlier in winter; U-4: Karlsplatz, follow *Karlsplatz* signs out of the station). Survey the lane of eateries at the end of the market nearest the Opera. The circa-1900 pub is inviting. Picnickers can buy supplies at the market and eat on nearby Karlsplatz (plenty of chairs facing the Karlskirche).

Connections

By Train

Vienna has two main train stations. The Westbahnhof (West Station) serves Munich, Salzburg, Melk, and Budapest. The Südbahnhof (South Station) serves Prague, Italy, and points east (though some Italy-bound trains go from the Westbahnhof). Trains don't always adhere to these generalizations, so always confirm which station your train leaves from. Looking ahead, Vienna is constructing a new main station that's due to start operating in 2011; it'll be near the current Südbahnhof and eventually take its place.

For general train information in Austria, call 051-717 (to get an operator, dial 2, then 2).

Westbahnhof (West Station): The Reisebüro am Bahnhof desk has maps, books hotels (for a pricey fee), sells the Vienna

Card (described on page 26), and answers questions (Mon–Fri 8:00–19:00, Sat 8:00–13:00, closed Sun). Nearby is a train info desk (daily 7:30–21:00). The Westbahnhof also has a grocery store (daily 5:30–23:00), ATMs, change offices, a post office, and storage facilities. Airport buses and taxis wait in front of the station.

To get to the city center (and most likely, your hotel), take the U-Bahn (subway) on the U-3 line (buy your ticket or transit pass—described under "Getting Around Vienna," near the beginning of this chapter—from a machine). Follow *U-3* signs down to the tracks (for Mariahilfer Strasse hotels or the center, direction: Simmering). If your hotel is along Mariahilfer Strasse, your stop is on this line (see page 82). If you're sleeping in the center or just can't wait to start sightseeing, ride five stops to Stephansplatz, escalate to the exit (direction: Stephansplatz), and you'll hit St. Stephen's Cathedral. From the cathedral, the TI is a five-minute stroll down the busy Kärntner Strasse pedestrian street.

Südbahnhof (South Station): To get from the Südbahnhof to Vienna's center, you can take tram #D to the Ring (departs every 5 min, stops right at the Opera). Bus #13A goes to Mariahilfer Strasse, where many of my recommended hotels are located. (You could also take the S- or U-Bahn, but the tram or bus are much easier.)

To get from downtown to the Südbahnhof in a hurry, take the U-3 to Südtiroler Platz and follow signs to the station (about a 5-min walk).

From Vienna by Train to: Salzburg (1–2/hr, 2.5–3 hrs), **Hallstatt** (hourly, 4 hrs, change in Attnang-Puchheim), **Innsbruck** (every 2 hrs, 5 hrs), **Budapest** (every 2 hours direct, 3 hrs; more with transfers), **Prague** (5/day direct, 4.5 hrs; more with 1 change, 5–6 hrs), **Munich** (3/day direct, 4.25 hrs; otherwise about hourly, 5–5.75 hrs, transfer in Salzburg), **Berlin** (8/day, most with 1 change, 9.5 hrs, some via Czech Republic; longer on night train), **Zürich** (nearly hourly, 9–10 hrs, 1 with changes in Innsbruck and Feldkirch, night train), **Ljubljana** (1 convenient early-morning direct train, 6 hrs; otherwise 6/day with change in Villach, Maribor, or Graz, 6–7 hrs), **Zagreb** (4/day, 5.5–7 hrs, 2 direct, others with 1–2 changes), **Kraków** (3 decent daytime options, 6.25 hrs direct or 7–8.5 hrs with 1–3 changes, plus a night train), **Warsaw** (2/day direct including 1 night train, 7.75–8.5 hrs), **Rome** (3/day, 13–15 hrs, plus several overnight options), **Venice** (1 direct/day, 10.5 hrs; 3/day, 10–12 hrs with changes; plus 1 direct night train, 12 hrs), **Frankfurt** (7/day direct, 7 hrs), **Paris** (7/day, 12–17 hrs, 1–3 changes, night train), **Amsterdam** (5/day, 11–14 hrs, 1–3 changes, 1 night train via Frankfurt).

By Plane

Vienna International Airport

The airport, 12 miles from the center, has easy connections to Vienna's various train stations (airport tel. 01/700-722-233, www .viennaairport.com).

To get from the airport to the center of town, your cheapest option is taking the S-Bahn commuter train to the central Wien-Mitte Bahnhof, on the east side of the Ring (S-7 yellow, €3.40, buy 2-zone ticket from machines on the platform, price includes any bus or S- or U-Bahn transfers, 2/hr, generally departs at :09 and :39, 24 min). You can also take the newer City Airport Train to the Wien-Mitte Bahnhof (CAT, follow green signs, €10, 2/hr, usually departs at :05 and :35, 16 min, www.cityairporttrain.com). From Wien-Mitte you can take the U-Bahn to Mariahilfer Strasse or other neighborhoods.

Express airport buses (parked immediately in front of the arrival hall, €6, 2/hr, 30 min, buy ticket from driver, note time to destination on curbside TV monitors) go conveniently to the Schwedenplatz U-Bahn station (for city-center hotels), the Westbahnhof (for Mariahilfer Strasse hotels), and the Südbahnhof, where it's easy to continue by taxi or public transportation (see "By Train," previous page).

Taxis into town cost about €35 (including the €11 airport surcharge); taxis also wait at the downtown terminus of each airport transit service. Hotels arrange for fixed-rate car service to the airport (€30, 30-min ride).

Bratislava Airport

The airport in nearby Bratislava, Slovakia—a hub for some low-cost flights—is just an hour away from Vienna. The fastest option for getting from Bratislava to Vienna is to take a Eurolines bus from the Bratislava Airport to the Erdberg stop of Vienna's U-3 subway line (9/day, €10, trip takes about an hour, book in advance, www.gratislava.at). A taxi from Bratislava Airport directly to Vienna costs €60–90 (depending on whether you use a cheaper Slovak or more expensive Austrian cab).

SALZBURG

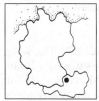

Salzburg is forever smiling to the tunes of Mozart and *The Sound of Music*. Thanks to its charmingly preserved old town, splendid gardens, Baroque churches, and Europe's largest intact medieval fortress, Salzburg feels made for tourism. It's a museum city with class. Vagabonds wish they had nicer clothes.

Even without Mozart and the von Trapps, Salzburg is steeped in history. In about A.D. 700, Bavaria gave Salzburg to Bishop Rupert in return for his promise to Christianize the area. Salzburg remained an independent city (belonging to no state) until Napoleon came in the early 1800s. Thanks in part to its formidable fortress, Salzburg managed to avoid the ravages of war for 1,200 years...until World War II. Much of the city was destroyed by WWII bombs (mostly around the train station), but the historic old town survived.

Eight million tourists crawl its cobbles each year. That's a lot of Mozart balls—and all that popularity has led to a glut of businesses hoping to catch the tourist dollar. Still, Salzburg is both a must and a joy.

Planning Your Time

While Salzburg's sights are rather mediocre, the town itself is a Baroque museum of cobbled streets and elegant buildings—simply a touristy stroller's delight. Even if your time is short, consider allowing half a day for the *Sound of Music* tour. The *S.O.M.* tour kills a nest of sightseeing birds with one ticket (city overview, *S.O.M.* sights, and a fine drive through the lakes).

You'd probably enjoy at least two nights in Salzburg—nights are important for swilling beer in atmospheric local gardens and attending concerts in Baroque halls and chapels. Seriously consider one of Salzburg's many evening musical events (a few are free, some are as cheap as €12, and most average €30–40).

A day trip from Salzburg to Hallstatt (the small-town highlight of the Salzkammergut Lake District—see next chapter) is doable, but involves about five hours for the round-trip transportation alone and makes for a very long day. An overnight in Hallstatt is better.

Orientation

(area code: 0662)

Salzburg, a city of 150,000 (Austria's fourth-largest), is divided into old and new. The old town, sitting between the Salzach River and its mini-mountain (Mönchsberg), holds nearly all the charm and most of the tourists. The new town, across the river, has its own share of sights and museums, plus some good accommodations.

Tourist Information

Salzburg has three helpful TIs (main tel. 0662/889-870, www.salzburg.info): at the **train station** (daily June–Aug 8:15–20:00, April–May and Sept–Oct 8:45–19:00, Nov–March 8:45–18:00, tel. 0662/8898-7340); on **Mozartplatz** in the old center (daily 9:00–18:00, July–mid-Sept until 19:00, closed Sun mid-Jan–Easter and Oct–mid-Nov, tel. 0662/889-870); and at the **Salzburg Süd park-and-ride** (generally open daily July–Aug 10:00–16:30 but sometimes longer hours, May–June Thu–Sat 10:00–16:30, Sept Mon–Sat 10:00–16:30, closed in winter, tel. 0662/8898-7360).

At any TI, you can pick up a free city-center map (the €0.70 map has a broader coverage and more information on sights, but probably isn't necessary), the Salzburg Card brochure (listing sights with current hours and prices), and a bimonthly schedule of events. Book a concert upon arrival. The TIs also book rooms for a €2.20 fee.

Salzburg Card: The TIs sell the Salzburg Card, which covers all your public transportation (including elevator and funicular) and admission to all the city sights (including Hellbrunn Castle and a river cruise). The card is pricey (€24/24 hrs, €32/48 hrs, €37/72 hrs, €2 cheaper Oct–April), but if you'd like to pop into all the sights, it can save money and enhance your experience. To analyze your potential savings, here are the major sights and what you'd pay without the card: Hohensalzburg Fortress and funicular-€10.50; Mozart's Birthplace and Residence-€10; Hellbrunn Castle-€8.50; Salzburg Panorama 1829-€2; Salzach River cruise-€13; 24-hour transit pass-€4.20. Busy sightseers can save plenty. Get this card, feel the financial pain once, and the city will be all yours.

Arrival in Salzburg

By Train: The Salzburg station is user-friendly. The TI is at track 2A. Downstairs at street level, you can store your luggage, buy tickets, and get train information. Bike rental is nearby (see "Getting Around Salzburg"). City buses depart from the lot facing the station (monitors clearly show each bus' destination—any bus heading for *Zentrum* stops near the main bridge in the old town, including buses #1, #3, #5, #6, and #25; get off at the first stop after you cross the river for most sights and city-center hotels, or just before the bridge for Linzergasse hotels). Figure €7 for a taxi to the center.

To walk downtown (15 minutes), leave the station ticket hall to the left, and walk straight down Rainerstrasse, which leads under the tracks past Mirabellplatz, turning into Dreifaltigkeitsgasse. From here, you can turn left onto Linzergasse for many of my recommended hotels, or cross the Staatsbrücke bridge for the old town (and more hotels). For a more dramatic approach, leave the station the same way but follow the tracks to the river, turn left, and walk the riverside path toward the fortress.

By Car: Coming on the A-1 from Vienna or Munich, take the A-10 toward Hallein and then take the next exit (Salzburg Süd) in the direction of Anif. First, you'll pass Hellbrunn Castle (and zoo), then the Salzburg Süd TI and a park-and-ride service—a smart place to park while visiting Salzburg. Park your car (€5), get sightseeing information and transit tickets from the TI (see above), and catch the shuttle bus into town (€1.80 for a single ticket, or covered by €4.20 *Tageskarte* day pass, both sold at the TI, more expensive if you buy tickets on board, every 5 min, bus #3, #8, or #28).

Mozart never drove in the old town, and neither should you. If you don't believe in park-and-rides, the easiest, cheapest, most central parking lot is the 1,500-car Altstadt lot in the tunnel under the Mönchsberg (€14/day, note your slot number and which of the twin lots you're in, tel. 0662/846-434). Your hotel may provide discounted parking passes.

Helpful Hints

Recommendations Skewed by Kickbacks: Salzburg is addicted to the tourist dollar, and it can never get enough. Virtually all hotels are on the take when it comes to concert and tour recommendations, influenced more by their potential kickback than by what's best for you. Take their advice with a grain of salt.

Internet Access: The Internet kiosk a few doors down from the Mozartplatz TI is well-located, but too expensive (€2/10 min). Cheaper places around the old town aren't hard to find. Two Internet cafés at the bottom of the cliff, between

Getreidegasse and the Mönchsberg lift, have good prices and hours (€2/hr, daily 10:00–22:00). Across the river, there's a big, handy Internet café on Theatergasse (near Mozart's Residence, €2/hr, daily 9:00–23:00), and plenty more near the station (including **Bubblepoint,** a modern launderette—see "Laundry" below). Readers of this book can get online free at the Panorama Tours terminal on Mirabellplatz (daily 8:00–18:00).

Post Office: A full-service post office is located in the heart of town, in the new Residenz (Mon–Fri 7:00–18:30, Sat 8:00–10:00, closed Sun).

Laundry: The launderette at the corner of Paris-Lodron-Strasse and Wolf-Dietrich-Strasse, near my recommended Linzergasse hotels, is handy (€10 self-service, €15 same-day full-service, Mon–Fri 7:30–18:00, Sat 8:00–12:00, closed Sun, tel. 0662/876-381). To do your laundry and email at the same time, head to **Bubblepoint** (wash and dry for €6, six Internet terminals, daily 7:00–23:00; with your back to the train station, take the first left for one block, then head right to Karl-Wurmb-Strasse 2; tel. 0664/471-1484).

Getting Around Salzburg

By Bus: Single-ride tickets for central Salzburg *(Einzelkarte–Kernzone)* are sold on the bus for €2. At machines and *Tabak/Trafik* shops, you can buy €1.80 single-ride tickets or a €4.20 day pass *(Tageskarte,* good for 24 hours, €5 if you buy it on the bus). To signal the driver that you want to get off, press the buzzer on the pole. Bus info: tel. 800-660-660.

By Bike: Salzburg is fun for cyclists. The following two bike-rental shops offer 20 percent off with a valid train ticket or Eurailpass—ask for it. **Top Bike** rents bikes from two outlets: at the river side of the train station (exit to the left and walk 50 yards), and on the river next to the Staatsbrücke (€6/2 hrs, €10/4 hrs, €15/24 hrs, usually daily April–June and Sept–Oct 10:00–17:00, July–Aug 9:00–19:00, closed Nov–March, tel. 06272/4656, mobile 0676-476-7259 and 0676-720-0047, www.topbike.at, Sabine).

Velo-Active rents bikes in the old town, just outside the TI on Mozartplatz (€4.50/1 hr, €7/2 hrs, €15/24 hrs; mountain bikes-€6/hr, €18/24 hrs; daily 9:00–18:00, until 19:00 July–Aug, but hours unreliable—you may have to call or let the Panorama Tours man nearby help you, shorter hours off-season and in bad weather, passport number for security deposit, tel. 0662/435-5950, mobile 0676-435-5950). Some of my recommended hotels and pensions rent bikes, and several of the B&Bs on Moosstrasse let guests use them for free).

By Funicular and Elevator: The old town is connected to the top of the Mönchsberg mountain (and great views) via funicular and elevator. The **funicular** *(Festungsbahn)* whisks you up to the imposing Hohensalzburg Fortress (included in castle admission, goes every few minutes). The **elevator** (labeled *MönchsbergAufzug*) on the east side of the old town propels you to the recommended Gasthaus Stadtalm café and hostel, the Museum of Modern Art, wooded paths, and more great views (€2 one-way, €3 round-trip, daily 8:30–19:00, Wed until 21:00; July–Aug daily until 1:00 in the morning, May–Sept starts running at 8:00).

By Taxi: Meters start at about €3 (from train station to your hotel, allow about €7). As always, small groups can taxi for about the same price as riding the bus.

By Buggy: The horse buggies *(Fiaker)* that congregate at Residenzplatz charge €36 for a 25-minute trot around the old town (German-only website: www.fiaker-salzburg.at).

Tours

Walking Tours—On any day of the week, you can take a two-language, one-hour guided walk of the old town without a reservation—just show up at the TI on Mozartplatz and pay the guide. The tours are informative, but you'll be listening to a half-hour of German (€8, daily at 12:15 and 14:00, tel. 0662/8898-7330). To save money (and avoid all that German), you can easily do it on your own using my self-guided walk—see next section.

Private Guides—**Christiana Schneeweiss** ("Snow White"), a hardworking young guide and art historian with a passion for fitting local history into the big picture, gives spirited private tours (€80/1 hr, €129/2 hrs, €150/3 hrs, tel. 0664/340-1757, www.kultur-tourismus.com, info@kultur-tourismus.com). Check her website for bike tours, private minibus tours, and more. **Bärbel Schalber,** one of Salzburg's senior guides, offers a two-hour walk packed with information and spicy opinions (€75 per family, €108 for a group of adults, tel. 0662/632-225, mobile 0664-412-3708, schalber.salzburg@aon.at). Salzburg has many other good guides (to book, call 0662/840-406).

▲▲Sound of Music Tour—I took this tour skeptically (as part of my research)—and liked it. It includes a quick but good general city tour, hits the *S.O.M.* spots (including the stately home, flirtatious gazebo, and grand wedding church), and shows you a lovely stretch of the Salzkammergut Lake District. This is worthwhile for *S.O.M.* fans and those who won't otherwise be going into the Salzkammergut. Warning: Many think rolling through the Austrian countryside with 30 Americans singing "Doe, a Deer" is pretty schmaltzy. Local Austrians don't understand all the commotion, and the audience is mostly native English speakers.

SALZBURG

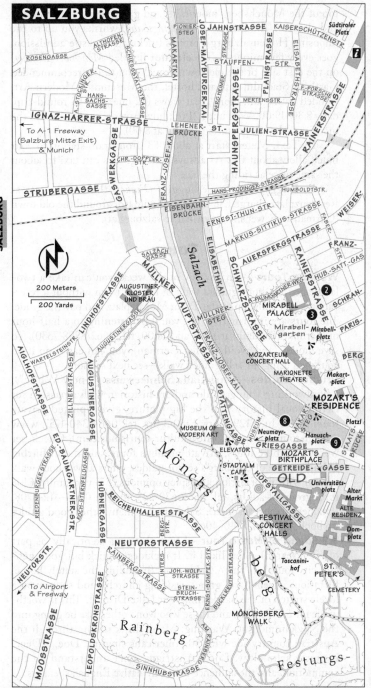

ROSENGASSE

PIONIER-STEG

JAHNSTRASSE

KAISERSCHÜTZENSTR.

Südtiroler Platz

ALTHOFEN-STRASSE

JOSEF-MAYBURGER-KAI

STAUFFEN-STR.

PLAINSTRASSE

ELISABETHSTRASSE

HANS-SACHS-GASSE

A.-STOCKINGER-STR.

SCHIESSSTÄTTSTRASSE

MAKARTKAI

BERGHEIMER STRASSE

HAUNSPERGSTRASSE

MERTENSSTR.

F.-PORSCHE-STRASSE

RAINERSTRASSE

IGNAZ-HARRER-STRASSE

To A-1 Freeway
(Salzburg Mitte Exit)
& Munich

LEHENER-BRÜCKE

ST.-JULIEN-STRASSE

GASWERKGASSE

CHR.-DOPPLER-STR.

FRANZ-JOSEF-KAI

HANS-PRODINGER-STRASSE

HUMBOLDTSTR.

STRUBERGASSE

EISENBAHN-BRÜCKE

ERNEST-THUN-STR.

MARKUS-SITTIKUS-STRASSE

AUERSPERGSTRASSE

WEISER-

FABER-

LINDHOFSTRASSE

SALZACHGASSE

ELISABETHKAI

Salzach

SCHWARZSTRASSE

RAINERSTRASSE

HUB.-SATT.-GAS

FRANZ-

200 Meters

200 Yards

AUGUSTINER-KLOSTER UND BRÄU

MÜLLNER HAUPTSTRASSE

MÜLLNER-STEG

B.-PAUMGARTNER-WEG

2

SCHRAN-

AIGLHOFSTRASSE

WARTELSTEINSTR.

AUGUSTINERGASSE

FRANZ-JOSEF-KAI

Mirabell-garten

MIRABELL PALACE

3

Mirabell-platz

PARIS-

BERG.

WILLNERSTRASSE

ILLIZ

GSTÄTTENGASSE

MOZARTEUM CONCERT HALL

MARIONETTE THEATER

Makart-platz

Mönchs-

MUSEUM OF MODERN ART

MOZART'S RESIDENCE

ED.-BAUMGARTNER-STR.

RIEDENBURGER STRASSE

KOCH-STERNFELDGASSE

HÜBNERGASSE

ELEVATOR

8

Neumayr-platz

GRIESGASSE

MAKARTSTEG

Platzl

RIEDENBURGER STRASSE

STADTALM CAFÉ

MOZART'S BIRTHPLACE

Hanusch-platz

9

STAATS-BRÜCKE

REICHENHALLER STRASSE

GETREIDE-GASSE

OLD

HOFSTALLGASSE

Universitäts-platz

Alter Markt

ALTE RESIDENZ

NEUTORSTRASSE

UNTERS-

RAINBERGSTRASSE

JOH.-WOLF-STRASSE

STEIN-BRUCH-STRASSE

BÜCKLREUTH STRASSE

ERNST-SOMPEK-STR.

FESTIVAL CONCERT HALLS

berg

Toscanini-hof

Dom-platz

ST. PETER'S CEMETERY

NEUTORSTR.

To Airport
& Freeway

MOOSSTRASSE

LEOPOLDSKRONSTRASSE

AM RAINBERG

Rainberg

SINNHUBSTRASSE

MÖNCHSBERG WALK

Festungs-

SALZBURG

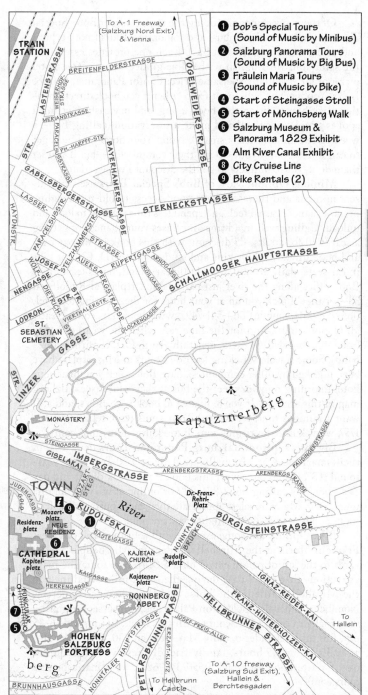

1 Bob's Special Tours (Sound of Music by Minibus)
2 Salzburg Panorama Tours (Sound of Music by Big Bus)
3 Fräulein Maria Tours (Sound of Music by Bike)
4 Start of Steingasse Stroll
5 Start of Mönchsberg Walk
6 Salzburg Museum & Panorama 1829 Exhibit
7 Alm River Canal Exhibit
8 City Cruise Line
9 Bike Rentals (2)

SALZBURG

Of the many companies doing the tour, consider Bob's Special Tours (usually uses a minibus) and Panorama Tours (more typical and professional, big 50-seat bus). Each one provides essentially the same tour (in English with a live guide, 4 hours, free hotel pick-up) for essentially the same price: €37 for Panorama, €40 for Bob's. You'll get a €5 discount from either if you book direct, mention Rick Steves, bring this book along, and pay cash. Getting a spot is simple—just call and make a reservation (calling Bob's a week or two in advance is smart). Note: Your hotel will be eager to call to reserve for you—to get their commission—but if you let them do it, you're unlikely to get the discount I've negotiated.

Minibus Option: Most of **Bob's Special Tours** use an eight-seat minibus and therefore have good access to old-town sights, promote a more casual feel, and spend less time waiting to load and unload. Calling well in advance increases your chances of getting a seat (€40 for adults, €5 discount with this book if you pay cash and book direct, €35 for kids and students with ID, €30 for kids in car seats, daily at 9:00 and 14:00 year-round, buses leave from Bob's office along the river just east of Mozartplatz at Rudolfskai 38—or they'll pick you up at your hotel for the morning tour, tel. 0662/849-511, mobile 0664-541-7492, www.bobstours.com). Nearly all of Bob's tours stop for the luge ride when the weather is dry (mountain bobsled—€4 extra, generally April–Oct, confirm beforehand). Some travelers looking for Bob's tours at Mozartplatz have been hijacked by other companies...have Bob's pick you up at your hotel (morning only) or meet the bus at their office (see Salzburg map in this section). If you're unable to book with Bob's, and still want a minibus tour, try **Kultur Tourismus** (€50, tel. 0664/340-1757, www.kultur-tourismus.com, info@kultur-tourismus.com).

Big-Bus Option: Salzburg Panorama Tours depart from their smart kiosk at Mirabellplatz daily at 9:30 and 14:00 year-round (€37, €5 discount with this book if you book direct and pay cash, book by calling 0662/874-029 or online at www.panorama tours.com). Many travelers appreciate their more businesslike feel, roomier buses, and slightly higher vantage point.

Bike Option: For some exercise with your tour, you can meet **Fräulein Maria** at the Mirabell Gardens (at Mirabellplatz 4, 50 yards to the left of palace entry) for a *S.O.M.* bike tour. The main attractions that you'll pass during the seven-mile pedal include the Mirabell Gardens, the horse pond, St. Peter's Cemetery, Nonnberg Abbey, Leopoldskron Palace and, of course, the gazebo (€24 includes bike, €2 discount with this book, €15 for kids 6–15 pay, €10 for kids under 6, daily May–Sept at 9:30, June–Aug also at 16:30, allow 3.5 hours, family-friendly, reservations required only for afternoon tours, tel. 0650/342-6297, www.mariasbicycle tours.com).

More Tours—Both Bob's and Panorama Tours also offer an extensive array of other day trips from Salzburg (Berchtesgaden/ Eagle's Nest, salt mines, and Salzkammergut lakes and mountains are the most popular, with the same discount—€5 off with this book if you book direct and pay cash). The tours are explained in their brochures, which litter hotel lobbies all over town.

City Cruise Line (a.k.a. Stadt Schiff-Fahrt) runs a basic 40-minute round-trip river cruise with recorded commentary (€13, 9/day July–Aug, 7/day in June, fewer Sept–Oct and April–May, no boats Nov–March). For a longer cruise, ride to Hellbrunn and return by bus (€16, 1–2/day April–Oct). Boats leave from the old-town side of the river just downstream of the Makartsteg bridge (tel. 0662/8257-6912). While views can be cramped, passengers are treated to a fun finale just before docking, when the captain twirls a fun "waltz."

Self-Guided Walk

▲▲▲Salzburg's Old Town

I've linked the best sights in the old town into this handy self-guided orientation walk. Any recommended restaurants mentioned are described more fully in "Eating," later in this chapter.

• *Begin in the heart of town, just up from the river, near the TI on...*

❶Mozartplatz

All the happy tourists around you probably wouldn't be here if not for the man honored by this statue—Wolfgang Amadeus Mozart (erected in 1842). Mozart spent much of his first 25 years (1756–1777) in Salzburg, the greatest Baroque city north of the Alps. But the city itself is much older: The Mozart statue actually sits on bits of Roman Salzburg. And the pink Church of St. Michael that overlooks the square dates from A.D. 800. The first Salzburgers settled right around here. Near you is the TI (with a concert box office), and just around the downhill corner is a pedestrian bridge leading over the Salzach River to the quiet and most medieval street in town, Steingasse (described on page 121).

• *Walk toward the cathedral and into the big square with the huge fountain.*

❷Residenzplatz

Important buildings ringed this square when it was the ancient Roman forum...and they still do. Salzburg's energetic Prince-Archbishop Wolf Dietrich (who ruled from 1587 to 1612) was raised in Rome, counted the Medicis as his buddies, and had grandiose Italian ambitions for Salzburg. After a convenient fire destroyed the cathedral, he set about building "the Rome of the North." This

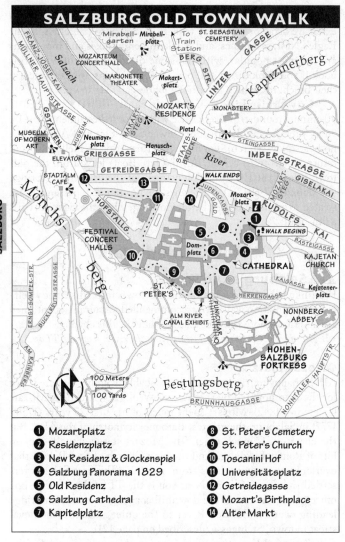

SALZBURG OLD TOWN WALK

SALZBURG

1. Mozartplatz
2. Residenzplatz
3. New Residenz & Glockenspiel
4. Salzburg Panorama 1829
5. Old Residenz
6. Salzburg Cathedral
7. Kapitelplatz
8. St. Peter's Cemetery
9. St. Peter's Church
10. Toscanini Hof
11. Universitätsplatz
12. Getreidegasse
13. Mozart's Birthplace
14. Alter Markt

square, with his new cathedral and palace, was the centerpiece of his Baroque dream city. A series of interconnecting squares—like you'll see nowhere else—make a grand processional way, leading from here through the old town.

For centuries, Salzburg's leaders were both important church officials *and* princes of the Holy Roman Empire, hence the title "prince-archbishop"—mixing sacred and secular authority. But Wolf Dietrich misplayed his hand, losing power and spending his last five years imprisoned up in the Salzburg castle.

The fountain is as Italian as can be, with a Triton matching Bernini's famous Triton Fountain in Rome. Lying on a busy trade route to the south, Salzburg was well aware of the exciting things going on in Italy. Things Italian were respected (as in colonial America, when a bumpkin would "stick a feather in his cap and call it macaroni"). Local artists even Italianized their names in order to raise their rates.

• *Along the left side of Residenzplatz (as you face the cathedral) is the...*

❸ New (Neue) Residenz and Glockenspiel

This former palace, long a government administration building, now houses the central post office, the Heimatwerk (a fine shop showing off all the best local handicrafts, Mon–Fri 9:00–18:00, Sat 9:00–17:00, closed Sun), the fascinating **Salzburg Panorama 1829** exhibit (definitely worth the €2 and described later), and the new **Salzburg Museum.** The first floor of this museum shows off various influential Salzburgers. The second floor explores Salzburg's history, particularly its longstanding reputation as a fairy-tale "Alpine Arcadia." While it's impressively well-done and described in English, the museum is only enjoyable to the extent that you're fascinated with the city—so most will find this merely a good rainy-day option (€7, €8 combo-ticket with Salzburg Panorama, both tickets about €2 cheaper on Sun, includes audioguide, Tue–Sun 9:00–17:00, Thu until 20:00, closed Mon except July–Aug and Dec—when it's open Mon 9:00–17:00, tel. 0662/620-808-700, www.smca.at).

The famous *Glockenspiel* rings atop the new Residenz. This bell tower has a carillon of 35 17th-century bells (cast in Antwerp) that chimes throughout the day and plays tunes (appropriate to the month) at 7:00, 11:00, and 18:00. There was a time when Salzburg could afford to take tourists to the top of the tower to actually see the big barrel with adjustable tabs turn (like a giant music-box mechanism)...pulling the right bells in the right rhythm. Notice the ornamental top: an upside-down heart in flames surrounding the solar system (symbolizing that God loves all of creation).

Look back, past Mozart's statue, to the 4,220-foot-high Gaisberg—the forested hill with the television tower. A road leads to the top for a commanding view. Its summit is a favorite destination for local nature-lovers and kids learning to ski.

• *Before continuing our walk, round the corner toward the back of the cathedral and drop into the...*

❹ Salzburg Panorama 1829

In the early 19th century, 360-degree "panorama" paintings of great cities or events were popular. These creations were even taken on extended road trips. Salzburg, at a stagnant stage in its development, had this circular view painted by Johann Michael Sattler: the city as seen from the top of its castle. When complete, it spent 10 years touring the great cities of Europe, showing off Salzburg's breathtaking setting. Today, the exquisitely restored painting, rated ▲, offers a fascinating look at the city in 1829. The river was slower and had beaches. The old town looks essentially as it does today, and Moosstrasse still leads into idyllic farm country. Paintings from that era of other great cities around the world are hung around the outside wall with numbers but without labels, as a kind of quiz game. A flier gives the cities' names on one side, and keys them to the numbers. See how many 19th-century cities you can identify (€2, €8 combo-ticket with Salzburg Museum, combo-ticket is about €2 cheaper on Sun, open daily 9:00–17:00, Thu until 20:00, Residenzplatz 9).

• *Backtrack into Residenzplatz and head to the opposite end from the new Residenz. This building is the...*

❺ Old (Alte) Residenz

Opposite the new Residenz is Wolf Dietrich's skippable palace, the old Residenz, which is connected to the cathedral by a sky-way. A series of ornately decorated rooms and an art gallery are open to visitors with time to kill (€8, €5 without gallery, Tue–Sun 10:00–17:00, closed Mon, tel. 0662/840-4510).

• *Walk under the prince-archbishop's skyway and step into Domplatz (Cathedral Square), where you'll find the...*

❻ Salzburg Cathedral (Salzburger Dom)

This cathedral, rated ▲▲, was one of the first Baroque buildings north of the Alps. It was consecrated in 1628, during the Thirty Years' War. (Pitting Roman Catholics against Protestants, this war devastated much of Europe and brought most grand construction projects to a halt.) Experts differ on what motivated the builders: to emphasize Salzburg's commitment to the Roman Catholic cause and the power of the Church here, or to show that there could be a peaceful alternative to the religious strife that was racking Europe at the time. Salzburg's archbishop was technically the top papal official north of the Alps, but the city managed to steer clear of the war. With its rich salt production, it had enough money to stay out of the conflict and carefully maintain its independence from the warring sides.

The dates on the iron gates refer to milestones in the church's history: In 774, the previous church (long since destroyed) was founded by St. Virgil, to be replaced in 1628 by the church you see today. In 1959, a partial reconstruction was completed, made necessary by a WWII bomb that had blown through the dome.

Domplatz is surrounded by the prince-archbishop's secular

administration buildings. The **statue of Mary** (1771) is looking away from the church, welcoming visitors. If you stand in the rear of the square, immediately under the middle arch, you'll see that she's positioned to be crowned by the two angels on the church facade.

Step inside the cathedral (donation requested; Easter–Oct Mon–Sat 9:00–18:00, Sun 13:00–18:00; Nov–Easter Mon–Sat 10:00–17:00, Sun 13:00–17:00). Enter the cathedral as if part of a festival procession—drawn toward the resurrected Christ by the brightly lit area under the dome, and cheered on by ceiling paintings of the Passion. The stucco, by a Milanese artist, is exceptional. Sit under the dome—surrounded by the tombs of ten 17th-century archbishops—and imagine all four organs playing, each balcony filled with musicians...glorious surround-sound. Mozart, who was the organist here for two years, would advise you that the acoustics are best in pews immediately under the dome. Study the symbolism of the decor all around you—intellectual, complex, and cohesive. Think of the altar in Baroque terms, as the center of a stage, with sunrays as spotlights in this dramatic and sacred theater. In the left transept, stairs lead down into the crypt *(Krypta)*, where you can see foundations of the earlier church, more tombs, and a tourist-free chapel (reserved for prayer) directly under the dome.

Built in just 14 years (1614–1628), the church boasts harmonious architecture. When Pope John Paul II visited in 1998, 5,000 people filled the cathedral (330 feet long and 230 feet tall). The baptismal font (dark bronze, left of the entry) is from the previous cathedral (basin from about 1320, although the lid is modern). Mozart was baptized here ("Amadeus" means "beloved by God"). Concert and Mass schedules are posted at the entrance; the Sunday Mass at 10:00 is famous for its music.

The **Cathedral Museum** (Dom Museum) has a rich collection of church art (entry at portico, €5, mid-May–Oct Mon–Sat 10:00–17:00, Sun 11:00–18:00, closed Nov–mid-May except during Advent, tel. 0662/8047-1870).

• *From the cathedral, exit left and walk toward the fortress into the next square.*

❼Kapitelplatz

Head past the underground public WCs (free, but small tip expected) to the giant **chessboard.** It's just under the golden orb topped by a man gazing up at the castle, trying to decide whether to walk up or shell out €10 for the funicular. Every year since 2002, a foundation has commissioned a different artist to create a new work of public art somewhere in the city; this is the piece from 2008. A small road leads uphill to the fortress (and fortress funicular; see arrow pointing to the *Steigkeller*).

Keep going across the square to the pond. This was a **horse bath,** the 18th-century equivalent of a car wash. Notice the puzzle above it—the artist wove the date of the structure into a phrase. It says, "Leopold the Prince Built Me," using the letters LLDVICMXVXI, which total 1732 (add it up...it works)—the year it was built. With your back to the cathedral, leave the square through a gate in the right corner that reads *zum Peterskeller.* It leads to a waterfall and St. Peter's Cemetery.

The **waterwheel** is part of a canal system that has brought water into Salzburg from Berchtesgaden, 16 miles away, since the 13th century. Climb uphill a few steps to feel the medieval water power. The stream, divided from here into smaller canals, was channeled through town to provide fire protection, to flush out the streets (Saturday morning was flood-the-streets day), and to power factories (there were more than 100 watermill-powered firms as late as the 19th century). Drop into the fragrant and traditional **bakery** at the waterfall. It's hard to beat their rock-like *Roggenbrot* (various fresh rolls for less than €1, Thu–Tue 7:00–17:30, Sat until 13:00, closed Wed). There's a good view of the funicular climbing up to the castle from here. For more on the canal system, check out the free **Alm River Canal exhibit** nearby (described on page 119).

• *Now find the* Katakomben *sign and step into...*

❽ St. Peter's Cemetery

This collection of lovingly tended mini-gardens abuts the Mönchberg's rock wall (free, silence is requested, daily April–Sept 6:30–19:00, Oct–March 6:30–18:00). Walk in about 50 yards to the intersection of lanes at the base of the cliff marked by a stone ball. (It's seemingly made-to-order for a little back-stretching break. Go ahead...I'll wait.) You're surrounded by three churches, each founded in the sixth century atop a pagan Celtic holy site. St. Peter's Church is closest to the stone ball. Notice the fine Romanesque stonework on the chapel nearest you, and the fancy rich guys' Renaissance-style tombs decorating its walls.

Wealthy as those guys were, they ran out of caring relatives. The graves surrounding you are tended by descendants of the deceased. In Austria, gravesites are rented, not owned. Rent bills are sent out every 10 years. If no one cares enough to make the payment, your remains are chucked. Iron crosses were much cheaper than tombstones. While the cemetery where the von Trapp family hid out in *The Sound of Music* was a Hollywood set, it was inspired by this one.

Look up the cliff. Legendary medieval hermit monks are said to have lived in the hillside—but "catacombs" they're not. For €1, you can climb lots of steps to see a few old caves, a chapel, and some fine views (May–Sept Tue–Sun 10:30–17:00, closed Mon; Oct–April Wed–Thu 10:30–15:30, Fri–Sun 10:30–16:00, closed Mon–Tue).

• *Continue downhill through the cemetery and out the opposite end. Just outside, hook right and drop into...*

❾St. Peter's Church

Just inside, enjoy a carved Romanesque welcome. Over the inner doorway, a fine tympanum shows Jesus on a rainbow flanked by Peter and Paul over a stylized Tree of Life and under a Latin inscription reading, "I am the door to life, and only through me can you find eternal life." Enter the nave and notice how the once purely Romanesque vaulting has since been iced with a sugary Rococo finish. Salzburg's only Rococo interior feels Bavarian (because it is—the fancy stucco work was done by Bavarian artists). Up the right side aisle is the tomb of St. Rupert, with a painting showing Salzburg in 1750 (one bridge, salt ships sailing the river, and angels hoisting barrels of salt to heaven as St. Rupert prays for his city). If you're here during the town's Ruperti-Kirtag festival in late September, you'll see candles and fresh flowers, honoring the city's not-forgotten saint. On pillars farther up the aisle are faded bits of 13th-century Romanesque frescos. Similar frescoes hide under Rococo whitewash throughout the church.

Leaving the church, notice the recommended Stiftskeller St. Peter restaurant (on the left), known for its Mozart Dinner Concert (described under "Music," later in this chapter). Charlemagne ate here in A.D. 803—allowing locals to claim it's the oldest restaurant in Europe. Opposite where you entered the square (look through the arch), you'll see St. Rupert waving you into the next square (early-20th-century Bauhaus-style dorms for student monks), with a modern crucifix (1926) on the far wall.

• *Walk through the archway next to the crucifix into...*

❿Toscanini Hof

This square faces the 1925 **Festival Hall**. The hall's three theaters seat 5,000. This is where Captain von Trapp nervously waited before walking onstage (in the movie, he sang "Edelweiss"), just before he escaped with his family. On the left is the city's 1,500-space, inside-the-mountain parking lot; ahead, behind the *Felsenkeller* sign, is a tunnel (generally closed) leading to the actual concert hall; and to the right is the backstage of a smaller hall where carpenters are often building stage sets (door open on hot days). The stairway leads to the top of the cliff and eventually to the recommended Stadtalm Café and hostel.

• *Walk downhill through Max-Reinhardt-Platz, to the right of the church and past the public WC, into...*

⓫Universitätsplatz

This square hosts an **open-air produce market**—Salzburg's live-liest (mornings Mon–Sat, best on Sat). Locals are happy to pay more here for the reliably fresh and top-quality produce. (These days, half of Austria's produce is grown organically.) The market really bustles on Saturday mornings, when the farmers are in town. Public marketplaces have fountains for washing fruit and vegetables. The fountain here—a part of the medieval water sys-tem—plummets down a hole and to the river. The sundial (over the water hole) is accurate (except for the daylight savings hour) and two-dimensional, showing both the time (obvious) and the date (less obvious). The fanciest facade overlooking the square (the yellow one) is the backside of Mozart's Birthplace (described on the next page).

• *Continue past the fountain to the end of the square, passing several characteristic and nicely arcaded medieval tunnels (on right) that con-nect the square to Getreidegasse. Cross the big road for a look at the giant horse troughs, adjacent to the prince's stables. Paintings show the various breeds and temperaments of horses in his stable. Like Vienna, Salzburg had a passion for the equestrian arts.*

Take two right turns and you're at the start of...

⓬Getreidegasse

This street, rated ▲▲, was old Salzburg's busy, colorful main drag. It's lined with *Schmuck* (jewelry) shops. Famous for its old wrought-iron signs (best viewed from this end), the architecture on the street still looks much as it did in Mozart's day—though its former elegance is now mostly gone, replaced by chain outlets.

On the right at #39, **Sporer** serves up homemade spirits (€1.40 per shot). This has been a family-run show for a century—fun-loving, proud, and English-speaking. *Nuss* is nut, *Marille* is apricot (typical of this region), the *Kletzen* cocktail is like a super-thick Baileys with pear, and *Edle Brande* are the stronger schnapps. The many homemade firewaters are in jugs at the end of the bar.

Continue down Getreidegasse, noticing the old doorbells—one per floor. At #40, **Eisgrotte** serves good ice cream. Across from Eisgrotte, a tunnel leads to the recommended **Balkan Grill** (signed as *Bosna Grill*), the local choice for the very best sausage in town. Farther along, you'll pass McDonald's (while required to keep its arches Baroque and low-key, it just couldn't hang anything less than the biggest sign on the street).

The knot of excited tourists and salesmen hawking goofy gimmicks marks the home of Salzburg's most famous resident. **Mozart's Birthplace** (Geburtshaus, ⓭ on map)—the house where Mozart was born, and where he composed many of his early works—is worth a visit for his true fans (described later). But for most, his Residence, across the river, is more interesting (described later in this chapter).

• *Continue on, past City Hall (Rathaus) and its clock tower, and turn right into...*

⑭Alter Markt

Here in Salzburg's old marketplace you'll find a sausage stand, the recommended **Café Tomaselli,** a fun **candy shop** at #7 (Mon–Fri 9:00–18:00, Sat 10:00–18:00, closed Sun), and, next door, the beautifully old-fashioned **Alte F.E. Hofapotheke** pharmacy— duck in discreetly to peek at the Baroque shelves and containers (be polite—the people in line are here for medicine, Mon–Fri 8:00–18:00, Sat 8:00–12:00, closed Sun, no photography).

• *Our walk is finished. From here, you can head up to the Hohensalzburg Fortress on the cliffs over the old town (listed under "Sights and Activities," next); or continue to some of the sights across the river. To reach those sights, head for the river, jog left (past the fast-food fish res- taurant and free WCs), climb to the top of the Makartsteg pedestrian bridge, and turn to page 119.*

Sights and Activities

▲Mozart's Birthplace (Geburtshaus)

Mozart was born here in 1756. It was in this building—the most popular Mozart sight in town—that he composed most of his boy-genius works. For fans, it's almost a pilgrimage. American artist Robert Wilson was recently hired to spiff up the exhibit, to make it feel more conceptual and less like a museum. But I was unimpressed. If you're tackling just one Mozart sight, skip this one. Instead, walk 10 minutes from here to Mozart's Residence (described later in this section, under "In the New Town, North of the River"), which provides a more informative visit. But if you want to max out on Mozart, a visit here is worthwhile.

Cost, Hours, Location: €6.50, or €10 for combo-ticket that includes Mozart's Residence, daily 9:00–17:00, July–Aug until 20:00, last entry 30 min before closing, Getreidegasse 9, tel. 0662/844-313.

⊙ Self-Guided Tour: Here's what you'll see as you shuffle through with the herd:

Room 1: Around a baby crib showing an infant both old and young (Mozart's music is timeless...get it?) are walls heavy with historic etchings, portraits, and documents. Most important: an engraving of the family (lower right) and a fine "portrait with a bird's nest" of Mozart, painted from life when he was nine years old (upper left).

Room 2: The living room shows off authentic family portraits:

Wolfgang's mom, dad, sister, and wife. Wolfgang composed his first pieces as a child on a clavichord (like the one in this room). A predecessor of the piano, it hit the strings with simple teeter-totter keys that played very softly...ideal for composers living in tight apartment quarters.

Room 3: The nursery is decorated like Mozart's music: light and free as a bird (hence the flying birds). Embedded in the walls are Mozart's personal possessions—his ring, silk wallet, and violin. He was born in this room, and the entire family slept here until Wolfgang was 14.

Room 4: Exactly what Mozart looked like is a bit of a mystery. Various portraits in this room give us something to go on.

Corridor: The neon phrase shows Mozart's juvenile sense of humor. It's a rhyme: *Madame Mutter, ich esse gerne Butter.* (Dear mother, I love to eat butter.) The next room is wallpapered with reproductions of actual circa-1840 photos of Mozart's wife and son (as an old man). More strange Wilson-designed rooms follow: Mozart loved to turn things upside-down—so the Salzburg cityscapes are that way, with stars on the floor. Downstairs, just before the shop, rooms dedicated to Mozart's operas play various video clips continuously.

Atop the Cliffs Above the Old Town

The main "sight" above town is the Hohensalzburg Fortress. But if you just want to enjoy the sweeping views over Salzburg, you have a couple of cheap options: Head up to the castle grounds on foot, take the elevator up the cliffs of Mönchsberg (explained under "Getting Around Salzburg," near the beginning of this chapter), or visit the castle in the evening on a night when they're hosting a concert (about 300 nights a year). This is the only time you can buy a funicular ticket without paying for the castle entrance—since the castle museum is closed, but the funicular is still running to bring up concert-goers.

▲▲**Hohensalzburg Fortress (Festung)**—Built on a rock (called Festungsberg) 400 feet above the Salzach River, this fortress was never really used. That's the idea. It was a good investment—so foreboding, nobody attacked the town for a thousand years. The city was never taken by force, but when Napoleon stopped by, Salzburg wisely surrendered. After a stint as a military barracks, the fortress was opened to the public in the 1860s by Emperor Franz Josef. Today, it remains one of Europe's mightiest castles, dominating Salzburg's skyline and offering incredible views.

Cost: Your daytime funicular ticket includes admission to the fortress grounds and all the museums inside—whether you want to see them or not (€10.50, €24.50 family ticket). Save money by walking up—the climb is much easier than it looks, and the

SALZBURG

views are fantastic. From the top you can opt to see the museums for €7, but many visitors are content to simply take in the grounds and views (free if you've walked up). If you'd rather take the funicular but want to skip the museums, head up the hill in the evening (within one hour of the museum's closing time, it's €6 one-way/€7.50 round-trip for funicular and entry to castle grounds; after closing time, the funicular is €3.60 round-trip).

Hours: The complex is open daily year-round (May–Sept 9:00–19:00, Oct–April 9:30–17:00, last entry 30 min before closing, tel. 0662/8424-3011). On nights when there's a concert, the castle grounds are free and open after the museum closes until 21:30.

Concerts: The fortress also serves as a venue for evening concerts (Festungskonzerte). For details, see "Music," later in this chapter.

Café: The café between the funicular station and the castle entry is a great place to nibble on apple strudel while taking in the jaw-dropping view.

Orientation: The fortress visit has three parts: a relatively dull courtyard with some fine views from its various ramparts; the fortress itself (with a required and escorted 45-minute audiotour); and the palace museum (by far the best exhibit of the lot). At the bottom of the funicular, you'll pass through an interesting little exhibit on the town's canal system (free, described at end of this listing).

◆ Self-Guided Tour: From the top of the funicular head to your right and down the stairs to bask in the view, either from the café or the view terrace a little farther along. Once you're done snapping photos, walk through to the castle grounds and go left, following the path up and around to reach the inner courtyard (labeled *Inneres Schloß*). Immediately inside, circling to the right (clockwise), you'll encounter cannons (still poised to defend Salzburg against an Ottoman invasion), the marionette exhibit, the palace museum, the Kuenburg bastion, scant ruins of a Romanesque church, the courtyard (with path down for those walking), toilets, shops, a restaurant, and the fortress tour.

• *Begin at the...*

Marionette Exhibit: Several fun rooms show off this local tradition, with three videos playing continuously: two with peeks at Salzburg's ever-enchanting Marionette Theater performances of Mozart classics (listed in "Music," later in this chapter), and one with a behind-the-scenes look at the action. Give the hands-on marionette a whirl.

• *Hiking through the former palace, you'll find the sight's best exhibits at the...*

Palace Museum (Festungsmuseum Carolino Augusteum): The second floor has exhibits on castle life, from music to torture. The top floor shows off fancy royal apartments, a sneak preview of the room used for the nightly fortress concerts, and the Rainier military museum, dedicated to the Salzburg regiments that fought in both World Wars.

Castle Courtyard: The courtyard was the main square of the castle residents, a community of a thousand—which could be self-sufficient when necessary. The square was ringed by the shops of craftsmen, blacksmiths, bakers, and so on. The well dipped into a rain-fed cistern. The church is dedicated to St. George, the protector of horses (logical for an army church) and decorated by fine red marble reliefs (c. 1502). Behind the church is the top of the old lift that helped supply the fortress. (From near here, steps lead back into the city, or to the mountaintop "Mönchsberg Walk," described later.) You'll also see the remains of a Romanesque chapel, which are well-described.

• *Near the chapel, turn left into the Kuenburg Bastion (once a garden) for fine city and castle views.*

Kuenburg Bastion: Notice how the castle has three parts: the original castle inside the courtyard, the vast whitewashed walls (built when the castle was a residence), and the lower, beefed-up fortifications (added for extra defense against the expected Ottoman invasion). Survey Salzburg from here and think about fortifying an important city by using nature. Mönchsberg (the cliffs to the left) and Festungsberg (the little mountain you're on) naturally cradle the old town, with just a small gate between the ridge and the river needed to bottle up the place. The new town across the river needed a bit of a wall arcing from the river to its hill. Back then, only one bridge crossed the Salzach into town, and it had a fortified gate.

• *Back inside the castle courtyard, continue your circle. The Round Tower (1497) helps you visualize the inner original castle.*

Fortress Interior: Tourists are allowed in this part of the fortified palace only with an escort. (They say that's for security, though while touring it, you wonder what they're protecting.) A crowd assembles at the turnstile, and every quarter-hour 40 people are issued their audioguides and let in for the escorted walk. You'll go one room at a time, listening to a 45-minute commentary. While the interior furnishings are mostly gone—taken by Napoleon—the rooms survived as well as they did because no one wanted to live here after 1500, so the building was never modernized. Your tour includes a room dedicated to the art of "excruciating questioning" ("softening up" prisoners, in current American military jargon)— filled with tools of that gruesome trade. The highlight is the commanding city view from the top of a tower.

• *After seeing the fortress, consider hiking down to the old town, or along the top of Mönchsberg (see "Mönchsberg Walk"). If you take the funicular down, keep an eye out for the...*

Alm River Canal Exhibit: At the base of the funicular, below the castle, is this fine little exhibit on how the river was broken into five smaller streams—powering the city until steam took up the energy-supply baton. Pretend it's the year 1200 and follow (by video) the flow of the water from the river through the canals, into the mills, and as it's finally dumped into the Salzach River (free, access from the bottom of the lift as you're leaving, or through amber shop next door if you're not riding the funicular).

▲**Mönchsberg Walk**—For a great 30-minute hike, exit the fortress by taking the steep lane down from the castle courtyard. At the first intersection, right leads into the old town, and left leads across the Mönchsberg. The lane leads 20 minutes through the woods high above the city (stick to the high lanes, or you'll end up back in town), taking you to the Gasthaus Stadtalm café (light meals, cheap beds—listed under both "Sleeping" and "Eating"). From the Stadtalm, pass under the medieval wall and walk left along the wall to a tableau showing how it once looked. Take the switchback to the right and follow the lane downhill to the Museum of Modern Art (described next), where the elevator zips you back into town (€2 one-way, €3 round-trip, daily 8:30–19:00, Wed until 21:00, July–Aug daily until 1:00 in the morning, May–Sept starts running at 8:00). If you stay on the lane past the elevator, you eventually pass the Augustine church that marks the rollicking Augustiner Bräustübl (see "Eating—Away from the Center," later in this chapter).

In 1669, a huge Mönchsberg landslide killed more than 200 townspeople. Since then the cliffs have been carefully checked each spring and fall. Even today, you might see crews on the cliff, monitoring its stability.

Museum of Modern Art on Mönchsberg—The modern-art museum on top of Mönchsberg, built in 2004, houses Salzburg's Rupertinum Gallery, plus special exhibitions. While the collection is not worth climbing a mountain for, the M32 restaurant has some of the best views in town (€8, €9.70 including elevator ticket, Tue–Sun 10:00–18:00, Wed until 20:00, closed Mon except during festival; restaurant open Tue–Sat 9:00–24:00, Sun 9:00–18:00, closed Mon except during festival; both at top of Mönchsberg elevator, tel. 0662/842-220, www.museumdermoderne.at).

In the New Town, North of the River

The following sights are across the river from the old town. I've connected them with walking instructions.

• *Begin at the Makartsteg pedestrian bridge, where you can survey the...*

Salzach River—Salzburg's river is called "salt river" not because it's salty, but because of the precious cargo it once carried—the salt mines of Hallein are just nine miles upstream. Salt could be transported from here all the way to the Danube, and on to the Mediterranean via the Black Sea. The riverbanks and roads were built when the river was regulated in the 1850s. Before that, the Salzach was much wider and slower-moving. Houses opposite the old town fronted the river with docks and "garages" for boats. The grand buildings just past the bridge (with their elegant promenades and cafés) were built on reclaimed land in the late 19th century, in the historicist style of Vienna's Ringstrasse.

Scan the cityscape. Notice all the churches. Salzburg, nick-named the "Rome of the North," has 38 Catholic churches (plus two Protestant churches and a synagogue). Find the five streams gushing into the river. These date from the 13th century, when the river was split into five canals running through the town to power its mills. The Stein Hotel (upstream, just left of next bridge), has a popular roof-terrace café (see "Stein Terrasse" listing, later in this section). Downstream, notice the Museum of Modern Art atop Mönchsberg, with a view restaurant and a faux castle (actually a water reservoir). The Romanesque bell tower with the green copper dome in the distance is the Augustine church, site of the best beer hall in town (the Augustiner Bräustübl—listed under "Eating").

• *Cross the bridge, pass the Café Bazar (a fine place for a drink—see page 141), walk two blocks inland, and take a left past the heroic statues into...*

▲**Mirabell Gardens and Palace (Schloss)**—The bubbly gardens laid out in 1730 for the prince-archbishop have been open to the public since 1850 (thanks to Emperor Franz Josef, who was rattled by the popular revolutions of 1848). The gardens are free and open until dusk. The palace is only open as a concert venue (explained later). The statues and the arbor (far left) were featured in *The Sound of Music*. Walk through the gardens to the palace. Look back, enjoy the garden/cathedral/castle view, and imagine how the prince-archbishop must have reveled in a vista that reminded him of all his secular and religious power. Then go around to the river side of the palace and find the horse.

The rearing **Pegasus statue** (rare and very well-balanced) is the site of a famous *Sound of Music* scene where the kids all danced before lining up on the stairs (with Maria 30 yards farther along). The steps lead to a small mound in the park (made of rubble from a former theatre, and today a rendezvous point for Salzburg's gay community).

Nearest the horse, stairs lead between two lions to a pair of tough dwarfs (early volleyball players with spiked mittens) wel-coming you to Salzburg's **Dwarf Park.** Cross the elevated walk (noticing the city's fortified walls) to meet statues of a dozen actual dwarfs who served the prince-archbishop—modeled after real people with real fashions in about 1600. This was Mannerist art, from the hyper-realistic age that followed the Renaissance.

There's plenty of **music,** both in the park and in the palace. A brass band plays free park concerts (May–Aug Sun at 10:30 and Wed with lighted fountains at 20:30, unless it's raining). To properly enjoy the lavish Mirabell Palace—once the prince-archbishop's summer palace, and now the seat of the mayor—get a ticket to a Schlosskonzerte (my favorite venue for a classical concert—see "Music," later in this chapter).

• *To visit Salzburg's best Mozart sight, go a long block southeast to Makartplatz, where you'll find...*

▲▲**Mozart's Residence (Wohnhaus)**—This reconstruction of Mozart's second home (his family moved here when he was 17) is the most informative Mozart sight in town. The English-language audioguide (included with admission, 90 min) provides fascinating insight into Mozart's life and music, with the usual scores, old pianos, and an interesting 30-minute film (#17 on your audioguide for soundtrack) that runs continuously (€6.50, or €10 for combo-ticket that includes Mozart's Birthplace in the old town, daily 9:00–17:00, July–Aug until 20:00, last entry 30 min before closing, allow at least one hour for visit, Makartplatz 8, tel. 0662/8742-2740).

In the main hall—used by the Mozarts to entertain Salzburg's high society—you can hear original instruments from Mozart's time. Mozart was proud to be the first in his family to compose a duet. Notice the family portrait (circa 1780) on the wall, showing Mozart with his sister Nannerl, their father, and their mother—who'd died two years earlier in Paris. Mozart also had silly crude bull's-eyes made for the pop-gun game popular at the time (licking an "arse," Wolfgang showed his disdain for the rigors of high society). Later rooms feature real artifacts that explore his loves, his intellectual pursuits, his travels, and more.

• *From here, you can walk a few blocks back to the main bridge (Staatsbrücke), where you'll find the Platzl, a square once used as a hay market. Pause to enjoy the kid-pleasing little fountain. Near the fountain (with your back to the river), Steingasse leads darkly to the right.*

▲**Steingasse Stroll**—This street, a block in from the river, was the only road in the Middle Ages going south over the Alps to Venice (this was the first stop north of the Alps). Today, it's wonderfully tranquil and free of Salzburg's touristy crush.

At #9, a plaque (of questionable veracity) shows where Joseph Mohr, who wrote the words to "Silent Night," was born—poor and illegitimate—in 1792. There is no doubt, however, that the popular Christmas carol was composed and first sung in the village of Oberndorf, just outside of Salzburg, in 1818. Stairs lead from near here up to a 17th-century Capuchin monastery.

On the next corner, the wall is gouged out. This scar was left even after the building was restored, to remind locals of the American GI who tried to get a tank down this road during a visit to the town brothel—two blocks farther up Steingasse. Inviting cocktail bars along here come alive at night (see "Steingasse Pub Crawl," near the end of this chapter).

At #19, find the carvings on the old door. Some say these are notices from beggars to the begging community (more numerous after post-Reformation religious wars, which forced many people out of their homes and towns)—a kind of "hobo code" indicating whether the residents would give or not. Trace the wires of the old-fashioned doorbells to the highest floors.

Farther on, you'll find a commanding Salzburg view across the river. Notice the red dome marking the oldest nunnery in the German-speaking world (established in 712) under the fortress and to the left. The real Maria from *The Sound of Music* taught in this nunnery's school. In 1927, she and Captain von Trapp were married in the church you see here (not the church filmed in the movie). He was 47. She was 22. Hmmmm.

From here look back, above the arch you just passed through, at part of the town's medieval fortification. The coat of arms on the arch is of the prince-archbishop who paid Bavaria a huge ransom to stay out of the Thirty Years' War (smart move). He then built this fortification (in 1634) in anticipation of rampaging armies from both sides.

Today, this street is for making love, not war. The Maison de Plaisir (a few doors down, at #24) has for centuries been a Salzburg brothel. But the climax of this walk is more touristic.

• *For a grand view, head back to the Platzl and the bridge, enter the Stein Hotel (left corner, overlooking the river), and ride the elevator to...*

Stein Terrasse—This café offers perhaps the best views in town (aside from the castle). Hidden from the tourist crush, it's a trendy, professional, local scene. You can discretely peek at the view, or enjoy a drink or light meal (small snacks, indoor/outdoor seating, Sun–Thu 9:00–24:00, Fri–Sat 9:00–1:00 in the morning).

• *Back at the Platzl and the bridge, you can head straight up Linzergasse (away from the river) into a neighborhood packed with recommended accommodations, as well as our final new-town sight...*

▲St. Sebastian Cemetery—Wander through this quiet place, so Baroque and so Italian (free, daily April–Oct 9:00–18:30, Nov–March 9:00–16:00, entry at Linzergasse 43 in summer; in winter go around the corner to the right, through the arch at #37, and around the building to the doorway under the blue seal). Mozart is buried in Vienna, his mom's in Paris, and his sister is in Salzburg's old town (St. Peter's)—but Wolfgang's wife Constanze

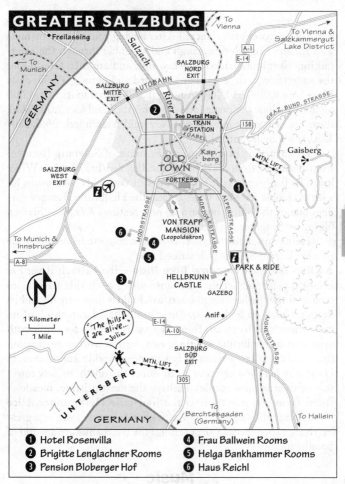

GREATER SALZBURG

To Vienna

To Vienna &
Salzkammergut
Lake District

Freilassing

Salzach River

GERMANY

To Munich

SALZBURG
NORD
EXIT

A-1
E-14

AUTOBAHN

SALZBURG
MITTE
EXIT

GRAZ. BUND. STRASSE

See Detail Map
TRAIN
STATION

Gaisberg

158

GABEL

Kap-
berg

OLD
TOWN

MTN. LIFT

SALZBURG
WEST
EXIT

FORTRESS

ALPENSTRASSE

MORZGERSTRASSE

MOOSSTRASSE

VON TRAPP
MANSION
(Leopoldskron)

PARK & RIDE

HELLBRUNN
CASTLE

To Munich &
Innsbruck

A-8

GAZEBO

Anif

AIGNERSTRASSE

1 Kilometer

1 Mile

N

"The hills
are alive...
~Julie

E-14
A-10

SALZBURG
SÜD
EXIT

MTN. LIFT

UNTERSBERG

305

GERMANY

To
Berchtesgaden
(Germany)

To Hallein

❶ Hotel Rosenvilla
❷ Brigitte Lenglachner Rooms
❸ Pension Bloberger Hof

❹ Frau Ballwein Rooms
❺ Helga Bankhammer Rooms
❻ Haus Reichl

("Constantia") and his father Leopold are buried here (from the black iron gate entrance on Linzergasse, walk 17 paces and look left). When Prince-Archbishop Wolf Dietrich had the cemetery moved from around the cathedral and put here, across the river, people didn't like it. To help popularize it, he had his own mausoleum built as its centerpiece. Continue straight past the Mozart tomb to this circular building (English description at door).

▲**Hellbrunn Castle**—About the year 1610, Prince-Archbishop Sittikus (after meditating on stewardship and Christ-like values) decided he needed a lavish palace with a vast and ornate garden purely for pleasure. He built this and just loved inviting his VIP guests out for fun with his trick fountains. Today, the visit is worthwhile for the garden full of clever fountains...and the sadistic joy the tour guide gets from soaking tourists. (Hint: When you see a wet place, cover your camera.) After buying your ticket, you must wait for the English tour, laugh and scramble through the entertaining 40-minute trick-water-toy tour, and are then free to tour the forgettable palace with an included audioguide (€8.50, daily May–Sept 9:00–17:30, July–Aug until 21:00—but tours from 18:00 on don't include the castle, mid-March–April and Oct 9:00–16:30, these are last tour times, closed Nov–mid-March, tel. 0662/820-3720, www.hellbrunn.at).

Hellbrunn is nearly four miles south of Salzburg (bus #25 from station or from Staatsbrücke bridge, 2–3/hr, 20 min). While it can be fun—especially on a hot day or with kids—for many, it's a lot of trouble for a few water tricks. The Hellbrunn Baroque garden, one of the oldest in Europe, now features *S.O.M.*'s "Sixteen Going on Seventeen" gazebo.

Hellbrunn makes a good 30-minute bike excursion along the riverbank from Salzburg (described next).

▲▲**Riverside or Meadow Bike Ride**—The Salzach River has smooth, flat, and scenic bike lanes along each side (thanks to medieval tow paths—cargo boats would float downstream and be dragged back up by horses). On a sunny day, I can think of no more shout-worthy escape from the city. The nearly four-mile path upstream to Hellbrunn Castle is easy, with a worthy destination (leave Salzburg on castle side). For a nine-mile ride, continue on to Hallein (where you can tour a salt mine; the north, or new town, side of river is most scenic). Perhaps the most pristine, meadow-filled farm-country route is the four-mile Hellbrunner Allee from Akademiestrasse. Even a quickie ride across town is a great Salzburg experience. In the evening, the riverbanks are a world of floodlit spires.

Music

▲▲**Salzburg Festival (Salzburger Festspiele)**—Each summer, from late July to the end of August, Salzburg hosts its famous Salzburg Festival, founded in 1920 to employ Vienna's musicians in the summer. This fun and festive time is crowded, but there are plenty of beds (except for a few August weekends). There are three big halls: the Opera and Orchestra venues in the Festival House, and the Landes Theater, where German-language plays are performed. Tickets for the big festival events are generally expensive (€50–600) and sell out well in advance (bookable from Jan). Most tourists think they're "going to the Salzburg Festival" by seeing smaller non-festival events that go on during the festival weeks. For these lesser events, same-day tickets are normally available (the ticket office on Mozartplatz, in the TI, prints a daily list of concerts and charges a 30 percent fee to book them). For specifics on this year's festival schedule and tickets, visit www.salzburg festival.at, or contact the Austrian National Tourist Office in the United States (tel. 212/944-6880, fax 212/730-4568, www.austria .info, travel@austria.info).

▲▲**Musical Events Year-Round**—Salzburg is busy through-out the year, with 2,000 classical performances in its palaces and churches annually. Pick up the events calendar at the TI (free, bimonthly). I've never planned in advance, and I've enjoyed great concerts with every visit. Whenever you visit, you'll have a number of concerts (generally small chamber groups) to choose from. Here are some of the more accessible events:

Concerts at Hohensalzburg Fortress (Festungskonzerte): Nearly nightly concerts—Mozart's greatest hits for beginners—are held atop Festungsberg, in the "prince's chamber" of the fortress, featuring small chamber groups (open seating after the first six more expensive rows, €31 or €38 plus €3.40 for the funicular; at 19:30, 20:00, or 20:30; doors open 30 min early, tel. 0662/825-858 to reserve, pick up tickets at the door). The medieval-feeling cham-ber has windows overlooking the city, and the concert gives you a chance to enjoy the grand city view and a stroll through the castle courtyard. (The funicular ticket costs €3.40 within an hour of the show—ideal for people who just want to ascend for the view.) For €51, you can combine the concert with a four-course dinner (starts two hours before concert).

Concerts at the Mirabell Palace (Schlosskonzerte): The nearly nightly chamber music concerts at the Mirabell Palace are performed in a lavish Baroque setting. They come with more sophisticated programs and better musicians than the fortress concerts. Baroque music flying around a Baroque hall is a happy bird in the right cage (open seating after the first five pricier rows, €29, usually at 20:00—but check flyer for times, doors open 1 hour ahead, tel. 0662/848-586, www.salzburger-schlosskonzerte.at).

"Five O'Clock Concerts" (5-Uhr-Konzerte): These con-certs—next to St. Peter's in the old town—are cheaper, since they feature young artists (€12, July–Sept Thu–Tue at 17:00, no con-certs Wed or Oct–June, 45–60 min, tel. 0662/8445-7619, www.5 -uhr-konzerte.com). While the series is formally named after the brother of Joseph Haydn, it offers music from various masters.

Mozart Piano Sonatas: St. Peter's Abbey hosts these concerts each weekend (€18, €9 for children, €45 for a family of four, Fri and Sat at 19:00 year-round, in the abbey's Romanesque Hall—a.k.a. Romanischer Saal, tel. 0664/423-5645). This short and inexpensive concert is ideal for families.

SALZBURG

Marionette Theater: Salzburg's much-loved marionette theater offers operas with spellbinding marionettes and recorded music. Music-lovers are mesmerized by the little people on stage (€18–35, nearly nightly at 17:00 or 19:30 June–Sept except Sun, also 3–4/week in May, some 14:00 matinees, box office open Mon–Sat 9:00–13:00 and 2 hours before shows, near the Mirabell Gardens and Mozart's Residence at Schwarzstrasse 24, tel. 0662/872-406, www.marionetten.at). For a sneak preview, check out the videos playing at the marionette exhibit up in the fortress.

Mozart Dinner Concert: For those who'd like some classical music but would rather not sit through a concert, Stiftskeller St. Peter offers a traditional candlelit meal with Mozart's greatest hits performed by a string quartet and singers in historic costumes gavotting among the tables. In this elegant Baroque setting, tourists clap between movements and get three courses of food (from Mozart-era recipes) mixed with three 20-minute courses of crowd-pleasing music (€48, Mozart-lovers with this guidebook pay €39 when booking direct, almost nightly at 20:00, dress is "smart casual," call to reserve at 0662/828-695, www.mozart dinnerconcert.com). When they run out of space, they book a second quartet to perform in the adjacent Haydn Zimmer. I find the ambience much nicer in the main Baroque Hall—when making the booking, get a promise that that's where you'll be seated. See restaurant listing under "Eating—In the Old Town," later in this chapter.

Sound of Salzburg Dinner Show: The show at the Sternbräu Inn (listed under "Eating") is Broadway in a dirndl with tired food. But it's a good show, and *Sound of Music* fans leave with hands red from clapping. A piano player and a hardworking quartet of singers wearing historical costumes perform an entertaining mix of *S.O.M.* hits and traditional folk songs (€46 for dinner, begins at 19:30). You can also come by at 20:30, pay €32, skip the dinner, and get the show. Those who book direct (not through a hotel) and pay cash get a 10 percent discount with this book (nightly mid-May–mid-Oct, Griesgasse 23, tel. 0662/826-617, www.soundof salzburgshow.com).

Music at Mass: Each Sunday morning, two great churches offer a Mass generally with glorious music. The Salzburg Cathedral is likely your best bet for fine music to worship by (10:00). The Franciscan church (9:00) is enthusiastic about its musical Masses, and St. Peter's Church also has music (10:30). See the Salzburg events guide for details.

Free Brass Band Concert: A traditional brass band plays in the Mirabell Gardens (May–Aug Sun at 10:30 and Wed at 20:30).

Sleeping

Finding a room in Salzburg, even during its music festival (mid-July–Aug), is usually easy. Rates rise significantly (20–30 percent) during the music festival, and sometimes around Easter and Christmas; these higher prices do not appear in the ranges I've listed. Many places charge 10 percent extra for a one-night stay.

In the New Town, North of the River

These listings, clustering around Linzergasse, are in a pleasant neighborhood (with easy parking) a 15-minute walk from the train station (for directions, see "Arrival in Salzburg," earlier in this chapter) and a 10-minute walk to the old town. If you're coming from the old town, simply cross the main bridge (Staatsbrücke) to the mostly traffic-free Linzergasse. If driving, exit the highway at Salzburg-Nord, follow Vogelweiderstrasse straight to its end, and turn right.

$$$ Altstadthotel Wolf-Dietrich, around the corner from Linzergasse on pedestrians-only Wolf-Dietrich-Strasse, is well-located (with half its rooms overlooking St. Sebastian Cemetery). With 27 tastefully plush rooms, it's the best value I could find for a big, stylish hotel (Sb-€85–105, Db-€140–190, price depends on size, family deals, €20–40 more during festival, complex pricing but readers of this book get a 10 percent discount on prevailing price—insist on this discount deducted from whatever price is offered that day, elevator, pool with loaner swimsuits, sauna, free DVD library, Wolf-Dietrich-Strasse 7, tel. 0662/871-275, fax 0662/871-2759, www.salzburg-hotel.at, office@salzburg-hotel.at). Their annex across the street has 14 equally comfortable rooms (but no elevator, and therefore slightly cheaper prices).

SALZBURG

Sleep Code

(€1 = about $1.40, country code: 43, area code: 0662)
S = Single, **D** = Double/Twin, **T** = Triple, **Q** = Quad, **b** = bathroom, **s** = shower only. Unless otherwise noted, credit cards are accepted and breakfast is included. All of these places speak English.

To help you sort easily through these listings, I've divided the rooms into three categories, based on the price for a standard double room with bath:

$$$ Higher Priced—Most rooms €90 or more.
  $$ Moderately Priced—Most rooms between €60–90.
    $ Lower Priced—Most rooms €60 or less.

SALZBURG

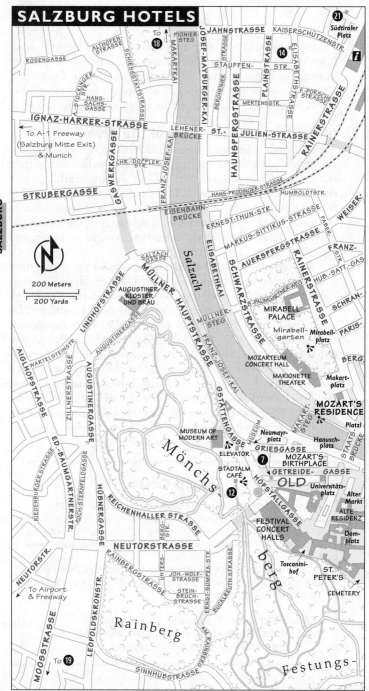

SALZBURG HOTELS

To A-1 Freeway
(Salzburg Mitte Exit)
& Munich

200 Meters
200 Yards

To Airport
& Freeway

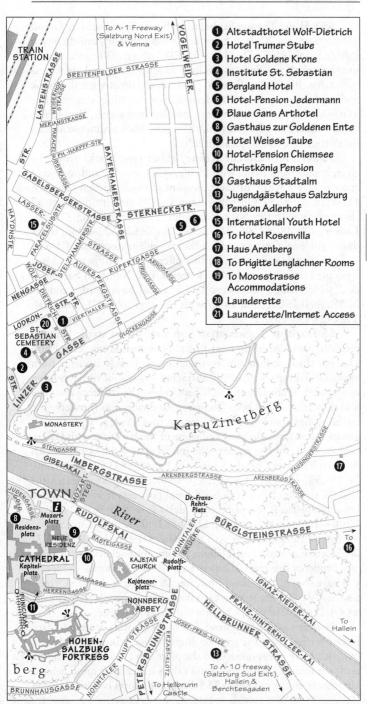

1. Altstadthotel Wolf-Dietrich
2. Hotel Trumer Stube
3. Hotel Goldene Krone
4. Institute St. Sebastian
5. Bergland Hotel
6. Hotel-Pension Jedermann
7. Blaue Gans Arthotel
8. Gasthaus zur Goldenen Ente
9. Hotel Weisse Taube
10. Hotel-Pension Chiemsee
11. Christkönig Pension
12. Gasthaus Stadtalm
13. Jugendgästehaus Salzburg
14. Pension Adlerhof
15. International Youth Hotel
16. To Hotel Rosenvilla
17. Haus Arenberg
18. To Brigitte Lenglachner Rooms
19. To Moosstrasse Accommodations
20. Launderette
21. Launderette/Internet Access

SALZBURG

$$$ Hotel Trumer Stube, three blocks from the river just off Linzergasse, has 20 clean, cozy rooms and a friendly, can-do owner (Sb-€65, Db-€105, Tb-€128, Qb-€147, about €30 more during music festival, top-floor rooms have lower ceilings and are €7 less expensive, 10 percent discount if you book direct with this book and pay cash—except during festival, non-smoking, elevator, free Wi-Fi except in top-floor rooms, free Internet access, Bergstrasse 6, tel. 0662/874-776, fax 0662/874-326, www.trumer-stube.at, info@trumer-stube.at, pleasant Silvia).

$$$ Hotel Goldene Krone, about five blocks from the river, is plain and basic, with 25 big, quiet, creaky, and well-kept rooms. Stay a while in their pleasant cliffside garden (Sb-€69, Db-€119, Tb-€159, Qb-€189, claim your 10 percent discount off these prices with this book, dim lights, elevator, parking-€12/day, Linzergasse 48, tel. 0662/872-300, fax 0662/8723-0066, www .hotel-goldenekrone.com, office@hotel-goldenekrone.com, Claudia and Günther Hausknost). Günther offers tours (€10/person, 2 hrs, 5 people minimum) and a "Rick Steves Two Nights in Salzburg" deal, which covers your room, a 24-hour Salzburg Card, a concert in Mirabell Palace, and a tour with Günther (Sb-€171, Db-€304, Tb-€429, Qb-€532).

$$ Institute St. Sebastian is in a somewhat sterile but very clean historic building next to St. Sebastian Cemetery. From October through June, the institute houses female students from various Salzburg colleges, and also rents 40 beds for travelers (men or women). From July through September, the students are gone and they rent all 100 beds (including 20 doubles) to travelers. The building has spacious public areas, a roof garden, a piano that guests are welcome to play, and some of the best rooms and dorm beds in town for the money. The immaculate doubles come with modern baths and head-to-toe twin beds (S-€33.50, Sb-€41.50, D-€53.50, Db-€67, Tb-€81, Qb-€96, €2.50/person extra for 1-night stay, includes very basic breakfast, elevator, self-service laundry-€4/load; reception open daily July–Sept 7:30–12:00 & 13:00–21:30, Oct–June 8:00–12:00 & 16:00–21:00; Linzergasse 41, enter through arch at #37, tel. 0662/871-386, fax 0662/8713-8685, www.st-sebastian-salzburg.at, office@st-sebastian-salzburg .at). Students like the €21 bunks in 4- to 10-bed dorms (€2 less if you have sheets, no lockout time, free lockers, free showers). You'll find self-service kitchens on each floor (fridge space is free; request a key). If you need parking, request it well in advance.

Pensions on Rupertgasse: These two hotels are about five blocks farther from the river on Rupertgasse, a breeze for drivers but with more street noise than the places on Linzergasse. They're both modern and well-run—good values if you don't mind being a bit away from the old town. **$$$ Bergland Hotel** is charming and

classy, with comfortable, neo-rustic rooms. It's a modern building, and therefore spacious and solid (Sb-€65, Db-€95, Tb-€117,
Qb-€140, elevator, Internet access, English library, bike rental-€6/
day, Rupertgasse 15, tel. 0662/872-318, fax 0662/872-3188, www
.berglandhotel.at, kuhn@berglandhotel.at, Kuhn family). The
similar, boutique-like **$$$ Hotel-Pension Jedermann,** a few
doors down, is tastefully done and comfortable, with an artsy
painted-concrete ambience and a backyard garden (Sb-€65–85,
Db-€90–130, Tb-€120–160, Qb-€160–200, much more during
festival, elevator, Internet access, Rupertgasse 25, tel. 0662/873-
2410, fax 0662/873-2419, www.hotel-jedermann.com, office
@hotel-jedermann.com, Herr und Frau Gmachl).

In or Above the Old Town

Most of these hotels are near Residenzplatz. While this area is
car-restricted, you're allowed to drive your car in to unload, pick
up a map and parking instructions, and head for the €14-per-day
garage in the mountain.

$$$ Blaue Gans Arthotel is ultra-modern and in the Old
Town, beautifully located at the far end of Getreidegasse. Its pub-
lic spaces feature contemporary Austrian art, and the 40 sleek,
thoughtfully designed rooms are decorated with local materials (Sb-
€115–125, standard Db-€135–160, bigger superior Db-€185–195,
fancier suites, extra bed-€35–40; prices €20–25 higher per person
during festival, around Christmas, and on holiday weekends; elevator, free Internet access and Wi-Fi, Getreidegasse 41, tel. 0662/842-
4910, fax 0662/8424-9175, www.blauegans.at, office@blauegans.at).

$$$ Gasthaus zur Goldenen Ente is in a 600-year-old
building with medieval stone arches and narrow stairs. Located
above a good, smoke-free restaurant, it's as central as you can be on
a pedestrian street in old Salzburg. The 17 rooms are modern and
newly renovated, and include classy amenities. While this hotel's
advertised rates are too high, travelers with this book get 10 per-
cent off—and prices may dip lower according to demand. Ulrike,
Franziska, and Anita run a tight ship for the absentee owners (most
of the year: Sb-€85, Db-€140; late July–Aug and Dec: Sb-€95,
Db-€160; extra person-€29, firm mattresses, non-smoking, eleva-
tor, free Internet access, Goldgasse 10, tel. 0662/845-622, fax
0662/845-6229, www.ente.at, hotel@ente.at.

$$$ Hotel Weisse Taube has 30 comfortable rooms in a
quiet, dark-wood, 14th-century building, well-located about a
block off Mozartplatz (Sb-€67–85, Db with shower-€98–138, bigger Db with bath-€119–162, 10 percent discount with this book
if you reserve direct and pay cash, elevator, Internet access, tel.
0662/842-404, fax 0662/841-783, Kaigasse 9, www.weissetaube.at,
hotel@weissetaube.at).

$$$ Hotel-Pension Chiemsee is a stony dollhouse nestled in a quiet lane just behind the cathedral. Hardworking Frau Höllbacher rents 10 big, beautifully renovated rooms and three suites (Sb-€48–58, Db-€88–98, Tb-€110–120; suite-€110 for 2 people, €28/person extra up to 5; during festival and Dec: Sb-€68, Db-€98–116, Tb-€120–130; these special Rick Steves prices available if you book direct and pay cash, Chiemseegasse 5, tel. 0662/844-208, fax 0662/8442-0870, www.hotel-ami.de/hotel /chiemsee, hotel-chiemsee@aon.at).

$$ Christkönig Pension makes you feel like a guest of the bishop because, in a sense...you are. With 20 rooms in a 14th-century church building just under the castle and behind the cathedral, this is where the bishop's visitors stay. It's a charming, quiet, convenient, and unique way to sleep well and affordably in the old center. Heavenly Frau Anna Huemer will take excellent care of you (S-€35, Ss-€41, Sb-€46, Ds-€68, Db-€80, suite for 2–4 people roughly €45/person, twin beds only, €3/person extra for 1-night stays, usually booked up during festival, cash only, Kapitelplatz 2a, tel. 0662/842-627, www.christkoenig-kolleg.at, christkoenig -pension@salzburg.co.at).

Hostels

For another hostel (on the other side of the river), see "International Youth Hotel," next page.

$ Gasthaus Stadtalm (a.k.a. the *Naturfreundehaus*) is a local version of a mountaineer's hut and a great budget alternative. Snuggled in a forest on the remains of a 15th-century castle wall atop the little mountain overlooking Salzburg, it has magnificent town and mountain views. While the 26 beds are designed-for-backpackers basic, the price and view are the best in town—with the right attitude, it's a fine experience (€18.50/person in 2-, 4-, and 6-bed dorms, same price for room with double bed; includes breakfast, sheets, and shower; lockers, 2 minutes from top of €2 Mönchsberg elevator, Mönchsberg 19C, tel. & fax 0662/841-729, www.diestadtalm.com—German only, info@diestadtalm.com, Peter). Once you've dropped your bags here, it's a five-minute walk down the cliffside stairs into Toscanini Hof, in the middle of the old town (path always lit).

$ Jugendgästehaus Salzburg, just steps from the old town center, is nevertheless removed from the bustle. While its dorm rooms are the standard crammed-with-beds variety—and the hallways will bring back high-school memories—the doubles and family rooms are modern, roomy, and bright, and a recent renovation has made the public spaces quite pleasant (bed in 8-person dorm-€20–22, Db-€65–68, Qs-€98–104, higher prices are for May–Sept, non-members pay €1.50 extra, includes breakfast and sheets, pay Internet access, free Wi-Fi, *The Sound of Music* plays daily; bike rental-€10/day, €6/half-day; free parking, just around the east side of the castle hill at Josef-Preis-Allee 18; from train station take bus #5 or #25 to the Justizgebäude stop, then head left one block along the bushy wall, cross Petersbrunnstrasse, find shady Josefs-Preis-Alle, and walk a few minutes to the end—the hostel is the big orange/green building on the right; tel. 0662/842-670, fax 0662/841-101, www.jfgh.at/salzburg.php, salzburg@jfgh.at). The new hotel at the back of the hostel isn't as cheap, but does offer more standard hotel amenities, such as TVs (Db-€82–96 depending on season, includes breakfast).

Near the Train Station

$$ Pension Adlerhof, a plain and decent old pension, is two blocks in front of the train station (left off Kaiserschutzenstrasse), but a 15-minute walk from the sightseeing action. It has a quirky staff, a boring location, and 30 stodgy-but-spacious rooms (Sb-€49–68, Db-€69–108, Tb-€93–123, Qb-€108–156, price depends on season and size of room, cash only, elevator, free Wi-Fi, limited free parking, Elisabethstrasse 25, tel. 0662/875-236, fax 0662/873-663, www.gosalzburg.com, adlerhof@pension-adlerhof.at).

$ International Youth Hotel, a.k.a. the "Yo-Ho," is the most lively, handy, and American of Salzburg's hostels. This easygoing place speaks English first; has cheap meals, 180 beds, lockers, tour discounts, and no curfew; plays *The Sound of Music* free daily at 10:30; runs a lively bar; and welcomes anyone of any age. The noisy atmosphere and lack of a curfew can make it hard to sleep (€18–19 in 4- to 8-bed dorms, €21–22 in dorms with bathrooms, D-€44, Ds-€56, Q-€76, Qs-€88, includes sheets, cheap breakfast, fee for Internet access and Wi-Fi, laundry-€4 wash and dry, 6 blocks from station toward Linzergasse and 6 blocks from river at Paracelsusstrasse 9, tel. 0662/879-649, fax 0662/878-810, www.yoho.at, office@yoho.at).

Four-Star Hotels in Residential Neighborhoods away from the Center

If you want plush furnishings, spacious public spaces, generous balconies, gardens, and free parking, consider the following places. These two modern hotels in nondescript residential neighborhoods are a fine value if you don't mind the 15-minute walk from the old town. While not ideal for train travelers, drivers in need of no-stress comfort for a home base should consider these.

$$$ Hotel Rosenvilla, close to the river, offers 14 rooms with bright furnishings, surrounded by a leafy garden (Sb-€79, Db-€128, bigger Db-€142, Db suite-€188, at least €30 more during festival, free Wi-Fi, Höfelgasse 4, tel. 0662/621-765, fax 0662/625-2308, www.rosenvilla.com, hotel@rosenvilla.com).

$$$ Haus Arenberg, higher up opposite the old town, rents 17 big, breezy rooms—most with generous balconies—in a quiet garden setting (Sb-€79–88, Db-€125–142, Tb-€148–158, Qb-€158–165, €25 more during music festival, Blumensteinstrasse 8, tel. 0662/640-097, fax 0662/640-0973, www.arenberg-salzburg .at, info@arenberg-salzburg.at, family Leobacher).

Private Rooms

These are generally roomy and comfortable, and come with a good breakfast, easy parking, and tourist information. Off-season, competition softens prices. While they are a bus ride from town, with a €4.20 transit day pass *(Tageskarte)* and the frequent service, this shouldn't keep you away. In fact, most homeowners will happily pick you up at the train station if you simply telephone them and ask. Most will also do laundry for a small fee for those staying at least two nights. I've listed prices for two nights or more—if staying only one night, expect a 10 percent surcharge. Most push tours and concerts to make money on the side. As they are earning a commission, if you go through them, you'll probably lose the discount I've negotiated for my readers who go direct.

Beyond the Train Station

$ Brigitte Lenglachner rents eight basic, well-cared-for rooms in her home in a quiet, suburban-feeling neighborhood that's a 25-minute walk, 10-minute bike ride, or easy bus ride away from the center. Frau Lenglachner serves breakfast in the garden (in good weather) and happily provides plenty of local information and advice (S-€25, D-€40, Db-€48, T-€53, Qb-€96, 5b-€113; apartment with kitchen-€56 for Db, €90 for Tb, €110 for Qb; easy and free parking, Scheibenweg 8, tel. & fax 0662/438-044, bedandbreakfast4u@yahoo.de). It's a 10-minute walk from station: Head for the river, cross the pedestrian Pioneer Bridge (Pioniersteg), turn right, and walk along the river to the third street (Scheibenweg). Turn left, and it's halfway down on the right.

On Moosstrasse

The busy street called Moosstrasse, which runs southwest of Mönchsberg (behind the mountain and away from the old town center), is lined with farmhouses offering rooms. To locate these places, see the map on page 123. Handy bus #21 connects Moosstrasse to the center frequently (Mon–Fri 4/hr until 19:00, Sat 4/hr until 17:00, evenings and Sun 2/hr, 20 min). To get to these pensions from the train station, take bus #1, #5, #6, or #25 to Makartplatz, where you'll change to #21. If you're coming from the old town, catch bus #21 from Hanuschplatz, just downstream of the Staatsbrücke bridge near the *Tabak* kiosk. Buy a €1.80

Einzelkarte–Kernzone ticket (for 1 trip) or a €4.20 *Tageskarte* (day pass, good for 24 hours) from the streetside machine and punch it when you board the bus. The bus stop you use for each place is included in the following listings. If you're driving from the center, go through the tunnel, continue straight on Neutorstrasse, and take the fourth left onto Moosstrasse. Drivers exit the autobahn at *Süd* and then head in the direction of *Grodig*.

$$ Pension Bloberger Hof, while more a hotel than a pension, is comfortable and friendly, with a peaceful, rural location and 20 farmer-plush, good-value rooms. It's the farthest out, but reached by the same bus #21 from the center. Inge and her daughter Sylvia offer a 10 percent discount to those who have this book, reserve direct, and pay cash (Sb-€50–60, Db-€70, big new Db with balcony-€90, Db suite-€120, extra bed-€20, family apartment with kitchen, non-smoking, free Internet access and Wi-Fi, restaurant for guests, free loaner bikes, free station pick-up if staying 3 nights, Hammerauer Strasse 4, bus stop: Hammerauer Strasse, tel. 0662/830-227, fax 0662/827-061, www.blobergerhof .at, office@blobergerhof.at).

$ Frau Ballwein offers four cozy, charming, and fresh rooms in two buildings, some with intoxicating view balconies (Sb-€35–37, Db-€55–60, Tb-€78, Qb-€80–85, prices depend on season, family deals, cash only, farm-fresh breakfasts amid her hanging teapot collection, non-smoking, small pool, 2 free loaner bikes, free parking, Moosstrasse 69-A, bus stop: Gsengerweg, tel. & fax 0662/824-029, www.haus-ballwein.at, haus.ballwein@gmx.net).

$ Helga Bankhammer rents four nondescript rooms in a farmhouse, with a real dairy farm out back (D-€46, Db-€52, no surcharge for 1-night stays, family deals, non-smoking, laundry about €6 per load, Moosstrasse 77, bus stop: Marienbad, tel. & fax 0662/830-067, www.privatzimmer.at/helga.bankhammer, bank hammer@aon.at).

$ Haus Reichl, with three good rooms at the end of a long lane, feels the most remote. Franziska offers free loaner bikes for guests (20-min pedal to the center) and bakes fresh cakes most days (Db-€60, Tb-€75, Qb-€92–97, cash preferred, doubles and triples have balcony and view, all have tea/coffee in room, non-smoking, between Ballwein and Bankhammer B&Bs, 200 yards down Reiterweg to #52, bus stop: Gsengerweg, tel. & fax 0662/826-248, www.privatzimmer.at/haus-reichl, haus.reichl@telering.at).

Eating

In the Old Town

Salzburg boasts many inexpensive, fun, and atmospheric eateries. I'm a sucker for big cellars with their smoky, Old World atmosphere, heavy medieval arches, time-darkened paintings, antlers, hearty meals, and plump patrons. Most of these restaurants are centrally located in the old town, famous with visitors, but also enjoyed by the locals.

Gasthaus zum Wilden Mann is *the* place if the weather's bad and you're in the mood for *Hofbräu* atmosphere and a hearty, cheap meal at a shared table in one small, smoky, well-antlered room. Notice the 1899 flood photo on the wall. For a quick lunch, get the *Bauernschmaus,* a mountain of dumplings, kraut, and peasant's meats (€10.50). Owner Robert—who runs the restaurant with Schwarzenegger-like energy—enjoys fostering a convivial ambience (you'll share tables with strangers) and serving fresh traditional cuisine at great prices. I simply love this place (€7–12 daily specials, Mon–Sat 11:00–21:00, closed Sun, 2 min from Mozart's Birthplace, enter from Getreidegasse 22 or from Griesgasse 17, tel. 0662/841-787).

Stiftskeller St. Peter has been in business for more than 1,000 years—it was mentioned in the biography of Charlemagne. It's classy and central as can be, serving uninspired traditional Austrian cuisine (€10–25 meals, daily 11:30–22:30, indoor/outdoor seating, next to St. Peter's Church at foot of Mönchsberg, restaurant tel. 0662/841-268). They host the Mozart Dinner Concert described in "Music" section, earlier in this chapter (€48, nearly nightly at 20:00, call 0662/828-6950 to reserve, ask about a discount if you book direct with this guidebook). Through the centuries, they've learned to charge for each piece of bread and don't serve free tap water.

St. Paul's Stub'n Beer Garden is tucked secretly away under the castle with a decidedly untouristy atmosphere. The food is better than a beer hall, and a young, Bohemian-chic clientele fills its two smoky, troll-like rooms and its idyllic, tree-shaded garden. *Kasnock'n* is a tasty mountaineers' pasta with cheese served in an iron pan with a side salad for €9—it's enough for two (€6–12 daily specials, €7–15 plates, Mon–Sat 17:00–22:30, open later for drinks only, closed Sun, Herrengasse 16, tel. 0662/843-220).

Fisch Krieg Restaurant, on the river where the fishermen used to sell their catch, is a great value. They serve fast, fresh, and inexpensive fish in a casual dining room—where trees grow through the ceiling—as well as great riverside seating (€2 fishwiches to go, self-serve €7 meals, salad bar, Mon–Fri 8:30–18:30, Sat 8:30–13:00 except July–Aug until 14:00, closed Sun, Hanuschplatz 4, tel. 0662/843-732).

Sternbräu Inn, a sloppy, touristy Austrian food circus, is a sprawling complex of popular eateries (traditional, Italian, self-serve, and vegetarian) in a cheery garden setting. Explore both courtyards before choosing a seat (Bürgerstube is classic, most restaurants open daily 9:00–24:00, enter from Getreidegasse 34, tel. 0662/842-140). One fancy, air-conditioned room hosts the Sound of Salzburg dinner show (described under "Music," earlier in this chapter).

Café Tomaselli (with its Kiosk annex across the way) has long been Salzburg's top place to see and be seen. While overpriced and often overcrowded, it is good for lingering and people-watching. Tomaselli serves light meals and lots of drinks, keeps long hours daily, and has fine seating on the square, a view terrace upstairs, and indoor tables. Despite its fancy inlaid wood paneling, 19th-century portraits, and chandeliers, it is surprisingly low-key (€3–7 entrées, daily 7:00–21:00, until 24:00 during music festival, Alter Markt 9, tel. 0662/844-488).

Saran Essbar is the product of hardworking Mr. Saran (from the Punjab), who cooks and serves with his heart. This delightful little eatery casts a rich orange glow under medieval vaults. Its fun menu is small (Mr. Saran is committed to both freshness and value), mixing Austrian (great schnitzel and strudel), Italian, Asian vegetarian, and salads (€9–12 meals, daily 11:00–22:00, often open later, a block off Mozartplatz at Judengasse 10, tel. 0662/846-628).

Bar Club Café Republic, a hip hangout for local young people near the end of Getreidegasse, feels like a theater lobby during intermission. It serves good food with smoky indoor and outdoor seating. It's ideal if you want something mod, untouristy, and un-wursty (trendy breakfasts 8:00–18:00, Asian and international menu, €7–12 plates, lots of hard drinks, daily until late, music with a DJ Fri and Sat from 23:00, salsa music on Tue night, no cover, Anton Neumayr Platz 2, tel. 0662/841-613).

Afro Cafe, between Getreidegasse and the Mönchsberg lift, is understandably popular with its student clientele. They serve tea, coffee, cocktails, and tasty food with a dose of '70s funk and a healthy sense of humor. The menu includes pan-African specialties—try the spicy chicken couscous—as well as standard soups and salads (€9–13 main dishes, Mon–Fri 10:00–24:00, Sat 9:00–24:00, closed Sun, between Getreidegasse and cliff face at Bürgerspitalplatz 5, tel. 0662/844-888).

Demel, the only outpost of Vienna's famed chocolatier (see page 37), is a wonderland of desserts that are as beautiful as they are delectable. Sink into the pink couches upstairs, or have them box up a treat for later (daily 9:00–19:00, near TI and cathedral at Mozartplatz 2, tel. 0662/840-358).

On the Cliffs Above the Old Town: **Gasthaus Stadtalm,** Salzburg's mountaineers' hut, sits high above the old town on the edge of the cliff with cheap prices, good food, and great views. If hiking across Mönchsberg, make this your goal (traditional food, salads, cliffside garden seating or cozy-mountain-hut indoor

SALZBURG RESTAURANTS

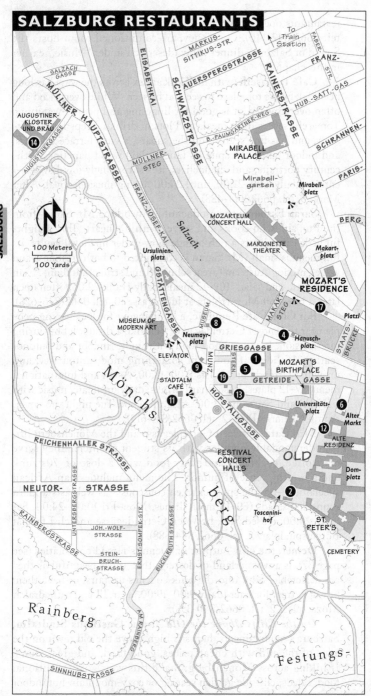

SALZBURG

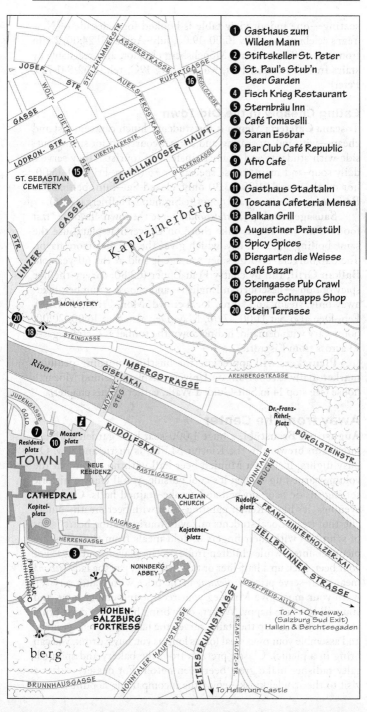

1 Gasthaus zum Wilden Mann
2 Stiftskeller St. Peter
3 St. Paul's Stub'n Beer Garden
4 Fisch Krieg Restaurant
5 Sternbräu Inn
6 Café Tomaselli
7 Saran Essbar
8 Bar Club Café Republic
9 Afro Cafe
10 Demel
11 Gasthaus Stadtalm
12 Toscana Cafeteria Mensa
13 Balkan Grill
14 Augustiner Bräustübl
15 Spicy Spices
16 Biergarten die Weisse
17 Café Bazar
18 Steingasse Pub Crawl
19 Sporer Schnapps Shop
20 Stein Terrasse

SALZBURG

seating—one indoor view table is booked for a decade of New Year's celebrations, daily 10:00–19:00, July–Aug until 24:00, 2 min from top of €3 round-trip Mönchsberg elevator, also reachable by stairs from Toscanini Hof, Mönchsberg 19C, tel. 0662/841-729, Peter).

Eating Cheaply in the Old Town

Toscana Cafeteria Mensa is the students' lunch canteen, fast and cheap—with indoor seating and a great courtyard for sitting outside with students and teachers instead of tourists. They serve a daily soup-and-main course special for €5 (Mon–Fri 9:00–15:00, hot meals served 11:00–13:30 only, closed Sat–Sun, behind the Residenz, in the courtyard opposite Sigmund-Haffnergasse 16).

Sausage stands *(Würstelstände)* serve the town's favorite "fast food." The best stands (like those on Universitätsplatz) use the same boiling water all day, which gives the weenies more flavor. The Salzburgers' favorite spicy sausage is sold at the 60-year-old **Balkan Grill,** run by chatty Frau Ebner (€2.80; survey the five spicy options—described in English—and choose a number; takeaway only, steady and sturdy local crowd, Mon–Fri 11:00–19:00, Feb–Dec also Sat 11:00–17:00, May–Dec also Sun 16:00–20:00, hours vary with demand, hiding down the tunnel at Getreidegasse 33 across from Eisgrotte).

Picnickers will appreciate the bustling morning **produce market** (daily except Sun) on Universitätsplatz, behind Mozart's house (see stop 14 in Self-Guided Walk, earlier in this chapter).

Away from the Center

Augustiner Bräustübl, a huge 1,000-seat beer garden within a monk-run brewery in the Kloster Mülln, is rustic and raw. On busy nights, it's like a Munich beer hall with no music but the volume turned up. When it's cool outside, you'll enjoy a historic setting inside beer-sloshed and smoke-stained halls. On balmy evenings, it's like a Renoir painting—but with beer breath—under chestnut trees. Local students mix with tourists eating hearty slabs of schnitzel with their fingers or cold meals from the self-serve picnic counter, while children frolic on the playground kegs. For your beer: Pick up a half-liter or full-liter mug, pay the lady (*schank* means self-serve price, *bedienung* is the price with waiter service), wash your mug, give Mr. Keg your receipt and empty mug, and you will be made happy. Waiters only bring beer; they don't bring food—instead, go up the stairs, survey the hallway of deli counters, and assemble your own meal (or, as long as you buy a drink, you can bring in a picnic). Classic pretzels from the bakery and spiraled, salty radishes make great beer even better. For dessert—after a visit to the strudel kiosk—enjoy the incomparable floodlit view of old Salzburg from the nearby Müllnersteg pedestrian bridge and a riverside stroll home (open daily 15:00–23:00, closed for lunch, Augustinergasse 4, tel. 0662/431-246). It's about a 15-minute walk along the river (with the river on your right) from the Staatsbrücke bridge. After passing the pedestrian Müllnersteg bridge, just after Café am Kai, follow the stairs up to a busy street, and cross it. From here, either continue up more stairs into the trees and around the small church (for a scenic approach to the monastery), or stick to the sidewalk as it curves around to Augustinergasse. Either way, your goal is the huge yellow building. Don't be fooled by second-rate gardens serving the same beer nearby.

North of the River, near Recommended Linzergasse Hotels

Spicy Spices is a trippy vegetarian-Indian restaurant where Suresh Syad serves tasty take-out curry and rice, samosas, organic salads, vegan soups, and fresh juices (€6.50 specials, Mon–Fri 10:30–21:30, Sat–Sun 12:00–21:30, Wolf-Dietrich-Strasse 1, tel. 0662/870-712).

Biergarten die Weisse, close to the hotels on Rupertgasse and away from the tourists, is a longtime hit with the natives. If a beer hall can be happening, this one—modern yet with antlers—is it. Their famously good beer is made right there; favorites include their fizzy wheat beer *(Weisse)* and their seasonal beers (on request). Enjoy the beer with their good, cheap traditional food in the great garden seating, or in the wide variety of indoor rooms— sports bar, young and noisy, or older and more elegant (daily specials, Mon–Sat 10:00–24:00, closed Sun, Rupertgasse 10, east of Bayerhamerstrasse, tel. 0662/872-246).

Café Bazar, overlooking the river between Mirabell Gardens and the Staatsbrücke bridge, is as close as you'll get to a Vienna coffee house in Salzburg. It's *the* venerable spot for a classy drink with an old-town-and-castle view (light meals, Mon–Sat 7:30– 23:00, Sun 9:00–18:00, Schwarzstrasse 3, tel. 0662/874-278).

Steingasse Pub Crawl

For a fun post-concert activity, crawl through medieval Steingasse's trendy pubs (all open until the wee hours). This is a local and hip scene, but accessible to older tourists: dark bars filled with well-dressed Salzburgers lazily smoking cigarettes and talking philosophy as avant-garde Euro-pop throbs on the soundtrack. Most of the pubs are in cellar-like caves...extremely atmospheric. (For more on Steingasse, see "Steingasse Stroll," page 121.) These four pubs are all within about 100 yards of each other. Start at the Linzergasse end of Steingasse.

Pepe Cocktail Bar, with Mexican decor and Latin music, serves Mexican snacks *con* cocktails (nightly 19:00–3:00 in the morning, live DJs Fri–Sat from 19:00, Steingasse 3, tel. 0662/873-662).

Shrimps, next door and less claustrophobic, is more a restaurant than a bar, serving creative international dishes (spicy shrimp sandwiches and salads, Tue–Sun 18:00–24:00, closed Mon, Steingasse 5, tel. 0662/874-484).

Saiten Sprung wins the "Best Atmosphere" award. The door is kept closed to keep out the crude and rowdy. Ring the bell and enter its hellish interior—lots of stone and red decor, with mountains of melted wax beneath age-old candlesticks and a classic soul music ambience. Stelios, who speaks English with Greek charm, serves cocktails, fine wine, and wine-friendly Italian antipasti (nightly 21:00–4:00 in the morning, Steingasse 11, tel. 0662/881-377).

Fridrich, a tiny place next door with lots of mirrors and a silver ceiling fan, specializes in wine. Bernd Fridrich is famous for his martinis, and passionate about Austrian wines and food (€5–12 small entrées, nightly from 18:00 in summer or 17:00 in winter, Steingasse 15, tel. 0662/876-218).

Connections

Salzburg's station, located so close to the German border, is covered not just by Austrian railpasses, but German ones as well—including the Bayern-Ticket (covers up to five people on all local trains in Bavaria for €27/day, not valid Mon–Fri before 9:00).

From Salzburg by Train to: Vienna (2/hr, 2.5–3 hrs), **Hallstatt** (hourly, 50 min to Attnang Puchheim, 20-min wait, then 90 min to Hallstatt), **Reutte** (hourly, 5 hrs, change either in Munich and Kempten, or in Innsbruck and Garmisch), **Munich** (2/hr, 1.5–2 hrs), **Füssen** (roughly hourly, 4 hrs, 1–2 changes), **Interlaken** (8/day, 8–9 hrs, 1–5 changes), **Venice** (5/day, 6–8 hrs, 1–3 changes, 2 good overnight connections), **Florence** (3/day, 8.5–9.5 hrs, 2 changes, 1 overnight connection via Villach), **Prague** (7/day, 6.5–7.5 hrs, 2 direct, no decent overnight connection). Train info: tel. 051-717 (to get an operator, dial 2, then 2).

Route Tips for Drivers

From Salzburg to Hallstatt: Get on the Munich–Wien autobahn (follow blue *A-1* signs), head for Vienna, exit at Thalgau (#274), and follow signs to *Hof, Fuschl,* and *St. Gilgen.* The Salzburg–Hallstatt road passes two luge rides (see Hallstatt chapter), St. Gilgen (pleasant but touristy), and Bad Ischl (the center of the Salzkammergut, with a spa, the emperor's villa if you need a Habsburg history fix, and a good **TI**—Mon–Fri 8:00–18:00, Sat 9:00–15:00, Sun 10:00–13:00, tel. 06132/277-570).

HALLSTATT
and the SALZKAMMERGUT

Commune with nature in Austria's Salzkammergut Lake District. "The hills are alive," and you're surrounded by the loveliness that has turned on everyone from Emperor Franz Josef to Julie Andrews. This is *Sound of Music* country. Idyllic and majestic, but not rugged, it's a gentle land of lakes, forested mountains, and storybook villages, rich in hiking opportunities and inexpensive lodging. Settle down in the postcard-pretty, lake-cuddling town of Hallstatt.

Planning Your Time

While there are plenty of lakes and charming villages in the Salzkammergut, Hallstatt is really the only one that matters. One night and a few hours to browse are all you'll need to fall in love. To relax or take a hike in the surroundings, give it two nights and a day. It's a relaxing break between Salzburg and Vienna.

Orientation

(area code: 06134)

Lovable Hallstatt is a tiny town bullied onto a ledge between a selfish mountain and a swan-ruled lake, with a waterfall ripping furiously through its middle. It can be toured on foot in about 15 minutes. The town is one of Europe's oldest, going back centuries before Christ. The symbol of Hallstatt, which you'll see all over town, consists of two adjacent spirals—a design based on jewelry found in Bronze Age Celtic graves high in the nearby mountains.

The charms of Hallstatt are the village and its lakeside setting. Go there to relax, nibble, wander, and paddle. While tourist

HALLSTATT

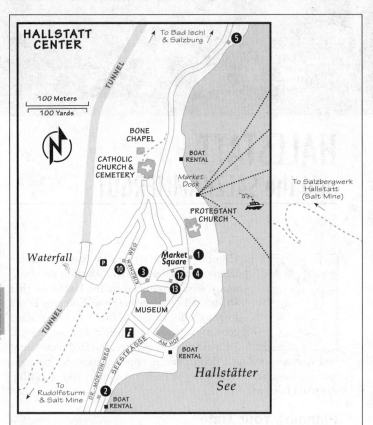

HALLSTATT CENTER

100 Meters
100 Yards

TUNNEL

To Bad Ischl & Salzburg

BONE CHAPEL

BOAT RENTAL

CATHOLIC CHURCH & CEMETERY

Market Dock

To Salzbergwerk Hallstatt (Salt Mine)

PROTESTANT CHURCH

Waterfall

P

Market Square

KIRCHEN WEG

MUSEUM

AM HOF

BOAT RENTAL

Hallstätter See

SEESTRASSE

DR. MORTON WEG

To Rudolfsturm & Salt Mine

BOAT RENTAL

TUNNEL

ECHERNTAL

ECHERNTALWEG

1 Hotel/Rest. Grüner Baum
2 Bräugasthof Hallstatt
3 Gasthof Zauner
4 Gasthof Simony
5 Pension Sarstein
6 Gasthof Pension Grüner Anger
7 Helga Lenz Rooms
8 Haus Trausner
9 Herta Höll Rooms
10 Gasthaus zur Mühle Hostel & Pizza
11 Strand Café
12 Ruth Zimmerman Pub
13 Internet Access (2)
14 Launderette/Campgrounds

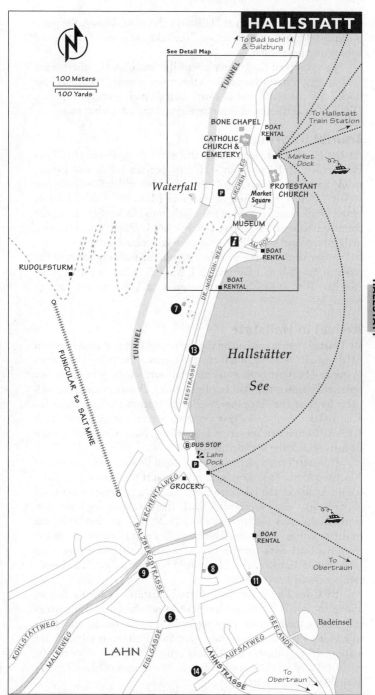

HALLSTATT

To Bad Ischl & Salzburg

See Detail Map

To Hallstatt Train Station

BONE CHAPEL

BOAT RENTAL

CATHOLIC CHURCH & CEMETERY

Market Dock

Waterfall

PROTESTANT CHURCH

Market Square

MUSEUM

BOAT RENTAL

BOAT RENTAL

RUDOLFSTURM

Hallstätter

See

FUNICULAR to SALT MINE

TUNNEL

WC

BUS STOP

Lahn Dock

GROCERY

BOAT RENTAL

To Obertraun

SALZBERGSTRASSE

ERCHENTALWEG

KOHLSTATTWEG

MALERWEG

EISLGASSE

LAHN

LAHNSTRASSE

AUFSATZWEG

SEELÄNDE

Badeinsel

To Obertraun

100 Meters

100 Yards

HALLSTATT

crowds can trample much of Hallstatt's charm in August, the place is almost dead in the off-season. The lake is famous for its good fishing and pure water.

Two tiny boat docks serve town: The "main" dock, where boats from the train station arrive, is in the center of town; the Lahn boat dock is on the south end of town, near a small grocery store (see "Eating," near the end of this chapter) and the town's bus stop.

Tourist Information

At the helpful TI, located on the main drag above the "Post Partner," Claudia and her staff can explain hikes and excursions, and find you a room (July–Aug Mon–Fri 9:00–17:00, Sat 10:00–14:00, closed Sun; Sept–June Mon–Fri 9:00–12:00 & 14:00–17:00, closed Sat–Sun; one block from Market Square, across from museum at Seestrasse 169, tel. 06134/8208, www.inneres -salzkammergut.at, hallstatt@inneres-salzkammergut.at).

In the summer, the TI offers 90-minute **walking tours** of the town in English and German (€4, May–Sept Sat at 10:00, July– Aug also Wed at 10:00, confirm schedule at TI). They can arrange private tours for €75.

Arrival in Hallstatt

By Train: If you're coming on the main train line that runs between Salzburg and Vienna, you'll change trains at Attnang-Puchheim to get to Hallstatt (you won't see Hallstatt on the schedules, but trains to Ebensee and Bad Ischl stop here). Day-trippers can check their bags at the Attnang-Puchheim station (follow signs for *Schliessfächer*, coin-op lockers are at the street, curbside near track 1, €2.50/24 hrs, a ticket serves as your key). Note: Connections can be fast—check the TV monitor.

Hallstatt's train station is a wide spot on the tracks across the lake from town. *Stefanie* (a boat) meets you at the station and glides scenically across the lake into town (€2.20, meets each train until about 18:30—don't arrive after that). The last departing boat-train connection leaves Hallstatt at about 18:00, and the first boat goes in the morning at 6:50 (9:20 on Sun). Once in Hallstatt, walk left from the boat dock for the TI and most hotels. Since there's no train station in town, the TI can help you find schedule information, or check www.oebb.at.

By Car: The main road skirts Hallstatt via a long tunnel above the town. Hallstatt has several numbered parking areas outside the town center. Parking lot #1 is in the tunnel above the town (often full mid-June–mid-Oct; swing through to check for a spot). If it's full, try lot #2, just after the tunnel, a lovely 10- to 20-minute lakeside walk from the town center. More lots are available away from town.

If you have a hotel reservation, the guard will let you drive into town to drop your bags; ask your hotel if it has any in-town parking when you book. Parking is free with a guest card (available from your hotel), and it's a laid-back system—just show your card later. Without a guest card, per-day parking is still quite reasonable (lot #1: €4.20/day, lot #2: €6/day; less after 14:00). Off-season (Nov–April), parking in town is easy and free.

Helpful Hints

Internet Access: Try **Hallstatt Umbrella Bar** (€4/hr, summers only, weather permitting—since it's literally under a big umbrella, halfway between Lahn boat dock and Museum Square at Seestrasse 145). You can get online all year at the **Lakeside Lounge** (€4/hr, daily 10:00–22:00, between Museum Square and Market Square at Badergraben 188).

Laundry: A small full-service **launderette** is at the campground up from the town's man-made island, Bade-Insel, just off the main road (about €8/load, mid-April–mid-Oct daily 8:00–12:00 & 14:00–20:00, closed off-season, tel. 06134/83224). In the center, **Hotel Grüner Baum** does laundry for non-guests (€13/load, on Market Square, see "Sleeping").

Bike Rental: See "Sights and Activities—Biking," later in this chapter.

Boat Rental: Two places rent electric boats; both rent from two locations in high season. **Riedler** is next to the main boat dock, and 75 yards past Bräugasthof (€14/hr, tel. 06134/8320). **Hemetsberger** is near Gasthof Simony, and the Lahn boat dock (€12/hr, tel. 06134/8228). Both are open daily until 19:00 in peak season and in good weather. Boats have two speeds: slow and stop (spend an extra €3/hr for faster 500-watt boats). Both places also rent rowboats and paddleboats.

Parks and Swimming: Green and peaceful lakeside parks line the south end of Lake Hallstatt. If you walk 10 minutes south of town to Hallstatt-Lahn, you'll find a grassy public park, playground, mini-golf, and swimming area *(Badestrand)* with the fun Bade-Insel play-island.

Views: For a great view over Hallstatt, hike above Helga Lenz's B&B as far as you like (see "Sleeping," later in this chapter), or climb any path leading up the hill. The 40-minute steep hike down from the salt mine (listed later in the chapter) gives the best views. While most visitors stroll the lakeside drag between the old and new parts of town, make a point to do the trip once by taking the more higgledy-piggledy high lane called Dr.-Morton-Weg.

Self-Guided Walk

Welcome to Hallstatt

• *This short walk starts at the dock.*

Boat Landing: There was a Hallstatt before there was a Rome. In fact, because of the importance of salt mining here, an entire epoch—the Hallstatt Era, from 800 to 400 B.C.—is named for this important spot. Through the centuries, salt was traded and people came and went by boat. You'll still see the traditional *Fuhr* boats, designed to carry heavy loads in shallow water.

Towering above the town is the Catholic church. Its faded St. Christopher—patron saint of travelers, with his cane and baby Jesus on his shoulder—watched over those sailing in and out. Until 1875, the town was extremely remote...then came a real road and the train. The good ship *Stefanie* shuttles travelers back and forth from here to the Hallstatt train station, immediately across the lake. The *Bootverleih* sign advertises boat rentals. By the way, *Schmuck* is not an insult...it's jewelry.

Notice the one-lane road out of town (below the church). Until 1966, when a bigger tunnel was built above Hallstatt, all the traffic crept single-file right through the town.

Look down the shore at the huge homes. Several families lived in each of these houses, back when Hallstatt's population was about double its present 1,000. Today, the population continues to shrink, and many of these generally underused houses rent rooms to visitors.

Parking is tight here in the tourist season. Locals and hotels have cards getting them into the prime town-center lot. From November through April, the barricade is lifted and anyone can park here. Hallstatt gets about three months of snow each winter, but the lake hasn't frozen over since 1981.

See any swans? They've patrolled the lake like they own it since the 1860s, when Emperor Franz Josef and Empress Sisi—the Princess Diana of her day (see page 47)—made this region their annual holiday retreat. Sisi loved swans, so locals made sure she'd see them here. During this period, the Romantics discovered Hallstatt, many top painters worked here, and the town got its first hotel. Today, that hotel (the big, derelict Haus Kranz facing the square) has an absentee owner and a floor plan so tangled that it's too expensive to renovate, so it just sits, looking ugly in the heart of Hallstatt.

Tiny Hallstatt has two big churches—Protestant (bordering the square on the left, with a grassy lakeside playground) and Catholic up above (with its fascinating bone chapel—described under "Sights and Activities," on page 151).

• *Walk over the town's stream, and pop into the...*

Protestant Church: In 1860, Emperor Franz Josef allowed non-Catholic Christians to build churches. Before that, they were allowed only to worship in low-key "houses of prayer." Back then, the Catholic Church was the church of royalty and the wealthy. The working class was more likely to be Protestant. As this was a mining town, it was quite Protestant. In 1863, the miners pooled their humble resources and built this fine church. Step inside (free and often open). It's very plain, emphasizing the pulpit and organ rather than fancy art and saints. Check out the portraits: Martin Luther (left of altar), the town in about 1865 with its new church (left wall), and a century of pastors.

• *Continue past the church to the...*

Market Square (Marktplatz): In 1750, a fire leveled this part of town. The buildings you see now are all late 18th-century and built of stone rather than flammable wood. The three big buildings on the left are government-subsidized housing (mostly for seniors and people with health problems). Take a close look at the two-dimensional, up-against-the-wall pear tree (it likes the sunwarmed wall). The statue features the Holy Trinity.

• *Continue a block past Gasthof Simony. At the first corner, just before the Gemeindeamt (City Hall), jog left across the little square and then right down the tiny lane marked* Am Hof, *which leads through an intimate bit of domestic town architecture, boat houses, lots of firewood, and maybe a couple of swans hanging out. The lane circles back to the main drag and the...*

Museum Square: Because 20th-century Hallstatt was of no industrial importance, it was untouched by World War II. But once upon a time, its salt was worth defending. High above, peeking out of the trees, is Rudolfsturm (Rudolf's Tower). Originally a 13th-century watchtower protecting the salt mines, and later the mansion of a salt-mine boss, it's now a restaurant with a great view. A zigzag trail connects the town with Rudolfsturm and the salt mines just beyond. The big, white houses by the waterfall were water-powered mills that once ground Hallstatt's grain. (If you hike up a few blocks, you'll see the river raging through town.)

Around you are the town's TI, post office, museum, City Hall, and Dachstein Sport Shop (described later). A statue recalls the mine manager who excavated prehistoric graves in about 1850. Much of the *Schmuck* sold locally is inspired by the jewelry found in the area's Bronze Age tombs.

The memorial wooden stairs in front of the museum are a copy of those found in Hallstatt's prehistoric mine—the original stairs are more than 2,500 years old. For thousands of years, people have been leaching salt out of this mountain. A brine spring sprung here, attracting Bronze Age people in about 1600 B.C. Later, they dug tunnels to mine the rock (which was 70 percent salt), dissolved it into a brine, and distilled out the salt—precious for preserving meat. For a look at early salt-mining implements and the town's story, visit the museum (described under "Sights and Activities").

Across from the TI, Pension Hallberg has a quirky hallway full of Nazi paraphernalia and other stuff found on the lake bed (€1). Only recently did local divers realize that, for centuries, the lake had been Hallstatt's garbage can. If something was *kaput,* locals would just toss it into the lake. In 1945, Nazi medals decorating German and Austrian war heroes suddenly became dangerous to own. Throughout the former Third Reich, hard-earned medals floated down to lonely lake beds, including Hallstatt's.

Under the TI is the "Post Partner"—a government-funded attempt to turn inefficient post offices into something more viable (selling souvenirs, renting bikes, and employing people with disabilities who otherwise wouldn't work). The *Fischerei* provides the town with its cherished fresh lake fish. The county allows two commercial fishermen on the lake. They spread their nets each morning and sell their catch here to town restaurants, or to any locals cooking up a special dinner (Mon–Fri 9:00–12:00, closed Sat–Sun).

• *Nearby, still on Museum Square, find the...*

Dachstein Sport Shop: During a renovation project, the builders dug down and hit a Celtic and ancient Roman settlement. Peek through the glass pavement on the covered porch to see where the Roman street level was. If the shop is open, pop in and go downstairs (free). You'll walk on Roman flagstones and see the small gutter that channeled water to power an ancient hammer mill (used to pound iron into usable shapes). In prehistoric times, people lived up by the mines. Romans were the first Hallstatt lakeside settlers. The store's owners are committed to sharing Hallstatt's fascinating history, and often display old town paintings and folk art.

• *From this square, the first right (after the bank) leads up a few stairs to...*

Dr.-Morton-Weg: House #26A dates from 1597. Follow the lane uphill to the left past more old houses. Until 1890, this was the town's main drag, and the lake lapped at the lower doors of these houses. Therefore, many main entrances were via the attic, from this level. Enjoy this back-street view of town. Just after the arch, near #133, check out the old tools hanging outside the workshop, and the piece of wooden piping. It's a section taken from the 25-mile wooden pipeline that carried salt brine from Hallstatt to Ebensee. This was in place from 1595 until the last generation, when the last stretch of wood was replaced by plastic piping. At the pipe, enjoy the lake view and climb down the stairs. From lake level, look back up at the striking traditional architecture (the fine woodwork on the left was recently rebuilt after a fire; parts of the old house on the right date to medieval times).

• *Your tour is finished. From here, you have boat rentals, the salt-mine tour, the town museum, and the Catholic church (with its bone chapel) all within a few minutes' walk.*

Sights and Activities

▲▲**Catholic Church and Bone Chapel**—Hallstatt's Catholic church overlooks the town from above. From near the main boat dock, hike up the covered wooden stairway and follow the *Kath. Kirche* signs. The lovely church has twin altars. The one on the left was made by town artists in 1897. The one on the right is more historic—dedicated in 1515 to Mary, who's flanked by St. Barbara (on right, patron of miners) and St. Catherine (on left, patron of foresters—a lot of wood was needed to fortify the many miles of tunnels, and to boil the brine to distill out the salt).

Behind the church, in the well-tended graveyard, is the 12th-century Chapel of St. Michael (even older than the church). Its bone chapel—or charnel house *(Beinhaus)*—contains more than 600 painted skulls. Each skull has been lovingly named, dated, and decorated (skulls with dark, thick garlands are oldest—18th century; those with flowers are more recent—19th century). Space was so limited in this cemetery that bones had only 12 peaceful, buried years here before making way for the freshly dead. Many of the dug-up bones and skulls ended up in this chapel. They stopped this practice in the 1960s, about the same time the Catholic Church began permitting cremation. But one woman (who died in 1983) managed to sneak her skull in later (dated 1995, under the cross, with the gold tooth). The skulls on the books are those of priests (€1, free English flier, daily May–Sept 10:00–18:00, Oct 10:00–16:00, closed Nov–April, tel. 06134/8279).

▲**Hallstatt Museum**—This pricey little museum tells the story of Hallstatt. It focuses on the Hallstatt Era (800–400 B.C.), when this village was the salt-mining hub of a culture that spread from France to the Balkans. Back then, Celtic tribes dug for precious salt, and Hallstatt was, as its name means, the "place of salt." While its treasures are the countless artifacts excavated from prehistoric gravesites around the mine, you'll get the whole gamut—with displays on everything from the region's flora and fauna to local artists and the surge in Hallstatt tourism during the Romantic Age. Everything's in German, and the skimpy €3 English guide is worth borrowing, but not buying (€7.50, May–Sept daily 9:00–18:00, shorter hours off-season, closed Mon–Tue Nov–March, adjacent to TI at Seestrasse 56, tel. 06134/828-015). On summer Tuesdays, when candlelit boats run, the museum stays open until 20:00 (see "candlelit boat rides" under "Nightlife," later in this chapter).

▲**Lake Trip**—For a quick boat trip, you can ride the *Stefanie* across the lake and back for €4.40. It stops at the tiny Hallstatt train station for 30 minutes (note return time in the boat's window), giving you time to walk to a hanging bridge (ask the captain to point you to the *Hängebrücke*—HENG-eh-brick-eh—a 10-minute lakeside stroll to the left). Longer lake tours are also available (€8/50 min, €9.50/75 min, sporadic schedules—especially off-season—so check chalkboards by boat docks for today's times). Those into relaxation can rent a sleepy electric motorboat to enjoy town views from the water (see "Helpful Hints," near the beginning of this chapter).

▲**Salt-Mine Tour**—If you have yet to tour a salt mine, consider visiting Hallstatt's, which claims to be the oldest in the world. First, you'll ride a steep funicular high above the town (€10 round-trip, €6 one-way, 4/hr, daily May–mid-Sept 9:00–18:00, mid-Sept–Oct 9:00–16:30, closed Nov–April). Then you'll hike 10 minutes to the mine (past excavation sites of many prehistoric tombs and a glass case with 2,500-year-old bones—but there's little to actually see). Report back 10 minutes before the tour time on your ticket, check your bag, and put on old miners' clothes. Then hike 200 yards higher in your funny outfit to meet your guide, who escorts your group down a tunnel dug in 1719. Inside the mountain, you'll watch a slide show, follow your guide through several caverns as you learn about mining techniques over the last 7,000 years, see a silly laser show on a glassy subterranean lake, peek at a few waxy cavemen with pickaxes, and ride the train out. The highlight for most is sliding down two banisters (the second one is longer and ends with a flash for an automatic souvenir photo that clocks your speed—see how you did compared to the rest of your group after the tour).

The presentation is very low-tech, as the mining company owns all three mine tours in the area and sees little reason to invest in the experience when they can simply mine the tourists. While the tour is mostly in German, the guide is required to speak English if you ask...so ask (salt-mine tour-€16, €22 combo-ticket for mine and funicular round-trip saves about €4, you can buy mine tickets at cable-car station—note the time and tour number on your ticket, daily May–mid-Sept 9:00–16:30, mid-Sept–Oct 9:00–15:00, closed Nov–April, the 16:00 funicular departure catches the last tour at 16:30, no children under age 4, arrive early or late to avoid summer crowds, dress for the constant 47-degree temperature, tel. 06132/200-2400). If you skip the funicular, the scenic 40-minute hike back into town is (with strong knees) a joy.

At the base of the funicular, notice train tracks leading to the Erbstollen tunnel entrance. This lowest of the salt tunnels goes many miles into the mountain, where a shaft connects it to the tunnels you just explored. Today, the salty brine from these tunnels flows 25 miles through the world's oldest pipeline—made of wood until quite recently—to the huge modern salt works (next to the highway) at Ebensee.

▲**Local Hikes**—Mountain-lovers, hikers, and spelunkers who use Hallstatt as their home base keep busy for days (ask the TI for ideas). A good, short, and easy walk is the two-hour round-trip up the Echern Valley to the Waldbachstrub waterfall and back: From the parking lot, follow signs to the salt mines, then follow the little wooden signs marked *Echerntalweg*. With a car, consider hiking around nearby Altaussee (flat, 3-hour hike) or along Grundlsee to Toplitzsee. Regular buses connect Hallstatt with Gosausee for a pleasant hour-long walk around that lake. Or consider walking nine miles halfway around Lake Hallstatt via the town of Steeg (boat to train station, walk left along lake and past idyllic farmsteads, returning to Hallstatt along the old salt trail, *Soleleitungsweg*); for a shorter hike, walk to Steeg along either side of the lake, and catch the train from Steeg back to Hallstatt's station. The TI can also recommend a great two-day hike with an overnight in a nearby mountain hut.

Biking—The best two bike rides take nearly the same routes as the hikes listed previously: up the Echern Valley, and around the lake (bikers do better going via Obertraun along the new lakeside bike path—start with a ride on the *Stefanie*). Two places in town rent bikes: **Post Partner** (the stamp-selling place formerly known as the post office; €5/2 hrs, €9/half-day, €13/day, €30/weekend rental—Fri–Mon, open Mon–Fri 8:00–12:00 & 14:30–16:00, closed Sat–Sun, on Museum Square, tel. 06134/8201) and **Hotel Grüner Baum** (€2.50/hr, €9/half-day, €16/day, on Market Square, see "Sleeping").

Near Hallstatt

▲▲**Dachstein Mountain Cable Car and Caves**—For a refreshing activity, ride a scenic cable car up a mountain to visit huge, chilly caves.

Dachstein Cable Car: From Obertraun, three miles beyond Hallstatt on the main road (or directly across the lake as the crow flies), a mighty gondola goes in three stages high up the Dachstein Plateau—crowned by Dachstein, the highest mountain in the Salzkammergut (9,800 feet). The first segment stops at Schönbergalm (4,500 feet, runs May–Oct), which has a mountain restaurant and two huge caves (described next). The second segment goes to the summit of Krippenstein (6,600 feet, runs mid-May–Oct). The third segment descends to Gjaidalm (5,800 feet, runs mid-June–Oct), where several hikes begin. For a quick high-country experience, Krippenstein is better than Gjaidalm. From

Salzkammergut

GERMANY

To Munich

A-8

Freilassing

TRAIN STATION

Salzburg

A-1

158

Fuschlsee

Mondsee

Mondsee

Schafberg

St. Gilgen

St. Wolfgang

Wolfgangsee

Untersberg

Hallein

305

AUSTRIA

A-10

162

Berchtesgaden

Kehlstein

HITLER'S EAGLE'S NEST

Königsee

Königsee

166

Bischofshofen

To Innsbruck

311

To Italy

HALLSTATT

Krippenstein, you'll survey a scrubby, limestone, karstic landscape (which absorbs, through its many cracks, the rainfall that ultimately carves all those caves) with 360-degree views of the surrounding mountains (round-trip cable-car ride to Schönbergalm and the caves-€15, to Krippenstein-€22, to Gjaidalm-€24; combo-ticket covering ride to Gjaidalm and entry to both caves-€35; cheaper family rates available, last cable car back down usually at

HALLSTATT

about 17:00, tel. 06131/51310, www.dachsteinwelterbe.at).

Giant Ice Caves (Riesen-Eishöhle, 4,500 feet): These were discovered in 1910. Today, guides lead tours in German and English on an hour-long, half-mile hike through an eerie, icy, subterranean world, passing limestone canyons the size of subway stations. The limestone caverns, carved by rushing water, are named for scenes from Wagner's operas—the favorite of the mountaineers who first came here. If you're nervous, note that the iron oxide covering the ceiling takes 5,000 years to form. Things are very stable.

At the lift station, report to the ticket window to get your cave appointment. The temperature is just above freezing, and although the 700 steps help keep you warm, bring a sweater. Allow 90 minutes, including the 10-minute hike up from the station (€10, €15 combo-ticket with Mammoth Caves, €35 combo-ticket covers the cable car up to Gjaidalm and entry to both caves, open May–Oct, hour-long tours start at 9:00, last tour at 15:30, stay in front and assert yourself to get English information, tel. 06131/51310).

Drop by the little free museum near the lift station—in a local-style wood cabin designed to support 200 tons of snow—to see the cave-system model, exhibits about its exploration, and info about life in the caves.

Mammoth Caves (Mammuthöhle): While huge and well-promoted, these are much less interesting than the ice caves and—for most—not worth the time. Of the 30-mile limestone labyrinth excavated so far, you'll walk a half-mile with a German-speaking guide (€10, €15 combo-ticket with ice caves, €35 combo-ticket covers the cable car up to Gjaidalm and entry to both caves, open May–Oct, hour-long tours in English and German 10:00–15:00, entrance a 10-min hike from lift station).

Combo-Ticket Tips: The several combo-tickets available generally won't save you any money over buying individual tickets. But if you're gung-ho enough to want to visit one or both caves, and plan to ride the cable car farther up the mountain, the €35 same-day combo-ticket makes sense (covers the cable car all the way to Gjaidalm and back, as well as entry to both caves; it's slightly cheaper to buy separate tickets if you're riding only to Krippenstein and skipping one of the caves).

Getting to Obertraun: The cable car to Dachstein leaves from the outskirts of Obertraun, across the lake from Hallstatt. To reach the Obertraun cable car from Hallstatt, the handiest and cheapest option is the bus (€1.70, 5–6/day, leaves from Lahn boat dock, drops you directly at cable-car station). Romantics can take the boat to Obertraun (€5, 5/day July–Aug, 4/day Sept–June, 15 min)—but it's a 40-minute hike from there to the lift station. The impatient can consider hitching a ride—virtually all cars leaving Hallstatt to the south will pass through Obertraun in a few minutes.

Returning to Hallstatt: Plan to leave by mid-afternoon. The last bus from the cable-car station back to Hallstatt (at 17:05 in summer) inconveniently leaves before the last cable car down—if you miss the bus, try getting a ride from a fellow cable-car passenger. Otherwise, you can either call a taxi (€13, ask cable-car staff for help), or simply walk back along the lakefront (about one hour).

Luge Rides (Sommerrodelbahnen) on the Hallstatt–Salzburg Road—If you're driving between Salzburg and Hallstatt, you'll pass two luge rides. Each is a ski lift that drags you backward up the hill as you sit on your go-cart. At the top, you ride the cart down the winding metal course. It's easy: Push to go, pull to stop, take your hands off your stick and you get hurt.

Each course is just off the road with easy parking. The ride up and down takes about 15 minutes. The one near Fuschlsee (closest to Salzburg, look for *Sommerrodelbahn* sign) is half as long and cheaper (€4.30/ride, 1,970 feet, tel. 06235/7297). The one near Wolfgangsee (look for *Riesenschutzbahn* sign) is a double course, more scenic with grand lake views (€6.40/ride, €43/10 rides, 4,265 feet, each track is the same speed, tel. 06137/7085). Courses are open May (or earlier) through October from 10:00 to 18:00 (Wolfgangsee luge also open July–Aug 9:30–20:00)—but generally closed in bad weather.

Nightlife

Locals would laugh at the thought. But if you do want some action after dinner, you do have a few options: **Gasthaus zur Mühle** (youth hostel with a rustic sports-bar ambience in its restaurant when drinks replace the food, open late, closed Tue Sept–mid-May, run by Ferdinand). Or, for your late-night drink, savor the Market Square from the trendy little pub called **Ruth Zimmermann,** where locals congregate with soft music, a good selection of drinks, two small rooms, and tables on the square (daily May–Sept 10:00–2:00 in the morning, Oct–April 11:00–2:00, tel. 06134/8306). In July and August, **candlelit boat rides** leave at 20:30 on Tuesday evenings (€12.50, €16 combo-ticket with Hallstatt Museum).

Sleeping

Hallstatt's TI can almost always find you a room (either in town or at B&Bs and small hotels outside of town—which are more likely to have rooms available and come with easy parking). Drivers, remember to ask if your hotel has in-town parking when you book your room.

Mid-July and August can be tight. Early August is worst. Hallstatt is not the place to splurge—some of the best rooms are *Privatzimmer,* just as nice and modern as the rooms in bigger hotels, at half the cost. In summer, a double bed in a private home costs about €50 with breakfast. It's hard to get a one-night advance reservation (try calling the TI for help). But if you drop in and they have a spot, one-nighters are welcome. Prices include breakfast, lots of stairs, and a silent night. *"Zimmer mit Aussicht?"*

Sleep Code

(€1 = about $1.40, country code: 43, area code: 06134)
S = Single, **D** = Double/Twin, **T** = Triple, **Q** = Quad, **b** = bathroom,
s = shower only. Unless otherwise noted, credit cards are
accepted, English is spoken, and breakfast is included.

    To help you sort easily through these listings, I've divided
the rooms into three categories, based on the price for a
standard double room with bath:

  $$$ **Higher Priced**—Most rooms €90 or more.
   $$ **Moderately Priced**—Most rooms between €50–90.
    $ **Lower Priced**—Most rooms €50 or less.

(TSIM-mer mit OWS-zeekt) means "Room with view?"—worth
asking for. Unlike many businesses in town, the cheaper places
don't take credit cards.

As most rooms here are in old buildings with well-cared-for
wooden interiors, dripping laundry is a no-no at Hallstatt pensions. Be especially considerate when hanging laundry over anything but tile—if you must wash larger clothing items here, ask
your host about using their clothesline.

$$$ Hotel Grüner Baum offers the priciest beds in town. Its
22 rooms are huge, each with a separate living area with modern
furnishings on ancient hardwoods. The owner, Monika, moved
in from Vienna and renovated this stately old hotel with urban
taste (suite-like Db-€130–200, price depends on view, 8 percent
discount with this book, family rooms, Internet access, laundry
service, closed in Nov, 20 yards from boat dock and overlooking
the lake and Market Square, tel. 06134/82630, fax 06134/826-344,
www.gruenerbaum.cc, contact@gruenerbaum.cc).

$$$ Bräugasthof Hallstatt is like a museum filled with
antique furniture and ancient family portraits. This creaky old
place—a former brewery with eight clean, cozy rooms—is run by
Virena and her daughter, Virena. Six of the rooms have gorgeous
little lakeview balconies (Sb-€50, Db-€90, Db with balcony-€95,
Tb-€130, free parking, just past TI on the main drag at Seestrasse
120, tel. 06134/8221, fax 06134/82214, www.brauhaus-lobisser
.com, info@brauhaus-lobisser.com, Lobisser family).

$$$ Gasthof Zauner is run by a friendly mountaineer, Herr
Zauner, whose family has owned it since 1893. The 13 pricey, pine-
flavored rooms on the inland side of the main square are decorated
with sturdy alpine-inspired furniture (sealed not with lacquer
but with wax, to let the wood breathe out its calming scent).
Lederhosen-clad Herr Zauner recounts tales of local mountaineer-

ing lore, including his own impressive ascents (Sb-€58, Db-€100, Db with lakeview-€108, cheaper mid-Oct–April, closed mid-Nov–mid-Dec, Marktplatz 51, tel. 06134/8246, fax 06134/82468, www .zauner.hallstatt.net, zauner@hallstatt.at).

$$$ Gasthof Simony is a well-worn, grandmotherly place on the square, with a lake view, balconies, ancient beds, creaky wood floors, slippery rag rugs, antique furniture, a lakefront garden for swimming, and a huge breakfast. Reserve in advance, and call if arriving late (S-€35, D-€55, Ds-€65, Db-€95, third person-€30–35 extra, cash only, kayaks for guests, Marktplatz 105, tel. & fax 06134/8231, www.hallstatt.net/gasthof/simony, info@gasthof -simony.at, Susanna Scheutz and grandson Valentin).

$$ Pension Sarstein is a big, flower-bedecked house right on the water. Its recently renovated rooms are bright, and all have lakeview balconies. You can swim from its plush and inviting lakeside garden (D-€50, Db-€65, Tb-€85; apartments with kitchen: Db-€65, Tb-€75, Qb-€85, apartment prices don't include breakfast; €3 extra per person for 1-night stay, cash only, fee for Internet access, 200 yards to the right of boat dock at Gosaumühlstrasse 83, tel. 06134/8217, fax 06134/20635, www.pension-sarstein.at.tf, pension.sarstein@aon.at, helpful Isabelle and Klaus Fischer).

$$ Gasthof Pension Grüner Anger is practical and modern, but located away from the medieval town center (a few blocks from the base of the salt-mine lift, and a 15-minute walk from the Market Square). It's big and quiet, with 11 rooms and no creaks or squeaks (Sb-€43–48, Db-€76–86, third person-€15, price depends on season, non-smoking, Internet access and Wi-Fi, free loaner bikes, free parking, Lahn 10, tel. 06134/8397, fax 06134/83974, www .anger.hallstatt.net, anger@aon.at, Sulzbacher family). If arriving by train, have the boat captain call Herr Sulzbacher, who will pick you up at the dock. They run a good-value restaurant, too.

$ Helga Lenz rents two fine *Zimmer* a steep five-minute climb above Dr-Morton-Weg (look for the green *Zimmer* sign). This large, sprawling, woodsy house has a nifty garden perch, wins the "Best View" award, and is ideal for those who sleep well in tree houses and don't mind the ascent from town (Db-€50, Tb-€72, €2 more per person for one-night stay, cash only, family room, closed Nov–March, Hallberg 17, tel. & fax 06134/8508, www.hallstatt .net/privatzimmer/helga.lenz, haus-lenz@aon.at).

$ Two places with *Privatzimmer* are a few minutes' stroll south of the center, just past the bus stop/parking lot and over the bridge. **Haus Trausner** has four clean, bright, new-feeling rooms adjacent to the Trausner family home (Ds/Db-€50, 2-night minimum for reservations, cash only, breakfast comes to your room, free parking, Lahnstrasse 27, tel. 06134/8710, trausner1@utanet .at, charming Maria Trausner makes you want to settle right in).

Herta Höll rents out three spacious, modern rooms on the ground floor of her modern riverside house crawling with kids (Db-€46, apartment for up to five-€60, €2 more per person for one-night stay, cash only, free parking, Malerweg 45, tel. 06134/8531, fax 06134/825-533, frank.hoell@aon.at).

$ *Hostel:* **Gasthaus zur Mühle Jugendherberge,** below the waterfall and along the gushing town stream, has 46 of the cheapest good beds in town (bed in 3- to 14-bed coed dorms-€14, D-€28, family quads, sheets-€4 extra, breakfast-€5, big lockers with a €15 deposit, closed Nov, reception closed Tue Sept–mid-May—so arrange in advance if arriving on Tue, below tunnel car park, Kirchenweg 36, tel. & fax 06134/8318, toeroe-f@hallstatt urlaub.at, Ferdinand Törö). It's also popular for its great, inexpensive pizza; see "Eating," next.

Eating

In this town, when someone is happy to see you, they'll often say, "Can I cook you a fish?" While everyone cooks the typical Austrian fare, your best bet here is trout. *Reinanke* trout is caught wild out of Lake Hallstatt and served the same day. You can enjoy good food inexpensively, with delightful lakeside settings. Restaurants in Hallstatt tend to have unreliable hours and close early on slow nights, so don't wait too long to get dinner. Most of the eateries listed below are run by hotels recommended under "Sleeping."

Restaurant Bräugasthof has great lakeside tables. You can feed the swans while your trout is being cooked. On a balmy evening, its lakeside dining offers the best ambience in town (€10–15 three-course meals, daily May–Oct 11:30–late, closed Nov–April, Seestrasse 120, tel. 06134/8221).

Hotel Grüner Baum is another lakefront option (Dec–Oct daily 8:00–22:00, closed Nov, at bottom of Market Square, tel. 06134/8263). Its **Restaurant zum Salzbaron** is an upscale place with tables overlooking the lake inside and out (elegant service, €15–20 plates). Its **Kaiserstüberl** is more casual and rustic, with a folksy feel, no lake views, and €10 meals.

Gasthof Zauner's classy restaurant lacks a lakeside setting, but it's well-respected for its grilled meat with "cracklings" and its fish. The service comes in lederhosen, the ivy is real, and most agree that the food is worth the few extra euros (daily 11:30–14:30 & 17:30–22:00, closed mid-Oct–mid Dec, at top of Market Square).

Gasthof Simony's Restaurant am See serves Austrian cuisine on a gorgeous lakeside terrace, as well as indoors (€10 entrées, Thu–Tue 11:30–20:00, until 21:00 June–Sept and on winter weekends, closed Wed).

Gasthaus zur Mühle serves the best pizza in town. Chow down cheap and hearty here with fun-loving locals and the youth-hostel crowd (€7 pizza, lots of Italian, some Austrian, daily in summer 11:00–14:00 & 17:00–21:00, closed Tue and no lunch Sept–mid-May, Kirchenweg 36, Ferdinand).

Strand Café, a local favorite, is a 10-minute lakeside hike away, near Bade-Insel, the town beach (€8–12 plates, plenty of alcohol, Tue–Sun April–mid-Sept 10:00–21:00, mid-Sept–Oct 11:30–14:00 & 16:30–20:00, closed Mon and Nov–March, great garden setting on the lake, Seelande 102, tel. 06134/8234). Despite Austria's recent ban on smoking in small restaurants, don't count on it being enforced.

Picnics and Cheap Eats: The **Zauner** bakery/butcher/grocer, great for picnickers, makes fresh sandwiches to go (Tue–Fri 7:00–12:00 & 15:00–18:00, Sat and Mon 7:00–12:00, closed Sun, uphill to the left from Market Square). The only **supermarket** is Konsum, in Lahn at the bus stop (Mon–Fri 7:30–12:00 & 15:00–18:00, Sat 7:30–12:00, closed Sun, July–Aug no midday break and until 17:00 on Sat, Sept–April closed Wed). The **snack stand** near the main boat dock sells *Döner Kebab* and so on for €3 (tables and fine lakeside picnic options nearby); another snack stand is near the Lahn boat/bus stop.

Connections

For tips for drivers coming here from Salzburg, see the end of the Salzburg chapter.

From Hallstatt by Train: Most travelers leaving Hallstatt are going to Salzburg or Vienna. In either case, you need to catch the shuttle boat (€2.20, departs 15 minutes before every train) to the little station across the lake, and then ride 90 minutes to **Attnang-Puchheim** (hourly from about 7:00 to 18:00). Trains are synchronized, so after a short wait in Attnang-Puchheim, you'll catch your connection to **Salzburg** (50 min) or **Vienna** (2.5 hrs). Train info: tel. 051-717 (to get an operator, dial 2, then 2).

By Bus: Some consider the bus ride from Hallstatt to **Salzburg** more scenic than the train, and just as practical (6–8/day, allow 3 hrs, €11.20, leaves from Lahn boat dock, no bus in icy weather, easy changes in Gosaumühle—a few minutes up the lake from Hallstatt—and in Bad Ischl, where you'll catch bus #150). The Hallstatt TI has a schedule.

HALLSTATT

BELGIUM

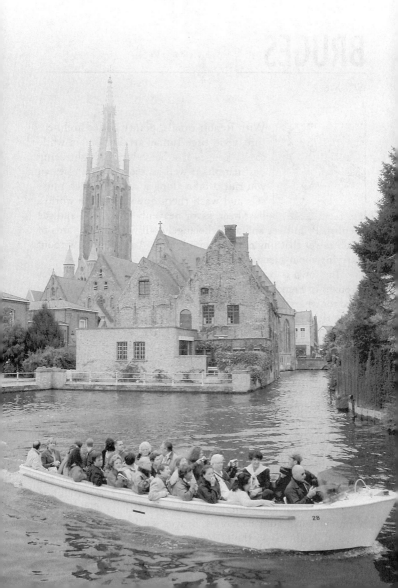

BRUGES

Brugge

With Renoir canals, pointy gilded architecture, vivid time-tunnel art, and stay-a-while cafés, Bruges is a heavyweight sightseeing destination, as well as a joy. Where else can you ride a bike along a canal, munch mussels and wash them down with the world's best beer, savor heavenly chocolate, and see Flemish Primitives and a Michelangelo, all within 300 yards of a bell tower that jingles every 15 minutes? And do it all without worrying about a language barrier?

The town is Brugge (BROO-ghah) in Flemish, and Bruges (broozh) in French and English. Its name comes from the Viking word for wharf. Right from the start, Bruges was a trading center. In the 11th century, the city grew wealthy on the cloth trade.

By the 14th century, Bruges' population was 35,000, as large as London's. As the middleman in the sea trade between northern and southern Europe, it was one of the biggest cities in the world and an economic powerhouse. In addition, Bruges had become the most important cloth market in northern Europe.

In the 15th century, while England and France were slugging it out in the Hundred Years' War, Bruges was the favored residence of the powerful Dukes of Burgundy—and at peace. Commerce and the arts boomed. The artists Jan van Eyck and Hans Memling had studios here.

But by the 16th century, the harbor had silted up and the economy had collapsed. The Burgundian court left, Belgium became a minor Habsburg possession, and Bruges' Golden Age abruptly ended. For generations, Bruges was known as a mysterious and dead city. In the 19th century, a new port, Zeebrugge, brought renewed vitality to the area. And in the 20th century, tourists discovered the town.

Today, Bruges prospers because of tourism: It's a uniquely well-preserved Gothic city and a handy gateway to Europe. It's no secret, but even with the crowds, it's the kind of place where you don't mind being a tourist.

Bruges' ultimate sight is the town itself, and the best way to enjoy it is to get lost on the back streets, away from the lace shops and ice-cream stands.

Planning Your Time

Bruges needs at least two nights and a full, well-organized day. Even non-shoppers enjoy browsing here, and the Belgian love of life makes a hectic itinerary seem a little senseless. With one day—other than a Monday, when the three museums are closed—the speedy visitor could do the Bruges blitz described below:

9:30	Climb the bell tower on Market Square.
10:00	Tour the sights on Burg Square.
11:30	Tour the Groeninge Museum.
13:00	Eat lunch and buy chocolates.
14:00	Take a short canal cruise.
14:30	Visit the Church of Our Lady and see Michelangelo's Madonna and Child.
15:00	Tour the Memling Museum.
16:00	Catch the De Halve Maan Brewery tour (note that their last tour runs at 15:00 in winter on weekdays).
17:00	Calm down in the Begijnhof courtyard.
18:00	Ride a bike around the quiet back streets of town or take a horse-and-buggy tour.
20:00	Lose the tourists and find dinner.

If this schedule seems insane, skip the bell tower and the brewery—or stay another day.

Overview

The tourist's Bruges—and you'll be sharing it—is less than one square mile, contained within a canal (the former moat). Nearly everything of interest and importance is within a convenient cobbled swath between the train station and Market Square (a 20-min walk). Many of my quiet, charming, recommended accommodations lie just beyond Market Square.

Tourist Information

The main tourist office, called **In&Uit** ("In and Out"), is in the big, red concert hall on the square called 't Zand (daily 10:00–18:00, take a number from the touch-screen machines and wait, 't Zand 34, tel. 050-448-686, www.brugge.be). The other TI is at the train station (Mon–Fri 10:00–17:00, Sat–Sun 10:00–14:00).

The TIs sell a great €1 *Bruges Visitors' Guide* with a map and listings of all the sights and services. You can also pick up a monthly English-language program called *events@brugge*. The TIs have information on train schedules and on the many tours available (see "Tours," later in this chapter). Many hotels give out free maps with more detail than the map the TIs sell.

Arrival in Bruges

By Train: Coming in by train, you'll see the bell tower that marks the main square (Market Square, the center of town). Upon arrival, stop by the train station TI to pick up the €1 *Bruges Visitors' Guide* (with map). The station lacks ATMs, but has lockers (€3–4, daily 6:00–24:00).

The best way to get to the town center is by **bus.** Buses #1, #3, #4, #6, #11, #13, #14, and #16 (all marked *Centrum*) go directly to Market Square. Simply hop on, pay €1.60 (€1.20 if you buy in advance at train station), and in four minutes, you're there. Buses #4 and #14 continue to the northeast part of town (to the windmills and recommended accommodations on Carmersstraat). The **taxi** fare from the train station to most hotels is about €8.

It's a 20-minute **walk** from the station to the center—no fun with your luggage. If you want to walk to Market Square, cross the busy street and canal in front of the station, head up Oostmeers, and turn right on Zwidzandstraat. You can rent a **bike** at the station for the duration of your stay, but other bike rental shops are closer to the center (see "Helpful Hints," below).

By Car: Park in front of the train station in the handy two-story garage for just €2.50 for 24 hours. The parking fee includes a round-trip bus ticket into town and back for everyone in your car. There are pricier underground parking garages at the square called 't Zand and around town (€10/day, all of them well-marked). Paid parking on the street in Bruges is limited to four hours. Driving in town is very complicated because of the one-way system. The best plan for drivers: Park at the train station, visit the TI, and rent a bike or catch a bus into town.

Helpful Hints

Market Days: Bruges hosts markets on Wednesday morning (Market Square) and Saturday morning ('t Zand). On Saturday, Sunday, and public holidays, a flea market hops along Dijver in front of the Groeninge Museum. The Fish Market sells souvenirs and seafood Tuesday through Saturday mornings until 13:00.

Shopping: Shops are generally open from 10:00 to 18:00. Grocery stores are usually closed on Sunday. The main shopping street, Steenstraat, stretches from Market Square to 't Zand Square. The **Hema** department store is at Steenstraat 73 (Mon–Sat 9:00–18:00, closed Sun).

Internet Access: Punjeb Internet Shop, just a block off Market Square, is a good place to get online (€1.50/30 min, daily 10:00–22:00, 4 Philipstockstraat).

Post Office: It's on Market Square near the bell tower (Mon–Fri 9:00–18:00, Sat 9:30–12:30, closed Sun, tel. 050-331-411).

Laundry: Bruges has three self-service launderettes, each a five-minute walk from the center; ask your hotelier for the nearest one.

Bike Rental: Koffieboontje Bike Rental, just under the bell tower on Market Square, is the handiest place to rent bikes (€4/1 hr, €8/4 hrs, €12/24-hr day; free city maps and child seats, daily 9:00–22:00, Hallestraat 4, tel. 050-338-027, www.hotel -koffieboontje.be). The €15 bike-plus-any-three-museums combo-ticket works only with this outfit (and can save enough to pay for lunch).

Fietsen Popelier Bike Rental is also good (€3.50/hr, €7/4 hrs, €10/day, 24-hour day is OK if your hotel has a safe place to store bike, daily 10:00–19:00, Mariastraat 26, tel. 050-343-262). Other rental places include the less-central **De Ketting** (cheap at €5/day, daily 9:00–18:30, Gentpoortstraat 23, tel. 050-344-196, www.deketting.be) and the **train station** (ticket window labeled *verhuring fietsen*, €9.50/day, €6.50/half-day after 14:00, €13 deposit, daily 7:00–19:30, blue lockers here for day-trippers leaving bags).

Best Town View: The bell tower overlooking Market Square rewards those who climb it with the ultimate town view.

Museum Tips: The TIs and participating museums sell a **museum combo-ticket** (any five museums for €15, 3-day validity period). Since the Groeninge and Memling museums each cost €8, art lovers will save money with this pass. Another combo-ticket offers any three museums and a one-day bike rental for €15 (get bike from Koffieboontje, listed above; sold at bike shop or TI, open-ended validity period). For information on all the museums, call 050-448-711 or visit www .brugge.be.

In Bruges, nearly all museums are open Tuesday through Sunday, year-round from 9:30 to 17:00, and are closed on Monday. If you're here on a Monday, you can still climb the bell-tower climb on Market Square, visit Begijnhof, take the De Halve Maan Brewery Tour, and visit the Basilica of the Holy Blood, City Hall's Gothic Room, and the chocolate

BRUGES

shops and museum. You can also join a boat, bus, or walking tour, or rent a bike and pedal into the countryside.

Getting Around Bruges

Most of the city is easily walkable, but you may want to take the bus or taxi between the train station and the city center at Market Square (especially if you have heavy luggage).

By Bus: A bus ticket is good for an hour (€1.20 if you buy in advance at train station, or €1.60 on the bus). While there are various day passes, there's really no need to buy one for your visit. Nearly all city buses go directly from the train station to Market Square and fan out from there; they then return to Market Square and go back to the train station. Note that buses returning to the train station from Market Square also leave from the library bus stop, a block off the square on nearby Kuiperstraat (every 5 min). Your key: Use buses that say either *Station* or *Centrum*.

By Taxi: You'll find taxi stands at the station and on Market Square (€8/first 2 km; to get a cab in the center, call 050-334-444).

Tours

Bruges

Bruges by Boat—The most relaxing and scenic (though not informative) way to see this city of canals is by boat, with the captain narrating. The city carefully controls this standard tourist activity, so the many companies all offer essentially the same thing: a 30-minute route (4/hr, daily 10:00–17:00), a price of €6.50, and narration in three or four languages. Qualitative differences are because of individual guides...not companies. Always let them know you speak English to ensure you'll understand the spiel. Two companies give a €1 discount with this book: Boten Stael (just over the canal from Memling Museum at Katelijnestraat 4, tel. 050-332-771) and Gruuthuse (Nieuwstraat 11, opposite Groeninge Museum, tel. 050-333-393).

City Minibus Tour—City Tour Bruges gives a rolling overview of the town in an 18-seat, two-skylight minibus with dial-a-language headsets and video support (€11.50, 50 min, pay driver). The tour leaves hourly from Market Square (10:00–20:00 in summer, until 18:00 in spring, until 17:00 in fall, less in winter, tel. 050-355-024, www.citytour.be). The narration, while clear, is slow-moving and a bit boring. But the tour is a lazy way to cruise past virtually every sight in Bruges.

Walking Tour—Local guides walk small groups through the core of town (€7, 2 hours, daily July–Aug, June and Sept Sat–Sun only, no tours Oct–May, depart from TI on 't Zand Square at 14:30—just drop in a few minutes early and buy tickets at the TI

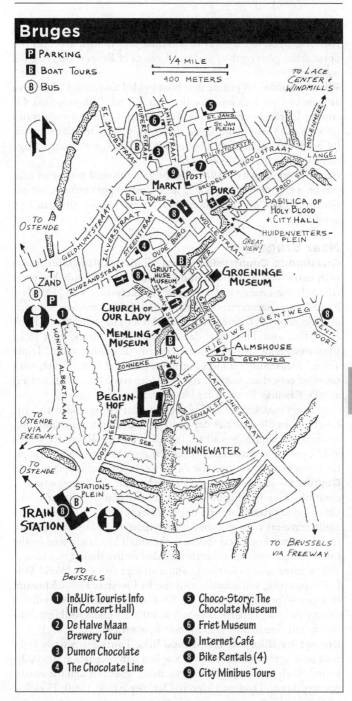

Bruges

P PARKING
B BOAT TOURS
Ⓑ BUS

1/4 MILE
400 METERS

TO LACE CENTER + WINDMILLS

① In&Uit Tourist Info (in Concert Hall)
② De Halve Maan Brewery Tour
③ Dumon Chocolate
④ The Chocolate Line
⑤ Choco-Story: The Chocolate Museum
⑥ Friet Museum
⑦ Internet Café
⑧ Bike Rentals (4)
⑨ City Minibus Tours

BRUGES

desk). Though earnest, the tours are heavy on history and given in two languages, so they may be less than peppy. Still, to propel you beyond the pretty gables and canal swans of Bruges, they're good medicine.

Private Guide—A private two-hour guided tour costs €60 (reserve at least one week in advance through TI, tel. 050-448-686). Or contact Christian and Danielle Scharle, who give two-hour walks for €60 and three-hour guided drives for €110 (Christian's mobile 0475-659-507, Danielle's mobile 0476-493-203, www.tourmanage mentbelgium.be, tmb@skynet.be).

Horse-and-Buggy Tour—The buggies around town can take you on a clip-clop tour (€30, 35 min; price is per carriage, not per person). When divided among four or five people, this can be a good value.

Near Bruges

Quasimodo Countryside Tours—This company offers those with extra time two entertaining, all-day, English-only bus tours through the rarely visited Flemish countryside. The "Flanders Fields" tour concentrates on WWI battlefields, trenches, memorials, and poppy-splattered fields (April–Oct Tue–Sun; Nov–March Sun, Tue, and Thu only; departs at 9:15, 8 hours, visit to In Flanders Fields Museum not included). The other tour, "Triple Treat," focuses on Flanders' medieval past and rich culture, with tastes of chocolate, waffles, and beer (departs Mon, Wed, and Fri at 9:15, 8 hours). Be ready for lots of walking.

Tours cost €55, or €45 if you're under 26 (includes a picnic lunch, 9- or 30-seat bus depending on demand, non-smoking, reservations required—call tel. 050-370-470 or toll-free tel. 0800-97525, www.quasimodo.be). After making a few big-hotel pickups, the buses leave town from the Park Hotel on 't Zand Square.

Daytours—Tour guide Nathan loves leading small groups on fascinating "Flanders Fields Battlefield" day trips. This tour is like Quasimodo's (listed above), but more expensive. The differences: eight travelers on a minibus rather than a big busload; pickup from any hotel or B&B (because the small bus is allowed in the town center); restaurant lunch included rather than a picnic; and a little more serious lecturing and a stricter focus on World War I. For instance, you actually visit the In Flanders Fields Museum in Ieper—Ypres in French (€65, €3 discount when booked direct using this book, departs Tue–Sun at 9:00, 8.5 hours, call 050-346-060 or toll-free 0800-99133 to reserve, www.visitbruges.org).

Bruges by Bike—**QuasiMundo Bike Tours** leads daily five-mile bike tours around the city (English only, departs at 10:00, 2.5 hours). Their other tour, "Border by Bike," goes through the nearby countryside to Damme (March–Oct, departs at 13:00, 15 miles,

4 hours). Either tour costs €22, but you'll get €3 off with this book (tel. 050-330-775, www.quasimundo.com). Both tours include bike rental, a light raincoat (if necessary), water, and a drink in a local café. Meet on Burg Square. If you already have a bike, you're welcome to join either tour for €14. Jos, who leads most departures, is a high-energy and entertaining guide.

Charming Mieke of **Pink Bear Bike Tours** leads small groups on an easy and delightful 3.5-hour guided pedal along a canal to the historic town of Damme and back, finishing with a brief tour of Bruges. English tours go daily through peak season and nearly daily the rest of the year (€20, €2 discount with this book, €14 if you already have a bike, meet at 10:25 under bell tower on Market Square, tel. 050-616-686, mobile 0476-744-525, www.pinkbear .freeservers.com).

For bike rental shops in Bruges, see "Helpful Hints," near the beginning of this chapter.

Sights and Experiences

These sights are listed in walking order, from Market Square to Burg Square to the cluster of museums around the Church of Our Lady to the Begijnhof (10-min walk from beginning to end, without stops).

▲**Market Square (Markt)**—Ringed by a bank, the post office, lots of restaurant terraces, great old gabled buildings, and the iconic bell tower, this is the modern heart of the city (most city buses run from near here to the train station—it's a block down Kuiperstraat at the library bus stop). Under the bell tower are two great Belgian-style french-fry stands, a quadrilingual Braille description of the old town, and a metal model of the tower. In Bruges' heyday as a trading center, a canal came right up to this square. Geldmuntstraat, just off the square, is a delightful street with many fun and practical shops and eateries.

▲▲**Bell Tower (Belfort)**—Most of this bell tower has presided over Market Square since 1300, serenading passersby with carillon music. The octagonal lantern was added in 1486, making it 290 feet high—that's 366 steps. The view is worth the climb and the €5 (daily 9:30–17:00, last entry 45 min before closing, €0.40 WC in courtyard).

▲▲**Burg Square**—This opulent square is Bruges' civic center, historically the birthplace of Bruges and the site of the ninth-century castle of the first count of Flanders. Today, it's an atmospheric place to take in an outdoor concert while surrounded by six centuries of architecture.

▲**Basilica of the Holy Blood**—Originally the Chapel of Saint Basil, this church is famous for its relic of the blood of Christ, which, according to tradition, was brought to Bruges in 1150 after the Second Crusade. The lower chapel is dark and solid—a fine example of Romanesque style. The upper chapel (separate entrance, climb the stairs) is decorated Gothic. An interesting treasury museum is next to the upper chapel (treasury entry-€1.50; April–Sept Thu–Tue 9:30–12:00 & 14:00–18:00, Wed 9:30–11:45 only; Oct–March Thu–Tue 10:00–12:00 & 14:00–16:00, Wed 10:00–11:45 only; Burg Square, tel. 050-336-792, www.holyblood.com).

▲**City Hall**—This complex houses several interesting sights. Your €2.50 ticket includes an audioguide; access to a room full of old town maps and paintings; the grand, beautifully restored **Gothic Room** from 1400, starring a painted and carved wooden ceiling adorned with hanging arches (daily 9:30–17:00, Burg 12); and the less impressive **Renaissance Hall** (Brugse Vrije), basically just one ornate room with a Renaissance chimney (daily 9:30–17:00, separate entrance—in corner of square at Burg 11a).

▲▲▲**Groeninge Museum**—This museum houses a world-class collection of mostly Flemish art, from Memling to Magritte. While there's plenty of worthwhile modern art, the highlights are the vivid and pristine Flemish Primitives. ("Primitive" here means "before the Renaissance.") Flemish art is shaped by its love of detail, its merchant patrons' egos, and the power of the Church. Lose yourself in the halls of Groeninge: Gaze across 15th-century canals, into the eyes of reassuring Marys, and through town squares littered with leotards, lace, and lopped-off heads (€8, includes audioguide, Tue–Sun 9:30–17:00, closed Mon, Dijver 12, tel. 050-448-743).

Gruuthuse Museum—Once a wealthy brewer's home, this 15th-century mansion is a sprawling smattering of everything from medieval bedpans to a guillotine. A fine museum, it's now in disarray—some rooms are closed until 2011 due to an extensive reorganization and renovation (€6, includes entry to apse in Church of Our Lady, Tue–Sun 9:30–17:00, closed Mon, Dijver 17, Bruges museums tel. 050-448-711, www.brugge.be).

▲▲**Church of Our Lady**—The church stands as a memorial to the power and wealth of Bruges in its heyday. A delicate *Madonna and Child* by Michelangelo is near the apse (to the right if you're facing the altar). It's said to be the only Michelangelo statue to leave Italy in his lifetime (thanks to the wealth generated by Bruges' cloth trade). If you like tombs and church art, pay to wander through the apse (Michelangelo viewing is free, art-filled apse-€2.50, covered by €6 Gruuthuse admission or €15 museum combo-ticket; church open Mon–Fri 9:30–17:00, Sat 9:30–16:45, Sun 13:30–17:00; museum and apse closed Mon; Mariastraat, www.brugge.be).

▲▲**Memling Museum/St. John's Hospital (Sint Janshospitaal)**—The former monastery/hospital complex has a fine museum in what was once the monks' church. It contains six much-loved paintings by the greatest of the Flemish Primitives, Hans Memling. His *Mystical Wedding of St. Catherine* triptych is a highlight, as is the miniature, gilded-oak shrine to St. Ursula (€8, includes fine audioguide, Tue–Sun 9:30–17:00, closed Mon, across the street from the Church of Our Lady, Mariastraat 38, Bruges museums tel. 050-448-711, www.brugge.be).

▲▲**Begijnhof**—Inhabited by Benedictine nuns, the Begijnhof courtyard (free and always open) almost makes you want to don a habit and fold your hands as you walk under its wispy trees and whisper past its frugal little homes. For a good slice of Begijnhof life, walk through the simple museum, the Beguine's House museum (€2, daily 10:00–17:00, shorter hours off-season, English explanations, museum is left of entry gate).

Minnewater—Just south of the Begijnhof is Minnewater, an idyllic world of flower boxes, canals, and swans.

Almshouses—Walking from the Begijnhof back to the town center, you might detour along Nieuwe Gentweg to visit one of about 20 almshouses in the city. At #8, go through the door marked *Godshuis de Meulenaere 1613* into the peaceful courtyard (free). This was a medieval form of housing for the poor. The rich would pay for someone's tiny room here in return for lots of prayers.

Bruges Experiences: Beer, Chocolate, Windmills, and Biking

▲▲**De Halve Maan Brewery Tour**—Belgians are Europe's beer connoisseurs. This fun, handy tour is a great way to pay your respects. The "Brugse Zot" is the only beer still brewed in Bruges, and the happy gang at this working-family brewery gives entertaining and informative, 45-minute tours in two languages. Avoid crowds by visiting at 11:00 or 15:00 (€5.50 includes a beer, lots of very steep steps, great rooftop panorama; tours run April–Oct daily on the hour 11:00–16:00, Sat until 17:00; Nov–March Mon–Fri 11:00 and 15:00 only, Sat–Sun on the hour 11:00–16:00; take a right down skinny Stoofstraat to #26 on Walplein, tel. 050-444-223, www.halvemaan.be).

During your tour, you'll learn that "the components of the beer are vitally necessary and contribute to a well-balanced life pattern. Nerves, muscles, visual sentience, and healthy skin are stimulated by these in a positive manner. For longevity and lifelong equilibrium, drink Brugse Zot in moderation!"

Their bistro, where you'll be given your included beer, serves quick, hearty lunch plates. You can eat indoors with the smell of hops, or outdoors with the smell of hops. This is a good place to wait for your tour or to linger afterward.

▲**Chocolate Shops**—Bruggians are connoisseurs of fine choco-late. You'll be tempted by chocolate-filled display windows all over town. While Godiva is the best big-factory/high-price/high-quality brand, there are plenty of smaller, family-run places in Bruges that offer exquisite handmade chocolates. Both of the following choco-latiers are proud of their creative varieties, generous with their samples, and welcome you to assemble a 100-gram assortment of five or six chocolates.

Dumon: Perhaps Bruges' smoothest and creamiest choco-lates are at Dumon (€2.10/100 grams). Madame Dumon and her children (Stefaan, Natale, and Christophe) make their top-notch chocolate daily and sell it fresh just off Market Square (Thu–Tue 10:00–18:00, closed Wed, old chocolate molds on display in base-ment, Eiermarkt 6, tel. 050-346-282). The Dumons don't provide English labels because they believe it's best to describe their chocolates in person—and they do it with an evangelical fervor. Try a small mix-and-match box to sample a few out-of-this-world flavors, and come back for more of your favorites.

The Chocolate Line: Locals and tourists alike flock to The Chocolate Line (pricey at €4.40/100 grams) to taste the *gas-tronomique* varieties concocted by Dominique Person—the mad scientist of chocolate. His unique creations include Havana cigar (marinated in rum, cognac, and Cuban tobacco leaves—so there-fore technically illegal in the US), lemongrass, lavender, ginger (shaped like a Buddha), saffron curry, spicy chili, and Moroccan mint. New combinations from Dominique's imagination are a Pop Rocks/cola chocolate, as well as "wine vinegar" chocolate (surpris-ingly good). The kitchen—busy whipping up 80 varieties—is on display in the back. Enjoy the window display, renewed monthly (daily 9:30–18:00, between Church of Our Lady and Market Square at Simon Stevinplein 19, tel. 050-341-090).

Choco-Story: The Chocolate Museum—This museum is rated ▲ for chocoholics. The Chocolate Fairy leads you through 2,600 years of chocolate history—explaining why, in the ancient Mexican world of the Mayas and the Aztecs, chocolate was considered the drink of the gods, and cocoa beans were used as a means of payment. With lots of artifacts well-described in English, the museum fills you in on the production of truffles, bonbons, hollow figures, and solid bars of chocolate. Then you'll view a delicious little video (8 min long, repeating continuously, alternating Flemish, French, and then English; peek into the theater to check the schedule. If you have time before the next English showing, visit the exhibits in the top room). Your finale is in the "demonstration room," where—after a 10-minute cook-ing demo—you get a taste (€6, €10 combo-ticket includes nearby Friet Museum, daily 10:00–17:00; where Wijnzakstraat meets Sint

Jansstraat at Sint Jansplein, 3-min walk from Market Square; tel. 050-612-237, www.choco-story.be).

Friet Museum—It's the only place in the world that enthusiastically tells the story of french fries, which, of course, aren't even French—they're Belgian. As there are no real artifacts, you could just Google "frites" and save the €6 entry fee (€10 combo-ticket includes Chocolate Museum, daily 10:00–17:00, Vlamingstraat 33, tel. 050-340-150, www.frietmuseum.be).

Windmills and Lace by the Moat—A 15-minute walk from the center to the northeast end of town brings you to four windmills strung along a pleasant grassy setting on the "big moat" canal. The St. Janshuysmolen **windmill** is open to visitors (€2, May–Aug daily 9:30–12:30 & 13:30–17:00, closed Sept–April, at the end of Carmersstraat, between Kruispoort and Dampoort, on Bruges side of the moat).

The **Folklore Museum,** in the same neighborhood, is cute but forgettable (€2, Tue–Sun 9:30–12:30 & 13:30–17:00, closed Mon, Balstraat 43, tel. 050-448-764). To find it, ask for the Jerusalem Church. On the same street is a lace shop with a good reputation, 't Apostelientje (Mon–Fri 9:30–18:00, Sat 10:00–17:00, Sun 10:00–13:00, Balstraat 11, tel. 050-337-860).

▲▲Biking—The Flemish word for bike is *fiets* (pronounced "feets"). While Bruges' sights are close enough for easy walking, the town is a treat for bikers, and a bike quickly gets you into dreamy back lanes without a hint of tourism. Take a peaceful evening ride through the town's nooks and crannies and around the outer canal. Consider keeping a bike for the duration of your stay—it's the way the locals get around in Bruges. Along the canal that circles the town, there is now a park with a delightful bike lane. Rental shops have maps and ideas (for rental options, see "Helpful Hints," near the beginning of this chapter).

Near Bruges

In Flanders Fields Museum—This World War I museum, about 40 miles southwest of Bruges, provides a moving look at the battles fought near Ieper (Ypres in French), where British losses totaled 60,000 dead and wounded in five weeks. Use its interactive computer displays to trace the wartime lives of individual soldiers and citizens. Powerful videos and ear-shattering audio complete the story (€8; April–mid-Nov daily 10:00–18:00; mid-Nov–March Tue–Sun 10:00–17:00, closed Mon and for three weeks in Jan; last entry one hour before closing, Grote Markt 34, Ieper, tel. 057-239-220, www.inflandersfields.be). From Bruges, catch a train to Ieper via Kortrijk (2 hrs), or take a tour (see "Tours," near the beginning of this chapter). Drivers take E-403 to Kortrijk, then A-19 to Ieper, following signs to *Bellewaerde*.

Sleeping

Bruges is a great place to sleep, with Gothic spires out your window, no traffic noise, and the cheerily out-of-tune carillon heralding each new day at 8:00 sharp. (Thankfully, the bell tower is silent from 22:00 to 8:00.) Most Bruges accommodations are located between the train station and the old center, with the most distant (and best) being a few blocks to the north and east of Market Square.

B&Bs offer the best value (listed after "Hotels," next). All are on quiet streets and (with a few exceptions) keep the same prices throughout the year.

Bruges is most crowded Friday and Saturday evenings from Easter through October, with July and August weekends being the worst. Many hotels charge a bit more on Friday and Saturday, and won't let you stay just one night if it's a Saturday.

Hotels

$$$ Hotel Heritage offers 24 rooms, with chandeliers that seem hung especially for you, in a solid and completely modernized old building with luxurious public spaces. Tastefully decorated and offering all the amenities, it's one of those places that does everything just right yet still feels warm and inviting—if you can afford it (Db-€192, superior Db-€238, deluxe Db-€286, includes breakfast, skipping their fine breakfast saves €17 per person, non-smoking, air-con, elevator, Internet access, sauna, tanning bed, fitness room, bike rental, Niklaas Desparsstraat 11, a block north of Market Square, tel. 050-444-444, fax 050-444-440, www.hotel-heritage.com, info@hotel-heritage.com). It's run by cheery and hardworking Johan and Isabelle Creytens.

$$$ Hotel Egmond is a creaky mansion located in the middle of the quietly idyllic Minnewater. Its eight 18th-century

---

Sleep Code

(€1 = about $1.40, country code: 32)
S = Single, **D** = Double/Twin, **T** = Triple, **Q** = Quad, **b** = bathroom, **s** = shower only. Everyone speaks English. Unless otherwise noted, credit cards are accepted.

To help you easily sort through these listings, I've divided the rooms into three categories, based on the price for a standard double room with bath:

$$$ Higher Priced—Most rooms €125 or more.
$$ Moderately Priced—Most rooms between €80–125.
$ Lower Priced—Most rooms €80 or less.

Bruges Accommodations

BRUGES

P PARKING
B BOAT TOURS

1 Hotels Heritage & Nicolas
2 To Hotel Egmond
3 Hotel Adornes
4 Hotel Patritius
5 Hotel Botaniek
6 Hotel ter Reien
7 Walwyck Cool Down Hotel
8 Hotel Cordoeanier
9 Hotel Cavalier
10 To Hotel de Pauw
11 To Hotel Imperial & Passage Hostel

12 Hotel Notre Dame
13 To Hotel 't Keizershof
14 Absoluut Verhulst B&B
15 B&B Setola
16 Dieltiens B&B
17 To Debruyne B&B
18 Gheeraert-Vandevelde B&B
19 't Geerwijn B&B
20 Royal Stewart B&B
21 Charlie Rockets Hostel
22 To Snuffel Backpacker Hostel

rooms are plain, with small modern baths shoehorned in, and the guests-only garden is just waiting for a tea party. This hotel is ideal for romantics who want a countryside setting—where you sleep surrounded by a park, not a city (Sb-€97, small twin Db-€103, larger Db-€125, Tb-€155, about €20 more Fri–Sat, parking-€10, Minnewater 15, tel. 050-341-445, fax 050-342-940, www.egmond .be, info@egmond.be).

$$ Hotel Adornes is small and classy—a great value situated in the most charming part of town. This 17th-century canalside house has 20 rooms with full modern bathrooms, free parking (reserve in advance), free loaner bikes, and a cellar lounge with games and videos (small Db-€120, larger Db-€140–150, Tb-€165, Qb-€175, includes breakfast, elevator, near Carmersstraat at St. Annarei 26, tel. 050-341-336, fax 050-342-085, www.adornes.be, info@adornes.be). Nathalie runs the family business.

$$ Hotel Patritius, family-run and centrally located, is a grand, circa-1830, Neoclassical mansion with hardwood oak floors in its 16 stately rooms. It features a plush lounge, a chandeliered breakfast room, and a courtyard garden. This is the best value in its price range (Db-€100–122 depending on size, €10 more Fri–Sat; Tb-€140, Qb-€165, €25 for extra bed, includes breakfast, coin-op laundry, parking-€7, garage parking-€12, Riddersstraat 11, tel. 050-338-454, fax 050-339-634, www.hotelpatritius.be, info @hotelpatritius.be, Garrett and Elvi Spaey).

$$ Hotel Botaniek, quietly located a block from Astrid Park, is a fine, pint-sized hotel with a comfy lounge, renting nine rooms (Db-€92 weekday special for my readers, €98 Fri–Sat; Tb-€120, Qb-€140, less for longer and off-season stays, free museum-discount card, elevator, Waalsestraat 23, tel. 050-341-424, fax 050-345-939, www.botaniek.be, info@botaniek.be, Yasmine).

$$ Hotel ter Reien is big and basic, with 26 rooms over-looking a canal in the town center (Db-€90–100, Tb-€110–130, Qb-€135–150, €10 off for viewless rooms, extra bed-€20, 10 percent Rick Steves discount if you ask when you reserve and show this book at check-in, includes breakfast, Internet access and Wi-Fi, Langestraat 1, tel. 050-349-100, fax 050-340-048, www.hotel terreien.be, info@hotelterreien.be, owners Diederik and Stephanie Pille-Maes).

$$ Walwyck Cool Down Hotel—a bit of modern comfort, chic design, and English verbiage in a medieval shell—is a new, nicely located hotel with 18 spacious rooms (Db-€90, includes breakfast, Wi-Fi, Leeuwstraat 8, tel. 050-616-360, www.walwyck .com, rooms@walwyck.com).

$ Hotel Cordoeanier, a charming family-run hotel, rents 22 bright, simple, well-worn rooms on a quiet street two blocks off Market Square. It's the best cheap hotel in town (Sb-€65–75,

Db-€70–85, twin Db–€80–95, Tb-€90–105, Qb-€110, Quint/b-€130, these cash-only prices valid with this book, Cordoeanierstraat 16–18, tel. 050-339-051, fax 050-346-111, www.cordoeanier.be, info@cordoeanier.be, run by Kris, Veerle, and family).

$ **Hotel Cavalier,** with more stairs than character, rents eight decent rooms and serves a hearty buffet breakfast in a once-royal setting (Sb-€55, Db-€65, Tb-€78, Qb-€90, two lofty "backpackers' doubles" on fourth floor-€42 or €47, includes breakfast, Kuipers-straat 25, tel. 050-330-207, fax 050-347-199, www.hotel cavalier.be, info@hotelcavalier.be, run by friendly Viviane De Clerck).

$ **Hotel de Pauw** is tall, skinny, and family-run, with eight straightforward rooms on a quiet street next to a church (Sb-€65, Db-€70–80, free and easy street parking, Sint Gilliskerkhof 8, tel. 050-337-118, fax 050-345-140, www.hoteldepauw.be, info @hoteldepauw.be, Philippe and Hilde).

$ **Hotel Nicolas** feels like an old-time boarding house that missed Bruges' affluence bandwagon. Its 14 big, plain rooms are a good value, and the location is ideal—on a quiet street a block off Market Square (Sb-€50, Db-€60–62, Tb-€73, includes breakfast, Niklaas Desparsstraat 9, tel. 050-335-502, fax 050-343-544, www.hotelnicolas.be, hotel.nicolas@telenet.be, Yi-Ling and Thomas).

$ **Hotel Imperial** is an old-school hotel with seven old-school rooms. It's simple and well-run in a charming building on a handy, quiet street. The fact that Paul Bernolet and Hilde don't use email fits its character (Db-€65–80, includes breakfast, Dweersstraat 24, tel. 050-339-014, fax 050-344-306).

$ **Hotel Notre Dame** is a humble and blocky little budget option, renting 12 decent rooms in the busy thick of things (Db-€70–75, includes breakfast, Mariastraat 3, tel. 050-333-193, fax 050-337-608, www.hotelnotredame.be, info@hotelnotredame.be).

Near the Train Station: $ **Hotel 't Keizershof** is a dollhouse of a hotel that lives by its motto, "Spend a night...not a fortune." It's simple and tidy, with seven small, cheery, old-time rooms split between two floors, with a shower and toilet on each (S-€25, D-€44, T-€66, Q-€80, includes breakfast, cash only, free and easy parking, laundry service-€7.50, Oostmeers 126, a block in front of station, tel. 050-338-728, www.hotelkeizershof.be, info @hotelkeizershof.be). The hotel is run by Stefaan and Hilde, with decor by their children, Lorie and Fien.

Bed-and-Breakfasts

These B&Bs, run by people who enjoy their work, offer a better value than hotels. Most families rent out their entire top floor—generally three rooms and a small sitting area. And most are mod and stylish, they're just in medieval shells. Each is central, with lots of stairs and €70 doubles you'd pay €100 for in a hotel. Most places charge €10 extra for one-night stays. It's possible to find parking on the street in the evening (pay 9:00–19:00, 2-hour maximum for metered parking during the day, free overnight).

$$ Absoluut Verhulst is a great, modern-feeling B&B in a 400-year-old house, run by friendly Frieda and Benno (Db-€90, huge and lofty suite-€120 for two, €140 for three, and €160 for four, €10 more for one-night stays, cash only, non-smoking, Wi-Fi, five-minute walk east of Market Square at Verbrand Nieuwland 1, tel. 050-334-515, www.b-bverhulst.com, b-b.verhulst@pandora.be).

$ B&B Setola, run by Lut and Bruno Setola, offers three modern expansive rooms and a spacious breakfast/living room on the top floor of their house. The family room has a fun loft (Sb-€60, Db-€70, €20 per extra person, €10 more for one-night stays, Wi-Fi, 5-min walk from Market Square, Sint Walburgastraat 12, tel. 050-334-977, fax 050-332-551, www.bedandbreakfast-bruges .com, setola@bedandbreakfast-bruges.com).

$ Koen and Annemie Dieltiens are a friendly couple who enjoy getting to know their guests while sharing a wealth of information on Bruges. You'll eat a hearty breakfast around a big table in their comfortable house (Sb-€60, Db-€70, Tb-€90, €10 more for one-night stays, cash only, Wi-Fi, Waalse Straat 40, three blocks southeast of Burg Square, tel. 050-334-294, www.bedand breakfastbruges.be, dieltiens@bedandbreakfastbruges.be).

$ Debruyne B&B, run by Marie-Rose and her architect husband, Ronny, offers three rooms with artsy, original decor (check out the elephant-size white doors—Ronny's design) and genuine warmth. If Gothic is getting old, this is refreshingly modern (Sb-€55, Db-€60, Tb-€90, €10 more for one-night stays, cash only, Internet access, seven-minute walk north of Market Square, two blocks from the little church at Lange Raamstraat 18, tel. 050-347-606, www.bedandbreakfastbruges.com, mietjedebruyne@yahoo .co.uk).

$ Paul and Roos Gheeraert-Vandevelde live in a Neoclassical mansion and rent three huge, bright, comfy rooms (Sb-€60, Db-€70, Tb-€90, two-night minimum stay required, cash only, strictly non-smoking, fridges in rooms, Internet access and Wi-Fi, Riddersstraat 9, 5-min walk east of Market Square, tel. 050-335-627, fax 050-345-201, www.bb-bruges.be, bb-bruges@skynet.be).

$ 't Geerwijn B&B, run by Chris de Loof, offers homey rooms in the old center. Check out the fun, lofty A-frame room upstairs (Ds/Db-€65, Tb-€75, pleasant breakfast room and a royal lounge, cash only, non-smoking, Geerwijnstraat 14, tel. 050-340-544, fax 050-343-721, www.geerwijn.be, chris.deloof@scarlet.be). Chris also rents an apartment that sleeps five (€100).

$ Royal Stewart B&B, run by Scottish Maggie and her husband, Gilbert, has three thoughtfully decorated rooms in a quiet, almost cloistered 17th-century house that was inhabited by nuns until 1953 (S-€45, D/Db-€62, Tb-€82, cash only, pleasant breakfast room, Genthof 25–27, 5-min walk from Market Square, tel. 050-337-918, fax 050-337-918, www.royalstewart.be, r.stewart @pandora.be).

Hostels

Bruges has several good hostels offering beds for around €15 in two- to eight-bed rooms. Breakfast is about €3 extra. The American-style **$ Charlie Rockets** hostel (and bar) is the liveliest and most central. The ground floor feels like a 19th-century sports bar, with a foosball-and-movie-posters party ambience. Upstairs is an industrial-strength pile of hostel dorms (90 beds, €16 per bed with sheets, 4–6 beds per room, D-€50, lockers, Hoogstraat 19, tel. 050-330-660, www.charlierockets.com). Other small, loose, and central places are **$ Snuffel Backpacker Hostel** (56 beds, €14–18 per bed includes sheets and breakfast, 4–14 beds per room, open 24/7, Ezelstraat 47, tel. 050-333-133, www.snuffel.be) and the minimal and funky **$ Passage** (€14, 4–7 beds per room, D-€50, Db-€65, prices include sheets, Dweerstraat 26, tel. 050-340-232, www.passagebruges.com, info@passagebruges.com).

Eating

Bruges' specialties include mussels cooked a variety of ways (one order can feed two), fish dishes, grilled meats, and french fries. Don't eat before 19:30 unless you like eating alone (or with other tourists).

Tax and service are always included in your bill (though a 5–10 percent tip is appreciated). You can't get free tap water; Belgian restaurateurs are emphatic about that. While tap water comes with a smile in Holland, France, and Germany, it's not the case in Belgium, where you'll either pay for water, enjoy the beer, or go thirsty.

You'll find plenty of affordable, touristy restaurants on floodlit squares and along dreamy canals. Bruges feeds 3.5 million tourists a year, and most are seduced by a high-profile location. These can be fine experiences for the magical setting and views, but the quality of food and service will likely be low. I wouldn't blame you for eating at one of these places, but I won't recommend any. I prefer the candle-cool bistros that flicker on back streets. Here are my favorites:

Rock Fort is a chic, eight-table spot with a modern, fresh coziness and a high-powered respect for good food. Two young

Bruges Restaurants

1. Rock Fort & Barsalon Tapas Bar
2. Pili Pili Restaurant
3. Rest. de Koetse
4. To Bistro de Bekoring
5. Bistro in den Wittenkop
6. Bistro den Amand & Medard Brasserie
7. The Flemish Pot
8. Lotus Vegetarian Restaurant
9. The Hobbit
10. To Tom's Diner
11. Café-Brasserie Craenenburg
12. 't Brugs Beertje Pub
13. De Garre Pub
14. L'Estaminet Restaurant
15. Herberg Vlissinghe Pub
16. Pub 't Gezelleke
17. Café Terrastje
18. Frituur Stands
19. Pickles Frituur
20. Laurenzino Waffles
21. Gelateria Da Vinci & Grocery

chefs, Peter Laloo and Hermes Vanliefde, give their French cui-sine a creative and gourmet twist. Reservations are required for dinner but not lunch. This place is a winner (€13 Mon–Fri lunch special with coffee, beautifully presented €19–24 dinner plates, fancy €49 fixed-price meal includes dessert, open Mon–Fri 12:00–14:30 & 18:30–23:00, closed Sat–Sun, great pastas and sal-ads, Langestraat 15, tel. 050-334-113). They also run the Barsalon restaurant next door.

Barsalon Tapas Bar, more than a tapas bar, is the brain-child of Peter Laloo from Rock Fort (listed previously), allowing him to spread his creative cooking energy. This long, skinny slice of L.A. thrives late into the evening with Bruges' beautiful people. Choose between the long bar, comfy stools, and bigger tables in back. Come early for fewer crowds. The playful menu comes with €6–10 "tapas" dishes taking you from Spain to Japan (three fill two hungry travelers) and more elaborate €14 plates. And don't over-look their daily "suggestions" board with some special wines by the glass and a "teaser" sampler plate of desserts. The €35 five-tapas special is a whole meal. Barsalon shares the same kitchen, hours, and dressy local clientele as the adjacent Rock Fort.

Pili Pili is a mod and inviting pasta eatery, where Gianna Santy handles the customers while husband Allan Hilverson pre-pares and serves pastas and great salads at good prices. It's clean, low-key, and brimming with quality food and snappy service (€10 lunch plate with wine, €8–10 pasta, Thu–Tue 12:00–14:30 & 18:00–22:30, closed Wed, Hoogstraat 17, tel. 050-491-149).

Restaurant de Koetse is a good bet for central, affordable, quality, local-style food. The feeling is traditional, a bit formal, and dressy yet accessible. The cuisine is Belgian and French, with an emphasis on grilled meat, seafood, and mussels (€28–37 three-course meals, €20–25 plates include vegetables and a salad, Fri–Wed 12:00–14:30 & 18:00–22:00, closed Thu, non-smoking section, Oude Burg 31, tel. 050-337-680, Piet).

Bistro de Bekoring, cute, candlelit, and Gothic, fills two almshouses and a delightful terrace with people thankful for good food. Rotund and friendly Chef Roland and his wife, Gerda, love to tempt the hungry—as the name of their bistro implies. They serve traditional Flemish food (especially eel and beer-soaked stew) from a small menu to people who like holding hands as they dine. Reservations are smart (€12 weekday lunch, €35 fixed-price dinners, €42 with wine, Wed–Sat 12:00–13:30 and from 18:30, closed Sun evening and Mon–Tue; out past the Begijnhof at Arsenaalstraat 53, tel. 050-344-157).

Bistro in den Wittenkop, very Flemish, is a stylishly clut-tered, laid-back, old-time place specializing in the local favorites. While Lieve cooks, her husband Daniel serves in a cool-and-jazzy, candlelit ambience (€35 three-course meal, €20–25 plates, Tue–Sat 12:00–14:00 & 18:00–21:30, closed Sun–Mon, reserve ahead, terrace in back in summer, Sint Jakobsstraat 14, tel. 050-332-059).

Bistro den Amand, with a plain interior and a few outdoor tables, exudes unpretentious quality the moment you step in. In this mussels-free zone, Chef Arnout is enthusiastic about vegetables as his busy wok and fun salads prove. It's on a busy pedestrian lane a half-block off the Market Square (€30 three-course meal, €20 plates; Mon–Tue and Thu–Sat 12:00–14:00 & 18:00–21:00, closed Wed and Sun; Sint-Amandstraat 4, tel. 050-340-122, An Vissers and Arnout Beyaert). Reservations are smart for dinner.

The Flemish Pot (a.k.a. The Little Pancake House) is a hard-working eatery serving up traditional peasant-style meals. They crank out pancakes (savory and sweet) and homemade *wafels* for lunch. Then, at 18:00, enthusiastic chefs Mario and Rik stow their waffle irons and pull out a traditional menu of vintage Flemish specialties served in little iron pots and skillets. Seating is tight and cluttered. You'll enjoy huge portions, refills from the hovering "fries maiden," and a good selection of local beers (€26–30 three-course meals, €16–24 plates, Wed–Sun 12:00–22:00, closed Mon–Tue, reservations smart, family-friendly, just off Geldmuntstraat at Helmstraat 3, tel. 050-340-086).

Lotus Vegetarian Restaurant serves serious lunch plates (€10 *plat du jour* offered daily), salads, and homemade chocolate cake in a bustling and upscale setting without a trace of tie-dye. To keep carnivorous spouses happy, they also serve several very good, politically correct (a.k.a. organic) meat dishes (Mon–Sat from 11:45, last orders at 14:00, closed Sun, cash only, just off north of Burg Square at Wapenmakersstraat 5, tel. 050-331-078).

The Hobbit, featuring an entertaining menu, is always busy with happy eaters. For a swinging deal, try the all-you-can-eat spareribs with bread and salad for €16.50. It's nothing fancy, just good, basic food in a fun, traditional grill house (daily 18:00–24:00, family-friendly, Kemelstraat 8–10, reservations smart, tel. 050-335-520).

Tom's Diner is a trendy, stark little "bistro eetcafé" in a quiet, cobbled residential area a 10-minute walk from the center. Young chef Tom gives traditional dishes a delightful modern twist. If you want to flee the tourists and experience a popular neighborhood joint, this is it—the locals love it (€17 plates, Thu–Tue 18:00–24:00, closed Wed, north of Market Square near Sint-Gilliskerk at West-Gistelhof 23, tel. 050-333-382).

Market Square Restaurants: Most tourists seem to be eating on Market Square with the bell tower high overhead and horse carriages clip-clopping by. The square is ringed by tourist traps with aggressive waiters expert at getting you to consume more than you intended. Still, if you order wisely, you can have a memorable meal or drink here on one of the finest squares in Europe at a reasonable price. Consider **Café-Brasserie Craenenburg,** with a straightforward menu, where you can get pasta and beer for €14 and spend all the time you want ogling the magic of Bruges (daily 7:30–24:00, Markt 16, tel. 050-333-402).

Cheap Eats: **Medard Brasserie,** just a block off Market Square, serves the cheapest hot meal in town—hearty meat spaghetti (big plate-€3, huge plate-€5.50, sit inside or out, daily 11:00–20:30, Sint Amandstraat 18, tel. 050-348-684).

Bars Offering Light Meals, Beer, and Ambience

My best budget-eating tip for Bruges: Stop into one of the city's atmospheric bars for a simple meal and a couple of world-class beers with great Bruges ambience. The last three pubs listed are in the wonderfully cozy *(gezellig)* quarter, northeast of Market Square.

The **'t Brugs Beertje** is young, convivial, and smoky. While any pub or restaurant carries the basic beers, you'll find a selection here of more than 300 types, including brews to suit any season. They serve light meals, including pâté, spaghetti, toasted sandwiches, and a traditional cheese plate. You're welcome to sit at the bar and talk with the staff (five cheeses, bread, and salad for €11; Thu–Tue 16:00–24:00, closed Wed, Kemelstraat 5, tel. 050-339-616, run by fun-loving manager Daisy).

De Garre is another good place to gain an appreciation of the Belgian beer culture. Rather than a noisy pub scene, it has a dressy, sit-down-and-focus-on-your-friend-and-the-fine-beer vibe. It's mature and cozy with tables, light meals (cold cuts, pâtés, and toasted sandwiches), and a selection of 150 beers (daily 12:00–24:00, additional seating up tiny staircase, off Breidelstraat between Burg and Markt, on tiny Garre alley, tel. 050-341-029).

L'Estaminet is a youthful, jazz-filled eatery, similar to one of Amsterdam's brown cafés. Don't be intimidated by its lack of tourists. Local students flock here for the Tolkien-chic ambience, hearty €9 spaghetti, and big dinner salads. Since this is Belgium, it serves more beer than wine. For outdoor dining under an all-weather canopy, enjoy the relaxed patio facing peaceful Astrid Park (Tue–Wed and Fri–Sun 11:30–24:00, Thu 16:00–24:00, closed Mon, Park 5, tel. 050-330-916).

Herberg Vlissinghe is the oldest pub in town (1515). Bruno keeps things simple and laid-back, serving simple plates (lasagna, grilled cheese sandwiches, and famous €8 angel-hair spaghetti) and great beer in the best old-time tavern atmosphere in town. This must have been the Dutch Masters' rec room. The garden outside comes with a *boules* court—free for guests to watch or play (Wed–Sat 11:00–24:00, Sun 11:00–19:00, closed Mon–Tue, Blekersstraat 2, tel. 050-343-737).

Pub 't Gezelleke lacks the mystique of the Vlissinghe, but it's a true neighborhood pub offering small, forgettable plates and a fine chance to drink with locals. Its name is an appropriate play on the word for cozy and the name of a great local poet (Mon–Fri 11:00–24:00, closed Sat–Sun, Carmersstraat 15, tel. 050-338-381, Peter and Gried).

Café Terrastje is a cozy pub serving light meals. Experience the grown-up ambience inside, or relax on the front terrace overlooking the canal and heart of the *gezellig* district (food served 12:00–21:00, open until 23:30, closed Thu, corner of Genthof and Langerei, tel. 050-330-919, Ian and Patricia).

Fries, Fast Food, and Picnics

Local french fries *(frites)* are a treat. Proud and traditional *frituurs* serve tubs of fries and various local-style shish kebabs. Belgians dip their *frites* in mayonnaise, but ketchup is there for the Yankees (along with spicier sauces). For a quick, cheap, hot, and scenic snack, hit a *frituur* and sit on the steps or benches overlooking Market Square (convenience benches are about 50 yards past the post office).

Market Square Frituur: Twin, take-away french fry carts are on Market Square at the base of the bell tower (daily 10:00–24:00). Skip the ketchup and have a sauce adventure. I find the cart on the left more user-friendly.

Pickles Frituur, a block off Market Square, is handy for sit-down fries. Its forte is greasy, fast, deep-fried Flemish fast food. The "menu 2" comes with three traditional gut bombs: shrimp, chicken, and "spicy gypsy" sausage (daily 11:30–24:00, at the corner of Geldmuntstraat and Sint Jakobstraat, tel. 050-337-957).

Delhaize-Proxy Supermarket is ideal for picnics. Its push-button produce pricer lets you buy as few as one mushroom (Mon–Sat 9:00–19:00, closed Sun, 3 blocks off Market Square on Geldmuntstraat). For midnight snacks, you'll find Indian-run corner grocery stores scattered around town.

Belgian Waffles and Ice Cream

While Americans think of "Belgian" waffles for breakfast, the Belgians (who don't eat waffles or pancakes for breakfast) think of *wafels* as Liège-style (dense, sweet, heated up, and eaten plain) and Brussels-style (lighter, often with powdered sugar or whipped cream and strawberries, served in teahouses only in the afternoons 14:00–18:00). You'll see waffles sold at restaurants and take-away stands. **Laurenzino** is a favorite with Bruges' teens when they get the waffle munchies. Their classic waffle with chocolate costs €2.50 (daily 10:00–23:00, across from Gelateria Da Vinci at Noordzandstraat 1, tel. 050-345-854).

Gelateria Da Vinci, the local favorite for homemade ice cream, has creative flavors and a lively atmosphere. As you approach, you'll see a line of happy lickers. Before ordering, ask to sample the Ferrero Rocher (chocolate, nuts, and crunchy cookie) and plain yogurt (daily 10:00–24:00, Geldmuntstraat 34, run by Sylvia from Austria).

Nightlife

Herberg Vlissinghe and **De Garre,** listed in "Eating," are great places to just nurse a beer and enjoy new friends.

Charlie Rockets is an American-style bar—lively and central—with foosball games, darts, and five pool tables (€9/hr) in the inviting back room. It also runs a youth hostel upstairs and therefore is filled with a young, international crowd (a block off Market Square at Hoogstraat 19). It's open nightly until 3:00 in the morning with non-stop rock 'n' roll.

Nighttime Bike Ride: Great as these pubs are, my favorite way to spend a late-summer evening in Bruges is in the twilight on a rental bike, savoring the cobbled wonders of its back streets, far from the touristic commotion.

Evening Carillon Concerts: The tiny courtyard behind the bell tower has a few benches where people can enjoy the free carillon concerts (generally Mon, Wed, and Sat at 21:00 in the summer; schedule posted on the wall).

Connections

Trains

From Bruges by Train to: Brussels (2/hr, usually at :31 and :57, 1 hr, €12.30), **Ghent** (2/hr, 40 min), **Ostende** (3/hr, 15 min), **Köln** (6/day, 3.5 hrs, change at Brussels Midi), **Paris** (1/day direct, about 2/hr via Brussels, 2.5 hrs on fast Thalys trains—it's best to book by 20:00 the day before), **Amsterdam** (hourly, 3.5–4 hrs, transfer at Antwerp Central or Brussels Midi; transfer can be timed closely—be alert and check with conductor), **Amsterdam's Schiphol Airport** (hourly, 3.5 hrs, transfer in Antwerp or Brussels), **Haarlem** (1–2/hr, 3.5 hrs, requires transfer). Train info: tel. 050/302-424.

Trains to London: Eurostar trains to London leave from platforms #1 and #2 at Brussels Midi. Arrive 30 minutes early to get your ticket validated and your luggage and passport checked by British authorities (similar to an airport check-in for an international flight).

Bruges is an ideal "Welcome to Europe" stop after London. For tips on getting to Bruges from London, and info on Eurostar fares, see "To Paris or Brussels via Eurostar Train" at the end of the London chapter.

Bus
By Bus to: London (cost can vary, but generally €35 one-way, €70 round-trip, about 9 hrs, Eurolines tel. 02-203-0707 in Brussels, www.eurolines.com).

CZECH REPUBLIC

PRAGUE

Praha

It's amazing what two decades of freedom can do. Prague has always been historic. Now it's fun, too. No other place in Europe has become so popular so quickly. And for good reason: Prague—the only Central European capital to escape the bombs of the last century's wars—is one of Europe's best-preserved cities. It's filled with sumptuous Art Nouveau facades, offers tons of cheap Mozart and Vivaldi concerts, and brews the best beer in Europe. Beyond its architecture and traditional culture, it's an explosion of pent-up entrepreneurial energy jumping for joy after 40 years of communist rule. Its low prices can cause you to jump for joy, too. Travel in Prague is like travel in Western Europe...20 years ago and (except for hotels) for half the price.

Planning Your Time

Prague demands a minimum of two full days (with three nights, or two nights and a night train) for a good introduction to the city. From Vienna, Berlin, and Munich, Prague is a four- to six-hour train ride by day (you also have the option of a longer night train from Munich). From Budapest, Warsaw, or Kraków, you can take a handy overnight train.

With two days in Prague, I'd spend one morning seeing the castle and another morning in the Jewish Quarter. Use your afternoons for loitering around the Old Town, Charles Bridge, and the Little Quarter, and split your nights between beer halls and live music. Keep in mind that Jewish Quarter sights close on Saturday. Some museums, mainly in the Old Town, are closed on Monday.

Orientation

Locals call their town "Praha" (PRAH-hah). It's big, with 1.2 million people, but focus on its relatively compact old center during a quick visit. As you wander, take advantage of brown street signs directing you to tourist landmarks. Self-deprecating Czechs note that while the signs are designed to help tourists (locals never use them), they're only printed in Czech. Still—thanks to the little icons—the signs can help smart visitors who are sightseeing on foot.

The Vltava River divides the west side (Castle Quarter and Little Quarter) from the east side (New Town, Old Town, Jewish Quarter, Main Train Station, and most of the recommended hotels).

Prague addresses come with references to a general zone. Praha 1 is in the old center on either side of the river. Praha 2 is in the new city, southeast of Wenceslas Square. Praha 3 and higher indicate a location farther from the center. Almost all of what I list here is in Praha 1 (unless noted otherwise).

Tourist Information

TIs are at several key locations: **Old Town Square** (in the Old Town Hall, just to the left of the Astronomical Clock; Easter–Oct Mon–Fri 9:00–19:00, Sat–Sun 9:00–18:00; Nov–Easter Mon–Fri 9:00–18:00, Sat–Sun 9:00–17:00; tel. 224-482-018), **Main Train Station** (generally same hours as Old Town Square TI, but closed Sun), and the castle side of **Charles Bridge** (Easter–Oct daily 10:00–18:00, closed Nov–Easter). For general tourist information in English, dial 12444 (Mon–Fri 8:00–19:00) or check the TIs' useful website: www.prague-info.cz.

The TIs offer maps, phone cards, a useful transit guide, information on guided walks and bus tours, and bookings for private guides, concerts, hotel rooms, and rooms in private homes.

Several monthly event guides—all of them packed with ads—include the *Prague Guide* (29 Kč), *Prague This Month* (free), and *Heart of Europe* (free, summer only). The English-language weekly *Prague Post* newspaper is handy for entertainment listings and current events (60 Kč at newsstands).

Arrival in Prague

As soon as you arrive, be sure to buy a city map, with trams and Metro lines marked and tiny sketches of the sights drawn in for ease in navigating (30–70 Kč, many different brands; sold at kiosks, exchange windows, and tobacco stands). It's a mistake to try doing Prague without a good map—you'll refer to it constantly. The *Kartografie Praha* city map, which shows all the tram lines and major landmarks, includes a castle diagram and a street index. It

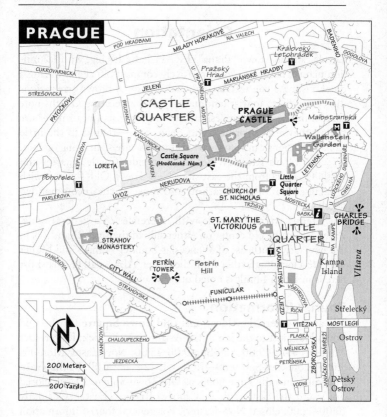

comes in two versions: 1:15,000 covers the city center, and 1:25,000 includes the whole city. The city center map is easier to navigate, and sufficient unless you're staying in the suburbs.

By Train

Prague has two international train stations. The Main Station (Hlavní Nádraží) serves all trains from Frankfurt, Salzburg, Munich, and Kraków; some trains from Vienna and Budapest; and most trains within the Czech Republic. The secondary station (Nádraží Holešovice, located north of the river) handles all trains from Berlin, most trains from Vienna and Budapest, and the high-speed SC Pendolino trains.

Upon arrival, get money. The stations have convenient ATMs (best rates). Avoid the exchange bureaus (rates are generally bad, but can vary—compare by asking at two windows what you'll get for $100). Then buy your map and confirm your departure plans. Those arriving on an international train may be met at the tracks by room hustlers, trying to snare tourists for cheap rooms. These can be a good value.

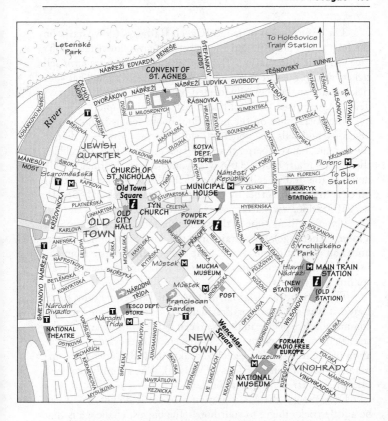

Main Station (Hlavní Nádraží): The station's creepy, low-ceilinged hall is the work of communist architects, who expanded a classy building to make it just big, painting it the compulsory dreary gray with reddish trim. An Italian firm is currently refitting the station to Western European standards, temporarily turning it into an overcrowded construction site with rare empty spaces filled by fancy clothing stores. An ATM is near the subway entrance. The station's baggage-storage counter is reportedly safer than the lockers.

The **Wasteels travel office** may offer friendly assistance or surly service, depending on which agent you get. You can drop by here upon arrival to get a transit ticket without using the ATM (they take euro coins), and to confirm and buy your outbound train tickets. They can help you figure out international train connections, and they sell train tickets to anywhere in Europe—with domestic stopovers if you like—along with tickets for fast local trains and cheap phone cards (no commission; Mon–Fri 9:00–17:00 or later, Sat 9:00–16:00, closed Sun, tel. 972-241-954, www.wasteels.cz). You can even leave your bags here for a short time.

The information office for Czech Railways (downstairs on the left) is less helpful, and the ticket windows downstairs don't give schedule information. The windows marked *vnitrostátní* sell tickets within the Czech Republic. You can also wait and get your tickets later at the centrally located office of the Czech Railways Travel Agency (see "Helpful Hints," later in this chapter).

The AVE office on the main floor books rooms in hotels and pensions, and sells taxi vouchers—for trips into town—at double the fair rate, but still better than you'd get directly from the cabbies themselves (daily 6:00–23:00; with your back to the tracks, walk down to the orange ceiling and past the "Meeting Point"—their office is in the left corner by the exit to the taxis; tel. 251-551-011, fax 251-555-156, www.avetravel.cz, ave@avetravel.cz).

If you're killing time at the station (or for a wistful glimpse of a more genteel age), go upstairs into the Art Nouveau hall. Here, under an elegant dome, you can sip coffee, enjoy music from the 1920s, watch boy prostitutes looking for work, and see new arrivals spilling into the city.

The station was originally named for Emperor Franz Josef. Later, it was renamed for President Woodrow Wilson (see the commemorative plaque in the main exit hall leading away from the tracks), because his promotion of self-determination led to the creation of the free state of Czechoslovakia in 1918. Under the communists (who weren't big fans of Wilson), it was bluntly renamed Hlavní Nádraží—"Main Station."

Even though the Main Station is basically downtown, it can be a little tricky to get to your hotel. The biggest challenge is that the **taxi** drivers at the train station are a gang of no-neck mafia thugs who wait around to charge an arriving tourist five times the regular rate. To get an honest cabbie, I'd walk a few blocks and hail one off the street; pay a premium for a voucher at the AVE office (see above); or call AAA Taxi (tel. 233-113-311) or City Taxi (tel. 257-257-257). A taxi should get you to your hotel for no more than 200 Kč (see "Getting Around Prague," later in this chapter).

A better option may be to take the **Metro.** It's dirt-cheap and easy, with very frequent departures. Once you're on the Metro, you'll wonder why you would ever bother with a taxi (inside station, look for the red M with two directions: Háje or Letňany). Get change at a newsstand or grocery, then buy a ticket from the automated machine by the Metro entrance. Validate your ticket in the yellow machines *before* you go down the stairs to the tracks. To get to hotels in the Old Town, catch a Háje-bound train to the Muzeum stop, then transfer to the green line (direction: Dejvická) and get off at either Můstek or Staroměstská; these stops straddle the Old Town. For more on using the Metro, see "Getting Around Prague," later in this chapter.

Rip-Offs in Prague

Prague's new freedom comes with new scams. There's no particular risk of violent crime, but green, rich tourists do get taken by con artists. Simply be on guard, particularly when traveling on trains (thieves thrive on overnight trains), changing money (tellers with bad arithmetic and inexplicable pauses while counting back your change), dealing with taxis (see "By Taxi," on page 200), paying in restaurants (see "Eating," later in this chapter), and in seedy neighborhoods.

Anytime you pay for something, make a careful note of how much it costs, how much you're handing over, and how much you expect back. Count your change. Someone selling you a phone card marked 190 Kč might first tell you it's 790 Kč, hoping to pocket the difference. If you call his bluff, he'll pretend that it never happened.

Plainclothes policemen "looking for counterfeit money" are con artists. Don't show them any cash or your wallet. If you're threatened with an inexplicable fine by a "policeman," conductor, or other official, you can walk away, scare him away by saying you'll need a receipt (which real officials are legally required to provide), or ask a passerby if the fine is legit. On the other hand, do not ignore the plainclothes inspectors on the Metro and trams who have shown you their badges.

Pickpockets can be little children or adults dressed as professionals—or even as tourists. They target Western visitors. Many thieves drape jackets over their arms to disguise busy fingers. Thieves work the crowded and touristy places in teams. They use mobile phones to coordinate their bumps and grinds. Be careful if anyone creates a commotion at the door of a Metro or tram car (especially around the Národní Třída and Vodičkova tram stops, or on the made-for-tourists tram #22)—it's a smokescreen for theft.

Car theft is also a big problem in Prague (many Western European car-rental companies don't allow their rentals to cross the Czech border). Never leave anything valuable in your car—not even in broad daylight on a busy street.

The sex clubs on Skořepka and Melantrichova streets, just south and north of Havelská Market, routinely rip off naive tourists and can be dangerous. They're filled mostly with young Russian women and German and Asian men. Lately this district has become the rage for British "stag" parties, for guys who are happy to fly cheaply to get to cheap beer and cheap thrills.

This all sounds intimidating. But Prague is safe. It has its share of petty thieves and con artists, but very little violent crime. Don't be scared—just be alert.

Or, if your hotel is close enough, consider **walking** (Wenceslas Square, a downtown landmark, is about a 10-minute walk away—turn left out of the station and follow Wilsonova street to the huge National Museum).

Holešovice Station (Nádraží Holešovice): This station, slightly farther from the center, is suburban mellow. The main hall has all the services of the Main Station in a more compact area. On the left are international and local ticket windows (open 24 hours), an information office, and an AVE office with last-minute accommodations (daily 12:00–20:00, tel. 972-224-660). On the right is a little-frequented café with Internet access (1 Kč/min, daily 8:00–19:30). Two ATMs are immediately outside the first glass doors, and the Metro is 50 yards to the right (follow signs toward *Vstup*, which means "entrance"; it's three stops to Hlavní Nádraží—the Main Station—or four stops to the city-center Muzeum stop). Taxis and trams are outside to the right (allow 200 Kč for a cab to the center). The airport bus (45 Kč, runs 2/hr) is outside to the left.

By Plane

Prague's modern, tidy, low-key **Ruzyně Airport,** located 12 miles (about 30 min) west of the city center, is as user-friendly as any airport in Western Europe or the US. The new Terminal 2 serves destinations within the EU except for Great Britain (no passport controls); Terminal 1 serves Great Britain and everywhere else. The airport has ATMs (avoid the change desks); desks promoting their transportation services (such as city transit and shuttle buses); kiosks selling city maps and phone cards; and a tourist service with few printed materials. Airport info: tel. 220-113-314, operator tel. 220-111-111.

Getting from the Airport to Downtown: It's easy. Leaving either airport terminal, you have five options, listed below from cheapest to priciest:

Dirt Cheap: Take bus #119 to the Dejvická Metro station, or #100 to the Zličín Metro station (20 min), then take the Metro into the center (20 Kč, info desk in airport arrival hall).

Budget: Take the airport express (AE) bus to Holešovice Station, then take the Metro into the center (bus runs daily 4:40–21:10, 2/hr, 30 min, 45 Kč, look for the AE sign in front of the terminal and pay the driver, www.czech-transport.com).

Moderate: Take the Čedaz minibus shuttle to Náměstí Republiky, across from Kotva department store (daily 5:30–21:30, 2/hr, pay 120 Kč directly to driver, info desk in arrival hall).

Expensive: Take a Čedaz minibus directly to your hotel, with a couple of stops likely en route (480 Kč for a group of up to four, tel. 220-114-286).

Splurge: Catch a taxi. Cabbies wait at the curb directly in front of the arrival hall. Airport taxi cabbies are honest but more expensive. Carefully confirm the complete price before getting in. It's a fixed rate of 600–700 Kč, with no meter.

Helpful Hints

Medical Help: A 24-hour pharmacy is at Palackého 5 (a block from Wenceslas Square, tel. 224-946-982). For standard assistance, there are two state hospitals in the center: the **General Hospital** (open daily 24 hours, moderate wait time, right above Karlovo Náměstí at U Nemocnice 2, Praha 2, use entry G, tel. 224-962-564); and the **Na Františku Hospital** (on the embankment next to Hotel InterContinental, Na Františku 1, go to the main entrance, for English assistance call Mr. Hacker between 8:00–14:00, tel. 222-801-278 or tel. 222-801-371—serious problems only). The reception staff may not speak English, but doctors do.

    For better-than-standard assistance in English (including dental service), consider the top-quality **Hospital Na Homolce** (less than 1,000 Kč for an appointment, from 8:00–16:00 call 252-922-146, for after-hours emergencies call 257-211-111; bus #167 from Anděl Metro station, Roentgenova 2, Praha 5). The **Canadian Medical Care Center** is a small, private clinic with English-speaking Czech staff at Veleslavínská 1 in Praha 6 (3,000 Kč for an appointment, 4,500 Kč for a house call, halfway between the city and the airport, tel. 235-360-133, after-hours emergency tel. 724-300-301).

    If a **massage** is all you need to cure your aches and pains, contact **Patrick Kočica,** an experienced Hoshino therapist (750 Kč/hr, mobile 722-070-703, www.asianhealingarts.org, patrick.kocica@hoshino.cz).

Internet Access: Internet cafés are well-advertised and scattered through the Old and New Towns. Consider **Bohemia Bagel** near the Jewish Quarter (see "Eating," later in this chapter). **Káva Káva Káva Coffee,** on the boundary between the Old and New Towns, is in the Platýz courtyard off Národní 37.

Bookstores: Prague has several enjoyable bookshops with English titles. **Anagram Bookshop,** in the Ungelt courtyard behind the Týn Church, sells books in English on a wide range of topics (Mon–Sat 10:00–20:00, Sun 10:00–19:00, Týn 4, tel. 224-895-737). **V Ráji,** next to Maisel Synagogue in the Jewish Quarter, is the flagship store of a small publishing house dedicated to books about Prague. They offer an assortment of photo publications, fairy tales, and maps (Maiselova 12, tel. 222-326-925). **Kiwi Map Store,** near Wenceslas Square, is one of Prague's best sources for maps (Mon–Fri 9:00–19:00,

Sat 9:00–14:00, closed Sun, Jungmanova 23, tel. 224-948-455; look for the *Kartografie Praha* city map (described under "Arrival in Prague," earlier in this chapter).

Laundry: A full-service laundry near most of the recommended hotels is at Karolíny Světlé 11 (200 Kč/8-pound load, wash and dry in 2 hours, Mon–Fri 7:30–19:00, closed Sat–Sun, 200 yards from Charles Bridge on Old Town side). Or surf the Internet while your undies tumble-dry at Korunní 14 (160 Kč/load wash and dry, Internet access-2 Kč/min, daily 8:00–20:00, near Náměstí Míru Metro stop, Praha 2).

Bike Rental: Prague has recently improved its network of bike paths, making bicycles a feasible option for exploring the center of the town and beyond (see www.prahounakole.cz/mapa for an updated map). Two bike-rental shops located near the Old Town Square are **Praha Bike** (daily 9:00–20:00, Dlouhá 24, mobile 732-388-880, www.prahabike.cz) and **City Bike** (daily 9:00–19:00, Králodvorská 5, mobile 776-180-284, www.citybike-prague.com). They rent bikes for about 400 Kč for four hours or 500 Kč per day (with a 2,000 Kč deposit) and also organize guided bike tours.

Train Tickets: Czech Railways Travel Agency is quick and helpful, with an English-speaking staff. Ask whether discounts are available for your journey, as the rail company has a complex scheme of special offers (Mon–Fri 9:00–17:00, closed Sat–Sun; in the Broadway Mall between Na Příkopě and Celetná streets, near the Powder Tower; inside the mall passageway by T.G.I. Friday's, look for blue neon *ČD* sign on your right; Na Příkopě 31, see map on page 204; tel. 972-243-071, www.cdtravel.cz, prodej@cdtravel.cz).

Best Views: Enjoy the "Golden City of a Hundred Spires" during the early evening, when the light is warm and the colors are rich. Good viewpoints include the terrace at the Strahov Monastery (above the castle), the top of St. Vitus Cathedral (at the castle), the top of either tower on Charles Bridge, the Old Town Square clock tower (has an elevator), the recommended Restaurant u Prince Terrace (see "Eating," later in this chapter), and the steps of the National Museum overlooking Wenceslas Square.

Getting Around Prague

You can walk nearly everywhere. But after you figure out the public transportation system, the Metro is slick, the trams fun, and the taxis quick and easy. For details, pick up the handy transit guide at the TI. City maps show the tram, bus, and Metro lines.

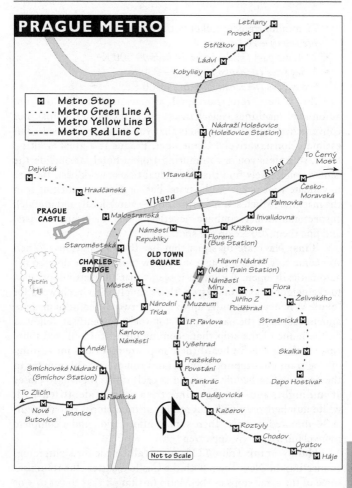

PRAGUE METRO

M	Metro Stop
· · · ·	Metro Green Line A
——	Metro Yellow Line B
- - - -	Metro Red Line C

Letňany

Prosek

Střížkov

Ládví

Kobylisy

Nádraží Holešovice
(Holešovice Station)

To Černý
Most

River

Dejvická

Vltavská

Česko-
Moravská

Hradčanská

Vltava

Palmovka

PRAGUE
CASTLE

Malostranská

Invalidovna

Náměstí
Republiky

Křižíkova

Florenc
(Bus Station)

Staroměstská

OLD TOWN
SQUARE

CHARLES
BRIDGE

Hlavní Nádraží
(Main Train Station)

Petřín
Hill

Můstek

Náměstí
Míru

Flora

Želivského

Národní
Třída

Muzeum

Jiřího Z
Poděbrad

Strašnická

I.P. Pavlova

Karlovo
Náměstí

Vyšehrad

Skalka

Anděl

Pražského
Povstání

Smíchovské Nádraží
(Smíchov Station)

Pankrác

Depo Hostivař

To Zličín

Radlická

Budějovická

Nové
Butovice

Jinonice

Kačerov

Roztyly

Chodov

Opatov

Háje

Not to Scale

PRAGUE

By Metro and Tram

Affordable and excellent public transit is perhaps the best legacy of the communist era (locals ride all month for 550 Kč). The three-line Metro system is handy and simple, but doesn't always get you right to the tourist sights (landmarks such as the Old Town Square and Prague Castle are several blocks from the nearest Metro stops). Trams rumble by every two or three minutes and take you just about anywhere.

Tickets: The trams and Metro work on the same tickets:

- 20-minute basic ticket with limited transfer options—18 Kč *základní s omezenou přestupností*. With this ticket, no transfers are allowed on trams and buses, but on the Metro, you can go up to five stops with one transfer (not valid for night trams or night buses).

- 75-minute transfer ticket with unlimited transfers *(základní přestupní)*—26 Kč.
- 24-hour pass *(jízdenka na 24 hodin)*—100 Kč.
- 3-day pass *(jízdenka na 3 dny)*—330 Kč.
- 5-day pass *(jízdenka na 5 dní)*—500 Kč.

Buy tickets from your hotel, at newsstand kiosks, or from automated machines (select ticket price, then insert coins). For convenience, buy all the tickets that you think you'll need—but estimate conservatively. Remember, Prague is a great walking town, so unless you're commuting from a hotel far outside the center, you'll likely find that individual tickets work best. Be sure to validate your ticket on the tram, bus, or Metro by sticking it in the machine (which stamps a time on it—watch locals and imitate). Inspectors routinely ambush ticketless riders (including tourists) and fine them 700 Kč on the spot.

Tips: Navigate by signs that list the end stations. When you come to your stop, push the yellow button if the doors don't automatically open. Although it seems that all Metro doors lead to the neighborhood of Výstup, that's simply the Czech word for "exit." When a tram pulls up to a stop, two different names are announced: first, the name of the stop you're currently at, followed by the name of the stop that's coming up next. Confused tourists, thinking they've heard their stop, are notorious for rushing off the tram one stop too soon. Trams run every 5–10 minutes in the daytime (a schedule is posted at each stop). The Metro closes at midnight, and the nighttime tram routes (identified with white numbers on blue backgrounds at tram stops) run all night at 30-minute intervals. There's more information and a complete route planner at www.dpp.cz/en.

Handy Tram: Tram #22 is practically made for sightseeing, connecting the New Town with the Castle Quarter. The tram uses some of the same stops as the Metro (making it easy to get to—or travel on from—the tram route). Of the many stops this tram makes, the most convenient are two in the New Town (Národní Třída Metro stop, between the bottom of Wenceslas Square and the river; and Národní Divadlo, at the National Theatre), two stops in the Little Quarter (Malostranské Náměstí and Malostranská Metro stop), and three stops above Prague Castle (Královský Letohrádek, Pražský Hrad, and Pohořelec; for details, see "Getting to Prague Castle—By Tram" on page 232).

By Taxi

Prague's taxis—notorious for hyperactive meters—are being tamed. New legislation is in place to curb crooked cabbies, and police will always take your side in an argument. Many cabbies are crooks who consider it a good day's work to take one sucker for a ride. You'll make things difficult for a dishonest cabbie by challenging an unfair fare.

While most hotel receptionists and guidebooks advise that you avoid taxis, I find Prague to be a great taxi town and use them routinely. With the local rate, they're cheap (read the rates on the door: drop charge starts at 36 Kč; per-kilometer charge—29 Kč; and waiting time per minute—5 Kč). The key is to be sure the cabbie turns on the meter at the #1 tariff (look for the word *sazba*, meaning "tariff," on the meter). Avoid cabs waiting at tourist attractions and train stations. To improve your odds of getting a fair meter rate—which starts only when you take off—call for a cab (or have your hotel or restaurant call one for you). AAA Taxi (tel. 233-113-311) and City Taxi (tel. 257-257-257) are the most likely to have English-speaking staff—and honest cabbies. I also find that hailing a passing taxi usually gets me a decent price, although at a slightly higher rate than when reserving by phone. If a cabbie surprises you at the end with an astronomical fare, simply pay 200 Kč, which should cover you for a long ride anywhere in the center. Then go into your hotel. On the miniscule chance that he follows you, the receptionist will back you up.

Tours

Walking Tours

Many small companies offer walking tours of the Old Town, the castle, and more. For the latest, pick up the walking tour fliers at the TI. Since guiding is a routine side-job for local university students, you'll generally get hardworking young guides at good prices. While I'd rather go with my own private guide (see below), public walking tours are cheaper (about 450 Kč for a 4-hour tour), cover themes you might not otherwise consider, connect you with other English-speaking travelers, and allow for spontaneity. The quality depends on the guide rather than the company. Your best bet is to show up at the Astronomical Clock a couple of minutes before 8:00, 10:00, or 11:00, then chat with a few of the umbrella-holding guides there. Choose the one you click with. Guides also have fliers advertising additional walks.

Private Guides

In Prague, hiring a local guide is particularly smart—they're twice as helpful for half the price compared to guides in Western Europe. Because prices are usually per hour (not per person), small groups can inexpensively hire a guide for several days. Guides meet you wherever you like, and tailor the tour to your interests. Visit their websites in advance for details on various walks, airport transfers, countryside excursions, and other services offered, and then make arrangements by email.

Šárka Kačabová, who uses her teaching background to help you comprehend Czech culture, has hand-picked a team of personable and knowledgeable guides for her company **Personal Prague Guide** (600 Kč/hr for 2–3 people, 800 Kč/hr for 4–8 people, mobile 777-225-205, www.prague-guide.info, saraguide@volny.cz).

Katka Svobodová, a hardworking anthropologist-historian-guide who knows her stuff, runs **Praguewalker,** which offers enthusiastic and friendly guides (600 Kč/hr for 2–3 people, 800 Kč/hr for 4–8 people, mobile 603-181-300, www.praguewalker.com, katerina @praguewalker.com).

Jana Hronková has a natural style—a welcome change from the more strict professionalism of some of the busier guides (mobile 732-185-180, janahronkova@hotmail.com). My readers also recommend **Renata Blažková,** who has a special interest in the history of Prague's Jewish Quarter (tel. 222-716-870, mobile 602-353-186, blazer@volny.cz), and **Martin Bělohradský,** whose main area of expertise lies in fine arts and architecture (martinb @uochb.cas.cz, mobile 723-414-565). These guides typically charge about 2,000–2,500 Kč for a half-day tour.

Athos Travel's licensed guides can lead you on a general sightseeing tour or fit the walk to your interests: music, Art Nouveau, architecture, and more (700 Kč/hr for 1–5 people, 800 Kč/hr for 5 or more people, arrange tour at least 24 hours in advance, tel. 241-440-571, www.a-prague.com/tours, info@athos.cz).

The **TI** also has plenty of private guides (rates for a 3-hour tour: 1,200 Kč/1 person, 1,400 Kč/2 people, 1,600 Kč/3 people, 2,000 Kč/4 people; desk at Old Town Square TI, arrange and pay in person at least 2 hours in advance, tel. 224-482-562, guides @pis.cz). Or get in touch with **Honza Vihan,** the co-author of *Rick Steves' Prague & the Czech Republic* (honzavihan@hotmail.com). For more listings of private guides, see www.guide-prague.cz.

Jewish-Themed Tours: Sylvie Wittmann, a native Czech Jew, has developed a diverse array of guides (some better than others) who aspire to bring Jewish traditions back to life in Prague. Consider her three-hour walking tour of the Jewish Quarter (880 Kč includes entry to the Jewish Museum and the Old-New Synagogue, May–Oct Sun–Fri at 10:30 and 14:00, Nov–Dec and mid-March–April Sun–Fri at 10:30 only, no tours Sat and Jan–mid-March) or her six-hour trip to Terezín Concentration Camp (1,150 Kč includes transportation and all entries, departs May–Oct daily at 10:00; mid-March–April and Nov–Dec no Mon, Wed, or Fri tours; Jan–mid-March by appointment only). All tours require prior reservation and meet in front of Hotel InterContinental at the end of Pařížská street (tel. & fax 222-252-472, mobile 603-168-427, www.wittmann-tours.com, sylvie@wittmann-tours.com).

Bus Tours

While I generally recommend cheap big-bus orientation tours for an efficient, once-over-lightly look at great cities, Prague just isn't built for bus tours. In fact, most bus tours of the city are walking tours that use buses for pick-ups and transfers. The sightseeing core (Castle Quarter, Charles Bridge, and the Old Town) are not accessible by bus. So if you insist on a bus, you're playing basketball with a catcher's mitt.

Bus tours make more sense for day trips out of Prague. Several companies have kiosks on Na Příkopě where you can comparison-shop. **Premiant City Tours** offers 20 different tours, including Terezín Concentration Camp, Karlštejn Castle, and Český Krumlov (1,750 Kč, 10 hrs), and a river cruise. The tours feature live guides and depart from near the bottom of Wenceslas Square at Na Příkopě 23. Get tickets at an AVE travel agency, your hotel, on the bus, or at Na Příkopě 23 (tel. 224-946-922, mobile 606-600-123, www.premiant.cz). Tour salespeople are notorious for telling you anything to sell a ticket. Some tours, especially those heading into the countryside, can be in as many as four different languages. Hiring a private guide, many of whom can drive you around in their car, can be a much better value (see previous page).

More Tours

Cruises—Prague isn't ideal for a boat tour because you'll spend half the time waiting to go through the locks. Still, the hour-long Vltava River cruises, which leave from near the castle end of Charles Bridge about hourly, are scenic and relaxing, though not informative (100–150 Kč).

▲**Paddleboat Cruises**—Renting a rowboat or paddleboat on the island by the National Theatre is a better way to enjoy the river. You'll float at your own pace among the swans and watch local lovers cruise by in their own paddleboats (40–60 Kč/hr, bring photo ID for deposit).

Sights

I've arranged Prague's sights per neighborhood: Old Town, New Town, Little Quarter, and Castle Quarter.

The Old Town (Staré Město)

From Prague's dramatic centerpiece, the Old Town Square, sightseeing options fan out in all directions. Get oriented on the square before venturing onward. You can learn about Jewish heritage in the Jewish Quarter (Josefov), a few blocks from the Old Town Square. Closer to the square, you'll find the quaint and historic Ungelt courtyard and Celetná street, which leads to the Museum of

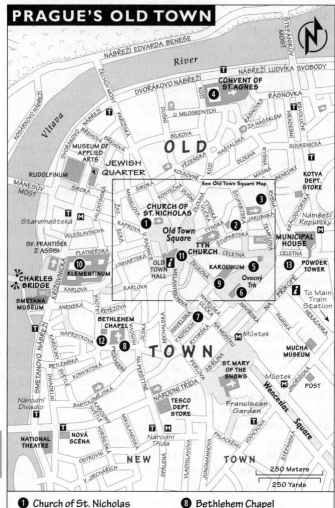

PRAGUE'S OLD TOWN

1. Church of St. Nicholas
2. Ungelt Courtyard & House at the Golden Ring
3. Church of St. James
4. St. Agnes Convent & Museum of Medieval Art
5. Museum of Czech Cubism
6. Estates Theatre
7. Havelská Market
8. Bethlehem Chapel
9. Charles University
10. Klementinum (National Library)
11. Old Town Hall & Astronomical Clock
12. Family Museum of Postcards
13. Czech Railways Travel Agency

PRAGUE

Czech Cubism and the landmark Estates Theatre. Nearby, Karlova street funnels all the tourists to the famous Charles Bridge. All of the sights described here are within a five-minute walk of the magnificent Old Town Square.

▲▲▲Old Town Square (Staroměstské Náměstí)

The focal point for most visits, Prague's Old Town Square is one of the city's top sights. This has been a market square since the 11th century. It became the nucleus of the Old Town (Staré Město) in the 13th century, when its Town Hall was built. Today, the old-time market stalls have been replaced by outdoor cafés and touristy horse buggies. But under this shallow surface, the square hides a magic power to evoke the history that has passed through here. The square's centerpiece is a memorial to Jan Hus.

• *Gawk your way to the square's centerpiece, the...*

Jan Hus Memorial: This monument, erected in 1915 (500 years after the Czech reformer's martyrdom by fire), symbolizes the long struggle for Czech freedom. Walk around the memorial. Jan Hus stands tall between two groups of people: victorious Hussite patriots and Protestants defeated by the Habsburgs in 1620. One of the patriots holds a chalice (cup); in the medieval Church, only priests could drink the wine at Communion. Since the Hussites fought for their right to take both the wine and the bread, the cup is their symbol. Hus looks proudly at the Týn Church (described on page 208), which became the headquarters and leading church of his followers. A golden chalice once filled the now-empty niche under the gold bas-relief of the Virgin Mary on the church's facade. After the Habsburg (and, therefore, Catholic) victory over the Czechs in 1620, the Hussite chalice was melted down and made into the image of Mary that shines from that spot high over the square today.

Behind the statue of Jan Hus, the bronze statue of a mother with her children represents the ultimate rebirth of the Czech nation. Because of his bold stance for independence in the way common people worship God, Hus was excommunicated and burned in Germany, a century before the age of Martin Luther.

• *Standing by Jan Hus, get oriented with a...*

Spin-Tour: Whirl clockwise to get a look at Prague's diverse architectural styles: Gothic, Renaissance, Baroque, Rococo, and Art Nouveau. Start with the green domes of the Baroque **Church of St. Nicholas.** Originally Catholic, now Hussite, this church is a popular venue for concerts. (There's another green-domed Church of St. Nicholas—also popular for concerts—by the same architect, across the Charles Bridge in the Little Quarter.) The Jewish Quarter (Josefov) is a few blocks behind the church, down the uniquely tree-lined Pařížská—"Paris street." (The quarter is

PRAGUE

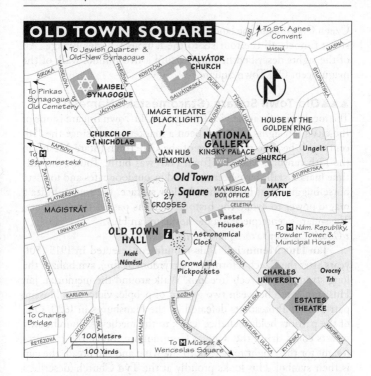

covered later in this chapter.) Pařížská, an eclectic cancan of mostly Art Nouveau facades, leads to a bluff that once sported a 100-foot-tall stone statue of Stalin. Demolished in 1962 after Khrushchev exposed Stalin's crimes, it was replaced in 1991 by a giant ticking **metronome**—partly to commemorate Prague's centennial exhibition (the 1891 exhibition is remembered by the Little Quarter's Eiffel-esque Petřín Tower), and partly to send the message that for every power, there's a time to go.

Spin to the right, past the Hus Memorial and the fine yellow Art Nouveau building. The large Rococo palace on the right (with a public WC in the courtyard) is part of the **National Gallery** and exhibits Asian art—particularly Chinese and Japanese works (Tue–Sun 10:00–18:00, closed Mon).

To the right, you can't miss the towering, Gothic **Týn Church** (pronounced "teen"), with its fanciful spires flanking the gold bas-relief of Mary. For 200 years after Hus' death, this was Prague's leading Hussite church (described in more detail later in this chapter). A narrow lane leading to the church's entrance passes the **Via Musica,** the most convenient ticket office in town (details listed under "Entertainment," later in this chapter). Behind the Týn Church is a gorgeously restored medieval courtyard called **Ungelt**. The row of pastel houses in front of Týn Church has a mixture of Gothic, Renaissance, and Baroque facades. To the right of these buildings, shop-lined **Celetná street** leads to a square called Ovocný Trh (with the Estates Theatre and Museum of Czech Cubism), and beyond that, to the Municipal House and Powder Tower in the New Town (all of these sights are covered later in this chapter).

Continue spinning right—with more gloriously colorful architecture—until you reach the pointed 250-foot-tall spire marking the 14th-century **Old Town Hall** (which has the only elevator-accessible tower in town—see "Clock Tour and Tower Climb," next page). The chunk of pink building attached to the tower of the Neo-Gothic City Hall is the town's memorial to bad losers. The building once stretched all the way to the Church of St. Nicholas. Then, in the last days of World War II (May 1945), German tanks knocked off this landmark—to the joy of many Prague citizens who considered it an ugly, oversized 19th-century stain on the medieval square. Across the square from the Old Town Hall (opposite the Astronomical Clock), touristy **Melantrichova street** leads directly to the New Town's Wenceslas Square, passing the craft-packed Havelská Market along the way.

• *Now wander across the square, toward the Old Town Hall Tower. Embedded in the pavement at the base of the tower (near the snack stand), you'll see...*

Twenty-Seven Crosses: These white inlaid crosses mark the spot where 27 Protestant nobles, merchants, and intellectuals were beheaded in 1621 after rebelling against the Catholic Habsburgs. The execution ended Czech independence for 300 years—and it's still one of the grimmest chapters in its history.

• *Looming behind the crosses is the Old Town Hall. Near the base of the tall tower, around the corner to the left, is Prague's famous...*

Astronomical Clock: Join the gang for the striking of the hour on the Town Hall clock, worth ▲▲ (daily 8:00–21:00, until 20:00 in winter). As you wait, see if you can figure out how the clock works.

With revolving disks, celestial symbols, and sweeping hands, this clock keeps several versions of time. Two outer rings show the hour: Bohemian time (gold Gothic numbers on black background, counts from sunset—find the zero, between 23 and 1...supposedly the time of tonight's sunset) and modern time (24 Roman numerals, XII at the top being noon, XII at the bottom being midnight). Five hundred years ago, everything revolved around the earth (the fixed middle background—with Prague marking the center, of course).

To indicate the times of sunrise and sunset, arcing lines and moving spheres combine with the big hand (a sweeping golden sun) and the little hand (a moon that spins to show various stages). Look for the orbits of the sun and moon as they rise through day (the blue zone) and night (the black zone).

If this seems complex to us, it must have been a marvel 500 years ago. Because the clock was heavily damaged during World War II, much of what you see today is a reconstruction. The circle below (added in the 19th century) shows the signs of the zodiac, scenes from the seasons of a rural peasant's life, and a ring of saints' names—one for each day of the year, with a marker showing today's special saint (at top).

Four statues flanking the clock represent the 15th-century outlook on time and prejudices. A Turk with a mandolin symbolizes hedonism, a Jewish moneylender is greed, and the figure staring into a mirror stands for vanity. All these worldly goals are vain in the face of Death, whose hourglass reminds us that our time is unavoidably running out.

At the top of the hour (don't blink—the show is pretty quick): First, Death tips his hourglass and pulls the cord, ringing the bell; then the windows open and the 12 apostles parade by, acknowledging the gang of onlookers; then the rooster crows; and then the hour is rung. Half the year, the hour is off because of daylight saving time (completely senseless to 15th-century clockmakers). At the top of the next hour, stand under the tower—protected by a line of banner-wielding concert salespeople in powdered wigs—and watch the tourists.

• To the left of the clock is Prague's main TI, which has an information desk and sells tickets for a pair of activities...

Clock Tour and Tower Climb: The main TI, to the left of the Astronomical Clock, contains an information desk and sells tickets for these two options: zipping up the Old Town Hall tower via elevator (60 Kč, Tue–Sun 9:00–17:30, Mon 11:00–17:30, fine views); or taking a 45-minute tour of the Old Town Hall, which includes a Gothic chapel and a close-up look at the inner guts of the Astronomical Clock (plus its statues of the 12 apostles; 50 Kč, 2/hr).

• Now that you're oriented, you can use this delightful square as your launchpad for the rest of Prague's Old Town sights...

▲Týn Church

Though this church has a long history, it's most notable for its 200-year-stint as the leading church of the Hussite movement (generally open to sightseers Tue–Sat 10:00–13:00 & 15:00–17:00). It was Catholic before the Hussites, and returned to Catholicism after the Hussites were defeated. As if to insult Hus and his doctrine of simplicity, the church's once elegant and pure Gothic columns are now encrusted with noisy Baroque altars. While Gothic, the church interior is uncharacteristically bright because of its clear Baroque windowpanes and whitewash. Read the church's story (posted in English, rear-left side) for a Catholic spin on the church's events—told with barely a mention of Hus. The fine 16th-century carved John the Baptist altar (right aisle) is worth a look. As you enjoy this church, try to ignore its unwelcoming signs—other than the Catholic-slanted history, the only English words you'll see here are commands that tell you what not to do.

Outside, on the side of the church facing Celetná street, find a statue of St. Mary resting on a temporary column against the wall. The Catholics are still waiting for a chance to reinstall St. Mary in the middle of the Old Town Square, where she stood for about 250 years until being torn down in 1918 by a mob of anti-Habsburg (and therefore anti-Catholic) demonstrators.

Behind Týn Church

▲**Ungelt Courtyard (Týnský Dvůr)**—Ever since the Old Town was established, the Ungelt courtyard—located directly behind the Old Town Square's Týn Church—has served as a hostel for foreign merchants, much like a Turkish caravanserai. Here the merchants (usually German) would store their goods and pay taxes before setting up stalls on the Old Town Square. Notice that there are only two entrances into the complex, for the purpose of guaranteeing the safety of goods and merchants. After decades of disuse, the courtyard had fallen into such disrepair by the 1980s that authorities considered demolishing it. Marvelously restored a few years ago, the Ungelt courtyard is now the most pleasant area in the Old Town for an outdoor coffee (try the recommended Ebel Coffee House; see "Eating—Cafés," later in this chapter), sorting through wooden crafts, and paging through English books (at Anagram Bookshop, described in "Helpful Hints," earlier in this chapter). Although Prague has undoubtedly lost some of its dreamy character to the booming tourist industry, places such as Ungelt stand as testimony to the miracles that money can work. Had the communists stayed in power for a few more years, Ungelt would have been a black hole by now. Ungelt also reminds us that Prague, for most of its history, has been a cosmopolitan center quite alien to the rest of the country.

House at the Golden Ring (Dům u Zlatého Prstenu)—This medieval townhouse displays a delightful collection of 20th-century Czech art. Its exterior has rectangular sgraffiti etchings (designs scratched out of one layer, revealing a different-colored layer beneath). Since 1900, Czech artists have been refining the subtle differences between dream, myth, and ideal. The English descriptions of each room psychoanalyze this demanding art, and recall the fact that Prague in the 1930s and 1960s was at the forefront of the European avant-garde. Notice the absence of Socialist Realism: The artists exhibited here chose deeply personal means of expression over regime-sponsored proclamations of universal optimism (90 Kč, Tue–Sun 10:00–18:00, closed Mon, just left of the entry into Ungelt courtyard as you approach it from the Old Town Square, Týnská 6, tel. 224-827-0224, www.citygallery prague.cz). There's a lively-with-students café in the courtyard.

Church of St. James (Kostel Sv. Jakuba)—Perhaps the most beautiful church in the Old Town, the Church of St. James is just behind Ungelt courtyard. The Minorite Order has occupied this church and the adjacent monastery almost as long as merchants have occupied Ungelt. A medieval city was a complex phenomenon: Side-by-side, there existed commerce, brothels, and a life of contemplation. (I guess it's not that much different from today.) Artistically, St. James (along with the Church of the Ascension of St. Mary at Strahov Monastery in the Castle Quarter—described later in this chapter) is a stunning example of how simple Gothic spaces could be transformed into sumptuous feasts of Baroque decoration. The blue light in the altar highlights one of Prague's most venerated treasures—the bejeweled Madonna Pietatis. Above the *pietà*, as if held aloft by hummingbird-like angels, is a painting of the martyrdom of St. James (free, daily 9:30–12:00 & 14:00–16:00).

As you leave, find the black and shriveled-up arm with clenched fingers (15 feet above and to the left of the door). According to legend, a thief attempted to rob the Madonna Pietatis from the altar, but his hand was frozen the moment he touched the statue. The monks had to cut off the arm in order for it to let go. The desiccated arm now hangs here as a warning—and the entire delightful story is posted nearby in English.

North of the Old Town Square, near the River

▲▲**Museum of Medieval Art**—The St. Agnes Convent houses the Museum of Medieval Art in Bohemia and Central Europe (1200–1550). The 14th century was Prague's Golden Age, and the religious art displayed in this Gothic space is a testament to the rich cultural life of the period. Each exquisite piece is well-lit and thoughtfully described in English. Follow the arrows on a chronological sweep through Gothic art history. The various Madonnas and saints were gathered here from churches all over Central Europe (100 Kč, Tue–Sun 10:00–18:00, closed Mon, two blocks northeast of the Spanish Synagogue, along the river at Anežská 12).

Princess Agnes founded this Clarist convent in the 13th century as the first hospital in Prague. Agnes was canonized by Pope John Paul II (who loved to promote the Slavic faithful) in 1989. Since local celebrations of her sainthood on November 26 coincided with the Velvet Revolution (the peaceful overthrow of the Communist government in 1989), Agnes has since been regarded as the patron of the renascent Czech democracy (you'll see her on the 50-Kč bill).

On Celetná Street, Toward the New Town

Celetná, a pedestrian-only street, is a convenient and relatively untouristy way to get from the Old Town Square to the New Town (specifically the Municipal House and Powder Tower). Along the way, at the square called Ovocný Trh, you'll find these sights.

Museum of Czech Cubism—Cubism was a potent force in Prague in the early 20th century. The fascinating Museum of Czech Cubism in the Black Madonna House (Dům u Černé Matky Boží) offers the complete Cubist experience: Cubist architecture (stand back and see how masterfully it makes its statement while mixing with its neighbors...then get up close and study the details), a great café (upstairs), a ground-floor shop, and, of course, a museum. On three floors, you'll see paintings, furniture, graphics, and architectural drafts by Czech Cubists. This building is an example of what has long been considered the greatest virtue of Prague's architects: the ability to adapt their grandiose plans to the existing cityscape (museum entry-100 Kč, Tue–Sun 10:00–18:00, closed Mon, corner of Celetná and Ovocný Trh at Ovocný Trh 19, tel. 224-301-003). If you're not interested in touring the museum itself, consider a drink in the similarly decorated upstairs Grand Café Orient (see "Eating—Cafés," later in this chapter).

Estates Theatre (Stavovské Divadlo)—Built by a nobleman in the 1770s, this Classicist building—gently opening its greenish walls onto Ovocný Trh—was the prime opera venue in Prague at a time when an Austrian prodigy was changing the course of music. Wolfgang Amadeus Mozart premiered *Don Giovanni* in this building, and personally directed many of his works here. Prague's theatergoers would whistle arias from Mozart's works on the streets the morning after they premiered. Today, part of the National Theatre group, the Estates Theatre, continues to produce *The Marriage of Figaro*, *Don Giovanni*, and occasionally *The Magic Flute*. For a more intimate encounter with Mozart, go to Villa Bertramka (described in "Entertainment," later in this chapter).

On Melantrichova Street

Skinny, tourist-clogged Melantrichova street leads directly from the Old Town Square's Astronomical Clock to the bottom of Wenceslas Square. But even along this most crowded of streets, a genuine bit of Prague remains...

▲**Havelská Market**—This open-air market, offering crafts and produce, was set up in the 13th century for the German trading community. Though heavy on souvenirs these days, the market still keeps hungry locals and vagabonds fed cheaply. It's ideal for a healthy snack; merchants are happy to sell a single vegetable or piece of fruit; and you'll find a washing fountain and plenty of inviting benches midway down the street. The market is also a fun place to browse for crafts. It's a homegrown, homemade kind of place; you'll often be dealing with the actual artist or farmer (market open daily 9:00–18:00, produce best on weekdays; more souvenirs, puppets, and toys on weekends). The many cafés and little eateries circling the market offer a fine and relaxing vantage point from which to view the action.

From Old Town Square to Charles Bridge

Karlova Street—Karlova street winds through medieval Prague from the Old Town Square to the Charles Bridge (it zigzags…just follow the crowds). This is a commercial gauntlet, and it's here that the touristy feeding frenzy of Prague is most ugly. Street signs keep you on track, and *Karlův most* signs point to the bridge. Obviously, you'll find few good values on this drag. Two favorite places providing a quick break from the crowds are just a few steps off Karlova on Husova street: **Cream and Dream Ice Cream** (Husova 12) and **U Zlatého Tygra,** a colorful pub that serves great, cheap beer in a classic and untouristy setting (Husova 17; see "Eating," later in this chapter).

▲**Klementinum**—The Czech Republic's massive National Library borders touristy Karlova street. The contrast could not be starker: Step out of the most souvenir-packed stretch of Eastern Europe, and enter into the meditative silence of Eastern Europe's biggest library. The Klementinum was built to house a college in the 1600s by the Jesuits, who had been invited to Prague by the Catholic Habsburgs to offset the influence of the predominantly Protestant Charles University nearby. The building was transformed into a library in the early 1700s, when the Jesuits took firm control of the university. Their books, together with the collections of several noble families (written in all possible languages… except Czech), form the nucleus of the National and University Library, which is now six million volumes strong. (Note that the Klementinum's Chapel of Mirrors is a popular venue for evening concerts.)

▲▲▲Charles Bridge (Karlův Most)

Among Prague's defining landmarks, this much-loved bridge offers one of the most pleasant and entertaining 500-plus-yard strolls in Europe. Enjoy the bridge at different times of day. (Although it's partially closed for renovation through 2010, it will remain crossable.) The bridge is most memorable early—before the crowds—

and late, during that photographers' "magic hour" when the sun is low in the sky.

At the Old Town end of the bridge, in a little square, is a statue of the bridge's namesake, **Charles IV.** This Holy Roman Emperor (Karlo Quatro—the guy on the 100-Kč bill) ruled his vast empire from Prague in the 14th century. He's holding a contract establishing Prague's university, the first in Northern Europe. This statue was erected in 1848 to celebrate the university's 500th birthday. The women around Charles' pedestal symbolize the university's four subjects: the arts, medicine, law, and theology. (From the corner by the busy street, many think the emperor's silhouette makes it appear as if he's peeing on the tourists. Which reminds me, public WCs are in the passageway opposite the statue.)

Bridges had been built on this spot before, as the remnant tower from Judith Bridge testifies (see the smaller of the two bridge towers at the far end). All were washed away by floods. After a major flood in 1342, Emperor Charles IV decided to commission an entirely new structure rather than repair the old one. Until the 19th century, this was Prague's only bridge that crossed the river.

Charles Bridge has long fueled a local love of legends—including one tied to numbers. According to medieval record, the bridge's foundation was laid in 1357. In the late 1800s, an amateur astronomer noticed a curious combination of numbers, leading to a popular theory about Charles IV. Charles is known to have been interested in numerology and astrology, and was likely aware of the significance of this date: the ninth of July at 5:31 in the morning. Written out in digits—as the year, month, day, hour, and minute—it's a numerical palindrome: 135797531. It's said that Charles must have chosen that precise moment (which also coincides with a favorable positioning of the earth and Saturn) to lay the foundation stone of the bridge. Further "corroboration" of this remarkable hypothesis was provided by the discovery that the end of the bridge on the Old Town side aligns perfectly with the tomb of St. Vitus (in the cathedral across the river) and the setting sun at summer solstice. In the absence of accurate 14th-century records, this intriguing proposition has delighted the modern Czech imagination. The number "135797531" is bound to remain celebrated as the adopted birthday of Prague's most beloved structure.

The magically aligned spot on the Old Town side is now occupied by the **bridge tower,** considered one of the finest Gothic gates anywhere. Contemplate the fine sculpture on the Old Town side of the tower, showing the 14th-century hierarchy of kings, bishops, and angels. Climbing the tower rewards you with wonderful views over the bridge (40 Kč, daily 10:00–19:00, as late as 22:00 in summer).

In the 17th century, there were no statues on the bridge—only a **cross,** which you can still see as part of the third sculpture on the right. The gilded Hebrew inscription celebrating Christ was paid for by a fine imposed on a Jew who mocked the cross.

The bronze Baroque statue depicting **John of Nepomuk**—a saint of the Czech people—draws a crowd (look for the guy with the five golden stars around his head, near the Little Quarter end of the bridge on the right). John of Nepomuk was a 14th-century priest to whom the queen confessed all her sins. According to a 17th-century legend, the king wanted to know his wife's secrets, but Father John dutifully refused to tell. He was tortured and eventually killed by being tossed off the bridge. When he hit the water, five stars appeared. The shiny plaque at the base of the statue depicts the priest-tossing. Devout pilgrims—from Mexico and Moravia alike—touch the engraving to make a wish come true. You get only one chance in life for this wish, so think carefully before you touch the saint. Notice the date on the inscription: This oldest statue on the bridge was unveiled in 1683, on the supposed 300th anniversary of the martyr's death.

The reason for John of Nepomuk's immense Baroque popularity and 1729 canonization remains contested. Some historians claim that at a time when the Czechs were being forcibly converted to Catholicism, Nepomuk became the rallying national symbol ("We will convert, but our patron must be Czech"). Others argue that Nepomuk was a propaganda figure used by Catholic leaders to give locals an alternative to Jan Hus. Statues like this one decorate squares and bridges throughout the country. The actual spot of the much-talked-about heave-ho is a few steps farther away from the castle—find the five points of the Orthodox cross between two statues on the bridge railing.

Most of the other Charles Bridge statues date from the late 1600s and early 1700s. Today, half of them are replicas—the originals are in city museums, out of the polluted air. At the far end of Charles Bridge, you reach the **Little Quarter.** For sights in this neighborhood, see page 227.

▲▲▲Jewish Quarter (Josefov)

Prague's Jewish Quarter neighborhood and its well-presented, profoundly moving museum tell the story of this region's Jews. For me, this is the most interesting collection of Jewish sights in Europe, and well worth seeing. The Jewish Quarter is an easy walk from Old Town Square, up delightful Pařížská street (next to the green-domed Church of St. Nicholas).

As the Nazis decimated Jewish communities in the region, Prague's Jews were allowed to collect and archive their treasures here. While the archivists were ultimately killed in concentration camps, their work survives. Seven sights scattered over

PRAGUE'S JEWISH QUARTER

a three-block area make up the tourists' Jewish Quarter. Six of the sights—all except the Old-New Synagogue—are called "The Museum" and are covered by one admission ticket. Your ticket comes with a map that locates the sights and lists admission appointments—the times you'll be let in if it's very busy. (Ignore the times unless it's really crowded.) You'll notice plenty of security (stepped up since 9/11).

Cost, Hours, Tours: To visit all seven sights, you'll pay 500 Kč (300 Kč for the six sights that make up the Museum, plus 200 Kč for the Old-New Synagogue). Museum sights open April–Oct Sun–Fri 9:00–18:00; Nov–March Sun–Fri 9:00–16:30; closed year-round on Sat—the Jewish Sabbath—and on Jewish holidays. Each sight is thoroughly and thoughtfully described in English, making a guided tour unnecessary for most visitors. Occasional guided walks in English start at the Maisel Synagogue (50 Kč, 3 hours, tel. 222-317-191).

Cemetery: The Old Jewish Cemetery—with its tightly packed, topsy-turvy tombstones—is, for many, the most evocative part of the experience. Unfortunately, there's no ticket just to see the cemetery, and they've closed off most free viewpoints. If the 300-Kč museum ticket is too steep for you and you just want a free peek at the famous cemetery, climb the steps to the covered porch of the Ceremonial Hall (but don't rest your chin on the treacherous railing).

Planning Your Time: The most logical start (if you'll be seeing everything) is to buy your ticket at Pinkas Synagogue and visit this most powerful memorial of the museum complex first. From there, walk through the Old Jewish Cemetery, which leads to the Ceremonial Hall and Klaus Synagogue. After visiting those, head over to the Old-New Synagogue, have a coffee break (nearby is the recommended Franz Kafka Café, described in "Eating," later in this chapter). Next, visit the museum-like Maisel Synagogue, and finally the Spanish Synagogue. (Note that Prague's fine Museum of Medieval Art, described earlier, is only a few blocks from the Spanish Synagogue.)

Art Nouveau and the New Josefov: Going from sight to sight in the Jewish Quarter, you'll walk through perhaps Europe's finest Art Nouveau neighborhood. Make a point to enjoy the circa-1900 buildings with their marvelous trimmings and oh-wow entryways. While today's modern grid plan has replaced the higgledy-piggledy medieval streets of old, Široká ("Wide Street") was and remains the main street of the ghetto.

Pinkas Synagogue (Pinkasova Synagóga)—A site of Jewish worship for 400 years, this synagogue is a poignant memorial to the victims of the Nazis. The walls are covered with the handwritten names of 77,297 Czech Jews who were sent from here to the gas chambers at Auschwitz and other camps. (As you ponder this sad sight, you'll hear the somber reading of the names alternating with a cantor singing the Psalms.) Hometowns are in gold and family names are in red, followed in black by the individual's first name, birthday, and last date known to be alive. Notice that families generally perished together. Extermination camps are listed on the east wall. Climb eight steps into the women's gallery. When the communists moved in, they closed the synagogue and erased virtually everything. With freedom, in 1989, the Pinkas Synagogue was reopened and the names were rewritten. (The names in poor condition near the ceiling are original.) Note that large tour groups may disturb this small memorial's compelling atmosphere between 10:00 and 12:00.

Upstairs is the **Terezín Children's Art Exhibit** (very well-described in English), displaying art drawn by Jewish children who were imprisoned at Terezín Concentration Camp and later perished. Terezín makes an emotionally moving day trip from Prague (the TI has details on tours and public transportation).

Old Jewish Cemetery (Starý Židovský Hřbitov)—From the Pinkas Synagogue, you enter one of the most wistful scenes in Europe—Prague's Old Jewish Cemetery. As you wander among 12,000 evocative tombstones, remember that from 1439 until 1787, this was the only burial ground allowed for the Jews of Prague. Tombs were piled atop each other because of limited space, the sheer number of graves, and the Jewish belief that the body should not be moved once buried. With its many layers, the cemetery became a small plateau. And as things settled over time, the tombstones got crooked. The Hebrew word for cemetery means "House of Life." Many Jews believe that death is the gateway into the next world. Pebbles on the tombstones are "flowers of the desert," reminiscent of the old days when rocks were placed upon the sand gravesite to keep the body covered. Wedged under some of the pebbles are scraps of paper that contain prayers.

Ceremonial Hall (Obřadní Síň)—Leaving the cemetery, you'll find a Neo-Romanesque mortuary house built in 1911 for the purification of the dead (on left). It's filled with a worthwhile exhibition, described in English, on Jewish medicine, death, and burial traditions. A series of crude but instructive paintings (hanging on walls throughout the house) show how the "burial brotherhood" took care of the ill and buried the dead. As all are equal before God, the rich and poor alike were buried in embroidered linen shrouds similar to the one you'll see on display.

Klaus Synagogue (Klauzová Synagóga)—This 17th-century synagogue (also near the cemetery exit) is the final wing of a museum devoted to Jewish religious practices. Exhibits on the ground floor explain the Jewish calendar of festivals. The central case displays a Torah (the first five books of the Bible) and solid silver pointers used when reading—necessary since the Torah is not to be touched. Upstairs is an exhibit on the rituals of Jewish life (circumcisions, bar and bat mitzvahs, weddings, kosher eating, and so on).

Old-New Synagogue (Staronová Synagóga)—For more than 700 years, this has been the most important synagogue and the central building in Josefov. Standing like a bomb-hardened bunker, it feels as though it has survived plenty of hard times. Stairs take you down to the street level of the 13th century and into the Gothic interior. Built in 1270, it's the oldest synagogue in Eastern Europe. Snare an attendant, who is likely to love showing visitors around. The separate, steep admission (see "Cost and Hours," next page) keeps many away, but even if you decide not to pay, you can see the exterior and a bit of the interior. (Go ahead...pop in and crane your cheapskate neck.)

The lobby (down the stairs, where you show your ticket) has two fortified old lockers—in which the most heavily taxed community in medieval Prague stored its money in anticipation of the taxman's arrival. As 13th-century Jews were not allowed to build, the synagogue was erected by Christians (who also built the St. Agnes Convent nearby). The builders were good at four-ribbed vaulting, but since that resulted in a cross, it wouldn't work for a synagogue. Instead, they made the ceiling using clumsy five-ribbed vaulting.

The interior is pure 1300s. The Shrine of the Ark in front is the focus of worship. The holiest place in the synagogue, it holds the sacred scrolls of the Torah. The old rabbi's chair to the right remains empty (notice the thin black chain) out of respect. The red banner is a copy of the one that the Jewish community carried through town during medieval parades. Notice the yellow-pointed hat within the Star of David (on the banner), which the pope ordered all Jewish men to wear in 1215. Twelve is a popular number (e.g., windows), because it symbolizes the 12 tribes of Israel. The horizontal slit-like windows are an 18th-century addition, allowing women to view the male-only services.

Cost and Hours: The Old-New Synagogue requires a separate 200-Kč admission that includes a worthwhile 10-minute tour—ask about it (Sun–Thu 9:30–18:00, Fri 9:30–17:00 or until sunset, closed Sat).

Maisel Synagogue (Maiselova Synagóga)—This synagogue was built as a private place of worship for the Maisel family during the 16th-century Golden Age of Prague's Jews. Maisel, the financier of the Habsburg king, had lots of money. The synagogue's interior is decorated Neo-Gothic. In World War II, it served as a warehouse for the accumulated treasures of decimated Jewish communities that Hitler planned to use for his "Museum of the Extinct Jewish Race." The one-room exhibit shows a thousand years of Jewish history in Bohemia and Moravia. Well-explained in English, topics include the origin of the Star of David, Jewish mysticism, the history of discrimination, and the creation of Prague's ghetto. Notice the eastern wall, with the Holy Ark containing the scroll of the Torah. The central case shows the silver ornamental Torah crowns that capped the scroll.

Spanish Synagogue (Španělská Synagóga)—Displays of Jewish history through the 18th, 19th, and tumultuous 20th centuries continue in this ornate, Moorish-style synagogue built in the 1800s. The upstairs is particularly intriguing, with circa-1900 photos of Josefov, an exhibit on the fascinating story of this museum and its relationship with the Nazi regime, and life in Terezín. The Winter Synagogue (also upstairs) shows a trove of silver worshipping aids gathered from countryside Jewish neighborhoods that were depopulated in the early 1940s, thus giving a sense of what the Nazis stockpiled.

The New Town (Nové Město)

Enough of pretty, medieval Prague—let's leap into the modern era. The New Town, with Wenceslas Square as its focal point, is today's urban Prague. This part of the city offers bustling boulevards and interesting neighborhoods. The New Town is the best place to view

PRAGUE'S NEW TOWN

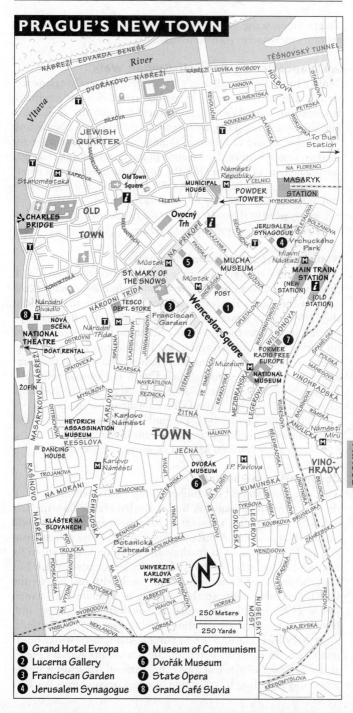

1 Grand Hotel Evropa
2 Lucerna Gallery
3 Franciscan Garden
4 Jerusalem Synagogue
5 Museum of Communism
6 Dvořák Museum
7 State Opera
8 Grand Café Slavia

Prague's remarkable Art Nouveau art and architecture and to learn more about its recent communist past.

▲▲Wenceslas Square Self-Guided Walk

More a broad boulevard than a square (until recently, trams rattled up and down its park-like median strip), this city landmark is named for King Wenceslas—featured both on the 20-Kč coin and the equestrian statue that stands at the top of the boulevard. Wenceslas Square (Václavské Náměstí) functions as a stage for modern Czech history: The creation of the Czechoslovak state was celebrated here in 1918; in 1968, the Soviets suppressed huge popular demonstrations here; and, in 1989, more than 300,000 Czechs and Slovaks converged here to claim their freedom.

• *Starting near the Wenceslas statue at the top (Metro: Muzeum), look to the building crowning the top of the square...*

National Museum (Národní Muzeum)

The museum stands grandly at the top. While its collection is dull, the building offers a powerful view, and the interior is richly decorated in the Czech Revival Neo-Renaissance style that heralded the 19th-century rebirth of the Czech nation. The light-colored patches in the museum's columns fill holes where Soviet bullets hit during the crackdown against the 1968 Prague Spring uprising. Masons—defying their communist bosses, who wanted the damage to be forgotten—showed their Czech spirit by intentionally mismatching their patches (80 Kč, daily May–Sept 10:00–18:00, Oct–April 9:00–17:00, halls of Czech fossils and animals).

The nearby Metro stop (Muzeum) is the crossing point of two Metro lines built with Russian know-how in the 1970s.

• *To the left of the National Museum (as you face it) is an ugly...*

Communist-Era Building

This structure housed the rubber-stamp Parliament back when they voted with Moscow. A Social Realist statue showing triumphant workers still stands at its base. Between 1994 and 2008 this building was home to Radio Free Europe. After communism fell, RFE lost some of its funding and could no longer afford its Munich headquarters. In gratitude for its broadcasts—which had kept the people of Eastern Europe in touch with real news—the Czech government offered this building to RFE for 1 Kč a year. But as RFE energetically beamed its American message deep into Islam from here, it drew attention—and threats—from Al-Qaeda. So in 2009 RFE moved to a new purpose-built, fortress-like headquarters at an easier-to-defend locale near Franz Kafka's grave, at the Želivského Metro station. The National Museum is in the process of installing its collection of non-Czech objects (such as

Greek and Roman art) inside this building, promising to turn it into a "window on the world."

• *In front of the National Museum is the equestrian...*

St. Wenceslas Statue

Wenceslas (Václav) is the "good king" of Christmas-carol fame. He was the wise and benevolent 10th-century Duke of Bohemia. A rare example of a well-educated and literate ruler, King Wenceslas I was credited by his people for Christianizing his nation and lifting up the culture. He astutely allied the Czechs with Saxony, rather than Bavaria, giving the Czechs a vote when the Holy Roman Emperor was selected (and therefore more political clout).

After his murder in 929, Wenceslas was canonized as a saint. He became a symbol of Czech nationalism and statehood—and remains an icon of Czech unity whenever the nation has to rally. Supposedly, when the Czechs face their darkest hour, Wenceslas will come riding out of Blaník Mountain (east of Prague) with an army of knights to rescue the nation. In 1620, when Austria stripped the Czechs of their independence, many people went to Blaník Mountain to see whether it had opened up. They did the same at other critical points in their history (in 1938, 1948, and 1968)—but Wenceslas never emerged. Although the Czech Republic is now safely part of NATO and the EU, Czechs remain realistic: If Wenceslas hasn't come out yet, the worst times must still lie ahead...

Study the statue. Wenceslas, on the horse, is surrounded by the four other Czech patron saints. Notice the focus on books. A small nation without great military power, the Czech Republic chose national heroes who enriched the culture by thinking, rather than fighting. This statue is a popular meeting point. Locals say, "I'll see you under the tail."

• *Now begin walking down the square. Thirty yards below the big horse is a small garden with a low-key...*

Memorial

This commemorates victims of communism, such as Jan Palach. In 1969, a group of patriots decided that an act of self-immolation would stoke the fires of independence. Jan Palach, a philosophy student who loved life—but wanted to live in freedom—set himself on fire on the steps of the National Museum for the cause of Czech independence. He died a few days later in a hospital ward. Czechs are keen on anniversaries, and huge demonstrations swept the city on the 20th anniversary of Palach's death. These protests led, 10 months later, to the overthrow of the Czech communist government in 1989.

This grand square is a gallery of modern architectural styles.

As you wander downhill, notice the fun mix, all post-1850: Romantic Neo-Gothic, Neo-Renaissance, and Neo-Baroque from the 19th century; Art Nouveau from about 1900; ugly Functionalism from the mid-20th century (the "form follows function" and "ornamentation is a crime" answer to Art Nouveau); Stalin Gothic from the 1950s "communist epoch" (a good example is the Jalta building, halfway downhill on the right); and the glass-and-steel buildings of the 1970s.

• *Walk a couple of blocks downhill through the real people of Prague (not tourists) to* **Grand Hotel Evropa**, *with its hard-to-miss, dazzling Art Nouveau exterior and plush café interior full of tourists. Stop for a moment to consider the events of...*

November of 1989

This huge square was filled every evening with more than 300,000 ecstatic Czechs and Slovaks who believed freedom was at hand. Assembled on the balcony of the building opposite Grand Hotel Evropa (look for the *Marks & Spencer* sign) were a priest, a rock star (famous for his unconventional style, which constantly unnerved the regime), Alexander Dubček (hero of the 1968 revolt), and Václav Havel (the charismatic playwright, newly released from prison, who was every freedom-loving Czech's Nelson Mandela). Through a sound system provided by the rock star, Havel's voice boomed over the gathered masses, announcing the resignation of the Politburo and saying that the Republic of Czechoslovakia's freedom was imminent. Picture that cold November evening, with thousands of Czechs jingling their keychains in solidarity, chanting at the government, "It's time to go now!" (To quell this revolt, government tanks could have given it the Tiananmen Square treatment—which had spilled patriotic blood in China just six months earlier. Locals believe that the Soviet head of state, Mikhail Gorbachev, must have made a phone call recommending a nonviolent response.) The wave of peaceful demonstrations, known as the "Velvet Revolution," ended later that year with the election of Václav Havel as the president of a free Czechoslovakia.

• *Immediately opposite Grand Hotel Evropa is the Lucerna Gallery (use entry marked Palác Rokoko and walk straight in).*

Lucerna Gallery

This grand mall retains some of its Art Deco glamour from the 1930s, with shops, theaters, a ballroom in the basement, and the fine Lucerna Café upstairs. You'll see a sculpture—called *Wenceslas Riding an Upside-Down Horse*—hanging like a swing from a glass dome. David Černý, who created the statue in 1999, is one of the Czech Republic's most original contemporary artists. Always aspiring to provoke controversy, Černý has painted a menacing

Russian tank pink, attached crawling babies to the rocket-like Žižkov TV tower, defecated inside the National Gallery to protest the policies of its director, and sunk a shark-like Saddam Hussein inside an aquarium. Inside are also a **Ticketpro box office** (with all available tickets, daily 9:30–18:00) and a lavish 1930s Prague cinema (under the upside-down horse, shows artsy films in Czech with English subtitles, or vice versa, 110 Kč).

Directly across busy Vodičkova street (with a handy tram stop) is the Světozor mall. Inside, you'll find the **World of Fruit Bar Světozor;** it's every local's favorite ice-cream joint. True to its name, the bar tops its ice cream with every variety of fruit. They sell cakes and milkshakes, too. Ask at the counter for an English menu.

• *Farther down the mall on the left is the entrance to the peaceful...*

Franciscan Garden (Františkánská Zahrada)

Its white benches and spreading rosebushes are a universe away from the fast beat of the city, which throbs behind the buildings that surround the garden.

Back on Wenceslas Square, if you're in the mood for a mellow hippie teahouse, consider a break at the recommended **Dobrá Čajovna** ("Good Teahouse") near the bottom of the square (#14—see "Eating," later in this chapter). Or, if you'd like an old-time wine bar, pop into the plain **Šenk Vrbovec** (nearby at #10); it comes with a whiff of the communist days, embracing the faintest bits of genteel culture from an age when refinement was sacrificed for the good of the working class. They serve traditional drinks, Czech keg wine, Moravian wines (listed on blackboard outside), *becherovka* (the 13-herb liqueur), and—only in autumn—*burčák* (this young wine tastes like grape juice turned halfway into wine).

The bottom of Wenceslas Square is called **Můstek,** which means "Bridge"; a bridge used to cross a moat here, allowing entrance into the Old Town (you can still see the original Old Town entrance down in the Metro station).

• *Running to the right from the bottom of Wenceslas Square is the street called Na Příkopě.*

Na Příkopě: Art Nouveau Prague

Meaning "On the Moat," this busy boulevard follows the line of the Old Town wall, leading to one of the wall's former gates, the Powder Tower. Along the way, it passes the Museum of Communism and a couple of Art Nouveau sights (all described later). City tour buses (details under "Tours," earlier in this chapter) leave from along this street, which offers plenty of shopping temptations (such as these malls: Slovanský Dům at Na Příkopě 22, and Černá Růže at Na Příkopě 12, next door to Mosers, which has a crystal showroom upstairs).

Stroll up Na Příkopě to take in two of Prague's best Art Nouveau sights: the Mucha Museum and the Municipal House. The first is on the street called Panská (turn right up the first street you reach as you walk up Na Příkopě from Wenceslas Square); the second is two blocks farther up Na Příkopě, next to the big, Gothic Powder Tower.

▲▲**Mucha Museum**—This is one of Europe's most enjoyable little museums. I find the art of Alfons Mucha (MOO-kah, 1860–1939) insistently likeable. See the crucifixion scene he painted as an eight-year-old boy. Read how this popular Czech artist's posters, filled with Czech symbols and expressing his people's ideals and aspirations, were patriotic banners that aroused the national spirit. And check out the photographs of his models. With the help of an abundant supply of slinky models, Mucha was a founding father of the Art Nouveau movement. Partly overseen by Mucha's grandson, the museum is two blocks off Wenceslas Square and wonderfully displayed on one comfortable floor (120 Kč, daily 10:00–18:00, well-described in English, Panská 7, tel. 224-233-355, www.mucha.cz). The included 30-minute video is definitely worthwhile (in English, generally at :15 and :45 past the hour—ask for the starting time); it describes the main project of Mucha's life—the *Slav Epic,* currently on display in Moravský Krumlov, a small Czech town to the east.

• *Coming back to Na Příkopě and continuing toward the Powder Tower, notice the Neo-Renaissance* **UniCredit Bank** *(formerly Živnostenská Banka, Prague's oldest banking institution) building on the corner of Nekázanka. It houses a modern bank with classy circa-1900 ambience (enter and peek into the main hall upstairs). At the end of Na Příkopě, you'll arrive at the...*

▲▲**Municipal House (Obecní Dům)**—The Municipal House is the "pearl of Czech Art Nouveau." Financed by cultural and artistic leaders, it was built (1905–1911) as a ceremonial palace to reinforce the self-awareness of the Czech nation. It features Prague's largest concert hall, a recommended Art Nouveau café (Kavárna Obecní Dům, see page 264), and two other restaurants. Pop in and wander around the lobby of the concert hall. Walk through to the ticket office on the ground floor. For the best look, including impressive halls and murals you won't see otherwise, take one of the regular hour-long **tours** (open daily 10:00–18:00; tours—150 Kč; generally at 10:15, 12:00, 14:00, and 16:00; in English 2/day, buy ticket from ground-floor shop where tour departs; tel. 222-002-101).

Standing in front of the Municipal House, you can survey four different styles of architecture. First, enjoy the colorful facade of the Municipal House itself—a mixture of Neo-Baroque and Art Nouveau. Featuring a goddess-like Praha presiding over a land of peace and high culture, the *Homage to Prague* mosaic on the building's striking facade stoked cultural pride and nationalist sentiment. Across the street, the classical fixer-upper from 1815 was the customs house, which has recently been turned into a giant stage for Broadway-style musicals. The stark national bank building (Česká Národní Banka) is textbook Functionalism from the 1930s. Farther away, across the square, former Neo-Romanesque barracks have been transformed into central Prague's biggest shopping mall and underground parking lot.

Powder Tower: The big, black Powder Tower (not worth touring inside) was the Gothic gate of the town wall, built to house the city's gunpowder. The decoration on the tower, portraying Czech kings, is the best 15th-century sculpture in town. If you go through the tower, you'll reach Celetná street, which leads past a few sights to the Old Town Square (see page 205).

Národní Třída: Communist Prague

From Můstek at the bottom of Wenceslas Square, you can head west on Národní Třída (in the opposite direction from Na Příkopě and the Art Nouveau sights) for an interesting stroll through urban Prague to the National Theatre and the Vltava River. But first, consider dropping into the Museum of Communism, a few steps down Na Příkopě (on the right).

▲▲**Museum of Communism**—This museum traces the story of communism in Prague: the origins, dream, reality, and nightmare; the cult of personality; and finally, the Velvet Revolution. Along the way, it gives a fascinating review of the Czech Republic's 40-year stint with Soviet economics, "in all its dreariness and puffed-up glory." You'll find propaganda posters, busts of communist All-Stars (Marx, Lenin, Stalin), and a photograph of the massive stone Stalin that overlooked Prague until 1962. Slices of communist life are re-created here, from a bland store counter to a typical classroom (with textbooks using Russia's Cyrillic alphabet—no longer studied—and a poem on the chalkboard that extols the virtues of the tractor). Don't miss the Jan Palach exhibit and the 20-minute video (plays continuously, English subtitles) that shows how the Czech people chafed under the big Red yoke from the 1950s through 1989 (180 Kč, daily 9:00–21:00, Na Příkopě 10, above a McDonald's and next to a casino—Lenin is turning over in his grave, tel. 224-212-966, www.muzeumkomunismu.cz).

• *Now head for the river (with your back to Wenceslas Square, go left down 28 Října to Národní Třída). Along the way, Národní Třída has a story to tell.*

Národní Třída and the Velvet Revolution—Národní Třída (National Street) is where you feel the pulse of the modern city. The street, which connects Wenceslas Square with the National Theatre and the river, is a busy thoroughfare running through the heart of urban Prague. In 1989, this unassuming boulevard played host to the first salvo of a Velvet Revolution that would topple the communist regime.

Make your way down Národní Třída until you hit the tram tracks (just beyond the Tesco department store). On the left, look for the photo of Bill Clinton playing saxophone, with Václav Havel on the side (this is the entrance to Reduta, Prague's best jazz club; next door are two recommended eateries, Café Louvre and Le Patio—see "Eating," later in this chapter). Just beyond that, you'll come to a short corridor with white arches. Inside this arcade is a simple memorial to the hundreds of students injured here by the police on November 17, 1989.

Along the Vltava River

I've listed these sights from north to south, beginning at the grand, Neo-Renaissance National Theatre, which is five blocks south of Charles Bridge and stands along the riverbank at the end of Národní Třída.

National Theatre (Národní Divadlo)—Opened in 1883 with Smetana's opera *Libuše,* this theater was the first truly Czech venue in Prague. From the very start, it was nicknamed the "Cradle of Czech Culture." The building is a key symbol of the Czech national revival that began in the late 18th century. In 1800, "Prag" was predominantly German. The Industrial Revolution brought Czechs from the countryside into the city, their new urban identity defined by patriotic teachers and priests. By 1883, most of the city spoke Czech, and the opening of this theater represented the birth of the modern Czech nation. It remains an important national icon: The state annually pours more subsidies into this theater than into all of Czech film production. It's the most beautiful venue in town for opera and ballet, often with world-class singers (described under "Entertainment," later in this chapter).

Next door (just inland, on Národní Třída) is the boxy, glassy facade of the **Nová Scéna.** This "New National Theatre" building, dating from 1983 (the 100th anniversary of the original National Theatre building), reflects the bold and stark communist aesthetic.

Across the street from the National Theatre is the former haunt of Prague's intelligentsia, **Grand Café Slavia,** a Viennese-style coffeehouse that is fine for a meal or drink with a view of the river (see "Eating," later in this chapter).

• *Just south of the National Theatre in the Vltava, you'll find...*

Prague's Islands—From the National Theatre, the Legions' Bridge (Most Legií) leads across the island called **Střelecký Ostrov.** Covered with chestnut trees, this island boasts Prague's best beach (on the sandy tip that points north to Charles Bridge). You might see a fisherman pulling out trout from a river that's now much cleaner than it used to be. Bring a swimsuit and take a dip just a stone's throw from Europe's most beloved bridge. In summer, the island hosts open-air movies (most in English or with English subtitles, nightly mid-July–early Sept at about 21:00, www.strelak.cz).

In the mood for boating instead of swimming? On the next island up, **Slovanský Ostrov,** you can rent a boat (40 Kč/hr for rowboats, 60 Kč/hr for paddleboats, bring a picture ID as deposit). A lazy hour paddling around Střelecký Ostrov—or just floating sleepily in the middle of the river surrounded by this great city's architectural splendor—is a delightful experience on a sunny day. It's cheap, easy fun (and it's good for you).

• *A 10-minute walk (or one stop on tram #17) from the National Theatre, beyond the islands, is Jirásek Bridge (Jiráskův Most), where you'll find the...*

Dancing House (Tančící Dům)—If ever a building could get your toes tapping, it would be this one, nicknamed "Fred and Ginger" by American architecture buffs. This metallic samba is the work of Frank Gehry (who designed the equally striking Guggenheim Museum in Bilbao, Spain, and Seattle's Experience Music Project). Eight-legged Ginger's wispy dress and Fred's metal mesh head are easy to spot. The building's top-floor restaurant, La Perle de Prague, is a fine place for a fancy French meal (VIPs often eat and drink here, reservation needed even to get into the elevator, tel. 221-984-160).

The Little Quarter (Malá Strana)

This charming neighborhood, huddled under the castle on the west bank of the river, is low on blockbuster sights but high on ambience. The most enjoyable approach from the Old Town is across Charles Bridge. From the end of the bridge (TI in tower), Mostecká street leads two blocks up to the Little Quarter Square (Malostranské Náměstí) and the huge Church of St. Nicholas. But before you head up there, consider a detour to Kampa Island (all described in this chapter).

Between Charles Bridge and Little Quarter Square
Kampa Island

One hundred yards before the castle end of the Charles Bridge, stairs on the left lead down to the main square of Kampa Island (mostly created from the rubble of the Little Quarter, which was destroyed in a 1540 fire). The island features relaxing pubs, a breezy park, hippies, lovers, a fine contemporary art gallery, and river access. From the main square, Hroznová lane (on the right) leads to a bridge. Behind the old mill wheel, notice the high-water marks from the flood of 2002. The water wheel is the last survivor of many that once lined the canal here. Each mill once had its own protective water spirit *(vodník)*. Today, only one wheel—and one spirit (Mr. Kabourek)—remains.

• *Fifty yards beyond the bridge (on the right, under the trees) is the...*

Lennon Wall (Lennonova Zeď)

While Lenin's ideas hung like a water-soaked trench coat upon the Czech people, rock singer John Lennon's ideas gave many locals hope and a vision. When Lennon was killed in 1980, a large wall was spontaneously covered with memorial graffiti. Night after night, the police would paint over the "All You Need Is Love" and "Imagine" graffiti. And day after day, it would reappear. Until independence came in 1989, travelers, freedom-lovers, and local hippies gathered here. Silly as it might seem, this wall is remembered as a place that gave hope to locals craving freedom. Even today, while the tension and danger associated with this wall is gone, people come here to imagine. *"John žije"* is Czech for "John lives." In the left-hand corner of the wall, a small gate leads to a quiet courtyard with a recommended outdoor café dedicated to John and George.

• *From here, you can continue up to the Little Quarter Square.*

On or near Little Quarter Square

The focal point of this neighborhood, the Little Quarter Square (Malostranské Náměstí) is dominated by the huge Church of St. Nicholas. Note that there's a handy Via Musica ticket office across from the church.

Church of St. Nicholas (Kostel Sv. Mikuláše)—When the Jesuits came to Prague, they found the perfect piece of real estate for their church and its associated school—right on Little Quarter Square. The church (built 1703–1760) is the best example of High Baroque in town. It's giddy with curves and illusions. The altar features a lavish gold-plated Nicholas, flanked by the two top Jesuits: the founder, St. Ignatius Loyola, and his missionary follower, St. Francis Xavier. Climb up the **gallery** through the staircase in the left transept for a close-up look at a collection of large canvases and illusionary frescoes by Karel Škréta, the greatest Czech Baroque painter. Notice that at first glance, the canvases are utterly dark. But as sunbeams shine through the window, various parts of the painting brighten up. Like a looking-glass, the image reflects the light, creating a play of light and darkness. This painting technique reflects a central Baroque belief: The world is full of darkness, and the only hope that makes it come alive comes from God. The church walls seem to nearly fuse with the sky, suggesting that happenings on earth are closely connected to heaven. Find St. Nick with his bishop's miter in the center of the ceiling, on his

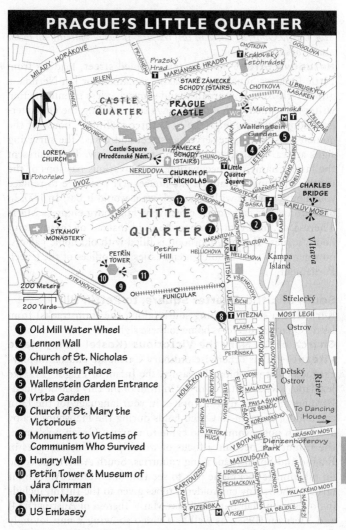

PRAGUE'S LITTLE QUARTER

1. Old Mill Water Wheel
2. Lennon Wall
3. Church of St. Nicholas
4. Wallenstein Palace
5. Wallenstein Garden Entrance
6. Vrtba Garden
7. Church of St. Mary the Victorious
8. Monument to Victims of Communism Who Survived
9. Hungry Wall
10. Petřín Tower & Museum of Jára Cimrman
11. Mirror Maze
12. US Embassy

way to heaven (60 Kč, church open daily 9:00–17:00, opens at 8:30 for prayer).

Tower Climb: For a good look at the city and the church's 250-foot dome, climb 215 steps up the bell tower (50 Kč, April–Oct daily 10:00–18:00, closed Nov–March, tower entrance is outside the right transept).

Concerts: The church is also an evening concert venue; tickets are generally on sale at the door (450 Kč, generally nightly except Tue at 18:00, www.psalterium.cz).

• *From here, you can hike 10 minutes uphill to the castle (and five more minutes to the Strahov Monastery). For information on these sights, see "The Castle Quarter," later in this chapter. If you're walking up to the castle, consider going via...*

Nerudova Street—This steep, cobbled street, leading from Little Quarter Square to the castle, is named for Jan Neruda, a gifted 19th-century journalist (and somewhat less talented fiction writer). It's lined with old buildings still sporting the character-istic doorway signs (e.g., the lion, three violinists, house of the golden suns) that once served as street addresses. The surviving signs are carefully restored and protected by law. They represent the family name, the occupation, or the various passions of the people who once inhabited the houses. (If you were to replace your house number with a symbol, what would it be?) In 1777, in order to collect taxes more effectively, Habsburg empress Maria Theresa decreed that numbers be used instead of these quaint house names. This neighborhood is filled with old noble palaces, now generally used as foreign embassies and offices of the Czech Parliament.

South of Little Quarter Square, to Petřín Hill

Karmelitská street, leading south (along the tram tracks) from Little Quarter Square, is home to these sights.

Church of St. Mary the Victorious (Kostel Panny Marie Vítězné)—This otherwise ordinary Carmelite church displays Prague's most worshiped treasure, the Infant of Prague (Pražské Jezulátko). Kneel at the banister in front of the tiny lost-in-gilded-Baroque altar, and find the prayer in your language (of the 13 in the folder). Brought to Czech lands during the Habsburg era by a Spanish noblewoman who came to marry a Czech nobleman, the Infant has become a focus of worship and miracle tales in Prague and Spanish-speaking countries. South Americans come on pilgrimage to Prague just to see this one statue. An exhibit upstairs shows tiny embroidered robes given to the Infant, includ-ing ones from Habsburg Empress Maria Theresa of Austria (1754) and Vietnam (1958), as well as a video showing a nun lovingly dressing the doll-like sculpture (free, Mon–Sat 9:30–17:30, Sun 13:00–17:00, English-language Mass Sun at 12:00, Karmelitská 9, www.pragjesu.com).

• *Continue a few more blocks down Karmelitská to the south end of the Little Quarter (where the street is called Újezd, roughly across the Legions' Bridge from the National Theatre). Here you find yourself at the base of...*

Petřín Hill—This hill, topped by a replica of the Eiffel Tower, features several unusual sights.

The figures walking down the steps in the hillside make up the **Monument to Victims of Communism Who Survived.** The monument's figures are gradually atrophied by the totalitarian regime. They do not die, but slowly disappear, one limb at a time. The statistics say it all: In Czechoslovakia alone, 205,486 people were imprisoned, 248 were executed, 4,500 died in prison, 327 were shot attempting to cross the border, and 170,938 left the country. To the left of the monument is the **Hungry Wall,** Charles IV's 14th-century equivalent of FDR's work-for-food projects. On the right (50 yards away) is the base of a handy **funicular**—hop on to reach Petřín Tower (uses 20-Kč tram/Metro ticket, runs daily, every 10–15 min from 8:00–22:00).

The summit of Petřín Hill is considered the best place in Prague to take your date for a romantic city view. Built for an exhibition in 1891, the 200-foot-tall **Petřín Tower** is a fifth the height of its Parisian big brother, which was built two years earlier. But, thanks to this hill, the top of the tower sits at the same elevation as the real Eiffel Tower. Climbing the 400 steps rewards you with amazing views over the city. Local wives drag their men to Petřín Hill each May Day to reaffirm their love with a kiss under a blooming sour-cherry tree.

In the tower's basement is the funniest sight in Prague, the **Museum of Jára Cimrman, Genius Who Did Not Become Famous.** The museum traces the (fictional) life of the greatest Czech who never lived, including pictures and English descriptions of the thinker's overlooked inventions (50 Kč includes tower and Cimrman museum, daily 10:00–22:00).

The **mirror maze** next door is nothing special, but fun to quickly wander through since you're already here (50 Kč, daily 10:00–22:00).

The Castle Quarter (Hradčany)

Looming above Prague, dominating its skyline, is the Castle Quarter. Prague Castle and its surrounding sights are packed with Czech history, as well as with tourists. In addition to the castle itself, I enjoy visiting the nearby Strahov Monastery—which has a fascinating old library and beautiful views over all of Prague.

Castle Square (Hradčanské Náměstí)—right in front of the castle gates—is at the center of this neighborhood. Stretching along the promontory away from the castle is a regal neighborhood that ends at the Strahov Monastery. Above the castle are the Royal Gardens, and below the castle are more gardens and lanes leading down to the Little Quarter.

Getting to Prague Castle

If you're not up for a hike, the tram offers a sweat-free ride up to the castle. Taxis are expensive, as they have to go the long way around (200 Kč).

PRAGUE

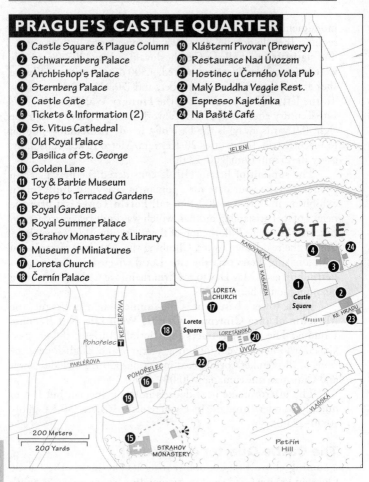

PRAGUE'S CASTLE QUARTER

1. Castle Square & Plague Column
2. Schwarzenberg Palace
3. Archbishop's Palace
4. Sternberg Palace
5. Castle Gate
6. Tickets & Information (2)
7. St. Vitus Cathedral
8. Old Royal Palace
9. Basilica of St. George
10. Golden Lane
11. Toy & Barbie Museum
12. Steps to Terraced Gardens
13. Royal Gardens
14. Royal Summer Palace
15. Strahov Monastery & Library
16. Museum of Miniatures
17. Loreta Church
18. Černín Palace
19. Klášterní Pivovar (Brewery)
20. Restaurace Nad Úvozem
21. Hostinec u Černého Vola Pub
22. Malý Buddha Veggie Rest.
23. Espresso Kajetánka
24. Na Baště Café

By Foot: Begin in the Little Quarter, just across Charles Bridge from the Old Town. Hikers can follow the main cobbled road (Mostecká) from Charles Bridge to Little Quarter Square, marked by the huge, green-domed Church of St. Nicholas. (The nearest Metro stop is Malostranská, from which Valdštejnská street leads down to Little Quarter Square.) From Little Quarter Square, hike uphill along Nerudova street (described on page 230). After about 10 minutes, a steep lane on the right leads to the castle. (If you continue straight, Nerudova becomes Úvoz and climbs to the Strahov Monastery.)

By Tram: Tram #22 takes you up to the castle. While you can catch the tram in various places, these three stops are particularly convenient: at the Národní Třída Metro stop (between Wenceslas Square and the National Theatre in the New Town); in front of the

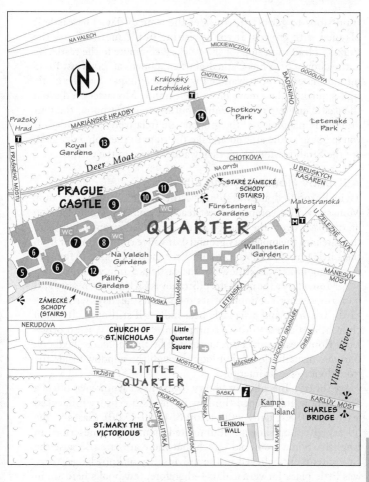

National Theatre (Národní Divadlo, on the riverbank in the New Town); and at Malostranská (the Metro stop in the Little Quarter). After rattling up the hill, these trams make three stops near the castle: Get off at **Královský Letohrádek** for the scenic approach to the castle (through the Royal Gardens); or stay on one more stop to get off at **Pražský Hrad** (most direct but least interesting—simply walk along U Prašného Mostu over the bridge into the castle); or go yet two more stops to **Pohořelec** to visit the Strahov Monastery before hiking down to the castle. To get to the monastery from this tram stop, follow the tram tracks uphill for 50 yards, enter the fancy gate on the left near the tall red-brick wall, and you'll see the twin spires of the monastery. The library entrance is in front of the church on the right.

Tram Tips: When you're choosing which of the castle's three tram stops to get off at, consider the time of day. The castle is plagued with crowds. If you're visiting in the morning, use the Pražský Hrad tram stop for the quickest commute to the castle. Be at the door of St. Vitus Cathedral when it opens at 9:00 (just 10–15 minutes later, it'll be swamped with tour groups). See the castle sights quickly, then move on to the Strahov Monastery. I'd avoid the castle entirely mid-morning, but by mid-afternoon, the tour groups are napping and the grounds are (relatively) uncrowded. If you're going in the afternoon, take the tram to the Pohořelec stop, see the Strahov Monastery, then wander down to the castle.

▲Strahov Monastery and Library

Twin Baroque domes high above the castle mark the Strahov Monastery. This complex is best reached from the Pohořelec stop on tram #22 (from the stop, go up the red-railed ramp and through the gate into the monastery grounds). If you're coming on foot from the Little Quarter, allow 15 minutes for the uphill hike. After seeing the monastery, hike down to the castle (a 5-min walk).

Monastery: The monastery (Strahovský Klášter Premonstrátů) had a booming economy of its own in its heyday, with vineyards, brewery, and a sizeable beer hall—all still open. Its main church, dedicated to the Assumption of St. Mary, is an originally Romanesque structure decorated by the monks in textbook Baroque (usually closed, but look through the window inside the front door to see its interior).

Library: The adjacent library (Strahovská Knihovna) offers a peek at how enlightened thinkers in the 18th century influenced learning (80 Kč, daily 9:00–12:00 & 13:00–17:00). Cases in the library gift shop show off illuminated manuscripts (described in English). Some are in old Czech, but these are rare. Because the Enlightenment believed in the universality of knowledge, there was little place for vernaculars—therefore, few books here are in the Czech language. Two rooms (seen only from the door) are filled with 10th- to 17th-century books, shelved under elaborately painted ceilings. The theme of the first and bigger hall is philosophy, with the history of man's pursuit of knowledge painted on the ceiling. The other hall focuses on theology. Notice the gilded locked case containing the *libri prohibiti* (prohibited books) at the end of the room. Only the abbot had the key, and you had to have his blessing to read these books—by writers such as Nicolas Copernicus and Jan Hus, and even including the French encyclopedia. As the Age of Enlightenment began to take hold in Europe at the end of the 18th century, monasteries still controlled the books. The hallway connecting these two library rooms was filled with cases illustrating the new practical approach to natural sciences. Find the dried-up elephant trunks, baby dodo bird (which became extinct in the 17th century), and one of the earliest models of an electricity generator.

Nearby Views: Just downhill from the monastery, past the venerable linden trees (a symbol of the Czech people) and through the gate, the views from the **monastery garden** are among the best in Prague. From the public perch below the tables, you can see St. Vitus Cathedral (the heart of the castle complex), the green dome of the Church of St. Nicholas (marking the center of the Little Quarter), the two dark towers fortifying both ends of Charles Bridge, and the fanciful black spires of the Týn Church (marking the Old Town Square). On the horizon is the modern **Žižkov TV and radio tower** (conveniently marking the liveliest nightlife zone in town). Begun in the 1980s, it was partly meant to jam Radio Free Europe's broadcast from Munich. By the time it was finished, communism was dead, and Radio Free Europe's headquarters had actually moved to Prague.

To reach the castle from Strahov Monastery, take Loretánská (the upper road, passing Loreta Square—see below); this is a more interesting route than the lower road, Úvoz, which takes you steeply downhill, below Castle Square (see Prague's Castle Quarter map in this section).

Or, for one more little sight, consider visiting the Museum of Miniatures. From the monastery garden viewpoint, backtrack through the gate to the big linden trees, and leave through a passage on your right. At the door is the miniscule...

Museum of Miniatures: You'll see 40 teeny exhibits, each under a microscope, crafted by an artist from St. Petersburg. Yes, you could fit the entire museum in a carry-on-size suitcase, but good things sometimes come in very, very small packages—it's fascinating to see minutiae such as a padlock on the leg of an ant. An English flier explains it all (entry-50 Kč, kids-20 Kč, daily 9:00–17:00).

On Loreta Square, Between Strahov Monastery and Castle Square

From the monastery, take Loretánská street to Loreta Square (Loretánské Náměstí). As you wander this road, you'll pass several mansions and palaces, and an important pilgrimage church.

Loreta Church—This church has been a hit with pilgrims for centuries, thanks to its dazzling bell tower, peaceful yet plush cloister, sparkling treasury, and much-venerated Holy House (110 Kč, Tue–Sun 9:00–12:15 & 13:00–16:30, closed Mon).

Once inside the entry, follow the one-way clockwise route. Strolling along the cloister, notice that the ceiling is painted with the many places Mary has miraculously appeared to the faithful in Europe.

In the garden-like center of the cloister stands the ornate **Santa Casa (Holy House),** considered by some pilgrims to be part of Mary's home in Nazareth. Because many pilgrims returning from the Holy Land docked at the Italian port of Loreto, it's called the Loreta Shrine. The Santa Casa is the "little Bethlehem" of Prague. It is the traditional departure point for Czech pilgrims setting out on the long, arduous journey to Europe's most important pilgrimage site, Santiago de Compostela, in northwest Spain. Inside, on the left wall, hangs what some consider to be an original beam from the house of Mary. It's overseen by a much-venerated statue of the Black Virgin. The Santa Casa itself might seem like a bit of a letdown, but consider that you're entering the holiest spot in the country for generations of believers.

The small Baroque church behind the Santa Casa is one of the most beautiful in Prague. The decor looks rich—but the marble and gold is all fake (tap the columns). From the window in the back, you can see a stucco relief on the Santa Casa that shows angels rescuing the house from a pagan attack in Nazareth and making a special delivery to Loreto in Italy.

Continue around the cloister. In the last corner is St. Bearded Woman (Svatá Starosta). This patron saint of unhappy marriages is a woman whose family arranged for her to marry a pagan man. She prayed for an escape, sprouted a beard...and the guy said, "No way." While she managed to avoid the marriage, it angered her father, who crucified her. The many candles here are from people suffering through unhappy marriages.

Take a left just before the exit and head upstairs, following signs to the treasury—a room full of jeweled worship aids (well-described in English). The highlight here is a monstrance (Communion wafer holder) from 1699, with more than 6,000 diamonds.

Enjoy the short carillon concert at the top of the hour; from the lawn in front of the main entrance, you can see the racks of bells being clanged. (At the exit, you'll see a schedule of English-language Masses and upcoming *pout'*—pilgrimages—departing from here.)

Castle Square (Hradčanské Náměstí)

This is the central square of the Castle Quarter. Enjoy the awesome city view and the two entertaining bands that play regularly at the gate. (If the Prague Castle Orchestra is playing, say hello to friendly, mustachioed Josef, and consider getting the group's terrific CD.) A café with dramatic city views called Espresso Kajetánka hides a few steps down, immediately to the right as you face the castle (see "Eating," near the end of this chapter). From here, stairs lead into the Little Quarter.

Castle Square was a kind of medieval Pennsylvania Avenue—the king, the most powerful noblemen, and the archbishop lived here. Look uphill from the gate. The Renaissance **Schwarzenberg Palace** (on the left, with the big rectangles scratched on the wall) was where the Rožmberks "humbly" stayed when they were in town from their Český Krumlov estates. The Schwarzenberg family inherited the Krumlov estates and aristocratic prominence in Bohemia, and stayed in the palace until the 20th century. The palace now houses the National Gallery's collection of Czech Baroque paintings, displayed in recently restored rooms that also have great views of the city (150 Kč, Tue–Sun 10:00–18:00, cheaper after 16:00, closed Mon).

The archbishop still lives in the yellow Rococo **palace** across the square (with the three white goose necks in the red field—the coat of arms of Prague's archbishops).

Through the portal on the left-hand side of the palace, a lane leads to the **Sternberg Palace** (Šternberský Palác), filled with the National Gallery's skippable collection of European paintings—including minor works by Albrecht Dürer, Peter Paul Rubens, Rembrandt, and El Greco (150 Kč, Tue–Sun 10:00–18:00, closed Mon).

The black Baroque sculpture in the middle of the square is a **plague column,** erected as a token of gratitude to the saints who saved the population from the epidemic, and an integral part of the main square of many Habsburg towns.

The statue marked *TGM* honors **Tomáš Garrigue Masaryk** (1850–1937), a university prof and a pal of Woodrow Wilson. At the end of World War I, Masaryk united the Czechs and the Slovaks into one nation and became its first president.

Prague Castle (Pražský Hrad)

For more than a thousand years, Czech leaders have ruled from Prague Castle. Today, Prague's Castle is, by some measures, the biggest on earth. Four stops matter, and all are explained here: St. Vitus Cathedral, Old Royal Palace, Basilica of St. George, and the Golden Lane.

Hours: Castle sights are open daily April–Oct 9:00–17:00, Nov–March 9:00–16:00, last entry 15 minutes before closing; grounds are open daily 5:00–23:00. St. Vitus Cathedral is closed Sunday mornings for Mass. Be warned that the cathedral can be unexpectedly closed due to special services—consider calling ahead to confirm (tel. 224-373-368 or 224-372-434). If you're not interested in entering the museums, you could try a nighttime visit—the castle grounds are safe, peaceful, floodlit, and open late.

Tickets: The cathedral is free. For the other castle sights, rather than buying the comprehensive long-tour ticket (350 Kč),

I recommend getting the short-tour ticket (250 Kč, covers the Old Royal Palace, Basilica of St. George, and the Golden Lane; buy in palace, Basilica, or the ticket offices on the two castle squares). To save time, skip the packed Golden Lane during the day, and return at night for a romantic, crowd-free visit (free before 9:00 and after 18:00).

Tours: Hour-long tours in English depart from the main ticket office about three times a day, but cover only the cathedral and Old Royal Palace (100 Kč plus entry ticket, tel. 224-373-368). You can rent an **audioguide** for 200 Kč (good all day) by picking it up at the main desk in the TI, located across from the cathedral entrance—show this book for the special Rick Steves rate. The audioguide also entitles you to priority entrance into the cathedral—when the line in front of the entrance is long, walk to the exit door on the right and show the audioguide to the guard to be let in.

Crowd-Beating Tips: Huge throngs of tourists turn the castle grounds into a sea of people during peak times (9:30–12:30). St. Vitus Cathedral is the most crowded part of the castle complex. If you're visiting in the morning, be at the cathedral entrance promptly at 9:00, when the doors open. For 10 minutes, you'll have the sacred space for yourself (after about 9:15, tour guides jockeying unwieldy groups from tomb to tomb turn the church into a noisy human traffic jam). Late afternoon is least crowded.

Castle Gate and Courtyards—Begin at Castle Square. From here, survey the castle—the tip of a 1,500-foot-long series of courtyards, churches, and palaces. The guard changes on the hour (5:00–23:00), with the most ceremony and music at noon.

Walk under the fighting giants, under an arch, through the passageway, and into the courtyard. The modern green awning with the golden-winged cat (just past the ticket office) marks the offices of the Czech president, who is elected by the parliament rather than by popular vote and serves as more of a figurehead than a power broker. The current president is Václav Klaus. His consistent politics have brought him popularity from like-minded Czechs, but bitter resentment from those who see him as incapable of considering points of view other than his own. Outside the Czech Republic, Klaus is known for his unconstructive criticism of the European Union and denunciation of the campaign against global warming (the reality of which he denies).

As you walk through another passageway, you'll find yourself facing...

▲▲▲St. Vitus Cathedral (Katedrála Sv. Víta)—The Roman Catholic cathedral symbolizes the Czech spirit—it contains the tombs and relics of the most important local saints and kings, including the first three Habsburg kings.

Cathedral Facade: Before entering, check out the facade.

What's up with the guys in suits carved into the facade below the big round window? They're the architects and builders who finished the church. Started in 1344, construction was stalled by wars and plagues. But, fueled by the 19th-century rise of Czech nationalism, Prague's top church was finished in 1929 for the 1,000th anniversary of the death of St. Wenceslas. While it looks all Gothic, it's actually two distinct halves: the original 14th-century Gothic around the high altar, and the modern Neo-Gothic nave. For 400 years, a temporary wall sealed off the functional, yet unfinished, cathedral.

Mucha Stained-Glass Window: Enter through the gate on the left with the fenced-off queuing area, and find the third window on the left. This masterful 1931 Art Nouveau window is by Czech artist Alfons Mucha (if you like this, you'll love the Mucha Museum in the New Town, listed earlier in this chapter).

Notice Mucha's stirring nationalism: Methodius and Cyril, widely considered the fathers of Slavic-style Christianity, are top and center. Cyril—the monk in black holding the Bible—brought the word of God to the Slavs. They had no written language in the ninth century—so he designed the necessary alphabet (Glagolitic, which later developed into Cyrillic). Methodius, the bishop, is shown baptizing a mythic, lanky, long-haired Czech man—a reminder of how he brought Christianity to the Czech people. Scenes from the life of Cyril on the left, and scenes from the life of Methodius on the right bookend the stirring and epic Slavic scene. In the center are a kneeling boy and a prophesying elder—that's young St. Wenceslas and his grandmother, St. Ludmila. In addition to being specific historical figures, these characters are also symbolic: The old woman, with closed eyes, stands for the past and memory, while the young boy, with a penetrating stare, represents the hope and future of a nation. Notice how master designer Mucha draws your attention to these two figures through the use of colors—the dark blue on the outside gradually turns into green, then yellow, and finally the gold of the woman and the crimson of the boy in the center. In Mucha's color language, blue stands for the past, gold for the mythic, and red for the future. Besides all the meaning, Mucha's art is simply a joy to behold. (And on the bottom, the tasteful little ad for *Banka Slavie,* which paid for the work, is hardly noticeable.)

Habsburg Emperor's Tomb: Continue circulating around the apse. The big royal tomb (within the black iron fence) is of the first Habsburg emperor. It dates from 1590, when Prague was a major Habsburg city.

Relief of Prague: As you walk around the high altar, study the fascinating carved-wood relief of Prague. It depicts the victorious Habsburg armies entering the castle after the Battle of White

Mountain, while the Protestant King Frederic escapes over the Charles Bridge (before it had any statues). Carved in 1630, 10 years after the famous event occurred, the relief also gives you a peek at Prague in 1620, stretching from the Týn Church to the cathedral (half-built at that time, up to where you are now). Notice that back then, the Týn Church was Hussite, so the centerpiece of its facade is not the Virgin Mary—but a chalice, symbol of Jan Hus' ideals. The old city walls—now replaced by the main streets of the city—stand strong. The Jewish Quarter (the slummy, muddy zone along the riverside below the bridge on the left) fills land no one else wanted.

Apse: Circling around the high altar, you pass graves of bishops, including the tomb of St. Vitus (behind the chair of the bishop). The stone sarcophagi contain kings from the Přemysl dynasty (12th–14th centuries). Locals claim the gigantic, shiny tomb of St. John of Nepomuk has more than a ton of silver (for more on St. John of Nepomuk, see page 214). After the silver tomb, look up at the royal box from where the king would attend Mass in his jammies (an elevated corridor connected his private apartment with his own altar-side box pew).

Look for the finely carved wood panel that gives a Counter-Reformation spin on the Wars of Religion. It shows the "barbaric" Protestant nobles destroying the Catholic icons in the cathedral after their short-lived victory.

Wenceslas Chapel: A fancy roped-off chapel (right transept) houses the tomb of St. Wenceslas, surrounded by precious 14th-century murals showing scenes of his life, and a locked door leading to the crown jewels. The Czech kings used to be crowned right here in front of the coffin, draped in red. The chapel is roped off because the wallpaper is encrusted with precious and semiprecious stones. (Lead us not into temptation.) You can view the chapel from either door (if the door facing the nave is crowded, duck around to the left to find a door that is most likely open).

Spire: You can climb 287 steps up the spire for one of the best views of the whole city (April–Oct daily 9:00–17:00 except Sun morning, last entry 45 minutes before closing, Nov–March closes at 16:00).

Back Outside the Cathedral: Leaving the cathedral, turn left (past the public WC). The **obelisk** was erected in 1928—a single piece of granite celebrating the 10th anniversary of the establishment of Czechoslovakia and commemorating the soldiers who fought for its independence. It was originally much taller, but broke in transit—an inauspicious start for a nation destined to last only 70 years. Up in the fat, green tower of the cathedral is the Czech Republic's biggest bell, nicknamed "Zikmund." In June of 2002, it cracked—and two months later, the worst flood in recorded history hit the city—which the locals saw as a sign. As a nation sandwiched between great powers, Czechs are deeply superstitious when it comes to the tides of history. Often feeling unable to influence the course of their own destiny, they helplessly look at events as we might look at the weather and other natural phenomena—trying to figure out what fate has in store for them next.

Find the 14th-century **mosaic** of the Last Judgment outside on the right transept. It was commissioned in the Italian style by King Charles IV, who was modern, cosmopolitan, and ahead of his time. Jesus oversees the action, as some go to heaven and some go to hell. The Czech king and queen kneel directly below Jesus and the six patron saints. On coronation day, they would walk under this arch, which would remind them (and their subjects) that even those holding great power are not above God's judgment. The royal crown and national jewels are kept in a chamber (see the grilled windows) above this entryway, which was the cathedral's main entry for centuries while the church remained uncompleted.

Across the square and 20 yards to the right, a door leads into the Old Royal Palace (in the lobby, there's a WC with a window shared by the men's and women's sections—meet your partner to enjoy the view).

Old Royal Palace (Starý Královský Palác)—Starting in the 12th century, this was the seat of the Bohemian princes. While extensively rebuilt, the **large hall** is late Gothic, designed as a multipurpose hall for the old nobility. It's big enough for jousts—even the staircase was designed to let a mounted soldier gallop in. It was filled with market stalls, giving nobles a chance to shop without actually going into town. In the 1400s, the nobility met here to elect their king. The tradition survived until modern times, as the parliament crowded into this room until the late 1990s to elect the Czechoslovak (and later Czech Republic) president. (The last three elections happened in another, far more lavish hall in the castle.) Look up at the flower-shaped, vaulted ceiling.

On your immediate right, enter the two small Renaissance rooms known as the **"Czech Office."** From these rooms (empty today except for their 17th-century porcelain heaters), two governors used to oversee the Czech lands for the Habsburgs in Vienna. In 1618, angry Czech Protestant nobles poured into these rooms and threw the two Catholic governors out of the window. An old law actually permits defenestration—throwing people (usually bad politicians) out of windows when necessary. Old prints on the wall show the second of Prague's many defenestrations. The two governors landed—fittingly—in a pile of horse manure. Even though they suffered only broken arms and bruised egos, this event kicked off the huge and lengthy Thirty Years' War.

Look down on the chapel from the end, and go out on the balcony for a fine Prague view. Is that Paris' Eiffel Tower in the distance? No, it's Petřín Tower—a fine place for a relaxing day at the park, offering sweeping views over Prague (described earlier in this chapter).

As you exit through the side door, pause at the door to consider the subtle yet racy little Renaissance knocker. Go ahead—play with it for a little sex in the palace (be gentle).

Across from the palace exit is the...

Basilica and Convent of St. George (Bazilika Sv. Jiří)—Step into the beautiful-in-its-simplicity Basilica of St. George to see Prague's best-preserved Romanesque church. Notice the characteristic double windows on the gallery, as well as the walls made of limestone (the rock that Prague rests on). In those early years, the building techniques were not yet advanced, and the ceiling is made of wood, rather than arched with stone. St. Wenceslas' grandmother, St. Ludmila, who established this first Bohemian convent, was reburied here in 973. Look for Gothic frescoes depicting this cultured woman (to the right of the altar space). The Baroque front—which dates from much later—was added on the exterior at the same time as the St. John of Nepomuk chapel (through which you exit the church). The scary-looking bones under the chapel altar are replicas—neither St. John's nor real.

Today, the **convent** next door houses the National Gallery's collection of 19th-century Czech paintings (150 Kč, Tue–Sun 10:00–18:00, closed Mon).

Continue walking downhill through the castle grounds. Turn left on the first street, which leads into the...

Golden Lane (Zlatá Ulička)—This street of old buildings, which originally housed goldsmiths, is jammed with tourists during the day and lined with overpriced gift shops. Franz Kafka lived briefly at #22. There's a deli/bistro at the top. In the morning (before 9:00) and at night (after 18:00 in summer, 17:00 in winter), the tiny street is free, empty, and romantic. Exit the lane through a corridor at the last house (#12).

Toy and Barbie Museum (Muzeum Hraček)—At the bottom of the castle complex, just after leaving the Golden Lane, a long, wooden staircase leads to two entertaining floors of old toys and dolls thoughtfully described in English. You'll see a century of teddy bears, 19th-century model train sets, and an incredible Barbie collection (the entire top floor). Find the buxom 1959 first edition, and you'll understand why these capitalistic sirens of material discontent weren't allowed here until 1989 (60 Kč, 120 Kč per family, not included in any castle tickets, daily 9:30–17:30, WC next to entrance).

After Your Castle Visit: Tourists squirt slowly through a fortified door at the bottom end of the castle. From there, you can follow the steep lane directly back to the riverbank...or turn right about halfway down the steps to visit the newly reopened **Fürstenberg Gardens,** with 3,500 flowering plants and 2,200 rose bushes (80 Kč, April–Oct daily from 10:00 until one hour before sunset). Either way you will end up at the Malostranská Metro station.

Or, as you walk out of the castle gate, you can take a hard right and stroll through the long, delightful park. Along the way, notice the modernist design of the **Na Valech Garden,** which was carried out by the court architect of the 1920s, Jože Plečnik of Slovenia.

Halfway through the long park is a viewpoint overlooking the terraced **Pálffy Gardens;** you can zigzag down through these gardens into the Little Quarter (80 Kč, April–Oct daily 10:00–18:00, closed Nov–March).

If you continue through the park all the way to Castle Square, you'll find two more options: a staircase leading down into the Little Quarter, or a cobbled street taking you to historic Nerudova street (described on page 230).

Congratulations. You've conquered the castle.

Entertainment

Prague booms with live and inexpensive theater, classical music, jazz, and pop entertainment. Everything is listed in several monthly cultural events programs (free at TIs) and in the *Prague Post* newspaper (60 Kč at newsstands).

You'll be tempted to gather fliers as you wander through the town. Don't bother. To really understand all your options (the street Mozarts are pushing only their concerts), drop by a **Via Musica** box office. There are two: One is next to Týn Church on the Old Town Square (daily 10:30–19:30, tel. 224-826-969), and the other is in the Little Quarter across from the Church of St. Nicholas (daily 10:30–18:00, tel. 257-535-568). The event schedule posted on the wall clearly shows everything that's playing today and tomorrow, including tourist concerts, Black Light Theater, and marionette shows, with photos of each venue and a map locating everything (www.viamusica.cz).

Ticketpro sells tickets for the serious concert venues and most music clubs (daily 8:00–12:00 & 12:30–16:30, Rytířská 31, between Havelská Market and Estates Theatre; also has a booth in Tourist Center at Rytířská 12, daily 9:00–20:00; English-language reservations tel. 296-329-999).

Consider buying concert tickets directly from the actual venues. You won't save money, but more of your money will go to the musicians.

PRAGUE

Locals dress up for the more "serious" concerts, opera, and ballet, but many tourists wear casual clothes—as long as you don't show up in shorts, sneakers, or flip-flops you'll be fine.

Black Light Theater

A kind of mime/modern dance variety show, Black Light Theater has no language barrier and is, for many, more entertaining than a classical concert. Unique to Prague, Black Light Theater originated in the 1960s as a playful and mystifying theater of the absurd. These days, aficionados and critical visitors lament that it's becoming a cheesy variety show, while others are uncomfortable with the sexual flavor of some acts. Still, it's an unusual theater experience that most enjoy. Shows last about 90 minutes. Avoid the first four rows, which get you so close that it ruins the illusion. Each theater has its own spin on what Black Light is supposed to be:

Ta Fantastika is traditional and poetic, with puppets and a little artistic nudity (*Aspects of Alice* nightly at 21:30, 650 Kč, reserved seating, near east end of Charles Bridge at Karlova 8, tel. 222-221-366, www.tafantastika.cz).

Image Theatre has more mime and elements of the absurd, with shows including *Clonarium*, *Fiction*, and *The Best of Image:* "It's precisely the fact that we are all so different that unites us" (shows nightly at 18:00 and 20:00, 480 Kč, open seating—arrive early to grab a good spot, just off Old Town Square at Pařížská 4, tel. 222-314-448, www.imagetheatre.cz).

Laterna Magica, in the big, glassy building next to the National Theatre, mixes Black Light techniques with film projection into a multimedia performance that draws Czech audiences (*Wonderful Circus, Rendezvous, Graffiti*, shows Mon–Sat at 20:00, no shows on Sun, 680 Kč, tel. 224-931-482, www.laterna.cz).

The other Black Light theaters advertised around town aren't as good.

Concerts

Each day, six to eight classical concerts designed for tourists fill delightful Old World halls and churches with music of the crowd-pleasing sort: Vivaldi, Best of Mozart, Most Famous Arias, and works by the famous Czech composer Antonín Dvořák. Concerts typically cost 400–1,000 Kč, start anywhere from 13:00 to 21:00, and last about an hour. Common venues are two buildings on the Little Quarter Square (the Church of St. Nicholas and the Prague Academy of Music in Liechtenstein Palace); in the Klementinum's Chapel of Mirrors; at the Old Town Square (in a different Church of St. Nicholas); and in the stunning Smetana Hall in the Municipal House. The artists vary from excellent to amateurish.

A sure bet is the jam session held every Monday at 17:00 at

St. Martin in the Wall, where some of Prague's best musicians gather to tune in and chat with each other (400 Kč, Martinská street, just north of the Tesco department store in the Old Town).

The **Prague Castle Orchestra,** one of Prague's most entertaining acts, performs regularly on Castle Square. This trio—Josef on flute, Radek on accordion, and Zdeněk on bass—plays a lively Czech mélange of Smetana, swing, old folk tunes, and 1920s cabaret songs. Look for them if you're visiting the castle and consider picking up their fun CD. They're also available for private functions (mobile 603-552-448, josekocurek@volny.cz).

Serious music-lovers should consider Prague's two top ensembles: The **Czech Philharmonic,** which performs in the classical Neo-Renaissance Rudolfinum (on Palachovo Náměstí, in the Jewish Quarter on the Old Town side of Mánes Bridge), and the **Prague Symphony Orchestra,** based in the gorgeous Art Nouveau Municipal House.

Both orchestras perform in their home venues about five nights a month from September through June. Most other nights these spaces are rented to agencies that organize tourist concerts of varying quality for double the price. Check first whether your visit coincides with either ensemble's performance.

One advantage of a tourist concert is that it allows you to experience music in one of Prague's best venues on the night of your choice. This is especially worth considering if you want to enjoy classical music in the Municipal House when the Symphony Orchestra isn't in town—but make sure your concert takes place in the building's Smetana Hall rather than in the much smaller Grégr Hall.

The Czech Philharmonic ticket office is at the Rudolfinum, on the right side under the stairs (250–1,000 Kč, open Mon–Fri 10:00–18:00, and until just before the show starts on concert days, tel. 227-059-352, www.ceskafilharmonie.cz, info@cfmail.cz).

The Prague Symphony Orchestra ticket office is on the right side of the **Municipal House,** on U Obecního Domu street opposite Hotel Paris (Mon–Fri 10:00–18:00, tel. 222-002-336, www.fok.cz, pokladna@fok.cz). A smaller selection of tickets is also available in the information office inside the Municipal House.

You'll find tickets for tourist concerts advertised and sold on the street in front of these buildings. Both the Rudolfinum and the Municipal House also act as chief venues for the Prague Spring, Prague Autumn, and Prague Proms music festivals (see "Festivals," next page).

During his frequent visits to Prague, Austrian Wolfgang Amadeus Mozart stayed with his friends in the beautiful, small, Neoclassical **Villa Bertramka,** now the Mozart Museum. Surrounded by a peaceful garden, the villa preserves the time when the Salzburg prodigy felt more appreciated in Prague than in Austria. Intimate concerts are held some afternoons and evenings, either in the garden or in the small concert hall (110 Kč, daily April–Oct 9:30–18:00, Nov–March 9:30–17:00, Mozartova 169, Praha 5; from Metro: Anděl, it's a 10-min walk—head to Hotel Mövenpick and then go up alley behind hotel; tel. 257-317-465, www.bertramka.cz).

Opera and Ballet

The **National Theatre** (Národní Divadlo, on the New Town side of Legií Bridge)—with a must-see Neo-Renaissance interior (listed on page 226)—is best for opera and ballet (shows from 19:00, 300–1,000 Kč, tel. 224-912-673, www.nationaltheatre.cz). The **Estates Theatre** (Stavovské Divadlo) is where Mozart premiered and personally directed many of his most beloved works. *Don Giovanni, The Marriage of Figaro,* and *The Magic Flute* are on the program a couple of times each month (shows from 20:00, 800–1,400 Kč, between the Old Town Square and the New Town on a square called Ovocný Trh, tel. 224-214-339, www.estatestheatre.cz). A handy ticket office for both of these theaters is in the little square (Ovocný Trh) behind the Estates Theatre, next to a pizzeria.

The **State Opera** (Státní Opera) operates on a smaller budget and is also not as architecturally rewarding as the National Theatre (shows at 19:00 or 20:00, 400–1,200 Kč, buy tickets at the theater, on 5 Května—the busy street between the Main Train Station and Wenceslas Square, see map on page 219, tel. 224-227-693, www .opera.cz).

Festivals

World-class musicians are in town during these musical festivals: **Prague Spring** (last three weeks of May, www.festival.cz), **Prague Autumn** (last half of Sept, www.pragueautumn.cz), and the newer **Prague Proms** (July–Aug, www.pragueproms.cz).

Shopping

Prague's entire Old Town seems designed to bring out the shopper in visitors. Puppets, glass, and ceramics are traditional. Shop your way from the Old Town Square up Celetná street to the Powder Tower, then along Na Příkopě to the bottom of Wenceslas Square (Václavské Náměstí). The city center is tourist-oriented—most locals do their serious shopping in the suburbs.

Celetná is lined with big stores selling all the traditional Czech goodies. Tourists wander endlessly here, mesmerized by the window displays. Celetná Crystal, about midway down the street, offers the largest selection of affordable crystal. You can have the glass safely shipped home directly from the shop.

Na Příkopě has a couple of good modern malls. The best is Slovanský Dům (daily 10:00–20:00, Na Příkopě 22), where you wander deep past a 10-screen multiplex into a world of classy restaurants and designer shops surrounding a peaceful, park-like inner courtyard. Another modern mall is Černá Růže (daily 10:00–20:00, Na Příkopě 12). Next door is Moser, which has a museum-like crystal showroom upstairs.

Národní Třída (National Street) is less touristy and lined with some inviting stores. The big Tesco department store in the middle sells anything you might need, from a pin for a broken watchband to a swimsuit (generally daily 9:00–21:00, Národní Třída 26).

Crystal: Along with shops on Celetná and Na Příkopě, a small square just off the Old Town Square, Malé Náměstí, is ringed by three major crystal retailers (generally open daily 10:00–20:00): Moser, Rott Crystal, and Crystalex (which claims to have "factory-direct" prices, at #6 on the square).

Czech Garnets: This extraordinary stone of fiery red color, with unique refractive—some claim even curative—properties, is found only in Bohemia. The characteristic design of garnet jewelry, with the jewels overwhelming the metal setting, became popular in the 1890s and remains so today. Although garnet jewelry is sold in most crystal shops, the **Turnov Granát Co-op** has the largest selection (with shops at Dlouhá 30 and Panská 1, www.granat.eu). It oversees its own mining and represents over 300 traditional goldsmiths and jewelers. If you buy garnet jewelry, make sure to ask your vendor for a certificate of authenticity—many shops sell glass imitations.

Sleeping

Peak season for hotels in Prague is late April, May, June, September, and early October. Easter and Christmas are the most crowded times, when prices are jacked up a bit. I've listed peak-time prices—if you're traveling in July or August, you'll find rates generally 15 percent lower, and from November through March, about 30 percent lower.

Room-Booking Services

Prague is awash with fancy rooms on the push list; private, small-time operators with rooms to rent in their apartments; and roving agents eager to book you a bed and earn a commission. You can save about 30 percent by showing up in Prague without a reservation and finding accommodations upon arrival. However, it can be a hassle, and you won't necessarily get your ideal choice. If you're coming in by train or car, you'll encounter booking agencies. They

Sleep Code

(25 Kč = about $1, country code: 420)
S = Single, **D** = Double/Twin, **T** = Triple, **Q** = Quad, **b** = bathroom,
s = shower only. Unless otherwise noted, credit cards are accepted, and breakfast and tax are included. Everyone listed here speaks English.

To help you sort easily through these listings, I've divided the rooms into three categories based on the price for a standard double room with bath:

$$$ Higher Priced—Most rooms 4,000 Kč or more.
$$ Moderately Priced—Most rooms between 3,000–4,000 Kč.
$ Lower Priced—Most rooms 3,000 Kč or less.

can almost always find you a reasonable room, and, if it's a private guest house, your host can even come and lead you to the place.

Athos Travel has a line on 200 properties (ranging from hostels to five-star hotels), 90 percent of which are in the historical center. To book a room, call them or use their handy website, which allows you to search for a room, based on various criteria (best to arrange in advance during peak season, can also help with last-minute booking off-season, tel. 241-440-571, fax 241-441-697, www.a-prague.com, info@a-prague.com). Readers report that Athos is aggressive with its business policies—while there's no fee to cancel well in advance, they strictly enforce penalties on cancellations within 48 hours.

AVE, at the Main Train Station (Hlavní Nádraží), is another booking service (daily 6:00–23:00). With the tracks at your back, walk down to the orange ceiling and past the "Meeting Point" (don't go downstairs)—their office is in the left corner by the exit to the rip-off taxis. Their display board shows discounted hotels, and they have a slew of hotels and small pensions available (2,000-Kč pension doubles in old center, 1,500-Kč doubles a Metro ride away). You can reserve by email, using your credit card as a deposit (tel. 251-551-011, fax 251-555-156, www.avetravel .cz, ave@avetravel.cz), or just show up at the office and request a room. Be clear on the location before you make your choice. They sell taxi vouchers for those who want the convenience of a ride from the train station's taxi stand, though they cost double the fair rate.

Lída Jánská's **Magic Praha** can help with accommodations (mobile 604-207-225, www.magicpraha.cz, magicpraha @magicpraha.cz; see "Helpful Hints," near the beginning of the chapter). Lída rents a well-located apartment with a river view near the Jewish Quarter.

Web-booking services, such as Priceline.com and Bidding fortravel.com, enable budget travelers to snare fancy rooms on the push list for half the rack rate. It's not unusual to find a room in a four-star hotel for 1,300 Kč—but keep in mind that many of these international business-class hotels are far from the city center.

Old Town Hotels and Pensions

You'll pay higher prices to stay in the Old Town, but for many travelers, the convenience is worth the expense. These places are all within a 10-minute walk of the Old Town Square.

$$$ Hotel Maximilian is a sleek, mod, 70-room place with Art Deco black design; big, plush living rooms; and all the business services and comforts you'd expect in a four-star hotel. It faces a church on a perfect little square just a short walk from the action (Db-4,500 Kč, extra bed-1,500 Kč, their "preferred rate" gives you a 14 percent discount if you lock in a reservation with no cancellation option, check online for lower rates, Internet access, Haštalská 14, tel. 225-303-111, fax 225-303-110, www.maximilianhotel.com, reservation@maximilianhotel.com).

$$$ Residence Retezova is on a central but delightfully quiet cobbled lane. Its medieval shell has been remodeled into nine elegant, plush, and spacious apartments—each one is unique. Stay away from ground-floor apartments in the summer—they tend to get stuffy (Db-3,400–5,200 Kč, large apartment-9,900 Kč for up to 6 people; free Internet access, Řetězová 9, tel. 222-221-800, fax 222-220-734, www.residenceretezova.com, info@residence retezova.com).

$$ Pension u Medvídků has 31 comfortably renovated rooms in a big, rustic, medieval shell with dark wood furniture. Upstairs, you'll find lots of beams—or, if you're not careful, they'll find you (Sb-2,300 Kč, Db-3,500 Kč, Tb-4,500 Kč, extra bed-500 Kč, "historical" rooms 10 percent more, apartment for 20 percent more, manager Vladimír promises readers of this book a 10 percent discount with cash if you book direct, Internet access, Na Perštýně 7, tel. 224-211-916, fax 224-220-930, www.umedvidku.cz, info @umedvidku.cz). The pension runs a popular beer-hall restaurant with live music most Fridays and Saturdays until 23:00—request an inside room for maximum peace.

$$ Green Garland Pension (U Zeleného Věnce), on the same quiet pedestrian street as Residence Retezova, has a warm and personal feel rare in the Old Town. Located in a thick 14th-century building with open beams, it has a blond-hardwood charm decorated with a woman's touch. Its nine rooms are clean and simply furnished (big Sb-2,900 Kč, Db-3,400 Kč, bigger Db-3,700 Kč,

HOTELS IN PRAGUE'S OLD TOWN

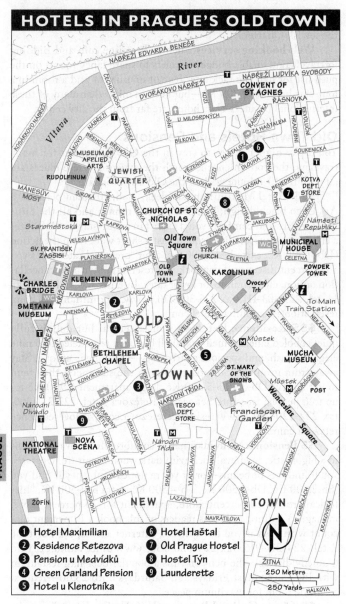

1. Hotel Maximilian
2. Residence Retezova
3. Pension u Medvídků
4. Green Garland Pension
5. Hotel u Klenotníka
6. Hotel Haštal
7. Old Prague Hostel
8. Hostel Týn
9. Launderette

Tb-4,400 Kč, 10 percent discount with cash, family suite, Internet access in lobby, Retězová 10, tel. 222-220-178, fax 224-248-791, www.uzv.cz, pension@uzv.cz).

$ Hotel u Klenotníka (At the Jeweler), with 11 modern, comfortable rooms in a plain building, is three blocks off the Old Town Square (Sb-2,000 Kč, small double-bed Db-2,750 Kč, bigger twin-bed Db-3,300 Kč, Tb-3,750 Kč, Marie and Helena promise 10 percent off when booking direct with this book, Wi-Fi, Rytířská 3, tel. 224-211-699, fax 224-221-025, www.uklenotnika.cz, info @uklenotnika.cz).

$ Hotel Haštal is next to Hotel Maximilian (listed above) on the same quiet, hidden square in the Old Town. A popular hotel back in the 1920s, it has been tactfully renovated to complement the neighborhood's vibrant circa-1900 architecture. Its 24 rooms are comfortable, but the walls are a bit thin (Sb-2,400 Kč, Db-2,800 Kč, extra bed-550 Kč, flexible online pricing based on occupancy—check for deals, air-con, Wi-Fi, Haštalská 16, tel. 222-314-335, www.hastal.com, info@hastal.com). The hotel's small restaurant is understandably popular with locals for its reasonably priced lunch specials and draft beer.

Under the Castle, in the Little Quarter

The first three listings are buried on quiet lanes deep in the Little Quarter, among cobbles, quaint restaurants, rummaging tourists, and embassy flags. The last is a 10-minute walk up the river on a quiet and stately street with none of the intense medieval cityscape of the others.

$$$ Vintage Design Hotel Sax recently remodeled its 22 rooms in a retro, meet-the-Jetsons fashion. With a fruity atrium and a distinctly modern, stark feel, this is a stylish, no-nonsense place (Sb-3,800–4,300 Kč, Db-4,000–4,500 Kč, Db suite-5,300 Kč, extra bed-1,000 Kč, 10 percent off with this book, elevator, Internet access, Jánský Vršek 3, tel. 257-531-268, fax 257-534-101, www.sax.cz, hotel@sax.cz).

$$ Dům u Velké Boty (House at the Big Boot), on a quiet square in front of the German Embassy, is the rare quintessential family hotel in Prague: homey, comfy, and extremely friendly. Charlotta, Jan, and their two sons treat every guest as a (thirsty) friend, and the wellspring of their stories never runs dry. Each of their 12 rooms is uniquely decorated, most in tasteful 19th-century Biedermeier style (tiny S-2,200 Kč, two D rooms that share a bathroom-2,650 Kč each, Db-3,400–3,900 Kč, extra bed-725 Kč, 10 percent off with advance reservation and this book, prices can be soft when slow, cash only, children up to 10 free—toys provided, free Internet access and Wi-Fi, Vlašská 30, tel. 257-532-088, www .bigboot.cz, info@bigboot.cz). While they don't include tax or

PRAGUE

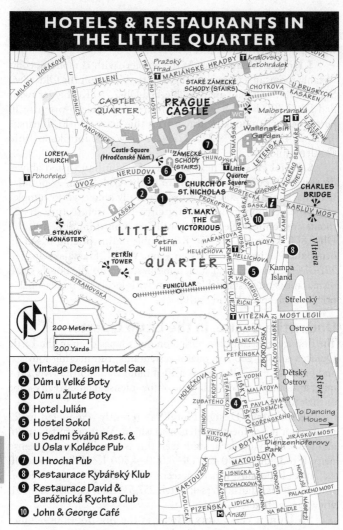

HOTELS & RESTAURANTS IN THE LITTLE QUARTER

1. Vintage Design Hotel Sax
2. Dům u Velké Boty
3. Dům u Žluté Boty
4. Hotel Julián
5. Hostel Sokol
6. U Sedmi Švábů Rest. & U Osla v Kolébce Pub
7. U Hrocha Pub
8. Restaurace Rybářský Klub
9. Restaurace David & Baráčnická Rychta Club
10. John & George Café

breakfast in their rates, I've included them in the prices for easy comparison. There's no hotel sign on the house—look for the splendid geraniums that Jan nurtures in the windows.

$$ Dům u Žluté Boty (House at the Yellow Boot) hides rustic wooden interiors behind colorful walls. Its seven rooms are each unique: Some preserve 16th-century wooden ceilings; some feel like mountain lodges; and others are a bit marred by an insensitive 1970s remodel. Top-floor rooms can get a bit stuffy during summer heat waves, although fans are provided (Sb-2,700 Kč, Db-3,300 Kč, Tb-3,800 Kč, extra bed-500 Kč, 15 percent discount with cash and this book, some thin walls, Internet access, Jánský Vršek 11, tel. 257-532-269, fax 257-534-134, www.zlutabota.cz, hotel @zlutabota.cz).

$$ Hotel Julián is an oasis of professional, predictable decency in an untouristy neighborhood. Its 32 spacious, fresh, well-furnished rooms and big, homey public spaces hide behind a noble Neoclassical facade. The staff is friendly and helpful (Sb-3,680 Kč, Db-3,980 Kč, Db suite-4,800 Kč, extra bed-900 Kč, discount for booking online, 15 percent discount off rack rate with this book, free tea and coffee in room, air-con, Wi-Fi, elevator, plush and inviting lobby, summer roof terrace has view of the Prague Castle, parking lot; Metro: Anděl, then an 8-min walk; or take tram #6, #9, #12, #20, or #58 for two stops; Elišky Peškové 11, Praha 5, reservation tel. 257-311-150, reception tel. 257-311-145, fax 257-311-149, www.julian.cz, casjul@vol.cz). Free lockers and a shower are available for those needing a place to stay after check out (for example, while waiting for an overnight train). Mike's Chauffeur Service, based here, is reliable and affordable (see "Connections—By Car with a Driver," at the end of this chapter).

Away from the Center

Moving just outside central Prague saves you money—and gets you away from the tourists and into some more workaday residential neighborhoods. The following listings (great values compared to the downtown hotels listed previously) are all within a 5- to 15-minute tram or Metro ride from the center.

Beyond Wenceslas Square

These hotels are in urban neighborhoods on the outer fringe of the New Town, beyond Wenceslas Square. But they're still within several minutes' walk of the sightseeing zone, and are well-served by trams.

$$$ Sieber Hotel, with 20 rooms, is a quality, four-star, business-class hotel in an upscale circa-1900 residential neighborhood (Vinohrady) that has recently become popular with Prague's expat community. They do a good job of being homey and welcoming (Sb-4,480 Kč, Db-4,780 Kč, extra bed-990 Kč, fourth night free, 20 percent discount with this book, 30 percent discount for last-minute reservations, air-con, elevator, Internet access, 3-min walk to Metro: Jiřího z Poděbrad, or tram #11, Slezská 55, Praha 3, tel. 224-250-025, fax 224-250-027, www.sieber.cz, reservations @sieber.cz).

$$ Hotel 16 is a sleek and modern business-class place with an intriguing Art Nouveau facade, polished cherry-wood elegance, high ceilings, and 14 fine rooms (Sb-2,800 Kč, Db-3,500 Kč, bigger Db-3,700 Kč, Tb-4,700 Kč, 10 percent discount with this book, triple-paned windows, back rooms facing the garden are quieter, air-con, elevator, Internet access, 10-min walk south of Wenceslas Square, Metro: I.P. Pavlova, Kateřinská 16, Praha 2, tel. 224-920-636, fax 224-920-626, www.hotel16.cz, hotel16 @hotel16.cz).

$ Hotel Anna offers 24 bright, simple, pastel rooms and basic service. It's a bit closer in—just 10 minutes by foot east of Wenceslas Square (Sb-2,000 Kč, Db-2,700 Kč, Tb-3,200 Kč, 10 percent discount with this book, special online offers, non-smoking rooms, elevator, Budečská 17, Praha 2, Metro: Náměstí Míru, tel. 222-513-111, fax 222-515-158, www.hotelanna.cz, sales@hotelanna .cz). They run a similar hotel (same standards and prices) nearby.

The Best Values, Farther from the Center

These accommodations are a 10- to 20-minute tram ride from the center, but once you make the trip, you'll see it's no problem—and you'll feel pretty smug saving $50 to $100 a night per double by not sleeping in the Old Town. The Šemíka and Lída are within a stone's throw of peaceful Vyšehrad Park, with a legendary castle on a cliff overlooking the Vltava River. The Adalbert is on the grounds of an ancient monastery and the Větrník is adjacent, with two of Prague's best-preserved natural areas (Star Park and Šárka) just a short walk away.

$$ Hotel Adalbert occupies an 18th-century building in the Břevnov Monastery (one of the Czech Republic's oldest monastic institutions, founded in 993). Meticulously restored after the return of the Benedictine monks in the 1990s, the monastery complex is the ultimate retreat for those who come to Prague for soul-searching or just wanting a quiet place away from the bustle. Join the monks for morning (7:00) and evening (18:00) Mass in the St. Margaret Basilica, a large and elegant Baroque church decorated with unusual simplicity. You can help yourself in the monastery fruit orchard, and eat in the atmospheric monastery pub (Klášterní Šenk). The hotel itself caters primarily to business clientele and takes ecology seriously: recycling, water conservation, and free tram tickets for guests. I prefer the first-floor rooms as some of the attic rooms—room numbers in the 200s—feel a bit cramped (Sb-2,600 Kč, Db-3,600 Kč, extra bed-1,050 Kč, ask for 10 percent Rick Steves discount when you reserve, Wi-Fi, free parking, halfway between city and airport at Markétská 1, Praha 6, tram #22 to Břevnovský Klášter; 5 min by tram beyond the castle, 20 min from Old and New Towns; tel. 220-406-170, fax 220-406-190, www .hoteladalbert.cz, info@hoteladalbert.cz).

$ Pension Větrník fills an attractive white-and-orange former 17th-century windmill in one of Prague's most popular residential areas, right next to the Břevnov Monastery and

HOTELS & RESTAURANTS IN THE NEW TOWN & BEYOND

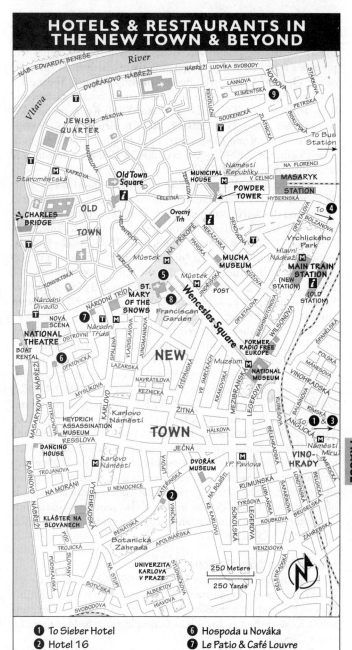

PRAGUE

1 To Sieber Hotel
2 Hotel 16
3 To Hotel Anna
4 To Hostel Elf
5 Restaurace u Pinkasů
6 Hospoda u Nováka
7 Le Patio & Café Louvre
8 Dobrá Čajovna Teahouse
9 Restaurant Červená Tabulka

midway between the airport and the city. The talkative owner, Miloš Opatrný, is a prizewinning Czech chef who once sailed the world, feeding cruise-ship passengers. On request, Miloš will prepare a feast you'll never forget. The six rooms here are the pride of the Opatrný family, who live on the upper floors. The garden has a good-hearted bear of a dog and a tennis court—rackets and balls are provided (Db-2,200 Kč, suite-3,300 Kč, extra bed-550 Kč, Internet access, U Větrníku 1, Praha 6; airport bus #179 stops near the house, tram #18 goes straight to Charles Bridge, both take 20 min; tel. 220-612-404, fax 220-513-390, www.vetrnik1722 .cz, pension@vetrnik1722.cz).

$ **Hotel u Šemíka,** named for a heroic mythical horse, offers 25 rooms in a quiet residential neighborhood just below Vyšehrad Castle and the Slavín cemetery where Dvořák, Mucha, and Čapek are buried. It's a 10-minute tram ride south of the Old Town (Sb-2,000 Kč, Db-2,650 Kč, apartment-3,350–3,700 Kč for 2–4 people, extra bed-600 Kč, ask for the "direct booking" Rick Steves 10 percent discount, Internet access; from the center, take tram #3, #17, or #21 to Výtoň, go under rail bridge, and walk 3 blocks uphill to Vratislavova 36; Praha 2, tel. 224-920-736, fax 224-911-602, www .usemika.cz, usemika@usemika.cz).

$ **Guest House Lída,** with 12 homey and spacious rooms, fills a big house in a quiet residential area farther inland, a 15-minute tram ride from the center. Jan, Jiří, and Jitka Prouza, who run the place, are a wealth of information and know how to make people feel at home (Sb-1,380 Kč, small Db-1,440 Kč, Db-1,760 Kč, Tb-2,110 Kč, Qb-2,530 Kč, cash only, family rooms, top-floor family suite with kitchenette, Internet access, parking garage-200 Kč/day, Metro: Pražského Povstání; exit Metro and turn left on Lomnického between the Metro station and big blue-glass ČSOB building, follow Lomnického for 500 yards, then turn left on Lopatecká, go uphill and ring bell at Lopatecká #26, no sign outside; Praha 4, tel. & fax 261-214-766, www.lidabb.eu, lida bb@seznam.cz). The Prouza brothers also rent four apartments across the river, an equal distance from the center (Db-1,600 Kč, Tb-1,900 Kč, Qb-2,100 Kč).

Hostels in the Center

It's tough to find a double for less than 3,000 Kč in the old center. But Prague has an abundance of fine hostels—each with a distinct personality, and each excellent in its own way for anyone wanting a 400-Kč dorm bed or an extremely simple, twin-bedded room for about 1,300 Kč.

$ **Old Prague Hostel** is a small and very friendly place with 70 beds on the second and third floors of an apartment building on a back alley near the Powder Tower. The spacious rooms were once apartment bedrooms, so it feels less institutional than most hostels. Hanging out in the comfy TV lounge/breakfast room, you'll feel like part of an international family. Older travelers would feel comfortable in this mellow place (D-1,400 Kč, bunk in 4- to 8-person room-400–500 Kč; includes breakfast, sheets, towels, lockers, and free Internet access; in summer reserve one month ahead, Benediktská 2, see map on page 250 for location, tel. 224-829-058, fax 224-829-060, www.oldpraguehostel.com, oldpraguehostel@seznam.cz).

$ Hostel Týn is hidden in a silent courtyard two blocks from the Old Town Square. Because the management is aware of its value, they don't bother being too friendly (D-1,240 Kč, T-1,410 Kč, bunk in 4- to 5-bed co-ed room-420 Kč, lockers, reserve one week ahead, Týnská 19, located on map on page 250, tel. 224-828-519, mobile 776-122-057, www.hostel-tyn.web2001.cz, backpacker@razdva.cz).

$ Hostel Elf, a 10-minute walk from the Main Train Station or one bus stop from the Florenc Metro station, is fun-loving, ramshackle, covered with noisy, self-inflicted graffiti, and the wildest of these hostels. They offer cheap, basic beds, a helpful staff, and lots of creative services—kitchen, free luggage room, free Internet access, laundry, no lockout, free tea, cheap beer, a terrace, and lockers (120 beds, D-1,100 Kč, bunk in 6- to 11-person room-320 Kč, includes sheets and breakfast, cash only, reserve four days ahead, Husitská 11, Praha 3, take bus #133 or #207 from Florenc Metro station for one stop to U Památníku, tel. 222-540-963, www.hostelelf.com, info@hostelelf.com).

$ Hostel Sokol, plain and institutional with 100 beds, is peacefully located just off park-like Kampa Island in the Tyrš House buildings (the seat of the Czech Sokol Organization). Big WWI hospital–style rooms are lined with single beds and lockers (D-900 Kč, bunk in 8- to 14-person room-350 Kč, cash only, no breakfast, easy to reserve without deposit by phone or email, open 24/7, kitchen, Nosticova 2, located on map on page 252, tel. 257-007-397, fax 257-007-340, www.sokol-cos.cz/index_en.htm, hostel@sokol-cos.cz). From the Main Train Station, ride tram #9 to Újezd. From the Holešovice station, take tram #12 to Hellichova. From either tram stop, walk 200 yards to the hostel.

Eating

A big part of Prague's charm is found in wandering aimlessly through the city's winding old quarters, marveling at the architecture, watching the people, and sniffing out fun restaurants. You can eat well here for very little money. What you'd pay for a basic meal in Vienna or Munich will get you a feast in Prague. In addition to meat-and-potatoes Czech cuisine, you'll find trendy, student-oriented bars and lots of fine ethnic eateries. For ambience, the options include traditional, dark Czech beer halls; elegant Art Nouveau dining rooms; and hip and modern cafés.

Watch out for scams. Many restaurants put more care into ripping off green tourists (and even locals) than into their cooking. Tourists are routinely served cheaper meals than what they ordered, given a menu with a "personalized" price list, charged extra for things they didn't get, or shortchanged. Speak Czech. Even saying "Hello" in Czech will get you better service. Avoid any menu without clear and explicit prices. Be careful of waiters padding the tab. Carefully examine your itemized bill and understand each line (a 10 percent service charge is sometimes added—in that case, there's no need to tip extra). Tax is always included in the price, so it shouldn't be tacked on later. Part with very large bills only if necessary, and deliberately count your change. Never let your credit card out of your sight. Make it a habit to get cash from an ATM to pay for your meals. (Credit cards can cost merchants as much as 10 percent.) Remember, there are two parallel worlds in Prague: the tourist town and the real city. Generally, if you walk two minutes away from the tourist flow, you'll find better value, atmosphere, and service.

I've listed these eating and drinking establishments by neighborhood. The most options—and highest prices—are in the Old Town. If you want a memorable splurge, see "Dining with Style," later in this section. For a light meal, consider one of Prague's many cafés (see "Cafés"). Many of the places listed here are handy for an efficient lunch, but may not offer fine evening dining. Others make less sense for lunch, but are great for a slow, drawn-out dinner. Read the descriptions to judge which is which.

Fun, Touristy Neighborhoods: Several areas are pretty and well-situated for sightseeing, but lined only with touristy restaurants. While these places are not necessarily bad values, I've listed only a few of your many options—just survey the scene in these spots and choose whatever looks best. Kampa Square, just off the Charles Bridge, feels like a small-town square. Havelská Market is surrounded by colorful little eateries, any of which give a fine perch for viewing the market scene while you munch. The massive Old Town Square is *the* place to nurse a drink or enjoy a meal while watching the tide of people, both tourists and locals, sweep back and forth. There's often some event on this main square, and its many restaurants provide tasty and relaxing vantage points.

Dining with a View: For great views, consider these options: **Restaurant u Prince Terrace** (rooftop dining above a fancy hotel, completely touristy but awesome views, recommended and described later in this section); the **Bellavista Restaurant** at Strahov Monastery; **Petřínské Terasy** and **Nebozízek** next to the funicular stop halfway up Petřín Hill; and the many overpriced but elegant places serving scenic meals along the riverbanks. For the best cheap riverside dinner, have a picnic on a paddleboat (see "Tours," near the beginning of this chapter). There's nothing like drifting down the middle of the Vltava River as the sun sets, while munching on a picnic meal and sipping a beer with your favorite travel partner.

In or near the Old Town
Characteristically Czech Places

With the inevitable closing of cheap student pubs (replaced by shops and hotels that make more money), it's getting difficult to find a truly Czech pub in the historic city center. Most Czechs no longer go to "traditional" eateries, preferring the cosmopolitan taste of the world to the mundane taste of sauerkraut. As a result, ancient institutions with "authentic" Czech ambience have become touristy—but they're still great fun, a good value, and respected by Czechs. Expect wonderfully rustic spaces, smoke, surly service, and reasonably good, inexpensive food. Understand every line on your bill.

Plzeňská Restaurace u Dvou Koček (By the Two Cats) is a typical Czech pub with cheap, no-nonsense, hearty Czech food and beer. Sandwiched between the two red-light-district streets, and now filled with tourists rather than Czechs, the restaurant somehow maintains its charm (200 Kč for three courses and beer, serving original Pilsner Urquell, piano or accordion music nightly until 23:00, under an arcade, facing a tiny square between Perlová and Skořepka streets, tel. 224-221-692).

Restaurace u Pinkasů, with a menu that reads like a 19th-century newspaper, is a Prague institution, founded in 1843. It's best in summer, when you sit in the garden behind the building, in the shade of the Gothic buttresses of the St. Mary of the Snows Church. But its waiters could win the award for the rudest service in town (daily 9:00–24:00, tucked in a courtyard near the bottom of Wenceslas Square, on the border between Old and New towns, located on map on page 255, Jungmannovo Náměstí 16, tel. 221-111-150).

Restaurace u Provaznice (By the Ropemaker's Wife) has all the Czech classics, peppered with the story of a once-upon-a-time-faithful wife. (Check the menu for details of the gory story.) It's less touristed and less expensive than the other restaurants in this area. Natives congregate here for their famously good "pig leg" with horseradish and Czech mustard (daily 11:00–24:00, a block into the Old Town from the bottom of Wenceslas Square at Provaznická 3, tel. 224-232-528).

RESTAURANTS IN THE OLD TOWN

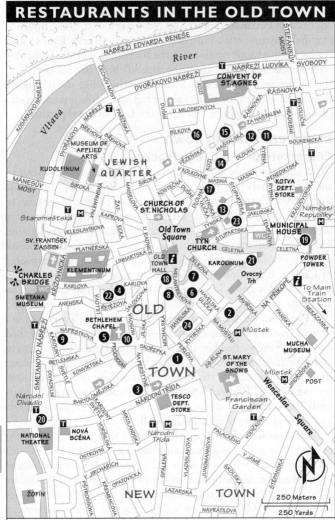

PRAGUE

1. Plzeňská Restaurace u Dvou Koček
2. Restaurace u Provaznice
3. U Medvídků Beer Hall
4. U Zlatého Tygra Pub
5. Restaurace u Betlémské Kaple
6. Česká Kuchyně Cafeteria
7. Restaurace Mlejnice
8. Country Life Vegetarian Rest.
9. Lehká Hlava Vegetarian Rest.
10. Klub Architektů
11. Dahab
12. Chez Marcel
13. Beas Indian Restaurant
14. Orange Moon
15. Molly Malone's Irish Pub
16. La Casa Blů
17. Bohemia Bagel
18. Restaurant u Prince Terrace
19. Municipal House Eateries
20. Grand Café Slavia
21. Grand Café Orient
22. Café Montmartre
23. Ebel Coffee House
24. Havelská Market

U Medvídků (By the Bear Cubs), which started out as a brewery in 1466, is now a flagship beer hall of the Czech Budweiser. The one large room is bright, noisy, touristy, and a bit smoky (daily 11:30–23:00, a block toward Wenceslas Square from Bethlehem Square at Na Perštýnì 7, tel. 224-211-916). The small beer bar next to the restaurant (daily 16:00–3:00 in the morning) is used by university students during emergencies—such as after most other pubs have closed.

U Zlatého Tygra (By the Golden Tiger) has long embodied the proverbial Czech pub, where beer turns strangers into kindred spirits, who cross the fuzzy line between memory and imagination as they tell their hilarious life stories to each other. Today, "the Tiger" is a buzzing shrine to one of its longtime regulars, the writer Bohumil Hrabal, whose fictions immortalize many of the colorful characters that once warmed the wooden benches here (daily 15:00–23:00, often jam-packed, just south of Karlova at Husova 17, tel. 222-221-111).

Hospoda u Nováka, behind the National Theatre (i.e., not so central), is emphatically Czech, with few tourists. It takes good care of its regulars (you'll see the old monthly beer tabs in a rack just inside the door). Nostalgic communist-era signs are everywhere. During that time, pubs like this were close-knit communities where regulars escaped from the depression of daily life. Today, the U Nováka is a bright and smoky hangout where you can still happily curse whatever regime you happen to live under. While the English menu lists the well-executed Czech classics, it doesn't list the cheap daily specials (daily 10:00–23:00, V Jirchářích 2, see map on page 255, tel. 224-930-639).

Restaurace u Betlémské Kaple, behind Bethlehem Chapel, is not "ye olde" Czech. It has light wooden decor, cheap lunch deals, and fish specialties that attract natives and visitors in search of a good Czech bite for Czech prices (daily 11:00–23:00, Betlémské Náměstí 2, tel. 222-221-639).

Česká Kuchyně (Czech Kitchen) is a blue-collar cafeteria serving steamy old Czech cuisine to a local clientele. It's fast, practical, cheap, and traditional as can be. There's no English inside, so—if you want apple charlotte, but not tripe soup—be sure to review the small English menu in the window outside before entering. Note the numbers of your preferred dishes, because they correspond to the Czech menu that you'll see inside. Pick up your tally sheet as you enter, grab a tray, point liberally to whatever you'd like, and keep the paper to pay as you exit. It's extremely cheap...unless you lose your paper (daily 9:00–20:00, very central, across from Havelská Market at Havelská 23, tel. 224-235-574).

Restaurace Mlejnice (The Mill) is a fun little pub strewn with farm implements and happy eaters, located just out of the tourist crush two blocks from the Old Town Square. They serve hardy traditional and modern Czech plates for 150–180 Kč. Reservations are smart in the evening (daily 11:00–24:00, between Melantrichova and Železná at Kožná 14, tel. 224-228-635).

Hip Restaurants

Country Life Vegetarian Restaurant is a bright, easy, non-smoking cafeteria with a well-displayed buffet of salads and hot veggie dishes. It's midway between the Old Town Square and the bottom of Wenceslas Square. They're serious about their vegetarianism, serving only plant-based, unprocessed, and unrefined food. Its dining area is quiet and elegantly woody for a cafeteria, with three tables and wicker chairs outside in the courtyard (Sun–Thu 9:00–20:30, Fri 9:00–17:00, closed Sat, through courtyard at Melantrichova 15/Michalská 18, tel. 224-213-366).

Lehká Hlava (Clear Head) Vegetarian Restaurant, tucked away on a cul-de-sac, has a mission to provide a "clear atmosphere for enjoying food." Sitting in an enchanted-forest setting, diners enjoy dishes from around the world. Reserve in advance for evenings (100–150-Kč plates, two-course 90-Kč daily special, no eggs, no smoke, lots of vegan dishes, daily 11:30–23:30, between Bethlehem Chapel and the river at Boršov 2, tel. 222-220-665).

Klub Architektů, next to Bethlehem Chapel, is a modern hangout in a medieval cellar that serves excellent original dishes, hearty salads, Moravian wines, and Slovak beer (daily, Betlémské Náměstí 169, tel. 224-401-214).

At **Le Patio,** on the big and busy Národní Třída, the first thing you'll notice are the many lanterns suspended from the ceiling—and the big ship moored out back (okay, just its hulking bow). Le Patio has a hip, continental feel, but for a place that also sells furniture (head straight back, and down the stairs), it definitely needs comfier dining chairs. The atmosphere is as pleasant and carefully designed as the dishes, with international fare from India, France, and points in between. There's always a serious vegetarian option available (200–350-Kč plates, daily 8:00–23:00, Národní 22, see map on page 255, tel. 224-934-375). Diners enjoy live music on Friday and Saturday nights (19:30–22:30).

Ethnic Eateries and Bars near Dlouhá Street

Dlouhá, the wide street leading away from the Old Town Square behind the Jan Hus Memorial (left of Týn Church), is lined with ethnic restaurants catering mostly to cosmopolitan locals. Within a couple of blocks, you can eat your way around the world. From Dlouhá, wander the Rámová/Haštalská area to survey a United Nations of eateries: You'll find Moroccan (**Dahab,** with some interesting hubbly-bubbly action at Dlouhá 33), French (**Chez**

Marcel at Haštalská 12 is understandably popular—with a fun-loving waitstaff), Afghan, Italian, and these five, which deserve special consideration:

Indian: **Beas** is a cheap vegetarian restaurant ruled by a Punjabi chef who concocts mild *thalis* (mixed platters in the style of the north Indian plains), and *dosas* (south Indian crêpes). Tucked away in a courtyard behind the Týn Church, this place is popular with university students (Mon–Sat 9:30–20:00, Sun 10:00–18:00, Týnská 19, mobile 608-035-727).

Thai: **Orange Moon** specializes in Thai curries, but you'll also find dishes from Myanmar (Burma) and India, served in a space delightfully decorated with artwork from Southeast Asia. This restaurant attracts a mixture of locals, expats, and tourists—as well as a mixture of wait-staff attitudes (daily 11:30–23:30, reservations recommended, Rámová 5, tel. 222-325-119).

Irish: **Molly Malone's Irish Pub,** hidden in a forgotten corner of the Jewish Quarter, may seem a strange recommendation in Prague—home of some of the world's best beer—but it has the kind of ambience that locals (and few tourists) seek out. Molly Malone's has been the expat and local favorite for Guinness ever since the Velvet Revolution enabled the Celts to return to one of their homelands. Worn wooden floors, dingy walls, and the Irish manager transport you right into the heart of blue-collar Dublin—which is, after all, a popular place for young Czechs to find jobs in the high-tech industry (Sun–Thu 11:00–1:00 in the morning, Fri–Sat 11:00–2:00 in the morning, U Obecního Dvora 4, tel. 224-818-851).

Latin American: **La Casa Blů,** with cheap lunch specials, Mexican plates, Staropramen beer, and greenish *mojitos,* is your Spanish village in Prague and one of the last student bastions in the Old Town. Painted in warm orange-and-red and guarded by creatures from Mayan mythology, La Casa Blů is packed nightly with smoke, guitar music, and a fusion of Czechs and Chileans (Mon–Sat 11:00–23:00, Sun 14:00–23:00, on the corner of Kozí and Bílkova, tel. 224-818-270).

North American: **Bohemia Bagel** is hardly authentic—exasperated Czechs insist that bagels have nothing to do with Bohemia. Owned by an American, this practical café caters mostly to youthful tourists, with good sandwiches (100–125 Kč), a little garden out back, and Internet access (1.50 Kč/min). If homesick, you'll love the menu, with everything from Philly cheesesteak to bacon and eggs (daily 7:00–24:00, Masná 2, tel. 224-812-560).

In the Jewish Quarter

These three eateries are well-located to break up a demanding tour of the Jewish Quarter—all within two blocks of each other on or near Široká (see map on page 215). Also consider the nearby ethnic eateries listed earlier.

Kolkovna, flagship of a franchise owned by Pilsner Urquell, is big and woody, yet modern, serving a fun mix of Czech and international cuisine—ribs, salads, cheese plates, and good beer (a bit overpriced but good energy, daily 11:00–24:00, across from Spanish Synagogue at V Kolkovně 8, tel. 224-819-701).

Franz Kafka Café, with a cool, dark, and woody interior strewn with historic photos of the ghetto and a few good sidewalk tables, is great for a relaxing salad, sandwich, snack, or drink (150-Kč salads, daily 10:00–21:00, one block from the cemetery at Široká 12).

Restaurace U Knihovny (By the Library), situated steps away from the City and National Libraries as well as the Pinkas Synagogue, is a favorite lunch spot for Czechs who work nearby. Their cheap daily lunch specials consist of seven imaginative variations on traditional Czech themes, the service is friendly, and the stylish red-brick interior is warm. Smoking is not permitted during lunch (daily 11:00–23:00, on the corner of Veleslavínova and Valentinská, mobile 732-835-876).

Dining with an Old Town Square View

Restaurant u Prince Terrace, in the five-star U Prince Hotel facing the Astronomical Clock, is designed for foreign tourists. A sleek elevator takes you to its rooftop, where every possible inch is used to serve good food (international with plenty of fish) from their open-air grill. The view is arguably the best in town—especially at sunset. The menu is a fun but overpriced mix, with photos that make ordering easy. Being in such a touristy spot, waiters are experts at nicking you with confusing menu charges; don't be afraid to confirm exact prices before ordering. This place is also great for just a drink at sunset or late at night (fine salads, 240–300-Kč plates, daily until 24:00, brusque staff, outdoor heaters when necessary, Staroměstské Náměstí 29, tel. 224-213-807—but no reservations possible).

Art Nouveau Splendor in the Municipal House

The Municipal House (Obecní Dům), the sumptuous Art Nouveau concert hall, has three restaurants: a café, a French restaurant, and a beer cellar (all at Náměstí Republiky 5). The dressy café, **Kavárna Obecní Dům,** is drenched in chandeliered, Art Nouveau elegance and offers the best value and experience here (light, pricey meals and drinks with great atmosphere and bad service, 250-Kč three-course special daily for lunch or dinner, open daily 7:30–23:00, live piano or jazz trio 16:00–20:00, tel. 222-002-763). The fine and formal French restaurant in the next wing oozes Mucha elegance (700–1,000-Kč meals, daily 12:00–16:00 & 18:00–23:00, tel. 222-002-777). The overpriced, touristy beer cellar is open daily 11:30–23:00.

Cafés

Dripping with history, these places are as much about the ambience as they are about the coffee. Most cafés also serve sweets and light meals.

Grand Café Slavia, across from the National Theatre (facing the Legií Bridge on Národní street), is a fixture in Prague, famous as a hangout for its literary elite. Today, it's tired and clearly past its prime, with an Art Deco interior, lousy piano entertainment, and celebrity photos on the wall. But its iconic status makes it a fun stop for a coffee—skip the food (daily 8:00–23:00, sit as near the river as possible, tel. 224-218-493). Notice the *Drinker of Absinthe* painting on the wall (and on the menu for 55 Kč)—with the iconic Czech writer struggling with reality.

Café Louvre is a longtime elegant favorite (opened in 1902) that still draws an energetic young crowd. From the big and busy Národní street, you walk upstairs into a venerable world of newspapers on sticks (including English) and waiters in vests and aprons. The back room has long been the place for billiard tables (100 Kč/hr). An English flier tells its history (200-Kč plates, 120-Kč two-course lunch offered 11:00–15:00, open daily 8:00–23:30, Národní 22, see map on page 255, tel. 224-930-949).

Grand Café Orient is just two flights up off busy Celetná street, yet a world away from the crush of tourism below. Located in the Black Madonna House, the café is upstairs from the Museum of Czech Cubism (listed on page 211) and fittingly decorated with a Cubist flair. With its stylish, circa-1910 decor toned to dark green, this space is full of air and light—and a good value as well (salads, sandwiches, great balcony seating, Mon–Fri 9:00–22:00, Sat–Sun 10:00–22:00, Ovocný Trh 19, at the corner of Celetná near the Powder Tower, tel. 224-224-240).

Café Montmartre, on a small street parallel to Karlova, combines Parisian ambience with unbeatable Czech prices. Dreamy Czech minds found their asylum here after Grand Café Slavia (listed above) and other longtime favorites either closed down or became stuck in their past. The main room is perfect for discussing art and politics, while the intimate room behind the courtyard is where you recite poetry to your date (Mon–Fri 9:00–23:00, Sat–Sun 12:00–23:00, Řetězová 7, tel. 222-221-244).

Ebel Coffee House, in the Ungelt courtyard behind the Týn Church, is the local Starbucks—priding itself on its wide assortment of fresh coffee from every coffee-growing country in the world, inviting cakes, and a colorful setting that delights the mind as much as the caffeine (daily 9:00–22:00, Týn 1, tel. 224-895-788).

John & George Café, in the courtyard on the other side of the Lennon Wall, is a secluded spot serving raspberry drinks, fresh sandwiches, and Italian coffee next to a flower garden, an English lawn, and one of the oldest trees in Prague (daily 11:00–22:00, Velkopřevorské Náměstí 4, look for small gate at left end of Lennon Wall, entrance to indoor seating area is another 20 yards to the left, see map on page 252, tel. 257-217-736).

Teahouses

Many Czech people are bohemian philosophers at heart and prefer the mellow, smoke-free environs of a teahouse to the smoky, traditional beer hall. Young Czechs are much more interested in traveling to exotic destinations like Southeast Asia, Africa, or Peru than to Western Europe, so the Oriental teahouses set their minds in vacation mode.

While there are teahouses all over town, a fine example in a handy locale is Prague's original one, established in 1991. **Dobrá Čajovna** (Good Teahouse), just a few steps off the bustle of Wenceslas Square, takes you into a very peaceful world that elevates tea to an almost religious ritual. At the desk, you'll be given an English menu and a bell. Grab a seat and study the menu, which lovingly describes each tea. The menu lists a world of tea (very fresh, prices by the small pot), "accompaniments" (such as Exotic Miscellany), and light meals "for hungry tea drinkers." When you're ready to order, ring your bell to beckon a tea monk—likely a member of the Lovers of Tea Society (Mon–Sat 10:00–21:30, Sun 14:00–21:30, near the base of Wenceslas Square, opposite McDonald's at Václavské Náměstí 14, tel. 224-231-480).

In the Little Quarter

These characteristic eateries are handy for a bite before or after your Prague Castle visit. For locations, see the map on page 252.

U Sedmi Švábů (By the Seven Roaches) is a touristy den where even the cuisine is medieval. Since America had not yet been discovered in the Middle Ages, you won't find any corn, potatoes, or tomatoes on the menu. The salty yellow things that come with the Krušovice beer are chickpeas. Carnivores thrive here: Try the skewered meats *(špíz u Sedmi Švábů),* flaming beef *(flambák),* or pork knuckle (daily 11:00–23:00, Janský Vršek 14, tel. 257-531-455).

U Osla v Kolébce (By the Donkey in the Cradle) fills a peaceful courtyard just a minute off the touristy hubbub of Nerudova. The laid-back scene consists of two restaurants with nearly identical simple menus, dominated by tasty sausages and salads (daily 10:00–22:00, Jánský Vršek 8, below Nerudova, next door to U

Sedmi Švábů, mobile 731-407-036).

U Hrocha (By the Hippo), a very authentic little pub packed with beer-drinkers and smoke, serves simple, traditional meals—basically meat starters with bread. Just below the castle near Little Quarter Square (Malostranské Náměstí), it's actually the haunt of many members of Parliament, which is located just around the corner (daily 12:00–23:00, chalkboard lists daily meals in English, Thunovská 10, tel. 257-533-389).

Restaurace Rybářský Klub, on Kampa Island overlooking the river, is run by the Society of Czech Fishermen and serves one of the widest and tastiest selections of freshwater fish in Prague, at reasonable prices. Dine on fish-cream soup, pike, trout, carp, or catfish under the imaginative artwork of Little Quarter painter Mr. Kuba. On warm evenings, late May through October, the Society fills its dock with tables—my choice for the best riverside dining in town (three-course meal for around 400 Kč, riverside menu not as extensive as indoor restaurant menu, daily 12:00–23:00, U Sovových Mlýnů 1, tel. 257-534-200).

In the Castle Quarter

To locate the following restaurants, see the map on page 232.

Klášterní Pivovar (Monastery Brewery), founded by an abbot in 1628 and reopened in 2004, has two large rooms, a pleasant courtyard, and typically unpleasant staff. This is the place to taste rare unpasteurized yeast beer, brewed on the premises. The wooden decor and circa-1900 newspaper clippings (including Habsburg Emperor Franz Josef's "Proclamation to My Nations," announcing the beginning of the First World War) evoke the era when Vienna was Europe's artistic capital, Prague was building its faux Eiffel Tower, and life moved much slower than today. To accompany the beer, try the beer-flavored cheese served on toasted black-yeast bread (daily 10:00–22:00, Strahovské Nádvoří 301, tel. 233-353-155). It's directly across from the entrance to the Strahov Library (not to be confused with the enormous, group-oriented Klášterní Restaurace next door, to the right).

Restaurace Nad Úvozem is hidden in the middle of a staircase that connects Loretánská and Úvoz streets. This secret spot, which boasts super views of Prague, offers decent food for surprisingly low prices, given its location. Try the roast beef in plum sauce (170 Kč). The service is slower when the restaurant is full, as the kitchen has limited space (daily 12:00–21:00; as you go down Loretánská watch for pans, scoops, and spoons hanging on chains on your right at #15; tel. 220-511-532). To discourage pub-goers from mingling with diners, the beer here is terribly overpriced (69 Kč).

Hostinec u Černého Vola (By the Black Ox) is a smoky, dingy old-time pub—its survival in the midst of all the castle splendor and tourism is a marvel. It feels like a kegger on the banks of the river Styx, with classic bartenders serving up Kozel beer (traditional "goat" brand with excellent darks) and beer-friendly light meals. The pub is located on Loretánská (no sign outside, sniff for cigarette smoke and look for the only house on the block without an arcade, daily 10:00–22:00, English menu on request, tel. 220-513-481).

Malý Buddha (Little Buddha) serves delightful food— especially vegetarian—and takes its theme seriously. You'll step into a mellow, low-lit escape of bamboo and peace to be served by people with perfect complexions and almost no pulse (Tue–Sun 13:00–22:30, closed Mon, non-smoking, between the castle and Strahov Monastery at Úvoz 46, tel. 220-513-894).

Espresso Kajetánka, just off Castle Square, has magnificent city views. It's a good-if-overpriced place for a drink or snack as you start or end your castle visit (daily 10:00–20:00, Ke Hradu, tel. 257-533-735).

Na Baště, more convenient but not as scenic, is in a garden through the gate to the left of the main castle entry. The outdoor seating, among Jože Plečnik's ramparts and obelisks, is the castle at its most peaceful (Sun–Thu 11:00–23:00, Fri–Sat 11:00–24:00, tel. 281-933-010).

Dining with Style

In Prague, a fancy candlelit dinner with fine wines and connoisseur-approved dishes costs more than most locals can afford—but it's still a bargain in comparison to similar restaurants in Paris or Dallas. I list only two such splurges: one aristocratic, Old World, and under the castle; one more modern, untouristy, and near the Old Town Square.

Restaurace David, with two little 18th-century rooms hiding on a small cobblestone street opposite the American Embassy in the Little Quarter, is my choice for a romantic splurge. The exquisite cuisine, a modern incarnation of traditional Czech dishes with French and European influences, ranges from game to roasted duck and liver. Your meal comes with the gourmet quotient of knives and fancy glasses, and graceful waiters serve you like an aristocrat—appropriate, considering the neighborhood. Reservations are recommended (most meals 600–1,000 Kč, open daily, Tržiště 21, see map on page 252, tel. 257-533-109).

Restaurant Červená Tabulka (Red Chalkboard) is in a low, nondescript townhouse in a quiet neighborhood outside of the tourist circus. Sit in the dressy candlelit interior or on the quiet and breezy cobbled courtyard. Either way, there's not a dumpling in sight. The menu features modern international dishes with a focus on fish (fine 300-Kč plates and gourmet presentation). The wines are excellent and a great value (daily 11:30–23:00, Lodecká

4, tel. 224-810-401). To get to the restaurant from the Municipal House, cross Náměstí Republiky and turn right onto Truhlářská; it's 200 yards down the street on the corner of quiet Petrské Náměstí Square (see map on page 255).

Connections

Centrally located Prague is a logical gateway between Western and Eastern Europe. Direct overnight trains connect Prague to Amsterdam, Frankfurt, and Zurich; and several daily trains leave from Vienna, Berlin, and Munich. From the East, Prague is connected with Budapest, Kraków, and Warsaw by convenient night trains. Remember that for all train connections, it's important to confirm which of Prague's stations to use. For information on Prague's airport, see "Arrival in Prague—By Plane," near the beginning of this chapter.

The Eurail Global pass and the Eurail Selectpass now cover the Czech Republic, as do more focused regional railpasses. Without a pass, tickets are cheap to buy as you go.

You'll find handy Czech train and bus schedules at www.idos .cz (train info tel. 221-111-122, little English spoken). You can make express or international reservations and buy tickets at the conveniently located **Czech Railways Travel Agency,** in the Broadway Mall between Na Příkopě and Celetná streets, near the Powder Tower (see map on page 204). Ask whether discounts are available for your journey, as the rail company has a complex scheme of special offers (Mon–Fri 9:00–17:00, closed Sat–Sun; quick, helpful, English-speaking staff; inside the mall passageway by T.G.I. Friday's, look for blue neon *ČD* sign on your right, Na Příkopě 31; tel. 972-243-071, www.cdtravel.cz, prodej@cdtravel.cz).

From Prague by Train to: Terezín (train to Bohušovice station, nearly hourly, 1–1.5 hrs; then 5-min taxi or bus ride), **Český Krumlov** (8/day, 1/day direct, 4 hrs—bus is faster, cheaper, and easier), **Berlin** (6/day, 4.5–5 hrs), **Munich** (2/day direct, 6 hrs, more with changes; 1 night train, 10 hrs), **Frankfurt** (almost hourly, 7–8.25 hrs), **Vienna** (5/day direct, 4.5 hrs, 5 more with 1 change, 5–6 hrs), **Budapest** (3/day, 7 hrs; 2 overnight trains, 8–9 hrs), **Kraków** (1 direct train/day, 7 hrs; more with 1–2 changes, 8 hrs), **Warsaw** (2/day direct including 1 night train, 9–10 hrs).

By Bus to: Terezín (hourly, 1 hr, from Florenc station), **Český Krumlov** (7/day, 3.5 hrs, some leave from Florenc station, including an easy direct 3-hr bus departing at about 8:15; others leave from Na Knížecí station—Metro Anděl, or Roztyly station— Metro Roztyly).

By Car with a Driver: Mike's Chauffeur Service is a reliable family-run company with fair and fixed rates around town and beyond. Friendly Mike's motto is, "We go the extra mile for you" (round-trip fares with waiting time included: Český Krumlov-4,000 Kč, Terezín-2,000 Kč, Karlštejn-1,800 Kč, plus 5 percent gas surcharge, these prices for up to 4 people, minivan for up to 6 and brand-new minibus for 7 also available, tel. 241-768-231, mobile 602-224-893, www.mike-chauffeur.cz, mike .chauffeur@cmail.cz). On the way to Krumlov, Mike will stop at no extra charge at Hluboká Castle or České Budějovice, where the original Bud beer is made. Mike offers a "Panoramic Transfer to Vienna" for 7,000 Kč (depart Prague at 8:00, arrive Český Krumlov at 10:00, stay up to 6 hrs, 1-hr scenic Czech riverside-and-village drive, then a 2-hr autobahn ride to your Vienna hotel, maximum 4 people). Mike also offers a similar "Panoramic Transfer to Budapest" for 10,000 Kč (2 hrs to Český Krumlov, then 1-hr scenic drive to Linz, followed by 5–6 hrs on expressway to Budapest).

FRANCE

PARIS

Paris—the City of Light—has been a beacon of culture for centuries. As a world capital of art, fashion, food, literature, and ideas, it stands as a symbol of all the fine things human civilization can offer. Come prepared to celebrate, rather than judge, the cultural differences, and you'll capture the romance and joie de vivre that Paris exudes.

Paris offers sweeping boulevards, chatty crêpe stands, chic boutiques, and world-class art galleries. Sip decaf with deconstructionists at a sidewalk café, then step into an Impressionist painting in a tree-lined park. Climb Notre-Dame and rub shoulders with the gargoyles. Cruise the Seine, zip up the Eiffel Tower, and saunter down avenue des Champs-Elysées. Master the Louvre and Orsay museums. Save some after-dark energy for one of the world's most romantic cities.

Planning Your Time

For three very busy but doable days in Paris, I've listed sights in descending order of importance in the planning sections below. Therefore, if you have only one day, just do Day 1; for two days, add Day 2; and so on. When planning where to plug in Versailles, remember that the Château is closed on Mondays and especially crowded on Sundays and Tuesdays—try to avoid these days.

Day 1
Morning: Follow this book's Historic Paris Walk, featuring Ile de la Cité, Notre-Dame, the Latin Quarter, and Sainte-Chapelle.
Afternoon: Tour the Louvre.

Evening: Enjoy the Trocadéro scene and a twilight ride up the Eiffel Tower.

Day 2
Morning: Wander the Champs-Elysées from the Arc de Triomphe down the grand avenue des Champs-Elysées to Tuileries Garden.

Midday: Cross the pedestrian bridge from the Tuileries Garden, then tour the Orsay Museum.

Afternoon: Tour the Rodin Museum, or the Army Museum and Napoleon's Tomb.

Evening: Cruise the Seine River, take Paris Vision's nighttime Illumination bus tour, or consider taking in a jazz club, cabaret, concert, or opera (see "Nightlife," later in this chapter).

Day 3
Morning: Ride the RER suburban train out to Versailles.

Afternoon: Stroll the Marais neighborhood.

Evening: Visit Montmartre and the Sacré-Cœur basilica.

Orientation

Paris (population of city center: 2,170,000) is split in half by the Seine River, divided into 20 arrondissements (proud and independent governmental jurisdictions), circled by a ring-road freeway (the *périphérique*), and speckled with Métro stations. You'll find Paris easier to navigate if you know which side of the river you're on, which arrondissement you're in, and which Métro stop you're closest to. If you're north of the river (the top half of any city map), you're on the Right Bank (Rive Droite). If you're south of it, you're on the Left Bank (Rive Gauche).

The bull's-eye of your Paris map is Notre-Dame, which sits on an island in the middle of the Seine. Most of your sightseeing will take place within five blocks of the river.

Arrondissements are numbered, starting at the Louvre and moving in a clockwise spiral out to the ring road. The last two digits in a Parisian zip code are the arrondissement number. The abbreviation for "Métro stop" is "Mo." In Parisian jargon, the

Paris Neighborhoods

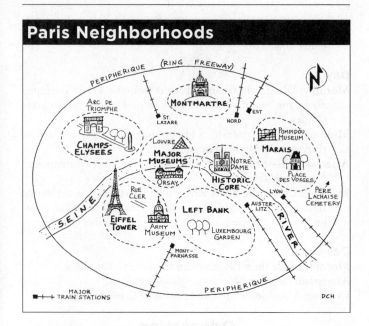

Eiffel Tower is on la Rive Gauche (the Left Bank) in the 7ème (7th arrondissement), zip code 75007, Mo: Trocadéro.

Paris Métro stops are used as a standard aid in giving directions, even for those not using the Métro. As you're tracking down addresses, these words and pronunciations will help: Métro (may-troh), *place* (plahs—square), *rue* (roo—road), *avenue* (ah-vuh-noo), *boulevard* (boo-luh-var), and *pont* (pohn—bridge).

Tourist Information

Paris tourist offices (abbreviated as **TI** in this book) have long lines, offer little information, and may charge for maps. But all you really need are this book and one of the freebie maps available at any hotel (or in the front of this book). Paris' TIs share a single phone number: 08 92 68 30 00 (from the US, dial 011 33 8 92 68 30 00).

If you must visit a TI, you can do so at several locations, including **Pyramides** (daily 9:00–19:00, at Pyramides Métro stop between the Louvre and Opéra), **Gares de Lyon and Nord** (both Mon–Sat 8:00–18:00, closed Sun), and **Montmartre** (daily 10:00–19:00, place du Tertre). The official website for Paris' TIs is www.parisinfo.com. Both **airports** have handy information offices (called ADP) with long hours and short lines (for more info, see "Connections," near the end of this chapter).

Pariscope: The weekly €0.40 *Pariscope* magazine (or one of its clones, available at any newsstand) lists museum hours, art exhibits, concerts, festivals, plays, movies, and nightclubs. Smart sightseers rely on this for the latest listings.

Other Publications: Look for the *Paris Times,* which provides helpful English information and fresh insights into living in Paris (available at English-language bookstores, French-American establishments, the American Church, and online at www.the paristimes.com). The *Paris Voice,* with snappy reviews of concerts, plays, and current events, is available only online at www.paris voice.com. For a schedule of museum hours and English museum tours, pick up the free *Musées, Monuments Historiques, et Expositions* booklet at any museum.

American Church and Franco-American Center: This interdenominational church—in the rue Cler neighborhood, facing the river between the Eiffel Tower and Orsay Museum—is a nerve center for the American émigré community. Worship services are at 9:00 and 11:00 on Sunday; the coffee hour after church and the free Sunday concerts (generally Sept–June at 17:00—but not every week) are a good way get a taste of émigré life in Paris (reception open Mon–Sat 9:00–12:00 & 13:00–22:00, Sun 14:30–19:00, 65 quai d'Orsay, Mo: Invalides, tel. 01 40 62 05 00, www.acparis.org). It's also a handy place to pick up free copies of *Paris Times* (above) and *France-USA Contacts* (an advertisement paper with info on housing and employment for the 30,000 Americans living in Paris, www.fusac.fr).

Arrival in Paris

For a comprehensive rundown of Paris' train stations and airports, see "Connections," near the end of this chapter.

Helpful Hints

Heightened Security *(Plan Vigipirate):* You may notice an abundance of police at monuments, on streets, and on the Métro, as well as security cameras at key sights. You'll go through quick and reassuring airport-like security checks at many major attractions. This is all part of Paris' anti-terror plan. The police are helpful, the security lines move quickly, and there are now fewer pickpocket problems on the Métro.

Theft Alert: Although the greater police presence has scared off some, troublesome thieves still thrive near famous monuments and on Métro and RER lines that serve high-profile tourist sights. Wear a money belt, put your wallet in your front pocket, loop your day bag over your shoulders, and keep a tight grip on your purse or shopping bag. Muggings are rare, but do occur. If you're out late, avoid the dark riverfront embankments and any place where the lighting is dim and pedestrian activity is minimal.

PARIS

Tourist Scams: Be aware of the latest scams, including these current favorites. The "found ring" scam involves an innocent-looking person who picks up a ring on the ground, and asks if you dropped it. When you say no, the person examines the ring more closely, then shows you a mark "proving" that it's pure gold. He offers to sell it to you for a good price—several times more than he paid for it before dropping it on the sidewalk.

In the "friendship bracelet" scam, a vendor approaches you and asks if you'll help him with a demonstration. He proceeds to make a friendship bracelet right on your arm. When finished, he asks you to pay for the bracelet he created just for you. And since you can't easily take it off on the spot, he counts on you feeling obliged to pay up.

Distractions by "salesmen" can also function as a smoke-screen for theft—an accomplice picks your pocket as you try to wriggle away from a pushy vendor.

In popular tourist spots (such as in front of Notre-Dame) young ladies politely ask if you speak English, then pretend to beg for money while actually angling to pick your pocket.

Street Safety: Parisian drivers are notorious for ignoring pedestrians. Look both ways (many streets are one-way) and be careful of seemingly quiet bus/taxi lanes. Don't assume you have the right of way, even in a crosswalk. When crossing a street, keep your pace constant and don't stop suddenly. By law, drivers can miss pedestrians by up to just one meter— a little more than three feet (1.5 meters in the countryside). Drivers carefully calculate your speed and won't hit you, provided you don't alter your route or pace.

Paris' "Vélib'" bike program, which offers short-term rentals to locals, means that more bikes than ever are on the roads. When crossing streets, beware of this silent transportation.

Paris Museum Pass: This worthwhile pass, covering most sights in Paris, is sold at TIs and museums. For detailed information, see page 295.

Museum Strategy: When possible, visit key museums first thing (when your energy is best) and save other activities for the afternoon. Remember, most museums require you to check daypacks and coats, and important museums have metal detectors that will slow your entry. The Louvre, Orsay, and Pompidou are open on selected nights, making for peaceful visits with fewer crowds.

Bookstores: There are many English-language bookstores in Paris, where you can pick up guidebooks (at nearly double their American prices). Most carry this book. My favorite is the friendly **Red Wheelbarrow Bookstore** in the Marais neighborhood, run by mellow Penelope (Mon–Sat 10:00–19:00, Sun 14:00–18:00, 22 rue St. Paul, Mo: St. Paul, tel. 01 48 04 75 08). Others include **Shakespeare and Company** (some used travel books, daily 12:00–24:00, 37 rue de la Bûcherie, across the river from Notre-Dame, Mo: St. Michel, tel. 01 43 26 96 50), **W. H. Smith** (Mon–Sat 10:00–19:00, closed Sun, 248 rue de Rivoli, Mo: Concorde, tel. 01 44 77 88 99), **Brentanos** (Mon–Sat 10:00–19:00, closed Sun, 37 avenue de l'Opéra, Mo: Opéra, tel. 01 42 61 52 50), and **Village Voice** (Mon 14:00–19:00, Tue–Sat 10:00–19:00, Sun 12:00–18:00, near St. Sulpice Church at 6 rue Princesse, tel. 01 46 33 36 47).

Public WCs: Public toilets are free (though it's polite to leave a small tip if there's an attendant). Modern, sanitary street-booth toilets provide both relief and a memory (don't leave small children inside unattended). The restrooms in museums are free and the best you'll find. Or walk into any sidewalk café like you own the place, and find the toilet in the back. Keep toilet paper or tissues with you, as some toilets are poorly supplied.

Parking: Most of the time, drivers must pay to park curbside (buy parking card at *tabac* shops—see below), but not at night (19:00–9:00), all day Sunday, or anytime in August, when many Parisians are on vacation. There are parking garages under Ecole Militaire, St. Sulpice Church, Les Invalides, the Bastille, and the Panthéon; all charge about €20–27 per day (it's cheaper per hour the longer you stay). Some hotels offer parking for less—ask.

Tobacco Stands *(Tabacs):* These little kiosks—usually just a counter inside a café—sell cards for parking meters, public-transit tickets (usually), postage stamps, and...oh yeah, cigarettes. To find one anywhere in Paris, just look for a *Tabac* sign and the red, cylinder-shaped symbol above some (but not all) cafés.

Getting Around Paris

Paris is easy to navigate. Your basic choices are Métro (in-city subway), RER (suburban rail tied into the Métro system), public bus, and taxi. (Also consider the hop-on, hop-off bus and boat tours, described under "Tours," later in this chapter.) You can buy tickets and passes at most *tabacs* (tobacco stands) and at Métro stations. While most Métro stations have staffed ticket windows, some smaller stations have only ticket-vending machines, for which you'll need coins (some take bills).

Public-Transit Tickets: The Métro, RER, and buses all work on the same tickets. (You can transfer between the Métro and RER on a single ticket, but combining a Métro or RER trip with

PARIS

a bus ride takes two tickets.) A **single ticket** costs €1.70. To save 25 percent, buy a *carnet* (kar-nay) of 10 tickets for €11.10 (that's €1.11 per ticket—€0.39 cheaper than a single ticket). It's less expensive for kids (ages 4–10 pay €5.50 for a *carnet*). *Carnets* can be shared between travelers.

Passes: The transit system has introduced a new chip-card, called the **Passe Navigo Découverte,** but for most tourists, *carnets* are still the better deal. The new Passe costs €22.50, runs Monday–Sunday (expires on Sun, even if you buy it on Fri), and requires a photo, which means it's not shareable. In contrast, two 10-packs of *carnets*—enough for most travelers staying a week—cost €22.80, are shareable, and don't expire until they're used.

If you do want the pass, ask for the *"Passe Navigo Découverte hebdomadaire"* (pahs nah-vee-go day-koo-vairt ehb-doh-mah-dair) and supply a small postage-stamp-size photo of yourself (bring your own, or use the €4 photo booths in major Métro stations). You buy a chip-embedded card (€5 one-time cost), then "load" a weekly value onto it (€16.50); this gives you free run of the bus and Métro system. At the Métro/bus turnstile, you scan your Passe to enter, and you're on your way.

The overpriced **Paris Visite** passes were designed for tourists and offer minor reductions at minor sights (1 day/€9, 2 days/€14, 3 days/€19, 5 days/€28), but you'll get a better value with a cheaper *carnet* of 10 tickets or a Passe Navigo Découverte.

By Métro

In Paris, you're never more than a 10-minute walk from a Métro station. Europe's best subway allows you to hop from sight to sight quickly and cheaply (runs daily 5:30–24:30 in the morning). Learn to use it. Color Métro maps are free at Métro stations, and included on freebie Paris maps at your hotel.

Beware of Pickpockets: Thieves dig the Métro. Be on guard. For example, if your pocket is picked as you pass through a turnstile, you end up stuck on the wrong side (after the turnstile bar has closed behind you) while the thief gets away. Stand away from Métro doors to avoid being a target for a theft-and-run just before the doors close. Any jostling or commotion—especially when boarding or leaving trains—is likely the sign of a thief or a team of thieves in action. Make any fare inspector show proof of identity (ask locals for help if you're not certain). Never show anyone your wallet.

How the Métro Works: To get to your destination, determine the closest "Mo" stop and which line or lines will get you there. The lines have numbers, but they're best known by their end-of-the-line stops. (For example, the La Défense/Château de Vincennes line, also known as line 1, runs between La Défense in the west and Vincennes in the east.) Once in the Métro station, you'll see blue-and-white signs directing you to the train going in your direction (e.g., *direction: La Défense*). Insert your ticket in the automatic turnstile, pass through, reclaim your ticket, and keep it until you exit the system (some stations require you to pass your ticket through a turnstile to exit). *Fare inspectors regularly check for cheaters and accept absolutely no excuses, so keep that ticket!*

Transfers are free and can be made wherever lines cross, providing you do so within 90 minutes. When you transfer, look for the orange *correspondance* (connection) signs when you exit your first train, then follow the proper direction sign.

Even though the Métro whisks you quickly from one point to another, be prepared to walk significant distances within stations to reach your platform (most noticeable when you transfer). Escalators are common, but they're often out of order. To limit excessive walking, avoid transferring at these sprawling stations: Montparnasse-Bienvenüe, Châtelet–Les Halles, Charles de Gaulle–Etoile, Gare du Nord, and Bastille.

Before taking the *sortie* (exit) to leave the Métro, check the helpful *plan du quartier* (map of the neighborhood) to get your bearings, locate your destination, and decide which *sortie* you want. At stops with several *sorties*, you can save lots of walking by choosing the best exit.

After you exit the system, toss or tear your used ticket so you don't confuse it with your unused ticket—they look virtually identical.

By RER

The RER (Réseau Express Régionale; air-ay-air) is the suburban arm of the Métro, serving outlying destinations (such as Versailles, Disneyland Paris, and the airports). These routes are indicated by thick lines on your subway map and identified by the letters A, B, C, and so on. Some routes are operated by France's railroad (SNCF) and are called Transilien; they function the same way and use the same tickets as the RER. For all of these trains, you need to insert your ticket in a turnstile to exit the system.

Within the city center, the RER works like the Métro, but can be speedier (if it serves your destination directly) because it makes fewer stops. Métro tickets and the Passe Navigo card are good on the RER when traveling in the city center. (You can transfer between the Métro and RER systems with the same ticket.) But to travel outside the city (to Versailles or the airport, for example), you'll need to buy a separate, more expensive ticket at the station window (or, to save time, at a ticket-vending machine) before boarding. Also, unlike the Métro, not every train stops at every station along the way; check the sign over the platform to see if your destination is listed as a stop (*"toutes les gares"* means it makes all stops along the way), or confirm with a local before you board.

By City Bus

Paris' excellent bus system is worth figuring out. Remember, even though buses use the same tickets as the Métro and RER, you can't use a single ticket to transfer between the systems—though you can transfer from one bus to another (within 90 minutes, though doesn't work with tickets bought on board). One ticket buys you a bus ride anywhere in central Paris—but if you leave the city center (shown as zone 1 on the diagram aboard the bus), you must validate a second ticket.

Buses don't seem as romantic as the famous Métro and are subject to traffic jams, but savvy travelers know that buses can have you swinging through the city like Tarzan in an urban jungle. Anywhere you are, you can generally see a bus stop, and every stop comes complete with all the information you need: a good city bus map, route maps showing exactly where each bus that uses this stop goes, a frequency chart and schedule, a *plan du quartier* map of the immediate neighborhood, and a *soirées* map explaining night service, if available. While the Métro shuts down about 24:30 in the morning, some buses continue much later (called *Noctilien* lines, www.noctilien.fr).

Enter buses through the front door. Punch your ticket in the machine behind the driver, scan your Passe Navigo, or pay the higher cash fare to get your ticket from the driver. (Remember: Tickets purchased from drivers do not allow transfers between buses). When you reach your destination, push the red button to signal you want a stop, then exit through the rear door. Even if you're not certain you've figured out the system, do some joy-riding (outside of rush hour: Mon–Fri 8:00–9:30 & 17:30–19:30). Be warned: Not all city buses are air-conditioned, so they can become rolling greenhouses on summer days. Handy bus-system maps *(plan des autobus)* are available in any Métro station (and in the €6 *Paris Pratique* map book sold at newsstands). Major stops are displayed on the side of each bus. I've also listed the handiest bus routes for each recommended hotel neighborhood (see "Sleeping," later in this chapter).

By Taxi

Parisian taxis are reasonable, especially for couples and families. The meters are tamper-proof. Fares and supplements (described in English on the rear windows) are straightforward and tightly regulated.

A taxi can fit three people comfortably, and cabbies are legally required to accept four passengers at a time (you'll be charged €3 extra for the fourth person). Groups of up to five can use a *grand taxi*, which must be booked in advance—ask your hotelier to call.

Rates: All Parisian taxis charge a €5.20 minimum. A 10-minute ride (e.g., Bastille to Eiffel Tower) costs about €12 (versus €1.11 per person to get anywhere in town using a *carnet* ticket on the Métro or bus). Higher rates are charged at rush hour and at night (17:00–10:00), all day Sunday, and to any of the airports. Your first bag is free; additional pieces of luggage are €1 each. To tip, round up to the next euro (at least €0.50).

How to Catch *un Taxi:* You can try waving down a taxi, but it's often easier to ask someone for the nearest taxi stand (*"Où est une station de taxi?"*; oo ay ewn stah-see-ohn duh taxi). Taxi stands are indicated by a circled "T" on good city maps, and on many maps in this book. When you summon a taxi by phone, the meter starts running as soon as the call is received, often adding €5 or more to the bill.

Taxis are tough to find during rush hour, when it's raining, and on Friday and Saturday nights, especially after the Métro closes (around 24:30 in the morning). If you need to catch a train or flight early in the morning, book a taxi the day before. Your hotelier can help.

By Bike

Paris is surprisingly good by bicycle. Riders enjoy plenty of bike lanes, and the extensive parks have bike-friendly paths that enable anyone on two wheels to get around easily. I biked along the river from Notre-Dame to the Eiffel Tower in 15 minutes. The tourist board has a fine "Paris à Vélo" map showing all the dedicated bike paths.

Fat Tire Bike Tours (listed under "Tours," next) rents bikes *sans* tour for independent types (€2.50/hr, €15/24 hrs, includes helmets and locks, credit-card imprint required for deposit, €4 discount with book for daily rental, daily 9:00–18:00, ask for their map of suggested routes, 24 rue Edgar Faure, Mo: Dupleix, tel. 01 56 58 10 54, www.fattirebiketoursparis.com).

Tours

By Bus

Bus Tours—Paris Vision offers bus tours of Paris, day and night (advertised in hotel lobbies). I'd consider a Paris Vision tour only for their night-time Illumination tour (see "Nightlife," later in this chapter). During the day, the hop-on, hop-off bus tours (listed immediately below) and the Batobus (see "By Boat," later in this section)—which both provide transportation between sights as well as commentary—are a better value.

Hop-on, Hop-off Bus Tours—Double-decker buses connect Paris' main sights while providing a basic running commentary, allowing you to hop on and hop off along the way. You get a disposable set of earplugs (dial English and listen to the so-so narration). You can get off at any stop, tour a sight, then catch a later bus. These are best in good weather, when you can sit up top. There are two companies: L'Open Tours and Les Cars Rouges; pick up their brochures showing routes and stops from any TI or on their buses. You can start either tour at just about any of the major sights, such as the Eiffel Tower, where both companies stop on avenue Joseph Bouvard.

L'Open Tours uses bright yellow buses and provides more extensive coverage (and slightly better commentary) on four different routes, rolling by most of the important sights in Paris. Their Paris Grand Tour (the green route) offers the best introduction. The same ticket gets you on any of their routes within the validity period. Buy your tickets from the driver (1 day-€29, 2 days-€32, kids 4–11 pay €15 for 1 or 2 days, allow 2 hours per tour). Two to four buses depart hourly from about 10:00 to 18:00; expect to wait 10–15 minutes at each stop (stops can be tricky to find—look for yellow signs; tel. 01 42 66 56 56, www.paris-opentour.com). A combo-ticket covers both the Batobus boats (described in "By Boat," below) and L'Open Tours buses (€44, kids under 12 pay €20, valid 3 days).

Les Cars Rouges' bright red buses offer largely the same service, with only one route and just nine stops, for less (recorded narration, adult-€24, kids 4–12 pay €12, good for 2 days, tel. 01 53 95 39 53, www.carsrouges.com).

By Boat

Seine Cruises—Several companies run one-hour boat cruises on the Seine (by far best at night).

Two companies are convenient to the rue Cler hotels: **Bateaux-Mouches** departs from pont de l'Alma's right bank and has the biggest open-top, double-decker boats. But this company often has too many tour groups, causing these boats to get packed (€10, kids 4–12 pay €5, tel. 01 40 76 99 99, www.bateaux-mouches.com).

Bateaux Parisiens has smaller covered boats with handheld audioguides, fewer crowds, and only one deck (€11, kids 4–11 pay €5, discounted half-price if you have a valid France or France–Switzerland railpass—does not use up a day of a flexipass, leaves from right in front of the Eiffel Tower, tel. 08 25 01 01 01, www.bateauxparisiens.com). Both companies run daily year-round (April–Oct 10:00–22:30, 2–3/hr; Nov–March shorter hours, runs hourly).

Vedettes du Pont Neuf offers essentially the same one-hour tour as Bateaux Parisiens, but starts and ends at Pont Neuf, closer to recommended hotels in the Marais and Luxembourg Garden neighborhoods. The boats feature a live guide whose delivery (in English and French) is as stiff as a recorded narration—and as hard to understand, given the quality of their sound system (€11, kids 4–12 pay €6, tip requested, nearly 2/hr, daily 10:30–22:30, tel. 01 46 33 98 38).

Hop-on, Hop-Off Boat Tour—**Batobus** allows you to get on and off as often as you like at any of eight popular stops along the Seine: Eiffel Tower, Champs-Elysées, Orsay/place de la Concorde, the Louvre, Notre-Dame, St. Germain-des-Prés, Hôtel de Ville, and Jardin des Plantes. Safety-conscious glass enclosures turn the boats into virtual ovens on hot days (1 day-€12, 2 days-€14, boats run June–Aug 10:00–21:30, mid-March–May and Sept–Oct 10:00–19:00, Nov–early-Jan and Feb–mid-March 10:30–16:30, no service last three weeks in Jan, every 15–20 minutes, 45 min one-way, 90 min round-trip, worthless narration). If you use this for getting around—sort of a scenic, floating alternative to the Métro—this can be worthwhile. But if you just want a guided boat tour, Batobus is not as good a value as the regular tour boats described earlier. A special combo-ticket covers L'Open Tours buses (described earlier) and Batobus boats (€40, kids under 12 pay €17, valid 3 days, www.batobus.com).

Low-Key Cruise on a Tranquil Canal—**Canauxrama** runs a lazy 2.5-hour cruise on a peaceful canal without the Seine in sight. Tours start from place de la Bastille and end at Bassin de la Villette (near Mo: Stalingrad). During the first segment of your trip, you'll pass through a long tunnel (built at the order of Napoleon in the early 19th century, when canal boats were vital for industrial transport). Once outside, you glide—not much faster than you can walk—through sleepy Parisian neighborhoods and slowly climb through four double locks as a guide narrates the trip in French and English (€15, departs at 9:45 and 14:30 across from Opéra Bastille, just below boulevard de la Bastille, opposite #50—where the canal meets place de la Bastille, tel. 01 42 39 15 00). The same tour also goes in the opposite direction (from Bassin de la Villette to place de la Bastille). It's OK to bring a picnic on board.

By Foot

Paris Walks—This company offers a variety of two-hour walks, led by British or American guides. Tours are thoughtfully prepared, and humorous. Don't hesitate to stand close to the guide to hear (€10–15, generally 2/day, private tours available, recorded English schedule tel. 01 48 09 21 40, www.paris-walks.com). Tours focus on the Marais (4/week), Montmartre (3/week), medieval

PARIS

Latin Quarter (Mon), Ile de la Cité/Notre-Dame (Mon), the "Two Islands" (Ile de la Cité and Ile St. Louis, Wed), *Da Vinci Code* sights (Wed), and Hemingway's Paris (Fri). Ask about their family-friendly tours. Call a day or two ahead to learn their schedule and starting point. Most tours don't require reservations, but specialty tours (such as the *Da Vinci Code* tour) require advance reservations and prepayment with credit card (not refundable if you cancel less than two days in advance).

Context Paris—These "intellectual by design" walking tours are led by docents (historians, architects, and academics) and cover both museums and neighborhoods, often with a fascinating theme (explained on their website). Try to book in advance, since groups are small and can fill up (limited to 6 participants, generally 3 hours long and €35–55 per person plus admissions, tel. 06 13 09 67 11, US tel. 888-467-1986, www.contextparis.com). They also offer private tours.

Classic Walks—If you'd prefer a more relaxed, low-brow walking tour, consider this outfit, run by Fat Tire Bike Tours (see "By Bike," below). Their 3.5-hour "Classic Walk" covers most major sights (€20, daily at 10:00, meet at office—see below). They also do two-hour walks on various themes and neighborhoods: Montmartre, French Revolution, World War II, *Da Vinci Code*, and Latin Quarter (€12, leave several times a week—see website for details, all walks get €2 discount with this book, 24 rue Edgar Faure, Mo: Dupleix, tel. 01 56 58 10 54, www.classicwalks paris.com).

Private Guides—For many, Paris merits hiring a Parisian as a personal guide. **Arnaud Servignat** is an excellent licensed local guide (€155/half-day, €260/day, also does car tours of the country-side around Paris for a little more, tel. 06 68 80 29 05, www .arnaud-servignat.com, arnotour@mac.com).

Elizabeth Van Hest is another highly likeable and capable guide (€175/half-day, €260/day, tel. 01 43 41 47 31, elisa.guide @gmail.com). **Thierry Gauduchon** is well worth his fee (€180/ half-day, €350/day, tel. 01 56 98 10 82, mobile 06 19 07 30 77, tgaud uchon@aol.com). **Sylvie Moreau** is also good, and charges the same as Elizabeth (mobile 06 87 02 80 67, silvmor@gmail.com).

By Bike

Fat Tire Bike Tours—A hardworking gang of young American expats runs an extensive program of bike, Segway tours, and walking tours, and rents bikes as well.

Their high-energy guides run four-hour bike tours of Paris, by day and by night. Reservations aren't necessary—just show up. On the day tour, you'll pedal with a pack of 10–20 riders, mostly in parks and along bike lanes, with a lunch stop in the Tuileries

Gardens (€26, show this book for a €4 per-person discount, maximum 2 discounts per book, English only, tours leave daily rain or shine at 11:00, April–Oct at 15:00 as well). Nighttime tours are more lively and include a boat cruise on the Seine (€28, €4 discount with this book, April–Oct daily at 19:00, March daily at 18:00, end of Feb and all of Nov Tue, Thu, and Sat–Sun at 18:00, no night tours Dec–mid-Feb). Both tours meet at the south pillar of the Eiffel Tower, where you'll get a short history lesson, then walk six minutes to the Fat Tire office to pick up bikes (helmets available upon request at no extra charge, office open daily 9:00–19:00, 24 rue Edgar Faure, Mo: Dupleix, tel. 01 56 58 10 54, toll-free from North America 866-614-6218, www.fattirebiketoursparis.com). They also run bike tours to Versailles and Giverny (reservations required, see website for details). Their office has Internet access with English keyboards.

Fat Tire's pricey four-hour **City Segway Tours**—on futuristic stand-up motorized scooters—are novel in that you learn to ride a Segway while exploring Paris (you'll get the hang of it after about half an hour). These tours take no more than eight people at a time, so reservations are required (€75, daily at 9:30, March–Nov also at 14:00, April–Oct also at 18:30, www.citysegwaytours.com).

Excursions from Paris

Many companies offer bus tours to regional sights, including all of the day trips described in this book. **Paris Vision** runs mass-produced, full-size bus and minivan tours to several popular regional destinations, including the Loire Valley, Champagne region, D-Day beaches, and Mont St. Michel. Minivan tours are more expensive, but more personal and given in English, and most offer convenient pickup at your hotel (€90–190/person). Their full-size bus tours are multilingual and cheaper than the minivan tours—worthwhile for some travelers simply for the ease of transportation to the sights (about €70, destinations include Versailles and Giverny). Paris Vision's full-size buses depart from 214 rue de Rivoli (Mo: Tuileries, tel. 01 42 60 30 01, www.parisvision.com).

PARIS

Self-Guided Walk

Historic Core of Paris Walk

(This information is distilled from the Historic Paris Walk chapter in *Rick Steves' Paris*, by Rick Steves, Steve Smith, and Gene Openshaw. A free audiotour version of this walk is available for people with iPods or other MP3 players at www.ricksteves.com and on iTunes.)

Allow four hours to do justice to this three-mile walk. Start where the city did—on the Ile de la Cité. Face Notre-Dame and

Historic Core of Paris

R I G H T   B A N K

TO LES HALLES

TO LOUVRE

RUE DE

BLVD SEBAST

TO POMPIDOU

QUAI DU LOUVRE

CHATELET (+ℝ)

TOUR ST. JACQUES

RENARD

TO PLACE BASTILLE

PONT NEUF

FINISH ⑮

S E I N E

PONT NEUF

RIVOLI

HOTEL DE VILLE

BOATS

⑭

⑬

QUAI DE L'HORLOGE

CHANGE

NOTRE DAME

QUAI DE L'HOTEL DE VILLE

B

TO ORSAY & PONT DES ARTS

PALAIS DE JUSTICE

⑫

SAINTE-CHAPELLE

⑩

CITÉ

MKT.

⑪

HOTEL DIEU HOSPITAL

WC

RUE DE LUTECE

RUE D'ARCOLE

PLACE ST. MICHEL

CRYPT

START

PLACE PARVIS

①

NOTRE-DAME

③

RUE ST. ANDRE-DES-ARTS

ℝ

⑨

PETIT PONT

HUCHETTE

⑥

B

④

②

QUAI TOURNELLE

PLACE ST. ANDRE-DES-ARTS

⑧

R. ST. SEVERIN

⑦

⑤

RUE GALANDE

LA GRANGE

ODEON

BLVD

RUE DE LA

RUE ST. JACQUES

MAUBERT MUTUALITE

TO ST. SULPICE

ST.

MICHEL

CLUNY

CLUNY MUSEUM

ST.

GERMAIN

R. MONGE

L E F T   B A N K

BLVD.

RUE ST. JACQUES

TO SORBONNE & LUXEMBOURG GARDEN

TO RUE MOUFFETARD

➡ WALKING TOUR ROUTE	
Ⓜ METRO STATION	Ⓑ BATOBUS BOAT STOP
Ⓡ RER STOP	⚘ VIEW

200 YARDS
200 METERS

DCH

① Point Zero	⑨ Place St. Michel
② Deportation Memorial	⑩ Sainte-Chapelle
③ Ile St. Louis	⑪ Cité Métro Stop
④ Left Bank Booksellers	⑫ Conciergerie
⑤ Medieval Paris	⑬ Place Dauphine
⑥ Shakespeare & Co. Bookstore	⑭ Statue of Henry IV
⑦ St. Séverin	⑮ Pont Neuf
⑧ Place St. André-des-Arts	

PARIS

follow the gray line on the Historic Core of Paris map.

• *To get to Notre-Dame, ride the Métro to Cité, Hôtel de Ville, or St. Michel and walk to the big square facing the cathedral. View it from the bronze plaque on the ground (30 yards from the central doorway) marked "Point Zero." You're standing at the center of France, the point from which all distances are measured...*

▲▲▲Notre-Dame Cathedral

This 700-year-old cathedral is packed with history and tourists. Study its sculpture and windows, take in a Mass, eavesdrop on guides, and walk all around the outside.

The **cathedral facade** is worth a close look. The church is dedicated to "Our Lady" (Notre-Dame). Mary is center stage—cradling Jesus, surrounded by the halo of the rose window. Adam is on the left and Eve is on the right.

Below Mary and above the arches is a row of 28 statues known as the Kings of Judah. During the French Revolution, these biblical kings were mistaken for the hated French kings. The citizens stormed the church, crying, "Off with their heads!" All were decapitated, but have since been recapitated.

Speaking of decapitation, look at the carving above the doorway on the left. The man with his head in his hands is St. Denis. Back when there was a Roman temple on this spot, Christianity began making converts. The fourth-century bishop of Roman Paris, Denis, was beheaded. But these early Christians were hard to keep down. The man who would become St. Denis got up, tucked his head under his arm, headed north, paused at a fountain to wash it off, and continued until he found just the right place to meet his maker: Montmartre. (Although the name "Montmartre" comes from the Roman "Mount of Mars," later generations—thinking of their beheaded patron, St. Denis—preferred a less pagan version, "Mount of Martyrs.") The Parisians were convinced of this miracle, Christianity gained ground, and a church soon replaced the pagan temple.

Medieval art was OK if it embellished the house of God and told biblical stories. For a fine example, move to the base of the central column (at the foot of Mary, about where the head of St. Denis could spit if he were really good). Working around from the left, find God telling a barely created Eve, "Have fun, but no apples." Next, the sexiest serpent I've ever seen makes apples à la mode. Finally, Adam and Eve, now ashamed of their nakedness, are expelled by an angel. This is a tiny example in a church covered with meaning.

Now move to the right and study the carving above the **central portal**. It's the end of the world, and Christ sits on the throne of Judgment (just under the arches, holding both hands up). Below

PARIS

him an angel and a demon weigh souls in the balance; the demon cheats by pressing down. The "good" stand to the left, gazing up to heaven. The "bad" ones to the right are chained up and led off to a six-hour tour of the Louvre on a hot day. The "ugly" ones must be the crazy, sculpted demons to the right, at the base of the arch.

Wander through the interior. You'll be routed around the ambulatory, much as medieval pilgrims would have been. Don't miss the rose windows filling each of the transepts. Back outside, walk around the church through the park on the riverside for a close look at the flying buttresses.

The Neo-Gothic, 300-foot **spire** is a product of the 1860 reconstruction. Around its base are apostles and evangelists (the green men) as well as Eugène-Emmanuel Viollet-le-Duc, the architect in charge of the work. Notice how the apostles look outward, blessing the city, while the architect (at top, seen from behind the church) looks up the spire, marveling at his fine work.

The **archaeological crypt** is a worthwhile 15-minute stop if you have a Paris Museum Pass (€3.50, covered by Museum Pass, Tue–Sun 10:00–18:00, closed Mon, enter 100 yards in front of cathedral). You'll see Roman ruins, trace the street plan of the medieval village, and see diagrams of how the earliest Paris grew and grew, all thoughtfully explained in English.

Cost, Hours, Location: Free, cathedral open daily 7:45–19:00; Treasury-€3, not covered by Museum Pass, Treasury open daily 9:30–17:30; audioguide-€5, ask about free English tours, normally Wed and Thu at 12:00, Sat at 14:30; Mo: Cité, Hôtel de Ville, or St. Michel; tel. 01 42 34 56 10, www.cathedraledeparis.com. On Good Friday and on the first Friday of the month at 15:00, the (physically underwhelming) relic known as Jesus' Crown of Thorns is on display.

Tower: You can climb to the top of the facade between the towers, and then to the top of the south tower, 400 steps total, for a grand view (€7.50, covered by Museum Pass but no bypass line for passholders, daily April–Sept 10:00–18:30—also June–Aug Sat–Sun until 23:00, Oct–March 10:00–17:30, last entry 45 min before closing; to avoid crowds in peak season, arrive before 10:00 or after 17:00).

• *Behind Notre-Dame, cross the street, and enter through the iron gate into the park at the tip of the island. Look for the stairs and head down to reach the...*

▲Deportation Memorial (Mémorial de la Déportation)

This memorial to the 200,000 French victims of the Nazi concentration camps draws you into their experience. As you descend the steps, the city around you disappears. Surrounded by walls,

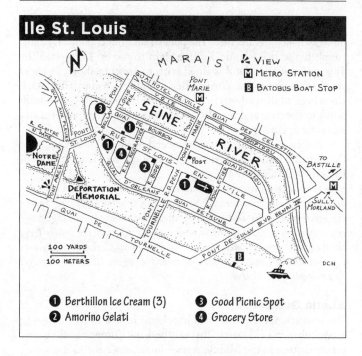

Ile St. Louis

♣ VIEW
Ⓜ METRO STATION
Ⓑ BATOBUS BOAT STOP

❶ Berthillon Ice Cream (3)   ❸ Good Picnic Spot
❷ Amorino Gelati   ❹ Grocery Store

you have become a prisoner. Your only freedom is your view of the sky and the tiny glimpse of the river below.

Enter the single-file chamber ahead. Inside, the circular plaque in the floor reads, "They went to the end of the earth and did not return." A hallway stretches in front of you, lined with 200,000 lighted crystals, one for each French citizen who died. Flickering at the far end is the eternal flame of hope. The tomb of the unknown deportee lies at your feet. Above, the inscription reads, "Dedicated to the living memory of the 200,000 French deportees sleeping in the night and the fog, exterminated in the Nazi concentration camps."

Above the exit as you leave is the message you'll find at other Holocaust sites: "Forgive, but never forget" (free, daily April–Sept 10:00–12:00 & 14:00–19:00, Oct–March 10:00–12:00 & 14:00–17:00, at the east tip of the island named Ile de la Cité, behind Notre-Dame and near Ile St. Louis, Mo: Cité, tel. 01 49 74 34 00).

• Back on street level, look across the river (north) to the island called...

Ile St. Louis

If the Ile de la Cité is a tug laden with the history of Paris, it's towing this classy little residential dinghy laden only with boutiques, famous sorbet shops, and restaurants (see "Eating," later in this chapter). This island wasn't developed until much later than the Ile de la Cité (17th century). What was a swampy mess is now harmonious Parisian architecture. The pedestrian bridge, pont St. Louis, connects the two islands, leading right to rue St. Louis-en-l'Ile. This spine of the island is lined with interesting shops. A short stroll takes you to the famous Berthillon ice cream parlor (#31). Loop back to the pedestrian bridge along the parklike quays (walk north to the river and turn left). This walk is about as peaceful and romantic as Paris gets.

Before walking to the opposite end of the Ile de la Cité, loop through the Latin Quarter (as indicated on the Historic Core of Paris map in this section).

• *From the Deportation Memorial, cross the bridge onto the Left Bank and enjoy the riverside view of Notre-Dame, window-shopping among the green book stalls and browsing through used books, vintage posters, and souvenirs. At the little park and church (over the bridge from the front of Notre-Dame), venture inland a few blocks, basically arcing through the Latin Quarter and returning to the island two bridges down at place St. Michel.*

▲Latin Quarter

The touristic fame of this neighborhood relates to its intriguing artsy, bohemian character. This was perhaps Europe's leading university district in the Middle Ages—home, since the 13th century, to the prestigious Sorbonne University. Back then, Latin was the language of higher education. And, since students here came from all over Europe, Latin served as their linguistic common denominator. Locals referred to the quarter by its language: Latin.

The neighborhood's main boulevards (St. Michel and St. Germain) are lined with far-out bookshops, street singers, and jazz clubs. While still youthful and artsy, the area has become a tourist ghetto filled with cheap North African eateries. The cafés that were once the haunts of great poets and philosophers are now the hangout of tired tourists. For colorful wandering or café sitting, afternoons and evenings are best (Mo: St. Michel).

Walking along rue St. Séverin, you can still see the shadow of the medieval sewer system (the street slopes into a central channel of bricks). In the days before plumbing and toilets, when people still went to the river or neighborhood wells for their water, flushing meant throwing it out the window. At certain times of day, maids on the fourth floor would holler, *"Garde de l'eau!"* ("Watch out for the water!") and heave it into the streets, where it would eventually be washed down into the Seine.

Consider a visit to the Cluny Museum for its medieval art and unicorn tapestries (see page 312).

Place St. Michel (facing the St. Michel bridge) is the traditional core of the Left Bank's artsy, liberal, hippie district of poets, philosophers, winos, and tourists. In less commercial times, place St. Michel was a gathering point for the city's malcontents and misfits. Here, in 1830, 1848, and again in 1871, the citizens took the streets from government troops, set up barricades *Les Mis*–style, and established the Paris Commune. During World War II, the locals rose up against their Nazi oppressors (read the plaques under the dragons at the foot of the St. Michel fountain). And in the spring of 1968, a time of social upheaval all over the world, young students battled riot batons and tear gas, took over the square, and declared it an independent state. Factory workers followed their call to arms and went on strike, toppling the de Gaulle government and forcing change. Eventually, the students were pacified, the university was reformed, and the Latin Quarter's original cobblestones were replaced with pavement, so future scholars could never again use the streets as weapons. Even today, whenever there's a student demonstration, it starts here.

• *From place St. Michel, look across the river and find the spire of the Sainte-Chapelle church and its weathervane angel nearby. Cross the river on pont St. Michel and continue along boulevard du Palais. On your left, you'll see the high-security doorway to Sainte-Chapelle. You'll need to pass through a metal detector to get into Sainte-Chapelle complex. (There are tentative plans for Sainte-Chapelle to have a shared entrance with the Conciergerie, described later on this walk.) Once you're past the extremely strict security, you'll find restrooms ahead on the left. The line into the church may be long (but you can bypass it with a Museum Pass, or by buying your ticket from the tabac shop across the street from the security entrance). Pick up an English info flier and enter the humble ground floor of...*

▲▲▲Sainte-Chapelle

This triumph of Gothic church architecture is a cathedral of glass like no other. It was speedily built between 1242 and 1248 for Louis IX (the only French king who is now a saint) to house the supposed Crown of Thorns. Its architectural harmony is due to the fact that it was completed under the direction of one architect in only five years—unheard of in Gothic times. (Notre-Dame took more than 200 years to build.)

The design clearly shows an *ancien régime* approach to worship. The low-ceilinged basement was for staff and other common folks—worshipping under a sky filled with painted fleurs-de-lis, a symbol of the king. Royal Christians worshipped upstairs. The ground-floor paint job, a 19th-century restoration, is a reasonably accurate copy of the original.

Climb the spiral staircase to the **Haute Chapelle.** Fill the place with choral music, crank up the sunshine, face the top of the altar, and really believe that the Crown of Thorns is there, and this

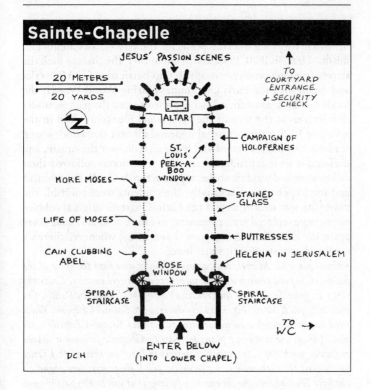

Sainte-Chapelle

JESUS' PASSION SCENES

20 METERS
20 YARDS

TO COURTYARD ENTRANCE & SECURITY CHECK

ALTAR

CAMPAIGN OF HOLOFERNES

ST. LOUIS' PEEK-A-BOO WINDOW

MORE MOSES

STAINED GLASS

LIFE OF MOSES

BUTTRESSES

CAIN CLUBBING ABEL

HELENA IN JERUSALEM

ROSE WINDOW

SPIRAL STAIRCASE

SPIRAL STAIRCASE

TO WC →

DCH

ENTER BELOW (INTO LOWER CHAPEL)

becomes one awesome space.

Fiat lux. "Let there be light." From the first page of the Bible, it's clear: Light is divine. Light shining through stained glass was a symbol of God's grace shining down to earth. Gothic architects used their new technology to turn dark stone buildings into lanterns of light. The glory of Gothic shines brighter here than in any other church.

There are 15 separate panels of stained glass (6,500 square feet—two-thirds of it 13th-century original), with more than 1,100 different scenes, mostly from the Bible.

The altar was raised up high to better display the relic—around which this chapel was built: the Crown of Thorns. The supposed crown cost King Louis three times as much as this church. Today, it is kept in the Notre-Dame Treasury and shown only on Good Friday and on the first Friday of the month at 15:00 (€7.50, €10 combo-ticket with Conciergerie—see next page, both covered by Museum Pass; daily March–Oct 9:30–18:00, Nov–Feb 9:00–17:00, last entry 30 min before closing, Mo: Cité, tel. 01 53 40 60 80).

• *Exit Sainte-Chapelle. Back outside, as you walk around the church exterior, look down to see the foundation and take note of how much Paris has risen in the 750 years since Sainte-Chapelle was built.*

Next door to Sainte-Chapelle is the...

Palais de Justice

Sainte-Chapelle sits within a huge complex of buildings that has housed the local government since ancient Roman times. It was the site of the original Gothic palace of the early kings of France. The only surviving medieval parts are the Sainte-Chapelle church and the Conciergerie prison.

Most of the site is now covered by the giant Palais de Justice, built in 1776, home of the French Supreme Court. The motto *Liberté, Egalité, Fraternité,* over the doors is a reminder that this was also the headquarters of the Revolutionary government.

• *Now pass through the big iron gate to the noisy boulevard du Palais. Cross the street to the wide pedestrian-only rue de Lutèce and walk about halfway down.*

Cité "Métropolitain" Stop and Flower Market

Of the 141 original early 20th-century subway entrances, this is one of only a few survivors—now preserved as a national art treasure. It marks Paris at its peak in 1900—on the cutting edge of Modernism, but with an eye for beauty. The curvy, plantlike ironwork is a textbook example of Art Nouveau, the style that rebelled against the erector-set squareness of the Industrial Age (e.g., Mr. Eiffel's tower).

The flower and plant market on place Louis Lépine is a pleasant detour. On Sundays, this square flutters with a busy bird market. And across the way is the Prefecture de Police, where Inspector Clouseau of *Pink Panther* fame used to work, and where the local resistance fighters took the first building from the Nazis in August of 1944, leading to the Allied liberation of Paris a week later.

• *Pause here to admire the view. Sainte-Chapelle is a pearl in an ugly architectural oyster. Double back to the Palais de Justice, turn right and enter the...*

▲Conciergerie

Though pretty barren inside, this former prison echoes with history. It's a gloomy place. Kings used it to torture and execute failed assassins. The leaders of the Revolution put it to similar good use. A tower along the river, called "The Babbler," was named for the painful sounds that leaked from it.

Marie-Antoinette was imprisoned here. During a busy eight-month period in the Revolution, she was one of 2,600 prisoners kept here on the way to the guillotine. You can see Marie-Antoinette's cell, which houses a collection of her mementos. In another room, a list of those made "a foot shorter at the top" by the "national razor" includes ex-King Louis XVI, Charlotte Corday (who murdered Jean-Paul Marat in his bathtub), and the chief revolutionary who got a taste of his own medicine, Maximilien de Robespierre (€6.50, €10 combo-ticket with Sainte-Chapelle, both covered by Museum Pass, daily April–Sept 9:30–18:00, Oct–March 10:00–17:00, last entry 30 min before closing, 4 boulevard du Palais, Mo: Cité, tel. 01 53 40 60 80, www.monum.fr).

• *Back outside, turn left on boulevard du Palais and head toward the river (north). On the corner is the city's oldest public clock. The mechanism of the present clock is from 1334, and even though the case is Baroque, it keeps on ticking.*

Turn left onto quai de l'Horloge and walk west along the river, past the round medieval tower called "The Babbler." The bridge up ahead is the pont Neuf, where we'll end this walk. At the first corner, veer left into a sleepy triangular square called place Dauphine. Marvel at how such coziness could be lodged in the midst of such greatness as you walk through the park to the end of the island (the departure point for Seine river cruises offered by Vedettes du Pont Neuf; see "Tours—By Boat," near the beginning of this chapter). At the equestrian statue of Henry IV, turn right onto the bridge and take refuge in one of the nooks on the Eiffel Tower side.

Pont Neuf

This "new bridge" is now Paris' oldest. Built during Henry IV's reign (about 1600), its 12 arches span the widest part of the river. The fine view includes the park on the tip of the island (note Seine tour boats), the Orsay Museum, and the Louvre. These turrets were originally for vendors and street entertainers. In the days of Henry IV, who originated the promise of "a chicken in every pot," this would have been a lively scene.

• *As for now, you can tour the Seine by boat, continue to the Louvre, or head to the...*

Paris Plage (Beach)

PARIS

The Riviera it's not, but this fanciful faux beach—assembled in summer along a two-mile stretch of the Seine on the Right Bank—is a fun place to stroll, play, and people-watch on a sunny day. Each summer since 2002, the Paris city government has shut down the embankment's highway and trucked in potted palm trees, hammocks, lounge chairs, and 2,000 tons of sand to create a colorful urban beach. You'll also find "beach cafés," climbing walls, prefab pools, trampolines, *boules,* a library, beach volleyball, badminton, and Frisbee areas in three zones: sandy, grassy, and wood-tiled. As you take in the playful atmosphere, imagine how much has changed here since the Middle Ages when this was a grimy fishing community (free, mid-July–mid-Aug daily 7:00–24:00, no beach off-season; on the Right Bank of the Seine, just north of the Ile de la Cité, between pont des Arts and pont de Sully).

Sights

Paris Museum Pass

In Paris, there are two classes of sightseers—those with a Paris Museum Pass, and those who stand in line. Serious sightseers save time and money by getting this pass.

Buying the Pass

The pass pays for itself with four admissions in two days, and lets you skip the ticket line at most sights (2 days/€32, 4 days/€48, 6 days/€64, no youth or senior discount). It's sold at the participating museums, monuments, and TIs (even at airports). Try to avoid buying the pass at a major museum (such as the Louvre), where the supply can be spotty and lines long. For more info, call 01 44 61 96 60 or visit www.parismuseumpass.com.

Tally up what you want to see from the list on page 297—and remember, an advantage of the pass is that you skip to the front of most lines, which can save hours of waiting, especially in summer. Note that at a few sights (including the Louvre, Sainte-Chapelle, and Notre-Dame's tower), everyone has to shuffle through the slow-moving baggage-check lines for security—but you still save time by avoiding the ticket line.

The pass isn't worth buying for children and teens, as most museums are free or discounted for those under 18 (teenagers may need to show ID as proof of age). Of the few museums that charge for children, some allow kids in free if their parent has a Museum Pass, while others charge admission, depending on age (the cutoff age varies from 5 to 18). The free directory that comes with your pass lists the current hours of sights, phone numbers, and the price that kids pay. If a sight is free for kids, they can skip the line with their passholder parents. (Paris' museums don't offer senior discounts.)

Think ahead to make the most of your pass. Validate it only when you're ready to tackle the covered sights on consecutive days. Make sure the sights you want to visit will be open (Mondays and Tuesdays are big days for museums to be closed). The Paris Museum Pass even covers most of Versailles (your other option for Versailles is the Le Passeport pass; see the top of the Versailles section, near the end of this chapter). On days that you don't have pass coverage, visit free sights as well as sights that aren't covered by passes.

Keep in mind that sights such as the Arc de Triomphe and Pompidou Center are open later in the evening, and that the

PARIS

Paris Sights

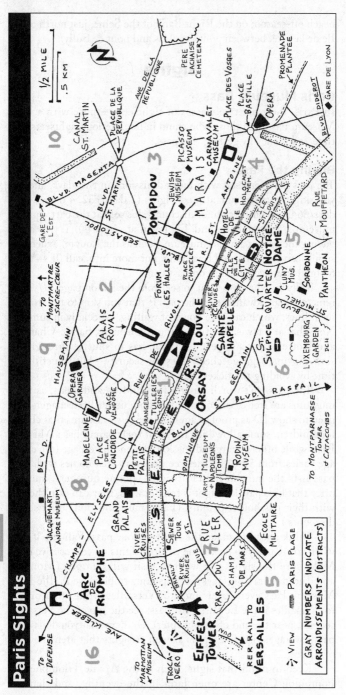

Louvre, Orsay, and Orangerie are open later on selected evenings, allowing you to stretch the day for your Paris Museum Pass.

What the Paris Museum Pass Covers

Most of the sights listed in this chapter are covered by the pass, but it does not cover: the Eiffel Tower, Montparnasse Tower, Marmottan Museum, Opéra Garnier, Notre-Dame Treasury, Jacquemart-André Museum, Grand Palais, La Défense and La Grande Arche, Catacombs, *Paris Story* film, Montmartre Museum, Sacré-Cœur's dome, Dalí Museum, Museum of Erotic Art, and the ladies of Pigalle.

Here's a list of some of the included sights and their admission prices without the pass:

Louvre (€9)	Paris Archaeological Crypt (€3.50)
Orsay Museum (€8)	Cluny Museum (€6.50)
Orangerie Museum (€7.50)	Pompidou Center (€10)
Sainte-Chapelle (€7.50)	Jewish Art and History Museum (€7)
Arc de Triomphe (€9)	National Maritime Museum (€6.50)
Rodin Museum (€6)	Sewer Tour (€4)
Army Museum (€8)	Quai Branly Museum (€8.50)
Conciergerie (€6.50)	Versailles (€22.50—€13.50 for
Panthéon (€7.50)	Château; €9 for Domaine de
Notre-Dame Tower (€7.50)	Marie-Antoinette)

Activating and Using the Pass

The pass isn't activated until the first time you use it (write the starting date on the pass).

To use your pass at sights, boldly walk to the front of the ticket line, hold up your pass, and ask the ticket-taker: *"Entrez, pass?"* (ahn-tray pahs). You'll either be allowed to enter at that point or you'll be directed to a special entrance. For major sights, such as the Louvre and Orsay museums, we've identified pass-holder entrances on the maps in this book.

With the pass, you'll pop freely into sights that you're walking by (even for a few minutes) that otherwise might not be worth the expense (e.g., the Conciergerie or Paris Archaeological Crypt).

Major Museums Neighborhood

Paris' grandest park, the Tuileries Garden, was once the private property of kings and queens. Today, it links the museums of the Louvre, Orangerie, Jeu de Paume, and the Orsay. And across from the Louvre are the tranquil, historic courtyards of the Palais Royal.

▲▲▲**Louvre (Musée du Louvre)**—This is Europe's oldest, biggest, greatest, and second-most-crowded museum (after the Vatican). Housed in a U-shaped, 16th-century palace (accentuated

Affording Paris' Sights

Paris is an expensive city for tourists, with lots of pricey sights, but—fortunately—lots of freebies, too. Smart budget-minded travelers begin by buying and getting the most out of a **Paris Museum Pass** (see page 295), while considering these frugal sightseeing options.

Free Museums: Some museums are always free, including the Carnavalet, Petit Palais, Victor Hugo's House, and Fragonard Perfume Museum. Many of Paris' most famous museums offer free entry on the first Sunday of the month, including the Louvre, Orsay, Rodin, Cluny, and Pompidou Center museums. You can also visit the Orsay Museum for free at 17:00, about 30 minutes before rooms start closing. One of the best everyday values is the Rodin Museum's garden, where you'll pay €1 to experience many of Rodin's finest works in a lovely outdoor setting.

Other Freebies: Many worthwhile sights don't charge entry, including the Notre-Dame Cathedral, Père Lachaise Cemetery, Deportation Memorial, Holocaust Memorial, Paris Plage (summers only), St. Sulpice Church (with its organ recital), and La Défense (though there is a charge to enter La Grande Arche).

Paris' glorious, entertaining parks are free, of course. These include Luxembourg Garden, Champ de Mars (under the Eiffel Tower), Tuileries Garden (between the Louvre and place de la Concorde), Palais Royal Courtyards, Jardin des Plantes, the Promenade Plantée walk, and Versailles' Gardens (except on summer weekends).

Reduced Price: Several museums offer a discount if you enter later in the day, including the Louvre (after 18:00 on Wed and Fri), Orsay (after 16:15), Army Museum (after 17:00), and Versailles' Château (after 15:00) and Domaine de Marie-Antoinette (after 16:00).

Free Concerts: Venues offering free or very cheap (€6-8) concerts include the American Church, Hotel des Invalides, Cluny

by a 20th-century glass pyramid), the Louvre is Paris' top museum and one of its key landmarks. It's home to *Mona Lisa, Venus de Milo,* and hall after hall of Greek and Roman masterpieces, medieval jewels, Michelangelo statues, and paintings by the greatest artists from the Renaissance to the Romantics (mid-1800s).

Touring the Louvre can be overwhelming, so be selective. Focus on the Denon wing (south, along the river), with Greek sculptures, Italian paintings (by Raphael and da Vinci), and—of course—French paintings (Neoclassical and Romantic). For extra credit, tackle the Richelieu wing (north, away from the river), with works from ancient Mesopotamia (today's Iraq), as well as French, Dutch, and Northern art; or the Sully wing (connecting the other two wings), with Egyptian artifacts and more French paintings.

Museum, St. Sulpice Church, Madeleine Church, and Notre-Dame Cathedral. For a listing of free concerts, check *Pariscope* magazine (under "Musique and Concerts Classiques") and look for events marked *entrée libre*).

Self-Guided Bus Tour: Instead of paying €25 for a tour company to give you an overview of Paris, ride city bus #69 for the price of a Métro ticket (runs daily except Sun). This scenic route crosses the city east–west, running between the Eiffel Tower and Père Lachaise Cemetery, and passes these great monuments and neighborhoods en route: Ecole Militaire, rue Cler, Les Invalides (Army Museum and Napoleon's Tomb), Louvre Museum, Ile de la Cité, Ile St. Louis, Hôtel de Ville, Pompidou Center, and the Marais. You don't have to do the whole enchilada; get on and off wherever you like (your ticket gives you 90 minutes if purchased at a Métro station). You can hop on Monday through Saturday, but avoid weekday rush hours (8:00–9:30 & 17:30–19:30), and hot days (no air-con). Evening bus rides are magical in months when it gets dark enough to see the floodlit monuments before the bus finishes running (last trip at 21:15). In the rue Cler area, catch bus #69 eastbound at the Eiffel Tower on avenue Joseph Bouvard (the first stop is at the southwestern end of the avenue, across from the Eiffel Tower) or along rue St. Dominique. In the Marais, catch the bus westbound on rues St. Antoine and Rivoli.

Good-Value Tours: At €10-15, Paris Walks' tours are a good value. The €10 Seine River cruises, best after dark, are also worthwhile. The Bus #69 Sightseeing Tour, which costs only the price of a transit ticket, could be the best deal of all.

Pricey...but worth it? Certain big-ticket items—primarily the Eiffel Tower, Louvre, and Versailles—are expensive and crowded, but offer once-in-a-lifetime experiences. Think of it like you would a spree in Vegas—budget in a little "gambling" money you expect to lose, then just relax...and enjoy.

Expect changes—the sprawling Louvre is constantly in flux. Rooms are periodically closed for renovation, and their paintings and sculpture are moved to new places within the museum. To find the artwork you're looking for, ask the nearest guard for its new location. Point to the photo in your book and ask, *"Où est, s'il vous plaît?"* (oo ay see voo play).

Cost: €9, €6 after 18:00 on Wed and Fri, free on first Sun of month, covered by Museum Pass. Tickets good all day and reentry allowed. Optional additional charges apply for temporary exhibits.

Hours: Wed–Mon 9:00–18:00, most wings stay open Wed and Fri until 21:45, closed Tue; galleries start closing 30 min early, last entry 45 min before closing; crowds worst on Sun, Mon, Wed, and mornings.

PARIS

Information: tel. 01 40 20 53 17, recorded info tel. 01 40 20 51 51, www.louvre.fr.

Location: At Palais Royal–Musée du Louvre Métro stop. (The old Louvre Métro stop, called Louvre-Rivoli, is farther from the entrance.)

Buying Tickets: Located under the pyramid, the self-serve ticket machines are faster to use than the ticket windows (machines accept euro notes, coins, and Visa cards). The *tabac* in the underground mall at the Louvre sells tickets to the Louvre, Orsay, and Versailles, plus Paris Museum Passes, for the same prices as elsewhere.

Crowd-Beating Tips: There is no grander entry than through the main entrance at the pyramid in the central courtyard, but metal detectors (not ticket-buying) create a long line at times. There are several ways to avoid the line:

If you have a Museum Pass, you can use the group entrance in the pedestrian passageway (labeled *Pavilion Richelieu*) between the pyramid and rue de Rivoli. It's under the arches, a few steps north of the pyramid; find the uniformed guard at the entrance, with the escalator down.

Otherwise, you can enter the Louvre from its (usually less crowded) underground entrance, accessed through the Carrousel du Louvre shopping mall. Enter the mall at 99 rue de Rivoli (the door with the red awning) or directly from the Métro stop Palais Royal–Musée du Louvre (stepping off the train, exit at the end of the platform, following signs to *Musée du Louvre–Le Carrousel du Louvre*).

Tours: The 90-minute English-language **guided tours** leave three times daily except Sun from the *Accueil des Groupes* area (normally at 11:00, 14:00, and 15:45; €5 plus your entry ticket, tour tel. 01 40 20 52 63). Digital **audioguides** provide eager students with commentary on about 130 masterpieces (€6, available at entries to the three wings, at the top of the escalators). I prefer the self-guided tour described below, which is also available as a free audiotour for people with iPods or other MP3 players (download from www.ricksteves.com or iTunes).

❍ Self-Guided Tour: Start in the Denon Wing and visit the highlights, in the following order (thanks to Gene Openshaw for his help with this).

Wander through the **ancient Greek and Roman works** to see the Parthenon frieze, Pompeii mosaics, Etruscan sarcophagi, and Roman portrait busts. Pop into the adjoining Sully Wing to see the lovely *Venus de Milo (Aphrodite)*. This goddess of love (c. 100 B.C., from the Greek island of Melos) created a sensation when she was discovered in 1820. Most "Greek" statues are actually later Roman copies, but Venus is a rare Greek original. She, like Golden Age

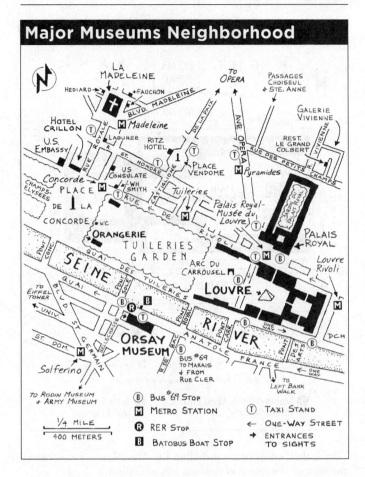

Major Museums Neighborhood

B Bus #69 Stop
M Metro Station
R RER Stop
B Batobus Boat Stop
T Taxi Stand
← One-Way Street
→ Entrances to Sights

1/4 MILE
400 METERS

Greeks, epitomizes stability, beauty, and balance. Later Greek art was Hellenistic, adding motion and drama. For a good example, see the exciting *Winged Victory of Samothrace* (*Victoire de Samothrace*, on the landing). This statue of a woman with wings, poised on the prow of a ship, once stood on a hilltop to commemorate a great naval victory. This is the *Venus de Milo* gone Hellenistic.

The **Italian collection** is on the other side of the *Winged Victory*. The key to Renaissance painting was realism, and for the Italians "realism" was spelled "3-D." Painters were inspired by the realism and balanced beauty of Greek sculpture. Painting a 3-D world on a 2-D surface is tough, and after a millennium of Dark Ages, artists were rusty. Living in a religious age, they painted mostly altarpieces full of saints, angels, Madonnas-and-bambinos, and crucifixes floating in an ethereal gold-leaf heaven. Gradually, though, they brought these otherworldly scenes down to earth.

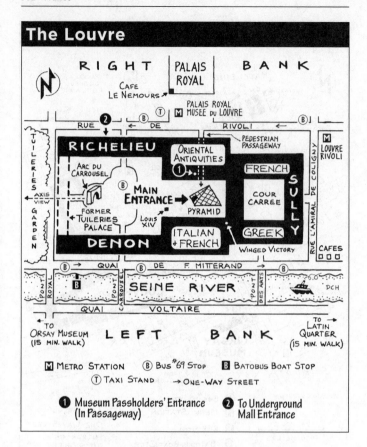

The Louvre

RIGHT   PALAIS   BANK
         ROYAL

CAFE
LE NEMOURS

PALAIS ROYAL
Ⓜ MUSÉE DU LOUVRE

Ⓑ Ⓣ Ⓜ

RUE ❷   ← DE   RIVOLI →   Ⓑ

PEDESTRIAN
PASSAGEWAY

RICHELIEU   ORIENTAL
            ANTIQUITIES ❶

ARC DU
CARROUSEL

Ⓑ MAIN
ENTRANCE →   PYRAMID

LOUIS
XIV

FORMER
TUILERIES
PALACE

ITALIAN
+ FRENCH

DENON

FRENCH

COUR
CARRÉE

GREEK

SULLY

WINGED VICTORY

Ⓜ LOUVRE
RIVOLI

RUE L'AMIRAL DE COLIGNY

CAFES

TUILERIES GARDEN

AXIS
VIEW

Ⓑ → QUAI   Ⓑ DE F. MITTERAND   Ⓑ

SEINE   RIVER

Ⓑ   DCH

PONT ROYAL   Ⓑ   PONT CARROUSEL   PONT DES ARTS

QUAI   VOLTAIRE

TO
ORSAY MUSEUM   LEFT   BANK   TO
(15 MIN. WALK)   LATIN
                                 QUARTER
                                 (15 MIN. WALK)

Ⓜ METRO STATION   Ⓑ BUS #69 STOP   Ⓑ BATOBUS BOAT STOP
Ⓣ TAXI STAND   → ONE-WAY STREET

❶ Museum Passholders' Entrance   ❷ To Underground
   (In Passageway)   Mall Entrance

(The Italian collection—including the *Mona Lisa*—are scattered throughout the rooms of the long Grand Gallery.)

Two masters of the Italian High Renaissance (1500–1600) were Raphael (see his *La Belle Jardinière,* showing the Madonna, Child, and John the Baptist) and Leonardo da Vinci. The Louvre has the greatest collection of Leonardos in the world—five of them, including the exquisite *Virgin, Child, and St. Anne,* the neighboring *Madonna of the Rocks,* and the androgynous *John the Baptist.* His most famous, of course, is the *Mona Lisa.*

The ***Mona Lisa*** (*La Joconde* in French) is in the Salle des Etats, midway down the Grand Gallery, on the right. After a €5 million renovation, Mona is behind glass on her own false wall.

Leonardo was already an old man when François I invited him to France. Determined to pack light, he took only a few paintings. One was a portrait of Lisa del Giocondo, the wife of a wealthy Florentine merchant. When Leonardo arrived, François I immediately fell in love with the painting and made it the

PARIS

centerpiece of the small collection of Italian masterpieces that would, in three centuries, become the Louvre museum. He called it *La Gioconda*—both her last name and a play on the Italian word for "happy woman." We know it as a contraction of the Italian for "my lady Lisa"—*Mona Lisa*. Warning: François I was impressed, but *Mona* may disappoint you. She's smaller and darker than you'd expect, located in a huge room, behind a glaring pane of glass.

Mona's overall mood is one of balance and serenity, but there's also an element of mystery. Her smile and long-distance beauty are subtle and elusive, tempting but always just out of reach, like strands of a street singer's melody drifting through the Métro tunnel. *Mona* doesn't knock your socks off, but she winks at the patient viewer.

Now for something **Neoclassical.** Exit behind *Mona Lisa* and turn right into the Salle Daru to find *The Coronation of Napoleon* by Jacques-Louis David. Neoclassicism, once the rage in France (1780–1850), usually features Greek subjects, patriotic sentiment, and a clean, simple style. After Napoleon quickly conquered most of Europe, he insisted on being made emperor (not merely king) of this "New Rome." He staged an elaborate coronation ceremony in Paris, and rather than let the pope crown him, he crowned himself. The setting is the Notre-Dame Cathedral, with Greek columns and Roman arches thrown in for effect. Napoleon's mom was also added, since she couldn't make it to the ceremony. A key on the frame describes who's who in the picture.

The **Romantic** collection, in an adjacent room (Salle Mollien), has works by Théodore Géricault *(The Raft of the Medusa)* and Eugène Delacroix *(Liberty Leading the People)*. Romanticism, with an emphasis on motion and emotion, is the complete flip side of Neoclassicism, though they both flourished in the early 1800s. Delacroix's *Liberty,* commemorating the stirrings of democracy in France, is also a fitting tribute to the Louvre, the first museum opened to the common rabble of humanity. The good things in life don't belong only to a small wealthy part of society, but to all. The motto of France is *"Liberté, Egalité, Fraternité"*—liberty, equality, and brotherhood.

Exit the room at the far end (past the café) and go downstairs, where you'll bump into the bum of a large, twisting male nude who looks like he's just waking up after a thousand-year nap. The two *Slaves* (1513–1515) by Michelangelo are a fitting end to this museum—works that bridge the ancient and modern worlds. Michelangelo, like his fellow Renaissance artists, learned from the Greeks. The perfect anatomy, twisting poses, and idealized faces look as if they could have been done 2,000 years earlier. Michelangelo said that his purpose was to carve away the marble to reveal the figures God had put inside. The *Rebellious Slave,* fighting against his bondage, shows the agony of that process and the ecstasy of the result.

Palais Royal Courtyards—Across from the Louvre are the pleasant courtyards of the stately Palais Royal. Although the palace is closed to the public, the courtyards are open. As you enter, you'll pass through a whimsical courtyard filled with stubby, striped columns and playful fountains (with fun, reflective metal balls) into another, curiously peaceful courtyard. This is where in-the-know Parisians come to take a quiet break, walk their poodles, or enjoy a rendezvous—surrounded by a serene arcade and a handful of historic restaurants.

Exiting the courtyard at the side facing away from the Seine brings you to the Galeries Colbert and Vivienne, good examples of shopping arcades from the early 1900s.

Cost, Hours, Location: Courtyards are free and always open. The Palais Royal is directly north of the Louvre on rue de Rivoli (Mo: Palais Royal–Musée du Louvre).

▲▲**Orangerie Museum (Musée de l'Orangerie)**—This Impressionist museum, lovely as a water lily, has recently reopened after years of renovation. Step out of the tree-lined, sun-dappled Impressionist painting that is the Tuileries Garden and into the Orangerie (oh-rahn-zheh-ree). You'll start with the museum's claim to fame: Claude Monet's water lilies. These large-scale paintings are displayed exactly as Monet intended them—surrounding you in oval-shaped rooms—so you feel immersed in his garden at Giverny. Then head downstairs to enjoy a little *bijou* of select works by Maurice Utrillo, Paul Cézanne, Pierre-Auguste Renoir, Henri Matisse, and Pablo Picasso.

Cost, Hours, Location: €7.50, under 18 free, covered by Museum Pass, audioguide-€5, Wed–Mon 9:00–18:00, closed Tue, located in Tuileries Garden near place de la Concorde, Mo: Concorde, tel. 01 44 77 80 07, www.musee-orangerie.fr.

▲▲▲**Orsay Museum (Musée d'Orsay)**—The Musée d'Orsay (mew-zay dor-say) houses French art of the 1800s (specifically, art from 1848 to 1914), picking up where the Louvre leaves off. For us, that means Impressionism. The Orsay houses the best general collection anywhere of Edouard Manet, Claude Monet, Pierre-Auguste Renoir, Edgar Degas, Vincent van Gogh, Paul Cézanne, and Paul Gauguin.

The museum shows art that is also both old and new, conservative and revolutionary. You'll start on the ground floor with the Conservatives and the early rebels who paved the way for the Impressionists. Here, sappy soft-focus Venuses (popular with the 18th-century bourgeoisie) are displayed alongside the grittier work of the Realists. For most visitors, the most important part of the museum is the Impressionist collection

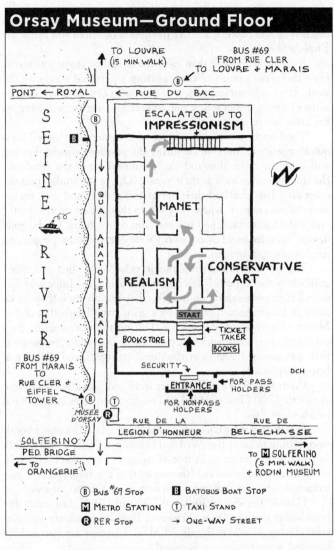

Orsay Museum—Ground Floor

TO LOUVRE
(15 MIN. WALK)

BUS #69
FROM RUE CLER
TO LOUVRE + MARAIS

Ⓑ

PONT ← ROYAL   ← RUE DU BAC

Ⓑ

S E I N E   R I V E R

QUAI ANATOLE FRANCE

ESCALATOR UP TO
IMPRESSIONISM

MANET

REALISM

CONSERVATIVE ART

START

BOOKSTORE

TICKET TAKER
BOOKS

SECURITY

DCH

ENTRANCE ← FOR PASS HOLDERS

FOR NON-PASS HOLDERS

BUS #69
FROM MARAIS
TO
RUE CLER +
EIFFEL TOWER

Ⓑ Ⓣ

MUSÉE D'ORSAY

Ⓡ

RUE DE LA
LEGION D'HONNEUR

RUE DE
BELLECHASSE

SOLFERINO
PED. BRIDGE

← TO
ORANGERIE

→
TO Ⓜ SOLFERINO
(5 MIN. WALK)
+ RODIN MUSEUM

Ⓑ BUS #69 STOP   Ⓑ BATOBUS BOAT STOP
Ⓜ METRO STATION   Ⓣ TAXI STAND
Ⓡ RER STOP   → ONE-WAY STREET

upstairs, where you can study many pictures you've probably seen in books, such as Renoir's *Dance at the Moulin de la Galette,* Monet's *Cathedral of Rouen,* James Abbott McNeill Whistler's *Portrait of the Artist's Mother,* Van Gogh's *The Church at Auvers-sur-Oise,* and Cézanne's *The Card Players.* As you approach these beautiful, easy-to-enjoy paintings, remember that there is more to this art than meets the eye.

Here's a primer on Impressionism: After the camera was invented, it threatened to make artists obsolete. A painter's original function was to record reality faithfully, like a journalist. Now a machine could capture a better likeness faster than you could say Etch-A-Sketch.

But true art is more than just painted reality. It gives us reality from the artist's point of view, putting a personal stamp on the work. It records not only a scene—a camera can do that—but the artist's impressions of that scene. Impressions are often fleeting, so the artist has to work quickly.

The Impressionist painters rejected camera-like detail for a quick style more suited to capturing the passing moment. Feeling stifled by the rigid rules and stuffy atmosphere of the Academy, the Impressionists took as their motto, "Out of the studio, into the open air." They grabbed their berets and scarves and took excursions to the country, where they set up their easels on riverbanks and hillsides, or sketched in cafés and dance halls. Gods, goddesses, nymphs, and fantasy scenes were out; common people and rural landscapes were in.

The quick style and simple subjects were ridiculed and called childish by the "experts." Rejected by the Salon, the Impressionists staged their own exhibition in 1874. They brashly took their name from an insult thrown at them by a critic, who laughed at one of Monet's impressions of a sunrise. During the next decade, they exhibited their own work independently. The public, opposed at first, was slowly drawn in by the simplicity, color, and vibrancy of Impressionist art.

Cost: €8, €5.50 Fri–Wed after 16:15 and Thu after 18:00, free at exactly 17:00 (Thu at 21:00) and on first Sun of month, covered by Museum Pass.

Free Entry near Closing Time: Right when the ticket booth stops selling tickets (Tue–Wed and Fri–Sun at 17:00, Thu at 21:00), you're welcome to scoot in free of charge. (They won't let you in much after that, however.) Remember that the Impressionist galleries upstairs start shutting down first, so go there right away.

Hours: Tue–Sun 9:30–18:00, Thu until 21:45, last entry one hour before closing (45 min before on Thu), Impressionist galleries start closing 45 min early, closed Mon. Tuesdays are particularly crowded, since the Louvre is closed.

Location: Above the RER-C stop called Musée d'Orsay; the nearest Métro stop is Solférino, three blocks southeast of the Orsay.

Bus #69 from the Marais neighborhood stops at the museum on the river side (quai Anatole France); from the rue Cler area, it stops behind the museum on the rue du Bac. From the Louvre, catch bus #69 along rue de Rivoli; otherwise, it's a lovely 15-minute walk through the Tuileries Garden and across the river on the pedestrian bridge to the Orsay. The museum is at 1 rue de la Légion d'Honneur. A taxi stand is in front of the entrance on quai Anatole France.

Information: The booth inside the entrance provides free floor plans in English. Tel. 01 40 49 48 14, www.musee-orsay.fr.

Tours: Audioguides are €6. English-language tours usually run at 11:30 daily (except Sun), cost €7, and take 90 minutes. Some tours are occasionally offered at other times (inquire when you arrive). A longer version of the self-guided tour described below is available as a free audio tour for people with an iPod or other MP3 player (download from www.ricksteves.com or iTunes).

Cuisine Art: There's a pricey but *très* elegant restaurant on the second floor, with affordable tea and coffee served 15:00–17:30. A simple fifth-floor café is sandwiched between the Impressionists; above it is an easy self-service place with sandwiches and drinks.

Eiffel Tower and Nearby

▲▲▲**Eiffel Tower (La Tour Eiffel)**—It's crowded and expensive, but this 1,000-foot-tall ornament is worth the trouble. Visitors to Paris may find *Mona Lisa* to be less than expected, but the Eiffel Tower rarely disappoints, even in an era of skyscrapers.

Built a hundred years after the French Revolution (and in the midst of an industrial one), the tower served no function but to impress. Bridge-builder Gustave Eiffel won the contest for the 1889 Centennial World's Fair by beating out such rival proposals as a giant guillotine. To a generation hooked on technology, the tower was the marvel of the age, a symbol of progress and human ingenuity. Indeed, despite its 7,000 tons of metal and 50 tons of paint, the tower is so well-engineered that it weighs no more per square inch at its base than a linebacker on tiptoes. Not all were so impressed, however; many found it a monstrosity. The writer Guy de Maupassant routinely ate lunch in the tower just so he wouldn't have to look at it.

Delicate and graceful when seen from afar, the Eiffel Tower is massive—even a bit scary—from close up. You don't appreciate the size until you walk toward it; like a mountain, it seems so close but takes forever to reach. There are three observation platforms, at 200, 400, and 900 feet; the higher you go, the more you pay. One elevator will take you to the first or second level (just stay on after first stop), but the third level has a separate elevator and line. Plan on at least 90 minutes if you want to go to the top and back. While being on the windy top of the Eiffel Tower is a thrill you'll never forget, the view is actually better from the second level because you're closer to the sights, and the monuments are more recognizable.

The stairs—yes, you can walk up to the second level—are next to the Jules Verne restaurant entrance (allow $300 per person for

Eiffel Tower and Nearby

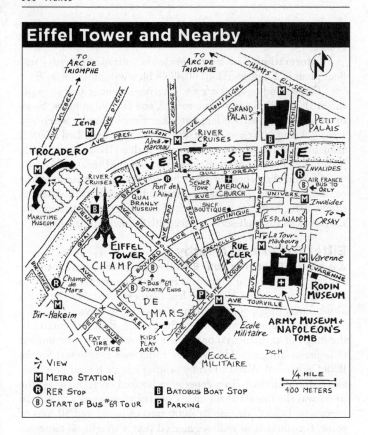

TO ARC DE TRIOMPHE
TO ARC DE TRIOMPHE
CHAMPS-ELYSEES
N

GRAND PALAIS
PETIT PALAIS

AVE. KLEBER
AVE. D'IENA
RUE GEORGE V
AVE. MONTAIGNE
AVE. CHURCHILL

Iéna

PRES. WILSON

TROCADERO

RIVER CRUISES
Alma Marceau

RIVE R   SE I N E

ALEX III

INVALIDES

MARITIME MUSEUM

RIVER CRUISES

QUAI D'ORSAY

SEWER TOUR
AMERICAN CHURCH

AIR FRANCE BUS TO ORLY

Pont de l'Alma
QUAI BRANLY MUSEUM

RUE COGNAC

SNCF BOUTIQUE

UNIVERS.

Invalides

TO ORSAY

AVE. RAPP

RUE C ST. DOMINIQUE

ESPLANADE

EIFFEL TOWER

AVE. DE LA BOURDONNAIS

RUE GRENELLE

RUE CLER

La Tour-Maubourg

Varenne

CHAMP

BLVD. DE LA TOUR

R. VARENNE

Champ de Mars

Bus #69 Starts/Ends

RODIN MUSEUM

Bir-Hakeim

AVE. DE SUFFREN

DE

MARS

AVE. DE LA MOTTE PICQUET

AVE. TOURVILLE

ARMY MUSEUM & NAPOLEON'S TOMB

DESAIX

FAURE

FAT TIRE OFFICE

KIDS' PLAY AREA

Ecole Militaire

DCH

ECOLE MILITAIRE

VIEW
METRO STATION
RER STOP
START OF BUS #69 TOUR

BATOBUS BOAT STOP
PARKING

¼ MILE
400 METERS

the restaurant, reserve three months in advance). As you ascend through the metal beams, imagine being a worker, perched high above nothing, riveting this giant erector set together.

The top level, called *le sommet* (900 feet), is tiny. (It can close temporarily without warning when it reaches capacity.) All you'll find here are wind and grand, sweeping views. The city lies before you, with a panoramic guide. On a good day, you can see for 40 miles.

The second level (400 feet) has the best views (up the short stairway, on the platform without the wire-cage barriers), souvenir shops, public telephones to call home, and a small stand-up café. While you'll save no money, consider taking the elevator up and the stairs down (five minutes from second level to first, five minutes more to ground) for good exercise and views.

The first level (200 feet) has exhibits, a post office (daily 10:00–19:00, cancellation stamp will read Eiffel Tower), a snack bar, WCs, and souvenirs. Read the informative signs (in English) describing the major monuments, see the entertaining free movie on the history of the tower, and don't miss a century of fireworks—including the entire millennium blast—on video. Then consider a drink or a sandwich overlooking all of Paris at the snack café (outdoor tables in summer) or at the city's best view bar/restaurant, **Altitude 95** (see "Eating," later in this chapter).

Seeing It All: If you don't want to miss a single level, here's a plan for getting the most out of your visit. Ride the lift to the second level, then immediately line up and catch the next lift to the top. Enjoy the views on top, then ride back down to the second level. Frolic there for a while and take in some more views. When you're ready, head to the first level by taking the stairs (no line) or lining up for the elevator. Explore the shops and exhibits on this level, have a snack, then take the stairs (best) or lift back to earth.

Cost, Hours, Location: €13 all the way to the top, €8 if you're going only up to the two lower levels, not covered by Museum Pass. You can skip the elevator line and climb the stairs to the first or second level for €4.50, or €3.50 if you're under 25. The elevators and stairs are both free going down. Daily mid-June–Aug 9:00–24:45 in the morning, Sept–mid-June 9:30–23:45, last ascent to top at 22:30 and to lower levels via elevator at 23:00 or by stairs at 18:30. Mo: Bir-Hakeim and Trocadéro or Champ de Mars–Tour Eiffel RER stop (each about a 10-min walk away). Tel. 01 44 11 23 23, www.tour-eiffel.fr.

If you climb the stairs, or buy a ticket only to one of the lower levels, you can buy your way up once you're in the tower—ticket booths and machines on the first and second levels sell supplements to go higher (with no penalty).

Tips: To avoid most crowds, go early (get in line by 8:45, before it opens) or late in the day (after 20:00 May–Aug, after 18:00 in off-season—see above for last ascent times). Weekends and holidays are worst. Weekdays off-season are not as crowded. A new online reservation system may debut in time for your trip, allowing you to book a half-hour time slot for your visit—check their website (www.tour-eiffel.fr). Ideally, you should arrive with some light and stay as it gets dark.

To pass the time in line, pick up whatever free reading material is available at the ground-level tourist stands.

Before or after your tower visit, you can catch the Bateaux Parisiens boat for a Seine cruise (near the base of Eiffel Tower, see "Tours—By Boat," earlier in this chapter, for details).

Best Views: The best place to view the tower is from Trocadéro Square to the north. It's a 10-minute walk across the river, a happening scene at night, and especially fun for kids. Consider arriving at the Trocadéro Métro stop for the view, then walking toward the tower. Another delightful viewpoint is the long, grassy field called Champ de Mars, to the south (great for picnics, though allowed only along side lawns). However impressive it may be by day, the tower is an awesome thing to see at twilight, when it becomes engorged with light, and virile Paris lies back and lets night be on top. When darkness fully envelops the city, the tower seems to climax—with a spectacular light show—at the top of each hour... for five minutes.

Quai Branly Museum (Museé du Quai Branly)—This is the best collection I've seen anywhere of so-called Primitive Art from Africa, Polynesia, Asia, and America. It's presented in a wild, organic, and strikingly modern building that's a sightseeing thrill in itself. This museum, opened in 2006, is still big news with locals. Masks, statuettes, musical instruments, clothes, voodoo dolls, and a variety of temporary exhibits and activities are artfully presented and exquisitely lit. It's not, however, accompanied by much printed English information—to really appreciate the exhibit, use the €5 audioguide. It's a 10-minute walk east (upriver) of the Eiffel Tower, along the river (€8.50, covered by Museum Pass, Tue–Sun 11:00–19:00, Thu–Sat until 21:00, closed Mon, 37 quai Branly, RER: Champ de Mars–Tour Eiffel or Pont de l'Alma, tel. 01 56 61 70 00, www.quaibranly.fr).

National Maritime Museum (Musée National de la Marine)— This extensive museum houses an amazing collection of ship models, submarines, torpedoes, cannonballs, *beaucoup* bowsprits, and naval you-name-it—including a small boat made for Napoleon. You'll find limited English information on the walls, but kids like the museum anyway (adults-€6.50, kids-€4.50, more during special exhibits, covered by Museum Pass, Wed–Mon 10:00–18:00, closed Tue, on left side of Trocadéro Square with your back to Eiffel Tower, tel. 01 53 65 69 53, www.musee-marine.fr).

▲Paris Sewer Tour (Les Egouts de Paris)—This quick, fascinating, and slightly stinky visit (a perfumed hanky helps) takes you along a few hundred yards of underground water tunnels in the world's first underground sewer system. Pick up the helpful English self-guided tour, then drop down into Jean Valjean's world of tunnels, rats, and manhole covers. (Victor Hugo was friends with the sewer inspector when he wrote *Les Misérables*.) You'll pass well-organized displays with helpful English information detailing the evolution of this amazing network. Over 1,500 miles of tunnels carry 317 million gallons of water daily through this underworld. It's the world's longest sewer system—so long, they say, that if it were laid out straight, it would stretch from Paris all the way to Istanbul. Don't miss the slide show, fine WCs just beyond the gift shop, and occasional tours in English.

Cost, Hours, Location: €4, covered by Museum Pass, May–Sept Sat–Wed 11:00–17:00, Oct–April Sat–Wed 11:00–16:00, closed Thu–Fri, located where pont de l'Alma greets the

Left Bank, Mo: Alma-Marceau, RER: Pont de l'Alma, tel. 01 53 68 27 81.

▲▲**Army Museum and Napoleon's Tomb (Musée de l'Armée)**—The emperor lies majestically dead inside several coffins under a grand dome glittering with 26 pounds of gold—a goose-bumping pilgrimage for historians. Napoleon is surrounded by the tombs of other French war heroes and fine military museums in the Hôtel des Invalides. Follow signs to the "crypt" to find Roman Empire–style reliefs that list the accomplishments of Napoleon's administration. The Army Museum's WWI exhibit is well presented in English and complements its interesting and worthwhile WWII rooms. The section on French military history ("Louis XIV to Napoleon III") has been under renovation recently; some parts may not be finished in time for your visit.

Cost, Hours, Location: €8, ticket covers Napoleon's Tomb and all museums within Les Invalides complex, includes audioguide for tomb, covered by Museum Pass, price drops to €6 an hour before closing time, always free for all military personnel with ID. Open daily April–Sept 10:00–18:00, mid-June–mid-Sept tomb stays open until 19:00, museum may be open Tue until 21:00, Oct–March until 17:00; last entry 30 min before closing, Oct–May closed first Mon of every month. The Hôtel des Invalides is at 129 rue de Grenelle; Mo: La Tour Maubourg, Varenne, or Invalides; tel. 01 44 42 38 77, www.invalides.org.

▲▲**Rodin Museum (Musée Rodin)**—This user-friendly museum is filled with passionate works by the greatest sculptor since Michelangelo. The entire museum is being gradually renovated over the next few years; pick up the essential museum map to guide you. Auguste Rodin (1840–1917) sculpted human figures on an epic scale, revealing through the body their deepest thoughts and feelings. Rodin's statues rise from the raw stone around them, driven by the life force. With missing limbs and scarred skin, these are prefab classics, making ugliness noble. Rodin's people are always moving restlessly. Even the famous *Thinker* is moving. Rodin worked with many materials—he chiseled marble (though not often), modeled clay, cast bronze, worked plaster, painted, and sketched. He often created different versions of the same subject in different media.

Rodin lived and worked in this mansion, renting rooms alongside Henri Matisse, the poet Rainer Maria Rilke (Rodin's secretary), and the dancer Isadora Duncan. Well-displayed in the mansion where the sculptor lived and worked, exhibits trace Rodin's artistic development, explain how his bronze statues were cast, and show some of the studies he created to work up to his masterpiece (the unfinished *Gates of Hell*). Learn about Rodin's tumultuous relationship with his apprentice and lover, Camille

Claudel. Mull over what makes his sculptures some of the most evocative since the Renaissance. For many, the gardens are the highlight of this museum. Here you'll find several of his greatest works, such as the *Thinker, Balzac,* the *Burghers of Calais,* and the *Gates of Hell.* The gardens are ideal for artistic reflection.

Cost, Hours, Location: €6, free on first Sun of the month, covered by Museum Pass. You'll pay €1 to get into the gardens only—which may be Paris' best deal, as many works are on display there (also covered by Museum Pass). Audioguides are €4, and baggage check is mandatory. Open April–Sept Tue–Sun 9:30–17:45, gardens close 18:45; Oct–March Tue–Sun 9:30–16:45, gardens close 17:00, last entry 30 min before closing, closed Mon. It's near the Army Museum and Napoleon's Tomb, 79 rue de Varenne, Mo: Varenne, tel. 01 44 18 61 10, www.musee-rodin.fr.

▲▲**Marmottan Museum (Musée Marmottan Monet)**—In this private, intimate, untouristy museum, you'll find the best collection anywhere of works by Impressionist headliner Claude Monet. Follow Monet's life through more than a hundred works, from simple sketches to the *Impression: Sunrise* painting that gave his artistic movement its start—and a name. You'll also enjoy large-scale canvases featuring the water lilies from his garden at Giverny.

Cost, Hours, Location: €8, not covered by Museum Pass, Tue 11:00–21:00, Wed–Sun 10:00–18:00, last entry 30 min before closing, closed Mon, 2 rue Louis Boilly, Mo: La Muette, tel. 01 44 96 50 33, www.marmottan.com. To get to the museum from the Métro stop, follow the brown museum signs six blocks down chaussée de la Muette through the park; pause to watch kids play on the old-time, crank-powered carousel.

Left Bank

Just opposite Notre-Dame, on the left bank of the Seine, is the Latin Quarter. (For more information and a walking tour, see the "Historic Core of Paris Walk," earlier in this chapter.)

▲▲**Cluny Museum (Musée National du Moyen Age)**—This treasure trove of Middle Ages (Moyen Age) art fills old Roman baths, offering close-up looks at stained glass, Notre-Dame carvings, fine goldsmithing and jewelry, and rooms of tapestries. The star here is the exquisite *Lady and the Unicorn* tapestry series: In five panels, a delicate, as-medieval-as-can-be noble lady introduces a delighted unicorn to the senses of taste, hearing, sight, smell, and touch.

Cost, Hours, Location: €6.50, free on first Sun of month, covered by Museum Pass, Wed–Mon 9:15–17:45, closed Tue, near corner of boulevards St. Michel and St. Germain at 6 place Paul Painlevé; Mo: Cluny–La Sorbonne, St. Michel, or Odéon; tel. 01 53 73 78 16, www.musee-moyenage.fr.

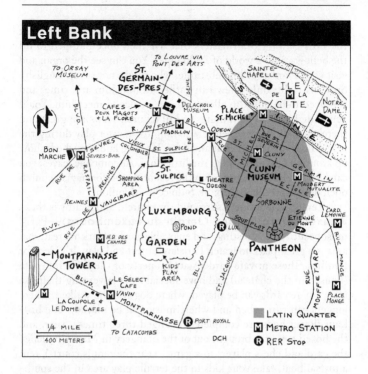

Left Bank

LATIN QUARTER
M METRO STATION
R RER STOP

St. Germain-des-Prés—A church was first built on this site in A.D. 452. The church you see today was constructed in 1163 and is all that's left of a once sprawling and influential monastery. The colorful interior reminds us that medieval churches were originally painted in bright colors. The surrounding area hops at night with venerable cafés, fire-eaters, mimes, and scads of artists (free, daily 8:00–20:00, Mo: St. Germain-des-Prés).

▲**St. Sulpice Church and Organ Concert**—Since it was featured in *The Da Vinci Code,* this grand church has become a trendy stop for the book's many fans. But the real reason to visit is to see and hear its intimately accessible organ. For pipe-organ enthusiasts, this is one of Europe's great musical treats. The Grand Orgue at St. Sulpice Church has a rich history, with a succession of 12 world-class organists—including Charles-Marie Widor and Marcel Dupré—that goes back 300 years. Widor started the tradition of opening the loft to visitors after the 10:30 service on Sundays. Daniel Roth (or his understudy) continues to welcome guests in three languages while playing five keyboards. (See www.danielrothsaintsulpice.org for his exact dates and concert plans.)

The 10:30–11:30 Sunday Mass (come appropriately dressed) is followed by a high-powered 25-minute recital. Then, just after noon, the small, unmarked door is opened (left of entry as you face

PARIS

the rear). Visitors scamper like sixteenth notes up spiral stairs, past the 19th-century Stairmasters that five men once pumped to fill the bellows, into a world of 7,000 pipes. You can see the organ and visit with Daniel (or his substitute, who might not speak English). Space is tight; only a few can gather around him at a time, and you need to be quick to allow others a chance to meet him. You'll generally have 20–30 minutes to kill (church views are great and there's a small lounge) before watching the master play during the next Mass; you can leave at any time. If you're late or rushed, show up around 12:30 and wait at the little door. As someone leaves, you can slip in, climb up, and catch the rest of the performance (church open daily 7:30–19:30, Mo: St. Sulpice or Mabillon).

Tempting boutiques surround the church, and nearby is the...

▲Luxembourg Garden (Jardin du Luxembourg)—Paris' most beautiful, interesting, and enjoyable garden/park/recreational area is a great place to watch Parisians at rest and play. It's ideal for families. These private gardens are property of the French Senate (housed in the château) and have special rules governing their use (e.g., where cards can be played, where dogs can be walked, where joggers can run, when and where music can be played). The brilliant flower beds are completely changed three times a year, and the boxed trees are brought out of the orangery in May. Challenge the card and chess players to a game (near the tennis courts), rent a toy sailboat, take your kids to the terrific play area in the southwest corner (small fee), or find a free chair near the main pond and take a breather (park open daily until dusk, Mo: Odéon, RER: Luxembourg).

The grand, Neoclassical-domed Panthéon, now a mausoleum housing the tombs of several great French figures, is just a block away.

If you enjoy the Luxembourg Garden and want to see more green spaces, you could visit the more elegant **Parc Monceau** (Mo: Monceau), the colorful **Jardin des Plantes** (Mo: Jussieu or Gare d'Austerlitz, RER: Gare d'Austerlitz), or the hilly and bigger **Parc des Buttes-Chaumont** (Mo: Buttes-Chaumont).

▲Panthéon—This dramatic Neoclassical monument celebrates France's illustrious history and people, balances Foucault's pendulum, and is the final home to many French VIPs. Step inside the vast building (360' by 280' by 270'). You'll trace the celebrated struggles of the French people (working clockwise around the church-like space): a martyred St. Denis picking up his head, St. Genevieve saving Paris from the Franks, St. Louis as king and crusader, Joan of Arc and her exploits, and so on.

Foucault's pendulum swings gracefully at the end of a 220-foot cable suspended from the towering dome. It was here in 1851 that the scientist Léon Foucault first demonstrated the rotation of the Earth. Watch as the pendulum's arc (appears to) shift as you and the earth rotate beneath it.

Stairs in the back lead down to the **crypt** where a pantheon of greats are buried, including famous French writers Victor Hugo *(Les Misérables, The Hunchback of Notre-Dame)*, and Alexandre Dumas *(The Three Musketeers, The Count of Monte Cristo)*. You'll also find the discoverers of radium, Polish-born Marie Curie and her French husband, Pierre, along with many others. An **exhibit** explores the building's fascinating history (good English descriptions). You can climb 206 steps to the **dome gallery** for fine views of the interior as well as the city (accessible only with an escort who leaves about every hour until 17:15—see schedule as you enter).

Cost, Hours, Location: €7.50, covered by Museum Pass, daily 10:00–18:30 in summer, until 18:00 in winter, last entry 45 minutes before closing (Mo: Cardinal Lemoine). Ask about occasional English tours or call ahead for schedule (tel. 01 44 32 18 00).

Montparnasse Tower (La Tour Montparnasse)—This 59-story superscraper—cheaper and easier to ascend than the Eiffel Tower—treats you to one of Paris' best views. (Some say the very best, as you can see the Eiffel Tower...and you can't see the Montparnasse Tower.) While there are plenty of dioramas identifying highlights of the star-studded vista, consider buying the €3 photo-guide, which makes a fun souvenir. As you zip up 56 floors in 38 seconds, watch the altimeter above the door. From the 56th floor, climb to the open terrace at the 59th floor to enjoy the surreal scene of a lonely man in a box, and a helipad surrounded by the window-cleaner track. Here, 690 feet above Paris, you can scan the city with the wind in your hair, noticing the lush courtyards hiding behind grand street fronts. Back inside and downstairs, you'll find a small, overpriced café, fascinating historic black-and-white photos, and a plush little theater playing a worthwhile video that celebrates the big views of this grand city (free, 12 min, shows continuously).

Cost, Hours, Location: €10, not covered by Museum Pass, daily April–Sept 9:30–23:30, Oct–March 9:30–22:30, disappointing after dark, entrance on rue de l'Arrivée, Mo: Montparnasse-Bienvenüe—from the Métro stay inside the station and simply follow the signs for "La Tour" (tel. 01 45 38 52 56, www.tour montparnasse56.com).

▲**Catacombs**—These underground tunnels contain the anonymous bones of six million permanent Parisians. In 1786, the citizens decided to relieve congestion and improve sanitary conditions by emptying the city cemeteries (which traditionally surrounded churches) into an official ossuary. They found the perfect locale in the many miles of underground tunnels from limestone quarries, which were, at that time, just outside the city. For decades, priests led ceremonial processions of black-veiled, bone-laden carts into the quarries, where the bones were stacked into piles five feet high and as much as 80 feet deep behind neat walls of skull-studded tibiae. Each transfer was complete when a plaque was placed, indicating the church and district where the bones came from and the date that they arrived. Note to wannabe Hamlets: An attendant checks your bag at the exit for stolen souvenirs. A flashlight is handy. Being under 6'2" is helpful.

Cost, Hours, Location: €7, not covered by Museum Pass, Tue–Sun 10:00–17:00, ticket booth closes at 16:00, closed Mon, 1 place Denfert-Rochereau, tel. 01 43 22 47 63. Take the Métro to Denfert-Rochereau, then find the lion in the big traffic circle; if he looked left rather than right, he'd stare right at the green entrance to the Catacombs. You'll exit at 36 rue Remy Dumoncel, far from where you started. If you walk to the right, to avenue du Général Leclerc, you'll be equidistant from Métro stops Alésia (walk left) and Mouton Duvernet (walk right).

Champs-Elysées and Nearby

▲▲**Champs-Elysées**—This famous boulevard is Paris' backbone, and has the greatest concentration of traffic. All of France seems to converge on the place de la Concorde, the city's largest square. The Tour de France bicycle race ends here, as do all parades (French or foe) of any significance. While the Champs-Elysées has become as international as it is local, a walk here is still a must.

In 1667, Louis XIV opened the first section of the street as a short extension of the Tuileries Garden. This year is considered the birth of Paris as a grand city. The Champs-Elysées soon became *the* place to cruise in your carriage. (It still is today—traffic can be jammed up even at midnight.) One hundred years later, the café scene arrived. It was on place de la Concorde that the guillotine took the lives of about 1,200 people—including King Louis XVI and Marie-Antoinette. Back then it was called the place de la Révolution.

From the 1920s until the 1960s, this boulevard was pure elegance. Parisians actually dressed up to come here. It was mainly residences, rich hotels, and cafés. Then, in 1963, the government pumped up the neighborhood's commercial metabolism by bringing in the RER (commuter underground). Suburbanites had easy access, and *pfft*—there went the neighborhood.

The *nouveau* Champs-Elysées, revitalized in 1994, has new benches and lamps, broader sidewalks, all-underground parking, and a fleet of green-suited workers who drive motorized street cleaners. Blink away the modern elements and it's not hard to imagine the boulevard pre-1963, with only the finest structures lining both sides all the way to the palace gardens.

Champs-Elysées and Nearby

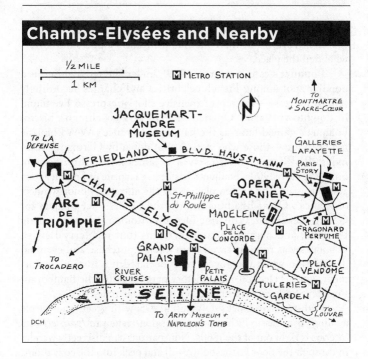

To saunter down the Champs-Elysées, take the Métro to the Arc de Triomphe, described later (Mo: Charles de Gaulle–Etoile; Métro stops every few blocks: Franklin D. Roosevelt, George V, and Charles de Gaulle–Etoile).

Inspect the fancy car dealerships—**Peugeot** at #136 (showing off its futuristic concept cars next to the classic models) and **Mercedes-Benz,** a block down at #118. In the 19th century, this was an area for horse stables; today, it's the district of garages, limo companies, and car dealerships. If you're serious about selling cars in France, you must have a showroom on the Champs-Elysées.

Next to Mercedes is the famous **Lido,** Paris' largest cabaret (and a multiplex cinema). You can walk all the way inside until 18:00 without a ticket. Check out the perky photos in the entryway, the R-rated videos, and the shocking prices. Paris still offers the kind of burlesque-type spectacles combining music, comedy, and scantily clad women that have been performed here since the 19th century. Movie-going on the Champs-Elysées provides another kind of fun, with theaters showing the very latest releases. Check to see if there are films you recognize, then look for the showings *(séances)*. A "v.o." *(version originale)* next to the time indicates the film will be shown in its original language.

The flagship store of leather-bag makers **Louis Vuitton** may be the largest single-brand luxury store in the world. Step inside.

PARIS

The store insists on providing enough salespeople to treat each customer royally—if there's a line, it means shoppers have overwhelmed the place.

Fouquet's café-restaurant (#99), under the red awning, is a popular spot among French celebrities and charges accordingly (€6 for espresso—the most expensive shot of espresso I've found in downtown Paris). Opened in 1899 as a coachman's bistro, Fouquet's gained fame as the hangout of France's WWI biplane fighter pilots—those who weren't shot down by Germany's infamous "Red Baron." It also served as James Joyce's dining room. Since the early 1900s, Fouquet's has been a favorite of French actors and actresses. The golden plaques by the entrance honor winners of France's Oscar-like film awards, the Césars—see plaques for Gérard Depardieu, Catherine Deneuve, Roman Polanski, Juliette Binoche, and many famous Americans (but not Jerry Lewis). Fouquet's was recently saved from foreign purchase and eventual destruction when the government declared it a historic monument. For his election-night victory party in 2007, the flamboyant President Sarkozy, and France's glitterati, celebrated here.

Ladurée (two blocks downhill at #75, with green-and-purple awning) is a classic 19th-century tea salon/restaurant/*pâtisserie*. Its interior is right out of the 1860s. Non-patrons can discreetly wander in through the door farthest downhill and peek into the cozy rooms upstairs. A coffee here is *très élégant* (only €3.50). The bakery sells traditional macaroons, cute little cakes, and gift-wrapped finger sandwiches to go (your choice of four mini-macaroons for €7.20).

▲▲▲**Arc de Triomphe**—Napoleon had the magnificent Arc de Triomphe commissioned to commemorate his victory at the battle of Austerlitz. There's no triumphal arch bigger (165 feet high, 130 feet wide). And, with 12 converging boulevards, there's no traffic circle more thrilling to experience—either from behind the wheel or on foot (take the underpass).

The foot of the arch is a stage on which the last two centuries of Parisian history have played out—from the funeral of Napoleon to the goose-stepping arrival of the Nazis, to the triumphant return of Charles de Gaulle after the Allied liberation. Examine the carvings on the pillars, featuring a mighty Napoleon and excitable Lady Liberty. Pay your respects at the Tomb of the Unknown Soldier (from World War I, at base of arch), where the flame is rekindled daily at 18:30.

The 284 steps lead to a cute museum about the arch, sweeping skyline panoramas, and a mesmerizing view down onto the traffic that swirls around the arch.

Cost, Hours, Location: Outside—free, always open. Interior—€9, free on first Sun of month Oct–March, free for kids under 18, covered by Museum Pass, daily April–Sept 10:00–23:00,

Oct–March 10:00–22:30, last entry 30 min before closing, place Charles de Gaulle, use underpass to reach arch, Mo: Charles de Gaulle–Etoile, tel. 01 55 37 73 77, www.monum.fr.

▲**Opéra Garnier**—This gleaming grand theater of the belle époque was built for Napoleon III and finished in 1875. While the building is huge, the actual auditorium seats only 2,000. The real show was before and after the performance, when the elite of Paris—out to see and be seen—strutted their elegant stuff in the extravagant lobbies. Think of the grand marble stairway as a theater itself. As you wander the halls and gawk at the decor, imagine the place filled with the beautiful people of its day. The massive foundations straddle an underground lake (inspiring the mysterious world of the *Phantom of the Opera*). Visitors can peek from two boxes into the actual red-velvet performance hall to view Marc Chagall's colorful ceiling (1964) playfully dancing around the eight-ton chandelier (guided tours take you into the performance hall). Note the box seats next to the stage—the most expensive in the house, with an obstructed view of the stage...but just right if you're here only to be seen.

The elitism of this place prompted a people's opera house to be built in the 1980s, symbolically on place de la Bastille, where the French Revolution started in 1789. This left the Opéra Garnier home only to ballet and occasional concerts. While the library/museum is of interest to opera buffs, anyone will enjoy the second-floor grand foyer and Salon du Glacier, iced with decor typical of 1900.

Cost, Hours, Location: €8, not covered by Museum Pass, daily 10:00–16:30, July–Aug until 18:00, closed during performances, 8 rue Scribe, Mo: Opéra, RER: Auber. To find out how get tickets to performances, see "Nightlife," later in this chapter.

Tours: English tours of the building run during summer and off-season weekends, usually at 11:30 and 14:00; call to confirm schedule (€12, includes entry, 90 min, tel. 01 40 01 17 89).

Nearby: The *Paris Story* film and Fragonard Perfume Museum (see next page) are on the left side of the Opéra, and the venerable Galeries Lafayette department store (its top-floor café has marvelous views) is just behind. Across the street, the illustrious Café de la Paix has been a meeting spot for the local glitterati for generations. If you can afford the coffee, this spot offers a delightful break.

***Paris Story* Film**—Simultaneously cheesy, entertaining, and pricey, this film offers a painless overview of the city's turbulent and brilliant past, covering 2,000 years in 45 fast-moving minutes. The theater's wide-screen projection and cushy chairs provide a break from bad weather and sore feet, and the movie usually works for kids, but don't go out of your way to get here.

Cost, Hours, Location: €10, kids-€6, family of four-€26, not covered by Museum Pass. Individuals get a 20 percent discount with this book in 2010 (no discount on family rate). The film shows on the hour daily 10:00–18:00. Next to Opéra Garnier at 11 rue Scribe, Mo: Opéra, tel. 01 42 66 62 06.

Fragonard Perfume Museum—Near Opéra Garnier, two perfume shops masquerade as museums. Either location will teach you a little about how perfume is made (ask for the English handout), but the one on rue Scribe smells even sweeter—and it's in a beautiful 19th-century mansion (both free, daily 9:00–18:00, at 9 rue Scribe and 30 rue des Capucines, tel. 01 47 42 04 56, www .fragonard.com).

▲▲Jacquemart-André Museum (Musée Jacquemart-André)—This thoroughly enjoyable museum (with an elegant café) showcases the lavish home of a wealthy, art-loving, 19th-century Parisian couple. After wandering the grand boulevards, get inside for an intimate look at the lifestyles of the Parisian rich and fabulous. Edouard André and his wife Nélie Jacquemart—who had no children—spent their lives and fortunes designing, building, and then decorating this sumptuous mansion. What makes the visit so rewarding is the excellent audioguide tour (in English, free with admission, plan on spending an hour with the audioguide). The place is strewn with paintings by Rembrandt, Botticelli, Uccello, Mantegna, Bellini, Boucher, and Fragonard—enough to make a painting gallery famous.

    Cost, Hours, Location: €10, not covered by Museum Pass, daily 10:00–18:00, at 158 boulevard Haussmann, Mo: Miromesnil or Saint-Philippe de Roule, bus #80 makes a convenient connection to Ecole Militaire, tel. 01 45 62 11 59, www.musee-jacquemart -andre.com.

    After Your Visit: Consider a break in the sumptuous museum tearoom, with delicious cakes and tea (daily 11:45–17:45). From here, walk north on rue de Courcelles to see Paris' most beautiful park, **Parc Monceau.**

Petit Palais (and its Musée des Beaux-Arts)—In this free museum, you'll find a broad collection of paintings and sculpture from the 1600s to the 1900s. It's a museum of second-choice art, but the building itself is impressive, and there are a few 19th-century diamonds in the rough, including pieces by Courbet and Monet. The Palais also has a pleasant garden courtyard and café (Wed–Sun 10:00–18:00, Tue 10:00–20:00 for temporary exhibits, closed Mon, across from Grand Palais on avenue Winston Churchill, just west of place de la Concorde, tel. 01 53 43 40 00, www.petitpalais.paris.fr).

Grand Palais—This grand exhibition hall, built for the 1900 World's Fair, is used for temporary exhibits. The building's

Industrial Age, erector-set, iron-and-glass exterior is grand, but the steep entry price is worthwhile only if the exhibit interests you. Get details on the current schedule from the TIs, in *Pariscope* (at any newsstand, in French), or from www.rmn.fr (usually €10, not covered by Museum Pass, Thu–Mon 10:00–20:00, Wed 10:00–22:00, last entry 45 min before closing, closed Tue and between exhibitions, avenue Winston Churchill, Mo: Rond Point or Champs-Elysées, tel. 01 44 13 17 17).

▲▲**La Défense and La Grande Arche**—While Paris keeps its historic center classic and skyscraper-free, this district, nicknamed "le petit Manhattan," offers an impressive excursion into modern-day economic superpower France. La Défense was conceived more than 60 years ago as a US-style forest of skyscrapers that would accommodate the business needs of the modern world. Today, La Défense is a thriving business and shopping center, home to 150,000 employees and 55,000 residents.

Take the Métro to the La Défense stop and start with **La Grande Arche de la Fraternité,** the centerpiece of this ambitious complex (inaugurated in 1989 on the 200th anniversary of the French Revolution). The place is big—Notre-Dame Cathedral could fit under its arch. The "cloud"—a huge canvas canopy under the arch—is an attempt to cut down on the wind-tunnel effect this gigantic building creates. Glass capsule elevators whisk you up to a grand open-air view, a thrilling 20-minute movie (with English subtitles) on the mammoth construction project, and models of the arch. Take advantage of its free Internet access (in the computer exhibit) and, if it's still there, check out the fascinating set of digital portraits by French artist Dimitri, illustrating *remanence*—"after imagery."

Cost, Hours, Location: La Grande Arche elevator-€9, kids-€7.50, family deals, not covered by Museum Pass, daily April–Sept 10:00–20:00, Oct–March until 19:00, RER or Mo: La Défense, follow signs to *La Grande Arche*, tel. 01 49 07 27 57, www.grande arche.com.

The Esplanade: La Défense is more than its eye-catching arch. Wander from the arch toward the city center along the Esplanade (a.k.a. "le Parvis") which is a virtual open-air modern art gallery, sporting pieces by Joan Miró (blue), Alexander Calder (red), and Yaacov Agam (the fountain with its colorful stripes and rhythmically dancing spouts), among others. *La Défense de Paris,* the statue that gave the area its name, recalls the 1871 Franco-Prussian war. Walking toward the Nexity Tower, you'll come to the Esplanade de la Défense Métro station, which zips you out of all this modernity and directly back into town.

PARIS

Marais Neighborhood and Nearby

The Marais neighborhood extends along the Right Bank of the Seine from the Pompidou Center to the Bastille. It contains more pre-revolutionary lanes and buildings than anywhere else in town and is more atmospheric than touristy. It's medieval Paris, and the haunt of the old nobility. This is how much of the city looked until, in the mid-1800s, Napoleon III had Baron Georges-Eugène Haussmann blast out the narrow streets to construct broad boulevards (wide enough for the guns and ranks of the army, too wide for revolutionary barricades), thus creating modern Paris. Originally a swamp *(marais)* during the reign of Henry IV, this area became the hometown of the French aristocracy. In the 17th century, big shots built their private mansions *(hôtels)* close to Henry IV's stylish place des Vosges. When strolling the Marais, stick to the west–east axis formed by rue Sainte-Croix de la Bretonnerie, rue des Rosiers (heart of Paris' Jewish community), and rue St. Antoine. On Sunday afternoons, this trendy area pulses with shoppers and café crowds.

▲**Place des Vosges**—Study the architecture in this grand square: nine pavilions (houses) per side. Some of the brickwork is real, some is fake. Walk to the center, where Louis XIII sits on a horse surrounded by locals enjoying their community park. Children frolic in the sandbox, lovers warm benches, and pigeons guard their fountains while trees shade this retreat from the glare of the big city. Henry IV built this centerpiece of the Marais in 1605. As he'd hoped, this turned the Marais into Paris' most exclusive neighborhood. Just like Versailles 80 years later, this was a magnet for the rich and powerful of France. With the Revolution, the aristocratic splendor of this quarter passed. The area became working-class, filled with gritty shops, artisans, immigrants, and a Jewish community. **Victor Hugo** lived at #6, and you can visit his house (free except during special exhibits—not worth paying for, Tue–Sun 10:00–18:00, last entry at 17:40, closed Mon, 6 place des Vosges, tel. 01 42 72 10 16). Leave the place des Vosges through the doorway at the southwest corner of the square (near the three-star Michelin restaurant l'Ambrosie) and pass through the elegant **Hôtel de Sully** (great example of a Marais mansion, grand courtyard open until 19:00, fine bookstore inside) to rue St. Antoine.

▲▲**Pompidou Center (Centre Pompidou)**—Europe's greatest collection of far-out modern art is housed in the Musée National d'Art Moderne, on the fourth and fifth floors of this colorful exhibition hall. The building itself is "exoskeletal" (like Notre-Dame or a crab), with its functional parts—the pipes, heating ducts, and escalator—on the outside, and the meaty art inside. It's the epitome of modern architecture, where "form follows function." Once ahead of its time, the 20th-century art displayed in this museum

Marais Neighborhood and Nearby

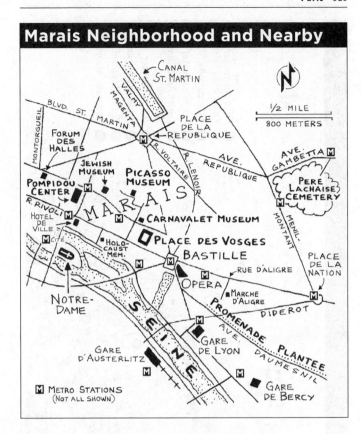

CANAL ST. MARTIN

½ MILE

800 METERS

PLACE DE LA REPUBLIQUE

BLVD. ST. MARTIN

VALMY

MAGENTA

MONTORGUEIL

FORUM DES HALLES

R. VOLTAIRE

R. LENOIR

AVE. REPUBLIQUE

AVE. GAMBETTA

JEWISH MUSEUM

PICASSO MUSEUM

PERE LACHAISE CEMETERY

POMPIDOU CENTER

R. RIVOLI

MARAIS

MENIL-MONTANT

HOTEL DE VILLE

CARNAVALET MUSEUM

CITÉ

HOLO-CAUST MEM.

PLACE DES VOSGES

BASTILLE

PLACE DE LA NATION

RUE D'ALIGRE

NOTRE-DAME

OPERA

MARCHE D'ALIGRE

DIDEROT

SEINE

PROMENADE PLANTEE

AVE. DAUMESNIL

GARE D'AUSTERLITZ

GARE DE LYON

M METRO STATIONS (NOT ALL SHOWN)

GARE DE BERCY

has been waiting for the world to catch up with it.

Enter on the fifth floor, show your ticket, and ask for a floor plan *(plan du musée)*. The 20th century—accelerated by technology and fragmented by war—was exciting and chaotic, and this art reflects the turbulence of that century of change. In this free-flowing and airy museum (with great views over Paris), you'll come face to face with works by Henri Matisse, Pablo Picasso, Marc Chagall, Salvador Dalí, Andy Warhol, Wassily Kandinsky, Max Ernst, Jackson Pollock, and many more. And after so many Madonnas-and-Children, a piano smashed to bits and glued to the wall is refreshing.

The Pompidou Center and the square that fronts it are lively, with lots of people, street theater, and activity inside and out—a perpetual street fair. Kids of any age enjoy the fun, colorful fountain (called *Homage to Stravinsky*) next to the Pompidou Center. Ride the escalator for a great city view from the top (ticket or Museum Pass required). If you need a light meal or snack, try the places lining the Stravinsky fountain: Dame Tartine and Crêperie

PARIS

Marais Neighborhood

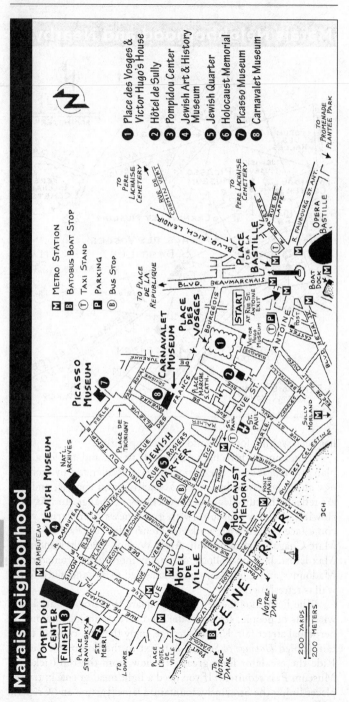

1 Place des Vosges &
Victor Hugo's House
2 Hôtel de Sully
3 Pompidou Center
4 Jewish Art & History
Museum
5 Jewish Quarter
6 Holocaust Memorial
7 Picasso Museum
8 Carnavalet Museum

M Metro Station
B Batobus Boat Stop
T Taxi Stand
P Parking
B Bus Stop

Beaubourg (to the right as you face the museum entrance; both have reasonable prices).

Cost, Hours, Location: €10, permanent collection covered by Museum Pass (but not special exhibitions), free on first Sun of month, Wed–Mon 11:00–21:00, ticket counters close at 20:00, closed Tue, Mo: Rambuteau or farther-away Hôtel de Ville, tel. 01 44 78 12 33, www.centrepompidou.fr.

▲▲**Jewish Art and History Museum (Musée d'Art et Histoire du Judaïsme)**—This fine museum, located in a beautifully restored Marais mansion, tells the story of Judaism throughout Europe, from the Roman destruction of Jerusalem to the theft of famous artworks during World War II. Displays illustrate the cultural unity maintained by this continually dispersed population. You'll learn about the history of Jewish traditions from bar mitzvahs to menorahs, and see the exquisite traditional costumes and objects central to daily life. Don't miss the explanation of "the Dreyfus affair," a major event in early 1900s French politics. You'll also see photographs of and paintings by famous Jewish artists, including Marc Chagall, Amedeo Modigliani, and Chaim Soutine. A small but moving section is devoted to the deportation of Jews from Paris during World War II.

Helpful audioguides and many English explanations make this an enjoyable history lesson (red numbers on small signs indicate the number you should press on your audioguide). Move along at your own speed.

Cost, Hours, Location: €7, more during special exhibits, includes audioguide, covered by Museum Pass, Mon–Fri 11:00–18:00, Sun 10:00–18:00, last entry one hour before closing, closed Sat, 71 rue du Temple, Mo: Rambuteau or Hôtel de Ville a few blocks farther away, tel. 01 53 01 86 60, www.mahj.org.

Jewish Quarter—Located along rue des Rosiers, the tiny yet colorful Jewish district of the Marais was once considered the largest in Western Europe. Today, while rue des Rosiers is lined with colorful Jewish shops and kosher eateries, the district is being squeezed by the trendy boutiques of modern Paris (visit any day but Saturday, when most businesses are closed—best on Sunday). If you're visiting at lunchtime, you'll be tempted by kosher pizza and plenty of cheap fast-food joints selling falafel "to go" *(emporter)*. The best falafel is at L'As du Falafel, with a bustling New York–deli atmosphere (at #34, sit-down or to go). The Sacha Finkelsztajn Yiddish bakery (at #27) is also good. The Jewish Quarter is also home to the Holocaust Memorial (described next).

Holocaust Memorial (Mémorial de la Shoah)—Commemorating the lives of the more than 76,000 Jews deported from France in World War II, this memorial's focal point is underground, where victims' ashes are buried. Displaying original deportation records, the museum takes you through the history of Jews in Europe and France, from medieval pogroms to the Nazi era (free, Sun–Fri 10:00–18:00, Thu until 22:00, closed Sat and certain Jewish holidays, 17 rue Geoffroy l'Asnier, tel. 01 42 77 44 72, www.memorialdelashoah.org).

▲▲**Picasso Museum (Musée Picasso)**—This museum is scheduled to close for renovations in September 2009 and remain closed for two years. When it reopens, it'll hold the world's largest collection of Picasso's paintings, sculptures, sketches, and ceramics, and includes his small collection of Impressionist art.

▲▲**Carnavalet Museum (Musée Carnavalet)**—The tumultuous history of Paris is well-portrayed in this hard-to-navigate museum, offering a good overview of everything from Louis XIV period rooms to Napoleon to the belle époque. The Carnavalet is housed in two Marais mansions connected by a corridor. The first half of the museum (pre-Revolution) dates from a period when people generally accepted the notion that some were born to rule, and most were born to be ruled. This section is difficult to follow (rooms numbered out of order, no English descriptions, and sections closed due to understaffing) so see it quickly, then concentrate your energy on the Revolution and beyond.

The Revolution is the museum's highlight. Fascinating exhibits cover this bloody period of French history, when atrocious acts were committed in the name of government "by, for, and of the people." The exhibits take you from events that led up to the Revolution to the storming of the 100-foot-high walls of the Bastille to the royal beheadings, and through the reigns of terror that followed. They then trace the rise and fall of Napoleon and end with the Paris Commune uprisings. While explanations are in French only, many displays are fairly self-explanatory.

Cost, Hours, Location: Free, Tue–Sun 10:00–18:00, closed Mon; avoid lunchtime (12:00–14:00), when many rooms close; 23 rue de Sévigné, Mo: St. Paul, tel. 01 44 59 58 58, www.carnavalet .paris.fr.

▲**Promenade Plantée Park**—This two-mile-long, narrow garden walk on a viaduct was once used for train tracks and is now a joy on foot. Part of the park is elevated. At times, you'll walk along the street until you pick up the next segment. The shops below the viaduct's arches (a creative use of once-wasted urban space) make for entertaining window-shopping.

Cost, Hours, Location: Free, opens Mon–Fri at 8:00, Sat–Sun at 9:00, closes at sunset. It runs from place de la Bastille (Mo: Bastille) along avenue Daumesnil to Saint-Mandé (Mo: Michel Bizot). From place de la Bastille (follow signs for *Sortie Opéra* or *Sortie rue de Lyon* from Bastille Métro station), walk down rue de Lyon with the Opéra immediately on your left. Find the steps up the red brick wall a block after the Opéra.

▲**Père Lachaise Cemetery (Cimetière du Père Lachaise)**—
Littered with the tombstones of many of the city's most illustrious
dead, this is your best one-stop look at Paris' fascinating, romantic
past residents. The tree-lined cemetery is enclosed by a massive wall
with peaceful, car-free lanes that encourage parklike meandering.
Named for Father *(Père)* La Chaise, whose job was listening to
Louis XIV's sins, the cemetery is relatively new, having opened in
1804 to accommodate Paris' expansion. Today, this city of the dead
(pop. 70,000) still accepts new residents, but real estate prices are
very high.

The 100-acre cemetery is big and confusing, with thousands of
graves and tombs crammed every which way, and only a few pathways to navigate by. The helpful €2 map (sold at the flower stores
located near either entry) will direct you to the graves of Frédéric
Chopin, Molière, Edith Piaf, Oscar Wilde, Gertrude Stein, Jim
Morrison, Héloïse and Abélard, and many more.

Cost, Hours, Location: Free, Mon–Sat 8:00–18:00, Sun
9:00–18:00, or until dusk if it falls before 18:00. It's down avenue
du Père Lachaise from Mo: Gambetta (also across the street from
the less-convenient Père Lachaise Métro stop and reachable via
bus #69). Tel. 01 55 25 82 10.

Montmartre

▲▲**Sacré-Cœur and Montmartre**—Stroll along Paris' highest
hilltop (420 feet) for a different perspective on the City of Light.
Walk in the footsteps of the people who've lived here—monks
stomping grapes (1200s), farmers grinding grain in windmills
(1600s), dust-coated gypsum miners (1700s), Parisian liberals
(1800s), modernist painters (1900s), and all the struggling artists,
poets, dreamers, and drunkards who came here for cheap rent,
untaxed booze, rustic landscapes, and cabaret nightlife. With
vineyards, wheat fields, windmills, animals, and a village tempo of
life, it was the perfect escape from grimy Paris.

The five-domed, Roman Byzantine–looking basilica of **Sacré-
Cœur** took 44 years to build (1875–1919). It stands on a foundation
of 83 pillars sunk 130 feet deep, necessary because the ground
beneath was honeycombed with gypsum mines. The exterior is
laced with gypsum, which whitens with age.

For an unobstructed panoramic view of Paris, climb 260
feet up the tight and claustrophobic spiral stairs to the top of
the dome (church free, daily 7:00–23:00; €5 to climb dome, not
covered by Museum Pass, daily June–Sept 9:00–19:00, Oct–May
10:00–18:00).

One block from the church, the **place du Tertre** was the
haunt of Henri de Toulouse-Lautrec and the original bohemians.

Today, it's mobbed with tourists and unoriginal bohemians, but it's still fun (to beat the crowds, go early in the morning). From here, follow rue des Saules (a block west), turn right, and find Paris' lone vineyard, and the Montmartre Museum (listed below).

To get to Montmartre, take the Métro to the Anvers stop (one more Métro ticket buys your way up the funicular and avoids the stairs, but the funicular may be closed for repairs) or the closer but less scenic Abbesses stop. A taxi to the top of the hill saves time and avoids sweat (costs about €10, €20 at night). For restaurant recommendations, see "Eating," later in this chapter.

Dalí Museum (L'Espace Dalí)—This beautifully lit black gallery (well-described in English) offers a walk through statues, etchings, and paintings by the master of surrealism. Don't miss the printed interview on the exit stairs (€10, not covered by Museum Pass, daily 10:00–18:30, 11 rue Poulbot, tel. 01 42 64 40 10, www.daliparis.com).

Montmartre Museum (Musée de Montmartre)—This 17th-century home re-creates the traditional cancan and cabaret Montmartre scene, with paintings, posters, photos, music, and memorabilia (€7, includes audioguide, not covered by Museum Pass, Tue–Sun 11:00–18:00, closed Mon, 12 rue Cortot, tel. 01 49 25 89 39, www.museedemontmartre.fr).

Pigalle—Paris' redlight district, the infamous "Pig Alley," is at the foot of Butte Montmartre. *Ooh la la.* It's more racy than dangerous. Walk from place Pigalle to place Blanche, teasing desperate barkers and fast-talking temptresses. In bars, a €150 bottle of cheap champagne comes with a friend. Stick to the bigger streets, hang onto your wallet, and exercise good judgment. Cancan can cost a fortune, as can con artists in topless bars. After dark, countless tour buses line the streets, reminding us that tour guides make big bucks by bringing their groups to touristy nightclubs like the famous Moulin Rouge (Mo: Pigalle or Abbesses).

Museum of Erotic Art (Musée de l'Erotisme)—Paris' sexy museum has five floors of risqué displays—mostly paintings and drawings—ranging from artistic to erotic to disgusting, with a few circa-1920 porn videos and a fascinating history of local brothels tossed in. It's in the center of the Pigalle red light district (€8, no... it's not covered by Museum Pass, daily 10:00–2:00 in the morning, 72 boulevard de Clichy, Mo: Blanche, tel. 01 42 58 28 73, www.musee-erotisme.com).

Nightlife

Paris is brilliant after dark. Save energy from your day's sightseeing and experience the City of Light lit. Whether it's a concert at the Sainte-Chapelle, a boat ride on the Seine, a walk in Montmartre, a hike up the Arc de Triomphe, or a late-night café, you'll see Paris come alive. Night walks in Paris are wonderful (and free). For a floodlit Seine river cruise, check out "Tours," near the beginning of this chapter.

The *Pariscope* magazine (available at most newsstands, in French) offers a complete weekly listing of music, cinema, theater, opera, and other special events. The *Paris Voice* website, in English, has a helpful monthly review of Paris entertainment (www.paris voice.com).

Music

Jazz Clubs—With a lively mix of American, French, and international musicians, Paris has been an internationally acclaimed jazz capital since World War II. You'll pay €12–25 to enter a jazz club (may include one drink; if not, expect to pay €5–10 per drink; beer is cheapest). See *Pariscope* magazine under "Musique" for listings, or, even better, the American Church's *Paris Voice* website for a good monthly review, or drop by the clubs to check out the calendars posted on their front doors. Music starts after 21:00 in most clubs. Some offer dinner concerts from about 20:30 on. Here are several good bets:

Caveau de la Huchette, a characteristic, old, jazz/dance club, fills an ancient Latin Quarter cellar with live jazz and frenzied dancing every night (admission about €11 on weekdays, €13 on weekends, €6 drinks, Tue–Sun 21:30–2:30 in the morning or later, closed Mon, 5 rue de la Huchette, Mo: St. Michel, recorded info tel. 01 43 26 65 05, www.caveaudelahuchette.fr).

For a spot teeming with late-night activity and jazz, go to the two-block-long rue des Lombards, at boulevard Sébastopol, midway between the river and the Pompidou Center (Mo: Châtelet). **Au Duc des Lombards** is one of the most popular and respected jazz clubs in Paris, with concerts nightly in a great, plush, 110-seat theater-like setting (admission about €20, cheap drinks, shows at 20:00 and 22:00, 42 rue des Lombards, tel. 01 42 33 22 88, www .ducdeslombards.fr). **Le Sunside,** run for 15 years by Stephane Portet, is just a block away. The club offers two little stages (ground floor and downstairs); one stage is devoted to contemporary world jazz, while the other features more traditional jazz—Dixieland and big band (concerts generally at 21:00, 60 rue des Lombards, tel. 01 40 26 21 25, www.sunset-sunside.com).

Old-Time Parisian Cabaret on Montmartre: Au Lapin Agile—This historic cabaret maintains the atmosphere of the heady days when bohemians would gather here to enjoy wine, song, and sexy jokes. For €24, you gather with about 25 French people in a dark room for a drink and as many as 10 different performers—mostly singers with a piano. Performers range from sweet and innocent Amélie types to naughty Maurice Chevalier types. While tourists are welcome, it's exclusively French, with no accommodation for English-speakers (non-French-speakers will be lost). You sit at carved wooden tables in a dimly lit room, taste the traditional drink (brandy with cherries), and are immersed in a true Parisian ambience. The soirée covers traditional French standards, love ballads, sea chanteys, and more. The crowd sings along, as it has here for a century (Tue–Sun 21:00–2:00 in the morning, closed Mon, best to reserve ahead, 22 rue des Saules, tel. 01 46 06 85 87, www.au-lapin-agile.com).

A Modern Cabaret near Canal St. Martin: Chez Raymonde—This club proves that the art of dinner cabaret is still alive in Paris. Your evening begins with a good three-course dinner (including apéritif, wine, a half-bottle of champagne, and coffee) in an intimate dining room, where you get to know your neighbors. Around 22:00, the maître d'hôtel and the chef himself kick off the performance with a waltz together. Then it's feather boas, song, and dance—audience participation is encouraged (€85–100/person, Fri–Sun evenings only, dinner starts at 20:00 and performance usually finishes about 23:00, reservations necessary, 119 avenue Parmentier, Mo: Goncourt, Parmentier, or République, tel. 01 43 55 26 27, www.chez-raymonde.com). On Sunday afternoons, you can also attend a performance over lunch (€70–85, starts at 12:30).

Classical Concerts—For classical music on any night, consult *Pariscope* magazine (check "Concerts Classiques" under "Musique" for listings of fee and free events) and look for posters at tourist-oriented churches.

From March through November, these churches regularly host concerts: St. Sulpice, St. Germain-des-Prés, Ste. Madeleine, St. Eustache, St. Julien-le-Pauvre, and Sainte-Chapelle. It's well worth the €25 entry for the pleasure of hearing Mozart or Vivaldi while surrounded by the stained glass of the tiny Sainte-Chapelle (unheated—bring a sweater). Pick up concert schedules and tickets during the day at the small ticket booth to the left of the chapel entrance. Or call 01 42 77 65 65 to reserve ahead; you can leave your message in English (just speak clearly and spell your name). Seats are unassigned, so arrive 30 minutes early to snare a good view. There are often two concerts per evening at 19:00 and 20:30; specify which one you want when you buy or reserve your ticket.

Look also for daytime concerts in parks, such as the Luxembourg Garden. Even the Galeries Lafayette department store offers concerts. Many concerts are free *(entrée libre)*, such as the Sunday atelier concert sponsored by the American Church (generally Sept–June at 17:00 but not every week, 65 quai d'Orsay, Mo: Invalides, RER: Pont de l'Alma, tel. 01 40 62 05 00).

PARIS

Opera—Paris is home to two well-respected opera venues. The **Opéra Bastille** is the massive modern opera house that dominates place de la Bastille. Come here for state-of-the-art special effects and modern interpretations of classic ballets and operas. In the spirit of this everyman's opera, unsold seats are available at a big discount to seniors and students 15 minutes before the show. Standing-room-only tickets for €15 are also sold for some performances (Mo: Bastille, tel. 01 43 43 96 96). The **Opéra Garnier,** Paris' first opera house, hosts opera and ballet performances. Come here for less expensive tickets and grand belle époque decor (Mo: Opéra).

Performance schedules are listed in *Pariscope* magazine, online (see below), and at the box offices. To get tickets for either opera house, call 08 92 89 90 90 (toll call, office closed Sun), or easier, reserve online at www.opera-de-paris.fr. You can also go direct to each opera's ticket office (open daily 11:00–18:00).

Night Walks

Go for an evening walk to best appreciate the City of Light. Break for ice cream, pause at a café, and enjoy the sidewalk entertainers as you join the post-dinner Parisian parade. Consider these suggestions:

▲▲▲**Trocadéro and Eiffel Tower**—This is one of Paris' most spectacular views at night. Take the Métro to the Trocadéro stop and join the party on place du Trocadéro for a magnificent view of the glowing Eiffel Tower. It's a festival of gawkers, drummers, street acrobats, and entertainers. Pass the fountains and cross the river to the base of the tower, worth the effort even if you don't go up (daily June–Aug until 24:45, Sept–mid-June until 23:45). See "Eiffel Tower and Nearby," page 307.

From the Eiffel Tower, you can stroll through Champ de Mars park past Frisbees, soccer balls, and romantic couples, and take the Métro home (Ecole Militaire stop, across avenue de la Motte-Picquet from far southeast corner of park). Or there's a handy RER stop (Champ de Mars–Tour Eiffel) two blocks west of the Eiffel Tower.

▲▲**Champs-Elysées and the Arc de Triomphe**—The avenue des Champs-Elysées glows after dark. Start at the Arc de Triomphe (observation deck open daily, April–Sept until 23:00, Oct–March until 22:30), then stroll down Paris' lively grand promenade. A right turn on avenue George V leads to the Bateaux-Mouches river cruises.

▲**Ile St. Louis and Notre-Dame**—This stroll features floodlit views of Notre-Dame and a taste of the Latin Quarter. Take the Métro (line 7) to the Pont Marie stop, then cross to Ile St. Louis. Turn right up rue St. Louis-en-l'Ile, stopping for dinner (or at least a Berthillon ice cream at #31 or Amorino Gelati at #47). Then cross pont St. Louis to Ile de la Cité, with a great view of Notre-Dame. Wander to the Left Bank on quai de l'Archevêché, and drop down to the river to the right for the best floodlit views. From May through September, you'll find fun bar-barges (daily until 2:00 in the morning, closed Oct–April, live music often Thu–Sun from 21:00). End your walk on place du Parvis Notre-Dame in front of Notre-Dame (on Sat–Sun in July–Aug, tower open until 23:00), or continue across the river to the Latin Quarter.

After-Dark Bus Tour

Several companies offer evening tours of Paris. I've described the company offering the most tours below. These trips are sold through your hotel (brochures in lobby) or directly at the offices listed below. You save no money by buying direct.

Paris Illumination Tours, run by Paris Vision, connect all the great illuminated sights of Paris with a 100-minute bus tour in 12 languages. The double-decker buses have huge windows, but the most desirable front seats are sometimes reserved for customers who've bought tickets for the overrated Moulin Rouge. Left-side seats are better. Visibility is fine in the rain.

Warning: These tours are not for everyone. You'll stampede on with a United Nations of tourists, get a set of headphones, dial up your language, and listen to a tape-recorded spiel (which is interesting, but includes an annoyingly bright TV screen and a pitch for the other, more expensive excursions). Uninspired as it is, the ride provides an entertaining, first-night overview of the city at its floodlit and scenic best. Bring your city map to stay oriented as you go. You're always on the bus, but the driver slows for photos at viewpoints (€26/person, kids under 12 ride free, 1.5 hours, departures 19:00–22:00 depending on time of year, usually April–Oct only, reserve 1 day in advance, arrive 30 min early to wait in line for best seats, departs from Paris Vision office at 214 rue de Rivoli, across the street from Mo: Tuileries, tel. 01 42 60 30 01, fax 01 42 86 95 36, www.parisvision.com). Skip their pricier minivan night tours.

Sleeping

I've focused most of my recommendations in three safe, handy, and colorful neighborhoods: the village-like rue Cler (near the Eiffel Tower), the artsy and trendy Marais (near place de la Bastille), and the lively and Latin yet classy Luxembourg (on the Left Bank). Before reserving, read the descriptions of the neighborhoods. Each offers different pros and cons, and your neighborhood is as important as your hotel for the success of your trip.

PARIS

Sleep Code

(€1 = about $1.40, country code: 33)
S = Single, **D** = Double/Twin, **T** = Triple, **Q** = Quad, **b** = bathroom,
s = shower only, * = French hotel rating system (0-4 stars).
Unless otherwise noted, hotel staff speak basic English and
breakfast is not included (but is usually optional).

To help you easily sort through these listings, I've divided
the rooms into three categories based on the price for a
standard double room with bath:

$$$ Higher Priced: Most rooms €150 or more.
$$ Moderately Priced: Most rooms between €100-150.
$ Lower Priced: Most rooms €100 or less.

Reserve ahead for Paris—the sooner, the better. Conventions clog Paris in September (worst), October, May, and June (very tough). There are unusually large crowds during holiday periods, so book your accommodations well in advance. In August, when Paris is quiet, some hotels offer lower rates to fill their rooms (if you're planning to visit Paris in the summer, consider spending extra for an air-conditioned room).

Old, characteristic, budget Parisian hotels have always been cramped. Retrofitted with toilets, private showers, and elevators (as most are today), they are even more cramped. Some hotels include the hotel tax (*taxe du séjour*, about €1 per person per day), though most will add this to your bill.

Recommended hotels have an elevator unless otherwise noted. Quad rooms usually have two double beds. Because rooms with double beds and showers are cheaper than rooms with twin beds and baths, room prices vary within each hotel.

Get advice from your hotel for safe parking. Consider long-term parking at either airport—Orly is closer and much easier for drivers to navigate than Charles de Gaulle. Garages are plentiful (€20–30/day, with special rates through some hotels). Curb parking is free at night (19:00–9:00), all day Sunday, and throughout the month of August. Self-serve launderettes are common; ask your hotelier for the nearest one (*"Où est un laverie automatique?"* ooh ay uh lah-vay-ree auto-mah-teek).

Rue Cler

Lined with open-air produce stands six days a week, rue Cler is a safe, tidy, village-like pedestrian street. It's so French that when I step out of my hotel in the morning, I feel like I must have been a poodle in a previous life. How such coziness lodged itself between the high-powered government district and the wealthy Eiffel

Tower and Les Invalides areas, I'll never know. This is a neighbor-hood of wide, tree-lined boulevards, stately apartment buildings, and lots of Americans. The American Church, American Library, American University, and many of my readers call this area home. Hotels here are relatively spacious and a good value, considering the elegance of the neighborhood and the higher prices of the more cramped hotels in other central areas. And for sightseeing, you're within walking distance of the Eiffel Tower, Army Museum, Seine River, and Orsay and Rodin museums.

Become a local at a rue Cler café for breakfast, or join the afternoon crowd for *une bière pression* (a draft beer). On rue Cler, you can eat and browse your way through a street full of pastry shops, delis, cheese shops, and colorful outdoor produce stalls. Afternoon *boules* (outdoor bowling) on the esplanade des Invalides is a relaxing spectator sport (look for the dirt area to the upper right as you face the front of Les Invalides). The manicured gardens behind the golden dome of the Army Museum are free, peaceful, and filled with flowers (at southwest corner of grounds, closes at about 19:00).

While hardly a happening nightlife spot, rue Cler offers many low-impact after-dark activities. Take an evening stroll above the river through the parkway between pont de l'Alma and pont des Invalides. For an after-dinner cruise on the Seine, it's a 15-min-ute walk to the river and the Bateaux-Mouches (see "Tours—By Boat," near the beginning of this chapter). For a post-dinner cruise on foot, saunter into Champ de Mars park to admire the glowing Eiffel Tower. For more ideas on Paris after hours, see previous sec-tion, "Nightlife."

The American Church and Franco-American Center is the community center for Americans living in Paris. They host inter-denominational worship services (every Sun at 9:00 and 11:00) and occasional concerts (most Sun at 17:00 Sept–June—but not every week), and distribute the useful *France-USA Contacts* and *Paris Times* (reception open Mon–Sat 9:00–12:00 & 13:00–22:00, Sun 14:30–19:00, 65 quai d'Orsay, Mo: Invalides, tel. 01 40 62 05 00, www.acparis.org).

Services: There's a large **post office** at the end of rue Cler on avenue de la Motte-Picquet, and a handy **SNCF train office** at 78 rue St. Dominique (Mon–Sat 8:30–19:30, closed Sun, get there when it opens to avoid a long wait). At both of these offices, take a number and wait your turn. A smaller post office is closer to the Eiffel Tower on avenue Rapp, one block past rue St. Dominique toward the river.

Markets: Cross Champ de Mars park to mix it up with bargain-hunters at the twice-weekly open-air market, **Marché Boulevard de Grenelle,** under the Métro, a few blocks southwest of Champ de Mars park (Wed and Sun until 12:30, between Mo: Dupleix and Mo: La Motte-Picquet-Grenelle). Two grocery stores, both on rue de Grenelle, are open until midnight: **Epicerie de la Tour** (at #197) and **Alimentation** (at corner with rue Cler). **Rue St. Dominique** is the area's boutique-browsing street.

Internet Access: Two Internet cafés compete in this neighborhood: **Com Avenue** is best (about €5/hr, shareable and multiuse accounts, Mon–Sat 10:00–20:00, closed Sun, 24 rue du Champ de Mars, tel. 01 45 55 00 07); **Cyber World Café** is more expensive but open later (about €7/hr, Mon–Sat 12:00–22:00, Sun 12:00–20:00, 20 rue de l'Exposition, tel. 01 53 59 96 54).

Laundry: Launderettes are omnipresent; ask your hotel for the nearest. Here are three handy locations: on rue Auguer (between rue St. Dominique and rue de Grenelle), on rue Amélie (between rue St. Dominique and rue de Grenelle), and at the southeast corner of rue Valadon and rue de Grenelle.

Métro Connections: Key Métro stops are Ecole Militaire, La Tour Maubourg, and Invalides. The RER-C line runs from the pont de l'Alma and Invalides stations, serving Versailles to the west; Auvers-sur-Oise to the north; and the Orsay Museum, Latin Quarter (St. Michel stop), and Austerlitz train station to the east.

Bus Routes: Smart travelers take advantage of these helpful bus routes (see "Rue Cler Hotels" map in this section for bus stop locations): Line #69 runs east–west along rue St. Dominique and serves Les Invalides, Orsay, Louvre, Marais, and Père Lachaise Cemetery (Mon–Sat only—no Sun service). Line #63 runs along the river (the quai d'Orsay), serving the Latin Quarter along boulevard St. Germain to the east (ending at Gare de Lyon), and Trocadéro and the Marmottan Museum to the west. Line #92 runs along avenue Bosquet, north to the Champs-Elysées and Arc de Triomphe (far better than the Métro) and south to the Montparnasse Tower and Gare Montparnasse. Line #87 runs on avenue de la Bourdonnais and serves St. Sulpice, Luxembourg Garden, the Sèvres-Babylone shopping area, the Bastille, and Gare de Lyon (also more convenient than Métro for these destinations). Line #28 runs on boulevard de la Tour Maubourg and serves Gare St. Lazare.

PARIS

Sleeping in the Rue Cler Neighborhood
(7th arrondissement, Mo: Ecole Militaire, La Tour–Maubourg, or Invalides)

Rue Cler is the glue that holds this handsome neighborhood together.

In the Heart of Rue Cler

Many of my readers stay in the rue Cler neighborhood. If you want to disappear into Paris, choose a hotel elsewhere. The first six hotels listed below are within Camembert-smelling distance of rue Cler; the others are within a 5- to 10-minute stroll. All hotels listed in the rue Cler area have elevators, air-conditioning, public Internet access terminals and Wi-Fi unless noted ("Wi-Fi only" means there's no computer available, but they do have Wi-Fi).

$$$ Hôtel Relais Bosquet*** is a professional place with generous public spaces and comfortable rooms that feature effective darkness blinds. The staff are politely formal and offer free breakfast (good buffet, including eggs and sausage) to anyone booking direct with this book in 2010 (standard Db-€170, bigger Db-€190, check website for special discounts, extra bed-€25, 19 rue du Champ de Mars, tel. 01 47 05 25 45, fax 01 45 55 08 24, www.relaisbosquet.com, hotel@relaisbosquet.com).

$$$ Hôtel du Cadran***, perfectly located a *boule* toss from rue Cler, welcomes you with a smart lobby, efficient staff, and stylish rooms featuring cool colors, mood lighting, and every comfort (Db-€205–230, 10 percent discount and free breakfast by entering the code "RickSteves" when you book by email or via their website, discount not valid for promotional rates on website; 10 rue du Champ de Mars, tel. 01 40 62 67 00, fax 01 40 62 67 13, www.hotelducadran.com, info@cadranhotel.com).

$$$ Hôtel de la Motte Picquet***, at the corner of rue Cler and avenue de la Motte-Picquet, is an intimate little place with plush rooms at fair prices (Sb-€150, standard Db-€160, bigger Db-€200, 30 avenue de la Motte-Picquet, tel. 01 47 05 09 57, fax 01 47 05 74 36, www.hotelmottepicquetparis.com, book@hotelmottepicquetparis.com).

$$ Hôtel Beaugency***, a solid value on a quieter street a short block off rue Cler, has 30 small rooms with standard furnishings and a lobby you can stretch out in (Sb-€105–115, Db-€115–155, 21 rue Duvivier, tel. 01 47 05 01 63, fax 01 45 51 04 96, www.hotel-beaugency.com, infos@hotel-beaugency.com, Christelle and Amel).

Warning: The next two hotels are super values, but very busy with my readers (reserve long in advance).

$$ Grand Hôtel Lévêque** faces rue Cler with red and gray tones, a singing maid, and a sliver-sized slow-dance elevator. This busy hotel has a convivial breakfast/hangout room and four floors. Half the rooms have been renovated and cost more (S-€62–74, Db-€95–132, Tb-€132–144, 29 rue Cler, tel. 01 47 05 49 15, fax 01 45 50 49 36, www.hotel-leveque.com, info@hotel-leveque.com, helpful Christophe and Lidwine).

$ Hôtel du Champ de Mars**, with adorable pastel rooms and serious owners Françoise and Stephane, is a cozy rue Cler option. This plush little hotel has a small-town feel from top to bottom. The rooms are snug but lovingly kept, and single rooms can work

Rue Cler Hotels

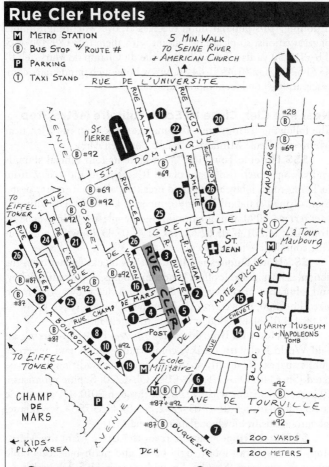

- Ⅿ Metro Station
- Ⓑ Bus Stop w/ Route #
- Ⓟ Parking
- Ⓣ Taxi Stand

5 Min. Walk to Seine River & American Church

① Hôtel Relais Bosquet
② Hôtel Beaugency
③ Grand Hôtel Lévêque
④ Hôtel du Champ de Mars
⑤ Hôtel de la Motte Picquet
⑥ Hôtels le Tourville & de Turenne
⑦ Hôtel Duquesne Eiffel
⑧ Hôtel La Bourdonnais
⑨ Hôtel de Londres Eiffel
⑩ Hôtel Eber Mars
⑪ Hôtel de la Tulipe
⑫ Hôtel Royal Phare
⑬ Hôtel Les Jardins d'Eiffel
⑭ Hôtel Muguet
⑮ Hôtel de l'Empereur
⑯ Hôtel du Cadran
⑰ Best Western Eiffel Park
⑱ Hôtel Kensington
⑲ Hôtel Prince
⑳ Hôtel St. Dominique
㉑ Hôtel de la Tour Eiffel
㉒ SNCF Office
㉓ Com Avenue Internet Café
㉔ Cyber World Internet Café
㉕ Late-Night Groceries (2)
㉖ Launderettes (3)

PARIS

as tiny doubles. It's an excellent value despite the lack of air-conditioning. This popular hotel receives an overwhelming number of reservations, so please be patient with them (Sb-€89, Db-€95, Tb-€119, 30 yards off rue Cler at 7 rue du Champ de Mars, tel. 01 45 51 52 30, fax 01 45 51 64 36, www.hotelduchampdemars.com, reservation@hotelduchampdemars.com).

Near Rue Cler, Close to Ecole Militaire Métro Stop

The following listings are a five-minute walk from rue Cler, near Métro stop Ecole Militaire or RER: Pont de l'Alma.

$$$ Hôtel le Tourville*****, despite its four official stars, is really a top-notch three-star place. It's intimate and classy, from its living-room lobby and vaulted breakfast area to its pretty pastel rooms (small standard Db-€190, superior Db-€250, Db with private terrace-€290, junior suite for 3–4 people-€450, 16 avenue de Tourville, tel. 01 47 05 62 62, fax 01 47 05 43 90, www.hoteltourville.com, hotel@tourville.com).

$$$ Hôtel Duquesne Eiffel*******, a few blocks farther from the action, is hospitable. It offers handsome rooms, a welcoming lobby, and a big, hot breakfast (Db-€170–210, price grows with room size, Tb-€230, breakfast-€13, 23 avenue Duquesne, tel. 01 44 42 09 09, fax 01 44 42 09 08, www.hde.fr, hotel@hde.fr).

$$$ Hôtel La Bourdonnais********* is *très* Parisian, mixing an Old World feel with creaky, comfortable rooms and generous public spaces. Its mostly spacious rooms are traditionally decorated (Sb-€140, Db-€175, Tb-€195, Qb-€220, Sophie promises a 10 percent discount with this book through 2010, 111 avenue de la Bourdonnais, tel. 01 47 05 45 42, fax 01 45 55 75 54, www.hotellabourdonnais.fr, hlb@hotellabourdonnais.fr).

$$ Hôtel Prince*****, across from the Ecole Militaire Métro stop, has a spartan lobby, ugly halls, and plain-but-acceptable rooms for the price (Sb-€83, Db with shower-€105, Db with tub-€120, Tb-€130, no Internet access, 66 avenue Bosquet, tel. 01 47 05 40 90, fax 01 47 53 06 62, www.hotelparisprince.com, paris@hotel-prince.com).

$$ Hôtel Eber Mars******* has larger-than-most rooms with weathered furnishings, oak-paneled public spaces, and a beam-me-up-Jacques, coffin-sized elevator (Sb-€100, Db-€118–138, Tb-€170, Qb-€190, 20 percent cheaper Nov–March and July–Aug, may have air-con in time for your visit, first breakfast free with this book in 2010, 117 avenue de la Bourdonnais, tel. 01 47 05 42 30, fax 01 47 05 45 91, www.hotelebermars.com, reservation@hotelebermars.com, manager Mr. Eber is a wealth of information for travelers).

$ Hôtel de Turenne******* is modest, with the cheapest air-conditioned rooms I've found and a colorful, open lobby. While the halls are frumpy and the rooms are *très* simple, the price is right. There are five true singles and several connecting rooms good for families (Sb-€69, Db-€79–92, Tb-€112, extra bed-€10, Wi-Fi only, 20 avenue de Tourville, tel. 01 47 05 99 92, fax 01 45 56 06 04, hotel.turenne.paris7@wanadoo.fr).

Near Rue Cler, Closer to Rue St. Dominique (and the Seine)

$$$ Hôtel de Londres Eiffel*** is my closest listing to the Eiffel Tower and Champ de Mars park. A good value, it offers immaculate, warmly decorated rooms, cozy public spaces, and a service-oriented staff. It's less convenient to the Métro (10-min walk) but handy to bus #69 and RER-C: Pont de l'Alma (Sb-€165, Db-€185, Db with Eiffel Tower view-€195–215, Tb-€245, check website for special rates, 1 rue Augereau, tel. 01 45 51 63 02, fax 01 47 05 28 96, www.londres-eiffel.com, info@londres-eiffel.com). The owners also have a good two-star hotel (Hôtel Apollon Montparnasse) in the Montparnasse area, with much lower rates—see www.londres-eiffel.com for details.

$$$ Hôtel de la Tulipe***, three blocks from rue Cler toward the river, is pricey but unique. The 20 small but artistically decorated rooms—each one different—come with stylish little bathrooms and surround a seductive, wood-beamed lounge and a peaceful, leafy courtyard (Db-€160, Tb-€180, two-room suite for up to five people-€280, friendly staff, no air-con, no elevator, 33 rue Malar, tel. 01 45 51 67 21, fax 01 47 53 96 37, www.paris-hotel-tulipe.com, hoteldelatulipe@wanadoo.fr).

$$ Hôtel St. Dominique** has fair rates, an inviting lobby, a small courtyard, and traditionally decorated rooms—most with minibars and floral wallpaper (Db-€140–160, extra bed-€20, no air-con, no elevator, Wi-Fi only, 62 rue St. Dominique, tel. 01 47 05 51 44, fax 01 47 05 81 28, www.hotelstdominique.com, saint-dominique.reservations@wanadoo.fr).

$ Hôtel de la Tour Eiffel** is a terrific two-star value on a quiet street near several of my favorite restaurants. The rooms are well-designed, spotless, and comfortable (snug Db-€79, bigger Db-€105–115, no air-con, Wi-Fi only, 17 rue de l'Exposition, tel. 01 47 05 14 75, fax 01 47 53 99 46, www.hotel-toureiffel.com, hte7@wanadoo.fr).

$ Hôtel Kensington** is a fine budget value close to the Eiffel Tower and run by elegant Daniele. It's an unpretentious place with mostly small, simple, but well-kept rooms (Sb-€62, Db-€79, big Db on back side-€94, Eiffel Tower views for those who ask, no air-con, no Internet access, 79 avenue de la Bourdonnais, tel. 01 47 05 74 00, fax 01 47 05 25 81, www.hotel-kensington.com, hk@hotel-kensington.com).

Near La Tour-Maubourg Métro Stop

The next three listings are within two blocks of the intersection of avenue de la Motte-Picquet and boulevard de la Tour Maubourg.

$$$ Hôtel Les Jardins d'Eiffel*, on a quiet street, feels like the modern motel it is, with professional service, its own parking garage (€24/day), and a spacious lobby. The 81 rooms are all designed for double occupancy (Sb/Db-€170–230; check website for special discounts; 8 rue Amélie, tel. 01 47 05 46 21, fax 01 45 55 28 08, www.hoteljardinseiffel.com, paris@hoteljardinseiffel.com).

$$ Hôtel Muguet, a peaceful, stylish, immaculate refuge, gives you three-star comfort for a two-star price. This delightful spot offers 43 tasteful rooms, a greenhouse lounge, and a small garden courtyard. The hands-on owner, Catherine, gives her guests a restful and secure home in Paris (Sb-€105, Db with one big bed-€135, twin Db-€135, small Db with view-€160, big Db with view and balcony-€190, Tb-€190, 11 rue Chevert, tel. 01 47 05 05 93, fax 01 45 50 25 37, www.hotelmuguet.com, muguet @wanadoo.fr, gentle Jacqueline runs reception).

$$ Hôtel de l'Empereur lacks intimacy, but it's spacious and a fair value. Its 38 pleasant rooms come with real wood furniture and views but some noise; fifth-floor rooms have small balconies and Napoleonic views (Db-€108, Tb-€135, Qb-€155, 2 rue Chevert, tel. 01 45 55 88 02, fax 01 45 51 88 54, www.hotel empereur.com, contact@hotelempereur.com).

Lesser Values in the Rue Cler Area

Given how fine this area is, these are acceptable last choices.

$$$ Best Western Eiffel Park* is a dead-quiet concrete business hotel with all the comforts, a relaxing lobby, 36 pleasant if unexceptional rooms, and a rooftop terrace (Db-€240, bigger "luxe" Db-€260, check online for promotional rates, 17 bis rue Amélie, tel. 01 45 55 10 01, fax 01 47 05 28 68, www.eiffelpark.com, reservation@eiffelpark.com).

$ Hôtel Royal Phare, facing the busy Ecole Militaire Métro stop, is humble and ideal for backpackers. The 34 basic, pink-pastel rooms are unimaginative but sleepable. Rooms on the courtyard are quietest, with peek-a-boo views of the Eiffel Tower from the fifth floor up (Sb-€76, Db with shower-€80–95, Db with tub-€100, Tb-€105, fridges in rooms, 40 avenue de la Motte-Picquet, tel. 01 47 05 57 30, fax 01 45 51 64 41, www.hotel-royalphare-paris.com, hotel-royalphare@wanadoo.fr, friendly manager Hocin).

Marais

Those interested in a more SoHo/Greenwich Village locale should make the Marais their Parisian home. Once a forgotten Parisian backwater, the Marais now is one of Paris' most popular residential, tourist, and shopping areas. This is jumbled, medieval Paris at its finest, where classy stone mansions sit alongside trendy bars, antiques shops, and fashion-conscious boutiques. The streets are a fascinating parade of artists, students, tourists, immigrants, and baguette-munching babies in strollers. The Marais is also known as a hub of the Parisian gay and lesbian scene. This area is *sans doute* livelier (and louder) than the rue Cler area.

In the Marais, you have these major sights close at hand: Picasso Museum, Carnavalet Museum, Victor Hugo's House, the Jewish Art and History Museum, and the Pompidou Center. You're also a manageable walk from Paris' two islands (Ile St. Louis and Ile de la Cité), home to Notre-Dame and Sainte-Chapelle. The Opéra Bastille, Promenade Plantée park, place des Vosges (Paris' oldest square), Jewish Quarter (rue des Rosiers), and nightlife-packed rue de Lappe are also walkable. (For Marais sights descriptions, see page 322; for the Opéra, see page 331.)

Most of my recommended hotels are located a few blocks north of the Marais' main east–west drag, rue St. Antoine/rue de Rivoli.

Tourist Information: The nearest TI is in Gare de Lyon (Mon–Sat 8:00–18:00, closed Sun, all-Paris TI tel. 08 92 68 30 00).

Services: Most banks and other services are on the main street, rue de Rivoli, which becomes rue St. Antoine. Marais **post offices** are on rue Castex and at the corner of rue Pavée and rue des Francs Bourgeois. There's a busy **SNCF Boutique** where you can take care of all train needs on rue St. Antoine at rue de Turenne (Mon–Sat 8:30–20:30, closed Sun). A quieter SNCF Boutique is nearer Gare de Lyon at 5 rue de Lyon (Mon–Sat 8:30–18:00, closed Sun).

Markets: The Marais has two good open-air markets: the sprawling **Marché de la Bastille,** around place de la Bastille (Thu and Sun until 12:30); and the more intimate, untouristy **Marché de la place d'Aligre** (Tue–Sun 9:00–12:00, closed Mon, cross place de la Bastille and walk about 10 blocks down rue du Faubourg St. Antoine, turn right at rue de Cotte to place d'Aligre; or, easier, take Métro line 8 from Bastille in the direction of Créteil-Préfecture, get off at the Ledru-Rollin stop, and walk a few blocks southeast). A small **grocery shop** is open until 23:00 on rue St. Antoine (near intersection with rue Castex). To shop at a Parisian Sears, find the **BHV** next to Hôtel de Ville.

Bookstore: The Marais is home to the friendliest English-language bookstore in Paris, **Red Wheelbarrow.** Penelope sells most of my guidebooks at good prices, and carries a great collection of other books about Paris and France for both adults and children (Mon–Fri 10:00–19:00, Sat 10:00–12:00 & 14:00–19:00, Sun 14:00–18:00, 22 rue St. Paul, Mo: St. Paul, tel. 01 48 04 75 08).

Internet Access: Try **Paris CY** (Mon–Sat 8:00–20:00, Sun 13:00–20:00, 8 rue de Jouy, Mo: St. Paul, tel. 01 42 71 37 37), or **Cyber Cube** (daily 10:00–22:00, 12 rue Daval, Mo: Bastille, tel. 01 49 29 67 67).

Laundry: There are many launderettes; ask your hotelier for the nearest. Here are four you can count on: on impasse Guéménée (north of rue St. Antoine), on rue du Plâtre (just west of rue du Temple), on rue du Petit Musc (south of rue St. Antoine), and on rue Daval (near Cyber Cube).

Métro Connections: Key Métro stops in the Marais are, from east to west: Bastille, St. Paul, and Hôtel de Ville (Sully-Morland, Pont Marie, and Rambuteau stops are also handy). Métro service to the Marais neighborhood is excellent, with direct service to the Louvre, Champs-Elysées, Arc de Triomphe, and La Défense (all on line 1); the rue Cler area and Opéra Garnier (line 8 from Bastille stop); and four major train stations: Gare de Lyon, Gare du Nord, Gare de l'Est, and Gare d'Austerlitz (all accessible from Bastille stop).

Bus Routes: Line #69 on rue St. Antoine takes you eastbound to Père Lachaise Cemetery and westbound to the Louvre, Orsay, and Rodin museums, plus the Army Museum, ending at the Eiffel Tower (Mon–Sat only—no Sun service). Line #86 runs down boulevard Henri IV, crossing Ile St. Louis and serving the Latin Quarter along boulevard St. Germain. Line #87 follows a similar route, but also serves Gare de Lyon to the east and the Eiffel Tower and rue Cler neighborhood to the west. Line #96 runs on rues Turenne and François Miron and serves the Louvre and boulevard St. Germain (near Luxembourg Garden), ending at Gare Montparnasse. Line #65 runs from Gare de Lyon up rue de Lyon, around place de la Bastille, and then up boulevard Beaumarchais to Gare de l'Est and Gare du Nord.

Taxis: You'll find taxi stands on place de la Bastille (where boulevard Richard Lenoir meets the square), on the south side of rue St. Antoine (in front of St. Paul Church), and a quieter one on the north side of rue St. Antoine (where it meets rue Castex).

PARIS

Sleeping in the Marais Neighborhood
(4th arrondissement, Mo: Bastille, St. Paul, and Hôtel de Ville)
The Marais runs from the Pompidou Center to the Bastille (a 15-min walk), with most hotels located a few blocks north of the main east–west drag, the rue de Rivoli/rue St. Antoine. It's about 15 minutes on foot from any hotel in this area to Notre-Dame, Ile St. Louis, and the Latin Quarter. Strolling home (day or night) from Notre-Dame along the Ile St. Louis is marvelous.

All hotels listed in the Marais neighborhood have elevators, air-conditioning, public Internet access terminals, and Wi-Fi unless otherwise noted.

Near Place des Vosges

$$$ Hôtel Castex*, a well-managed place with tiled floors and dark wood accents, is well-situated on a quiet street near place de la Bastille. A clever system of connecting rooms allows families total privacy between two rooms, each with its own bathroom. The 30 rooms are narrow but tasteful; it's a good value year-round. Your fourth night is free in August and from November through February, except around New Year's (Sb-€120, Db-€150, Tb-€220, just off place de la Bastille and rue St. Antoine at 5 rue Castex, Mo: Bastille, tel. 01 42 72 31 52, fax 01 42 72 57 91, www.castexhotel .com, info@castexhotel.com).

$$ Hôtel Bastille Spéria*, a short block off place de la Bastille, offers business-type service. The walls are thin, but the 42 well-configured rooms are modern and comfortable, with big beds (Sb-115, Db-€140–178, child's bed-€20, good buffet breakfast-€13, 1 rue de la Bastille, Mo: Bastille, tel. 01 42 72 04 01, fax 01 42 72 56 38, www.hotel-bastille-speria.com, info@hotel-bastille -speria.com).

$$ Hôtel Saint-Louis Marais is a little hotel on a quiet residential street between the river and rue St. Antoine. The lobby is inviting and the 19 rooms have character (a few are at street level), but there's no air-conditioning, no elevator, and no Internet access (small Db-€115, standard Db-€140, Tb-€160, parking-€20, 1 rue Charles V, Mo: Sully Morland, tel. 01 48 87 87 04, fax 01 48 87 33 26, www.saintlouismarais.com, marais@saintlouishotels.com).

$$ Hôtel du 7ème Art, two blocks south of rue St. Antoine toward the river, is a young, carefree, Hollywood-nostalgia place with a full-service café-bar and Charlie Chaplin murals (but no elevator and pay Wi-Fi). Its 23 good-value rooms have brown 1970s decor, but are comfortable enough. The large rooms are American-spacious (small Db-€93, standard Db-€105, large Db-€120–150, Tb-€140–170, extra bed-€20, 20 rue St. Paul, Mo: St. Paul, tel. 01 44 54 85 00, fax 01 42 77 69 10, www.paris-hotel-7art.com, hotel 7art@wanadoo.fr).

$ Grand Hôtel Jeanne d'Arc, a lovely little hotel with thoughtfully appointed rooms, is ideally located for (and very popular with) connoisseurs of the Marais. It's a fine value and worth booking way ahead (three months in advance, if possible). Sixth-floor rooms have views, and corner rooms are wonderfully bright in the City of Light—though no rooms have air-conditioning and there's no Internet access. Rooms on the street can be noisy until the bars close (Sb-€62–89, Db-€89, larger twin

Marais Hotels

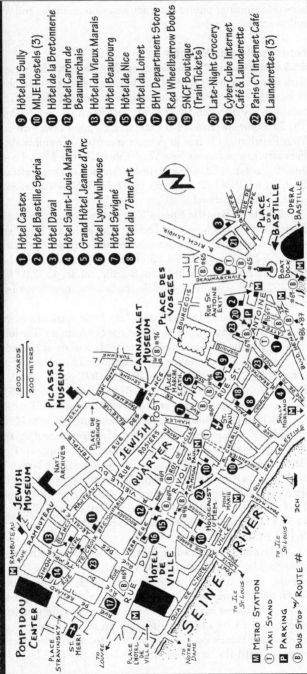

1. Hôtel Castex
2. Hôtel Bastille Spéria
3. Hôtel Daval
4. Hôtel Saint-Louis Marais
5. Grand Hôtel Jeanne d'Arc
6. Hôtel Lyon-Mulhouse
7. Hôtel Sévigné
8. Hôtel du 7ème Art

9. Hôtel du Sully
10. MIJE Hostels (3)
11. Hôtel de la Bretonnerie
12. Hôtel Caron de Beaumarchais
13. Hôtel du Vieux Marais
14. Hôtel Beaubourg
15. Hôtel de Nice
16. Hôtel du Loiret
17. BHV Department Store
18. Red Wheelbarrow Books
19. SNCF Boutique (Train Tickets)
20. Late-Night Grocery
21. Cyber Cube Internet Café & Launderette
22. Paris CY Internet Café
23. Launderettes (3)

M Metro Station
T Taxi Stand
P Parking
B Bus Stop w/ Route #

Db-€116, Tb-€146, good Qb-€160, 3 rue de Jarente, Mo: St. Paul, tel. 01 48 87 62 11, fax 01 48 87 37 31, www.hoteljeannedarc.com, information@hoteljeannedarc.com).

$ Hôtel Lyon-Mulhouse**, well-managed by gregarious Nathalia, is located on a busy street barely off place de la Bastille. While less intimate than some, it is a solid deal, with pleasant, relatively large rooms—five are true singles with partial Eiffel Tower views (Sb-€70, Db-€100, Tb-€130, Qb-€150, pay Wi-Fi, 8 boulevard Beaumarchais, Mo: Bastille, tel. 01 47 00 91 50, fax 01 47 00 06 31, www.1-hotel-paris.com, hotelyonmulhouse @wanadoo.fr).

$ Hôtel Daval**, an unassuming place with good rates on the lively side of place de la Bastille, is ideal for night owls. Ask for a quieter room on the courtyard side (Sb-€72, Db-€85, Tb-110, Qb-€125, 21 rue Daval, Mo: Bastille, tel. 01 47 00 51 23, fax 01 40 21 80 26, www.hoteldaval.com, hoteldaval@wanadoo.fr, Didier).

$ Hôtel Sévigné**, run by straight-faced owner Monsieur Mercier, is a snappy little hotel with lavender halls and 30 tidy, comfortable rooms at good prices (Sb-€68, Db-€81–92, Tb-€104; one-night, no-refund policy for any cancellation; no Internet access, 2 rue Malher, Mo: St. Paul, tel. 01 42 72 76 17, fax 01 42 78 68 26, www.le-sevigne.com, contact@le-sevigne.com).

$ Hôtel du Sully, sitting right on rue St. Antoine, is nothing fancy, but it is cheap. The entry is long and narrow, and the rooms are dimly lit but sleepable (Db-€65, Tb-€80, no elevator, no air-con, no Internet access, 48 rue St. Antoine, Mo: St. Paul, tel. 01 42 78 49 32, fax 01 44 61 76 50, www.sullyhotelparis.com, sullyhotel @orange.fr, run by friendly Monsieur Zeroual).

$ *MIJE Youth Hostels:* The Maison Internationale de la Jeunesse et des Etudiants (MIJE) runs three classy old residences that make a budget traveler's dream come true. Each is well-maintained, with simple, clean, single-sex (unless your group takes a whole room), one- to four-bed rooms for travelers of any age. The hostels are **MIJE Fourcy** (biggest and loudest, €11 dinners available with a membership card, 6 rue de Fourcy, just south of rue de Rivoli), **MIJE Fauconnier** (no elevator, 11 rue du Fauconnier), and **MIJE Maubisson** (smallest and quietest, no outdoor terrace, 12 rue des Barres). None has double beds or air-conditioning; all have private showers in every room (all prices per person: Sb-€49, Db-€36, Tb-€32, Qb-€30, credit cards accepted, includes breakfast but not towels, required membership card-€2.50 extra/person, 7-day maximum stay, rooms locked 12:00–15:00, curfew at 1:00 in the morning). They all share the same contact information (tel. 01 42 74 23 45, fax 01 40 27 81 64, www.mije.com, info @mije.com) and Métro stop (St. Paul). Reservations are accepted (six weeks ahead online, ten days ahead by phone)—though you must show up by noon, or call the morning of arrival to confirm a later arrival time.

Near the Pompidou Center

These hotels are farther west, closer to the Pompidou Center than to place de la Bastille. The Hôtel de Ville Métro stop works well for all of these hotels, unless a closer stop is noted.

$$$ Hôtel Caron de Beaumarchais*** feels like a fluffy folk museum with 20 sweet little rooms and a lobby cluttered with bits from an elegant 18th-century Marais house. Short antique collectors should sleep here (small Db in back-€152, larger Db facing the front-€170, Wi-Fi only, 12 rue Vieille du Temple, tel. 01 42 72 34 12, fax 01 42 72 34 63, www.carondebeaumarchais.com, hotel @carondebeaumarchais.com).

$$ Hôtel de la Bretonnerie*,** three blocks from the Hôtel de Ville, makes a fine Marais home. It has a warm, welcoming lobby, chic decor, and 29 tastefully appointed rooms with an antique, open-beam warmth (perfectly good standard "classic" Db-€130, bigger "charming" Db-€160, Db suite-€190, Tb/Qb-€190, Tb/ Qb suite-€210, no air-con, between rue Vieille du Temple and rue des Archives at 22 rue Ste. Croix de la Bretonnerie, tel. 01 48 87 77 63, fax 01 42 77 26 78, www.bretonnerie.com, hotel @bretonnerie.com).

$$ Hôtel du Vieux Marais,** with a quirky owner and modern rooms that should all be renovated by the time you get there, is tucked away on a quiet street two blocks east of the Pompidou Center. Say *bonjour* to friendly bulldog Leelou, who runs the small lobby (Sb-€100–115, Db-€120–155, extra bed-€23, Wi-Fi only, just off rue des Archives at 8 rue du Plâtre, Mo: Rambuteau or Hôtel de Ville, tel. 01 42 78 47 22, fax 01 42 78 34 32, www.vieuxmarais .com, hotel@vieuxmarais.com).

$$ Hôtel Beaubourg*** is a good three-star value on a quiet street in the shadow of the Pompidou Center. The lounge is inviting, and the 28 rooms are wood-beam comfy (standard Db-€140, bigger twin Db-€160, rates vary wildly by season, 11 rue Simon Le Franc, Mo: Rambuteau, tel. 01 42 74 34 24, fax 01 42 78 68 11, www.hotelbeaubourg.com, reservation@hotelbeaubourg.com).

$$ Hôtel de Nice,** on the Marais' busy main drag, is a turquoise-and-fuchsia "Marie-Antoinette-does-tie-dye" spot. Its narrow halls are littered with paintings and layered with carpets, and its 23 Old World rooms have thoughtful touches and tight bathrooms. Twin rooms, which cost the same as doubles, are larger and on the street side—but have effective double-paned windows (Sb-€85, Db-€115, Tb-€140, extra bed-€20, no Internet access, reception on second floor, 42 bis rue de Rivoli, tel. 01 42 78 55 29,

fax 01 42 78 36 07, www.hoteldenice.com, contact@hoteldenice
.com, laissez-faire management).

$ Hôtel du Loiret* is a centrally located (some noise) and
rare Marais budget hotel. If you can get past the lobby, you'll be
surprised at how much better the rooms are (S with WC across
hall-€50, Db-€70–90, Tb-€100, no air-con, 8 rue des Mauvais
Garçons, tel. 01 48 87 77 00, fax 01 48 04 96 56, www.hotel-loiret
.fr, hotelduloiret@hotmail.com).

In the Historic Core, on Ile St. Louis

The peaceful, residential character of this river-wrapped island,
its brilliant location, and its homemade ice cream have drawn
Americans for decades, allowing hotels to charge dearly. There
are no budget values here, but the island's coziness and proximity
to the Marais, Notre-Dame, and the Latin Quarter help compen-
sate for higher rates. All of the following hotels are on the island's
main drag, rue St. Louis-en-l'Ile, where I list several restaurants
(see "Eating," later in this chapter). Use Mo: Pont Marie or Sully-
Morland.

$$$ Hôtel du Jeu de Paume**, occupying a 17th-century
tennis center, is the most expensive hotel I list in Paris. When you
enter its magnificent lobby, you'll understand why. Greet Scoop,
le chien, then take a spin in the glass elevator for a half-timbered-
tree-house experience. The 30 quite comfortable rooms are care-
fully designed and *très* tasteful, though small for the price (you're
paying for the location and public spaces—check for deals on their
website). Most rooms face a small garden; all are pin-drop peace-
ful (standard Db-€285, larger Db-€370, deluxe Db-€450, 54 rue
St. Louis-en-l'Ile, tel. 01 43 26 14 18, fax 01 40 46 02 76, www
.jeudepaumehotel.com, info@jeudepaumehotel.com).

$$$ Hôtel de Lutèce** charges top euro for its island address
but comes with a sit-a-while wood-paneled lobby, a fireplace, and
warmly designed rooms. Twin rooms are larger and the same price
as double rooms (Db-€195, Tb-€235, 65 rue St. Louis-en-l'Ile, tel.
01 43 26 23 52, fax 01 43 29 60 25, www.hoteldelutece.com, info
@hoteldelutece.com).

$$$ Hôtel des Deux-Iles** is bright and colorful, with mar-
ginally smaller rooms (Db-€180, Wi-Fi only, 59 rue St. Louis-
en-l'Ile, tel. 01 43 26 13 35, fax 01 43 29 60 25, www.2iles.com,
hotel.2iles@free.fr).

$$$ Hôtel Saint-Louis** has less personality but good
rooms with parquet floors and comparatively good rates (Db-
€145–160, extra bed-€50, Wi-Fi only, 75 rue St. Louis-en-l'Ile, tel.
01 46 34 04 80, fax 01 46 34 02 13, www.hotelsaintlouis.com, slouis
@noos.fr).

PARIS

In the Historic Core, on Ile de la Cité

$$ Hôtel Dieu Hospitel Paris is the only Paris hotel with an Ile de la Cité address. It's located in the oldest city hospital of Paris, on the square in front of Notre-Dame (find the hospital on the map on page 286). Originally intended to receive families of patients, it now offers rooms for tourists, too. To get a spot in this prime location in front of Notre-Dame, with only 14 rooms, you'll need to book well in advance. You'll be surprised by the modern, comfortable decor and may even forget you're in a hospital (Sb-€104, Db-€115, some rooms have peek-a-boo views of Notre-Dame, 1 place du Parvis, tel. 01 44 32 01 00, www.hotel -hospitel.com, hospitelhoteldieu@wanadoo.fr). Enter the hotel's main entrance, turn right, follow signs to wing B2, and take the elevator to the sixth floor.

Luxembourg Garden

This neighborhood revolves around Paris' loveliest park and offers quick access to the city's best shopping streets and grandest café-hopping. Sleeping in the Luxembourg area offers a true Left Bank experience without a hint of the low-end commotion of the nearby Latin Quarter tourist ghetto. The Luxembourg Garden, boulevard St. Germain, Cluny Museum, and Latin Quarter are all at your doorstep. Here you get the best of both worlds: youthful Left Bank energy and the classic trappings that surround the monumental Panthéon and St. Sulpice Church. Hotels in this central area are more expensive than in other neighborhoods I list.

Having the Luxembourg Garden at your back door allows strolls through meticulously cared-for flowers, a great kids' play area, and a purifying escape from city traffic. Place St. Sulpice offers an elegant, pedestrian-friendly square and quick access to some of Paris' best boutiques. Sleeping in the Luxembourg area also puts several movie theaters at your fingertips (at Métro stop: Odéon), as well as lively cafés on boulevard St. Germain, rue de Buci, rue des Canettes, place de la Sorbonne, and place de la Contrescarpe, all of which buzz with action until late.

Services: The nearest **TI** is across the river in Gare de Lyon (Mon–Sat 8:00–18:00, closed Sun, all-Paris TI tel. 08 92 68 30 00). There are two useful **SNCF boutiques** for easy train reservations and ticket purchase: at 79 rue de Rennes and at 54 boulevard Saint-Michel (Mon–Sat 8:30–18:00, closed Sun).

Markets: The colorful street market at the south end of rue Mouffetard is a worthwhile 10- to 15-minute walk from these hotels (Tue–Sat 8:00–12:00 & 15:30–19:00, Sun 8:00–12:00, closed Mon, five blocks south of place de la Contrescarpe, Mo: Place Monge).

Bookstore: The **Village Voice** bookstore carries a full selection of English-language books (including mine), and is near St.

Hotels and Restaurants on Ile St. Louis

VIEW

M METRO STATION

B BATOBUS BOAT STOP

1 Hôtel du Jeu de Paume

2 Hôtel de Lutèce & Grocery

3 Hôtel des Deux-Iles

4 Hôtel Saint-Louis

5 Le Tastevin Rest.

6 Café Med

7 La Brasserie de l'Ile St. Louis

8 Rests. Nos Ancêtres les Gaulois & La Taverne du Sergeant Recruteur

9 Berthillon Ice Cream (3)

10 Amorino Gelati

11 Good Picnic Spot

Sulpice (Mon 14:00–19:00, Tue–Sat 10:00–19:00, Sun 12:00–18:00, 6 rue Princesse, tel. 01 46 33 36 47, www.villagevoicebook shop.com).

Internet Access: You'll find it at **Le Milk** (always open, between the Luxembourg Garden and Panthéon at 17 rue Soufflot).

Métro Connections: Métro lines 10 and 4 serve this area (10 connects to the Austerlitz train station, and 4 runs to the Montparnasse, Est, and Nord train stations). Neighborhood stops are Cluny–La Sorbonne, Mabillon, Odéon, and St. Sulpice. RER-B (Luxembourg station is handiest) provides direct service to Charles de Gaulle airport and Gare du Nord trains, and access to Orly airport via the Orlybus (transfer at Denfert-Rochereau).

Bus Routes: Buses #63, #86, and #87 run eastbound through this area on boulevard St. Germain, and westbound along rue des Ecoles, stopping on place St. Sulpice. Lines #63 and #87 provide direct connections west to the rue Cler area. Line #63 also serves the Orsay, Army, Rodin, and Marmottan museums to the west and Gare de Lyon to the east. Lines #86 and #87 run east to the Marais, and #87 continues to Gare de Lyon.

Sleeping in the Luxembourg Garden Area

(5th and 6th arrondissements, Mo: St. Sulpice, Mabillon, Odéon, and Cluny–La Sorbonne; RER: Luxembourg)

While it takes only 15 minutes to walk from one end of this neighborhood to the other, I've located the hotels by the key monument they are close to (St. Sulpice Church, the Odéon Theater, and the Panthéon). Most hotels are within a five-minute walk of the Luxembourg Garden (and none is more than 15 minutes away).

All hotels listed in the Luxembourg Garden area have elevators, air-conditioning, public Internet access terminals, and Wi-Fi unless otherwise noted.

Hotels near St. Sulpice Church

These hotels are all within a block of St. Sulpice Church and two blocks from famous boulevard St. Germain. This is nirvana for boutique-minded shoppers—and you'll pay extra for the location. Métro stops St. Sulpice and Mabillon are equally close.

$$$ Hôtel de l'Abbaye**** is a lovely refuge just west of Luxembourg Garden; it's a find for well-heeled connoisseurs of this area. The hotel's four-star luxury includes refined lounges inside and out, with 44 sumptuous rooms and every amenity at surprisingly reasonable rates (Db-€220, bigger Db-€335, suites and apartments available for €390–425, includes breakfast, 10 rue Cassette, tel. 01 45 44 38 11, fax 01 45 48 07 86, www.hotel-abbaye .com, hotel.abbaye@wanadoo.fr).

$$$ Hôtel Relais St. Sulpice***, on the small street just behind St. Sulpice Church, is a dark little boutique hotel with a cozy lounge and 26 pricey and stylish rooms, most surrounding a leafy glass atrium. Top-floor rooms get more light and are worth requesting (Db-€180–215 depending on size, sauna free for guests, Wi-Fi only, 3 rue Garancière, tel. 01 46 33 99 00, fax 01 46 33 00 10, www.relais-saint-sulpice.com, relaisstsulpice@wanadoo.fr).

$$$ Hôtel la Perle*** is a spendy pearl in the thick of the lively rue des Canettes, a block off place St. Sulpice. At this snappy, modern, business-class hotel, sliding glass doors open onto the traffic-free street, and you're greeted by a fun lobby built around a central bar and atrium (standard Db-€185, bigger Db-€205, luxury Db-€235, check website or call for last-minute deals within five days of your stay, 14 rue des Canettes, tel. 01 43 29 10 10, fax 01 46 34 51 04, www.hotellaperle.com, booking@hotellaperle.com).

$$ Hôtel Bonaparte**, an unpretentious place wedged between boutiques, is a few steps from place St. Sulpice. While the 29 Old World rooms don't live up to the handsome entry, they're adequately comfortable and generally spacious, with big bathrooms and molded ceilings (Sb-€100–120, Db-€133–155, big Db-€165, Tb-€175, includes breakfast, 61 rue Bonaparte, tel. 01 43 26 97 37,

Hotels and Restaurants near St. Sulpice and the Odéon Theater

Ⓑ Bus Stop
Ⓜ Metro Station

DCH

❶ Hôtel de l'Abbaye
❷ Hôtel Relais St. Sulpice
❸ Hôtel la Perle
❹ Hôtel Bonaparte
❺ Hôtel le Récamier
❻ Hôtel le Relais Médicis
❼ Hôtel Michelet Odéon

❽ La Crêpe Rit du Clown
❾ Le Bistrot Henri IV
❿ Lou Pescadou-Chez Julien Rest.
⓫ Chez Georges
⓬ Village Voice Books
⓭ To Internet Café & Panthéon

fax 01 46 33 57 67, www.hotelbonaparte.fr, reservation@hotel bonaparte.fr, helpful Fréderic and Eric at reception).

$$ Hôtel le Récamier**, romantically tucked in the corner of place St. Sulpice, feels like grandma's house—but it may soon close for renovation (call ahead to check). For now, it has flowery wallpaper, dark halls, and clean, simple rooms, but renovation may change the decor. Regardless, the location is ideal (pre-renovation rates: S-€100, Sb-€120, D-€100, Db-€125, bigger Db-€140–150, Tb-€165, Qb-€190, no air-con, no Internet access, 3 bis place St. Sulpice, tel. 01 43 26 04 89, fax 01 46 33 27 73, hotelrecamier @wanadoo.fr).

Near the Odéon Theater

These two hotels are between the Odéon Métro stop and Luxembourg Garden (five blocks east of St. Sulpice), and may have rooms when others don't. In addition to the Odéon Métro stop, the RER-B Luxembourg stop is a short walk away.

$$$ Hôtel Relais Médicis*** is perfect in every way—if you've always wanted to live in a Monet painting and can afford it. Its 16 rooms surround a fragrant little garden courtyard and fountain, giving you a countryside break fit for a Medici in the heart of Paris. This delightful refuge is tastefully decorated with floral Old World charm, and is permeated with thoughtfulness (Sb-€172, Db-€208–228, deluxe Db-€258, Tb-€298, €30 cheaper mid-July–Aug and Nov–March, includes extravagant continental breakfast, faces the Odéon Theater at 23 rue Racine, tel. 01 43 26 00 60, fax 01 40 46 83 39, www.relaismedicis.com, reservation @relaismedicis.com, eager-to-help Isabelle runs reception).

$$ Hôtel Michelet Odéon** sits shyly in a corner of place de l'Odéon with big windows on the world. It's a decent value in this pricey area, with 24 spacious-but-simple rooms with modern decor and views of the square (Db-€105–130, Tb-€165, Qb-€185, no air-con, pay Wi-Fi, 6 place de l'Odéon, tel. 01 53 10 05 60, fax 01 46 34 55 35, www.hotelmicheletodeon.com, hotel@michelet odeon.com).

Near the Panthéon and Rue Mouffetard

The last two listings are cheap dives, but in a great area.

$$ Hôtel des Grandes Écoles*** is idyllic. A private cobbled lane leads to three buildings that protect a flower-filled garden courtyard, preserving a sense of tranquility rare in this city. Its 51 rooms are French-countryside pretty, spotless, and reasonably spacious, but have no air-conditioning. This romantic spot is deservedly popular, so call well in advance (Db-€115–140 depending on size, extra bed-€20, parking garage-€30, Wi-Fi only, 75 rue du Cardinal Lemoine, Mo: Cardinal Lemoine, tel. 01 43 26 79 23, fax

01 43 25 28 15, www.hotel-grandes-ecoles.com, hotel.grandes.ecoles @wanadoo.fr, mellow Marie speaks English, Mama does not).

$$ Hôtel des 3 Collèges** greets clients with a sterile lobby, claustrophobic hallways, and unimaginative rooms with low ceilings...but decent rates (small Sb-€80, small Db-€110, bigger Db-€130–150, Tb-€132–165, pay Wi-Fi only, 16 rue Cujas, tel. 01 43 54 67 30, fax 01 46 34 02 99, www.3colleges.com, hotel@3colleges .com).

$ Hôtel Cluny Sorbonne** is welcoming and a good deal. It's located in the thick of things across from the famous university and below the Panthéon. Rooms are clean and comfortable, with wood furnishings (standard Db-€95, really big Db-€160, no air-con, 8 rue Victor Cousin, tel. 01 43 54 66 66, fax 01 43 29 68 07, www.hotel-cluny.fr, cluny@club-internet.fr).

$ Hôtel Central*, wedged between two cafés, has a smoky, dingy reception, a steep, slippery stairway, dumpy beds, and mildewed rooms. Bottom line: It's youth-hostel cheap, but with a charm only romantic hobos will appreciate. All rooms have showers, but toilets are down the hall (Ss-€33–38, Ds-€46–51, cash only, no elevator, no air-con, no Internet access, 6 rue Descartes, Mo: Cardinal Lemoine, tel. 01 46 33 57 93). Do your best to get a smile out of Madame Pilar, who doesn't speak English.

$ Young & Happy Hostel is easygoing, well-run, and English-speaking, with Internet access, kitchen facilities, and acceptable hostel conditions. It sits dead-center in the rue Mouffetard bar, café, and people action...which can be good or bad (all rates per person: bunk in 4- to 10-bed dorms-€24, 3- to 5-bed dorms-€26, double rooms-€28, includes breakfast, sheets-€2.50, credit cards accepted, no air-con, no lockers but safety box at reception, rooms closed 11:00–16:00 but reception stays open, no curfew, 80 rue Mouffetard, Mo: Place Monge, tel. 01 47 07 47 07, fax 01 47 07 22 24, www.youngandhappy.fr, smile@youngandhappy.fr).

Farther Away from the Seine, at the Bottom of Rue Mouffetard

These hotels, away from the Seine and other tourists in an appealing workaday area, offer more room for your euro. They require a longer walk or Métro ride to sights, but often have rooms when other accommodations are booked up. Rue Mouffetard is the bohemian soul of this area, running south from its heart—place de la Contrescarpe—to rue de Bazeilles. Two thousand years ago, it was the principal Roman road south to Italy. Today, this small, meandering street has a split personality. The lower half thrives in the daytime as a pedestrian shopping street. The upper half sleeps during the day but comes alive after dark, teeming with bars, restaurants, and nightlife. Use Métro stops

Hotels and Restaurants near the Pantheon

Ⓜ METRO STATION
Ⓡ R.E.R. STOP

1 Hôtel Cluny Sorbonne
2 Hôtel des 3 Collèges
3 Hôtel des Grandes Ecoles
4 Port-Royal-Hôtel
5 Hôtel de L'Espérance
6 Hôtel de France
7 Hôtel Central
8 Young & Happy Hostel
9 Hotel des Mines
10 Restaurant Perraudin
11 Le Soufflot Café
12 Place de la Sorbonne Eateries
13 Restaurant Polidor
14 Brasserie Bouillon Racine

15 Café Delmas
16 Le Mouffetard Café
17 Les Papillons Restaurant
18 Cave de Bourgogne
19 Internet Café
20 SNCF Boutique

PARIS

Censier-Daubenton or Les Gobelins.

$$ Hôtel de France**, on a busy street, offers modest but comfortable rooms. Its substantial makeover, including the addition of air-conditioning, should be done in time for your visit; this means the information below may change. Currently, the best and quietest rooms are *sur la cour* (on the courtyard), though streetside rooms are acceptable (Sb-€95, Db-€100–115, Tb-€140, 108 rue Monge, Mo: Censier-Daubenton, tel. 01 47 07 19 04, fax 01 43 36 62 34, www.hotelfrancequartierlatin.com, hotel.de.fce @wanadoo.fr).

$ Port-Royal-Hôtel* has only one star, but don't let that fool you. Its 46 rooms are polished top to bottom and have been well-run by the same proud family for 68 years. You could eat off the floors of its spotless, comfy rooms...but you won't find air-conditioning, Internet access, or Wi-Fi. Ask for a room away from the street (S-€41–55, D-€55, Db-€79–89 depending on size, big shower down the hall-€3, cash only, nonrefundable cash deposit required, on busy boulevard de Port-Royal at #8, Mo: Les Gobelins, tel. 01 43 31 70 06, fax 01 43 31 33 67, www.hotelportroyal.fr, portroyal hotel@wanadoo.fr).

$ Hôtel de L'Espérance** is a terrific two-star value. It's quiet, pink, and cushy, with feminine rooms and canopy beds (Sb-€75–80, Db-€80–90, Tb-€107, no Internet access, 15 rue Pascal, Mo: Censier-Daubenton, tel. 01 47 07 10 99, fax 01 43 37 56 19, www.hoteldelesperance.fr, hotel.esperance@wanadoo.fr).

On the South Side of Luxembourg Garden

$ Hôtel des Mines** is less central but worth the walk. Its 50 well-maintained rooms are a good value and come with updated bathrooms and a welcoming lobby (standard Db-€100, bigger Db-€100–120, Tb-€144, Qb-€170, check for Web deals, between Luxembourg and Port-Royal stations on the RER-B line, a 10-min walk from Panthéon, one block past Luxembourg Garden at 125 boulevard St. Michel, tel. 01 43 54 32 78, fax 01 46 33 72 52, www .hoteldesminesparis.com, hotel@hoteldesminesparis.com).

Near Place de la République

(10th and 11th arrondissements, Mo: République, Oberkampf)
The three budget accommodations below are in the neighborhood north of the Marais, between place de la République and Canal St. Martin. This area is untouristy, young, and *très* international (read "melting pot"). It's definitely unpolished (and edgy to some) and more remote—but if you can put up with some rough edges and don't mind using the Métro and buses for all your sightseeing, you'll find some good deals here.

PARIS

Hotels near Place de la République

Ⓜ -Metro Station

200 YARDS
200 METERS

TO
GARE
DU NORD
& GARE
DE L'EST

ST. LOUIS
HOSPITAL

N

CANAL
ST. MARTIN

QUAI DE LANCRY
QUAI DE MARSEILLE
QUAI DE VALMY
QUAI DE JEMMAPES

BLVD. MAGENTA

RUE ALBERT THOMAS

R. BEAUREPAIRE
R. DIEU
R. LEON JOUHAUX
TOUR DIC

Jacques
Bonsergent Ⓜ

Ⓜ

④ Post

R. ALBERT
RUE BICHAT
R. DU TEMPLE
AVE. PARMENTIER
RUE DE LA FONTAINE DU ROI
FOLIE MERICOURT
PIERRE LEVÉE
RICHARD LENOIR
R. LENOIR BLVD.

Goncourt
Ⓜ

RUE DU FAUBOURG DU TEMPLE

③ Hostel Absolute Paris

ST.
MARTIN Ⓜ

PLACE
DE LA
RÉPUBLIQUE

Ⓜ
Ⓜ

Ⓜ République

RUE DU FAUBOURG

JULES FERRY BLVD.

AVE. DE LA RÉPUBLIQUE

②

①

TURBIGO
Ⓜ

Post
Temple

BLVD. DU TEMPLE
BLVD.

RUE BERANGER
R. DEP. THOUARS
R. DUPUIS
RUE CHARLOT
R. DE TURENNE
RUE DE BRETAGNE

R. TIMBAUD

TO
PERE
LACHAISE
CEMETERY

Oberkampf
Ⓜ

R. CRUS-

RUE OBERKAMPF

R. DU TEMPLE
RUE AMELO
COM.

Filles du
Calvaire Ⓜ

PASSAGE
AMELOT

VOLTAIRE

R. PIERRE FOREN
RUE DE

10 MIN. WALK
TO MARAIS ↓

DCH

R. ST. SEBASTIEN

TO PLACE
BASTILLE

① Hôtel de Nevers
② Auberge de Jeunesse Jules
Ferry (Hostel)

③ Hostel Absolute Paris
④ La Marine Restaurant

$ Hôtel de Nevers* is a cheap one-star hotel with a historic elevator and pretty good rooms for the price, despite the dim lighting (D-€44–50 with free shower down the hall, Ds-€55, Db-€65, Tb-€75, Qb-€84, 53 rue de Malte, tel. 01 47 00 56 18, fax 01 43 57 77 39, www.hoteldenevers.com, reservation@hoteldenevers.com).

$ Auberge de Jeunesse Jules Ferry is a relaxed youth hostel right on the parkway that runs above Canal St. Martin. Arrive before 10:00 or book online to be assured a room (€22 per bunk in pleasant, sink-equipped 2-, 4-, or 6-bed rooms, higher rates for non-members; small lockers available, rooms closed 10:30–14:00, 8 boulevard Jules Ferry, tel. 01 43 57 55 60, fax 01 43 14 82 09, www .hihostels.com).

$ Hostel Absolute Paris is part two-star hotel, part four-beds-per-room hostel. It faces the canal and is filled with backpackers. The rooms are industrial-strength clean and adequate—but worth considering only if you want dorm-style accommodations (€24 each in 4-bed room with private bathroom, Db-€85, Tb-€100, includes breakfast, Internet access, 1 rue de la Fontaine du Roi, tel. 01 47 00 47 00, fax 01 47 00 47 02, www.absolute-paris.com, bonjour@absolute-paris.com).

Eating

The Parisian eating scene is kept at a rolling boil. Entire books (and lives) are dedicated to the subject. Paris is France's wine-and-cuisine melting pot. While it lacks a style of its own (only French onion soup is truly Parisian), it draws from the best of France. Paris could hold a gourmets' Olympics and import nothing.

Cafés are happy to serve a *plat du jour* (garnished plate of the day, about €12–18) or a chef-like salad (about €10–12) day or night, while restaurants expect you to enjoy a full dinner. Restaurants open for dinner at about 19:00, and small local favorites get crowded after 21:00. Most of the restaurants listed below accept credit cards. Smokers dominate outside tables.

To save money, go to bakeries for quick take-out lunches, or stop at a café for a lunch salad or *plat du jour,* but linger longer over dinner. To save even more, consider picnics (tasty take-out dishes available at *charcuteries*).

Good Picnic Spots: The Palais Royal (across place du Palais Royal from the Louvre) is a good spot for a peaceful, royal picnic, as is the little triangular Henry IV park on the west tip of Ile de la Cité. The pedestrian pont des Arts bridge, across from the Louvre, has great views and plentiful benches, as does the Champ de Mars park below the Eiffel Tower (no picnicking in central area of park, however). For great people-watching, try the Pompidou Center (by the *Homage to Stravinsky* fountains), the elegant place

Restaurant Price Code

To help you choose among these listings, I've divided the restaurants into three categories, based on the price for a typical
meal without wine.

$$$ Higher Priced—Most meals €35 or more.
 $$ Moderately Priced—Most meals between €20-35.
  $ Lower Priced—Most meals less than €20.

des Vosges (closes at dusk), the gardens behind Les Invalides, and
the Tuileries and Luxembourg gardens (parks close at dusk).

Restaurants

My recommendations are centered around the same great neighborhoods for which I list accommodations (see previous section);
you can come home exhausted after a busy day of sightseeing and
have a good selection of restaurants right around the corner. And
evening is a fine time to explore any of these delightful neighborhoods, even if you're sleeping elsewhere. Most restaurants I've
listed in these areas have set-price meals *(menus)* between €15 and
€30. In most cases, the few extra euros you pay are well-spent, and
open up a variety of better choices. You decide.

   If you are traveling outside of Paris, save your splurges for the
countryside, where you'll enjoy regional cooking for less money.
Many Parisian department stores have huge supermarkets hiding
in the basement and top-floor cafeterias that offer affordable, low-
risk, low-stress, what-you-see-is-what-you-get meals.

Rue Cler Neighborhood

The rue Cler neighborhood caters to its residents. Its eateries, while
not destination places, have an intimate charm. I've provided a full
range of choices from cozy ma-and-pa diners to small and trendy
boutique restaurants to classic, big bistros. You'll generally find
great dinner *menus* for €20–30, *plats du jour* for about €14–18, and
meal-sized salads for €10–12. Eat early with tourists or late with
locals. For all restaurants listed in this area, use the Ecole Militaire
Métro stop (unless another station is listed).

Close to Ecole Militaire, Between Rue de la
Motte-Picquet and Rue de Grenelle

$$$ Le Florimond is good for a special occasion. The setting,
while spacious and quiet, is also intimate and welcoming. Locals
come for classic French cuisine with elegant indoor or breezy
streetside seating. Friendly English-speaking Laurent—whose

playful ties change daily—serves one small room of tables gracefully and loves to help with suggestions. Try the explosively tasty
stuffed cabbage (€36 *menu*, closed Sun, reservations smart, good
house wine by the carafe, affordable wine selection, 19 avenue de la
Motte-Picquet, tel. 01 45 55 40 38).

$$ Restaurant Pasco, perched elegantly overlooking Les
Invalides, is semi-dressy, with a special enthusiasm for fish. The
owner, Pasco Vignes, attracts a local clientele with his modern
Mediterranean cuisine, generously endowed with olive oil. While
there's some outdoor seating, I'd come here for the red-brick-cozy
interior (€20 *plats*, €20–34 *menus*, daily, reservations smart, 74
boulevard de la Tour Maubourg, Mo: La Tour Maubourg, tel. 01
44 18 33 26).

$$ La Terrasse du 7ème is a sprawling, happening café with
grand outdoor seating and a living room–like interior with comfy
love seats. Located on a corner, it overlooks a busy intersection with
a constant parade of people. Chairs are set up facing the street, as
a meal here is like dinner theater—and the show is slice-of-life
Paris. Consider their Spring Plate for an adventurous gourmet
starter (€16 daily *plats*, no fixed-price *menu*, good €13 *salade niçoise*,
daily until at least 24:00 and sometimes until 2:00 in the morning,
at École Militaire Métro stop, tel. 01 45 55 00 02).

$$ Café le Bosquet is a modern, chic Parisian brasserie with
dressy waiters and your choice of the mod-elegant interior or
sidewalk tables on a busy street. Come here for a bowl of French
onion soup, or a full three-course *menu* with good fish and meat
choices. Say *bonsoir* to owner Jean-François, who likes to be called
Jeff. Escargots are great here; the house red wine is plenty good,
too (€15 *plats*, closed Sun, reservations smart Fri–Sat, fun menu
includes vegetarian options, corner of rue du Champ de Mars and
avenue Bosquet, 46 avenue Bosquet, tel. 01 45 51 38 13).

$ Café du Marché boasts the best seats, coffee, and prices
on rue Cler. The owner's philosophy: Brasserie on speed—crank
out good food at great prices to trendy locals and savvy tourists.
It's high-energy, with waiters who barely have time to smile...
très Parisian. This place is ideal if you want to eat an inexpensive,
one-course meal among a commotion of people and are willing to
go with the small, fresh menu. The chalkboard lists your choices:
good, hearty €10 salads or more filling €10 *plats du jour* (Mon–Sat
11:00–23:00, Sun 11:00–17:00, arrive before 19:30 for dinner—it's
packed at 21:00, and service can be slow; free water served without
a grimace, at the corner of rue Cler and rue du Champ de Mars, at
38 rue Cler, tel. 01 47 05 51 27).

$ Tribeca Italian Restaurant, next door to Café du Marché,
is run by the same people with essentially the same formula. They
offer similar (if not even better) value and more space, a calmer

Rue Cler Restaurants

RUE DE L'UNIVERSITE

↑ 5 MIN. WALK
TO SEINE RIVER
+ AMERICAN CHURCH

N

ST. PIERRE

RUE MALAR

RUE NICOT

ST. DOMINIQUE

COMTE

TOUR MAUBOURG

RUE AMELIE

RUE NICOT

La Tour-Maubourg

M

RUE CLER

BOSQUET

R. DE L'EXPO

RUE

AUGEREAU

GRENELLE

R. DUVIVIER

RUE PSICHARI

ST. JEAN

DE VALADON

RUE CLER

DE MARS

RUE DU CHAMP

RUE BOURDONNAIS

↖ TO EIFFEL TOWER + ⑧

CHAMP DE MARS

← KIDS' PLAY AREA

DE LA MOTTE PICQUET

CHEVET

DE LA TOUR

RUE

POST

Ecole Militaire

M

M

DUQUESNE

AVE DE TOURVILLE

DCH

AVENUE

ARMY MUSEUM + NAPOLEON'S TOMB

Ⓜ METRO STATION

200 YARDS
200 METERS

1. Le Florimond
2. Restaurant Pasco
3. La Terrasse du 7ème
4. Café le Bosquet
5. Café du Marché & Tribeca Italian Rest.
6. Crêperie Ulysée en Gaule
7. Petite Brasserie PTT
8. To Altitude 95 Rest. & Jules Verne Restaurant
9. Au Petit Tonneau
10. La Fontaine de Mars
11. Le P'tit Troquet
12. Billebaude Bistro
13. Chez Agnès
14. L'Ami Jean
15. Chez Pierrot
16. Café Constant
17. La Varangue
18. La Gourmandise Pizzeria
19. Real McCoy
20. Late-Night Groceries (2)
21. Julien's Bakery
22. Café la Roussillon
23. O'Brien's Pub

PARIS

ambience, and more patient service. This family-friendly eatery offers €12 pizzas and €12 Italian *plats*.

$ Crêperie Ulysée en Gaule offers the best cheap seats on rue Cler. Their crêpes are €3–10 to go, with no extra charge to sit for readers of this book if you buy a drink. The Ulysée family—Stephanos, Chrysa, Marcos, and English-speaking Vassilis—seem to make friends with all who drop by for a bite. The family loves to serve Greek dishes, and their excellent crêpes are your least expensive rue Cler hot meal (open daily, 28 rue Cler, tel. 01 47 05 61 82).

Between Rue de Grenelle and the River

$$$ Altitude 95 is in the Eiffel Tower, 95 meters (about 300 feet) above the ground. Reserve a month in advance for a view table (€36 lunches, €65 dinners, daily 12:00–21:45, dinner seatings nightly at about 19:00 and 21:00, bar open until 23:00; before you ascend to dine, drop by the booth between the north/*nord* and east/*est* pillars to buy your Eiffel Tower ticket and pick up a pass that enables you to skip the line; Mo: Bir-Hakeim or Trocadéro, RER: Champ de Mars-Tour Eiffel, tel. 01 45 55 20 04, fax 01 47 05 94 40). Also in the Eiffel Tower is the even more expensive **Jules Verne Restaurant**.

$$$ Au Petit Tonneau is a souvenir of old Paris. Fun-loving owner-chef Madame Boyer prepares everything herself, wearing her tall chef's hat like a crown as she rules from her family-style kitchen. The small, plain dining room doesn't look like it's changed in the 26 years she's been in charge. Her steaks and lamb are excellent (€8–10 starters, €18 *plats*, open daily, 20 rue Surcouf, Mo: La Tour Maubourg, tel. 01 47 05 09 01).

$$$ La Fontaine de Mars is a longtime favorite for locals, charmingly situated on a classic, tiny Parisian street and jumbled square. It's a happening scene, with tables jammed together for the serious business of good eating. Reserve in advance for a table on the ground floor (or in summer on the square), or eat upstairs without the fun street-level ambience (€20 *plats du jour,* superb foie gras, open nightly, where rue de l'Exposition and rue St. Dominique meet, 129 rue St. Dominique, tel. 01 47 05 46 44).

$$ Le P'tit Troquet, a petite eatery taking you back to the Paris of the 1920s, is gracefully and earnestly run by Dominique. The fragile elegance here makes you want to hug a flapper. Dominique is particularly proud of her foie gras and lamb, and of her daughter's breads and pastries. The delicious, three-course €32 *menu* comes with traditional choices. Its delicate charm and gourmet flair make this restaurant a favorite of connoisseurs (opens at 18:00, closed Sun, reservations smart, 28 rue de l'Exposition, tel. 01 47 05 80 39).

$$ La Casa Campana is the place to try if you're craving Italian food and don't want to leave the neighborhood. The gentle owners recently moved to Paris from southern Italy, bringing their tasty and unspoiled cuisine with them. The handmade raviolis are *bellisimo* (*menus* start at €20, open daily, near other recommended restaurants at 20 rue de l'Exposition, tel. 01 45 51 37 71).

$$ Billebaude, run by patient Pascal, is an authentic Parisian bistro where the focus is on what's fresh and meats from the hunt (€29 *menu*, closed Sun–Mon, 29 rue de l'Exposition, tel. 01 45 55 20 96).

$$ Chez Agnès, the smallest of my recommended Paris restaurants, is not for everyone. It's tiny, flowery, family-style, and filled with kisses on the cheek. Eccentric but sincere Agnès (a French-Tahitian Rosie O'Donnell) does it all—cooking in her minuscule kitchen and serving, too. Agnès, who cooks "French with an exotic twist" and clearly loves her work, makes children feel right at home. Don't come for a quick dinner (€23 *menu*, closed Mon, 1 rue Augereau, tel. 01 45 51 06 04).

$$ L'Ami Jean offers excellent Basque specialties at fair prices. The chef has made his reputation on the quality of his cuisine. Arrive by 19:30 or call ahead (€33 *menu*, closed Sun–Mon, 27 rue Malar, Mo: La Tour Maubourg, tel. 01 47 05 86 89).

$$ Chez Pierrot is a warm, welcoming bistro with 12 tables served by smiling Linda. On a quiet street, it offers large portions of traditional fare—try the beef stew (€18 *plats*, €12 big salads, daily, 9 rue Amélie, tel. 01 45 51 50 08).

$ Café Constant is a tiny, cool, two-level place that feels more like a small bistro–wine bar than a café. They serve delicious and affordably priced dishes in a fun setting to a well-established clientele (€14 *plats*, closed Sun–Mon, corner of rue Augereau and rue St. Dominique, next to recommended Hôtel Londres Eiffel).

$ La Varangue is an entertaining one-man show featuring English-speaking Philippe, who ran a French catering shop in Pennsylvania for three years. He lives upstairs, and has found his niche serving a mostly American clientele who are all on a first-name basis. The food is cheap and basic (don't come here for high cuisine), the tables are few, and he opens early (at 17:30). Norman Rockwell would dig his tiny dining room—with the traditional kitchen sizzling just over the counter. Philippe is so fun and accessible that you are welcome to join him in the kitchen and help cook your meal. Try his snails and chocolate cake...but not together (€12 *plats*, €17.50 *menu*, always a vegetarian option, closed Sun, 27 rue Augereau, tel. 01 47 05 51 22).

$ La Gourmandise is a tiny, friendly pizzeria across the street from La Varangue. Its good, cheap pizza is ideal for kids (closed Sun, eat in or take out, 28 rue Augereau, tel. 01 45 55 45 16).

Picnicking in Rue Cler

Rue Cler is a moveable feast that gives "fast food" a good name. The entire street is clogged with connoisseurs of good eating. Only the health-food store goes unnoticed. A festival of food, the street is lined with people whose lives seem to be devoted to their specialty: polished produce, rotisserie chicken, crêpes, or cheese.

For a magical picnic dinner at the Eiffel Tower, assemble it in no fewer than five shops on rue Cler. Then lounge on the best grass in Paris, with the dogs, Frisbees, a floodlit tower, and a cool breeze in the Champ de Mars park (but keep off the grass in the center—mayor's orders).

Asian delis (generically called *Traiteur Asie*) provide tasty, low-stress, low-price take-out treats (€6 dinner plates, the one on rue Cler near rue du Champ de Mars has tables). **Crêperie Ulysée en Gaule** (described earlier), the Greek restaurant on rue Cler across from Grand Hôtel Lévêque, sells take-away crêpes. **Real McCoy** is a little shop selling American food and sandwiches (closed Sun, 194 rue de Grenelle). There's a small **late-night grocery** at 197 rue de Grenelle (open daily until midnight), and another where rues Cler and Grenelle cross. For excellent baguettes and sandwiches, try **Julien's** bakery at 85 rue St. Dominique.

Breakfast in Rue Cler

Hotel breakfasts, while convenient, are generally not a good value. For a great rue Cler start to your day, drop by the **Petite Brasserie PTT,** where Jerome and Alexi promise Rick Steves readers a *deux pour douze* breakfast special (2 "American" breakfasts—juice, a big coffee, croissant, bread, ham, and eggs—for €12; closed Sun, a two-minute walk from most area hotels, opposite 53 rue Cler).

Nightlife in Rue Cler

This sleepy neighborhood is not ideal for night owls, but there are a few notable exceptions. **Café du Marché** and **La Terrasse du 7ème** (both listed earlier) are busy with a Franco-American crowd until at least midnight, as is the younger **Café la Roussillon** (occasional happy hours 18:00–20:00—but every hour seems happy, €10 salads, €13 *plats,* fine for a French pub atmosphere, corner of rue de Grenelle and rue Cler). **O'Brien's Pub** is a relaxed Parisian rendition of an Irish pub, full of Anglophones (77 avenue St. Dominique, Mo: La Tour Maubourg).

In the Marais Neighborhood

The trendy Marais is filled with locals enjoying good food in colorful and atmospheric eateries. The scene is competitive and changes all the time. I've listed an assortment of eateries—all handy to recommended hotels—that offer good food at reasonable prices, plus a memorable experience.

Dining on Romantic Place des Vosges

On this square, which offers Old World Marais elegance, you'll find several different eateries (use Bastille or St. Paul Métro stop). Enjoy a square stroll around the entire arcade—fun art galleries alternate with enticing restaurants. Choose the restaurant that best fits your mood and budget; all have arcade seating and provide big space-heaters to make outdoor dining during colder months an option. Also consider a drink or dessert on the square at Café Hugo or Nectarine after eating elsewhere.

$$$ Ma Bourgogne is a classic old eatery where you'll sit under warm arcades in a whirlpool of Frenchness, as bow-tied and black-aproned waiters serve you traditional French specialties: blood-red steak, lots of French fries, escargot, and great red wine. While service comes with few smiles, the staff of this venerable Marais fixture enjoy their work and care about your experience. Monsieur Cougourou (koo-gah-roo), who's run this place since de Gaulle was sniveling at Americans, offers anyone with this book a free *amuse-bouche* ("amusement for your mouth") of steak tartare. This is your ideal chance to try this "raw spiced hamburger" delicacy without dedicating an entire meal to it...and the quality here is famous (€35 *menu*, daily, dinner reservations smart, cash only, at northwest corner at #19, tel. 01 42 78 44 64).

$$ At Les Bonnes Soeurs, barely off the square, Cecile and Alexandra cater to a somewhat younger and more local clientele by mixing modern and traditional fare with fun ambience (*plats* from €16, no *menu*, daily, 8 rue du pas de la Mule, tel. 01 42 74 55 80).

$ Nectarine is small and demure—with a wicker, pastel, and feminine atmosphere. This peaceful teahouse serves healthy €10 salads, quiches, and €12–14 *plats du jour* day and night. Its menu lets you mix and match omelets and crêpes, and the huge desserts are splittable (daily, at #16, tel. 01 42 77 23 78).

$ Café Hugo, named for the square's most famous resident, is best for drinks only, as the cuisine does not live up to its setting (daily, at #22).

Near the Bastille

To reach these restaurants, use the Bastille Métro stop.

$$ Brasserie Bofinger, an institution for over a century, is famous for fish and traditional cuisine with Alsatian flair. You're surrounded by brisk, black-and-white-attired waiters. The sprawling interior features elaborately decorated rooms reminiscent of the Roaring Twenties. Eating under the grand 1919 *coupole* is a memorable treat (as is using the "historic" 1919 WC downstairs).

Marais Restaurants

1. Ma Bourgogne
2. Nectarine & Café Hugo
3. Brasserie Bofinger
4. Chez Janou
5. Les Bonnes Soeurs
6. La Bastoche
7. Vins des Pyrénées
8. Au Temps des Cerises
9. Au Bourguignon du Marais
10. L'Ebouillanté
11. Restaurante Sant Antonio
12. BHV Cafeteria
13. Place du Marché Ste. Catherine Eateries
14. L'Enoteca Wine Bar
15. Camille Brasserie
16. Le Rouge Gorge
17. Chez Marianne
18. L'As du Falafel
19. Bistrot les Sans Culottes
20. Au Petit Fer à Cheval & La Belle Hortense
21. La Perla Bar
22. Le Pick-Clops Bar Rest.

M METRO STATION
T TAXI STAND
P PARKING

PARIS

Check out the boys shucking and stacking seafood platters out front before you enter. Their €32 three-course *menu*, while not top cuisine, is a good value. If you've always wanted one of those picturesque seafood platters, this is a good place—you can take the standard platter or create one à la carte (open daily and nightly, fun kids' menu, 5 rue de la Bastille, don't be confused by the lesser "Petite" Bofinger across the street, tel. 01 42 72 87 82).

$$ Chez Janou, a Provençal bistro, tumbles out of its corner building and fills its broad sidewalk with happy eaters. At first glance, you know this is a find. Don't let the trendy and youthful crowd intimidate you—it's relaxed and charming, with helpful and patient service. While the curbside tables are inviting, I'd sit inside (with very tight seating) to immerse myself in the happy commotion. The style is French Mediterranean, with an emphasis on vegetables (€15–18 *plats du jour* that change with the season, daily from 19:45, 2 blocks beyond place des Vosges at 2 rue Roger Verlomme, tel. 01 42 72 28 41). They're proud of their 81 different varieties of *pastis* (licorice-flavored liqueur, €3.50 each, browse the list above the bar).

$$ La Bastoche (Parisian slang for "the Bastille") is cozy and welcoming. Step down into an 18th-century building with exposed timbers and a great mural of the storming of the old prison, and choose from a nice selection of traditional French fare at good prices. Caring owners Sylvie and Lise work hard to please (€23 3-course *menu*, daily, 7 rue St. Antoine, one block away from the Bastille, tel. 01 48 04 84 34).

$$ Vins des Pyrénées ("Wines of the Pyrenees") is a fun bistro that attracts a young, lively crowd with its convivial setting, varying *menus* with lots of choices, reasonable wine list, and hardworking, English-speaking owner, Olivier. Don't come here for a romantic dinner (€15–20 *plats*, daily, 25 rue Beautreillis, tel. 01 42 72 64 94).

$ Au Temps des Cerises is a *très* local wine bar, with a woody 1950s atmosphere, tight seating, and wads of character. While they serve three-course, €15 lunch *menus*, I'd come here for wine and heavy munchies pre- or post-dinner—or even for dinner. "Dinner" is limited to bread, dry sausage, cheese, and wine served by goateed Yves and his wife, Michele. While full plates of cold cuts run around €13, a small mixed plate of cheese (€5), meat (€5), and a carafe of good wine (€4–8) surrounded by the intimate Old World ambience can make a good light meal (Mon–Sat until about 22:00, closed Sun, at rue du Petit-Musc and rue de la Cerisaie).

Closer to Hôtel de Ville

These eateries, near the Pompidou Center, appear on the Marais Restaurants map in this section. To reach them, use the Hôtel de Ville Métro stop.

$$$ Au Bourguignon du Marais is an attractive wine bar–bistro for Burgundy-lovers, where excellent wines (available by the glass) blend with a good selection of well-designed dishes and efficient service (Philippe is clearly in charge). The *œufs en meurette* were the best I've ever had, and the *bœuf bourguignon* could feed two (€10–14 starters, €18–22 *plats,* closed Sun–Mon, indoor and outdoor seating, 52 rue Francois Miron, tel. 01 48 87 15 40).

$ L'Ebouillanté is a breezy crêperie-café, romantically situated near the river on a broad, cobbled lane behind a church. With great outdoor seating and an artsy, cozy interior, it's ideal for an inexpensive and relaxing tea, snack, or lunch—or for dinner on a warm evening. Try a *brick,* the light-hearted chef's specialty (think beefy crêpe). The salads and desserts are also good (€13 *plats,* €15 2-course *menu,* Tue–Sun 12:00–22:00, closed Mon, 6 rue des Barres, tel. 01 42 71 09 69).

$ Restaurante Sant Antonio is bustling and cheap, serving up €10 pizzas and salads on a fun Marais square (daily, barely off rue de Rivoli on place du Bourg Tibourg).

$ BHV Department Store's fifth-floor cafeteria provides nice views, an escape from the busy streets below, and no-brainer, point-and-shoot cafeteria cuisine (Mon–Sat 11:30–18:00, closed Sun, at intersection of rue du Temple and rue de la Verrerie, one block from Hôtel de Ville).

In the Heart of the Marais
These are closest to the St. Paul Métro stop.

$$ On place du Marché Ste. Catherine: This small, romantic square, just off rue St. Antoine, is an international food festival cloaked in extremely Parisian, leafy-square ambience. On a balmy evening, this is clearly a neighborhood favorite, with a handful of restaurants offering €20–30 meals. Study the square, and you'll find two popular French bistros (**Le Marché** and **Au Bistrot de la Place,** each with €23 3-course *menus,* tight seating indoors and out, both open daily) and other inviting eateries serving a variety of international food—Russian, Korean, Italian, and so on. You'll eat under the trees, surrounded by a futuristic-in-1800 planned residential quarter.

$$ L'Enoteca is a high-spirited, half-timbered spot serving affordable Italian cuisine (no pizza) with a tempting *antipasti* bar. It's a relaxed, open setting with busy, blue-aproned waiters serving two floors of local eaters (€15 pastas, €20 *plats,* €30 3-course *menu,* open daily, across from L'Excuse at rue St. Paul and rue Charles V, 25 rue Charles V, tel. 01 42 78 91 44).

$ Camille, a traditional corner brasserie, is a neighborhood favorite with great indoor and sidewalk seating. Its waiters serve €13 salads and very French *plats du jour* (€20) from the chalkboard list to a down-to-earth but sophisticated clientele (daily, 24 rue des Francs Bourgeois at corner of rue Elzévir, tel. 01 42 72 20 50).

$ Le Rouge Gorge's relaxed wine bar and bistro is 10-table cozy. Come for a meal (€16–20 dinner *plats* based on monthly themes), a coffee, or a glass of wine. Friendly François, the owner, will send you downstairs to the *cave* (cellar) to choose your wine; there are different prices for take-out wine purchases (closed Sun, 8 rue St. Paul, tel. 01 48 04 75 89).

$ Several hardworking **Asian fast-food eateries,** great for a €6 meal, line rue St. Antoine.

On Rue des Rosiers in the Jewish Quarter

To reach the Jewish Quarter, use the St. Paul Métro stop.

$ Chez Marianne, a neighborhood fixture, offers classic Jewish meals and Parisian atmosphere. Choose from several indoor zones with a cluttered wine shop/deli ambience, or sit outside. You'll select from two dozen "Zakouski" elements to assemble your €15 plate (great vegetarian options, eat cheap with a €6 falafel sandwich, or even cheaper with takeout, long hours daily, corner of rue des Rosiers and rue des Hospitalieres St. Gervais, tel. 01 42 72 18 86). For takeout, pay inside first and get a ticket before you order outside.

$ L'As du Falafel rules the falafel scene in the Jewish quarter. Monsieur Isaac, the "Ace of Falafel" here since 1979, brags he's got "the biggest pita on the street...and he fills it up." Apparently, it's Lenny Kravitz's favorite, too. Your inexpensive Jewish cuisine comes on plastic plates, in a bustling setting that seems to prove he's earned his success. While the €6.50 "special falafel" is the big hit, many Americans enjoy his lighter chicken version *(poulet grillé)* or the tasty and filling *assiette de falafel*. Their take-out service draws a constant crowd; the interior is air-conditioned (day and night until late, closed Sat, 34 rue des Rosiers).

Picnicking in the Marais

Picnic at peaceful place des Vosges (closes at dusk) or on the Ile St. Louis *quais* (see next page). Stretch your euros at the basement supermarket of the **Monoprix** department store (closed Sun, near place des Vosges on rue St. Antoine). You'll find a small **grocery** open until 23:00 near 48 rue St. Antoine.

Nightlife in the Marais

The best scene for hard-core night owls is the dizzying array of wacky eateries, bars, and dance halls on **rue de Lappe.** This street is what the Latin Quarter aspires to be. Just east of the stately place de la Bastille, it's one of the wildest nightspots in Paris and not for everyone. Sitting amid the chaos like a Van Gogh painting is the popular, old-time **Bistrot les Sans Culottes.**

Trendy cafés and bars—popular with gay men—also cluster on rue Vieille du Temple, rue des Archives, and rue Ste. Croix de la Bretonnerie (closing at about 2:00 in the morning). You'll find a line of bars and cafés providing front-row seats for the buff parade on rue Vieille du Temple, a block north of rue de Rivoli (the horseshoe-shaped **Au Petit Fer à Cheval** bar-restaurant and the atmospheric **La Belle Hortense** bookstore/wine bar are the focal points of the action). Nearby, rue des Rosiers bustles with youthful energy, but there are no cafés to observe from. **Vins des Pyrénées** (described earlier) is young and fun—find the small bar in the back. **La Perla** is full of Parisian yuppies in search of the perfect margarita (26 rue François Miron).

$ Le Pick-Clops bar-restaurant is a happy peanuts-and-lots-of-cocktails diner with bright neon, loud colors, and a garish local crowd. It's perfect for immersing yourself in today's Marais world—a little boisterous, a little edgy, a little gay, fun-loving, easygoing...and no tourists. Sit inside, on old-fashioned diner stools, or streetside to watch the constant Marais parade. The name means "Steal the Cigarettes"—but you'll pay €10 for your big salad (daily 7:00–24:00, 16 rue Vieille du Temple, tel. 01 40 29 02 18).

The most enjoyable peaceful evening may be simply donning your floppy "three musketeers" hat and slowly strolling around place des Vosges, window-shopping the art galleries.

Ile St. Louis

The Ile St. Louis is a romantic and peaceful neighborhood where you can amble around for plenty of promising dinner possibilities. Cruise the island's main street for a variety of options, from cozy *crêperies* to Italian eateries (intimate pizzerias and upscale) to typical brasseries (a few with fine outdoor seating facing the bridge to Ile de la Cité). After dinner, sample Paris' best sorbet and stroll across to the Ile de la Cité to see Notre-Dame illuminated, or enjoy a scenic drink on the deck of a floating café moored under Notre-Dame's right transept. All these listings line the island's main drag, rue St. Louis-en-l'Ile (see map on page 349; to get here, use the Pont Marie Métro stop). Consider skipping dessert to enjoy a stroll licking the best ice cream in Paris (described under "Ice-Cream Dessert," next page).

$$$ Le Tastevin is an intimate mother-and-son-run restaurant serving top-notch traditional French cuisine with white-tablecloth, candlelit, gourmet elegance under heavy wooden beams. The romantic setting (and the elegantly romantic local couples enjoying the place) makes you naturally whisper. The three-course *menus* start at about €38 and offer plenty of classic choices that change with the season to ensure freshness (daily, reserve for late-evening dining, good wine list, 46 rue St. Louis-en-l'Ile, tel. 01 43 54 17 31; owner Madame Puisieux and her gentle son speak just enough English).

$$$ Medieval Theme Restaurants: La Taverne du Sergeant Recruteur, famous for its rowdy, medieval-cellar atmosphere, is ideal for hungry warriors and their wenches who like to swill hearty wine. For as long as anyone can remember, they've served up a rustic all-you-can-eat buffet with straw baskets of raw veggies and bundles of sausage (cut whatever you like with your dagger), massive plates of pâté, a meat course, and all the wine you can stomach for €41. The food is just food; burping is encouraged. If you want to eat a lot, drink a lot of wine, be surrounded by tourists, and holler at your friends while receiving smart-aleck buccaneer service, this food fest can be fun. And it comes with a historic twist: The "Sergeant Recruiter" used to get young Parisians drunk and stuffed here, then sign them into the army (daily from 19:00, #37 rue St. Louis-en-l'Ile, tel. 01 43 54 75 42). Next door, **Nos Ancêtres les Gaulois** is a bit goofier and grittier, and serves the same basic formula. As the name implies ("Our Ancestors the Gauls"), this place makes barbarians feel right at home (tel. 01 46 33 66 07). You might swing by both and choose the..."ambience" is not quite the right word...that fits your mood.

$$ La Brasserie de l'Ile St. Louis is situated at the prow of the island's ship as it faces Ile de la Cité, offering purely Alsatian cuisine (try the *choucroute garni* for €18), served in a Franco-Germanic setting with no-nonsense brasserie service. This is a good balmy-evening perch for watching the Ile St. Louis promenade—or, if it's chilly, the interior is plenty characteristic for a memorable night out (closed Wed, no reservations, 55 quai de Bourbon, tel. 01 43 54 02 59).

$ Café Med, near the pedestrian bridge to Notre-Dame at #77, has inexpensive salads, crêpes, and a €13–20 *menu* served in a tight but cheery setting (open daily, limited wine list, tel. 01 43 29 73 17). Two similar *crêperies* are just across the street.

Riverside Picnic

On sunny lunchtimes and balmy evenings, the *quai* on the Left Bank side of Ile St. Louis is lined with locals who have more class than money, spreading out tablecloths and even lighting candles for elegant picnics. And tourists can enjoy the same budget meal. There's a handy grocery store at #67 on the main drag (Wed–Mon until 22:00, closed Tue) that has tabouli and other simple, cheap, take-away dishes for your picnicking pleasure.

Ice-Cream Dessert

Half the people strolling Ile St. Louis are licking an ice-cream cone, because this is the home of *les glaces Berthillon*. The original

Berthillon shop, at 31 rue St. Louis-en-l'Ile, is marked by the line of salivating customers (closed Mon–Tue). Another Berthillon shop is across the street, and there's one more around the corner on rue Bellay (all are located on map on page 349). The three shops are so popular that the wealthy people who can afford to live on this fancy island complain about the congestion they cause. For a less famous but at least as tasty treat, the homemade Italian gelato a block away at **Amorino Gelati** is giving Berthillon competition (no line, bigger portions, easier to see what you want, and they offer little tastes—Berthillon doesn't need to, 47 rue St. Louis-en-l'Ile, tel. 01 44 07 48 08). Having some of each is not a bad thing.

Luxembourg Neighborhood

Sleeping in the Luxembourg neighborhood puts you near many appealing dining and after-hours options. Because my hotels in this area cluster around the Panthéon and St. Sulpice Church, I've organized restaurant listings the same way. Restaurants near the Panthéon tend to be calm, those around St. Sulpice more boisterous; it's a short walk from one area to the other. Anyone sleeping in this area is close to the inexpensive eateries that line the always-bustling rue Mouffetard.

Near the Panthéon

For locations, see the map on page 354. These eateries are served by the Cluny–La Sorbonne Métro stop and the RER-B Luxembourg station.

$$ Restaurant Perraudin is a welcoming, family-run, red-checkered-tablecloth eatery understandably popular with tourists. Friendly Monsieur Correy serves classic *cuisine bourgeoise* with an emphasis on Burgundian dishes in air-conditioned comfort. The decor is vintage turn-of-the-20th-century, with big mirrors and old wood paneling (€19 lunch *menus*, €30 dinner *menus*, *bœuf bourguignon* is a specialty here, between the Panthéon and Luxembourg Garden at 157 rue St. Jacques, tel. 01 46 33 15 75).

$ Le Soufflot Café, between the Panthéon and Luxembourg Garden, is well-positioned for afternoon sun. It has a nifty library-like interior, lots of outdoor tables, point-blank views of the Panthéon, and friendly service (Frédéric and Serge are owners). The cuisine is café-classic: good €10 salads, omelets, and *plats du jour* (daily, a block below the Panthéon on the right side of rue Soufflot as you walk toward Luxembourg Garden, tel. 01 43 26 57 56).

$ *Place de la Sorbonne:* This cobbled and green square, with a small fountain facing the Sorbonne University just a block from the Cluny Museum, offers several opportunities for a quick outdoor lunch or light dinner. At the tiny **Baker's Dozen,** you'll pay take-away prices for salads and sandwiches you can sit down to eat (€5 salad and quiche special, Mon–Sat until 17:00, closed Sun). **Café de l'Ecritoire** is a typical, lively brasserie with happy diners enjoying €11 salads, €13 *plats*, and fine square seating (daily, tel. 01 43 54 60 02). **Patios,** with appealing decor inside and out, seems more popular. It serves inexpensive Italian fare, including pizza (daily until late).

Near the Odéon Theater

To reach these, use the Odéon Métro stop.

$$ Brasserie Bouillon Racine takes you back to 1906 with an Art Nouveau carnival of carved wood, stained glass, and old-time lights reflected in beveled mirrors. The over-the-top decor, energetic waiters, and affordable menu combine to give it an inviting conviviality. Check upstairs before choosing a table. Their roast suckling pig (€18) is a house favorite. There's good beer on tap and a fascinating history on the menu (€18 *plats,* €29 *menu,* traditional French with lots of fish and meat, daily 12:00–14:00 & 19:00–23:00, 3 rue Racine, tel. 01 44 32 15 60, Phillipe).

$$ La Méditerranée is all about fish in a pastel and dressy setting...with similar clientele. The scene and the menu are sophisticated while accessible, and the view of the Odéon is *formidable.* The sky-blue tablecloths and the lovingly presented dishes add to the romance (€18–27 *plats,* €32 3-courses *menus,* open daily, smart to book ahead, facing the Odéon at 2 place de l'Odéon, tel. 01 43 26 02 30).

$ Restaurant Polidor, a bare-bones neighborhood fixture since the 19th century, is much-loved for its unpretentious quality cooking, fun old-Paris atmosphere, and fair value. Stepping inside, you know this is a winner—noisy, happy diners sit tightly at shared tables as waiters chop and serve fresh bread. The selection features classic bourgeois *plats* from every corner of France; their *menu fraicheur* is designed for lighter summer eating (€12–15 *plats,* €20–30 3-course *menus,* daily 12:00–14:30 & 19:00–23:00, cash only, no reservations, 41 rue Monsieur-Le-Prince, tel. 01 43 26 95 34, Amelia).

On Rue Mouffetard

Lying several blocks behind the Panthéon, rue Mouffetard is a conveyer belt of comparison-shopping eaters with wall-to-wall budget options (fondue, crêpes, Italian, falafel, and Greek). Come here to sift through the crowds and eat a less expensive meal (you get what you pay for). This street stays up late and likes to party (particularly around place de la Contrescarpe). The gauntlet begins on top, at thriving place de la Contrescarpe, and ends below where rue

Mouffetard stops at St. Médard Church. Both ends offer fun cafés where you can eat, drink, and watch the action. The upper stretch is pedestrian and touristic; the bottom stretch is purely Parisian. Anywhere between is no-man's land for consistent quality. Still, strolling with so many fun-seekers is enjoyable, whether you eat or not. To get here, use the Censier-Daubenton Métro stop.

$ **Café Delmas,** at the top of rue Mouffetard on picturesque place de la Contrescarpe, is *the* place to see and be seen. Come here for a before- or after-dinner drink on the broad outdoor terrace, or for typical but pricey café cuisine (€15 salads, €20 *plats,* great chocolate ice cream, open daily).

$ **Le Mouffetard,** a traditional café with a lively location in the heart of rue Mouffetard, is good for an inexpensive lunch or dinner (€13 lunches, €16 2-course *menus,* closed Sun evening and all day Mon, 116 rue Mouffetard, tel. 01 43 31 42 50).

$ Bar-restaurant **Les Papillons** is a down-and-dirty local diner where a few outdoor tables tangle with pedestrians and no one seems to care (€12 *plats,* closed Sun–Mon, 129 rue Mouffetard, tel. 01 43 31 66 50).

$ **Cave de Bourgogne** is *très* local and serves reasonably priced café fare at the bottom of rue Mouffetard. Outside has picture-perfect tables on a raised terrace; inside is warm and cozy (€13–16 *plats,* specials listed on chalkboards, daily, 144 rue Mouffetard).

Near St. Sulpice Church
Rue des Canettes and Rue Guisarde: For an entirely different experience, roam the streets between the St. Sulpice Church and boulevard St. Germain, abounding with restaurants, *crêperies,* wine bars, and jazz haunts (use Mo: St. Sulpice). Find rue des Canettes and rue Guisarde, and window-shop the many French and Italian eateries—most with similar prices, but each with a slightly different feel. For tasty crêpes, try $ **La Crêpe Rit du Clown** (Mon–Sat 12:00–23:00, closed Sun, 6 rue des Canettes, tel. 01 46 34 01 02). For good ambience and above-average bistro fare in a zone where every restaurant looks the same, consider $$ **Le Bistrot Henri IV** (daily, only indoor seating, 6 rue Princesse, tel. 01 46 33 51 12) or $$ **Lou Pescadou–Chez Julien** (daily, some outdoor seating, 16 rue Mabillon, tel. 01 43 54 56 08).

And for a bohemian pub lined with black-and-white photos of the artsy and revolutionary French '60s, have a drink at **Chez Georges.** Sit in a cool little streetside table nook, or venture downstairs to find a hazy, drippy-candle, traditionally French world in the Edith Piaf–style dance cellar (cheap drinks from old-fashioned menu, Tue–Sat 14:00–2:00 in the morning, closed Sun–Mon and in Aug, 11 rue des Canettes).

Eating Elsewhere in Paris
Along Canal St. Martin, North of République
Escape the crowded tourist areas and enjoy a breezy canalside experience. Take the Métro to place de la République and walk down rue Beaurepaire to Canal St. Martin. There you'll find a few worthwhile cafés with similarly reasonable prices. **$ La Marine** is a good choice (daily, 55 bis quai de Valmy, tel. 01 42 39 69 81). In the summertime, most bars and cafés offer beer and wine to go *(à emporter)*, so you can take it to the canal's edge and picnic there with the young locals.

In the Galerie Vivienne, behind the Palais Royal
$$ Le Grand Colbert, appropriately located in the elegant Galerie Vivienne, gives its clients the feel of a luxury restaurant at moderate prices. It's a stylish, grand brasserie with hurried waiters, leather booths, and brass lamps, serving all the classic dishes from steak *frites* to escargots (*menus* from €41, daily, 4 rue Vivienne, Mo: Palais Royal/Musée du Louvre or Pyramides, tel. 01 42 86 82 38).

Near the Louvre
$ Café le Nemours, a staunchly Parisian fixture serving pricey but good light lunches, is tucked into the corner of the Palais Royal adjacent to the Comédie Française. With elegant brass and Art Deco style, and outdoor tables under an arcade two minutes from the pyramid, it's a great post-Louvre retreat (fun and filling €11 salads, open daily; leaving the Louvre, cross rue de Rivoli and veer left to 2 place Colette—see Louvre map on page 302; Mo: Palais Royal, tel. 01 42 61 34 14).

Near Opéra Garnier
$ Bouillon Chartier is a noisy, old, classic eatery. It's named for the bouillon it served the neighborhood's poor workers back in 1896, when its calling was to provide an affordable warm meal for those folks. Workers used to eat *à la gamelle* (from a tin lunchbox). That same spirit—complete with surly waiters and a cheap menu—survives today. Among more than 300 simple seats and 15 frantic waiters, you can still see the restaurant's napkin drawers for its early regulars (€18 *menus,* daily 11:30–15:00 & 18:00–22:00, east of the Opéra Garnier near boulevard Poissonniere, 7 rue de Faubourg-Montmartre, Mo: Grands Boulevards, tel. 01 47 70 86 29).

Montmartre
Montmartre is extremely touristy, with many mindless mobs following guides to cancan shows. But the ambience is undeniably fun, and an evening up here overlooking Paris is a quintessential

experience in the City of Light. The steps in front of Sacré-Cœur are perfect for a picnic with a view. Along the touristy main drag (near place du Tertre and just off it), several fun piano bars serve crêpes with great people-watching. To reach this area, use the Anvers Métro stop.

$$ Restaurant Chez Plumeau, just off jam-packed place du Tertre, is touristy yet moderately priced, with formal service but great seating on a tiny, characteristic square (elaborate €16 salads, €16–20 plats, closed Wed, place du Calvaire, tel. 01 46 06 26 29).

$ L'Eté en Pente Douce hides under generous branches below the crowds on a classic neighborhood corner. It features fine indoor and outdoor seating, €10 *plats du jour* and salads, vegetarian options, and good wines (daily, 23 rue Muller, many steps below Sacré-Cœur to the left as you leave, down the stairs below the WC, tel. 01 42 64 02 67).

Dinner Cruises
The following companies all offer dinner cruises (reservations required). Bateaux Mouches and Bateaux Parisiens have the best reputations and the highest prices. They offer multicourse meals and music in aircraft-carrier-size dining rooms with glass tops and good views. For both, proper dress is required—no denim, shorts, or sport shoes; Bateaux Mouches requires a jacket and tie for men. The main difference between these companies is the ambience: Bateaux Mouches offers violin and piano to entertain your romantic evening, while Bateaux Parisiens boasts a lively atmosphere with a singer, band, and dance floor.

Bateaux Mouches, started in 1949, is hands-down the most famous. You can't miss its sparkling port on the north side of the river at pont de l'Alma. The boats usually board 19:30–20:15, depart at 20:30, and return at 22:45 (€130/person, RER: Pont de l'Alma tel. 01 42 25 96 10, www.bateauxmouches.com).

Bateaux Parisiens leaves from Port de la Bourdonnais, just east of the bridge under the Eiffel Tower. Begin boarding at 19:45, leave at 20:30, and return at 23:00 (€100–145/person, 3 price tiers, depends on seating, tel. 08 25 62 75 13, www.bateauxparisiens.com). The middle level is best. Pay the few extra euros to get seats next to the windows—it's more romantic and private, with sensational views.

Le Capitaine Fracasse offers the budget option (€50/person, €70 with wine; tables are first-come, first-serve, so get there early; boarding times vary by season and day of week, closed Mon, walk down stairs in the middle of Bir Hakeim bridge near the Eiffel Tower to Iles aux Cygne, Mo: Champs de Mars-Tour Eiffel, tel. 01 46 21 48 15, www.croisiere-paris.com).

Connections

Trains

Paris is Europe's rail hub, with six major train stations and one minor one, each serving different regions: Gare de l'Est (eastbound trains), Gare du Nord (northern France and Europe), Gare St. Lazare (northwestern France), Gare d'Austerlitz (southwestern France and Europe), Gare de Lyon (southeastern France and Italy), Gare Montparnasse (northwestern France and TGV service to France's southwest), and a smaller station, Gare de Bercy, the departure point for most night trains to Italy. Any train station has schedule information, can make reservations, and sells tickets for any destination. Unless you happen to pass a station in your sightseeing, buying tickets is handier from an SNCF neighborhood office. It's worth the small fee.

All six main train stations have banks or change offices, ATMs, train information desks, telephones, cafés, newsstands, and clever pickpockets. Because of security concerns, not all have baggage checks.

Each station offers two types of rail service: long distance to other cities, called *Grandes Lignes* (major lines); and suburban service to outlying areas, called *banlieue* or RER. Both *banlieue* and RER trains serve outlying areas and the airports; the only difference is that *banlieue* lines are operated by SNCF (France's train system, called Transilien) and RER lines are operated by RATP (Paris' Métro and bus system). You may also see ticket windows identified as *Ile de France*. This is for Transilien (SNCF) trains serving destinations outside Paris in the Ile de France region (usually no more than an hour from Paris).

Paris train stations can be intimidating, but if you slow down, avoid peak times, take a deep breath, and ask for help, you'll find them manageable and efficient. Bring a pad of paper for clear communication at ticket/info windows. All stations have helpful *accueil* (information) booths; the bigger stations have roving helpers, usually in red vests. They're capable of answering rail questions more quickly than the information or ticket windows.

Paris' Stations

Métro and RER trains, as well as buses and taxis, are well-marked at every station. When arriving by Métro, follow signs for *Grandes Lignes–SNCF* to find the main tracks.

Gare du Nord

Key Destinations Served by Gare du Nord *Grandes Lignes*:
Bruges (about 2/hr, 2.5 hrs, change in Brussels), **Amsterdam** (nearly hourly, 4–5 hrs, change in Brussels), **Copenhagen** (7/day,

Paris Train Stations

Paris Train Stations & Destinations

1. **Gare Nord:** To London, Brussels, Amsterdam & N. France (also Chantilly & Auvers-sur-Oise)

2. **Gare Montparnasse:** To SW France (Languedoc & Dordogne), Loire Valley, Brittany (also Chartres) & Mont St. Michel

3. **Gare de Lyon:** To Italy & SE France (Burgundy, Alps, Provence & Riviera; also Fontainebleau & Melun/Vaux-le-Vicomte)

4. **Gare de Bercy:** Night trains to Italy

5. **Gare de l'Est:** To NE France (Reims, Champagne & Alsace), S. Germany, Switzerland & Austria

6. **Gare St. Lazare:** To Normandy (also Vernon/Giverny)

7. **Gare d'Austerlitz:** To SW France, Loire Valley & Spain

PARIS

14–18 hrs, two night trains), and **London** via Eurostar Chunnel train (12–15/day, 2.5 hrs, for details, see "To Paris or Brussels via Eurostar Train" near the end of the London chapter). Routes via **Brussels** (e.g., to Amsterdam and Bruges) require taking the pricey Thalys train, which has the monopoly on the rail route between Paris and Brussels; for details and tips, see "Connections" at the end of the Amsterdam chapter.

By *Banlieue*/RER Lines: **Charles de Gaulle Airport** (4/hr, 30 min, runs 5:00–24:00, track 4).

Gare Montparnasse
Key Destinations Served by Gare Montparnasse: Chartres (10/day, 1 hr, *banlieue* lines), **Madrid** (3/day, 13.5 hrs, one overnight via Irun, more night trains from Gare d'Austerlitz), and **Lisbon** (1/day, 21.5 hrs via Irun or Madrid).

Gare de Lyon
Key Destinations Served by Gare de Lyon: Avignon (9/day in 2.5 hrs to Avignon TGV station, 5/day in 3.5 hrs to Avignon Centre-Ville station, more connections with change—3–4 hrs), **Arles** (17/day, 2 direct TGVs in 4 hrs, 15 with change in Avignon in 5 hrs), **Nice** (10/day, 6 hrs, may require change, 11-hr night train possible out of Gare d'Austerlitz), **Venice** (3/day, 4/night, 10–13 hrs with change in Milan; 1 direct overnight, 13 hrs, important to reserve ahead), **Rome** (3/day, 13–16 hrs, plus several overnight options, important to reserve ahead), **Interlaken** (nearly hourly, 6.5 hrs, night train possible via Basel from Gare de l'Est), and **Barcelona** (3/day, 9 hrs, 1–2 changes; night train possible from Gare d'Austerlitz).

Gare de Bercy
This smaller station handles some night train service to Italy (Mo: Bercy, one stop east of Gare de Lyon on line 14).

Gare de l'Est
Key Destinations Served by Gare de l'Est: Munich (4/day, 6–7 hrs, some require changes), **Interlaken** (night train possible via Basel with changes at 5:00 and 8:00), **Vienna** (7/day, 12–17 hrs, 1–3 changes, night train), **Zürich** (2/day direct, 4 hrs; 7/day with changes, 5–6.5 hrs; night train), **Berlin** (6/day, 8–9 hrs, 1–2 changes, many via Belgium; 1 direct night train, 11.25 hrs) and **Prague** (5/day, 12–18 hrs, night train possible via Berlin).

Gare St. Lazare
Key Destinations Served by Gare St. Lazare: Bayeux (11/day, 2.5 hrs, 3 require change in Caen), **Caen** (14/day, 2 hrs), and **Pontorson/Mont St. Michel** (2/day, 4–5.5 hrs, via Caen; more trains from Gare Montparnasse).

Gare d'Austerlitz
Key Destinations Served by Gare d'Austerlitz: Versailles (via RER line C, 4/hr, 30–40 min), **Barcelona** (1/night, 12 hrs; day

trains from Gare de Lyon), and **Madrid** (2/night, 13 hrs direct, 16 hrs via Irun; day trains from Gare Montparnasse).

Airports

Charles de Gaulle Airport

Paris' primary airport has three terminals: T-1, T-2, and T-3. Most flights from the US use T-1 or T-2. To see which terminal serves your airline, check your ticket, or contact the airport (toll tel. 3950, www.adp.fr). Pickpockets prey on jet-lagged tourists on shuttles between terminals, and on RER trains. Don't take an unauthorized taxi from the men greeting you on arrival; official taxi stands are well-signed.

Transportation Between Charles de Gaulle Airport and Paris: Efficient public-transportation routes, taxis, and airport shuttle vans link the airport's terminals with central Paris. All are well-marked, and stops are centrally located at all terminals. If you're carrying lots of baggage—or are just plain tired—taxis are well worth the extra cost (avoid the airport shuttle vans going in the airport-to-Paris direction).

Roissy-Buses run every 15–20 minutes to the Opéra Métro stop (€8.50, runs 6:30–21:00, 50 min, buy ticket on bus). You'll arrive at a bus stop on rue Scribe on the left side of the Opéra building. To get to the Métro entrance, turn left out of the bus and walk counterclockwise around the Opéra to the front. The Métro station entrance is on the island in the middle of the square. For rue Cler hotels, take Métro line 8 (direction: Balard) to La Tour Maubourg or Ecole Militaire. For hotels in the Marais neighborhood, take line 8 (direction: Créteil Préfecture) to the Bastille stop. You can also take a taxi (about €12) to any of my listed hotels from behind the Opéra (the stand is in front of Galeries Lafayette department store).

Air France buses serve central Paris and continue to Orly Airport (at least 2/hr, 5:45–23:00). Allow 45 minutes to the Arc de Triomphe and Porte Maillot; 45 minutes to the Gare de Lyon train station; and 60 minutes to Montparnasse Tower/train station. To reach Marais hotels from the Gare de Lyon, take Métro line 1 (direction: La Défense) to the Bastille, St. Paul, or Hôtel de Ville stops; or walk 10 minutes up rue de Lyon to place de la Bastille. A ticket costs €15 one-way, €24 round-trip (pay driver).

Taxis run about €50 for up to three people (more if traffic is bad). Your hotel can call for a taxi to the airport. Specify that you want a real taxi *(un taxi normal),* and not a limo service that costs €20 more (and gives your hotel a kickback).

Airport vans also go straight to and from your hotel, but are not a good option to take from the airport to Paris; you have to book them in advance even though you don't know exactly when you'll arrive (getting baggage, going through customs). However, they are a good budget option *to* the airport (particularly for single travelers or families of four or more, as that's too many for a taxi). If your hotel does not work with a van service, reserve directly (book at least a day in advance—most hoteliers will make the call for you). Airport vans cost about €35 for one person, €45 for two, and €55 for three. **Golden Air** is reliable (from Paris to Charles de Gaulle: €27 for one person, €17 per person for two; from Charles de Gaulle to Paris: €35 for one person, €20 per person for two; tel. 01 43 62 82 75, fax 01 48 18 08 68, www.paris-airport-shuttle -limousine.com, goldenair@wanadoo.fr).

Sleeping at or near Charles de Gaulle Airport

Hôtel Ibis**, outside the Charles de Gaulle-1 RER stop, is huge and offers standard and predictable accommodations (Db-€95–120, near *navette* stop, free and fast shuttle bus to all terminals, tel. 01 49 19 19 19, fax 01 49 19 19 21, www.ibishotel.com, h1404@accor.com).

Novotel*** is next door and the next step up. Book early for the best rates (Db-€120–170, can rise to €260 for last-minute rooms, tel. 01 49 19 27 27, fax 01 49 19 27 99, www.novotel.com, h1014@accor.com). Both have simple restaurants.

Orly Airport

This airport feels small. It's good for rental-car pickup and drop-off, as it's closer to Paris and far easier to navigate than Charles de Gaulle Airport.

Transportation Between Orly Airport and Paris: Several efficient public-transportation routes, taxis, and a couple of airport vans link Orly with central Paris. The gate locations listed below apply to Orly Sud, but the same transportation services are available from both terminals.

Air France buses (outside Gate K) run to Montparnasse train station (with many Métro lines) and to the Invalides Métro stop (€9 one-way, €14 round-trip, 4/hr, 40 min to Invalides). These buses are handy for those staying in or near the rue Cler neighborhood (from Invalides bus stop, take the Métro to La Tour Maubourg or Ecole Militaire to reach recommended hotels). Remember that to continue on the Métro, you'll need to buy a separate ticket (for ticket types and prices, see "Getting Around Paris," near the beginning of this chapter).

Jetbus (outside Gate H, €5.70, 4/hr) is the quickest way to the Paris Métro and a good way to the Marais and Luxembourg Garden neighborhoods. Take the Jetbus to the Villejuif–Louis Aragon Métro stop. To reach the Marais neighborhood, take the Métro to the Sully-Morland stop. For the Luxembourg area, take the same train to the Censier-Daubenton or Place Monge stop. If taking the Jetbus from the Marais to the airport, make sure before you board the Métro that your train is going to Villejuif–Louis Aragon (not Mairie d'Ivry), as the route splits at the end of the line.

The **Orlybus** (outside Gate H, €6.20, 3/hr) takes you to the Denfert-Rochereau RER-B line and the Métro, offering Métro access to central Paris, including the Luxembourg Area and Notre-Dame Cathedral, as well as the Gare du Nord train station.

Taxis are to the far right as you leave the terminal, at Gate M. Allow €28–38 with bags for a taxi into central Paris.

Airport vans are good for single travelers or families of four or more (too many for a taxi) if going from Paris to the airport (see opposite page for a company to contact; from Orly, figure about €23/1 person, €30/2 people, less per person for larger groups and kids).

Beauvais Airport

Budget airlines such as Ryanair use this airport, offering dirt-cheap airfares, but leaving you 50 miles north of Paris. Still, this small airport has direct buses to Paris (see below). It's ideal for drivers who want to rent a car here and head to Normandy or north to Belgium (airport tel. 08 92 68 20 66, www.aeroportbeauvais.com; Ryanair tel. 08 92 68 20 73, www.ryanair.com).

Transportation Between Beauvais Airport and Paris: Buses depart from the airport about 20 minutes after flights arrive and take 90 minutes to reach Paris. Buy your ticket at the little kiosk to the right as you exit the airport (€14). Buses wait nearby and depart once they are full (baggage goes underneath), and arrive at Porte Maillot on the west edge of Paris, which has a Métro and RER stop. The closest taxi stand is across the street at Hôtel Concorde LaFayette.

Buses depart Paris for Beauvais Airport three hours and 15 minutes before scheduled flight departures. Catch the bus at Porte Maillot in the parking lot on boulevard Pershing next to Hôtel Concorde LaFayette. Arrive with enough time to purchase your bus ticket before boarding (Beauvais Airport tel. 08 92 68 20 66, www.aeroportbeauvais.com).

Trains connect Beauvais' city center and Paris' Gare du Nord (20/day, 80 min).

Taxis run from Beauvais Airport to Paris: €130 to central Paris, €12 to Beauvais' train station or city center.

Versailles

Every king's dream, Versailles was the residence of the French king and the cultural heartbeat of Europe for about 100 years—until the Revolution of 1789 ended the notion that God deputized some people to rule for him on Earth. Louis XIV spent half a year's income of Europe's richest country turning his dad's hunting lodge into a palace fit for a divine monarch. Louis XV and Louis XVI spent much of the 18th century gilding Louis XIV's lily. In 1837, about 50 years after the royal family was evicted, King Louis Philippe opened the palace as a museum. Europe's next-best palaces are Versailles wannabes.

Visiting Versailles can seem daunting because of its size and hordes of visitors. But it's easy. Arm yourself with a pass to skip ticket-buying lines and arrive early to avoid the crowds. I've provided all the details in "Orientation," next.

Orientation

Cost: I recommend buying either a Paris Museum Pass or Versailles' "Le Passeport" Pass, both of which give you access to the most important parts of the complex (see "Passes," later in this section).

You can also buy individual tickets to each of the three different sections:

1. The **Château,** the main palace, costs €13.50 (€10 after 15:00, under 18 always free, includes audioguide). Your Château ticket includes the King's and Queen's State Apartments (with the famous Hall of Mirrors), the Royal Chapel, the Opera House, and several lesser rooms.

2. The **Domaine de Marie-Antoinette,** the estate of the queen, costs €9 April–Oct; €5 after 16:00 and Nov–March; under 18 always free. This ticket gives you access to the far part of the Gardens and entry into several small palaces: the queen's Hamlet, the Grand and Petit Trianons, and a smattering of nearby buildings.

3. The **Gardens** are free, except on weekends April–Sept, when the fountains blast and the price is €8 (see "Fountain Spectacles," later in this section).

Passes: Smart travelers arrive at Versailles with one of these two passes in hand. Either pass can save you money—and both allow you to skip the long ticket-buyer lines (though everyone must endure the security check before entering the palace).

The **Paris Museum Pass** covers the Château and the Domaine de Marie Antoinette (a €22.50 value). The Paris Museum Pass

Versailles

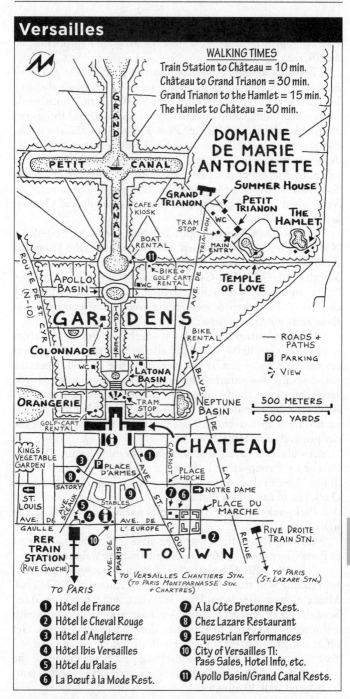

WALKING TIMES
Train Station to Château = 10 min.
Château to Grand Trianon = 30 min.
Grand Trianon to the Hamlet = 15 min.
The Hamlet to Château = 30 min.

GRAND CANAL

PETIT CANAL

DOMAINE DE MARIE ANTOINETTE

SUMMER HOUSE
GRAND TRIANON
PETIT TRIANON
THE HAMLET
CAFE & KIOSK
TRAM STOP
WC
MAIN ENTRY
BOAT RENTAL
AVE. DE TRIANON
BIKE & GOLF CART RENTAL
WC
TEMPLE OF LOVE
APOLLO BASIN
ROUTE DE ST. CYR (N-10)
GAR · DENS
TAPIS VERT
BIKE RENTAL
COLONNADE
WC
WC
BLVD DE
ROADS & PATHS
P PARKING
VIEW
LATONA BASIN
ORANGERIE
TRAM STOP
NEPTUNE BASIN
500 METERS
500 YARDS
GOLF-CART RENTAL
KING'S VEGETABLE GARDEN
CHATEAU
AVE. CARNOT
ST. LOUIS
AVE. DE SATORY
Hôtel de France ①
P PLACE D'ARMES
③
⑧
PLACE HOCHE
AVE. ST. CLOUD
⑦ ⑥
② NOTRE DAME
PLACE DU MARCHE
STABLES ⑨
AVE. DE SCEAUX ⑤
④
AVE. DE GAULLE
⑩
AVE. DE L'EUROPE
T O W N
② RIVE DROITE TRAIN STN.
REINE
AVE. DE PARIS
RER TRAIN STATION (RIVE GAUCHE)
TO PARIS
TO VERSAILLES CHANTIERS STN. (TO PARIS MONTPARNASSE STN. & CHARTRES)
TO PARIS (ST. LAZARE STN.)

① Hôtel de France
② Hôtel le Cheval Rouge
③ Hôtel d'Angleterre
④ Hôtel Ibis Versailles
⑤ Hôtel du Palais
⑥ La Bœuf à la Mode Rest.
⑦ A la Côte Bretonne Rest.
⑧ Chez Lazare Restaurant
⑨ Equestrian Performances
⑩ City of Versailles TI: Pass Sales, Hotel Info, etc.
⑪ Apollo Basin/Grand Canal Rests.

PARIS

does not include audioguides and does not cover the Gardens on Fountain Spectacle weekends. For Paris Museum Pass pricing and details, see page 295.

The **Le Passeport** one-day pass is a good deal if you don't have a Paris Museum Pass and you want to see the whole shebang. Le Passeport covers your entrance to the Château, Domaine de Marie-Antoinette, and Gardens. It also covers several things not covered by the Paris Museum Pass: audioguides and the weekend Fountain Spectacles. You can buy Le Passeport at any FNAC department store in Paris, or at the Versailles TI or Château box office. In April–Oct, Le Passeport costs €20 Mon–Fri, €25 Sat–Sun; Nov–March it's €16 Tue–Sun. This pass is a poor value on Mon, when only the Domaine de Marie-Antoinette and Gardens are open.

Hours: The **Château** is open Tue–Sun April–Oct 9:00–18:30, Nov–March 9:00–17:30, closed Mon year-round. The **Domaine de Marie-Antoinette** is open daily April–Oct 12:00–18:30, Nov–March 9:00–17:30. The **Gardens** are generally open daily from 9:00 to sunset (17:30 to 21:30), except on Sat in summer when they close at 18:00 to prepare for evening events. Last entry to all of these areas is one hour before closing.

Crowd Control: From May through September, Versailles is a zoo between 10:00–13:00, and all day Tue and Sun. For fewer crowds, go early or late. If you go early, arrive by 9:00 (when the palace opens), and tour the Château first, then the Gardens. If you arrive later, tour the Gardens first and the Château after 13:00 when crowds dissipate (except on Tue and Sun, when the place is packed from open to close). Note that the last guided tours of the day generally depart by 15:00.

Avoid ticket-buying lines altogether by using a Paris Museum Pass or Le Passeport, or by booking a guided tour (see "Guided Tours," later in this section). Everyone must wait in the security-check line to enter the Château.

Pickpocket Alert: Assume pickpockets are working the tourist crowds.

Getting There: The town of Versailles is 30 minutes southwest of Paris. The palace is a 10-minute walk from the train station.

Take the **RER-C train** (4/hr, 30–40 min one-way, €6 round-trip) from any of these RER stops: Gare d'Austerlitz, St. Michel, Musée d'Orsay, Invalides, Pont de l'Alma, and Champ de Mars. Scan the list of departing trains. Any train whose name starts with a V (e.g., "Vick") goes to Versailles; don't board other trains. Get off at the last stop, which is Versailles R.G., or "Rive Gauche." Exit through the turnstiles by inserting your ticket. To reach the palace, turn right out of the train station, then left at the first boulevard, and walk 10 minutes.

All trains leaving Versailles from the Rive Gauche station serve all downtown Paris RER stops on the C line.

Taxis for the 30-minute ride between Versailles and Paris cost about €55.

By **car,** it's a 30-minute drive to reach Versailles from Paris, if the traffic's not bad. Get on the *périphérique* freeway that circles Paris, and take the toll-free A13 autoroute toward Rouen. Follow signs into Versailles, then look for *château* signs and park in the huge pay lot (€4.50/2 hrs, €8/4 hrs, €12/8 hrs, free 19:30–8:30).

Information: Visit Versailles' good website before you go: www.chateauversailles.fr. Versailles has two information offices: the town's official TI (helpful, less crowded), and one at the palace. Both sell Paris Museum Passes and Le Passeport. You'll pass the town TI on your walk from the main RER station to the palace; it's just past the Pullman Hôtel (daily April–Sept 9:00–19:00, Oct–March 9:00–18:00, tel. 01 39 24 88 88). The Château's information office is on the left side of the Château courtyard (as you face the Château, tel. 08 10 81 16 14). The useful *Versailles Orientation Guide* brochure (free at either information office) explains your sight-seeing options.

Guided Tours: The primary 90-minute English guided tour includes commentary from trained guides, access to a few extra rooms (the interior of the Royal Chapel, some private apartments— the line-up varies), and it's a good way to skip ticket-buying lines if you don't have a pass. The guided tours are long, but those with an appetite for palace history enjoy them.

Skip the tours hawked as you leave the train station; book directly at the Château. Reserve your tour upon arrival (tours can sell out by 13:00) at the information office in the Château court-yard (€7.50 plus Château admission or pass, 90 min, departing roughly every 45 min 10:00–15:00). Don't wait in the ticket-buying line—instead, walk to the front of the line, where you'll find the guided-tour desk to the right.

Audioguide Tours: Audioguides are available at the entrances to the Château and Domaine de Marie-Antoinette. They're free with Le Passeport or individual Château or Domaine tickets. With the Paris Museum Pass, the Château audioguide costs €6 (€10 on Fountain Spectacle weekends); the Domaine audioguide is €4.

A free Rick Steves audioguide tour of the most important rooms of the King's and Queen's State Apartments is available for users of iPods and other MP3 players at www.ricksteves.com. You may also want to check out the podcasts at www.podibus.com /versailles.

Length of This Day Trip: With the usual lines, allow 90 minutes for the Château, two hours for the Gardens, and another hour for the Domaine de Marie-Antoinette. Add another two hours for round-trip transit, plus another hour for lunch...and Versailles is a full day trip from Paris. On a half-day visit, tour the Château, then spend an hour in the Gardens and skip the Domaine de Marie-Antoinette.

Baggage Check: There's a free checkroom at the main entrance—use it to check forbidden items (food, big bags, baby carriages, and so on). Strollers are not allowed inside the Château, so today's a good day for parents to either hire a babysitter or carry their toddler in a backpack with a child-seat.

Services: Reminiscent of the days when dukes urinated behind the potted palm trees, WCs at the Château are few and far between, and come with long lines. Use the public WC just before the palace gates, or find one of several in the Gardens.

Cuisine Art: A cafeteria and WCs are to the right of the Château's main entrance. Sandwich kiosks and cafés are scattered about the Gardens, including a good range of restaurants near the Apollo Basin and canal.

In the **town,** restaurants are on the street to the right of the parking lot (as you face the Château), though the best eateries line the lively market square, place du Marché, in the town center. A handy McDonald's is immediately across from the train station (WC without crowds, Internet café next door). An appealing assortment of reasonable restaurants line rue de Satory between the station and the palace.

Photography: Allowed indoors without a flash.

Fountain Spectacles: On spring and summer weekends, loud classical music fills the king's backyard, and the Gardens' fountains are in full squirt. Louis XIV had his engineers literally reroute a river to fuel these gushers. Even by today's standards, they are impressive.

The fountains run April–Sept Sat–Sun 11:00–12:00 & 15:30–17:00, with the finale from 17:20–17:30. On these "spray days," the Gardens cost €8. (Pay at the ticket booth near the golf-cart rental in the Gardens; covered by Le Passeport but not Paris Museum Pass; not included in individual Château ticket.) Pick up the helpful *Les Grandes Eaux Musicales* brochure and ask about the various evening spectacles (Sat in July–Aug).

Starring: Louis XIV, Marie-Antoinette, and the *ancien régime*.

Overview

The main sights to see at Versailles are the Château (the palace), the landscaped Gardens in the "backyard," and the small palaces of the Domaine de Marie-Antoinette. If your time is limited, stick to the Château and the Gardens just outside. It's a 30-minute walk from the Château, through the Gardens, to the heart of the

Domaine at the far end (longer if you stop along the way).

In the Château, the highlights are the King's and Queen's State Apartments, the Opera House, and the Chapel. (These rooms are labeled the "Red Itinerary" and "Blue Itinerary" by Versailles' curators.)

Welcome to Versailles

This commentary, which leads you through the various attractions at Versailles, covers just the basics. If you don't have *Rick Steves' Paris* (buy in the US or at any of the English-language bookstores listed in this book), the guidebook called *The Châteaux, the Gardens, and Trianon* gives a more detailed room-by-room rundown (sold at Versailles).

Stand in the courtyard and face the palace. If you need to buy a ticket (or want to book a tour), go to the box office on the far left side of the courtyard. If you already have a ticket or pass, read the section below, then enter the Château through the modern glass entry just left of center (expect a line).

The Château: Enter the palace and take a one-way walk through the State Apartments from the **King's Wing,** past the dazzling 700 seat **Opera House,** by the intimate, two-tiered **Royal Chapel,** and through glamorous ballrooms. You'll also see a billiard room, a royal make-out room, the Swiss bodyguard room, Louis' official bedroom, and his grand throne room (the **Apollo Room**)—with a 10-foot-tall canopied throne, and war rooms. You'll finish in the magnificent **Hall of Mirrors**—250 feet long, with 17 arched mirrors matching 17 windows looking out upon royal garden views. The mirrors—a luxury at the time—reflect an age when beautiful people loved to look at themselves. In another age altogether, this was the room in which the Treaty of Versailles was signed, ending World War I.

Before leaving, stop by the **Hall of Battles,** the long room filled with murals depicting the great battles of France (not always open—in the History of France Galleries).

Getting Around the Gardens: It's a 30-minute **walk** from the palace down to the Grand Canal and past the two Trianon palaces to the Hamlet—the heart of the Domaine de Marie-Antoinette. Allow more time if you stop along the way. A rental **bike** gives you the most freedom to explore the Gardens economically (€6.50/hr, near the Grand Canal, kid-size bikes available). The fast-looking, slow-moving *petit train* (tram) leaves from behind the Château (north side) and serves the Grand Canal and the Domaine. You can hop on and off as you like (€6, 4/hr, three stops, worthless commentary). Another option is to rent a **golf cart** for a drive through the gardens (€28/hr, audioguide-€1.20, rent at Orangerie side of palace or down by the canal, shuts off automatically if you diverge from prescribed route).

Palace Gardens: The Gardens offer a world of royal amusements. Outside the palace and to the left is the Orangerie. The warmth from the Sun King was so great that he could even grow orange trees in chilly France. Louis XIV had a thousand of these to amaze his visitors. In winter, they were kept in the greenhouses that surround the courtyard. On sunny days, they were wheeled out in their silver planters and scattered around the grounds. With the palace behind you, the grounds stretch out—it seems—forever. A promenade leads from the palace to the Grand Canal, an artificial lake that, in Louis' day, was a mini-sea with nine ships, including a 32-cannon warship. France's royalty floated up and down the canal in imported Venetian gondolas.

Domaine de Marie-Antoinette (Marie-Antoinette's Estate): Versailles began as an escape from the pressures of kingship. But in a short time, the palace became as busy as Paris ever was. Louis XIV needed an escape from his escape and built a smaller palace out in the boonies. Later, his successors retreated still farther into the garden and built a fantasy world of simple pleasures, allowing them to ignore the real world that was crumbling all around them.

The beautifully restored **Grand Trianon Palace** is as sumptuous as the main palace, but much smaller. With its pastel-pink colonnade and more human scale, this is a place you'd like to call home. Nearby are the **French Pavilion** and the **Petit Trianon,** which has a fine Neoclassical exterior. Despite her bad public reputation, Marie-Antoinette was a sweet girl from Vienna who never quite fit in with the fast, sophisticated crowd at Versailles. Here at the Petit Trianon, she could get away and re-create the simple home life she remembered from her childhood.

You can almost see princesses bobbing gaily in the branches as you walk through the enchanting forest, past the white marble **Temple of Love** to the queen's fake-peasant **Hamlet** *(le Hameau).* Marie-Antoinette's happiest days were spent at the Hamlet, under a bonnet, tending her perfumed sheep and manicured gardens in a thatch-happy wonderland.

Lesser Sights near the Palace

The King's Vegetable Garden (Le Potager du Roi)—When Louis XIV demanded fresh asparagus in the middle of winter, he got it, thanks to his vegetable garden. The 22-acre garden—still productive—is open to visitors. Stroll through symmetrically laid-out plots planted with vegetables both ordinary and exotic, among thousands of fruit trees. The garden is surrounded by walls and sunk below street level to create its own microclimate. Overseeing the central fountain is a statue of the agronomist Jean de la Quintinie, who wowed Louis XIV's court with Versailles-sized produce. Even today, the garden sprouts 20 tons of vegetables and 50 tons of fruit a year, which you can buy in season (€4.50 on weekdays, €6.50 on weekends, April–Oct daily 10:00–18:00, closed Nov–March, 10 rue du Maréchal Joffre).

The Equestrian Performance Academy (Academie du Spectacle Equestre)—The art of horseback riding has returned to Versailles. On most weekends from May through mid-December, you can watch rigorous training sessions, or enjoy choreographed performances—including "equestrian fencing"—performed to classical music (training sessions-€11, 60 min, Sat–Sun only at 11:15; musical shows-€25, Sun and some Thu at 15:00 plus Sat at 20:00 May–July and at 18:00 Sept–Dec, maybe also Tue–Sun mid-Feb–mid-March and April, but schedule is sporadic—check website for closure dates and extra performances). The stables (Grandes Ecuries) are across the parking square from the Château, next to the post office. For information, call 01 39 02 07 14. For reservations, call 08 92 68 18 91 or visit www.acadequestre.fr.

PROVENCE

This magnificent region is shaped like a giant wedge of quiche. From its sunburned crust, fanning out along the Mediterranean coast from Nîmes to Nice, it stretches north along the Rhône Valley to Orange. The Romans were here in force and left many ruins—some of the best anywhere. Seven popes, artists such as Vincent van Gogh and Paul Cézanne, and author Peter Mayle all enjoyed their years in Provence. This destination features a splendid recipe of arid climate (except for occasional vicious winds, known as the mistral), oceans of vineyards, dramatic scenery, captivating cities, and adorable hill-capping villages.

Explore France's greatest Roman ruin, the Pont du Gard. Spend your starry, starry nights where Van Gogh did, in Arles. Uncover its Roman past, then find the linger-longer squares and café corners that inspired Vincent. Youthful but classy, Avignon bustles in the shadow of its brooding Palace of the Popes.

Planning Your Time

Make Arles or Avignon your sightseeing base, particularly if you have no car. Arles has a blue-collar quality and good-value hotels, while Avignon (three times larger than Arles) feels sophisticated and offers more nightlife and shopping. Italophiles prefer smaller Arles, while poodles pick urban Avignon.

You'll want a full day for sightseeing in Arles (best on Wed or Sat, when the morning market rages), a half-day for Avignon, and a day or two for the villages and sights in the countryside.

Provence

Getting Around Provence

By Car: The region is made-to-order for a car. The yellow Michelin Local maps #332 and #340 are a godsend. Avignon (pop. 100,000) is a headache for drivers; Arles (pop. 35,000) is easier. Be wary of thieves: Park only in well-monitored spaces and leave nothing valuable in your car.

   By Train or Bus: Travelers relying on public transportation might find their choices limited. Public transit is good between cities and decent to some towns, but marginal at best to the villages.

Frequent trains link Avignon and Arles (about 20 min between each). The Pont du Gard is also connected by bus from Avignon.

Tours of Provence

Wine Safari—Dutchman Mike Rijken runs a one-man show, taking travelers through the region he adopted 20 years ago. Mike came to France to train as a chef, later became a wine steward, and has now found his calling as a driver/guide. His English is fluent, and while his focus is wine and wine villages, Mike knows the region thoroughly and is a good teacher of its history (€55/half-day, €100/day, priced per person; tel. 04 90 35 59 21, mobile 06 19 29 50 81, www.winesafari.net, mikeswinesafari@wanadoo.fr).

Imagine Tours—Unlike most tour operators, this is a non-profit organization with a focus on cultural excursions. It offers personal-ized tours allowing visitors to discover the "true heart of Provence." The itineraries adapt to your interests, and the volunteer guides will meet you at your hotel or the departure point of your choice (€150/half-day, €275/day, prices are for up to 4 people, tel. & fax 04 90 24 84 26, mobile 06 89 22 19 87, www.imagine-tours.net).

Wine Uncovered—Passionate Englishman (is that an oxymoron?) Oliver Hickman takes small groups on focused tours of selected wineries in the villages near Vaison la Romaine. Oliver is serious about French wine, knows his subject matter inside and out, and wants to help you learn. He offers in-depth tastings at two winer-ies for €40 per person (his minimum fee is €110) and full-day tours for €70 per person. If you need transportation, he can help arrange it (tel. 06 75 10 10 01, www.wine-uncovered.com, oliver.hickman @wine-uncovered.com).

François Marcou—For a fun and distinctly French perspective on wines of the Côtes du Rhône region, François offers different itineraries each day. He is based in Avignon and will pick up trav-elers at their hotel, the TI, or the train station (€75 per person for all-day wine tours that include 4–5 tastings, tel. 06 28 05 33 84, www.avignon-wine-tour.com, avignon.wine.tour@modulonet.fr).

Visit Provence—Based in Avignon, this company provides a variety of guided tours to most destinations covered in this book. They have eight-seat minivans and English commentary (about €60/half-day, €100/day; they'll pick you up at your hotel in Avignon). Ask about their cheaper big-bus excursions, or consider hiring a van and driver for your own private use (plan on €210/half-day, €400/day, tel. 04 90 14 70 00, check website for current destinations, www.provence-reservation.com).

Arles

By helping Julius Caesar defeat Marseille, Arles (pronounced "arl") earned the imperial nod and was made an important port city. With the first bridge over the Rhône River, Arles was a key stop on the Roman road from Italy to Spain, the Via Domitia. After reigning as the seat of an important archbishop and a trading center for centuries, the city became a sleepy backwater of little importance in the 1700s. Vincent van Gogh settled here a hundred years ago, but left only a chunk of his ear (now gone). American bombers destroyed much of Arles in World War II as the townsfolk hid out in its underground Roman galleries. But today Arles thrives again, with its evocative Roman ruins, an eclectic assortment of museums, made-for-ice-cream pedestrian zones, and squares that play hide-and-seek with visitors. It's an understandably popular home base from which to explore Provence.

Orientation

Arles faces the Mediterranean, turning its back on Paris. While the town is built along the Rhône, it almost completely ignores the river. That's all for the best, since it is the part of Arles most damaged by Allied bombers in World War II (and is therefore the least appealing today).

Landmarks hide in Arles' medieval tangle of narrow, winding streets. Virtually everything is close—but first-time visitors can walk forever to get there. Hotels have good, free city maps, and Arles provides helpful street-corner signs that point you toward sights and hotels. Racing cars enjoy Arles' medieval lanes, turning sidewalks into tightropes and pedestrians into leaping targets.

Tourist Information

The **main TI** is on the ring road boulevard des Lices, at esplanade Charles de Gaulle (April–Sept daily 9:00–18:45; Oct–March Mon–Sat 9:00–16:45, Sun 10:00–13:00; tel. 04 90 18 41 20, www .arlestourisme.com). There's also a **train station TI** (Mon–Fri 9:00–13:00 & 14:00–16:45, closed Sat–Sun). At either TI, pick up the city map, note the bus schedules (in books on the TI desks), and get English information on nearby destinations such as the Camargue wildlife area. Ask about "bullgames" (Provence's more humane version of bullfights—see "Events in Arles," later in the chapter) and walking tours of Arles. They sell a €1 brochure describing several walks in Arles, including one that locates Van Gogh's "easels." Both TIs charge €1 to reserve hotel rooms.

Arrival in Arles

By Train: The train station is on the river, a 10-minute walk from the town center (baggage storage nearby—see "Helpful Hints," below). Before heading into town, get what you need at the train station TI.

To reach the town center, turn left out of the train station and walk 10 minutes; or wait for the free Starlette bus (3/hr, Mon–Sat only) at the shelter across the street. Taxis generally wait out front, but if you don't see any, call the posted telephone numbers (rates are fixed, allow about €10 to any of my recommended hotels).

By Bus: The central Centre-Ville bus station is a few blocks below the main TI, located on the ring road at 16–24 boulevard Georges Clemenceau.

By Car: Arles' only parking garage is Parking des Lices, near the TI on boulevard des Lices (€7/24 hrs). Most hotels have parking nearby—ask for detailed directions (it's only €3/24 hrs at most meters). For most hotels, first follow signs to *Centre-Ville*, then *Gare SNCF* (train station). You'll come to a big roundabout (place Lamartine) with a Monoprix department store to the right. You can park for free along the city wall and find your hotel on foot; the hotels I list are no more than a 10-minute walk away (best not to park here overnight due to theft concerns and markets on Wed and Sat). Courageous drivers can plunge into the narrow streets between the two stumpy towers via rue de la Calade, and follow signs to their hotel. Again, theft is a big problem; leave nothing in your car, and trust your hotelier's advice on where to park.

Helpful Hints

Market Days: The big markets are on Wednesdays and Saturdays.

Meetings and Festivals: An international photo event jams hotels in early July.

Internet Access: Cyber Café Taxiphone will make you feel like you've gone to Morocco (daily 10:00–22:00, 31 rue Augustin Tardieu).

Baggage Storage and Bike Rental: Recommended Hôtel Régence (see "Sleeping," page 406) will store your bags for €3–5 each (7:30–22:00 mid-March–mid-Nov, closed in winter). They also rent bikes (€6/hr, €14/day, one-way rentals within Provence possible, same hours as baggage storage). Ask about their electric bikes—handy on windy days.

Laundry: There's a launderette at 12 rue Portagnel (daily 7:00–21:30, you can stay later to finish if you're already inside, English instructions).

Car Rental: Avis is at the train station (tel. 04 90 96 82 42), and **Europcar** and **Hertz** are downtown (2 bis avenue Victor Hugo, Europcar tel. 04 90 93 23 24, Hertz tel. 04 90 96 75 23).

Local Guide: Charming **Jacqueline Neujean,** an excellent guide, knows Arles and nearby sights intimately and loves her work (€90/2 hrs, tel. 04 90 98 47 51).

English Book Exchange: A small exchange is available at **Soleilei** ice-cream shop (see page 408).

Language and Cooking Courses: Food- or language-lovers enjoy classes offered by outgoing American (and Arles resident) Madeleine Vedel and her French husband, Eric. In addition to renting out rooms (see Maison d'Hôtes en Provence on page 404), they present a wide range of cooking and language-learning experiences: Pick wild asparagus, hunt mushrooms, harvest grapes at an organic winery, or make chocolate (www.cuisineprovencale.com).

Public Pools: Arles has three public pools (indoor and outdoor). Ask at the TI or your hotel.

Boules: The local *"boul*ing alley" is by the river on place Lamartine. After their afternoon naps, the old boys congregate here for a game of *pétanque*—it's fun to watch this popular local pastime.

Getting Around Arles

In this flat city, everything's within walking distance. Only the Ancient History Museum requires a long walk (take a taxi for €10, or a public bus for €0.80—details in museum listing under "Sights," next). The elevated riverside promenade provides Rhône views and a direct route to the Ancient History Museum (to the southwest) and the train station (to the northeast). Keep your head up for *Starry Night* memories, but eyes down for decorations by dogs with poorly trained owners.

Arles' **taxis** charge a set fee of about €10, but nothing except the Ancient History Museum is worth a taxi ride. To call a cab, dial 04 90 96 90 03.

The free **Starlette bus** circles the town (3/hr, Mon–Sat only), but is useful only for access to the train station.

Sights

The worthwhile **Monument Pass** *(le pass monuments)* covers almost all of Arles' sights (adults-€13.50, kids under 18-€12, sold at each sight except the Arlaten Folk Museum; Fondation Van Gogh discounted, but not fully covered). The less-tempting €9 *Circuit Romain* ticket covers Arles' four Roman sights, but not the Ancient History Museum. With no pass, you'll pay €3–6 per sight. While any sight is worth a few minutes, many aren't worth the individual admission.

Start at the Ancient History Museum for a helpful overview

(drivers should try to do this museum on their way into Arles), then dive into the city-center sights. Remember, many sights stop selling tickets 30–60 minutes before closing (both before lunch and at the end of the day).

▲▲Ancient History Museum (Musée de l'Arles et de la Provence Antiques)

Begin your town visit here—it's Roman Arles 101. Located on the site of the Roman chariot racecourse (the arc of which is built into the parking lot), this air-conditioned, all-on-one-floor museum is just west of central Arles along the river. Models and original sculptures (with almost no English translations) re-create the Roman city, making workaday life and culture easier to imagine.

Cost, Hours, Location: €5.50, daily April–Oct 9:00–19:00, Nov–March 10:00–17:00, presqu'île du Cirque Romain.

Information: Ask for the English booklet, which provides some background on the collection, and find out whether there are any free English tours (usually daily July–Sept at 17:00, 90 min). Tel. 04 90 18 88 88, www.arles-antique.cg13.fr.

Getting There: To reach the museum by **foot** from the city center (a 25-min walk), turn left at the river and take the riverside path to the big, modern building just past the new bridge. The **taxi** ride costs €10 (museum can call a taxi for your return). **Bus** #1 gets you within a five-minute walk (€0.80, 3/hr, daily except Sun). Catch the bus in Arles on boulevard des Lices, then get off at the Musée de l'Arles Antique stop and follow the signs (to your left as you step off the bus).

⊙Self-Guided Tour: Find the impressive row of pagan and early-Christian sarcophagi (from the second to fifth centuries). These would have lined the Via Aurelia outside the town wall. In the early days of the Church, Jesus was often portrayed beardless and as the good shepherd, with a lamb over his shoulder (see relief at end of ramp, #41).

Next, you'll see models of every Roman structure in (and near) Arles. These are the highlight for me, as they breathe life into buildings as they looked 2,000 years ago. Find the Forum (still the center of town, though only two columns survive today); the floating bridge (over the widest, and therefore slowest, part of the river); the Arena (with its movable stadium cover, which sheltered spectators from sun or rain); and the Circus, or chariot racecourse. While long gone, the racecourse must have been like Rome's Circus Maximus in its day—its obelisk is now the center-piece of Arles' place de la République.

Finally, check out the 3-D model of the aqueduct of Barbegal, with its 16 waterwheels and eight grain mills cascading down a nearby hillside (well worth a side-trip if you have a car).

Arles

Van Gogh Sights
1. Place Lamartine
2. Starry Night Over the Rhône View Easel
3. Fondation Van Gogh
4. Place du Forum (Café Van Gogh)
5. Espace Van Gogh

Other
6. Europcar & Hertz Car Rentals
7. Launderette
8. Avis Car Rental & Bike Rental
9. Internet Café

100 YARDS
100 METERS

← VAN GOGH WALKING TOUR
★ FORUM SQUARE
P PARKING
B BUS STOP
View

TO LES BAUX, FONTVIEILLE & AVIGNON

TO TRAIN STATION

MONO-PRIX

PLACE LAMAR.

PETANQUE

GATE

RUE JULES FERRY

RHONE

RUE LAMARTINE

RUE JOUVEAU

RUE CAVALERIE

R.L. BLUM

PLACE VOLTAIRE R. CONDOR.

REATTU MUSEUM

TO ANCIENT HISTORY MUSEUM

QUAI MARX DORMOY

QUAI LAMARTINE

RUE DU GRAND PRIEURE

RUE DU QUATRE SEPT.

RUE R. AMPH.

R. TARDIEU

RUE PORTAGNEL

R. REFUGE

DR. FANTON

RUE SAUVAGE

RUE DES SUISSES

RUE DE HOTEL DE VILLE

ENTER

ROMAN ARENA

NOTRE DAME

R. LIBERTE

ARLATEN FOLK MUSEUM

RUE DES ARENES

R. DIDEROT

FOND. V.G.

R. BALZE

RUE CALADE

ST. TROPHIME

PLACE REPUB.

RUE REPUBLIQUE

WC

ANCIENT CITY WALLS

CLASSICAL THEATER

DE CLOITRE

PORTE DE LAURE

JARDIN D'ETE

CLOISTER

MONTEE VAUBAN

BUS STN.

B

ESPACE VAN GOGH

BLVD. DES LICES

V. HUGO

TO ANCIENT HISTORY MUSEUM

POST & TAXIS

PLAYGROUND

BD. E. COMBES

R. E. FASSIN

TO LES AYLSCAMPS CEMETERY

DCH

PROVENCE

The model of the Roman city shows that an emphasis on sports—with the Arena and huge racecourse—is not unique to modern America. It also illustrates how little Arles seems to have changed over two millennia, with warehouses still on the opposite side of the river and houses clustered around the city center.

All of the museum's statues are original, except for the greatest—the *Venus of Arles,* which Louis XIV took a liking to and had moved to Versailles. It's now in the Louvre—and, as locals say, "When it's in Paris...bye-bye." Jewelry, fine metal and glass artifacts, and well-crafted mosaic floors make it clear that Roman Arles was a city of art and culture.

In Central Arles

Ideally, visit these sights in the order listed below. I've included some walking directions to connect the dots.

▲▲**Forum Square (Place du Forum)**—Named for the Roman forum that once stood here, this square was the political and religious center of Roman Arles. Still lively, this café-crammed square is a local watering hole and popular for a *pastis* (see "Eating," page 406). The bistros on the square, while no place for a fine dinner, can put together a good-enough salad or *plat du jour*—and when you sprinkle on the ambience, that's €10 well spent.

At the corner of Grand Hôtel Nord-Pinus, a plaque shows how the Romans built a foundation of galleries to make the main square level. The two columns are all that survive from the upper story of the entry to the Forum. Steps leading to the entrance are buried (the Roman street level was about 20 feet below you).

The statue on the square is of **Frédéric Mistral** (1830–1914). This popular poet, who wrote in the local dialect rather than in French, was a champion of Provençal culture. After receiving the Nobel Prize in Literature in 1904, Mistral used his prize money to preserve and display the folk identity of Provence. He founded the regional folk museum (see "Arlaten Folk Museum," later in this section) at a time when France was rapidly centralizing. (The local mistral wind—literally, "master"—has nothing to do with his name.)

The **bright-yellow café**—called Café Van Gogh today, but previously named Café la Nuit—is famous as the subject of one of Vincent van Gogh's most famous works in Arles. While his painting showed the café in a brilliant yellow from the glow of gas lamps, the facade was bare limestone, just like the other cafés on this square. The café's current owners have painted it to match Van Gogh's version...and to cash in on the Vincent-crazed hordes who pay too much to eat or drink here.

• *Walk a block to rue du Hôtel de Ville, turn right, and you'll find the big...*

PROVENCE

Republic Square (Place de la République)—This square used to be called "place Royale"...until the French Revolution. The obelisk was the centerpiece of Arles' Roman Circus. The lions at its base are the symbol of the city, whose slogan is (roughly) "the gentle lion." Find a seat and watch the peasants—pilgrims, locals, and street musicians. There's nothing new about this scene.

• *Overlooking this square is...*

▲▲**St. Trophime Church**—Named after a third-century bishop of Arles and located on a large square, this church sports the finest Romanesque main entrance (west portal) I've seen anywhere.

Like a Roman triumphal arch, the church facade trumpets the promise of Judgment Day. The tympanum (the semicircular area above the door) is filled with Christian symbolism. Christ sits in majesty, surrounded by symbols of the four evangelists: Matthew (the winged man), Mark (the winged lion), Luke (the ox), and John (the eagle). The 12 apostles are lined up below Jesus. It's Judgment Day...some are saved and others aren't. Notice the condemned (on the right)—a chain gang doing a sad bunny-hop over the fires of hell. For them, the tune trumpeted by the three angels above Christ is not a happy one. Below the chain gang, St. Stephen is being stoned to death, with his soul leaving through his mouth and instantly being welcomed by angels. Ride the exquisite detail back to a simpler age. In an illiterate medieval world, long before the vivid images of our Technicolor time, this was a neon billboard over the town square.

There's no charge to enter the church (daily April–Sept 9:00–12:00 & 14:00–18:30, Oct–March 9:00–12:00 & 14:00–17:00). Just inside the door on the right, a handy chart locates the interior highlights and helps explain the carvings you just saw on the tympanum.

Tour the church counterclockwise. The tall, 12th-century Romanesque nave is decorated by a set of tapestries showing scenes from the life of Mary (17th-century, from French town of Aubusson). Amble around the Gothic apse. Just to the left of the high altar, check out the relic chapel—with its fine golden boxes that hold long-venerated bones of obscure saints. Farther down is a chapel built on an early-Christian sarcophagus from Roman Arles (dated about A.D. 300). The heads were lopped off during the French Revolution.

This church is a stop on the ancient pilgrimage route to Santiago de Compostela in northwest Spain. For 800 years, pilgrims on their way to Santiago have paused here...and they still do today. As you leave, notice the modern-day pilgrimages advertised on the far right near the church's entry.

• *Leaving the church, turn left, then left again through a courtyard to enter the cloisters.*

The adjacent **cloisters** are interesting, with many small columns that were scavenged from the ancient Roman theater. Enjoy the sculpted capitals, the rounded 12th-century Romanesque arches, and the pointed 14th-century Gothic ones. On the second floor, you'll walk an angled rooftop designed to catch rainwater—notice the slanted gutter that channeled the water into a cistern (€3.50, daily March–Oct 9:00–18:00, Nov–Feb 10:00–17:00).

• *To get to the next sight, face the church, walk left, then take the first right on rue de la Calade.*

Classical Theater (Théâtre Antique)—This first-century B.C. Roman theater once seated 10,000. In the Middle Ages, it served as a convenient town quarry—precious little of the original theater survives (though considerable effort is ongoing to rebuild sections of the seating area).

Walk to a center aisle and pull up a stone seat. To appreciate its original size, look to the upper-left side of the tower and find the protrusion that supported the highest of three seating levels. Today, 3,000 can attend events here. Two lonely Corinthian columns look out from the stage over the audience. The orchestra section is defined by a semicircular pattern in the stone. Stepping up onto the left side of the stage, look down to the slender channel that allowed the curtain to disappear below, like magic. Go backstage and browse through broken bits of Rome, and loop back to the entry behind the grass (€3; June–Aug daily 9:30–12:30 & 14:00–18:30; April–May and Sept Tue–Sun 9:00–12:00 & 14:00–17:30, closed Mon; Oct–March Tue–Sun 9:00–12:00 & 14:00–16:30, closed Mon). Budget travelers can peek over the fence from rue du Cloître, and see just about everything for free.

• *A block uphill is the...*

▲▲▲Roman Arena (Amphithéâtre)—Nearly 2,000 years ago, gladiators fought wild animals here to the delight of 20,000 screaming fans. Today, local daredevils still fight wild animals here—"bullgame" posters around the Arena advertise upcoming spectacles (see "Bullgames," under the next section, "Events in Arles"). A lengthy restoration process is well underway, giving the amphitheater an almost bleached-teeth whiteness.

In Roman times, games were free (sponsored by city bigwigs) and fans were seated by social class. The many exits allowed for rapid dispersal after the games—fights would break out among frenzied fans if they couldn't leave quickly. Through medieval times and until the early 1800s, the arches were bricked up and the stadium became a fortified town—with 200 humble homes crammed within its circular defenses. Three of the medieval towers survive (the one above the ticket booth is open and rewards those who climb it with a good view). To see two still-sealed arches—complete with cute medieval window frames—turn right as you leave, walk to the Andaluz restaurant, and look back to the second floor (€5.50, daily May–Sept 9:00–18:00, March–April and Oct 9:00–12:00 & 14:00–18:00, Nov–Feb 10:00–12:00 & 14:00–16:30).

• *Turn left out of the Arena and walk uphill to find the...*

▲▲**Fondation Van Gogh**—A refreshing stop for any art-lover, and especially interesting to Van Gogh fans, this small gallery features works by contemporary artists who pay homage to Vincent through thought-provoking interpretations of his works. Many pieces are explained in English by the artists. The black-and-white photographs (both art and shots of places that Vincent painted) complement the paintings. Unfortunately, this collection is often on the road July through September, when non–Van Gogh material is on display here (€7, €5 with Monument Pass; great collection of Van Gogh souvenirs, prints, and postcards for sale in gift shop; April–June daily 10:00–18:00; July–Sept daily 10:00–19:00; Oct–March Tue–Sun 11:00–17:00, closed Mon; facing Arena at 24 bis rond-point des Arènes, tel. 04 90 49 94 04, www.fondation vangogh-arles.org).

• *The next two sights are back across town. The Arlaten Folk Museum is close to place du Forum, and the Réattu Museum is near the river.*

▲**Arlaten Folk Museum (Musée Arlaten/Museon Arlaten)**— Built on the remains of the Roman Forum (first century A.D., see the courtyard), this museum houses the treasures of daily Provençal life. It was given to Arles by Nobel Prize winner Frédéric Mistral (see "Forum Square," earlier in this section). Mistral's vision was to give locals an appreciation of their cultural roots, presented in tableaux that unschooled villagers could understand—"a veritable poem for the ordinary people who cannot read." The museum offers a unique and intimate look at local folk culture from the 18th and 19th centuries. As it's undergoing a massive renovation, only about a quarter of the collection is on display. A visit is still worthwhile, and a well-done English handout explains the entire collection (€1; June–Aug daily 9:30–12:30 & 14:00–18:30; April–May and Sept Tue–Sun 9:00–12:00 & 14:00–17:30, closed Mon; Oct–March Tue–Sun 9:00–12:00 & 14:00–16:30, closed Mon; last entry one hour before closing, 29 rue de la République, tel. 04 90 96 08 23, www.museonarlaten.fr).

A one-way route takes you through several rooms showing old costumes, religious objects, and popular traditions, watched over by guards in traditional dress. The last room holds two dioramas, the museum's pride and joy. The first diorama shows "the great supper"—a Provençal feast served on Christmas Eve before midnight Mass. It's 1860, and everything on the table is locally produced. Traditionally, 13 sweets—for Jesus and the 12 apostles—were served. Grandma and grandpa warm themselves in front of the fireplace; grandpa pours wine on a log for good luck in the coming year. In the second display, a wealthy mom is shown with her newborn. Her friends visit with gifts that represent the four physical and moral qualities hoped for in a new baby—good as bread, full as an egg, wise as salt, and straight as a match. The cradle is fully stocked with everything needed to raise an infant in 1888.

Réattu Museum (Musée Réattu)—Housed in a beautiful 15th-century mansion, this mildly interesting, mostly modern art collection includes 57 Picasso drawings (some two-sided and all done in a flurry of creativity—I liked the bullfights best), a room of Henri Rousseau's Camargue watercolors, and an unfinished painting by the Neoclassical artist Jacques Réattu...but none with English explanations (€4, €2 extra for special exhibits, daily July–mid-Sept 10:00–19:00, March–June and mid-Sept–Oct 10:00–12:30 & 14:00–17:30, Nov–Feb 13:00–17:00, last entry 30 min before closing for lunch or at end of day, 10 rue du Grand Prieuré, tel. 04 90 96 37 68).

Events In Arles

▲▲**Wednesday and Saturday Markets**—Twice a week in the morning, Arles' ring road erupts into an open-air market of fish, flowers, produce, and you-name-it. The Wednesday market runs along boulevard Emile Combes, between place Lamartine and bis avenue Victor Hugo; the segment nearest place Lamartine is all about food, and the upper half features clothing, tablecloths, purses, and so on. On the first Wednesday of the month, it's a flea market, with less produce. The Saturday market is along boulevard des Lices near the TI. Join in, buy flowers, try the olives, sample some wine, and swat a pickpocket. Both markets are open until 12:00.

▲▲**Bullgames (Courses Camarguaises)**—Occupy the same seats that fans have used for nearly 2,000 years, and take in Arles' most memorable experience—the *courses camarguaises* in the ancient Arena. These nonviolent "bullgames" are more sporting than bloody Spanish bullfights. The bulls of Arles (who, locals stress, "die of old age") are promoted in posters even more boldly than their human foes. In the bullgame, a ribbon *(cocarde)* is laced between the bull's horns. The *razeteur,* with a special hook, has 15 minutes to snare the ribbon. Local businessmen encourage a *razeteur* (dressed in white with a red cummerbund) by shouting out how much money they'll pay for the *cocarde*. If the bull pulls a good stunt, the band plays the famous "Toreador" song from *Carmen.* The following day, newspapers report on the games, including how many *Carmens* the bull earned.

Three classes of bullgames—determined by the experience of

Sleep Code

(€1 = about $1.40, country code: 33)
S = Single, **D** = Double/Twin, **T** = Triple, **Q** = Quad, **b** = bathroom,
s = shower only, ***** = French hotel rating system (0–4 stars).
Unless otherwise noted, credit cards are accepted and English
is spoken.

To help you sort easily through these listings, I've divided
the rooms into three categories based on the price for a
standard double room with bath:

$$$ Higher Priced—Most rooms €80 or more.
$$ Moderately Priced—Most rooms between €55–80.
$ Lower Priced—Most rooms €55 or less.

---

the *razeteurs*—are advertised in posters: The *course de protection* is
for rookies. The *trophée de l'Avenir* comes with more experience.
And the *trophée des As* features top professionals. During Easter and
the fall rice harvest festival *(Féria du Riz)*, the Arena hosts actual
Spanish bullfights (look for *corrida*) with outfits, swords, spikes,
and the whole gory shebang. Bullgame tickets run €5–15, while
bloody bullfights *(corrida)* are pricier (€12–80). Schedules change
every year—ask at the TI or check online at www.arenes-arles
.com (in 2009, the bullgames were every Wed at 17:00 June–Aug).

Don't pass on a chance to see *Toro Piscine*, a silly spectacle for
warm summer evenings where the bull ends up in a swimming
pool (uh-huh...get more details at TI). Nearby villages stage *courses
camarguaises* in small wooden bullrings nearly every weekend; the
TI has the latest schedule.

Sleeping

Hotels are a great value here; many are air-conditioned, though
few have elevators. The Calendal, Musée, and Régence hotels offer
exceptional value.

$$$ Hôtel le Calendal*** is a seductive place located between
the Arena and Classical Theater. You enter through a handsome
terrace into an expertly run hotel with comfy lounges and a lovely
palm-shaded courtyard. Enjoy the great €11 buffet breakfast,
and have lunch in the courtyard or at the inexpensive sandwich
bar (daily 12:00–15:00). There's a children's play area, and a new
pool and "spa" with a Jacuzzi and a Turkish bath—and they even
have my Provence video on DVD in the lobby. The comfortable
rooms come in all shapes and sizes (smallest Db-€54, standard
Db-€80–95, Db with balcony-€98–115, price depends on room

PROVENCE

size, air-con, Wi-Fi and four free laptops for guests, reserve ahead for parking-€10, just above Arena at 5 rue Porte de Laure, tel. 04 90 96 11 89, fax 04 90 96 05 84, www.lecalendal.com, contact @lecalendal.com).

$$$ Hôtel d'Arlatan***, built on the site of a Roman basilica, is classy in every sense of the word. It has sumptuous public spaces, a tranquil terrace, a designer pool, a turtle pond, and antique-filled rooms, most with high, wood-beamed ceilings and stone walls. In the lobby of this 15th-century building, a glass floor looks down into Roman ruins (smallest Db-€90, standard Db-€105–125, bigger Db-€125–160, Db/Qb suites-€180–250, excellent buffet breakfast-€13, air-con, bathrobes, ice machines, elevator, Wi-Fi, parking-€13–16, 1 block below place du Forum at 26 rue Sauvage, tel. 04 90 93 56 66, fax 04 90 49 68 45, www.hotel-arlatan.fr, hotel -arlatan@wanadoo.fr).

$$ Hôtel du Musée** is a quiet and affordable manor-home hideaway tucked deep in Arles (tricky to find by car). This delightful refuge comes with 28 air-conditioned rooms, a flowery two-tiered courtyard, and snazzy art-gallery lounges. Lighthearted Claude and English-speaking Laurence, the gracious owners, are eager to help (Sb-€45–50, Db-€55–70, Tb-€70–80, Qb-€85, Wi-Fi and a laptop available for guests, garage-€10, follow signs to *Réattu Museum* to 11 rue du Grand Prieuré, tel. 04 90 93 88 88, fax 04 90 49 98 15, www.hoteldumusee.com, contact@hoteldu musee.com).

$$ Hôtel de la Muette**, with reserved owners Brigitte and Alain, is a good choice. Located in a quiet corner of Arles, this low-key hotel is well-kept, with stone walls, wood beams, and air-conditioning. The just-renovated rooms are very sharp (Db-€65–70, Tb-€68–75, Qb-€85, buffet breakfast with eggs-€8, Internet access and Wi-Fi, garage-€7, 15 rue des Suisses, tel. 04 90 96 15 39, fax 04 90 49 73 16, www.hotel-muette.com, hotel.muette@wanadoo.fr).

$$ Maison d'Hôtes en Provence, run by engaging American Madeleine and her soft-spoken French husband Eric, combines an interesting B&B experience—four spacious and funky-but-comfy rooms—with optional Provençal cooking workshops. Foodies should check out their website for its affordable range of gourmet classes (Db-€70–75, extra person-€15, good family room, across from launderette at 11 rue Portagnel, tel. & fax 04 90 49 69 20, www.cuisineprovencale.com, actvedel@wanadoo.fr).

$$ Hôtel le Cloître** was originally the cloister provost's residence. Caring owners Jean-François and Agnes run a warm, ramshackle place with 30 simple but homey rooms. The best rooms are on the first floor, while cheaper rooms are on the second floor (Ss or Ds-€44, Sb or Db-€51, bigger Db-€65–70, Tb-€75, Qb-€85, no

Arles Hotels and Restaurants

1. Hôtel le Calendal
2. Hôtel d'Arlatan
3. Hôtel du Musée
4. Hôtel de la Muette
5. Maison d'Hôtes en Provence
6. Hôtel le Cloître
7. Hôtel Régence
8. Hôtel Acacias
9. Hôtel Voltaire
10. To Mas du Petit Grava

11. Restaurants Le 16, Au Bryn du Thym & La Paillotte
12. Bistrot à Vins Restaurant
13. La Cuisine de Comptoir Rest.
14. Café de la Major (Coffee/Tea)
15. Le Grillon Rest.
16. L'Atelier & A Côté Restaurants
17. Soleilei Ice Cream

PROVENCE

air-con, no elevator, Internet access and Wi-Fi, parking-€5, closed Nov–mid-March, 16 rue du Cloître, tel. 04 90 96 29 50, fax 04 90 96 02 88, www.hotelcloitre.com, hotel_cloitre@hotmail.com).

$$ Hôtel Acacias**, just off place Lamartine and inside the old city walls, is a modern pastel paradise. Its smallish, well-maintained, well-priced rooms have all the comforts (Sb or Db-€48–58, larger Db-€62–72, extra bed-€15, air-con, elevator, Wi-Fi, 1 rue Marius Jouveau, tel. 04 90 96 37 88, fax 04 90 96 32 51, www.hotel-acacias.com, contact@hotel-acacias.com).

$ Hôtel Régence**, about the best deal in Arles, has a riverfront location, immaculate and comfortable Provençal rooms, good beds, safe parking, and easy access to the train station (Db-€45–55, Tb-€55–65, Qb-€65–75, good buffet breakfast-€6, choose river view or quieter courtyard rooms, most rooms have showers, air-con, no elevator but only two floors, Internet access and Wi-Fi; from place Lamartine, turn right immediately after passing between towers to reach 5 rue Marius Jouveau; tel. 04 90 96 39 85, fax 04 90 96 67 64, www.hotel-regence.com, contact @hotel-regence.com). The gentle Nouvions also rent bikes.

$ Hôtel Voltaire* rents 12 small and spartan rooms with ceiling fans and nifty balconies overlooking a caffeine-stained square. Located a block below the Arena, it's perfect for starving artists. Smiling owner "Mr." Ferran (fur-ran) loves the States (his dream is to travel there), and hopes you'll add to his postcard collection (D-€30, Ds-€34, Db-€40, 1 place Voltaire, tel. 04 90 96 49 18, fax 04 90 96 45 49, levoltaire@aol.com). They also serve lunch and dinner (see "Eating," next).

Eating

You can dine well in Arles on a modest budget—in fact, it's hard to blow a lot on dinner here (most of my listings have fixed-price meals—*menus*—for €22 or less). The bad news is that restaurants here change regularly, so double-check my suggestions. Most places I list have outdoor seating. Before dinner, go local on place du Forum and enjoy a *pastis*. This anise-based apéritif is served straight in a glass with ice, plus a carafe of water—dilute to taste.

For **picnics,** a big, handy Monoprix supermarket/department store is on place Lamartine (Mon–Sat 8:30–19:25, closed Sun).

On or near Place du Forum

Great atmosphere and mediocre food at fair prices await on place du Forum. By all accounts, the garish, yellow Café Van Gogh is worth avoiding. A half-block below the Forum, on rue du Dr. Fanton, lies a lineup of more tempting restaurants (including the first four listed below).

Le 16, with warm ambience inside and out, is an affordable place to enjoy a fresh salad (€9, bright and creative) or a one-course dinner (their "bull and red rice" is popular). They also offer a daily *plat du jour,* a two-course €14 *formule,* and a seasonal *menu* (closed Sat–Sun, 16 rue du Dr. Fanton, tel. 04 90 93 77 36).

Au Bryn du Thym, almost next door, has long been reliable and specializes in traditional Provençal cuisine. Arrive early for an outdoor table, and let Madame Colombaud take care of you (€19 *menu,* closed Tue, 22 rue du Dr. Fanton, tel. 04 90 49 95 96).

La Paillotte, a few doors down, features soft tablecloths under wood-beamed comfort inside, a terrace outside, and fine regional cuisine at affordable prices. It's quite popular with tourists (€18–30 *menus,* closed Wed, 28 rue du Dr. Fanton, tel. 04 90 96 33 15).

Bistrot à Vins is for wine addicts who enjoy matching food and drink. You'll dine to light jazz at this cozy *bistrot,* which is well-run by affable Ariane. She speaks enough English and offers simple, tasty dishes (€10–16) designed to highlight her reasonably priced wines—many available by the glass. Try the veal with mashed potatoes (indoor dining only, closed Mon–Tue, 2 rue du Dr. Fanton, tel. 04 90 52 00 65).

At **La Cuisine de Comptoir,** locals abandon Provençal décor and pretend they're urbanites in Paris. This cool little bistro (indoor tables only) serves light €9 *tartine* dinners—a cross between pizza and bruschetta served with soup or salad (closed Sun, just off place du Forum's lower end at 10 rue de la Liberté, tel. 04 90 96 86 28).

Café de la Major is the place to go to recharge with some serious coffee or tea (closed Sun, 7 bis rue Réattu, tel. 04 90 96 14 15).

Near the Roman Arena

For about the same price as on place du Forum, you can enjoy regional cuisine with a point-blank view of the Arena. Because they change regularly, the handful of (mostly) outdoor eateries that overlook the Arena are pretty indistinguishable.

Le Grillon—with good salads, crêpes, and *plats du jour* for €9–12—has been the most reliable (closed Wed, at the top of Arena on rond point des Arènes, tel. 04 90 96 70 97).

Hôtel le Calendal (recommended in "Sleeping," previous section) serves lunch in its lovely courtyard (€15, daily 12:00–15:00) or delicious little sandwiches for €2 each (three makes a good meal) at its small café.

Hôtel Voltaire (recommended in "Sleeping," previous section) serves a nothing-fancy three-course dinner (or lunch) for €11 and hearty salads for €8–10—try the *salade fermière* (1 place Voltaire, tel. 04 90 96 49 18).

A Gastronomic Dining Experience

One of France's most recognized chefs, Jean-Luc Rabanel, has created a sensation with two different-as-night-and-day dining options 50 yards from place de la République (at 7 rue des Carmes). They sit side by side, both offering indoor and terrace seating.

L'Atelier is so intriguing that people travel great distances just for the experience. Diners fork over €80 (at lunch, you'll spoon out €50) and trust the chef to create a memorable meal...which he does. There is no menu, just an onslaught of delicious taste sensations served on artsy dishes. Don't plan on a quick dinner and don't come for the setting—it's a contemporary, shoebox-shaped dining room, but several outdoor tables are also available. The get-to-know-your-neighbor atmosphere means you can't help but join the party (closed Mon–Tue, best to book ahead, friendly servers will hold your hand through this palate-widening experience, tel. 04 90 91 07 69, www.rabanel.com).

A Côté saddles up next door offering a wine bar/bistro ambience and top-quality cuisine for far less. Here you can sample the famous chef's talents for as little as €6 (tapas plate) or as much as €30 (3-course *menu*). You'll also find reasonable prices for wine (from €3 a glass) and a helpful staff (daily, tel. 04 90 47 61 13).

And for Dessert...

Soleilei has Arles' best ice cream, with all-natural ingredients and unusual flavors such as *fadoli*—olive oil. There's also a shelf of English books for exchange (open daily, across from recommended Le 16 restaurant at 9 rue du Dr. Fanton).

Connections

From Arles by Train to: Paris (17/day, 2 direct TGVs—4 hrs, 15 with transfer in Avignon—5 hrs), **Avignon Centre-Ville** (11/day, 20 min, less frequent in the afternoon), **Nîmes** (9/day, 30 min), **Nice** (11/day, 3.75–4.5 hrs, most require transfer in Marseille), **Barcelona** (2/day, 6 hrs, transfer in Montpellier), **Italy** (3/day, transfer in Marseille and Nice; from Arles, it's 4.5 hrs to Ventimiglia on the border, 8 hrs to Milan, 9.5 hrs to Cinque Terre, 11 hrs to Florence, and 13 hrs to Venice or Rome).

From Arles Train Station to Avignon TGV Station: If you're connecting from Arles to the TGV in Avignon, it's easiest to take the bus directly from Arles' train station to Avignon's TGV station (11/day, 1 hr). Another option—which takes the same amount of time, but adds more walking—is to take the regular train from Arles to Avignon's Centre-Ville station, then catch the *navette* (shuttle bus) to the TGV station from there.

From Arles Bus Station to: **Nîmes** (6/day, 1 hr). The bus station is at 16–24 boulevard Georges Clemenceau (2 blocks below main TI, next to Café le Wilson). Bus info: tel. 04 90 49 38 01 (unlikely to speak English).

Avignon

Famous for its nursery rhyme, medieval bridge, and brooding Palace of the Popes, contemporary Avignon (ah-veen-yohn) bustles and prospers behind its mighty walls. During the 68 years (1309–1377) that Avignon starred as the *Franco Vaticano,* it grew from a quiet village into a thriving city. With its large student population and fashionable shops, today's Avignon is an intriguing blend of medieval history, youthful energy, and urban sophistication. Street performers entertain the international crowds who fill Avignon's ubiquitous cafés and trendy boutiques. If you're here in July, be prepared for big crowds and higher prices, thanks to the rollicking theater festival. (Reserve your hotel far in advance.) Clean, sharp, and popular with tourists, Avignon is more impressive for its outdoor ambience than for its museums and monuments. See the Palace of the Popes, and then explore the city's thriving streets and beautiful vistas from the parc des Rochers des Doms.

Orientation

The cours Jean Jaurès, which turns into rue de la République, runs straight from the Centre-Ville train station to place de l'Horloge and the Palace of the Popes, splitting Avignon in two. The larger eastern half is where the action is. Climb to the parc des Rochers des Doms for the town's best view, tour the pope's immense palace, lose yourself in Avignon's back streets, and find a shady square to call your own. Avignon's shopping district fills the traffic-free streets where rue de la République meets place de l'Horloge.

Tourist Information

The main TI is between the Centre-Ville train station and the old town, at 41 cours Jean Jaurès (April–Oct Mon–Sat 9:00–18:00—until 19:00 in July, Sun 9:00–17:00; Nov–March Mon–Fri 9:00–18:00, Sat 9:00–17:00, Sun 10:00–12:00; tel. 04 32 74 32 74, www.avignon-tourisme.com). From April through mid-October, a branch TI office, called Espace Ferruce, is open at St. Bénezet Bridge (daily 10:00–13:00 & 14:00–18:00, but it can be slow with just one person working).

At either TI, get the good tear-off map and pick up the free and handy *Guide Pratique* (info on car and bike rentals, hotels, apartment rentals, and museums). Also pick up the free **Avignon Passion Pass** (valid 15 days, for up to five people). Get the pass stamped when you pay full price at your first sight, and then receive reductions at the others (for example, €2 less at the Palace of the Popes and €3 less at the Petit Palais). The discounts add up—always show your Passion Pass when buying a ticket. The pass comes with the Avignon "Passion" map and guide, which includes several good (but tricky-to-follow) walking tours.

Arrival in Avignon

By Train

Avignon has two train stations: TGV (linked to downtown by frequent shuttle buses) and Centre-Ville.

TGV Station (Gare TGV): This shiny new station is on the outskirts of town. There is no baggage storage here (though you can store your bags at the Centre-Ville station, described below). To pick up a **rental car,** take the south exit *(sortie sud)* to find the *location de voitures* (for driving directions to other destinations from this station, see "By Car," later in this section).

To get to the city center, the best and most inexpensive option is to take the *navette*/**shuttle bus** (marked *Navette/Avignon Centre;* €1.20, buy ticket from driver, 3/hr, 15 min). To find the bus stop, leave the station by the north exit *(sortie nord),* walk down the stairs, and find the long bus shelter to the left. In downtown Avignon, you'll arrive at a stop located three blocks from the city's main TI and two blocks from Centre-Ville station (just inside the city walls, in front of the post office on cours Président Kennedy— see Avignon map on opposite page). A **taxi** ride between the TGV station and downtown Avignon costs about €14.

If you're heading from the Avignon TGV station to the **Arles train station,** you can catch a direct SNCF bus from the same TGV stop (11/day, 1 hr, schedule available at any information booth inside the TGV station).

Centre-Ville Station (Gare Avignon Centre-Ville): All non-TGV trains (and a few TGV trains) serve the central station. You can store bags here—exit the station to the left and look for *consignes* sign (daily May–Sept 6:00–22:00, Oct–April 7:00–19:00). To reach the town center, walk out of the train station and through the city walls onto cours Jean Jaurès. The TI is three blocks down, at #41.

By Bus

The dingy bus station *(gare routière)* is 100 yards to the right of Centre-Ville station as you leave (beyond and below Ibis Hôtel).

Avignon

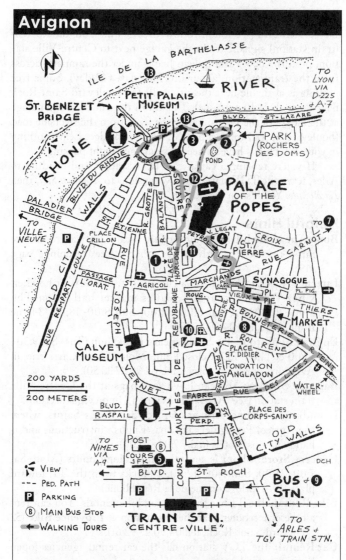

ILE DE LA BARTHELASSE

TO LYON VIA D-225 & A-7

RIVER

St. Benezet Bridge

Petit Palais Museum

BLVD. ST-LAZARE

PARK (ROCHERS DES DOMS)

POND

RHONE

FERRULE

PALACE SQUARE

BLVD. DU RHONE

WALLS

PALACE OF THE POPES

DALADIER BRIDGE

TO VILLE-NEUVE

OLD CITY

PLACE CRILLON

ST. ETIENNE

PASSAGE L'ORAT.

ST. AGRICOL

RUE JOSEPH VERNET

R. GROTTES

R. BALANCE

PLACE DE L'HORLOGE

R. DE LA REPUBLIQUE

V. LEGAT

PEYROL

CROIX

ST. PIERRE

RUE CARNOT

TO

MARCHANDS

ROUG.

VIEUX

PL.

R. FOURB.

R. BONNETERIE

SYNAGOGUE

PL. PIG.

PIE

R. THIERS

MARKET

R. ROI RENE

CALVET MUSEUM

PLACE ST. DIDIER

R. FAU-CON.

FONDATION ANGLADON

RUE DES LICES

WATER-WHEEL

R. TEINT.

200 YARDS
200 METERS

BLVD. RASPAIL

FABRE

PERD.

PLACE DES CORPS-SAINTS

OLD CITY WALLS

TO NIMES VIA A-9

Post

COURS JFK

ST. MICHEL

BLVD. ST. ROCH

DCH

BUS & STN.

COURS

TRAIN STN. "CENTRE-VILLE"

TO ARLES & TGV TRAIN STN.

VIEW
--- PED. PATH
P PARKING
B MAIN BUS STOP
WALKING TOURS

1 Start of Welcome to Avignon Walk
2 Views & Orientation Table
3 Best View of Bridge & Stairs to Ramparts
4 Hôtel la Mirande (Start of Discovering Back Streets Walk)
5 TGV Shuttle & Bus #11 Stop
6 Launderette
7 To Shakespeare Bookshop
8 Chez W@M Internet Café
9 Provence Bike Rental
10 Shopi Grocery
11 City Hall
12 Tourist Train Stop
13 Shuttle Boat Stops (2)

By Car

Drivers entering Avignon follow *Centre-Ville* and *Gare SNCF* (train station) signs. Park in the garage next to Centre-Ville station, or at the new Parking Jean Juarès under the ramparts across from the train station (about €10/half-day, €13/day). Some free parking is available near the city walls (on boulevard Saint-Roch near Porte de la République). To park in the underground garage at the Palace of the Popes, follow the signs from the riverside road (boulevard St. Lazare) just past St. Bénezet Bridge. Leave nothing in your car. Hotels have advice for smart overnight parking.

If you're renting a car at the TGV station and heading to Arles, leave the TGV station following signs to *Avignon Sud*, then *La Rocade*. You'll soon see exits to Arles.

Helpful Hints

Book Ahead for July: During the July theater festival, rooms are rare—reserve very early or stay in Arles (see "Sleeping," page 419).

Internet Access: The TI has a current list, or ask your hotelier. **Chez W@M** is near Les Halles market hall (Mon–Thu 8:00–20:00, Fri–Sat 8:00–23:00, Sun 8:00–18:00, 34 rue Bonneterie, tel. 04 90 86 19 03).

English Bookstore: Try **Shakespeare Bookshop** (Tue–Sat 9:30–12:00 & 14:00–18:30, closed Sun–Mon, 155 rue Carreterie, in Avignon's northeast corner, tel. 04 90 27 38 50).

Baggage Storage: You can leave your bags at the Centre-Ville train station (see "Arrival in Avignon," in previous section).

Laundry: The launderette at 66 place des Corps-Saints, where rue Agricol Perdiguier ends, has English instructions and is handy to most hotels (daily 7:00–20:00).

Grocery Store: Shopi is central and has long hours (Mon–Sat 7:00–21:00, Sun 9:00–12:00, 2 blocks from the TI, toward place de l'Horloge on rue de la République).

Bike Rental: The TI has the latest on bike rentals. You can rent a bike or a scooter near the bus station at **Provence Bike** (52 boulevard Saint-Roch, tel. 04 90 27 92 61).

Car Rental: The TGV station has the car-rental agencies (open long hours daily).

Shuttle Boat: A free shuttle boat plies back and forth across the river (as it did in the days when the town had no functioning bridge) from near St. Bénezet Bridge (daily July–Aug 11:00–21:00, Sept–June roughly 10:00–12:30 & 14:00–18:00, 3/hr). It drops you on the peaceful Ile de la Barthelasse, with its riverside restaurant (see "Eating—Across the River," later in this chapter), grassy walks, and bike rides with city views. If you stay on the island for dinner, check the schedule for the last return boat—or be prepared for a pleasant 25-minute walk back to town.

Commanding City Views: Walk or drive across Daladier Bridge (pont Daladier) for a great view of Avignon and the Rhône River (there's a good walking path across the bridge, along the river). You can enjoy other impressive vistas from the top of parc des Rochers des Doms, from the tower cafeteria in the Palace of the Popes, and from the end of the famous, broken St. Bénezet Bridge.

Tours

Walking Tours—The TI offers informative, two-hour English walking tours of Avignon (€10, discounted with Avignon Passion Pass, €15 includes a tour of the Pope's Palace; April–Oct daily at 10:00, Nov–March on Sat only; depart from main TI, Sun departures from ticket room at Palace of the Popes; themes vary daily).

Tourist Trains—Two little trains, designed for tired tourists, leave regularly from the Palace of the Popes (mid-March–mid-Oct daily 10:00–19:00). One does a town tour (€7, 3/hr, 45 min, English commentary) and the other choo-choos you sweat-free to the top of the park, high above the river (€1 one-way, schedule depends on demand, no commentary).

Guided Excursions—Several minivan tour companies based in Avignon offer tours to destinations around Provence, including the Pont du Gard (about €60–75 per person for all-day tours). See "Tours of Provence," near the beginning of this chapter, or ask the TI to book you a tour.

Self-Guided Walk

▲▲Welcome to Avignon

Before starting this walk—which connects the city's top sights—be sure to pick up the Avignon Passion Pass at the TI, then show it when entering each attraction to receive discounted admission (explained under "Tourist Information" on page 409).

• *Start your tour where the Romans did, on place de l'Horloge, in front of City Hall (Hôtel de Ville).*

Place de l'Horloge

This café square was the town forum during Roman times and the market square through the Middle Ages. (Restaurants here come with ambience, but marginal-quality meals.) Named for a medieval clock tower that the City Hall now hides, this square's present popularity arrived with the trains in 1854.

• *Walk uphill past the carousel (public WCs behind). You'll see the Palace of the Popes looming large over the buildings. Veer right at the street's end, and continue into...*

Palace Square (Place du Palais)

This grand square is surrounded by the Palace of the Popes, the Petit Palais, and the cathedral. In the 1300s, the Vatican moved the entire headquarters of the Catholic Church to Avignon. The Church bought Avignon and gave it a complete makeover. Along with clearing out vast spaces like this square and building this three-acre palace, the Church erected more than three miles of protective wall, with 39 towers, "appropriate" housing for cardinals (read: mansions), and residences for the entire Vatican bureaucracy. The city was Europe's largest construction zone. Avignon's population grew from 6,000 to 25,000 in short order. (Today, 13,000 people live within the walls.) The limits of pre-papal Avignon are outlined on city maps: Rues Joseph Vernet, Henri Fabre, des Lices, and Philonarde all follow the route of the city's earlier defensive wall.

The Petit Palais (Little Palace) seals the uphill end of the square and was built for a cardinal; today, it houses medieval paintings (museum described next). The church just to the left of the Palace of the Popes is Avignon's cathedral. It predates the Church's purchase of Avignon by 200 years. Its small size reflects Avignon's modest, pre-papal population. The gilded Mary was added in 1854, when the Vatican established the doctrine of her Immaculate Conception. Mary is purposefully taller than the Palace of the Popes. The Vatican never accepted what it called the "Babylonian Captivity," and had a bad attitude about Avignon long after the pope was definitively back in Rome.

Directly across the square from the palace's main entry stands a cardinal's residence built in 1619. Its fancy Baroque facade was a visual counterpoint to the stripped-down Huguenot aesthetic of the age. During this time, Provence was a hotbed of Protestantism—but, buried within this region, Avignon was a Catholic stronghold.

Notice the stumps in front of the Conservatoire National de Musique. Nicknamed *bites,* slang for the male anatomy, they effectively keep cars from double-parking in areas designed for people. Many of the metal ones slide up and down by remote control to let privileged cars come and go.

• *You can visit the massive Palace of the Popes (described later in this section) now, but it works better to visit that palace at the end of this walk.*

Now is a good time to take in the...

Petit Palace Museum (Musée du Petit Palais)

This palace displays the Church's collection of mostly medieval Italian painting (including one delightful Botticelli) and sculpture. All 350 paintings deal with Christian themes. A visit here before going to the Palace of the Popes helps furnish and populate that otherwise barren building (€6; June–Sept Wed–Mon 10:00–13:00 & 14:00–18:00, closed Tue; Oct–May Wed–Mon 9:30–13:00 & 14:00–17:30, closed Tue; at north end of Palace Square, tel. 04 90 86 44 58).

• *From Palace Square, we'll head up to the rocky hilltop where Avignon was first settled, then down to the river. With this short loop, you can enjoy a park, hike to a grand river view, walk a bit of the wall, and visit Avignon's beloved* **broken bridge**—*an experience worth* ▲▲. *Begin by hiking (or taking the tourist train—see previous section, "Tours") up to the...*

▲▲Parc des Rochers des Doms

While the park itself is a delight—with a sweet little café and public WCs—don't miss the climax: a panoramic view of the Rhône River Valley and the broken bridge. You'll find a huge terrace in the north side of the park, with an orientation table and information plaques, but views that are inferior to the smaller viewpoint described below (park gates open daily April–Sept 7:30–20:00, Oct–March 7:30–18:00).

For the best views (and the favorite make-out spot for local teenagers), find the small terrace across the grass from the park café and behind the odd zodiac display. An orientation table explains the view. On a clear day, the tallest peak you see, with its white limestone cap, is Mont Ventoux ("Windy Mountain"). St. André Fortress (across the river) was built by the French in 1360, shortly after the pope moved to Avignon, to counter the papal incursion into this part of Europe. The castle was in the kingdom of France. Avignon's famous bridge was a key border crossing, with towers on either end—one French and one Vatican. The one across the river is the Tower of Phillip the Fair (described under next section, "More Sights").

• *From this viewpoint, take the stairs to the left (closed at night) down to the tower. As the stairs spiral down, just before St. Bénezet Bridge, catch a glimpse of the...*

Ramparts

The only bit of the rampart you can walk on is just beyond the tower (access from St. Bénezet Bridge). When the pope came in the 1360s, small Avignon had no town wall...so he built one. What you see today was restored in the 19th century.

• *When you come out of the tower on street level, exit outside the walls and walk left, going under the bridge to find the bridge's entrance.*

▲▲St. Bénezet Bridge (Pont St. Bénezet)

This bridge, whose construction and location were inspired by a shepherd's religious vision, is the "pont d'Avignon" of nursery-rhyme fame. The ditty (which you've probably been humming all day) dates back to the 15th century: *Sur le pont d'Avignon, on y danse, on y danse, sur le pont d'Avignon, on y danse tous en rond* ("On the bridge of Avignon, we will dance, we will dance, on the bridge of Avignon, we will dance all in a circle").

But the bridge was a big deal even outside of its kiddie-tune fame. Built between 1171 and 1185, it was the only bridge crossing the mighty Rhône in the Middle Ages. It was damaged several times by floods and subsequently rebuilt, until 1668, when most of it was knocked down by a disastrous icy flood. The townsfolk decided not to rebuild this time, and for more than a century, Avignon had no bridge across the Rhône. While only four arches survive today, the original bridge was huge: Imagine a 22-arch, 3,000-foot-long bridge extending from Vatican territory to the lonely Tower of Philip the Fair, which marked the beginning of France. A Romanesque chapel on the bridge is dedicated to St. Bénezet. While there's not much to see on the bridge, the audioguide included with your ticket tells a good story. It's also fun to be in the breezy middle of the river with a fine city view.

Cost and Hours: €4, €12 combo-ticket includes Palace of the Popes, same hours as the Palace of the Popes (see below), last entry one hour before closing, tel. 04 90 27 51 16. The ticket booth is housed in what was a medieval hospital for the poor (funded by bridge tolls). Admission includes a small museum about the song of Avignon's bridge and your only chance to walk a bit of the ramparts (enter both from the tower).

• *To get to the Palace of the Popes from here, exit left, then turn left again back into the walls and walk to the end of the short street, then turn right following signs to* Palais des Papes. *After a block, look for the brown signs leading you left under the passageway, and up the stairs to Palace Square and the...*

▲▲Palace of the Popes (Palais des Papes)

In 1309, a French pope was elected (Pope Clement V). At the urging of the French king, His Holiness decided he'd had enough of unholy (and dangerous) Italy. So he loaded up his carts and moved to Avignon for a secure rule under a supportive king. The Catholic Church literally bought Avignon (then a two-bit town), and popes resided here until 1403. Meanwhile, Italians demanded a Roman pope, so from 1378 on, there were twin popes—one in Rome and one in Avignon—causing a schism in the Catholic Church that wasn't fully resolved until 1417.

A visit to the mighty yet barren papal palace comes with an audioguide that leads you along a one-way route and does a credible job of overcoming the lack of furnishings. It teaches the basic history while allowing you to tour at your own pace.

As you wander, ponder that this palace—the largest surviving Gothic palace in Europe—was built to accommodate 500 people as the administrative center of the Vatican and home of the pope. This was the most fortified palace of the age (remember, the pope left Rome to be more secure). You'll walk through the pope's personal quarters (frescoed with happy hunting scenes), see models of how the various popes added to the building, and learn about its state-of-the-art plumbing. The rooms are huge. The "pope's chapel" is twice the size of the adjacent Avignon cathedral.

While the last pope checked out in 1417, the Vatican owned Avignon until the French Revolution in 1789. During this interim period, the pope's "legate" (official representative...normally a nephew) ruled Avignon from this palace. Avignon residents, many of whom had come from Rome, spoke Italian for a century after the pope left, making it a linguistic island within France. In the Napoleonic age, the palace was a barracks, housing 1,800 soldiers. You can see cuts in the wall where high ceilings gave way to floor beams. Climb the tower (Tour de la Gâche) for a grand view and windswept café.

A room at the end of the tour (called *la boutellerie*) is dedicated to the region's wines, of which they claim the pope was a fan. Sniff "Le Nez du Vin"—a black box with 54 tiny bottles designed to develop your "nose." (Blind-test your travel partner.) The nearby village of Châteauneuf-du-Pape is where the pope summered in the 1320s. Its famous wine is a direct descendant of his wine. You're welcome to taste here (€6 for three fine wines and souvenir tasting cup).

Cost and Hours: €9.50, €12 combo-ticket includes St. Bénezet Bridge, daily mid-March–Oct 9:00–19:00, until 20:00 July and Sept, until 21:00 in Aug, Nov–mid-March 9:30–17:45, last entry one hour before closing, tel. 04 90 27 50 74, www.palais-des-papes.com.

• *After you finish, you'll exit at the rear of the palace. To return to Palace Square, make two rights after exiting the palace.*

More Sights

Avignon's Back Streets
Most of the following sights line Avignon's back streets, an enjoyable wander from the exit of the Palace of the Popes.

PROVENCE

Avignon's Synagogue—Jews first arrived in Avignon with the Diaspora (exile) of the first century. Avignon's Jews were nicknamed "the Pope's Jews" because of the protection that the Vatican offered to Jews expelled from France. While this synagogue dates from the 1220s, in the mid-19th century it was completely rebuilt in a Neoclassical, Greek-temple style by a non-Jewish architect. This is the only synagogue under a rotunda that you'll see anywhere. The ark holding the Torah is in the east, next to a list of the Jews who were deported from here to Auschwitz in 1942, after Vichy France was overtaken by the Nazis. To visit the synagogue, press the buzzer and friendly Rabbi Moshe Amar will be your guide (Mon–Fri 10:00–12:00 & 15:00–17:00, closed Sat–Sun, 2 place Jerusalem, tel. 04 90 55 21 24).

Rue des Teinturiers—This "Street of the Dyers" is Avignon's headquarters for all that's hip. You'll pass the Grey Penitents chapel about three small bridges down. The upper facade shows the GPs, who dressed up in robes and pointy hoods to do their anonymous good deeds back in the 13th century (long before the KKK dressed this way).

As you stroll, you'll see the work of amateur sculptors, who have carved whimsical car barriers out of limestone. Earthy cafés, galleries, and a small stream (a branch of the Sorgue River) with waterwheels line this tie-dyed street. This was the cloth industry's dyeing and textile center in the 1800s. Those stylish Provençal fabrics and patterns you see for sale everywhere started here, after a pattern imported from India.

For trendy restaurants on this atmospheric street, see "Eating," later in this chapter.

• *Farther down rue des Teinturiers, you'll come to the...*

Waterwheel—Standing here, imagine the Sorgue River—which hits the mighty Rhône in Avignon—being broken into several canals in order to turn 23 such wheels. In about 1800, waterwheels powered the town's industries. The little cogwheel above the big one could be shoved into place, kicking another machine into gear behind the wall. Across from the wheel at #41 is **La Cave Breysse,** offering regional wines by the glass and good lunch fare (see "Eating," later in this chapter).

Elsewhere in Avignon

Fondation Angladon-Dubrujeaud—Visiting this museum is like being invited into the elegant home of a rich and passionate art collector. It mixes a small but enjoyable collection of art from Post-Impressionists (including Paul Cézanne, Vincent van Gogh, Honoré Daumier, Edgar Degas, and Pablo Picasso) with re-created art studios and furnishings from many periods. It's a quiet place with a few superb paintings (€6; May–Nov Tue–Sun 13:00–18:00, closed Mon; Dec–April Wed–Sun 13:00–18:00, closed Mon–Tue; 5 rue Laboureur, tel. 04 90 82 29 03, www.angladon.com).

Calvet Museum (Musée Calvet)—This fine-arts museum impressively displays its good collection, and now provides an English-language audioguide with admission (€6; June–Sept Wed–Mon 10:00–18:00, closed Tue; Oct–May Wed–Mon 10:00–12:00 & 13:00–18:00, closed Tue; in the quieter western half of town at 65 rue Joseph Vernet, antiquities collection a few blocks away at 27 rue de la République—same hours and ticket, tel. 04 90 86 33 84, www.musee-calvet.org).

Near Avignon, in Villeneuve-lès-Avignon

▲**Tower of Philip the Fair (Tour Philippe-le-Bel)**—Built to protect access to St. Bénezet Bridge in 1307, this massive tower offers the finest view over Avignon and the Rhône basin. It's best late in the day (€2; April–Sept daily 10:00–12:30 & 14:00–18:30; March and Oct–Nov Tue–Sat 10:00–12:30 & 14:00–17:00, closed Sun–Mon; closed Dec–Feb; tel. 04 32 70 08 57). To reach the tower from Avignon, you can drive (5 min, cross Daladier Bridge, follow signs to *Villeneuve-lès-Avignon*); take a boat (Bateau-Bus departs from Mireio Embarcadère near Daladier Bridge); or take bus #11 (2/hr, catch bus in front of post office on cours Président Kennedy—see Avignon map earlier in this chapter).

Sleeping

Hotel values are better in Arles. Avignon is particularly popular during its July festival, when you must book ahead (expect inflated prices). Also note that only a few hotels have elevators—specifically, the first three listed near place de l'Horloge.

Near Avignon's Centre-Ville Station

The first three listings are a 10-minute walk from the Centre-Ville train station; turn right off cours Jean Jaurès on rue Agricol Perdiguier.

$$ Hôtel Colbert** is Avignon's best two-star hotel and a good midrange bet, with well-maintained and nicely decorated rooms in many sizes. Your efficient hosts—Patrice, Annie, and *le chien* Brittany—care for this restored manor house, with its warm public spaces and sweet little patio (Sb-€45–60, small Db-€60, bigger Db-€78, Tb-€98, air-con, Wi-Fi, parking-€9, 7 rue Agricol Perdiguier, tel. 04 90 86 20 20, fax 04 90 85 97 00, www.lecolbert -hotel.com, contact@avignon-hotel-colbert.com).

$$ Hôtel le Splendid* rents 17 simple but cheery rooms with wood floors and small but sharp bathrooms (Sb-€42–48, Db-€60, bigger Db with air-con-€70, Tb with air-con-€80, three

Avignon Hotels

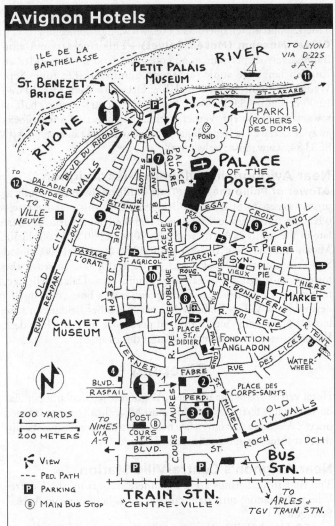

ILE DE LA BARTHELASSE

RIVER

TO LYON VIA D-225 & A-7 & ⑪

Petit Palais Museum

St. Benezet Bridge

RHONE

BLVD. ST-LAZARE

PARK (ROCHERS DES DOMS)

POND

BLVD. DU RHONE

R. FER

CITY WALLS

ST. ETIENNE

R. GROTTES

⑦

PALACE SQUARE

R. B. LANCE

Palace of the Popes

TO VILLE-NEUVE

DALADIER BRIDGE

TO ⑫

LOULLE

RUE

⑤

PLACE DE L'HORLOGE

PEY.

LEGAT

⑥

CROIX

R. CARNOT

⑨

St. Pierre

OLD RAMPART

PASSAGE L'ORAT.

ST. AGRICOL

RUE JOSEPH

⑩

MARCH.

ROUG.

RUE FOURB.

SYN.

VIEUX

PL. PIE

R. THIERS

MARKET

R. BONNETERIE

RUE TEINT

RUE DE LA REPUBLIQUE

⑧

R. ROI RENE

Calvet Museum

VERNET

PLACE ST. DIDIER

3 PILCONS

Fondation Angladon

RUE DES LICES

WATER-WHEEL

N

BLVD. RASPAIL

④

FABRE

②

PLACE DES CORPS-SAINTS

OLD CITY WALLS

200 YARDS
200 METERS

JAURES

PERD.

③ ①

ST. MICHEL

ROCH

DCH

TO NIMES VIA A-9

POST Ⓑ

COURS JFK

BLVD.

COURS

ST.

BUS STN.

View
--- Ped. Path
P Parking
Ⓑ Main Bus Stop

P

P

TRAIN STN. "CENTRE-VILLE"

TO ARLES & TGV TRAIN STN.

❶ Hôtel Colbert
❷ Hôtel du Parc
❸ Hôtel le Splendid
❹ Hôtel Boquier
❺ Hôtel d'Europe
❻ Hôtel Mercure Cité des Papes
❼ Hôtel Pont d'Avignon

❽ Hôtel de Blauvac
❾ Hôtel Médiéval
❿ Villa Agapè B&B
⓫ To Le Clos du Rempart Rooms & Lumani B&B
⓬ To Jardin de Bacchus Rooms & Auberge Bagatelle Hostel

Db apartments-€90, extra person-€10, discounts for stays longer than one week, 17 rue Agricol Perdiguier, tel. 04 90 86 14 46, fax 04 90 85 38 55, www.avignon-splendid-hotel.com, contacthotel @infonie.fr).

$ Hôtel du Parc* is a spotless value with white walls, tiny bathrooms, and stone accents. It's scrupulously managed by entertaining Avignon native Madame Rous, who bakes her own bread and pastries for breakfast—and even made the bedspreads by hand (S-€29, Ss-€39, D-€40, Ds-€48–56, Ts-€67, no TVs or phones, tel. 04 90 82 71 55, fax 04 90 85 64 86, http://perso.modulonet .fr/hoduparc, hotel.parc@modulonet.fr). This place is cheaper and homier than Hôtel le Splendid, across the street.

$ At Hôtel Boquier**, engaging Madame Sendra offers 12 quiet, good-value rooms under wood beams (small Db-€55, bigger Db-€68, Tb-€78, Qb-€90, extra bed-€10, air-con, Internet access and Wi-Fi, parking-€7, near the TI at 6 rue du portail Boquier, tel. 04 90 82 34 43, fax 04 90 86 14 07, www.hotel-boquier.com, contact@hotel-boquier.com).

In the Center, near Place de l'Horloge

$$$ Hôtel d'Europe****, with Avignon's most prestigious address, lets peasants sleep royally—if you get one of the 10 surprisingly reasonable "standard rooms." Enter a fountain-filled courtyard, linger in the lounges, and savor every comfort. The hotel is located on the handsome place Crillon, near the river (standard Db-€175, first-class Db-€350, superior Db-€495, breakfast-€25, elevator, Internet access, garage-€16, near Daladier Bridge at 12 place Crillon, tel. 04 90 14 76 76, fax 04 90 14 76 71, www.heurope.com, reservations@heurope.com). The hotel's restaurant is Michelin-rated (one star) and serves an upscale €50 *menu* in its formal dining room or front courtyard.

$$$ Hôtel Mercure Cité des Papes*** is a modern chain hotel within spitting distance of the Palace of the Popes. It has 89 smartly designed small rooms (Sb-€115, Db-€130–170, many rooms have views over place de l'Horloge, air-con, elevator, 1 rue Jean Vilar, tel. 04 90 80 93 00, fax 04 90 80 93 01, www.mercure .com, h1952@accor.com).

$$$ Hôtel Pont d'Avignon***, just inside the walls near St. Bénezet Bridge, is part of the same chain as the Hôtel Mercure Cité des Papes, with the same prices for its 87 rooms (direct access to a garage makes parking easier than at the other Mercure hotel, elevator, on rue Ferruce, tel. 04 90 80 93 93, fax 04 90 80 93 94, www.mercure.com, h0549@accor.com).

$$ At Hôtel de Blauvac**, friendly owner Veronica manages 16 mostly spacious, plush-carpeted, high-ceilinged rooms (many with an additional upstairs loft). It's a faded old manor home with

PROVENCE

a sky-high atrium. Its location near the pedestrian zone means reliable noise at night (Sb-€70–80, Db-€75–85, Tb-€90–100, Qb-€105, €10 less off-season, Internet access, 1 block off rue de la République at 11 rue de la Bancasse, tel. 04 90 86 34 11, fax 04 90 86 27 41, www.hotel-blauvac.com, blauvac@aol.com).

$$ Hôtel Médiéval** is burrowed deep a few blocks from the Church of St. Pierre. Built as a cardinal's home, this massive stone mansion has a small garden and friendly-as-they-get Mike at the helm. It has 35 wood-paneled, air-conditioned, unimaginative rooms (Sb-€49, Db-€59–74, bigger Db or Tb-€83–90, kitchenettes available but require 3-night minimum stay, Wi-Fi, 5 blocks east of place de l'Horloge, behind Church of St. Pierre at 15 rue Petite Saunerie, tel. 04 90 86 11 06, fax 04 90 82 08 64, www.hotel medieval.com, hotel.medieval@wanadoo.fr).

Chambres d'Hôte

$$$ Villa Agapè, just off busy place de l'Horloge (right in the center of town), is an oasis of calm and good taste. Run by friendly Madame de La Pommeraye, the villa has three handsomely decorated rooms, a peaceful courtyard, lovely public spaces, and a soaking pool to boot (Db-€100–150, extra person-€30, includes breakfast, 2-night minimum, closed in July, Internet access and Wi-Fi, from place de l'Horloge it's one block down on left above the pharmacy at 13 rue St. Agricol—ring buzzer, tel. & fax 04 90 85 21 92, mobile 06 07 98 71 30, www.villa-agape.com, michele @villa-agape.com). For a weeklong stay, ask about renting her entire house, where you get Madame's room, study, and kitchen (€2,500–3,300).

$$$ At **Le Clos du Rempart,** Madame Assad, another Parisian refugee, rents two rooms and one apartment on a pleasant courtyard decorated in a Middle Eastern theme, complete with a hammock. It's less central but close enough for many (Db-€100–140 depending on season and room size, 2-bedroom apartment for 4 with kitchen-€175–230, apartment cheaper by the week, includes breakfast, air-con, Wi-Fi, 1 parking spot in garage, inside the walls east of the Pope's Palace at 35–37 rue Crémade—call or check website for directions, tel. & fax 04 90 86 39 14, www.clos durempart.com, aida@closdurempart.com).

$$$ Lumani provides the ultimate urban refuge just inside the city walls, a 15-minute walk from the Pope's Palace. In this graceful old manor house, gentle Elisabeth and Jean welcome guests to their art-gallery-cum-bed-and-breakfast that surrounds a fountain-filled courtyard with elbow room. She paints, he designs buildings, and both care about your experience in Avignon. The five rooms are decorated with flair; no two are alike and all overlook the shady garden (small Db-€100, big Db-€130, Db suites-€160, extra person-€25, includes breakfast, Internet access and Wi-Fi, music studio, parking-€10 or easy on street, 37 rue de Rempart St Lazare, tel. 04 90 82 94 11, www.avignon-lumani.com, lux @avignon-lumani.com).

On the Outskirts of Town

$ Auberge Bagatelle's hostel offers dirt-cheap beds, a lively atmosphere, café, grocery store, launderette, great views of Avignon, and campers for neighbors (D-€40, dorm bed-€17, across Daladier Bridge on Ile de la Barthelasse, bus #10 from main post office, tel. 04 90 86 71 31, fax 04 90 27 16 23, www.aubergebagatelle.fr, auberge.bagatelle@wanadoo.fr).

Near Avignon

$$ At **Jardin de Bacchus,** just 15 minutes northwest of Avignon and convenient to the Pont du Gard, enthusiastic and English-speaking Christine and Erik offer three rooms in their rural farmhouse overlooking little Tavel's famous vineyards (Db-€75–80, 2-night minimum or add €20, fine dinner possible, Wi-Fi, tel. 04 66 90 28 62, www.provence-escapade.fr, jardindebacchus@free.fr). Ask about their cooking classes.

Eating

Skip the overpriced places on place de l'Horloge (L'Opéra Café and La Civette near the carousel are the least of the evils here) and find a more intimate location for your dinner. Avignon has many delightful squares filled with tables ready to seat you.

Near the Church of St. Pierre

The church divides two enchanting squares. One is quiet and intimate, the other is lively.

L'Epicerie, sitting alone on an intimate square, serves the highest-quality and highest-priced cuisine around the Church of St. Pierre (€20–25 *plats,* closed Sun off-season, cozy interior good in bad weather, 10 place St. Pierre, tel. 04 90 82 74 22).

On Place des Châtaignes: Pass under the arch by L'Epicerie restaurant and enter enchanting place des Châtaignes, with a tasty commotion of tables from four restaurants. The first you'll come to is **La Goulette,** featuring Tunisian specialties like couscous and *tagine* (slow-cooked meals in a special pot from €15, closed Mon, tel. 04 90 86 06 69). **Crêperie du Cloître** sells cheap salads and dinner crêpes (closed Sun–Mon, cash only). **Restaurant Nem,** tucked in the corner, is Vietnamese and family-run (*menus* from €12, cash only). **Pause Gourmande** is a small lunch-only eatery with €9 *plats du jour* and always has a veggie option (closed Sun).

Avignon Restaurants

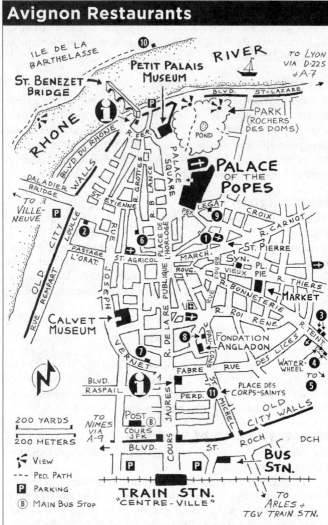

① Restaurants near Church of St. Pierre

② Place de Crillon Restaurants

③ La Cave Breysse Wine Bar & Restaurant l'Empreinte

④ Woolloomooloo Restaurant

⑤ To Restaurant Numéro 75

⑥ L'Isle Sonnante Restaurant

⑦ La Compagnie des Comptoirs Restaurant

⑧ Le Caveau du Théâtre Rest.

⑨ Hôtel la Mirande Restaurant

⑩ Le Bercail Restaurant

⑪ Place des Corps-Saints Restaurants

PROVENCE

Place Crillon

This large and trendy square just off the river attracts a stylish crowd. Several cafés offer inexpensive bistro fare with *menus* from €16, *plats* from €12, and many tables to choose from. **Restaurant les Artistes** seems most popular (€16 *menu,* daily until 22:30, 21 place Crillon, tel. 04 90 82 23 54), while **Café Le Crillon** is most refined and more pricey (closed Sun).

Place des Corps-Saints

You'll find several relaxed and reasonable eateries with tables sprawling under big plane tress on this shady square. **Cuisine et Comptoire** attracts the café crowd (closed Sun, tel. 04 90 82 18 39), though I enjoy the €10 pizzas and friendly service at **Le Pili** (daily, tel. 04 90 27 39 53).

Rue des Teinturiers

This "happening" street has a wonderful concentration of eateries popular with the natives, and justifies the long walk. It's a youthful and trendy area, recently spiffed up with a canalside ambience and little hint of tourism. I'd survey the eateries listed here before choosing.

La Cave Breysse is a fun and colorful pause before dinner. Midday or evening, Christine and Tim would love to serve you a fragrant €2.50 glass of regional wine. Choose from the blackboard by the bar that lists all the bottles open today, then join the gang outside by the canal. In the evening, this place is a hit with the young local crowd for its wine (flexible hours, usually Tue–Sat 12:00–14:30 & 18:00–22:30, closed Sun–Mon, no food in evening; across from waterwheel at 41 rue des Teinturiers).

L'Empreinte is good for North African cuisine. Choose a table in its tent-like interior, or sit canalside on the cobbles (copious couscous for €13–20, take-out and veggie options available, open daily, 33 rue des Teinturiers, tel. 04 32 76 31 84).

Woolloomooloo was named, Dada-style, for the aboriginal term for "little black kangaroo." It's a funky and young-spirited eatery...think Van Gogh drunk on rum-and-fruit punch. The food—while slopped together from a precooked buffet—is hearty, creative, and a fair value. You'll mix and match from a very fun menu (2 courses-€22, 3 courses-€28, 3 courses matched with 3 wines-€36, open daily, frequent jazz evenings, 16 rue des Teinturiers, tel. 04 90 85 28 44).

Restaurant Numéro 75 is worth the walk (just past where the cobbles end on rue de Teinturiers), filling the Pernod mansion (of *pastis* liquor fame) and a large, romantic courtyard with outdoor tables. The menu is limited to Mediterranean cuisine, but everything's *très* tasty. It's best to go with the options offered by your young, black-shirted server (2-course lunch *menu* with wine and coffee-€20; dinner *menus:* appetizer and main course or main course and dessert-€27, 3 courses-€33; Mon–Sat 12:00–14:00 & 20:00–22:00, closed Sun, 75 rue Guillaume Puy, tel. 04 90 27 16 00).

Elsewhere in Avignon

At **L'Isle Sonnante,** join chef Boris and his wife Anne to dine intimately in their formal and charming one-room *bistrot.* You'll choose from a small menu offering only fresh products and be served by owners who care (*menus* from €27, closed Sun–Mon, 100 yards from the carousel on place de l'Horloge at 7 rue Racine, tel. 04 90 82 56 01, best to book ahead).

La Compagnie des Comptoirs is the brainchild of famous twin-brother chefs who established a following in southern France with their inventive cuisine. Enter a white world of cool bars, sleek interiors, and a grand courtyard (the restaurant's highlight). This is where young Avignon professionals meet to enjoy foods from the Mediterranean basin (allow €45 for dinner with wine, or enjoy the same cuisine and ambience for far less at lunch—€10–12 *plats du jour,* 83 rue Joseph Vernet, tel. 04 90 85 99 04).

Le Caveau du Théâtre invites relaxed diners to share a glass of wine or dinner at one of their sidewalk tables, or to come inside and enjoy the carefree interior (€13 *plats,* €18 *menus,* fun ambience for free, closed Sun, 16 rue des Trois Faucons, tel. 04 90 82 60 91).

Hôtel la Mirande is the ultimate Avignon splurge. Reserve ahead here for understated elegance and Avignon's top cuisine (€35 lunch *menu,* €105 dinner tasting *menu;* closed Tue–Wed—but for a price break, dine in the kitchen with the chef on these "closed" days for €85 including wine; behind Palace of the Popes, 4 place de la Mirande, tel. 04 90 86 93 93, fax 04 90 86 26 85).

Across the River

Le Bercail offers a fun opportunity to get out of town (barely) and take in *le fresh air* with a terrific riverfront view of Avignon, all while enjoying inexpensive Provençal cooking served in big portions. Book ahead, as this restaurant is popular (*menus* from €16, serves late, daily April–Oct, tel. 04 90 82 20 22).

To get there, take the small shuttle boat (located near St. Bénezet Bridge) to the Ile de la Barthelasse, turn right, and walk five minutes. As the boat usually stops running at about 18:00 (except in July–Aug, when it runs until 21:00), you can either taxi home or walk 25 minutes along the pleasant riverside path and over Daladier Bridge.

Connections

Trains

Remember, there are two train stations in Avignon: the suburban TGV station and the Centre-Ville station in the city center (€1.20 shuttle buses connect to both stations, buy ticket from driver, 3/ hr, 15 min). Only the Centre-Ville station has baggage storage (see "Arrival in Avignon," earlier in this chapter). Car rental is available at the TGV station. Some cities, such as Paris, are served both by slower local trains (including some slower TGV trains) from the Centre-Ville station and by faster TGV trains from the TGV station; I've listed the most convenient stations for each trip.

From Avignon's Centre-Ville Station by Train to: Arles (11/ day, 20 min, less frequent in the afternoon), **Nîmes** (14/day, 30 min), **Lyon** (10/day, 2 hrs, also from TGV station—see below), **Barcelona** (2/day, 6 hrs, transfer in Montpellier).

From Avignon's TGV Station to: Arles (by SNCF bus, 11/ day, 1 hr), **Nice** (20/day, 13 of which are via TGV, 4 hrs, most require transfer in Marseille), **Lyon** (12/day, 1.5 hrs, also from Centre-Ville station—see above), **Paris'** Gare de Lyon (9/day in 2.5 hrs, 6/day in 3–4 hrs with change), **Paris'** Charles de Gaulle airport (7/day, 3 hrs).

Buses

The bus station *(gare routière)* is just past and below the Ibis Hôtel, to the right as you exit the train station (information desk open Mon–Fri 10:15–13:00 & 14:00–18:00, Sat 8:00–12:00, closed Sun, tel. 04 90 82 07 35). Nearly all buses leave from this station. The biggest exception is the SNCF bus service from the Avignon TGV station to Arles (see above). The Avignon TI has schedules. Service is reduced or nonexistent on Sundays and holidays. Check your departure time beforehand and make sure to verify your destination with the driver.

From Avignon to Pont du Gard: Buses go to this famous old aqueduct (3/day, 50 min, departs from bus station, usually from stall #11), but the schedule doesn't work well for day-trippers from Avignon; instead, consider a taxi one-way and bus back (see "Getting to the Pont du Gard—By Taxi" in the following section).

Pont du Gard

Throughout the ancient world, aqueducts were flags of stone that heralded the greatness of Rome. A visit to the Pont du Gard still works to proclaim the wonders of that age. This perfectly preserved Roman aqueduct was built as the critical link of a 30-mile canal that, by dropping one inch for every 350 feet, supplied nine million gallons of water per day (about 100 gallons per second) to Nîmes—one of ancient Europe's largest cities. Though most of the aqueduct is on or below the ground, at the Pont du Gard it spans a canyon on a massive bridge—one of the most remarkable surviving Roman ruins anywhere.

Getting to the Pont du Gard

The famous aqueduct is between Remoulins and Vers-Pont du Gard on D-981, 17 miles from Nîmes and 13 miles from Avignon.

By Car: Pont du Gard is an easy 25-minute drive due west of Avignon on N-100 and D-981 (follow signs to *Nîmes*, then *Pont du Gard*) and 45 minutes northwest of Arles (via Tarascon). The handy Rive Gauche parking is off D-981 (the road from Remoulins to Uzès). (Parking is also available on the Rive Droite side, but it's farther away from the museum.) If going to Arles from Pont du Gard, follow signs to *Nîmes* (not Avignon), then follow D-986.

By Bus: Buses run to the Pont du Gard (on the Rive Gauche side) from Avignon, Nîmes, and Uzès, but schedules are not well-coordinated. Consider this plan: Take the 12:05 bus from Avignon, arriving at Pont du Gard at 12:50, then take the 14:45 bus from there to Nîmes (where trains run hourly back to Avignon).

Most buses stop at the traffic roundabout 300 yards from the aqueduct. In summer and on weekends, however, buses usually drive into the Pont du Gard site and stop at the parking lot's ticket booth. You can confirm where the bus stops at the parking booth inside the Pont du Gard site.

At the roundabout, the stop for buses coming from Avignon and Nîmes is on the side opposite of Pont du Gard; the stop for buses to Nîmes and to Avignon is on the same side as Pont du Gard (see Pont du Gard map). Make sure you're waiting for the bus on the correct side of the traffic circle, and use your hand to signal the bus to stop for you (otherwise, it'll chug on by). Buy your ticket when you get on, and verify your destination with the driver.

By Taxi: From Nîmes or Avignon, it's about €42 for a taxi ride to Pont du Gard (tel. 04 66 29 40 11). If you're staying in Avignon and only want to see the Pont du Gard (and not Nîmes or Uzès), consider splurging on a taxi to the aqueduct in the morning, then take the early afternoon bus back.

Orientation

There are two riversides to Pont du Gard: the Left Bank (Rive Gauche) and Right Bank (Rive Droite). Park on the Rive Gauche, where you'll find the museums, ticket booth, ATM, cafeteria, WCs, and shops—all built into a modern plaza. You'll see the aqueduct in two parts: first the fine museum complex, then the actual river gorge spanned by the ancient bridge.

Cost: While it's free to see the aqueduct itself, the optional activities cost extra: parking (€5), museum (€7), corny film (€4), and a kids' space called *Ludo* (€5, scratch-and-sniff experience in English of various aspects of Roman life and the importance of water). The extensive outdoor *garrigue* natural area, featuring historic crops and landscapes of the Mediterranean, is free (though €4 buys you a helpful English booklet). All these attractions are designed to give the sight more meaning—and they do—but for most visitors, only the museum is worth paying for. Those on a budget can skip the pay sights, just pay €5 for parking, and enjoy the aqueduct for free.

The €12 **combo-ticket** (€9 for kids ages 6–17) covers all sights and parking, and includes the €4 booklet to the *garrigue* natural area. If you want to see all the sights, this is a good value. Families save with the €24 **family ticket** (covers 2 parents and up to 4 kids). If you get a combo-ticket, check the movie schedule; the romancing-the-aqueduct 25-minute film is silly, but it offers good information in a flirtatious French-Mediterranean style...and a cool, entertaining, and cushy break.

For an extra €6, you can rent an **audioguide** for detailed explanations of the aqueduct in English.

Hours: The museum is open May–Sept Tue–Sun 9:30–19:00, Mon 13:00–19:00; Oct–April closes at 17:00; closed two weeks in Jan. The aqueduct itself is free and open until 1:00 in the morning, as is the parking lot. Tel. 08 20 90 33 30, www.pontdugard.fr.

Canoe Rental: Consider seeing Pont du Gard by canoe. Collias Canoes will pick you up at Pont du Gard (or elsewhere, if prearranged) and shuttle you to the town of Collias. You'll float down the river to the nearby town of Remoulins, where they'll pick you up and take you back to Pont du Gard (€18/person, €9/child under 12, usually 2 hrs though you can take as long as you like, good idea to reserve the day before in July–Aug, tel. 04 66 22 85 54).

Plan Ahead for Swimming: Pont du Gard is perhaps best

Pont du Gard

PONT DU GARD

— ROAD
--- PATH
↗ VIEW
🅿 PARKING

GARRIGUE NATURAL AREA

TO REMOULINS & NÎMES

🅿 (RIVE DROITE) DON'T PARK HERE

MUSEUM COMPLEX
CINEMA, LUDO (KIDS' SPACE), INFO, SHOP, WC & RESTAURANT

❸

🅿 (RIVE GAUCHE) PARK HERE

GARDON RIVER

D-981

D-981

TO UZÈS

❷

❶ ← ROUNDABOUT

TO REMOULINS, NÎMES, AVIGNON, ARLES & A-9 FREEWAY

❶ Bus Stop from Avignon & Nîmes
❷ Bus Stop to Avignon & Nîmes
❸ Bus Stop (Summer & Weekends)

NOT TO SCALE: MUSEUM TO PONT DU GARD IS A 5-MINUTE WALK

DCH

enjoyed on your back and in the water—bring along a swimsuit, and sandals for the rocks.

Sights

▲**Museum**—The state-of-the-art museum's multimedia approach (well-presented in English) shows how water was an essential part of the Roman "art of living." You'll see examples of lead pipes, faucets, and siphons; walk through a rock quarry; and learn how they moved those huge rocks into place and how those massive arches were made. While actual artifacts from the aqueduct are few, the exhibit shows the immensity of the undertaking as well as the payoff. Imagine the excitement as this extravagant supply of water finally tumbled into Nîmes. A relaxing highlight is the scenic video helicopter ride along the entire 30-mile course of the structure, from its start at Uzès all the way to the Castellum in Nîmes.

▲▲▲**Viewing the Aqueduct**—A park-like path leads to the aqueduct. Until a few years ago, this was an actual road—adjacent

PROVENCE

to the aqueduct—that had spanned the river since 1743. Before you cross the bridge, pass under it and hike about 300 feet along the riverbank for a grand viewpoint from which to study the second-highest standing Roman structure. (Rome's Colosseum is only 6 feet taller.)

This was the biggest bridge in the whole 30-mile-long aqueduct. It seems exceptional because it is: The arches are twice the width of standard aqueducts, and the main arch is the largest the Romans ever built—80 feet (so it wouldn't get its feet wet). The bridge is about 160 feet high and was originally about 1,100 feet long. Today, 12 arches are missing, reducing the length to 790 feet.

While the distance from the source (in Uzès) to Nîmes was only 12 miles as the eagle flew, engineers chose the most economical route, winding and zigzagging 30 miles. The water made the trip in 24 hours with a drop of only 40 feet. Ninety percent of the aqueduct is on or under the ground, but a few river canyons like this required bridges. A stone lid hides a four-foot-wide, six-foot-tall chamber lined with waterproof mortar that carried the stream for more than 400 years. For 150 years, this system provided Nîmes with good drinking water. Expert as the Romans were, they miscalculated the backup caused by a downstream corner, and had to add the thin extra layer you can see just under the lid to make the channel deeper.

The appearance of the entire gorge changed in 2002, when a huge flood flushed lots of greenery downstream. Those floodwaters put Roman provisions to the test. Notice the triangular-shaped buttresses at the lower level—designed to split and divert the force of any flood *around* the feet of the arches rather than *into* them. The 2002 floodwaters reached the top of those buttresses. Anxious park rangers winced at the sounds of trees crashing onto the ancient stones...but the arches stood strong.

The stones that jut out—giving the aqueduct a rough, unfinished appearance—supported the original scaffolding. The protuberances were left, rather than cut off, in anticipation of future repair needs. The lips under the arches supported wooden templates that allowed the stones in the round arches to rest on something until the all-important keystone was dropped into place. Each stone weighs four to six tons. The structure stands with no mortar—taking full advantage of the innovative Roman arch, made strong by gravity.

Walk across the bridge for a closer look. Across the river, a high trail (marked *panorama*) leads upstream and offers commanding views. On the exhibit side of the structure, a trail marked *Accès l'Aqueduc* leads up to surviving stretches of the aqueduct. For a peaceful walk alongside the top of the aqueduct (where it's on land and no longer a bridge), follow the red-and-yellow markings.

Remains of this part are scant because of medieval cannibalization—frugal builders couldn't resist the precut stones as they constructed local churches. The ancient quarry (about a third of a mile downstream on the exhibit side) may be open to the public by the time you visit.

NICE on the FRENCH RIVIERA

La Côte d'Azur

A hundred years ago, celebrities from London to Moscow flocked to the French Riviera to socialize, gamble, and escape the dreary weather at home. Belle époque resorts now also cater to budget vacationers at France's most sought-after fun-in-the-sun destination.

Some of the Continent's most stunning scenery and intriguing museums lie along this strip of land—as do millions of heat-seeking tourists. Evenings on the Riviera, a.k.a. the Côte d'Azur, were made for a stroll and outdoor dining.

My favorite home base is Nice, the region's capital and France's fifth-largest city. With convenient train and bus connections to most regional sights, it's practical for train travelers. Urban Nice has a full palette of world-class museums, a grand beachfront promenade, and a seductive old town (and all the drawbacks of a major city: traffic, crime, pollution, etc.). Nice also has the best selection of hotels in all price ranges, and good nightlife options. A car is a headache in Nice, though it's easily stored at one of the many pricey parking garages.

Getting Around the Riviera

Nice is perfectly situated for exploring the Riviera by public transport. Villefranche-sur-Mer, Antibes, and Cannes are all within a one-hour bus or train ride of each other. Boats go from Nice to Monaco and St-Tropez.

By Bus and Train: Many key Riviera destinations are connected by direct bus or train service from Nice, and some are served by both. Since bus fare is only €1, the pricier train is a better choice only when it saves you time (which it generally does—there is no faster way to move about the Riviera than by train). All trains

The French Riviera

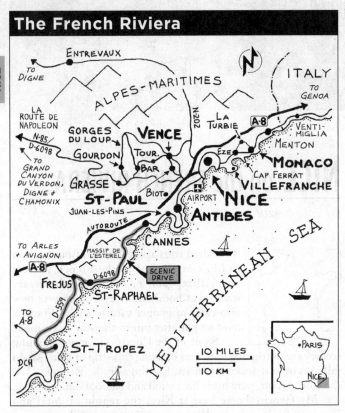

serving Nice arrive at and depart from the Nice-Ville station.

You make the call—both modes of transportation work well. All prices are one-way. The following bus frequencies are for Monday–Saturday. Sundays either have limited or no service.

Destination	Bus from Nice	Train from Nice
Villefranche	4/hr, 20 min	2/hr, 10 min, €1.80
Cap Ferrat	every 40 min, 30 min (no service on Sun)	none
Monaco	4/hr, 45 min	2/hr, 20 min, €3.40
Antibes	2–4/hr, 1–1.5 hrs	2/hr, 15–30 min, €3.90
Cannes	2–4/hr, 1.5–1.75 hrs	2/hr, 30–40 min, €6

By Minivan Excursion: A tour with lively **Sylvie Di Cristo**, who loves to teach about the area's culture and history, is a splurge worth considering (€170/person for 2–3 people, €120/person for 4–6 people, car or minivan, 2-person minimum, mobile 06 09 88

83 83, www.azur-guides.net, sylvie.di.cristo@wanadoo.fr). The TI and most hotels have information on other minivan excursions from Nice (€50–60/half-day, €80–110/day). **Med-Tour** is one of many (tel. 04 93 82 92 58 or 06 73 82 04 10, www.med-tour.com); **Tour Azur** is a bit pricier (tel. 04 93 44 88 77, www.tourazur.com); and **Revelation Tours** specializes in English excursions (tel. 04 93 53 69 85, www.revelation-tours.com). All companies also offer private tours by the day or half-day (check with them for their outrageous prices, about €90/hr).

By Boat: From June to mid-September, Trans Côte d'Azur offers scenic trips from Nice to Monaco and Nice to St-Tropez. Boats leave in the morning and return in the evening, giving you all day to explore your destination. Drinks and WCs are available on board. Boats to **Monaco** depart at 9:30 and return at 18:00 (€28 round-trip, 45 min each way, June–Sept Tue, Thu, and Sat only). Boats to **St-Tropez** depart at 9:00 and return at 19:00 (€50 round-trip, 2.5 hrs each way; July–Aug Tue–Sun, no boats Mon; late June and early Sept Tue, Thu, and Sun only). Reservations are required for both boats, and tickets for St-Tropez often sell out, so book a few days ahead (tel. 04 92 00 42 30, fax 04 92 00 42 31, www.trans-cote-azur.com). The boats leave from Nice's port, bassin des Amiraux, just below Castle Hill—look for the blue ticket booth *(billeterie)* on quai de Lunel (see map on page 437). The same company also runs one-hour round-trip cruises along the coast to Cap Ferrat (see "Tours," later in this chapter).

Nice

Nice (sounds like "niece"), with its spectacular Alps-to-Mediterranean surroundings, eternally entertaining seafront promenade, and intriguing museums, is an enjoyable big-city highlight of the Riviera. In its traffic-free old city, Italian and French flavors mix to create a spicy Mediterranean dressing. Nice may be nice, but it's hot and jammed in July and August—reserve ahead and get a room with air-conditioning *(une chambre avec climatisation)*. Everything you'll want to see in Nice is within walking distance, or a short bus or tram ride away.

Orientation

Most recommended sights and hotels are between the train station and the beach, near avenue Jean Médecin or boulevard Victor Hugo. It's a 20-minute walk (or a €10 taxi ride) from the train station to the beach, and a 20-minute walk along the promenade from the fancy Hôtel Negresco to the heart of Old Nice.

You can also hop aboard the new tramway (the first of three planned lines is finally running). A quick 10-minute (€1) ride takes you through the center of the city, connecting the train station, Old Nice, and the bus station. All city and regional buses cost only €1 per trip, making this one of the cheapest and easiest cities in France to get around (see "Getting Around Nice," later in this section).

Tourist Information

Nice's helpful TI has three locations: at the **airport** (in Terminal 1, daily 8:00–21:00, closed Sun off-season), next to the **train station** (usually busy; summer Mon–Sat 8:00–20:00, Sun 9:00–18:00; rest of year Mon–Sat 9:00–19:00, Sun 10:00–17:00), and facing the **beach** at 5 promenade des Anglais (usually quiet, daily 9:00–18:00, until 20:00 July–Aug, closed Sun off-season, tel. 08 92 70 74 07—costs €0.34/min, www.nicetourisme.com). Pick up the thorough *Practical Guide to Nice,* information on day trips (such as city maps and details on boat excursions), and a free Nice map (or find a better one at your hotel).

Arrival in Nice

By Train: All trains stop at Nice's main station, Nice-Ville (also called Gare Thiers, baggage storage at the far right with your back to the tracks, lockers open daily 7:00–21:45, left luggage desk Mon–Sat 8:45–12:00 & 14:00–15:45, closed Sun). This is one busy station, and theft is a problem, so never leave your bags unattended.

Turn left out of the station to find a branch of the **TI** a few steps away. Continue a few more blocks for the Gare Thiers **tram stop** (this will take you to place Masséna, the old city, and bus station). Board the tram on the near side of the street (the one heading toward the right, direction Pont Michel; see "Getting Around Nice," later in this section). Many of my recommended **hotels** are a 10- to 15-minute walk down the same street (see "Sleeping— Between Nice Etoile and the Sea" later in this chapter).

To find **car rental** offices and more recommended **hotels,** turn right out of the station. To get to the hotels, cross avenue Thiers, then walk down the steps by Hôtel Interlaken. If you'd rather head to the beach, continue past these hotels and keep walking down avenue Durante as it turns into rue des Congrés to reach the heart of Nice's beachfront promenade.

For **taxis** or for **buses to the airport,** walk straight out of the train station. You'll find taxis in the first lane, express airport bus #99 in the second lane, and local airport bus #23 in the third lane.

NICE

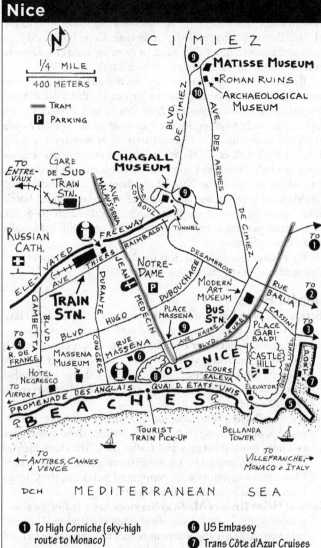

Nice

N

1/4 MILE
400 METERS

— TRAM
P PARKING

CIMIEZ

MATISSE MUSEUM
ROMAN RUINS
ARCHAEOLOGICAL
MUSEUM

BLVD. DE CIMIEZ
AVE. DES ARENES
AVE. DE CIMIEZ

TO
ENTRE-
VAUX

GARE
DE SUD
TRAIN
STN.

AVE. MALAUSSENA

CHAGALL
MUSEUM

AVE. COMBOUL

FREEWAY

TUNNEL

RUSSIAN
CATH.

RAIMBALDI

DESAMBROIS

TO
1

ELEVATED AVE. THIERS

JEAN MEDECIN

DURANTE

NOTRE-
DAME

DUBOUCHAGE

MODERN
ART
MUSEUM

RUE
BARLA

TO
2

GAMBETTA BLVD.

HUGO

P

PLACE
MASSENA

BUS
STN.

CASSINI

PLACE
GARI-
BALDI

TO
3

TRAIN
STN.

BLVD

CONGRES

RUE
MASSENA

AVE. FAURE

BLVD JAURES

CASTLE
HILL

QUAI DE LUNEL

PORT

TO
4
R. DE
FRANCE

MASSENA
MUSEUM

OLD NICE

TO
AIRPORT

HOTEL
NEGRESCO

PROMENADE DES ANGLAIS

COURS
SALEYA

QUAI D. ETATS-UNIS

ELEVATOR

TO
7

B E A C H E S

BELLANDA
TOWER

5

TOURIST
TRAIN PICK-UP

TO
ANTIBES, CANNES
& VENCE

DCH

TO
VILLEFRANCHE,
MONACO & ITALY

MEDITERRANEAN   SEA

1 To High Corniche (sky-high route to Monaco)

2 To Middle Corniche (middle route, best for Monaco & Eze-le-Village)

3 To Low Corniche (low route to Villefranche-sur-Mer & Cap Ferrat)

4 To Fine Arts Museum

5 World War II Monument

6 US Embassy

7 Trans Côte d'Azur Cruises

8 Le Grand Tour Bus Departure Point & Albert I Park

9 Bus #22 Stops (3)

10 Bus #17 Stops

By Bus: Nice's bus station *(gare routière)* is sandwiched between boulevard Jean Jaurès and avenue Félix Faure, next to the old city. The station has no baggage storage. Cross boulevard Jean Jaurès and enter teeming Old Nice, or cross avenue Félix Faure to get to my recommended hotels near Nice Etoile.

By Car: Driving into the city on the autoroute from the west, take the first Nice exit (for the airport—called Côte d'Azur, Central) and follow signs for *Nice Centre* and *Promenade des Anglais.* (Be ready to cross three left lanes of traffic as soon as you get off the autoroute.) Try to avoid arriving at rush hour (usually Mon–Fri 8:00–9:30 & 17:00–19:30), when promenade des Anglais grinds to a halt. Hoteliers know where to park (allow €14–20/day). The parking garage at the Nice Etoile shopping center on avenue Jean Médecin is pricey but near many of my recommended hotels (ticket booth on third floor, about €20/day, €10–12 20:00–8:00). All on-street parking is metered (9:00–18:00 or 19:00), but usually free all day on Sunday.

By Plane: For information on Nice's handy airport, see "Connections," at the end of this chapter.

Helpful Hints

Theft Alert: Nice has more than its share of pickpockets. Have nothing important on or around your waist, unless it's in a money belt tucked out of sight (thieves target fanny packs); don't leave anything visible in your car; be wary of scooters when standing at intersections; don't leave things unattended on the beach while swimming; and stick to main streets in Old Nice after dark.

Events: The Riviera is famous for staging major events. Unless you're actually taking part in the festivities, these events give you only room shortages and traffic jams. The three biggies are the Nice Carnival (www.nicecarnaval.com), Grand Prix of Monaco (www.yourmonaco.com/grand_prix), and the Cannes Film Festival (www.festival-cannes.fr).

Medical Help: Riviera Medical Services has a list of English-speaking physicians for anywhere along the Riviera. They can help you make an appointment or call an ambulance (tel. 04 93 26 12 70, www.rivieramedical.com).

Sightseeing Tips: On Mondays, the following sights are closed: the Modern and Contemporary Art Museum, Fine Arts Museum, and cours Saleya market. On Tuesdays, the Chagall, Matisse, and Archaeological museums are closed. Nice's city museums are free of charge (except the Chagall Museum and the Russian Cathedral).

Internet Access: There's no shortage of places to get online in Nice—they're everywhere. Ask at your hotel, or just look up as you walk (keep your eye out for the @ symbol).

English Bookstore: The Cat's Whiskers has an eclectic selection of novels and regional travel books, including mine. Say *bonjour* to mellow owner Linda (Tue–Sat 10:00–12:00 & 14:00–19:00, closed Sun–Mon, 26–30 rue Lamartine—located on Nice Hotels map in "Sleeping," later in this chapter, tel. 04 93 80 02 66).

Laundry: You'll find launderettes everywhere in Nice—ask your hotelier for the nearest one. The self-service **Point Laverie** is centrally located (daily 8:00–20:00, at the corner of rue Alberti and rue Pastorelli, next to Hôtel Vendôme—see Nice Hotels map in "Sleeping").

Grocery Store: The big **Monoprix** on avenue Jean Médecin and rue Biscarra has it all, including a deli counter, bakery, and cold drinks (closed Sun, see Nice Restaurants map in "Eating," later in this chapter). You'll also find many small grocery stores (some open Sun and/or until late hours) near my recommended hotels.

Renting a Bike (and Other Wheels): Roller Station rents bikes (*vélos*, €5/hr, €10/half-day, €15/day), inline skates (*rollers*, €6/day), Razor-type scooters (*trotinettes*, €6/half-day, €9/day), and skateboards (€6/half-day, €9/day). You'll need to leave your ID as a deposit (daily 9:30–19:00, July–Aug until 20:00, next to yellow awnings of Pailin's Asian restaurant at 49 quai des Etats-Unis—see Old Nice Hotels and Restaurants map in "Sleeping," another location at 10 rue Cassini near place Garibaldi, tel. 04 93 62 99 05, owner Eric).

Car Rental: Renting a car is easiest at Nice's airport, which has offices for all the major companies. You'll also find most companies represented at Nice's train station.

English Radio: Tune into Riviera-Radio at FM 106.5.

Views: For panoramic views, climb Castle Hill (listed in "Sights"), or take a one-hour boat trip (listed in "Tours").

Rocky Beaches: To make life tolerable on the rocks, swimmers should buy a pair of the cheap plastic beach shoes sold at many shops (flip-flops fall off in the water). Try **Go Sport** (daily 10:00–19:00, 13 place Masséna—see Old Nice Hotels and Restaurants map in "Sleeping").

Getting Around Nice

While you can walk to most attractions in Nice, the bus and tram can be useful. Both are covered by the same single-ride €1 ticket (good for 74 min in one direction, including transfers between bus and tram; can't be used for a round-trip). An all-day pass is €4 (valid on local buses and trams, as well as buses to nearby destinations—see "Getting Around the Riviera," earlier in this chapter).

The **bus** is handy to reach the Chagall and Matisse museums and maybe to the Russian Cathedral. Make sure to validate your ticket in the machine just behind the driver—watch to see how locals do it.

Nice's **tramway** runs along avenue Jean Médecin and boulevard Jean Jaurès. This handy tram connects the main train station (Gare Thiers stop), place Masséna (Masséna stop, a few blocks' walk from the sea), Old Nice (Opéra–Vieille Ville), the bus station (Cathédrale–Vieille Ville), and the Modern and Contemporary Art Museum (Place Garibaldi).

Taking the tram in the direction of Pont Michel will take you from the train station toward the beach and bus station (direction Las Planas goes the other way). Buy tickets at the machines on the platforms (coins only, no credit cards, choose the English flag to change the display language, spin the round knob and push the green button, red button to cancel). Once you're on the tram, don't forget to validate your ticket by inserting it into the top of the white box, then reclaiming it.

Taxis are handy for getting to Nice's outlying sights, and worth it if you're nowhere near a bus or tram stop (figure €10–12 from promenade des Anglais). They normally pick up only at taxi stands *(tête de station)*, or you can call 04 93 13 78 78.

The hokey **tourist train** gets you up Castle Hill (see "Tours," next).

Tours

Bus Tour—Le Grand Tour Bus provides a hop-on, hop-off service on an open-deck bus with headphone commentary. There are two routes: The red route (2/hr, about 90 min) includes promenade des Anglais, old port, Cap de Nice, and the Chagall and Matisse museums on Cimiez Hill. The less-frequent blue route (6/day) includes the Russian Cathedral, the promenade, and more of modern Nice (€20/1-day pass, €23/2-day pass, cheaper for seniors and students, €10 for last tour of the day at about 18:00, some hotels offer €2 discounts—ask at your hotel, buy tickets on bus, main stop is near where promenade des Anglais and quai des Etats-Unis meet, across from plage Beau Rivage—look for signs, tel. 04 92 29 17 00). This tour is a pricey way to get to the Chagall and Matisse museums, but it's a good option if you also want a city overview tour. If you want to use this bus to go to the Russian Cathedral, make sure to check the schedule, as it may be faster to walk.

Tourist Train—For €7 (or €3 for children under 9), you can spend 40 embarrassing minutes on the tourist train tooting along the promenade, through the old city, and up to Castle Hill. This is a sweat-free way to get to Castle Hill...but so is the elevator, which is much cheaper (every 30 min, daily 10:00–18:00, June–Aug until 19:00, recorded English commentary, meet train near Le Grand Tour Bus stop on quai des Etats-Unis, tel. 04 93 62 85 48).

▲**Boat Cruise**—Here's your chance to join the boat parade and see Nice from the water. On this one-hour, star-studded tour, you'll cruise in a comfortable, yacht-size vessel to Cap Ferrat and past Villefranche-sur-Mer, then return to Nice with a final lap along promenade des Anglais. It's a scenic and worthwhile trip (the best views are from the seats on top). French (and sometimes English-speaking) guides play Robin Leach, pointing out mansions owned by some pretty famous people, including Elton John (just as you leave Nice, it's the soft-yellow square-shaped place right on the water), Sean Connery (on the hill above Elton, with rounded arches and tower), Microsoft mogul Paul Allen (in saddle of Cap Ferrat hill, above yellow-umbrella beach with sloping red-tile roof), and Mick Jagger (between Cap Ferrat and Villefranche-sur-Mer, pink place hidden by trees). I wonder if this gang ever hangs out together...(€13; May–Oct Tue–Sun 2/day, usually at 11:00 and 15:00, no boats Mon; March–April Tue–Wed, Fri, and Sun at 15:00; no boats Nov–Feb; call ahead to verify schedule, arrive 30 min early to get best seats, drinks and WCs available). For directions to the dock and contact information, see "Getting Around the Riviera—By Boat," page 435.

Walking Tours—The TI on promenade des Anglais organizes weekly walking tours of Old Nice in French and English (€12, May–Oct only, usually Sat morning at 9:30, 2.5 hours, reservations necessary, depart from TI, tel. 08 92 70 74 07).

Nice's cultural association (Centre du Patrimoine) offers incredibly cheap €3 on-demand walks on varying themes (in English, minimum 3 people). Call 04 92 00 41 90 or 06 76 98 67 82 a few days ahead to make a reservation. Most tours start at their office at 75 quai des Etats-Unis; look for the red plaque next to Musée des Ponchettes (see Old Nice map in "Sleeping").

Les Petits Farcis Cooking Tour and Classes—Canadian food-journalist-turned-Francophile Rosa Jackson is making a Mediterranean splash with her one- and four-day cooking classes in Old Nice. Her single-day classes include a morning trip to the open-air market for picking up ingredients, and an afternoon session, where you'll learn what to do with your purchases. Her four-day courses focus exclusively on the art of cooking (1 day-€200, 4 days-€480, tel. 06 81 67 41 22, www.petitsfarcis.com). Ask about the farm tours she organizes to meet the producers themselves.

Self-Guided Walk

A Scratch-and-Sniff Walk Through Old Nice

• *See the map on page 455, and start at Nice's main market square, the...*

Cours Saleya (koor sah-lay-yuh): Named for its broad exposure to the sun *(soleil)*, this commotion of color, sights, smells, and people has been Nice's main market square since the Middle Ages (produce market held Tue–Sun until 13:00—on Mon, an antique market takes center stage). Amazingly, part of this square was a parking lot until 1980, when the mayor of Nice had an underground garage built.

Stroll down the center of the cours. The first section is devoted to the plants and flowers that seem to grow effortlessly and everywhere in this ideal climate. Carnations, roses, and jasmine are local favorites in what has been the Riviera's biggest flower market since the 19th century. The boisterous produce section trumpets the season with mushrooms, strawberries, white asparagus, zucchini flowers—whatever's fresh gets top billing.

Place Pierre Gautier (also called Plassa dou Gouvernou—bilingual street signs include the old Niçoise language, an Italian dialect) is where the actual farmers set up stalls to sell their produce and herbs directly.

Continue down the center of cours Saleya, stopping when you see La Cambuse restaurant on your left. In front, hovering over the black barrel fire with the paella-like pan on top, is the self-proclaimed Queen of the Market, Thérèse (tehr-ehz). When she's not looking for a husband, Thérèse is cooking *socca*, Nice's chickpea crêpe specialty. Spend €2 for a wad of *socca* (careful—it's hot, but good). If she doesn't have a pan out, that means it's on its way (watch for the frequent scooter deliveries). Wait in line...or else it'll be all gone when you return.

• *Continue down cours Saleya. The fine golden building at the end is where Henri Matisse lived for 17 years. Turn left at the Café des Ponchettes, and head down...*

Rue de la Poissonnerie: Look up at the first building on your right. Adam and Eve are squaring off, each holding a zucchini-like gourd. This scene (post-apple) represents the annual rapprochement in Nice to make up for the sins of a too-much-fun Carnival (Mardi Gras). Nice residents have partied hard during Carnival for more than 700 years. A few doors down, on the left, find the small church dedicated to St. Rita, the patron saint of desperate causes. She holds a special place in locals' hearts, and this church is the most popular in Nice.

• *Turn right on the next street, where you'll pass Old Nice's most happening café/bar (Distilleries Ideales), with a lively happy hour (18:00–*

20:00) and a Pirates of the Caribbean–style interior. Now turn left on "Right" Street (rue Droite), and enter an area that feels like a Little Naples.

Rue Droite: In the Middle Ages, this straight, skinny street provided the most direct route from wall to wall, or river to sea. Stop at Esipuno's bakery (at place du Jésus) and say bonjour to the friendly folks. Thirty years ago, this baker was voted the best in France—the trophies you see were earned for bread making, not bowling. His son now runs the place. Notice the firewood stacked by the oven. Farther along, at #28, Thérèse (whom you met earlier) cooks her socca in the wood-fired oven before she carts it to her barrel on cours Saleya. The balconies of the mansion in the next block mark the Palais Lascaris (1647, gorgeous at night), a rare souvenir from one of Nice's most prestigious families (free, Wed–Mon 10:00–18:00, closed Tue, worth touring for a peek at 1700s Baroque Italian high life). Look up and make faces back at the guys under the balconies.

• Turn left on the rue de la Loge, then left again on rue Centrale, to reach...

Place Rossetti: The most Italian of Nice's piazzas, place Rossetti feels more like Rome than Nice. This square comes alive after dark. Fenocchio is popular for its many gelato flavors. Walk to the fountain and stare back at the church. This is the Cathedral of St. Réparate—an unassuming building for a major city's cathedral. The cathedral was relocated here in the 1500s, when Castle Hill was temporarily converted to military-only use. The name comes from Nice's patron saint, a teenage virgin named Réparate whose martyred body floated to Nice in the fourth century, accompanied by angels. The interior gushes Baroque. Remember that Baroque was a response to the Protestant Reformation. With the Catholic Church's "Counter-Reformation," the theatrical energy of churches was cranked up—with reenergized, high-powered saints and eye-popping decor.

• Our walk is over. Castle Hill is straight up the stepped lane opposite the cathedral (described in "Sights").

Activities

▲**Wheeling the Promenade**—Get a bike and ride along the coast in both directions (about 30 min each way). **Roller Station** rents bikes, in-line skates, and mini-scooters (see "Helpful Hints," earlier in this chapter). Both of the following paths start along promenade des Anglais.

The path to the west stops just before the airport at perhaps the most scenic boules courts in France. Stop and watch the old-timers while away their afternoon tossing those shiny metal balls.

Heading east, you'll round the hill—passing a scenic cape and the town's memorial to both world wars—to the harbor of Nice, with a chance to survey some fancy yachts. Pedal around the harbor and follow the coast past the Corsica ferry terminal (you'll need to carry your bike up a flight of steps). From there, the path leads to an appealing tree-lined residential district.

Relaxing at the Beaches—Nice is where the masses relax on the rocks. After settling into the smooth pebbles, you can play beach volleyball, table tennis, or *boules;* rent paddleboats, personal watercraft, or windsurfing equipment; explore ways to use your zoom lens as a telescope; or snooze on comfy beach beds with end tables. To rent a spot on the beach, compare rates, as prices vary—beaches on the east end of the bay are usually cheaper (mattress and *chaise longue*-€12–18, umbrella-€5, towel-€3). Many hotels have special deals with certain beaches for discounted rentals (check with your hotel for details). Consider lunch in your bathing suit (€10–12 salads and pizzas in bars and restaurants all along the beach). For a peaceful cup of coffee by the sea, stop here first thing in the morning before the crowds hit. *Plage Publique* signs explain the 15 beach no-nos (translated in English).

While Nice's beaches are traditionally rocky, a few years ago a small sandy area appeared toward the Italy end of the bay.

Sights

▲▲▲Along the Promenade des Anglais

Welcome to the Riviera. There's something for everyone along this four-mile-long seafront circus. Watch the Europeans at play, admire the azure Mediterranean, anchor yourself on a blue seat, and prop your feet up on the made-to-order guardrail. Later in the day, come back to join the evening parade of tans along the promenade.

The broad sidewalks of promenade des Anglais ("walkway of the English") were financed by wealthy English tourists who wanted a safe place to stroll and admire the view. In 1822, the walk was paved in marble for aristocrats who didn't want to dirty their shoes or smell the fishy gravel. For now, stroll like the belle époque English aristocrats for whom the promenade was built.

Start at the pink-domed Hôtel Negresco, then cross to the sea and end your promenade at Castle Hill. The following sights are listed in the order you'll pass them. This walk is ideally done at sunset (as a pre-dinner stroll).

Hôtel Negresco—Nice's finest hotel (also a historic monument) offers the city's most expensive beds (€460 minimum for a sea view, see "Sleeping," later in this section), and a free "museum" interior (always open—provided you're dressed decently, absolutely no

NICE

beach attire). March straight through the lobby (as if you're staying there) into the exquisite Salon Royal. The chandelier hanging from the Eiffel-built dome is made of 16,000 pieces of crystal. It was built in France for the Russian czar's Moscow palace... but because of the Bolshevik Revolution in 1917, he couldn't take delivery. Read the explanation of the dome and saunter around counterclockwise: The bucolic scene, painted in 1913 for the hotel, sets the tone. Nip into the toilets for either a turn-of-the-century powder room or a Battle of Waterloo experience. The chairs nearby were typical of the age (cones of silence for an afternoon nap sitting up).

Bay of Angels (Baie des Anges)—Grab a blue chair and face the sea. The body of Nice's patron saint, Réparate, was supposedly escorted into this bay by angels in the fourth century. To your right is where you might have been escorted into France—Nice's airport, built on a massive landfill. On that tip of land way beyond the runway is Cap d'Antibes. Until 1860, Antibes and Nice were in different countries—Antibes was French, but Nice was a protectorate of the Italian kingdom of Savoy-Piedmont, a.k.a. the Kingdom of Sardinia. (During that period, the Var River—just west of Nice—was the geographic border between these two peoples.) In 1850, locals spoke Italian and ate pasta. As Italy was uniting, the region was given a choice: Join the new country of Italy or join France (which was enjoying good times under the rule of Napoleon III). The vast majority voted in 1860 to go French...and voilà!

The green hill to your left is Castle Hill. Farther left lies Villefranche-sur-Mer (marked by the tower at land's end, and home to lots of millionaires), then Monaco (which you can't see, with more millionaires), then Italy (with lots of, uh, Italians). Behind you are the foothills of the Alps (Alpes Maritimes), which gather threatening clouds, ensuring that the Côte d'Azur enjoys sunshine more than 300 days each year. While half a million people live here, pollution is carefully treated—the water is routinely tested and very clean. Stroll the promenade with the sea starboard, and read about "Relaxing at the Beaches" (listed in the previous section, "Activities").

Albert I Park—The park was named for the Belgian king who enjoyed wintering here. While the English came first, the Belgians and Russians were also huge fans of 19th-century Nice. The 1960 statue in the park commemorates Nice's being part of France for 100 years. If you detour from the promenade into the park and continue down the center of the grassy strip, you'll be walking over Nice's river, the Paillon (covered since the 1800s). For centuries, this river was Nice's natural defense to the north and west (the sea protected the south, and Castle Hill defended the east). Imagine the fortified wall ran along its length from the hills behind you to the sea. With the arrival of tourism in the 1800s, Nice expanded over and beyond the river.

Castle Hill (Colline du Château)—This hill—in an otherwise flat city center—offers sensational views over Nice, the port (to the east), the foothills of the Alps, and the Mediterranean. The city of Nice was first settled here by Greeks circa 400 B.C. In the Middle Ages, a massive castle stood there, with turrets, high walls, and soldiers at the ready. With the river guarding one side and the sea the other, this mountain fortress seemed strong—until Louis XIV leveled it in 1706. Nice's medieval seawall ran along the lineup of two-story buildings below. Today, you'll find a waterfall, a playground, two cafés (fair prices), and a cemetery—but no castle—on Castle Hill. The views are best early or at sunset, or whenever the weather's really clear (park closes at 20:00 in summer, earlier off-season). You can get to the top by foot, by elevator (€0.70 one-way, €1.10 round-trip, runs daily 10:00–19:00, until 20:00 in summer, next to beachfront Hôtel Suisse), or by tourist train (described under "Tours," earlier in this chapter). Up top, you'll find cafés and an extensive play area for kids.

Nice's port, where you'll find Trans Côte d'Azur's boat cruises (described near the beginning of this chapter, in "Getting Around the Riviera—By Boat"), is just below on the east edge of Castle Hill.

Museums

To bring culture to the masses, the city of Nice has nixed the entry fee to all municipal museums—so it's free to enter any of the sights listed below, except the Chagall Museum and the Russian Cathedral. Amazing. The first two museums (Chagall and Matisse) are a long walk northeast of Nice's city center, and because they're on the same bus line (in the same direction), it makes sense to visit them at the same time. From place Masséna, the Chagall Museum is a 30-minute walk, and the Matisse Museum is a 60-minute walk.

▲▲▲Chagall Museum (Musée National Marc Chagall)—Even if you're suspicious of modern art, this museum—with the largest collection of Chagall's work in captivity anywhere—is a delight. After World War II, Chagall returned from the US to settle in nearby Vence. Between 1954 and 1967, he painted a cycle of 17 large murals designed for, and donated to, this museum. These paintings, inspired by the biblical books of Genesis, Exodus, and the Song of Songs, make up the "nave," or core, of what Chagall called the "House of Brotherhood."

Each painting is a lighter-than-air collage of images that draw from Chagall's Russian-folk-village youth, his Jewish heritage, biblical themes, and his feeling that he existed somewhere between heaven and earth. He believed that the Bible was a synonym for nature, and that color and biblical themes were key ingredients for understanding God's love for his creation. Chagall's brilliant blues and reds celebrate nature, as do his spiritual and folk themes. On your way out, be sure to visit the three Chagall stained-glass windows in the auditorium (depicting God's creation of the universe).

Cost, Hours, Location: €7, free first Sunday of the month (but crowded), can cost a little more during special exhibits, free to anyone under 25; open Wed–Mon 10:00–17:00, May–Oct until 18:00, closed Tue year-round; avenue Docteur Ménard, tel. 04 93 53 87 20, www.musee-chagall.fr.

Services: An idyllic garden café (open April–Oct) with fair prices awaits in the corner of the museum grounds. A spick-and-span WC is next to the ticket desk (there's one inside, too).

Getting to the Chagall Museum: You can reach the museum by bus or on foot. **Bus #22** serves the Chagall Museum from place Masséna (5/hr Mon–Sat, 3/hr Sun, €1; stop faces eastbound on rue Gioffredo, a block east of Galeries Lafayette—see Old Nice Hotels and Restaurants map in "Sleeping"). The museum's bus stop (called Musée Chagall, shown on the bus shelter) is on boulevard de Cimiez (walk uphill from the stop to find the museum). To **walk** from central Nice to the Chagall Museum, go to the train-station end of avenue Jean Médecin and turn right onto boulevard Raimbaldi. Walk four long blocks along the elevated road, then turn left onto avenue Raymond Comboul, and follow *Musée Chagall* signs.

Leaving the Museum: Taxis usually wait outside the museum. To take **bus #22** back to downtown Nice, turn right out of the museum, then make another right down boulevard de Cimiez, and catch the bus on the near side of the street. To continue on to the Matisse Museum, catch bus #22 using the uphill stop, located across the street. To **walk** to the train station from the museum, turn left out of the museum, then left again on the street behind it. Look for the staircase on your left (leading down), cross under the freeway, then turn right to reach the station.

▲**Matisse Museum (Musée Matisse)**—This museum, worth ▲▲▲ for his fans, contains the world's largest collection of Henri Matisse paintings. It offers a painless introduction to the artist, whose style was shaped by Mediterranean light and by fellow Côte d'Azur artists Pablo Picasso and Pierre-Auguste Renoir. The collection is scattered through several rooms with a few worthwhile works, though it lacks a certain *je ne sais quoi* when compared to the Chagall Museum.

Henri Matisse, the master of leaving things out, could suggest a woman's body with a single curvy line—leaving it to the viewer's mind to fill in the rest. Ignoring traditional 3-D perspective, he used simple dark outlines saturated with bright blocks of color to create recognizable but simplified scenes, all composed into a decorative pattern to express nature's serene beauty. You don't look

NICE

"through" a Matisse canvas, like a window; you look "at" it, like wallpaper.

Matisse understood how colors and shapes affect us emotionally. He could create either shocking, clashing works (Fauvism) or geometrical, balanced, harmonious ones (later works). While other modern artists reveled in purely abstract design, Matisse (almost) always kept the subject matter at least vaguely recognizable. He used unreal colors and distorted lines not just to portray what an object looks like, but to express the object's inner nature (even inanimate objects). Meditating on his paintings helps you connect with nature—or so Matisse hoped.

Cost, Hours, Location: Free, Wed–Mon 10:00–18:00, closed Tue, 164 avenue des Arènes de Cimiez, tel. 04 93 81 08 08, www .musee-matisse-nice.org. The museum is set in an olive grove amid the ruins of the Roman city of Cemenelum.

Getting to the Matisse Museum: It's a long uphill walk from the city center. Take the bus (details below) or a cab (about €12 from promenade des Anglais). Once here, walk into the park to find the pink villa. **Buses #22** and **#17** offer frequent service to the Matisse Museum from just off place Masséna on rue Gioffredo (Masséna Guitry stop, a block east of the Galeries Lafayette department store—see Old Nice Hotels and Restaurants map in "Sleeping"; €1 for the trip). Get off at the Arènes–Matisse bus stop.

Leaving the Museum: When leaving the museum, find the stop for bus #22 (which has more frequent service downtown and stops en route at the Chagall Museum) by exiting the park and crossing boulevard de Cimiez, where the two roads meet (the stop is on boulevard de Cimiez, not avenue des Arènes de Cimiez—see map on page 437). The stop for bus #17 (less frequent, no Chagall stop) also faces downhill, but it's on avenue des Arènes de Cimiez. Confusing, I know.

Modern and Contemporary Art Museum (Musée d'Art Moderne et d'Art Contemporain)—This ultramodern museum features an explosively colorful, far-out, yet manageable permanent collection (on the second floor) of mostly American and European art from the 1960s and 1970s. The exhibits include a few works by Andy Warhol, Roy Lichtenstein, and Jean Tinguely, and small models of Christo's famous wrappings. Several of Niki de Saint Phalle's works are almost huggable. The temporary exhibits can be as appealing to modern-art-lovers as the permanent collection— ask the TI what's playing.

Cost, Hours, Location: Free, Tue–Sun 10:00–18:00, closed Mon, about a 15-minute walk from place Masséna, near bus station on promenade des Arts, tel. 04 93 62 61 62, www.mamac-nice.org.

Molinard Perfume Museum—The Molinard family has been making perfume in Grasse (about an hour's drive from Nice) since

1849. Their Nice store has a small museum in the back that illustrates the story of their industry. Back when people believed water spread the plague (Louis XIV supposedly bathed less than once a year), doctors advised people to rub fragrances into their skin and then powder their body. Back then, perfume was a necessity of everyday life.

Room 1 shows photos of the local flowers used in perfume production. Room 2 shows the earliest (18th-century) production method. Petals would be laid on a bed of animal fat. After baking in the sun, the fat would absorb the essence of the flowers. Petals would be replaced daily for two months until the fat was saturated. Models and old photos show the later distillation process (660 pounds of lavender would produce only a quarter-gallon of essence). Perfume is "distilled like cognac and then aged like wine." Room 3 shows the desk of a "nose" (top perfume creator). Of the 150 real "noses" in the world, more than 100 are French. You are welcome to enjoy the testing bottles before heading into the shop.

Cost, Hours, Location: Free, daily 10:00–19:00, sometimes closed Mon off-season, just between beach and place Masséna at 20 rue St. François de Paule—see Old Nice Hotels and Restaurants map in "Sleeping," tel. 04 93 62 90 50, www.molinard.com.

Other Nice Museums—All of these museums are acceptable rainy-day options, and free of charge.

The **Fine Arts Museum** (Musée des Beaux-Arts), located in a sumptuous villa with lovely gardens, houses 6,000 works from the 17th to 20th centuries, and will satisfy your need for a fine-arts fix (free, Tue–Sun 10:00–18:00, closed Mon, 3 avenue des Baumettes, western end of Nice, take bus #38 from the bus station, tel. 04 92 15 28 28, www.musee-beaux-arts-nice.org).

The **Archaeological Museum** (Musée Archéologique) displays various objects from the Romans' occupation of this region. It's convenient—just below the Matisse Museum—but has little of interest to anyone but ancient Rome aficionados. You also get access to the Roman bath ruins...which are, sadly, overgrown with weeds (free, very limited information in English, Wed–Mon 10:00–18:00, closed Tue, near Matisse Museum at 160 avenue des Arènes de Cimiez, tel. 04 93 81 59 57, www.musee-archeologique -nice.org).

The **Masséna Museum** (Musée Masséna) features 18th- and 19th-century paintings (mostly by artists from Nice), local porcelain, and other collections relevant to the city's tumultuous history (free, Wed–Mon 10:00–18:00, closed Tue, 35 promenade des Anglais, tel. 04 93 91 19 10).

▲Russian Cathedral

Nice's Russian Orthodox church—claimed to be the finest outside Russia—is worth a visit. Five hundred rich Russian families
wintered in Nice in the late 19th century. Since they couldn't pray
in a Catholic church, the community needed a worthy Orthodox
house of worship. Czar Nicholas I's widow provided the land
(which required tearing down her house), and Czar Nicholas II
gave this church to the Russian community in 1912. (A few years
later, Russian comrades—who didn't winter on the Riviera—
assassinated him.) Here in the land of olives and anchovies, these
proud onion domes seem odd. But, I imagine, so did those old
Russians.

Step inside (pick up English info sheet). The one-room interior is filled with icons and candles, and the old Russian music
adds to the ambience. The wall of icons (iconostasis) divides things
between the spiritual world and the temporal world of the worshippers. Only the priest can walk between the two worlds, by
using the "Royal Door." Take a close look at items lining the front
(starting in the left corner). The angel with red boots and wings—
the protector of the Romanov family—stands over a symbolic tomb
of Christ. The tall, black, hammered-copper cross commemorates
the massacre of Nicholas II and his family in 1918. Notice the Jesus
icon to the right of the Royal Door. According to a priest here,
as worshippers meditate, staring deep into the eyes of Jesus, they
enter a lake where they find their soul. Surrounded by incense,
chanting, and your entire community...it could happen. Farther
to the right, the icon of the unhappy-looking Virgin and Child
is decorated with semiprecious stones from the Ural Mountains.
Artists worked a triangle into each iconic face—symbolic of the
Trinity.

Cost, Hours, Location: €3, daily 9:00–12:00 & 14:30–18:00,
until 17:00 off-season, chanted services Sat at 17:30 or 18:00, Sun
at 10:00, no tourist visits during services, no short shorts, 17 boulevard du Tzarewitch, tel. 04 93 96 88 02. The park around the
church stays open at lunch and makes a fine setting for picnics.

Getting to the Russian Cathedral: From the train station, it's
a 10-minute walk; exit the station to the right onto avenue Thiers,
turn right on avenue Gambetta, and follow signs to the cathedral.
Or, from the station, take any bus heading west on avenue Thiers
and get off at avenue Gambetta (a few stops away).

Nightlife

Promenade des Anglais, cours Saleya, and rue Masséna are all
worth an evening walk. Nice's bars play host to one of the Riviera's
most happening late-night scenes, full of jazz, rock, and heat-

seeking singles. Most activity focuses on Old Nice, near place Rossetti and along rue Droite. **Distilleries Ideales** is a fine place to start or end your evening, with a lively, international crowd and a fun interior (where rues de la Poissonnerie and Barillerie meet, happy hour 18:00–20:00). Just down the street, **Wayne's Bar** is a happening spot for the younger, English-speaking backpacker crowd (15 rue Préfecture). The plush bar at **Hôtel Negresco** is fancy-cigar old English.

Plan on a cover charge or expensive drinks when music is involved. If you're out very late, avoid walking alone. Nice is well-known for its lively after-dark action.

Sleeping

Don't look for charm in Nice. Go for modern and clean, with a central location and, in summer, air-conditioning. The rates listed here are for April through October. Prices generally drop €10–20 from November through March, but go sky-high during the Nice Carnival, Monaco's Grand Prix, and the Cannes Film Festival. Between the Grand Prix and the film festival, the second half of May is very tight every year. June is convention month, and Nice is one of Europe's top convention cities. Reserve early if visiting May through August, especially during these times. For parking, ask your hotelier (several have limited private parking), or see "Arrival in Nice—By Car," earlier in this chapter.

I've divided my sleeping recommendations into three areas: between the train station and Nice Etoile shopping center (easy access to the train station and Old Nice via the sleek new tram-way, 20-min walk to promenade des Anglais); between Nice Etoile and the sea (east of avenue Jean Médecin, great access to Old Nice

Sleep Code

(€1 = about $1.40, country code: 33)
S = Single, **D** = Double/Twin, **T** = Triple, **Q** = Quad, **b** = bathroom, **s** = shower only, ***** = French hotel rating (0-4 stars). Hotels speak English, have elevators, and accept credit cards unless otherwise noted.

To help you sort easily through these listings, I've divided the rooms into three categories based on the price for a standard double room with bath:

　$$$ **Higher Priced**—Most rooms €100 or more.
　$$ **Moderately Priced**—Most rooms between €70-100.
　$ **Lower Priced**—Most rooms €70 or less.

NICE

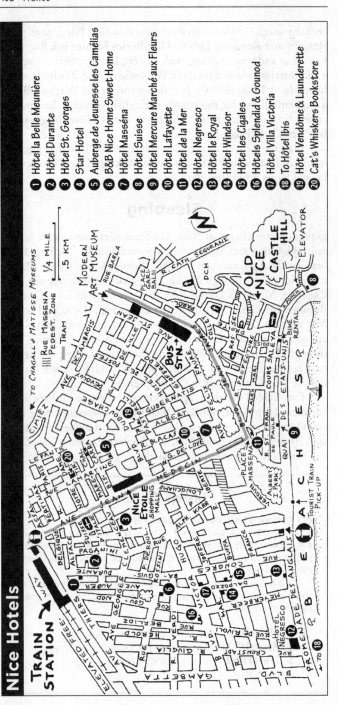

Nice Hotels

1. Hôtel la Belle Meunière
2. Hôtel Durante
3. Hôtel St. Georges
4. Star Hotel
5. Auberge de Jeunesse les Camélias
6. B&B Nice Home Sweet Home
7. Hôtel Masséna
8. Hôtel Suisse
9. Hôtel Mercure Marché aux Fleurs
10. Hôtel Lafayette
11. Hôtel de la Mer
12. Hôtel Negresco
13. Hôtel le Royal
14. Hôtel Windsor
15. Hôtels les Cigales
16. Hôtels Splendid & Gounod
17. Hôtel Villa Victoria
18. To Hôtel Ibis
19. Hôtel Vendôme & Launderette
20. Cat's Whiskers Bookstore

and the sea at quai des Etats-Unis); and between boulevard Victor Hugo and the sea (a somewhat classier area, offering better access to promenade des Anglais but longer walks to the train station and Old Nice). I've also listed a hotel near the airport.

Most hotels I list have public Internet access in the lobby and/or Wi-Fi for laptop users.

Between the Train Station and Nice Etoile

This area offers Nice's cheapest sleeps, though most hotels near the station ghetto are overrun, overpriced, and loud. These are the pleasant exceptions (most are near avenue Jean Médecin). They're listed in order of proximity from the train station, going toward the beach.

$ Hôtel la Belle Meunière, in a fine old mansion built for Napoleon III's mistress, offers cheap beds and private rooms just a block below the train station. Lively and youth-hostel-esque, this place attracts budget-minded travelers of all ages with frumpy-but-adequate rooms and charismatic Madame Marie-Pierre presiding. Tables in the front yard greet guests and provide opportunities to meet other travelers (bunk in 4-bed dorm-€23 with private bath, €18 with shared bath, Db-€60, includes breakfast, 21 avenue Durante, tel. 04 93 88 66 15, fax 04 93 82 51 76, www.belle meuniere.com, hotel.belle.meuniere@cegetel.net).

$$ Hôtel Durante,** run by smiling Nathalie, feels like a Mediterranean villa, with its cheery and way-orange facade, spacious central courtyard, and cool bathroom tiles. Rooms are good enough, and the price is right (Db-€71–79, bigger Db-€100–150, Tb-€130–150, air-con, 16 avenue Durante, tel. 04 93 88 84 40, fax 04 93 87 77 76, www.hotel-durante.com, info@hotel-durante .com).

$$ Hôtel St. Georges** is big and bright, with a backyard garden, reasonably clean and comfortable high-ceilinged rooms, orange tones, blue halls, fair rates, and friendly reception (Sb-€78, Db-€93, Tb with 3 separate beds-€115, extra bed-€20, air-con, 7 avenue Georges Clémenceau, tel. 04 93 88 79 21, fax 04 93 16 22 85, www.hotelsaintgeorges.fr, contact@hotelsaintgeorges.fr).

$$ Star Hotel** is a fair budget option. Rooms are small and bare-bones, with air-conditioning and surprisingly firm beds (Sb-€55–60, Db-€65–80, Tb-€85–95, no elevator—rooms on 4 floors, 14 rue Biscarra, tel. 04 93 85 19 03, fax 04 93 13 04 23, www.hotel -star.com, info@hotel-star.com).

$ Auberge de Jeunesse les Camélias is a laid-back youth hostel in a grand building with a fine location. Rooms accommodate between four and seven people (136 beds in all) and come with showers and sinks—WCs are down the hall. Reservations must be made via the website in advance, or on the same day by phone. In high season, call by 10:00 (€21/bed, €3 extra without hostel membership, rooms closed 11:00–15:00 but can leave bags, includes breakfast, Internet access, laundry, kitchen, safes, bar, 3 rue Spitalieri, tel. 04 93 62 15 54,www.hihostels.com, nice -camelias@fuaj.org, Isabelle at the desk and Bernard at the helm).

$ B&B Nice Home Sweet Home is a great value. Gentle Genevieve Levert rents out three spacious rooms and one small single in her home. Her rooms are simply decorated, with high ceilings, big windows, lots of light, and sitting areas where you can spread out. One room comes with private bath; otherwise, it's just like at home...down the hall (S-€31–38, D-€61–70, Db-€65–75, Tb-€74–84, Q-€80–90, includes breakfast, air-con units available in summer, no elevator, washer/dryer-€5, use of fridge, 35 rue Rossini at intersection with rue Auber, 2nd floor, tel. 06 19 66 03 63, www.nicehomesweethome.com, glevert@free.fr).

Between Nice Etoile and the Sea

$$$ Hôtel Masséna********, in a classy building a few blocks from place Masséna, is a stylish business hotel showcasing 100 rooms with every amenity at almost-reasonable rates (small Db-€120–150, larger Db-€140–190, still larger Db-€200–270, extra bed-€30, some non-smoking rooms, check website or call same day for special rates—prices drop when hotel is not full, reserve parking ahead-€25/day, 58 rue Gioffredo, tel. 04 92 47 88 88, fax 04 92 47 88 89, www.hotel-massena-nice.com, info@hotel-massena -nice.com).

$$$ Hôtel Suisse*******, below Castle Hill, has Nice's best ocean and city views for the money, and is surprisingly quiet given the busy street below. Rooms are quite comfortable, the decor is classy, and the staff is professional. There's no reason to sleep here if you don't land a view, so I've listed prices only for view rooms—many of which have balconies (Db-€155–195, extra bed-€36, breakfast-€15, 15 quai Rauba Capeu, tel. 04 92 17 39 00, fax 04 93 85 30 70, www .hotels-ocre-azur.com, hotel.suisse@hotels-ocre-azur.com).

$$$ Hôtel Mercure Marché aux Fleurs******* is a chain hotel ideally situated across from the sea and behind cours Saleya. It offers smallish yet tastefully designed rooms (some with beds in a loft). Prices are reasonable, though rates vary dramatically over the season (Db-€115–140, Db suite-€200, sea view-€50 extra, air-con, 91 quai des Etats-Unis, tel. 04 93 85 74 19, fax 04 93 13 90 94, h0962@accor.com). Don't confuse this Mercure with the six others in Nice.

$$$ Hôtel Vendôme******* gives you a whiff of the belle époque, with pink pastels, high ceilings, and grand staircases in a mansion set off the street. That whiff could be sharper (many tour groups stay here and the rooms seem a tad tired), but the location

Old Nice Hotels and Restaurants

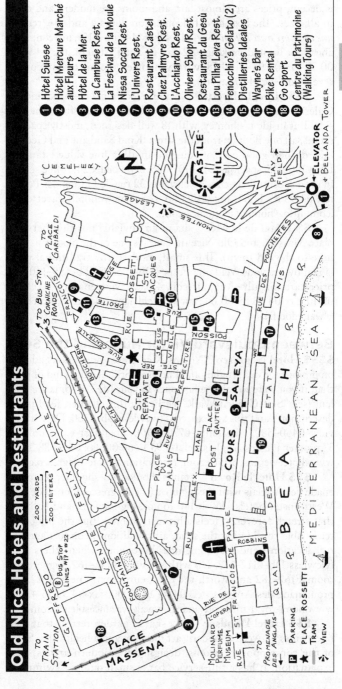

1. Hôtel Suisse
2. Hôtel Mercure Marché aux Fleurs
3. Hôtel de la Mer
4. La Cambuse Rest.
5. La Festival de la Moule
6. Nissa Socca Rest.
7. L'Univers Rest.
8. Restaurant Castel
9. Chez Palmyre Rest.
10. L'Acchiardo Rest.
11. Oliviera Shop/Rest.
12. Restaurant du Gesù
13. Lou Pilha Leva Rest.
14. Fenocchio's Gelato (2)
15. Distilleries Ideales
16. Wayne's Bar
17. Bike Rental
18. Go Sport
19. Centre du Patrimoine (Walking Tours)

is decent, prices are almost fair, and rooms are modern and come in all sizes. The best have balconies (on floors 4 and 5)—request *une chambre avec balcon* (Sb-€111, Db-€144, Tb-€159, air-con, book ahead for limited parking-€12/day, 26 rue Pastorelli, tel. 04 93 62 00 77, fax 04 93 13 40 78, www.vendome-hotel-nice.com, contact @vendome-hotel-nice.com).

$$$ Hôtel Lafayette***, in a nice location a block behind the Galeries Lafayette department store, looks average from the outside. But inside it's homey, with 18 well-designed, mostly spacious rooms, all one floor up from the street. Kind Sandrine and Georges take darned good care of you—all in all, a fine value (standard Db-€100–115, spacious Db-€105–125, extra bed-€24, coffee service in rooms, central air-con, no elevator, 32 rue de l'Hôtel des Postes, tel. 04 93 85 17 84, fax 04 93 80 47 56, www.hotellafayettenice .com, info@hotellafayettenice.com).

$$ Hôtel de la Mer** sits in an enviable position between place Masséna and Old Nice (in fact, it's one of the closest listings here to the old town). This small, modest, *très* traditional place is run by gracious Madame Ferry (Db-€75–95, Tb-€85–140, top prices are for July–Aug, air-con, 4 place Masséna, tel. 04 93 92 09 10, fax 04 93 85 00 64, www.hoteldelamernice.com, hotel.mer @wanadoo.fr).

Between Boulevard Victor Hugo and the Sea

$$$$ Hôtel Negresco**** owns Nice's most prestigious address on promenade des Anglais and knows it. Still, it's the kind of place that, if you were to splurge just once in your life... Rooms are opulent (see "Self-Guided Walk," earlier in this chapter, for further description), and tips are expected (viewless Db-€360, Db with sea view-€460–580, view suite-€770–1,900, breakfast-€35, cool bar, 37 promenade des Anglais, tel. 04 93 16 64 00, fax 04 93 88 35 68, www.hotel-negresco-nice.com, reservations@hotel-negresco.com).

$$$ Hôtel le Royal*** stands shoulder-to-shoulder on promenade des Anglais with the big boys (the Negresco, Concorde, and Westminster hotels). With 140 rooms, big lounges, and hallways that stretch forever, it feels a bit institutional. But the prices are reasonable considering the solid, air-conditioned comfort and terrific location—and they sometimes have rooms when others don't (viewless Db-€112–132, Db with sea view-€142–162, bigger view room-€162–182 and worth the extra euros, extra person-€25, 23 promenade des Anglais, tel. 04 93 16 43 00, fax 04 93 16 43 02, www.hotel-royal-nice.cote.azur.fr, royal@vacancesbleues.com).

$$$ Hôtel Windsor*** is a snazzy garden retreat that feels like a cross between a modern-art museum and a health spa. Some of the contemporary rooms, designed by modern artists, defy explanation. It has a full-service bar, a small outdoor swimming

pool and gym (both free for guests), an €11 sauna, €55 massages, and light, full meal service in the cool, shaded garden area (standard Db-€120, bigger Db-€150, big Db with balcony-€175, extra bed-€20, rooms over garden worth the higher price, air-con, Internet access, 11 rue Dalpozzo, tel. 04 93 88 59 35, fax 04 93 88 94 57, www.hotelwindsornice.com, reservation@hotelwindsornice .com).

$$$ Hôtel les Cigales*** is one of my favorites. It's a smart little pastel place with tasteful decor, 19 plush rooms (most with tub-showers), air-conditioning, and a nifty upstairs terrace, all well-managed by friendly Mr. Valentino, with Veronique and Elaine. Book directly through the hotel and show this book for a surprise treat on arrival (standard Db-€90–129, big Db-€115–140, Tb-€150, €30 more during major events, extra bed-€20, 16 rue Dalpozzo, tel. 04 97 03 10 70, fax 04 97 03 10 71, www.hotel-les cigales.com, info@hotel-lescigales.com).

$$$ Hôtel Splendid**** is a worthwhile splurge if you miss your Marriott. The panoramic rooftop pool, Jacuzzi, bar, restaurant, and breakfast room almost justify the cost...but throw in comfortable rooms (four of the six floors are non-smoking), a free gym, spa services, and air-conditioning, and you're as good as home. Check their website for deals (Db-€225, deluxe Db with terrace-€265, suites-€355–395, free breakfast if you stay at least 3 nights, 10 percent off for weeklong stays, parking-€22/day, 50 boulevard Victor Hugo, tel. 04 93 16 41 00, fax 04 93 16 42 70, www.splendid-nice.com, info@splendid-nice.com).

$$$ Hôtel Gounod*** is behind Hôtel Splendid, and because the two share the same owners, Gounod's guests are allowed free access to Splendid's pool, Jacuzzi, and other amenities. Don't let the lackluster lobby fool you. Most rooms are richly decorated, with high ceilings and air-conditioning—though quality can vary (Db-€155, palatial 4-person suites-€250, parking-€15/day, 3 rue Gounod, tel. 04 93 16 42 00, fax 04 93 88 23 84, www.gounod -nice.com, info@gounod-nice.com).

$$$ Hôtel Villa Victoria*** is nicely managed by cheery Marlena, who welcomes travelers into this classy old building with a green awning and an attractive lobby overlooking a generous garden. Rooms are traditional and well-kept, with space to stretch out (Db-€115–160, Tb-€135–175, suites-€160–210, pricier rooms face the garden, breakfast-€15, air-con, parking-€15, 33 boulevard Victor Hugo, tel. 04 93 88 39 60, fax 04 93 88 07 98, www.villa -victoria.com).

Closer to the Airport

$$ Hôtel Ibis** offers a handy port-in-the-storm outlet for those with early flights or just stopping in for a single night (Db-€75–90

when no special events in town, 359 promenade des Anglais, tel. 04 89 88 30 30, fax 04 93 21 19 43, reception@ibisnice.com).

Eating

Remember, you're in a resort. Go for ambience and fun, and lower your palate's standards. Italian is a low-risk and local cuisine. The restaurants listed below are concentrated in neighborhoods close to my recommended hotels, though you should focus your dining energy on Old Nice. Several offer fixed-price, multi-course meals *(menus)*. Promenade des Anglais is ideal for picnic dinners on warm, languid evenings. Old Nice has the best and busiest dining atmosphere, while the Nice Etoile area is more convenient and offers a good range of choices. To feast cheaply, eat on rue Droite in Old Nice, or explore the area around the train station. For terribly touristy trolling, wander the wall-to-wall places lining rue Masséna. Yuck.

In Old Nice

Nice's dinner scene converges on cours Saleya (koor sah-lay-yuh), which is entertaining enough in itself to make the generally mediocre food a good deal. It's a fun, festive place to compare tans and mussels. Even if you're eating elsewhere, wander through here in the evening. For locations, see the Old Nice map.

La Cambuse is a small island of refinement for those who want to dine on cours Saleya—and the one place along here that doesn't try to reel in passersby. Owner Gregory is swimming upstream in his effort to provide quality cuisine with attentive service in this touristy area. Split a starter like the filling *petits farcis niçois* (stuffed vegetables), then order your own *plat* (€13 starters, €18–24 *plats*, open daily, 5 cours Saleya, tel. 04 93 80 82 40).

La Festival de la Moule is a relatively cheap place that's all about mussels. For just €11, you get all-you-can-eat mussels and fries (across the square from la Cambuse, 20 cours Saleya, tel. 04 93 62 02 12).

Nissa Socca offers good, cheap Italian cuisine and a lively atmosphere in a small room a few blocks from cours Saleya. Indoor tables are usually steamy—arrive early to land a table outside (€9 pizza, €10 pastas, €15–24 *menus*, Mon–Sat from 19:00, closed Sun, a block off place Rossetti on rue Ste. Réparate, tel. 04 93 80 18 35).

L'Univers, a block off place Masséna, earned a Michelin star while maintaining a warm ambience. This elegant place is as relaxed as a "top" restaurant can be, from its casual decor to the tasteful dinnerware. When the artfully presented food arrives, you know this is high cuisine (*menus* from €44, closed Sun, 53 boulevard Jean Jaurès, tel. 04 93 62 32 22, plumailunivers@aol.com).

NICE

Restaurant Castel is your best eat-on-the-beach option. Dining here, you almost expect Don Ho to grab a mic. You're right on the beach below Castle Hill, perfectly positioned to watch evening swimmers get in their last laps as the sky turns pink and city lights flicker on. The views are unforgettable; you can even have lunch at your beach chair if you've rented one (€10/half-day, €14/day). Dinner here is best, so arrive before sunset and linger long enough to merit the few extra euros the place charges (€13–16 salads and pastas, €20–24 main dishes, open daily, 8 quai des Etats-Unis, tel. 04 93 85 22 66).

Dining Cheap *à la Niçoise*

Try at least one of these five places—not just because they're terrific budget options, but primarily because they offer authentic *niçoise* cuisine.

Chez Palmyre is as real as it gets. Your hostess Madame Palmyre shuffles between her small kitchen and the seven-table dining room. The four-course *menu* is only €13, and the cuisine could not be more homemade (closed Sun, cash only, 5 rue Droite, tel. 04 93 85 72 32).

L'Acchiardo, in the heart of Old Nice, does a good job mixing a loyal local and tourist clientele. Its simple, hearty, *niçoise* cuisine is served for fair prices in a homey setting overseen by gentle Monsieur Acchiardo (€13 dinner *plats,* cash only, closed Sat–Sun, 38 rue Droite, tel. 04 93 85 51 16).

Oliviera is all about the French olive. This shop/restaurant sells a wide variety of oils, offers free tastings, and serves a menu of dishes paired with specific oils (just like a wine pairing). Owner Nadim, who speaks excellent English, knows all of his producers personally and provides great "Olive Oil 101" explanations with his tastings (it's nice if you buy something afterwards). You'll feel how passionate he is about his products, and once you come to taste, you'll want to stay and eat (€14–22 main dishes, Tue–Sat 10:00–22:00, closed Sun–Mon, 8 bis rue du Collet, tel. 04 93 13 06 45, www.oliviera.com).

Restaurant du Gesù, a happy-go-lucky budget eatery, squeezes plastic tables into a slanting square deep in the old city (sailors accustomed to dining at an angle will feel right at home). Arrive early or join the mobs waiting for an outside table; better yet, have fun in the soccer-banner–draped interior. The *raviolis sauce daube* is popular (€9 pizzas, €10 pastas, closed Sun, 1 place du Jésus, tel. 04 93 62 26 46).

Lou Pilha Leva offers a fun, *très* cheap lunch or dinner option with *niçoise* specialties and outdoor-only benches. Order your food from one side and drinks from the other (open daily, located where rue de la Loge and Centrale meet in Old Nice).

NICE

Nice Restaurants

1. Rue Biscarra Eateries
2. Bistrot les Viviers
3. L'Ovale Rest. & La Cantine de Lulu
4. La Maison de Marie Rest.
5. La Part des Anges Wine Bar
6. Il Vino Ino Rest. & Cave de L'Origine Wine Bar
7. Chantecler Restaurant
8. Restaurant d'Angleterre
9. Voyageur Nissart Rest.
10. Monoprix Grocery Store
11. Bus #98 to Airport
12. Bus #22 to Chagall & Matisse Mus. & Bus #17 to Matisse Museum
13. Buses #99 & 23 to Airport

TRAIN STATION

TO CHAGALL & MATISSE MUSEUMS

Rue Massena Pedest. Zone

TRAM

¼ MILE

.5 KM

MODERN ART MUSEUM

OLD NICE

CASTLE HILL

ELEVATOR

Nice Étoile Shopping Mall

Tourist Train Pick-up

BUS STN.

PAGANINI

Hotel Negresco

BEACHES

PROMENADE DES ANGLAIS

And for Dessert...

Gelato-lovers should save room for the tempting ice cream stands in Old Nice. For instance, **Fenocchio** serves up 86 flavors, from tomato to lavender to avocado—which is actually pretty good (daily until 23:30, two locations in Old Nice: on place Rossetti and on rue de la Poissonnerie).

Eating near Nice Etoile

If you're not up for eating in Old Nice, try one of these spots around the Nice Etoile shopping mall.

On Rue Biscarra: Laid-back cafés line up along the broad sidewalk on rue Biscarra (just east of avenue Jean Médecin behind Nice Etoile, all closed Sun). **L'Authentic, Le Vin sur Vin,** and **Le Cenac** are all reasonable enough. **Le Vin sur Vin** seems most popular as a restaurant and wine bar (tel. 04 93 92 93 20), though **L'Authentic** is also good, with memorable owners (burly Philippe and sleek Laurent), daily specials, €19 *menus,* and reasonable pasta dishes (live music some Fri and Sat nights, 18 bis rue Biscarra, tel. 04 93 62 48 88).

Bistrot les Viviers appeals to those who require attentive service, silver warming covers, and authentic *niçoise* cuisine. At this cozy splurge, allow €65 per person for wine and three courses, or consider lunch (€17 *menus*). It has two different settings (with the same prices): a formal restaurant and a more relaxed *bistrot* next door. Reserve for the atmospheric *bistrot*. Fish is the chef's forte (closed Sun, 5-min walk west of avenue Jean Médecin at 22 rue Alphonse Karr, tel. 04 93 16 00 48).

L'Ovale is a find. How this ever-so-local and rugby-loving café survives in a tourist mecca, I'll never know. It's run by Nice's nicest couple, Jean-Marc and Jacqueline, who serve quality food at respectable prices. Join the lively local crowd and dine inside on big *plats* for €11. Consider their specialty, *cassoulet* (€36 for two people), or enjoy *la planche de charcuterie* as a meaty, filling first course (excellent €15 3-course *menu,* closed Sun, air-con, 29 rue Pastorelli, tel. 04 93 80 31 65).

La Maison de Marie is a surprisingly high-quality refuge off touristy rue Masséna, where most other places serve mediocre food to tired travelers. Enter through a deep-red arch to a bougainvillea-draped courtyard, and enjoy the fair prices and good food that draw locals and out-of-towners alike. The interior tables are as appealing as those in the courtyard (*menus* from €21, open daily, look for the square red flag at 5 rue Masséna, tel. 04 93 82 15 93).

La Cantine de Lulu is small and charming. This Czech-owned restaurant serves homemade recipes from Nice and Prague (closed Sat–Mon, 26 rue Alberti, tel. 04 93 62 15 33).

NICE

La Part des Anges, an atmospheric wine shop with a few tables in the back, serves a decent but limited menu and a large selection of wines (open daily for lunch, Fri–Sat only for dinner, reserve ahead, 17 rue Gubernatis, tel. 04 93 62 69 80).

Near Promenade des Anglais

Il Vino Ino, a block from promenade des Anglais, has street appeal. This lively, reasonably priced eatery serves only Italian food amid cheery decor, either indoors or out (closed Sun, 33 rue de la Buffa, tel. 04 93 87 94 25).

Cave de L'Origine, run by kind Isabelle and Carlo, is a quality food shop *(épicerie)* and wine bar that also serves a small menu selection. Carlo enjoys talking about his all-natural wines and other products, as he knows all the farmers personally. Stop by for a glass of wine, to peruse the shop, or to reserve a table for a meal (open Tue–Sat for lunch, Thu–Sat for dinner, reservations smart; shop open Tue–Sat 10:00–20:00, closed Sun–Mon; 3 rue Dalpozzo, tel. 04 83 50 09 60).

Chantecler has Nice's most prestigious address—inside the Hôtel Negresco. This is everything a luxury restaurant should be: elegant, soft, and top-quality. If your trip is ending in Nice, call or email for reservations—you've earned this splurge *(menus* from €90, closed Mon–Tue, 37 promenade des Anglais, tel. 04 93 16 64 00, chantecler@hotel-negresco.com).

Near the Train Station

These two places are hardly undiscovered—they're listed in many other guidebooks—but they deserve their acclaim.

Restaurant d'Angleterre is ideal for hungry travelers on a tight budget. For €15, you get a filling three-course dinner with tasty choices and great service (indoor and outdoor tables, closed Sun–Mon, 25 rue d'Angleterre, tel. 04 03 88 64 48).

Voyageur Nissart has blended budget cuisine with cool Mediterranean ambience and friendly service since 1908 (€17 *menus,* closed Mon, 19 rue d'Alsace-Lorraine, tel. 04 93 82 19 60).

Connections

For basic train, bus, and boat schedules from Nice to nearby towns, see "Getting Around the Riviera," near the beginning of this chapter. Note that most long-distance train connections to other French cities require a change in Marseille.

From Nice by Train to: Marseille (18/day, 2.5 hrs), **Arles** (11/day, 3.75–4.5 hrs, most require transfer in Marseille or Avignon), **Avignon** (20/day, 13 of which are via TGV, 4 hrs, a few direct, most require transfer in Marseille), **Paris'** Gare de Lyon (10/day,

6 hrs, may require change; 11-hr night train goes to Paris' Gare d'Austerlitz), **Munich** (4/day, 12–13 hrs with 2–4 transfers, night trains possible via Italy), **Interlaken** (6/day, 9.25–10.75 hrs, 3–5 transfers), **Florence** (6/day, 7–9 hrs, 1–3 transfers), **Venice** (5/day, 8–9 hrs, all require transfers), **Barcelona** (2/day, 11–12 hrs).

Nice's Airport

Nice's easy-to-navigate airport (Aéroport de Nice Côte d'Azur) is on the Mediterranean, a 20–30-minute drive west of the city center. Planes leave about hourly to Paris (1-hr flight, about the same price as a train ticket, check www.easyjet.com for the cheapest flights to Paris' Orly airport). The two terminals (Terminal 1 and Terminal 2) are connected by frequent shuttle buses *(navettes)*. Both terminals have banks, ATMs, taxis, baggage storage, and buses to Nice. The TIs for Nice and Monaco are in Terminal 1 (tel. 08 20 42 33 33 or 04 89 88 98 28, www.nice.aeroport.fr).

Taxis into the center are expensive, charging €30 to Nice hotels (10 percent more from 19:00–7:00 and all day Sunday). Taxis stop outside door *(Porte)* A-1 at Terminal 1 and outside *Porte* A-3 at Terminal 2. Notorious for overcharging, Nice taxis are not always so nice. If your fare for a ride into town is much higher than €30 (or €33 at night or on Sun), refuse to pay the overage. If this doesn't work, tell the cabbie to call a *gendarme* (police officer). It's always a good idea to ask for a receipt *(reçu)*.

Airport shuttle vans work with some of my recommended hotels, but they only make sense when going *to* the airport, not when arriving. Unlike taxis, shuttle vans offer a fixed price that doesn't rise on Sundays, early mornings, or evenings. Prices are best for groups (figure €25 for one person, and only a little more for additional people). Keet Business is a good option (€25/shuttle for 2–4 people, tel. 06 60 33 20 54, www.keet-business.com), or ask your hotelier for recommendations.

Three bus lines connect the airport with the city center, offering good alternatives to high-priced taxis and shuttles. **Bus #99** (airport express) runs from both terminals to Nice's main train station (€4, 2/hr, 8:00–21:00, 30 min, drops you within a 10-min walk of many recommended hotels). To take this bus *to* the airport, catch it right in front of the train station (departs on the half-hour). If your hotel is within walking distance of the station, #99 is a breeze. **Bus #98** serves both terminals, and runs along promenade des Anglais to Nice's main bus station *(gare routière)*, which is near Old Nice (€4, 3/hr, from the airport 6:00–23:00, to the airport until 21:00, no service on Sun, 30 min). The slower, cheaper local **bus #23** serves only Terminal 1, and makes every stop between the airport and train station (€1, 3/hr, 6:00–20:00, 40 min, direction: St. Maurice). For all buses, buy tickets in the information office just outside either terminal, or from the driver. To reach the bus information office and stops at Terminal 1, turn left after passing customs and exit the doors at the far end. Buses serving Terminal 2 stop across the street from the exit. If you take bus #98 or #99, hang on to your €4 ticket—it's good all day on any public bus and the tramway in Nice, and for buses between Nice and nearby towns (for details, see page "Getting Around the Riviera," near the beginning of the chapter).

GERMANY

BAVARIA AND TIROL

Füssen • King's Castles • Reutte, Austria

Two hours south of Munich, between Germany's Bavaria and Austria's Tirol, is a timeless land of fairy-tale castles, painted buildings shared by cows and farmers, and locals who still yodel when they're happy.

In Germany's Bavaria, tour "Mad" King Ludwig II's ornate Neuschwanstein Castle, Europe's most spectacular. Just over the border in Austria's Tirol, explore the ruined Ehrenberg Castle and scream down the mountain on an oversized skateboard.

My favorite home base for exploring Bavaria's castles is actually in Austria, in the town of Reutte (see page 484). Füssen, in Germany, is a handier home base for train travelers.

Planning Your Time

While Germans and Austrians vacation here for a week or two at a time, the typical speedy American traveler will find two days' worth of sightseeing. With a car and more time, you could enjoy three or four days.

By Public Transportation: Train travelers can use Füssen as a base and bus or bike the three miles to Neuschwanstein. Reutte is connected by bus with Füssen (except Sat–Sun; taxi €30 one-way). If you're based in Reutte, you can bike to the Ehrenberg ruins (just outside Reutte) and to Neuschwanstein Castle/Tegelberg luge (90 min). A one-way taxi from Reutte to Neuschwanstein costs about €35. Or, if you stay at the recommended Gutshof zum Schluxen hotel (in Pinswang, Austria—see page 492), it's a one-hour hike through the woods to Neuschwanstein.

FÜSSEN AND REUTTE AREA

To Munich via Buchloe • Romantic Road to Rothenburg • Steingaden • ECHELSBACHER BRIDGE (GORGE)

To Kempten • Wies • WIESKIRCHE • Saulgrub

Forggensee • A-7 • 17 • 23

See Füssen Map • LUGE • Tegelberg • Ober-ammergau

Füssen • Schwangau • NEUSCHWANSTEIN • LINDERHOF • To Munich

Unterpinswang • HOHENSCHWANGAU • Ettal

REUTTNER BERGBAHN • See Reutte Map • GERMANY

Reutte • Eibsee • Garmisch-Partenkirchen • 187

198 • EHRENBERG RUINS • Plansee • AUSTRIA • Grainau

Lech River • Bichlbach • 179 • Zugspitze 2973 m

Stanzach • Lermoos • Ehrwald • LUGE

Namlos • Blindsee • Biberwier

NARROW ROAD • Fernpass • REST STOP

Fallerschein • Nassereith • Telfs

5 Kilometers • 179

5 Miles • To Zürich • A-12 • Stams • To Innsbruck

BAVARIA AND TIROL

Getting Around the Füssen/Reutte Area

By Public Transportation: Local bus service in the region is spotty for sightseeing. If you're rushed and without wheels, Reutte is probably not worth the trouble. Note that the bus connections listed below are for summer weekdays; on weekends and out of season, frequency plummets. Confirm all bus schedules locally: Check the big board at the bus stop across from the Füssen train station, check online at www.rva-bus.de, or call 08362/939-0505.

From Füssen: Füssen is connected by hourly train with **Munich** (2-hour trip, some with transfer in Buchloe). Füssen is three miles from Ludwig's castles (Neuschwanstein and Hohen-schwangau), easily reachable by bus (or by bike—see page 478).

From Füssen, handy buses connect to **Ludwig's castles** and the **Tegelberg luge** (buses #73 and #78, 2/hr, 10 min). To reach **Reutte,** you can take the bus (#74, Mon–Fri 6/day—but only 4 return buses/day, no buses at all Sat–Sun, less off-season, 35 min, €3.40) or a taxi (€30).

From Reutte: Reutte is the most challenging home base for non-drivers. It's a 35-minute bus ride from Füssen (Mon–Fri 6/day, none Sat–Sun, less off-season, €3.40; taxis from Reutte to Ludwig's castles are €35 one-way; to Füssen, €30). There are only four return buses (from Reutte back to Füssen), but Reutte is planning a more regular bus service to Füssen and the sights across the border—ask your hotel for the latest information.

By Bike: This is great biking country. Shops in or near train stations rent bikes for €8–15 per day. The ride from Reutte to Neuschwanstein and the Tegelberg luge (90 min) is a natural.

Füssen

Dramatically situated under a renovated castle on the lively Lech River, Füssen is a handy home base for exploring the region. Füssen has been a strategic stop since ancient times. Its main street sits on the Via Claudia Augusta, which crossed the Alps (over the Brenner Pass) in Roman times. The town was the southern terminus of a medieval trade route, now known among modern tourists as the "Romantic Road." Today, while Füssen is overrun by tourists in the summer, few venture to the back streets...where you'll find the real charm. Apart from my self-guided walk (see next page) and the City Museum, there's little to do here. It's just a pleasant small town with a big history and lots of hardworking people in the tourist business.

Halfway between Füssen and the border (as you drive, or a woodsy walk from the town) is the **Lechfall,** a thunderous waterfall (with a handy WC).

Orientation

(area code: 08362)
Füssen's train station is a few blocks from the TI, the town center (a cobbled shopping mall), and all my hotel listings (see "Sleeping," page 474).

Tourist Information
The TI is in the center of town (June–mid-Sept Mon–Fri 9:00–18:00, until 17:00 off-season, Sat 10:00–14:00, Sun 10:00–12:00, one free Internet terminal, 3 blocks down Bahnhofstrasse from station, tel. 08362/93850, www.fuessen.de). If necessary, the TI can help you find a room. After hours, the little self-service info pavilion near the front of the TI features an automated room-finding service (7:00–24:30).

Arrival in Füssen

From the train station (lockers available, €2–3), exit to the left and walk a few straight blocks to the center of town and the TI. Buses leave from the station to Neuschwanstein (2/hr) and Reutte (6/day Mon–Fri in summer).

Helpful Hints

Internet Access: Beans & Bytes is the best place to get online, with fast terminals and good drink service (€1/30 min, Wi-Fi, Skype, disc-burning for your photos, daily 10:00–22:00, down the pedestrian alley off the main drag at Reichenstrasse 33, tel. 08362/926-8960).

Bike Rental: Bike Station, sitting right where the train tracks end, outfits sightseers with good bikes and tips on two-wheeled fun in the area (€8/24 hrs, April–Sept Mon–Fri 9:00–18:00, Sat 10:00–14:00, Sun 9:00–12:00 in good weather, closed Oct–March, mobile 0176-2205-3080).

Car Rental: Peter Schlichtling, in the town center, rents cars for reasonable prices (€62/day, includes insurance, Mon–Fri 8:00–18:00, Sat 9:00–12:00, closed Sun, Kemptener Strasse 26, tel. 08362/922-122, www.schlichtling.de).

Auto Osterried/Europcar rents at similar prices, but is an €8 taxi ride away from the train station. Their cheapest car is a fun-to-try SmartCar going for about €40 per day (daily 8:00–19:00, across river from Füssen at Tiroler Strasse 65, tel. 08362/6381).

Local Guide: Silvia Beyer speaks English and knows the region very well (silliby@web.de, mobile 0160-901-13431).

Self-Guided Walk

Welcome to Füssen

For most, Füssen is just a touristy home base for visiting Ludwig's famous castles. But the town has a rich history and hides some evocative corners, as you'll see when you follow this short orientation walk. Throughout the town, "City Tour" information plaques explain points of interest in English. Use them to supplement the information I've provided.

• Begin at the square in front of the TI, three blocks from the train station.

Kaiser-Maximilian-Platz: The entertaining "Seven Stones" fountain on this square (in front of the TI) was built in 1995 to celebrate Füssen's 700th birthday. The stones symbolize community, groups of people gathering, conviviality...each is different, with "heads" nodding and talking. It's granite on granite. The moving heads are not connected, and nod only with waterpower. While

BAVARIA AND TIROL

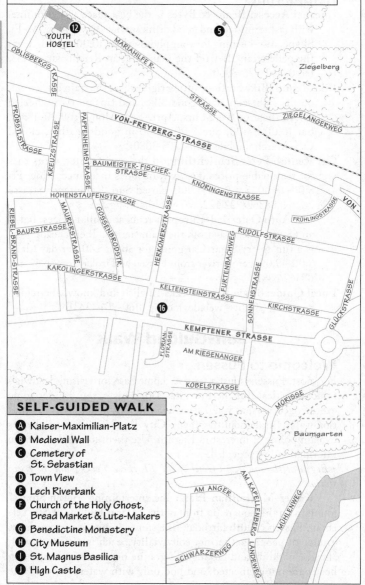

1 Hotel/Rest. Kurcafe
2 Hotel Hirsch
3 Hotel Sonne
4 Altstadthotel zum Hechten & Rest. Ritterstub'n
5 Suzanne's B&B
6 Hotel Bräustüberl
7 Gasthof Krone
8 House LA
9 Allgäuer Gästehaus
10 To Magdalena Höbel
11 Haus Peters
12 Youth Hostel
13 Aquila das Rest.
14 Markthalle Food Court
15 Bike Rental
16 Car Rental
17 To Car Rental
18 Internet Café

YOUTH HOSTEL
Ziegelberg
OBLISBERGSTRASSE
MARIAHILFE R.
STRASSE
ZIEGELANGERWEG
PROBSTLSTRASSE
KREUZBSTRASSE
PAPPENHEIMSTRASSE
VON-FREYBERG-STRASSE
BAUMEISTER-FISCHER-STRASSE
KNÖRINGENSTRASSE
VON-
HOHENSTAUFENSTRASSE
HERKOMERSTRASSE
COSSENBRODSTR.
FRÜHLINGSTRASSE
RIEBEL-BRAND-STRASSE
BAURSTRASSE
MAURERSTRASSE
RUDOLFSTRASSE
FURTENBACHWEG
KAROLINGERSTRASSE
KELTENSTEINSTRASSE
SONNENSTRASSE
KIRCHSTRASSE
GLÜCKSTRASSE
KEMPTENER STRASSE
FLORIAN-STRASSE
AM RIESENANGER
KOBELSTRASSE
MORISSE
Baumgarten
AM ANGER
AM KAPELLENBERG
LANDEWEG
MÜHLENWEG
SCHWÄRZERWEG

SELF-GUIDED WALK

A Kaiser-Maximilian-Platz
B Medieval Wall
C Cemetery of St. Sebastian
D Town View
E Lech Riverbank
F Church of the Holy Ghost, Bread Market & Lute-Makers
G Benedictine Monastery
H City Museum
I St. Magnus Basilica
J High Castle

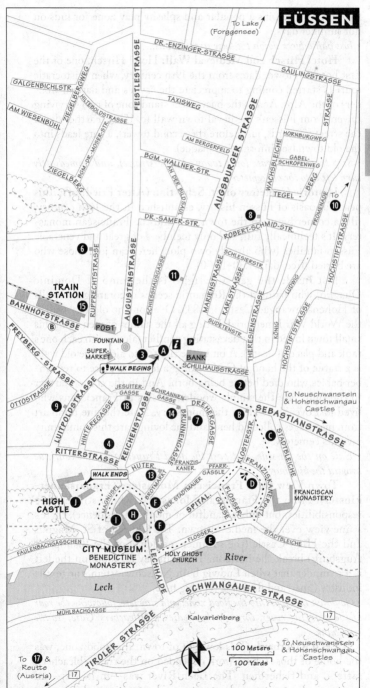

FÜSSEN

To Lake (Forggensee)

DR.-ENZINGER-STRASSE

FEISTLESTRASSE

GALGENBICHLSTR.

AM WIESENBÜHL

ZIEGELBERGWEG

HILTEBOLDSTRASSE

BGM.-DR.-MOSER-STR.

TAXISWEG

SÄULINGSTRASSE

AUGSBURGER STRASSE

WACHSBLEICHE

HORNBURGWEG

GABEL-SCHROFENWEG

AM BERGERFELD

BGM.-WALLNER-STR.

ZIEGELBERG

AN DER BILDSÄULE

TEGEL-BERG

STRASSE

PROMENADE

To **10**

DR.-SAMER-STR.

ROBERT-SCHMID-STR.

8

HOCHSTIFTSTRASSE

6

SCHIESSHAUSGASSE

SCHLESIERSTR.

MARIENSTRASSE

KARLSTRASSE

THERESIENSTRASSE

KÖNIG LUDWIG

11

TRAIN STATION

RUPPRECHTSTRASSE

AUGUSTENSTRASSE

SUDETENSTR.

HOCHSTIFTSTRASSE

BAHNHOFSTRASSE

B

15

POST

1

FREYBERG-STRASSE

FOUNTAIN

SUPERMARKET

WALK BEGINS

3 **A**

i **P**

BANK

SCHULHAUSSTRASSE

2

OTTOSTRASSE

9

LUITPOLDSTRASSE

JESUITER-GASSE

HINTEREGASSE

SCHRANNEN-GASSE

REICHENSTRASSE

18

DREHERGASSE

14 **7**

B

To Neuschwanstein & Hohenschwangau Castles

SEBASTIANSTRASSE

C

STADTBLEICHE

RITTERSTRASSE

4

HUTER-GASSE

BRUNNENGASSE

FRANZIS-KANER-GÄSSLE

13

PFARR-GASSE

KLOSTERSTR.

FRANZISKANERPLATZ

D

FRANCISCAN MONASTERY

WALK ENDS

MAGNUSPL.

BROTMARKT

F

AN DER STADTMAUER

SPITAL-GASSE

FLOSSER-GASSE

HIGH CASTLE

J

I **H**

G

F

FAULENBACHGASSSCHEN

CITY MUSEUM BENEDICTINE MONASTERY

LECHHALDE

HOLY GHOST CHURCH

E

STADTBLEICHE

FLOSSER-STR.

River

Lech

MÜHLBACHGASSE

SCHWANGAUER STRASSE

Kalvarienberg

17

To **17** & Reutte (Austria)

TIROLER STRASSE

17

N

100 Meters

100 Yards

To Neuschwanstein & Hohenschwangau Castles

BAVARIA AND TIROL

frozen in winter, it's a popular and splashy play zone for kids on hot summer days.

• *Just half a block down the busy street stands...*

Hotel Hirsch and Medieval Wall: Hotel Hirsch, one of the first hotels in town, dates from the 19th century, when aristocratic tourists started coming to appreciate the castles and natural wonders of the Alps. Across the busy street stands one of two surviving towers from Füssen's medieval town wall (c. 1515). Farther down the street (50 yards, just before the second tower), a gate leads into the old town (see information plaque).

• *Step through the gate (onto today's Klosterstrasse), and immediately turn left into the old cemetery.*

Historic Cemetery of St. Sebastian (Alter Friedhof): This peaceful oasis of Füssen history, established in the 16th century, fills a corner between the town wall and the Franciscan monastery. It's technically full, and only members of great and venerable Füssen families (who already own plots here) can join those who are buried (free, daily 7:30–19:00).

Just inside the gate (on right) is the tomb of Dominic Quaglio, who painted the Romantic scenes decorating the walls of Hohenschwangau Castle in 1835. Over on the old city wall is the World War I memorial, listing all the names of men from this small town killed in that devastating conflict (along with each one's rank and place of death). A bit to the right, also along the old wall, is a statue of the hand of God holding a fetus—a place to remember babies who died before being born. And in the corner, farther to the right, are the simple wooden crosses of Franciscans who lived just over the wall in the monastery. Note the fine tomb art from many ages collected here, and the loving care this community gives its cemetery.

• *Exit on the far side, just past the dead Franciscans, and continue toward the big church.*

Town View from Franciscan Monastery (Franziskaner-kloster): From the Franciscan Monastery (which still has big responsibilities, but only a handful of monks in residence), there's a fine view over the medieval town. The Church of St. Magnus and the High Castle (the summer residence of the Bishops of Augsburg) break the horizon. The chimney (c. 1886) on the left is a reminder that when Ludwig built Neuschwanstein, the textile industry (linen and flax) was very big here.

• *Go down the steps into the flood zone, and stay left, following the roar of the charging river, through the medieval "Bleachers' Gate," to the riverbank.*

Lech Riverbank: This low end of town, the flood zone, was the home of those whose work depended on the river—bleachers, rafters, and fishermen. The Lech River was—in its day—an expressway to Augsburg (about 70 miles to the north). Around the year 1500, the rafters established the first professional guild in Füssen. As Füssen was on the Via Claudia, cargo from Italy passed here en route to big German cities farther north. Rafters would assemble rafts, and pile them high with goods—or with people needing a lift. If the water was high, they could float all the way to Augsburg in as little as one day. There they'd disassemble their raft and sell off the lumber along with the goods they'd carried, then make their way home to raft again. Today you'll see no water sports here, as there's a hydroelectric plant just downstream.

• *Walk upstream a bit, and head inland immediately after crossing under the bridge.*

Church of the Holy Ghost, Bread Market, and Lute-Makers: Climbing uphill, you pass the colorful Church of the Holy Ghost (Heilig-Geist-Spitalkirche) on the left. As this was the church of the rafters, their patron, St. Christopher, is prominent on the facade. Today it's the church of Füssen's old folks' home (it's adjacent—notice the easy-access skyway).

Farther up the lane (opposite the entry to the big monastery) is Bread Market Square (Brotmarkt), with its fountain honoring the famous 16th-century lute-making family, the Tieffenbruckers. In its day, Füssen was a huge center of violin- and lute-making, with about 200 workshops. Today only two survive.

• *Backtrack and enter the courtyard in the huge monastery just across the street.*

Benedictine Monastery (Kloster St. Mang): From 1717 until secularization in 1802, this was the powerful center of town. Today the courtyard is popular for concerts, and the building houses the City Hall and City Museum (and a public WC).

City Museum: This is Füssen's one must-see sight (€2.50, €3 includes castle gallery; April–Oct Tue–Sun 11:00–17:00, closed Mon; Nov–March Fri–Sun 13:00–16:00, closed Mon–Thu; tel. 08362/903-146). Pick up the loaner English translations and follow the one-way route. In the St. Anna Chapel, you'll see the famous *Dance of Death.* This was painted shortly after a plague devastated the community in 1590. It shows 20 social classes, each dancing with the Grim Reaper—starting with the pope and the emperor. The words above say, essentially, "You can say yes or you can say no, but you must ultimately dance with death." Leaving the chapel, you walk over the metal lid of the crypt. Farther on, exhibits illustrate the rafting trade and violin- and lute-making (with a complete workshop). The museum also includes an exquisite *Festsaal* (main festival hall), an old library, a textile factory, and a Ludwig's "castle dream room."

• *Leaving the courtyard, hook left around the monastery and uphill. The square tower marks...*

St. Magnus Basilica (Basilika St. Mang): St. Mang (or Magnus) is Füssen's favorite saint. In the eighth century, he worked miracles all over the area with his holy rod. For centuries, pilgrims came from far and wide to enjoy art depicting the great works of St. Magnus. Above the altar dangles a glass cross containing his relics (including that holy stick). Just inside the door is a chapel remembering a much more modern saint—Franz Seelos (1819–1867), the local boy who went to America (Pittsburg and New Orleans) and lived such a saintly life that in 2000 he was made a saint. If you're in need of a miracle, fill out one of the cards next to the candles.

• *From the church, a lane leads high above, into the castle courtyard.*

High Castle (Hohes Schloss): This castle, long the summer residence of the Bishop of Augsburg, houses a painting gallery. Its courtyard is interesting for the striking perspective tricks painted onto its flat walls. From below the castle, the city's main drag (once the Roman Via Claudia and now Reichenstrasse) leads from a grand statue of St. Magnus past lots of shops, cafés, and strolling people to Kaiser-Maximilian-Platz and the TI...where you began.

Sleeping

(country code: 49, area code: 08362)
Though I prefer sleeping in Reutte (see page 484), convenient Füssen is just three miles from Ludwig's castles and offers a cobbled, riverside retreat. It's very touristy, but it has plenty of rooms. All recommended accommodations are within a few blocks of the train station and the town center. Parking is easy at the station. Prices listed are for one-night stays. Most hotels give about 5 to 10 percent off for two-night stays—always request this discount. Competition is fierce, and off-season prices are soft. High season is mid-June through September. Rooms are generally about 12 percent less in shoulder season and much cheaper in off-season. To locate these hotels, see the Füssen map earlier in this chapter.

$$$ Hotel Kurcafe is deluxe, with 30 spacious rooms and all of the amenities. The standard rooms are comfortable, and the newer, bigger rooms have elegant touches and fun decor—such as canopy drapes and cherubic frescoes over the bed (Sb-€89, standard Db-€109–125, bigger Db-€135–149 depending on size, Tb-€135, Qb-€149, 4-person suite-€179–209, high prices are for July–Aug, €10 more for weekends and holidays, you'll likely save money by booking via their website, elevator, Internet access, parking-€5/day, a block from station at Bahnhofstrasse 4, tel. 08362/930-180, fax 08362/930-1850, www.kurcafe.com, info@kurcafe.com, Norbert and the Schöll family).

Sleep Code

(**€1 = about $1.40, Germany country code: 49, Austria country code: 43**)

S = Single, **D** = Double/Twin, **T** = Triple, **Q** = Quad, **b** = bathroom, **s** = shower only. Unless otherwise noted, credit cards are accepted, English is spoken, and breakfast is included. The €1.35 per person, per night "tourist tax" is not included in these rates.

To help you sort easily through these listings, I've divided the rooms into three categories, based on the price for a standard double room with bath:

$$$ Higher Priced—Most rooms €100 or more.
$$ Moderately Priced—Most rooms between €60–100.
$ Lower Priced—Most rooms €60 or less.

$$$ Hotel Hirsch is a big, romantic, old tour-class hotel with 53 rooms on the main street in the center of town. Their standard rooms are fine, and their theme rooms are a fun splurge (Sb-€65–85, standard Db-€110–140, theme Db-€140–170, price depends on room size and demand, cheaper Nov–March and during slow times, family rooms, elevator, free parking, Kaiser-Maximilian-Platz 7, tel. 08362/93980, fax 08362/939-877, www.hotelhirsch.de, info @hotelhirsch.de).

$$$ Hotel Sonne, in the heart of town, rents 51 stylish and spacious rooms (Sb-€93–109, Db-€93–159, Tb-€118–148, Qb-€164–200, higher prices are for huge rooms in the newer wing, cheaper Oct–mid-May, elevator, Internet access, free sauna, parking-€4/day, kitty-corner from TI at Prinzregentenplatz 1, tel. 08362/9080, fax 08362/908-100, www.hotel-sonne.de, info @hotel-sonne.de).

$$ Altstadthotel zum Hechten, with 35 rooms, offers all the modern comforts in a friendly, traditional building right under Füssen Castle in the old-town pedestrian zone (Sb-€57, Db-€90, Tb-€117, Qb-€140, request Rick Steves discount, beds can be short, fun miniature bowling alley in basement, free parking with this book; from TI, walk down pedestrian street and take second right to Ritterstrasse 6; tel. 08362/91600, fax 08362/916-099, www.hotel-hechten.com, hotel.hechten@t-online.de, Pfeiffer and Tramp families).

$$ Suzanne's B&B is run by a plainspoken, no-nonsense American woman who strikes some travelers as a brusque drill sergeant. Suzanne runs a tight ship, offering travel advice, local cheese, a children's yard, garden, and bright, woody, spacious rooms (Db-€90, huge Db with waterbed and balcony-€110,

Tb-€120, Qb-€156, suite sleeps up to 10, cash only, non-smoking, €8/day bike rental; exit station right and backtrack 2 blocks along tracks, cross tracks at Venetianerwinkel to #3; tel. 08362/38485, fax 08362/921-396, www.suzannes.de, svorbrugg@t-online.de).

$$ Hotel Bräustüberl has 17 decent rooms at fair rates attached to a gruff, musty, old beer hall. Don't expect much service (Db-€84, cash only, Rupprechtstrasse 5, 1 block from station, tel. 08362/7843, fax 08362/923-951, www.brauereigasthof-braeu stueberl.de, brauereigasthof-fuessen@t-online.de).

Füssen's Budget Beds

$ Gasthof Krone, a rare bit of pre-glitz Füssen in the pedestrian zone, has dumpy halls and stairs and 12 big, worn time-warp rooms (S-€31, D-€58, extra bed-€26, extra bed for kids under 12-€20, €3 more per person for 1-night stays, closed Nov–June; from TI, head down pedestrian street and take first left to Schrannengasse 17; tel. 08362/7824, fax 08362/37505, www.krone-fuessen.de, info @krone-fuessen.de).

$ House LA offers nine basic, clean rooms at rock-bottom prices near the town center (4-bed dorms-€18/bed, Db-€42, Wachsbleichstrasse 2, mobile 0170-624-8610, www.housela.de, info@housela.de). They also rent four very basic rooms and one apartment at Welfenstrasse 39 (D-€40, light breakfast served in room).

$ Allgäuer Gästehaus has four cheap and slightly run-down rooms on a busy street near the center of town (Db-€54, Luitpoldstrasse 10, tel. 08362/926-8425, hdnet@web.de).

$ Magdalena Höbel, your quintessential German grand-mother, rents two double rooms in a quiet neighborhood about a 10-minute walk from the train station. Magdalena speaks some English (D-€36, Frauensteinweg 42c, tel. 08362/2950).

$ Füssen Youth Hostel, a fine, German-run place, welcomes travelers, especially younger ones (bed in 2- to 6-bed dorm rooms-€20, D-€56, €3 more for non-members, includes breakfast and sheets, guests over age 26 pay €4 penalty for being so old, laundry-€3.20/load, cheap dinners, office open 7:00–12:00 & 17:00–23:00, until 22:00 off-season, from station backtrack 10 min along tracks, Mariahilfer Strasse 5, tel. 08362/7754, fax 08362/2770, www.fuessen.jugendherberge.de, jhfuessen@djh-bayern.de).

Eating

Aquila das Restaurant serves modern international dishes in a simple, traditional *Gasthaus* setting with great seating outside on the delightful little Brotmarkt square (€10 plates, serious salads, daily from 11:30 and from 17:00, Brotmarkt 9, tel. 08362/6253).

Restaurant Ritterstub'n offers delicious, reasonably priced fish, salads, veggie plates, and a fun kids' menu. They have three eating zones: dressy in front, casual in back, and courtyard. Demure Gabi serves while her husband cooks standard Bavarian fare (€5 lunch specials, €6–12 plates, Tue–Sun 11:30–14:30 & 17:30–23:00, closed Mon, Ritterstrasse 4, tel. 08362/7759).

Schenke & Wirtshaus (inside the Altstadthotel zum Hechten) dishes up hearty, traditional Bavarian fare. They specialize in pike *(Hecht)* pulled from the Lech River, served with a tasty fresh-herb sauce (€8–13 plates, salad bar, cafeteria ambience, daily 10:00–22:00, Ritterstrasse 6, tel. 0836/91600).

Hotel Kurcafe's fine restaurant, right on Füssen's main traffic circle, has good weekly specials. Choose between a traditional dining room and a pastel winter garden, and enjoy the live Bavarian zither music most Fridays and Saturdays during dinner (open daily 11:30–14:30 & 17:30–21:30, Bahnhofstrasse 4, tel. 08362/930-180).

Markthalle, just across the street from Gasthof Krone, is a fun food court offering a wide selection of reasonably priced, wurst-free food. Located in an old warehouse from 1483, it's now home to a fishmonger; Chinese, Turkish, and Italian delis; a fruit stand; a bakery; and a wine bar. Buy your food from one of the vendors, park yourself at any one of the tables, then look up and admire the Renaissance ceiling (Mon–Fri 7:30–18:30, Sat 7:30–14:00, closed Sun, corner of Schrannengasse and Brunnengasse).

Gelato: **Hohes Schloss Italian Ice Cream** is a good gelateria on the main drag, with cheap ice cream to go and an inviting perch for a coffee or dessert while people-watching (Reichenstrasse 14).

Picnic Supplies: Bakeries and *Metzgers* (butcher shops) abound and frequently have ready-made sandwiches. For groceries, try the **Plus** supermarket at the roundabout on your way into town from the train station (Mon–Sat 8:30–20:00, closed Sun).

Connections

From Füssen to: Neuschwanstein (bus #73 or #78, departs from train station, continues to Tegelberg lift station after castles, 2/hr, 10 min, €2 one-way, €3.50 round-trip; taxis cost €10 one-way), **Reutte** (bus #74, Mon–Fri 6 buses/day, none Sat–Sun, 35 min, €3.40 one-way; taxis cost €30 one-way), **Munich** (hourly trains, 2 hrs, some change in Buchloe), **Salzburg** (hourly, 4 hrs, 1–2 changes). Train info: tel. 11861 (€0.60/min).

Romantic Road Buses: The northbound Romantic Road bus departs Füssen at 8:00; the southbound bus arrives in Füssen at 19:00 (bus stops at train station). A railpass gets you a 20 percent discount on the Romantic Road bus (without using up a day of a flexipass).

The King's Castles

The most popular tourist destinations in Bavaria are the "King's Castles" *(Königsschlösser)*. The older Hohenschwangau, King Ludwig's boyhood home, is less touristy but more historic. The more dramatic Neuschwanstein, which inspired Walt Disney, is the one everyone visits. I'd recommend visiting both, and planning some time to hike above Neuschwanstein to Mary's Bridge—and if you enjoy romantic hikes, down through the gorge below. With fairy-tale turrets in a fairy-tale alpine setting built by a fairy-tale king, these castles are understandably a huge hit.

Getting There

If arriving by **car**, note that road signs in the region refer to the sight as *Königsschlösser*, not Neuschwanstein. There's plenty of parking (all lots-€4.50). The first lots require more walking. Drive right through Touristville and past the ticket center, and park in lot #4 by the lake for the same price.

From **Füssen**, those without cars can catch the twice-hourly **bus** #73 or #78 (€2 one-way, €3.50 round-trip, 10 min, catch bus at train station), take a **taxi** (€10 one-way), or ride a rental **bike** (two level miles).

From **Reutte,** take bus #74 to the Füssen train station (Mon–Fri 4/day, none Sat–Sun, €3.40, 35 min), then hop on bus #73 or #78 to the castle.

For a romantic twist, hike or mountain-bike from the trailhead at the recommended hotel **Gutshof zum Schluxen** in Pinswang, Austria (see page 492; they rent bikes). When the dirt road forks at the top of the hill, go right (downhill), cross the Austria-Germany border (marked by a sign and deserted hut), and follow the narrow paved road to the castles. It's a 60- to 90-minute hike or a great circular bike trip (allow 30 min; cyclists can return to Schluxen from the castles on a different 30-min bike route via Füssen).

Sights

For all the logistics, see "Visiting the Castles," later in this section.

▲▲▲Hohenschwangau Castle

Standing quietly below Neuschwanstein, the big, yellow Hohenschwangau (hoh-en-SHVAHN-gow) Castle was Ludwig's boyhood home. Originally built in the 12th century, it was ruined by Napoleon. Ludwig's father, King Maximilian II, rebuilt it in 1830. Hohenschwangau ("High Land of the Swans") was used by the royal family as a summer hunting lodge until 1912. This was

Ludwig's boyhood escape.

The interior decor is harmonious, cohesive, and original—all done in 1835, with paintings inspired by Romantic themes. The Wittelsbach family (which ruled Bavaria for nearly seven centuries) still owns the place (and lived in the annex—today's shop—until the 1970s). As you tour the castle, imagine how the paintings must have inspired young Ludwig. For 17 years, he followed the construction of his dream castle from his dad's place—you'll see the telescope still set up and directed at Neuschwanstein.

The excellent 30-minute tours give a better glimpse of Ludwig's life than the more-visited and famous Neuschwanstein Castle tour. Tours here are smaller (35 people rather than 60) and more relaxed.

▲▲▲Neuschwanstein Castle

Imagine "Mad" King Ludwig as a boy, climbing the hills above his dad's castle, Hohenschwangau, dreaming up the ultimate fairy-tale castle. Inheriting the throne at the young age of 18, he had the power to make his dream concrete and stucco. Neuschwanstein (noy-SHVAHN-shtine) was designed by a theater set designer first...then by an architect. It looks medieval, but it's modern iron-and-brick construction with a sandstone veneer—only about as old as the Eiffel Tower. It feels like something you'd see at a home show for 19th-century royalty. Built from 1869 to 1886, it's the epitome of the Romanticism popular in 19th-century Europe. Construction stopped with Ludwig's death (only a third of the interior was finished), and within six weeks, tourists were paying to go through it.

Today, guides herd groups of 60 through the castle, giving an interesting—if rushed—30-minute tour. You'll go up and down more than 300 steps, through lavish rooms based on Wagnerian opera themes, the king's gilded-lily bedroom, and his extravagant throne room. You'll visit 15 rooms with their original furnishings and fanciful wall paintings. After the tour, before you descend to the king's kitchen, see the 20-minute video about the king's life and passions accompanied by Wagner's music (next to the café, alternates between English and German, schedule board at the entry says what's playing and what's on deck). After the kitchen (state of the art for this high-tech king in its day), you'll see a room lined with fascinating drawings (described in English) of the castle plans, construction, and drawings from 1883 of Falkenstein—a whimsical, over-the-top, never-built castle that makes Neuschwanstein look stubby. Falkenstein occupied Ludwig's fantasies the year he died.

Visiting the Castles

Cost: Each castle costs €9, a *Königsticket* for both castles costs €17, and children under 18 (accompanied by an adult) are admitted free.

Hours: Both castles are open April–Sept daily from 9:00 with last tour departing at 18:00, Oct–March daily from 10:00 with last tour at 16:00.

Getting Tickets for the Castles: Every tour bus in Bavaria converges on Neuschwanstein, and tourists flush in each morning from Munich. A handy reservation system (described next page) sorts out the chaos for smart travelers. Tickets come with admission times. To tour both castles, you must do Hohenschwangau first (logical, since this gives a better introduction to Ludwig's short life). You'll get two tour times: Hohenschwangau and then, two hours later, Neuschwanstein. If you miss your appointed tour time, you can't get in.

A **ticket center** for both castles is located at street level between the two (daily April–Sept 8:00–17:00, Oct–March 9:00–15:00, last tickets sold for Neuschwanstein one hour before closing, for Hohenschwangau 30 min before closing). Arrive by 8:00 in summer, and you'll likely be touring by 9:00. During August, tickets for English tours can run out by 16:00.

Reservations: While chaotic crowd scenes are largely a thing of the past, it's smart to reserve in peak season (July–Sept, especially Aug). Reservations cost €2 per person per castle, and you should make them a minimum of 24 hours in advance by phone (tel. 08362/930-830), email (info@ticket-center-hohenschwangau .de), or online (www.ticket-center-hohenschwangau.de).

Tour Procedure: You must pick up tickets well before the appointed entry time (30 min before your Hohenschwangau tour, one hour before your Neuschwanstein tour). Why the long wait? Many of the businesses serving tourists are owned by the old royal family...so they require more waiting time than necessary in the hope that you'll spend more money. The same applies to the minimum allowable time between the two castle tours: two hours. After completing the Hohenschwangau tour, this leaves you with about 45 minutes to kill. Ask for the minimum between tours. If they give you a longer gap, request less downtime.

For each castle, tourists jumble at the entry, waiting for their ticket number to light up on the board. When it does, power through the mob (most waiting there are holding higher numbers) and go to the turnstile. Warning: You must use your ticket while your number is still on the board. If you space out while waiting for a polite welcome, you'll miss your entry window and never get in.

Getting to the Castles: From the ticket booth, Hohenschwangau is an easy 10-minute climb, and Neuschwanstein is a steep 30-minute hike. To minimize hiking to Neuschwanstein, you can take a shuttle bus (leaves every few minutes from in front of Hotel Lisl, just above ticket office and to the left) or a horse-drawn carriage (in front of Hotel Müller, just above ticket office and to the right), but neither gets you to the castle doorstep. The shuttle bus drops you off near Mary's Bridge, leaving you a steep, 10-minute downhill walk to the castle—be sure to see the view from Mary's Bridge before hiking down (€1.80 one-way, the €2.60 round-trip is not worth it since you have to hike uphill to the bus stop for your return trip). Carriages (€5 up, €2.50 down) are slower than walking and stop below Neuschwanstein, leaving you a five-minute uphill hike. Here's the most economic and least strenuous plan: Ride the bus to Mary's Bridge for the view, hike down to Neuschwanstein, and then catch the horse carriage from the castle back down to the parking lot.

Services: The helpful TI, bus stop, ATM, WC (€0.50), and telephones cluster around the main intersection (**TI** open daily May–Sept 11:00–19:00, Oct–April 11:00–17:00, tel. 08362/819-765, www.schwangau.de).

Eating: The "village" at the foot of Europe's Disney castle feeds off the droves of hungry, shop-happy tourists. The Bräustüberl cafeteria serves the cheapest grub (€4 gut-bomb meals, often with live folk music, from 11:30). The Alpsee lake is ideal for a picnic, but there are no grocery shops nearby. Your best bet is to get food to go from one of the many bratwurst stands (between the ticket center and TI) or a sandwich at the shop adjacent the ticket booth. Enjoy a lazy lunch at the lakeside park or in one of the old-fashioned rowboats (rented by the hour in summer).

Near the Castles

Mary's Bridge (Marienbrücke)—Before or after the Neuschwanstein tour, climb up to Mary's Bridge to marvel at Ludwig's castle, just as Ludwig did. This bridge was quite an engineering accomplishment 100 years ago. From the bridge, the frisky can hike even higher to the *Beware—Danger of Death* signs and an even more glorious castle view. (Access to the bridge is closed in bad winter weather, but many travelers walk around the barriers to get there—at their own risk, of course.) For the most interesting descent from Neuschwanstein (15 min longer but worth it, especially with new steel walkways and railings that make the slippery area safer), follow signs to the Pöllat Gorge *(Pöllatschlucht)*.

▲Tegelberg Gondola—Just north of Neuschwanstein is a fun play zone around the mighty Tegelberg Gondola. For €16 round-trip (€10 one-way), you can ride the lift to the 5,500-foot summit (daily 9:00–17:00, closed Nov, 4/hr, last ride at 16:30, in bad weather call first to confirm, tel. 08362/98360; remember, buses #73 and #78 from Füssen continue from the castles to Tegelberg). On a clear day, you get great views of the Alps and Bavaria and the vicarious thrill of watching hang gliders and paragliders leap into airborne ecstasy. Weather permitting, scores of adventurous Germans line up and leap from the launch ramp at the top of the lift. With someone leaving every two or three minutes, it's great for spectators. Thrill-seekers with exceptional social skills may talk themselves into a tandem ride with a paraglider. From the top of Tegelberg, it's a steep and demanding 2.5-hour hike down to Ludwig's castle. (Avoid the treacherous trail directly below the gondola.) At the base of the gondola, you'll find a playground, a cheery eatery, the stubby remains of an ancient Roman villa, and a luge ride (below).

▲Tegelberg Luge—Next to the Tegelberg Gondola is a luge *(Sommerrodelbahn)* course. A luge is like a bobsled on wheels. This stainless-steel track is heated, so it's often dry and open, even when drizzly weather shuts down the concrete luges. A funky cable system pulls riders (in their sleds) to the top without a ski lift. Push the stick forward to go faster, pull back to apply brakes, keeping both hands on your stick. To avoid getting into a bumper-to-bumper traffic jam, let the person in front of you get way ahead before you start. You'll emerge from the course with a windblown hairdo and a smile-creased face (€2.50/ride, 6-ride sharable card-€10, July–Sept daily 10:00–18:00, otherwise same hours as gondola, in winter sometimes opens late due to wet track, in bad weather call first to confirm, no children under 6, tel. 08362/98360).

Sleeping

In Hohenschwangau, near Neuschwanstein Castle

(€1 = about $1.40, country code: 49, area code: 08362)

Inexpensive farmhouse B&Bs abound in the Bavarian countryside around Neuschwanstein, offering drivers a decent value. Look for *Zimmer Frei* signs ("room free," or vacancy). The going rate is about €50–65 for a double, including breakfast.

$$ Alpenhotel Meier is a small, family-run hotel with 18 rooms in a bucolic setting within walking distance of the castles, just beyond the lower parking lot (Sb-€48–58, perfectly fine older Db-€80, newer Db-€88, Tb-€110, these are book-direct prices, all rooms have porches or balconies—some with castle views, family rooms, elevator, sauna, free parking, just before tennis courts at Schwangauer Strasse 37, tel. 08362/81152, fax 08362/987-028, www.alpenhotel-allgaeu.de, info@alpenhotel-allgaeu.de, Frau Meier).

$ Beim "Landhannes," a 200-year-old working dairy farm run by Connie Schon, rents six creaky but sunny rooms, and keeps flowers on the balconies, big bells and antlers in the halls, and cows in the yard (Sb-€30, Db-€60, 20 percent discount for 3 or more nights, apartment with kitchen, cash only, poorly signed in the village of Horn on the Füssen side of Schwangau, look for the farm down a tiny lane through the grass 100 yards in front of Hotel Kleiner König, Am Lechrain 22, tel. 08362/8349, www .landhannes.de, mayr@landhannes.de).

$ Sonnenhof is a big, woody, old house with four spacious, traditionally decorated rooms (all with balconies) and a cheery garden. It's a 15-minute walk through the fields to the castles (S-€35, D-€50, Db-€60, cash only; at Pension Schwansee on the Füssen-Neuschwanstein road, follow the small lane 100 yards to Sonnenweg 11; they'll pick you up from the train station if you request ahead, tel. 08362/8420, Frau Görlich).

Reutte, Austria

Reutte (ROY-teh, with a rolled *r*), a relaxed Austrian town of 5,700, is located 20 minutes across the border from Füssen. While overlooked by the international tourist crowd, it's popular with Germans and Austrians for its climate. Doctors recommend its "grade 1" air. I like Reutte for the opportunity to simply be in a real community. As an example of how the town is committed to its character, real estate can be sold only to those using it as a primary residence. (Many formerly vibrant alpine towns made a pile of money but lost their sense of community by becoming resorts. They allowed wealthy foreigners—who just drop in for a week or two a year—to buy up all the land, and are now shuttered up and dead most of the time.)

Reutte's one claim to fame with Americans: As Nazi Germany was falling in 1945, Hitler's top rocket scientist, Werner von Braun, joined the Americans (rather than the Russians) in Reutte. You could say that the American space program began here.

Reutte isn't featured in any other American guidebook. While its generous sidewalks are filled with smart boutiques and lazy coffeehouses, its charms are subtle. It was never rich or important. Its castle is ruined, its buildings have painted-on "carvings," its churches are full, its men yodel for each other on birthdays, and its energy is spent soaking its Austrian and German guests in *Gemütlichkeit*. Most guests stay for a week, so the town's attractions are more time-consuming than thrilling.

Orientation

(country code: 43, area code: 05672)

Tourist Information

Reutte's TI is a block in front of the train station (Mon–Fri 8:00–12:00 & 14:00–17:00, no midday break July–Aug, Sat 8:30–12:00, closed Sun, tel. 05672/62336, www.reutte.com). Go over your sightseeing plans, ask about a folk evening, pick up city and biking maps and the *Sommerprogramm* events schedule (in German only), and ask about discounts with the hotel guest cards. Their free informational booklet has a good self-guided town walk.

Arrival in Reutte

If you're coming by car from Germany, skip the north *(Nord)* exit and take the south *(Süd)* exit into town. For parking in town, blue lines denote pay-and-display spots. There is a free lot (P-1) near the train station on Muhlerstrasse.

While Austria requires a **toll sticker** *(Vignette)* for driving on its highways (€8/10 days, buy at the border, gas stations, car-rental agencies, or *Tabak* shops), those just dipping into Tirol from Bavaria do not need one.

Helpful Hints

Internet Access: There's a **call shop** at Untermarkt 22 in the town center (Tue–Sun 11:00–22:00, closed Mon), and **Café Alte Post** at Untermarkt 15 has Internet access. Otherwise, rely on your hotel.

Laundry: There isn't an actual launderette in town, but the recommended hotels Maximilian and Ernberg let even non-guests use their self-service machines (see listings in "Sleeping," later in this chapter).

Bike Rental: Try **Intersport** (€15/day, Mon–Fri 9:00–18:00, Sat 9:00–17:00, closed Sun, Lindenstrasse 25, tel. 05672/62352), or check at Hotel Maximilian (listed in "Sleeping").

Car Rental: Autoreisen Köck rents cars at Muhlerstrasse 12 (€80/24 hrs, tel. 05672/62233).

"Nightlife": Reutte is pretty quiet. For any action at all, there's a strip of bars, dance clubs, and Italian restaurants on Lindenstrasse.

Sights and Activities

▲▲Ehrenberg Castle Ensemble (Festungsensemble Ehrenberg)

If Neuschwanstein was the medieval castle dream, Ehrenburg is the medieval castle reality. Just a mile outside of Reutte are the brooding ruins of four castles that once made up the largest fort in Tirol. This impressive "castle ensemble" was built to defend against the Bavarians and to bottle up the strategic Via Claudia trade route, which cut through the Alps as it connected Italy and Germany. Today, these castles have become a European "castle museum," showing off 500 years of military architecture in one swoop. The European Union is helping fund the project (paying a third of its €9 million cost) because it promotes the heritage of a multinational region—Tirol—rather than a country.

The complex has four parts: the fortified Klause toll both on the valley floor, the oldest castle on the first hill above (Ehrenberg), a mighty and more modern castle high above (Schlosskopf, built in the age when cannon positioned there made the original castle vulnerable), and a smaller fourth castle across the valley (Fort Claudia, an hour's hike away). All four were a fortified complex once connected by walls. Signs posted throughout the castle complex help visitors find their way and explain some background on

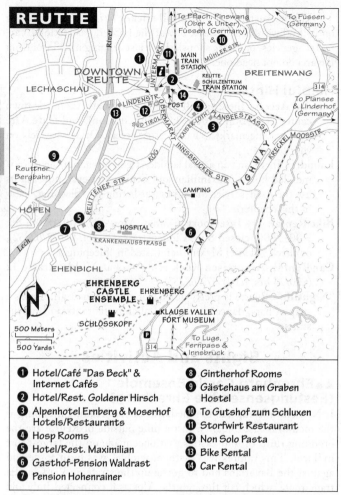

REUTTE

To Pflach, Pinswang (Ober & Unter) Füssen (Germany) & ⑩

To Füssen (Germany)

River

UNTERMARKT

MÜHLER STR.

MAIN TRAIN STATION

DOWNTOWN REUTTE

LECHASCHAU

REUTTE-SCHULZENTRUM TRAIN STATION

BREITENWANG

314

LINDENSTR.

OBERMARKT

POST

KAISER LOTH.

PLANSEESTRASSE

To Plansee & Linderhof (Germany)

SÜD TIROL

INNSBRUCKER STR.

KRECKELMOOSSTR.

KÖG.

To Reuttner Bergbahn

REUTTENER STR.

HIGHWAY

CAMPING

HÖFEN

Lech

HOSPITAL

KRANKENHAUSSTRASSE

MAIN

EHENBICHL

EHRENBERG CASTLE ENSEMBLE

EHRENBERG

SCHLOSSKOPF

KLAUSE VALLEY FORT MUSEUM

P

To Luge, Fernpass & Innsbruck

314

500 Meters

500 Yards

① Hotel/Café "Das Beck" & Internet Cafés
② Hotel/Rest. Goldener Hirsch
③ Alpenhotel Ernberg & Moserhof Hotels/Restaurants
④ Hosp Rooms
⑤ Hotel/Rest. Maximilian
⑥ Gasthof-Pension Waldrast
⑦ Pension Hohenrainer
⑧ Gintherhof Rooms
⑨ Gästehaus am Graben Hostel
⑩ To Gutshof zum Schluxen
⑪ Storfwirt Restaurant
⑫ Non Solo Pasta
⑬ Bike Rental
⑭ Car Rental

the region's history, geology, geography, culture, flora, and fauna. (While the castles are free and open all the time, the museum and multimedia show at the fort's parking lot charge admission.)

Getting to the Castle Ensemble: The Klause, Ehrenberg, and Schlosskopf castles are on the road to Lermoos and Innsbruck. These are a pleasant walk or a short bike ride from Reutte; bikers can use the *Radwanderweg* along the Lech River (the TI has a good map).

▲**Klause Valley Fort Museum**—Historians estimate that about 10,000 tons of precious salt passed through this valley (along the route of Rome's Via Claudia) each year in medieval times, so it's no wonder the locals built this complex of fortresses and castles.

Beginning in the 14th century, the fort controlled traffic and levied tolls on all who passed. Today, these scant remains hold a museum and a theater with a multimedia show (€8 for museum, €11 combo-ticket also includes multimedia show, €18 family pass for 2 adults and any number of kids, daily 10:00–17:00, closed Nov–mid-Dec, tel. 05672/62007, www.ehrenberg.at).

While there are no real artifacts here (other than the sword used in A.D. 2008 to make me the honorary First Knight of Ehrenberg), the clever, kid-friendly **museum** takes one 14th-century decade (1360–1370) and attempts to bring it to life. It's a hands-on experience, well-described in English. You can try on a set of armor (and then weigh yourself), see the limited vision knights had to put up with when wearing their helmet, empathize with victims of the plague, and join a Crusade.

The **multimedia show** takes you on a 30-minute spin through the 2,000-year history of this valley's fortresses, with images projected on the old stone walls and modern screens (generally in German, in English at 13:00 or sometimes by request).

▲▲**Ehrenberg Ruins**—Ehrenberg, a 13th-century rock pile, provides a super opportunity to let your imagination off its leash. Hike up 30 minutes from the parking lot of the Klause Valley Fort Museum for a great view from your own private ruins. Ehrenberg (which means "Mountain of Honor") was the first castle here, built in 1296. Thirteenth-century castles were designed to stand boast-fully tall. With the advent of gunpowder, castles dug in. (Notice the 18th-century **ramparts** around you.)

Approaching Ehrenberg Castle, look for the small **door** to the left. It's the night entrance (tight and awkward, and therefore safer against a surprise attack). Entering this castle, you go through two doors. Castles allowed step-by-step retreat, giving defenders time to regroup and fight back against invading forces.

Before climbing to the top of the castle, follow the path around to the right to a big, grassy courtyard with commanding views and a fat, newly restored **turret.** This stored gunpowder and held a big cannon that enjoyed a clear view of the valley below. In medieval times, all the trees approaching the castle were cleared to keep an unobstructed view.

Look out over the valley. The pointy spire marks **Breitenwang,** which was a stop on the ancient Via Claudia. In A.D. 46, there was a Roman camp there. In 1489, after the Reutte bridge crossed the Lech River, Reutte (marked by the onion-domed church) was made a market town and eclipsed Breitenwang in importance. Any gliders circling? They launch from just over the river in Höfen.

For centuries, this castle was the seat of government—ruling an area called the "judgment of Ehrenberg" (roughly the same as today's "district of Reutte"). When the emperor came by, he stayed here. In 1604, the ruler moved downtown into more comfortable quarters, and the castle was no longer a palace.

Now climb to the top of Ehrenberg Castle. Take the high ground. There was no water supply here—just kegs of wine, beer, and a cistern to collect rain.

Ehrenberg repelled 16,000 Swedish soldiers in the defense of Catholicism in 1632. Ehrenberg saw three or four other battles, but its end was not glorious. In the 1780s, a local businessman bought the castle in order to sell off its parts. Later, in the late 19th century, when vagabonds moved in, the roof was removed to make squatting miserable. With the roof gone, deterioration quickened, leaving only this evocative shell and a whiff of history.

▲**Schlosskopf**—From Ehrenberg, you can hike up another 30 minutes to the mighty Schlosskopf ("Castle Head"). When the Bavarians captured Ehrenberg in 1703, the Tiroleans climbed up to the bluff above it to rain cannonballs down on their former fortress. In 1740, a mighty new castle—designed to defend against modern artillery—was built on this sky-high strategic location. By the end of the 20th century, the castle was completely overgrown with trees—you literally couldn't see it from Reutte. But today the trees are shaved away, and the castle has been excavated. In 2008, the Castle Ensemble project, led by local architect Armin Walch, opened the site with English descriptions and view platforms. One spot gives spectacular views of the strategic valley. The other looks down on the older Ehrenberg Castle ruins, illustrating the strategic problems presented with the advent of cannon.

In Reutte

Reutte Museum (Museum Grünes Haus)—Reutte's city museum, offering a quick look at the local folk culture and the story of the castles, is more cute than impressive. Perhaps someday a little English will bring more meaning to the exhibits (€2, May–Oct Tue–Sun 10:00–16:00, closed Mon and Nov–April, in the bright-green building on Untermarkt, around corner from Hotel Goldener Hirsch, tel. 05672/72304, www.museum-reutte.at).

▲▲**Tirolean Folk Evening**—Ask the TI or your hotel if there's a Tirolean folk evening scheduled. During the summer (July–Aug), nearby towns (such as Höfen on Tuesdays) occasionally put on an evening of yodeling, slap dancing, and Tirolean frolic. These are generally free and worth the short drive. Off-season, you'll have to do your own yodeling. There are also weekly folk concerts featuring the local choir or brass band in Reutte's Zeiller Platz (free, July–Aug only, ask at TI). For listings of these and other local events, pick up a copy of the German-only *Sommerprogramm* schedule at the TI.

Sleeping

In and near Reutte

(€1 = about $1.40, country code: 43, area code: 05672)

Reutte is a mellow Füssen with fewer crowds and easygoing locals with a contagious love of life. Come here for a good dose of Austrian ambience and lower prices. While it's workable on public transit, staying here makes most sense for those with a car. Reutte is popular with Austrians and Germans, who come here year after year for one- or two-week vacations. The hotels are big, elegant, and full of comfy, carved furnishings and creative ways to spend lots of time in one spot. They take great pride in their restaurants, and the owners send their children away to hotel-management schools. All include a great breakfast, but few accept credit cards. Most hotels give about a 5 percent discount for stays of two nights or longer.

The Reutte TI has a list of 50 private homes that rent out generally good rooms *(Zimmer)* with facilities down the hall, pleasant communal living rooms, and breakfast. Most charge €20 per person per night, and the owners speak little or no English. As these are family-run places, it is especially important to cancel in advance if your plans change. I've listed a few favorites below, but the TI can always find you a room when you arrive.

Reutte is surrounded by several distinct "villages" that basically feel like suburbs—many of them, such as Breitenwang, are within easy walking distance of the Reutte town center. If you want to hike through the woods to Neuschwanstein Castle, stay at Gutshof zum Schluxen (listed on page 492). To locate the recommended accommodations, see the Reutte map.

In Central Reutte

$$ Hotel "Das Beck" offers 16 clean, sunny rooms (many with balconies) filling a modern building in the heart of town. It's a great value, and guests are personally taken care of by Hans, Inge, Tamara, and Pipi. Enjoy their homemade marmalade at breakfast in the open kitchen/coffee bar or on the pleasant patio. Their small café offers tasty snacks and specializes in Austrian and Italian wines. Expect good conversation overseen by Hans (Sb-€45, Db-€68, Tb suite-€89, Qb suite-€106, Internet access free for Rick Steves readers, free parking, they'll pick you up from the train station, Untermarkt 11, tel. 05672/62522, fax 05672/625-2235, www.hotel-das-beck.at, info@hotel-das-beck.at).

$$ Hotel Goldener Hirsch, located in the center of Reutte just two blocks from the station, is a grand old hotel with 56 rooms and one lonely set of antlers (Sb-€58–62, Db-€85–90, Db suite-€90–98, Tb-€125–135, Qb-€140–145, 2-night discounts, elevator, tel. 05672/62508, fax 05672/625-087, www.goldener-hirsch.at, info@goldener-hirsch.at; Monika, Helmut, and daughters Vanessa and Nina).

In Breitenwang

Right next door to Reutte is the older and quieter village of Breitenwang (with good *Zimmer* and a fine bakery). It's a 20-minute walk from the Reutte train station: At the post office roundabout, follow Planseestrasse past the onion-dome church to the pointy straight-dome church near the two hotels. The Hosps—as well as other B&Bs—are along unmarked Kaiser-Lothar-Strasse, the first right past this church. If your train stops at the tiny Reutte-Schulzentrum station, hop out here—you're just a five-minute walk from here.

$$ Alpenhotel Ernberg is run with great care by friendly Hermann, who combines Old World elegance with modern touches. Nestle in for some serious coziness among the carved-wood eating nooks, tiled stoves, and family-friendly backyard (Sb-€45, Db-€84, less for longer stays, self-service laundry for €7—also available for non-guests, restaurant, Planseestrasse 50, tel. 05672/71912, fax 05672/191-240, www.ernberg.at, info @ernberg.at).

$$ Moserhof Hotel has 30 new-feeling rooms plus an elegant dining room (Sb-€52, Db-€88, extra bed-€35, most rooms have balconies, elevator, restaurant, free parking, Planseestrasse 44, tel. 05672/62020, fax 05672/620-2040, www.hotel-moserhof.at, info @hotel-moserhof.at, Hosp family).

$ Walter and Emilie Hosp rent three rooms in a comfortable, quiet, and modern house two blocks from the Breitenwang church steeple. You'll feel like you're staying at Grandma's (D-€40, or €36 for 4 nights or more, T-€60, Q-€80, cash only, Kaiser-Lothar-Strasse 29, tel. 05672/65377).

In Ehenbichl, near the Ehrenberg Ruins

The next listings are a bit farther from central Reutte, a couple of miles upriver in the village of Ehenbichl (under the Ehrenberg ruins). From central Reutte, go south on Obermarkt and turn right on Kög, which becomes Reuttener Strasse, following signs to Ehenbichl.

$$ Hotel Maximilian is a great value. It includes free bicycles, table tennis, a children's playroom, a pool table, and the friendly service of Gabi, Monika, and the rest of the Koch family. They host many special events, and their hotel has lots of wonderful extras such as a sauna and a piano (Sb-€48–52, Db-€76–84, ask for these special Rick Steves prices when you reserve, family deals, elevator, free Internet access and Wi-Fi, laundry service for €12—or €16 for non-guests, good restaurant, tel. 05672/62585, fax 05672/625-8554, www.maxihotel.com, info@hotelmaximilian.at). They rent cars to guests only (one Renault, one VW van—€0.72/km, book in advance) and bikes to anyone (€6/half-day, €10/day).

$ Gasthof-Pension Waldrast, separating a forest and a meadow, is run by the farming Huter family. The place feels hauntingly quiet and has no restaurant, but it's inexpensive and offers 10 nice rooms with generous sitting areas and castle-view balconies (Sb-€37, Db-€60, Tb-€75, Qb-€95; cash only, all rooms non-smoking, free parking; about a mile from Reutte, just off main drag toward Innsbruck, past campground and under castle ruins on Ehrenbergstrasse; tel. & fax 05672/62443, www.waldrasttirol .com, info@waldrasttirol.com, Gerd).

$ Pension Hohenrainer, a big, quiet, no-frills place, is a good value with 12 modern rooms and some castle-view balconies (Sb-€25–30, Db-€49–55, €3 per person extra for one-night stays, cheaper for longer stays and in April–June and Sept–Oct, cash only, family rooms, non-smoking rooms, free Internet access, restaurant across the street, follow signs up the road behind Hotel Maximilian into village of Ehenbichl, tel. 05672/62544 or 05672/63262, fax 05672/62052, www.hohenrainer.at, hohenrainer@aon.at).

$ Gintherhof is a working farm that provides its guests with fresh milk, butter, and bacon. Christl and Rudi Ginther offer geranium-covered balconies, six nice rooms with carved-wood ceilings, and a Madonna in every corner (Db-€46–50, Unterried 7, just up the road behind Hotel Maximilian, tel. 05672/67697, www .gintherhof.com, gintherhof@aon.at).

A Hostel Across the River

$ The homey **Gästehaus am Graben hostel** has 2–6 beds per room and includes breakfast and sheets. It's lovingly run by the Reyman family—Frau Reyman, Rudi, and Gabi keep the 50-bed place traditional, clean, and friendly, and they serve guests a great €7 dinner. This is a super value less than two miles from Reutte, and the castle views are fantastic. If you've never hosteled and are curious (and have a car or don't mind a bus ride), try it. If traveling with kids, this is a great choice. The double rooms are hotel-grade, and they accept non-members of any age (dorm bed-€22, bunk-bed D-€44, hotel-style Db-€56, cash only, non-smoking rooms, laundry service, no curfew, closed April and Nov–mid-Dec; from downtown Reutte, cross bridge and follow main road left along river, or take the bus—hourly until 19:30, ask for Graben stop, no buses Sun; Graben 1, tel. 05672/626-440, fax 05672/626-444, www.hoefen.at, info@hoefen.at).

In Pinswang

The village of Pinswang is closer to Füssen (and Ludwig's castles), but still in Austria.

$$ Gutshof zum Schluxen gets the "Remote Old Hotel in an Idyllic Setting" award. This family-friendly working farm offers rustic elegance draped in goose down and pastels, and a chance to pet a rabbit and feed the deer. Its picturesque meadow setting will turn you into a dandelion picker, and its proximity to Neuschwanstein will turn you into a hiker; the castle is just an hour's hike away—see page 479 (Sb-€45, Db-€78, extra person-€22, 5 percent discount for stays of 3 or more nights, self-service laundry, mountain-bike rental, restaurant, fun bar, between Reutte and Füssen in village of Pinswang, free pick-up from Reutte or Füssen, call ahead if you'll arrive after 18:00, tel. 05677/8903, fax 05677/890-323, www.schluxen.com, welcome @schluxen.com).

Eating

In Reutte

The hotels here take great pride in serving local cuisine at reasonable prices to their guests and the public. Rather than go to a cheap restaurant, eat at a hotel. Most offer €8–14 dinners from 18:00 to 21:00 and are closed one night a week. Reutte itself has plenty of inviting eateries, including traditional, ethnic, fast food, grocery stores, and delis.

Since hospitality is such a big part of the local scene, **hotel restaurants** are generally your best bet for a good meal. Hotel Goldener Hirsch, Alpenhotel Ernberg, Moserhof Hotel, and Hotel Maximilian all offer fine restaurants (see each listing under "Sleeping," earlier in this section).

Storfwirt is *the* place for a quick and cheap lunch or light dinner. You can get the usual sausages here, as well as baked potatoes and salads (€5–8 daily meals, salad bar, always something for vegetarians, Mon–Fri 8:30–15:00, Sat 9:00–14:30, closed Sun, Schrettergasse 15, tel. 05672/62640).

Non Solo Pasta, just off the traffic circle, is a local favorite for Italian food (€7 pizzas, €7–10 entrées, Mon–Fri 11:30–14:00 & 18:00–23:00, Sat 18:00–23:00, closed Sun, Lindenstrasse 1, tel. 05672/72714).

Picnic Supplies: **Billa** supermarket has everything you'll need (across from TI, Mon–Fri 8:00–19:00, Sat 8:00–17:00, closed Sun).

Connections

From Reutte by Train to: Garmisch (every 2 hrs, 1 hr), **Munich** (every 2 hrs, 2.5 hrs, change in Garmisch), **Salzburg** (9/day, 4.5 hrs, 2 changes).

By Bus to: Füssen (Mon–Fri 4/day, none Sat–Sun, 35 min, €3.40, buses depart from in front of the train station, pay driver). Taxis cost €30 one-way to Füssen, or €35 to the King's Castles.

ROTHENBURG

Rothenburg ob der Tauber

In the Middle Ages, when Frankfurt and Munich were just wide spots on the road, Rothenburg ob der Tauber was a free imperial city. With a whopping population of 6,000, it was one of Germany's largest. Today, it's the country's best-preserved medieval walled town, enjoying tremendous tourist popularity without losing its charm.

During Rothenburg's heyday, from 1150 to 1400, it was a strategic stop on the trade routes between northern and southern Europe. That route is now Germany's "Romantic Road," linking Frankfurt to Munich through a medieval heartland strewn with picturesque villages, farmhouses, onion-domed churches, and walled cities. Rothenburg is the cream of the crop.

Today, Rothenburg's great trade is tourism: Two-thirds of the townspeople are employed to serve you. While 2.5 million people visit each year, a mere 500,000 spend the night. Rothenburg is yours after dark, when the groups vacate and the town's floodlit cobbles wring some romance out of any travel partner.

Too often, Rothenburg brings out the shopper in visitors before they've had a chance to see the historic town. True, this is a fine place to do your German shopping, but appreciate Rothenburg's great history and sights, too.

Planning Your Time

If time is short, you can make just a two- to three-hour midday stop in Rothenburg, but the town is really best appreciated after the day-trippers have gone home. Spend at least one night in Rothenburg (hotels are cheap). With two nights and a day, you'll be able to see more than the essentials and actually relax a little.

Rothenburg

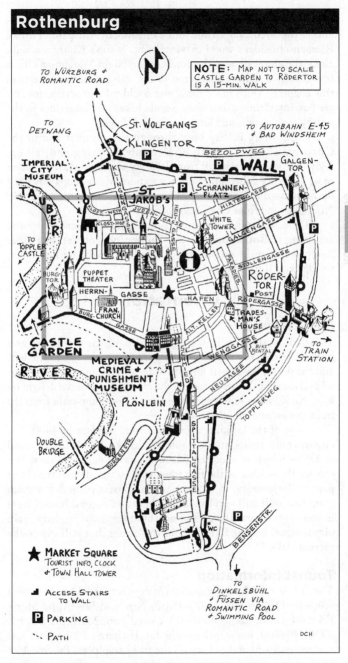

NOTE: MAP NOT TO SCALE
CASTLE GARDEN TO RÖDERTOR
IS A 15-MIN. WALK

TO WÜRZBURG &
ROMANTIC ROAD

TO DETWANG

ST. WOLFGANGS

KLINGENTOR

TO AUTOBAHN E-45
& BAD WINDSHEIM

BEZOLDWEG

WALL

GALGEN-TOR

IMPERIAL CITY MUSEUM

SCHRANNEN-PLATZ

HIRTENGASSE

ST. JAKOB'S

KLINGENGASSE

KLOST.-WETH

KLOST-HOF

JUDEN-GASSE

HEU-GASSE

WHITE TOWER

GALGENGASSE

PARADIES

STOLLENGASSE

TO TOPPLER CASTLE

BURG-TOR

PUPPET THEATER

HERRN- GASSE

FRAN. CHURCH

BURG- GASSE

HAFEN

ALT. KELLER

RÖDER-TOR Post

RÖDERGASSE

TRADES-MAN'S HOUSE

BIKE RENTAL

TO TRAIN STATION

CASTLE GARDEN

RIVER

MEDIEVAL CRIME & PUNISHMENT MUSEUM

PLÖNLEIN

SCHMIED GASSE

WENGGASSE

NEUGASSE

TOPPLERWEG

DOUBLE BRIDGE

BURGENSTR.

SPITTALGASSE

WC

BENSENSTR.

TO DINKELSBÜHL & FÜSSEN VIA ROMANTIC ROAD & SWIMMING POOL

★ MARKET SQUARE
TOURIST INFO, CLOCK & TOWN HALL TOWER

⬛ ACCESS STAIRS TO WALL

🅿 PARKING

⋱ PATH

DCH

ROTHENBURG

Rothenburg in one day is easy, with four essential experiences: the Medieval Crime and Punishment Museum, Tilman Riemenschneider's wood carving in St. Jakob's Church, a walk along the city wall, and the entertaining Night Watchman's Tour (the first two sights are covered in my self-guided walk, later in this chapter). With more time, you could take in several mediocre but entertaining museums, scenic hikes and bike rides in the nearby countryside, and lots of cafés and shops.

Rothenburg is very busy through the summer and in the Christmas Market month of December. Spring and fall are a joy, but it's pretty bleak from January through March—when most locals are hibernating or on vacation. Many shops stay open on Sundays during the tourist season, but close on Sundays in November and from Christmas to Easter.

There are several Rothenburgs in Germany, so make sure you are going to **Rothenburg ob der Tauber** (not "ob der" any other river); people really do sometimes drive or ride the train to other, nondescript Rothenburgs by accident.

Orientation

(area code: 09861)

To orient yourself in Rothenburg, think of the town map as a human head. Its nose—the castle garden—sticks out to the left, and the skinny lower part forms a wide-open mouth, with the hostel and some of the best hotels in the chin. The town is a delight on foot. No sights or hotels are more than a 15-minute walk from the train station or each other.

Most of the buildings you'll see were in place by 1400. The city was born around its long-gone castle—built in 1142, destroyed in 1356—which was located where the castle garden is now. You can see the shadow of the first town wall, which defines the oldest part of Rothenburg, in its contemporary street plan. A few gates from this wall still survive. The richest and biggest houses were in this central part. The commoners built higgledy-piggledy (read: picturesque) houses farther from the center, but still inside the present walls.

Tourist Information

The TI is on Market Square (May–Oct and Dec Mon–Fri 9:00–18:00, Sat–Sun 10:00–15:00; Nov and Jan–April Mon–Fri 9:00–17:00, Sat 10:00–13:00, closed Sun; Marktplatz 2, tel. 09861/404800, www.rothenburg.de). If there's a long line, just raid the rack where they keep all the free pamphlets. The free *Map & Guide* comes with a walking guide to the town. The free *RoTour* monthly magazine lists all the events and entertainment (in

German only; also look for current concert listing posters here and at your hotel). Ask about the daily English walking tour at 14:00 (€6, April–Oct and Dec; see next section, "Tours"). The TI has one free Internet terminal (15-min maximum). Visitors who arrive after closing can check the handy map highlighting which hotels have rooms available, with a free direct phone connection to them; it's just outside the door. A pictorial town map is available free with this book at the Friese shop, two doors west from the TI (toward St. Jakob's Church; see "Shopping," later in this chapter).

Arrival in Rothenburg

By Train: It's a 10-minute walk from the station to Rothenburg's Market Square (following the brown *Altstadt* signs, exit left from station, turn right on Ansbacher Strasse, and head straight into the Middle Ages). Day-trippers can leave luggage in station lockers (€1–2, on platform) or at a local shop (try the Friese shop on Market Square, or Passage 12—see "Shopping"). Arrange train and *couchette*/sleeper reservations at the combined ticket office and travel agency in the station (€0.50 charge for questions without ticket purchase, Mon–Fri 9:00–18:00, Sat 9:00–13:00, closed Sun, tel. 09861/7711). Free WCs are behind the snack bar next door to the station. Taxis wait at the station (€5 to any hotel).

By Car: While much of the town is closed to traffic, anyone with a hotel reservation can drive in and through pedestrian zones to get to their hotel. But driving in town can be a nightmare, with many narrow, one-way streets. If you're packing light, just park outside the walls and walk five minutes to the center. Parking lots line the town walls: P1 costs €5 per day; P5 and the south half of P4 are free. Only those with a hotel reservation can park within the walls after hours (but not during festivals). The easiest way to enter and leave Rothenburg is generally via Spitalgasse and the Spitaltor (south end).

Helpful Hints

Festivals: *Biergartens* spill out into the street and Rothenburgers dress up in medieval costumes to celebrate Mayor Nusch's Meistertrunk victory (see story of the draught that saved the town under "Meistertrunk Show" on page 501, more info at www.meistertrunk.de). The Reichsstadt festival every September celebrates Rothenburg's history.

Christmas Market: Rothenburg is dead in November, January, and February, but December is its busiest month—the entire town cranks up the medieval cuteness with concerts and costumes, shops with schnapps, stalls filling squares, hot spiced wine, giddy nutcrackers, and mobs of earmuffed Germans. Christmas markets are big all over Germany, and

Rothenburg's is considered one of the best. The festival takes place each year during Advent. Virtually all sights listed in this chapter are open longer hours during these four weeks. Try to avoid Saturdays and Sundays, when big-city day-trippers really clog the grog.

Internet Access: When it comes to getting online, Rothenburg is still pretty medieval. Only some hotels have Internet access, and many have no phones in the rooms. **Inter@Play,** the only Internet café in town, has eight fast terminals (€3/hr, daily 8:00–24:00, 18 and older only, 2 blocks down Hafengasse from Market Square and around the corner to the left at Milchmarkt 3—see Rothenburg Self-Guided Walk map in this chapter, tel. 09861/935-599). The **TI** has one free terminal for brief use (maximum 15 min). The **Passage 12** souvenir shop offers free use of the computer at their desk upstairs (see "Shopping," later in this chapter).

Laundry: A handy launderette is near the station, off Ansbacher Strasse (€5.50/load, includes soap, English instructions, opens at 8:00, last load Mon–Fri at 18:00, Sat at 14:00, closed Sun, Johannitergasse 9, tel. 09861/2775).

Haircuts: At **Salon Wack** (pronounced *vack*, not *wack*), Horst and his team speak English and welcome both men and women (€17.50 for men, €27–32.50 for women, Tue–Fri 8:00–12:00 & 13:30–18:00, Sat 8:30–14:00, closed Sun–Mon, in the old center just off Wenggasse at Goldene Ringgasse 8, tel. 09861/7834).

Swimming: Rothenburg has a fine swimming complex, with a heated outdoor pool *(Freibad)* from mid-May to mid-September, and an indoor pool and sauna the rest of the year. It's about 15 minutes' walk south of Spitaltor along the main road toward Dinkelsbühl (adults-€3.50, kids-€2, swimsuit and towel rental-€2.50 each; outdoor pool open Fri–Tue 9:00–20:00, Wed 6:30–20:00, Thu 10:00–20:00; indoor pool open Mon 14:00–21:00, Tue–Thu 9:00–21:00, Fri–Sun 9:00–18:00; Nördlinger Strasse 20, tel. 09861/4565, www.stadtwerke -rothenburg.de).

Bike Rental: You can rent a bike and follow the suggested route described under "Sights and Activities: Near Rothenburg." **Fahrradhaus Krauss** is a big bike shop that rents eight-gear bikes. It's cheap, reliable, and right in the old town (€5/6 hrs, €10/24 hrs, no helmets, Tue–Fri 9:00–18:00, Sat 9:00–13:00, closed Sun–Mon, Wenggasse 42, tel. 09861/3495).

Tours

▲▲Night Watchman's Tour—This tour is flat-out the most entertaining hour of medieval wonder anywhere in Germany. The Night Watchman (a.k.a. Hans-Georg Baumgartner) jokes like a medieval Jerry Seinfeld as he lights his lamp and takes tourists on his rounds, telling slice-of-gritty-life tales of medieval Rothenburg (€6, free for kids, Easter–Dec nightly at 20:00, in English, meet at Market Square, www.nightwatchman.de). This is the best evening activity in town.

Old Town Historic Walk—The TI offers 90-minute guided walking tours in English (€6, April–Oct and Dec daily at 14:00, Jan–March Sat only at 11:00, no tours in Nov, departs from Market Square). While the Night Watchman's Tour is fun, take this tour for the serious side of Rothenburg's history, and to make sense of the town's architecture. The tours are completely different, and it would be a shame not to take advantage of this informative tour just because you took the other.

Local Guides—A local historian can really bring the ramparts alive. Prices are standardized (€60/90 min, €78/2 hrs). **Gisela Vogl** (tel. 09861/4957, werner.vogl@t-online.de) and **Anita Weinzierl** (tel. 09868/7993, anitaweinzierl@aol.com) are both good. **Martin Kamphans,** a potter, also works as a guide (tel. 09861/7941, www.stadtfuehrungen-rothenburg.de, kamphans@t-online.de). Or you can reserve a guide by sending an email to the TI (info@rothenburg.de; also click "Guided Tours" at www.rothenburg.de).

Horse-and-Buggy Rides—These farm boys, who are generally about as charming as their horses, give a relaxing 30-minute clip-clop through the old town, starting from Market Square or Schrannenplatz. Good luck negotiating a fair price (private buggy for €30–50, or wait for one to fill up for €10 per person).

Self-Guided Walk

Welcome to Rothenburg

This one-hour circular walk weaves Rothenburg's top sights together.

• *Start the walk on Market Square.*

Market Square Spin-Tour

Stand at the bottom of Market Square (10 feet below the wooden post on the corner) and spin 360 degrees clockwise, starting with the Town Hall tower. Now do it again, this time more slowly, following these notes:

Town Hall and Tower: Rothenburg's tallest spire is the **Town Hall tower** (Rathausturm). At 200 feet, it stands atop the old

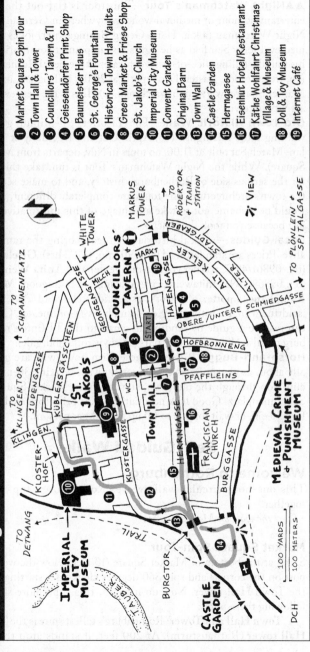

ROTHENBURG

Rothenburg Self-Guided Walk

1. Market Square Spin Tour
2. Town Hall & Tower
3. Councillors' Tavern & TI
4. Geissendörfer Print Shop
5. Baumeister Haus
6. St. George's Fountain
7. Historical Town Hall Vaults
8. Green Market & Friese Shop
9. St. Jakob's Church
10. Imperial City Museum
11. Convent Garden
12. Original Barn
13. Town Wall
14. Castle Garden
15. Herrngasse
16. Eisenhut Hotel/Restaurant
17. Käthe Wohlfahrt Christmas Village & Museum
18. Doll & Toy Museum
19. Internet Café

Town Hall, a white, Gothic, 13th-century building. Notice the tourists enjoying the best view in town from the black top of the tower (€2 and a rigorous but interesting climb, 214 steps, narrow and steep near the top—watch your head, April–Oct daily 9:30–12:30 & 13:00–17:00, closed Nov–March, enter on Market Square through middle arch of new Town Hall). After a fire burned down part of the original building, a new Town Hall was built alongside what survived of the old one (fronting the square). This half of the rebuilt complex is in the Renaissance style from 1570.

Meistertrunk Show: At the top of Market Square stands the proud Councillors' Tavern (clock tower from 1466). In its day, the city council—the rich guys who ran the town government—drank here. Today, it's the TI and the focus of most tourists' attention when the little doors on either side of the clock flip open and the wooden figures (from 1910) do their thing. Be on Market Square at 11:00, 12:00, 13:00, 14:00, 15:00, 20:00, 21:00, or 22:00 for the ritual gathering of the tourists to see the less-than-breathtaking reenactment of the Meistertrunk ("Master Draught") story:

In 1631, the Catholic army took the Protestant town and was about to do its rape, pillage, and plunder thing. As was the etiquette, the mayor had to give the conquering general a welcoming drink. The general enjoyed a huge tankard of local wine. Feeling really good, he told the mayor, "Hey, if you can drink this entire three-liter tankard of wine in one gulp, I'll spare your town." The mayor amazed everyone by drinking the entire thing, and Rothenburg was saved.

While this is a nice story, it was dreamed up in the late 1800s for a theatrical play designed (effectively) to promote a romantic image of the town. In actuality, if Rothenburg was spared, it happened because it bribed its way out of a jam. It was occupied and ransacked several times in the Thirty Years' War, and it never recovered—which is why it's such a well-preserved time capsule today.

For the best show, don't watch the clock; watch the open-mouthed tourists gasp as the old windows flip open. At the late shows, the square flickers with camera flashes.

Bottom of Market Square: On the bottom end of the square, the cream-colored building on the corner has a fine **print shop** (upstairs—see "Romantic Prints" under "Shopping"). Adjoining that is the **Baumeister Haus,** featuring a famous Renaissance facade with statues of the seven virtues and the seven vices—the former supporting the latter. The statues are copies; the originals are in the Imperial City Museum (described later on this walk). The green house below that is the former home of the 15th-century Mayor Toppler (it's now the recommended Gasthof Goldener Greifen).

Keep circling to the big 17th-century **St. George's fountain.** The long metal gutters slid, routing the water into the villagers' buckets. Rothenburg had an ingenious water system. Built on a rock, it had one real source above the town, which was plumbed to serve a series of fountains; water flowed from high to low through Rothenburg. Its many fountains had practical functions beyond providing drinking water (some were stocked with fish on market days and during times of siege). Water was used for fighting fires, and because of its plentiful supply—and its policy of requiring relatively wide lanes as fire breaks—the town never burned entirely, as so many neighboring villages did.

Two fine buildings behind the fountain show the old-time lofts with warehouse doors and pulleys on top for hoisting. All over town, lofts were filled with grain and corn. A year's supply was required by the city so they could survive any siege. The building behind the fountain is an art gallery showing off work by members of the local artists' association (free, Tue–Sun 14:00–18:00, closed Mon). To the right is Marien Apotheke, an old-time pharmacy mixing old and new in typical Rothenburg style.

The broad street running under the Town Hall tower is **Herrngasse.** The town originated with its castle (built in 1142 but now long gone; only the castle garden remains). Herrngasse connected the castle to Market Square. The last leg of this circular walking tour will take you from the castle garden up Herrngasse to where you now stand. For now, walk a few steps down Herrngasse and stand by the arch under the Town Hall tower (between the new and old town halls). On the left wall are the town's measuring rods—a reminder that medieval Germany was made of 300 independent little countries, each with its own weights and measures. Merchants and shoppers knew that these were the local standards: the rod (4.3 yards), the *Schuh* (or shoe, roughly a foot), and the *Ell* (from elbow to fingertip—four inches longer than mine...try it). Notice the protruding cornerstone. These are all over town—originally to protect buildings from reckless horse carts (and vice versa).

• *Under the arch, you'll find the...*

▲Historical Town Hall Vaults (Historiengewölbe)

This grade-schoolish little museum gives a waxy but interesting look at Rothenburg during the Catholics-vs.-Protestants Thirty Years' War. With helpful English descriptions, it offers a look at "the fateful year 1631," a replica of the mythical Meistertrunk tankard, and a dungeon complete with three dank cells and some torture lore (€2, April–Oct daily 9:30–17:30, closed Nov–March, tel. 09861/86751).

• *Leaving the museum, turn left (past a much-sketched and photo-*

graphed venerable door), and walk through the courtyard to a square called...

Green Market (Grüner Markt)

Once a produce market, this is now a parking lot that fills with Christmas shops during December. Notice the clay-tile roofs. These "beaver tail" tiles became standard after thatched roofs were outlawed to prevent fires. Today, all of the town's roofs are made of these. The little fences keep the snow from falling, and catch tiles that blow off during storms. The free public WC is on your left, the recommended **Friese shop** (see "Shopping") is on your right, and straight ahead is St. Jakob's Church.

Outside the church, you'll see 14th-century statues (mostly original) showing Jesus praying at Gethsemane, a common feature of Gothic churches. The artist is anonymous, because in the Gothic age (pre–Albrecht Dürer) artists were just nameless craftspeople working only for the glory of God. Five yards to the left (on the wall), notice the nub of a sandstone statue—a rare original, looking pretty bad after 500 years of weather and, more recently, pollution. Most original statues are now in the city museum. The better-preserved statues you see on the church are copies.

• *If it's your wedding day, take the first entrance. Otherwise, use the second (downhill) door to enter...*

▲▲St. Jakob's Church (St. Jakobskirche)

Built in the 14th century, this church has been Lutheran since 1544. The interior was "purified" by Romantics in the 19th century—cleaned of everything Baroque or not original, and refitted in the Neo-Gothic style. (For example, the baptismal font and the pulpit above the second pew *look* Gothic, but are actually Neo-Gothic.) The stained-glass windows behind the altar (most colorful in the morning light) are originals from the 1330s. Entrance costs €2 (April–Oct and Dec Mon–Sat 9:00–17:15, Sun 10:45–17:15; Nov and Christmas–March daily 10:00–12:00 & 14:00–16:00; free helpful English info sheet, concerts and tour schedule posted on the door). There are guided tours in English for no extra charge on Saturdays at 15:00.

At the back of the church, take the stairs that lead up behind the pipe organ. In the loft, you'll find the artistic highlight of Rothenburg and perhaps the most wonderful wood carving in all of Germany: the glorious 500-year-old, 35-foot-high *Altar of the Holy Blood.* Tilman Riemenschneider, the Michelangelo of German woodcarvers, carved this from 1499 to 1504 to hold a precious rock-crystal capsule, set in a cross that contains a scrap of tablecloth miraculously stained in the shape of a cross by a drop of communion wine. It's a realistic commotion, showing that

Riemenschneider—while a High Gothic artist—was ahead of his time. Below, in the scene of the Last Supper, Jesus gives Judas a piece of bread, marking him as the traitor, while John lays his head on Christ's lap. Everything is portrayed exactly as described in the Bible. On the left: Jesus enters Jericho, with the shy tax collector Zacchaeus looking on from his tree. Notice the fun attention to detail—down to the nails on the horseshoe. On the right: Jesus prays in the Garden of Gethsemane. Notice how Judas, with his big bag of cash, could be removed from the scene—illustrated by photos on the wall nearby—as was the tradition for the four days leading up to Easter.

Head back down the stairs to the church's main hall. Go up front to take a close look at the main altar (from 1466, by Friedrich Herlin). Below Christ are statues of six saints. St. James (Jakob in German) is the one with the shell. He's the saint of pilgrims, and this church was a stop on the medieval pilgrimage route to Santiago ("St. James" in Spanish) de Compostela in Spain. Study the painted panels—ever see Peter with spectacles? Around the back of the altarpiece (upper left) is a painting of Rothenburg's Market Square in the 15th century—looking much like it does today, with the exception of the full-Gothic Town Hall (as it was before the big fire of 1501). Notice Christ's face on the veil of Veronica (center of back side). It follows you as you walk from side to side—it must have given the faithful the religious heebie-jeebies four centuries ago.

The small altar to the left is also worth a look. It's a century older than the main altar. Notice the unusual Trinity: the Father and Son are literally bridged by a dove, which represents the Holy Spirit. Stepping back, you can see that Jesus is standing on a skull—clearly "overcoming death."

Before leaving the front of the church, notice the old medallions above the carved choir stalls. They feature the coats of arms of Rothenburg's leading families and portraits of city and church leaders.

• *Leave the church and, from its outside steps, walk around the corner to the right and under the chapel (built over the road). Go two blocks down Klingengasse and stop at the corner of Klosterhof Street. Looking down Klingengasse, you see the...*

Klingentor

This cliff tower was Rothenburg's water reservoir. From 1595 until 1910, a copper tank high in the tower provided clean spring water (pumped up by river power) to the privileged. To the right of Klingentor is a good stretch of wall rampart to walk. To the left, the wall is low and simple, lacking a rampart because it guards only a cliff. Now find the shell decorating a building on the street

corner next to you. That's the symbol of St. James (pilgrims commemorated their visit to Santiago de Compostela with a shell),
indicating that this building is associated with the church.

• *Turn left down Klosterhof, passing the shell and, on your right, the
colorful Altfränkische Weinstube am Klosterhof (see "Eating," near the
end of this chapter), to reach the...*

▲▲Imperial City Museum (Reichsstadt-Museum)

You'll get a scholarly sweep through Rothenburg's history at this
museum, housed in the former Dominican convent. Cloistered
nuns used the lazy Susan embedded in the wall (to the right of
museum door) to give food to the poor without being seen.

Highlights include *The Rothenburg Passion*, a 12-panel series
of paintings from 1492 showing scenes leading up to Christ's crucifixion (in the *Konventsaal*); an exhibit of Jewish culture through
the ages in Rothenburg *(Judaika)*; a 14th-century convent kitchen
(Klosterküche) with a working model of the lazy Susan and a massive
chimney; romantic paintings of the town *(Gemäldegalerie)*; the fine
Baumann collection of weapons and armor; and sandstone statues
from the church and Baumeister Haus (the seven vices and seven
virtues). Follow the *Rundgang Tour* signs (€3.50, daily April–Oct
9:30–17:30, Nov–March 13:00–16:00, English info sheet and
descriptions, Klosterhof 5, tel. 09861/939-043, www.reichsstadt
museum.rothenburg.de).

• *Leaving the museum, go around to the right and into the Convent
Garden (when locked at night, continue straight to the T-intersection
and see the barn three doors to the right).*

Convent Garden

This spot is a peaceful place to work on your tan...or mix a poi-
soned potion (free, same hours as museum). Enjoy the herb garden. Monks and nuns, who were responsible for concocting herbal
cures in the olden days, often tended herb gardens. Smell (but
don't pick) the *Pfefferminze, Juniper* (gin), *Chamomilla* (disinfec-
tant), and *Origanum*. Don't smell the plants in the poison corner
(potency indicated by the number of crosses...like spiciness stars in
a Chinese restaurant).

• *Exit opposite from where you entered, angling left through the nuns'
garden (site of the now-gone Dominican church), eventually leaving
via an arch at the far end. Looking to your left, you'll see the back end
of an...*

Original Barn

This is the back side of a complex that fronts Herrngasse. Medieval
Germans often lived in large structures like this that were like
small villages in themselves, with a grouping of buildings and

open spaces. The typical design included a house, a courtyard, a stable, a garden, and, finally, a barn. Notice how the bulging wall is corseted by a brace with iron washers. Crank on its nuts and the building will stand up straight.

• *Now go downhill to the...*

Town Wall

This part of the wall (view through bars, look to far right) takes advantage of the natural fortification provided by the cliff, and is therefore much smaller than the ramparts. Angle left along the wall to the big street (Herrngasse), then right under the Burgtor tower. Notice the tiny "eye of the needle" door cut into the big door. If trying to get into town after curfew, you could bribe the guard to let you through this door (which was small enough to keep out any fully armed attackers).

• *Step through the gate and outside the wall. Look around and imagine being locked out in the year 1400. This was a wooden drawbridge (see the chain slits above). Notice the "pitch nose" mask—designed to pour boiling Nutella on anyone attacking. High above is the town coat of arms: a red castle (roten Burg).*

Castle Garden (Burggarten)

The garden before you was once that red castle (destroyed in the 14th century). Today, it's a picnic-friendly park. The chapel (50 yards into the park on the left) is the only bit of the original castle to survive. It's now a memorial to local Jews killed in a 1298 slaughter. A few steps beyond that is a grapevine trellis that provides a fine picnic spot. If you walk all the way out to the garden's far end, you'll find a great viewpoint (well past the tourists, and considered the best place to kiss by romantic local teenagers). But the views of the lush Tauber River Valley below are just as good from the top end of the park. Facing the town, on the left, a path leads down to the village of Detwang (you can see the church spire below)—a town even older than Rothenburg (for a walk to Detwang, see "A Walk in the Countryside," under "Sights and Activities: Near Rothenburg"). To the right is a fine view of the fortified Rothenburg and the "Tauber Riviera" below.

• *Return to the tower, cross carefully under the pitch nose, and hike back up Herrngasse to your starting point.*

Herrngasse

Many towns have a Herrngasse, where the richest patricians and merchants (the *Herren*) lived. Predictably, it's your best chance to see the town's finest old mansions. Strolling back to Market Square, you'll pass the old-time puppet theater (German only, on left), the Franciscan church (from 1285, oldest in town, on right), and the hippie Sawasdee shop (where the Night Watchman spends his days dreaming of his next trip to Thailand while his girlfriend sells what they've imported, as well as "Night Watchman mementos," Herrngasse 23). The house at #18 is the biggest patrician house on the street. The family, which has lived here for three centuries, disconnected the four old-time doorbells. Their door—big enough to allow a carriage in (with a human-sized door cut into it)—is typical of the age. To see the traditional house-courtyard-stables-garden-barn layout, pop into either #14 (now an apartment block) or—if that's closed—the shop across the street, at #11. The Hotel Eisenhut, Rothenburg's fanciest, is worth a peek inside. The Käthe Wohlfahrt Christmas shops (at Herrngasse 1 and 2, see "Shopping") are your last, and perhaps greatest, temptations before reaching your starting and ending point: Market Square.

Sights and Activities

Museums Within a Block of Market Square

▲▲**Medieval Crime and Punishment Museum (Mittel-alterliches Kriminalmuseum)**—This museum is the best of its kind, specializing in everything connected to medieval criminal justice. Learn about medieval police, medieval criminal law, and above all, instruments of punishment and torture—even a special cage complete with a metal gag for nags. The museum is more eclectic than its name, and includes exhibits on general history, superstition, biblical art, and temporary displays in a second building. Follow the yellow arrows—the one-way traffic system makes it hard to double back. Exhibits are tenderly described in English (€3.80, daily April–Oct 9:30–18:00, Nov and Jan–Feb 14:00–16:00, Dec and March 10:00–16:00, last entry 45 min before closing, fun cards and posters, Burggasse 3–5, tel. 09861/5359, www.kriminal museum.rothenburg.de).

▲**Doll and Toy Museum (Puppen- und Spielzeugmuseum)**—These two floors of historic *Kinder* cuteness are a hit with many. Pick up the free English binder (just past the entry curtain) for an extensive description of the exhibits (€4, family ticket-€10, daily March–Dec 9:30–18:00, Jan–Feb 11:00–17:00, just off Market Square, downhill from the fountain at Hofbronnengasse 11–13, tel. 09861/7330, www.spielzeugmuseum.rothenburg.de).

▲**German Christmas Museum (Deutsches Weihnachts-museum)**—This excellent museum, upstairs in the giant Käthe Wohlfahrt Christmas Village shop, tells the history of Christmas decorations. There's a unique and thoughtfully described collection of Christmas-tree stands, mini-trees sent in boxes to WWI soldiers at the front, early Advent calendars, old-time Christmas cards, and a look at tree decorations through the ages—including the Nazi era and when you were a kid. The museum is not just a ploy to get shoppers to spend more money, but a serious collection managed by professional curator Felicitas Höptner (€4, April–Dec daily 10:00–17:30, Jan–March Sat–Sun 10:00–17:30 and irregularly on weekdays, Herrngasse 1, tel. 09861/409-365, www.german christmasmuseum.com).

More Sights and Activities in Rothenburg

▲▲**Walk the Wall**—Just longer than a mile and a half around, providing great views and a good orientation, this walk can be done by those under six feet tall and without a camera in less than an hour. The hike requires no special sense of balance. This walk is covered and is a great option in the rain. Photographers will stay very busy, especially before breakfast or at sunset, when the lighting is best and the crowds are fewest. You can enter or exit the ramparts at nearly every tower. The best fortifications are in the Spitaltor (south end). Climb the Rödertor en route (described next). The names you see along the way are people who donated money to rebuild the wall after World War II, and those who've recently donated €1,000 per meter for the maintenance of Rothenburg's heritage.

▲**Rödertor**—The wall tower nearest the train station is the only one you can climb. It's worth the 135 steps for the view and a short but fascinating rundown on the bombing of Rothenburg in the last weeks of World War II, when the east part of the city was destroyed (€1.50, pay at top, unreliable hours, usually open April–Oct daily 10:00–16:00, closed Nov–March, WWII photos have English translations). If you climb this, you can skip the more claustrophobic Town Hall tower climb.

▲▲**The Allergic-to-Tourists Wall and Moat Walk**—For a quiet and scenic break from the tourist crowds and a chance to appreciate the marvelous fortifications of Rothenburg, consider this hike: From the Castle Garden, go right and walk outside the wall to Klingentor. At Klingentor, climb up to the ramparts and walk on the wall past Galgentor to Rödertor. Then descend, leave the old town, and hike through the park (once the moat) down to Spitaltor. Explore the fortifications here before hiking a block up Spitalgasse, turning left to pass the youth hostel, popping back outside the wall, and heading along the upper scenic reaches of the "Tauber Riviera" and above the vineyards back to the Castle Garden.

▲**Tradesman's House (Alt-Rothenburger Handwerkerhaus)**—See the everyday life of a Rothenburger in the town's heyday in this restored 700-year-old home (€2.20; Easter–Oct Mon–Fri 11:00–17:00, Sat–Sun 10:00–17:00; Nov–Dec daily 14:00–16:00; closed Jan–Easter; Alter Stadtgraben 26, near Markus Tower, tel. 09861/94280).

ROTHENBURG

St. Wolfgang's Church—This fortified Gothic church is built into the medieval wall at Klingentor. Its dungeon-like passages and shepherd's-dance exhibit are pretty lame (€1.50, April–Sept Wed–Mon 10:00–13:00 & 14:30–17:00, Oct Wed–Mon 10:00–16:00, closed Tue and Nov–March).

Near Rothenburg

▲▲ **Walk in the Countryside**—From the *Burggarten* (castle garden), head into the Tauber Valley. With your back to town, go down the hill, exiting the castle garden on your left. Once outside of the wall, walk around, keeping the castle and town on your right. The trail becomes really steep, taking you down to the wooden covered bridge on the valley floor. Across the bridge, the road goes left to Toppler Castle and right (downstream, with a pleasant parallel footpath) to Detwang.

Toppler Castle (Topplerschlösschen) is cute, skinny, sky-blue, and 600 years old. It was the castle/summer home of the medieval Mayor Toppler. The tower's top looks like a house—a sort of tree fort for grownups. It's in a farmer's garden, and it's open whenever he's around and willing to let you in (€1.50, normally Fri–Sun 13:00–16:00, closed Mon–Thu and Nov, 1 mile from town center at Taubertalweg 100, tel. 09861/7358). People say the mayor had this valley-floor escape to get people to relax about leaving the fortified town...or to hide a mistress.

To extend your stroll, walk back to the bridge and follow the river downstream to the peaceful village of **Detwang.** One of the oldest villages in Franconia, Detwang dates from 968. Like Rothenburg, it has a Riemenschneider altarpiece in its church.

Franconian Bike Ride—To get a fun, breezy look at the countryside around Rothenburg, rent a bike from Fahrradhaus Krauss (see "Helpful Hints," near the beginning of this chapter). For a pleasant half-day pedal, escape the old town through Rödertor, bike along Topplerweg to Spitaltor, and follow the curvy road down into the Tauber Riviera. Turn right at the yellow *Leutzenbronn* sign to cross the double-arcaded bridge. From here a peaceful road follows the river downstream to **Detwang,** passing the cute Topplerschlösschen (described above). From Detwang, follow the main road to the old mill, and turn left to follow the *Liebliches Taubertal* bike path signs as far up the Tauber River (direction: Bettwar) as you like. After 2.5 miles, you'll arrive in the sleepy farming town of **Bettwar;** claim a spot among the chickens and the apple trees for a picnic or have a drink at one of the two restaurants in town.

Franconian Open-Air Museum (Fränkisches Freiland-museum)—A 20-minute drive from Rothenburg—in the undiscovered "Rothenburgy" town of Bad Windsheim—is an open-air folk museum that, compared with others in Europe, is a bit humble. But it tries very hard and gives you the best look around at traditional rural Franconia (€5, daily mid-March–Sept 9:00–18:00, Oct–mid-Dec 10:00–16:00, closed mid-Dec–mid-March, last entry one hour before closing, tel. 09841/66800, www.freilandmuseum.de).

Shopping

Be warned...Rothenburg is one of Germany's best shopping towns. Do it here and be done with it. Lovely prints, carvings, wine glasses, Christmas-tree ornaments, and beer steins are popular. Rödergasse is the old town's everyday shopping street. There is also a modern shopping center across the street from the train station.

Christmas Souvenirs

Rothenburg is the headquarters of the **Käthe Wohlfahrt** Christmas trinkets empire, which is spreading across the half-timbered reaches of Europe. In Rothenburg, tourists flock to two Käthe Wohlfahrt stores (at Herrngasse 1 and 2, just off Market Square). Start with the **Christmas Village** (Weihnachtsdorf) at Herrngasse 1. This Christmas wonderland is filled with enough twinkling lights to require a special electrical hookup. You're greeted by instant Christmas mood music (best appreciated on a hot day in July) and American and Japanese tourists hungrily filling little woven shopping baskets with €5–8 goodies to hang on their trees. Let the spinning flocked tree whisk you in, but pause at the wall of Steiffs, jerking uncontrollably and mesmerizing little kids. (OK, I admit it, my Christmas tree sports a few KW ornaments.) The **Christmas Museum** upstairs is described in the previous section). The smaller **Christmas Market** (Weihnachtsmarkt), across the street at Herrngasse 2, specializes in finely crafted wooden ornaments. A third, much smaller store is at Untere Schmiedgasse 19 (all stores open Mon–Sat 9:00–18:00, May–Dec also most Sun 10:00–18:00, Jan–April generally closed Sun, tel. 09861/4090, www.wohlfahrt.com or www.bestofchristmas.com). Käthe started the business in Stuttgart in 1964, and it's now run by her son Harald Wohlfahrt, who lives in Rothenburg.

Traditional German Souvenirs

The **Friese shop** has been welcoming readers of this book for more than 20 years (on the smaller square just off Market Square, west of TI, on corner across from free public WC). Cuckoo with friendliness, trinkets, and souvenirs, they give shoppers with this book tremendous service: a 10 percent discount, 19 percent sales tax deducted if you have purchases mailed, and a free pictorial map (normally €1.50). Anneliese Friese, who runs the place with her sons Frankie and Berni and grandson Rene, charges only her cost for shipping, and lets tired travelers leave their bags in her back room for free. If he's not busy, ask Rene to show you pictures of the local American football team he played on. For fewer crowds and more attentive service, visit after 14:00 (Mon–Sat 8:30–17:00, Sun 10:00–17:00, Grüner Markt 8, tel. 09861/7166, fax 09861/936-619, friese-kabalo@gmx.de).

Passage 12, a huge, more commercial souvenir shop with a vast selection of steins, knives, and noisy clocks, is locked in tooth-gnashing competition with the Friese shop. It's just a block below Market Square at Obere Schmiedgasse 12 (April–Dec Mon–Sat 9:00–19:00, Sun 10:00–19:00; Jan–March Mon–Sat 10:00–18:00, usually closed Sun; tel. 09861/8196). Customers can check their email for free upstairs, use the WC, and stash their bags in lockers in the storage room.

Werkstattladen Lebenshilfe sells tasteful, original, unconventional souvenirs made in sheltered workshops by Germans with disabilities. It's a tiny shop down the side street behind Herrngasse 10 (daily 10:30–18:00, Jan–April closed Sun, Kirchgasse 1, tel. 09861/938-401).

Romantic Prints: The Ernst Geissendörfer print shop has sold fine prints, etchings, and paintings here since 1908. Enter through the teddy bear shop on the lower corner of Market Square, and go up the stairs in the back of the store (May–Dec Mon–Sat 11:00–18:00, Sun 11:00–17:00; Jan–April Mon–Sat 11:00–18:00, closed Sun; Obere Schmiedgasse 1 at corner of Hafengasse, go up one floor, tel. 09861/2005, www.geissendoerfer.de).

Wine Stuff: For characteristic wine glasses, winemaking gear, and the real thing from the town's oldest winemakers, drop by the **Weinladen am Plönlein** (daily 10:00–18:00, Untere Schmiedgasse 27—for info on wine-tasting, see "Wine-Drinking in the Old Center" under "Eating," later in this chapter). Although Rothenburg is technically in Bavaria, the region around Rothenburg is called *Franken* (Franconia). You'll recognize Franconian wines by the shape of the bottle—short, stubby, and round.

Books: A good bookstore is **Rothenburger Büchermarkt** at Rödergasse 3, on the corner of Alter Stadtgraben (Mon–Sat 9:00–18:30, Sun 11:00–18:00, Jan–April closed Sun).

Mailing Your Goodies Home: You can get handy yellow €2.50 boxes at the old town **post office** (Mon–Fri 9:00–13:00 & 14:00–17:30, Sat 9:00–12:00, closed Sun, inside photo shop at Rödergasse 11). The main post office is in the shopping center across from the train station.

Pastries: Those who prefer to eat their souvenirs browse the *Bäckereien* (bakeries). Their succulent pastries, pies, and cakes are pleasantly distracting...but skip the bad-tasting Rothenburger *Schneeballen*. Unworthy of the heavy promotion they receive, *Schneeballen* are bland pie crusts crumpled into a ball and dusted with powdered sugar or frosted with sticky-sweet glop. There's little reason to waste calories on a *Schneeball* when you can enjoy a curvy *Mandelhörnchen* (almond crescent), a triangular *Nussecke* (nut bar), a round *Florentiner* cookie, a couple of fresh *Krapfen* (like jelly doughnuts), or even just a soft, warm German pretzel.

Sleeping

Rothenburg is crowded with visitors, but most are day-trippers. Except for the rare Saturday night and during festivals (see "Helpful Hints," near the beginning of this chapter), finding a room is easy throughout the year. If you want to splurge, you'll snare the best value by paying extra for the biggest and best rooms at the hotels I recommend.

Many hotels and guest houses will pick up tired heavy-packers at the station. If you're driving and unable to find where you're sleeping, stop and give them a call. They will likely come rescue you. Keep your key when out late. Rothenburg's hotels are small, and often lock the front entrance at about 22:00, asking you to let yourself in through a side door.

You may be greeted at the station by *Zimmer* skimmers who have rooms to rent. If you have reservations, resist them and honor your reservation. But if you haven't booked ahead, you could try talking one of these eager beavers into giving you a bed-and-breakfast room for a youth-hostel price. Be warned: These people are notorious for taking you to distant hotels and then charging you for the ride back if you decline a room. The automated hotel vacancy board at the TI (described under

---

Sleep Code

(€1 = about $1.40, country code: 49, area code: 09861)
S = Single, **D** = Double/Twin, **T** = Triple, **Q** = Quad, **b** = bathroom, **s** = shower only. Unless otherwise noted, credit cards are accepted, English is spoken, and breakfast is included.

To help you sort easily through these listings, I've divided the rooms into three categories, based on the price for a standard double room with bath:

  $$$ **Higher Priced**—Most rooms €85 or more.
    $$ **Moderately Priced**—Most rooms between €55-85.
     $ **Lower Priced**—Most rooms €55 or less.

"Orientation," near the beginning of this chapter) is another option for those without reservations.

In the Old Town

$$$ Hotel Kloster-Stüble, deep in the old town near the castle garden, is my classiest listing. Rudolf does the cooking, while Erika—his fun and energetic first mate—welcomes guests. Twenty-one rooms fill two medieval buildings, connected by a modern atrium. The hotel is just off Herrngasse on a tiny side street (Sb-€55–75, traditional Db-€85, bigger and more modern Db-€115, Tb-€110–130, see website for suites and family rooms, kids under age 5 free, Internet access and Wi-Fi, Heringsbronnengasse 5, tel. 09861/938-890, fax 09861/6474, www.klosterstueble.de, hotel @klosterstueble.de).

$$$ Hotel Spitzweg is a rustic-yet-elegant 1536 mansion (never bombed or burned) with 10 big rooms, open beams, and endearing hand-painted antique furniture. It's run by gentle Herr Hocher, whom I suspect is the former Wizard of Oz—now retired and in a very good mood (Db-€85, family rooms, non-smoking, elegant breakfast room, free parking, Internet access at nearby hotel, Paradeisgasse 2, tel. 09861/94290, fax 09861/1412, www .hotel-spitzweg.de, info@hotel-spitzweg.de).

$$$ Hotel Gerberhaus is warmly run by Inge and Kurt and daughter Deborah, who mix modern comforts into 20 bright and airy rooms while maintaining a sense of half-timbered elegance. Enjoy the pleasant garden in back (Sb-€60–75, Db-€74–110, Tb-€129–139, Qb-€145, prices depend on room size; 2-room apartment with kitchen-€120/2 people, €155/4 people; 10 percent off the second and subsequent nights and a free *Schneeball* if you pay cash, non-smoking, 4 rooms have canopied 4-poster *Himmel* beds, Internet access, laundry-€7, Spitalgasse 25, tel. 09861/94900, fax 09861/86555, www.gerberhaus.rothenburg.de, gerberhaus @t-online.de). The downstairs café and *Biergarten* serve good soups, salads, and light lunches.

$$ Gasthof Goldener Greifen, once Mayor Toppler's home, is a big, traditional, 600-year-old place with 15 large rooms and all the comforts. It's run by a helpful family staff and creaks with rustic splendor (small Sb-€38, Sb-€48, small Db-€65, big Db-€77–82, Tb-€97–102, Qb-€117–122, 10 percent off for 3-night stays, non-smoking, full-service laundry-€8, free and easy parking, half a block downhill from Market Square at Obere Schmiedgasse 5, tel. 09861/2281, fax 09861/86374, www.gasthof-greifen-rothenburg .de, info@gasthof-greifen-rothenburg.de, Brigitte and Klingler family). The family also has a couple of loaner bikes free for guests, and runs a good restaurant, serving meals in the back garden or dining room.

Rothenburg Accommodations

NOTE: MAP NOT TO SCALE
CASTLE GARDEN TO RÖDERTOR
IS A 15-MIN. WALK

TO WÜRZBURG &
ROMANTIC ROAD

TO
DETWANG

St. WOLFGANGS

KLINGENTOR

TO AUTOBAHN E-45
& BAD WINDSHEIM

BEZOLDWEG

WALL

GALGEN-
TOR

IMPERIAL
CITY
MUSEUM

ST.
JAKOB'S

SCHRANNEN-
PLATZ

HIRTENGASSE

TAUBER

WHITE
TOWER

GALGENGASSE

TO
TOPPLER
CASTLE

STOLLENGASSE

BURG-
TOR

PUPPET
THEATER

RÖDER-
TOR

Post

HERRN-   GASSE

RÖDERGASSE

TRADES-
MAN'S
HOUSE

FRAN.
CHURCH

HAFEN

CASTLE
GARDEN

WENGGASSE

TO
TRAIN
STATION

RIVER

NEUGASSE

MEDIEVAL
CRIME &
PUNISHMENT
MUSEUM

PLÖNLEIN

TOPPLERWEG

DOUBLE
BRIDGE

SPITTALGASSE

★ – MARKET SQUARE
TOURIST INFO, CLOCK
& TOWN HALL TOWER

◢ – ACCESS STAIRS
TO WALL

🅿 – PARKING

⋅⋅⋅ – PATH

WC

BENSENSTR.

TO
DINKELSBÜHL
& FÜSSEN VIA
ROMANTIC ROAD
& SWIMMING POOL

DCH

1 Hotel Kloster-Stüble
2 Hotel Spitzweg
3 Hotel Gerberhaus
4 Gasthof Goldener Greifen
5 Hotel Altfränkische
   Weinstube am Klosterhof
6 Pension Elke
7 Hotel Café Uhl
8 Gästehaus Flemming

9 Gästehaus Viktoria
10 Gästehaus Raidel
11 Pension Pöschel
12 Frau Liebler Rooms
13 Rossmühle Youth Hostel
14 Hotel Hornburg
15 To Pension Fuchsmühle
16 Bike Rental

$$ Hotel Altfränkische Weinstube am Klosterhof is *the* place for well-heeled bohemians. Mario, Hanne, and their lovely daughter Viktoria rent six cozy rooms above their dark and evocative pub in a 600-year-old building. It's an upscale, *Lord of the Rings* atmosphere, with TVs, modern showers, open-beam ceilings, and canopied four-poster beds (Sb-€48, Db-€59, bigger Db-€69, Db suite-€79, Tb-€79, prefer cash, kid-friendly, Wi-Fi, off Klingengasse at Klosterhof 7, tel. 09861/6404, fax 09861/6410, www.romanticroad.com/altfraenkische-weinstube). Their pub is a candlelit classic—and a favorite with locals, serving hot food to Hobbits until 22:30, and closing at 1:00 in the morning. Drop by on Wednesday evening (19:00–24:00) for the English Conversation Club (see "Meet the Locals" at the end of the "Eating" section).

$$ Pension Elke, run by spry Erich Endress and his son Klaus, rents 12 bright, airy, and comfy rooms above the family grocery store. Guests who jog are welcome to join Klaus on his half-hour run around the city every evening at 19:30 (S-€28, Sb-€38, D-€42–48, Db-€60–65, price depends on room size, extra bed-€15, cash only, Internet access; reception in grocery store until 19:00, otherwise go around corner to back of building and ring bell at top of stairs; near Markus Tower at Rödergasse 6, tel. 09861/2331, fax 09861/935-355, www.pension-elke-rothenburg.de, info@pension-elke-rothenburg.de).

$$ Hotel Café Uhl offers 12 fine rooms over a bakery (Sb-€35–58, Db-€58–78, Tb-€78–92, Qb-€92–118, price depends on room size, reception in café, pay Internet access, parking-€6/day, closed Jan, Plönlein 8, tel. 09861/4895, fax 09861/92820, www.hotel-uhl.de, info@hotel-uhl.de, Paul and Robert the baker).

$$ Gästehaus Flemming has seven tastefully modern, fresh, and comfortable rooms and a peaceful garden behind St. Jakob's Church (Sb-€47, Db-€62, Tb-€84, cash only, non-smoking, Klingengasse 21, tel. 09861/92380, fax 09861/976-384, www.gaestehaus-flemming.de, gaestehaus-flemming@t-online.de, Regina).

$$ Gästehaus Viktoria is a cheery little place right next to the town wall. Its three rooms overflow with furniture, ribbons, and silk flowers, and lovely gardens surround the house (Db-€59–69, larger Db suite-€79, ask about family specials, free Wi-Fi, a block from Klingentor at Klingenschutt 4, tel. 09861/87682, www.romanticroad.com/gaestehaus-viktoria, gaestehaus-viktoria@gmx.de).

$$ Gästehaus Raidel rents 12 rooms in a 500-year-old house filled with beds and furniture, all handmade by friendly Norry Raidel himself. The ramshackle ambience makes me want to sing the *Addams Family* theme song—but the place has a rare, time-passed family charm (S-€24, Sb-€39, D-€49, Db-€59, Tb-€70, cash only, Wenggasse 3, tel. 09861/3115, Norry asks you to use the reservations form at www.romanticroad.com/raidel). Norry, who plays in a Dixieland band, has invented a fascinating hybrid saxophone/trombone called the Norryphone...and loves to jam.

$ Pension Pöschel is simple and friendly, with six plain rooms in a concrete but pleasant building, and an inviting garden out back. Only one room has a private shower and toilet (S-€22, D-€40, Db-€45, T-€55, Tb-€60, small kids free, cash only, non-smoking, Wenggasse 22, tel. 09861/3430, www.pensionpoeschel .de, pension.poeschel@t-online.de, Bettina).

$ Frau Liebler rents two large, modern, ground-floor rooms with kitchenettes. They're great for those looking for real privacy— you'll have your own room fronting a quiet cobbled lane just below Market Square. She also rents a two-bedroom apartment (Db-€40, apartment-€50, extra bed-€10, breakfast-€5, cash only, non-smoking, laundry-€5, behind Christmas shop at Pfäffleinsgässchen 10, tel. 09861/709-215, fax 09861/709-216).

$ Rossmühle Youth Hostel, run since 1981 by Eduard Schmitz, rents 186 beds in two buildings. While it's mostly four- to six-bed dorms, this charming hostel also has 15 doubles. Reception is in the droopy-eyed building—formerly a horse mill, it was used when the old town was under siege and the river-powered mill was inaccessible (dorm bed-€20, bunk-bed Db-€45, those over 26 pay €4 extra unless traveling with a family, includes breakfast and sheets, all-you-can-eat dinner-€6, pay Internet access, self-serve laundry including soap-€5, entrance on Rossmühlgasse, tel. 09861/94160, fax 09861/941-620, www.rothenburg.jugend herberge.de, jhrothenburg@djh-bayern.de).

Outside the Wall

$$$ Hotel Hornburg, a grand 1903 mansion, is close to the train station, a two-minute walk outside the wall. With groomed grounds, gracious sitting areas, and 10 spacious, tastefully decorated rooms, it's a super value (Sb-€58–79, Db-€78–108, Tb-€100–130, ground-floor rooms, non-smoking, family-friendly, avoid if you're allergic to dogs, free Internet access, expensive Wi-Fi, parking-€5/day; if walking, exit station and go straight on Ludwig-Siebert-Strasse, then turn left on Mannstrasse until you're 100 yards from town wall; if driving, the hotel is across from parking lot P4; Hornburgweg 28, at intersection with Mannstrasse, tel. 09861/8480, fax 09861/5570, www.hotel-hornburg.de, info@hotel -hornburg.de, friendly Gabriele and Martin).

$$ Pension Fuchsmühle is a guest house in a renovated old mill on the river below the castle end of Rothenburg, across from the Toppler Castle. It feels rural, but is a pleasant (though steep) 15-minute hike to Market Square, and a €10 taxi ride from the train station. Alex and Heidi Molitor, a young couple, run a book-lined café on summer weekends and offer a free look at the mill (in use until 1989). Eight bright, modern, light-wood rooms fill the building's three floors (Sb-€45, Db-€65, Tb-€90, Qb-€115, 6-bed apartment-€160, extra bed-€25, less for longer stays at some times of year, includes healthy farm-fresh breakfasts—or €9 less per person if you don't want breakfast, non-smoking, pay Wi-Fi, parking, flashlights provided for your walk back after dark, Taubertalweg 103, tel. 09861/92633, fax 09861/933895, www.fuchsmuehle.de, fuchsmuehle@t-online.de).

Eating

Many restaurants take a mid-afternoon break, and stop serving lunch at 14:00 and dinner as early as 20:00. My recommendations are all within a five-minute walk of Market Square. While all survive on tourism, many still feel like local hangouts. Your choices are typical German or ethnic. Any bakery will sell you a sandwich for a couple euros.

Traditional German Restaurants

Gasthof Goldener Greifen is in a historic building just off the main square. The Klingler family serves quality Franconian food at a good price...and with a smile. The wood is ancient and polished from generations of happy use, and the ambience is practical rather than posh—and that's just fine with me (€7–15 entrées, €12 three-course daily specials, super-cheap kids' meals, Mon–Sat 11:30–21:30, Sun 11:30–14:00, Obere Schmiedgasse 5, tel. 09861/2281).

Hotel Restaurant Klosterstüble, on a small street off Herrngasse near the castle garden, is a classy place for delicious and beautifully presented traditional cuisine. Chef Rudy's food is better than his English, so head waitress Erika makes sure communication goes smoothly. The shady terrace is nice on a warm summer evening. I prefer their traditional dining room to the stony, sleek, modern room (€7–17 main dishes, daily 11:00–14:00 & 18:00–21:00, Heringsbronnengasse 5, tel. 09861/938-890).

Bürgerkeller is a typical European cellar restaurant with a quiet, calming atmosphere, medieval murals, and pointy pikes. Without a burger in sight (*Bürger* means "townsman"), Harry Terian and his family pride themselves on quality local cuisine, offering a small but inviting menu and reasonable prices. Harry likes oldies, and you're welcome to look over his impressive playlist and request your favorite music (€6–13 entrées, cash only, Thu–Tue 11:30–14:00 & 18:00–21:00, closed Wed, a few sidewalk tables, near bottom of Herrngasse at #24, tel. 09861/2126).

Altfränkische Weinstube am Klosterhof seems designed

Rothenburg Restaurants

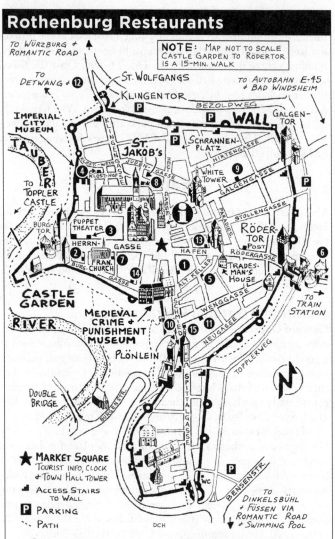

NOTE: MAP NOT TO SCALE
CASTLE GARDEN TO RÖDERTOR
IS A 15-MIN. WALK

TO WÜRZBURG &
ROMANTIC ROAD

TO DETWANG &

ST. WOLFGANGS

KLINGENTOR

TO AUTOBAHN E-45
& BAD WINDSHEIM

BEZOLDWEG

WALL

GALGEN-TOR

IMPERIAL
CITY
MUSEUM

SCHRANNEN-PLATZ

HIRTENGASSE

TAUBER

ST. JAKOB'S

JUDEN-GASSE

KLOST.-WEITH.

KLOST.-HOFG.

WHITE
TOWER

HEUGASSE

GALGENGASSE

TO TOPPLER CASTLE

BURG-TOR

PUPPET THEATER

HERRN-

GASSE

FRAN.-CHURCH

PARADIES.

STOLLENGASSE

RÖDER-TOR

Post

RÖDERGASSE

TRADES-MAN'S HOUSE

TO TRAIN STATION

CASTLE GARDEN

MEDIEVAL CRIME & PUNISHMENT MUSEUM

HAFEN

ALT KELLER

SCHMIED

WENGGASSE

RIVER

PLÖNLEIN

NEUGASSE

TOPPLERWEG

DOUBLE BRIDGE

BURGENSTR.

SPITALGASSE

TO DINKELSBÜHL & FÜSSEN VIA ROMANTIC ROAD & SWIMMING POOL

BENSENSTR.

WC

DCH

★ **MARKET SQUARE**
TOURIST INFO, CLOCK & TOWN HALL TOWER

◢ **ACCESS STAIRS TO WALL**

P **PARKING**

⋰ **PATH**

1. Gasthof Goldener Greifen
2. Hotel Restaurant Klosterstüble
3. Bürgerkeller
4. Altfränkische Weinstube am Klosterhof
5. Altstadt-Café Alter Keller
6. Gasthof Rödertor & Beer Garden
7. Eisenhut Restaurant
8. Reichs-Küchenmeister
9. Pizzeria Roma
10. China-Restaurant Peking
11. Döner Kebab Shop
12. To Unter den Linden Beer Garden
13. Eis Café D' Isep (Ice Cream)
14. Trinkstube zur Hölle
15. Restaurant Glocke

ROTHENBURG

for gnomes to celebrate their anniversaries. At this very dark pub, classically candlelit in a 600-year-old building, Mario whips up gourmet pub grub (€6–12 entrées, hot food served 18:00–22:30, closes at 1:00 in the morning, off Klingengasse at Klosterhof 7, tel. 09861/6404). If you'd like dinner company, drop by on Wednesday evening, when the English Conversation Club has a big table reserved from 19:00 on (see "Meet the Locals," later in this section). You'll eat well and with new friends—both travelers and locals.

Altstadt-Café Alter Keller is just right for a light meal near the main square, but tucked away from the crowds. Eat indoors under walls festooned with old pots and jugs, or outdoors on a quiet little square. Herr Hufnagel, a baker and pastry chef, whips up a tempting array of cakes, pies, and giant meringue cookies, while gracious Christine makes sure you understand your options (€3 goulash soup with bread, €5–7 main dishes, Sat–Thu 11:00–20:00, Sun 11:00–18:00, closed Fri, Alter Keller 8, tel. 09861/2268).

Gasthof Rödertor, just outside the wall through the Rödertor gate, is a lively place where Rothenburgers go for a hearty meal at a good price. Their passion is potatoes—the menu is dedicated to spud cuisine. Try a €6.50 plate of *Schupfnudeln,* potato noodles with sauerkraut and bacon (€6–12 entrées, daily 11:30–14:00 & 17:30–22:30, Ansbacher Strasse 7, tel. 09861/2022). They also run a popular *Biergarten* (see "Beer Gardens," next page).

Eisenhut Restaurant, in Hotel Eisenhut, is a fine place for a dress-up splurge with surprisingly reasonable prices. You'll enjoy elegantly presented dishes, both traditional and international, with formal service. Sit in their royal dining room or on their garden sun terrace (€18–26 main dishes, fixed-price meals from €26, daily 11:00–23:00, Herrngasse 3, tel. 09861/7050).

Reichs-Küchenmeister is a forgettable, big-hotel restaurant, but on a balmy evening, its pleasant, tree-shaded terrace overlooking St. Jakob's Church is hard to beat. Their €12.50 *Vesperbrett* plate is a fine selection of cold cuts (€9–20 main dishes, daily 11:00–22:00, Kirchplatz 8, tel. 09861/9700).

Breaks from Pork and Potatoes

Pizzeria Roma is the locals' favorite for €6.50 pizza and pastas with good Italian wine. The Magrini family moved here from Tuscany in 1970 (many Italians immigrated to Germany in those years), and they've been cooking pasta for Rothenburg ever since (Thu–Tue 11:30–24:00, closed Wed and mid-Aug–mid-Sept, Galgengasse 19, tel. 09861/4540, Ricardo).

China-Restaurant Peking, at the Plönlein, has €5–7 two-course lunch specials (Mon–Sat only), and its noisy streetside tables have a fine tower view (daily 11:30–15:00 & 17:00–23:00, Plönlein 4, tel. 09861/938-738).

The *Döner Kebab* shop at Wenggasse 4, just off Untere Schmiedgasse, serves cheap and tasty food to go. This tiny place offers what must be the best €3 hot meal in Rothenburg (Mon–Sat 11:00–20:00, closed Sun).

Picnic Goodies: A small **grocery store** is in the center of town at Rödergasse 6 (Mon–Fri 7:30–19:00, Sat 7:30–18:00, April–Dec also Sun 10:00–18:00, closed Sun Jan–March). **Supermarkets** are outside the wall: Exit the town through Rödertor, turn left through the cobbled gate, and cross the parking lot to reach the Edeka supermarket (Mon–Fri 8:00–20:00, Sat 8:00–18:00, closed Sun); or head to the even bigger Kaufland in the shopping center across from the train station (Mon–Sat 7:00–20:00, closed Sun).

Beer Gardens (Biergartens)

Rothenburg's *Biergartens* can be great fun, but they're open only when the weather is balmy.

Unter den Linden, a bohemian yet family-friendly *Biergarten* in the valley along the river, is worth the 20-minute hike on a pleasant evening (daily in season with decent weather, 10:00–21:00 and sometimes later, self-service food and good beer, call first to confirm it's open, tel. 09861/5909). As it's in the valley on the river, it's cooler than Rothenburg; bring a sweater. Take a right outside the Burgtor, then a left on the footpath toward Detwang; it's at the bottom of the hill on the left.

Gasthof Rödertor, just outside the wall through the Rödertor gate, runs a backyard *Biergarten* that's great for a rowdy crowd, cheap food, and good beer (May–Sept daily 17:00–24:00, look for wooden gate, tel. 09861/2022). If the *Biergarten* is closed, their indoor restaurant (described earlier) is a good value.

Dessert

Eis Café D' Isep, with a pleasant "Venetian minimal" interior, is the town's ice-cream parlor, serving up cakes, drinks, fresh-fruit ice cream, and fancy sundaes. Their sidewalk tables are great for lazy people-watching (daily 9:30–22:00, closed mid-Oct–mid-Feb, 1 block off Market Square at Hafengasse 17, run by Paolo and Paola D'Isep).

Wine-Drinking in the Old Center

Trinkstube zur Hölle ("Hell") is dark and foreboding, offering a thick wine-drinking atmosphere, pub food, and a few main dishes. It's small and can get painfully touristy in summer (daily 17:00–24:00, closed Sun Jan–March, a block past Medieval Crime and Punishment Museum on Burggasse, with the devil hanging out front, tel. 09861/4229).

Mario's **Altfränkische Weinstube am Klosterhof** (listed

under "Traditional German Restaurants," earlier in this section) is the liveliest place, and a clear favorite with locals for an atmospheric drink or late meal. When every other place is asleep, you're likely to find good food, drink, and energy here.

Eisenhut, behind the fancy hotel of the same name on Herrngasse, is a good bet for gentle and casual *Biergarten* ambience within the old center (also listed under "Traditional German Restaurants," earlier in this section).

Restaurant Glocke, a *Weinstube* (wine bar) popular with locals, is run by Rothenburg's oldest winemakers, the Thürauf family. The menu, which has a very extensive wine list, is in German only because the friendly staff wants to explain your options in person. Their €4.40 deal, which lets you sample five Franconian wines, is popular (€8–17 entrées, Mon–Sat 11:00–23:00, Sun 11:00–14:00, Plönlein 1, tel. 09861/958-990).

Meet the Locals—English Conversation Club

For a rare chance to mix it up with locals who aren't selling anything, bring your favorite slang and tongue twisters to the English Conversation Club at Mario's Altfränkische Weinstube am Klosterhof (Wed 19:00–24:00; see restaurant listing under "Traditional German Restaurants," on earlier in this section). This group of intrepid linguists has met more than 1,000 times. Hermann the German and his sidekick Wolfgang are regulars. Consider arriving early for dinner, or after 21:00, when the beer starts to sink in, the crowd grows, and everyone seems to speak that second language a bit more easily.

Connections

Reaching Rothenburg ob der Tauber by Train: A tiny branch train line connects Rothenburg to the outside world via **Steinach** in 14 minutes (generally hourly from Rothenburg at :06 and from Steinach at :35). If you plan to arrive in Rothenburg in the evening, note that the last train from Steinach to Rothenburg departs at about 20:30. All is not lost if you arrive in Steinach after the last train—there's a subsidized taxi service to Rothenburg (cheaper for the government than running an almost-empty train). To use this handy service, called AST *(Anrufsammeltaxi),* make an appointment with a participating taxi service (call 09861/2000 or 09861/7227) at least an hour in advance (2 hours ahead is better), and they'll drive you from Steinach to Rothenburg for the train fare (about €3.60/person) rather than the regular €25 taxi fare.

Train connections in Steinach are usually quick and efficient (trains to and from Rothenburg generally use track 5). The station at Steinach is not staffed, but has touch-screen terminals for fare and schedule information and ticket sales. Visit the ticket office in Rothenburg, or as a last resort call for train info at tel. 11861 (€0.60/min).

From Rothenburg by Train to: Würzburg (hourly, 1.25 hrs), **Nürnberg** (hourly, 1–1.5 hrs, change in Ansbach), **Munich** (hourly, 2.5–3 hrs, 1–2 changes), **Frankfurt** (hourly, 2.5–3 hrs, change in Würzburg), **Frankfurt Airport** (hourly, 3–3.5 hrs, change in Würzburg), **Berlin** (hourly, 5.5 hrs, 2 changes). Remember, all destinations also require a change in Steinach.

From Rothenburg by Bus: The Romantic Road bus stops at Schrannenplatz in Rothenburg once a day (early May–late Oct) on its way between Frankfurt and Füssen (and vice versa; www .romanticroadcoach.de).

RHINE VALLEY

Best of the Rhine • Bacharach • St. Goar

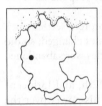

The Rhine Valley is storybook Germany, a fairy-tale world of legends and robber-baron castles. Cruise the most castle-studded stretch of the romantic Rhine as you listen for the song of the treacherous Loreley. For hands-on thrills, climb through the Rhineland's greatest castle, Rheinfels, above the town of St. Goar. Spend your nights in a castle-crowned village, either Bacharach or St. Goar.

Planning Your Time

For a good look at the Rhine, cruise in, tour a castle or two, sleep in a medieval town, and take the train out. If you have limited time, cruise less and explore Rheinfels Castle. Both Bacharach and St. Goar are an easy 90-minute train ride or drive from Frankfurt Airport, and make a good first or last stop for air travelers.

Ideally, spend two nights here, sleep in Bacharach, cruise the best hour of the river (from Bacharach to St. Goar), and tour the Rheinfels Castle. Those with more time can ride the riverside bike path.

The Best of the Rhine

Ever since Roman times, when this was the empire's northern boundary, the Rhine has been one of the world's busiest shipping rivers. You'll see a steady flow of barges with 1,000- to 2,000-ton loads. Tourist-packed buses, hot train tracks, and highways line both banks.

Many of the castles were "robber-baron" castles, put there by petty rulers (there were 300 independent little countries in medieval Germany, a region about the size of Montana) to levy tolls on passing river traffic. A robber baron would put his castle on, or even in, the river. Then, often with the help of chains and a tower on the opposite bank, he'd stop each ship and get his toll. There were 10 customs stops in the 60-mile stretch between Mainz and Koblenz alone (no wonder merchants were early proponents of the creation of larger nation-states).

Some castles were built to control and protect settlements, and others were the residences of kings. As times changed, so did the lifestyles of the rich and feudal. Many castles were abandoned for more comfortable mansions in the towns.

Most Rhine castles date from the 11th, 12th, and 13th centuries. When the pope successfully asserted his power over the German emperor in 1076, local princes ran wild over the rule of their emperor. The castles saw military action in the 1300s and 1400s, as emperors began reasserting their control over Germany's many silly kingdoms.

The castles were also involved in the Reformation wars, in which Europe's Catholic and Protestant dynasties fought it out using a fragmented Germany as their battleground. The Thirty Years' War (1618–1648) devastated Germany. The outcome: Each ruler got the freedom to decide if his people would be Catholic or Protestant, and one-third of Germany was dead. (Production of Gummi bears ceased entirely.)

The French—who feared a strong Germany and felt the Rhine was the logical border between them and Germany—destroyed most of the castles prophylactically (Louis XIV in the 1680s, the Revolutionary army in the 1790s, and Napoleon in 1806). Many were rebuilt in Neo-Gothic style in the Romantic Age—the late 1800s—and today are enjoyed as restaurants, hotels, hostels, and museums.

Getting Around the Rhine

The Rhine flows north from Switzerland to Holland, but the scenic stretch from Mainz to Koblenz hoards all the touristic charm. Studded with the crenellated cream of Germany's castles, it bustles

Rhine Overview

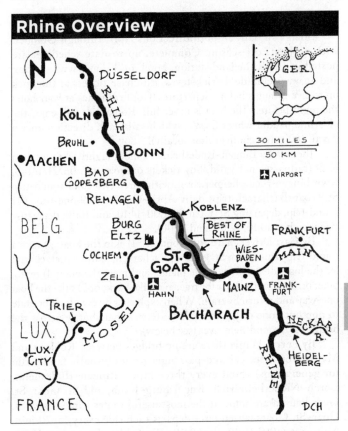

with boats, trains, and highway traffic. Have fun exploring with a mix of big steamers, tiny ferries *(Fähre)*, trains, and bikes.

By Boat: While some travelers do the whole Mainz–Koblenz trip by boat (5.5 hours downstream, 8.5 hours up), I'd just focus on the most scenic hour—from St. Goar to Bacharach. Sit on the top deck with your handy Rhine map-guide (or the kilometer-keyed tour in this chapter) and enjoy the parade of castles, towns, boats, and vineyards.

Two boat companies take travelers along this stretch of the Rhine. Most travelers sail on the bigger, more expensive, and romantic Köln–Düsseldorfer (K-D) Line (free with a German railpass or any Eurailpass that covers Germany, but uses up a day of any flexipass; otherwise about €9 for the first hour, then progressively cheaper per hour; recommended Bacharach–St. Goar trip: €9.90 one-way, €12.10 round-trip, bikes-€2.50; discounts: Mon and Fri—half-price for seniors over 60, Tue—bicyclists travel 2 for the price of 1; tel. 06741/1634 in St. Goar, tel. 06743/1322 in

Bacharach, www.k-d.com).

Boats run daily in both directions April through October, with no boats off-season. Complete, up-to-date schedules are posted in any Rhineland station, hotel, or TI; at www.k-d.com; and at www.euraide.de/ricksteves. Purchase tickets at the dock up to five minutes before departure. (Confirm times at your hotel the night before.) The boat is never full. Romantics will enjoy the old-time paddle-wheel *Goethe*, which sails each direction once a day (€1.60 extra, confirm time locally).

The smaller Bingen–Rüdesheimer Line is slightly cheaper than K-D (railpasses not valid, buy tickets on boat, tel. 06721/14140, www.bingen-ruedesheimer.com), with three two-hour round-trip St. Goar–Bacharach trips daily April–October (€9 one-way, €11 round-trip; departing St. Goar at 11:00, 14:10, and 16:10; departing Bacharach at 10:10, 12:00, and 15:00).

By Car: Drivers have these options: 1) skip the boat; 2) take a round-trip cruise from St. Goar or Bacharach; 3) draw pretzels and let the loser drive, prepare the picnic, and meet the boat; 4) rent a bike, bring it on the boat for free, and bike back; or 5) take the boat one-way and return by train. When exploring by car, don't hesitate to pop onto one of the many little ferries that shuttle across the bridgeless-around-here river (see below).

By Ferry: While there are no bridges between Koblenz and Mainz, you'll see car-and-passenger ferries (usually family-run for generations) about every three miles. Bingen–Rüdesheim, Lorch–Niederheimbach, Engelsburg–Kaub, and St. Goar–St. Goarshausen are some of the most useful routes (times vary; St. Goar–St. Goarshausen ferry departs each side every 15–20 min, Mon–Sat 6:00–21:00, Sun 8:00–21:00, May–Sept until 23:00; one-way fares: adult-€1.30, car and driver-€3.30, pay on the boat; www.faehre-loreley.de). For a fun little jaunt, take a quick round-trip with some time to explore the other side.

By Bike: You can bike on either side of the Rhine, but for a designated bike path, stay on the west side, where a 35-mile path runs between Koblenz and Bingen. The six-mile stretch between St. Goar and Bacharach is smooth and scenic, but mostly along the highway. The bit from Bacharach to Bingen hugs the riverside and is road-free. Either way, biking is a great way to explore the valley. Many hotels provide free or cheap bikes to guests; in Bacharach, anyone can rent bikes at Hotel Hillen (€12/day for non-guests, see "Helpful Hints" in Bacharach section).

Consider biking one-way and taking the bike on the riverboat back, or designing a circular trip using the fun and frequent shuttle ferries. A good target might be Kaub (where a tiny boat shuttles sightseers to the better-from-a-distance castle on the island) or Rheinstein Castle.

By Train: Hourly milk-run trains down the Rhine hit every town (St. Goar–Bacharach, 12 min; Bacharach–Mainz, 60 min; Mainz–Koblenz, 90 min). Some train schedules list St. Goar but not Bacharach as a stop, but any schedule listing St. Goar also stops at Bacharach. Tiny stations are not staffed—buy tickets at the platform machines (user-friendly, takes paper money). Prices are cheap (for example, €3 between St. Goar and Bacharach); consider the Rhineland-Pfalz-Ticket, which covers travel on milk-run trains for up to five people (€26, not good before 9:00 on weekdays). Express trains speed past the small towns, taking only 50 minutes between Koblenz and Mainz.

Self-Guided Tour

▲▲▲Rhine Blitz Tour by Train or Boat

One of Europe's great train thrills is zipping along the Rhine enjoying this blitz tour. Or, even better, do it relaxing on the deck of a Rhine steamer, surrounded by the wonders of this romantic and historic gorge. This quick and easy tour (you can cut in anywhere) skips most of the syrupy myths filling normal Rhine guides. You can follow along on a train, bike, car, or boat. By train or boat, sit on the left (river) side going south from Koblenz. While nearly all the castles listed are viewed from this side, train travelers need to clear a path to the right window for the times I yell, "Cross over!"

You'll notice large black-and-white kilometer markers along the riverbank. I erected these years ago to make this tour easier to follow. They tell the distance from the Rhinefalls, where the Rhine leaves Switzerland and becomes navigable. Now the river-barge pilots have accepted these as navigational aids as well. We're tackling just 36 miles (58 km) of the 820-mile-long (1,320-km) Rhine. Your Rhine Blitz Tour starts at Koblenz and heads upstream to Bingen. If you're going the other direction, it still works. Just hold the book upside-down.

Km 590—Koblenz: This Rhine blitz starts with Romantic Rhine thrills—at Koblenz. Koblenz is not a nice city (it was hit hard in World War II), but its place as the historic *Deutsche Eck* (German corner)—the tip of land where the Mosel joins the Rhine—gives it a certain historic charm. Koblenz, from the Latin for "confluence," has Roman origins. If you stop here, take a walk through the park, noticing the reconstructed memorial to the *Kaiser*. Across the river, the yellow Ehrenbreitstein Castle now houses a hostel. It's a 30-minute hike from the station to the Koblenz boat dock.

Km 585—Lahneck Castle (Burg Lahneck): Above the modern autobahn bridge over the Lahn River, this castle *(Burg)*

The Best of the Rhine

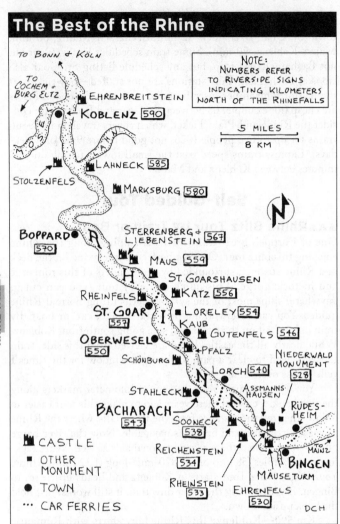

NOTE: NUMBERS REFER TO RIVERSIDE SIGNS INDICATING KILOMETERS NORTH OF THE RHINEFALLS

TO BONN & KÖLN

TO COCHEM + BURG ELTZ

EHRENBREITSTEIN

◄ KOBLENZ 590

5 MILES
8 KM

N

LAHNECK 585

STOLZENFELS

MARKSBURG 580

BOPPARD 570

R

STERRENBERG & LIEBENSTEIN 567

MAUS 559

H

ST. GOARSHAUSEN

RHEINFELS

KATZ 556

ST. GOAR 557

I

LORELEY 554

KAUB

GUTENFELS 546

OBERWESEL 550

PFALZ

SCHÖNBURG

N

NIEDERWALD MONUMENT 528

LORCH 540

STAHLECK

E

ASSMANNS-HAUSEN

RÜDES-HEIM

BACHARACH 543

SOONECK 538

TO MAINZ

REICHENSTEIN 534

BINGEN

MÄUSETURM

RHEINSTEIN 533

EHRENFELS 530

DCH

🏰 CASTLE
▪ OTHER MONUMENT
● TOWN
⋯ CAR FERRIES

RHINE VALLEY

was built in 1240 to defend local silver mines; the castle was ruined by the French in 1688 and rebuilt in the 1850s in Neo-Gothic style. Burg Lahneck faces another Romantic rebuild, the yellow Schloss Stolzenfels (out of view above the train, a 10-min climb from tiny parking lot, open for touring, closed Mon). Note that a *Burg* is a defensive fortress, while a *Schloss* is mainly a showy palace.

Km 580—Marksburg Castle: This castle (black and white, with the three modern chimneys behind it, just before the town of Spay) is the best-looking of all the Rhine castles and the only surviving medieval castle on the Rhine. Because of its command-ing position, it was never attacked in the Middle Ages (though it was captured by the US Army in March of 1945). It's now open as a museum with a medieval interior second only to the Mosel's Burg Eltz. The three modern smokestacks vent Europe's biggest car-battery recycling plant just up the valley.

Km 570—Boppard: Once a Roman town, Boppard has some impressive remains of fourth-century walls. Notice the Roman towers and the substantial chunk of Roman wall near the train station, just above the main square.

If you visit Boppard, head to the fascinating church below the main square. Find the carved Romanesque crazies at the doorway. Inside, to the right of the entrance, you'll see Christian symbols from Roman times. Also notice the painted arches and vaults. Originally most Romanesque churches were painted this way. Down by the river, look for the high-water *(Hochwasser)* marks on the arches from various flood years. (You'll find these flood marks throughout the Rhine and Mosel valleys.)

Km 567—Sterrenberg Castle and Liebenstein Castle: These are the "Hostile Brothers" castles across from Bad Salzig. Take the wall between the castles (actually designed to improve the defenses of both castles), add two greedy and jealous brothers and a fair maiden, and create your own legend. Burg Liebenstein is now a fun, friendly, and affordable family-run hotel (9 rooms, Db-€115, suite-€140, giant king-and-the-family room-€215, easy parking, tel. 06773/308 or 06773/251, www.castle-liebenstein.com, hotel -burg-liebenstein@rhinecastles.com, Nickenig family).

Km 560: While you can see nothing from here, a 19th-century lead mine functioned on both sides of the river, with a shaft actu-ally tunneling completely under the Rhine.

Km 559—Maus Castle (Burg Maus): The Maus (mouse) got its name because the next castle was owned by the Katzenelnbogen family. (*Katz* means "cat.") In the 1300s, it was considered a state-of-the-art fortification...until Napoleon had it blown up in 1806 with state-of-the-art explosives. It was rebuilt true to its original plans in about 1900. Today, the castle hosts a falconry show (€8, Tue–Sun at 11:00 and 14:30, also at 16:30 on Sun, closed Mon, 20-min walk up, tel. 06771/7669, www.burg-maus.de).

Km 557—St. Goar and Rheinfels Castle: Cross to the other side of the train. The pleasant town of St. Goar was named for a sixth-century hometown monk. It originated in Celtic times (really old) as a place where sailors would stop, catch their breath, send home a postcard, and give thanks after surviving the seductive and treacherous Loreley crossing. St. Goar is worth a stop to explore its mighty Rheinfels Castle. (For information, a self-guided castle tour, and accommodations, see St. Goar section of this chapter.)

Km 556—Katz Castle (Burg Katz): Burg Katz (Katzen-elnbogen) faces St. Goar from across the river. Together, Burg Katz (built in 1371) and Rheinfels Castle had a clear view up and down the river, effectively controlling traffic. There was absolutely no duty-free shopping on the medieval Rhine. Katz got Napoleoned in 1806 and rebuilt in about 1900.

Today, the castle is shrouded by intrigue and controversy. In 1995, a wealthy and eccentric Japanese man bought it for about $4 million. His vision: to make the castle—so close to the Loreley that Japanese tourists are wild about—an exotic escape for his countrymen. But the town wouldn't allow his planned renovation of the historic (and therefore protected) building. Stymied, the frustrated investor just abandoned his plans. Today, Burg Katz sits empty...the Japanese ghost castle.

Below the castle, notice the derelict grape terraces—worked since the eighth century, but abandoned only in the last genera-tion. The Rhine wine is particularly good because the local slate absorbs the heat of the sun and stays warm all night, resulting in sweeter grapes. Wine from the flat fields above the Rhine gorge is cheaper and good only as table wine. The wine from the steep side of the Rhine gorge—harder to grow and harvest—is tastier and more expensive.

About Km 555: A statue of the Loreley, the beautiful-but-deadly nymph (see next listing for legend), combs her hair at the end of a long spit—built to give barges protection from vicious ice floes that until recent years would rage down the river in the win-ter. The actual Loreley, a cliff (marked by the flags), is just ahead.

Km 554—The Loreley: Steep a big slate rock in centu-ries of legend and it becomes a tourist attraction—the ultimate Rhinestone. The Loreley (flags and visitors center on top, name painted near shoreline), rising 450 feet over the narrowest and deepest point of the Rhine, has long been important. It was a holy site in pre-Roman days. The fine echoes here—thought to be ghostly voices—fertilized legend-tellers' imaginations.

Because of the reefs just upstream (at kilometer 552), many ships never made it to St. Goar. Sailors (after days on the river) blamed their misfortune on a *wunderbares Fräulein,* whose long blond hair almost covered her body. Heinrich Heine's *Song of Loreley* (the CliffsNotes version is on local postcards) tells the story of a count who sent his men to kill or capture this siren after she distracted his horny son, causing him to drown. When the sol-diers cornered the nymph in her cave, she called her father (Father Rhine) for help. Huge waves, the likes of which you'll never see today, rose from the river and carried Loreley to safety. And she has never been seen since.

But alas, when the moon shines brightly and the tour buses

RHINE VALLEY

are parked, a soft, playful Rhine whine can still be heard from the Loreley. As you pass, listen carefully ("Sailors...sailors...over my bounding mane").

Km 552—The Seven Maidens: Killer reefs, marked by red-and-green buoys, are called the "Seven Maidens." Okay, one more goofy legend: The prince of Schönburg Castle (*über* Oberwesel—described below) had seven spoiled daughters who always dumped men because of their shortcomings. Fed up, he invited seven of his knights to the castle and demanded that his daughters each choose one to marry. But they complained that each man had too big a nose, was too fat, too stupid, and so on. The rude and teasing girls escaped into a riverboat. Just downstream, God turned them into the seven rocks that form this reef. While this story probably isn't entirely true, there's a lesson in it for medieval children: Don't be hard-hearted.

Km 550—Oberwesel: Cross to the other side of the train. Oberwesel was a Celtic town in 400 B.C., then a Roman military station. It now boasts some of the best Roman-wall and medieval-tower remains on the Rhine, and the commanding Schönburg Castle. Notice how many of the train tunnels have entrances designed like medieval turrets—they were actually built in the Romantic 19th century. Okay, back to the river side.

Km 546—Gutenfels Castle and Pfalz Castle, the Classic Rhine View: Burg Gutenfels (see white-painted *Hotel* sign) and the shipshape Pfalz Castle (built in the river in the 1300s) worked very effectively to tax medieval river traffic. The town of Kaub grew rich as Pfalz raised its chains when boats came, and lowered them only when the merchants had paid their duty. Those who didn't pay spent time touring its prison, on a raft at the bottom of its well. In 1504, a pope called for the destruction of Pfalz, but the locals withstood a six-week siege, and the castle still stands. Notice the overhanging outhouse (tiny white room—with faded medieval stains—between two wooden ones). Pfalz (also known as Pfalzgrafenstein) is tourable but bare and dull (€3 ferry from Kaub, €3 entry; March–Oct Tue–Sun 10:00–18:00, until 17:00 in March, closed Mon; Nov and Jan–Feb Sat–Sun 10:00–17:00, closed Mon–Fri; closed Dec; last entry one hour before closing, tel. 0172/262-2800).

In Kaub, on the riverfront directly below the castles, a green statue honors the German general Gebhard von Blücher. He was Napoleon's nemesis. In 1813, as Napoleon fought his way back to Paris after his disastrous Russian campaign, he stopped at Mainz—hoping to fend off the Germans and Russians pursuing him by controlling that strategic bridge. Blücher tricked Napoleon. By building the first major pontoon bridge of its kind here at the Pfalz Castle, he crossed the Rhine and outflanked the French. Two years later, Blücher and Wellington teamed up to defeat Napoleon once and for all at Waterloo.

Km 544—"The Raft Busters": Immediately before Bacharach, at the top of the island, buoys mark a gang of rocks notorious for busting up rafts. The Black Forest, upstream from here, was once poor, and wood was its best export. Black Foresters would ride log booms down the Rhine to the Ruhr (where their timber fortified coal-mine shafts) or to Holland (where logs were sold to shipbuilders). If they could navigate the sweeping bend just before Bacharach and then survive these "raft busters," they'd come home reckless and likely horny—the German folkloric equivalent of American cowboys after payday.

Km 543—Bacharach and Stahleck Castle (Burg Stahleck): Cross to the other side of the train. The town of Bacharach is a great stop (see details and accommodations in the next section). Some of the Rhine's best wine is from this town, whose name likely derives from "altar to Bacchus." Local vintners brag that the medieval Pope Pius II ordered Bacharach wine by the cartload. Perched above the town, the 13th-century Burg Stahleck is now a hostel.

Km 540—Lorch: This pathetic stub of a castle is barely visible from the road. Check out the hillside vineyards. These vineyards once blanketed four times as much land as they do today, but modern economics have driven most of them out of business. The vineyards that do survive require government subsidies. Notice the small car ferry (3/hr, 10 min), one of several along the bridgeless stretch between Mainz and Koblenz.

Km 538—Sooneck Castle: Cross back to the other side of the train. Built in the 11th century, this castle was twice destroyed by people sick and tired of robber barons.

Km 534—Reichenstein Castle and **Km 533—Rheinstein Castle:** Stay on the other side of the train to see two of the first castles to be rebuilt in the Romantic era. Both are privately owned, tourable, and connected by a pleasant trail.

Km 530—Ehrenfels Castle: Opposite Bingerbrück and the Bingen station, you'll see the ghostly Ehrenfels Castle (clobbered by the Swedes in 1636 and by the French in 1689). Since it had no view of the river traffic to the north, the owner built the cute little *Mäuseturm* (mouse tower) on an island (the yellow tower you'll see near the train station today). Rebuilt in the 1800s in Neo-Gothic style, it's now used as a Rhine navigation signal station.

Km 528—Niederwald Monument: Across from the Bingen station on a hilltop is the 120-foot-high Niederwald monument, a memorial built with 32 tons of bronze in 1877 to commemorate "the reestablishment of the German Empire." A lift takes tourists to this statue from the famous and extremely touristy wine town of Rüdesheim.

From here, the Romantic Rhine becomes the industrial Rhine, and our tour is over.

Bacharach

Once prosperous from the wine and wood trade, Bacharach (BAHKH-ah-rahkh, with a guttural *kh* sound) is now just a pleasant half-timbered village of a thousand people working hard to keep its tourists happy.

Orientation

Tourist Information

The TI, on the main street in the Posthof courtyard next to the church, will store bags for day-trippers (April–Oct Mon–Fri 9:00–17:00, Sat–Sun 10:00–15:00; Nov–March Mon–Fri 9:00–12:00, closed Sat–Sun; Oberstrasse 45, from train station turn right and walk 5 blocks down main street with castle high on your left, tel. 06743/919-303, www.bacharach.de or www.rhein-nahe-touristik .de, Herr Kuhn and his team).

Helpful Hints

Shopping: The **Jost** German gift store, across the main square from the church, carries most everything a souvenir-shopper could want (from beer steins to cuckoo clocks). The Josts offer a 10 percent discount to readers of this book who pay cash, and can ship things to the US (March–Oct Mon–Fri 8:30–18:00, Sat 8:30–17:00, Sun 10:00–16:00; Nov–Feb shorter hours and closed Sun; Blücherstrasse 4, tel. 06743/1224, www.phil-jost -germany.com, phil.jost@t-online.de).

Internet Access: The Rhine's cheapest Internet café is in the basement of the Lutheran-church-run kindergarten at Koblenzer Strasse 10, a few doors past the Altes Haus (€1/hr, Mon–Tue and Thu–Fri 16:00–21:00, closed Sat–Sun and Wed). The TI has a coin-op terminal (€0.50/15 min).

Post Office: It's inside a shop, at Oberstrasse 37 between the train station and the TI (Mon–Fri 9:00–12:00 & 14:00–18:00, Sat 9:00–12:00, closed Sun).

Grocery Store: Across from the Altes Haus is a **Nahkauf,** a basic grocery store (Mon–Fri 8:00–12:30 & 14:00–18:00, Sat 8:00–15:00, closed Sun, Oberstrasse 46).

Bike Rental: While many hotels loan bikes to guests, the only real bike-rental business in the town center is run by Erich at Hotel Hillen (see listing on page 540). He rents 25 bikes daily from 9:00 until dark (€12/day for non-guests, €7/day for guests, Langstrasse 18, tel. 06743/1287).

Local Guides and Walking Tours: Get acquainted with Bacharach by taking a walking tour. Charming **Herr Rolf Jung,** retired headmaster of the Bacharach school, is a superb English-speaking guide who loves sharing his town's story with Americans (€30, 90 min, call to reserve, tel. 06743/1519). **Manuela Mades** (tel. 06743/2759), **Birgit Wessel** (tel. 06743/937-514), and Aussie **Joanne Augustin,** who works at the youth hostel (tel. 06743/919-300, mobile 0179-231-1389), also give good tours. If none of the above is available, call the TI for advice, or take my self-guided walk (see below). On Saturdays at 11:00 from May to October, the TI offers a 90-minute walking tour (€4.50) in German only.

Self-Guided Walk

Welcome to Bacharach

• *Start at the Köln–Düsseldorfer ferry dock (next to a fine picnic park).*

View the town from the parking lot—a modern landfill. The Rhine used to lap against Bacharach's town wall, just over the present-day highway. Every few years the river floods, covering the highway with several feet of water. The **castle** on the hill is now a youth hostel. Two of the town's original 16 towers are visible from here (up to five if you look really hard). The huge roadside wine keg declares that this town was built on the wine trade.

Reefs farther upstream forced boats to unload upriver and reload here. Consequently, in the Middle Ages, Bacharach became the biggest wine-trading town on the Rhine. A riverfront crane hoisted huge kegs of prestigious "Bacharach" wine (which, in practice, was from anywhere in the region). The tour buses next to the dock and the flags of the biggest spenders along the highway remind you that today's economy is basically founded on tourism.

• *Before entering the town, walk upstream through the riverside park.*

This park was laid out in 1910 in the English style: Notice how the trees were planted to frame fine town views, highlighting the most picturesque bits of architecture. Until recently, stepping on the grass was *verboten.* The dark, sad-looking monument—its "eternal" flame long snuffed out—is a war memorial. The German psyche is permanently scarred by war memories. Today, many Germans would rather avoid monuments like this, which revisit the dark periods before Germany became a nation of pacifists. Take a close look at the monument. Each panel honors sons of Bacharach who died for the Kaiser: in 1864 against Denmark, in 1870 against France, in 1914 during World War I. The military

Bacharach

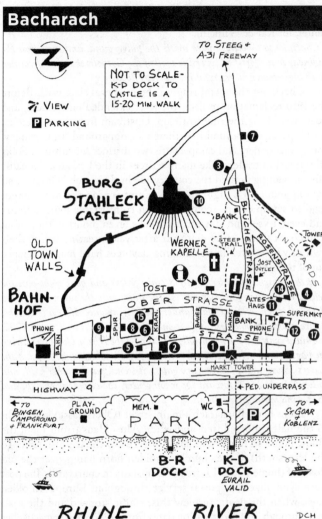

Not to Scale—K-D dock to Castle is a 15-20 min. walk

View

P Parking

TO STEEG & A-31 FREEWAY

BURG STAHLECK CASTLE

OLD TOWN WALLS

BAHN-HOF

BANK

WERNER KAPELLE

STEEP TRAIL

VINEYARDS

TOWER

JOST OUTLET

POST

OBER STRASSE

ALTES HAUS

SUPERMKT.

PHONE

SPUR

BAHN

KRAN

BAUER

LANG

STRASSE

MARKT

BANK

PHONE

MARKT TOWER

HIGHWAY 9

PED. UNDERPASS

TO BINGEN, CAMPGROUND & FRANKFURT

PLAY-GROUND

MEM.

PARK

WC

P

TO St GOAR & KOBLENZ

B-R DOCK

K-D DOCK EURAIL VALID

RHINE RIVER

DCH

RHINE VALLEY

1. Rhein Hotel & Stüber Rest.
2. Hotel/Rest. Kranenturm
3. Pension im Malerwinkel
4. Pension Binz
5. Hotel Hillen & Bike Rental
6. Pension Lettie
7. Pension Winzerhaus
8. Ursula Orth B & B
9. Irmgard Orth B & B
10. Jugendherberge Stahleck Hostel
11. Altes Haus Restaurant
12. Kurpfälzische Münze Restaurant
13. Eis Café Italia
14. Bastian's Weingut zum Grüner Baum
15. Weingut Karl Heidrich
16. Old Posthof
17. Internet Café

Maltese cross—flanked by classic German helmets—has a *W* at its center, for Kaiser Wilhelm.

• *Continue to where the park meets the playground, and then cross the highway to the fortified riverside wall of the Catholic church—decorated with high-water marks recalling various floods.*

Check out the metal ring on the medieval slate wall. Before the 1910 reclamation project, the river extended out to here, and boats would use the ring to tie up. Upstream from here, there's a trailer park, and beyond that there's a campground. In Germany, trailer vacationers and campers are two distinct subcultures. Folks who travel in trailers, like many retirees in the US, are a nomadic bunch, hauling around the countryside in their mobile homes and paying about €6 a night to park. Campers, on the other hand, tend to set up camp—complete with comfortable lounge chairs and even TVs—and stay put for weeks, even months. They often come back to the same plot year after year, treating it like their own private estate. These camping devotees have made a science out of relaxing.

• *At the church, go under the 1858 train tracks and hook right past the yellow floodwater yardstick and up the stairs onto the town wall. Atop the wall, turn left and walk under the long arcade. After a few steps, notice a well on your left. This is one of 40 such wells that, until 1900, provided water to the townsfolk. You'll pass the Rhein Hotel (see listing on page 538; hotel is before the Markt tower, which marks one of the town's 15 original 14th-century gates), descend, pass another well, and follow Marktstrasse toward the town center, the two-tone church, and the town's main intersection.*

From here, Bacharach's main street (Oberstrasse) goes right to the half-timbered, red-and-white Altes Haus (from 1368, the oldest house in town) and left 400 yards to the train station. To the left (south) of the church, a golden horn hangs over the old **Posthof** (home to the TI, free WC upstairs in courtyard). The post horn symbolizes the postal service throughout Europe. In olden days, when the postman blew this, traffic stopped and the mail sped through. This post station dates from 1724, when stagecoaches ran from Köln to Frankfurt and would change horses here, Pony Express–style.

Step past the old oak doors into the courtyard—once a carriage house and inn that accommodated Bacharach's first VIP visitors. Notice the fascist eagle (from 1936, on the left as you enter; a swastika once filled its center) and the fine view of the church and a ruined chapel above. The Posthof is on a charming square. Spin around to enjoy the higgledy-piggledy building style.

Two hundred years ago, Bacharach's main drag was the only road along the Rhine. Napoleon widened it to fit his cannon wagons. The steps alongside the church lead to the castle. Return to the church, passing the Italian ice-cream café (Eis Café Italia), where friendly Mimo serves his special invention: Riesling wine–flavored gelato (see "Eating," page 541).

Inside the Protestant church (April–Oct daily 9:30–18:00, closed Nov–March, English info on table near door), you'll find Grotesque capitals, brightly painted in medieval style, and a mix of round Romanesque and pointed Gothic arches. To the left of the altar, some medieval frescoes survive where an older Romanesque arch was cut by a pointed Gothic one.

• *Continue down Oberstrasse to the **Altes Haus**.*

Notice the 14th-century building style—the first floor is made of stone, while upper floors are half-timbered (in the ornate style common in the Rhine Valley). Some of its windows still look medieval, with small, flattened circles as panes (small because that's all that glass-blowing technology of the time would allow), pieced together with molten lead. Frau Weber welcomes visitors to enjoy the fascinating ground floor of her Altes Haus, with its evocative old photos and etchings (consider eating here later—see "Eating," page 541).

• *Keep going down Oberstrasse to the **old mint** (Münze), marked by a crude coin in its sign.*

Across from the mint, the Bastian family's wine garden is the liveliest place in town after dark (see "Wine-Tasting" on page 542). Above you in the vineyards stands a lonely white-and-red tower—your destination.

At the next street, look right and see the mint tower, painted in the medieval style (illustrating that the Dark Ages weren't really *that* dark), and then turn left. Wander 30 yards up Rosenstrasse to the **well.** Notice the sundial and the wall painting of 1632 Bacharach with its walls intact. (The town is working to reconstruct the wall's missing sections—you may be able to walk the whole length of the wall in 2010.) Climb the tiny-stepped lane behind the well up into the vineyard and to the tall tower. The slate steps lead to a small path through the vineyard that deposits you at a viewpoint atop the stubby remains of the old town wall. If the tower's open, hike to its top floor for the best view.

A grand medieval town spreads before you. For 300 years (1300–1600), Bacharach was big (population 4,000), rich, and politically powerful.

From this perch you can see the chapel ruins and six surviving **city towers.** Visually trace the wall to the castle. The castle was actually the capital of Germany for a couple of years in the 1200s. When Holy Roman Emperor Frederick Barbarossa went away to fight the Crusades, he left his brother (who lived here) in charge of his vast realm. Bacharach was home of one of seven electors who voted for the Holy Roman Emperor in 1275. To protect their own power, these elector-princes did their best to choose the weakest guy on the ballot. The elector from Bacharach helped select a two-bit prince named Rudolf von Habsburg (from a no-name castle in Switzerland). The underestimated Rudolf brutally silenced the robber barons along the Rhine and established the mightiest dynasty in European history. His family line, the Habsburgs, ruled much of Central and Eastern Europe from Vienna until 1918.

Plagues, fires, and the Thirty Years' War (1618–1648) finally did in Bacharach. The town, with a population of about a thousand, has slumbered for several centuries. Today, the castle houses commoners—40,000 overnights annually by youth hostelers.

In the mid-19th century, painters such as J. M. W. Turner and writers such as Victor Hugo were charmed by the Rhineland's romantic mix of past glory, present poverty, and rich legend. They put this part of the Rhine on the old Grand Tour map as the "Romantic Rhine." Victor Hugo pondered the ruined 15th-century chapel that you see under the castle. In his 1842 travel book, *Rhein Reise (Rhine Travels)*, he wrote, "No doors, no roof or windows, a magnificent skeleton puts its silhouette against the sky. Above it, the ivy-covered castle ruins provide a fitting crown. This is Bacharach, land of fairy tales, covered with legends and sagas." If you're enjoying the Romantic Rhine, thank Victor Hugo and company.

• *To get back into town, take the level path away from the river that leads along the once-mighty wall up the valley past the next tower. Then cross the street into the parking lot. Pass Pension Malerwinkel on your right, being careful not to damage the old arch with your head. Follow the creek past a delightful little series of half-timbered homes and cheery gardens known as "Painters' Corner" (Malerwinkel). Resist looking into some pervert's peep show (on the right) and continue downhill back to the village center. Nice work.*

Sleeping

(area code: 06743)

Ignore guest houses and restaurants posting *Recommended by Rick Steves* signs. If they're not listed in the current edition of this book, I do not recommend them. Parking in Bacharach is simple along the highway next to the tracks (3-hour daytime limit is generally not enforced) or in the boat parking lot. For locations, see the Bacharach map earlier in this chapter.

$$$ Rhein Hotel, with 14 spacious and comfortable rooms, is classy, well-run, decorated with a modern flair, and overlooks the river. Since it's right on the train tracks, its river- and train-side rooms come with four-paned windows and air-conditioning. This place has been in the Stüber family for six generations (Sb-€55,

Sleep Code

(€1 = about $1.40, country code: 49)
S = Single, **D** = Double/Twin, **T** = Triple, **Q** = Quad, **b** = bathroom,
s = shower only. All hotels speak some English. Breakfast
is included and credit cards are accepted unless otherwise
noted.

To help you sort easily through these listings, I've divided
the rooms into three categories, based on the price for a
standard double room with bath:

$$$ Higher Priced—Most rooms €80 or more.
$$ Moderately Priced—Most rooms between €60–80.
$ Lower Priced—Most rooms €60 or less.

The Rhine is an easy place for cheap sleeps. B&Bs and
Gasthäuser with €25 beds abound (and normally discount
their prices for longer stays). Rhine-area hostels offer €17 beds
to travelers of any age. Each town's TI is eager to set you up,
and finding a room should be easy any time of year (except
for winefest weekends in Sept and Oct). Bacharach and St.
Goar, the best towns for an overnight stop, are 10 miles apart,
connected by milk-run trains, riverboats, and a riverside bike
path. Bacharach is a much more interesting town, but St. Goar
has the famous castle (for St. Goar recommendations, see
page 551).

RHINE VALLEY

Db-€90, cheaper for longer stays, half-board option, non-smoking,
free loaner bikes for guests, Wi-Fi, directly inland from the K-D
boat dock at Langstrasse 50, tel. 06743/1243, fax 06743/1413, www
.rhein-hotel-bacharach.de, info@rhein-hotel-bacharach.de). For a
culinary splurge, consider dining here (see next section).

$$ Hotel Kranenturm, offering castle ambience without
the climb, combines hotel comfort with *Privatzimmer* coziness
right downtown. Run by hardworking Kurt Engel and his intense
but friendly wife, Fatima, this hotel is part of the medieval for-
tification. Its former *Kran* (crane) towers are now round rooms.
When the riverbank was higher, cranes on this tower loaded bar-
rels of wine onto Rhine boats. While just 15 feet from the train
tracks, a combination of medieval sturdiness, triple-paned win-
dows, and included earplugs makes the riverside rooms sleepable
(Sb-€39–45, small Db-€56–62, regular Db-€58–65, Db in huge
tower rooms with castle and river views-€72–80, Tb-€83–95,
Qb great for families with small kids-€100–115, honeymoon
special-€85–105, lower price May–Oct with 3-night stay and
Nov–April with 2-night stay, family deals, cash preferred, Rhine
views come with train noise, back rooms are quiet, non-smoking,

showers can be temperamental, kid-friendly, good breakfast, pay Internet access, free Wi-Fi, laundry service-€12.80, Langstrasse 30, tel. 06743/1308, fax 06743/1021, www.kranenturm.com, hotel -kranenturm@t-online.de). Kurt, a good cook, serves €8–14 dinners.

$$ Pension im Malerwinkel sits like a grand gingerbread house that straddles the town wall in a quiet little neighborhood so charming it's called "Painters' Corner" *(Malerwinkel)*. The Vollmer family's 20-room place is super-quiet and comes with a sunny garden on a brook, views of the vineyards, and easy parking (Sb-€38, Db-€62 for 1 night, €56 for 2 nights, €53 for 3 nights or more, cash only, some rooms have balconies, no train noise, non-smoking, bike rental-€6/day; from Oberstrasse, turn left at the church, and stay to the left of the babbling brook until you reach Blücherstrasse 41; tel. 06743/1239, fax 06743/93407, www.im-malerwinkel.de, pension@im-malerwinkel.de, Armin and Daniela).

$$ Pension Binz offers four large, bright, plainly furnished rooms in a good location with no train noise (Sb-€35, Db-€60, third person-€18, slightly cheaper for 3 nights or more, apartment with kitchen but no breakfast and 2-night minimum-€65, Koblenzer Strasse 1, tel. 06743/1604, fax 06743/937-9916, pension .binz@freenet.de, warm Carla speaks a little English).

$ Hotel Hillen, a block south of the Hotel Kranenturm, has a little less charm and similar train noise (with the same ultra-thick windows). It offers spacious rooms, good food, and friendly owners (S-€30, Sb-€35, D-€40, Ds-€45, Db-€50, Tb-€65, Qb-€80, prices are for a 2-night minimum, €5 more for 1-night stays, closed mid-Nov–mid-March, family rooms, Langstrasse 18, tel. 06743/1287, fax 06743/1037, hotel-hillen@web.de, kind Iris speaks some English). The Hillen also rents bikes (see "Helpful Hints," earlier in this chapter).

$ At Pension Lettie, effervescent and eager-to-please Lettie offers four bright rooms. Lettie speaks English (she worked for the US Army before they withdrew) and does laundry for €10.50/ load (Sb-€38, Db-€53, Tb-€70, Qb-€90, 5b-€105, pricier if you book through TI, €3–5 discount for 2-night stays, 10 percent more if paying with credit card, strictly non-smoking, buffet breakfast with waffles and eggs, no train noise, pay Wi-Fi, a few doors inland from Hotel Kranenturm, Kranenstrasse 6, tel. 06743/2115, fax 06743/947564, pension.lettie@t-online.de).

$ Pension Winzerhaus, a 10-room place run by friendly Sybille and Stefan, is outside the town walls, 200 yards up the side-valley road from the town gate, directly under the vineyards. Though you can't hear the train, there is slight noise from passing cars. The rooms are simple, clean, and modern, and parking is easy (Sb-€30, Db-€49, Tb-€65, Qb-€75, cash only, non-smoking, 3 free loaner bikes for guests, Blücherstrasse 60, tel. 06743/1294, winzerhaus@gmx.de).

$ Orth *Zimmer:* Delightful sisters-in-law run two fine little B&Bs across the lane from each other (from station, walk down Oberstrasse, turn right on Spurgasse, and look for *Orth* sign). **Ursula Orth** rents five rooms, speaks a smidge of English, and is proud of her homemade jam (Sb-€22, Db-€37, Tb-€45, cash only, rooms 4 and 5 on ground floor, Spurgasse 3, tel. 06743/1557). **Irmgard Orth** rents three fresh rooms, two of which share a bathroom on the hall. She speaks even less English but is exuberantly cheery and serves homemade honey with breakfast (S-€22, D-€34–35, Db-€37, cash only, Spurgasse 2, look for beehive signs, tel. 06743/1553). Their excellent prices assume you're booking direct, instead of through the TI.

$ Jugendherberge Stahleck hostel is a 12th-century castle on the hilltop—500 steps above Bacharach—with a royal Rhine view. Open to travelers of any age, this is a gem with 168 beds and a private modern shower and WC in most rooms. The steep 20-minute climb on the trail from the town church is worth it for the view, even if you're not sleeping there. The hostel serves hearty €6.50 all-you-can-eat buffet dinners, and its pub serves cheap local wine and snacks until midnight. To reach the hostel with luggage from the train station, call an €8 taxi at 06743/1653 or 06743/1418 (€17.40 dorm beds with breakfast and sheets, non-members-€3.10 extra, couples can share one of five €46 Db, no smoking in rooms, pay Internet access, laundry-€5.50, dorm beds normally available but call and leave your name—they'll hold a bed until 18:00, tel. 06743/1266, fax 06743/2684, www.diejugendherbergen.de, bacharach@diejugendherbergen.de). If driving, don't go in the driveway; park on the street and walk 200 yards.

Eating

Restaurants

You can easily find inexpensive (€10–15), atmospheric restaurants offering indoor and outdoor dining. There's also a cozy pizzeria and a *Döner Kebab* joint (daily until 23:00) on the main street.

The Rhein Hotel's **Stüber Restaurant** is Bacharach's best top-end choice. Chef Andreas Stüber is the sixth generation to prepare regional, seasonal plates, served on river- and track-side seating or indoors with a spacious wood-and-white-tablecloth elegance. Consider their €14 William Turner pâté sampler plate, named after the British painter who liked Bacharach (€9–19 entrées, March–mid-Dec Wed–Mon 12:00–14:00 & 17:30–21:00, closed Tue and mid-Dec–Feb, call to reserve on weekends or for an outdoor table, facing the K-D boat dock just below the center of town, Langstrasse 50, tel. 06743/1243).

Altes Haus, the oldest building in town (see page 537), serves reliably good food with Bacharach's most romantic atmosphere. Find the cozy little dining room with photos of the opera singer who sang about Bacharach, adding to its fame (€9–15 entrées, Easter–Nov Thu–Tue 12:00–15:30 & 18:00–23:00, closed Wed and Dec–Easter, dead center by the church, tel. 06743/1209).

Kurpfälzische Münze, while more expensive than Altes Haus, is a popular standby for lunch or a drink on its sunny terrace or in its pubby candlelit interior (main dishes-€7–14 at lunch and €10–20 at dinner, daily 10:00–22:00; in the old mint, a half-block down from Altes Haus; tel. 06743/1375).

Hotel Kranenturm is another good value, with hearty dinners (Kurt prides himself on his *Sauerbraten*—marinated beef with potato dumplings and red cabbage) and good main-course salads. If you're a train-spotter, sit on their track-side terrace and trade travel stories with new friends over dinner, letting screaming trains punctuate your conversation. If you prefer charming old German decor, sit inside (€8–14 main dishes, open 6 days a week 17:00–21:00—closed day varies, see hotel listing in previous section, "Sleeping"). Kurt and Fatima are your hosts.

Eis Café Italia, on the main street and run by friendly Mimo Calabrese, is known for its refreshing, not-too-sweet Riesling-flavored gelato. Notice the big sundae bowls on the shelves. To enjoy your *Eis* German-style, sit down and order ice cream off the menu, or just stop by for a cone before an evening stroll (€0.70/scoop, no tastes offered, April–mid-Oct daily 10:00–22:00, closed off-season, opposite Posthof at Oberstrasse 48).

Wine-Tasting

Bacharach is proud of its wine. Two places in town—Bastian's rowdy and rustic Grüner Baum, and sophisticated Weingut Karl Heidrich—offer visitors an inexpensive chance to join in on the fun. Each creates carousels of local wines that small groups of travelers (who don't mind sharing a glass) can sample and compare.

At **Bastian's Weingut zum Grüner Baum,** groups of 2–6 people pay €14 for a wine carousel of 15 glasses—14 different white wines and one lonely rosé—and a basket of bread. Your mission: Team up with others who have this book to rendezvous here after dinner. Spin the Lazy Susan, share a common cup, and discuss the taste. Doris Bastian insists: "After each wine, you must talk to each other." They offer soup and cold cuts, and good ambience indoors and out (Mon–Wed and Fri from 13:00, Sat–Sun from 12:00, closed Thu and Feb–mid-March, just past Altes Haus, tel. 06743/1208). To make a meal of a carousel, consider the *Käse Teller* (7 different cheeses, including *Spundekäse*, the local soft cheese).

Weingut Karl Heidrich is a fun, family-run wine shop and *Stube* in the town center (at Oberstrasse 18, near Hotel Kranenturm), where Markus proudly shares his family's wine while passionately explaining its fine points to travelers. They offer a variety of carousels with six wines and bread (€10), which are ideal for the more sophisticated wine-taster (Easter–Oct Thu–Tue 11:00–22:00, closed Wed and Nov–Easter, tel. 06743/93060).

Connections

Milk-run trains stop at Rhine towns each hour starting as early as 6:00, connecting at Mainz and Koblenz to trains farther afield. Trains between St. Goar and Bacharach depart at about :20 after the hour in each direction (€3, buy tickets from the machine in the unstaffed stations). The ride times listed below are calculated from Bacharach; for St. Goar, the difference is only 12 minutes. Train info: tel. 11861 (€0.60/min).

From Bacharach by Train to: St. Goar (hourly, 12 min), **Moselkern** near Burg Eltz (hourly, 1.75 hrs, change in Koblenz), **Cochem** (hourly, 1.5 hrs, change in Koblenz), **Trier** (hourly, 2.5 hrs, change in Koblenz), **Köln** (hourly, 1.75 hrs, change in Koblenz), **Frankfurt Airport** (hourly, 1.25–1.5 hrs, most change in Mainz or Bingen), **Frankfurt** (hourly, 1.5–2 hrs, change in Mainz or Bingen), **Rothenburg ob der Tauber** (every 2 hrs, 4–5 hrs, 3–4 changes), **Munich** (hourly, 5 hrs, 2 changes), **Berlin** (hourly, 5.5–6.5 hrs, 1–3 changes), **Amsterdam** (6/day, 5 hrs, 2 changes).

RHINE VALLEY

St. Goar

St. Goar is a classic Rhine town. Its hulk of a castle overlooks a half-timbered shopping street and leafy riverside park, busy with sightseeing ships and contented strollers. Rheinfels Castle, once the mightiest on the Rhine, is the single best Rhineland ruin to explore. From the riverboat docks, the main drag—a dull pedestrian mall without history—cuts through town before ending at the road up to the castle.

While the town of St. Goar itself isn't much more than a few hotels and restaurants—and is less interesting than Bacharach—it still makes a good base for hiking or biking the region. A tiny car ferry will shuttle you back and forth across the busy Rhine from here. (One of my favorite pastimes in St. Goar is chatting with friendly Heike at the K-D boat kiosk.) For train connections, see Bacharach's "Connections."

Orientation

Tourist Information

The helpful St. Goar TI, which books rooms and stores bags for free, is on the pedestrian street, three blocks from the K-D boat dock and train station (May–Sept Mon–Fri 9:00–12:30 & 13:30–18:00, Sat 10:00–12:00, closed Sun; April and Oct Mon–Fri until 17:00, closed Sat–Sun; Nov–March Mon–Thu until 17:00, Fri 9:00–14:00, closed Sat–Sun; from train station, go downhill around church and turn left, Heerstrasse 86, tel. 06741/383, www.st-goar.de).

Helpful Hints

Picnics: St. Goar's waterfront park is hungry for a picnic. You can buy picnic fixings at the tiny **St. Goarer Stadtladen** grocery store on the pedestrian street (Mon–Fri 8:00–18:00, Sat 8:00–13:00, closed Sun, Heerstrasse 106).

Shopping: The helpful Montag family runs two shops (one specializes in steins and the other in cuckoo clocks) and a hotel, all at the base of the castle hill road. The stein shop under the hotel has Rhine guides, fine steins, and copies of this year's *Rick Steves' Germany* guidebook (April–Oct daily 8:30–18:00). Both shops offer 10 percent off any of their souvenirs (including Hummels) for travelers with this book (€5 minimum purchase). On-the-spot VAT refunds cover about half of your shipping costs (if you're not shipping, they'll give you a VAT form to claim your refund at airport). Another good souvenir shop is across from the K-D boat dock.

Internet Access: Hotel Montag offers very expensive coin-op access (€7.50/hr, 6 terminals, Heerstrasse 128, tel. 06741/1629). If you're headed to nearby Bacharach, Internet is cheaper there (see "Helpful Hints" at top of Bacharach section, earlier in this chapter).

Bike Rental: Goarbike, run by Herr Langhans, is five doors from the train station (€6/6 hrs, €11.50/day, April–Oct Mon–Fri 9:00–13:00 & 18:00–20:00, Sat–Sun 9:00–20:00, go right as you exit station, tel. 06741/1735).

Parking: There's a free lot at the downstream end of town.

Sights

▲▲▲Rheinfels Castle

Sitting like a dead pit bull above St. Goar, this mightiest of Rhine castles rumbles with ghosts from its hard-fought past. Burg Rheinfels *was* huge—once the biggest castle on the Rhine (built in 1245). It withstood a siege of 28,000 French troops in 1692. But

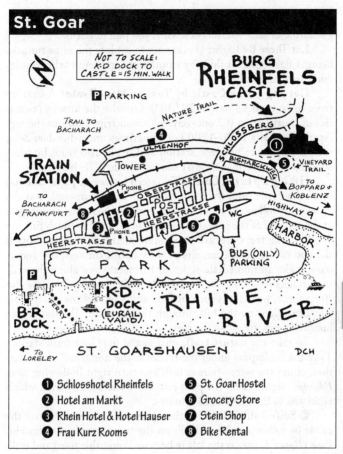

St. Goar

NOT TO SCALE:
KD DOCK TO
CASTLE = 15 MIN. WALK

P PARKING

TRAIL TO
BACHARACH

NATURE TRAIL

BURG
RHEINFELS
CASTLE

SCHLOSSBERG

TRAIN
STATION

TOWER

ULMENHOF

BISMARCKWEG

VINEYARD
TRAIL

TO
BACHARACH
& FRANKFURT

Phone

OBERSTRASSE

POST

HEERSTRASSE

TO
BOPPARD &
KOBLENZ

HIGHWAY 9

HEERSTRASSE

Phone

WC

HARBOR

HEERSTRASSE

P A R K

BUS (ONLY)
PARKING

P

K·D
DOCK
(EURAIL
VALID)

RHINE
RIVER

B·R
DOCK

To
LORELEY

ST. GOARSHAUSEN

DCH

RHINE VALLEY

1 Schlosshotel Rheinfels
2 Hotel am Markt
3 Rhein Hotel & Hotel Hauser
4 Frau Kurz Rooms

5 St. Goar Hostel
6 Grocery Store
7 Stein Shop
8 Bike Rental

in 1797, the French Revolutionary army destroyed it. For years, the castle was used as a source of building stone, and today—while still mighty—it's only a small fraction of its original size. This hollow but interesting shell offers your single best hands-on ruined-castle experience on the river.

Cost and Hours: €4, family card-€10; mid-March–Oct daily 9:00–18:00, last entry at 17:00; Nov–mid-March Sat–Sun only 11:00–17:00, last entry at 16:00—weather permitting; tel. 06741/7753, in winter 06741/383, www.burg-rheinfels.com.

Tours and Information: Call in advance or gather 10 English-speaking tourists and beg to get an English tour—perhaps from Günther, the "last knight of Rheinfels" (tel. 06741/7753). Otherwise, follow my self-guided tour (next page). The castle map is mediocre; the €2 English booklet is better, with history and illustrations. If it's damp, be careful of slippery stones. A handy

WC is immediately across from the ticket booth (check out the guillotine urinals—stand back when you pull to flush).

Let There Be Light: If planning to explore the mine tunnels, bring a flashlight, or do it by candlelight (museum sells candles with matches, €0.50).

Getting to the Castle by Taxi or Mini-Train: A taxi up from town costs €5 (tel. 06741/7011). Or take the kitschy "tschu-tschu" tourist train (€2 one-way, €3 round-trip, 7 min to the top, April–Oct daily 10:00–17:00 but sometimes unpredictable, 2/hr, runs from square between station and dock, also stops by beer-stein shop, complete with lusty music, mobile 0171-496-3762).

Hiking Up to the Castle: Two steep but scenic paths take you up to the castle from the town (allow 15–20 minutes up). You can also simply follow the main road up through the railroad underpass at the top end of the pedestrian street, but it's not as much fun.

To take the **vineyard trail,** start at the beer-stein shop at the end of the pedestrian street, walk uphill through the under-pass, make an immediate right on Bismarcksweg along the railroad tracks following the *Fussweg Burg Rheinfels* and yellow *Zur Burg* signs, pass the youth hostel, and then follow the yellow *Zur Burg* signs up the hill through the vineyard. The last couple hundred yards are along the road.

To take the **nature trail,** start at the St. Goar train station. Take the underpass under the tracks at the north end of the station, climb the steep stairs uphill, and turn right (following *Burg Rheinfels* signs) along the path just above the old city wall, which takes you to the castle in 10 minutes.

❷ Self-Guided Tour: Rather than wander aimlessly, visit the castle by following this tour: From the ticket gate, walk straight. Pass *Grosser Keller* on the left (where we'll end this tour) and walk through an internal gate past the *zu den gedeckten Wehrgängen* sign on the right (where we'll pass later) uphill to the museum (open 10:00–12:30 & 13:00–17:30, included in castle entry) in the only finished room of the castle. The museum is pleasant, with good English descriptions, but it's not as important as seeing the castle itself—skip the museum if you're short on time.

❶ Museum and Castle Model: The seven-foot-tall carved stone immediately inside the door (marked *Keltische Säule von Pfalzfeld*)—a tombstone from a nearby Celtic grave—is from 400 years before Christ. There were people here long before the Romans...and this castle. Find the old wooden library chair near the tombstone. If you smile sweetly, the man behind the desk may demonstrate—pull the chair's back forward and it becomes stairs for accessing the highest shelves.

The sweeping castle history exhibit in the center of the room is well-described in English. The massive fortification was the only

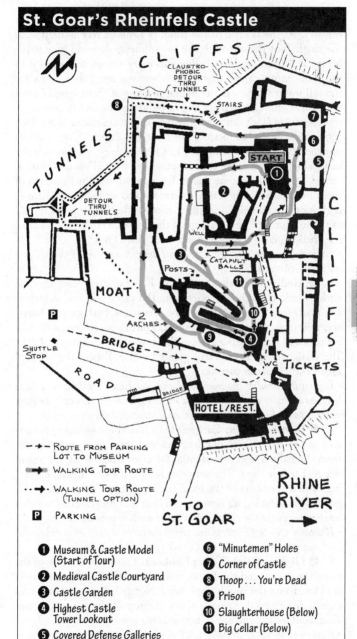

St. Goar's Rheinfels Castle

CLIFFS

CLAUSTRO-PHOBIC DETOUR THRU TUNNELS

STAIRS

START
1

TUNNELS

7
6
5

8

DETOUR THRU TUNNELS

2

CLIFFS

WELL

3

CATAPULT BALLS

POSTS

11

MOAT

10

2 ARCHES

9

4

BRIDGE

SHUTTLE STOP

ROAD

BRIDGE

WC TICKETS

HOTEL/REST.

CLIFFS

- - → ROUTE FROM PARKING LOT TO MUSEUM

➡ WALKING TOUR ROUTE

···→ WALKING TOUR ROUTE (TUNNEL OPTION)

P PARKING

RHINE RIVER →

TO ST. GOAR

RHINE VALLEY

1 Museum & Castle Model (Start of Tour)
2 Medieval Castle Courtyard
3 Castle Garden
4 Highest Castle Tower Lookout
5 Covered Defense Galleries

6 "Minutemen" Holes
7 Corner of Castle
8 Thoop . . . You're Dead
9 Prison
10 Slaughterhouse (Below)
11 Big Cellar (Below)

Rhineland castle to withstand Louis XIV's assault during the 17th century. At the far end of the room is a model reconstruction of the castle (not the one with the toy soldiers) showing how much bigger it was before French Revolutionary troops destroyed it in the 18th century. Study this. Find where you are. (Hint: Look for the tall tower.) This was the living quarters of the original castle, which was only the smallest ring of buildings around the tiny central courtyard (13th century). The ramparts were added in the 14th century. By 1650, the fortress was largely complete. Ever since its destruction by the French in the late 18th century, it's had no military value. While no WWII bombs were wasted on this ruin, it served St. Goar as a stone quarry for generations. The basement of the museum shows the castle pharmacy and an exhibit of Rhine-region odds and ends, including tools and an 1830 loom. Don't miss the photos of ice-breaking on the Rhine. While once routine, ice-breaking hasn't been necessary here since 1963.

· *Exit the museum and walk 30 yards directly out, slightly uphill into the castle courtyard.*

❷ **Medieval Castle Courtyard:** Five hundred years ago, the entire castle circled this courtyard. The place was self-sufficient and ready for a siege, with a bakery, pharmacy, herb garden, brewery, well (top of yard), and livestock. During peacetime, 300–600 people lived here; during a siege, there would be as many as 4,000. The walls were plastered and painted white. Bits of the original 13th-century plaster survive.

· *Continue through the courtyard and out Erste Schildmauer, turn left into the next courtyard, and walk straight to the two old, wooden, upright posts. Find the pyramid of stone catapult balls on your left.*

❸ **Castle Garden:** Catapult balls like these were too expensive not to recycle—they'd be retrieved after any battle. Across from the balls is a well—essential for any castle during the age of sieges. Look in. Spit. The old posts are for the ceremonial baptizing of new members of the local trading league. While this guild goes back centuries, it's now a social club that fills this court with a huge wine party the third weekend of each September.

· *If weary, skip to #5; otherwise, climb the cobbled path up to the castle's best viewpoint—up where the German flag waves.*

❹ **Highest Castle Tower Lookout:** Enjoy a great view of the river, the castle, and the forest. Remember, the fortress once covered five times the land it does today. Notice how the other castles (across the river) don't poke above the top of the Rhine canyon. That would make them easy for invading armies to see.

· *Return to the catapult balls, walk down the road, go through the tunnel, veer left through the arch marked zu den gedeckten Wehrgängen ("to the covered defense galleries"), go down two flights of stairs, and turn left into the dark, covered passageway. From here, we will begin a rectangular walk taking us completely around (counterclockwise) the perimeter of the castle.*

❺ & ❻ Covered Defense Galleries with "Minutemen" Holes: Soldiers—the castle's "minutemen"—had a short commute: defensive positions on the outside, home in the holes below on the left. Even though these living quarters were padded with straw, life was unpleasant. A peasant was lucky to live beyond age 45.

• *Continue straight through the dark gallery and to the corner of the castle, where you'll see a white painted arrow at eye level. Stand with your back to the arrow on the wall.*

❼ Corner of Castle: Look up. A three-story, half-timbered building originally rose beyond the highest stone fortification. The two stone tongues near the top just around the corner supported the toilet. (Insert your own joke here.) Turn around and face the wall. The crossbow slits below the white arrow were once steeper. The bigger hole on the riverside was for hot pitch.

• *Follow that white arrow along the outside to the next corner. Midway you'll pass stairs on the right leading down* zu den Minengängen *(sign on upper left). Adventurers with flashlights can detour here (see "Optional Detour—Into the Mine Tunnels," at the end of this listing). You may come out around the next corner. Otherwise, stay with me, walking level to the corner. At the corner, turn left.*

❽ Thoop...You're Dead: Look ahead at the smartly placed crossbow slit. While you're lying there, notice the stonework. The little round holes were for scaffolds used as they built up. They indicate this stonework is original. Notice also the fine stonework on the chutes. More boiling pitch...now you're toast, too.

• *Continue along the castle wall around the corner. At the gray railing, look up the valley and uphill where the sprawling fort stretched. Below, just outside the wall, is land where attackers would gather. The mine tunnels are under there, waiting to blow up any attackers (see next page).*

Keep going along the perimeter, jog left, go down five steps and into an open field, and walk toward the wooden bridge. You may detour here into the passageway (on right) marked 13 Halsgraben. *The "old" wooden bridge is actually modern. Angle left through two arches (before the bridge) and through the rough entry to the* Verliess *(prison) on the left.*

❾ Prison: This is one of six dungeons. You just walked through an entrance prisoners only dreamed of 400 years ago. They came and went through the little square hole in the ceiling. The holes in the walls supported timbers that thoughtfully gave as many as 15 residents something to sit on to keep them out of the filthy slop that gathered on the floor. Twice a day, they were given bread and water. Some prisoners actually survived longer than two years in here. While the town could torture and execute, the castle had permission only to imprison criminals in these dungeons.

Consider this: According to town records, the two men who spent the most time down here—2.5 years each—died within three weeks of regaining their freedom. Perhaps after a diet of bread and water, feasting on meat and wine was simply too much.

• *Continue through the next arch, under the white arrow, then turn left and walk 30 yards to the* Schlachthaus.

❿ Slaughterhouse: Any proper castle was prepared to survive a six-month siege. With 4,000 people, that's a lot of provisions. The cattle that lived within the walls were slaughtered in this room. The castle's mortar was congealed here (by packing all the organic waste from the kitchen into kegs and sealing it). Notice the drainage gutters. "Running water" came through from drains built into the walls (to keep the mortar dry and therefore strong... and less smelly).

• *Back outside, climb the modern stairs to the left. A skinny, dark passage (yes, that's the one) leads you into the...*

⓫ Big Cellar: This *Grosser Keller* was a big pantry. When the castle was smaller, this was the original moat—you can see the rough lower parts of the wall. The original floor was 13 feet deeper. The drawbridge rested upon the stone nubs on the left. When the castle expanded, the moat became this cellar. Halfway up the walls on the entrance side of the room, square holes mark spots where timbers made a storage loft, perhaps filled with grain. In the back, an arch leads to the wine cellar (sometimes blocked off) where finer wine was kept. Part of a soldier's pay was wine...table wine. This wine was kept in a single 180,000-liter stone barrel (that's 47,550 gallons), which generally lasted about 18 months.

The count owned the surrounding farmland. Farmers got to keep 20 percent of their production. Later, in more liberal feudal times, the nobility let them keep 40 percent. Today, the German government leaves the workers with 60 percent...and provides a few more services.

• *You're free. Climb out, turn right, and leave. For coffee on a terrace with a great view, visit Schlosshotel Rheinfels, opposite the entrance (WC at base of steps).*

Optional Detour—Into the Mine Tunnels: In about 1600, to protect their castle, the Rheinfellers cleverly booby-trapped the land just outside their walls by building tunnels topped with thin slate roofs and packed with explosives. By detonating the explosives when under attack, they could kill hundreds of invaders. In 1626, a handful of underground Protestant Germans blew 300 Catholic Spaniards to—they figured—hell. You're welcome to wander through a set of never-blown-up tunnels. But be warned: It's 600 feet long, assuming you make no wrong turns; it's pitch-dark, muddy, and claustrophobic, with confusing dead-ends; and you'll never get higher than a deep crouch. It cannot be done without a light (candles available at entrance). At stop #6 of the above tour, follow the stairs on the right leading down *zu den Minengängen* (sign on upper left).

The *Fuchsloch* sign welcomes you to the foxhole. Walk level (take no stairs) past the first steel railing (where you hope to emerge later) to the second steel railing. Climb down. The "highway" in this foxhole is three feet high. The ceiling may be painted with a white line indicating the correct path. Don't venture into the narrower side aisles. These were once filled with the gunpowder. After a small decline, take the second right. At the T-intersection, go right (uphill). After about 10 feet, go left. Take the next right and look for a light at the end of the tunnel. Head up a rocky incline under the narrowest part of the tunnel and you'll emerge at that first steel railing. The stairs on the right lead to freedom. Cross the field, walk under the bigger archway, and continue uphill toward the old wooden bridge. Angle left through two arches (before the bridge) and through the rough entry to the *Verliess* (prison) on the left. Rejoin the tour here at stop #9.

Sleeping

(€1 = about $1.40, country code: 49, area code: 06741)
Parking in St. Goar is tight; ask at your hotel.

$$$ Schlosshotel Rheinfels ("Rheinfels Castle Hotel") is the town splurge. Part of the castle, but in a purpose-built new building, this luxurious 60-room place is good for those with money and a car (Db-€165–225 depending on river views and balconies, extra adult bed-€65, extra bed for kids ages 12–18-€45, extra bed for kids ages 7–11-€30, kids under age 7 free, elevator, non-smoking rooms, Internet access, free Wi-Fi, indoor pool and sauna, dressy restaurant, free parking, Schlossberg 47, tel. 06741/8020, fax 06741/802-802, www.schloss-rheinfels.de, info@schloss-rheinfels.de).

$$ Hotel am Markt, well-run by Herr and Frau Velich, is rustic and a good deal, with all the modern comforts. It features a hint of antler with a pastel flair, 18 bright rooms, and a good restaurant. It's a good value and a stone's throw from the boat dock and train station (S-€40, Sb-€50, standard Db-€65, bigger riverview Db-€80, cheaper March–mid-April and Oct, closed Nov–Feb, Markt 1, tel. 06741/1689, fax 06741/1721, www.hotel-am-markt-sankt-goar.de, hotel.am.markt@gmx.de).

$$ Rhein Hotel, two doors away and run by the Velichs' energetic son Gil (a trained chef), has 10 rooms of similar quality and its own restaurant (Sb-€50, Db-€65–85, higher price is for Rhine-view rooms with balcony, non-smoking, free Wi-Fi at reception, closed mid-Nov–Feb, Heerstrasse 71, tel. 06741/981-240,

fax 06741/981-267, www.rheinhotel-st-goar.de, info@rheinhotel
-st-goar.de).

$ Hotel Hauser, across the square from Hotel am Markt,
is another good deal, warmly run by another Frau Velich. Its 12
simple rooms sit over a fine restaurant (S-€22, D-€46, Db-€54,
great Db with Rhine-view balconies-€58, cash preferred, à la
carte half-pension-€14, expensive Wi-Fi in lounge, Heerstrasse 77,
tel. 06741/333, fax 06741/1464, www.hotelhauser.de, hotelhauser
@t-online.de).

$ Frau Kurz offers St. Goar's best B&B, renting three
delightful rooms (sharing 2.5 bathrooms) with refrigerators,
bathrobes, a breakfast terrace, garden, fine view, and homemade
marmalade (S-€28, D-€48, 2-night minimum, cash only, non-
smoking, free and easy parking, honor your reservation or call to
cancel, Ulmenhof 11, tel. & fax 06741/459, www.gaestehaus-kurz
.de, jeanette.kurz@superkabel.de). It's a memorably steep five-
minute hike from the train station: Exit left from the station, take
an immediate left at the yellow phone booth, pass under the tracks,
go up the stairs, and follow the zigzag path, turning right through
an archway onto Ulmenhof; #11 is just past the tower.

$ St. Goar Hostel, the big beige building down the hill
from the castle, rents 18 doubles and piles of beds in 4- to 10-bed
dorms. It has a well-run, strong, institutional atmosphere with a
22:30 curfew (but you can borrow the key) and hearty €6 dinners
(dorm beds-€15, D-€36, includes breakfast, non-members-€3.10
extra, non-smoking, expensive Wi-Fi, all ages welcome, open
all day, Bismarckweg 17, tel. 06741/388, fax 06741/2869, st-goar
@diejugendherbergen.de). It's a fairly level 10-minute walk from
the train station: Veer left and go all the way down narrow, red-
brick Oberstrasse, then turn left through the underpass and make
an immediate right on Bismarcksweg, following the red *Jugendherberge* signs.

Eating

Hotel am Markt serves tasty traditional meals with plenty of game
and fish (specialties include marinated roast beef and homemade
cheesecake) at fair prices with good atmosphere and service (€9–16
main dishes, March–Oct daily 8:00–21:00, closed Nov–Feb,
Markt 1, tel. 06741/1689).

Schlosshotel Rheinfels is your Rhine splurge, with an
incredible view terrace in an elegant, dressy setting. As it's at the
hilltop castle, you'll have to hike, taxi, or drive up (€18–21 main
dishes, €36 three-course fixed-price meals, daily 12:00–14:00 &
18:30–21:00, call to reserve a window table, tel. 06741/8020; see
also hotel listing). Their downstairs **Burgschänke** has no view,

but is family-friendly and cheaper (€9–12 main dishes, Sun–Thu 11:00–18:00, Fri–Sat 11:00–21:00, tel. 06741/802-806).

Other Options: There are a couple of Italian places in town and plenty of ways to gather a picnic to enjoy on the riverside park. For more options, take the quick train to Bacharach, which leaves and returns hourly (last train at 22:00).

BERLIN

No tour of Germany is complete without a look at its historic and reunited capital. Over the last decade, Berlin has been a construction zone. Standing over ripped-up tracks and under a canopy of cranes, visitors witnessed the rebirth of a great European capital. Today, as we enjoy the thrill of walking over what was the Wall and through the well-patched Brandenburg Gate, it's clear that history is not contained in some book, but is an exciting story that we are a part of. Historians find Berlin exhilarating.

Berlin had a tumultuous 20th century. After the city was devastated in World War II, it was divided by the Allied powers: The American, British, and French sectors became West Berlin, and the Soviet sector, East Berlin. In 1948 and 1949, the Soviet Union tried to starve the Western half into submission, but the siege was foiled by the United States' Berlin Airlift, which flew in supplies from Frankfurt. The East–West division was set in stone in 1961, when the East German government boxed in West Berlin by building the Berlin Wall. The Wall stood for 28 years. In 1990, less than a year after the Wall fell, the two Germanys—and the two Berlins—officially became one. When the dust settled, Berliners from both sides of the once-divided city faced the monumental challenge of reunification.

While the work is far from over, a new Berlin has emerged. Berliners joke that they don't need to go anywhere because their city's always changing. Spin a postcard rack to see what's new. A five-year-old guidebook on Berlin covers a different city.

Reunification has had its negative side, and locals are fond of saying, "The Wall survives in the minds of some people." Some "Ossies" (impolite slang for Easterners) miss their security. Some

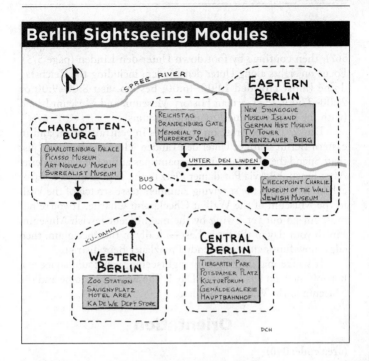

Berlin Sightseeing Modules

N

SPREE RIVER

CHARLOTTEN-BURG
CHARLOTTENBURG PALACE
PICASSO MUSEUM
ART NOUVEAU MUSEUM
SURREALIST MUSEUM

EASTERN BERLIN
NEW SYNAGOGUE
MUSEUM ISLAND
GERMAN HIST MUSEUM
TV TOWER
PRENZLAUER BERG

REICHSTAG
BRANDENBURG GATE
MEMORIAL TO
MURDERED JEWS

UNTER DEN LINDEN

BUS 100

CHECKPOINT CHARLIE
MUSEUM OF THE WALL
JEWISH MUSEUM

KU-DAMM

WESTERN BERLIN
ZOO STATION
SAVIGNYPLATZ
HOTEL AREA
KADEWE DEPT STORE

CENTRAL BERLIN
TIERGARTEN PARK
POTSDAMER PLATZ
KULTURFORUM
GEMÄLDEGALERIE
HAUPTBAHNHOF

DCH

"Wessies" miss their easy ride (military deferrals, subsidized rent, and tax breaks). For free spirits, walled-in West Berlin was a citadel of freedom within the East.

The city government has been eager to charge forward, with little nostalgia for anything that was Eastern. Big corporations and the national government have moved in, and the dreary swath of land that was the Wall and its notorious "death strip" has been transformed. City planners have boldly made Berlin's reunification and the return of the national government a good opportunity to make Berlin a great capital once again.

Today, Berlin feels like the nuclear fuel rod of a great nation. It's so vibrant with youth, energy, and an anything-goes-and-anything's-possible buzz that Munich feels spent in comparison. Berlin is both extremely popular and surprisingly affordable. As a tourist attraction, it's booming. But the city is so spread out, you'll often feel like you have the place to yourself.

Planning Your Time

Because of Berlin's inconvenient location, try to enter and/or leave by either night train or plane. I'd give Berlin at least two days and spend them this way:

Day 1: Begin your day getting oriented to this huge city: Either take the 10:00 "Discover Berlin" guided walking tour offered by Original Berlin Walks (see page 564) or follow my "Do-It-Yourself Orientation Tour" by bus to the Reichstag (page 567), then continue by foot down Unter den Linden (page 575). Focus on sights along Unter den Linden, including the Reichstag dome (most crowded 10:00–16:00; best to visit 8:00–9:00 or 21:00–22:00), the German History Museum, and Museum Island (with the Pergamon and Egyptian museums).

Day 2: Concentrate on the sights in central Berlin, and in eastern Berlin south of Unter den Linden. Here's a plan to do just that: Spend the morning with the paintings at the Gemäldegalerie. After lunch, hike via Potsdamer Platz to the Topography of Terror exhibit and along the surviving Zimmerstrasse stretch of the Wall to the Museum of the Wall at Checkpoint Charlie. If you're not museum-ed out yet, swing by the magnificent Jewish Museum. Finish your day in the lively East—ideally in the once glum, then edgy, now fun-loving and trendy Prenzlauer Berg district.

If you're maximizing your sightseeing, you could squeeze a hop-off, hop-on bus tour into Day 1. The Reichstag dome and the Museum of the Wall are open late.

Orientation

(area code: 030)

Berlin is huge, with 3.4 million people. But the tourist's Berlin can be broken into three digestible chunks:

1. Eastern Berlin has the highest concentration of notable sights and colorful neighborhoods. Near the famous Brandenburg Gate, you'll find the Reichstag building, Pariser Platz, and the new Holocaust Memorial. From the Brandenburg Gate, the famous Unter den Linden boulevard runs eastward through the former East Berlin, passing the marvelous German History Museum and Museum Island (Pergamon Museum, Egyptian Museum, and Berlin Cathedral) on the way to Alexanderplatz (TV Tower). The intersection of Unter den Linden and Friedrichstrasse is emerging as the new center of the city. South of Unter den Linden, you'll find the delightful Gendarmenmarkt square, most Nazi sites (including the Topography of Terror exhibit), the Jewish Museum, the best Wall-related sights (Museum of the Wall at Checkpoint Charlie, and East Side Gallery), and the colorful Turkish neighborhood of Kreuzberg. North of Unter den Linden are these worth-a-wander neighborhoods: around Oranienburger Strasse (Jewish Quarter and New Synagogue), Hackescher Markt, and Prenzlauer Berg (several recommended hotels and a very lively restaurant/nightlife zone).

2. Central Berlin is dominated by the giant Tiergarten park. South of the park are Potsdamer Platz and the Kulturforum museum cluster (including the Gemäldegalerie, New National Gallery, Musical Instruments Museum, and Philharmonic Concert Hall). To the north, the huge Hauptbahnhof (main train station) straddles the former Wall in what was central Berlin's no-man's-land.

3. Western Berlin centers on the Bahnhof Zoo (Zoo train station) and the grand Kurfürstendamm boulevard, nicknamed "Ku'damm" (transportation hub, tours, information, shopping, and recommended hotels). The East is all the rage. But the West, while staid in comparison, is bouncing back—with lots of big-name stores and destination restaurants that keep the area buzzing. During the Cold War, this "Western Sector" was the hub for Western visitors. Capitalists visited the West, with a nervous side-trip beyond the Wall into the grim and foreboding East. (Cubans, Russians, Poles, and Angolans stayed behind the Wall and did their sightseeing in the East.) Remnants of this Iron Curtain–era Western focus have left today's visitors with a stronger focus on the Ku'damm and Bahnhof Zoo than the district really deserves.

Tourist Information

With any luck, you won't have to use Berlin's TIs—they're for-profit agencies working for the city's big hotels, which colors the information they provide. TI branches, appropriately called "info-stores," are unlikely to have the information you need (tel. 030/250-025, www.berlin-tourist-information.com). You'll find them at the **Hauptbahnhof** train station (daily 8:00–22:00, by main entrance on Europaplatz), **Ku'damm** (Kurfürstendamm 21, in the glass-and-steel Neues Kranzler Eck building, Mon–Sat 10:00–20:00, Sun 10:00–18:00, shorter hours in winter), the **Reichstag** (on Scheidemannstrasse, daily April–Oct 8:00–20:00, Nov–March 10:00–18:00), and the **Brandenburg Gate** (daily April–Oct 9:30–19:00, Nov–March 10:00–19:00).

Skip the TI's €1 map, and instead pick up any of the walking tour companies' brochures—they include better maps for free (most hotels also provide free city maps). While the TI does sell the three-day Museumspass (described next), it's also available at major museums. If you take a walking tour, your guide is likely a better source of nightlife or shopping tips than the TI. The TI offers a €3 room-finding service (but only to hotels that give them kickbacks—many don't).

Museum Passes: The three-day **Museumspass** (Schaulust MuseenBerlin) gets you into 70 museums (including the national museums and most of the recommended biggies) on three consecutive days for €19. As you'll routinely pay €5–8 per admission, this pays for itself in a hurry. And you'll enjoy the ease of popping in and out of museums that you might not otherwise want to pay for. Buy it at the TI or any participating museum. Note that if a museum is closed on one of the days of your Museumsspass, you have access to that museum on a fourth day to make up for lost time. The pass won't, however, enable you to skip lines: Many museums want passholders to stand in line to get a free ticket that lets you through the turnstile. The €12 **Museum Island Pass** (Standortkarte Museumsinsel) covers all the museums on the island (otherwise €8 each) and is a fine value—but for €7 more, the three-day Museumsspass gives you triple the days and many more entries. TIs also sell the **Welcome Card,** a transportation pass that also gives some museum discounts (see "Getting Around Berlin," later in this section).

Local Publications: Various magazines can help make your time in Berlin more productive (all available at the TI and most at newsstands). *Berlin Programm* is a comprehensive German-language monthly, especially strong in high culture, that lists upcoming events and museum hours (€2, www.berlin-programm .de). *Berlin To Go* is a sketchier German/English, TI-produced bimonthly magazine offering timely features on Berlin and a partial calendar of events (€1). *Exberliner Magazine* is the only real English monthly (published mostly for expat Americans, but very helpful for curious travelers). It has an edgy, youthful focus and gives a fascinating insider's look at this fast-changing city (€2, www.exberliner.com).

Arrival in Berlin
By Train
Berlin's newest and grandest train station is **Berlin Hauptbahnhof** (main train station, a.k.a. simply "der Bahnhof"). All long-distance trains now arrive at Europe's biggest, mostly underground train station. Tracks 1–8 are underground, while tracks 11–16 are a floor above ground level (along with the S-Bahn).

It's a "transfer station"—unique for its major lines coming in at right angles—where the national train system meets the city's train system (S-Bahn). It's also the home of 80 shops with long hours—some locals call the station a "shopping mall with trains" (daily 8:00–22:00, even Sunday). The Kaisers supermarket (above track 2) is handy for assembling a picnic for the ride.

Services: While the station has no lockers, the Gepäck Center is an efficient and secure deposit service (€4/day per bag, always open, on the upper level—signed as *UG* or *+1,* directly under track 14). The WC Center (public toilets) is next to the Virgin Megastore.

Train Information: The station has two DeutscheBahn *Reisezentrum* information counters (one upper level, one lower—just follow signs; both open daily 6:00–22:00). If you're staying in the West, keep in mind that the info center at the Bahnhof Zoo station is just as good and much less crowded.

EurAide is an English-speaking information desk with answers to your questions about train travel around Europe. It operates from a single counter in the lower-level *Reisezentrum* (labeled *-1*, not *+1*; follow signs to tracks 5–6). It's American-run, so communication is simple. This is an especially good place to make fast-train and *couchette* reservations for later in your trip. EurAide also gives out a helpful, free city map (April–Sept daily 10:00–20:00; Oct–March Mon–Fri 11:00–19:00, closed Sat–Sun; www.euraide.com).

Getting into Town: While taxis and buses await outside the station, the S-Bahn is probably your best means of connecting to your destination within Berlin. The crosstown express S-Bahn line connects the station with my recommended hotels in a few minutes. It's simple: All S-Bahn trains are on tracks 15 and 16 at the top of the station. All trains on track 15 go east (toward the Ostbahnhof and Hackescher Markt), and trains on track 16 go west (toward Bahnhof Zoo and Savignyplatz). Your train ticket or railpass into the station covers you on your connecting S-Bahn ride into town (and your ticket out includes the transfer via S-Bahn to the Hauptbahnhof). U-Bahn rides are not covered by tickets or railpasses.

If you're sleeping in the West, catch any train on track 16 to Savignyplatz, and you're a five-minute walk from your hotel (see Western Berlin map in "Sleeping," later in this chapter). Savignyplatz is one stop after **Bahnhof Zoo** (rhymes with "toe," a.k.a. Bahnhof Zoologischer Garten), the once-grand train hub now eclipsed by the Hauptbahnhof. Nowadays it's useful mainly for its shops, uncrowded train-information desk, and BVG transit office (outside the entrance, amid the traffic).

If you're sleeping in eastern Berlin, take any train on track 15 two stops to Hackescher Markt, then catch tram #M1 north (see Prenzlauer Berg map in "Sleeping").

By Plane

For information on reaching the city center from Berlin's airports, see "Connections" at the end of this chapter.

Helpful Hints

Medical Help: "Call a Doc" is a non-profit referral service designed for tourists (tel. 01804-2255-2362, phone answered 24 hours a day, www.calladoc.com). Payment is arranged between you and the doctor, and is likely far more affordable than similar care in the US. The US Embassy also has a list of local English-speaking doctors (www.usembassy.de).

Museum Hours: Many major Berlin museums are closed on Monday. All national museums, including the Pergamon and Gemäldegalerie (plus others as noted in "Sights," later in this chapter), are free for the last four hours on Thursdays (for example, if it closes at 18:00, it's free from 14:00 on; www.museen-berlin.de).

Monday Activities: Since many museums close on Monday, save the day for Berlin Wall sights, the Reichstag dome, my "Do-It-Yourself Orientation Tour" and strolling Unter den Linden, walking/bus tours, the Jewish Museum, churches, the zoo, or shopping (the Kaufhaus des Westens—KaDeWe—department store is a sight in itself). Be aware that when Monday is a holiday—as it is several times a year—museums are open then and closed Tuesday.

Addresses: Many Berlin streets are numbered with odd and even numbers on the same side of the street, often with no connection to the other side (for example, Ku'damm #212 can be across the street from #14). To save steps, check the white street signs on curb corners; many list the street numbers covered on that side of the block.

Internet Access: You'll find Internet access in most hotels and hostels, as well as at small Internet cafés all over the city. The **easyInternetcafé** outlets—generally paired with Dunkin' Donuts (daily 6:00–23:00)—have handy locations, including Hardenbergplatz 2 (across from Bahnhof Zoo, next to McDonald's), Ku'damm 224 (10-min walk from Bahnhof Zoo, near several recommended hotels), and Rathaus-Passagen (on Alexanderplatz). Buy a ticket at the self-service machines and follow the English instructions. Unused time can be used at any branch in Berlin for up to a week.

Bookstore: Berlin Story, a big, fun bookshop, has the best selection anywhere in town of English-language books on Berlin. They also have a fascinating, free little museum in the back with a model of Unter den Linden from 1930 and a room showing a good 25-minute Berlin history video (in English). The shop has a knowledgeable staff and stocks an amusing mix of knickknacks and East Berlin nostalgia souvenirs (daily 10:00–20:00, Unter den Linden 26, tel. 030/2045-3842, www.berlinstory.de).

Laundry: Schnell und Sauber Waschcenter is a chain of handy launderettes, with a location in western Berlin's Charlottenburg at Kaiserdamm 100 (while waiting, grab a beer at Alt-Berlin, a locals-only pub next door), and another in eastern Berlin at Torstrasse 115, around the corner from the Circus Hostel (€5–9/load wash and dry, daily 6:00–23:00). Also near my recommended hotels in Prenzlauer Berg, try **Eco-Express**

Waschsalon (€4–9/load wash and dry, daily 6:00–22:00, self- or full-serve, attached café, Danziger Strasse 7).

Travel Agency: Last Minute Flugbörse can help you find a flight in a hurry (discount flights, no train tickets, in Europa Center near Bahnhof Zoo, Mon–Sat 10:00–20:00, closed Sun, tel. 030/2655-1050, www.lastminuteflugboerse.de). **American Express** is a few blocks off Unter den Linden at Friedrichstrasse 172 (sells train tickets for €4 service fee, Mon–Fri 9:00–19:00, Sat 10:00–14:00, closed Sun, tel. 030/201-7400).

Getting Around Berlin

Berlin's sights spread far and wide. Right from the start, commit yourself to the city's fine public-transit system.

By Subway and Bus: Berlin's many modes of transportation are consolidated into one system that uses the same tickets: U-Bahn (*Untergrund-Bahn*, Berlin's subway), S-Bahn (*Schnell-Bahn*, or "fast train," mostly above ground and with fewer stops), *Strassenbahn* (streetcars, called "trams" by locals), and buses. Here are your options:

• A basic ticket *(Einzelfahrschein)* for two hours of travel in one direction on buses or subways—€2.10. It's easy to make this ticket stretch to cover several rides...as long as they're all in the same direction.

• A cheap, short-ride ticket *(Kurzstrecke)* for a single short ride of six bus stops or three subway stations (one transfer allowed)—€1.20.

• A four-trip ticket *(4-Fahrten-Karte)*, four basic tickets at a small discount—€8.

• A day pass *(Tageskarte)* covering zones A and B, the city proper—€6.10 (good until 3:00 the morning after). (For longer stays, a 7-day pass—*Sieben-Tage-Karte*—is also available for €26.20, or buy 2 WelcomeCards, described next.) The *Kleingruppenkarte* lets groups of up to five travel all day for €16.

• The **WelcomeCard** covers transportation, and gives you a 25 percent discount on lots of minor and a few major museums (including Checkpoint Charlie), sightseeing tours (including 25 percent off the recommended Original Berlin Walks), and music and theater events. The central-Berlin version covers transit zones A and B (€16.50/48 hrs, €21.50/72 hrs). The card is valid for an adult and up to three kids younger than 14. If you plan to cover a lot of ground using public transportation during a two- or three-day visit, this is usually the best transit deal.

Buy your U- and S-Bahn tickets from machines at stations. (They are also sold at BVG pavilions at train stations, airports, and the TI, and aboard trams and buses—drivers give change.) *Erwachsener* means "adult"—anyone 14 or older. Don't be afraid of the automated machines: First select the type of ticket you want, then load in the coins or paper bills. As you board the bus or tram, or enter the subway system, punch your ticket in a red or yellow clock machine to validate it (or risk a €40 fine; for an all-day or multi-day pass, validate it only the first time you ride). Within Berlin, Eurailpasses are good only on S-Bahn connections from the train station when you're arriving, and to the station when you're departing.

The S-Bahn crosstown express is a river of public transit through the heart of the city, in which many lines converge on one basic highway. Get used to this and you'll leap within a few minutes between: Savignyplatz (hotels), Bahnhof Zoo (Ku'damm, bus #100, walking tour meeting spot), the Hauptbahnhof (all major trains in and out of Berlin), Friedrichstrasse (heart of Unter den Linden), Hackescher Markt (Museum Island, hotels, restaurants, nightlife), and Alexanderplatz (eastern end of Unter den Linden).

Sections of the U- or S-Bahn sometimes close temporarily for repairs. In this situation, a bus route often replaces the train (*Ersatzverkehr*, or "replacement transportation").

Berlin's public transit is operated by BVG (except the S-Bahn, run by Deutsche Bahn). Bus schedules are available on the helpful BVG website, www.bvg.de.

By Taxi: Taxis are easy to flag down, and taxi stands are common. A typical ride within town costs €8–10, and a crosstown trip (for example, Bahnhof Zoo to Alexanderplatz) will run you about €15.

Money-Saving Taxi Tip: For any ride of less than two kilometers (about a mile), you can save several euros if you take advantage of the *Kurzstrecke* (short-stretch) rate. To get this rate, it's important that you flag the cab down on the street—not at or even near a taxi stand. Also, you must ask for the *Kurzstrecke* rate as soon as you hop in: Confidently say *"Kurzstrecke, bitte"* (KOORTS-shtreh-keh BIT-teh), and your driver will flip the meter to a fixed €3.50 rate.

By Bike: Flat Berlin is a very bike-friendly city, but be careful—Berlin's motorists don't brake for bicyclists (and bicyclists don't brake for pedestrians). Fortunately, some roads and sidewalks have special red-painted bike lanes. Just don't ride on the regular sidewalk—it's *verboten*.

In western Berlin, you can rent good bikes at the **Bahnhof Zoo** left-luggage counter, next to the lockers at the back of the station (€10/day, €23/3 days, €35/7 days; bikes come with lock, air pump, and mounted basket; daily 7:00–21:00, there's a limited supply of bikes and they've been known to run out). In the East, **Fahrradstation** near the Friedrichstrasse S-Bahn station has a huge number of bikes (€15/day, April–Oct daily 8:00–20:00;

Berlin

½ MILE
1 KM

...... COURSE OF FORMER WALL
+•+ ELEVATED S-BAHN LINE + STATION

TO PRENZLAUER BERG
T.V. TOWER
ALEXANDER-PLATZ
KARL-MARX-ALLEE
RATHAUS
NIKOLAI CHURCH
TO OSTBAHNHOF TRAIN STN. + EAST SIDE GALLERY
ORANIENSTR.
KREUZBERG
CANAL
HACK. MARKT.
DOM
MUSEUM ISLAND
MITTE
UNTER DEN LINDEN
STRASSE
MUSEUM OF THE WALL AT CHECKPOINT CHARLIE
KOCHSTR.
JEWISH MUSEUM BERLIN
LINDENSTR.
NEW SYNAGOGUE
ORANIENBURG
BRANDENBURG GATE
MEMORIAL TO MURDERED JEWS OF EUROPE
LEIPZIG STRASSE
REMAINS OF WALL
POTSDAMER PLATZ
REICHSTAG
EBERT
LIB.
POTSDAMER STRASSE
LANDWEHR
PCH
HAUPT-BAHNHOF
17 JUNI
TIERGARTEN
GEMÄLDEGALERIE
GERMAN RESIST. MUSEUM
New NAT'L GALLERY
KURFÜRSTEN STR.
KLEIST STR.
DES
STRASSE
SPREE R.
VICTORY COLUMN
BAUHAUS MUSEUM
ZOO
EUROPA CENTER
KaDeWe STORE
MEMORIAL CHURCH
CHARLOTTENBURG
ERNST REUTER PLATZ
BISMARCKSTR.
KANTSTR.
SAVIGNY-PLATZ
BAHNHOF ZOO
HARD.
KÜ'DAMM
LIETZEN STR.
KOLLWITZ MUSEUM

BERLIN

Nov–March Mon–Fri 10:00–19:00, Sat 10:00–16:00, closed
Sun; leave the S-Bahn station via Friedrichstrasse exit, turn left
on Dorotheenstrasse and walk 500 yards, and you'll find it at
the entrance to the parking garage at Dorotheenstrasse 30; tel.
030/2045-4500).

Tours

▲▲▲Walking Tours

Berlin is an ideal city to get to know with a walking tour. The city
is a battle zone of extremely competitive and creative walking-
tour companies, all offering employment to American and British
expats and students and cheap, informative tours to visiting travelers. Unlike many other European countries, Germany has no
regulations controlling who can give city tours. Berlin is home to a
large number of expatriates and academics, and it seems that every
year some of them get together and form a new tour company.
Some of these upstarts run great tours, but you'll generally get the
best quality with one of the more established companies. All give
variations on the same themes, including a general introductory
walk, Hitler and Nazi sites walk, and a communism walk. The
youth-oriented outfits also do nightly pub crawls. For details, see
the various websites. Here's my take on the current situation:

Original Berlin Walks—This is the most established operation,
with tours aiming at a clientele that's curious about the city's history. They don't offer "free tours" or pub crawls, and their guides are
professionals. I've enjoyed the help of O.B.W.'s high-quality, high-
energy guides for many years, and routinely hire them when my
tour groups are in town. I'm always impressed with founder Nick
Gay's ability to assemble guides of such high caliber. Tours generally cost €12 (€9 with WelcomeCard, or €10 if you're under 26).

There's no need to reserve ahead—just show up. All tours
meet at the taxi stand in front of the Bahnhof Zoo, and start at
10:00 unless otherwise noted. The Discover Berlin and Jewish
Life tours have a second departure point 30 minutes later opposite
eastern Berlin's Hackescher Markt S-Bahn station, outside the
Weihenstephaner Restaurant; if you're staying in the East, save
time by showing up here.

Discover Berlin, their flagship introductory walk, covers the
birthplace of the city, Museum Island, then heads up Unter den
Linden, stops at the Reichstag, and then goes on to Checkpoint
Charlie (no interior visits, 4 hrs, English only, daily year-round,
meet at 10:00 at Bahnhof Zoo, April–Oct also daily at 14:30).
Other tours include: **Infamous Third Reich Sites** (April–Oct Tue
and Thu at 10:00, Sat at 14:30, Sun at 10:00; less frequently off-
season—check their website or pick up a flier for the schedule);

Jewish Life in Berlin (April–Oct Mon at 10:00 at Bahnhof Zoo); and **Nest of Spies** (April–Oct only, Sat at 12:30). Many of the Third Reich and Jewish history sights are difficult to pin down without these excellent walks.

You can confirm these starting times at EurAide or by phone with Nick or his wife and business partner, Serena (tel. 030/301-9194, www.berlinwalks.de, info@berlinwalks.de). They can also arrange private guides (€150/3 hrs).

Insider Tour—This feisty company, in business since 1998, has already become well-established. They offer essentially the same itineraries as Original Berlin Walks, as well as hugely success-ful pub crawls (€12, nightly, with profit supplemented by fea-tured bars—for details see "Nightlife," later in this chapter). The basic introductory city walks leave daily at 10:30 and 15:00 from Coffeemamas at Hackescher Markt S-Bahn station—just show up (€12, 4 hours, no afternoon tours Nov–March, will also pick you up 30 min before tour start from McDonald's opposite Bahnhof Zoo, www.insidertour.com).

New Berlin Tours—The newest of the established tour companies is New Berlin, which targets a younger crowd and offers free intro-ductory tours. Their guides make their money off of tips, cross-selling their specialty tours. The idea: You take their introductory walk for free, then choose—if you wish—to take any of their other walks (€10–12 each, roughly the same list of itineraries as O.B.W. and Insider Tour, including a nightly pub crawl—see "Nightlife," later in this chapter). They publish a practical, free Berlin map. The basic introductory city walks leave daily at 11:00 and 13:00 (free but tip expected, 3.5 hrs, meet at Starbucks at Brandenburg Gate/Pariser Platz, or 30 min earlier from Dunkin' Donuts opposite Bahnhof Zoo, just show up). For all the details, see their magazine or visit www.newberlintours.com.

Brewer's Berlin Tours—For a more exhaustive (or, for some, exhausting) walking tour of Berlin, consider Brewer's Berlin Tours. These are run by Terry (retired from the British diplomatic service—he worked at the embassy in East Berlin) and his well-trained and engaging staff (all native English speakers). Their All-Day Berlin tours are legendary for their length, and best for those with a long attention span and a serious interest in Berlin (€12, tour lasts 8 hours or more and covers the entire old center, departs daily at 10:30 year-round from Bandy Brooks ice cream shop at Friedrichstrasse U- and S-Bahn station, tel. 030/2248-7435, mobile 0177-388-1537, www.brewersberlintours.com). Just show up.

Berlin Underground Association (Berliner Unterwelten Verein)—Much of Berlin's history lies beneath the surface, and this group has an exclusive agreement with the city to explore and research what is hidden underground. Their one-of-a-kind tour

BERLIN

of a WWII air-raid bunker features a chilling explanation of the air war over Berlin (April–Oct Mon–Thu at 11:00, Nov–March Mon and Thu at 11:00). They also have access to the inside of the Humboldthain air defense tower (April–Oct Thu at 13:00) and to a completely stocked and fully functional nuclear emergency bunker (Sat–Mon at 13:00). The English tours are usually led by Nick Jackson, one of the best tour guides in the city (all tours cost €9, meet in the hall of the Gesundbrunnen U-Bahn/S-Bahn station, follow signs to *Humboldthain/Brunnenstrasse* exit and walk up the stairs to their office, www.berlinerunterwelten.de, tel. 030/4991-0517). Nick also gives private tours by arrangement (mobile 0176-8318-8521).

Bus Tours

Full-Blown Bus Tours—Severin & Kühn offers a long list of bus tours in and around Berlin; their three-hour "Big Berlin Tour" is a good introduction (€22, daily at 10:00 and 14:00, two stops: Checkpoint Charlie and Brandenburg Gate, live guides in two languages, departs from Ku'damm 216, buy ticket at bus, tel. 030/880-4190, www.severin-kuehn-berlin.de).

Hop-on, Hop-off City Circle Tours—Several companies cooperate so that you can make a circuit of the city with unlimited hop-on, hop-off privileges (about 14 stops) on buses with boring recorded commentary (€20, 4/hr, daily 10:00–18:00, last bus leaves all stops at 16:00, 2-hr loop). Just hop on where you like and pay the driver. On a sunny day, when some convertible double-decker buses go topless, these are a photographer's delight, cruising slowly by just about every major sight in town. In the winter (Nov–March), the buses come only twice an hour and the last departure is at 15:00.

Bike Tours

Fat Tire Bike Tours—Choose among three different four-hour, six-mile tours (€20 each): City Tour (daily March–Nov at 11:00, June–Aug also at 16:00), Berlin Wall Tour (mid-May–Sept Mon, Thu, and Sat at 10:30), and Third Reich Tour (mid-May–Sept Wed, Fri, and Sun at 10:30). For any tour, meet at the TV Tower at Alexanderplatz (no need to reserve for the Wall or Third Reich tours, tel. 030/2404-7991, fax 030/2404-8837, www.fattirebike toursberlin.com, info@fattirebiketoursberlin.com).

New Berlin Tours—The young guides who offer New Berlin's free walking tours also give quite good four-hour bike tours (€14, daily at 11:30 and 15:00, meet on the corner of Oranienburger Strasse and Tucholskystrasse, S-Bahn: Oranienburger Strasse, no need to reserve, for contact info see "Walking Tours," earlier in this section).

Self-Guided Tour

Do-It-Yourself Orientation Tour: Bus #100 from Bahnhof Zoo to the Reichstag

This tour narrates the route of convenient bus #100, which connects my recommended hotel neighborhood in western Berlin with the sights in eastern Berlin. If you have the €20 and two hours for a hop-on, hop-off bus tour (described earlier), take that instead. But this short €2.10 bus ride provides a fine city introduction. Bus #100 is a sightseer's dream, stopping at Bahnhof Zoo, the Berlin Zoo, Victory Column (Siegessäule), Reichstag, Brandenburg Gate, Unter den Linden, Pergamon Museum, and Alexanderplatz. While you could ride it to the end, it's more fun to get out at the Reichstag and walk down Unter den Linden at your own pace (using my commentary on page 575). When combined with the self-guided walk down Unter den Linden, this tour merits ▲▲▲. Before you take this bus into eastern Berlin, consider checking out the sights in western Berlin (see page 597).

The Tour Begins: Buses start from Hardenbergplatz in front of Bahnhof Zoo. Buses come every 10 minutes, and single tickets are good for two hours—so take advantage of hop-on-and-off privileges. Climb aboard, stamp your ticket (giving it a starting time), and grab a seat on top. This is about a 15-minute ride. The upcoming stop will light up on the reader board inside the bus.

● On your left and then straight ahead you'll see the bombed-out hulk of the **Kaiser Wilhelm Memorial Church,** with its postwar sister church (described on page 598) and the **Europa Center.** This shopping district, once the center of West Berlin, is still a bustling people zone with big department stores nearby. When the Wall came down, East Berliners flocked to this area's department stores (especially KaDeWe, described on page 599). Soon after, the biggest, swankiest new stores were built in the East. Now the West is trying to win those shoppers back by building even bigger and better shopping centers around the Europa Center.

● At the stop in front of Hotel Palace: On the left, the elephant gates mark the entrance to the **Berlin Zoo** and its aquarium (described on page 600).

● Cruising down Kurfürstenstrasse, you'll pass several Asian restaurants—a reminder that, for most, the best food in Berlin is not German. Turning left, with the huge Tiergarten park in the distance ahead, you'll cross a canal and see the famous **Bauhaus Archive** behind the trees on the right (hard to see—it's the off-white, blocky building with scoopy roof ducts). The Bauhaus movement ushered in a new age of modern architecture that emphasized function over beauty, giving rise to blocky steel-and-glass skyscrapers in big cities around the world. On the left is Berlin's new embassy row. The big turquoise wall marks the communal home of all five Nordic embassies. This building is "green," run entirely on solar power.

❷ The bus enters a 400-acre park called the **Tiergarten,** packed with cycling paths, joggers, and—on hot days—nude sunbathers. Straight ahead, the **Victory Column** (Siegessäule, with the gilded angel, described on page 592) towers above this vast city park that was once a royal hunting grounds, now nicknamed the "green lungs of Berlin."

❷ A block after leaving the Victory Column (on the left) is the 18th-century, late-Rococo **Bellevue Palace.** Formerly the official residence of the Prussian (and later German) crown prince, and at one time a Nazi VIP guest house, it's now the residence of the federal president (whose power is mostly ceremonial—the chancellor wields the real power). If the flag's out, he's in.

❷ Driving along the Spree River, look left for the next sights: This park area was a residential district before World War II. Now it's filled with the buildings of the **national government.** The huge brick "brown snake" complex was built to house government workers—but it didn't sell, so now its apartments are available to anyone. A metal Henry Moore sculpture entitled *Butterfly* floats in front of the slope-roofed House of World Cultures (Berliners have nicknamed this building "the pregnant oyster"). The modern tower (next on left) is a carillon with 68 bells (from 1987).

❷ Leap out at the Platz der Republik stop. (While you could continue on bus #100, it's better on foot from here.) Through the trees on the left you'll see Germany's new and sprawling **Chancellery.** Started during the more imperial rule of Helmut Kohl, it's now considered overly grand. The big open space is the **Platz der Republik,** where the Victory Column stood until Hitler moved it. The Hauptbahnhof (Berlin's vast main train station, marked by its tall tower with the *DB* sign) is across the field between the Chancellery and the Reichstag. Watch your step—excavators found a 250-pound, undetonated American bomb here.

❷ Just down the street stands an old building with a new dome...the **Reichstag.**

Sights

Eastern Berlin

I've arranged the following sights in the order of a convenient self-guided orientation walk, picking up where my "Do-It-Yourself Orientation Tour" (previous section) leaves off. Allow a comfortable hour for this walk from the Reichstag to Alexanderplatz, including time for lingering (but not museum stops).

Eastern Berlin

--- FORMER COURSE OF THE WALL

400 YARDS
400 METERS

BERLIN WALL DOCUMENTATION CENTER

PRENZLAUER BERG

Eberswalder Strasse
U DANZIGER.

Bernauer Str.

Nord-bahnhof

Zinn.-Str.

NATURAL HIST. MUSEUM

Senefelder-platz

Rosenthaler Platz

Rosa-Lux.-Platz

TOR STRASSE

INVALIDEN-

Oranien- STR.

Oranienburger Tor

NEW SYNAGOGUE

Weinmeister

Münz

Hack. Markt

ALEXANDER-PLATZ

OTTO BRAUN-STR.

TO HAUPTBAHNHOF & BAHNHOF ZOO

MUSEUM ISLAND

Friedrich strasse

MITTE

Alexander-platz

KARL-MARX-ALLEE

REICHSTAG

SPREE

Unter den Linden

UNTER DEN LINDEN

Jänn-brücke

STR. DES 17 JUNI

FRANZ.
Franz.str.

RIVER

TO EASTSIDE GALLERY & OSTEL HOSTEL

BRANDENBURG GATE

MEMORIAL TO MURDERED JEWS OF EUROPE

GENDARMEN-MARKT

Mohren-str.
Stadtmitte

Mark. Museum

KÖPEN.

Heinrich-Heine-Str.

POTSDAMER PLATZ

Potsdamer Platz

LEIPZIGER

ZIMMERSTR.

Spittel-markt

TOPOGRAPHY OF TERROR

MUSEUM OF THE WALL AT CHECKPOINT CHARLIE

KOCH

Kochstr.

RITTER-

ORANIENSTR.

Moritzpl.

Anhalter Bahnhof

JEWISH MUSEUM BERLIN

GITSCHINER- STRASSE

Prinzenstr.

Kottbusser Tor

LANDWEHR CANAL

U U-BAHN STN.
S S-BAHN STN.

KREUZBERG

DCH

BERLIN

Near the Brandenburg Gate

▲▲▲**Reichstag Building**—The parliament building—the heart of German democracy—has a short but complicated and emotional history. When it was inaugurated in the 1890s, the last emperor, Kaiser Wilhelm II, disdainfully called it the "house for chatting." It was from here that the German Republic was proclaimed in 1918. In 1933, this symbol of democracy nearly burned down. While the Nazis blamed a communist plot, some believe that Hitler himself (who needed what we'd call today a "new Pearl Harbor") planned the fire, using it as a handy excuse to frame the communists and grab power. As World War II drew to a close, Stalin ordered his troops to take the Reichstag from the Nazis by May 1 (the workers' holiday). More than 1,500 Nazis (mostly French SS troops) made their last stand here—extending World War II by two days. On April 30, 1945, it fell to the Red Army. It was hardly used from 1933 to 1999. For the building's 101st birthday in 1995, the Bulgarian-American artist Christo wrapped it in silvery-gold cloth. It was then wrapped again—in scaffolding—and rebuilt by British architect Lord Norman Foster into the new parliamentary home of the Bundestag (Germany's lower house, similar to the US House of Representatives). To many Germans, the proud resurrection of the Reichstag symbolizes the end of a terrible chapter in German history.

The **glass cupola** rises 155 feet above the ground. Its two sloped ramps spiral 755 feet to the top for a grand view. Inside the dome, a cone of 360 mirrors reflects natural light into the legislative chamber below. Lit from inside at night, this gives Berlin a memorable nightlight. The environmentally friendly cone also helps with air circulation, drawing hot air out of the legislative chamber (no joke) and pulling in cool air from below.

Cost, Hours, Location: Free, daily 8:00–24:00, last entry at 22:00, most crowded 10:00–16:00 (wait in line to go up—good street musicians, metal detectors, no big luggage allowed, some hour-long English tours when parliament is not sitting), Platz der Republik 1, S- or U-Bahn: Friedrichstrasse or Unter den Linden, tel. 030/2273-2152, www.bundestag.de.

Crowd-Beating Tips: Berlin is now Germany's biggest tourist attraction. Lines at the Reichstag can be terrible. If possible, visit between 8:00 and 9:00 or between 21:00 and 22:00. Pick up the English flier just before the security checkpoint to have something to read as you wait. The skip-the-line entrance is under the grand front porch on the right. If you're here with a child (younger than 8 years old) or a frail person, or have reservations for the Dachgarten rooftop restaurant, you can get in without a wait. To reserve at the restaurant, call 030/2262-9933 (€58 three-course meals, lunch from €15, dinner from €20, daily 9:30–16:30 & 18:30–24:00).

◆ **Self-Guided Tour:** As you approach the building, look above the door, surrounded by stone patches from WWII bomb damage, to see the motto and promise: *Dem Deutschen Volke* ("To the German People"). The open, airy lobby towers 100 feet high, with 65-foot-tall colors of the German flag. See-through glass doors show the **central legislative chamber.** The message: There will be no secrets in government. Look inside. The seats are "Reichstag blue," a lilac-blue color designed by the architect to brighten the otherwise gray interior. Spreading his wings behind the podium is the *Bundestagsadler* (a.k.a. "the fat hen"), a stylized German eagle representing the Bundestag (each branch of government has its own symbolic eagle). Notice the doors marked "Yes," "No," and "Abstain"...an homage to the Bundestag's traditional "sheep jump" way of counting votes by exiting the chamber through the corresponding door (although for critical issues, all 669 members vote with electronic cards).

Ride the elevator to the base of the glass **dome.** Take time to study the photos and read the circle of captions—an excellent exhibit telling the Reichstag story. Then study the surrounding architecture: a broken collage of new on old, torn between antiquity and modernity, like Germany's history. Notice the dome's giant and unobtrusive sunscreen that moves as necessary with the sun. Peer down through the skylight to look over the shoulders of the elected representatives at work. For Germans, the best view from here is down—keeping a close eye on their government.

Start at the ramp nearest the elevator and wind up to the top of the **double ramp.** Take a 360-degree survey of the city as you hike: First, the big park is the **Tiergarten,** the "green lungs of Berlin." Beyond that is the **Teufelsberg,** or "Devil's Hill" (built of rubble from the destroyed city in the late 1940s, and famous during the Cold War as a powerful ear of the West—notice the telecommunications tower on top). Knowing the bombed-out and bulldozed story of their city, locals say, "You have to be suspicious when you see the nice, green park." Find the **Victory Column** (Siegessäule, moved by Hitler in the 1930s from in front of the Reichstag to its present position in the Tiergarten). Next, scenes of the new Berlin spiral into your view—**Potsdamer Platz,** marked by the conical glass tower that houses Sony's European headquarters. The yellow building to the right is the Berlin Philharmonic Concert Hall, marking the museums at the Kulturforum. Continue circling left, and find the green chariot atop the **Brandenburg Gate.** The new **Memorial to the Murdered Jews of Europe** stretches south of the Brandenburg Gate. Next, you'll see **former East Berlin** and the city's next huge construction zone, with a forest of 300-foot-tall skyscrapers in the works. Notice the TV Tower (featuring the Pope's Revenge—explained on page 584), the Berlin Cathedral's massive dome, the red tower of the City Hall, the golden dome of the New Synagogue, and the Reichstag's **Dachgarten Restaurant** (see "Crowd-Beating Tips," previous page).

Follow the train tracks in the distance to the left toward Berlin's huge main train station, the **Hauptbahnhof.** Just in front of it, alone in a field, is the Swiss Embassy. It used to be surrounded by buildings, but now it's the only one left. Complete your spin-tour with the blocky **Chancellery,** nicknamed by Berliners "the washing machine." It may look like a pharaoh's tomb, but it's the office and home of Germany's most powerful person, the chancellor (currently Angela Merkel).

Memorial to Politicians Who Opposed Hitler—As you leave the Reichstag, look for the row of slate slabs imbedded in the ground by the park across from the main entry (looks like a fancy slate bicycle rack). This is a memorial to the 96 politicians (the equivalent of our members of Congress) who were murdered and persecuted because their politics didn't agree with Chancellor Hitler's. They were part of the Weimar Republic, the weak and ill-fated attempt at post-WWI democracy in Germany. These were the people who could have stopped Hitler...so they became his first victims. Each slate slab remembers one man—his name, party (mostly KPD—Communists, and SPD—Social Democrats), and date and location of death—generally in concentration camps. (*KZ* stands for "concentration camp.") They are honored here, in front of the building in which they worked.

To the Brandenburg Gate: Let's continue our walk and cross what was the Berlin Wall, the 100-mile long barrier erected by the communist government to "protect" East Berlin from the Western world. Leaving the Reichstag, return to the busy road and walk around the building. At the rear of the building (across the street, at the edge of the park) is a small memorial to some of the East Berliners who died trying to cross the Wall. Look at the faces of these exceptionally free spirits. The Wall was built on August 13, 1961. Of these people—many of whom died within months of the wall's construction—most died trying to swim the river to freedom. In the park just behind this memorial, another memorial is planned. It will remember the Roma (Gypsy) victims of the Holocaust. (The Roma, as disdained by the Nazis as the Jews were, lost the same percentage of their population to Hitler.)

The Brandenburg Gate is ahead. Stay on the park side of the street for a better view of the gate. As you cross at the light, notice the double row of **cobblestones**—it goes around the city, marking where the Wall used to stand. (You could go directly to the Jewish memorial from here, but we'll go through the Brandenburg Gate first, then reach the memorial through Pariser Platz.)

▲▲**Brandenburg Gate (Brandenburger Tor)**—The historic Brandenburg Gate (1791) was the grandest, and is the last survivor, of 14 gates in Berlin's old city wall (this one led to the neighboring region of Brandenburg). The gate was the symbol of Prussian Berlin...and later the symbol of a divided Berlin. It's crowned by a majestic four-horse chariot with the Goddess of Peace at the reins. Napoleon took this statue to the Louvre in Paris in 1806. After the Prussians defeated Napoleon and got it back (1813), she was renamed the Goddess of Victory.

The gate sat unused, part of a sad circle dance called the Wall, for more than 25 years. Now postcards all over town show the ecstatic day—November 9, 1989—when the world enjoyed the sight of happy Berliners jamming the gate like flowers on a parade float. Pause a minute and think about struggles for freedom—past and present. (There's actually a special room built into the gate for this purpose.) Around the gate, look at the information boards with pictures of how much this area changed throughout the 20th century. The latest chapter: The shiny white gate was completely restored in 2002 (but you can still see faint patches marking war damage). The TI within the gate is open daily (April–Oct 9:30–19:00, Nov–March 10:00–19:00, S-Bahn: Unter den Linden).

The Brandenburg Gate, the center of old Berlin, sits on a major boulevard running east to west through Berlin. The western segment, called Strasse des 17 Juni (named for a workers' uprising against the DDR government in 1953), stretches for four miles from the Brandenburg Gate and Victory Column to the Olympic Stadium. But we'll follow this city axis in the opposite direction, east, walking along what is known as Unter den Linden—into the core of old imperial Berlin and past what was once the palace of the Hohenzollern family who ruled Prussia and then Germany. The palace—the reason for just about all you'll see—is a phantom sight, long gone (though the facade—which we'll see later on this walk—is now being partially rebuilt). Alexanderplatz, which marks the end of this walk, is near the base of the giant TV Tower hovering in the distance.

Ponder the fact that you're standing in what was the so-called "death strip." Now cross through the gate, into...

▲**Pariser Platz**—"Parisian Square," so named after the Prussians defeated Napoleon in 1813, was once filled with important government buildings—all bombed to smithereens in World War II. For decades, it was an unrecognizable, deserted no-man's-land. But now, sparkling new banks, embassies (the French Embassy rebuilt where it was before WWII), a palace of coffee (Starbucks), the small Kennedys Museum (described later), and a swanky rebuilt hotel have filled in the void. The winners of World War II got prime real estate: The American, French, British, and Soviet (now Russian) embassies are all on or near this square.

Face the gate and look to your left. The **US Embassy** moved back here in 2008. This new embassy has been controversial: For safety's sake, Uncle Sam wanted it away from other buildings, but the Germans preferred it in its original location. A compromise was reached, building the embassy by the gate—but routing roads farther from it (at the expense of American taxpayers) to reduce the security risk. Throughout the world, American embassies are the most fortified buildings in town.

BERLIN

Just to the left, the **DZ Bank building** is by Frank Gehry, the unconventional American architect famous for Bilbao's organic Guggenheim Museum, Prague's Dancing House, Seattle's Experience Music Project, Chicago's Millennium Park, and Los Angeles' Walt Disney Concert Hall. Gehry fans might be surprised at the DZ Bank building's low profile. Structures on Pariser Platz are designed to be bland so as not to draw attention away from the Brandenburg Gate. (The glassy facade of the Academy of Arts, next to Gehry's building, is controversial for drawing attention to itself.) For your fix of the good old Gehry, step into the lobby and check out its undulating interior. It's a fish—and you feel like you're both inside and outside of it. Gehry's vision is explained on a nearby plaque.

The **Academy of Arts** (Akademie der Kunst), with its notorious glass facade, is next door. Its doors lead to a mall (daily 10:00–22:00), which leads directly to the vast...

▲▲Memorial to the Murdered Jews of Europe (Denkmal für die Ermordeten Juden Europas)—The new Holocaust memorial, consisting of 2,711 gravestone-like pillars and completed in 2005, is an essential stop for any visit to Berlin. This is the first formal German government–sponsored Holocaust memorial. Jewish American architect Peter Eisenman won the competition for the commission (and built it on time and on budget—€27 million). It's controversial for the focus—just Jews. The government promises to make memorials to the other groups targeted by the Nazis.

The pillars are made of hollow concrete, each chemically coated for easy removal of graffiti. The number of pillars, symbolic of nothing, is simply how many fit on the provided land.

Is it a labyrinth...symbolic cemetery...intentionally disorienting? The meaning is entirely up to the visitor to derive. The idea is for you to spend time pondering this horrible chapter in human history.

The pondering takes place under the sky. For the learning, go under the field of concrete pillars to the state-of-the-art information center (there may be a short line because visitors must go through a security check). This studies the Nazi system of extermination, humanizes the victims, traces stories of individual families and collects vivid personal accounts, and lists 200 different places of genocide (all well-explained in English, free, Tue–Sun 10:00–20:00, closed Mon, last entry 45 min before closing, S-Bahn: Unter den Linden or Potsdamer Platz, tel. 030/2639-4336, www.stiftung-denkmal.de). The €3 audioguide augments the experience.

The location—where the Wall once stood—is coincidental. It's just a place where lots of people will experience it. Nazi propagandist Joseph Goebbels' bunker was discovered during the work and left buried under the northeast corner of the memorial. Hitler's bunker is just 200 yards away, under a nondescript parking lot. Such Nazi sites are intentionally left hidden to discourage neo-Nazi elements from creating shrines.

Before leaving the area, consider ducking into the nearby **Mythos Germania** exhibit, which displays a model of "Germania," the creepy fascist-utopian city that Hitler hoped would replace Berlin (a city he'd never liked). Recently discovered documents have revealed how detailed these plans were. To see the full model upstairs you've got to pay the admission fee, but anyone's welcome to the foyer to peek at a model of the "Great Hall"—a building that would have dwarfed the Brandenburg Gate (€6, foyer free, daily 11:00–19:00, Gertrud-Kolmar-Strasse 14, tel. 030/4991-0517).

Now backtrack to Pariser Platz (through the yellow building). Across the square, consider dropping into the...

Kennedys Museum—This crisp new private enterprise facing the Brandenburg Gate recalls Kennedy's Germany trip in 1963, with great photos and video clips as well as a photographic shrine to the Kennedy clan in America. It's a small, overpriced, yet delightful experience with interesting mementos—such as JFK's notes with the phonetic "ish bin ein Bear lee ner." Jacqueline Kennedy commented on how strange it was that this was her husband's most quotable quote (€7, €3.50 to a broad array of visitors—dream up a discount and ask for it, daily 10:00–18:00, Pariser Platz 4a, tel. 030/2065-3570).

Leave Pariser Platz and begin strolling...

▲▲Along Unter den Linden

Unter den Linden is the heart of former East Berlin. In Berlin's good old days, Unter den Linden was one of Europe's grand boulevards. In the 15th century, this carriageway led from the palace to the hunting grounds (today's big Tiergarten). In the 17th century, Hohenzollern princes and princesses moved in and built their palaces here so they could be near the Prussian emperor.

Named centuries ago for its thousand linden trees, this was the most elegant street of Prussian Berlin before Hitler's time, and the main drag of East Berlin after his reign. Hitler replaced the venerable trees—many 250 years old—with Nazi flags. Popular discontent actually drove him to replant linden trees. Today, Unter den Linden is no longer a depressing Cold War cul-de-sac, and its pre-Hitler strolling café ambience is returning. Notice how it is divided, roughly at Friedrichstrasse, into a business section that stretches toward the Brandenburg Gate, and a culture section that spreads out toward Alexanderplatz. Frederick the Great wanted culture, mainly the opera and the university, closer to his palace, and to keep business (read: banks) farther away, near the city walls.

BERLIN

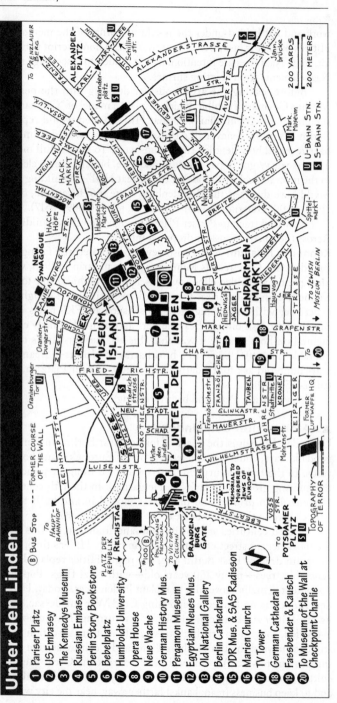

Unter den Linden

ⓑ Bus Stop   — — — FORMER COURSE OF THE WALL

1 Pariser Platz
2 US Embassy
3 The Kennedys Museum
4 Russian Embassy
5 Berlin Story Bookstore
6 Bebelplatz
7 Humboldt University
8 Opera House
9 Neue Wache
10 German History Mus.
11 Pergamon Museum
12 Egyptian/Neues Mus.
13 Old National Gallery
14 Berlin Cathedral
15 DDR Mus. & SAS Radisson
16 Marien Church
17 TV Tower
18 German Cathedral
19 Fassbender & Rausch
20 To Museum of the Wall at
   Checkpoint Charlie

200 YARDS
200 METERS

Ⓤ U-Bahn Stn.   Ⓢ S-Bahn Stn.

As you walk toward the giant TV Tower, the big building you see jutting out into the street on your right is the **Hotel Adlon.** It hosted such notables as Charlie Chaplin, Albert Einstein, and Greta Garbo. This was where Garbo said, "I want to be alone" during the filming of *Grand Hotel.* And, perhaps fresher in your memory, this is where Michael Jackson shocked millions by dangling his little baby over the railing (second balcony up, center of facade). Destroyed by Russians just after World War II, the grand Adlon was rebuilt in 1996. See how far you can get inside.

Descend into the Unter den Linden S-Bahn station ahead of you. It's one of Berlin's former **ghost subway stations.** During the Cold War, most underground train tunnels were simply blocked at the border. But a few Western lines looped through the East. To make a little hard Western cash, the Eastern government rented the use of these tracks to the West, but the stations (which happened to be in East Berlin) were strictly off-limits. For 28 years, the stations were unused, as Western trains slowly passed through, seeing only eerie DDR (East German) guards and lots of cobwebs. Literally within days of the fall of the Wall, these stations were reopened, and today they are a time warp (looking essentially as they did when built in 1931, with dreary old green tiles and original signage). Walk along the track (the walls are lined with historic photos of the Reichstag through the ages) and exit on the other side, following signs to *Russische Botschaft* (the Russian Embassy).

The **Russian Embassy** was the first big postwar building project in East Berlin. It's built in the powerful, simplified, Neoclassical style that Stalin liked. While not as important now as it was a few years ago, it's immense as ever. It flies the Russian white, blue, and red. Find the hammer-and-sickle motif decorating the window frames—a reminder of the days when this was the USSR embassy.

Continuing past the Aeroflot airline offices, look across Glinkastrasse to the right to see the back of the **Komische Oper** (Comic Opera; program and view of ornate interior posted in window). While the exterior is ugly, the fine old theater interior—amazingly missed by WWII bombs—survives.

Back on the main drag, at #26, is a great bookstore, **Berlin Story.** In addition to a wide range of English-language books, this shop has a free museum (with a model of 1930s Unter den Linden) and a 25-minute English film about the history of Berlin (daily 10:00–20:00; for more details, see "Helpful Hints," near the beginning of the chapter). This is also a good opportunity to pick up some nostalgic knickknacks from the Cold War. The West lost no time in consuming the East; consequently, some are feeling a wave of *Ost*-algia for the old days of East Berlin. In 2006 local elections, nearly half of East Berlin's voters—and 6 percent of

West Berliners—voted for the extreme left party, which has ties to the bygone Communist Party.

One symbol of that era has been given a reprieve. As you continue to Friedrichstrasse, look at the DDR-style pedestrian lights, and you'll realize that someone had a sense of humor back then. The perky red and green men—*Ampelmännchen*—were under threat of replacement by the far less jaunty Western signs. Fortunately, after a 10-year court battle, the DDR signals will be kept after all.

At **Friedrichstrasse,** look right. Before the war, the Unter den Linden/Friedrichstrasse intersection was the heart of Berlin. In the 1920s, Berlin was famous for its anything-goes love of life. This was the cabaret drag, a springboard to stardom for young and vampy entertainers like Marlene Dietrich. (Born in 1901, Dietrich starred in the first German "talkie" and then headed straight to Hollywood.) Over the last few years, this boulevard—lined with super department stores (such as Galeries Lafayette) and big-time hotels (such as the Hilton and Regent)—has slowly begun to replace Ku'damm as the grand commerce and café boulevard of Berlin. (More recently, the West is retaliating with some new stores of its own.) Across from Galeries Lafayette is American Express (handy for any train-ticket needs—see "Helpful Hints," near the beginning of the chapter). Consider detouring to Galeries Lafayette, with its cool marble and glass waste-of-space interior (Mon–Sat 9:30–20:00, closed Sun; belly up to its amazing ground-floor viewpoint, or have lunch in its basement cafeteria—see page 613).

If you continued down Friedrichstrasse, you'd wind up at the sights listed in "South of Unter den Linden," on page 585—including the Museum of the Wall at Checkpoint Charlie (a 10-min walk from here). But for now, continue along Unter den Linden. You'll notice big, colorful **water pipes** around here, and throughout Berlin. As long as the city remains a gigantic construction zone, it will be laced with these drainage pipes—key to any building project. Berlin's high water table means any new basement comes with lots of pumping out.

The **VW Automobil Forum** shows off the latest models from the many car companies owned by VW (free, corner of Friedrichstrasse and Unter den Linden, VW art gallery in the basement).

Continue down Unter den Linden a few more blocks, past the large equestrian statue of Frederick II ("the Great"), and turn right into the square called **Bebelplatz.** Stand on the glass window in the center.

Frederick the Great—who ruled from 1740 to 1786—established Prussia not just as a military power, but as a cultural and intellectual heavyweight, as well. This square was the center of the "new Rome" that Frederick envisioned. His grand palace was just down the street; now it's a construction zone (see "Site of the Palace of the Republic" on page 583).

Look down through the glass you're standing on (center of Bebelplatz): The room of empty bookshelves is a memorial to the notorious Nazi **book burning.** It was on this square in 1933 that staff and students from the university threw 20,000 newly forbidden books (like Einstein's) into a huge bonfire on the orders of the Nazi propaganda minister Joseph Goebbels. A memorial plaque nearby reminds us of the prophetic quote by the German Jewish poet Heinrich Heine. In 1820, he said, "When you start by burning books, you'll end by burning people." A century later, his books were among those that went up in flames on this spot.

Great buildings front Bebelplatz. Survey the square counterclockwise:

Humboldt University, across Unter den Linden, is one of Europe's greatest. Marx and Lenin (not the brothers or the sisters) studied here, as did the Grimms (both brothers) and more than two-dozen Nobel Prize winners. Einstein, who was Jewish, taught here until taking a spot at Princeton in 1932 (smart guy).

The former **state library** is where Vladimir Lenin studied during much of his exile from Russia. If you climb to the second floor of the library and go through the door opposite the stairs, you'll see a 1968 vintage stained-glass window depicting Lenin's life's work with almost biblical reverence. On the ground floor is Tim's Canadian Deli, a great little café with light food, student prices, and garden seating (€2 plates, Mon–Sat 7:00–20:00, closed Sun, easy WC).

The **German State Opera** was bombed in 1941, rebuilt to bolster morale and to celebrate its centennial in 1943, and bombed again in 1945.

The round, Catholic **St. Hedwig's Church**—nicknamed the "upside-down teacup"—was built by the pragmatic Frederick the Great to encourage the integration of Catholic Silesians after his empire annexed their region in 1815. (St. Hedwig is the patron saint of Silesia, a region now shared by Germany, Poland, and the Czech Republic.) When asked what the church should look like, Frederick literally took a Silesian teacup and slammed it upside-down on a table. Like all Catholic churches in Berlin, St. Hedwig's is not on the street, but stuck in a kind of back lot—indicating inferiority to Protestant churches. You can step inside the church to see the cheesy DDR government renovation.

Continue down Unter den Linden. The next square on your right holds the **Opera House.** The Opernpalais, preening with fancy prewar elegance, hosts the pricey Operncafé. With the best desserts and the longest dessert bar in Europe, it's popular with Berliners for *Kaffee und Kuchen* (see "Eating—In Eastern Berlin," later in this chapter).

Cross Unter den Linden to the university side. The Greek-temple-like building set in the small, chestnut-tree-filled park is the **Neue Wache** (the emperor's "New Guardhouse," from 1816). When the Wall fell, this memorial to the victims of fascism was transformed into a new national memorial. Look inside, where a replica of the Käthe Kollwitz statue, *Mother with Her Dead Son,* is surrounded by thought-provoking silence. This marks the tombs of Germany's unknown soldier and the unknown concentration camp victim. The inscription in front reads, "To the victims of war and tyranny." Read the entire statement in English (on wall, left of entrance). The memorial, open to the sky, incorporates the elements—sunshine, rain, snow—falling on this modern-day *pietà.*

After the Neue Wache, the next building you'll see is Berlin's pink-yet-formidable Zeughaus, or arsenal. Dating from 1695, it's considered the oldest building on the boulevard and now houses the...

▲▲▲German History Museum (Deutsches Historisches Museum)—This fantastic museum is a two-part affair: the pink former Prussian arsenal building, and the I. M. Pei–designed annex. The main building (fronting Unter den Linden) houses the permanent collection. Two huge rectangular floors are packed with more than 8,000 artifacts telling the story of Germany—making this the top history museum in town. Historical objects, photographs, and models are intermingled with multimedia stations to help put everything in context. The first floor traces German history from 1 B.C. to 1918, with exhibits on early cultures, the Middle Ages, Reformation, Thirty Years' War, German Empire, and World War I. Exhibits on the ground floor continue with the Weimar Republic, Nazism, World War II, Allied occupation, and a divided Germany, wrapping up with reunification and a quick look at Germany today (€5, daily 10:00–18:00, excellent €3 audioguide has six hours of info for you to choose from, tel. 030/2030-4751, www.dhm.de).

For architecture buffs, the big attraction is the Pei annex behind the history museum, which complements the museum with often-fascinating temporary history exhibits. From the old building (with the Pei glass canopy over its courtyard), take a tunnel to the new wing, emerging under a striking glass spiral staircase that unites four floors with surprising views and lots of light. It's here that you'll experience why Pei—famous for his glass pyramid at Paris' Louvre—is called the "perfector of classical modernism," "master of light," and a magician of uniting historical buildings with new ones. (If the museum is closed, or you don't have a ticket, venture down the street—Hinter dem Giesshaus—to the left of the museum to see the Pei annex from the outside.)

Back on Unter den Linden, head toward the **Spree River.** Just before the bridge, wander left along the canal through a tiny but colorful arts-and-crafts market (weekends only; a larger flea market is just outside the Pergamon Museum). Canal tour boats leave from here (€7, 1 hour, departures on the half-hour, tour in German only but so dull it hardly matters). Continue up the riverbank two blocks and cross the Spree at the footbridge, which takes you to...

Museum Island (Museumsinsel)

This island, home of Berlin's first museum, is undergoing a formidable renovation. The grand vision is to integrate the city's major museums with a grand entry and tunnels that will lace the complex together (intended completion date: 2015). The complex was originally built in about 1871, when Germany was newly unified as one nation—and when Berlin was calling itself the "Athens on the Spree River." Today, its imposing Neoclassical buildings host five grand museums: the Pergamon (classical antiquities), the Neues Museum (housing the Egyptian Museum, with the bust of Queen Nefertiti), the Old National Gallery (19th-century German Romantic painting), the Bode Museum (European statuary through the ages, coins, and Byzantine art), and the Altes Museum (ancient artifacts). The museums function as one with the same prices, phone number, and a €12 combo-ticket that's far better than buying individual €8 entries (all are also included in the city's €19 Museumspass; Pergamon, Neues, Bode, and Altes museums open daily 10:00–18:00, Thu until 22:00, free on Thu after 18:00; Old National Gallery open same hours except closed Mon; tel. 030/2090-5577, www.museumsinsel-berlin.de). Since the Neues Museum's renovation is still underway at the time of this writing, expect that some details may change by the time you visit. The nearest S-Bahn station is Hackescher Markt.

Consider visiting any of these museums, and other Museum Island attractions (mentioned later), before continuing our walk. Once you're finished, skip over to "Museum Island to Alexanderplatz," next, to resume the self-guided tour.

▲▲**Pergamon Museum**—This world-class museum, part of Berlin's Collection of Classical Antiquities (Antikensammlung), stars the fantastic Pergamon Altar. From a second-century B.C. Greek temple, the altar shows the Greeks under Zeus and Athena beating the giants in a dramatic pig pile of mythological mayhem. Check out the action spilling onto the stairs. The Babylonian Ishtar Gate (glazed blue tiles from the sixth century B.C.) and many ancient Greek and Mesopotamian treasures are also impressive. (Renovation work might take the altar and/or the Ishtar Gate off display during your visit—check online or with the TI for the latest.) The superb "Pergamon in 30 Minutes" audioguide (free with admission, but €4 during free Thu extended hours) covers the museum's highlights and broadens your experience by introducing you to wonders you might not otherwise notice.

▲▲**Neues Museum**—This newly rebuilt museum contains one of the world's top collections of Egyptian art. The curator welcomes you on the included audioguide and encourages a broader approach to the museum than just seeing its claim to fame, the bust of Queen Nefertiti (described next). The fine audioguide celebrates new knowledge about ancient Egyptian civilization and offers fascinating insights into workaday Egyptian life as it describes the vivid papyrus collection, slice-of-life artifacts, and dreamy wax portraits decorating mummy cases.

But let's face it: The main reason to visit is to enjoy one of the great thrills in art appreciation—gazing into the still-young-and-beautiful face of 3,000-year-old **Queen Nefertiti,** the wife of King Akhenaton. This bust of Queen Nefertiti (c. 1340 B.C.) is the most famous piece of Egyptian art in Europe. Discovered in 1912, Nefertiti—with all the right beauty marks: long neck, symmetrical face, and just the right makeup—is called "Berlin's most beautiful woman." The bust never left its studio, but served as a master model for all other portraits of the queen. (That's probably why the left eye was never inlaid.) Buried for more than 3,000 years, she was found in the early 1900s by a German team who, by agreement with the Egyptian government, got to take home any workshop models they found. Although this bust is not particularly representative of Egyptian art in general, it has become a symbol for Egyptian art by popular acclaim.

Old National Gallery (Alte Nationalgalerie)—This gallery, behind the Altes Museum and across from the Neues Museum, is designed to look like a Greek temple. It shows mostly paintings: three floors with French and German Impressionists on the second, and Romantic German paintings (which I find most interesting) on the top (audioguide is free).

Lustgarten—For 300 years, the island's big central square has flip-flopped between being a military parade ground and a people-friendly park, depending upon the political tenor of the time. In 1999, it was made into a park again (read the history posted in corner opposite church). On a sunny day, it's packed with relaxing locals and is one of Berlin's most enjoyable public spaces.

Berlin Cathedral (Berliner Dom)—This century-old church towers over Museum Island (€5 includes access to dome gallery, not covered by Museum Island ticket, Mon–Sat 9:00–20:00, Sun 12:00–20:00, until 19:00 in winter, www.berliner-dom.de; many organ concerts—generally Sat at 20:00, tickets about €10 always available at the door, tel. 030/2026-9136). Inside, the great reformers (Luther, Calvin, and company) stand around the brilliantly restored dome like stern saints guarding their theology. Frederick I rests in an ornate tomb (right transept, near entrance to dome). The 270-step climb to the outdoor dome gallery is tough, but offers pleasant, breezy views of the city at the finish line (last entry 45 min before closing). The crypt downstairs is not worth a look.

Site of the Palace of the Republic—Across Unter den Linden from Berlin Cathedral is a construction site that once held the decrepit Palace of the Republic—formerly East Berlin's parliament building/futuristic entertainment complex, and a symbol of the communist days. Much of Frederick the Great's earlier palace actually survived World War II, but was replaced by the communists with this blocky Soviet-style building. The landmark building fell into disrepair after reunification, and was eventually dismantled in 2007. After long debate, the German Parliament decided to construct a building that will include the rebuilt facade of the old palace. Investing a huge sum, they will create a huge new public venue to be filled with museums, shops, galleries, and concert halls.

Museum Island to Alexanderplatz

Continue walking down Unter den Linden. Before crossing the bridge (and leaving Museum Island), look right. The pointy twin spires of the 13th-century Nikolai Church mark the center of medieval Berlin. This Nikolaiviertel (*Viertel* means "quarter") was restored by the DDR and was trendy in the last years of socialism. Today, it's a lively-at-night riverside restaurant district.

As you cross the bridge, look left in the distance to see the gilded **New Synagogue dome,** rebuilt after WWII bombing (see "North of Unter den Linden," later in this section).

Across the river to the left of the bridge is the giant **SAS Radisson Hotel** and shopping center, with a huge aquarium in the center. The elevator goes right through the middle of a deep-sea world. (You can see it from the unforgettable Radisson hotel lobby—tuck in your shirt and walk past the guards with the confidence of a guest who's sleeping there.) Here in the center of the old communist capital, it seems that capitalism has settled in with a spirited vengeance.

At the river side of the SAS Radisson Hotel, the little **DDR Museum** offers an interesting peek at a humbler life before capitalism took hold. You'll crawl through a Trabant car, see a DDR kitchen, and be surrounded by former DDR residents reminiscing about the bad old days (steep €5.50 admission, daily 10:00–22:00, Karl-Liebknecht Strasse 1, tel. 030/847-123-731).

In the park immediately across the street (a big jaywalk from the Radisson) are grandfatherly statues of **Marx and Engels** (nicknamed by locals "the old pensioners"). Surrounding them are stainless-steel monoliths with evocative photos that show the struggles of the workers of the world.

Walk toward **Marien Church** (from 1270, an artist's rendering helps you follow the interesting but very faded old "Dance of Death" mural which wraps around the narthex inside the door), just left of the base of the TV Tower. The big, redbrick building past the trees on the right is the **City Hall,** built after the revolution of 1848 and arguably the first democratic building in the city.

The 1,200-foot-tall **TV Tower** (Fernsehturm) offers a fine view from halfway up (€9.50, daily March–Oct 9:00–24:00, Nov–Feb 10:00–24:00). The tower offers a handy city orientation and an interesting view of the flat, red-roofed sprawl of Berlin—including a peek inside the city's many courtyards *(Höfe)*. Consider a kitschy trip to the observation deck for the view and lunch in its revolving restaurant (mediocre food, €12 plates, horrible lounge music, reservations smart for dinner, tel. 030/242-3333). It's very retro and somewhat trendy these days, so expect a line for the elevator. Built (with Swedish know-how) in 1969, the tower was meant to show the power of the atheistic state at a time when DDR leaders were having the crosses removed from church domes and spires. But when the sun shined on their tower—the greatest spire in East Berlin—a huge cross was reflected on the mirrored ball. Cynics called it "The Pope's Revenge." East Berliners dubbed the tower the "Tele-Asparagus." They joked that if it fell over, they'd have an elevator to the West.

Farther east, pass under the train tracks into **Alexanderplatz.** This area—especially the Kaufhof department store—was the commercial pride and joy of East Berlin. Today, it's still a landmark, with a major U- and S-Bahn station.

Our orientation stroll is finished. For a ride through workaday eastern Berlin, with its Lego-hell apartments (dreary even with their new facelifts), hop back on bus #100 from here. It loops five minutes to the end of the line and then, after a couple minutes' break, heads on back. (This bus retraces your route, finishing at Bahnhof Zoo.) Or consider extending this foray into eastern Berlin to...

Karl-Marx-Allee

The buildings along Karl-Marx-Allee in East Berlin (just beyond Alexanderplatz) were completely leveled by the Red Army in 1945. As an expression of their adoration to the "great Socialist Father" (the "cult of Stalin" was in full gear), the DDR government decided to rebuild the street better than ever (the USSR provided generous subsidies) and made it intentionally one meter wider than the Champs-Elysées. They named it Stalinallee. Today, this street, done in the bold "Stalin Gothic" style so common in Moscow in the 1950s, has been restored, renamed after Karl Marx, and lined with "workers' palaces"—providing a rare look at Berlin's communist days. Distances are a bit long for convenient walking, but you can cruise Karl-Marx-Allee by taxi, or ride the U-Bahn to Strausberger Platz (which was built to resemble an Italian promenade) and walk to Frankfurter Tor, reading the good information posts along the way. Notice the Social Realist reliefs on the buildings and the lampposts, which incorporate the wings of a phoenix (rising from the ashes) in their design.

The **Café Sibylle,** just beyond the Strausberger Platz U-Bahn station, is a fun spot for a coffee, traditional DDR ice-cream treats, and a look at its free, informal museum that tells the story of the most destroyed street in Berlin. While the humble exhibit is nearly all in German, it's fun to see the ear and half a moustache from what was the largest statue of Stalin in Germany (the centerpiece of the street until 1961) and a few intimate insights into apartment life in a DDR flat. The café is known for its good coffee and *Schwedeneisbecher mit Eierlikor*—an ice-cream sundae with a shot of liqueur, popular among those nostalgic for communism (daily 10:00–20:00, Karl-Marx-Allee 72, at intersection with Koppenstrasse, a block from U-Bahn: Strausberger Platz, tel. 030/2935-2203).

Heading out to Karl-Marx-Allee (just beyond the TV Tower), you're likely to notice a giant colorful **mural** decorating a blocky communist-era skyscraper. This was the Ministry of Education, and the mural is a tile mosaic trumpeting the accomplishments of the DDR's version of "No Child Left Behind."

South of Unter den Linden

The following sights—heavy on Nazi and Wall history—are listed roughly north to south (as you reach them from Unter den Linden).

▲▲**Gendarmenmarkt**—This delightful and historic square is bounded by twin churches, a tasty chocolate shop, and the Berlin Symphony's concert hall (designed by Karl Friedrich Schinkel, the man who put the Neoclassical stamp on Berlin). In summer, it hosts a few outdoor cafés, *Biergarten*s, and sometimes concerts. Wonderfully symmetrical, the square is considered by Berliners to be the finest in town. The name of the square—part French and part German (after the *Gens d'Armes,* Frederick the Great's royal guard who were headquartered here)—reminds us that in the 17th century, a fifth of all Berliners were French émigrés, Protestant Huguenots fleeing Catholic France. Back then, tolerant Prussia was a magnet for the persecuted. These émigrés vitalized Berlin with new ideas and know-how.

The German Cathedral (described below) on the square has an exhibit worthwhile for history buffs. The French Cathedral (Französischer Dom) offers a humble museum on the Huguenots (€2, Tue–Sun 12:00–17:00, closed Mon, U-Bahn: Französische Strasse or Stadtmitte). Fun fact: Neither of these churches are true cathedrals, as they never contained a bishop's throne; their German title of *Dom* (cathedral) is actually a mistranslation from the French word *dôme* (cupola).

Fassbender & Rausch, on the corner near the German Cathedral, claims to be Europe's biggest chocolate store. After 150 years of chocolate-making, this family-owned business proudly displays its sweet delights—250 different kinds—on a 55-foot-long buffet. Truffles are sold for about €0.60 each—it's fun to compose a fancy little eight-piece box of your own for about €5 (daily 10:00–20:00, corner of Mohrenstrasse at Charlottenstrasse 60, tel. 030/2045-8440). Upstairs is an elegant hot chocolate café with fine views.

Gendarmenmarkt is buried in what has recently emerged as Berlin's new "Fifth Avenue" shopping district. For the ultimate in top-end shops, find the corner of Jägerstrasse and Französische Strasse and wander through the Quartier 206 (Mon–Fri 10:30–19:30, Sat 10:00–18:00, closed Sun, www.quartier206.com).

▲**German Cathedral (Deutscher Dom)**—This cathedral, bombed flat in the war and rebuilt only in the 1980s, houses the thought-provoking *Milestones, Setbacks, Sidetracks (Wege, Irrwege, Umwege)* exhibit, which traces the history of the German parliamentary system. The parliament-funded exhibit—while light on actual historical artifacts—is well done and more interesting than it sounds. It takes you quickly from the revolutionary days of 1848 to the 1920s, and then more deeply through the tumultuous 20th century. There are no English descriptions, but you can follow the essential, excellent, and free 90-minute English audioguide or buy the wonderfully detailed €10 guidebook. If you think this museum is an attempt by the German government to develop a more sophisticated and educated electorate in the interest of stronger democracy, you're exactly right. Germany knows (from its own troubled history) that a dumbed-down electorate, manipulated by clever spin-meisters and sound-bite media blitzes, is a dangerous thing (free, May–Sept Tue–Sun 10:00–19:00, Oct–April Tue–Sun 10:00–18:00, closed Mon year-round, on Gendarmenmarkt just off Friedrichstrasse, tel. 030/2273-0431).

▲▲▲**Museum of the Wall at Checkpoint Charlie (Mauermuseum Haus am Checkpoint Charlie)**—While the famous border checkpoint between the American and Soviet sectors is long gone, its memory is preserved by one of Europe's most interesting, though cluttered, museums. During the Cold War, the House at Checkpoint Charlie stood defiantly—spitting distance from the border guards—showing off all the clever escapes over, under, and through the Wall. Today, while the drama is over and hunks of the Wall stand like victory scalps at its door, the museum still tells a gripping history of the Wall, recounts the many ingenious escape attempts (early years—with a cruder wall—saw more escapes), and includes plenty of video coverage of those heady days when people-power tore down the Wall (€12.50, assemble 20 tourists and get in for €7.50 each, €3 audioguide, discount with WelcomeCard but not covered by Museumspass, cash only, daily 9:00–22:00, U-6 to Kochstrasse or—better from Zoo—U-2 to Stadtmitte, Friedrichstrasse 43–45, tel. 030/253-7250, www .mauermuseum.de). If you're pressed for time, this is a good after-dinner sight. With extra time, consider the "Hear We Go" audioguide about the Wall that takes you outside the museum (€7, 90 min, leave ID as deposit).

▲▲**Checkpoint Charlie Street Scene**—Where Checkpoint Charlie once stood, notice the thought-provoking post with larger-than-life posters of a young American soldier facing east and a young Soviet soldier facing west. The area has become a Cold War freak show. The rebuilt guard station now hosts two actors playing American guards who pose for photos. Across the street is Snack Point Charlie. The old checkpoint was not named for a person, but because it was checkpoint number three—as in Alpha (at the East–West German border, a hundred miles west of here), Bravo (as you enter Berlin proper), and Charlie (the most famous because it was where most foreigners would pass). A fine photo exhibit stretches down the street with great English descriptions telling the story of the Wall. While you could get this information from a book, it's poignant to stand here in person and ponder the gripping history of this place. A few yards away (on Zimmerstrasse), a glass panel describes the former checkpoint. From there, a double row of cobbles in Zimmerstrasse traces the former path of the Wall. These innocuous cobbles run throughout the city, even through some modern buildings.

Follow the cobbles one very long block to Wilhelmstrasse, a surviving stretch of Wall, and the...

Topography of Terror (Topographie des Terrors)—The park behind the Zimmerstrasse/Wilhelmstrasse bit of Wall marks the site of the command center of Hitler's Gestapo and SS. Because of the horrible things planned here, the rubble of these buildings will always be left as rubble. The SS, Hitler's personal bodyguards, grew to become a state-within-a-state, with its talons in every corner of German society. Along an excavated foundation of the building, an exhibit tells the story of National Socialism and its victims in Berlin (free, info booth open daily May–Sept 10:00–20:00, Oct–April 10:00–18:00 or until dark, tel. 030/2548-6703, www.topographie.de). Posted information is in both German and English, but the free English audioguide is helpful (available only until 18:45 in summer).

Across the street (facing the Wall) is the **German Finance Ministry** (Bundesministerium der Finanzen). Formerly the headquarters of the Nazi Luftwaffe (Air Force), this is the only major Hitler-era government building that survived the war's bombs. The communists used it to house their—no joke—Ministry of Ministries. Walk up Wilhelmstrasse (to the north) to see an entry gate (on your left) that looks much like it did when Germany occupied nearly all of Europe. On the north side of the building (farther up Wilhelmstrasse, at corner with Leipziger Strasse) is a wonderful example of communist art. The mural, Max Lingner's *Aufbau der Republik* (*Building the Republic*, 1953), is classic Socialist Realism, showing the entire society—industrial laborers, farm workers, women, and children—all happily singing the same patriotic song. This was the communist ideal. For the reality, look at the ground in the courtyard in front of the mural to see an enlarged photograph from a 1953 uprising here against the communists... quite a contrast.

▲▲▲Jewish Museum Berlin (Jüdisches Museum Berlin)—This museum is one of Europe's best Jewish sights. The highly conceptual building is a sight in itself, and the museum inside—an overview of the rich culture and history of Europe's Jewish community—is excellent. The Holocaust is appropriately remembered, but it doesn't overwhelm this celebration of Jewish life. Even though the museum is in a nondescript residential neighborhood (a 10-min walk from the Hallesches Tor U-Bahn station or the Checkpoint Charlie museum), it's well worth the trip.

Designed by American architect Daniel Libeskind (who is redeveloping New York City's World Trade Center site), the zinc-walled building's zigzag shape is pierced by voids symbolic of the irreplaceable cultural loss caused by the Holocaust. Enter through the 18th-century Baroque building next door, then go through an underground tunnel to reach the museum interior.

Before you reach the exhibit, your visit starts with three memorial spaces. Underground, follow the Axis of Exile to a disorienting slanted garden with 49 pillars. Then the Axis of Holocaust leads to an eerily empty tower shut off from the outside world. A detour near the bottom of the long stairway leads to the "Memory Void," a thought-provoking space of "fallen leaves": heavy metal faces that you walk on, making un-human noises with each step.

Finally, climb the stairs to the top of the museum, from where you stroll chronologically through the 2,000-year story of Judaism in Germany. The exhibit, on two floors, is engaging. Interactive bits (for example, spell your name in Hebrew) make it lively for kids. English explanations interpret both the exhibits and the design of the very symbolic building.

Cost and Hours: €5, covered by Museumspass, discount with WelcomeCard, daily 10:00–20:00, Mon until 22:00, last entry one hour before closing, closed on Jewish holidays. Tight security includes bag check and metal detectors. If you're here in December, be sure to check out their "Hannumas" holiday market. Tel. 030/2599-3300, www.jmberlin.de.

Getting There: Ride U-Bahn line 1, 6, or 15 to Hallesches Tor, take the exit marked *Jüdisches Museum,* exit straight ahead, then turn right on Franz-Klühs-Strasse. The museum is a five-minute walk ahead on your left, at Lindenstrasse 9.

Eating: The museum has a good, but not kosher, café/restaurant (€9 daily specials, lunch served 12:00–16:00, snacks at other times, tel. 030/2593-9760).

East Side Gallery—The biggest remaining stretch of the Wall is now "the world's longest outdoor art gallery." It stretches for nearly a mile and is covered with murals painted by artists from around the world. The murals are routinely whitewashed so new ones can be painted. This segment of the Wall makes another poignant walk. For a quick look, take the S-Bahn to the Ostbahnhof station (follow signs to Stralauerplatz exit; once outside, TV Tower will be to your right; go left and at next corner look to your right—the Wall is across the busy street). The gallery is slowly being consumed by developers. If you walk the entire length of the East Side Gallery, you'll find a small Wall souvenir shop at the end and a bridge crossing the river to a subway station at Schlesisches Tor (in Kreuzberg). The bridge, a fine example of Brandenburg Neo-Gothic brickwork, has a fun neon "rock, paper, scissors" installment poking fun at the futility of the Cold War.

Kreuzberg—This district—once abutting the dreary Wall and inhabited mostly by poor Turkish guest laborers and their families—is still run-down, with graffiti-riddled buildings and plenty of student and Turkish street life. It offers a gritty look at melting-pot Berlin, in a city where original Berliners are as rare as old buildings. Berlin is the fourth-largest Turkish city in the world, and Kreuzberg is its "downtown." But to call it a "little Istanbul" insults the big one. You'll see *Döner Kebab* stands, shops decorated with spray paint, and mothers wrapped in colorful scarves looking like they just got off a donkey in Anatolia. But lately, an influx of immigrants from many other countries has diluted the Turkish-ness of Kreuzberg. Berliners come here for fun ethnic eateries. For a dose of Kreuzberg without getting your fingers dirty, joyride on bus #129 (catch it near Jewish Museum). For a colorful stroll, take the U-Bahn to Kottbusser Tor and wander—ideally on Tuesday and Friday between 12:00 and 18:00, when the Turkish Market sprawls along the Maybachufer riverbank.

North of Unter den Linden

While there are few major sights to the north of Unter den Linden, this area has some of Berlin's trendiest, most interesting neighborhoods.

▲**New Synagogue (Neue Synagogue)**—A shiny gilded dome marks the New Synagogue, now a museum and cultural center on Oranienburger Strasse. Only the dome and facade have been restored—a window overlooks the vacant field marking what used to be the synagogue. The largest and finest synagogue in Berlin before World War II, it was desecrated by Nazis on "Crystal Night" (Kristallnacht) in 1938, bombed in 1943, and partially rebuilt in 1990. Inside, past tight security, there's a small but moving exhibit on the Berlin Jewish community through the centuries with some good English descriptions (ground floor and first floor). On its facade, the *Vergesst es nie* message—added by East Berlin Jews in 1966—means "Never forget." East Berlin had only a few hundred Jews, but now that the city is reunited, the Jewish community numbers about 12,000 (€3; March–Oct Sun–Mon 10:00–20:00, Tue–Thu 10:00–18:00, Fri 10:00–17:00, closed Sat; Nov–Feb Sun–Thu 10:00–18:00, Fri 10:00–14:00, closed Sat; Oranienburger Strasse 28/30, U-Bahn: Oranienburger Tor, tel. 030/8802-8300 and press 1, www.cjudaicum.de).

Cheer things up 50 yards away with every local kid's favorite traditional candy shop—**Bonbonmacherei**—where you can see candy being made the old-fashioned way (at Oranienburger Strasse 32, in another example of a classic Berlin courtyard).

A block from the synagogue, walk 50 yards down Grosse Hamburger Strasse to a little park. This street was known for 200 years as the "street of tolerance" because the Jewish community donated land to Protestants so that they could build a church. Hitler turned it into the "street of death" *(Todes Strasse)*, bulldozing 12,000 graves of the city's oldest Jewish cemetery and turning a Jewish nursing home into a deportation center. Because of the small but growing radical Muslim element in Berlin, and a smattering of persistent neo-Nazis, several police officers and an Israeli secret agent keep watch over this park and the Jewish high school nearby.

▲**Oranienburger Strasse**—Berlin is developing so fast, it's impossible to predict what will be "in" from year to year. The area around Oranienburger Strasse is definitely trendy (but is being challenged by hip Friedrichshain, farther east, and Prenzlauer

Berg, described later). While the area immediately around the synagogue is dull, 100 yards away things get colorful. The streets behind Grosse Hamburger Strasse flicker with atmospheric cafés, *Kneipen* (pubs), and art galleries. At night (from about 20:00), techno-prostitutes line Oranienburger Strasse. Prostitution is decriminalized here, but there's a big debate about taxation. Since they don't get unemployment insurance, why should they pay taxes?

Hackescher Markt—This area, in front of the S-Bahn station by the same name, is a great people scene day and night. The brick trestle supporting the train track is another classic example of the city's Brandenburg Neo-Gothic brickwork. Most of the brick archways are now filled with hip shops, which have official—and newly trendy—addresses such as "S-Bahn Arch #9, Hackescher Markt." Within 100 yards of the S-Bahn station, you'll find Hackesche Höfe (see below), recommended Turkish and Bavarian restaurants, walking-tour and pub-crawl departure points, and tram #M1 to Prenzlauer Berg.

Hackesche Höfe (a block in front of the Hackescher Markt S-Bahn station) is a series of eight courtyards bunny-hopping through a wonderfully restored 1907 *Jugendstil* building. Berlin's apartments are organized like this—courtyard after courtyard leading off the main roads. This complex is full of trendy restaurants (including a good Turkish place, Hasir—see "Eating—In Eastern Berlin," later in this chapter), theaters, and cinema (playing movies in their original languages). This is a wonderful example of how to make huge city blocks livable. Two decades after the Cold War, this area has reached the final evolution of East Berlin's urban restoration—this is where Prenzlauer Berg is heading. (These courtyards also serve a useful lesson for visitors: Much of Berlin's charm hides off the street front.)

▲**Prenzlauer Berg**—Young, in-the-know locals agree that "Prenzl'berg" is one of Berlin's most colorful neighborhoods (roughly between Helmholtzplatz and Kollwitzplatz and along Kastanienallee, U-Bahn: Senefelderplatz and Eberswalder Strasse; or take the S-Bahn to Hackescher Markt and catch tram #M1 north). This part of the city was largely untouched during World War II, but its buildings slowly rotted away under the communists. Since the Wall fell, it's been overrun with laid-back hipsters, energetic young families, and clever entrepreneurs who are breathing life back into its classic old apartment blocks, deserted factories, and long-forgotten breweries. While it's no longer "up-and-coming," but on the road to gentrification, Prenzlauer Berg is a celebration of life and a joy to stroll through. The area feels strangely wholesome and family-friendly, as former ruffians with tattoos, piercings, and an appetite for the cutting-edge life are now

BERLIN

responsible young parents. Though it's a few blocks farther out than the neighborhoods described earlier, it's a fun area to explore and have a meal or spend the night.

Natural History Museum (Museum für Naturkunde)—This museum is worth a visit just to see the largest dinosaur skeleton ever assembled. While you're there, meet "Bobby" the stuffed ape (€4, Tue–Fri 9:30–17:00, Sat–Sun 10:00–18:00, closed Mon, last entry 30 min before closing, U-Bahn line 6 to Zinnowitzer Strasse, Invalidenstrasse 43, tel. 030/2093-8591, www.museum .hu-berlin.de).

Berlin Wall Documentation Center (Dokumentations-zentrum Berliner Mauer)—The last surviving complete "Wall system" (with both sides of its Wall and its no-man's-land, or "death strip," all still intact) is now part of a sober little memorial and "Doku-Center." Though it's directed at German-speakers and far from other sights, it's handy enough to the S-Bahn that any Wall aficionado will find it worth a quick visit. The Documentation Center has a photo gallery and rooftop viewpoint (accessible by elevator), from which you can view the "Wall system." It's poignantly located where a church was destroyed to make way for the Wall; today, a memorial chapel has been built where the church once stood (free, April–Oct Tue–Sun 10:00–18:00, Nov–March until 17:00, closed Mon year-round, Bernauer Strasse 111, tel. 030/464-1030, www.berliner-mauer-dokumentationszentrum .de). Take the S-Bahn to Nordbahnhof and walk 200 yards along Bernauer Strasse, which is still lined with a long chunk of Wall.

Central Berlin

Tiergarten Park and Nearby

Berlin's "Central Park" stretches two miles from Bahnhof Zoo to the Brandenburg Gate.

Victory Column (Siegessäule)—The Tiergarten's centerpiece, the Victory Column, was built to commemorate the Prussian defeat of Denmark in 1864...then reinterpreted after the defeat of France in 1870. The pointy-helmeted Germans rubbed it in, decorating the tower with French cannons and paying for it all with francs received as war reparations. The three lower rings commemorate Bismarck's victories. I imagine the statues of Moltke and other German military greats—which lurk in the trees nearby—goose-stepping around the floodlit angel at night. Originally standing at the Reichstag, in 1938 the tower was moved to this position and given a 25-foot lengthening by Hitler's architect Albert Speer, in anticipation of the planned re-envisioning of Berlin as "Germania"—the capital of a world-wide Nazi empire. Streets leading to the circle are flanked by surviving Nazi guardhouses—built in the bold style that fascists loved. At the memorial's first

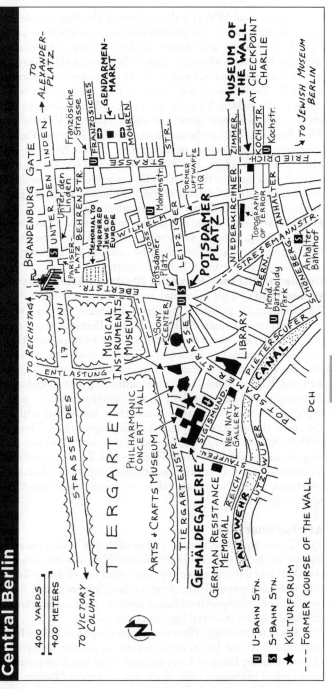

Central Berlin

400 YARDS
400 METERS

TO VICTORY COLUMN

Ⓤ U-Bahn Stn.
Ⓢ S-Bahn Stn.
★ KULTURFORUM
- - - FORMER COURSE OF THE WALL

TIERGARTEN

STRASSE DES 17 JUNI

ENTLASTUNG

TO REICHSTAG

BRANDENBURG GATE

UNTER DEN LINDEN

Unter den Linden

Pariser-Platz
EBERTSTR.
BEHREN-STR.

Französische Strasse

FRANZÖSISCHE

GENDARMEN-MARKT

MOHREN

TO ALEXANDER-PLATZ

Memorial to Murdered Jews of Europe

Mohrenstr.

W I L H E L M S T R A S S E

Vossstr.

Potsdamer Platz

LEIPZIGER

Former Luftwaffe HQ

POTSDAMER PLATZ

STR.

ZIMMER.

KOCHSTR.

Kochstr.

MUSEUM OF THE WALL
AT CHECKPOINT CHARLIE

FRIEDRICH

TO JEWISH MUSEUM BERLIN

MUSICAL INSTRUMENTS MUSEUM

Sony Center

STRESEMANNSTR.

Topography of Terror

NIEDERKIRCHNER

ANHALTER

BERNBURGER STR.

SCHÖNEBERGER STR.

Anhalter Bahnhof

Mend.-Bartholdy Park

LIBRARY

PIETERSCUFER

CANAL

POTS

UFER

PHILHARMONIC CONCERT HALL

SIGISMUND-STR.

TIERGARTENSTR.

STAUFFEN.

New Natl. Gallery

REICH

ARTS + CRAFTS MUSEUM

GEMÄLDEGALERIE

GERMAN RESISTANCE MEMORIAL

LANDWEHR

LÜTZOWUFER

DCH

BERLIN

level, notice how WWII bullets chipped the fine marble columns. More recently, the column has been the epicenter of the Love Parade (a city-wide techno-hedonist street party) and the backdrop for Barack Obama's summer 2008 visit to Germany as a presidential candidate. Climbing its 285 steps earns you a breathtaking Berlin-wide view and a close-up look at the gilded bronze statue of the goddess Victoria (go ahead, call her "the chick on a stick"—everybody here does). You might recognize Victoria from Wim Wenders' 1987 art-house classic *Wings of Desire*, or the *Stay (Faraway, So Close!)* video he directed for U2 (€2.20; April–Sept Mon–Thu 9:30–18:30, Fri–Sun 9:30–19:00; Oct–March daily 9:30–17:30; closes in the rain, WCs for paying guests only, no elevator, bus #100, tel. 030/8639-8560). From the tower, the grand Strasse des 17 Juni leads east to the Brandenburg Gate.

Flea Market—A colorful flea market with great antiques, more than 200 stalls, collector-savvy merchants, and fun German fast-food stands thrives weekends on Strasse des 17 Juni (Sat–Sun 6:00–16:00, right next to S-Bahn: Tiergarten).

German Resistance Memorial (Gedenkstätte Deutscher Widerstand)—This memorial and museum, just south of the Tiergarten, tells the story of several organized German resistance movements against Hitler. The Bendlerblock was a military headquarters where an ill-fated attempt to assassinate Hitler was plotted (the actual attempt occurred in Rastenburg, eastern Prussia; the event is dramatized in the 2009 Tom Cruise film *Valkyrie*). Claus Schenk Graf von Stauffenberg and several of his co-conspirators were shot here in the courtyard. While posted explanations are in German only and there are no real artifacts, the spirit that haunts the place is multilingual (free, Mon–Fri 9:00–18:00, Thu until 20:00, Sat–Sun 10:00–18:00, free and good English audioguide with passport, €3 printed English translation, no crowds, near Kulturforum at Stauffenbergstrasse 13, enter in courtyard, door on left, main exhibit is on third floor, bus #M29, tel. 030/2699-5000).

▲Potsdamer Platz

The "Times Square of Berlin," and possibly the busiest square in Europe before World War II, Potsdamer Platz was cut in two by the Wall and left a deserted no-man's-land for 40 years. Today, this immense commercial/residential/entertainment center, sitting on a futuristic transportation hub, is home to the European corporate headquarters of several big-league companies.

The new Potsdamer Platz was a vision begun in 1991, when it was announced that Berlin would resume its position as capital of Germany. Sony, Daimler-Chrysler, and other major corporations have turned the square once again into a center of Berlin. Like great Christian churches were built upon pagan holy grounds, Potsdamer Platz—with its corporate logos flying high and shiny above what was the Wall—trumpets the triumph of capitalism.

While Potsdamer Platz tries to give Berlin a common center, the city has always been—and remains—a collection of towns. Locals recognize 28 distinct neighborhoods that may have grown together but still maintain their historic orientation. While Munich has the single dominant Marienplatz, Berlin will always have Savignyplatz, Kreuzberg, Prenzlauer Berg, and so on. In general, Berliners prefer these characteristic neighborhoods to an official city center. They're unimpressed by the grandeur of Potsdamer Platz, and consider it simply a good place for movies, with overpriced, touristy restaurants.

While most of the complex just feels big (the arcade is like any huge, modern, American mall), the entrance to the complex and Sony Center are worth a visit, and German-film buffs will enjoy the Deutsche Kinemathek museum (described later).

For an overview of the new construction, and a scenic route to the Sony Center, start at the Bahnhof Potsdamer Platz (east end of Potsdamer Strasse, S- and U-Bahn: Potsdamer Platz, exit following *Leipziger Platz* signs to see the best view of skyscrapers as you emerge). Find the green hexagonal clock tower with the traffic lights on top. This is a replica of the first automatic traffic light in Europe, which once stood at the six-street intersection of Potsdamer Platz. On either side of Potsdamer Strasse, you'll see enormous cubical entrances to the new underground Potsdamer Platz train station. Near these entrances, notice the slanted glass cylinders sticking out of the ground. The mirrors on the tops of the tubes move with the sun to collect light and send it underground (saving piles of euros in energy costs). A line in the pavement indicates where the Berlin Wall once stood. Notice also the slabs of the Wall re-erected where the Wall once stood. Imagine when the first piece was cut out (see photo and history on nearby panel). These hang at the gate of Fort Capitalism...look up at the towering corporate headquarters: Market forces have won a clear victory. Now descend into one of the train station entrances and follow signs to *Sony Center*.

You'll come up the escalator into the **Sony Center** under a grand canopy (designed to evoke Mount Fuji). At night, multicolored floodlights play on the underside of this tent. Office workers and tourists eat here by the fountain, enjoying the parade of people. The modern Bavarian Lindenbräu beer hall—the Sony boss wanted a *Bräuhaus*—serves traditional food (€5–16, daily 11:00–24:00, big salads, three-foot-long taster boards of eight different beers, tel. 030/2575-1280). The adjacent Josty Bar is built around a surviving bit of a venerable hotel that was a meeting place for Berlin's rich and famous before the bombs (expensive, daily 10:00–24:00, tel. 030/2575-9702). CineStar is a rare cinema that plays mainstream movies in their original language (www .cinestar.de).

▲**Deutsche Kinemathek Film and TV Museum**—This exhibit is the most interesting place to visit in the Sony Center. Your admission ticket gets you into several floors of exhibits (third floor is permanent exhibits, first and fourth floor are temporary exhibits) made meaningful by the included (and essential) English audioguide. The film section takes you from the German film industry's beginnings, with emphasis on the Weimar Republic period in the 1920s, when Berlin rivaled Hollywood (*Metropolis* was a 1927 German production). Three rooms are dedicated to Marlene Dietrich, and another section features Nazi use of film as propaganda. The TV section tells the story of *das Booben Tube* from its infancy (when it was primarily used as a Nazi propaganda tool) to today. The 30-minute kaleidoscopic review—kind of a frantic fast-forward montage of greatest hits in German TV history—is great fun even if you don't understand a word of it (it plays all day long, with 10-minute breaks). Upstairs is a TV archive where you can dial through a wide range of new and classic German TV standards (€6, includes 90-min audioguide, Tue–Sun 10:00–18:00, Thu until 20:00, closed Mon, tel. 030/2474-9888). The Kino Arsenal theater downstairs shows offbeat artistic films in their original language.

Across Potsdamer Strasse, you can ride what's billed as "the fastest elevator in Europe" to skyscraping rooftop views at the **Panaromapunkt.** You'll travel at nearly 30 feet per second to the top of the 300-foot-tall Kollhoff Tower. Its sheltered but open-air view deck provides a fun opportunity to survey Berlin's ongoing construction from above (€3.50, daily 11:00–20:00, last lift at 19:30, closed Mon in winter, in red-brick building at Potsdamer Platz 1, tel. 030/2529-4372, www.panoramapunkt.de).

Kulturforum

Just west of Potsdamer Platz, with several top museums and Berlin's concert hall—home of the world-famous Berlin Philharmonic orchestra—is the city's cultural heart (admission to all Kulturforum sights covered by a single €8 "Standortkarte Kulturforum" combo-ticket or the Museumspass; phone number for all museums: tel. 030/266-2951). Of its sprawling museums, only the Gemäldegalerie is a must (S- or U-Bahn to Potsdamer Platz, then walk along Potsdamer Platz; or from Bahnhof Zoo, take bus #200 to Philharmonie).

▲▲▲**Gemäldegalerie**—Germany's top collection of 13th-through 18th-century European paintings (more than 1,400 canvases) is beautifully displayed in a building that's a work of art in itself. Follow the excellent free audioguide. The North Wing starts with German paintings of the 13th to 16th centuries, including eight by Albrecht Dürer. Then come the Dutch and Flemish—Jan van Eyck, Pieter Brueghel, Peter Paul Rubens, Anthony van Dyck, Frans Hals, and Jan Vermeer. The wing finishes with German, English, and French 18th-century art, such as Thomas Gainsborough and Antoine Watteau. An octagonal hall at the end features an impressive stash of Rembrandts. The South Wing is saved for the Italians—Giotto, Botticelli, Titian, Raphael, and Caravaggio (free Thu after 18:00, open Tue–Sun 10:00–18:00, Thu until 22:00, closed Mon, clever little loaner stools, great salad bar in cafeteria upstairs, Matthäikirchplatz 4).

New National Gallery (Neue Nationalgalerie)—This features 20th-century art, with ever-changing special exhibits (Tue–Fri 10:00–18:00, Thu until 22:00, Sat–Sun 11:00–18:00, closed Mon, café downstairs, Potsdamer Strasse 50).

Museum of Arts and Crafts (Kunstgewerbemuseum)—Wander through a thousand years of applied arts—porcelain, fine *Jugendstil* furniture, Art Deco, and reliquaries. There are no English descriptions and no crowds (Herbert-von-Karajan-Strasse 10).

▲Musical Instruments Museum (Musikinstrumenten Museum)—This impressive hall is filled with 600 exhibits from the 16th century to modern times. Wander among old keyboard instruments and funny-looking tubas. There's no English, aside from a €0.10 info sheet, but it's fascinating if you're into pianos (Tue–Fri 9:00–17:00, Thu until 22:00, Sat–Sun 10:00–17:00, closed Mon, low-profile white building east of the big, yellow Philharmonic Concert Hall, tel. 030/254-810).

Philharmonic Concert Hall—Poke into the lobby of Berlin's yellow Philharmonic building and see if there are tickets available during your stay (ticket office open Mon–Fri 15:00–18:00, Sat–Sun 11:00–14:00, must purchase tickets in person, box office tel. 030/2548-8132). You can often get inexpensive and legitimate tickets sold on the street before the performance. The interior is famous for its extraordinary acoustics. Even from the outside, this is a remarkable building, designed by a nautical engineer to look like a ship—notice how different it looks from each angle.

Western Berlin

Throughout the Cold War, Western travelers—and most West Berliners—got used to thinking of western Berlin's Kurfürstendamm boulevard as the heart of the city. But those days have gone the way of the Wall. With the huge changes the city has undergone since 1989, the real "city center" is now, once again, Berlin's historic center (the Mitte district, around Unter den Linden and Friedrichstrasse). While western Berlin has long had the best infrastructure to support your visit, and still works well as a home base, it's no longer the obvious base from which to explore Berlin. And after the new Hauptbahnhof essentially put the Bahnhof Zoo out of business in 2006, the area was left with an identity crisis. Now, almost 20 years after reunification, the west side is back and has fully embraced its historical role as a chic, classy suburb. There are a few interesting sights here, all within walking distance of Bahnhof Zoo and the Savignyplatz hotels.

For a detailed map of this area, see the Western Berlin map in the "Sleeping" section, later in this chapter.

▲**Kurfürstendamm**—Western Berlin's main drag, Kurfürstendamm boulevard (nicknamed "Ku'damm"), starts at Kaiser Wilhelm Memorial Church and does a commercial cancan for two miles. In the 1850s, when Berlin became a wealthy and important capital, her new rich chose Kurfürstendamm as their street. Bismarck made it Berlin's Champs-Elysées. In the 1920s, it became a chic and fashionable drag of cafés and boutiques. During the Third Reich, as home to an international community of diplomats and journalists, it enjoyed more freedom than the rest of Berlin. Throughout the Cold War, economic subsidies from the West made sure that capitalism thrived on Ku'damm. And today, while much of the old charm has been hamburgerized, Ku'damm is still a fine place to enjoy elegant shops (around Fasanenstrasse), department stores, and people-watching.

▲**Kaiser Wilhelm Memorial Church (Gedächtniskirche)**— This church was originally dedicated to the first emperor of Germany. Reliefs and mosaics show great events in the life of Germany's favorite *Kaiser,* from his coronation in 1871 to his death in 1888. The church's bombed-out ruins have been left standing as a memorial to the destruction of Berlin in World War II (free, Mon–Sat 10:00–16:00, closed Sun, Breitscheidplatz, S-Bahn: Zoologischer Garten or U-Bahn: Wittenbergplatz, www.gedaechtniskirche.com).

Under a Neo-Romanesque mosaic ceiling, a small exhibit features interesting photos about the bombing and before-and-after models of the church. As you enter the church, turn immediately right to find a simple charcoal sketch of the Virgin Mary wrapped in a shawl. During the Battle of Stalingrad, German combat surgeon Kurt Reuber rendered the Virgin on the back of a stolen Soviet map to comfort the men in his care. On the right are the words "Light, Life, Love" from the gospel of John; on the left, "Christmas in the cauldron 1942"; and at the bottom, "Fortress Stalingrad." Though Reuber died in captivity a year later, his sketch had been flown out of Stalingrad on the last medical evacuation flight, and post-war Germany embraced it as a symbol of the wish for peace. Copies of the drawing, now known as the *Stalingrad Madonna,* hang in the Berlin Cathedral, in England's Coventry, and in Russia's Volgograd (formerly Stalingrad), as a sign of reconciliation between the nations.

After the war, some Berliners wanted to tear down the church and build it anew. Instead, it was decided to keep the ruin as a memorial, and stage a competition to design a modern add-on section. The winning selection—the short, modern building (1961) next to the church—offers a world of 11,000 little blue windows (free, daily 9:00–19:00). The blue glass was given to the church by the French as a reconciliation gift. For more information on both churches, pick up the English booklet (€2.60).

The lively square between the churches and the Europa Center (a once-impressive, shiny high-rise shopping center built as a showcase of Western capitalism during the Cold War) usually attracts street musicians.

The Story of Berlin—Filling most of what seems like a department store right on Ku'damm (at #207), this sprawling history exhibit is a business venture making money by telling the stormy 800-year story of Berlin in a creative way. While there are almost no real historic artifacts, the exhibit does a good job of cobbling together many dimensions of the life and tumultuous times of this great city. However, for similar information, the German History Museum on Unter den Linden is a far better use of your time and money (see page 580).

▲**Käthe Kollwitz Museum**—This local artist (1867–1945), who experienced much of Berlin's stormiest century, conveys some powerful and mostly sad feelings about motherhood, war, and suffering through the stark faces of her art. This small yet fine collection (the only one in town of Kollwitz's work) consists of three floors of charcoal drawings, topped by an attic with a handful of sculptures (€5, €1 pamphlet has necessary English explanations of a few major works, daily 11:00–18:00, a block off Ku'damm at Fasanenstrasse 24, U-Bahn: Uhlandstrasse, tel. 030/882-5210, www.kaethe-kollwitz.de).

▲**Kaufhaus des Westens (KaDeWe)**—The "Department Store of the West" celebrated its 100th birthday in 2007. With a staff of 2,100 to help you sort through its vast selection of 380,000 items, KaDeWe claims to be the biggest department store on the Continent. You can get everything from a haircut and train ticket (basement) to souvenirs (third floor). The theater and concert box office on the sixth floor charges an 18 percent booking fee, but they know all your options (cash only). The sixth floor is a world of gourmet taste treats. The biggest selection of deli and exotic food in Germany offers plenty of classy opportunities to sit down and eat. Ride the glass elevator to the seventh floor's glass-domed Winter Garden self-service cafeteria—fun but pricey (Mon–Fri 10:00–20:00, Sat 9:30–20:00, closed Sun, S-Bahn: Zoologischer Garten or U-Bahn: Wittenbergplatz, tel. 030/21210, www.kadewe .de). The Wittenbergplatz U-Bahn station (in front of KaDeWe) is a unique opportunity to see an old-time station. Enjoy its interior.

Berlin Zoo (Zoologischer Garten Berlin)—More than 1,400 different kinds of animals call Berlin's famous zoo home...or so the zookeepers like to think. The recent big hit here is Knut, a young polar bear who first made headlines for being born in captivity, but quickly became an international star after he was abandoned by his mother and raised by zookeepers. Germans also enjoy seeing the pandas at play (straight in from the entrance). I enjoy seeing the Germans at play (€11 for zoo, €12 for world-class aquarium, €18 for both, children half-price, daily mid-March–mid-Oct generally 9:00–19:00, mid-Oct–mid-March generally 9:00–17:00, aquarium closes 30 min earlier; feeding times—*Fütterungszeiten*—posted on map just inside entrance, the best feeding show is the sea lions— generally at 15:30; enter near Europa Center in front of Hotel Palace or opposite Bahnhof Zoo on Hardenbergplatz, Budapester Strasse 34, tel. 030/254-010, www.zoo-berlin.de). Nearby, you may see construction underway for the "Great Berlin Wheel," a London Eye–esque Ferris wheel that will whisk visitors 610 feet above the city. Planned to be up and running in late 2010, it'll be the world's tallest—if Beijing, currently building a 680-foot wheel, doesn't finish first. Will Berlin meet its goal? Wheel see.

Erotic Art Museum—This offers two floors of graphic art (especially East Asian), old-time sex-toy knickknacks, and a special exhibit on the queen of German pornography, the late Beate Uhse. This amazing woman, a former test pilot for the Third Reich and groundbreaking purveyor of condoms and sex ed in the 1950s, was the female Hugh Hefner of Germany and CEO of a huge chain of porn shops. She is famously credited with bringing sex out of the bedroom, and onto the kitchen table (€6, Mon–Sat 9:00–24:00, Sun 13:00–24:00, last entry at 23:00, hard-to-beat gift shop, at corner of Kantstrasse and Joachimstalerstrasse, a block from Bahnhof Zoo, tel. 030/8862-6613). If you just want to see sex, you'll see much more for half the price in a private video booth next door.

Nightlife

Berlin is a happening place for nightlife—whether it's nightclubs, pubs, jazz music, cabaret, hokey-but-fun German variety shows, theater, or concerts.

Sources of Entertainment Info: *Berlin Programm* lists a non-stop parade of concerts, plays, exhibits, and cultural events (€2, in German, www.berlin-programm.de); *Exberliner Magazine* (€2, www.exberliner.com) and the TI-produced *Berlin To Go* (€1) have less information, but are in English (all sold at kiosks and TIs). For the young and determined sophisticate, *Zitty* and *Tip* are the top guides to alternative culture (in German, sold at kiosks). Also pick up the free schedules *Flyer* and *030* in bars and clubs.

Visit KaDeWe's ticket office for your music and theater options (sixth floor, 18 percent fee but access to all tickets; see page 599). Ask about "competitive improvisation" and variety shows.

Western Berlin Jazz—To enjoy live music near my recommended Savignyplatz hotels in western Berlin, consider **A Trane Jazz Club** (all jazz, great stage and intimate seating, €7–18 cover depending on act, opens at 21:00, live music nightly 22:00–2:00 in the morning, Bleibtreustrasse 1, tel. 030/313-2550) and **Quasimodo Live** (mix of jazz, rock, and blues, €5–12 cover, Tue–Sat from 22:00, closed Sun–Mon, Kantstrasse 12A, under Delphi Cinema, tel. 030/312-8086, www.quasimodo.de).

Berliner Rock and Roll—Berlin has a vibrant rock and pop scene, with popular venues at the Spandau Citadel and at the outdoor Waldbühne ("Woods Stage"). Check out what's playing on posters in the U-Bahn, in *Zitty*, or at any ticket agency. Great Berlin bands include Wir Sind Helden, The Beatsteaks, Jennifer Rostock, and the funky ska band Seeed.

Cabaret—Bar Jeder Vernunft offers modern-day cabaret a short walk from the recommended hotels in western Berlin. This variety show—under a classic old tent perched atop a modern parking lot—is a hit with German speakers, but can still be worthwhile for those who don't speak the language (as some of the music shows are in a sort of "Denglish"). Even some Americans perform here periodically. Tickets are generally about €20, and shows change regularly (performances start Mon–Sat at 20:30, Sun at 20:00, Wed is non-smoking, seating can be a bit cramped, south of Ku'damm at Schaperstrasse 24, tel. 030/883-1582, www.bar-jeder -vernunft.de).

German Variety Show—To spend an evening enjoying Europe's largest revue theater, consider Revue Berlin at the Friedrichstadt Palast. This super-kitschy German Moulin Rouge–type show basically depicts the history of Berlin, and is choreographed in a funny and musical way that's popular with the Lawrence Welk–type German crowd (€17–61, Tue–Sat 20:00, Sat–Sun also at 16:00, no shows Mon, U-Bahn: Oranienburger Tor, tel. 030/2326-2326, www.friedrichstadtpalast.de).

Nightclubs and Pubs—Oranienburger Strasse's trendy scene (page 590) is being eclipsed by the action at Friedrichshain (farther east). To the north, you'll find the hip Prenzlauer Berg neighborhood, packed with everything from smoky pubs to small art bars and dance clubs (best scene is around Helmholtsplatz, U-Bahn: Eberswalder Strasse; see page 591).

Dancing—Cut a rug at **Clärchens Ballhaus,** an old ballroom that's been a Berlin institution since 1913. At some point everyone in Berlin comes through here, as the dance hall attracts an eclectic Berlin-in-a-nutshell crowd of grannies, elegant women in evening dresses, yuppies, scenesters, and hippies. The music (swing, waltz, tango, or cha-cha) changes every day, with live music on Friday and Saturday (daily from 10:00 until the last person goes home, in the heart of the Auguststrasse gallery district at Auguststrasse 24, S-Bahn: Oranienburger Strasse, tel. 030/282-9295, www.ballhaus.de). Dancing lessons are also available (€8, Mon–Tue and Thu at 19:00, 90 min). The restaurant serves decent food and good pizzas.

Art Galleries—Berlin, a magnet for new artists, is a great city for gallery visits. Galleries—many of which stay open late—welcome visitors who are "just looking." The most famous gallery district is in eastern Berlin's Mitte neighborhood, along **Auguststrasse** (branches off from Oranienburger Strasse at the Tacheles building). Check out the Berlin outpost of the edgy-yet-accessible art of the New Leipzig movement at **Galerie Eigen+Art** (Tue–Sat 11:00–18:00, closed Sun–Mon, Auguststrasse 26, tel. 030/280-6605, www.eigen-art.com). The other gallery area is in western Berlin, along **Fasanenstrasse**.

Pub Crawls—Insider Tour and New Berlin Tours each offer €12 pub crawls (or, some would say, "pub brawls"). Insider Tour leaves at 20:30 from Hackescher Markt; New Berlin Tours leaves at 21:00 from the Oranienburger Strasse S-Bahn station. Those who show up early are treated to a warm-up keg. After the recent (unrelated) binge-drinking death of a German teenager, the tours enforce an 18-year-old minimum. A new marketing slogan for one organization: "Our mission: To show you Berlin's great nightlife...not to hospitalize you." Both tours generally visit four bars and two clubs, and provide a great way to get drunk with new English-speaking friends from around the world while getting a peek at Berlin's bar scene...or at least how its bars look when invaded by 50 loud tourists.

Sleeping

When in Berlin, I sleep in the former West, on or near Savignyplatz. While Bahnhof Zoo and Ku'damm are no longer the center of Berlin, the trains, TI, and walking tours are all still handy to the Zoo. And the streets around the tree-lined Savignyplatz (a 10-min walk behind the station) have a neighborhood charm. While towering new hotels are being built in the new center,

---

Sleep Code

(€1 = about $1.40, country code: 49, area code: 030)
S = Single, **D** = Double/Twin, **T** = Triple, **Q** = Quad, **b** = bathroom, **s** = shower only. Unless otherwise noted, credit cards are accepted, English is spoken, and breakfast is included.

To help you sort easily through these listings, I've divided the rooms into three categories, based on the price for a standard double room with bath:

$$$ Higher Priced—Most rooms €125 or more.
$$ Moderately Priced—Most rooms between €85–125.
$ Lower Priced—Most rooms €85 or less.

---

simple, small, friendly, good-value places abound here. My listings are generally located a couple of flights up in big, run-down buildings. Inside, they're clean, quiet, and spacious enough so that their well-worn character is actually charming. Rooms in back are on quiet courtyards.

For those interested in staying in a livelier, more colorful district, I've also listed some suggestions in eastern Berlin's youthful and increasingly popular Prenzlauer Berg neighborhood.

Berlin is packed and hotel prices go up on holidays, including Green Week in mid-January, Easter weekend, the first weekend in May, Ascension weekend in May, German Unity Day (Oct 3), Christmas, and New Year's. Keep in mind that many hotels have limited staff after 20:00, so if you're planning to arrive after that, let the hotel know in advance.

In Western Berlin: Near Savignyplatz and Bahnhof Zoo

These hotels and pensions are a 5- to 15-minute walk from Bahnhof Zoo and Savignyplatz (with S- and U-Bahn stations). Asking for a quieter room in back gets you away from any street noise. The area has an artsy charm going back to the cabaret days in the 1920s, when it was the center of Berlin's gay scene. Of the accommodations listed in this area, Pension Peters offers the best value for budget travelers.

$$$ Hotel Askanischerhof is the oldest B&B in Berlin, posh as can be with 16 sprawling, antique-furnished living rooms you can call home. Photos on the walls brag of famous movie-star guests. Frau Glinicke offers Old World service and classic Berlin atmosphere (Sb-€105, Db-€125, extra bed-€25, elevator, free parking, Ku'damm 53, tel. 030/881-8033, fax 030/881-7206, www.askanischer-hof.de, info@askanischer-hof.de).

Western Berlin

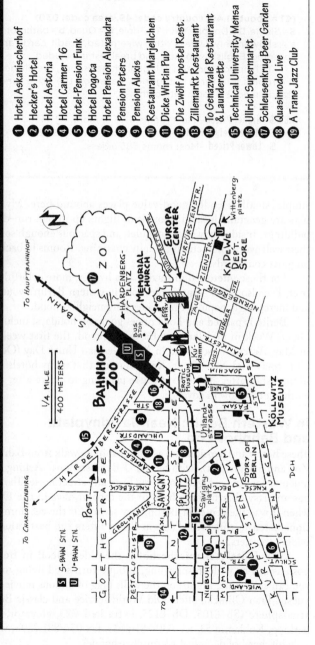

1 Hotel Askanischerhof
2 Hecker's Hotel
3 Hotel Astoria
4 Hotel Carmer 16
5 Hotel-Pension Funk
6 Hotel Bogota
7 Hotel Pension Alexandra
8 Pension Peters
9 Pension Alexis
10 Restaurant Marjellchen
11 Dicke Wirtin Pub
12 Die Zwölf Apostel Rest.
13 Zillemarkt Restaurant
14 To Genazvale Restaurant & Launderette
15 Technical University Mensa
16 Ullrich Supermarkt
17 Schleusenkrug Beer Garden
18 Quasimodo Live
19 A Trane Jazz Club

S S-BAHN STN
U U-BAHN STN

$$$ Hecker's Hotel is an ultra-modern, four-star business hotel with 69 rooms and all the sterile Euro-comforts (Sb-€125, Db-€150, all rooms €200 during conferences but generally only €100 July–Aug, breakfast-€15, non-smoking rooms, elevator, parking-€9–12/day, between Savignyplatz and Ku'damm at Grolmanstrasse 35, tel. 030/88900, fax 030/889-0260, www.heckers-hotel.com, info@heckers-hotel.com).

$$$ Hotel Astoria is a friendly, three-star, business-class hotel with 32 comfortably furnished rooms and affordable summer and weekend rates (high-season Db-€108–160; prices drop to Db-€70–94 during low season of July–Aug and Nov–Feb—check their website for deals; breakfast-€10 extra, non-smoking floors, elevator, Internet access, parking-€5/day, around corner from Bahnhof Zoo at Fasanenstrasse 2, tel. 030/312-4067, fax 030/312-5027, www.hotelastoria.de, info@hotelastoria.de).

$$ Hotel Carmer 16, with 30 bright and airy (if a bit dated) rooms, is both business-like and homey, and has an inviting lounge and charming balconies (Db-€93–160, ask for Rick Steves discount, extra person-€20, some rooms have balconies, elevator and a few stairs, Carmerstrasse 16, tel. 030/3110-0500, fax 030/3110-0510, www.hotel-carmer16.de, info@hotel-carmer16.de).

$$ Hotel-Pension Funk, the former home of a 1920s silent-movie star, is delightfully quirky. Kind manager Herr Michael Pfundt offers 14 elegant old rooms with rich Art Nouveau furnishings (S-€34–57, Ss-€41–75, Sb-€52–82, D-€62–82, Ds-€93, Db-€98–105, extra person-€23, cash preferred, a long block south of Ku'damm at Fasanenstrasse 69, tel. 030/882-7193, fax 030/883-3329, www.hotel-pensionfunk.de, berlin@hotel-pensionfunk.de).

$$ Hotel Bogota is a once-elegant old slumbermill renting 115 rooms in a sprawling old maze of a building that used to house the Nazi Chamber of Culture. Today, pieces of the owner's modern-art collection lurk around every corner (S-€44, Ss-€57, Sb-€72, D-€69, Ds-€77, Db-€98, extra bed-€22, children under 12 free, elevator, 10-min walk from Savignyplatz at Schlüterstrasse 45, tel. 030/881-5001, fax 030/883-5887, www.hotelbogota.de, hotel-bogota@t-online.de).

$$ Hotel Pension Alexandra has 11 pleasant rooms on a tree-lined street between Savignyplatz and Ku'damm. Expect the usual high ceilings and marble entryway found in these turn-of-the-century buildings, but with added touches—most rooms and the elegant breakfast room are decorated with original antique furniture (Ss-€69, Sb-€89, Ds-€95, Db-€105–120, lower prices off-season, extra bed-€35, Wielandstrasse 32, tel. 030/881-2107, fax 030/885-77818, www.hotelalexandra.de, info@hotelalexandra.de, Frau Kuhn and Mariane).

BERLIN

$ Pension Peters, run by a German-Swedish couple, is sunny and central, with a cheery breakfast room. Decorated sleek Scandinavian, with each of its 37 rooms renovated, it's a winner (S-€36, Ss-€47, Sb-€55, D-€51, Ds-€68, Db-€75–78, extra bed-€10, up to 2 kids under 13 free with 2 paying adults, family room, cash preferred, Internet access, 10 yards off Savignyplatz at Kantstrasse 146, tel. 030/3150-3944, fax 030/312-3519, www.pension-peters -berlin.de, info@pension-peters-berlin.de, Annika and Christoph). The same family also rents apartments in Prenzlauer Berg (ideal for small groups and longer stays; see Steiner Apartments, listed under "In Eastern Berlin," below).

$ Pension Alexis is a classic Old World four-room pension in a stately 19th-century apartment run by Frau and Herr Schwarzer (who speak just enough English). The shower and toilet facilities are old and cramped, but this, more than any other Berlin listing, has you feeling at home with a faraway grandmother (S-€43, D-€67, T-€97, Q-€128, 2-night minimum, cash only, big rooms, Carmerstrasse 15, tel. 030/312-5144).

In Eastern Berlin: Prenzlauer Berg

If you want to sleep in the former East Berlin, set your sights on the youthful, colorful, and fun Prenzlauer Berg district (or "Prenzl'berg" for short). After decades of neglect, this corner of the East has quickly come back to life. Gentrification has brought Prenzlauer Berg great hotels, tasty ethnic and German eateries (see "Eating—In Eastern Berlin"), and a happening nightlife scene. Think of all the graffiti as just some people's way of saying they care. The huge and impersonal concrete buildings are now enlivened with a street fair of fun little shops and eateries. Prenzlauer Berg is about a mile and a half north of Alexanderplatz, roughly between Kollwitzplatz and Helmholtzplatz, and to the west, along Kastanienallee (known affectionately as "Casting Alley" for its extra share of beautiful people). The closest U-Bahn stops are Senefelderplatz at the south end of the neighborhood and Eberswalder Strasse at the north end. Or, for less walking, take the S-Bahn to Hackescher Markt, then catch tram #M1 north.

$$$ Myer's Hotel is a boutique-hotel splurge renting 52 simple, small, but elegant rooms. The gorgeous public spaces include a patio and garden. Details done right and impeccable service set this place apart. This peaceful hub—off a quiet courtyard and tree-lined street, just a five-minute walk from Kollwitzplatz or the nearest U-Bahn stop (Senefelderplatz)—makes it hard to believe you're in a capital city (Sb-€79–139, Db-€99–189, price depends on size of room, Metzer Strasse 26, tel. 030/440-140, fax 030/4401-4104, www.myershotel.de, info@myershotel.de).

BERLIN

Prenzlauer Berg Neighborhood

FORMER COURSE OF WALL

Eberswalder Str.

STADIUM

ALLEE PAPPEL-

LYCHENER STR.

HELMHOLTZ-PLATZ

DUNCKER STR.

EBERSWALDER STR.

BERNAUER STR.

SCHWEDTER STR.

KASTANIEN ALLEE

ALLEE

DANZIGER STRASSE

SREDZKISTR.

STRASSE

ARKONA-PLATZ

CHORINER STRASSE

WEINBERGSWEG

WÖRTHER STR.

KOLLWITZ-PLATZ

HAUSER.

KOLLWITZ

STRASSE

MARIENBURG

STRASSE

WINSTRASSE

GREIFSWALDER STRASSE

PAST.

HUFE-

Rosenthaler Platz

BRUNN

METZER

PRENZLAUER

SCHÖN

Senefelder-platz

CEMETERY

TORSTR.

ROSEN.

LINIENSTR.

Rosa-Luxemburg-platz

PRENZ. BERG

AM FRIEDRICHS.

VOLKSPARK FRIEDRICHS-HAIN

FRIEDENSSTR.

Wein-meister-strasse

MÜNZSTR.

MOLLSTRASSE

LIEBKNECHTSTR.

ALEX.

BRAUNSTR.

ORANIEN.

DIRCKSEN

T.V. TOWER

KARL.

OTTO

KARL-MARX ALLEE

HACKESCHER MARKT

ALEXANDER-PLATZ

To UNTER DEN LINDEN

DCH

U U-BAHN STOP

S S-BAHN STOP

+ M-1 TRAM

400 YARDS

400 METERS

1. Myer's Hotel
2. Hotel Jurine
3. Hotel Kastanienhof
4. Hotel Transit Loft
5. EastSeven Hostel
6. Steiner Apartments
7. Gugelhof Restaurant
8. Metzer Eck
9. Prater Biergarten

10. Zum Schusterjungen Speisegaststätte & Launderette
11. La Bodeguita del Medio Cuban Bar Restaurant
12. Knoppke's Imbiss
13. Kauf Dich Glücklich
14. Walking Tour & Pub Crawl Departure Point
15. To Berlin Wall Documentation Center, Nordbahnhof S-Bahn & Natural History Museum

$$ Hotel Jurine (yoo-REEN) is a pleasant 53-room business-style hotel whose friendly staff aims to please. Enjoy the breakfast buffet surrounded by modern art, or relax in the lush backyard (Sb-€75, Db-€105, Tb-€135, extra bed-€37, prices can zoom up during conventions, check website for discounts in July–Aug, breakfast-€14, parking garage-€13/day, Schwedter Strasse 15, 10-min walk to U-Bahn: Senefelderplatz, tel. 030/443-2990, fax 030/4432-9999, www.hotel-jurine.de, mail@hotel-jurine.de).

$$ Hotel Kastanienhof is a basic, less-classy hotel offering 35 sleepable but slightly overpriced rooms (Sb-€79, Db-€105, reception closed 22:00–6:30, 40 yards from the M1 tram stop at Kastanienallee 65, tel. 030/443-050, fax 030/4430-5111, www.kastanienhof.biz, info@kastanienhof.biz).

$ Hotel Transit Loft is technically a hostel, but feels more like an upscale budget hotel. Located in a refurbished factory, it offers clean, bright, modern, new-feeling, mostly blue rooms with an industrial touch. The reception—staffed by friendly, hip Berliners—is open 24 hours, with a bar serving drinks all night long (4- to 6-bed dorms-€21/bed, Sb-€62, Db-€72, Tb-€96, includes sheets and breakfast, no age limit, cheap Internet access, fully wheelchair-accessible, Emmanuelkirchstrasse 14A, U-Bahn: Alexanderplatz then tram M4 to Hufelandstrasse and walk 50 yards, tel. 030/4849-3773, fax 030/4405-1074, www.transit-loft.de, loft@hotel-transit.de).

$ EastSeven Hostel rents the best cheap beds in Prenzlauer Berg. It's sleek and modern, with all the hostel services and more: 24-hour reception, inviting lounge, fully equipped guests' kitchen, lockers, garden, and bike rental. Children are welcome. While most hostels—especially in Prenzlauer Berg—are annoyingly youthful to people over 30, easygoing people of any age are comfortable here (S-€37, D-€50, T-€63, €17 for a bed in a 4-, 5-, or 6-bed dorm, bathrooms always down the hall, one-time €3 fee for sheets, free Internet access and Wi-Fi, laundry-€5, 100 yards from U-Bahn: Senefelderplatz at Schwedter Strasse 7, tel. 030/9362-2240, www.eastseven.de, info@eastseven.de).

$ Steiner Apartments, run by Pension Peters, are nine well-located, modern, and comfortable apartments near Hackescher Markt (Sb-€55, Db-€70, Tb-€80, Qb-€90, cash only, up to 2 children under 13 sleep free with 2 paying adults, fully equipped as if you live there, Linienstrasse 60—enter on Gormannstrasse, 350 yards from S-Bahn: Hackescher Markt, even closer to U-Bahn: Rosenthaler Platz, www.pension-peters-berlin.de, info@pension-peters-berlin.de; to book, contact Pension Peters, listed on page 606).

Hostels

Berlin is known among budget travelers for its fun, hip hostels. Here are some good bets. The first one is south of Bahnhof Zoo, the next two are in Prenzlauer Berg, and the last is in Friedrichshain.

$ Studentenhotel Meininger 10 (€14/bed in 8-bed dorms, D-€46, includes sheets, no curfew, elevator, free parking, near City Hall on JFK Platz, Meininger Strasse 10, a 200-yard walk from U-Bahn: Rathaus Schöneberg, tel. 030/7871-7414, www.meininger-hostels.de).

$ Circus is a brightly colored, well-run place with 230 beds, a Dylanesque ambience, and a bar downstairs (€18/bed in 4- to 8-bed dorms, S-€33, Sb-€46, D-€50, Db-€62, T-€63, Q-€76, 2-person apartment with kitchen-€77, 4-person apartment-€134, sheets-€2, breakfast-€5, no curfew, Internet access; U-Bahn: Rosenthaler Platz, Weinbergsweg 1a; tel. 030/2839-1433, www.circus-berlin.de, info@circus-berlin.de).

$ Mitte's Backpacker Hostel (€15/bed in 32-bed dorms, S-€30–35, D-€48–56, T-€63, Q-€80, sheets-€2.50, no breakfast, could be cleaner, no curfew, Internet access, English newspapers, laundry, bike rental, U-Bahn: Zinnowitzer Strasse, Chauseestrasse 102, tel. 030/2839-0965, fax 030/2839-0935, www.backpacker.de, reservation@backpacker.de).

$ Ostel is a fun, retro-1970s-DDR apartment building that recreates the lifestyle and interior design of a country relegated to the dustbin of history. All the furniture and room decorations have been meticulously collected and restored to their former social-ist glory—only the psychedelic wallpaper is a replica. Guests buy ration vouchers (€3.50 per person) for breakfast in the attached restaurant. Kitschy and tacky, sure—but also clean and memo-rable (€9 for a bed in a 4- or 6-bed "Pioneer Camp" room, S-€33, Sb-€40, D-€54, Db-€61, 4-person apartments-€120, Wi-Fi, free bike rental, free parking, free collective use of the people's own barbeque, right behind Ostbahnhof station on the corner of Strasse der Pariser Kommune at Wriezener Karree 5, tel. 030/2576-8660, www.ostel.eu, contact@ostel.eu).

BERLIN

Eating

Don't be too determined to eat "Berlin-style." The city is known only for its mildly spicy sausage. Still, there is a world of restaurants to choose from in this ever-changing city. Your best approach may be to select a neighborhood, rather than a particular restaurant.

Colorful pubs—called *Kneipen*—offer light, quick, and easy meals and the fizzy local beer, *Berliner Weiss*. Ask for it *mit Schuss* for a shot of fruity syrup in your suds. Germans—especially

Berliners—consider their food old-school; when they go out to eat, they're not usually looking for the "traditional local" fare many travelers are after. Nouveau German is California cuisine with scant memories of wurst, kraut, and pumpernickel. In 2008, Berlin banned smoking in restaurants.

If the kraut is getting the wurst of you, try one of the many Turkish, Italian, and Balkan restaurants. Eat cheap at *Imbiss* snack stands, bakeries (sandwiches), and falafel/kebab counters. Train stations have grocery stores, as well as bright and modern fruit-and-sandwich bars.

In Western Berlin
Near Savignyplatz
Many good restaurants are on or within 100 yards of Savignyplatz, near my recommended western Berlin hotels. Take a walk and survey these; continue your stroll along Bleibtreustrasse to discover many trendier, more creative little eateries.

Restaurant Marjellchen is a trip to East Prussia. Dine in a soft, jazzy elegance in one of two six-table rooms. While it doesn't have to be expensive (€25 for two courses), plan to go the whole nine yards here, as this can be a great Prussian experience with a great and caring service. The menu is inviting, and the Königsberg meatballs are the specialty. Reservations are smart (daily 17:00–23:30, family-run, Mommsenstrasse 9, tel. 030/883-2676).

Dicke Wirtin is a pub with traditional old-Berlin *Kneipe* atmosphere, six good beers on tap, and good, solid home cooking at reasonable prices—such as their famously cheap *Gulaschsuppe* (€3.40). Their interior is fun and pubby; their streetside tables are also inviting (€5 daily specials, open daily from 12:00 with dinner served from 18:00, just off Savignyplatz at Carmerstrasse 9, tel. 030/312-4952).

Die Zwölf Apostel ("The Twelve Apostles") is trendy for good Italian food. Choose between indoors with candlelit ambience, outdoors on a sun-dappled patio, or overlooking the people-parade on its pedestrian street. A dressy local crowd packs this restaurant for excellent €10 pizzas and €15–30 meals (open 24 hours daily, cash only, immediately across from Savignyplatz S-Bahn entrance, Bleibtreustrasse 49, tel. 030/312-1433).

Zillemarkt Restaurant, which feels like an old-time Berlin *Biergarten,* serves traditional Berlin specialties in the garden or in the rustic candlelit interior. Their *Berliner Allerlei* is a fun way to sample a bit of nearly everything (for a minimum of two people...but it can feed up to five). They have their own microbrew (€10 meals, daily 12:00–24:00, near the S-Bahn tracks at Bleibtreustrasse 48A, tel. 030/881-7040).

Genazvale ("Best Friends") serves traditional fare from the Republic of Georgia, and is popular with Berlin's immigrant Russian community. Sample some Georgian wines—virtually impossible to find in North America—and try their warm *catchapuri* (cheese bread) or a delicious plate of *chinkali* (cheese dumplings). The best way to enjoy Georgian food is to order several appetizers and split a main dish, which is usually grilled meat or stew (€8–15 main dishes, daily 17:00–23:00, live music and dancing on Georgian holidays, on the corner of Kantstrasse at Windscheidstrasse 14, tel. 030/4508-6026).

Technical University Mensa, a student cafeteria with impossibly cheap prices, puts you in a modern university scene with fine food and good indoor or streetside seating (€5 meals, Mon–Fri 11:00–15:30, closed Sat–Sun, general public entirely welcome, cheap coffee bar downstairs with Internet access, just north of Uhlandstrasse at Hardenbergstrasse 34).

Ullrich Supermarkt is the neighborhood grocery store (Mon–Sat 9:00–22:00, Sun 11:00–22:00, Kantstrasse 7, under the tracks near Bahnhof Zoo). There's plenty of fast food near Bahnhof Zoo and on Ku'damm.

Near Bahnhof Zoo

Schleusenkrug beer garden is hidden in the park between the Bahnhof Zoo and Tiergarten stations. Choose from an ever-changing self-service menu of huge salads, pasta, and some German dishes. English breakfast is served until 15:00 (€7–12 plates, €3–5 grill snacks, daily 10:00–24:00, Müller-Breslau-Strasse; standing in front of Bahnhof Zoo, turn left and follow the path into the park between the zoo and train tracks; tel. 030/313-9909).

Self-Service Cafeterias: The top floor of the famous department store, KaDeWe, holds the Winter Garden Buffet view cafeteria, and its sixth-floor deli/food department is a picnicker's nirvana. Its arterials are clogged with more than 1,000 kinds of sausage and 1,500 types of cheese (Mon–Fri 10:00–20:00, Sat 9:30–20:00, closed Sun, U-Bahn: Wittenbergplatz). Wertheim department store, a half block from Kaiser Wilhelm Memorial Church, has cheap food counters in the basement and a city view from its self-service cafeteria, Le Buffet, located up six banks of escalators (Mon–Sat 9:30–20:00, closed Sun, U-Bahn: Ku'damm). Marche, a chain that's popped up in big cities all over Germany, is another inexpensive, self-service cafeteria within a half-block of Kaiser Wilhelm Memorial Church (Mon–Thu 8:00–22:00, Fri–Sat 8:00–24:00, Sun 10:00–22:00, plenty of salads, fruit, made-to-order omelets, Ku'damm 14, tel. 030/882-7578).

BERLIN

In Eastern Berlin
Along Unter den Linden

These eateries are listed as you'll reach them as you walk along Unter den Linden from west to east.

At the Opera House (Opernpalais): The **Operncafé** is perhaps the classiest coffee stop in Berlin, with a selection of 50—count 'em: 50—different decadent desserts (daily 8:00–24:00, across from university and war memorial at Unter den Linden 5, tel. 030/202-683). The **Schinkel Klause Biergarten** serves good €9–14 meals on its shady terrace with a view of the Unter den Linden scene when sunny, or in its cellar otherwise (daily 11:30–24:00).

Near the Pergamon Museum: Georgenstrasse, a block behind the Pergamon Museum and under the S-Bahn tracks, is lined with fun eateries filling the arcade of the train trestle—close to the sightseeing action but in business mainly for students from nearby Humboldt University. **Deponie3** is a trendy Berlin *Kneipe* usually filled with students. Garden seating in the back is nice if you don't mind the noise of the S-Bahn passing directly above you. The interior is a cozy, wooden wonderland of a bar with several inviting spaces. They serve basic sandwiches, salads, traditional Berlin dishes, and hearty daily specials (€3–7 breakfasts, €5–11 lunches and dinners, open daily from 9:00, sometimes live music, Georgenstrasse 5, tel. 030/2016-5740). A branch of **Die Zwölf Apostel** is nearby (daily until 24:00, described earlier under "Near Savignyplatz").

In the Heart of Old Berlin's Nikolai Quarter: The *Nikolaiviertel* marks the original medieval settlement of Cölln, which would eventually become Berlin. The area was destroyed during the war, but rebuilt for Berlin's 750th birthday in 1987. The whole area has a cute, cobbled, and characteristic old town...Middle Ages meets Socialist Realism. Today, the district is pretty soulless by day, but is a popular restaurant zone at night. **Bräuhaus Georgbrau** is a thriving beer hall serving homemade suds on a picturesque courtyard overlooking the Spree River. Eat in the lively and woody but mod-feeling interior, or outdoors with fun riverside seating—thriving with German tourists. It's a good place to try one of the few typical Berlin dishes: *Eisbein* (boiled ham hock) with sauerkraut and mashed peas with bacon (€9.99 with a beer and schnapps). The statue of St. George once stood in the courtyard of Berlin's old castle—until the Nazis deemed it too decadent and not "German" enough, and removed it (cheap plates, three-foot-long sampler board with a dozen small glasses of beer, daily 10:00–24:00, 2 blocks south of Berlin Cathedral and across the river at Spreeufer 4, tel. 030/242-4244).

South of Unter den Linden, near Gendarmenmarkt

The twin churches of Gendarmenmarkt seem to be surrounded by people in love with food. The lunch and dinner scene is thriving with upscale restaurants serving good cuisine at highly competitive prices to local professionals. If in need of a quick-yet-classy lunch, stroll around the square and along Charlottenstrasse.

Lutter & Wegner Restaurant is well-known for its Austrian cuisine (*Schnitzel* and *Sauerbraten*) and popular with businesspeople. It's dressy, with fun sidewalk seating or a dark and elegant interior (two-course lunch with wine-€15 Mon–Fri, €20 Sat–Sun; fixed-price gourmet dinner-€34, daily 11:00–24:00, Charlottenstrasse 56, tel. 030/202-9540).

Maredo Argentine Steak Restaurant, a family-friendly chain restaurant, is generally a good value with a fine €6.20 salad bar that can make a healthy and cheap meal (behind French Cathedral at Gendarmenmarkt, at Charlottenstrasse 57, tel. 030/2094-5230).

Galeries Lafayette Food Circus is a festival of fun eateries in the basement of the landmark department store (Mon–Sat 10:00–20:00, closed Sun, U-Bahn: Französische Strasse).

Turkish and Bavarian Cuisine at Hackescher Markt

Hasir Turkish Restaurant is your chance to dine with candles, hardwood floors, and happy Berliners as snappy Turkish waiters bring plates piled high with meaty Anatolian specialties. As Berlin is one of the world's largest Turkish cities, it's no wonder you can find some good Turkish restaurants here. But while most locals think of Turkish food as fast and cheap, this is a dining experience. The restaurant, in a courtyard next to the Hackesche Höfe shopping complex, offers indoor and outdoor tables filled with an enthusiastic local crowd (€14 plates, huge and splittable portions, daily from 11:30 until late, a block from the Hackescher Markt S-Bahn station at Oranienburger Strasse 4, tel. 030/2804-1616).

Weihenstephaner Bavarian Restaurant serves upmarket Bavarian traditional food for around €15 a plate, offers an atmospheric cellar and a busy people-watching street-side terrace, and, of course, has excellent beer (daily 11:00–24:00, Neue Promenade 5 at Hackescher Markt, tel. 030/2576-2871).

In Prenzlauer Berg

Prenzlauer Berg is packed with fine restaurants—German, ethnic, and everything in between. (For more on this district, see page 591.) Before making a choice, I'd spend half an hour strolling and browsing through this bohemian wonderland of creative eateries. **Kollwitzplatz** is an especially good area to prowl for dinner—this square, home of the DDR student resistance in 1980s, is now trendy and upscale. With its leafy playground park in the center, it's a good place for up-market restaurants. Walk the square and choose. Just about every option offers sidewalk seats in the summer—these are great on a balmy evening. Nearby **Helmholtzplatz** (especially Lychener Strasse) is a somewhat younger, hipper, and edgier place to eat and drink.

Gugelhof, right on Kollwitzplatz, is the Prenzlauer Berg stop for visiting dignitaries. It's an institution famous for its Alsatian German cuisine. You'll enjoy French quality with German proportions. It's highly regarded with a boisterous and enthusiastic local crowd filling its minimalist yet classy interior (3-course-meal-€25, daily from 16:00, reservations required during peak times, where Knaackstrasse meets Kollwitzplatz, tel. 030/442-9229).

Metzer Eck is a time-warp *Kneipe* with a family tradition dating to 1913 and a cozy charm. It serves cheap basic typical Berlin food with Czech Budvar beer on tap (€5–7 meals, daily from 18:00, Metzer Strasse 33, on the corner of Metzer Strasse and Strassburger Strasse, tel. 030/442-7656).

Prater Biergarten offers two great eating opportunities: a rustic restaurant indoors and a mellow, shady, super-cheap, and family-friendly beer garden outdoors—each proudly pouring its own microbrew. In the beer garden—Berlin's oldest—you step up to the counter and order (simple €3–5 plates and an intriguing selection of beer munchies). The restaurant serves serious traditional *Biergarten* cuisine and good salads (€8–14 plates, Mon–Sat 18:00–24:00, Sun 12:00–24:00, cash only, Kastanienallee 7, tel. 030/448-5688).

Zum Schusterjungen Speisegaststätte ("The Cobbler's Apprentice") is a classic old-school, German-with-attitude eatery that retains its circa-1986 DDR decor. Famous for its schnitzel and filling €7–8 meals, it's a no-frills place with quality ingredients and a strong local following. It serves the eating needs of those Berliners lamenting the disappearance of solid traditional German cooking amid the flood of ethnic eateries (small 40-seat dining hall, daily 11:00–24:00, corner of Lychener Strasse and Danziger Strasse 9, tel. 030/442-7654).

La Bodeguita del Medio Cuban Bar Restaurant is purely fun-loving Cuba—Christmas lights, graffiti-caked walls, Che Guevara posters, animated staff, and an ambience that makes you want to dance. Come early to eat or late to drink. It seems the waiters know the regulars' drinks. This restaurant has been here for more than a decade—and in fast-changing Prenzlauer Berg, that's an eternity. Cuban ribs and salad for €7 is a hit (€4–10 tapas, struggle with a menu in German and Spanish, puff a Cuban cigar, daily 17:00–24:00, 1 block from U-Bahn: Eberswalder Strasse at Lychener Strasse 6, tel. 030/4171-4276).

Knoppke's Imbiss, a super-cheap German-style hot-dog

stand, has been a Berlin institution for over 70 years—it was family-owned even during DDR times. Berliners say Knoppke's cooks up the city's best *Currywurst* (grilled hot dog with curry-infused ketchup, €2). There are a few tables under a nearby tent for sit-down wurst-munching (Mon–Sat 6:00–20:00, closed Sun; Kastanienallee dead-ends at the elevated train tracks, and under them you'll find Knoppke's at Schönhauser Allee 44A). Don't be fooled by the Currystation at the foot of the stairs coming out of the station; Knoppke's is actually across the street, under the tracks.

For Dessert: **Kauf Dich Glücklich** makes a great capper to a Prenzlauer Berg dinner. It serves an enticing array of sweet Belgian waffles and ice cream in a candy-sprinkled, bohemian, retro setting under WWII bullet holes on a great Prenzlauer Berg street (daily until late, indoor and outdoor seating, Oderberger Strasse 44—it's the only un-renovated building on the street, tel. 030/4435-2182).

Connections

Trains

Berlin used to have several major train stations. But now that the Hauptbahnhof has emerged as the single, massive central station, all the others have wilted into glorified subway stations. Virtually every long-distance train passes through the Hauptbahnhof—ignore the other stations.

EurAide is an agent of the German Railroad that sells high-speed- and overnight-train reservations, with staff that can answer your travel questions in English (located in the Hauptbahnhof; see "Arrival in Berlin," near the beginning of this chapter).

From Berlin by Train to: Dresden (every 2 hrs, more with a transfer in Leipzig, 2.25 hrs), **Frankfurt** (hourly, 4 hrs), **Bacharach** (hourly, 5.5–6.5 hrs, 1–3 changes), **Würzburg** (hourly, 4 hrs, 1 change in Fulda or Hannover), **Nürnberg** (hourly, 4.5 hrs), **Munich** (hourly, 5.75–6.25 hrs), **Köln** (hourly, 4.5 hrs), **Amsterdam** (3/day direct, 3 more with change in Duisberg, 6.5 hrs), **Budapest** (3/day, 13 hrs; these go via Czech Republic and Slovakia, where Eurailpass is not valid, for an overnight you need to go to Vienna and then change), **Copenhagen** (5/day, 6.5 hrs, reservation required, change in Hamburg; also consider the direct overnight train-plus-ferry route to Malmö, Sweden, which is just 20 min from Copenhagen—covered by a railpass that includes Germany or Sweden), **London** (5/day, 10–11.5 hrs, 2 changes—but you're better off flying cheap on easyJet or Air Berlin, even if you have a railpass—see next page), **Paris** (9/day, 8–9 hrs, 1–2 changes, 1 direct 12-hr night train, many connections go via Belgium), **Zürich** (hourly, 8.5 hrs, 1 direct 12-hr night train), **Prague** (6/day, 4.5–5 hrs, no overnight trains), **Warsaw** (3/day, 6 hrs, 1 night

BERLIN

train; reservations required on all Warsaw-bound trains), **Kraków** (1/day direct, 2 more with transfer in Warsaw, 10 hrs, 1 night train), **Vienna** (8/day, most with 1 change, 9.5 hrs, some via Czech Republic—for second-class ticket, Eurailers pay an extra €40; the Berlin–Vienna via Passau train avoids Czech Republic—nightly at 20:55—as do connections with a change in Nürnberg or Munich). It's wise but not required to reserve in advance for trains to or from Amsterdam or Prague. Train info: tel. 11861 (€0.60/min). Before buying a ticket for any long train ride from Berlin (over 7 hours), consider taking a cheap flight instead (buy it well in advance to get a super fare).

Eurailpasses don't cover the Czech Republic, so if you're headed to Prague you need to buy a ticket for the Czech portion of the trip. You can either buy that in the station before leaving Berlin (€14), or save about €5 by buying it directly from the Czech conductor. (German stations charge twice what Czechs do for Czech tickets; note that you can only buy tickets on board on long-distance trains—if you go to Prague indirectly via a milk-run train, you can be fined heavily for boarding without a ticket.)

There are **night trains** from Berlin to these cities: Munich, Frankfurt, Köln, Brussels, Paris, Vienna, Kraków, Warsaw, Malmö, Basel, and Zürich. There are no night trains from Berlin to anywhere in Italy or Spain. A *Liegeplatz*, or *couchette* berth (€13–36), is a great deal; inquire at EurAide at the Hauptbahnhof for details. Beds generally cost the same whether you have a first- or second-class ticket or railpass. Trains are often full, so reserve your *couchette* a few days in advance from any travel agency or major train station in Europe.

The **Berlin–Paris night train** goes through Belgium. If you're using a railpass, either the pass must include Benelux, or you'll have to pay extra for the Belgian segment of the trip (roughly €50 in second class).

Berlin's Two Airports

Tegel Airport handles most flights from the United States and Western Europe (4 miles from center, no subway trains, catch the faster bus #X9 to Bahnhof Zoo, or bus #109 to Ku'damm and Bahnhof Zoo for €2.10; bus #TXL goes between Tegel Airport, the Hauptbahnhof, and Alexanderplatz in eastern Berlin; taxi from Tegel Airport costs €15 to Bahnhof Zoo, €25 to Alexanderplatz). Flights from the east and discount airlines usually arrive at **Schönefeld Airport** (12.5 miles from center, 3-min walk to S-Bahn station where you catch the regional express train into the city—going direct to Savignyplatz, Hauptbahnhof, and Hackescher Markt, railpass valid, taxi €35 to city center). The central telephone number for both airports is 01805-000-186. For

British Air, tel. 01805-266-522; Delta, tel. 01803-337-880; SAS, tel. 01805-117-002; Lufthansa, tel. 01803-803-803.

Berlin, the New Discount Airline Hub: Berlin's Schönefeld Airport is now the Continental European hub for discount airlines such as easyJet (with lots of flights to Spain, Italy, Eastern Europe, the Baltics, and more—book long in advance to get the incredible €30-and-less fares, www.easyjet.com). Ryanair (www.ryanair .com) and Air Berlin (www.airberlin.com) are also making the London–Berlin trip (and other routes) dirt-cheap, so consider this option before booking an overnight train. Consequently, British visitors to the city are now outnumbered only by Americans.

BERLIN

British Air, tel. 01805-266-522; Delta, tel. 01803-337-880; SAS, tel. 01805-117-002; Lufthansa, tel. 01803-803-803.

Berlin, the New Discount Airline Hub: Berlin's Schönefeld Airport is now the Continental European hub for discount airlines such as easyJet (with lots of flights to Spain, Italy, Eastern Europe, the Baltics, and more—book long in advance to get the incredible €30 and-less fares. www.easyjet.com), Ryanair (www.ryanair.com) and Air Berlin (www.airberlin.com) are also making the London–Berlin trip (and other routes) dirt-cheap, so consider this option before booking an overnight train. Consequently, British visitors to the city are now outnumbered only by Americans.

GREAT
BRITAIN

LONDON

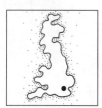

London is more than 600 square miles of urban jungle. With eight million people—who don't all speak English—it's a world in itself and a barrage on all the senses. On my first visit I felt extremely small.

London is more than its museums and landmarks. It's a living, breathing, thriving organism...a coral reef of humanity. The city has changed dramatically in recent years, and many visitors are surprised to find how "un-English" it is. White people are now a minority in major parts of the city that once symbolized white imperialism. Arabs have nearly bought out the area north of Hyde Park. Chinese take-outs outnumber fish-and-chips shops. Eastern Europeans pull pints in British pubs. Many hotels are run by people with foreign accents (who hire English chambermaids), while outlying suburbs are home to huge communities of Indians and Pakistanis. It's a city of eight million separate dreams, inhabiting a place that tolerates and encourages them. With the English Channel Tunnel making travel between Britain and the Continent easier than ever, many locals see even more holes in their bastion of Britishness. London is learning—sometimes fitfully—to live as a microcosm of its formerly vast empire.

With just a few days here, you'll get no more than a quick splash in this teeming human tidal pool. But with a good orientation, you'll find London manageable and fun. You'll get a sampling of the city's top sights, history, and cultural entertainment, and a good look at its ever-changing human face.

Blow through the city on the open deck of a double-decker orientation tour bus, and take a pinch-me-I'm-in-London walk through the West End. Ogle the crown jewels at the Tower

London's Neighborhoods

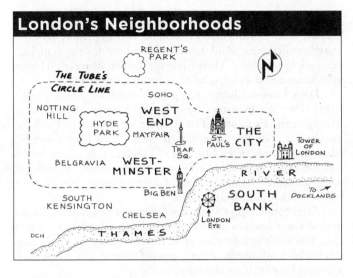

of London, hear the chimes of Big Ben, and see the Houses of Parliament in action. Cruise the Thames River, and take a spin on the London Eye. Hobnob with the tombstones in Westminster Abbey, and visit with Leonardo, Botticelli, and Rembrandt in the National Gallery. Enjoy Shakespeare in a replica of the Globe Theatre, then marvel at a glitzy, fun musical at a modern-day theater. Whisper across the dome of St. Paul's Cathedral, and rummage through our civilization's attic at the British Museum. And sip your tea with pinky raised and clotted cream dribbling down your scone.

Planning Your Time

The sights of London alone could easily fill a trip to Britain. It's worth at least four busy days. If you're flying in, consider starting your trip in Bath and making London your British finale. Especially if you hope to enjoy a play or concert, a night or two of jet lag is bad news.

Here's a suggested schedule:

Day 1: 9:00—Tower of London (crown jewels first, then Beefeater tour, then White Tower); 12:00—Munch a sandwich on the Thames while cruising from the Tower to Westminster Bridge; 13:00—Follow the self-guided Westminster Walk (see page 640) with a quick visit to the Churchill Museum and Cabinet War Rooms; 15:30—Trafalgar Square and National Gallery; 17:30—Visit the Britain and London Visitors Centre near Piccadilly, planning ahead for your trip; 18:30—Dinner in Soho. Take in a play or 19:30 concert at St. Martin-in-the-Fields.

Day 2: 9:00—Take a double-decker hop-on, hop-off bus

tour (start at Victoria Street and hop off for the Changing of the Guard); 11:30–Buckingham Palace (guards change most days, but worth confirming); 13:00–Covent Garden for lunch, shopping, and people-watching; 14:30–Tour the British Museum. Have a pub dinner before a play, concert, or evening walking tour.

Days 3 and 4: Choose among these remaining London high-lights: Tour Westminster Abbey, British Library, Imperial War Museum, the two Tates (Tate Modern on the South Bank for modern art, Tate Britain on the North Bank for British art), St. Paul's Cathedral, or the Museum of London; take a spin on the London Eye or a cruise to Greenwich; do some serious shopping at one of London's elegant department stores or open-air markets; or take another historic walking tour.

After considering London's major tourist destinations, I have pruned them down to just the most important (or fun) for a first visit. You won't be able to see all of these, so don't try. You'll keep coming back to London. After dozens of visits myself, I still enjoy a healthy list of excuses to return.

Orientation

(area code: 020)

To grasp London more comfortably, see it as the old town in the city center without the modern, congested sprawl. The Thames River runs roughly west to east through the city, with most of the visitor's sights on the North Bank. Mentally, maybe even physi-cally with a pair of scissors, trim down your map to include only the area between the Tower of London (to the east), Hyde Park (west), Regent's Park (north), and the South Bank (south). This is roughly the area bordered by the Tube's Circle Line. This three-mile stretch between the Tower and Hyde Park (about a 90-min walk) looks like a milk bottle on its side (see map opposite), and holds 80 percent of the sights mentioned in this chapter.

London is a collection of neighborhoods:

The City: Shakespeare's London was a walled town clustered around St. Paul's Cathedral. Today, The City is the modern finan-cial district.

Westminster: This neighborhood includes Big Ben, Parliament, the Churchill Museum and Cabinet War Rooms, Westminster Abbey, and Buckingham Palace, the grand govern-ment buildings from which Britain is ruled.

The West End: Lying between Westminster and The City (that is, at the "west end" of the original walled town), this is the center of London's cultural life. Trafalgar Square has major muse-ums. Piccadilly Circus and Leicester Square host tourist traps,

Greater London

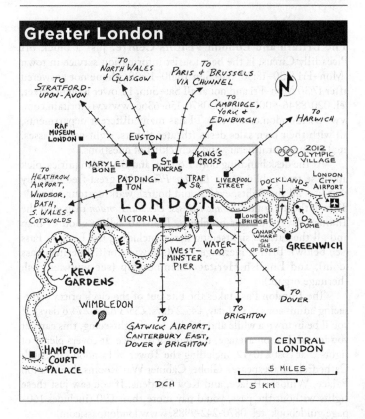

To NORTH WALES & GLASGOW

To PARIS & BRUSSELS VIA CHUNNEL

To STRATFORD-UPON-AVON

To CAMBRIDGE, YORK & EDINBURGH

To HARWICH

RAF MUSEUM LONDON

EUSTON

St. PANCRAS

KING'S CROSS

2012 OLYMPIC VILLAGE

MARYLE-BONE

To HEATHROW AIRPORT, WINDSOR, BATH, S. WALES & COTSWOLDS

PADDING-TON

TRAF. SQ.

LIVERPOOL STREET

DOCKLANDS

LONDON CITY AIRPORT

LONDON

VICTORIA

LONDON BRIDGE

O2 DOME

THAMES

WEST-MINSTER PIER

WATER-LOO

CANARY WHARF on ISLE OF DOGS

GREENWICH

KEW GARDENS

WIMBLEDON

To GATWICK AIRPORT, CANTERBURY EAST, DOVER & BRIGHTON

To BRIGHTON

To DOVER

HAMPTON COURT PALACE

DCH

CENTRAL LONDON

5 MILES

5 KM

cinemas, and nighttime glitz. Soho and Covent Garden are thriving people zones housing theaters, restaurants, pubs, and boutiques.

The South Bank: The entire south bank of the Thames River used to be a run-down, generally ignored area, but now it's the hottest real estate in town, with upscale restaurants, major new sightseeing attractions, and pedestrian bridges allowing easy access from the rest of London.

Residential Neighborhoods to the West: Though they lack major tourist sights, the neighborhoods of Mayfair, South Kensington, Notting Hill, Chelsea, and Belgravia are home to the city's wealthy and trendy, as well as to many shopping streets and enticing restaurants.

The Docklands and the East End: London's new Manhattan has sprung up far to the east, around Canary Wharf. Energized by big businesses migrating here from the old center of town, and selected as the site for much of the 2012 Olympics, the Docklands and the East End are fast becoming an essential part of any London visit.

LONDON

Tourist Information

The Britain and London Visitors Centre, just a block off Piccadilly Circus, is the best tourist information service in town (Mon–Fri 9:30–18:30, Sat–Sun 10:00–16:00, phone not answered after 17:30 Mon–Fri and not at all Sat–Sun, 1 Lower Regent Street, tel. 020/8846-9000, toll tel. 0870-156-6366, www.visitbritain.com, www.visitlondon.com). This TI has many different departments, all with their own sales desks (theater tickets, sightseeing passes, etc.). Bring your itinerary and a checklist of questions.

At the desk handling both London and Britain inquiries, pick up these free publications: *London Planner* (a great free monthly that lists all the sights, events, and hours), walking-tour schedule fliers, a theater guide, *London Buses: Central London* map, and the Thames River Services brochure. The staff sells a good £1 map and all the various sightseeing deals, including the London Pass (see below), British Heritage Pass (see www.britishheritagepass .com), and English Heritage membership (see www.english -heritage.org.uk).

The **London Pass** takes the bite out of the city's pricey sightseeing admissions (£32/1 day, £45/2 days, £55/3 days, £74/6 days). If you'll be in town a while and doing a lot of sightseeing, this can get you into sights, on average, for about half-price. It covers plenty of sights that cost £10–12, including the Tower of London, St. Paul's Cathedral, Shakespeare's Globe, Cabinet War Rooms, Kensington Palace, Windsor Palace, and Kew Gardens. If you saw just these sights without the pass, you'd pay more than £90 (includes 160-page guidebook, tel. 0870-242-9988, www.londonpass.com).

The entertainment desk to the left of the pink desk sells tickets to plays (20 percent booking fee), plus long-distance bus tickets and passes, train tickets (convenient for reservations), and Fast Track tickets to some of London's attractions. The Fast Track tickets, which allow you to skip the queue at the sights at no extra cost, are worthwhile for places that sometimes have long ticket lines, such as the Tower of London, the London Eye, and Madame Tussauds Waxworks. (If you'll be going to the Waxworks, buy tickets here, since—at £20—they're cheaper than at the sight itself.) There's also a Rail Europe section handling train rides or train passes on the Continent.

After grazing through the great leaflet racks, head upstairs for more brochures, Internet access (£1/15 min), and comfy chairs where you can read or get organized. While the Visitors Centre books rooms, you can avoid their £5 booking fee by calling hotels direct (see "Sleeping," later in this chapter).

If you visit only one TI, make it this one, the Britain and London Visitors Centre. Unfortunately, London's Tourist Information Centres (which represent themselves as TIs at major train and bus stations and airports) are now simply businesses selling advertising space to companies with fliers to distribute.

Arrival in London

By Train: London has nine train stations, all connected by the Tube (subway) and all with ATMs, exchange offices, and luggage storage. From any station, ride the Tube or taxi to your hotel.

By Bus: The bus ("coach") station is one block southwest of Victoria Station (which has a TI and a Tube entrance).

By Plane: For detailed information on getting from London's airports to downtown London, see "Connections," near the end of this chapter.

Helpful Hints

Theft Alert: The Artful Dodger is alive and well in London. Be on guard, particularly on public transportation and in places crowded with tourists. Tourists, considered naive and rich, are targeted. More than 7,500 handbags are stolen annually at Covent Garden alone. Wear your money belt.

Pedestrian Safety: Cars drive on the left side of the road, so before crossing a street, I always look right, look left, then look right again just to be sure. Many crosswalks are even painted with instructions, reminding their foreign guests to "Look right" or "Look left."

Medical Problems: Local hospitals have 24-hour-a-day emergency care centers where any tourist who needs help can drop in and, after a wait, be seen by a doctor. Your hotel has details. St. Thomas' Hospital, immediately across the river from Big Ben, has a fine reputation.

Internet Access: The **easyInternetcafé** chain offers hundreds of computers per store (generally daily 8:00–22:00, £2/hr, £3.50/24 hrs). You'll find branches at Trafalgar Square (456 Strand), Bayswater (Queensway, second floor of Whiteley's Shopping Centre), Oxford Street (#358, opposite Bond Street Tube station), and Kensington High Street (#160–166).

Travel Bookstores: Located in Covent Garden, **Stanfords Travel Bookstore** is good, and stocks my latest titles (Mon, Wed, and Fri 9:00–19:30, Tue 9:30–19:30, Thu 9:00–20:00, Sat 10:00–19:00, Sun 12:00–18:00, 12–14 Long Acre, Tube: Covent Garden, tel. 020/7836-1321, www.stanfords.co.uk).

Two impressive **Waterstone's** bookstores have the biggest collection of travel guides in town: on Piccadilly (Mon–Sat 10:00–22:00, Sun 12:00–18:00, 203 Piccadilly, tel. 020/7851-2400) and on Trafalgar Square (Mon–Sat 9:30–21:00, Sun 12:00–18:00, with Costa Café on second floor, tel. 020/7839-4411).

Affording London's Sights

London is, in many ways, Europe's most expensive city, with the dubious distinction of having some of the world's most expensive admission prices. Fortunately, many of its best sights are free.

Free Museums: Many of the city's biggest and best museums won't cost you a dime. Free sights include the British Museum, British Library, National Gallery, National Portrait Gallery, Tate Britain, Tate Modern, Wallace Collection, Imperial War Museum, Victoria and Albert Museum, Natural History Museum, Science Museum, National Army Museum, Sir John Soane's Museum, the Museum of London, and on the outskirts of town, the Royal Air Force Museum London.

Several museums, such as the British Museum, request a donation of a few pounds, but whether you contribute or not is up to you. If I spend money for an audioguide, I feel fine about not otherwise donating. If that makes you uncomfortable, give £1.

Free Churches: Smaller churches let worshippers (and tourists) in free. The big sightseeing churches—Westminster Abbey and St. Paul's—charge steep admission fees, but offer free evensong services daily. Westminster Abbey offers free organ recitals most Sundays at 17:45. At St. Paul's, admission is half-price if you go after 15:30 (but does not include dome).

Other Freebies: There are plenty of free performances, such as lunch concerts at St. Martin-in-the-Fields (see page 648) and summertime movies at The Scoop amphitheater near City Hall (Tube: London Bridge, schedule at www.morelondon.com—click on "The Scoop"). There's no charge to enjoy the pageantry of the Changing of the Guard, rants at Speaker's Corner in Hyde Park, displays at Harrods, and the people-watching scene at Covent Garden. It's free to view the legal action at Old Bailey and the legislature at work in the Houses of Parliament. And you can get into a bit of the Tower of London by attending Sunday services in the Tower's chapel (chapel access only).

Good-Value Tours: The £7 city walking tours with professional guides are one of the best deals going. And with the new free walking tours, you always get at least your money's worth. Hop-on, hop-off big-bus tours (£19–24), while expensive,

Baggage Storage: Train stations have replaced their lockers with more-secure left-luggage counters. Each bag must go through a scanner (just like at the airport), so lines can be long. Expect long waits in the morning to check in (up to 45 min) and in the afternoon to pick up (each item-£6.50/24 hours, daily 7:00–24:00). You can also store bags at the airports (£5/day). If leaving London and returning later, you may be able to leave a box or bag at your hotel for free—assuming you'll be staying there again.

provide a great overview, and include free boat tours as well as city walks. A one-hour Thames ride costs £7.20 one-way, but generally comes with an entertaining commentary. A three-hour bicycle tour is about £15–18.

Pricey...But Worth It? Big-ticket sights worth their admission fees are Kew Gardens (£13), Shakespeare's Globe Theatre (£10.50), and the Cabinet War Rooms, with its fine Churchill Museum (£12). The London Eye is becoming a London must-see (£15.50), and the Vinopolis wine museum provides a classy way to get a buzz and call it museum-going (£19.50 entry includes five small glasses of wine).

While Kensington Palace (£12.30) and Hampton Court Palace (£13) are expensive, they are well-presented and a reasonable value if you have a real interest in royal history. The Queen charges big time to open her palace to the public: Buckingham Palace (£15.50, Aug–Sept only) and her art gallery and carriage museum (adjacent to the palace, about £8 each) are expensive but interesting. Madame Tussauds Waxworks is pricey but still fun and popular (£25, but £16 after 17:00).

Many smaller museums cost only around £5. My favorites include the Courtauld Gallery (free on Mon until 14:00) and the Wellington Museum at Apsley House (£5.50).

Not Worth It: Gimmicky, overpriced, bad-value enterprises include the London Dungeon (£20) and the Dalí Universe (great location next to the popular London Eye, but for £12, skip it).

Theater: Compared with Broadway's prices, London theater is a bargain. Seek out the freestanding "tkts" booth at Leicester Square to get discounts from 25–50 percent (though not necessarily for the hottest shows; see page 673). A £5 "groundling" ticket for a play at Shakespeare's Globe is the best theater deal in town (see page 668). Tickets to the Open Air Theatre at north London's Regent's Park start at £10 (see page 674).

These days, London doesn't come cheap. But with its many free museums and affordable plays, this cosmopolitan, cultured city offers days of sightseeing thrills without requiring you to pinch your pennies (or your pounds).

LONDON

Time Zone Difference: Remember that Britain is one hour earlier than most of continental Europe.

Getting Around London

To travel smart in a city this size, you must get comfortable with public transportation. London's excellent taxis, buses, and subway (Tube) system make a private car unnecessary. An £8 congestion charge levied on any private car entering the city center has been effective in cutting down traffic jam delays and bolstering London's public transit. The revenue raised subsidizes the buses, which are now cheaper, more frequent, and even more user-friendly than before. Today, the vast majority of vehicles in the city center are buses, taxis, and service trucks. (Drivers: For all the details on the congestion charge, see www.cclondon.com.)

By Tube

London's subway system (called the Tube or Underground, but never "subway," which refers to a pedestrian underpass) is one of this planet's great people-movers, and often the fastest long-distance transport in town (runs Mon–Sat about 5:00–24:00, Sun about 7:00–23:00).

Start by studying a Tube map (free at any Tube station, and included with most London maps). Each line has a name (such as Circle, Northern, or Bakerloo) and two directions (indicated by the end-of-the-line stops). Find the line that will take you to your destination, and figure out roughly what direction (north, south, east, or west) you'll need to go to get there.

You can use paper tickets, Travelcards, or an Oyster card to pay for your journey (see sidebar on page 630). At the Tube station, feed your paper ticket or Travelcard into the turnstile, reclaim it, and hang on to it—you'll need it to get through the turnstile at the end of your journey. If using a plastic Oyster card, touch the card to the yellow card reader when you enter and exit the station.

Find your train by following signs to your line and the (general) direction it's headed (such as Central Line: east). Since some tracks are shared by several lines, you'll need to double-check before boarding a train: First, make sure your destination is one of the stops listed on the sign at the platform. Also, check the electronic signboards that announce which train is next, and make sure the destination (the end-of-the-line stop) is the one you want. Some trains, particularly on the Circle and District lines, split off for other directions, but each train has its final destination marked above its windshield. When in doubt, ask a local or a blue-vested staff person for help.

Trains run roughly every 3–10 minutes. If one train is absolutely packed and you notice another to the same destination is coming in three minutes, you can wait to avoid the sardine experience. The system can be fraught with construction delays and breakdowns, so pay attention to signs and announcements explaining necessary detours. The Circle Line is notorious for problems. Rush hours (8:00–10:00 and 16:00–19:00) can be packed and sweaty. Bring something to do to make your waiting time productive. If you get confused, ask for advice at the information window located before the turnstile entry.

Remember that you can't leave the system without feeding

London

Oyster Cards and Travelcards

London has the most expensive public transit in the world—you will definitely save money on your Tube and bus rides using a multi-ride pass. There are two similar but distinct options: Oyster cards and Travelcards (details online at www.tfl.gov.uk, click "Tickets"). As a bonus, you can use either type of card to get a 33 percent discount on most Thames cruises.

Oyster Cards

Oyster cards are the standard, smart way to economically ride the Tube, buses, and Docklands Light Railway (DLR). You buy a plastic card (embedded with a computer chip) and prepay for fare credit. Fares are automatically deducted each time you travel. On each type of transport, you simply touch the card to the yellow card reader at the turnstile/entrance, it flashes green, and you've paid your fare. (You'll need the card to exit the Tube and DLR turnstiles, but not to exit buses.)

With an Oyster card you'll pay only £1.50–2 per ride on the Tube (in Zones 1–6 off-peak) instead of £4 per ride with a full-fare ticket. For the bus, it's £1 versus £2. A price cap guarantees you'll never pay more than the One-Day Travelcard price within a 24-hour period (see "One-Day Travelcard," opposite page). An Oyster card is worth considering if you'll be in London for even a few days, and is especially handy if you're not sure you'll ride enough each day to justify a Travelcard. Buy Oyster cards at ticket offices in Tube stations.

With the standard **pay-as-you-go Oyster card,** you load up your Oyster with however much credit you want (there's no minimum, but I recommend starting with £10). When your balance gets low, add another £5 or £10 (at a ticket window or machine) to keep riding. To see how much credit remains on your card, swipe it at any automatic ticket machine. You can also see a record of all your travels (and what you paid). Try it. Pay-as-you-go Oyster balances never expire (though they need reactivating every two years); you can use the card whenever you're in London, or lend it to someone else. The only downside is that you pay a £3 one-time refundable deposit for the card itself (you can turn in your card for the £3 refund at any ticket window, but allow 20 minutes for the process).

The **Seven-Day Oyster card** is another good possibility to consider, even for a visit as short as four days. The least expensive version is £25.80, and covers unlimited peak-time travel through Zones 1 and 2 (no deposit required, cards covering more zones are also available).

Travelcards

A paper Travelcard works like a traditional ticket: You buy it at any Tube station ticket window or machine, then feed it into a turnstile (and retrieve it) to enter and exit the Tube. On a bus, just show it to the driver when you get on. If you take at least two rides a day, a Travelcard is a better deal than buying individual tickets. Like the Oyster card, Travelcards are valid on the Tube, buses, and Docklands Light Railway. The following fares are for Zones 1 and 2; pricier versions covering more zones are also available.

The **One-Day Travelcard** gives you unlimited travel for a day. The regular price is £7.20, but an "off-peak" version is £5.60 (good for travel starting after 9:30 on weekdays and anytime on weekends). A One-Day Travelcard for Zones 1–6, which includes Heathrow Airport, costs £14.80; the restricted off-peak version costs £7.50.

The **Three-Day Travelcard** for £18.40 costs about 15 percent less than three One-Day "peak" Travelcards, and is also good any time of day. Most travelers staying three days will easily take enough Tube and bus rides to make this worthwhile. Three-Day Travelcards are not available in an "off-peak" version. Buying three One-Day "off-peak" Travelcards will save you a few pence, but you'll only be able to travel after 9:30 on weekdays.

Which Pass to Buy?

Trying to decide between an Oyster and a Travelcard? Here's what I recommend:

- For one to two days, get a One-Day Travelcard each day.
- For three consecutive days, buy a Three-Day Travelcard.
- For four consecutive days, either buy a Three-Day Travelcard plus an extra One-Day Travelcard as needed (total £25.60), or a Seven-Day Oyster card (£25.80).
- For five or more days in a row, a Seven-Day Oyster card is usually your best bet. But if you aren't sure if you'll ride enough each day to justify the expense, get the pay-as-you-go Oyster card instead.

Other Discounts

Groups of 10 or more adults can travel all day on the Tube for £3.70 each (but not on buses). Kids 12–17 pay £1 when part of a group of 10.

Families: A paying adult can take up to four kids (aged 10 and under) for free on the Tube and Docklands Light Railway all day, every day. In the Tube, use the manual gate, rather than the turnstiles, to be waved in. Families with children 11–15 also save with the "Kid for a Quid" promotion: Any adult with a Travelcard can buy an off-peak One-Day Travelcard for up to four kids 15 or younger for only £1 (a "quid") each.

your ticket or Travelcard to the turnstile or touching your Oyster card to an electronic reader. If you have a single-trip paper ticket, the turnstile will eat your now-expired ticket; if it's a Travelcard, it will spit your still-valid card back out. Save walking time by choosing the best street exit—check the maps on the walls or ask any station personnel. For Tube and bus information, visit www .tfl.gov.uk (and check out the journey planner).

Any ride in Zones 1–6 (the center of town all the way out to Heathrow Airport) costs a steep £4 for adults paying cash. If you plan to ride the Tube and buses more than twice in one day, you'll save money by getting a Travelcard.

If you do buy a single Tube ticket, you can avoid ticket-window lines in stations by using the coin-op or credit-card machines; practice on the punchboard to see how the system works (hit "Adult Single" and your destination). These tickets are valid only on the day of purchase.

Tube Etiquette

- When waiting at the platform, get out of the way of those exiting the train. Board only after everyone is off.
- Avoid using the hinged seats near the doors of some trains when the car is jammed; they take up valuable standing space.
- In a crowded train, try not to block the exit. If you're blocking the door when the train stops, step out of the car and to the side, let others off, then get back on.
- Talk softly in the cars. Listen to how quietly Londoners communicate and follow their lead.
- On escalators, stand on the right and pass on the left (even though Brits do the opposite behind the wheel). But note that in some passageways or stairways, you might be directed to walk on the left (same as car direction).
- When leaving a station, hold the door for the person behind you.

By Bus

Riding city buses doesn't come naturally to many travelers, but if you make a point to figure out the system you'll swing like Tarzan through the urban jungle of London. Pick up the free *London Buses: Central London* at a transport office, TI, or some major museums for a fine map listing all the bus routes best for sightseeing.

The first step in mastering the bus system is learning how to decipher the bus-stop signs. Find a bus stop and study the signs mounted on the pole next to the stop. You'll see a chart listing (alphabetically) the destinations served by buses that pick up at this spot or nearby; the names of the buses; and alphabet letters

Handy Bus Routes

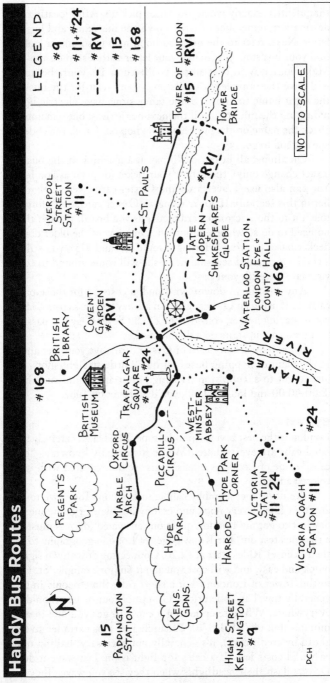

LONDON

NOT TO SCALE

that identify exactly where the buses pick up. After locating your destination, remember or write down the bus name and bus stop letter. Next, refer to the neighborhood map (also on the pole) to find your bus stop. Just match your letter with a stop on the map. Make your way to that stop—you'll know it's yours because it will have the same letter on its pole—and wait for the bus with the right name to arrive. Some fancy stops have electric boards indicating the minutes until the next bus arrives; but remember to check the name on the bus before you hop on. Crack the code and you're good to go.

On almost all buses, you'll pay at a machine at the bus stop (exact change only), then show your ticket (or pass) as you board. You can also use Travelcards and Oyster cards (see sidebar earlier in this section). If you're using an Oyster card, don't forget to touch it to the electronic card reader as you board, though there's no need to do so when you hop off. On a few of the older double-decker buses (serving "Heritage" routes #9 and #15), you still pay a conductor; take a seat and he or she will come around to collect your fare or verify your pass.

Any bus ride in downtown London costs £2 for those paying cash; £1 if using an Oyster card. An all-day bus pass costs £3.80. If you're staying longer, consider the £13.80 Seven-Day bus pass. The best views are upstairs on a double-decker.

If you have a Travelcard or Oyster card, save your feet and get in the habit of hopping buses for quick little straight shots, even just to get to a Tube stop. During bump-and-grind rush hours (8:00–10:00 and 16:00–19:00), you'll go faster by Tube.

By Taxi

London is the best taxi town in Europe. Big, black, carefully regulated cabs are everywhere. (While historically known as "black cabs," some of London's official taxis are now covered with wildly colored ads.)

I've never met a crabby cabbie in London. They love to talk, and they know every nook and cranny in town. I ride in one each day just to get my London questions answered (drivers must pass a rigorous test on "The Knowledge" of London geography to earn their license). Rides start at £2.20. Connecting downtown sights is quick and easy, and will cost you about £6 (for example, St. Paul's to the Tower of London). For a short ride, three people in a cab generally travel at Tube prices. Groups of four or five should taxi everywhere. While telephoning a cab will get you one in a few minutes (tel. 0871-871-8710; £2 surcharge, plus extra fee to book ahead by credit card), it's generally not necessary; hailing one is easy and costs less. If a cab's top light is on, just wave it down. Drivers flash their headlights when they see you wave. They have a tiny turning radius, so you can hail cabs going in either direction. If waving doesn't work, ask someone where you can find a taxi stand.

Don't worry about meter cheating. Licensed British cab meters come with a sealed computer chip and clock that ensures you'll get the regular tariff #1 most of the time (Mon–Fri 6:00–20:00), tariff #2 during "unsociable hours" (Mon–Fri 20:00–22:00 and Sat–Sun 6:00–22:00), and tariff #3 at night (nightly 22:00–6:00) and on holidays. (Rates go up about 15–20 percent with each higher tariff.) All extra charges are explained in writing on the cab wall. The only way a cabbie can cheat you is by taking a needlessly long route. Another pitfall is taking a cab when traffic is bad to a destination efficiently served by the Tube. On a recent trip to London, I hopped in a taxi at South Kensington for Waterloo Station and hit bad traffic. Rather than spending 20 minutes and £2–4 on the Tube, I spent 40 minutes and £16 in a taxi.

Tip a cabbie by rounding up (maximum 10 percent). If you over-drink and ride in a taxi, be warned: Taxis charge £40 for "soiling" (a.k.a. pub puke).

Tours

▲▲▲Hop-on, Hop-off Double-Decker Bus Tours

Two competitive companies (Original and Big Bus) offer essentially the same two tours of the city's sightseeing highlights, with nearly 30 stops on each route. One tour has buses with live (English-only) guides, and a second (sometimes slightly different route) comes with tape-recorded, dial-a-language narration. These two-hour, once-over-lightly bus tours drive by all the famous sights, providing a stress-free way to get your bearings and see the biggies. With a good guide and nice weather, sit back and enjoy the entire two hours. Narration is important—so hop on and hop off to see the sights or to change guides (if yours is more boring than entertaining).

Buses run about every 10–15 minutes in summer, every 20 minutes in winter, and operate daily (from about 9:00 until early evening in summer, until late afternoon in winter). These buses stop at a core group of sights regardless of which overview tour you're on: Victoria Station, Marble Arch, Piccadilly Circus, Trafalgar Square, the Tower of London, and elsewhere.

In addition to the overview tours, both Original and Big Bus include a narrated Thames boat tour covered by the same ticket (buy ticket from driver, credit cards accepted at major stops such as Victoria Station, ticket good for 24 hours, bring a sweater and a camera). Big Bus tours are a little bit more expensive (£24), while

Original tours are cheaper (£19 with this book) and nearly as good. Pick up a map from any flier rack or from one of the countless salespeople, and study the complex system. Note: If you start at Victoria Station at 9:00, you'll finish near Buckingham Palace in time to see the Changing of the Guard at 11:30; ask your driver for the best place to hop off. Sunday morning—when the traffic is light and many museums are closed—is a fine time for a tour. The last full loop leaves Victoria Station at 17:00. Unless you're using the bus tour mainly for hop-on, hop-off transportation, consider saving money by taking a night tour (described below).

Original London Sightseeing Bus Tour: For a live guide on the city highlights tour, look for a yellow triangle on the front of the bus. A red triangle means a longer, tape-recorded multilingual tour that includes Madame Tussauds—avoid it, unless you have kids who'd enjoy the entertaining recorded kids' tour. Green, black, and purple triangle routes link major train stations to the central routes, while a blue triangle connects far-flung museums. All routes are covered by the same ticket. Keep it simple and just take the city highlights tour (£24, £21 after £3 discount with this book, limit two discounts per book, they'll rip off the corner of this page—raise bloody hell if they don't honor this discount, also online deals, ticket good for 24 hours, tel. 020/8877-1722, www.theoriginaltour.com). Your ticket includes a City Cruises "River Red Rover" all-day river cruise ticket (normally £10; for details see "Cruises: To Greenwich," later in this chapter).

Big Bus London Tours: For £24 (£20 if you book a specific date), you get the same basic overview tours: Red buses come with a live guide, while the blue route has a recorded narration and a longer path around Hyde Park. Your ticket includes coupons for three silly one-hour London walks, as well as the scenic and usually entertainingly guided Thames boat ride between Westminster Pier, the Tower of London, and Greenwich (normally £6.40). The pass and extras are valid for 24 hours. These pricier tours tend to have better, more dynamic guides than Original, and more departures as well—meaning shorter waits for those hopping on and off (daily 8:30–18:00, winter until 16:30, from Victoria Station, tel. 020/7233-9533, www.bigbus.co.uk).

At Night: The London by Night Sightseeing Tour operates two routes, but after hours, with none of the extras (e.g., walks, boat tours), and at a lower price. While the narration can be pretty lame, the views at twilight are grand (though note that it stays light out late on summer nights). Their West End Tour drives by more biggies than their City Tour. Each tour costs £14 and lasts 90 minutes. You can pay the driver when you board (at any of the stops on their route, such as the London Eye, where the two routes intersect); or buy tickets at the Victoria Station or Paddington

Station TIs; or save £4 by booking on their website (April–Dec only, West End Tour normally departs 19:30, 20:30, and 21:30 from Victoria Station, only at 20:30 in winter; Taxi Road, at front of station near end of Wilton Road, tel. 020/8545-6109, www.london -by-night.net). For a memorable and economical evening, munch a scenic picnic dinner on the top deck. There are plenty of take-away options within the train stations and near the various stops.

▲▲Walking Tours

Several times a day, top-notch local guides lead (often big) groups through specific slices of London's past. Schedule fliers litter the desks of TIs, hotels, and pubs. *Time Out* lists many, but not all, scheduled walks. Simply show up at the announced location, pay £7, and enjoy two chatty hours of Dickens, the Plague, Shakespeare, Legal London, the Beatles, Jack the Ripper, or whatever is on the agenda.

London Walks: The dominant company lists its extensive daily schedule in a beefy, plain black-and-white *London Walks* brochure and on their website. Their two-hour walks cost £7 (cash only, walks offered year-round—even Christmas, private tours for groups-£100, tel. 020/7624-3978, for a recorded listing of today's walks call 020/7624-9255, www.londonwalks.com). They also run Explorer day trips, a good option for those with limited time and transportation (£12 plus £10–40 for transportation and admission costs, cash only, different trip daily: Stonehenge/Salisbury, Oxford/Cotswolds, York, Bath, and so on; fewer offered in winter).

Sandemans New London Tours: The same outfit making waves on the Continent employs English-speaking students to give London tours. Their fast-moving, youthful tours are light, irreverent, entertaining, and fun. One of their tours—Royal London—is free (daily at 11:00, 2.5–3 hours, meet at Wellington Arch, Tube: Hyde Park Corner, Exit 2; they push for tips at the end and cross-promote their evening pub crawl). Their other tours include Old City (£9, daily at 10:00, meet at the sundial opposite the Tower Hill Tube station exit); Grim Reapers (£9, daily at 14:00, also meets at Tower Hill Tube sundial); and a pub crawl (£12, Tue–Sat at 19:30, meet at Belushi's at 9 Russell Street, Tube: Covent Garden). Look for the guides in their red T-shirts (www.newlondon-tours.com).

The Beatles: Fans of the still–Fabulous Four can take one of two Beatles walks (London Walks, above, has 5/week; Big Bus, page 636, includes a daily walk with their bus tour). For a photo op, go to Abbey Road and walk the famous crosswalk (at intersection with Grove End Road, Tube: St. John's Wood). The Beatles Store is at 231 Baker Street (daily 10:00–18:30, next to Sherlock Holmes Museum, Tube: Baker Street, tel. 020/7935-4464, www.beatles storelondon.co.uk).

Jack the Ripper: Each walking-tour company seems to make most of its money with "haunted" and Jack the Ripper tours. Many guides are historians and would rather not lead these lightweight tours—but tourists pay more for gore (the ridiculously juvenile London Dungeon is one of the city's top sights). You'll find plenty of Ripper tours. For a little twist, you might consider the scary walk given by the Yeoman Warders of the Tower of London. In Ripping Yarns' "Tour from Hell," the Beefeaters get in on the haunted-walk action, offering their own Jack the Ripper tour (£7, nightly at 18:45 at Tower Hill Tube station, mobile 07813-559-301, www.jack-the-ripper-tours.com).

Private Guides—Standard rates for London's registered guides usually run about £120 for four hours, and £180 or more for eight hours (tel. 020/7780-4060, www.touristguides.org.uk, www.blue -badge.org.uk). Consider **Sean Kelleher** (£120/half-day, £200/day, tel. 020/8673-1624, mobile 07764-612-770, seankelleher @btinternet.com) or **Britt Lonsdale** (£150/half-day, £220/day, great with families, tel. 020/7386-9907, mobile 07813-278-077, brittl@btinternet.com).

Drivers: Robina Brown leads tours for small groups in her Toyota Previa (£250/half-day, £410–540/day, prices vary by destination, tel. 020/7228-2238, www.driverguidetours.com, robina @driverguidetours.com). **Janine Barton** provides a similar driver-and-guide tour and similar prices (tel. 020/7402-4600, jbsiis @aol.com), and offers a 15 percent discount to readers of this book. Robina and Janine's services are particularly helpful for wheelchair-using travelers who want to see more of London.

London Duck Tours

A bright-yellow amphibious WWII-vintage vehicle (the model that landed troops on Normandy's beaches on D-Day) takes a gang of 30 tourists past some famous sights on land—Big Ben, Trafalgar Square, Piccadilly Circus—then splashes into the Thames for a cruise. All-in-all, it's good fun at a rather steep price. The live guide works hard, and it's kid-friendly to the point of goofiness (£19, 2/hr, daily 10:00–17:30, 75 min—45 min on land and 30 min in the river, £2.50 online booking fee, these book up in advance, departs from Chicheley Street—you'll see the big ugly vehicle parked 100 yards behind the London Eye, Tube: Waterloo or Westminster, tel. 020/7928-3132, www.londonducktours.co.uk).

Bike Tours

London, like Paris, is committed to making more bike paths and many of its best sights can be laced together with a pleasant pedal through its parks.

London Bicycle Tour Company: Three tours covering London are offered daily from their base at Gabriel's Wharf on the south bank of the Thames. Sunday is the best, as there is less car traffic (Central Tour—£14.95, daily at 10:30, 6 miles, 2.5 hours, includes Westminster, Covent Garden, and St. Paul's; West Tour—£17.95, Sat–Sun at 12:00, 9 miles, 3.5 hours, includes Waterloo and Victoria stations, Hyde Park, Buckingham Palace, and Covent Garden; East Tour—£17.95, Sat–Sun at 14:00, 9 miles, 3.5 hours, includes south side of the river to Tower Bridge, then The City to the East End). They also rent bikes (office open daily 10:00–18:00, west of Blackfriars Bridge on the South Bank, 1A Gabriel's Wharf, tel. 020/7928-6838, www.londonbicycle.com).

Fat Tire Bike Tours: Daily bike tours cover the highlights of downtown London. The spiel is light and irreverent rather than scholarly, but the price is right. This is a fun way to see the sights and enjoy the city on two wheels (£16, daily June–Aug at 11:00 and 15:30, March–May and Sept–Nov at 11:00, Dec–Feb by reservation only, 4 hours, pay when you show up—no reservation needed except in winter, Queensway Tube station, mobile 078-8233-8779, www.fattirebiketourslondon.com).

▲▲Cruises

Boat tours with entertaining commentaries sail regularly from many points along the Thames. It's a bit confusing, since there are several companies offering essentially the same trip. Your basic options are downstream (to the Tower and Greenwich), upstream (to Kew Gardens), and round-trip scenic tour cruises. Most people depart from the Westminster Pier (at the base of Westminster Bridge under Big Ben). You can catch many of the same boats (with less waiting) from Waterloo Pier at the London Eye across the river. For pleasure and efficiency, consider combining a one-way cruise (to Kew, Greenwich, or wherever) with a Tube ride back.

Buy boat tickets at the small ticket offices on the docks. While individual Tube and bus tickets don't work on the boats, an Oyster card or Travelcard can snare you a 33 percent discount on most cruises (just show the card when you pay for the cruise). Children and seniors get discounts. You can purchase drinks and scant, pricey snacks onboard. Clever budget travelers pack a picnic and munch while they cruise.

Here are some of the most popular cruise options:

To the Tower of London: City Cruises boats sail 30 minutes to the Tower from Westminster Pier (£6.40 one-way, £7.80 round-trip, one-way included with Big Bus London tour; covered by £10 "River Red Rover" ticket that includes Greenwich—see next paragraph; daily April–Oct roughly 10:00–21:00, until 18:00 in winter, every 20 min).

To Greenwich: Two companies—City Cruises and the

Thames River Services—head to Greenwich from Westminster Pier. The companies' prices are the same, though **City Cruises** offers a few more alternatives (£7.50 one-way, £9.80 round-trip; or get their £10 all-day hop-on, hop-off "River Red Rover" ticket to have option of getting off at the London Eye and Tower of London—included with Original London bus tour; daily April–Oct generally 10:00–17:00, less off-season, every 40 min, 70 min to Greenwich; also departs for Greenwich from the pier at the Tower of London for less: £6.40 one-way, £7.80 round-trip, 30 min; tel. 020/7740-0400, www.citycruises.com). The **Thames River Services** goes to Greenwich from Westminster Pier a bit more frequently and a little quicker (£7.50 one-way, £9.80 round-trip, April–Oct 10:00–16:00, July–Aug until 17:00, daily 2/hr; Nov–March shorter hours and runs every 40 min; 60 min to Greenwich, tel. 020/7930-4097, www.thamesriver services.co.uk).

Round-Trip Cruises: The London Eye operates its own "River Cruise Experience," offering a 40-minute live-guided circular tour from Waterloo Pier (£12, reservations recommended, departures daily 12:45–18:45 generally at :45 past each hour, April–Oct also at 10:45 and 11:45, tel. 0870-443-9185, www.londoneye.com).

From Tate to Tate: The Tate Boat service for art-lovers connects the Tate Modern and Tate Britain in 18 scenic minutes, stopping at the London Eye en route (£5 one-way or £12 for a day ticket; discounted with Travelcard, buy ticket at gallery desk or onboard, departing every 40 min from 10:00–17:00, 18-min trip, tel. 020/7887-8008).

On Regent's Canal: Consider exploring London's canals by taking a cruise on historic Regent's Canal in north London. The good ship *Jenny Wren* offers 90-minute guided canal boat cruises from Walker's Quay in Camden Town through scenic Regent's Park to Little Venice (£7.50, April–Oct daily at 12:30 and 14:30, Sat–Sun also at 16:30, Walker's Quay, 250 Camden High Street, 3-min walk from Tube: Camden Town, tel. 020/7485-4433, www .walkersquay.com). While in Camden Town, stop by the popular, punky Camden Lock Market to browse through trendy arts and crafts (daily 10:00–18:00, busiest on weekends, a block from Walker's Quay).

Self-Guided Walk

Westminster Walk

Just about every visitor to London strolls along historic Whitehall from Big Ben to Trafalgar Square. Under London's modern traffic and big-city bustle lie two thousand fascinating years of history. This three-quarter-mile, self-guided orientation walk (see

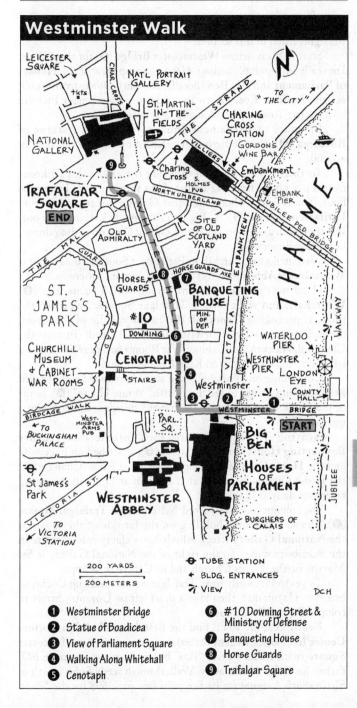

Westminster Walk

LEICESTER SQUARE

NAT'L PORTRAIT GALLERY

CHAR. CROSS

ST. MARTIN-IN-THE-FIELDS

THE STRAND

TO "THE CITY"

CHARING CROSS STATION

GORDON'S WINE BAR

NATIONAL GALLERY

VILLIERS ST.

Charing Cross

S. HOLMES PUB

Embankment

EMBANK. PIER

JUBILEE PED. BRIDGE

⑨

NORTHUMBERLAND

TRAFALGAR SQUARE END

OLD ADMIRALTY

THE MALL

LITTLE WHITEHALL

SITE OF OLD SCOTLAND YARD

EMBANKMENT

T H A M E S

ST. JAMES'S PARK

GUARDS

Horse Guards

⑧

HORSE GUARDS AVE

⑦

BANQUETING HOUSE

VICTORIA EMBANKMENT

WALKWAY

CHURCHILL MUSEUM & CABINET WAR ROOMS

HORSE GUARDS ROAD

#10 DOWNING

⑥

MIN. OF DEF.

WATERLOO PIER

WESTMINSTER PIER

CENOTAPH

⑤

PARL. ST.

STAIRS

④

Westminster

LONDON EYE

COUNTY HALL

③

②

①

BIRDCAGE WALK

WEST-MINSTER ARMS PUB

PARL. SQ.

WESTMINSTER BRIDGE

START

TO BUCKINGHAM PALACE

VICTORIA ST.

BIG BEN

St James's Park

WESTMINSTER ABBEY

HOUSES OF PARLIAMENT

JUBILEE

TO VICTORIA STATION

BURGHERS OF CALAIS

200 YARDS

200 METERS

⚓ TUBE STATION
✝ BLDG. ENTRANCES
🏞 VIEW

DCH

① Westminster Bridge
② Statue of Boadicea
③ View of Parliament Square
④ Walking Along Whitehall
⑤ Cenotaph
⑥ #10 Downing Street & Ministry of Defense
⑦ Banqueting House
⑧ Horse Guards
⑨ Trafalgar Square

LONDON

Westminster Walk map) gives you a whirlwind tour and connects the sights listed in this section.

Start halfway across **Westminster Bridge** (❶) for that "Wow, I'm really in London!" feeling. Get a close-up view of the **Houses of Parliament** and **Big Ben** (floodlit at night). Downstream you'll see the **London Eye.** Down the stairs to Westminster Pier are boats to the Tower of London and Greenwich.

En route to Parliament Square, you'll pass a **statue of Boadicea** (❷), the Celtic queen defeated by Roman invaders in A.D. 60.

To thrill your loved ones (or bug the envious), call home from a pay phone near Big Ben at about three minutes before the hour. You'll find a phone on Great George Street, across from **Parliament Square** (❸). As Big Ben chimes, stick the receiver outside the booth and prove you're in London: Ding dong ding dong... dong ding ding dong.

Wave hello to Churchill in Parliament Square. To his right is **Westminster Abbey** with its two stubby, elegant towers.

Head north up Parliament Street, which turns into (❹) **Whitehall,** and walk toward Trafalgar Square. You'll see the thought-provoking **Cenotaph** (❺) in the middle of the street, reminding passersby of Britain's many war dead. To visit the Churchill Museum and Cabinet War Rooms (see page 645), take a left before the Cenotaph, on King Charles Street.

Continuing on Whitehall, stop at the barricaded and guarded **#10 Downing Street** to see the British "White House" (❻), home of the prime minister. Break the bobby's boredom and ask him a question.

Nearing Trafalgar Square, look for the 17th-century **Banqueting House** across the street (❼); described on page 646, and the **Horse Guards** (❽) behind the gated fence (Changing of the Horse Guards Mon–Sat at 11:00, Sun at 10:00, dismounting ceremony daily at 16:00).

The column topped by Lord Nelson marks **Trafalgar Square** (❾). The stately domed building on the far side of the square is the **National Gallery** (free), which has a classy café upstairs in the Sainsbury wing. To the right of the National Gallery is **St. Martin-in-the-Fields Church** and its Café in the Crypt.

To get to Piccadilly from Trafalgar Square, walk up Cockspur Street to Haymarket, then take a short left on Coventry Street to colorful **Piccadilly Circus.**

Near Piccadilly you'll find the **Britain and London Visitors Centre** (on Lower Regent Street) and piles of theaters. **Leicester Square** (with its half-price "tkts" booth for plays, see page 673) thrives just a few blocks away. Walk through seedy **Soho** (north of Shaftesbury Avenue) for its fun pubs (see page 698 for the "Food is Fun" dinner crawl). From Piccadilly or Oxford Circus, you can take a taxi, bus, or the Tube home.

Sights

▲▲▲Westminster Abbey

The greatest church in the English-speaking world, Westminster Abbey is the place where England's kings and queens have been crowned and buried since 1066. A thousand years of English history—3,000 tombs, the remains of 29 kings and queens, and hundreds of memorials to poets, politicians, and warriors—lie within its stained-glass splendor and under its stone slabs. Like a stony refugee camp huddled outside St. Peter's Pearly Gates, this place has many stories to tell. The steep admission includes an excellent audioguide, worthwhile if you have the time and interest. To experience the church more vividly, take a live tour, or attend evensong or an organ concert (see below). You can even have a sandwich or bowl of soup in the cloister...but you can't take photos.

Two tiny **museums** ring the cloisters: the Chapter House (where the monks held their daily meetings, notable for its fine architecture, stained glass, and faded but well-described medieval art), and the Abbey Museum (which tells of the abbey's history, royal coronations, and burials). Look into the impressively realistic eyes of Henry VII's funeral effigy (one of a fascinating series of wax-and-wood statues that, for three centuries, graced royal coffins during funeral processions).

The church hosts **evensong** performances daily, sung every night but Wednesday, when it is spoken (Mon–Fri at 17:00, Sat–Sun at 15:00) and often has a free 30-minute **organ recital** on Sunday at 17:45.

Cost, Hours, Location: £12, £28 family ticket; both include excellent audioguide and admission to the cloisters and Abbey Museum; free church entry for worshippers; Abbey open Mon–Fri 9:30–16:30, Sat 9:30–14:30, Wed until 19:00, last entry one hour before closing, closed Sun to sightseers but open for services; Abbey Museum open daily 10:30–16:00, cloisters open daily 8:00–18:00, free access to cloisters through Dean Court (near west entrance); £3 guided tours—up to 6/day in summer, Tube: Westminster or St. James's Park, info desk tel. 020/7222-5152, www.westminster-abbey.org.

The main entrance, on the Parliament Square side, often has a sizable line; visit early, during lunch, or late to avoid tourist hordes. Mid-mornings are most crowded, while weekdays after 14:30 are less congested; come then and stay for the 17:00 evensong (but note that on Wed the service is not sung). Since the church is often closed to the public for special services, it's wise to call first.

Between the Abbey and Trafalgar Square

▲▲**Houses of Parliament (Palace of Westminster)**—This Neo-Gothic icon of London, the royal residence from 1042–1547, is now the meeting place of the legislative branch of government. The Houses of Parliament are located in what was once the Palace of Westminster—long the palace of England's medieval monarchs—until it was largely destroyed by fire in 1834. The palace was rebuilt in the Victorian Gothic style (a move away from Neoclassicism back to England's Christian and medieval heritage, true to the Romantic Age) and completed in 1860.

Tourists are welcome to view debates in either the bickering House of Commons or the genteel House of Lords. You're only allowed inside when Parliament is in session, indicated by a flag flying atop the Victoria Tower. While the actual debates are generally quite dull, it is a thrill to be inside and see the British government inaction (both Houses usually open Mon–Tue 14:30–22:30, Wed–Thu 11:30–17:50, Fri 9:30–15:00, closed Sat–Sun, generally less action and no lines after 18:00, Tube: Westminster, tel. 020/7219-4272; see www.parliament.uk for schedule). The House of Lords has more pageantry, shorter lines, and less interesting debates (tel. 020/7219-3107 for schedule, and visit www.parliament live.tv for a preview).

Visiting the Houses of Parliament: Enter the venerable HOP midway along the west side of the building (across from Westminster Abbey); to find the entrance, follow the people and signs, or ask a guard. As you enter, you'll be asked if you want to visit the House of Commons or the House of Lords. Inquire about the wait. If there's a long line for the House of Commons and you just want a quick look inside the grand halls of this grand building, start with the House of Lords. Once inside you can switch if you like.

Just past security, you enter the vast and historic **Westminster Hall,** which survived the 1834 fire. The hall was built in the 11th century, and its famous self-supporting hammer-beam roof was added in 1397. Racks of brochures here explain how the British government works, and plaques describe the hall. The Jubilee Café, open to the public, has live video feeds showing exactly what's going on in each house. Just seeing the café video is a fun experience (and can help you decide which house—if either—you'd like to actually see). Walking through the hall and up the stairs, you'll enter the busy world of government with all its high-powered goings-on.

Houses of Parliament Tours: In August and September, you can get a behind-the-scenes peek at the royal chambers of both houses with a tour led by a Blue Badge guide (£12, 75 min; Aug Mon–Tue and Fri–Sat 9:15–16:30, Wed–Thu 13:15–16:30; Sept Mon and Fri–Sat 9:15–16:30, Tue–Thu 13:15–16:30; confirm times

LONDON

in advance, to book a spot ahead—avoiding waits and guarantee-ing a spot—use Keith Prowse ticket service, tel. 0844-209-0382, US tel. 800-669-8687, www.keithprowse.com, no booking fee).

The **Jewel Tower**—across the street from the Parliament building's St. Stephen's Gate—is the only other part of the old Palace of Westminster to survive (besides Westminster Hall). It contains a fine little exhibit on Parliament (first floor—history, sec-ond floor—Parliament today) with a 25-minute video and lonely, picnic-friendly benches (£2.90, daily April–Oct 10:00–17:00, Nov–March 10:00–16:00, tel. 020/7222-2219).

Big Ben, the clock tower (315 feet high), is named for its 13-ton bell, Ben. The light above the clock is lit when the House of Commons is sitting. The face of the clock is huge—you can actually see the minute hand moving. For a good view of it, walk halfway over Westminster Bridge.

▲▲▲**Churchill Museum and Cabinet War Rooms**—This is a fascinating walk through the underground headquarters of the British government's fight against the Nazis in the darkest days of the Battle for Britain. The 27-room nerve center of the British war effort was used from 1939 to 1945. Churchill's room, the map room, and other rooms are just as they were in 1945. For all the blood, sweat, toil, and tears details, pick up the excellent, essential, and included audioguide at the entry and follow the 60-minute tour; be patient—it's well worth it.

Don't bypass the Churchill Museum (entrance is a half-dozen rooms into the exhibit), which shows the man behind the famous cigar, bowler hat, and V-for-victory sign—allow an hour for that museum alone. It shows his wit, irascibility, work ethic, American ties, writing talents, and drinking habits. A long touch-the-screen timeline lets you zero in on events in his life from birth (November 30, 1874) to his appointment as prime minister in 1940. It's all the more amazing considering that, in the 1930s, the man who would become my vote for greatest statesman of the 20th century was considered a washed-up loony ranting about the growing threat of fascism (£12, daily 9:30–18:00, last entry one hour before closing; on King Charles Street, 200 yards off Whitehall, follow the signs, Tube: Westminster; tel. 020/7930-6961, www.iwm.org.uk). The museum's gift shop is great for anyone nostalgic for the 1940s.

If you're hungry, get your rations at the Switch Room café (in the museum, daily 10:00–17:00) or, for a nearby pub lunch, try the Westminster Arms (food served downstairs, on Storey's Gate, a couple of blocks south of Cabinet War Rooms).

Horse Guards—The Horse Guards change daily at 11:00 (10:00 on Sun), and there's a colorful dismounting ceremony daily at 16:00. The rest of the day, they just stand there—terrible for video cameras (on Whitehall, between Trafalgar Square and

#10 Downing Street, Tube: Westminster). While Buckingham Palace pageantry is canceled when it rains, the Horse Guards change regardless of the weather.

▲**Banqueting House**—England's first Renaissance building was designed by Inigo Jones around 1620. It's one of the few London landmarks spared by the 1698 fire and the only surviving part of the original Palace of Whitehall. Don't miss its Rubens ceiling, which, at Charles I's request, drove home the doctrine of the legitimacy of the divine right of kings. In 1649—divine right ignored—Charles I was beheaded on the balcony of this building by a Cromwellian Parliament. Admission includes a restful 20-minute audiovisual history, which shows the place in banqueting action; a 30-minute audio tour—interesting only to history buffs; and a look at the exquisite banqueting hall (£4.50, Mon–Sat 10:00–17:00, closed Sun, last entry at 16:30, subject to closure for government functions, aristocratic WC, immediately across Whitehall from the Horse Guards, Tube: Westminster, tel. 020/3166-6154, www.hrp.org.uk). Just up the street is Trafalgar Square.

Trafalgar Square

▲▲**Trafalgar Square**—London's recently renovated central square, the climax of most marches and demonstrations, is a thrilling place to simply hang out. Lord Nelson stands atop his 185-foot-tall fluted granite column, gazing out toward Trafalgar, where he lost his life but defeated the French fleet. Part of this 1842 memorial is made from his victims' melted-down cannons. He's surrounded by spraying fountains, giant lions, hordes of people, and—until recently—even more pigeons. A former London mayor, Ken Livingstone, nicknamed "Red Ken" for his passion for an activist government, decided that London's "flying rats" were a public nuisance and evicted Trafalgar Square's venerable seed salesmen (Tube: Charing Cross).

▲▲▲**National Gallery**—This displays Britain's top collection of European paintings from 1250–1900—including works by Leonardo, Botticelli, Velázquez, Rembrandt, Turner, van Gogh, and the Impressionists. The huge collection traces European art history through medieval holiness, Renaissance realism, Dutch detail, Baroque excess, British restraint, and colorful French Impressionism. Cruise like an eagle with wide eyes for the big picture, seeing how each style progresses into the next. The audio-guide tour (suggested £3.50 donation) is one of the finest I've used in Europe.

Cost, Hours, Location: Free admission, daily 10:00–18:00, Wed until 21:00; last entry to special exhibits 45 min before closing, free one-hour overview tours daily at 11:30 and 14:30. Photography is prohibited. It's on Trafalgar Square (Tube: Charing Cross or

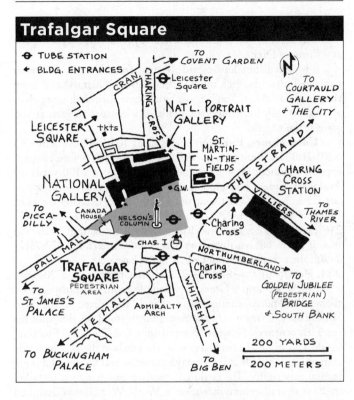

Trafalgar Square

- ⊕ TUBE STATION
- ← BLDG. ENTRANCES

TO COVENT GARDEN
Leicester Square
TO COURTAULD GALLERY & THE CITY
CRAN.
CHARING CROSS
NAT'L. PORTRAIT GALLERY
LEICESTER SQUARE   tkts
ST. MARTIN-IN-THE-FIELDS
THE STRAND
CHARING CROSS STATION
NATIONAL GALLERY
G.W.
VILLIERS
TO THAMES RIVER
TO PICCA-DILLY
CANADA House
NELSON'S COLUMN
Charing Cross
PALL MALL
CHAS. I
NORTHUMBERLAND
TRAFALGAR SQUARE
PEDESTRIAN AREA
Charing Cross
TO GOLDEN JUBILEE (PEDESTRIAN) BRIDGE & SOUTH BANK
TO ST. JAMES'S PALACE
THE MALL
ADMIRALTY ARCH
WHITEHALL
TO BUCKINGHAM PALACE
TO BIG BEN
200 YARDS
200 METERS

Leicester Square, recorded info tel. 020/7747-2885, switchboard tel. 020/7839-3321, www.nationalgallery.org.uk).

Eateries: The excellent-but-pricey café in the museum's restaurant, called the National Dining Rooms, is a good spot to split afternoon tea (£5 savory tarts, £15 afternoon tea, £20 plates, tea served 15:00–17:00, located in Sainsbury Wing, tel. 020/7747-2525). The National Café and the Espresso Bar are less expensive options on the ground floor near the Getty entrance.

▲▲**National Portrait Gallery**—Put off by halls of 19th-century characters who meant nothing to me, I used to call this "as interesting as someone else's yearbook." But a selective walk through this 500-year-long *Who's Who* of British history is quick and free, and puts faces on the story of England. The collection is well-described, not huge, and in historical sequence, from the 16th century on the second floor to today's royal family on the ground floor.

Some highlights: Henry VIII and wives; several fascinating portraits of the "Virgin Queen" Elizabeth I, Sir Francis Drake, and Sir Walter Raleigh; the only real-life portrait of William Shakespeare; Oliver Cromwell and Charles I with his head on; self-portraits and other portraits by Gainsborough and Reynolds;

the Romantics (Blake, Byron, Wordsworth, and company); Queen Victoria and her era; and the present royal family, including the late Princess Diana.

The excellent audioguide tours (free, but £2 donation requested) describe each room (or era in British history) and more than 300 paintings. You'll learn more about British history than art and actually hear interviews with 20th-century subjects as you stare at their faces.

Cost, Hours, Location: Free, daily 10:00–18:00, Thu–Fri until 21:00, last entry to special exhibits 45 min before closing, excellent audioguide—£2 suggested donation. It's 100 yards off Trafalgar Square (around corner from National Gallery, opposite Church of St. Martin-in-the-Fields, Tube: Charing Cross or Leicester Square, tel. 020/7306-0055, recorded info tel. 020/7312-2463, www.npg.org.uk). The elegant Portrait Restaurant on the top floor is pricey but has fine views (reservations smart, tel. 020/7312-2490); the cheaper Portrait Café is in the basement.

▲**St. Martin-in-the-Fields**—This church, built in the 1720s with a Gothic spire atop a Greek-type temple, is an oasis of peace on the wild and noisy Trafalgar Square. St. Martin cared for the poor. "In the fields" was where the first church stood on this spot (in the 13th century), between Westminster and The City. Stepping inside, you still feel a compassion for the needs of the people in this community—the church serves the homeless and houses a Chinese community center. The strikingly modern east window, installed in 2008 to replace one damaged in World War II, was designed by Iranian-born artist Shirazeh Houshiary. A free flier provides a brief yet worthwhile self-guided tour (church entry free, donations welcome, open daily, Tube: Charing Cross, tel. 020/7766-1100).

The church is famous for its **concerts.** Consider a free lunchtime concert (Mon, Tue, and Fri at 13:00), an evening concert (£6–25, at 19:30 Thu–Sat and on some Tue), or live jazz in the church's café (£5–8, Wed at 20:00). See the church's website for the concert schedule (www.smitf.org).

After a two-year renovation, a new, freestanding glass pavilion opened in 2008 to the left of the church. The pavilion serves as the entrance to the church's underground areas, including the concert ticket office, a gift shop, brass-rubbing center, and the fine support-the-church Café in the Crypt (listed at the top of the "Restaurants" section later in this chapter).

Piccadilly, Soho, and Covent Garden

For a "Food is Fun" dinner crawl from Covent Garden to Soho, see page 698.

▲▲**Piccadilly Circus**—London's most touristy square got its name from the fancy ruffled shirts—*picadils*—made in the

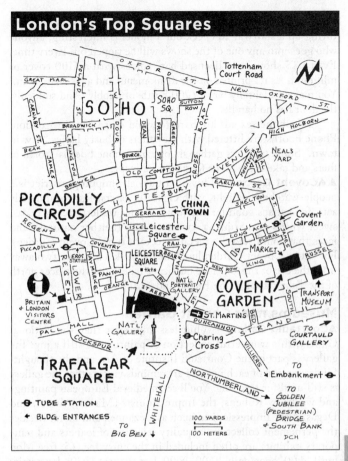

London's Top Squares

neighborhood long ago. Today, the square, while pretty grotty, is surrounded by fascinating streets swimming with youth on the rampage. For overstimulation, drop by the extremely trashy **Trocadero Center** for its Funland virtual-reality games, nine-screen cinema, and 10-lane bowling alley (admission to Trocadero is free; individual attractions cost £2–10; located between Coventry and Shaftesbury, just off Piccadilly, Tube: Piccadilly Circus). Chinatown, to the east, swelled when the former British colony of Hong Kong was returned to China in 1997, but is now threatened by developers. Nearby Shaftesbury Avenue and Leicester Square teem with fun-seekers, theaters, Chinese restaurants, and street singers.

Soho—North of Piccadilly, seedy Soho has become seriously trendy and is well worth a gawk. But Soho is also London's red-light district, where "friendly models" wait in tiny rooms up dreary stairways, and voluptuous con artists sell strip shows. While venturing up a stairway to check out a model is interesting, anyone who goes into any one of the shows will be ripped off. Every time. Even a £5 show in a "licensed bar" comes with a £100 cover or minimum (as it's printed on the drink menu) and a "security man." You may accidentally buy a £200 bottle of bubbly. And suddenly, the door has no handle.

Telephone sex ads are hard to avoid these days in London. Phone booths are littered with racy fliers of busty ladies "new in town." Some travelers gather six or eight phone booths' worth of fliers and take them home for kinky wallpaper.

▲▲Covent Garden—This boutique-ish shopping district is a people-watcher's delight, with cigarette eaters, Punch-and-Judy acts, food that's good for you (but not your wallet), trendy crafts, sweet whiffs of marijuana, two-tone hair (neither natural), and faces that could set off a metal detector (Tube: Covent Garden). For better Covent Garden lunch deals, walk a block or two away from the eye of this touristic hurricane (check out the places north of the Tube station along Endell and Neal Streets).

Museums near Covent Garden

▲Courtauld Gallery—While less impressive than the National Gallery, this wonderful collection of paintings is still a joy. The gallery is part of the Courtauld Institute of Art, and the thoughtful description of each piece of art reminds visitors that the gallery is still used for teaching. You'll see medieval European paintings and works by Rubens, the Impressionists (Manet, Monet, and Degas), Post-Impressionists (such as Cézanne), and more. Besides the permanent collection, a quality selection of loaners and temporary exhibits are often included in the entry fee (£5, free Mon until 14:00, open daily 10:00–18:00, last entry at 17:30; downstairs cafeteria, lockers, and WC; bus #6, #9, #11, #13, #15, or #23 from Trafalgar Square; Tube: Temple or Covent Garden, tel. 020/7845-4600 or 020/7848-2777, recorded info tel. 020/7848-2526, www.courtauld.ac.uk).

The Courtauld Gallery is located at Somerset House, a grand 18th-century civic palace that offers a marvelous public space and a riverside terrace (between the Strand and the Thames). The palace once held the national registry that recorded Britain's births, marriages, and deaths: "...where they hatch 'em, match 'em, and dispatch 'em." Step into the courtyard to enjoy the fountain. Go ahead...walk through it. The 55 jets get playful twice an hour. In the winter, this becomes a popular ice-skating rink with a toasty café for viewing (www.somerset-house.org.uk).

▲London Transport Museum—This newly renovated museum is fun for kids and thought-provoking for adults. Whether you're cursing or marveling at the buses and Tube, the growth of Europe's third-biggest city (after Moscow and Istanbul) has been made possible by its public transit system. An elevator transports you back to 1800, when horse-drawn vehicles ruled the road. London invented the notion of a public bus traveling a set route that anyone could board without a reservation. Next, you descend to the first floor and the world's first underground Metro system, which used steam-powered locomotives (the Circle Line, c. 1865). On the ground floor, horses and trains are quickly replaced by motorized vehicles (cars, taxis, double-decker buses, streetcars), resulting in 20th-century congestion. How to deal with it? In 2003, car drivers were slapped with a congestion charge. Today, a half-billion people ride the Tube every year. Learn how city planners hope to improve efficiency with better tracks and more coverage of the expanding East End. Finally, an exhibit lets you imagine four different scenarios for the year 2055 depending on the choices you make today. Will fresh strawberries in December destroy the planet? (£10—actually £8 but they include a £2 "donation"—a weird way to extract a premium out of visitors, Sat–Thu 10:00–18:00, Fri 11:00–21:00, last entry 45 min before closing, pleasant upstairs café with Covent Garden view, in southeast corner of Covent Garden courtyard, Tube: Covent Garden, tel. 020/7379-6344, recorded info tel. 020/7565-7299, www.ltmuseum.co.uk).

North London

▲▲▲**British Museum**—Simply put, this is the greatest chronicle of civilization...anywhere. A visit here is like taking a long hike through Encyclopedia Britannica National Park. Entering on Great Russell Street, you'll step into the Great Court, the glass-domed hub of a two-acre cultural complex containing restaurants, shops, and lecture halls plus the Reading Room.

The most popular sections of the museum fill the ground floor: Egyptian, Assyrian, and ancient Greek, with the famous Elgin Marbles from the Athenian Parthenon. Huge winged lions (which guarded an Assyrian palace 800 years before Christ) guard these great galleries. For a brief tour, connect these ancient dots:

Start with the **Egyptian** artifacts. Wander from the Rosetta Stone past the many statues. At the end of the hall, climb the stairs to mummy land.

Back at the winged lions, explore the dark, violent, and mysterious **Assyrian** rooms. The Nimrud Gallery is lined with royal propaganda reliefs and wounded lions (from the ninth century B.C.).

The most modern of the ancient art fills the **Greek** section. Find Room 11, behind the winged lions, and start your walk through Greek art history with the simple and primitive Cycladic fertility figures. Later, painted vases show a culture really into

North London

partying. The finale is the Elgin Marbles. The much-wrangled-over bits of the Athenian Parthenon (from about 450 B.C.) are even more impressive than they look. To best appreciate these ancient carvings, take the audioguide tour (see the end of this listing).

Be sure to venture upstairs to see artifacts from **Roman Britain** (Room 50) that surpass anything you'll see at Hadrian's Wall or elsewhere in Britain. Nearby, the Dark Age Britain exhibits offer a worthwhile peek at that bleak era; look for the Sutton Hoo Burial Ship artifacts from a seventh-century royal burial on the east coast of England (Room 41). A rare Michelangelo cartoon (preliminary sketch) is in Room 90.

The **Great Court** is Europe's largest covered square—bigger than a football field. This people-friendly court—delightfully spared from the London rain—was for 150 years one of London's great lost spaces...closed off and gathering dust. While the vast British Museum wraps around the court, its centerpiece is the stately **Reading Room,** famous as the place Karl Marx hung out while formulating his ideas on communism and writing *Das Kapital*. It is normally free and open to the quiet public, but sometimes hosts special exhibits.

Cost, Hours, Location: The British Museum is free (but donation of $5, £3, or €5 requested; temporary exhibits extra, daily 10:00–17:30, Thu–Fri until 20:30—but only a few galleries open

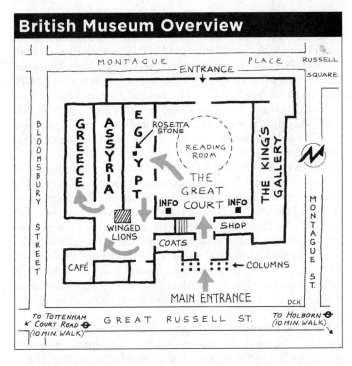

British Museum Overview

after 17:30, least crowded weekday late afternoons, Great Russell Street, Tube: Tottenham Court Road, tel. 020/7323-8000, www .thebritishmuseum.org).

Tours: The various eyeOpener tours are free (generally run every half-hour 10:30–15:30, 35 min); each one is different, focusing on one particular subject within the museum. The Highlights tours are expensive but meaty (£8, 90 min, at 10:30, 13:00, and 15:00). There are also several different audioguide tours (£3.50, £5.50/double set, must leave photo ID), including Museum Highlights (90 min), the Parthenon Sculptures (60 min), and Family Tours (length varies; "Bodies, Beasts, and Boardgames," narrated by Stephen Fry, is particularly good).

▲▲▲**British Library**—Here, in just two rooms called "The Treasures of the British Library," are the literary gems of Western civilization, from early bibles to Shakespeare's *Hamlet* to the Magna Carta to Lewis Carroll's *Alice's Adventures in Wonderland*. You'll see the Lindisfarne Gospels transcribed on an illuminated manuscript, as well as Beatles' lyrics scrawled on the back of a greeting card. The British Empire built its greatest monuments out of paper. And it's with literature that England made her lasting contribution to civilization and the arts (free but donations appreciated, Mon–Fri 9:30–18:00, Tue until 20:00,

Sat 9:30–17:00, Sun 11:00–17:00; see map on page 652; 75-min tours for £8 of library and building usually offered Mon, Wed, and Fri at 15:00, Sat at 10:30 and 15:00, Sun at 11:30 and 15:00; call 020/7412-7639 to confirm and reserve; helpful free computers supply extra info; Tube: King's Cross, from station walk a block west to 96 Euston Road, St. Pancras and Euston Tube stations are nearby; buses #10, #30, #73, #91, #205, #390, or #476; tel. 020/7412-7000, www.bl.uk). The ground-floor café is next to a vast, fun pull-out stamp collection, and the self-service cafeteria upstairs serves good hot meals.

▲Wallace Collection—Sir Richard Wallace's fine collection of 17th-century Dutch Masters, 18th-century French Rococo, medieval armor, and assorted aristocratic fancies fills the sumptuously furnished Hertford House on Manchester Square. From the rough and intimate Dutch life-scapes of Jan Steen to the pink-cheeked Rococo fantasies of François Boucher, a wander through this little-visited mansion makes you nostalgic for the days of empire (free, daily 10:00–17:00, £3 audioguide; guided tours available—but call to confirm times; just north of Oxford Street on Manchester Square, Tube: Bond Street, tel. 020/7563-9500, www.wallace collection.org).

▲Madame Tussauds Waxworks—This is gimmicky and expensive but dang good. The original Madame Tussaud did wax casts of heads lopped off during the French Revolution (such as Marie-Antoinette's). She took her show on the road and ended up in London in 1835. And now it's much easier to be featured. The gallery is one big photo-op—a huge hit with the kind of travelers who skip the British Museum. After looking a hundred famous people in their glassy eyes and surviving a silly hall of horror, you'll board a Disney-type ride and cruise through a kid-pleasing "Spirit of London" time trip. Your last stop is the auditorium for a 12-minute stage show (runs every 15 min). They've dumped anything really historical (except for what they claim is the blade that beheaded Marie-Antoinette) because "there's no money in it and we're a business." Now, it's all about squeezing Brad Pitt's bum, gambling with George Clooney, and partying with Beyoncé, Kylie, Britney, and Posh. The unpopular Gordon Brown is the first prime minister in 150 years not to be immortalized in wax.

Cost, Hours, Location: £25, £35 combo-ticket with London Eye; kids-£21 or £25 with London Eye. From 17:00 to closing, it's £16, kids-£11 (does not include London Eye). Children under 5 are always free. Open mid-July–Aug daily 9:00–18:00; Sept–mid-July Mon–Fri 9:30–17:30, Sat–Sun 9:30–18:00; Marylebone Road, Tube: Baker Street. Their website (www.madame-tussauds .com) explains a few ways to whittle down the cost of this pricey waxtravaganza.

Sir John Soane's Museum—Architects and fans of eclectic knickknacks love this quirky place, as do Martha Stewarts and lovers of Back Door sights. Tour this furnished home on a bird-chirping square and see 19th-century chairs, lamps, and carpets, wood-paneled nooks and crannies, and stained-glass skylights. The townhouse is cluttered with Soane's (and his wife's) collection of ancient relics, curios, and famous paintings, including Hogarth's series on *The Rake's Progress* (read the fun plot) and several excellent Canalettos. In 1833, just before his death, Soane established his house as a museum, stipulating that it be kept as nearly as possible in the state he left it. If he visited today, he'd be entirely satisfied. You'll leave wishing you'd known the man (free, Tue–Sat 10:00–17:00, first Tue of the month also 18:00–21:00, closed Sun–Mon, good £1 brochure, £5 guided tours Sat at 11:00, 13 Lincoln's Inn Fields, quarter-mile southeast of British Museum, Tube: Holborn, tel. 020/7405-2107).

Cartoon Museum—This humble but interesting museum is located in the shadow of the British Museum. While its three rooms are filled with British cartoons unknown to most Americans, the satire of famous bigwigs and politicians—from Napoleon to Margaret Thatcher, the Queen, and Tony Blair—shows the power of parody to deliver social commentary. Upstairs, you'll see pages spanning from *Tarzan* to *Tank Girl*—interesting only to comic-book diehards (£4, Tue–Sat 10:30–17:30, Sun 12:00–17:30, closed Mon, 35 Little Russell Street—go one block south of the British Museum on Coptic Street and make a left, Tube: Tottenham Court Road, tel. 020/7580-8155, www.cartoon museum.org).

Pollock's Toy Museum—This rickety old house, with glass cases filled with toys and games lining its walls and halls, is a time-warp experience that brings back childhood memories to people who grew up without batteries or computer chips. While the museum is small, you could spend a lot of time here, squinting at the fascinating toys and dolls that entertained the children of 19th- and early 20th-century England. The included information is great. The story of Theodore Roosevelt refusing to shoot a bear cub while on a hunting trip was celebrated in 1902 cartoons, resulting in a new, huggable toy: the Teddy Bear. It was popular for good reason—it could be manufactured during World War I without rationed products; it coincided with the new belief that soft toys were good for a child's development; it was an acceptable "doll for boys"; and it's *the* toy children keep long after they've grown up (£5, kids-£2, Mon–Sat 10:00–17:00, closed Sun, 1 Scala Street, Tube: Goodge Street, tel. 020/7636-3452, www.pollocks toymuseum.com).

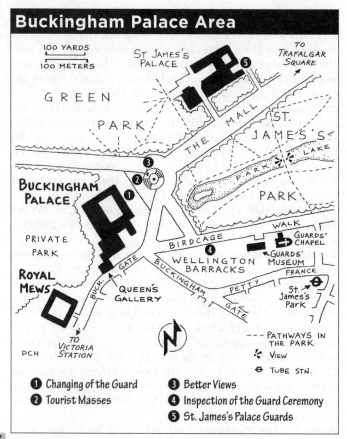

Buckingham Palace Area

```
100 YARDS
100 METERS
```

ST JAMES'S PALACE

TO TRAFALGAR SQUARE

G R E E N

P A R K

THE MALL

ST. JAMES'S

PARK LAKE

BUCKINGHAM PALACE

PRIVATE PARK

ROYAL MEWS

BUCK. GATE

QUEEN'S GALLERY

BIRDCAGE WALK

BUCKINGHAM GATE

WELLINGTON BARRACKS

PETTY FRANCE

GUARDS' CHAPEL

GUARDS' MUSEUM

St. James's Park

TO VICTORIA STATION

DCH

N

--- PATHWAYS IN THE PARK

VIEW

TUBE STN.

1 Changing of the Guard
2 Tourist Masses
3 Better Views
4 Inspection of the Guard Ceremony
5 St. James's Palace Guards

Buckingham Palace

▲**Buckingham Palace**—This lavish home has been Britain's royal residence since 1837. When the queen's at home, the royal standard flies (a red, yellow, and blue flag); otherwise the Union Jack flaps in the wind. Recently, the queen has opened her palace to the public—but only in August and September, when she's out of town (£15.50 for state apartments and throne room, Aug–Sept only, daily 9:45–18:00, last admission 15:45; only 8,000 visitors a day—to get an entry time, come early or for £1.25 extra you can book ahead by phone or online; Tube: Victoria, tel. 020/7766-7300, www.royalcollection.org.uk).

▲**Queen's Gallery at Buckingham Palace**—Queen Elizabeth's 7,000 paintings make up the finest private art collection in the world, rivaling Europe's biggest national art galleries. It's actually a collection of collections, built on by each successive monarch since the 16th century. She rotates her paintings, enjoying some of them privately in her many palatial residences while sharing others with her subjects in public galleries in Edinburgh and London. Small, thoughtfully presented, and always exquisite displays fill the handful of rooms open to the public in a wing of Buckingham Palace. As you're in "the most important building in London," security is tight. You'll see a temporary exhibit and the permanent "treasures"—which come with a room full of "antique and personal jewelry." Compared to the crown jewels at the Tower, it may be Her Majesty's bottom drawer—but it's still a dazzling pile of diamonds. Temporary exhibits change about twice a year, and are lovingly described by the included audioguide. While the admission tickets come with an entry time, this is only enforced during rare days when crowds are a problem (£8.50, £15.50 with Royal Mews, daily 10:00–17:30, last entry one hour before closing, Tube: Victoria, tel. 020/7766-7301 but Her Majesty rarely answers). Men shouldn't miss the mahogany-trimmed urinals.

Royal Mews—The Queen's working stables, or "mews," are open to visitors. The visit is likely to be disappointing (you'll see four horses out of the Queen's 30, a fancy car, and a bunch of old carriages) unless you follow the included guided tour, in which case it's thoroughly entertaining—especially if you're interested in horses and/or royalty. The 40-minute tours go twice an hour and finish with the Gold State Coach (c. 1760, 4 tons, 4 mph). Queen Victoria said absolutely no cars. When she died, in 1901, the mews got its first Daimler. Today, along with the hay-eating transport, the stable is home to five Rolls-Royce Phantoms, with one on display (£7.50, £15.50 with Queen's Gallery, Aug–Sept Sat–Thu 10:00–17:00, March–July and Oct Sat–Thu 11:00–16:00, last entry 45 min before closing, closed Fri and Nov–Feb, Buckingham Palace Road, Tube: Victoria, tel. 020/7766-7302).

▲▲Changing of the Guard at Buckingham Palace—The guards change with much fanfare at around 11:30 almost daily from May through July, and every other day for the rest of the year (odd days in Aug, even days in Sept, and so on; no band in very wet weather). Call 020/7766-7300 for the day's plan, or check www.royalcollection.org.uk (click "Visit," then "Changing the Guard"). Then hop into a big black taxi and say, "Buck House, please" (a.k.a. Buckingham Palace).

Most tourists just mob the palace gates for a peek at the Changing of the Guard, but those who know the drill will enjoy the event more. Here's the lowdown on what goes down: It's just after 11:00, and the on-duty guards—actually working at nearby St. James's Palace—are ready to finish their shift. At 11:15, these tired guards, along with the band, head out to the Mall, and then take a right turn for Buckingham Palace. Meanwhile, their replacement guards—fresh for the day—gather at 11:00 at their

Wellington Barracks, 500 yards east of the palace (on Birdcage Walk), for a review and inspection. At 11:30, they also head for Buckingham Palace. As both the tired and fresh guards converge on the palace, the Horse Guard enters the fray, marching down the Mall from the Horse Guard Barracks on Whitehall. At 11:45, it's a perfect storm of Red Coat pageantry, as all three groups converge. Everyone parades around, the guard changes (passing the regimental flag, or "color") with much shouting, the band plays a happy little concert, and then they march out. A few minutes later, fresh guards set up at St. James's Palace, the tired ones dress down at the barracks, and the tourists disperse.

Stake out the high ground on the circular Victoria Monument for the best overall view. Or start early either at St. James's Palace or the Wellington Barracks (the inspection is in full view of the street) and stride in with the band. The marching troops and bands are colorful and even stirring, but the actual Changing of the Guard is a nonevent. It is interesting, however, to see nearly every tourist in London gathered in one place at the same time. Afterwards, stroll through nearby St. James's Park (Tube: Victoria, St. James's Park, or Green Park).

West London

▲**Hyde Park and Speakers' Corner**—London's "Central Park," originally Henry VIII's hunting grounds, has more than 600 acres of lush greenery, a huge man-made lake, the royal Kensington Palace and Orangery, and the ornate neo-Gothic Albert Memorial across from the Royal Albert Hall. On Sundays from just after noon until early evening, Speakers' Corner offers soapbox oratory at its best (Tube: Marble Arch). Characters climb their stepladders, wave their flags, pound emphatically on their sandwich boards, and share what they are convinced is their wisdom. Regulars have resident hecklers—who know their lines and are always ready with a verbal jab or barb. "The grass roots of democracy" is actually a holdover from when the gallows stood here and the criminal was allowed to say just about anything he wanted to before he swung. I dare you to raise your voice and gather a crowd—it's easy to do.

The **Princess Diana Memorial Fountain** honors the "People's Princess" who once lived in nearby Kensington Palace. The low-key circular stream is in the eastern part of the park, near the Serpentine Gallery. (Don't be confused by signs to the Diana Princess of Wales Memorial Playground, also found within the park.)

▲**Apsley House (Wellington Museum)**—Having beaten Napoleon at Waterloo, the Duke of Wellington was once the most famous man in Europe. He was given London's ultimate address, #1 London. His newly refurbished mansion offers one of London's

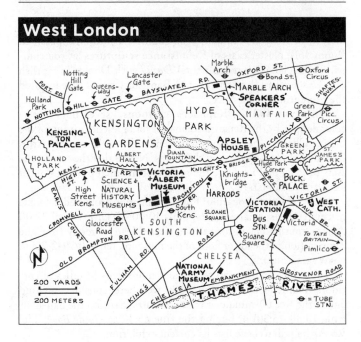

West London

best palace experiences. An 11-foot-tall marble statue (by Canova) of Napoleon, clad only in a fig leaf, greets you. Downstairs is a small gallery of Wellington memorabilia, including a pair of Wellington boots, which the duke popularized (the Brits still call rubber boots "wellies"). The lavish upstairs shows off the duke's fine collection of paintings, including works by Velázquez and Steen (£5.50, Wed–Sun 10:00–17:00 in summer, until 16:00 in winter, closed Mon–Tue, well-described by included audioguide, 20 yards from Hyde Park Corner Tube station, tel. 020/7499-5676, www.english-heritage.org.uk). Hyde Park's pleasant and picnic-wonderful rose garden is nearby.

▲▲**Victoria and Albert Museum**—The world's top collection of decorative arts (vases, stained glass, fine furniture, clothing, jewelry, carpets, and more) is a surprisingly interesting assortment of crafts from the West as well as Asian and Islamic cultures.

The V&A grew out of the Great Exhibition of 1851, that ultimate festival celebrating the greatness of Britain. After much support from Queen Victoria and Prince Albert, it was renamed after the royal couple, and its present building was opened in 1909.

Many visitors start with the **British Galleries** (upstairs)—a one-way tour stretching through 400 years of high-class British lifestyles, almost a museum in itself.

In Room 46A are the plaster casts of **Trajan's Column,** a copy of Rome's 140-foot spiral relief telling the story of the conquest of Romania. (The V&A's casts are copies made for the benefit of 19th-century art students who couldn't afford a railpass.) **In** Room 46B, plaster casts of **Renaissance sculptures** let you compare Michelangelo's monumental *David* with Donatello's girlish *David;* see also Ghiberti's bronze Baptistery doors that inspired the Florentine Renaissance.

In Room 48A are **Raphael's "cartoons,"** seven huge watercolor designs by the Renaissance master for tapestries meant for the Sistine Chapel. The cartoons were sent to Brussels, cut into strips (see the lines), and placed on the looms. Notice that the scenes, the Acts of Peter and Paul, are the reverse of the final product (lots of left-handed saints).

Cost, Hours, Location: Free, £3 donation requested, possible pricey fee for special exhibits, daily 10:00–17:45, Fri until 22:00 (Tube: South Kensington, a long tunnel leads directly from the Tube station to the lower floor of the museum, tel. 020/7942-2000, www.vam.ac.uk).

The museum has 150 rooms and more than 12 miles of corridors. While just wandering works well here, consider catching one of the free 60-minute orientation **tours** (daily on the half-hour from 10:30–15:30) or buying the fine £5 *V&A Guide Book*. The V&A's helpful website lists its current exhibitions.

▲**Natural History Museum**—Across the street from Victoria and Albert, this mammoth museum is housed in a giant and wonderful Victorian, Neo-Romanesque building. Built in the 1870s specifically for the huge collection (50 million specimens), it has two halves: the Life Galleries (creepy-crawlies, human biology, "our place in evolution," and awesome dinosaurs) and the Earth Galleries (meteors, volcanoes, earthquakes, and so on). Exhibits are wonderfully explained, with lots of creative, interactive displays. Pop in, if only for the wild collection of dinosaurs and the roaring *Tyrannosaurus rex* (free, possible fee for special exhibits, daily 10:00–17:50, last entry at 17:30, occasional tours, a long tunnel leads directly from South Kensington Tube station to museum, tel. 020/7942-5000, exhibit info and reservations tel. 020/7942-5011, www.nhm.ac.uk).

▲**Science Museum**—Next door to the Natural History Museum, this sprawling wonderland for curious minds is kid-perfect. It offers hands-on fun, from moonwalks to deep-sea exploration, with trendy technology exhibits, an IMAX theater (£7.50, kids-£6), cool rotating themed exhibits, and a revamped kids' zone on the third floor (free entry, daily 10:00–18:00, Exhibition Road, Tube: South Kensington, tel. 0870-870-4868, www.science museum.org.uk).

▲▲**Kensington Palace**—In 1689, King William and Queen Mary moved their primary residence from Whitehall in central

London to the more pristine and peaceful village of Kensington (now engulfed by London). With a little renovation help from Sir Christopher Wren, they turned an existing house into Kensington Palace, which was the center of English court life until 1760, when the royal family moved into Buckingham Palace. Since then, lesser royals have bedded down in Kensington Palace (as Princess Diana did from her 1981 marriage to Prince Charles until her death in 1997). The palace, while still functioning as a royal residence, also welcomes visitors with an impressive string of historic royal apartments and a few rooms of queens' dresses and ceremonial clothing (late 19th and 20th centuries). Enjoy a re-created royal tailor and dressmaker's workshop, the 17th-century splendor of the apartments of William and Mary, and the bed where Queen Victoria was born (fully clothed). The displays are wonderfully described by the included audioguide. The empty, unfurnished Apartment 1A, the former home of Princess Margaret, is skippable (£12.30, daily 10:00–18:00, until 17:00 in winter, last entry one hour before closing, a 10-min hike through Kensington Gardens from either Queensway or High Street Kensington Tube station, tel. 0870-751-5170, www.hrp.org.uk). Garden enthusiasts enjoy popping into the secluded Sunken Garden, 50 yards from the exit.

Consider afternoon tea at the nearby Orangery, built as a greenhouse for Queen Anne in 1704 (tea served 15:00–18:00, choose £13 "Orangery tea" or £18 champagne tea, small portions, about 20 yards from the palace—see map on page 659, tel. 020/7938-1406).

Victoria Station—From underneath this station's iron-and-glass canopy, trains depart for the south of England and Gatwick Airport. While Victoria Station is famous and a major Tube stop, few tourists actually take trains from here—most just come to take in the exciting bustle. It's a fun place to just be a "rock in a river" teeming with commuters and services. The station is surrounded by big red buses and taxis, travel agencies, and lousy eateries. It's next to the main bus station (National Express) and the best inexpensive B&Bs in town.

Westminster Cathedral—This largest Catholic church in England, just a block from Victoria Station, is striking but not very historic or important to visit. Opened in 1903, it has a brick neo-Byzantine flavor (surrounded by glassy office blocks). While it's definitely not Westminster Abbey, half the tourists wandering around inside seem to think it is. The highlight is the lift to the viewing gallery atop its bell tower (fine view, £3 for the lift, tower open daily 9:30–12:30 & 13:00–17:00, cathedral sometimes open longer hours for Mass; 5-min walk from Victoria Station or take bus #11, #24, #148, #211, or #507 to museum's door; just off Victoria Street, Tube: Victoria).

National Army Museum—This museum is not as awe-inspiring as the Imperial War Museum, but it's still fun, especially for kids into soldiers, armor, and guns. And while the Imperial War Museum is limited to wars of the 20th century, this tells the story of the British army from 1415 through the Bosnian conflict and Iraq, with lots of Red Coat lore and a good look at Waterloo. Kids enjoy trying on a Cromwellian helmet, seeing the skeleton of Napoleon's horse, and peering out from a WWI trench through a working periscope (free, daily 10:00–17:30, follow arrows in carpet to stay on track, bus #239 from Victoria Station stops at museum's door, Royal Hospital Road, Chelsea, Tube: Sloane Square, tel. 020-7730-0717, www.national-army-museum.ac.uk).

East London: The City

▲▲**The City of London**—When Londoners say "The City," they mean the one-square-mile business center that 2,000 years ago was Roman Londinium. The outline of the Roman city walls can still be seen in the arc of roads from Blackfriars Bridge to Tower Bridge. Within The City are 23 churches designed by Sir Christopher Wren, mostly just ornamentation around St. Paul's Cathedral. Today, while home to only 5,000 residents, The City thrives with more than 500,000 office workers coming and going daily. It's a fascinating district to wander on weekdays, but since almost nobody actually lives there, it's dull in the evenings and on Saturday and Sunday.

▲**Old Bailey**—To view the British legal system in action—lawyers in little blond wigs speaking legalese with a British accent—spend a few minutes in the visitors' gallery at the Old Bailey, called the "Central Criminal Court." Don't enter under the dome; signs point you to the two visitors' entrances (free, generally Mon–Fri 9:45–12:45 & 14:00–16:30 depending on caseload, closed Sat–Sun, reduced hours in Aug; no kids under 14; no bags, mobile phones, or cameras, but small purses OK; Eddie at Bailey's Café across the street at #30 stores bags for £2; 2 blocks northwest of St. Paul's on Old Bailey Street, follow signs to public entrance, Tube: St. Paul's, tel. 020/7248-3277).

▲▲▲**St. Paul's Cathedral**—Wren's most famous church is the great St. Paul's, its elaborate interior capped by a 365-foot dome. The crypt (included with admission) is a world of historic bones and memorials, including Admiral Nelson's tomb and interest-ing cathedral models. Stroll down the same nave Prince Charles and Lady Diana walked on their 1981 wedding day. Imagine how they felt making the hike to the altar with the world watching. Sit under the second-largest dome in the world and eavesdrop on guided tours.

Since World War II, St. Paul's has been Britain's symbol

East London: The City

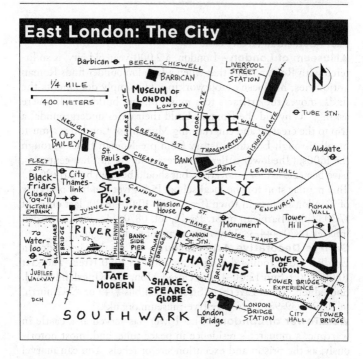

of resistance. Despite 57 nights of bombing, the Nazis failed to destroy the cathedral, thanks to the St. Paul's volunteer fire watch, who stayed on the dome. Today you can climb the dome for a great city view and some fun in the Whispering Gallery—where the precisely designed barrel of the dome lets sweet nothings circle audibly around to the opposite side.

The **evensong** services are free, but nonpaying visitors are not allowed to linger afterward (Mon–Sat at 17:00, Sun at 15:15, 40 min). Restoration of the cathedral's organ should be finished in time for your visit—check to see if the traditional free Sunday evening **organ recitals** have resumed (previously at 17:00).

Cost, Hours, Location: £10, includes church entry and dome climb; £5 between 15:30–16:00 but you can't climb dome; Mon–Sat 8:30–16:30, last church entry at 16:00, last dome entry at 15:30, closed Sun except for worship. No photography is allowed. Guided 90-minute "super tours" of the cathedral and crypt cost £3 (Mon–Sat at 11:00, 11:30, 13:30, and 14:00—confirm schedule at church or call 020/7236-4128; £4 for 60-min audioguide that covers 17 stops, available Mon–Sat 9:15–15:30). A good café and a pricier restaurant are in the crypt (Tube: St. Paul's, Mansion House, or Cannon Street; buses #4, #11, #15, #17, #23, #26, #76, #100, or #172; tel. 020/7236-4128, recorded info tel. 020/7246-8348, www.stpauls.co.uk). Careful: Tourist maps show a "St. Paul's

Church" near Covent Garden, but you're heading instead for St. Paul's Cathedral, farther east.

▲**Museum of London**—London, a 2,000-year-old city, is so littered with Roman ruins that when a London builder finds Roman antiquities, he doesn't stop working. He simply documents the finds, moves the artifacts to a museum, and builds on. If you're asking, "Why did the Romans build their cities underground?" a trip to the creative and entertaining Museum of London is a must. Stroll through London history from pre-Roman times through the 1600s. (The lower galleries, representing the last few centuries, have been closed for renovation, but should be open by early 2010.) This regular stop for the local school kids gives the best overview of London history in town (free, daily 10:00–18:00, last entry at 17:30, Tube: Barbican or St. Paul's, tel. 0870-444-3852, recorded info tel. 0870-444-3851, www.museumoflondon.org.uk).

Geffrye Decorative Arts Museum—Walk through a dozen English front rooms dating from 1600 to 1990 (free, Tue–Sat 10:00–17:00, Sun 12:00–17:00, closed Mon, 136 Kingsland Road, Shoreditch, Tube: Liverpool Street, then bus #149 or #242 north, tel. 020/7739-9893, www.geffrye-museum.org.uk).

▲▲▲**Tower of London**—The Tower has served as a castle in wartime, a monarch's residence in peace time, and, most notoriously, as the prison and execution site of rebels. You can marvel at the crown jewels, take a witty Beefeater tour, and ponder the executioner's block that dispensed with troublesome heirs to the throne and a couple of Henry VIII's wives (£16.50, family-£46; March–Oct Tue–Sat 9:00–17:30, Sun–Mon 10:00–17:30; Nov–Feb Tue–Sat 9:00–16:30, Sun–Mon 10:00–16:30; last entry 30 min before closing, the long but fast-moving ticket lines are worst on Sun, no photography allowed of jewels or in chapels, Tube: Tower Hill, tel. 0870-751-5177, recorded info tel. 0870-756-6060, booking tel. 0870-756-7070). Avoid long lines by buying your ticket online (www.hrp.org.uk), at any London TI, at the Trader's Gate gift shop down the steps from the Tower Hill Tube stop, or at the Welcome Centre to the left of the normal ticket line (credit card only). After your visit, consider taking the boat to Greenwich from here (see "Cruises—To Greenwich" on page 639).

On Sunday morning, visitors are welcome on the grounds for free to worship in the **Royal Chapel**—you get in with no lines but can only see the chapel (11:00 service with fine choral music, meet at west gate at 10:45, dress for church).

The pageantry-filled **Ceremony of the Keys** is held every night at precisely 21:30, when the Tower of London is locked up (as it has been for the last 700 years). To attend this free 30-minute event, you need to request an invitation at least two months before your visit. For details, go to www.hrp.org.uk and select

"Tower of London," then "What's On" and "Ceremony of the Keys" (but note that some readers report that it's difficult to get the required International Reply Coupons from their local U.S. post office).

More Sights near the Tower—The best remaining bit of London's **Roman Wall** is just north of the tower (at the Tower Hill Tube station). The impressive Tower Bridge is freshly painted and restored; for more information on this neo-Gothic maritime gateway to London, you can visit the **Tower Bridge Experience** for its 1894–1994 history exhibit and a peek at its Victorian engine room (£6, family-£14 and up, daily 10:00–18:30, last entry at 17:30, good view, poor value, enter at the northwest tower, tel. 020/7403-3761, for bridge-lifting schedule call 020/7940-3984, www.tower bridge.org.uk). The chic **St. Katharine Dock,** just east of Tower Bridge, has private yachts, mod shops, and the classic old Dickens Inn, fun for a drink or pub lunch. Across the bridge is the South Bank, with the upscale Butlers Wharf area, City Hall, museums, and the Jubilee Walkway.

South London, on the South Bank

▲▲**Jubilee Walkway**—The South Bank is a thriving arts and cultural center tied together by this riverside path, a popular, pub-crawling pedestrian promenade called the Jubilee Walkway. Stretching from Tower Bridge past Westminster Bridge, it offers grand views of the Houses of Parliament. On a sunny day, this is the place to be to see London out strolling. Start at Westminster Bridge and enjoy the promenade. The walkway hugs the river except just east of London Bridge, where it cuts inland for a couple of blocks (www.jubileewalkway.org.uk).

City Hall—The glassy, egg-shaped building near the south end of Tower Bridge is London's City Hall, designed by Sir Norman Foster, the architect who worked on London's Millennium Bridge and Berlin's Reichstag. City Hall is where London's mayor works (blonde, flamboyant, conservative Boris Johnson), along with the Assembly representatives of the city's 25 districts. An interior spiral ramp allows visitors to watch and hear the action below in the Assembly Chamber; ride the lift to the second floor (the highest visitors can go) and spiral down. The Visitors Centre on the lower ground floor has a handy cafeteria (Visitors Centre open Mon–Fri 8:00–20:00, Tube: London Bridge station plus 10-min walk, or Tower Hill station plus 15-min walk; the Hall occasionally opens up for public tours—call or check website to confirm tour times and opening hours, tel. 020/7983-4100, www.london.gov.uk/gla /city_hall).

▲▲▲**London Eye**—This giant Ferris wheel, which towers above London opposite Big Ben, was built by British Airways. It's now

The South Bank

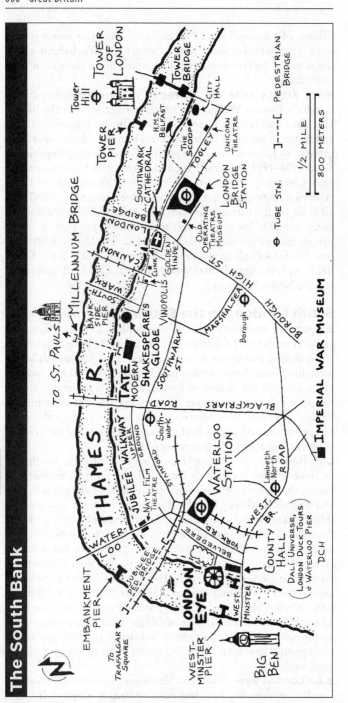

run in an extremely commercial way by Merlin Entertainment, which also operates the London Dungeon and Madame Tussauds Waxworks.

London's answer to the Eiffel Tower is the world's highest observational wheel. While the experience is memorable, London doesn't have much of a skyline and the price is borderline outrageous. But whether you ride or not, the wheel is a sight to behold. Designed like a giant bicycle wheel, it's a pan-European undertaking: British steel and Dutch engineering, with Czech, German, French, and Italian mechanical parts. It's also very "green," running extremely efficiently and virtually silently. Twenty-five people ride in each of its 32 air-conditioned capsules for the 30-minute rotation (each capsule has a bench, but most people stand); you go around only once. From the top of this 450-foot-high wheel—the highest public viewpoint in the city—even Big Ben looks small. The London Eye's original five-year lease has been extended to 25 years, and it looks like it will become a permanent fixture on the London skyline. Thames boats come and go from here using the Waterloo Pier at the foot of the wheel.

Cost, Hours, Location: £15.50, or £35 combo-ticket with Madame Tussauds Waxworks, £10 extra buys a Fast Track ticket that lets you jump the queue, daily June–Sept 10:00–21:00, Oct–Christmas and mid-Jan–May 10:00–20:00, closed Christmas–mid-Jan for annual maintenance, Tube: Waterloo or Westminster. If you want to book a ticket (with an assigned time) in advance, call 0870-500-0600, or save 10 percent by booking online at www .londoneye.com.

Dalí Universe—Cleverly located next to the hugely popular London Eye, this overpriced exhibit features 500 works of mind-bending art by Salvador Dalí. It's not worth it for most, unless you like Surrealism and want to learn about Dalí (£12, £2.50 audioguide, daily 9:30–19:00, last entry one hour before closing, Tube: Waterloo or Westminster, tel. 020/7620-2720, www.the daliuniverse.co.uk). The Dalí Universe currently also has a secondary show, "Picasso: Art of a Genius."

▲▲**Imperial War Museum**—This impressive museum covers the wars of the last century, from heavy weaponry to love notes and Vargas Girls, from Monty's Africa campaign tank to Schwartzkopf's Desert Storm uniform. You can trace the development of the machine gun, watch footage of the first tank battles, see one of more than a thousand V2 rockets Hitler rained on Britain in 1944 (each with more than a ton of explosives), hold your breath through the gruesome WWI trench experience, and buy WWII-era toys in the fun museum shop. The "Secret War" section gives a fascinating peek into the intrigues of espionage in World Wars I and II. The section on the Holocaust is one of the best on the subject anywhere. Rather than glorify war, the museum does its best to shine a light on the powerful human side of one of mankind's most persistent traits (free, daily 10:00–18:00, 2 hours is enough time for most visitors, often guided tours on weekends—ask at info desk, £3.50 audioguide, interesting bookshop, Tube: Lambeth North or bus #12 from Westminster, tel. 020/7416-5320 or 020/7416-5321, www.iwm.org.uk).

The museum is housed in what was the Royal Bethlam Hospital. Also known as "the Bedlam asylum," the place was so wild it gave the world a new word for chaos. Back in Victorian times, locals—without reality shows and YouTube—came here for their entertainment. The asylum was actually open to the paying public on weekends.

▲▲▲**Tate Modern**—Dedicated in the spring of 2000, the striking museum across the river from St. Paul's opened the new century with art from the old one. Its powerhouse collection of Monet, Matisse, Dalí, Picasso, Warhol, and much more is displayed in a converted powerhouse. Each year, the main hall features a different monumental installation by a prominent artist (free but £3 donations appreciated, fee for special exhibitions, daily 10:00–18:00, Fri–Sat until 22:00—a good time to visit, audioguide-£2, children's audioguide-£1; free guided tours at 11:00, 12:00, 14:00, and 15:00—confirm at info desk; view restaurant on top floor; cross the Millennium Bridge from St. Paul's; Tube: London Bridge plus a 10-min walk; Blackfriars Tube stop is also nearby but closed through 2011; or connect by Tate Boat ferry from Tate Britain for £4 one-way, discounted with Travelcard; switchboard tel. 020/7887-8888, recorded info tel. 020/7887-8008, www.tate.org.uk).

▲**Millennium Bridge**—The pedestrian bridge links St. Paul's Cathedral and the Tate Modern across the Thames. This is London's first new bridge in a century. When it first opened, the $25 million bridge wiggled when people walked on it, so it promptly closed for an $8 million, 20-month stabilization; now it's stable and open again (free). Nicknamed the "blade of light" for its sleek minimalist design (370 yards long, four yards wide, stainless steel with teak planks), the bridge has clever aerodynamic handrails that deflect wind over the heads of pedestrians.

▲▲**Shakespeare's Globe**—The original Globe Theatre has been rebuilt, half-timbered and thatched, as it was in Shakespeare's time. (This is the first thatched roof in London since they were outlawed after the Great Fire of 1666.) The Globe originally accommodated 2,200 seated and another 1,000 standing. Today, slightly smaller and leaving space for reasonable aisles, the theater holds 900 seated and 600 groundlings. Its promoters brag that the theater melds "the three A's"—actors, audience, and architecture—

with each contributing to the play.

The complex has three parts: the museum, the theater itself, and the box office. The Globe's museum on Shakespeare is the world's largest, with interactive displays and film presentations, a sound lab, a script factory, and costumes. The working theater hosts authentic old-time performances of Shakespeare's plays (generally 14:00 and 19:30—but confirm). For details on seeing a play, see "Entertainment," later in this chapter.

You can tour the theater only when there are no plays going on—it's worth planning ahead for these excellent actor-led guided tours. On performance days (when you can't tour the Globe Theatre), you can still see the museum, but you'll tour the nearby Rose Theatre instead (£10.50 includes museum and tour; tickets good all day; complex open daily 9:00–17:00; museum and tours May–Sept daily 9:00–17:00—tours offered only in morning in summer, Oct–April daily 10:00–17:00—tours run all day in winter; tours go every 15–30 min; on the South Bank directly across Thames over Southwark Bridge from St. Paul's, Tube: Mansion House or London Bridge plus a 10-min walk; tel. 020/7902-1400 or 020/7902-1500, www.shakespeares-globe.org).

The Globe Café is open daily (10:00–17:30, tel. 020/7902-1433).

▲▲**Old Operating Theatre Museum and Herb Garret**—Climb a tight and creaky wooden spiral staircase to a church attic where you'll find a garret used to dry medicinal herbs, a fascinating exhibit on Victorian surgery, cases of well-described 19th-century medical paraphernalia, and a special look at "anesthesia, the defeat of pain." Then you stumble upon Britain's oldest operating theater, where limbs were sawed off way back in 1821 (£5.45, daily 10:30–17:00, closed Dec 15–Jan 5, 9A St. Thomas Street, Tube: London Bridge, tel. 020/7188-2679, www.thegarret.org.uk).

▲▲**Vinopolis: City of Wine**—While it seems illogical to have a huge wine museum in London, Vinopolis makes a good case. Built over a Roman wine store and filling the massive vaults of an old wine warehouse, the museum offers an excellent audioguide with a light yet earnest history of wine to accompany your sips of various reds and whites, ports, and champagnes. Allow some time, as the audioguide takes 90 minutes—and the sipping can slow things down wonderfully. This place is popular. Booking ahead for Friday and Saturday nights is a must (£19.50–32.50 tour options, each includes five wine tastes and audioguide; some packages also include tastes of whiskey, beer, or absinthe; open Mon and Thu–Fri 12:00–22:00, Sat 11:00–21:00, Sun 12:00–18:00, closed Tue–Wed, last entry 2.5 hours before closing, between the Globe and Southwark Cathedral at 1 Bank End, Tube: London Bridge, tel. 0870-241-4040 or 020/7940-8322, www.vinopolis.co.uk).

South London, on the North Bank

▲▲**Tate Britain**—One of Europe's great art houses, Tate Britain specializes in British painting from the 16th century through modern times. The museum has a good representation of William Blake's religious sketches, the Pre-Raphaelites' realistic art, and J. M. W. Turner's swirling works (free, £2 donation requested, daily 10:00–17:50, last entry at 17:00, fine and necessary £3.50 audioguide; free tours: normally Mon–Fri at 11:00 on the 16th, 17th, and 18th centuries; at 12:00 on the 19th century; at 14:00 on Turner; and at 15:00 on the 20th century; Sat–Sun at 12:00 and 15:00—highlights; call to confirm schedule, kids' activities on weekends, no photography allowed; Tube: Pimlico, then 7-min walk; or arrive directly at museum by taking the Tate Boat ferry from Tate Modern or London Eye—£4 one-way, discounted with Travelcard, or bus #88 from Oxford Circus or #87 from National Gallery; recorded info tel. 020/7887-8008, office tel. 020/7887-8888, www.tate.org.uk).

▲**Kew Gardens**—For a fine riverside park and a palatial green-house jungle to swing through, take the Tube or the boat to every botanist's favorite escape, Kew Gardens. While to most visitors the Royal Botanic Gardens of Kew are simply a delightful opportunity to wander among 33,000 different types of plants, to the hard-working organization that runs the gardens, it's a way to promote understanding and preservation of the botanical diversity of our planet. The Kew Tube station drops you in an herbal little busi-ness community, a two-block walk from Victoria Gate (the main garden entrance). Pick up a map brochure and check at the gate for a monthly listing of best blooms.

Garden-lovers could spend days exploring Kew's 300 acres. For a quick visit, spend a fragrant hour wandering through three buildings: the **Palm House,** a humid Victorian world of iron, glass, and tropical plants built in 1844; a **Waterlily House** that Monet would swim for; and the **Princess of Wales Conservatory,** a modern greenhouse with many different climate zones grow-ing countless cacti, bug-munching carnivorous plants, and more. The latest addition to the gardens is the **Rhizotron and Xstrata Treetop Walkway,** a 200-yard-long scenic steel walkway that puts you high in the canopy 60 feet above the ground (£13, discounted to £12 one hour before closing, £5 for Kew Palace only; April–Aug Mon–Fri 9:30–18:30, Sat–Sun 9:30–19:30; until 17:30 Sept–Oct, until 16:15 Nov–Jan, until 17:00 Feb–March, last entry to gardens 30 min before closing, galleries and conservatories close at 17:30 in high season—earlier off-season, free tours daily at 11:00 and 14:00, children's activities, £4 narrated floral 35-min joyride on little train departs on the hour until 16:00 from Victoria Gate, Tube: Kew Gardens, boats run between Kew Gardens and Westminster Pier, tel. 020/8332-5000, www.kew.org). For a sun-dappled lunch, walk 10 minutes from the Palm House to the Orangery (£6 hot meals, daily 10:00–17:30).

Entertainment

Theater (a.k.a. "Theatre")

London's theater rivals Broadway's in quality and beats it in price. Choose from 200 offerings—Shakespeare, musicals, comedy, thrillers, sex farces, cutting-edge fringe, revivals starring movie celebs, and more. London does it all well. I prefer big, glitzy—even bombastic—musicals over serious chamber dramas, simply because London can deliver the lights, sound, dancers, and multimedia spectacle I rarely get back home.

Most theaters, marked on tourist maps (also see map on next page), are found in the West End between Piccadilly and Covent Garden. Box offices, hotels, and TIs offer a handy free *London Theatre Guide* (also at www.londontheatre.co.uk) and *Entertainment Guide*. From home, it's easy to check www.official londontheatre.co.uk or the American magazine *Variety* for the latest on what's currently playing in London.

Performances are nightly except Sunday, usually with one or two matinees a week (Shakespeare's Globe is the rare theater that does offer performances on Sun, mid-May–Sept). Tickets range from about £11 to £55. Matinees are generally cheaper and rarely sell out.

To book a seat, simply call the theater box office directly, ask about seats and available dates, and buy a ticket with your credit card. You can call from the US as easily as from London. Arrive about 30 minutes before the show starts to pick up your ticket and to avoid lines.

For a booking fee, you can reserve online. Most theater websites link you to a preferred ticket vendor, usually www.ticket master.co.uk or www.seetickets.com. Keith Prowse ticket service is also handy by phone or online (US tel. 800-669-8687, British tel. 0844-209-0382, www.keithprowse.com).

While booking through an agency is quick and easy, prices are inflated by a standard 25 percent fee. Ticket agencies (whether in the US, at London's TIs, or scattered throughout the city) are scalpers with an address. If you're buying from an agency, look at the ticket carefully (your price should be no more than 30 percent over the printed face value; the 17.5 percent VAT—value-added tax—is already included in the face value), and understand where you're sitting according to the floor plan (if your view is restricted, it will state this on the ticket; for floor plans of the various theaters, see www.theatremonkey.com). Agencies are worthwhile only if a

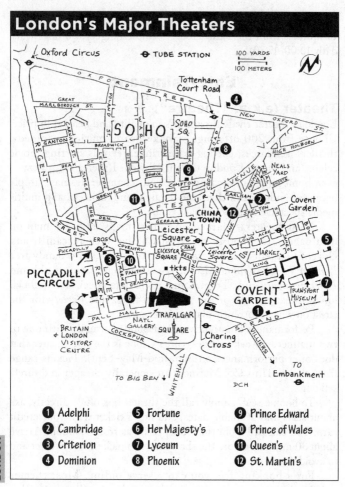

London's Major Theaters

- ❶ Adelphi
- ❷ Cambridge
- ❸ Criterion
- ❹ Dominion
- ❺ Fortune
- ❻ Her Majesty's
- ❼ Lyceum
- ❽ Phoenix
- ❾ Prince Edward
- ❿ Prince of Wales
- ⓫ Queen's
- ⓬ St. Martin's

show you've just got to see is sold out at the box office. They scarf up hot tickets, planning to make a killing after the show is sold out. US booking agencies get their tickets from another agency, adding even more to your expense by involving yet another middleman. Many tickets sold on the street are forgeries. Although some theaters have booking agencies handle their advance sales, you'll stand a good chance of saving money and avoiding the middleman by simply calling the box office directly to book your tickets (international phone calls are cheap and credit cards make booking a snap).

Theater Lingo: Stalls (ground floor), dress circle (first balcony), upper circle (second balcony), balcony (sky-high third balcony), slips (cheap seats on the fringes). Many cheap seats have a restricted view (behind a pillar).

Cheap Theater Tricks: Most theaters offer cheap returned tickets, standing-room, matinee, and senior or student standby deals. These "concessions" are indicated with a "conc" or "s" in the listings. Picking up a late return can get you a great seat at a cheap-seat price. If a show is "sold out," there's usually a way to get a seat. Call the theater box office and ask how.

If you don't care where you sit, the absolutely cheapest seats (obstructed view or nosebleed section) can be found at the box office, and generally cost less than £20 per ticket. Many theaters are so small that there's hardly a bad seat. After the lights go down, scooting up is less than a capital offense. Shakespeare did it.

Half-Price "tkts" Booth: This famous ticket booth at **Leicester Square** sells discounted tickets for top-price seats to shows on the push list the day of the show only (£2.50 service charge per ticket, Mon–Sat 10:00–19:00, Sun 12:00–15:30, matinee tickets from noon, lines often form early, list of shows available online, www.tkts.co.uk). Most tickets are half-price; other shows are discounted 25 percent.

Here are some sample prices: A top-notch seat to *Chicago* costs £52.50 bought directly from the theater; the same seat costs £28.75 at Leicester (LESS-ter) Square. The cheapest balcony seat (bought from the theater) is £20. Half-price tickets can be a good deal, unless you want the cheapest seats or the hottest shows. But check the board; occasionally they sell cheap tickets to good shows. For example, a first-class seat to the long-running *Les Misérables* (which rarely sells out) costs £55 when bought from the theater ticket office, but you'll pay £30 at the tkts booth. Note that the real half-price booth (with its "tkts" name) is a freestanding kiosk at the edge of the garden in Leicester Square. Several dishonest outfits nearby advertise "official half-price tickets"; avoid these.

West End Theaters: The commercial (non-subsidized) theaters cluster around Soho (especially along Shaftesbury Avenue) and Covent Garden. With a centuries-old tradition of pleasing the masses, these present London theater at its glitziest.

Royal Shakespeare Company: If you'll ever enjoy Shakespeare, it'll be in Britain. The RSC performs at various theaters around London and in Stratford year-round. To get a schedule, contact the RSC (Royal Shakespeare Theatre, Stratford-upon-Avon, tel. 01789/403-444, www.rsc.org.uk).

Shakespeare's Globe: To see Shakespeare in a replica of the theater for which he wrote his plays, attend a play at the Globe. This round, thatch-roofed, open-air theater performs the plays much as Shakespeare intended (with no amplification). The play's the thing from May through October (usually Tue–Sat 14:00 and 19:30, Sun either 13:00 and 18:30 or 16:00 only, sometimes Mon 19:30, tickets can be sold out months in advance). You'll pay £5 to stand and £15–33 to sit (usually on a backless bench; only a few rows and the pricier Gentlemen's Rooms have seats with backs; £1 cushions and £3 add-on back rests are considered a good investment by many). The £5 "groundling" tickets—while open to rain—are most fun. Scurry in early to stake out a spot on the stage's edge leaning rail, where the most interaction with the actors occurs. You're a crude peasant. You can lean your elbows on the stage, munch a picnic dinner, or walk around. I've never enjoyed Shakespeare as much as here, performed as it was meant to be in the "wooden O." Plays can be long. Many groundlings leave before the end. If you like, hang out outside an hour before the finish and beg or buy a ticket from someone leaving early (groundlings are allowed to come and go).

For information on plays or £10.50 tours of the theater and museum (see page 668), contact the theater at tel. 020/7902-1500 or 020/7902-1500 (or see www.shakespeares-globe.org). To reserve tickets for plays, call or drop by the box office (Mon–Sat 10:00–20:00, box office phone answered on Sun, at Shakespeare's Globe at New Globe Walk entrance, tel. 020/7401-9919). You can also reserve online (£1–2.20 booking fee per ticket).

The theater is on the South Bank, directly across the Thames over the Millennium Bridge from St. Paul's Cathedral (Tube: Mansion House or London Bridge). The Globe is inconvenient for public transport, but the courtesy phone in the lobby gets a minicab in minutes. (These minicabs have set fees—e.g., £8 to South Kensington—but generally cost less than a metered cab and provide fine and honest service.) During theater season, there's a regular supply of black cabs outside the main foyer on New Globe Walk.

Outdoor Theater in Summer: Enjoy Shakespearean drama and other plays under the stars at the **Open Air Theatre,** in leafy Regent's Park in north London. Munching is allowed: You can bring your own picnic; order à la carte from a menu at the theater; or pre-order a £16 picnic supper from the theater at least one week in advance (tickets £10–40; season runs June–mid-Sept, box office open late March–late May Mon–Sat 10:00–18:00, closed Sun; late May–mid-Sept Mon–Sat 10:00–20:00, Sun 16:00–20:00 on performance days only; order tickets online after mid-Jan or by phone at tel. 0870-060-1811, £1 booking fee by phone, no fee if ordering online or in person; grounds open 90 min prior to evening performances, 30 min prior for matinees; 10-min walk north of Baker Street Tube, near Queen Mary's Gardens within Regent's Park; detailed directions and more info at www.openairtheatre.org).

Fringe Theater: London's rougher evening-entertainment scene is thriving, filling pages in *Time Out*. Choose from a wide range of fringe theater and comedy acts (generally £5).

Classical Music

Concerts at Churches

For easy, cheap, or free concerts in historic churches, check TI listings for **lunch concerts,** especially:

- St. Bride's Church, with free lunch concerts twice a week at 13:15 (generally Tue, Wed, or Fri—confirm by phone or online, church tel. 020/7427-0133, www.stbrides.com).
- St. James at Piccadilly, with 50-minute concerts on Monday, Wednesday, and Friday at 13:10 (suggested donation £3, info tel. 020/7381-0441, www.st-james-piccadilly.org).
- St. Martin-in-the-Fields, offering free concerts on Monday, Tuesday, and Friday at 13:00 (church tel. 020/7766-1100, www.smitf.org).

St. Martin-in-the-Fields also hosts fine **evening concerts** by candlelight (£6–25, at 19:30 Thu–Sat, sometimes Tue) and live jazz in its underground Café in the Crypt (£5–8, Wed after 20:00, church tel. 020/7766-1100, www.smitf.org).

Evensong and Organ Recitals at Churches

Evensong services are held at several churches, including:

- St. Paul's Cathedral (Mon–Sat at 17:00, Sun at 15:15).
- Westminster Abbey (Mon–Tue and Tue–Fri at 17:00, Sat–Sun at 15:00; there's a service on Wed, but it's spoken, not sung).

Free **organ recitals** are held on Sunday at 17:45 in Westminster Abbey (30 min, tel. 020/7222-7110). Many other churches have free concerts; ask for the *London Organ Concerts Guide* at the TI.

Prom Concerts and Opera

For a fun classical event (mid-July–early Sept), attend a **Prom Concert** (shortened from "Promenade Concert") during the annual festival at the Royal Albert Hall. Nightly concerts are offered at give-a-peasant-some-culture prices to "Promenaders"—those willing to stand throughout the performance (£5 standing-room spots sold at the door, £7 restricted-view seats, Tube: South Kensington, tel. 020/7589-8212, www.bbc.co.uk/proms).

Some of the world's best **opera** is belted out at the prestigious Royal Opera House, near Covent Garden (box office tel. 020/7304-4000, www.royalopera.org), and at the less-formal Sadler's Wells Theatre (Rosebery Avenue, Islington, Tube: Angel, info tel. 020/7863-8198, box office tel. 0844-412-4300, www.sadlerswells.com).

Tours

Guided **walks** are offered several times a day. London Walks is the most established company (tel. 020/7624-3978, www.walks.com). Daytime walks vary: ancient London, museums, legal London,

Dickens, Beatles, Jewish quarter, Christopher Wren, and so on. In the evening, expect a more limited choice: ghosts, Jack the Ripper, pubs, or a literary theme. Get the latest from a TI, fliers, or *Time Out.* Show up at the listed time and place, pay £7, and enjoy the two-hour tour. For more options, see page 637.

To see the city illuminated at night, consider a **bus** tour. A one-hour London by Night Sightseeing Tour leaves every evening from Victoria Station and other points (see page 636).

Summer Evenings Along the South Bank

If you're visiting London in summer, consider the South Bank.

Take a trip around the **London Eye** while the sun sets over the city (Ferris wheel spins until 22:00). Then cap your night with an evening walk along the pedestrian-only **Jubilee Walkway,** which runs east–west along the river. It's where Londoners go to escape the heat. This pleasant stretch of the walkway—lined with pubs and casual eateries—goes from the London Eye past Shakespeare's Globe to Tower Bridge (you can walk in either direction; see www.jubileewalkway.com for maps and Tube stops).

If you're in the mood for a movie, take in a flick at the **National Film Theatre,** located just across from Waterloo Bridge on the South Bank. Run by the British Film Institute, the state-of-the-art theater shows Hollywood films (both new and classic), as well as art cinema (£8.60, Tube: Waterloo or Embankment, box office tel. 020/7928-3232, check www.bfi.org.uk for schedules).

Farther east along the South Bank is **The Scoop**—an outdoor amphitheater next to City Hall. It's a good spot for outdoor movies, concerts, and theater productions throughout the summer—with Tower Bridge as a scenic backdrop. These events are free, nearly nightly, and family-friendly. The schedule usually includes movies three nights a week in June, twice-daily musical and dance performances in July, and nightly theater in August and September, with most events beginning at 19:00. For the latest event schedule, see www.morelondon.com and click on "The Scoop" (next to City Hall, Riverside, The Queen's Walkway, Tube: London Bridge).

Cruises

During the summer, boats sail as late as 21:00 between Westminster Pier (near Big Ben) and the Tower of London. (For details, see page 639.)

A handful of outfits run Thames River evening cruises with four-course meals and dancing. London Showboat offers the best value (£70, April–Oct Wed–Sun, Nov–March Thu–Sat, 3 hours, departs at 19:00 from Westminster Pier and returns by 22:30, reservations necessary, tel. 020/7740-0400, www.citycruises.com).

LONDON

For more on cruising, get the *Thames River Services* brochure from a London TI.

Sleeping

London is perhaps Europe's most expensive city for rooms. Cheaper rooms are relatively dumpy. Don't expect £130 cheeriness in an £80 room. For £70 (about $110), you'll get a double with breakfast in a safe, cramped, and dreary place with minimal service and the bathroom down the hall. For £90 (about $145), you'll get a basic, clean, reasonably cheery double in a usually cramped, cracked-plaster building with a private bath, or a soulless but comfortable room without breakfast in a huge Motel 6–type place. My London splurges, at £150–260 ($240–415), are spacious, thoughtfully appointed places good for entertaining or romancing. Off-season, it's possible to save money by arriving late without a reservation and looking around. Competition softens prices, especially for multi-night stays. Check hotel websites for special deals. All of Britain's accommodations are now non-smoking. Street noise is a fact of life in London; if you're concerned, request a room in the back.

Hearty English or generous buffet breakfasts are included unless otherwise noted, and TVs are standard in rooms, but may come with only the traditional four British channels (no cable).

Reserve your London room as soon as you can commit to a date. To call a London hotel from the US or Canada, dial 011-44-20 (London's area code without the initial zero), then the local eight-digit number.

Online Hotel Deals for London

Given the high hotel prices and relatively weak dollar, consider turning to the Internet to help score a hotel deal. Various websites list rooms in high-rise three- and four-star business hotels. You'll give up the charm and warmth of a family-run establishment, and breakfast will probably not be included, but you might find the price is right.

Start by checking the websites of several big hotel chains to get an idea of typical rates and to check for online-only deals. Big London hotel chains include the following: Millennium/Copthorne (www.millenniumhotels.com), Thistle Hotels (www.thistlehotels.com), Intercontinental/Holiday Inn (www.ichotelsgroup.com), Radisson (www.radisson.com), and Red Carnation (www.redcarnationhotels.com). For specific recommendations for London, see "London's Chain Hotels," on the next page.

Auction-type sites (such as www.priceline.com) can be great for matching flexible travelers with empty hotel rooms, often at

LONDON

Sleep Code

(£1 = about \$1.60, country code: 44, area code: 020)
S = Single, **D** = Double/Twin, **T** = Triple, **Q** = Quad, **b** = bathroom,
s = shower only. Unless otherwise noted, credit cards are accepted and prices include a generous breakfast.

To help you easily sort through these listings, I've divided the rooms into three categories, based on the price for a double room with bath:

\$\$\$ Higher Priced—Most rooms £110 or more.
\$\$ Moderately Priced—Most rooms between £70-110.
\$ Lower Priced—Most rooms £70 or less.

---

prices well below the hotel's normal rates. Don't feel you have to start as high as the site's suggested opening bid. (For more about the complicated world of online bidding strategies and success stories from other travelers, see www.biddingfortravel.com or www.betterbidding.com.) Warning: Scoring a deal this way may require more patience and flexibility than you have, but if you enjoy shopping for cars, you'll probably like this, too.

Other favorite accommodation discount sites for London mentioned by my readers include www.londontown.com (an informative site with a discount booking service), http://athomein london.co.uk and www.londonbb.com (both list central B&Bs), www.lastminute.com, www.visitlondon.com, http://roomsnet .com, and www.eurocheapo.com. Read candid reviews of London hotels at www.tripadvisor.com. And check the "Graffiti Wall" at www.ricksteves.com for the latest tips and discoveries.

For a good overview on finding London hotel deals, go to www.smartertravel.com and click "Travel Guides," then "London."

London's Chain Hotels

These places are well run and offer elevators, 24-hour reception, and all the modern comforts in a no-nonsense, practical package. With the notable exception of my second listing, they are often located on busy streets in dreary train-station neighborhoods, so use common sense after dark and wear your money belt. The doubles for £80–100 are a great value for London. Breakfast is always extra. Online bookings are often the easiest way to make reservations, and will generally net you a discount.

\$\$\$ Jurys Inn Islington rents 200 compact, comfy rooms near King's Cross station (Db/Tb-£110–120, some discounted rooms available online, 2 adults and 2 kids under age 12 can share

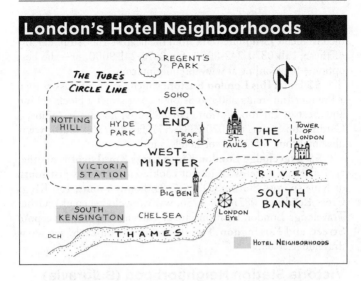

London's Hotel Neighborhoods

1 room, 60 Pentonville Road, Tube: Angel, tel. 020/7282-5500, fax 020/7282-5511, www.jurysinns.com).

$$ Premier Inn London County Hall, literally down the hall from a $400-a-night Marriott Hotel, fills one end of London's massive former County Hall building. This family-friendly place is wonderfully located near the base of the London Eye and across the Thames from Big Ben. Its 313 efficient rooms come with all the necessary comforts (Db-£104–114 for 2 adults and up to 2 kids under age 16, book in advance, no-show rooms are released at 15:00, some easy-access rooms, 500 yards from Westminster Tube stop and Waterloo Station, Belvedere Road, central reservations tel. 0870-242-8000, reception desk tel. 0870-238-3300, you can fax 020/7902-1619 but you might not get a response, easiest to book online at www.premierinn.com).

$$ Premier Inn London Southwark, with 59 rooms, is near Shakespeare's Globe on the South Bank (Db for up to 2 adults and 2 kids-£85–92, Bankside, 34 Park Street, tel. 0870-990-6402, www.premierinn.com).

$$ Premier Inn King's Cross, with 276 rooms, is just east of King's Cross station (Db-£90–110, 26–30 York Way, tel. 0870-990-6414, fax 0870-990-6415, www.premierinn.com).

Other **$$ Premier Inns** charging £90–110 per room include **London Euston** (big, blue, Lego-type building packed with families on vacation, on handy but noisy street, 141 Euston Road, Tube: Euston, tel. 0870-238-3301), **London Kensington** (11 Knaresboro Place, Tube: Earl's Court or Gloucester Road, tel. 0870-238-3304), and **London Putney Bridge** (£81–93, farther out, 3 Putney Bridge Approach, Tube: Putney Bridge, tel.

0870-238-3302). Avoid the **Tower Bridge** location, which is an inconvenient, 15-minute walk from the nearest Tube stop. For any of these, call 0870-242-8000, fax 0870-241-9000, or—the best option—book online at www.premierinn.com.

$$ Hotel Ibis London Euston, which feels a bit classier than a Premier Inn, rents 380 rooms on a quiet street a block behind and west of Euston Station (Db-£89–109, no family rooms, 3 Cardington Street, tel. 020/7388-7777, fax 020/7388-0001, www.ibishotel.com, h0921@accor-hotels.com).

$$ Travelodge London Kings Cross Royal Scot is another typical chain hotel with lots of cookie-cutter rooms just south of King's Cross Station (Db-£77–95, family rooms, 100 Kings Cross Road, tel. 0871-984-6256, www.travelodge.co.uk). Other Travelodge London locations are at **Covent Garden, Liverpool Street,** and **Farringdon.** For all the details on each, see www.travelodge.co.uk.

Victoria Station Neighborhood (Belgravia)

The streets behind Victoria Station teem with little moderately priced (for London) B&Bs. It's a safe, surprisingly tidy, and decent area without a hint of the trashy, touristy glitz of the streets in front of the station. West of the tracks is Belgravia, where the prices are a bit higher and your neighbors include Andrew Lloyd Webber and Margaret Thatcher (her policeman stands outside 73 Chester Square). East of the tracks is Pimlico—cheaper and just as handy, but the rooms can be a bit dowdier. Decent eateries abound (see "Eating: Near Recommended Victoria Station Accommodations," later in this chapter).

All the recommended hotels are within a five-minute walk of the Victoria Tube, bus, and train stations. On hot summer nights, request a quiet back room. Nearby is the 400-space Semley Place NCP **parking garage** (£30/day, possible discounts with hotel voucher, just west of the Victoria Coach Station at Buckingham Palace Road and Semley Place, tel. 0870-242-7144, www.ncp.co.uk). The handy **Pimlico Launderette** is about five blocks southwest of Warwick Square (daily 8:00–19:00, self-service or full service, south of Sutherland Street at 3 Westmoreland Terrace, tel. 020/7821-8692). **Launderette Centre** is a block north of Warwick Square (Mon–Fri 8:00–22:00, Sat–Sun until 19:30, £7 wash and dry, £9 for full-service, 31 Churton Street, tel. 020/7828-6039).

$$$ Lime Tree Hotel, enthusiastically run by Charlotte and Matt, comes with 28 spacious and thoughtfully decorated rooms and a fun-loving breakfast room (Sb-£80–85, Db-£110–140, Tb-£145–175, family room-£165–190, £5 Internet access—but free for my readers, Wi-Fi, small lounge opens into quiet garden, 135 Ebury Street, tel. 020/7730-8191, www.limetreehotel.co.uk,

Victoria Station Neighborhood

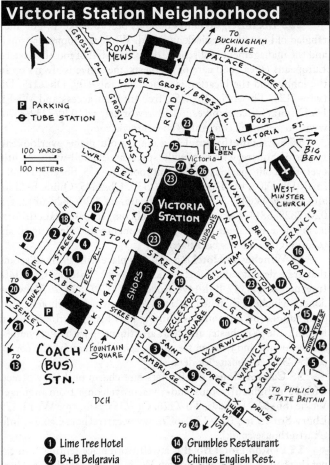

1. Lime Tree Hotel
2. B+B Belgravia
3. Elizabeth Hotel & Jubilee Hotel
4. Cartref House & Lynton Hotel B&Bs
5. Luna Simone Hotel
6. Morgan House
7. Winchester Hotel
8. Cherry Court Hotel
9. Bakers Hotel
10. easyHotel Victoria
11. Ebury Wine Bar
12. Jenny Lo's Tea House
13. To La Poule au Pot Rest.
14. Grumbles Restaurant
15. Chimes English Rest. & Cider Bar
16. The Jugged Hare Pub
17. Seafresh Fish Rest.
18. La Bottega Deli
19. St. George's Tavern
20. To The Duke of Wellington Pub
21. The Belgravia Pub
22. The Thomas Cubitt Pub
23. Grocery Stores (4)
24. Launderettes (2)
25. Bus Tours – Day (2)
26. Bus Tours – Night
27. Tube, Taxis & City Buses

LONDON

info@limetreehotel.co.uk, trusty Alan covers the night shift).

$$$ B&B Belgravia has done its best to make a tight-and-tangled old guesthouse sleek and mod. While the rooms are small and the management is absentee, the young staff of mostly Eastern Europeans takes good care of its guests, the coffee is always on in the lobby, and the location is unbeatable (Sb-£99, Db-£115, Db twin-£125, Tb-£145, Qb-£155, free Internet access and Wi-Fi, DVD library, loaner bikes, 64 Ebury Street, tel. 020/7259-8570, www.bb-belgravia.com, info@bb-belgravia.com).

$$$ Elizabeth Hotel is a stately old place overlooking Eccleston Square, with fine public spaces and 37 well-worn, slightly overpriced but spacious and decent rooms (S-£55, Sb-£85, D-£85, small Db-£103, big Db-£115, Tb-£130, Qb-£145, Quint/b-£150, air-con-£9, Wi-Fi, 37 Eccleston Square, tel. 020/7828-6812, fax 020/7828-6814, www.elizabethhotel.com, info@elizabethhotel.com). The Elizabeth also rents apartments that sleep up to six (£230/night, includes breakfast).

$$ Winchester Hotel is a well-run place with 19 small rooms that are a decent value for the price (Db-£89, Tb-£115, Qb-£140, Internet access, 17 Belgrave Road, tel. 020/7828-2972, www.londonwinchesterhotel.co.uk, info@londonwinchesterhotel.co.uk, commanded by no-nonsense Jimmy plus his crew: Juanita and Karim). The Winchester also rents apartments—with kitchenettes, sitting rooms, and beds on the quiet back side—around the corner (£125–230, see website for details).

$$ Cartref House B&B offers rare charm on Ebury Street, with 10 delightful rooms and a warm welcome from manager Vickie (Sb-£70, Db-£95, Tb-£126, Qb-£155, fans, free Wi-Fi, 129 Ebury Street, tel. 020/7730-6176, www.cartrefhouse.co.uk, info@cartrefhouse.co.uk).

$$ Lynton Hotel B&B is a well-worn place renting 12 inexpensive rooms with small pre-fab WCs. It's a fine value, exuberantly run by brothers Mark and Simon Connor (D-£75, Db-£85, free Wi-Fi, 113 Ebury Street, tel. 020/7730-4032, www.lyntonhotel.co.uk, mark-and-simon@lyntonhotel.co.uk).

$$ Luna Simone Hotel rents 36 fresh and spacious rooms with modern bathrooms. It's a well-managed place, run for over 30 years by twins Peter and Bernard and son Mark, and they seem to still enjoy their work (Sb-£65, Db-£90, Tb-£110, Qb-£130, discount with cash, free Internet access and Wi-Fi, corner of Charlwood Street and Belgrave Road at 47 Belgrave Road, tel. 020/7834-5897, www.lunasimonehotel.com, lunasimone@talk21.com).

$$ Morgan House rents 11 good rooms and is entertainingly run, with lots of travel tips and friendly chat from owner Rachel Joplin and her staff, Danilo and Fernanda (S-£52, D-£72, Db-£92,

T-£92, family suites-£112–132 for 3–4 people, Wi-Fi, 120 Ebury Street, tel. 020/7730-2384, www.morganhouse.co.uk, morgan house@btclick.com).

$ Cherry Court Hotel, run by the friendly and industrious Patel family, rents 12 very small, basic, incense-scented rooms in a central location (Sb-£48, Db-£55, Tb-£80, Qb-£95, Quint/b-£110, paying with credit card costs 5 percent extra, fruit-basket breakfast in room, air-con, laundry, free Internet access and Wi-Fi, peaceful garden patio, 23 Hugh Street, tel. 020/7828-2840, fax 020/7828-0393, www.cherrycourthotel.co.uk, info@cherrycourthotel.co.uk).

$ Jubilee Hotel is a well-run slumber mill with 24 tiny rooms and many tiny beds. It's a bit musty and its windows only open a few inches, but the price is right (S-£35, Sb-£50, tiny D-£50, tiny Db-£60, Db-£65, Tb-£75, Qb-£95, ask for the 5 percent Rick Steves discount, free Internet access and Wi-Fi, 31 Eccleston Square, tel. 020/7834-0845, www.jubileehotel.co.uk, stay@jubilee hotel.co.uk, Bob Patel).

$ Bakers Hotel is a well-worn cheapie, with 10 tight rooms, but it's well-located and offers youth hostel prices and a small breakfast (S-£30, D-£50, T-£60, family room-£65–70, £5 more Fri–Sat, 126 Warwick Way, tel. 020/7834-0729, www.bakershotel .co.uk, reservations@bakershotel.co.uk, Amin Jamani).

$ easyHotel Victoria is a radical concept—offering what you need to sleep well and safe—and no more. Their 77 rooms fit the old floor plan, so some rooms are tiny windowless closets, while others are quite spacious. All rooms are well-ventilated and come with an efficient "bathroom pod"—just big enough to take care of business. Prices are the same for one person or two. You get two towels, soap and shampoo, and a clean bed—no breakfast, no fresh towels, and no daily cleaning. Rooms range from £25 to £65, depending on their size and when you book: "The earlier you book, the less you pay" (reserve only through website, 36 Belgrave Road, tel. 020/7834-1379, www.easyhotel.com, victoriastaff@easyhotel.com). They also have branches at South Kensington, Paddington, and Heathrow and Luton airports (see their website for details).

"South Kensington," She Said, Loosening His Cummerbund

To stay on a quiet street so classy it doesn't allow hotel signs, surrounded by trendy shops and colorful restaurants, call "South Ken" your London home. Shoppers like being a short walk from Harrods and the designer shops of King's Road and Chelsea. When I splurge, I splurge here. Sumner Place is just off Old Brompton Road, 200 yards from the handy South Kensington Tube station (on Circle Line, two stops from Victoria Station, direct Heathrow

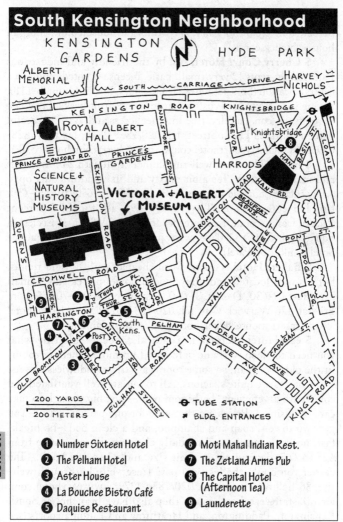

South Kensington Neighborhood

KENSINGTON GARDENS

HYDE PARK

ALBERT MEMORIAL

HARVEY NICHOLS

SOUTH CARRIAGE DRIVE

KENSINGTON ROAD

KNIGHTSBRIDGE

ROYAL ALBERT HALL

Knightsbridge

PRINCE CONSORT RD.

PRINCE'S GARDENS

HARRODS

SCIENCE & NATURAL HISTORY MUSEUMS

VICTORIA & ALBERT MUSEUM

BEAUFORT GDNS.

EXHIBITION ROAD

ENNISMORE GDNS.

TREVOR

HANS RD.

SLOANE

BASIL

HANS

CROMWELL ROAD

QUEEN'S

BROMPTON ROAD

WALTON STREET

PONT ST.

CADOGAN

THURLOE PL.

THURLOE SQUARE

THUR. ST.

CROM. PL.

❾ QUEENS

❷

❺

South Kens.

PELHAM

DRAYCOTT

CADOGAN ST.

HARRINGTON

❼ ❻

❹

Post

ONSLOW SQ.

ROAD

SLOANE AVE.

AVE.

KING'S ROAD

QUEEN'S GATE

❶

SUMNER PL.

❸

OLD BROMPTON ROAD

ONSLOW

PELHAM ST.

FULHAM ROAD

SYDNEY

200 YARDS
200 METERS

⊖ TUBE STATION
✷ BLDG. ENTRANCES

❶ Number Sixteen Hotel
❷ The Pelham Hotel
❸ Aster House
❹ La Bouchee Bistro Café
❺ Daquise Restaurant
❻ Moti Mahal Indian Rest.
❼ The Zetland Arms Pub
❽ The Capital Hotel (Afternoon Tea)
❾ Launderette

connection). The handy **Wash & Dry launderette** is on the corner of Queensberry Place and Harrington Road (Mon–Fri 7:30–21:00, Sat 9:00–20:00, Sun 10:00–19:00, bring 50p and £1 coins).

$$$ Number Sixteen, for well-heeled travelers, has over-the-top formality and class packed into its 42 rooms, plush lounges, and tranquil garden. It's in a labyrinthine building, with modern decor throughout—perfect for an urban honeymoon (Db-£165—but soft, ask for discounted "seasonal rates" especially in July–Aug, breakfast buffet in the garden-£17, elevator, 16 Sumner Place, tel. 020/7589-5232, fax 020/7584-8615, US tel. 800-553-6674, www.firmdalehotels.com, sixteen@firmdale.com).

$$$ The Pelham Hotel, a 52-room business-class hotel with a pricey mix of pretense and style, is not quite sure which investment company owns it. It's genteel, with low lighting and a pleasant drawing room among the many perks (Sb-£170, Db-£190–260, breakfast extra, lower prices Aug and weekends, Web specials can include free breakfast, air-con, expensive Internet access and Wi-Fi, elevator, gym, 15 Cromwell Place, tel. 020/7589-8288, www.pelhamhotel.co.uk, reservations@pelhamhotel.co.uk).

$$$ Aster House, run by friendly and accommodating Simon and Leonie Tan, has a sumptuous lobby, lounge, and breakfast room. Its rooms are comfy and quiet, with TV, phone, and air-conditioning. Enjoy breakfast or just lounging in the whisper-elegant Orangery, a Victorian greenhouse (Sb-£120, Db-£180, bigger Db-£225, 5 percent off for five or more nights with cash, check website for specials, VAT not included, pay Internet access and Wi-Fi, 3 Sumner Place, tel. 020/7581-5888, fax 020/7584-4925, www.asterhouse.com, asterhouse@btinternet.com). Simon and Leonie offer free loaner mobile phones to their guests.

Notting Hill and Bayswater Neighborhoods

Residential Notting Hill has quick bus and Tube access to downtown, and, for London, is very "homely" (Brit-speak for cozy). It's also peppered with trendy bars and restaurants, and is home to the historic Coronet movie theater, as well as the famous Portobello Road Market (Mon–Wed and Fri–Sat 8:00–18:30, sparse on Mon, closes at 13:00 on Thu, closed Sun, tel. 020/7229-8354, www.portobelloroad.co.uk).

Popular with young international travelers, Bayswater's Queensway street is a multicultural festival of commerce and eateries. The neighborhood does its dirty clothes at **Galaxy Launderette** (£6 self-service, £8 full-service, daily 8:00–20:00, staff on hand with soap and coins, 65 Moscow Road, at corner of St. Petersburgh Place and Moscow Road, tel. 020/7229-7771). For **Internet access,** you'll find several stops along busy Queensway, and a self-serve bank of easyInternetcafé computer terminals on the food circus level of the Whiteleys Shopping Centre (daily 8:30–24:00, corner of Queensway and Porchester Gardens).

Near Kensington Gardens Square

Several big old hotels line the quiet Kensington Gardens Square (not to be confused with the much bigger Kensington Gardens), a block west of bustling Queensway, north of Bayswater Tube station. These hotels are quiet for central London.

$$$ Phoenix Hotel, a Best Western modernization of a 125-room hotel, offers American business-class comforts; spacious,

Notting Hill and Bayswater Neighborhoods

⊖ TUBE STN.

1/4 MILE

400 METERS

1. Phoenix Hotel
2. Vancouver Studios & Princes Square Guest Accommodation
3. Kensington Gardens Hotel
4. Westland Hotel
5. London Vicarage Hotel
6. To Norwegian YWCA
7. Maggie Jones Restaurant
8. The Churchill Arms Pub & Thai Kitchens
9. The Prince Edward Pub
10. Café Diana
11. Royal China Restaurant
12. Whiteleys Mall Food Court
13. Spar Market
14. The Orangery (Afternoon Tea)
15. Launderette

plush public spaces; and big, fresh, modern-feeling rooms. Its prices—which range from fine value to rip-off—are determined by a greedy computer program, with huge variations according to expected demand. See their website and book online to save money (Db-£90–150, continental breakfast, elevator, impersonal staff, 1–8 Kensington Gardens Square, tel. 020/7229-2494, fax 020/7727-1419, US tel. 800-528-1234, www.phoenixhotel.co.uk, info@phoenixhotel.co.uk).

$$$ Vancouver Studios offers 45 modern rooms with fully equipped kitchenettes (utensils, stove, microwave, and fridge) rather than breakfast (small Sb-£79, Db-£125, Tb-£170, extra bed-£15, 10 percent discount for week-long stay or more, welcoming lounge and garden, near Kensington Gardens Square at 30 Princes Square, tel. 020/7243-1270, fax 020/7221-8678, www .vancouverstudios.co.uk, info@vancouverstudios.co.uk).

$$ Kensington Gardens Hotel laces 17 pleasant rooms together in a tall, skinny building with lots of stairs and no elevator (S-£50–55, Sb-£55–59, Db-£79, Tb-£97; book by phone or email for these special Rick Steves prices, rather than through the pricier website; continental breakfast included at sister hotel next door, Wi-Fi, 9 Kensington Gardens Square, tel. 020/7221-7790, fax 020/7792-8612, www.kensingtongardenshotel.co.uk, info @kensingtongardenshotel.co.uk, Rowshanak).

$$ Prince's Square Guest Accommodation is a big, impersonal 50-room place that's well-located, practical, and a good value, especially with its cash discount (Sb-£60–65, Db-£85–95, £10 per night cash discount, 23–25 Prince's Square, tel. 020/7229-9876, www.princessquarehotel.co.uk, info@princessquarehotel.co.uk).

Near Kensington Gardens

$$$ Westland Hotel is comfortable, convenient (5-min walk from Notting Hill neighborhood), and feels like a wood-paneled hunting lodge, with a fine lounge. The rooms are spacious, recently refurbished, and quite plush. Their £130 doubles are the best value (Sb-£110, Db-£130, deluxe Db-£152, cavernous deluxe Db-£172, sprawling Tb-£165–193, gargantuan Qb-£186–220, Quint/b-£234, elevator, garage-£12/day; between Notting Hill Gate and Queensway Tube stations, 154 Bayswater Road; tel. 020/7229-9191, fax 020/7727-1054, www.westlandhotel.co.uk, reservations @westlandhotel.co.uk, Jim and Nora ably staff the front desk).

$$$ London Vicarage Hotel is family-run, understandably popular, and elegantly British in a quiet, classy neighborhood. It has 17 rooms furnished with taste and quality, a TV lounge, and facilities on each floor. Mandy and Richard maintain a homey and caring atmosphere (S-£52, Sb-£88, D-£88, Db-£114, T-£109, Tb-£145, Q-£116, Qb-£160, 20 percent less in winter—check website, 8-min walk from Notting Hill Gate and High Street Kensington Tube stations, near Kensington Palace at 10 Vicarage Gate, tel. 020/7229-4030, fax 020/7792-5989, www.london vicaragehotel.com, vicaragehotel@btconnect.com).

Near Holland Park
$ Norwegian YWCA (Norsk K.F.U.K.)—where English is definitely a second language—is for women 30 and under only (and men 30 and under with Norwegian passports). Located on a quiet, stately street, it offers a study, TV room, piano lounge, and an open-face Norwegian ambience (goat cheese on Sundays!). They have mostly quads, so those willing to share with strangers are most likely to get a bed (July–Aug: Ss-£36, shared double-£35/bed, shared triple-£30/bed, shared quad-£26/bed, includes breakfast and sack lunch; includes dinner Sept–June; 52 Holland Park, tel. 020/7727-9346, www.kfukhjemmet.org.uk, kontor@kfukh jemmet.org.uk). With each visit, I wonder which is easier to get—a sex change or a Norwegian passport?

Other Neighborhoods
North of Marble Arch: **$$$ The 22 York Street B&B** offers a casual alternative in the city center, renting 10 stark, hardwood, comfortable rooms (Sb-£89, Db-£120, two-night minimum, continental breakfast served at big communal table, Internet access and Wi-Fi, inviting lounge; from Baker Street Tube station, walk 2 blocks down Baker Street and take a right, 22 York Street; tel. 020/7224-2990, www.22yorkstreet.co.uk, mc@22yorkstreet.co.uk, energetically run by Liz and Michael Callis).

$$$ The Sumner Hotel, in a 19th-century Georgian townhouse, is located a few blocks north of Hyde Park and Oxford Street, a busy shopping destination. Decorated with fancy modern Italian furniture, this swanky place packs in all the extras (Db-£130–145, extra bed-£30, includes breakfast, free Wi-Fi, 54 Upper Berkeley Street just off Edgware Road, Tube: Marble Arch, tel. 020/7723-2244, fax 0870-705-8767, www.thesumner.com, hotel @thesumner.com, manager Peter).

Near Covent Garden: **$$$ Fielding Hotel,** located on a charming, quiet pedestrian street just two blocks east of Covent Garden, offers 24 no-frills rooms and a fine location (Db-£105–125, Db with sitting room-£150, pricier rooms are bigger with better bathrooms, no breakfast, no kids under 7, 4 Broad Court, Bow Street, tel. 020/7836-8305, fax 020/7497-0064, www.the fieldinghotel.co.uk, reservations@thefieldinghotel.co.uk, manager Graham Chapman).

Near Buckingham Palace: **$$ Vandon House Hotel,** run by Central College in Iowa, is packed with students most of the year, but its 32 rooms are rented to travelers from late May through August at great prices. The rooms, while institutional, are comfy, and the location is excellent (S-£45, D-£69, Db-£89, Tb-£99, Qb-£118, only twin beds, elevator, Internet access and Wi-Fi, on a tiny road 3-min walk west of St. James's Park Tube station or 7-min walk from Victoria Station, near east end of Petty France Street at 1 Vandon Street, tel. 020/7799-6780, www.vandonhouse .com, info@vandonhouse.com).

Near Euston Station and the British Library: The **$$$ Methodist International Centre (MIC),** a modern, youthful Christian hotel and conference center, fills its lower floors with international students and its top floor with travelers. The 28 rooms are modern and simple yet comfortable, with fine bathrooms, phones, and desks. The atmosphere is friendly, safe, clean, and controlled; it also has a spacious lounge and game room (Sb-£140, deluxe Sb-£165, Db-£153, deluxe Db-£178; Sb-£95 and Db-£108 with £116 membership; check website for specials, elevator, Wi-Fi, on a quiet street a block west of Euston Station, 81–103 Euston Street—not Euston Road, Tube: Euston Station, tel. 020/7380-0001, www.micentre.com, acc@micentre.com). From June through August, when the students are gone, they also rent simpler twin rooms (S or D-£45, includes one breakfast, extra breakfast-£12.50).

Hostels

$ London Central Youth Hostel is the new flagship of London's hostels, with 300 beds and all the latest in security and comfortable efficiency. Families and travelers of any age will feel welcome in this wonderful facility. You'll pay the same price for any bed in a 4- to 8-bed single-sex dorm—with or without private bathroom—so try to grab one with a bathroom (£18–30 per bunk bed—fluctuates with demand, £3/night extra for non-members, breakfast-£4; includes sheets, towel and locker; families or groups welcome to book an entire room, free Wi-Fi, members' kitchen, laundry, book long in advance, between Oxford Street and Great Portland Street Tube stations at 104 Bolsover Street, tel. 0870-770-6144, www.yha .org.uk, londoncentral@yha.org.uk).

$ St. Paul's Youth Hostel, near St. Paul's, is clean, modern, friendly, and well-run. Most of the 190 beds are in shared, single-sex bunk rooms (bed-£15–26 depending on number of beds in room and demand, twin D-£61, bunk-bed Q-£90, non-members pay £3 extra, includes breakfast, cheap meals, open 24 hours, 36 Carter Lane, Tube: St. Paul's, tel. 020/7236-4965, www.yha.org .uk, city@yha.org.uk).

$ A cluster of three **St. Christopher's Inn** hostels, south of the Thames near London Bridge, have cheap dorm beds (£19–22,

161–165 Borough High Street, Tube: Borough or London Bridge, tel. 020/7407-1856, www.st-christophers.co.uk).

Dorms

$ The **University of Westminster** opens up its dorm rooms to travelers during summer break, from mid-June through mid-September. Located in several high-rise buildings scattered around central London, the rooms—some with private bathrooms, others with shared bathrooms nearby—come with access to well-equipped kitchens and big lounges (S-£26–35, Sb-£30–43, D-£40–60, Db-£59–75, apartment Sb-£48–80, apartment Db-£58–90, weekly rates, tel. 020/7911-5181, www.wmin.ac.uk/comserv, unilet vacations@westminster.ac.uk).

$ **University College London** also has rooms for travelers from mid-June until mid-September (S-£27–30, D-£54, breakfast extra, minimum 3-night stay, www.ucl.ac.uk/residences).

$ **Ace Hotel,** a budget hotel set in a residential neighborhood within four townhouses, has contemporary decor (£18–27 per bed in 3- to 8-bed dorms, bunk-bed D-£53–57, bunk-bed Db-£57–61, Db with patio-£99, pay Internet access, lounge and garden, 16–22 Gunterstone Road, West Kensington, tel. 020/7602-6600, www.ace-hotel.co.uk, reception@ace-hotel.co.uk).

Heathrow and Gatwick Airports

At or near Heathrow Airport: It's so easy to get to Heathrow from central London, I see no reason to sleep there. But if you do, $ **easyHotel** is your cheapest bet (described on page 683, www.easyhotel.com). $$ **Yotel,** also at the airport, has small sleep dens that offer a place to catch a quick nap (four hours from £37.50), or to stay overnight (tiny "standard cabin"—£59/8 hours, "premium cabin"—£82/8 hours; cabins sleep 1–2 people; price is per cabin not person). Prices vary by day, week, and time of year, so check their website. All rooms are only slightly larger than a double bed, and have private bathrooms and free Internet access and Wi-Fi. Windowless rooms have oddly purplish lighting (Heathrow Terminal 4, tel. 020/7100-1100, www.yotel.com, customer @yotel.com).

Near Heathrow Airport: $$ **Heathrow Ibis** is a chain hotel offering predictable value (Db-£77, Db-£52 on Fri–Sun, check website for specials as low as £42, breakfast-£6.95, pay Internet access and Wi-Fi, 112–114 Bath Road; take free local bus #105, #111, or #140 from airport's Central Bus Station, or the £4 "Hotel Hoppa" shuttle bus #6 from any terminal except Terminal 4—runs 3/hr; tel. 020/8759-4888, fax 020/8564-7894, www.ibishotel.com, h0794@accor-hotels.com).

At or near Gatwick Airport: $$ Yotel, with small rooms, has a branch right at the airport (Gatwick South Terminal, see prices and contact info in Heathrow listing, previous page).

$$ Barn Cottage, a converted 16th-century barn, sits in the peaceful countryside, with a tennis court, swimming pool, and a good pub just two blocks away. It has two wood-beamed rooms, antique furniture, and a large garden that makes you forget Gatwick is 10 minutes away (S-£55, D-£75, cash only, Church Road, Leigh, Reigate, Surrey, tel. 01306/611-347, warmly run by Pat and Mike Comer). Don't confuse this place with others of the same name; this Barn Cottage has no website. A taxi from Gatwick to here runs about £14; the Comers can take you to the airport or train station for about £10.

$$ Gatwick Airport Central Premier Inn rents cheap rooms (Db-£75, £67 Fri–Sun, £2 shuttle bus from airport—must reserve in advance, Longbridge Way, North Terminal, tel. 0870-238-3305, frustrating phone tree, www.premierinn.com).

$ Gatwick Airport Travelodge has budget rooms two miles from the airport (Db-£57, breakfast extra, Wi-Fi, Church Road, Lowfield Heath, Crawley, £3 "Hotel Hoppa" shuttle bus from airport, tel. 0871-984-6031, www.travelodge.co.uk).

For Longer Stays

Staying in London a week or longer? Consider the advantages that come with renting a furnished apartment, or "flat" as the British say. Complete with a small, equipped kitchen and living room, this option can also sometimes work for families or groups on shorter visits. Among the many organizations ready to help, the following have been recommended by local guides and readers: www.perfectplaceslondon.co.uk; www.london33.com; www.london-house.com; www.gowithit.co.uk; www.nghapartments.co.uk; www.holiday-rentals.co.uk; www.touristapartments.com; and www.regentsuites.com.

Sometimes you can save money by renting directly from the apartment owner (check www.vrbo.com). Readers also report success using Craig's List (http://london.craigslist.co.uk; search within "holiday rentals").

Read the conditions of rental carefully and ask lots of questions. If a certain amenity is important to you (such as Wi-Fi or a washing machine in the unit) ask specifically about it and what to do if it stops working. Plot the location carefully (plug the address into http://maps.google.com) and remember to factor in travel time and costs from outlying neighborhoods to central London. Finally, it's a good idea to buy trip cancellation/interruption insurance, as many weekly rentals are non-refundable.

Eating

In London, the sheer variety of foods—from every corner of its former empire and beyond—is astonishing. You'll be amazed at the number of hopping, happening new restaurants of all kinds.

If you want to dine (as opposed to eat), drop by a London newsstand to get a weekly entertainment guide or an annual restaurant guide (both have extensive restaurant listings). Visit www.london-eating.co.uk or www.squaremeal.co.uk for more options.

The thought of a £40 meal in Britain generally ruins my appetite, so my London dining is limited mostly to easygoing, fun, inexpensive alternatives. I've listed places by neighborhood—handy to your sightseeing or hotel. Considering how expensive London can be, if there's any good place to cut corners to stretch your budget, it's by eating cheaply.

Pub grub is the most atmospheric budget option. Many of London's 7,000 pubs serve fresh, tasty buffets under ancient timbers, with hearty lunches and £7–9 dinners.

Ethnic restaurants—especially Indian and Chinese—are popular, plentiful, and cheap. Most large museums (and many churches) have inexpensive, cheery cafeterias. Of course, picnicking is the fastest and cheapest way to go. Good grocery stores and sandwich shops, fine park benches, and polite pigeons abound in Britain's most expensive city.

London (and all of Britain) is now smoke-free, thanks to a recent smoking ban. Expect restaurants and pubs that sell food to be non-smoking indoors, with smokers occupying patios and doorways outside.

Restaurants

Near Trafalgar Square

These places are within about 100 yards of Trafalgar Square. To locate the following restaurants, see the map on the opposite page.

St. Martin-in-the-Fields Café in the Crypt is just right for a tasty meal on a monk's budget—maybe even on a monk's tomb. You'll dine sitting on somebody's gravestone in an ancient crypt. While their enticing buffet line is kept stocked all day, their cheap sandwich bar is generally sold out by 13:30 (£6–8 cafeteria plates, Mon–Tue 8:00–20:00, Wed–Sat 8:00–22:30, Sun 12:00–18:30, profits go to the church, underneath Church of St. Martin-in-the-Fields on Trafalgar Square, Tube: Charing Cross, tel. 020/7839-4342 or 020/7766-1100). Wednesday evenings at 20:00 come with a live jazz band (£5–8 tickets). While here, check out the concert schedule for the busy church upstairs (or visit www.smitf.org).

The Chandos Pub's Opera Room floats amazingly apart

Central London Eateries

1. St. Martin-in-the-Fields Café in the Crypt
2. The Chandos Pub's Opera Room
3. Gordon's Wine Bar
4. The Lord Moon of the Mall Pub
5. Stockpot & Woodland South Indian Vegetarian Restaurant
6. West End Kitchen
7. Criterion Restaurant
8. Just Falafs
9. To The Food Balcony, Joe Allen, Livebait & PJ's Bar and Grill
10. Ristorante Zizzi
11. Belgo Centraal
12. Yo! Sushi
13. Wagamama Noodle Bar
14. Busaba Eathai Thai Rest. & Côte Restaurant
15. Y Ming Chinese Rest.
16. Andrew Edmunds Rest.
17. Mildred's Vegetarian Rest., Thai & Chinese Buffet & Fernandez & Wells
18. Neal's Yard Eateries
19. Food for Thought Café
20. To The Princess Louise Pub

LONDON

from the tacky crush of tourism around Trafalgar Square. Look for it opposite the National Portrait Gallery (corner of William IV Street and St. Martin's Lane) and climb the stairs to the Opera Room. This is a fine Trafalgar rendezvous point and wonderfully local pub. They serve traditional, plain-tasting £6–7 pub meals—meat pies are their specialty. The ground-floor pub is stuffed with regulars and offers snugs (private booths), the same menu, and more serious beer drinking (kitchen open daily 11:00–19:00, order and pay at the bar, tel. 020/7836-1401).

Gordon's Wine Bar, with a simple, steep staircase leading into a candlelit 15th-century wine cellar, is filled with dusty old bottles, faded British memorabilia, and local nine-to-fivers. At the "English rustic" buffet, choose a hot meal or a hearty (and split-table) plate of cheeses, various cold cuts, and pickles (£7.50). Then step up to the wine bar and consider the many varieties of wine and port available by the glass. This place is passionate about port. The low, carbon-crusted vaulting deeper in the back seems to intensify the Hogarth-painting atmosphere. While it's crowded, you can normally corral two chairs and grab the corner of a table. On hot days, the crowd spills out into a leafy back patio (arrive before 17:30 to get a seat, Mon–Sat 11:00–23:00, Sun 12:00–22:00, 2 blocks from Trafalgar Square, bottom of Villiers Street at #47, Tube: Embankment, tel. 020/7930-1408, manager Gerard Menan).

The Lord Moon of the Mall pub, the best place on Whitehall, has real ales on tap and good, cheap pub grub, including a two-meals-for-the-price-of-one deal (£8 anytime). This kid-friendly pub fills a great old former Barclays Bank building a block down Whitehall from Trafalgar Square (daily 9:00–23:00, 18 Whitehall, tel. 020/7839-7701). Nearby are several cheap cafeterias and pizza joints.

Cheap Eating near Piccadilly

Hungry and broke in the theater district? Head for Panton Street (off Haymarket, 2 blocks southeast of Piccadilly Circus), where several hardworking little places compete, all seeming to offer a three-course meal for about £8.50. Peruse the entire block (vegetarian, Pizza Express, Moroccan, Thai, Chinese, and two famous eateries) before making your choice. **Stockpot** is a mushy-peas kind of place, famous and rightly popular for its edible, cheap meals (daily 7:00–23:00, 38 Panton Street, cash only). The **West End Kitchen** (across the street at #5, same hours and menu) is a direct competitor that's also well-known and just as good. Vegetarians prefer the **Woodland South Indian Vegetarian Restaurant.**

The palatial **Criterion** serves a special £15 two-course French fixed-price meal (or £18 for three courses) for lunch and early dinner, under gilded tiles and chandeliers in a dreamy Byzantine church setting from 1880. It's right on Piccadilly Circus but a world away from the punk junk. The house wine is great, as is the food. After 19:00, the menu becomes really expensive. Anyone can drop in for coffee or a drink (Mon–Sat 12:00–14:30 & 17:30–23:30, Sun 12:00–15:30 & 17:30–22:30, tel. 020/7930-0488).

The Wolseley is the grand 1920s showroom of a long-defunct British car. While the last Wolseley drove out with the Great Depression, today this old-time bistro bustles with formal waiters serving traditional Austrian and French dishes in an elegant black-marble-and-chandeliers setting fit for its location next to the Ritz. While the food can be unexceptional, prices are reasonable, and the presentation and setting are grand. Reservations are a must (£16 plates, cheaper burger-and-sandwich menu available, Mon–Fri 7:00–24:00, Sat 8:00–24:00, Sun 8:00–23:00, 160 Piccadilly, tel. 020/7499-6996). They're popular for their fancy cream tea (£9.50, served 15:30–17:30).

Near Covent Garden

Covent Garden bustles with people and touristy eateries. While the area feels overrun, there are some decent options.

Just Falafs is a healthy fast-food option in the chaos of Covent Garden. Located in the southeast corner, where rows of outdoor café tables line the tiny shop, they offer falafel sandwiches with yummy vegetarian-friendly extras (£6 sandwiches, daily until about 21:00, 27b Covent Gardens Square, tel. 020/7622-6262).

The Food Balcony, with great people-watching overlooking the Jubilee Market Piazza, is a sticky food circus of ethnic places serving £6 meals on disposable plates and wobbly plastic tables (closes at 18:30). A handy Wagamama Noodle Bar is around the corner on Tavistock Street (see description under "Hip Eating from Covent Garden to Soho," next page).

Joe Allen, tucked in a basement a block away, serves modern international cuisine with both style and hubbub. Downstairs off a quiet street with candles and white tablecloths, it's comfortably spacious and popular with the theater crowd (meals for about £30, £15 two-course specials until 18:45, piano music after 21:00, 13 Exeter Street, tel. 020/7836-0651).

Livebait Restaurant is an upscale fish-and-chips place with an elegant yet simple tiled interior. Their forte is fresh and well-prepared fish (£15 main courses, specials before 19:00, closed Sun, 21 Wellington Street, tel. 020/7836-7161).

Ristorante Zizzi is a fun, top-end Italian chain with a crisp contemporary atmosphere, an open pizza oven adding warmth and action, and a sharp local clientele (£5–10 pizzas and pastas, great chicken Caesar salads, daily 12:00–24:00, 20 Bow Street, tel. 020/7836-6101).

PJ's Bar and Grill, a tired diner which seems to be a hit with locals, serves decent "modern European" food. It's family-friendly, with more intimate seating in the back (£10–15 meals, closed Sun, 30 Wellington Street, 020/7240-7529).

Hip Eating from Covent Garden to Soho

London has a trendy, Generation X scene that most Beefeater-seekers miss entirely. These restaurants are scattered throughout the hipster, gay, and strip-club district (see map on page 693), teeming each evening with fun-seekers and theater-goers. Even if you plan to dine elsewhere, it's a treat to wander around this lively area.

Beware of the extremely welcoming women standing outside the strip clubs (especially on Great Windmill Street). Enjoy the sales pitch—but only fools fall for the "£5 drink and show" lure. They don't get back out without emptying their wallets...literally.

Belgo Centraal serves hearty Belgian specialties in a vast, 400-seat underground lair. It's a seafood, chips, and beer emporium dressed up as a mod-monastic refectory—with noisy acoustics and waiters garbed as Trappist monks. The classy restaurant section is more comfortable and less rowdy, but usually requires reservations. It's often more fun to just grab a spot in the boisterous beer hall, with its tight, communal benches (no reservations accepted). The same menu and specials work on both sides. Belgians claim they eat as well as the French and as heartily as the Germans. Specialties include mussels, great fries, and a stunning array of dark, blond, and fruity Belgian beers. Belgo actually makes Belgian things trendy—a formidable feat (£10–14 meals; Mon–Sat 12:00–23:00, Sun 12:00–22:30, Mon–Fri £5–6.30 "beat the clock" meal specials 17:00–18:30—the time you order is the price you pay—including main dishes, fries, and beer; no meal-splitting after 18:30, and you must buy food with beer; daily £6.50 lunch special 12:00–17:00; 2 kids eat free for each parent ordering a regular entrée; 1 block north of Covent Garden Tube station at intersection of Neal and Shelton Streets, 50 Earlham Street, tel. 020/7813-2233).

Yo! Sushi is a futuristic Japanese-food-extravaganza experience. It's pricey—those plates add up fast. But it's a memorable experience, complete with thumping rock, Japanese cable TV, and a 195-foot-long conveyor belt—the world's longest sushi bar. For £1 you get unlimited tea or water (from spigot at bar, with or without gas). Snag a bar stool and grab dishes as they rattle by (priced by color of dish; check the chart: £1.75–5 per dish, £1.50 for miso soup, daily 12:00–23:00, 2 blocks south of Oxford Street, where Lexington Street becomes Poland Street, 52 Poland Street, tel. 020/7287-0443). If you like Yo!, keep an eye out for other locations around town, which include a handy branch a block from the London Eye on Belvedere Road, as well an outlet in Whiteleys Mall on Queensway (listed later in this section under "Near Recommended Notting Hill B&Bs and Bayswater Hotels").

Wagamama Noodle Bar is a noisy pan-Asian organic slurpa-thon. As you enter, check out the kitchen and listen to the roar of the basement, where benches rock with happy eaters. Everybody sucks. Stand against the wall to feel the energy of all this "positive eating." Portions are huge and splitting is allowed (£7–12 meals, daily 11:30–23:00, crowded after 19:00, 10A Lexington Street, tel. 020/7292-0990 but no reservations taken). If you like this place, handy branches are all over town, including one near the British Museum (Streatham Street), High Street Kensington (#26), in Harvey Nichols (109 Knightsbridge), Covent Garden (Tavistock Street), Leicester Square (Irving Street), Piccadilly Circus (Norris Street), Fleet Street (#109), and between St. Paul's and the Tower of London (22 Old Broad Street).

Busaba Eathai Thai Restaurant is a hit with locals for its snappy service, casual-yet-high-energy ambience, and good, inex-pensive Thai cuisine. You'll sit communally around big, square, 16-person hardwood tables or in two-person tables by the win-dow—with everyone in the queue staring at your noodles. They don't take reservations, so arrive by 19:00 or line up (£10–14 meals, daily 12:00–23:00, 106 Wardour Street, tel. 020/7255-8686).

Côte Restaurant is a contemporary French bistro chain, serv-ing good-value French cuisine at the right prices (£10 *plats rapide*, £12 mains, daily, 124–126 Wardour Street, tel. 020/7287-9280).

Y Ming Chinese Restaurant—across Shaftesbury Avenue from the ornate gates, clatter, and dim sum of Chinatown—has dressy European decor, serious but helpful service, and authentic Northern Chinese cooking (good £10 meal deal offered 12:00–18:00—last order at 18:00, £7–10 plates, open Mon–Sat 12:00–23:45, closed Sun, 35 Greek Street, tel. 020/7734-2721, Jackman).

Andrew Edmunds Restaurant is a tiny candlelit place where you'll want to hide your camera and guidebook and act as local as possible. This little place—with a jealous and loyal clientele—is the closest I've found to Parisian quality in a cozy restaurant in London. The modern European cooking and creative seasonal menu are worth the splurge (£25 meals, daily 12:30–15:00 & 18:00–22:45, come early or call ahead, request ground floor rather than basement, 46 Lexington Street in Soho, tel. 020/7437-5708).

Mildred's Vegetarian Restaurant, across from Andrew Edmunds, has cheap prices, an enjoyable menu, and a plain-yet-pleasant interior filled with happy eaters (£7 meals, Mon–Sat 12:00–23:00, closed Sun, vegan options, 45 Lexington Street, tel. 020/7494-1634).

Thai and Chinese Buffet is a tiny all-you-can-eat joint that feels classier than others (£6 for lunch or dinner, 41 Lexington Street). Their £3.50 take-away boxes make a very cheap, light to-go meal that can feed two people.

Fernandez & Wells is a delightfully simple little wine, cheese, and ham bar. Drop in and grab a stool as you belly up to the big wooden bar. Share a plate of top-quality cheeses and/or Spanish or French hams with fine bread and oil, while sipping a nice glass of wine and talking with Juan or Toby (daily 11:00–22:00, quality sandwiches at lunch, wine/cheese/ham bar after 16:00, 43 Lexington Street, tel. 020-7734-1546).

Neal's Yard is *the* place for cheap, hip, and healthy eateries near Covent Garden. The neighborhood is a tabouli of fun, hippie-type cafés. One of the best is the vegetarian **Food for Thought,** packed with local health nuts (good £5 vegetarian meals, £7.50 dinner plates, Mon–Sat 12:00–20:30, Sun 12:00–17:00, 2 blocks north of Covent Garden Tube station, 31 Neal Street, near Neal's Yard, tel. 020/7836-0239).

The Soho "Food is Fun" Three-Course Dinner Crawl: For a multicultural, movable feast, consider eating (or splitting) one course and enjoying a drink at each of these places. Start around 17:30 to avoid lines, get in on early-bird specials, and find waiters willing to let you split a meal. Prices, while reasonable by London standards, add up. Servings are large enough to share. All are open nightly. Arrive at 17:30 at **Belgo Centraal** and split the early-bird dinner special: a kilo of mussels, fries, and dark Belgian beer. At **Yo! Sushi,** have beer or sake and a few dishes. Slurp your last course at **Wagamama Noodle Bar.** For dessert, people-watch at Leicester Square.

Near Recommended Victoria Station Accommodations

I've enjoyed eating at these places, a few blocks southwest of Victoria Station. See the map on page 681.

Ebury Wine Bar, filled with young professionals, provides a cut-above atmosphere, delicious £15–18 mains, and a £15.50 two-course special from 18:00–20:00. In the delightful back room, the fancy menu features modern European cuisine with a French accent; at the wine bar, find a cheaper bar menu that's better than your average pub grub. This is emphatically a "traditional wine bar," with no beers on tap (daily 11:00–23:00, reserve after 20:00, at intersection of Ebury and Elizabeth Streets, near bus station, 139 Ebury Street, tel. 020/7730-5447).

Jenny Lo's Tea House is a simple, budget place serving up reliably tasty £7–8 eclectic Chinese-style meals to locals in the know. While the menu is small, everything is high quality. Jenny clearly learned from her father, Ken Lo, one of the most famous Cantonese chefs in Britain, whose fancy place is just around the corner (Mon–Fri 12:00–15:00 & 18:00–22:00, Sat 18:00–22:00, closed Sun, cash only, 14 Eccleston Street, tel. 020/7259-0399).

La Poule au Pot, ideal for a romantic splurge, offers a classy, candlelit ambience with well-dressed patrons and expensive but fine country-style French cuisine (£18 lunch specials, £25 dinner plates, daily 12:30–14:30 & 18:45–23:00, Sun until 22:00, £50 for dinner with wine, leafy patio dining, reservations smart, end of Ebury Street at intersection with Pimlico Road, 231 Ebury Street, tel. 020/7730-7763).

Grumbles brags it's been serving "good food and wine at non-scary prices since 1964." Offering a delicious mix of "modern eclectic French and traditional English," this hip and cozy little place with four nice sidewalk tables is *the* spot to eat well in this otherwise workaday neighborhood (£8–16 plates, £10 early-bird special, daily 12:00–14:30 & 18:00–23:00, reservations wise, half a block north of Belgrave Road at 35 Churton Street, tel. 020/7834-0149). Multitaskers take note: The self-service launderette across the street is open evenings.

Chimes English Restaurant and Cider Bar comes with a fresh country-farm ambience, serious ciders (rare in London), and very good, traditional English food. Experiment with the cider—it's legal here...just barely (£13 two-course meals, hearty salads, daily 12:00–15:00 & 17:30–22:15, 26 Churton Street, tel. 020/7821-7456).

The Jugged Hare, a 10-minute walk from Victoria Station, is a pub in a lavish old bank building, its vaults replaced by tankards of beer and a fine kitchen. They have a fun, traditional menu with more fresh veggies than fries, and a plush and vivid pub scene good for a meal or just a drink (£8–10 meals, daily 12:00–21:30, 172 Vauxhall Bridge Road, tel. 020/7828-1543).

Seafresh Fish Restaurant is the neighborhood place for plaice—either take-out on the cheap or eat-in, enjoying a chrome-and-wood mod ambience with classic and creative fish-and-chips cuisine. While Mario's father started this place in 1965, it feels like the chippie of the 21st century (meals-£5 to go, £8–13 to sit, Mon–Fri 12:00–15:00 & 17:00–22:30, Sat 12:00–22:30, closed Sun, 80 Wilton Road, tel. 020/7828-0747).

La Bottega is an Italian delicatessen that fits its upscale Belgravia neighborhood. It offers tasty, freshly cooked pastas (£5.50), lasagnas, and salads at its counter (lasagna and salad meal-£8), along with great sandwiches (£3) and a good coffee bar with pastries. While not cheap, it's fast (order at the counter) and the ingredients would please an Italian chef (Mon–Sat 8:00–18:00, closed Sun, on corner of Ebury and Eccleston Streets, tel. 020/7730-2730, managed by Aghi from Bergamo). Grab your meal to go or enjoy the good Belgravia life with locals, either sitting inside or on the sidewalk.

St. George's Tavern is *the* pub for a meal in this neighborhood. They serve dinner from the same fun menu in three zones: on the sidewalk to catch the sun and enjoy some people-watching, in the sloppy pub, and in a classier back dining room (£7–10 meals, proud of their sausages, breakfast from 10:00, dinner served 17:00–22:00, corner of Hugh Street and Belgrave Road, tel. 020/7630-1116).

Drinking Pubs that Serve Food: If you want to have a pub meal or just enjoy a drink surrounded by an interesting local crowd, consider three pubs in the neighborhood, each with a distinct character: **The Duke of Wellington** is a classic neighborhood pub with forgettable grub, woodsy sidewalk seating, and an inviting interior (closed Sun, 63 Eaton Terrace, tel. 020/7730-1782). **The Belgravia Pub** is a sports bar with burgers, a stark interior, and a little outdoor garden (daily, corner of Ebury Street and South Eaton Place at 152 Ebury Street, tel. 020/7730-6040). **The Thomas Cubitt Pub,** packed with young professionals, is the neighborhood's trendy new "gastro pub," great for a drink or pricey meals (44 Elizabeth Street, tel. 020/7730-6060).

Cheap Eats: For groceries, a handy **Marks & Spencer Simply Food** is inside Victoria Station (Mon–Sat 7:00–24:00, Sun 8:00–22:00), along with a **Sainsbury's Market** (daily 6:00–23:00, at rear entrance, on Eccleston Street). A larger **Sainsbury's Market** is on Wilton Road, to the side of the station (daily 6:00–24:00). There are a string of good ethnic restaurants on Wilton Road (near the Seafresh Fish Restaurant, recommended on the previous page). For affordable if forgettable meals, try the row of cheap little eateries on Elizabeth Street.

Near Recommended Notting Hill B&Bs and Bayswater Hotels

The road called Queensway is a multi-ethnic food circus, lined with lively and inexpensive eateries. See the map on page 686.

Maggie Jones, a £40 splurge, is where Charles Dickens meets Ella Fitzgerald—exuberantly rustic and very English with a 1940s-jazz soundtrack. You'll get solid English cuisine, including huge plates of crunchy vegetables, served by a young and casual staff. It's pricey, but the portions are huge (especially the meat and fish pies—their specialty). You're welcome to save lots by splitting your main course. The candlelit upstairs is the most romantic, while the basement is kept lively with the kitchen, tight seating, and lots of action. If you eat well once in London, eat here—and do it quick, before it burns down (daily 12:30–14:30 & 18:30–23:00, reservations recommended, 6 Old Court Place, just east of Kensington Church Street, near High Street Kensington Tube stop, tel. 020/7937-6462).

The Churchill Arms pub and **Thai Kitchens** (same location) are local hangouts, with good beer and a thriving old-English ambience in front, and hearty £6 Thai plates in an enclosed patio in the back. You can eat the Thai food in the tropical hideaway or in the atmospheric pub section. The place is festooned with Churchill memorabilia and chamber pots (including one with Hitler's mug on it—hanging from the ceiling farthest from Thai Kitchen—sure to cure the constipation of any Brit during World War II). Arrive by 18:00 or after 21:00 to avoid a line. During busy times, diners are limited to an hour at the table (daily 12:00–22:00, 119 Kensington Church Street, tel. 020/7792-1246).

The Prince Edward serves good grub in a quintessential pub setting (£7–10 meals, Mon–Sat 12:00–15:00 & 18:00–22:00, Sun 12:00–20:00, plush-pubby indoor seating or sidewalk tables, family-friendly, free Wi-Fi, 2 blocks north of Bayswater Road at the corner of Dawson Place and Hereford Road, 73 Prince's Square, tel. 020/7727-2221).

Café Diana is a healthy little eatery serving sandwiches, salads, and Middle Eastern food. It's decorated—almost shrine-like—with photos of Princess Diana, who used to drop by for pita sandwiches (daily 8:00–22:30, 5 Wellington Terrace, on Bayswater Road, opposite Kensington Palace Garden Gates—where Di once lived, tel. 020/7792-9606).

Royal China Restaurant is filled with London's Chinese, who consider this one of the city's best eateries. It's dressed up in black, white, and gold, with candles, brisk waiters, and fine food (£7–11 dishes, daily 12:00–23:00, dim sum until 16:45, 13 Queensway, tel. 020/7221-2535).

Whiteleys Mall Food Court offers a fun selection of ethnic and fast-food chain eateries among Corinthian columns, and a multi-screen theater in a delightful mall (Mon–Sat 10:00–20:00, Sun 12:00–18:00; options include Yo! Sushi, good salads at Café Rouge, pizza, Starbucks, and a coin-op Internet place; second floor, corner of Porchester Gardens and Queensway).

Supermarket: **Europa** is a half-block from the Notting Hill Gate Tube stop (Mon–Sat 8:00–23:00, Sun 12:00–18:00, near intersection with Pembridge Road, 112 Notting Hill Gate). The smaller **Spar Market** is at 18 Queensway (Mon–Sat 7:00–24:00, Sun 9:00–24:00), and **Marks & Spencer** can be found in Whiteleys Mall (Mon–Sat 10:00–20:00, Sun 12:00–18:00).

Near Recommended Accommodations in South Kensington

Popular eateries line Old Brompton Road and Thurloe Street (Tube: South Kensington), and a huge variety of cheap eateries are clumped around the Tube station. See the map on page 684. The **Tesco Express** grocery store is handy for picnics (daily 7:00–24:00, 54 Old Brompton Road).

La Bouchee Bistro Café is a classy, hole-in-the-wall touch of France—candlelit and woody—serving an early-bird two-course £11.50 dinner weekdays from 17:30–18:30 and £17 *plats du jour* all *jour* (daily 12:00–15:00 & 17:30–23:00, 56 Old Brompton Road, tel. 020/7589-1929).

Daquise, an authentic-feeling 1930s Polish time warp, is ideal if you're in the mood for kielbasa and kraut. It's likeably dreary—fast, cheap, family-run—and a much-appreciated part of the neighborhood (£10 meals, £8 weekday lunch special includes wine, daily 11:30–23:00, 20 Thurloe Street, tel. 020/7589-6117).

Moti Mahal Indian Restaurant, with minimalist-yet-classy mod ambience and attentive service, serves delicious Indian and Bangladeshi cuisine. Chicken *jalfrezi* and butter chicken are the favorites (£10 dinners, daily 12:00–23:00, 3 Glendower Place, tel. 020/7584-8428, Rahmat).

The Zetland Arms serves good pub meals in a classic pub atmosphere on its noisy and congested ground floor, and in a more spacious and comfy upstairs—used only in the evenings (same menu throughout, £6–10 meals, food served Mon–Sat 12:00–21:00, 2 Bute Street, tel. 020/7589-3813).

Elsewhere in London

Between St. Paul's and the Tower: **The Counting House,** formerly an elegant old bank, offers great £8–10 meals, nice homemade meat pies, fish, and fresh vegetables. The fun "nibbles menu" is available after 17:00 (Mon–Fri 12:00–22:00, closed Sat–Sun, gets really busy with the buttoned-down 9-to-5 crowd after 12:15, near Mansion House in The City, 50 Cornhill, tel. 020/7283-7123).

Near St. Paul's: **De Gustibus Sandwiches** is where a top-notch artisan bakery meets the public, offering fresh you-design-it sandwiches, salads, and soups with simple seating or take-out picnic sacks (great parks nearby), just a block below St. Paul's (Mon–Fri 7:00–17:00, closed Sat–Sun, from church steps follow signs to youth hostel a block downhill, 53–55 Carter Lane, tel. 020/7236-0056).

Near the British Library: Drummond Street (running just west of Euston Station) is famous in London for very cheap and good Indian vegetarian food. Consider **Chutneys** (124 Drummond, tel. 020/7388-0604) and **Ravi Shankar** (133 Drummond, tel.

020/7388-6458) for a good thali (both generally open daily until 21:30, later Fri–Sat).

Connections

Airports

Heathrow Airport

Heathrow Airport is the world's third busiest, after Atlanta and Chicago O'Hare. Think about it: 68 million passengers a year on 470,000 flights from 185 destinations riding 90 airlines, like some kind of global maypole dance. Read signs, ask questions. For Heathrow's airport, flight, and transfers information, call the switchboard at 0870-000-0123 (www.heathrowairport.com).

Heathrow has five terminals: T-1 (mostly domestic flights, with some European); T-2 (mainly European flights), T-3 (mostly flights from the US); T-4 (British Airways transatlantic flights and BA flights to Paris, Amsterdam, and Athens; also Northwest and Qantas Airlines); and T-5 (British Airways flights only). Taxis know which terminal you'll need. If you're taking the Tube to the airport, note that some Piccadilly Line subway cars post which airlines are served by which terminals. Otherwise, check your plane ticket or call your airline in advance to confirm which terminal your flight will use. Allow extra time to get to T-4 and T-5.

Each terminal has an airport information desk, car-rental agencies, exchange bureaus, ATMs, a pharmacy, a **VAT refund desk** (tel. 020/8910-3682; you must present the VAT claim form from the retailer here to get your tax rebate on items purchased in Britain; and **baggage storage** (£6.50/item for 24 hours, daily 6:00–23:00 at each terminal). Get online 24 hours a day at Heathrow's **Internet access points** (at each terminal—T-4's is on the mezzanine level) and with a laptop at pay-as-you-go wireless "hotspots"—including many hosted by T-Mobile—in its departure lounges. There are **post offices** in T-2 and T-4. Each terminal has cheap **eateries** (such as the cheery Food Village self-service cafeteria in T-3).

Heathrow's small **TI** (tourist info shop), even though it's a for-profit business, is worth a visit to pick up free information: a simple map, the *London Planner,* and brochures (daily 8:30–18:00, 5-min walk from T-3 in Tube station, follow signs to Underground; bypass queue for transit info to reach window for London questions). Have your partner stay with the bags at the terminal while you head over to the TI. There's also an airport info desk in the arrivals concourse of each terminal (generally open daily 7:00–21:30).

If you're taking the Tube into London, buy a one-day Travelcard or Oyster card to cover the ride (see next page).

LONDON

Getting to London from Heathrow Airport

You have several options for traveling the 14 miles between Heathrow Airport and downtown London. For one person on a budget, the Tube or bus is cheap but slow. To speed things up though you'll spend a little more; combining the Heathrow Connect train with either a Tube or taxi ride (between Paddington Station and your hotel) is nearly as fast and less than half the cost of taking a cab the whole way. For groups of four or more, a taxi is faster and easier, as well as cheaper.

By Tube (Subway): For £4, the Tube takes you to downtown London in 50–60 minutes on the Piccadilly Line, with stops at (among others) South Kensington, Leicester Square, and King's Cross Station (6/hr; depending on your destination, may require a transfer). Even better, buy a One-Day Travelcard that covers your trip into London and all your Tube travel for the day (£14.80 covers peak times, £7.50 "off-peak" card starts at 9:30, less-expensive Travelcards cover the city center only). If you're staying four or more days, consider an Oyster card. For information on both types of passes, see "Oyster Cards and Travelcards" on page 630. Buy tickets or cards at the Tube station ticket window. You can hop on the Tube at any terminal. If taking the Tube to the airport, note that Piccadilly Line subway cars post which airlines are served by which terminals.

If you're taking the Tube from downtown London to the airport, note that the Piccadilly Line trains don't stop at every terminal on every run. Trains either go to T-4, T-1, T-2, and T-3 (in that order); or T-1, T-2, T-3, and T-5 (so allow extra time if going to T-4 or T-5). Check before you board.

By Bus: Most buses depart from the outside common area called the Central Bus Station. It serves T-1, T-2, and T-3, and is a 5-minute walk from any of these terminals. To get to T-4 or T-5 from the Central Bus Station, go inside, go downstairs, and follow signs to take the Tube to your terminal (free, but runs only every 15–20 min to those terminals).

National Express has regular service from Heathrow's Central Bus Station to Victoria Coach Station in downtown London, near several of my recommended hotels. While slow, the bus is affordable and convenient for those staying near Victoria Station (£4, 1–3/hr, 45–75 min, tel. 0871-781-8181—calls are 8p/min, www.nationalexpress.com).

By Train: Two different trains run between Heathrow Airport and London's Paddington Station. At Paddington Station, you're in the thick of the Tube system, with easy access to any of my recommended neighborhoods—Notting Hill Gate is just two Tube stops away. The **Heathrow Connect** train is the slightly slower, much cheaper option serving T-1, T-2, T-3, and T-4; you can get to

T-5 if you transfer at T-1, T-2, or T-3 (£6.90 one-way, 2/hr, 25 min, tel. 0845-678-6975, www.heathrowconnect.com). The **Heathrow Express** train is blazing fast (15 min to downtown from T-1, T-2, and T-3; and 21 min from T-5) and runs more frequently (4/hr), but it's pricey (£16.50 "express class" one-way, £32 round-trip, ask about discount promos at ticket desk, kids under 16 ride half-price, under 5 ride free, buy ticket before you board or pay a £3 surcharge to buy it on the train, covered by BritRail pass, daily 5:10–23:25, tel. 0845-600-1515, www.heathrowexpress.co.uk). At the airport, you can use either the Heathrow Express or Heathrow Connect as a free transfer between terminals.

By Taxi: Taxis from the airport cost about £45–70 to west and central London (one hour). For four people traveling together, this can be a deal. Hotels can often line up a cab back to the airport for about £30–40. For the cheapest taxi to the airport, don't order one from your hotel. Simply flag down a few and ask them for their best "off-meter" rate.

Getting to Bath from Heathrow Airport

By Bus: Direct buses run daily from Heathrow to Bath (£18, 10/day direct, 2–3 hours, more frequent but slower with transfer in London, tel. 0871-781-8181, 8p/min, www.nationalexpress.com). BritRail passholders may prefer the 2.5-hour Heathrow–Bath bus/train connection via Reading (£9.50 for bus with pass, rail portion free with pass, otherwise £53 total for travelers without a BritRail pass, payable at desk in terminal, tel. 0118-957-9425, www.railair.com). First catch the twice-hourly RailAir Link shuttle bus to Reading (RED-ding), then hop on the twice-hourly express train to Bath. Factoring in the connection in Reading—which can add at least an hour to the trip—the train is a less convenient option than the direct bus to Bath. Also consider taking a minibus with Alan Price (see www.celtichorizons.com). For more bus information, see "By Bus," opposite page.

Gatwick Airport

More and more flights, especially charters, land at Gatwick Airport, halfway between London and the South Coast (recorded airport info tel. 0870-000-2468).

Getting to London: Gatwick Express trains—clearly the best way into London from here—shuttle conveniently between Gatwick and London's Victoria Station (£17.90, £30.80 round-trip, 4/hr during day, 1–2/hr at night, 30 min, runs 5:00–24:00 daily, can purchase tickets on train at no extra charge, tel. 0845-850-1530, www.gatwickexpress.co.uk). If you're traveling with two or three other adults, buy your tickets at the station before boarding, and you'll travel for the price of two. The only restriction on this impressive deal is that you have to travel together. So if you see another couple in line, get organized and save 50 percent.

You can save a few pounds by taking Southern rail line's slower and less frequent shuttle between Gatwick's South Terminal and Victoria Station (£10.90, up to 4/hr, hourly 24:00–4:00, 45 min, tel. 0845-127-2920, www.southernrailway.com). A train also runs from Gatwick to St. Pancras International Station (£8.90, 8/hr, 50–60 min, www.firstcapitalconnect.co.uk), useful for travelers taking the Eurostar train (to Paris or Brussels) or staying in the St. Pancras/King's Cross neighborhood.

Getting to Bath: To get to Bath from Gatwick, you can catch a bus to Heathrow and take the bus to Bath from there (see previous page). By train, the best Gatwick–Bath connection involves a transfer in Reading (about hourly, 2.5 hrs; avoid transfer in London, where you'll likely have to change stations).

Connecting London's Airports

The **National Express Airport** service offers direct bus connections from **Heathrow** to **Gatwick Airport** (1–4/hr, 1.25–1.5 hrs or more, depending on traffic), departing just outside arrivals at all terminals (£19.50 one-way, £36.50 round-trip). To make a flight connection between Heathrow and Gatwick, allow three hours between flights.

More and more travelers are taking advantage of cheap flights out of London's smaller airports. A handy National Express bus runs between Heathrow, Gatwick, Stansted, and Luton airports—easier than having to cut through the center of London. Buses are frequent (less so between Stansted and Luton); for instance, the Heathrow–Luton bus runs hourly (£19 one-way, £23.50 round-trip, 1.25–1.5 hours direct). Check schedules at www.national express.com (tel. 0871-781-8181—calls are 8p/min).

Trains and Buses

Britain is covered by a myriad of rail systems (owned by different companies), which together are called National Rail. London, the country's major transportation hub, has a different train station for each region. St. Pancras International Station handles the Eurostar to Paris or Brussels. King's Cross and Euston stations cover northeast England, North Wales, and Scotland. Paddington covers west and southwest England (including Bath) and South Wales. For information, call 0845-748-4950 (or visit www.nationalrail.co.uk or www.eurostar.com; £5 booking fee for telephone reservations). New simplified names for rail fares were recently introduced across the National Rail network: "Advance," "Anytime," and "Off-Peak." Note that for security reasons, stations offer a baggage-storage service (£6.50/bag for 24 hours) rather than lockers; because of long security lines, it can take a while to check or pick up your bag (for more details, see "Helpful Hints," near the beginning of this chapter).

By Train
To Paris or Brussels via Eurostar Train

From St. Pancras Station to: Paris (12–15/day, 2.5 hrs), **Bruges** (via Brussels: 10/day, 2.5 hrs to Brussels Midi; then transfer, backtracking to Bruges: 2/hr, 1 hr, entire trip is covered by same Eurostar ticket). Arrive at least 30 min early; security procedures for the Eurostar are similar to airport check-in.

Eurostar Fares: Eurostar fares are reasonable but complicated. Prices vary depending on how far ahead you reserve, whether you can live with restrictions, and whether you're eligible for any discounts (children, youths, seniors, and railpass holders all qualify). Rates are lowest for round-trips.

Fares can change without notice, but typically a **one-way, full-fare ticket** (with no restrictions on refundability) runs about $425 first-class and $310 second-class. Accepting more restrictions lowers the price substantially (figure $90–200 for second class, one-way), but these **cheaper seats** sell out quickly. Those traveling with a railpass that covers Britain or France (for Paris trips) or Belgium (for Brussels trips) should look first at the **passholder** fare (about $90–160 for second-class, one-way Eurostar trips). Eurostar tickets between London and Brussels include travel to/from any Belgian city at no additional cost within 24 hours of the Brussels Eurostar arrival or departure (not valid on Thalys express trains). Just show the Eurostar ticket when boarding the other train(s).

You can check the latest fares and book tickets by phone or online in the US (order online at www.ricksteves.com/rail /eurostar.htm, prices listed in dollars; or order by phone at US tel. 800-EUROSTAR), or in Europe (www.eurostar.com, prices listed in euros; French tel. 08 92 35 35 39, Belgian tel. 02-528-2828). While tickets are usually cheaper if purchased in the US, fares offered in Europe follow different discount rules—so it can be worth it to check www.eurostar.com before purchasing. If you buy from a US company, you'll pay for ticket delivery in the US. In Europe, you can buy your Eurostar ticket at any major train station in any country or at any travel agency that handles train tickets (expect a booking fee).

Fares and rules may have changed by the time you visit, however, as Eurostar's monopoly on the cross-channel route expires at the beginning of 2010; Air France plans to start a competing high-speed rail service between London and Paris in late 2010.

To Points West in Britain

From Paddington Station to: Bath (2/hr, 1.5 hrs; also consider a guided Evan Evans tour by bus—see "By Bus," below); **Oxford** (2–5/hr, 1–1.5 hrs, possible transfer in Didcot or Reading), **Penzance** (about hourly, 5–6 hrs, possible change in Plymouth), and **Cardiff** (2/hr, 2 hrs).

To Points North in Britain

From King's Cross Station: Trains run at least hourly, stopping in **York** (2–2.25 hrs), **Durham** (3 hrs), and **Edinburgh** (4.5 hrs). Trains to **Cambridge** also leave from here (2/hr, 1–1.5 hrs).

From Euston Station to: Conwy (10/day, 3.25–4 hrs, transfer in Chester or Crewe), **Liverpool** (1/hr, 2.5 hrs direct), **Blackpool** (2/hr, 3 hrs, transfer at Preston), **Keswick** (10/day, 4–5 hrs, transfer to bus at Penrith), **Glasgow** (1–2/hr, 4.5–5 hrs direct, some may leave from King's Cross Station).

From London's Other Stations

Trains run between London and **Canterbury,** leaving from Charing Cross Station and arriving in Canterbury West, as well as from London's Victoria Station and arriving in Canterbury East (2/hr, 1.5–2 hrs).

Direct trains leave for **Stratford-upon-Avon** from Marylebone Station, located near the southwest corner of Regents Park (every 2 hrs, 2–2.5 hrs).

Other Destinations: Dover (2/hr, 2 hrs, one direct from Victoria Station, one from Charing Cross Station—sometimes with transfer), **Brighton** (1–2/hr direct, 50 min, from Victoria Station; also several other connections to different London stations, some requiring transfers), **Portsmouth** (2–4/hr, 1.5–2 hrs, almost all depart from Waterloo Station, a few a day depart from Victoria Station), and **Salisbury** (2/hr, 1.5 hrs, direct from Waterloo Station).

By Bus

National Express' excellent bus service is considerably cheaper than the train, and a fine option for destinations within England (call 0871-781-8181—calls are 8p/min, or visit www.national express.com or the bus station a block southwest of Victoria Station).

To Bath: The National Express bus leaves from Victoria Station nearly hourly (a little over 3 hrs, one-way-£18, round trip-£27.50).

To get to Bath via Stonehenge, consider taking a guided bus tour from London to Stonehenge and Bath, and abandoning the tour in Bath (be sure to confirm that Bath is the last stop). **Evan**

Evans' tour is £69 and includes admissions. The tour leaves from the Victoria Coach station every morning at 8:45 (you can stow your bag under the bus), stops in Stonehenge (45 min), and then stops in Bath for lunch and a city tour before returning to London (offered year-round). You can book the tour at the Victoria Coach station or the Evan Evans office (258 Vauxhall Bridge Road, near Victoria Coach station, tel. 020/7950-1777, US tel. 866-382-6868, www.evanevans.co.uk, reservations@evanevanstours.co.uk).

Golden Tours also runs a fully guided Stonehenge–Bath tour (£39, does not include admissions; runs Mon, Wed, and Fri–Sat; departs from Fountain Square, located across from Victoria Coach Station, tel. 020/7233-7030, US tel. 800-548-7083, www.golden tours.co.uk, reservations@goldentours.co.uk). Another similarly priced day trip hits Oxford, Stratford, and Warwick.

To Other Destinations: Oxford (2–4/hr, 1.75–2.25 hrs), **Cambridge** (hourly direct, 2 hrs), **Canterbury** (hourly, 2–2.5 hrs), **Dover** (hourly, about 3 hrs), **Penzance** (5/day direct, 9 hrs), **Cardiff** (every 2–3 hrs direct, 3.25 hrs), **Liverpool** (7/day direct, 5–6 hrs), **Blackpool** (5/day direct, 6–6.5 hrs), **York** (4/day direct, 5.25 hrs), **Durham** (4/day direct, 6–7.5 hrs), **Glasgow** (2/day direct, 8.5 hrs, train is a much better option), **Edinburgh** (3/day direct, 8.5–9.5 hrs, go via train instead).

LONDON

BATH

The best city to visit within easy striking distance of London is Bath—just a 90-minute train ride away. Two hundred years ago, this city of 85,000 was the trendsetting Hollywood of Britain. If ever a city enjoyed looking in the mirror, Bath's the one. It has more "government-listed" or protected historic buildings per capita than any other town in England. The entire city, built of the creamy warm-tone limestone called "Bath stone," beams in its cover-girl complexion. An architectural chorus line, it's a triumph of the Georgian style. Proud locals remind visitors that the town is routinely banned from the "Britain in Bloom" contest to give other towns a chance to win. Bath's narcissism is justified. Even with its mobs of tourists (2 million per year) and greedy prices, Bath is a joy to visit.

Long before the Romans arrived in the first century, Bath was known for its mineral hot springs. The importance of Bath has always been shaped by the healing allure of its 116°F hot springs. Romans called the popular spa town Aquae Sulis. The town's importance carried through Saxon times, when it had a huge church on the site of the present-day abbey and was considered the religious capital of Britain. Its influence peaked in 973 with King Edgar's sumptuous coronation in the abbey. Later, Bath prospered as a wool town.

Bath then declined until the mid-1600s, languishing to just a huddle of huts around the abbey, with hot, smelly mud and 3,000 residents, oblivious to the Roman ruins 18 feet below their dirt floors. In fact, with its own walls built upon ancient ones, Bath was no bigger than that Roman town. Then, in 1687, Queen Mary, fighting infertility, bathed here. Within 10 months she gave birth

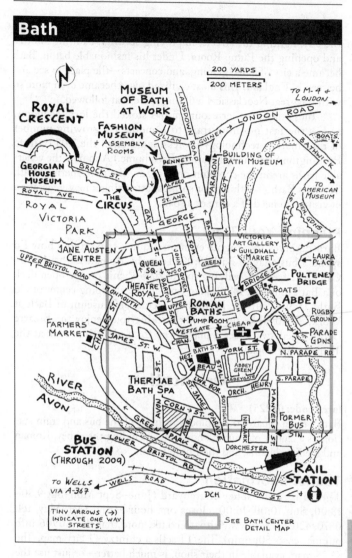

Bath

TINY ARROWS (→) INDICATE ONE WAY STREETS.

☐ SEE BATH CENTER DETAIL MAP

to a son...and a new age of popularity for Bath.

The revitalized town boomed as a spa resort. Ninety percent of the buildings you'll see today are from the 18th century. Local architect John Wood was inspired by the Italian architect Andrea Palladio to build a "new Rome." The town bloomed in the Neoclassical style, and streets were lined not with scrawny sidewalks but with wide "parades," upon which the women in their stylishly wide dresses could spread their fashionable tails.

Beau Nash (1673–1762) was Bath's "master of ceremonies."

He organized both the daily regimen of aristocratic visitors and the city, lighting the streets, improving security, banning swords, and opening the Pump Room. Under his fashionable baton, Bath became a city of balls, gaming, and concerts—the place to see and be seen in England. This most civilized place became even more so with the great Neoclassical building spree that followed.

These days, modern tourism has stoked the local economy, as has the fast morning train to London. (A growing number of information-technology professionals catch the 7:05 train to Paddington Station while calling Bath home.) And now the venerable baths are in the spotlight once again. The new Thermae Bath Spa taps Bath's soothing hot springs, attracting a new generation of visitors in need of a cure or a soak.

Planning Your Time

Bath deserves two nights even on a quick trip. Here's how I'd spend a busy day in Bath: 9:00–Tour the Roman Baths; 10:30–Catch the free city walking tour; 12:30–Picnic on the open deck of a Bath tour bus; 14:00–Free time in the shopping center of old Bath; 15:30–Tour the Fashion Museum or Museum of Bath at Work, 20:00–Take the evening walking tour, enjoy the Bizarre Bath comedy walk, see a play, or go for a nighttime soak at the Thermae Bath Spa.

Orientation

(area code: 01225)
Bath's town square, three blocks in front of the bus and train station, is a cluster of tourist landmarks, including the abbey, Roman and medieval baths, and the Pump Room.

Tourist Information

The TI is in the abbey churchyard (June–Sept Mon–Sat 9:30–18:00, Sun 10:00–16:00, closes one hour earlier Oct–May, tel. 0870-420-1278, www.visitbath.co.uk, note that their 0906 info number costs 50p/min). The TI sells a chintzy £1 city map. The £1.25 map, available in their shop, is much better—or just use the one included in the free *Bath Visitors' Guide and Map*. While you're at the TI, browse through scads of fliers, books, and maps, or ask them to book you a room (£3 charge). They don't bother to print an events flier, so look at the local paper or their daily events board.

Arrival in Bath

The Bath **train station** has a national and international tickets desk and a privately run travel agency masquerading as a TI. Immediately surrounding the train station is a sea of construc-

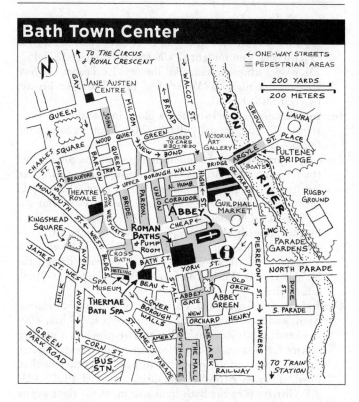

Bath Town Center

To THE CIRCUS & ROYAL CRESCENT

← ONE-WAY STREETS
▨ PEDESTRIAN AREAS

200 YARDS
200 METERS

JANE AUSTEN CENTRE

GAY
QUEEN
JOHN
MILSOM
WALCOT ST.
BROAD
AVON
GROVE
LAURA PLACE

CHARLES SQUARE
WOOD
QUIET
GREEN
CLOSED TO CARS 8:30-18:30
VICTORIA ART GALLERY
ARGYLE ST.
PULTENEY BRIDGE

QUEEN
BARTON
NEW
BOND
BRIDGE
GR. PARADE
BOATS

PRINCES
BEAUFORT
TRIM
UPPER BOROUGH WALLS
HIGH ST.
RIVER

MONMOUTH ST.
THEATRE ROYALE
CLOSE
WESTGATE
BRIDE
PARSON
UNION
N. HUMB.
CORRIDOR
ABBEY
GUILDHALL MARKET
RUGBY GROUND

KINGSMEAD SQUARE
WEST
ST.
BLDGS.
CROSS BATH
ROMAN BATHS & PUMP ROOM
CHEAP
BATH ST.
PIERREPONT ST.
WC
PARADE GARDENS

JAMES ST. WEST
AVON
ST.
HETLING
BEAU
YORK ST.
NORTH PARADE

MILK ST.
AVON
SPA MUSEUM
THERMAE BATH SPA
LOWER BOROUGH WALLS
ABBEY GATE
ABBEY GREEN
OLD ORCH.
DUKE ST.
S. PARADE

GREEN PARK ROAD
CORN ST.
ST. JAMES'S PARADE
SOUTHGATE
NEW ORCHARD
HENRY
NEWARK
MANVERS ST.
TO TRAIN STATION

BUS STN.
THE MALL
RAILWAY

tion, as Bath gets a new mall and underground parking garage (due to be complete in 2011). To get to the TI from the train station, walk two blocks up Manvers Street and turn left at the triangular "square," following the small TI arrow on a signpost.

The **bus station** is immediately in front of the train station. (Because of the construction, Bath's **bus station** was moved to a temporary location on Corn Street in 2009. It should be back near the train station in time for your visit—but if it's not, you'll find temporary station at the southwest corner of town, a few blocks from the train station and town center.)

My recommended B&Bs are all within a 10- to 15-minute walk or a £4–5 taxi ride from either station.

Helpful Hints

Festivals: Bath hosts book, music, and theater festivals in the spring, including the **Bath Literature Festival** (www.bathlit fest.org.uk), the **Bath International Music Festival** (classical, folk, jazz, contemporary; www.bathmusicfest.org.uk), and the eclectic **Bath Fringe Festival** (theater, walks, talks, bus trips; www.bathfringe.co.uk). The **Jane Austen Festival** unfolds genteelly in late September (www.janeausten.co.uk). Bath's festival box office sells tickets for most events, and can tell you exactly what's on tonight (2 Church Street, tel. 01225/462-231, www.bathfestivals.org.uk). The city's local paper, the *Bath Chronicle*, publishes a "What's On" event listing on Fridays (www.thisisbath.com).

Internet Access: Try **@Internet,** a block in front of the train station (£1/20 min, daily 10:00–22:00, Manvers Street, tel. 01225/443-181).

Laundry: Spruce Goose Launderette is around the corner from the recommended Brocks Guest House, on the pedestrian lane called Margaret's Buildings (bring lots of £0.20 and £1 coins, self-service daily 8:00–21:00, full-service Mon–Fri 9:00–13:00—but book ahead, tel. 01225/483-309). Anywhere ... ~~Speedy Wash~~ can pick up your laundry for same-day service (£10/bag, Mon–Fri 7:30–17:30, most hotels work with them, tel. 01225/427-616). East of Pulteney Bridge, the humble **Lovely Wash** is on Daniel Street (daily 9:00–21:00, self-service only).

Car Rental: Enterprise and **Thrifty** are each handy to central Bath, and have roughly the same rates (£40/24 hrs, £80/weekend, £130–160/week). **Enterprise** provides a pick-up service for customers to and from their hotels (extra charge for one-way rentals, promises to beat any other deal in town, at Lower Bristol Road outside Bath, tel. 01225/443-311). **Thrifty** is in the Bath train station, to the right as you exit (tel. 01225/442-911). **National/Alamo** is a £7 taxi ride from the train station, but will do one-way rentals (at Brass Mill Lane—go west on Upper Bristol Road, tel. 01225/481-982). **Europcar** advertises that it's in Bath, but it's actually a 20-minute taxi ride outside of town. **Avis** is a mile from the Bristol train station; you'd need to rent a car to get there. Most offices close Saturday afternoon and all day Sunday, which complicates weekend pick-ups. Ideally, take the train or bus from downtown London to Bath, and rent a car as you leave Bath, rather than from within London.

BATH

Tours

Of Bath

▲▲▲**Walking Tours**—Free two-hour tours are offered by **The Mayor's Corps of Honorary Guides,** led by volunteers who want to share their love of Bath with its many visitors (as the city's mayor first did when he took a group on a guided walk back in the 1930s). Their chatty, historical, and gossip-filled walks are essential for your understanding of this town's amazing Georgian social scene.

How else will you learn that the old "chair ho" call for your sedan chair evolved into today's "cheerio" farewell? Tours leave from in front of the Pump Room (free, no tips, year-round Sun–Fri at 10:30 and 14:00, Sat at 10:30 only; evening walks offered May–Sept on Tue and Fri at 19:00; tel. 01225/477-411). Advice for theatergoers: When your guide stops to talk outside the Theatre Royal, skip out for a moment, pop into the box office, and see about snaring a great deal on a play for tonight (see "Nightlife," later in this chapter, for details).

For a **private tour**, call the local guides' bureau (£60/2 hrs, tel. 01225/337-111). For **Ghost Walks** and **Bizarre Bath** tours, see "Nightlife," later in this chapter.

▲▲**City Bus Tours**—City Sightseeing's hop-on, hop-off bus tours zip through Bath. Jump on a bus anytime at one of 17 signposted pick-up points, pay the driver, climb upstairs, and hear recorded commentary about Bath. City Sightseeing has two routes: a 50-minute downtown tour (unintelligible audio recording on half the buses, live guides on the other half—choose the latter), and a 45-minute "Skyline" route outside of town (all live guides, stops near the American Museum—15-min walk). On a sunny day, this is a multitasking tourist's dream come true: You can munch a sandwich, work on a tan, snap great photos, and learn a lot, all at the same time. Save money by doing the bus tour first—ticket stubs get you minor discounts at many sights (£10, ticket valid for 2 days and both tour routes, generally 4/hr daily in summer from 9:30–19:00, in winter from 10:00–15:00).

Taxi Tours—Local taxis, driven by good talkers, go where big buses can't. A group of up to four can rent a cab for an hour (about £20) and enjoy a fine, informative, and—with the right cabbie—entertaining private joyride. It's probably cheaper to let the meter run than to pay for an hourly rate, but ask the cabbie for advice.

Sights

In Bath's Town Center

▲▲▲**Roman and Medieval Baths**—In ancient Roman times, high society enjoyed the mineral springs at Bath. From Londinium, Romans traveled so often to Aquae Sulis, as the city was called, to "take a bath" that finally it became known simply as Bath. Today, a fine museum surrounds the ancient bath. It's a one-way system leading you past well-documented displays, Roman artifacts, mosaics, a temple pediment, and the actual mouth of the spring, piled high with Roman pennies. Enjoy some quality time looking into the eyes of Minerva, goddess of the hot springs. The included audioguide makes the visit easy and plenty informative. For those with a big appetite for Roman history, in-depth 40-minute guided tours leave from the end of the museum at the edge of the actual bath (included with ticket, on the hour, a poolside clock is set for the next departure time). The water is greenish because of algae—don't drink it. You can revisit the museum after the tour (£11, £14 combo-ticket includes Fashion Museum—a £4 savings, family ticket available, daily July–Aug 9:00–22:00, March–June and Sept–Oct 9:00–18:00, Nov–Feb 9:30–17:30, last entry one hour before closing, tel. 01225/477-784, www.romanbaths.co.uk). The museum and baths are fun to visit in the evening in summer—romantic, gas-lit, and all yours.

After touring the Roman Baths, stop by the attached Pump Room for a spot of tea, or to gag on the water.

▲Pump Room—For centuries, Bath was forgotten as a spa. Then, in 1687, the previously barren Queen Mary bathed here, became pregnant, and bore a male heir to the throne. A few years later, Queen Anne found the water eased her painful gout. Word of its wonder waters spread, and Bath earned its way back on the aristocratic map. High society soon turned the place into one big pleasure palace. The Pump Room, an elegant Georgian hall just above the Roman Baths, offers visitors their best chance to raise a pinky in this Chippendale grandeur. Above the newspaper table and sedan chairs, a statue of Beau Nash himself sniffles down at you. Drop by to sip coffee or tea or to enjoy a light meal (daily 9:30–12:00 for coffee and £6–8 breakfast, 12:00–14:30 for £18 lunches, 14:30–16:30 for £18 traditional afternoon tea, £7 tea/coffee and pastry also available in the afternoons, open for dinner July–Aug only; live music daily—string trio 10:00–12:00, piano 12:45–14:30, string trio in high season or piano in winter 15:00–17:00; tel. 01225/444-477). For just the price of a coffee (£3), you're welcome to drop in anytime—except during lunch—to enjoy the music and atmosphere.

The Spa Water: This is your chance to eat a famous (but forgettable) "Bath bun" and split a drink of the awful curative water (£0.50, free with a ticket to the baths). The water comes from the King's Spring and is brought to you by an appropriately attired server, who explains that the water is 10,000 years old, pumped from nearly 100 yards deep, and marinated in wonderful minerals. Convenient public WCs (which use plain old tap water) are in the entry hallway that connects the Pump Room with the baths.

▲Thermae Bath Spa—After simmering unused for a quarter-century, Bath's natural thermal springs once again offer R&R for the masses. The state-of-the-art spa is housed in a complex of three buildings that combine historic structures with controversial new glass-and-steel architecture. And that's not the only controversy associated with the spa: Renovations were delayed by years and went millions over budget, putting Bath in a financial hole that the

BATH

town now seems to be paying for by cutting corners on the rest of its attractions.

Is the Thermae Bath Spa worth the time and money? The experience is pretty pricey and humble compared to similar German and Hungarian spas. Because you're in a tall, modern building in the city center, it lacks a certain old-time elegance. Jets are very limited, and the only water toys you'll see are big foam noodles. There's no cold plunge—the only way to cool off between steam rooms is to step onto a small, unglamorous balcony. The Royal Bath's two pools are essentially the same, and the water isn't particularly hot in either—in fact, the main attraction is the rooftop view from the top one (best with a partner or as a social experience).

If you do visit, bring your own swimsuit and come for a couple of hours (Fri night and Sat afternoon are most crowded). Or consider an evening visit, when—on a chilly day—Bath's twilight glows through the steam from the rooftop pool. The only natural thermal spa in the UK, Thermae also has all the "pamper thyself" extras—massages, mud wraps, and various healing-type treatments, including "watsu"—water shiatsu (£40–70 extra).

Cost: The cheapest spa pass is £22 for two hours, which gains you access to the Royal Bath's large ground-floor "Minerva Bath"; the four steam rooms and the waterfall shower; and the view-filled, open-air rooftop thermal pool. If you want to stay longer, it's £32/4 hrs and £52/day (towels-£3, robes-£4, slippers-£2). The much-hyped £35 Twilight Session Package includes three hours and a meal (one plate, drink, robes, towel, and slippers). This package's appeal is not the mediocre meal, but to be on top of the building at a magical hour (which you can do for less money at the regular rate).

Hours: Generally open daily 9:00–22:00, last entry at 19:30.

Location and Information: It's 100 yards from the Roman and Medieval Baths, on Beau Street. Tel. 01225/331-234, book treatments at www.thermaebathspa.com. There's a salad-and-smoothies café for guests.

Cross Bath: This renovated, circular Georgian structure across the street from the main spa provides a simpler and less-expensive bathing option. It has a hot-water fountain that taps directly into the spring, making its water temperature higher than the spa's (£13/90 min, daily 10:00–17:00, changing rooms, no access to Royal Bath).

Spa Museum: Also across the street in the Hetling Pump Room, this free one-room exhibit explains the story of the spa (Mon–Sat 10:00–17:00, Sun 10:00–16:00, £2 audioguide).

▲**Abbey**—The town of Bath wasn't much in the Middle Ages, but an important church has stood on this spot since Anglo-Saxon times. King Edgar I was crowned here in 973, when the church was much bigger (before the bishop packed up and moved to Wells). Dominating the town center, today's abbey—the last great medieval church of England—is 500 years old and a fine example of Late Perpendicular Gothic, with breezy fan vaulting and enough stained glass to earn it the nickname "Lantern of the West." The glass, red-iron gas-powered lamps, and heating grates on the floor are all remnants of the 19th century. The window behind the altar shows 52 scenes from the life of Christ. A window to the left of the altar shows Edgar's coronation (worth the £2.50 donation; April–Oct Mon–Sat 9:00–18:00, Sun 13:00–14:30 & 16:30–17:30; Nov–March Mon–Sat 9:00–16:30, Sun 13:00–14:30; handy flier narrates a self-guided 19-stop tour, www.bathabbey.org).

Posted on the door is the schedule for concerts, services, and **evensong** (Sun at 15:30 year-round, plus most Sat in Aug at 17:00). The facade (c. 1500, but mostly restored) is interesting for some of its carvings. Look for the angels going down the ladder. The statue of Peter (to the left of the door) lost his head to mean iconoclasts; it was re-carved out of his once super-sized beard. Take a moment to appreciate the abbey's architecture from the Abbey Green square.

A small but worthwhile exhibit, the abbey's **Heritage Vaults** tell the story of Christianity in Bath since Roman times (free, Mon–Sat 10:00–16:00, last entry at 15:30, closed Sun, entrance just outside church, south side).

▲**Pulteney Bridge, Parade Gardens, and Cruises**—Bath is inclined to compare its shop-lined Pulteney Bridge to Florence's Ponte Vecchio. That's pushing it. But to best enjoy a sunny day, pay about £1 to enter the Parade Gardens below the bridge (April–Sept daily 10:00–dusk, shorter hours off-season, includes deck chairs, ask about concerts held some Sun at 15:00 in summer, tel. 01225/394-041). Taking a siesta to relax peacefully at the riverside provides a wonderful break (and memory).

Across the bridge at Pulteney Weir, tour boat companies run **cruises** (£7, £3.50 one-way, up to 7/day if the weather's good, 60 min to Bathampton and back, WCs onboard, tel. 01225/312-900). Just take whatever boat is running. Avon Cruisers actually stop in Bathampton (allowing you to hop off and walk back). Boats come with picnic-friendly sundecks.

Guildhall Market—The little shopping mall, located across from Pulteney Bridge, is a frumpy time warp in this affluent town—fun for browsing and picnic shopping. Its cheap Market Café is recommended under "Eating," later in this chapter.

Victoria Art Gallery—The one-room gallery, next to Guildhall Market, is filled with paintings from the 18th and 19th centuries (free, includes audioguide, Tue–Sat 10:00–17:00, Sun 13:30–17:00, closed Mon, WC, www.victoriagal.org.uk).

Near Royal Crescent and the Circus

▲▲**Royal Crescent and the Circus**—If Bath is an architectural cancan, these are the knickers. These first Georgian "condos" by John Wood (the Elder and the Younger) are well-explained by the city walking tours. "Georgian" is British for "Neoclassical," or dating from the 1770s. As you cruise the Crescent, pretend you're rich. Then pretend you're poor. Notice the "ha ha fence," a drop-off in the front yard that acted as a barrier, invisible from the windows, for keeping out sheep and peasants. The refined and stylish **Royal Crescent Hotel** sits unmarked in the center of the crescent. You're welcome to (politely) drop in to explore its fine ground-floor public spaces and back garden. A gracious and traditional tea is served in the garden out back (£13 cream tea, £23 afternoon tea, daily 15:00–17:00, sharing is OK, reserve a day in advance in summer, tel. 01225/823-333).

Picture the round Circus as a coliseum turned inside out. Its Doric, Ionic, and Corinthian capital decorations pay homage to its Greco-Roman origin, and are a reminder that Bath (with its seven hills) aspired to be "the Rome of England." The frieze above the first row of columns has hundreds of different panels, each representing the arts, sciences, and crafts. The first floor was high off the ground, to accommodate aristocrats on sedan chairs and women with sky-high hairdos. The top floors, with tiny round windows, were the servants' quarters. While the building fronts are uniform, the backs are higgledy-piggledy, infamous for their "hanging loos." Stand in the middle of the Circle among the grand plane trees, on the capped old well. Imagine the days when there was no indoor plumbing, and the servant girls gathered here to fetch water—this was gossip central. If you stand on the well, your clap echoes three times around the circle (try it).

▲**Georgian House at No. 1 Royal Crescent**—This museum (corner of Brock Street and Royal Crescent) offers your best look into a period house. Your visit is limited to four roped-off rooms, but if you take your time and talk to the docents stationed in each room, it's worth the £5 admission to get behind one of those classy Georgian facades. The docents are determined to fill you in on all the fascinating details of Georgian life...like how high-class women shaved their eyebrows and pasted on carefully trimmed strips of furry mouse skin in their place. On the bedroom dresser sits a bowl of black beauty marks and a head-scratcher from those pre-shampoo days. Fido spent his days on the kitchen treadmill powering the rotisserie (mid-Feb–Oct Tue–Sun 10:30–17:00, Nov Tue–Sun 10:30–16:00, last entry 30 min before closing, closed Mon and Dec–mid-Feb, £2 guidebook available, no photos, "no stiletto heels, please," tel.

01225/428-126, www.bath-preservation-trust.org.uk). Its WC is accessible from the street (under the entry steps, across from the exit and shop).

▲▲Fashion Museum—Housed within Bath's Assembly Rooms, this museum displays four centuries of fashion, organized by theme (bags, shoes, underwear, wedding dresses, and so on). Follow the included audioguide tour, and allow about an hour—unless you pause to lace up a corset and try on a hoop underdress (£7, £14 combo-ticket covers Roman Baths—saving you £4, family ticket available, daily March–Oct 10:30–18:00, Nov–Feb 11:00–17:00, last entry one hour before closing, on-site self-service café, tel. 01225/477-789, www.fashionmuseum.co.uk).

The **Assembly Rooms,** which you can see for free en route to the museum, are big, grand, empty rooms. Card games, concerts, tea, and dances were held here in the 18th century, before the advent of fancy hotels with grand public spaces made them obsolete. Note the extreme symmetry (pleasing to the aristocratic eye) and the high windows (assuring privacy). After the Allies bombed the historic and well-preserved German city of Lübeck, the Germans picked up a Baedeker guide and chose a similarly lovely city to bomb: Bath. The Assembly Rooms—gutted in this wartime tit-for-tat by WWII bombs—have since been restored to their original splendor. (Only the chandeliers are original.)

Below the Fashion Museum (to the left as you leave, 20 yards away) is one of the few surviving sets of **iron house hardware.** "Link boys" carried torches through the dark streets, lighting the way for big shots in their sedan chairs as they traveled from one affair to the next. The link boys extinguished their torches in the black conical "snuffers." The lamp above was once gas-lit. The crank on the left was used to hoist bulky things to various windows (see the hooks). Few of these sets survived the dark days of the WWII Blitz, when most were collected, melted down, and turned into weapons to power the British war machine. (Not long ago, these well-meaning Brits finally found out that all of their patriotic extra commitment to the national struggle had been for naught, since the metal ended up in junk heaps.)

▲▲Museum of Bath at Work—This is the official title for Mr. Bowler's Business, a 1900s engineer's shop, brass foundry, and fizzy-drink factory with a Dickensian office. It's just a pile of meaningless old gadgets—until the included audioguide resurrects Mr. Bowler's creative genius. Featuring other Bath creations through the years, including a 1914 car and the versatile plasticine (proto-Play-Doh), the museum serves as a vivid reminder that there was an industrial side to this spa town. Don't miss the fine "Story of Bath Stone" in the basement (£5, April–Oct daily 10:30–17:00, Nov–March weekends only, last entry at 16:00, 2 steep blocks up

Russell Street from Assembly Rooms, tel. 01225/318-348, www
.bath-at-work.org.uk).

Jane Austen Centre—This exhibition focuses on Jane Austen's
tumultuous, sometimes-troubled five years in Bath (circa 1800,
during which time her father died), and the influence the city had
on her writing. While the exhibit is a hit with "Jane-ites," there is
little of historic substance here. You'll walk through a Georgian
townhouse that she didn't live in (one of her real addresses in Bath
was a few houses up the road, at 25 Gay Street), and see mostly
enlarged reproductions of things associated with her writing.
The museum describes various places from two novels set in Bath
(*Persuasion* and *Northanger Abbey*). After a live intro (15 min, 2/
hr) explaining how this romantic but down-to-earth woman dealt
with the silly, shallow, and arrogant aristocrats' world, where "the
doing of nothings all day prevents one from doing anything," you
see a 15-minute video and wander through the rest of the exhibit
(£6.50; March–Oct daily 9:45–17:30, July–Aug Thu–Sat until 19:30;
Nov–Feb Sun–Fri 11:00–16:30, Sat 9:45–17:30; between Queen's
Square and the Circus at 40 Gay Street, tel. 01225/443-000, www
.janeausten.co.uk). Jane Austen–themed walking tours of the city
begin across from the Roman Baths and end at the Centre (£5, 90
min, Sat–Sun at 11:00, ask at the Centre for more information—no
reservation necessary).

Building of Bath Collection—This offers an intriguing look
behind the scenes at how the Georgian city was actually built,
though its opening days are limited, and it may close in 2010—call
ahead before visiting (£4, Sat–Mon 10:30–17:00, closed Nov–mid-
April, north of the city center on a street called "The Paragon," tel.
01225/333-895, www.bath-preservation-trust.org.uk).

Outer Bath

▲**American Museum**—I know, you need this in Bath like you
need a Big Mac. The UK's only museum dedicated to American
history, this may be the only place that combines Geronimo and
Groucho Marx. While it has thoughtful exhibits on the history
of Native Americans and the Civil War, the museum's heart
is with the decorative arts and cultural artifacts that reveal how
Americans lived from colonial times to the mid-19th century.
Each of the 18 completely furnished rooms (from a plain 1600s
Massachusetts dining/living room to a Rococo Revival explosion
in a New Orleans bedroom) is hosted by eager guides, waiting to
fill you in on the everyday items that make domestic Yankee history
surprisingly interesting. (In the Lee Room, look for the original
mouse holes, lovingly backlit, in the floor boards.) One room is a
quilter's nirvana. You can easily spend an afternoon here, enjoying
the surrounding gardens, arboretum, and trails (£7.50, April–Oct

Tue–Sun 12:00–17:00, last entry one hour before closing, closed
Mon and Nov–March, at Claverton Manor, tel. 01225/460-503,
www.americanmuseum.org). The museum is outside of town and a
headache to reach if you don't have a car (10–15-min walk from bus
#18 or the hop-on, hop-off bus stop).

Activities

Walking—The Bath Skyline Walk is a six-mile wander around
the hills surrounding Bath (leaflet at TI). Plenty of other scenic
paths are described in the TI's literature. For additional options,
get *Country Walks around Bath,* by Tim Mowls (£4.50 at TI or
bookstores).

Hiking the Canal to Bathampton—An idyllic towpath leads
from the Bath train station, along an old canal to the sleepy village
of Bathampton. Immediately behind the station, cross the footbridge and find where the canal hits the river. Turn left, noticing
the series of Industrial Age locks, and walk along the towpath,
giving thanks that you're not a horse pulling a barge. In less than
an hour you'll be in Bathampton, where a classic pub awaits with a
nice lunch and cellar-temp beer.

Boating—The Bath Boating Station, in an old Victorian boat-
house, rents rowboats, canoes, and punts (£7 per person/first
hour, then £2/additional hour, April–Sept daily 10:00–18:00,
closed off-season, Forester Road, 1 mile northeast of center, tel.
01225/312-900, www.bathboating.co.uk).

Swimming and Kids' Activities—The Bath Sports and Leisure
Centre has a fine pool for laps as well as lots of water slides. Kids
have entertaining options in the mini-gym "Active Zone" area,
which includes a rock wall (£3.50, daily 8:00–22:00 but kids' hours
are limited, call for open swim times, just across North Parade
Bridge, tel. 01225/462-565, www.aquaterra.org).

Shopping—There's great browsing between the abbey and the
Assembly Rooms (Fashion Museum). Shops close at 17:30, some
have longer hours on Thursday, and many are open on Sunday
(11:00–17:00). Explore the antiques shops lining Bartlett Street,
just below the Assembly Rooms.

Nightlife

For an up-to-date list of events, pick up the local newspaper,
the *Bath Chronicle,* on Fridays, when the "What's On" schedule
appears (www.thisisbath.com). Younger travelers may enjoy the
party-ready bar, club, and nightlife recommendations at www
.itchybath.co.uk.

▲▲▲**Bizarre Bath Street Theater**—For an immensely entertaining walking-tour comedy act "with absolutely no history or culture," follow Dom, J. J., or Noel Britten on their creative and entertaining Bizarre Bath walk. This 90-minute "tour," which plays off local passersby as well as tour members, is a belly laugh a minute (£8, or £6 for Rick Steves readers, includes some minor discounts in town, April–Oct nightly at 20:00, smaller groups Mon–Thu, heavy on magic, careful to insult all minorities and sensitivities, just racy enough but still good family fun, leaves from The Huntsman pub near the abbey, confirm at TI or call 01225/335-124, www.bizarrebath.co.uk).

▲**Theatre Royal Performance**—The 18th-century 800-seat Theatre Royal, newly restored and one of England's loveliest, offers a busy schedule of London West End–type plays, including many "pre-London" dress-rehearsal runs (£15–32, shows generally start at 19:30 or 20:00, box office open Mon–Sat 10:00–20:00, Sun 12:00–20:00, tel. 01225/448-844, www.theatreroyal.org.uk). Forty nosebleed spots on a bench (misnamed "standby seats") go on sale at noon on the day of each performance (£5, pay cash at box office or call and book with credit card, 2 tickets maximum). Or you can snatch up any unsold seat in the house for £10–15 a half-hour before "curtain up."

A handy cheap sightseers' tip: During the free Bath walking tour (see "Tours," near the beginning of this chapter), your guide stops here. Pop into the box office, ask what's playing tonight, and see if there are many seats left. If the play sounds good and if plenty of seats remain unsold, you're fairly safe to come back 30 minutes before curtain time to buy a ticket at that cheaper price. Oh...and if you smell jasmine, it's the ghost of Lady Grey, a mistress of Beau Nash.

Evening Walks—Take your choice: comedy (Bizarre Bath, described above), history, or ghost tour. The free city history walks (a daily standard described under "Tours," near the beginning of this chapter) are offered on some summer evenings (2 hours, May–Sept Tue and Fri at 19:00, leave from Pump Room). Ghost Walks are a popular way to pass the after-dark hours (£6, 90 min, unreliably April–Oct Mon–Sat at 20:00, Fri only in winter, leave from The Garrick's Head pub to the left and behind Theatre Royal as you face it, tel. 01225/350-512, www.ghostwalksofbath.co.uk).

Pubs—Most pubs in the center are very noisy, catering to a rowdy twentysomething crowd. But on the top end of town you can still find some classic old places with inviting ambience and live music. These are listed in order from closest to farthest away:

The Old Green Tree, the most convenient of all these pubs, is a rare traditional pub right in the town center (locally brewed real ales, no children, Green Street, tel. 01225/448-259; also recommended under this chapter's "Eating" section, for lunch).

The Star Inn is much appreciated by local beer-lovers for its fine ale and "no machines or music to distract from the chat." It's a "spit 'n' sawdust" place, and its long bench, nicknamed "death row," still comes with a complimentary pinch of snuff from tins on the ledge. Try the Bellringer Ale, made just up the road (Mon–Fri 12:00–15:00 & 17:30–24:00, Sat–Sun 12:00–24:00, no food served, 23 The Vineyards, top of The Paragon/A4 Roman Road, tel. 01225/425-072, generous and friendly welcome from Paul, who runs the place).

The Bell has a jazzy, pierced-and-tattooed, bohemian feel, but with a mellow older crowd. They serve pizza on the large concrete terrace out back in summer, and there's some kind of activity nearly every night, usually involving live music (Mon–Sat 11:00–23:00, Sun 12:00–10:30, sandwiches served all day, 103 Walcot Street, tel. 01225/460-426).

Summer Nights at the Baths—In July and August, you can stretch your sightseeing day at the Roman Baths, open nightly until 22:00 (last entry 21:00), when the gas lamps flame and the baths are far less crowded and more atmospheric. To take a dip yourself, consider popping in to the new Thermae Bath Spa (last entry at 19:30; see page 716).

Sleeping

Bath is a busy tourist town. Accommodations are expensive, and low-cost alternatives are rare. By far the best budget option is the YMCA—it's central, safe, simple, and very well-run, with plenty of twin rooms available (see listing on page 729). To get a good B&B, make a telephone reservation in advance. Competition is stiff, and it's worth asking any of these places for a weekday, three-nights-in-a-row, or off-season deal. Friday and Saturday nights are tightest (with many rates going up by about 25 percent)—especially if you're staying only one night, since B&Bs favor those lingering longer. If staying only Saturday night, you're very bad news to a B&B hostess. If you're driving to Bath, stowing your car near the center will generally cost £8 a day, though farther-out places may have parking. Almost every place provides Wi-Fi at no charge to its guests.

B&Bs near the Royal Crescent

These listings are all a 15-minute uphill walk or an easy £4–5 taxi ride from the train station. Or take any hop-on, hop-off bus tour from the station, get off at the stop nearest your B&B (likely Royal Avenue—confirm with driver), check in, then finish the tour later

---

Sleep Code

(£1 = about $1.60, country code: 44, area code: 01225)
S = Single, **D** = Double/Twin, **T** = Triple, **Q** = Quad, **b** = bathroom, **s** = shower only. Unless otherwise noted, credit cards are accepted.

To help you sort easily through these listings, I've divided the rooms into three categories based on the price for a standard double room with bath:

$$$ Higher Priced—Most rooms £90 or more.
$$ Moderately Priced—Most rooms between £60–90.
$ Lower Priced—Most rooms £60 or less.

---

in the day. The Marlborough Lane places have easier parking, but are less centrally located.

$$$ The Town House, overlooking the Assembly Rooms, is genteel, deluxe, and homey, with three fresh, mod rooms that have a hardwood stylishness. In true B&B style, you'll enjoy a gourmet breakfast at a big family table with the other guests (Db-£94–100 or £110–120 Fri–Sat, 2-night minimum, Wi-Fi, 7 Bennett Street, tel. & fax 01225/422-505, www.thetownhousebath.co.uk, stay @thetownhousebath.co.uk, Alan and Brenda Willey).

$$ Brocks Guest House has six rooms in a Georgian town-house built by John Wood in 1765. Located between the prestigious Royal Crescent and the courtly Circus, it was redone in a way that would make the great architect proud (Db-£79–87, Tb-£99, Qb-£115, prices go up about 10 percent Fri–Sat, Wi-Fi, little top-floor library, 32 Brock Street, tel. 01225/338-374, fax 01225/334-245, www.brocksguesthouse.co.uk, brocks@brocksguesthouse .co.uk, run by Sammy and her husband Richard).

$$ Parkside Guest House has five thoughtfully appointed Edwardian rooms—tidy, clean, and homey, with nary a doily in sight—and a spacious back garden (Db-£75, this price is for Rick Steves readers, 11 Marlborough Lane, tel. & fax 01225/429-444, www.parksidebandb.co.uk, post@parksidebandb.co.uk, Erica and Inge Lynall).

$$ Elgin Villa rents five comfy, nicely maintained rooms (Ss-£38, Sb-£55, Ds-£60, Db-£80, Tb-£96, Qb-£120, more expensive for Sat-only stay, discount for 3 nights, includes substantial un-fried breakfast, Wi-Fi, parking, 6 Marlborough Lane, tel. 01225/424-557, www.elginvilla.co.uk, stay@elginvilla.co.uk, Anna).

$$ Cornerways B&B, located on a noisy street, is simple and well-worn, with three rooms and old-fashioned homey touches (Db-£65–75, 15 percent discount with this book and 3-night stay, Wi-Fi, DVD library, free parking, 47 Crescent Gardens, tel. 01225/422-382, www.cornerwaysbath.co.uk, info@corner waysbath.co.uk, Sue Black).

B&Bs East of the River

These listings are a 10-minute walk from the city center. While generally a better value, they are less conveniently located.

$$$ Villa Magdala rents 18 stately, hotelesque rooms in a freestanding Victorian townhouse opposite a park. In a city that's so insistently Georgian, it's fun to stay in a mansion that's decorated so enthusiastically Victorian (Db-£95–105, £10 more Fri–Sat, fancier rooms and family options described on website, inviting lounge, Wi-Fi, parking, in quiet residential area on Henrietta Street, tel. 01225/466-329, fax 01225/483-207, www.villamagdala .co.uk, office@villamagdala.co.uk; Mike, Shirley, Roy, and Lois).

$$ The Ayrlington, next door to a lawn-bowling green, has 14 attractive rooms with Asian decor, and hints of a more genteel time. Though this well-maintained hotel fronts a busy street, it's quiet and tranquil. Rooms in the back have pleasant views of sports greens and Bath beyond. For the best value, request a standard double with a view of Bath (standard Db-£80, fancy Db-£100, big deluxe Db-£130, prices spike 30 percent Fri–Sat, see website for specifics, Wi-Fi, fine garden, easy parking, 24–25 Pulteney Road, tel. 01225/425-495, fax 01225/469-029, www.ayrlington.com, mail@ayrlington.com). If you stay here three weeknights, you get a free pass to the Thermae Bath Spa (worth £22/person).

$$ Holly Villa Guest House, with a cheery garden, six bright rooms, and a cozy TV lounge, is enthusiastically and thoughtfully run by chatty, friendly Jill and Keith McGarrigle (Ds-£60, small Db-£65, big Db-£70, Tb-£95, cash only, Wi-Fi, easy parking; 8-min walk from station and city center—walk over North Parade Bridge, take the first right, and then take the second left to 14 Pulteney Gardens; tel. 01225/310-331, www.hollyvilla.com, jill @hollyvilla.com).

$$ 14 Raby Place is another good value, mixing Georgian glamour with homey warmth and modern, artistic taste within its five rooms. Muriel Guy—a no-high-tech Luddite—keeps things simple and endearingly friendly. She's a fun-loving live wire who serves organic food for breakfast (S-£35, Db-£70, Tb-£80, cash only; 14 Raby Place—go over bridge on North Parade Road, left on Pulteney Road, cross to church, Raby Place is first row of houses on hill; tel. 01225/465-120).

In the City Center

$$$ Three Abbey Green Guest House, with seven rooms, is newly renovated, bright, fresh, and located in a quiet, traffic-free

Bath Accommodations

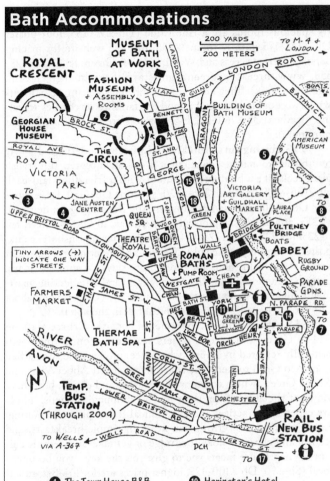

1. The Town House B&B
2. Brocks Guest House
3. To Parkside Guest House & Elgin Villa
4. Cornerways B&B
5. Villa Magdala
6. To The Ayrlington
7. To Holly Villa Guest House
8. To 14 Raby Place
9. Three Abbey Green Guest House
10. Harington's Hotel
11. Abbey House Apartments
12. Pratt's Hotel
13. The Henry Guest House
14. Parade Park Hotel
15. Travelodge Bath Central
16. YMCA
17. White Hart Hostel
18. St. Christopher's Inn
19. Library (Internet Access)

courtyard only 50 yards from the abbey and the Roman Baths. Its spacious rooms are a fine value (Db-£95–135, four-poster Db-£145–175, family rooms-£135–165, see website for pricing details, Internet access and Wi-Fi, 3 Abbey Green, tel. 01225/428-558, www.threeabbeygreen.com, stay@threeabbeygreen.com, Sue and Derek). They also rent several self-catering apartments with two double beds each, good for families or couples traveling together (Qb-£160–195, higher prices are for Fri–Sat, 2-night minimum).

$$$ **Harington's Hotel** rents 13 fresh, modern, and newly refurbished rooms on a quiet street in the town center. This stylish place feels like a boutique hotel, but with a friendlier, laid-back vibe (Sb-£108, standard Db-£120, superior Db-£130, large superior Db-£140, prices vary substantially depending on demand, Wi-Fi, attached restaurant-bar open all day, 10 Queen Street, tel. 01225/461-728, fax 01225/444-804, www.haringtonshotel.co.uk, post@haringtonshotel.co.uk). Melissa and Peter offer a 5 percent discount with this book for three-night stays except on Fridays, Saturdays, and holidays. They also rent several self-catering apartments down the street that can sleep up to five (Db-£115 plus about £10/person, includes continental breakfast in the hotel).

$$$ **Abbey House Apartments** consist of three flats on Abbey Green and several others scattered around town—all tastefully restored by Laura (who, once upon a time, was a San Francisco Goth rocker). The apartments, called Abbey View and Abbey Green (which comes with a washer and dryer), both have views of the abbey from their nicely equipped kitchens. These are especially practical and economical if you plan on cooking. Laura provides everything you need for simple breakfasts, and it's fun and cheap to stock the fridge or get take-away ethnic cuisine. When Laura meets you to give you the keys, you become a local (Sb-£90, Db-£100–125, higher prices are for Fri–Sat, rooms can sleep four with Murphy and sofa beds, apartments clearly described on website, Wi-Fi, Abbey Green, tel. 01225/464-238, www.laurastownhouseapartments.co.uk, laura@laurastownhouse apartments.co.uk).

$$$ **Pratt's Hotel** is as proper and olde English as you'll find in Bath. Its creaks and frays are aristocratic. Even its public places make you want to sip a brandy, and its 46 rooms are bright and spacious. Since it's in the city center, occasionally it can get noisy—request a quiet room, away from the street (Sb-£90, Db-£140, advance reservations get highest rate, drop-ins after 16:00 often snare Db for £80, dogs-£7.50 but children under 14 free, attached restaurant-bar, elevator, 4 blocks from station on South Parade, tel. 01225/460-441, fax 01225/448-807, www.forest dale.com, pratts@forestdale.com).

$$ Parade Park Hotel rents 35 modern, basic rooms in a very central location (straight pricing: S-£40, D-£55, small Db-£70, large Db-£90, Tb-£100, Qb-£120, no Wi-Fi, lots of stairs, lively bar downstairs and noisy seagulls, 10 North Parade, tel. 01225/463-384, fax 01225/442-322, www.paradepark.co.uk, info@paradepark.co.uk).

$$ Royal York Travelodge, which offers 66 American-style, characterless-yet-comfortable rooms, worries B&Bs with its reasonable prices. As it's located in a late-night party zone, request a room on the third floor—especially on weekends (Db/Tb/Qb-£75 on weeknights, £95 Fri–Sat, as low as £26 on weeknights if you book online in advance, up to 2 kids sleep free, breakfast extra, 1 York Building at George Street, new location being built near the station, tel. 01225/442-061, central reservation tel. 08700-850-950, www.travelodge.co.uk). This is especially economical for families of four (who enjoy the Db price).

$$ Henry Guest House is a simple, vertical place, renting eight clean rooms. It's friendly, well-run, and just two blocks in front of the train station (S-£40, Db-£80 or £90 Fri–Sat, extra bed-£10, family deals, Wi-Fi, 6 Henry Street, tel. 01225/424-052, www.thehenry.com, stay@thehenry.com). Steve and Liz also rent two self-catering apartments nearby that sleep four comfortably, and up to eight with cots and a sleeper couch (Db-£90, email for group prices).

Bargain Accommodations

Bath's Best Budget Beds: **$** The **YMCA,** centrally located on a leafy square, has 200 beds in industrial-strength rooms—all with sinks and prison-style furnishings. The place is a godsend for budget travelers—safe, secure, quiet, and efficiently run. With lots of twin rooms and no double beds, this is the only easily accessible budget option in downtown Bath (S-£27, twin D-£42, T-£54, Q-£61, dorm beds-£15, £2/person more Fri–Sat, WCs and showers down the hall, includes continental breakfast, cheap lunches, lockers, Internet access, dorms closed 10:00–14:00, down a tiny alley off Broad Street on Broad Street Place, tel. 01225/325-900, fax 01225/462-065, www.bathymca.co.uk, stay@bathymca.co.uk, run by Maggie King and Rob Lane).

Sloppy Backpacker Dorms: **$** **White Hart Hostel** is a simple nine-room place offering adults and families good, cheap beds in two- to six-bed dorms (£15/bed, D-£40, Db-£70, family rooms, kitchen, fine garden out back, 5-min walk behind train station at Widcombe—where Widcombe Hill hits Claverton Street, tel. 01225/313-985, www.whitehartbath.co.uk, run by Jo). The White Hart also has a pub with a reputation for decent food. **$** **St. Christopher's Inn,** in a prime central location, is part of a

BATH

chain of low-priced, high-energy hubs for backpackers looking for beds and brews. Their beds are so cheap because they know you'll spend money on their beer (46 beds in 4- to 12-bed rooms-£20, D-£50, higher prices on weekends or if you don't book online, Internet access, laundry, lounge with video, lively "Belushi's" pub and bar downstairs, 9 Green Street, tel. 01225/481-444, www .st-christophers.co.uk).

Eating

Bath is bursting with eateries. There's something for every appetite and budget—just stroll around the center of town. A picnic dinner of deli food or take-out fish-and-chips in the Royal Crescent Park or down by the river is ideal for aristocratic hoboes. The restaurants I recommend are small and popular—reserve a table on Friday and Saturday evenings. Most pricey little bistros offer big savings with their two- and three-course lunches and "pre-theater" specials. In general, you can get two courses for £10 at lunch or £12 in the early evening (compared to £15 for a main course after 18:30 or 19:00). Restaurants advertise their early-bird specials, and as long as you order within the time window, you're in for a cheap meal.

Romantic French and English

Tilley's Bistro, popular with locals, serves healthy French, English, and vegetarian meals with candlelit ambience. New owners Dawn and Dave make you feel as if you are guests at a special dinner party in their elegant living room. Their fun menu lets you build your own meal, and there's an interesting array of £7 starters. If you cap things off with the cheese plate and a glass of the house port, you'll realize that's a passion of Dave's (Mon–Sat 12:00–14:30 & 18:00–22:30, closed Sun, reservations smart, 3 North Parade Passage, tel. 01225/484-200).

The Garrick's Head is an elegantly simple gastro-pub right around the corner from the Theatre Royal, with a pricey restaurant on one side and a bar serving affordable snacks on the other. You're welcome to eat from the bar menu, even if you're in the fancy dining room or outside enjoying some great people-watching (Mon–Sat 11:00–21:00, Sun 12:00–21:00, 8 St. John's Place, tel. 01225/318-368).

The Circus Café and Restaurant is a relaxing little eatery serving rustic European cuisine. They have a romantic interior, with a minimalist modern atmosphere, and four tables on the peaceful street (£7 lunches, £12 dinner plates, open Mon–Sat from 12:00 for lunch and from 18:00 for dinner, closed Sun, 34 Brock Street, tel. 01225/466-020).

Bath Restaurants

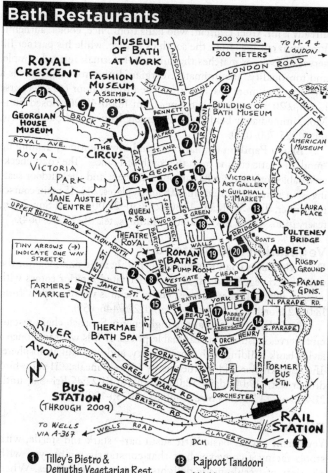

1. Tilley's Bistro & Demuths Vegetarian Rest.
2. The Garrick's Head
3. The Circus Café & Rest.
4. Casanis French Bistro-Rest.
5. Bistro Papillon
6. Loch Fyne Restaurant
7. Yen Sushi
8. Thai Balcony Restaurant
9. Ocean Pearl Oriental Buffet & Waitrose Supermarket
10. Wagamama
11. Martini Restaurant
12. Ask Restaurant
13. Rajpoot Tandoori
14. Yak Yeti Yak
15. Boston Tea Party & Seafoods Fish & Chips
16. Chandos Deli
17. Crystal Palace Pub
18. The Old Green Tree
19. The Cornish Bakehouse
20. Guildhall Market
21. Royal Crescent Hotel (Afternoon Tea)
22. The Star Inn
23. The Bell
24. Marks & Spencer & Café Revive

BATH

Casanis French Bistro-Restaurant just opened and is already a hit. Chef Laurent, who hails from Nice, cooks "authentic Provençal cuisine" from the south of France, while his partner Jill serves. The decor matches the cuisine—informal, relaxed, simple, and top-quality. The intimate Georgian dining room upstairs is a bit nicer and more spacious than the ground floor (£12 2-course lunch, £20 3-course early dinner from 18:00–19:00, closed Sun–Mon, immediately behind the Assembly Rooms at 4 Saville Row, tel. 01225/780-055).

Bistro Papillon is small, fun, and unpretentious, dishing up "modern-rustic cuisine from the south of France." The cozy, checkered-tablecloth interior has an open kitchen, and the outdoor seating is on a fine pedestrian lane (£8 lunch plates, £13–15 main courses for dinner, Tue–Sat 12:00–14:30 & 18:30–22:00, closed Sun–Mon, reservations smart, 2 Margaret's Buildings, tel. 01225/310-064).

Vegetarian and Seafood

Demuths Vegetarian Restaurant is highly rated and ideal for the well-heeled vegetarian. Its stark, understated interior comes with a vegan vibe (£15 main dishes, entire menu is vegan, nightly from 18:00, 2 North Parade Passage, tel. 01225/446-059).

Loch Fyne Restaurant, a high-energy Scottish chain restaurant, serves fresh fish at reasonable prices. It fills what was once a lavish bank building with a bright, airy, and youthful atmosphere. The open kitchen adds to the energy (£10–18 meals, £11 early-bird dinner until 19:00, daily 12:00–22:00, until 22:45 Fri–Sat, until 21:45 Sun, 24 Milsom Street, tel. 01225/750-120).

Ethnic

Yen Sushi is your basic little sushi bar—stark and sterile, with stools facing a conveyor belt that constantly tempts you with a variety of freshly made delights on color-coded plates. When you're done, they tally your plates and give you the bill (£1.50–3.50 plates, you can fill up for £12 or so, closed Mon, 11 Bartlett Street, tel. 01225/333-313).

Thai Balcony Restaurant's open, spacious interior is so plush, it'll have you wondering, "Where's the Thai wedding?" While locals debate which of Bath's handful of Thai restaurants serves the best food or offers the lowest prices, there's no doubt that Thai Balcony's fun and elegant atmosphere makes for a memorable and enjoyable dinner (£8 2-course special, £8–9 plates, daily 12:00–14:00 & 18:00–22:00, reservations smart on weekends, Saw Close, tel. 01225/444-450).

Ocean Pearl Oriental Buffet is famous for being the restaurant Asian tourists eat at repeatedly. It offers a practical 40-dish all-you-can-eat buffet in the modern Podium Shopping Centre and spacious seating in a high, bright dining hall overlooking the river. You'll pay £6.50 for lunch, £13 for dinner, or you can fill up a take-away box for just £4 (daily 12:00–14:30 & 18:00–22:30, in the Podium Shopping Centre on Northgate Street, tel. 01225/331-238).

Wagamama, a stylish, youthful, and modern chain of noodle shops, continues its quest for world domination. There's one in almost every mid-sized city in the UK, and after you've sampled their udon noodles, fried rice, or curry dishes, you'll know why. Diners enjoy huge portions in a sprawling, loud, and modern hall. Bowls are huge enough for light eaters on a tight budget to share (£7–9 meals, Mon–Sat 12:00–23:00, Sun 12:00–22:00, good vegetarian options, 1 York Buildings, George Street, tel. 01225/337-314).

Martini Restaurant, a hopping, purely Italian place, has class and jovial waiters. It offers a very good eating value (£12–16 entrées, £7–9 pizzas, daily 12:00–14:30 & 18:00–22:30, plenty of veggie options, daily fish specials, extensive wine list, reservations smart on weekends, 9 George Street, tel. 01225/460-818; Mauro, Nunzio, Franco, and chef Luigi).

Ask Restaurant is part of a chain of Italian eateries, serving standard-quality pizza and pasta in a big 200-seat place with a loud and happy local crowd (£7 pizza and pasta, good salads, daily 12:00–23:00, George Street but entrance on Broad Street, tel. 01225/789-997).

Rajpoot Tandoori serves—by all assessments—the best Indian food in Bath. You'll hike down deep into a cellar, where the plush Indian atmosphere and award-winning cooking make paying the extra pounds palatable. The seating is tight and the ceilings low, but it's air-conditioned (£8 3-course lunch special, £10 plates, £20 dinners, daily 12:00–14:30 & 18:00–23:00, 4 Argyle Street, tel. 01225/466-833, Ali).

Yak Yeti Yak is a fun Nepalese restaurant, with both Western and sit-on-the-floor seating. Sera and his wife, Sarah, along with their cheerful, hardworking Nepali team, cook up great traditional food (and plenty of vegetarian plates) at prices a sherpa could handle (£6–7 lunches, £4 veggie plates, £7 meat plates, £15 fixed-price dinner for carnivores, £12 for vegetarians, daily 12:00–14:00 & 17:00–22:30, 5 Pierrepont Street, tel. 01225/442-299).

Simple Options

Light Meals: **Boston Tea Party** feels like a Starbucks—if there were only one. It's fresh and healthy, serving extensive breakfasts, light lunches, and salads. The outdoor seating overlooks a busy square (daily 7:30–19:00, 19 Kingsmead Square, tel. 01225/313-901). **Chandos Deli** has good coffee and tasty £6–7 sandwiches made on artisan breads. This upscale but casual eight-table place

BATH

serves breakfast and lunch to dedicated foodies who don't want to pay too much (Mon–Sat 9:00–17:00, closed Sun, 12 George Street, tel. 01225/314-418).

Pubs: **Crystal Palace Pub** is an inviting place just a block away from the abbey, facing the delightful little Abbey Green. With a focus on food rather than drink, they serve "pub grub with a Continental flair" in three different spaces, including a picnic-table back patio (£8–10 meals, daily 12:00–21:00, last order by 20:00, no kids after 16:30, Abbey Green, tel. 01225/482-666). **The Old Green Tree,** in the old town center, serves satisfying lunches to locals in a characteristic pub setting. As Bath is not a good pub-grub town, this is likely the best you'll do in the center (real ales on tap, lunch 12:00–15:00 only, no children, can be crowded on weekend nights, 12 Green Street, tel. 01225/448-259).

Fast Food: **Seafoods Fish & Chips** is respected by lovers of greasy fried fish in Bath. There's diner-style and outdoor seating, or you can get your food to go (£4–5 meals, Mon–Sat 11:30–21:00, takeout until 22:00, closed Sun, 38 Kingsmead Square, tel. 01225/465-190). **The Cornish Bakehouse,** near the Guildhall Market, has freshly baked £2 take-away pasties (open until 17:30, off High Street at 11A The Corridor, tel. 01225/426-635). Munch your picnic while enjoying buskers from a bench on the Abbey Square.

Produce Market and Café: **Guildhall Market,** across from Pulteney Bridge, has produce stalls with food for picnickers. At its inexpensive **Market Café,** you can slurp a curry or sip a tea while surrounded by stacks of used books, bananas on the push list, and honest-to-goodness old-time locals (£4 meals including fried breakfasts all day, Mon–Sat 8:00–17:00, closed Sun, a block north of the abbey, on High Street).

Supermarkets: **Waitrose,** at the Podium Shopping Centre, is great for picnics, with a good salad bar (Mon–Fri 8:30–20:00, Sat 8:30–19:00, Sun 11:00–17:00, just west of Pulteney Bridge and across from post office on High Street). **Marks & Spencer,** near the train station, has a grocery at the back of its department store, and the pleasant, inexpensive **Café Revive** on the top floor (Mon–Fri 8:30–19:00, Sat 8:30–18:00, Sun 11:00–17:00, Stall Street).

Connections

Bath's train station is called Bath Spa (train info: tel. 0845-748-4950). The National Express bus office is just west of the train station, in the area called South Gate (Mon–Sat 8:00–17:30, closed Sun, bus info tel. 0870-580-8080, www.nationalexpress.com).

From London to Bath: To get from London to Bath and see Stonehenge to boot, consider an all-day organized **bus tour** from

London (and skip out of the return trip; see "By Bus" on page 708).

From Bath to London: You can catch a **train** to London's Paddington Station (2/hr, 1.5 hrs, £46 one-way after 9:30, www.firstgreatwestern.co.uk), or save money—but not time—by taking the National Express **bus** to Victoria Station (direct buses nearly hourly, a little over 3 hours, one-way-£18, round-trip-£27.50).

From Heathrow to Bath: See page 705.

From Bath to London's Airports: You can reach **Heathrow** directly and easily by National Express bus (10/day, 2–3 hrs, £18 one-way, tel. 0871-781-8181) or by a train-and-bus combination (take twice-hourly train to Reading, catch twice-hourly airport shuttle bus from there, allow 2.5 hours total, £53, cheaper for BritRail passholders). Or take the Celtic Horizons minibus to Heathrow; see www.celtichorizons.com.

You can get to **Gatwick** by train (about hourly, 2.5 hrs, £40 one-way, transfer in Reading) or by bus (about hourly, 4.5 hrs, £25 one-way, transfer at Heathrow Airport).

Between Bristol Airport and Bath: Located about 20 miles west of Bath, this airport is closer than Heathrow, but they haven't worked out good connections to Bath yet. From Bristol Airport, your most convenient options are to take a taxi (£35) or take a tour with Alan Price (www.celtichorizons.com). Otherwise, you can hop aboard the Bristol International Flyer (city bus #330 or #331), which takes you to the Temple Meads train station (£8, 2–4/hr, 30 min, buy bus ticket at airport info counter or from driver, tell driver you want the Temple Meads train station). At the Temple Meads station, check the departure boards for trains going to the Bath Spa station (4/hr, 15 min, £6). To get from Bath to Bristol Airport, just reverse these directions: Take the train to Temple Meads, then catch the International Flyer bus.

From Bath by Train to: Salisbury (2/hr, 1 hr), **Portsmouth** (hourly, 2.25 hrs), **Exeter** (2–3/hr, 1.75–3 hrs, 1–2 transfers), **Penzance** (1–3/hr, 4.5–6 hrs, 1–3 transfers), **Moreton-in-Marsh** (hourly, 2 hrs, 1–3 transfers), **York** (hourly, 4.5–5 hrs, 1–2 transfers in Bristol or London), **Oxford** (hourly, 1.5 hrs, transfer in Didcot).

BATH

Rome

DCH

TERMINI (MAIN STN.)

BATHS OF DIOCLETIAN

V. GIOLITTI

SAN GIOVANNI IN LATERANO

HOLY STAIRS

NAT'L MUSEUM

VIA VIT. EM.

MERULANA

SAN CLEM.

S. STEFANO

VIANO

PIAZZA

V. FIRENZE

PIAZZA REP.

S. MARIA MAGGIORE

VIA LANZA

ST. PETER-IN-CHAINS

VIA LABICANA

VIA S.GIOVANNI LAT.

OLD CITY WALLS

SETTEMBRE

TRITONE

CAPPUCCIN CRYPT

U.S. EMB.

VIA BARB.

V. CONT.

VIA MILANO

VIA CAVOUR

VIA SERPENTI

CAVOUR

COLOSSEUM

BATHS OF CARACALLA

GREG

BORGHESE GALLERY

VILLA BORGHESE GARDENS

VIA VENETO

V. SISTINE

SPAGNA

SPAN. STEPS

VIA DEL BABUINO

TREVI

IMP. FORUM

VIA DEI FORI IMP.

ROMAN FORUM

CAP. HILL.

PALATINE HILL RUINS

CIRCUS MAX.

FLAMINIO

PIAZZA DEL POPOLO

CORSO

PIAZZA COLONNA

PIAZZA DELLA ROT.

PANTHEON

PIAZZA VEN.

VICTOR EM. MON.

LARGO ARG.

GHETTO

TO TESTACCIO & E.U.R.

P. PAL.

P. GARI.

TIBER

T I B E R

P. CAVOUR

PIAZZA RISORGIMENTO

VIA COLA DI RIENZO

PIAZZA CAVOUR

P. UMB.

VIA CRESCENZIO

CASTEL SANT'ANGELO

P. ANG.

P. VIT.

CORSO VIT. EM.

VIA CORONARI

P. AOSTA

PIAZZA NAVONA

CAMPO DE' FIORI

P. FARNESE

LUNGOTEVERE

S. MARIA

VIA LUNG.

PIAZZA BELLI

TRASTEVERE

PORTA PORTESE MKT.

CESARE GUILIO

LEPANTO

T I B E R

OTTAVIANO

VIA OTTAVIANO

VIA ANDREA DORIA

VIA LEONE

VIA CANDIA

VIALE VATICANO

VAT. MUSEUM

ST. PETERS

VATICAN CITY

TUNNEL

VIA CAVALLEGGERI

VIA AURELIA

VIA CONC.

GIANICOLO

LUNGO

VIA MURA

AURELIE

CIPRO

VIA PIS

400 YARDS
400 METERS

N

Ⓜ METRO STATION

ROME

through ancient Rome's Forum and Colosseum. Savor Europe's most sumptuous building, the Borghese Gallery, and take an early evening "Dolce Vita Stroll" down the Via del Corso with Rome's beautiful people. Enjoy an after-dark walk from Campo de' Fiori to the Spanish Steps, lacing together Rome's Baroque and bubbly nightspots. Dine well at least once.

Planning Your Time

Rome is wonderful, but it's huge (pop. 2.6 million) and exhausting. On a first-time visit, many travelers find that Rome is best done quickly—Italy is more charming elsewhere. But whether you're here for a day or a week, you won't be able to see all of Rome's attractions, so don't try—you'll keep coming back to Rome. After several dozen visits, I still have a healthy list of excuses to return.

Rome in a Day: Some people actually try to "do" Rome in a day. Crazy as that sounds, if all you have is a day, it's one of the most exciting days Europe has to offer. See Vatican City (two hours in the Vatican Museum and Sistine Chapel—if the line's not too long—then one hour in St. Peter's), taxi over the river to the Pantheon, then hike over Capitol Hill, through the Forum, and to the Colosseum. Have dinner on Campo de' Fiori and dessert on Piazza Navona. (With typical crowds, you'll likely have to skip the Vatican Museum. But the rest is entirely doable.) Note: If you only want a day in Rome, consider side-tripping in from Orvieto or Florence, and maybe before the night train to Venice.

Rome in Two to Three Days: On the first day, do the "Caesar Shuffle" from the Colosseum to the Forum, then over Capitol Hill to the Pantheon. After a siesta, join the locals strolling from Piazza del Popolo to the Spanish Steps (see the "Dolce Vita Stroll," later in this chapter). On the second day, see Vatican City (St. Peter's, climb the dome, tour the Vatican Museum). Have dinner on the atmospheric Campo de' Fiori, then walk to the Trevi Fountain and Spanish Steps (see my "Night Walk Across Rome," also later in this chapter). With a third day, add the Borghese Gallery (reservations required) and the National Museum of Rome.

Orientation

Sprawling Rome actually feels manageable once you get to know it. The old core, with most of the tourist sights, sits in a diamond formed by the Termini train station (in the east), the Vatican (west), Villa Borghese Gardens (north), and the Colosseum (south). The Tiber River runs through the diamond from north to south. In the center of the diamond sits Piazza Venezia, a busy square and traffic hub. It takes about an hour to walk from the Termini train station to the Vatican.

Rome's Neighborhoods

VATICAN MUSEUM
VATICAN CITY
ST. PETER'S

PIAZZA DEL POPOLO

NORTH ROME

VILLA BORGHESE

BORGHESE GALLERY

"SHOPPING TRIANGLE"

SPANISH STEPS

TERMINI
NAT'L. MUSEUM
TRAIN STATION

PANTHEON NEIGHBORHOOD (HEART OF ROME)

PIAZZA VENEZIA

CAPITOL HILL
FORUM

PILGRIM'S ROME

TIBER RIVER

ANCIENT ROME

SAN GIOVANNI IN LATERANO

STA. MARIA
TRASTEVERE

COLOSSEUM

TESTACCIO

SOUTH OF TESTACCIO

SOUTH ROME

APPIAN WAY

E.U.R.

NOT TO SCALE

DCH

Think of Rome as a series of neighborhoods, huddling around major landmarks. The sights listed in this chapter are arranged according to neighborhood.

Ancient Rome: In ancient times, this was home for the grandest buildings of a city of a million people. Today, the best of the classical sights stand in a line from the Colosseum to the Forum to the Pantheon.

Pantheon Neighborhood (The Heart of Rome): The Pantheon anchors the neighborhood I like to call the "Heart of Rome." It stretches eastward from the Tiber River through Campo de' Fiori and Piazza Navona, past the Pantheon to the Trevi Fountain.

North Rome: With the Spanish Steps, Villa Borghese Gardens, and trendy shopping streets (Via Veneto and the "shopping triangle"), this is a more modern, classy area.

Vatican City: Located west of the Tiber, it's a compact world of its own, with two great, huge sights: St. Peter's Basilica and the Vatican Museum.

Trastevere: This seedy, colorful, wrong-side-of-the-river neighborhood is village Rome. It's the city at its crustiest—and perhaps most "Roman."

Termini: Though light on sightseeing highlights, the train station neighborhood has many recommended hotels and public-transportation connections.

Pilgrim's Rome: Several prominent churches dot the area south of the Termini train station.

Southeast Rome: South of the city center, you'll find the Appian Way, home of the catacombs.

Within each of these neighborhoods, you'll find elements from the many layers of Rome's 2,000-year history: the marble ruins of ancient times; tangled streets of the medieval world; early Christian churches; grand Renaissance buildings and statues; Baroque fountains and church facades; 19th-century apartments; and 20th-century boulevards choked with traffic.

Since no one is allowed to build taller than St. Peter's dome, and virtually no buildings have been constructed in the city center since Mussolini got distracted in 1938, Rome has no modern skyline. The Tiber River is basically ignored—after the last floods (1870), the banks were built up very high, and Rome turned its back on its naughty river.

Tourist Information

While Rome has several tourist information offices, the dozen or so TI kiosks scattered around the town at major tourist centers are handy and just as helpful. If all you need is a map, forget the TI and get one at your hotel or at a newsstand kiosk.

Rome's single best source of up-to-date tourist information is its call center, answered by English-speakers. Dial 06-0608 (answered daily 9:00–22:30, press 2 for English). You can call to book museum tickets, sightseeing passes (explained on page 746), and theater tickets using your credit card. There's usually only a minimal €1.50 fee (no fee for the Roma Pass), and you can generally order from several months in advance up until the day before your visit.

At Fiumicino Airport, the TIs are in Terminal C (daily 8:00–19:00) and Terminal B (daily 8:15–19:00, has brochures on walking itineraries but not much else).

Inside the Termini train station, there's a poorly marked TI (walk along track 24, go through the doors at the baggage-check sign, TI is just past the post office; if you get off the train far enough down the tracks you'll see the *sottopassaggio* shortcut—go down the stairs, walk toward track 24, then take the elevator up).

Smaller TIs (daily 9:00–18:00) include kiosks near the Forum (on Piazza del Tempio della Pace), in Trastevere (on Piazza Sonnino), on Via Nazionale (at Palazzo delle Esposizioni), at Castel Sant'Angelo (at Piazza Pia), at Santa Maria Maggiore Church, at Piazza Navona (at Piazza delle Cinque Lune), and near the Trevi Fountain (at Via del Corso and Via Minghetti).

At any TI, ask for a city map and a listing of sights and hours (in the free *Museums of Rome* booklet). The TIs don't offer room-booking services. If a commercial info-center offers to book you a room, just say no—you'll save money by booking direct.

The *Evento* booklet, given out free at TIs, has English-language pages that list the month's cultural events on art, museums, and music. *Roma c'è* is a cheap little weekly entertainment guide with a useful English section (in the back) on music, art, events, and nightclubs (€1.50, new edition every Wed, sold at newsstands, www.romace.it).

Websites on Rome: Check out www.whatsoninrome.com (events and news), www.romaturismo.com (music, exhibitions, and events), www.wantedinrome.com (job openings and real estate, but also festivals and exhibitions), and www.vatican.va (the pope's website).

Arrival in Rome

By Train at Termini Station: Rome's main train station is a buffet of tourist services: TI (daily 8:00–21:00, poorly marked, 100 yards down track 24 near baggage deposit), train info office (daily 7:00–21:00), ATMs, late-hours banks, 24-hour thievery, cafés (VyTA, on the track 1 side of the station, offers healthful sandwiches) and two good self-service cafeterias (Ciao is upstairs, with fine views and seating; Food Village Chef Express is on the track level, daily 11:00–22:30). Borri Books, near the front of the station, sells books in English, including popular fiction, Italian history and culture, and kids' books, plus maps upstairs (daily 7:00–23:00). In the modern mall downstairs, a grocery on the track 1 side of the station also sells useful electronics (daily 7:00–22:00). There are two pharmacies (both open daily 7:30–22:00, at track 1 and downstairs below track 24). Baggage deposit is along track 24 downstairs (€4 for up to 5 hours, €0.60/hr thereafter, daily 6:00–24:00, follow signs, pass through double doors, and take elevator). The post office is on the ground floor, above the baggage deposit (Mon–Fri 8:00–19:00, Sat 8:00–13:15, closed Sun). The "Leonardo Express" train to Fiumicino Airport usually runs from track 24 (see "Rome's Airports," near the end of this chapter).

Termini is also a local transportation hub. The city's two Metro lines (A and B) intersect at the Termini Metro station (downstairs). Buses (including Rome's hop-on, hop-off bus tours—see "Tours" later in this chapter) leave from the square directly in front of the main station hall. Taxis queue in front; avoid con men hawking "express taxi" services in unmarked cars (only use ones marked with the word *taxi* and a phone number). To avoid the long taxi line, simply hike out past the buses to the main street and

Greater Rome

TO VITERBO

TO FLORENCE

VIA FLAMINIA

VIA CASSIA S·2

VIA SALARIA

RING FREEWAY →
GRANDE RACCORDO ANULARE

OLYMPIC STADIUM→

CATACOMBS OF PRISCILLA

A·1

TO TIVOLI S·5

CENTRAL ROME

TIBURTINA TRAIN & BUS STN.

A·24

TO CIVITAVECCHIA

VIA AURELIA S·1

VATICAN

TERMINI TRAIN STN.

TO L'AQUILA

HYDRO-MANIA WATER PARK

●COLOSSEUM

PORTA PORTESE FLEA MKT.

VIA APPIAN WAY

CATACOMBS

A·1

TO FIUMICINO (DA VINCI) AIRPORT

A·12

TESTACCIO & PYRAMID

S. PAUL'S✚

BATHS OF CARA-CALLA

TO NAPLES

TIBER RIVER

VIA OSTIENSE

S-8

●E.U.R.

RING FREEWAY

CIAMPINO AIRPORT

●OSTIA ANTICA

TO BEACH

5 MILES

5 KM

= SEE DETAIL MAPS

DCH

hail one. The station has some sleazy sharks with official-looking business cards; avoid anybody selling anything unless they're in a legitimate shop at the station.

From the Termini train station, most of my accommodation listings are easily accessible by foot (for hotels near the Termini train station) or by Metro (for hotels in the Colosseum and Vatican neighborhoods).

By Train or Bus at Tiburtina Station: Rome's second-largest train station is located in the city's northeast corner. In general, slower trains (from Milan, Bolzano, Bologna, Udine, and Reggio di Calabria) and some night trains (from Munich, Milan, Venice, Innsbruck, and Udine) use Tiburtina, as does the night bus to Fiumicino airport. However, Tiburtina has recently been redeveloped for high-speed rail, which may be running in time for your trip. At the time of this writing, direct night trains from Paris and Vienna use the Termini station.

Tiburtina is better known as a hub for bus service to/from destinations all across Italy (including Assisi and Siena). Buses depart from the piazza in front of the station. Ticket offices are located in the piazza and around the corner on Circonvallazione Nomentana.

Within the train station are a currency-exchange office and a 24-hour grocery. Tiburtina station is on Metro line B, with easy connections to the Termini train station (a straight shot, four stops away) and the entire Metro system. Or take bus #492 from Tiburtina to various city-center stops (such as Piazza Barberini, Piazza Venezia, and Piazza Cavour) and the Vatican neighborhood.

By Plane: For information on Rome's airports and connections into the city, see "Rome's Airports" at the end of this chapter.

Helpful Hints

Sightseeing Tips: Avid sightseers can save money by buying the Roma Pass (see page 746). To avoid lines at the Colosseum and Forum, buy a Roma Pass (online, by phone, or at a less-crowded sight), or buy a combo-ticket online and print it out (see "Avoiding Lines" on page 775). If you want to see the Borghese Gallery, remember to reserve ahead (explained in listing under "Sights," later in this chapter). To bypass the long Vatican Museum line, reserve your ticket in advance (see page 804).

Audiotours: Users of iPods and other MP3 players can download free audiotours of the Colosseum, Roman Forum, Pantheon, Sistine Chapel, and St. Peter's Basilica from my website, www.ricksteves.com.

Internet Access: If your hotel doesn't offer free or cheap Internet access, your hotelier can point you to the nearest Internet café. Remember to bring your passport, which you may be asked to show before getting online.

Bookstores: These stores (all open daily) sell travel guidebooks—**Borri Books** (at the Termini train station), two handy locations of **Feltrinelli International** (one at Largo Argentina and the other just off Piazza della Repubblica at Via Vittorio Emanuele Orlando 84, tel. 06-482-7878), **Almost Corner Bookshop** in Trastevere (Via del Moro 45, tel. 06-583-6942), and the **Anglo American Bookshop** (a few blocks south of the Spanish Steps at Via della Vite 102, tel. 06-679-5222).

Laundry: Your hotelier can direct you to the nearest launderette. The **ondablu** launderette chain comes with Internet access (€2/hr, about €7 to wash and dry a 15-pound load, usually

Tips on Sightseeing in Rome

Sightseeing Passes: Rome offers several passes to help you save money. For most visitors, the Roma Pass is the clear winner.

The **Roma Pass** costs €20 and is valid for three days, covering public transportation and free or discounted entry to Roman sights. You get free admission to your first two sights (where you also get to skip the ticket line), and then a discount on the rest within the three-day window. Sights covered (or discounted) by the pass include the following: Colosseum/Palatine Hill/Roman Forum, Borghese Gallery (though you still must make a reservation and pay the €2 booking fee), Capitoline Museums, Castel Sant'Angelo, Ara Pacis, Museum of Roman Civilization, Etruscan Museum, Baths of Caracalla, Trajan's Market, some of the Appian Way sights. The pass also covers all four branches of the National Museum of Rome, considered as a single "sight": Palazzo Massimo (the main branch), Museum of the Bath at the Baths of Diocletian (Roman inscriptions), Crypta Balbi (medieval art), and Palazzo Altemps (so-so sculpture collection).

If you'll be visiting any two of the major sights in a three-day period, get the pass. It's sold at participating sights, online (www.romapass.it or www.pierreci.it), by phone (TI call-center tel. 06-0608), and at the TIs at the airport and Termini train station (includes map and brochure listing additional discounts). Sometimes the sights run out of passes, so if you see the pass for sale, buy it. The pass can also be purchased at *tabacchi* and newsstands inside Termini station.

Validate your Roma Pass by writing your name and validation date on the card. Then insert it directly into the turnstile at your first two (free) sights. At other sights, show it at the ticket office to get your reduced *(ridotto)* price—about 30 percent off.

To get the most of your pass, visit the two most expensive sights first—for example, the Colosseum (€11) and the National Museum (€10). Definitely use it to bypass the long ticket line at the Colosseum. For sights that normally sell a combined ticket (such as the Colosseum-Palatine-Roman Forum or the four National Museum branches), visiting the combined sight counts as a single entry.

The Roma Pass also includes a three-day transit pass. Write your name and birth date on the transit pass, validate it in the machine on your first bus or Metro ride, and you can take unlimited rides until midnight of the third day.

The more expensive (€25) **Roma and Più Pass** isn't useful for most visitors, as it includes sights and transportation in outlying areas of Rome.

Those visiting several ancient sights should also consider the **Archeologia Card.** It costs €22, is valid for seven days, and covers many of the biggies: the Colosseum, Palatine Hill, Roman Forum, Baths of Caracalla, Tomb of Cecilia Metella (on Appian Way), Villa of the Quintilli (barren Roman villa on the outskirts of Rome), and all four branches of the National Museum. This combo-ticket saves you money if you plan to visit at least three of the major sights, such as the Colosseum, National Museum of Rome, and the Baths of Caracalla (sold at participating sights).

If buying both a Roma Pass and Archeologia Card, use your free Roma Pass entries for sights *not* covered by the Archeologia Card (such as the Borghese Gallery and Capitoline Museums).

Museums: Plan ahead. The marvelous Borghese Gallery requires **reservations** well in advance (for specifics, see page 794). You can reserve tickets online to avoid the long lines at the Vatican Museum (see page 804).

Museum **hours** can vary. Get a current listing of opening times from one of Rome's TIs—ask for the free booklet *Museums of Rome*. On holidays, expect shorter hours or closures.

Churches: Churches offer amazing art (often free). They open early (around 7:00-7:30), close for lunch (roughly 12:00-15:00), and close late (about 19:00). Kamikaze tourists maximize their sightseeing hours by visiting churches before 9:00 and seeing the major sights that stay open during the siesta (St. Peter's, Colosseum, Forum, Capitoline Museums, and National Museum of Rome).

Many churches have "modest dress" requirements, which means no bare shoulders, miniskirts, or shorts—for men, women, or children. However, this dress code is only strictly enforced at St. Peter's (and at St. Paul's Outside the Walls, south of the city center). Elsewhere, you'll see many tourists in shorts (but not skimpy shorts) touring churches.

Spend money for light: A coin box near a piece of art in a church often illuminates the art for a coin (allowing a better photo). Some churches also have coin-operated audioboxes that describe the art and history. Consider these expenses a worthwhile donation.

Picnic Discreetly: Rome is cracking down on public drinking and snacking at its major sights. They've imposed a fine for these activities, but it'll likely be difficult to enforce. Still, it's smart to keep a low profile or choose an untouristed piazza for your picnic.

open daily 8:00–22:00, near Termini train station at Via Principe Amedeo 70b, tel. 06-474-4647).

Travel Agencies: You can get train tickets and railpass-related reservations and supplements at travel agencies, avoiding a trip to a train station. The cost is often the same, though sometimes there's a minimal charge. Your hotelier will know of a convenient agency nearby. The **American Express** office near the Spanish Steps sells train tickets and makes reservations for no extra fee (Mon–Fri 9:00–17:30, Sat 9:00–12:30, closed Sun, Piazza di Spagna 38, tel. 06-67641).

Dealing with (and Avoiding) Problems

Theft Alert: With sweet-talking con artists meeting you at the station, well-dressed pickpockets on buses, and thieving gangs of children at the ancient sites, Rome is a gauntlet of rip-offs. While it's nowhere near as bad as it was a few years ago, and pickpockets don't want to hurt you—they usually just want your money—green or sloppy tourists will be scammed. Thieves strike when you're distracted. Don't trust kind strangers. Keep nothing important in your pockets. Be most on guard while boarding and leaving buses and subways. Thieves crowd the door, then stop and turn while others crowd and push from behind. The sneakiest thieves are well-dressed businessmen (generally with something in their hands); lately many are posing as tourists with fanny packs, cameras, and even Rick Steves guidebooks. Scams abound: Don't give your wallet to self-proclaimed "police" who stop you on the street, warn you about counterfeit (or drug) money, and ask to see your cash. If a bank machine eats your ATM card, see if there's a thin plastic insert with a tongue hanging out that thieves use to extract it.

If you know what to look out for, the gangs of children picking the pockets and handbags of naive tourists are no threat, but an interesting, albeit sad, spectacle. Groups of city-stained children (just 8–10 years old—too young to be prosecuted, but old enough to rip you off) troll through the tourist crowds around the Colosseum, Forum, Piazza della Repubblica, and train and Metro stations. Watch them target tourists who are overloaded with bags or distracted with a video camera. The kids look like beggars and hold up newspapers or cardboard signs to confuse their victims. They scram like stray cats if you're on to them. A fast-fingered mother with a baby is often nearby. The terrace above the bus stop near the Colosseo Metro stop is a fine place to watch the action...and maybe even pick up a few moves of your own.

Reporting Losses: To report lost or stolen passports and documents, or to make an insurance claim, you must file a police report (at Termini train station, with Polizia at track 1 or with Carabinieri at track 20; offices are also at Piazza Venezia). To replace a passport, file the police report, then go to your embassy (see page 1251). For information on how to report missing credit cards, see page 11.

Emergency Numbers: Police—tel. 113. Ambulance—tel. 118.

Pedestrian Safety: While petty crime is common in the city center, violent crime is very rare. Your main concern in Rome is crossing streets safely, using extreme caution. Scooters don't need to stop at red lights, and even cars exercise what drivers call the "logical option" of not stopping if they see no oncoming traffic. As noisy, gasoline-powered scooters are replaced by electric ones, they'll be quieter (hooray) but more dangerous for pedestrians. Follow locals like a shadow when you cross a street (or spend a good part of your visit stranded on curbs). When you do cross alone, don't be a deer in the headlights. Find a gap in the traffic and walk with confidence while making eye contact with approaching drivers—they won't hit you if they can tell where you intend to go.

Staying/Getting Healthy: The siesta is a key to survival in summertime Rome. Lie down and contemplate the extraordinary power of gravity in the Eternal City. I drink lots of cold, refreshing water from Rome's many drinking fountains (the Forum has three).

There's a pharmacy (marked by a green cross) in every neighborhood. Pharmacies stay open late in the Termini train station (daily 7:30–22:00, downstairs below track 24) and at Piazza dei Cinquecento 51 (open 24 hours daily, next to Termini train station on the corner of Via Cavour, tel. 06-488-0019).

Embassies can recommend English-speaking doctors. Consider MEDline, a 24-hour home-medical service (tel. 06-808-0995, doctors speak English). Anyone is entitled to free emergency treatment at public hospitals. The hospital closest to the Termini train station is Policlinico Umberto 1 (entrance for emergency treatment on Via Lancisi, translators available, Metro: Policlinico). The American Hospital, a private hospital on the edge of town, is accustomed to helping Yankees (Via Emilio Longoni 69, tel. 06-22-551).

Getting Around Rome

Sightsee on foot, by city bus, by Metro, or by taxi. I've grouped your sightseeing into walkable neighborhoods. Make it a point to visit sights in a logical order. Needless backtracking wastes precious time.

The public transportation system, which is cheap and efficient, consists primarily of buses, a few trams, and the two underground Metro lines. Consider it part of your Roman experience.

Buying Tickets

All public transportation uses the same ticket (€1, valid for one Metro ride—including transfers underground—plus unlimited city buses and *elettrico* buses during a 1.25-hour period); you can also buy an all-day bus/Metro pass (€4, good until midnight), a three-day pass (€11), or a one-week pass (€16—about the same cost of two taxi rides).

You can buy tickets and passes at some newsstands, tobacco shops (*tabacchi,* marked by a black-and-white *T* sign), and major Metro stations and bus stops, but not on board. It's smart to stock up on tickets early, or to buy an all-day pass or a Roma Pass (which includes a three-day transit pass—see sidebar earlier in this chapter). That way, you don't have to run around searching for an open *tabacchi* when you spot your bus approaching. Metro stations rarely have human ticket-sellers, and the machines are often either broken or require exact change (it helps to insert your smallest coin first).

Validate your ticket by sticking it in the Metro turnstile (brown stripe facing toward you and angled down) or in the machine when you board the bus—watch others and imitate. If the validation machine won't work, you can ride with your ticket unstamped, but you must write the date, time, and bus number on it, or risk getting fined. For more information, visit www.atac.roma.it, or call 800-431-784.

Buses (especially the touristy #64) and the Metro are havens for thieves and pickpockets. Assume any commotion is a thief-created distraction. If one bus is packed, there's likely a second one on its tail with far fewer crowds and thieves. Once you know the bus system, it's easier than searching for a cab.

By Metro

The Roman subway system (Metropolitana, or Metro) is simple, with two clean, cheap, fast lines—A and B—that intersect at the Termini train station (Line A runs Mon–Sat 5:30–22:00, Sun 6:30–22:00; Line B runs Sun–Thu 5:30–23:00, Fri–Sat 5:30–1:30 in the morning). The subway's first and last compartments are generally the least crowded.

You'll notice lots of big holes in the city as a new line is built. Line C, from the Colosseum to Largo Argentina, will likely be done in 2020.

While much of Rome is not served by its skimpy subway, the following stops are helpful.

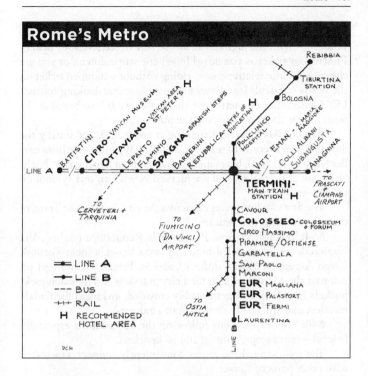

Rome's Metro

Termini (intersection of lines A and B): Termini train station, National Museum of Rome, and recommended hotels

Repubblica (line A): Baths of Diocletian/Octagonal Hall, Via Nazionale, and recommended hotels

Barberini (line A): Cappuccin Crypt and Trevi Fountain

Spagna (line A): Spanish Steps, Villa Borghese, and classy shopping area

Flaminio (line A): Piazza del Popolo, start of recommended "Dolce Vita Stroll" down Via del Corso

Ottaviano (line A): St. Peter's and Vatican City

Cipro (line A): Vatican Museum and recommended hotels

Tiburtina (line B): Tiburtina train and bus station

Colosseo (line B): Colosseum, Roman Forum, bike rental, and recommended hotels

By Bus

The Metro is handy, but it won't get you everywhere—take the bus. Bus routes are clearly listed at the stops. TIs usually don't have bus maps, but with some knowledge of major stops and this diagram, you won't necessarily need one (though if you do want a route map, buy it from *tabacchi* shops; bus info: tel. 06-57-003, usually not in English).

Tickets have a barcode and must be stamped on the bus in the yellow box with the digital readout (be sure to retrieve your ticket). Punch your ticket as you board (magnetic stripe down), or you are cheating. While relatively safe, riding without a stamped ticket on the bus is stressful. Inspectors fine even innocent-looking tourists €52. General bus etiquette (not always followed) is to board at the front or rear doors and exit out the middle.

Regular bus lines start running at about 5:30, and during the day, they run every 5–10 minutes. After 23:30, and sometimes earlier (such as on Sun), buses are less frequent but dependable. Night buses are also reliable, and are marked N with an owl symbol on the bus-stop signs.

The first two bus routes cut across the city, linking the Termini train station with the Vatican:

#64: Termini station, Piazza della Repubblica (sights), Via Nazionale (recommended hotels), Piazza Venezia (near Forum), Largo Argentina (near Pantheon), and St. Peter's Basilica (get off just past the tunnel). Ride it for a city overview and to watch pickpockets in action (can get horribly crowded, awkward for female travelers uncomfortably close to male strangers).

#40: This express bus following the #64 route is especially helpful—fewer stops, crowds, and pickpockets.

The following three routes conveniently connect Trastevere with other parts of Rome:

#H: This express bus connects Termini station and Trastevere, with a few stops on Via Nazionale (for Trastevere, get off at Piazza Belli, just after crossing the Tiber River).

#8: This tram connects Largo Argentina with Trastevere (get off at Piazza Belli).

#23 and #280: Links Vatican with Trastevere, stopping at Porta Portese (Sunday flea market), Trastevere (Piazza Belli), Castel Sant'Angelo, and Vatican Museum (nearest stop is Via Leone IV).

Here are other useful routes:

#62: Largo Argentina to St. Peter's Square.

#81: San Giovanni in Laterano, Largo Argentina, and Piazza Risorgimento (Vatican).

#85 and #87: Piazza Venezia, Colosseum, San Clemente, and San Giovanni in Laterano.

#492: Tiburtina (train and bus stations), Piazza Barberini, Piazza Venezia, Piazza Cavour (Castel Sant'Angelo), and Piazza Risorgimento (Vatican).

#714: Termini train station, Santa Maria Maggiore, San Giovanni in Laterano, and Terme di Caracalla (Baths of Caracalla).

These cute *elettrico* minibuses wind through the narrow streets

Rome's Public Transportation

TO M BATTISTINI
CIPRO
Vatican Museum
OTTAVIANO
M
492
23 280
LEPANTO
M
TIBER
CASTEL SANT'ANGELO
40
492
St. Peter's
GIANICOLO TERMINAL
116
64
FLAMINIO
M
117
PIAZZA DEL POPOLO
SPAGNA
M
117
Spanish Steps
116
492
Trevi
Pantheon
116
64·40
Largo Argentina
PIAZZA NAVONA
62
64·40
Campo de' Fiori
116
23 280
Sta. Maria Trastevere
PIAZZA MASTAI
PORTA PORTESE
23 280
8
H
P. BELLI
Circus Maximus
TO EUR + LAURENTINA
CIRCO MASSIMO
M
Borghese Museum
6
116
VIA VENETO
BARBERINI
M
REPUBBLICA
M
64·40·170
H
117
H
Capitol Hill
Victor Emmanuel Mon.
Forum + Palatine Hill
COLOSSEO
M
Colosseum
117
TO TIBURTINA + REBIBBIA
TO M
CASTRO PRETORIO
M
492
Baths of Dio.
64 40 H
714
TERMINI (TRAIN STATION)
TO TIBURTINA BUS + TRAIN STN.
TO FIUMICINO (DA VINCI) AIRPORT, FLORENCE, NAPLES, ETC.
Nat'l. Mus.
S. Maria Maggiore
CAVOUR
M
714
VITTORIO EMANUELE
M
MANZONI
M
San Giovanni Lat.
117
S. GIOVANNI
TO M ANAGNINA

¼ MILE
400 M.

N

M — METRO A
M — METRO B
64 — BUS ROUTES
117 — ELETTRICO MINIBUS ROUTES
116 —
8 — TRAM
B · · B — BOATS

ROME

of old and interesting neighborhoods, and are great for transport or simple joyriding:

Elettrico #116: Through the medieval core of Rome: Ponte Vittorio Emanuele II (near Castel Sant'Angelo) to Campo de' Fiori, then to Piazza Barberini via the Pantheon, and finally through the scenic Villa Borghese Gardens.

Elettrico #117: San Giovanni in Laterano, Colosseo, Via dei Serpenti, Trevi Fountain, Piazza di Spagna, and Piazza del Popolo.

By Taxi

I use taxis in Rome more often than in other cities. They're reasonable and useful for efficient sightseeing in this big, hot metropolis. Taxis start at about €2.50, then charge about €1 per kilometer (surcharges: €1 on Sun, €2.75 for nighttime hours of 22:00–7:00, €1 for luggage, tip by rounding up to the nearest euro). Sample fares: Termini train station to Vatican-€9; Termini train station to Colosseum-€6; Colosseum to Trastevere-€7. From the airport to anywhere in central Rome is a strictly fixed €40 rate (up to four people and their bags). Three or four companions with more money than time should taxi almost everywhere. It's tough to wave down a taxi in Rome. Find the nearest taxi stand by asking a passerby or a clerk in a shop, *"Dov'è una fermata dei taxi?"* (doh-VEH OO-nah fehr-MAH-tah DEHee TAHK-see). Some taxi stands are listed on my maps. To save time and energy, have your hotel or restaurant call a taxi for you; the meter starts when the call is received (generally adding a euro or two to the bill). To call a cab on your own, dial 06-4994 or 06-88177. It's routine for Romans to ask the waiter in a restaurant to call a taxi when they ask for the bill. The waiter will tell you how many minutes you have to enjoy your coffee.

Late at night, taxis are more expensive and hard to get. Don't try to hail one—go to a taxi stand. Beware of corrupt taxis. If hailing a cab on the street, be sure the meter is restarted when you get in (should be around €2.50, or around €5 if you or your hotelier phoned for the taxi). Many meters show both the fare and the time elapsed during the ride—and some tourists pay €10 for an eight-and-a-half-minute trip (more than the fair meter rate). When you arrive at the train station or airport, beware of hustlers conning naive visitors into unmarked rip-off "express taxis." Only use official taxis, with a *taxi* sign and phone number marked on the door. By law, they must display a multilingual official price chart. If you have any problems with a taxi, point to the chart and ask the cabbie to explain it to you. Making a show of writing down the taxi number (to file a complaint) can motivate a driver to quickly settle the matter. Tired travelers arriving at the airport might find it less stressful to take the airport shuttle to their hotel or catch the train to the Termini train station and take the Metro or a cheaper taxi from there (for details on the shuttle and train, see "Connections," near the end of this chapter).

By Bike

Biking in the big city of Rome can speed up sightseeing or simply be an enjoyable way to explore. Though Roman traffic can be stressful, Roman drivers are respectful of cyclists. The best rides are on small streets in the city center. A bike path along the banks of the Tiber River makes a good 20-minute ride (easily accessed from the ramps at Porta Portese and Ponte Regina Margherita near Piazza del Popolo). Get a bike with a well-padded seat—the little stones that pave Roman streets are unforgiving.

Top Bike Rental and Tours is professionally run by Roman bike enthusiasts who want to show off their city. Your rental comes with a handy map that suggests a route and indicates less-trafficked streets. Ciro and Riccardo also offer three- to four-hour-long guided tours around the city and the ancient Appian Way; check their website for days and prices (rental: €10/half-day, €15/day, more for mountain bikes, best to reserve in advance via email; bike tours: €15 plus bike rental fees, reservations required; leave ID for deposit, from Santa Maria Maggiore TI kiosk, take Via Olmata and turn left one block down, Via dei Quattro Canti 40, tel. 06-488-2893, www.topbikerental.com, info@topbikerental.com).

Cool Rent, near the Colosseo Metro stop, is cheaper but less helpful (€3/hr, €10/day, 3-person bike cart €10/hr, daily 9:30–20:00, €100 cash or driver's license for deposit, 10 yards to the right as you exit the Metro). A second outlet is just off Via del Corso (on Largo di Lombardi, near corner of Via del Corso and Via della Croce).

By Car with Driver

You can hire your own private car with driver through **Autoservizi Monti Concezio,** run by gentle, capable, and English-speaking Ezio (car-€35/hr, minibus-€40/hr, 3-hour minimum, mobile 335-636-5907 or 349-674-5643, www.montitours.com, concemon @tiscali.it).

Tours

Rome has many highly competitive tour companies. I've listed some here, but without a lot of details on their offerings. Before your trip, spend some time on their websites to get to know your options, as each company has a particular teaching and guiding personality. Some are highbrow, and others are less scholarly. It's sometimes required, and always smart, to book a spot in advance (easy online). The following companies all offer Vatican Museum tours—which, if you didn't book tickets online, can be a convenient (if pricey) way to skirt that museum's exasperating lines, provided they use licensed guides (confirm before booking). While it may seem like a splurge to have a local or an American expat show you around, it's a treat that can suddenly turn brutal Rome into your friend.

Having said that, I must add that we get a lot of negative feedback on most of these tour companies. Readers report that their advertising can be misleading, and that scheduling mishaps are not uncommon. Especially considering the costliness of these guided tours, budget travelers should consider the alternative of simply following the self-guided tours in this chapter, or using my free Rome audiotours covering the Colosseum, the Roman Forum, the Pantheon, St. Peter's Basilica, and the Sistine Chapel (downloadable at www.ricksteves.com on your iPod or other MP3 player). If you don't mind me in your ear, they're hard to beat: Nobody will stand you up, the quality is reliable (if not live), you can take the tour exactly when you like, and it's free.

Context Rome—Americans Paul Bennett and Lani Bevacqua offer informative walking tours for travelers with longer-than-average attention spans. Their orientation walks lace together lesser-known sights from antiquity to the present. Tours vary in length from 2–4 hours and range in price from €35–75. Try to book in advance, since their groups are limited to six and fill up fast (tel. 06-482-0911, US tel. 888-467-1986, www.contextrome.com). They also offer orientation chats in your hotel that can be well worth the price (€65/1 hour). Similar Context programs are offered in Venice, Florence, Naples, London, and Paris. See their website for other creative Context teaching initiatives.

Enjoy Rome—This English-speaking information service offers five different walking tours (€27 plus entry fees, 3 hours, groups limited to 25, reserve by phone or online). It also provides a free, useful city guide and an informative website (Mon–Fri 8:30–19:00, Sat 8:30–14:00, closed Sun, 3 blocks north of Termini train station, Via Marghera 8a, tel. 06-445-1843, fax 06-445-0734, www.enjoyrome.com, info@enjoyrome.com).

Rome Walks—The licensed guides give tours in fluent English to small groups (2–10 people). Sample tours include Colosseum/Forum/Palatine Walk (€51, includes admission to Colosseum, 3 hours), Scandal Tour (€40, 3 hours to dig up the dirt on Roman emperors, royalty, and popes), Vatican City Walk (€58, includes admission to Vatican Museum, 4 hours), Twilight Rome Evening Walk (€25, all the famous squares that offer lively people scenes, 2 hours), and a Jewish Ghetto and Trastevere Walk (€40, explore the back streets of Rome, 3 hours). They also do pricier, private tours to more far-flung places such as Orvieto (for wine and olives), Ostia Antica, the Appian Way, and the Catacombs (mobile 347-795-5175, www.romewalks.com, info@romewalks.com, Annie Frances Gray).

Roman Odyssey—This expat-led tour company offers various tours, led by native English speakers who are licensed guides. Tours have a maximum of 15 participants. Sample tours are their Ancient Rome walk (€25, Colosseum entrance extra, 3 hours) and Vatican Museum tour (€55, museum admission included, you get to skip the Vatican line, 4 hours, ask about Rick Steves discount, €60/hr for private guides, tel. 06-580-9902, mobile 328-912-3720, www.romanodyssey.com, Rahul).

Through Eternity—This company offers several walking tours, all led by native English speakers who strive to bring the history to life. The tours, which run nearly daily and are limited to groups of 15, do not include entry fees to museums or sights. Sample tours are St. Peter's and the Vatican Museum (€46, 5 hours); the Colosseum and Roman Forum (€30, 3 hours); and Rome at Twilight (€30, nightly). Their more unusual tours are "Underground Rome," which explores the layers of ancient churches above and below ground, ending in Trastevere (€30, 3 hours); and "Secret Rome," which includes a visit to the National Museum of Rome, Santa Maria Maggiore, and other churches (€30, 3 hours). If you book by phone or online, the company offers a 10 percent Rick Steves discount for most of their tours and 20 percent for the Underground Rome and Secret Rome tours (tel. 06-700-9336, mobile 347-336-5298, www.through eternity.com, info@througheternity.com, Rob Allyn).

Angel Tours—This gang of hardworking Irish Italo-philes mix light narrative with their charming gift of gab. They generally do a free 19:00 Pantheon tour, hoping the charm and quality of the guide will encourage people to take the rest of that evening walk or book another tour. Note that these guides are not licensed or that knowledgeable about history—these tours are just for fun. Their website lists tours and departure times (€25 plus entry fees, €15 for students, 2–3 hours, English only, groups limited to 15, tel. 06-7720-3048, mobile 348-734-1850, www.angeltoursrome .com, Sean).

Artviva: The Original & Best Walking Tours—Their "Rome in One Glorious Day Package" consists of a four-hour walking introduction to Rome in the morning, and a Vatican Museum tour in the afternoon for €90 (March–Nov Mon, Wed, Fri, and Sat; ask for Rick Steves discount when you reserve). Check their website for all their tours, prices, and times. Groups are small (maximum of 14) and booking is necessary (tel. 055-264-5033 during day or mobile 329-613-2730 from 18:00–20:00, also private tours year-round, www.italy.artviva.com, staff@artviva.com).

Private Guides—Consider a personal tour. Any of the tour companies I list can provide a guide (about €60/hr). I work with Francesca Caruso, a licensed Italian guide who speaks excellent English, loves to teach and share her appreciation of her city, and has contributed generously to this chapter. She has a broad range of expertise and can tailor a walk to your interests, and enjoys working with my readers (€50/hr, chris.fra@mclink.it).

The following licensed, independent local guides are also excellent and will tailor tours to your interests. Each guide charges a set fee for small groups: Carla Zaia (engaging Roman teacher, €180/half-day, mobile 349-759-0723, chrisecarla@tiscali.it); Sara Magister (a Roman with her doctorate in art history who wrote a book on Renaissance Rome, €50/hr, up to 10 people, tel. 06-583-6783, mobile 339-379-3813, a.magister@iol.it); and Jason Spiehler (Louisiana native with a Masters in Roman art history from Yale, €55/hr, mobile 340-798-0585, toursofrome@hotmail.com).

Hop-on, Hop-off Tours—Several different agencies, including the ATAC public bus company, run hop-on, hop-off tours around Rome. These tours are constantly evolving and offer varying combinations of sights. While you can grab one (and pay as you board) at any stop, the Termini train station and Piazza Venezia are handy hubs. Although the city is perfectly walkable and traffic jams can make the bus dreadfully slow, these open-top bus tours remain popular. Several tour companies offer essentially the same deal.

Trambus Open 110 seems to be the best. It's operated by the ATAC city bus lines, and offers an orientation tour on big red double-decker buses with an open-air upper deck. In less than two hours, you'll have 80 sights pointed out to you (with a next-to-worthless recorded narration). While you can hop on and off, the service can be erratic (mobbed midday, not ideal in bad weather) and it can be very slow in heavy traffic. It's best to think of this as a two-hour quickie orientation with scant information and lots of images. The 11 stops include Via Veneto, Via Tritone, Ara Pacis, Piazza Cavour, St. Peter's Square, Corso Vittorio Emanuele (for Piazza Navona), Piazza Venezia, Colosseum, and Via Nazionale. Bus #110 departs every 10 minutes (runs daily 8:00–20:00, tel. 06-684-0901, www.trambusopen.com). Buy the €16 ticket as you board (or at platform E in front of Termini train station).

Archeobus is an open-top bus also operated by ATAC that runs hourly from the Termini train station out to the Appian Way (with stops at the Colosseum, Baths of Caracalla, San Callisto, San Sebastian, the Tomb of Cecilia Metella, and the Aqueduct Park). This is a handy way to see the sights down this ancient Roman road, but it can be frustrating for various reasons—sparse narration, sporadic service, and not ideal for hopping on and off (€13, €24 combo-ticket with Trambus, daily 9:00–16:00, hourly departures from Termini train station and Piazza Venezia, tel. 06-684-0901). A similar bus laces together all the Christian sights.

Self-Guided Walks

Here are three walks that give you a moving picture of Rome, an ancient yet modern city. You'll walk through history ("Roman Forum Walk"), take a refreshing early-evening stroll ("The Dolce Vita Stroll"), and enjoy the thriving night scene ("Night Walk Across Rome").

Roman Forum Walk

The Forum was the political, religious, and commercial center of the city. Rome's most important temples and halls of justice were here. This was the place for religious processions, political demonstrations, elections, important speeches, and parades by conquering generals. As Rome's empire expanded, these few acres of land became the center of the civilized world.

Cost, Hours, Location: €11 combo-ticket includes Colosseum and Palatine Hill, daily 8:30 until one hour before sunset (April–Sept until 19:00, Oct until 18:15, Nov–Feb until 16:15, March until 16:30), last entry one hour before closing. Metro: Colosseo, tel. 06-3996-7700. There's a €4 unexciting yet informative audioguide that helps decipher the rubble, but you'll have to return it to the Forum entrance on Via dei Fori Imperiali instead of being able to exit directly to Capitol Hill or the Colosseum. Official guided tours in English run once a day at around 13:00 (€4, 45 min, confirm time at ticket office). Street vendors at several ancient sites sell small *Rome: Past and Present* books with plastic overlays that restore the ruins (includes DVD, marked €25, offer less). A TI is near the Via dei Fori Imperiali entrance (near Basilica Aemilia).

• *Walk through the entrance, located on Via dei Fori Imperiali, and stroll down the hill to the main road: the Via Sacra. Take a left down the Via Sacra and amble all the way to the...*

❶ **Arch of Titus (Arco di Tito):** This arch commemorated the Roman victory over the province of Judaea (Israel) in A.D. 70. The Romans had a reputation as benevolent conquerors who tolerated the local customs and rulers. All they required was allegiance to the empire, shown by worshipping the emperor as a god. No problem for most conquered people, who already had half a dozen gods on their prayer lists anyway. But Israelites believed in only one god, and it wasn't the emperor. Israel revolted. After a short but bitter war, the Romans defeated the rebels, took Jerusalem, destroyed their temple (leaving only the foundation wall—today's revered "Wailing Wall"), and brought home 50,000 Jewish slaves... who were forced to build this arch (and the Colosseum).

Roman Forum Walk

- M METRO STN.
- TO GAUL
- CAPITOL HILL
- STEPS TO CAPITOL HILL
- PIAZZA VENEZIA
- ⑬
- EXIT
- ⑪ ⑫
- ⑭
- ⑩
- FORUM SQUARE ③
- VIA SAN TEODORO
- WC
- ④
- ⑥
- ⑧
- ⑦
- ⑨
- MAIN ENTRANCE
- VIA SACRA
- ⑤
- TICKET OFFICE & WC
- FORUM
- ②
- FORI IMPERIALI
- DEI
- "WATCH ROME GROW" MAPS
- CIRCUS MAXIMUS
- PALATINE HILL
- TO CLIMB PALATINE HILL
- DIRECT TO FORUM
- TICKET OFFICE
- ①
- EXIT
- VIA
- PCH
- VIA DI SAN GREGORIO
- TO CARTHAGE
- ARCH OF CONSTANTINE
- COLOSSEUM
- COLOSSEO M

1. Arch of Titus
2. Basilica of Constantine
3. The Forum's Main Square
4. Temple of Julius Caesar
5. Temple of Antoninus Pius & Faustina
6. Basilica Aemilia
7. Caligula's Palace
8. Temple of Vesta
9. House of the Vestal Virgins
10. The Curia
11. Rostrum
12. Arch of Septimius Severus
13. Temple of Saturn
14. Column of Phocas

• *Backtrack down the Via Sacra into the Forum. After about 50 yards, turn right and follow a path uphill to the three huge arches of the…*

❷ **Basilica of Constantine (a.k.a. Basilica Maxentius):** Yes, these are big arches. But they represent only one-third of the original Basilica of Constantine, a mammoth hall of justice. The arches were matched by a similar set along the Via Sacra side (only a few squat brick piers remain). Between them ran the central hall, which was spanned by a roof 130 feet high—about 55 feet higher than the side arches you see. (The stub of brick you see sticking up began an arch that once spanned the central hall.) The hall itself was as long as a football field, lavishly furnished with colorful inlaid marble, a gilded bronze ceiling, and statues, and filled with strolling Romans. At the far (west) end was an enormous marble statue of Emperor Constantine on a throne. (Pieces of this statue, including a hand the size of a man, are on display in Rome's Capitoline Museums.)

The basilica was begun by the emperor Maxentius, but after he was trounced in battle (described in Arch of Constantine listing under "Sights" later in this chapter), the victor—Constantine—completed the massive building. No doubt about it, the Romans built monuments on a more epic scale than any previous Europeans, wowing their "barbarian" neighbors.

• *Now stroll deeper into the Forum, downhill along the Via Sacra, through the trees. Many of the large basalt stones under your feet were walked on by Caesar Augustus 2,000 years ago. Pass by the only original bronze door still swinging on its ancient hinges (green, on right) and continue between ruined buildings until the Via Sacra opens up to a flat, grassy area.*

❸ **The Forum's Main Square:** The original Forum, or main square, was this flat patch about the size of a football field, stretching to the foot of Capitol Hill. Surrounding it were temples, law courts, government buildings, and triumphal arches.

Rome was born right here. According to legend, twin brothers Romulus (Rome) and Remus were orphaned in infancy and raised by a she-wolf on top of Palatine Hill. Growing up, they found it hard to get dates. So they and their cohorts attacked the nearby Sabine tribe and kidnapped their women. After they made peace, this marshy valley became the meeting place and then the trading center for the scattered tribes on the surrounding hillsides.

The square was the busiest and most crowded—and often the seediest—section of town. Besides the senators, politicians, and currency exchangers, there were even sleazier types—souvenir hawkers, pickpockets, fortune-tellers, gamblers, slave marketers, drunks, hookers, lawyers, and tour guides.

The Forum is now rubble, but imagine it in its prime: blinding white marble buildings with 40-foot-high columns and shining bronze roofs; rows of statues painted in realistic colors; processional chariots rattling down the Via Sacra. Mentally replace tourists in T-shirts with tribunes in togas. Imagine the buildings towering and the people buzzing around you while an orator gives a rabble-rousing speech from the Rostrum. If things still look like just a pile of rocks, at least tell yourself, "But Julius Caesar once leaned against these rocks."

• At the near (east) end of the main square (the Colosseum is to the east) are the foundations of a temple now capped with a peaked wood-and-metal roof.

❹ The Temple of Julius Caesar (Tempio del Divo Giulio, or "Ara di Cesare"): Julius Caesar's body was burned on this spot (under the metal roof) after his assassination. Peek behind the wall into the small apse area, where a mound of dirt usually has fresh flowers—given to remember the man who, more than any other, personified the greatness of Rome.

Caesar (100–44 b.c.) changed Rome—and the Forum—dramatically. He cleared out many of the wooden market stalls and began to ring the square with even grander buildings. Caesar's house was located behind the temple, near that clump of trees. He walked right by here on the day he was assassinated ("Beware the Ides of March!" warned a street-corner Etruscan preacher).

Though he was popular with the masses, not everyone liked Caesar's urban design or his politics. When he assumed dictatorial powers, he was ambushed and stabbed to death by a conspiracy of senators, including his adopted son, Brutus ("Et tu, Brute?").

The funeral was held here, facing the main square. The citizens gathered, and speeches were made. Mark Antony stood up to say (in Shakespeare's words), "Friends, Romans, countrymen, lend me your ears. I come to bury Caesar, not to praise him." When Caesar's body was burned, the citizens who still loved him threw anything at hand on the fire, requiring the fire department to come put it out. Later, Emperor Augustus dedicated this temple in his name, making Caesar the first Roman to become a god.

• Behind and to the left of the Temple of Julius Caesar are the 10 tall columns of the...

❺ Temple of Antoninus Pius and Faustina: The Senate built this temple to honor Emperor Antoninus Pius (a.d. 138–161) and his deified wife, Faustina. The 50-foot-tall Corinthian (leafy) columns must have been awe-inspiring to out-of-towners who grew up in thatched huts. Although the temple has been inhabited by a church, you can still see the basic layout—a staircase led to a shaded porch (the columns), which admitted you to the main building (now a church), where the statue of the god sat. Originally, these columns supported a triangular pediment decorated with sculptures.

Picture these columns, with gilded capitals, supporting brightly painted statues in the pediment, and the whole building capped with a gleaming bronze roof. The stately gray rubble of today's Forum is a faded black-and-white photograph of a 3-D Technicolor era.

The building is a microcosm of many of the changes that occurred after Rome fell. In medieval times, the temple was pillaged. Note the diagonal cuts high on the marble columns—a failed attempt by scavengers to cut through the pillars to pull them down for their precious stone. (Vinegar and rope cut marble... but because vinegar also eats through rope, they abandoned the attempt.) In 1550, a church was housed inside the ancient temple. The door shows the street level at the time of Michelangelo. The long staircase was underground until excavated in the 1800s.

• *There's a ramp next to the Temple of A. and F. Walk halfway up it and look to the left to view the...*

❻ **Basilica Aemilia:** A basilica was a covered public forum, often serving as a Roman hall of justice. In a society that was as legal-minded as America is today, you needed a lot of lawyers—and a big place to put them. Citizens came here to work out matters such as inheritances and building permits, or to sue somebody.

Notice the layout. It was a long, rectangular building. The stubby columns all in a row form one long, central hall flanked by two side aisles. Medieval Christians required a larger meeting hall for their worship services than Roman temples provided, so they used the spacious Roman basilica as the model for their churches. Cathedrals from France to Spain to England, from Romanesque to Gothic to Renaissance, all have the same basic floor plan as a Roman basilica.

• *Return again to the Temple of Julius Caesar. To the right of the temple are the three tall Corinthian columns of the Temple of Castor and Pollux. Beyond that is Palatine Hill—the corner of which may have been...*

❼ **Caligula's Palace (a.k.a. the Palace of Tiberius):** Emperor Caligula (ruled A.D. 37–41) had a huge palace on Palatine Hill overlooking the Forum. It actually sprawled down the hill into the Forum (some supporting arches remain in the hillside).

Caligula was not a nice person. He tortured enemies, stole senators' wives, and parked his chariot in disabled spaces. But Rome's luxury-loving emperors only added to the glory of the Forum, with each one trying to make his mark on history.

• *To the left of the Temple of Castor and Pollux, find the remains of a small, white, circular temple.*

❽ **The Temple of Vesta:** This is perhaps Rome's most sacred spot. Rome considered itself one big family, and this temple represented a circular hut, like the kind that Rome's first families lived in. Inside, a fire burned, just as in a Roman home. And back in the days before lighters and butane, you never wanted your fire to go out. As long as the sacred flame burned, Rome would stand. The flame was tended by priestesses known as Vestal Virgins.

• *Around the back of the Temple of Vesta, you'll find two rectangular brick pools. These stood in the courtyard of the...*

❾ **House of the Vestal Virgins:** The Vestal Virgins lived in a two-story building surrounding a long central courtyard with these two pools at one end. Rows of statues depicting important Vestal Virgins flanked the courtyard. This place was the model—both architecturally and sexually—for medieval convents and monasteries.

Chosen from noble families before they reached the age of 10, the six Vestal Virgins served a 30-year term. Honored and revered by the Romans, the Vestals even had their own box opposite the emperor in the Colosseum.

As the name implies, a Vestal took a vow of chastity. If she served her term faithfully—abstaining for 30 years—she was given a huge dowry and allowed to marry. But if they found any Virgin who wasn't a virgin, she was strapped to a funeral car, paraded through the streets of the Forum, taken to a crypt, given a loaf of bread and a lamp...and buried alive. Many women suffered the latter fate.

• *Return to the Temple of Julius Caesar and head to the Forum's west end (opposite the Colosseum). As you pass alongside the big open space of the Forum's main square, consider how the piazza is still a standard part of any Italian town. It has reflected and accommodated the gregarious and outgoing nature of the Italian people since Roman times.*

Stop at the big, well-preserved brick building (on right) with the triangular roof and look in.

❿ **The Curia (Senate House):** The Curia was the most important political building in the Forum. While the present building dates from A.D. 283, this was the site of Rome's official center of government since the birth of the republic. Three hundred senators, elected by the citizens of Rome, met here to debate and create the laws of the land. Their wooden seats once circled the building in three tiers; the Senate president's podium sat at the far end. The marble floor is from ancient times. Listen to the echoes in this vast room—the acoustics are great.

Rome prided itself on being a republic. Early in the city's history, its people threw out the king and established rule by elected representatives. Each Roman citizen was free to speak his mind and have a say in public policy. Even when emperors became the supreme authority, the Senate was a power to be reckoned with. The Curia building (A.D. 280) is well-preserved, having been used as a church since early Christian times. In the 1930s, it was restored and opened to the public as a historic site. (Note: Although Julius

Caesar was assassinated in "the Senate," it wasn't here—the Senate was temporarily meeting across town.)

A statue and two reliefs inside the Curia help build our mental image of the Forum. The statue, made of porphyry marble in about A.D. 100 (with its head, arms, and feet now missing), was a tribute to an emperor, probably Hadrian or Trajan. The two relief panels may have decorated the Rostrum. Those on the left show people (with big stone tablets) standing in line to burn their debt records following a government amnesty. The other shows the distribution of grain (Rome's welfare system), some buildings in the background, and the latest fashion in togas.

• *Go back down the Senate steps and find the 10-foot-high wall at the base of Capitol Hill, marked...*

⓫ Rostrum (Rostra): Nowhere was Roman freedom more apparent than at this "Speaker's Corner." The Rostrum was a raised platform, 10 feet high and 80 feet long, decorated with statues, columns, and the prows of ships *(rostra).*

On a stage like this, Rome's orators, great and small, tried to draw a crowd and sway public opinion. Mark Antony rose to offer Caesar the laurel-leaf crown of kingship, which Caesar publicly (and hypocritically) refused while privately becoming a dictator. Men such as Cicero railed against the corruption and decadence that came with the city's newfound wealth. In later years, daring citizens even spoke out against the emperors, reminding them that Rome was once free. Picture the backdrop that these speakers would have had—a mountain of marble buildings piling up on Capitol Hill.

• *The big arch to the right of the Rostrum is the...*

⓬ Arch of Septimius Severus: In imperial times, the Rostrum's voices of democracy would have been dwarfed by images of empire such as the huge, six-story-high Arch of Septimius Severus (A.D. 203). The reliefs commemorate the African-born emperor's battles in Mesopotamia. Near ground level, see soldiers marching captured barbarians back to Rome for the victory parade. Despite Severus' efficient rule, Rome's empire was crumbling under the weight of its own corruption, disease, decaying infrastructure, and the constant attacks by foreign "barbarians."

• *Pass underneath the Arch of Septimius Severus and turn left. On the slope of Capitol Hill are the eight remaining columns of the...*

⓭ Temple of Saturn: These columns framed the entrance to the Forum's oldest temple (497 B.C.). Inside was a humble, very old wooden statue of the god Saturn. But the statue's pedestal held the gold bars, coins, and jewels of Rome's state treasury, the booty collected by conquering generals.

• *Standing here, at one of the Forum's first buildings, look east at the lone, tall...*

ROME

❹ **Column of Phocas:** This is the Forum's last monument (A.D. 608), a gift from the powerful Byzantine Empire to a fallen empire—Rome. Given to commemorate the pagan Pantheon's becoming a Christian church, it's like a symbolic last nail in ancient Rome's coffin. After Rome's 1,000-year reign, the city was looted by Vandals, the population of a million-plus shrank to about 10,000, and the once-grand city center—the Forum—was abandoned, slowly covered up by centuries of silt and dirt. In the 1700s, an English historian named Edward Gibbon overlooked this spot from Capitol Hill. Hearing Christian monks singing at these pagan ruins, he looked out at the few columns poking up from the ground, pondered the "Decline and Fall of the Roman Empire," and thought, "Hmm, that's a catchy title...."

• *There are several ways to exit the Forum:*

1. Exiting past the Arch of Titus lands you at the Arch of Constantine and Colosseum.

2. Exiting near the Arch of Septimius Severus and Mamertine Prison gets you to the stairs up to Capitol Hill.

3. Though the Forum entrance on Via dei Fori Imperiali is not officially an exit, guards will usually let you exit here.

The Dolce Vita Stroll

This is the city's chic stroll, from Piazza del Popolo (Metro: Flaminio) down a wonderfully traffic-free section of Via del Corso, and up Via Condotti to the Spanish Steps each evening around 18:00. Saturdays and Sundays are best; leave earlier than 18:00 if you plan to visit the Ara Pacis, which closes at 19:00.

Shoppers, people-watchers, and flirts on the prowl fill this neighborhood of some of Rome's most fashionable stores (open after siesta 16:30–19:30). While both the crowds and the shops along Via del Corso have gone downhill recently, elegance survives in the grid of streets between this street and the Spanish Steps.

To get to **Piazza del Popolo,** where the stroll starts, take Metro line A to Flaminio and walk south to the square. Delightfully car-free, Piazza del Popolo is marked by an obelisk that was brought to Rome by Augustus after he conquered Egypt. (It used to stand in the Circus Maximus.) In medieval times, this area was just inside Rome's main entry. For more background on the square, see page 796.

The Baroque church of **Santa Maria del Popolo** is worth popping into (Mon–Sat until 19:00, Sun until 19:30, next to gate in old wall on north side of square). Inside, look for Raphael's Chigi Chapel (KEE-gee, second chapel on left) and two paintings by Caravaggio (the side paintings in the Cerasi Chapel, left of altar). See the listing on page 796 for more information.

From Piazza del Popolo, shop your way down **Via del Corso.** If you need a rest or a viewpoint, join the locals sitting on the steps

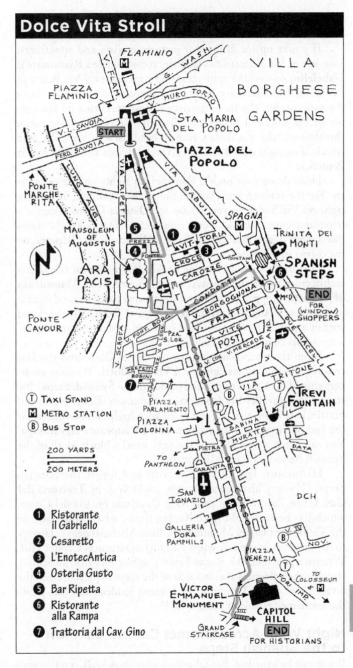

Dolce Vita Stroll

FLAMINIO
V. FLAM.
V. G. WASH.

VILLA BORGHESE GARDENS

PIAZZA FLAMINIO

V. MURO TORTO

START

Sta. Maria del Popolo

V. L. SAVOIA

FERD. SAVOIA

PIAZZA DEL POPOLO

VIA BABUINO

PONTE MARGHERITA

CONG. AUG.

VIA RIPETTA

SPAGNA
M

TRINITÀ DEI MONTI

MAUSOLEUM OF AUGUSTUS

FREZZA

❶ ❷
V. VITTORIA
V. CROCE
❸
V. CAROZZE
CONDOTTI
V. BORGOGNONA
V. FRATTINA
V. VITE
POST
V. CON. V. MERCEDE

SPANISH STEPS ❻
McD
T
END
FOR (WINDOW) SHOPPERS

❺
❹
PONTE

ARA PACIS

PONTE CAVOUR

V. SCROFA
V. FONT. BORG.
PZA. S. LOR.
V. MARZ.

❼
PREFETTI
ROSINI

PIAZZA PARLAMENTO

CORSO

PIAZZA COLONNA

V. CON.
V. MERCEDE
AND
V. MACE
V. TRITONE

TREVI FOUNTAIN
T
Ⓑ
T
T

Ⓣ TAXI STAND
Ⓜ METRO STATION
Ⓑ BUS STOP

200 YARDS
200 METERS

PIETRA
V. SABINA
MURATTE
DATA

TO PANTHEON

CARAVITA

SAN IGNAZIO

DCH

❶ Ristorante il Gabriello
❷ Cesaretto
❸ L'EnotecAntica
❹ Osteria Gusto
❺ Bar Ripetta
❻ Ristorante alla Rampa
❼ Trattoria dal Cav. Gino

GALLERIA DORA PAMPHILJ

PIAZZA VENEZIA

Ⓑ
V. IV
NOV.

TO COLOSSEUM + Ⓜ

FORI IMP.

VICTOR EMMANUEL MONUMENT

CAPITOL HILL
END
FOR HISTORIANS

GRAND STAIRCASE

ROME

of various churches along the street. The stroll continues down Via del Corso, but there are some fun detours off the main drag:

If you're up for dinner, or just some wine and appetizers, turn left at Via Vittorio to reach the recommended **Ristorante il Gabriello,** or pass the restaurant and turn right on Via Bocca di Leone for two wine bars: laid-back **Cesaretto,** and, farther down the same street, the more touristy **L'EnotecAntica** (at the corner of Via Bocca di Leone and Via della Croce). If you've taken this detour, take Via della Croce to head back to Via del Corso (you'll turn right out of L'EnotecAntica). Cross the street to Via Pontefici.

Head down west on Via Pontefici for sights and more eateries. For the eateries, walk behind the modern building by turning right on Via Soderini; you'll soon see **Osteria Gusto** (nice for a wine-and-cheese break). For a cappuccino that looks and tastes like a work of art, head down Via della Frezza to **Bar Ripetta,** on the corner of Via Ripetta.

Historians should continue on Via Pontefici past the fascist architecture to see the massive, rotting, round-brick **Mausoleum of Augustus,** topped with overgrown cypress trees. Beyond it, next to the river, is Augustus' **Ara Pacis** (Altar of Peace), now enclosed within a protective glass-walled museum (listed under "Sights" later in this chapter, closed Mon).

From the mausoleum, return to Via del Corso and the 21st century, continuing straight until **Via Condotti.** Window shoppers should take a left to join the parade to the **Spanish Steps.** The streets that parallel Via Condotti to the south (Borgognona and Frattini) are more elegant, and filled with high-end boutiques. At the end of the walk is the recommended **Ristorante alla Rampa.** You can catch a taxi home at the taxi stand a block south of the Spanish Steps (at Piazza Mignonelli).

Historians: Ignore Via Condotti and forget the Spanish Steps. (Hungry historians, though, could drop by **Trattoria dal Cav. Gino,** described on page 837). Continue on Via del Corso, which has been straight since Roman times, a half-mile down to the Victor Emmanuel Monument. Climb Michelangelo's stairway to his glorious (especially when floodlit) square atop Capitol Hill. Whether you take the Rome From the Sky elevator, or simply stand at the balconies at either side of the mayor's palace, catch the lovely views of the Forum as the horizon reddens and cats prowl the unclaimed rubble of ancient Rome.

Night Walk Across Rome: Campo de' Fiori to the Spanish Steps

Rome can be grueling. But taking an after-dark walk is a fine way to mix romance into all the history, enjoy the cool of the evening, and enliven everything with some of Europe's best people-watching. My favorite nighttime stroll laces together Rome's floodlit nightspots and fine urban spaces with real-life theater vignettes.

Sitting so close to a Bernini fountain that traffic noises evaporate; jostling with local teenagers to see all the gelato flavors; observing lovers straddling more than the bench; jaywalking past *polizia* in flak-proof vests; and marveling at the ramshackle elegance that softens this brutal city for those who were born here and can imagine living nowhere else—these are the flavors of Rome best tasted after dark.

Start this mile-long walk at the **Campo de' Fiori** (Field of Flowers), my favorite outdoor dining room after dark (see "Eating—In the Heart of Rome," later in this chapter). The center of the great, colorful square, Campo de' Fiori, is marked with the statue of Giordano Bruno, an intellectual heretic who was burned on this spot in 1600. Bruno overlooks a busy produce market in the morning and strollers after sundown. This neighborhood is still known for its free spirit and occasional demonstrations. When the statue of Bruno was erected in 1889, local riots overcame Vatican protests against honoring a heretic. Bruno faces his nemesis, the Vatican Chancellery (the big white building in the corner a bit to his right), while his pedestal reads, "And the flames rose up." Check out the reliefs on the pedestal for scenes from Bruno's trial and execution.

At the east end of the square (behind Bruno), the ramshackle apartments are built right into the old outer wall of ancient Rome's mammoth Theater of Pompey. This entertainment complex covered several city blocks, stretching from here to Largo Argentina. Julius Caesar was assassinated in the Theater of Pompey, where the Senate was renting space.

The square is lined with and surrounded by fun eateries. Bruno faces **Ristorante la Carbonara,** the only real restaurant on the square. The **Forno,** next door to the left (Mon–Sat 7:30–14:30 & 16:45–20:00, closed Sun), is a popular place for hot and tasty take-out *pizza bianco*. Step in to at least observe the frenzy as pizza is sold hot out of the oven. You can order an *etto* (100 grams) by pointing, then take your snack to the counter to pay. The many bars lining the square are fine for drinks and people-watching. Late at night on weekends, the place is packed with beer-drinking kids, turning what was once a charming medieval square into one vast Roman street party.

If Bruno did a hop, step, and jump forward, then turned right on Via dei Baullari and marched 200 yards, he'd cross the busy Corso Vittorio Emanuele; then, continuing another 150 yards on Via Cuccagna, he'd find **Piazza Navona**. Rome's most interesting night scene features street music, artists, fire-eaters,

ROME

Night Walk Across Rome

TO PIAZZA DEL POPOLO

VILLA BORGHESE

SPAGNA

S. TRINITÀ MONTI

MAUSOLEUM OF AUGUSTUS

ARA PACIS

SPANISH STEPS END

PIAZZA MIG.

PONTE CAVOUR

PONTE UMBERTO

TI BER

PONTE CAVOUR

LUNGOTEVERE MARZIO

ANCIENT STADIUM ENTRANCE

SAN LUIGI (CARAVAGGIO)

CORONARI

TRE SCALINI

RIVERS FTN

PIAZZA NAVONA

PIAZZA PASQUINO

CITY MUSEUM

CAMPO DE' FIORI   START

PALAZZO FARNESE

TO TRASTEVERE

PREF.

PIAZZA COLONNA

UFF. VICARIO

AQUIRO

SALV. GIUST.

SEMINARIO

PANTHEON

STA. MARIA SOPRA MINERVA

POST

TREVI FOUNTAIN

TRITONE

DATARIA

SABINA

MURATTE

VIA DEL

SAN IGNAZIO

GALLERIA DORA PAMPHILJ

PIAZZA VENEZIA

GESÙ

LARGO ARGENTINA RUINS (+CAT HOSPICE)

CAPITOL HILL

FORUM

V.E. MON.

TO COLOSSEUM

FORI IMPERIALI

Ⓣ Taxi Stand
Ⓜ Metro Station
Ⓑ Bus Stop

200 YARDS
200 METERS

DCH

local Casanovas, ice cream, fountains by Bernini, and outdoor cafés (worthy of a splurge if you've got time to sit and enjoy Italy's human river).

This oblong square retains the shape of the original racetrack that was built by the emperor Domitian. (To see the ruins of the original entrance, exit the square at the far—or north—end, then take an immediate left, and look down to the left 25 feet below the current street level.) Since ancient times, the square has been a center of Roman life. In the 1800s, the city would flood the square to cool off the neighborhood.

The **Four Rivers Fountain** in the center is the most famous fountain by the man who remade Rome in Baroque style, Gian Lorenzo Bernini. Four burly river gods (representing the four continents that were known in 1650) support an Egyptian obelisk that once stood on the ancient Appian Way. The water of the world gushes everywhere. The Nile has his head covered, since the headwaters were unknown then. The Ganges holds an oar. The Danube turns to admire the obelisk, which Bernini had moved here from a stadium on the Appian Way. And the Rio de la Plata from Uruguay tumbles backward in shock, wondering how he ever made the top four. Bernini enlivens the fountain with horses plunging through the rocks and exotic flora and fauna from these newly discovered lands. Homesick Texans may want to find the armadillo. (It's the big, weird armor-plated creature behind the Plata River statue.)

The Plata river god is gazing upward at the church of St. Agnes, worked on by Bernini's former-student-turned-rival, Francesco Borromini. Borromini's concave facade helps reveal the dome and epitomizes the curved symmetry of Baroque. Tour guides say that Bernini designed his river god to look horrified at Borromini's work. Or maybe he's shielding his eyes from St. Agnes' nakedness, as she was stripped before being martyred. But either explanation is unlikely, since the fountain was completed two years before Borromini even started work on the church.

At the **Tre Scalini** bar (near the fountain), sample some *tartufo* "death by chocolate" ice cream, world-famous among connoisseurs of ice cream and chocolate alike (€5 to go, €10 at a table, open daily). Or get it cheaper next door (to the south) at **Ai Tre Tartufi** and chose from white chocolate or dark chocolate. Admire a painting by a struggling artist, and listen to the white noise of gushing water and exuberant café-goers.

Leave Piazza Navona directly across from the Tre Scalini bar, go east past rose peddlers and palm readers, jog left around the guarded building, and follow the brown sign to the Pantheon. The Pantheon is straight down Via del Salvatore. (There's a cheap pizza place on the left a few yards before you reach the piazza, and a WC at the McDonald's.)

Sit for a while under the floodlit and moonlit portico of the **Pantheon.** The 40-foot, single-piece granite columns of the Pantheon's entrance show the scale that the ancient Romans built on. The columns support a triangular, Greek-style roof with an inscription that says "M. Agrippa" built it. In fact, it was built *(fecit)* by Emperor Hadrian (A.D. 120), who gave credit to the builder of an earlier structure. This impressive entranceway gives no clue that the greatest wonder of the building is inside—a domed room that inspired later domes, including Michelangelo's St. Peter's and Filippo Brunelleschi's Duomo (in Florence).

With your back to the Pantheon, veer to the right down Via Orfani, toward the Albergo Abruzzi. On the right, you'll see a sign for **Tazza d'Oro Casa del Caffè,** one of Rome's top coffee shops, which dates back to the days when this area was licensed to roast coffee beans. Locals come here for its fine *granita di caffè con panna* (coffee slush with cream). Look back at the fine view of the Pantheon from here. Then take Via Orfani uphill to Piazza Capranica.

Piazza Capranica is home to the big, plain, Florentine Renaissance–style Palazzo Capranica (directly opposite as you enter the square). Big shots, like the Capranica family, built towers on their palaces—not for any military use, but just to show off. Leave the piazza to the right of the palace, between the palace and the church. The street Via Aquiro leads to a sixth-century B.C. **Egyptian obelisk** (taken as a trophy by Augustus after his victory in Egypt over Mark Antony and Cleopatra). The obelisk was set up as a sundial. Walk the zodiac markings to the front door of the guarded parliament building.

To your right is Piazza Colonna, where we're heading next—unless you like gelato...

A short detour to the left (past Albergo National) brings you to Rome's most famous *gelateria*. **Giolitti's** is cheap for take-out or elegant and splurge-worthy for a sit among classy locals (open daily until past midnight, Via Uffici del Vicario 40); get your gelato in a cone *(cono)* or cup *(coppetta)*.

Piazza Colonna features a huge second-century column. Its reliefs depict the victories of Emperor Marcus Aurelius over the barbarians. When Marcus died in A.D. 180, the barbarians began to get the upper hand, beginning Rome's long three-century fall. The big, important-looking palace houses the headquarters for the deputies (or cabinet) of the prime minister. The **Via del Corso** is named for the Berber horse races—without riders—that took place here during Carnevale until the 1800s when a horse trampled a man to death in front of a horrified queen. Historically the street was filled with meat shops. When it became Rome's first gas-lit street in the 1800s, these butcher shops were banned and replaced by classier boutiques, jewelers, and antique dealers. Nowadays most of Via del Corso is closed to traffic every evening and becomes a wonderful parade of Romans out for a stroll (see previous walk, "The Dolce Vita Stroll").

Cross Via del Corso, Rome's noisy main drag. Turn left under the portico to enter the Y-shaped Galleria del Sordi shopping gallery, forking to the right and exiting onto Via Sabini. (But if you're here past 20:00, the shops are closed; instead, cross Via del Corso at the crosswalk and then head straight on Via dei Sabini). Head down Via dei Sabini to the roar of the water, light, and people of the Trevi Fountain.

The **Trevi Fountain** shows how Rome took full advantage of the abundance of water brought into the city by its great aqueducts. This watery Baroque avalanche was completed in 1762 by Nicola Salvi, hired by a pope who was celebrating the reopening of the ancient aqueduct that powers it. Salvi used the palace behind the fountain as a theatrical backdrop for the figure of "Ocean," who represents water in every form. The statue surfs through his wet kingdom—with water gushing from 24 spouts and tumbling over 30 different kinds of plants—while Triton blows his conch shell.

The magic of the square is enhanced by the fact that no streets directly approach it. You can hear the excitement as you approach, and then—*bam!*—you're there. The scene is always lively, with lucky Romeos clutching dates while unlucky ones clutch beers. Romantics toss a coin over their shoulder, thinking it will give them a wish and assure their return to Rome. That may sound silly, but every year I go through this tourist ritual...and it actually seems to work.

Take some time to people-watch (whisper a few breathy *bello*s or *bella*s) before leaving. There's a peaceful zone at water level on the far right.

Facing the fountain, take the street on the right (Via della Stamperia) and cross the busy Via del Tritone. Continue 100 yards and veer right at Via S. Andrea, a street that changes its name to Via Propaganda before ending at the **Piazza di Spagna,** with the very popular Spanish Steps. The piazza is named for the Spanish Embassy to the Vatican, which has been here for 300 years. It's been the hangout of many Romantics over the years (Keats, Wagner, Openshaw, Goethe, and others). The British poet John Keats pondered his mortality, then died in the pink building on the right side of the steps. Fellow Romantic Lord Byron lived across the square at #66.

The Sinking Boat Fountain at the foot of the steps, built by Bernini or his father, Pietro, is powered by an aqueduct. All of Rome's fountains are aqueduct-powered; their spurts are determined by the water pressure provided by the various aqueducts.

This one, for instance, is much weaker than Trevi's gush.

The piazza is a thriving night scene. Window-shop along Via Condotti, which stretches away from the steps. This is where Gucci and other big names cater to the trendsetting jet set.

Our walk is finished. If you'd like to head up to the top of the steps sweat-free, there's a free elevator just outside the Spagna Metro stop (elevator closes at 21:00; Metro stop is to the left of the Spanish Steps). Afterwards, you can zip home on the Metro (usually open until 22:00); or, if you'd prefer, grab a taxi at the north or south side of the piazza.

Sights

I've clustered Rome's sights into walkable neighborhoods, some quite close together (see map on page 741). For example, the Colosseum and the Forum are a few minutes' walk from Capitol Hill; a 10-minute walk beyond that is the Pantheon. I like to group these sights into one great day, starting at the Colosseum and ending at the Pantheon.

Ancient Rome
The core of the ancient city, where the grandest monuments were built, is between the Colosseum and Capitol Hill. To the north, this ancient area flows into the Renaissance at Capitol Hill, then into the modern era at Piazza Venezia.

The Colosseum and Nearby
▲▲▲Colosseum (Colosseo)—This 2,000-year-old building is the classic example of Roman engineering. The Romans pioneered the use of concrete and the rounded arch, which enabled them to build on this tremendous scale. While the essential structure is Roman, the four-story facade is decorated with the three types of Greek columns—Doric (ground level), Ionic (second story), Corinthian, and, on the top, half-columns with a mix of all three. Built when the Roman Empire was at its peak in A.D. 80, the Colosseum represents Rome at its grandest. The Flavian Amphitheater (Anfiteatro Flavio, its real name) was an arena for gladiator contests and public spectacles. When killing became a spectator sport, the Romans wanted to share the fun with as many people as possible, so they stuck two semicircular theaters together to create a freestanding amphitheater. The outside (where slender cypress trees stand today) was decorated with a 100-foot-tall bronze statue of Nero that gleamed in the sunlight. In a later age, the colossal structure was nicknamed a "coloss-eum," the wonder of its age. It could accommodate 50,000 roaring fans (100,000 thumbs). The whole thing was topped with an enormous canvas

awning that could be hoisted across by armies of sailors to provide shade for the spectators—the first domed stadium. This was where ancient Romans—whose taste for violence was the equal of modern America's—enjoyed their *Dirty Harry* and *Terminator*. Gladiators, criminals, and wild animals fought to the death in every conceivable scenario. The new bit of reconstructed Colosseum floor gives you an accurate sense of the original floor and the subterranean warren where animals were held, then lifted up in elevators. Released at floor level, the animals would pop out from behind blinds into the arena—the gladiator didn't know where, when, or by what he'd be attacked.

Cost, Hours, Location: €11 combo-ticket includes Palatine Hill and Roman Forum, ticket valid two days—one entry per sight. It's also covered by the €20 Roma Pass—see page 746. The Colosseum is open daily 8:30 until one hour before sunset (April–Sept until 19:00, Oct until 18:15, Nov–Feb until 16:15, March until 16:30). Last entry is one hour before closing.

A dry but fact-filled audioguide is available just past the turnstiles (€4.50 for 2 hours of use). A handheld **videoguide** senses where you are in the site and plays related video clips (€5.50, pick up after turnstiles). Guided 45-minute to one-hour **tours** in English depart nearly hourly between 9:45 and 17:15 (€4, purchase inside the Colosseum near the ticket counter at windows marked *Visite Guidate*). Taking the official Colosseum tour allows you to skip the ticket line. Metro: Colosseo. Information tel. 06-3996-7700.

Vendors outside the entrance sell handy little *Rome: Past and Present* books with plastic overlays to un-ruin the ruins (marked €25 with DVD, price soft so offer less). Tiny, crowded WCs are inside; the better, bigger, and cleaner WC is behind the Colosseum (facing ticket entrance, go right; WC is under stairway). Caution: For a fee, the incredibly crude modern-day gladiators snuff out their cigarettes and pose for photos. They take easy-to-swindle tourists for too much money. Watch out if you tangle with these guys (they're armed...and accustomed to getting as much as €100 from naive tourists). If you go for it, €4–5 for one photo usually keeps them appeased.

Avoiding Lines: The lines in front of the Colosseum are for buying tickets and for security checks, not for actually entering the sight. While everyone has to wait in the security line to go through the metal detectors, once you're through that—if you have your ticket already—stay to the left and muscle your way past the ticket-buying crowd to go directly to the turnstile, which never has a line. You'll likely save lots of time if you get your ticket in advance using one of these alternatives:

1. Consider buying the €20 Roma Pass or €22 Archeologia

Card at a less-crowded sight, and then use it to bypass the ticket-buying line at the Colosseum; you can insert your pass directly into the turnstile. Note: You can buy a Roma Pass at the *tabacchi* shop in the Colosseo Metro station; at the entrance to Palatine Hill; or at the entrance to the Forum (as well as online or by phone). For details on these passes, see page 746.

2. Buy and print your ticket online, choosing the day you'll visit and paying a €1.50 booking fee (www.ticketclic.it). Note that "free tickets" are valid only for EU citizens with ID.

3. Buy your ticket at the less-crowded Palatine Hill entrance on Via di San Gregorio (facing the Forum, with Colosseum at your back, go left down the street). Technically, the Palatine Hill entry is "entrance-only," but this rule is not strictly enforced, meaning you could buy the ticket, exit, and head straight back to the Colosseum.

4. Purchase a €4 guided tour. Tickets for official tours, offered hourly by the Colosseum's guides, are available inside the Colosseum near the ticket counter. Tell the guard that you want to purchase a guided tour and he will usher you toward the ticket booth.

Private walking-tour guides (or their American assistants) linger outside the Colosseum, offering tours that include the admission fee and allow you to skip the line. This will cost you a few extra euros (€21 for two-hour tours of the Colosseum, Palatine Hill, and Forum, including the €11 ticket), but can save time; however, unscrupulous private guides might tell you that there's a long line, when really there's no line at all. They might say the Palatine Hill and Forum are included in their tour, only to give just a few minutes of commentary. (They purchase a group Colosseum ticket, but say "ciao" after the Colosseum tour, leaving you to buy a new ticket for Palatine Hill and the Forum.) Also note that you may buy a tour ticket to save time, only to get stuck waiting for the guide to sell enough tickets to assemble a group.

▲**Arch of Constantine**—If you are a Christian, were raised a Christian, or simply belong to a so-called "Christian nation," ponder this arch. It marks one of the great turning points in history— the military coup that made Christianity mainstream. In A.D. 312, Emperor Constantine defeated his rival Maxentius in the crucial Battle of the Milvian Bridge. The night before, he had seen a vision of a cross in the sky. Constantine—whose mother and sister were Christians—became sole emperor and legalized Christianity. With this one battle, a once-obscure Jewish sect with a handful of followers was now the state religion of the entire Western world. In A.D. 300, you could be killed for being a Christian; later, you could be killed for not being one. Church enrollment boomed.

This newly restored arch is like an ancient museum. It's

decorated entirely with recycled carvings originally made for other buildings. By covering it with exquisite carvings of high Roman art—works that glorified previous emperors—Constantine put himself in their league. Hadrian is featured in the round reliefs, with Marcus Aurelius in the square reliefs higher up. The big statues on top are of Trajan and Augustus. Originally, Augustus drove a chariot similar to the one topping the modern Victor Emanuel II monument. Fourth-century Rome may have been in decline, but Constantine clung to its glorious past.

▲**St. Peter-in-Chains Church (San Pietro in Vincoli)**—Built in the fifth century to house the chains that held St. Peter, this church is most famous for its Michelangelo statue. Check out the much-venerated chains under the high altar, then focus on mighty Moses (free, daily 8:00–12:30 & 15:00–19:00, until 18:00 in winter, modest dress required; the church is a 15-minute, uphill, zigzag walk from the Colosseum, or a shorter, simpler walk from the Cavour Metro stop—exiting the Metro stop, go up the steep flight of steps, take a right at the top, and walk a block to the church). Note that this isn't the famous St. Peter's Basilica, which is in the Vatican City.

Pope Julius II commissioned Michelangelo to build a massive tomb, with 48 huge statues, crowned by a grand statue of this egomaniacal pope. The pope had planned to have his tomb placed in the center of St. Peter's Basilica. When Julius died, the work had barely been started, and no one had the money or necessary commitment to Julius to finish the project. In 1542, some of the remnants of the tomb project were brought to St. Peter-in-Chains and pieced together by Michelangelo's assistants. Some of the best statues ended up elsewhere, like the *Prisoners* in Florence, and the *Slaves* in the Louvre. *Moses* and the *Slaves* are the only statues Michelangelo personally completed for the project. Flanking *Moses* are the Old Testament sister-wives of Jacob, Leah (to our left) and Rachel, both begun by Michelangelo but probably finished by pupils.

This powerful statue of Moses—mature Michelangelo—is worth studying. The artist worked on it in fits and starts for 30 years. Moses has received the Ten Commandments. As he holds the stone tablets, his eyes show a man determined to stop his tribe from worshipping the golden calf and idols...a man determined to win salvation for the people of Israel. Why the horns? Centuries ago, the Hebrew word for "rays" was mistranslated as "horns."

Nero's Golden House (Domus Aurea)—The sparse underground remains of Emperor Nero's "Golden House" are a faint shadow of their ancient grandeur. In its heyday, the gold-leaf-encrusted residence was huge, with its original entrance all the way over at the Arch of Titus in the Forum. Nero's massive estate once sprawled across the valley (where the Colosseum now stands) and up the hill. Unfortunately, the Golden House is closed indefinitely. Even when open, it's in a sad state of ruin, more historically significant than interesting—unless you're an archaeologist. Nero (ruled A.D. 54–68) was Rome's most notorious emperor. He killed his own mother, kicked his pregnant wife to death, and crucified St. Peter. When Rome burned in A.D. 64, Nero was accused of setting the fire to clear land for his domestic building needs. The Romans rebelled, the Senate declared him a public enemy, and his only noble option was suicide. With the help of a slave, Nero stabbed himself in the neck, crying, "What an artist dies in me!" (closed indefinitely, for more information visit www.pierreci.it or call 06-3996-7700).

The Roman Forum and Nearby

▲▲▲**Roman Forum (Foro Romano)**—This is ancient Rome's birthplace and civic center, and the common ground between Rome's famous seven hills. As just about anything important that happened in ancient Rome happened here, it's arguably the most important piece of real estate in Western civilization. While only a few fragments of that glorious past remain, history-seekers find plenty to ignite their imaginations amid the half-broken columns and arches (€11 combo-ticket includes Colosseum and Palatine Hill, daily 8:30 until one hour before sunset, Metro: Colosseo, tel. 06-3996-7700). See my "Roman Forum Walk," earlier in this chapter.

▲▲▲**Palatine Hill (Monte Palatino)**—The hill above the Forum is jam-packed with history—"the huts of Romulus and Remus," the huge Imperial Palace, the House of Livia and Augustus (with four rooms of frescoes recently opened to the public), and a view of the Circus Maximus—but there are only scant remains of rubble left to tell the story.

We get our word "palace" from this hill, where the emperors chose to live. The Palatine Hill was once so filled with palaces that later emperors had to build out. (Looking up at it from the Forum, you see the substructure that supported these long-gone palaces.) The Palatine museum contains statues and frescoes that help you imagine the luxury of the imperial Palatine. From the pleasant garden, you'll get an overview of the Forum. On the far side, look down into an emperor's private stadium and then beyond at the dusty Circus Maximus, once a chariot course. Imagine the cheers, jeers, and furious betting.

While many tourists consider Palatine Hill just extra credit after the Forum, it offers an insight into the greatness of Rome that's well worth the effort. (And, if you're visiting the Colosseum or Forum, you've got a ticket whether you like it or not.)

Ancient Rome

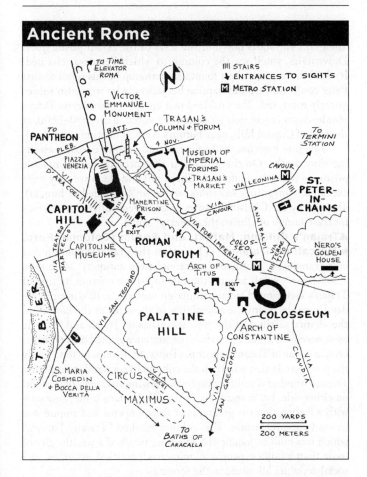

To Time Elevator Roma

Victor Emmanuel Monument

Trajan's Column + Forum

STAIRS
ENTRANCES TO SIGHTS
M METRO STATION

To Pantheon

Piazza Venezia

Batt.
4 Nov.

Museum of Imperial Forums + Trajan's Market

Cavour M

Via Leonina

To Termini Station

St. Peter-in-Chains

Capitol Hill

Mamertine Prison

Via D'Aracoeli

Pleb.

Exit

Roman Forum

Via Cavour

Via Fori Imperiali

Annibaldi

Colosseo M

Via Terme Tito

Nero's Golden House

Capitoline Museums

Via Teatro Marcello

Arch of Titus

Exit

Tiber

Via San Teodoro

Palatine Hill

Colosseum

Arch of Constantine

Via Claudia

S. Maria Cosmedin + Bocca della Verità

Circus Maximus

Via Cerchi

Via di San Gregorio

200 YARDS
200 METERS

To Baths of Caracalla

Cost, Hours, Location: €11 combo-ticket includes Roman Forum and Colosseum (ticket valid two days—one entry per site). It's also covered by the Roma Pass—see page 746. Buy a ticket or pass here to avoid lines at the Colosseum. It's open daily from 8:30 until one hour before sunset (April–Sept until 19:00, Oct until 18:15, Nov–Feb until 16:15, March until 16:30). Last entry is one hour before closing. The entrance is on Via di San Gregorio (facing the Forum with the Colosseum at your back, it's down the street to your left).

Audioguides cost €4 (must leave ID). Guided tours in English are offered once daily at 11:30 (€4, 45 min); ask for information at the ticket booth.

▲**Mamertine Prison**—This 2,500-year-old, cistern-like prison, which once held the bodies of Saints Peter and Paul, is worth a look. When you step into the room, ignore the modern floor and look up at the hole in the ceiling, from which prisoners were lowered. Then take the stairs down to the level of the actual prison floor. Downstairs, you'll see the column to which Peter was chained. It's said that a miraculous fountain sprang up in this room so that Peter could convert and baptize his jailers, who were also subsequently martyred. The upside-down cross commemorates Peter's upside-down crucifixion (donation requested, daily 9:00–19:00, at the foot of Capitol Hill, near Forum's Arch of Septimius Severus).

Imagine humans, amid fat rats and rotting corpses, awaiting slow deaths. On the walls near the entry are lists of notable prisoners (Christian and non-Christian) and the ways they were executed: *strangolati, decapitato, morto per fame* (died of hunger). The sign by the Christian names reads, "Here suffered, victorious for the triumph of Christ, these martyr saints."

▲**Trajan's Column, Market, and Forum (Colonna, Foro, e Mercati de Traiano)**—This offers the grandest column and best example of "continuous narration" from antiquity. More than 2,500 figures scroll around the 140-foot-high column, telling of Trajan's victorious Dacian campaign (circa A.D. 103, in present-day Romania), from the assembling of the army at the bottom to the victory sacrifice at the top. The ashes of Trajan and his wife were once held in the base while the sun once glinted off a polished bronze statue of Trajan at the top. (Today, St. Peter is on top.) Study the propaganda that winds up the column like a scroll, trumpeting Trajan's wonderful military exploits. Viewing balconies once stood on either side, but it seems likely that Trajan fans came away only with a feeling that the greatness of their emperor and empire was beyond comprehension. This column marked "Trajan's Forum," which was built to handle the shopping needs of a wealthy city of more than a million people. Commercial, political, religious, and social activities all mixed in the forum.

Nestled into the cutaway curve of Quirinal Hill is the semicircular brick complex of Trajan's Market. It was likely part shopping mall, part warehouse, and part administration building, though some archaeologists recently suggested it may have contained mostly government offices.

Paying the admission fee gets you inside Trajan's Market, Trajan's Forum, and the new **Museum of the Imperial Forums.** The museum features discoveries from the forums of several different emperors, as they remodeled and built over previous structures (€6.50, Tue–Sun 9:00–19:00, last entry one hour before closing, closed Mon, tel. 06-992-3521, Via IV Novembre 94, www.mercati ditraiano.it).

Trajan's Column is just a few steps off Piazza Venezia, on Via dei Fori Imperiali, across the street from the Victor Emmanuel Monument. The Museum of the Imperial Forums is uphill from the column. Trajan's Forum stretches southeast of the column toward the Colosseo Metro stop and the Colosseum itself.

Time Elevator Roma—This cheesy and overpriced show is really just for kids. The 45-minute, multi-screen show jolts you through the centuries. Equipped with headphones, you get nauseated in a comfortable, air-conditioned theater as the history of Rome unfolds before you—from the founding of the city, through its rise and fall, to its Renaissance rebound, and up to the present (€11, daily 10:30–19:30, shows at the bottom of each hour, no kids under 39 inches, just off Via del Corso, a 3-min walk from Piazza Venezia at Via dei S.S. Apostoli 20, tel. 06-9774-6243, www.time-elevator.it).

Capitol Hill Area

Of Rome's famous seven hills, this is the smallest, tallest, and most famous—home of the ancient Temple of Jupiter and the center of city government for 2,500 years. There are several ways to get to the top of Capitol Hill. (While I call it "Capitol Hill" for simplicity, it's correctly called "Capitoline Hill," and the piazza on top is called the Campidoglio). If you're coming from the north (from Piazza Venezia), take Michelangelo's impressive stairway to the right of the big, white Victor Emmanuel Monument. Coming from the southeast (the Forum), take the steep staircase near the Arch of Septimius Severus. From near Trajan's Forum along Via dei Fori Imperiali, take the winding road. All three converge at the top, in the square called Campidoglio (kahm-pee-DOHL-yoh).

▲**Capitol Hill Square (Campidoglio)**—This square atop the hill, once the religious and political center of ancient Rome, is still the home of the city's government. In the 1530s, the pope called on Michelangelo to reestablish this square as a grand center. Michelangelo placed the ancient equestrian statue of Marcus Aurelius as the square's focal point. Effective. (The original statue is now in the adjacent museum.) The twin buildings on either side are the Capitoline Museums. Behind the replica of the statue is the mayoral palace (Palazzo Senatorio).

Michelangelo intended that people approach the square from his grand stairway off Piazza Venezia. From the top of the stairway, you see the new Renaissance face of Rome, with its back to the Forum. Michelangelo gave the buildings the "giant order"—huge pilasters make the existing two-story buildings feel one-storied and more harmonious with the new square. Notice how the statues atop these buildings welcome you and then draw you in.

The terraces just downhill (past either side of the mayor's palace) offer grand views of the Forum. To the left of the mayor's palace is a copy of the famous *She-Wolf* statue on a column. Farther down is *il nasone* ("the big nose"), a refreshing water fountain.

Capitol Hill and Piazza Venezia

Legend:
- ■ CAPITOLINE MUSEUMS
- → ENTRY POINT TO SIGHTS
- Ⓜ METRO STATION
- Ⓣ TAXI STAND
- Ⓑ BUS STOP

Map labels:
- S. APOST.
- TIME ELEVATOR ROMA
- CORSO
- VIA BATTISTI
- Ⓑ #64, 40
- VIA PLEBISCITO
- ❽
- Ⓣ
- PALAZZO VENEZIA
- PIAZZA
- Ⓑ
- VENEZIA
- S. MARCO
- TRAJAN'S COLUMN
- TRAJAN'S
- TO GESÙ & PANTHEON
- Ⓑ #64
- VIA D'ARACOELI
- #110
- Ⓑ
- VICTOR EMMANUEL MONUMENT
- CAFÉ
- ❶❶
- FORUM
- Ⓣ
- VIA DEI FORI IMPERIALI
- STA. MARIA ARACOELI
- ❻
- GRAND STAIRCASE
- ❼
- PALAZZO NUOVO
- ❾
- ❶
- ❸
- TO COLOSSEUM & Ⓜ
- STATUE
- ❹
- VIA TEATRO MARCELLO
- TO ❿
- PIAZZA CAFFARELLI
- ❷
- MAMERTINE PRISON
- PUBLIC CAFÉ ENTRANCE
- ❺
- EXIT
- CAFÉ
- TABULARIUM
- ARCH OF SEPTIMIUS SEVERUS
- ❺
- PALAZZO SENATORIO
- ROMAN
- PALAZZO DEI CONSERVATORI
- SAN TEODORO
- FORUM
- DCH

100 YARDS
100 METERS

1. Campidoglio (Main Square)
2. Capitoline Museums Entrance
3. Copy of She-Wolf Statue
4. "Il Nasone" Water Fountain
5. Views of Forum
6. Shortcut to Victor Emmanuel Monument
7. Shortcut to Santa Maria in Aracoeli Church
8. Mussolini's Balcony
9. Michelangelo's Grand Staircase
10. To Teatro Marcello Ruins
11. Rome from the Sky

ROME

Block the spout with your fingers, and water spurts up for drinking. Romans joke that a cheap Roman boy takes his date out for a drink at *il nasone*. Near the *She-Wolf* statue is the staircase leading to a shortcut to the Victor Emmanuel Monument.

Shortcut to Victor Emmanuel Monument: A clever little "back door" gives you access from the top of Capitol Hill directly to the top of the Victor Emmanuel Monument, saving lots of uphill stair-climbing. Near the *She-Wolf* statue (to the left of the mayoral palace), climb the wide set of stairs (the highest set of stairs you see), pass through the iron gate at the top of the steps, and enter the small unmarked door at #13 on the right. You'll soon emerge on a café terrace at the top of the monument with vast views. The shortcut gives you easy access to several sights: the Rome from the Sky elevator, Museum of the Risorgimento (both listed under "Victor Emmanuel Monument," page 785), and Santa Maria in Aracoeli (described on the next page).

▲▲**Capitoline Museums (Musei Capitolini)**—This museum encompasses two buildings (Palazzo dei Conservatori and Palazzo Nuovo), connected by an underground passage that leads to the vacant Tabularium and panoramic views of the Roman Forum (€8, open Tue–Sun 9:00–20:00, closed Mon, last entry one hour before closing; good €5 audioguide, tel. 06-8205-9127, www.musei capitolini.org).

To identify the museum's two buildings, face the equestrian statue (with your back to the grand stairway). The Palazzo Nuovo is on your left, the Palazzo dei Conservatori (where you buy your ticket and start your self-guided tour) is on your right, closer to the river. Ahead is the Palazzo Senatorio (mayoral palace, not open to public); below it—and out of sight—is the Tabularium.

Buy your ticket and consider renting the good €5 audioguide at the Palazzo dei Conservatori entrance.

The **Palazzo dei Conservatori** is one of the world's oldest museums, founded in 1471 when a pope gave ancient statues to the citizens of Rome. In the courtyard, enjoy the massive chunks of Constantine: his head, hand, and foot. When intact, this giant held the place of honor in the Basilica of Constantine in the Forum. The museum is worthwhile, with lavish rooms and several great statues. You'll see the 13th-century *Capitoline Wolf* (the little statues of Romulus and Remus were added in the Renaissance). Don't miss the *Boy Extracting a Thorn* and the enchanting *Commodus as Hercules*. Behind Commodus is a statue of his dad, Marcus Aurelius, on a horse. The greatest surviving equestrian statue of antiquity, this was the original centerpiece of the square (where a copy stands today). While most such pagan statues were destroyed by Dark Age Christians, Marcus was mistaken for Constantine (the first Christian emperor) and therefore spared.

The second-floor café, Caffè Capitolino, has a splendid patio offering city views. It's lovely at sunset (public entrance for non-museum-goers off Piazza Caffarelli).

Go downstairs to the **Tabularium.** Built in the first century B.C., these sturdy rooms once held the archives of ancient Rome. The word Tabularium comes from "tablet," on which the Romans wrote their laws. You won't see any tablets, but you will see a superb head-on view of the Forum from the windows.

Leave the Tabularium and enter the **Palazzo Nuovo,** which houses mostly portrait busts of forgotten emperors. But it also has two must-see statues: the *Dying Gaul* and the *Capitoline Venus* (both on the first floor up).

Santa Maria in Aracoeli—This church is built on the site where Emperor Augustus (supposedly) had a premonition of the coming of Mary and Christ standing on an "altar in the sky" *(Ara Coeli).* The church is Rome in a nutshell, where you can time-travel across 2,000 years by standing in one spot (daily 9:00–12:00 & 14:30–17:30). It's atop Capitol Hill, squeezed between the Victor Emmanuel Monument and the square called Campidoglio. While dedicated pilgrims climb up the long, steep staircase from street level (the right side of Victor Emmanuel monument, as you face it), casual sightseers prefer to enter through the "back door," on the shortcut between the Capitoline Museums and Victor Emmanuel monument (described on the previous page): As you climb the stairs from Campidoglio to the shortcut, look for a sign that points left to *Santa Maria in Aracoeli.*

Piazza Venezia

This vast square, dominated by the big, white Victor Emmanuel Monument, is a major transportation hub and the focal point of modern Rome. (The square will be dug up for years—Metro line C is under construction, and when anything of archaeological importance is uncovered, progress is interrupted.) Stand with your back to the monument and look down the Via del Corso, the city's axis, surrounded by Rome's classiest shopping district. In the 1930s, Benito Mussolini whipped up Italy's nationalistic fervor from a balcony above the square (with your back to Victor Emmanuel Monument, it's the less-grand balcony on the left). Fascist masses filled the square screaming, "Four more years!"—or something like that. Mussolini created boulevard Via dei Fori Imperiali to open up views of the Colosseum in the distance to impress his visiting friend, Adolf Hitler. Mussolini lied to his people, mixing fear and patriotism to push his country to the right and embroil the Italians in expensive and regrettable wars. In 1945, they shot and hanged Mussolini from a meat hook in Milan.

Circling around the right side of the Victor Emmanuel

Monument, look down into the ditch on your left to see the ruins of an ancient apartment building from the first century A.D.; part of it was transformed into a tiny church (faded frescoes and bell tower). Rome was built in layers—almost everywhere you go, there's an earlier version beneath your feet. (The hop-on, hop-off Trambus Open 110 stops just across the busy intersection from here.)

Continuing on, you reach two staircases leading up Capitol Hill. One is Michelangelo's grand staircase up to the Campidoglio. The longer of the two leads to the Santa Maria in Aracoeli church, a good example of the earliest style of Christian churches (described on previous page). The contrast between this climb-on-your-knees ramp to God's house and Michelangelo's elegant stairs illustrates the changes Renaissance humanism brought civilization.

From the bottom of Michelangelo's stairs, look right several blocks down the street to see a condominium actually built upon the surviving ancient pillars and arches of Teatro Marcello.

Victor Emmanuel Monument—This oversize monument to Italy's first king, built to celebrate the 50th anniversary of the country's unification in 1870, was part of Italy's push to overcome the new country's strong regionalism and to create a national identity. The scale of the monument is over-the-top. The 43-foot-long statue of the king on the horse is the biggest equestrian statue in the world. The king's moustache is over five feet wide, and a person could fit into the horse's hoof. Open to the public, the structure offers a grand view of the Eternal City (free, 242 punishing steps to the top—unless you take the shortcut from Capitol Hill, described on page 783).

Locals love to hate the "Altar of the Nation." Romans think of the 200-foot-high, 500-foot-wide monument not as an altar of the fatherland, but as "the wedding cake," "the typewriter," or "the dentures." It wouldn't be so bad if it weren't sitting on a priceless acre of ancient Rome and if they had chosen better marble (this is in-your-face white and picks up the pollution horribly). Soldiers guard Italy's Tomb of the Unknown Soldier as the eternal flame flickers.

The Victor Emmanuel Monument also houses a little-visited **Museum of the Risorgimento,** which explains the movement and war that led to the unification of Italy in 1870 (free, daily 9:30–18:00, café).

▲Rome from the Sky—This elevator, located near the top of the Victor Emmanuel Monument next to the outdoor café, zips you to the rooftop for the grandest, 360-degree view of the center of Rome (even better than from the top of St. Peter's dome). Helpful panoramic diagrams describe the skyline, with powerful binoculars available for zooming in on particular sights. Go in late afternoon, when it's beginning to cool off and Rome glows (€7, May–Sept Mon–Thu 9:30–19:30, Fri–Sat 9:30–23:30, Sun

9:30–20:30; Oct–April Mon–Thu 9:30–18:30, Fri–Sun 9:30–19:30; follow signs inside the Victor Emmanuel Monument to *ascensori panoramici* or take the shortcut from Capitol Hill).

Pantheon Neighborhood: The Heart of Rome

I like to call the area around the Pantheon the "Heart of Rome." This neighborhood stretches eastward from the Tiber River through Campo de' Fiori and Piazza Navona, past the Pantheon to the Trevi Fountain. Besides the neighborhood's ancient sights and historic churches, it's also the place that gives Rome its urban-village feel. Wander narrow streets, sample the many shops and eateries, and gather with the locals in squares marked by a bubbling fountain. Exploring is especially good in the evening, when the restaurants bustle and streets are jammed with foot-traffic. For more on nocturnal sightseeing, see my "Night Walk Across Rome," earlier in this chapter.

Getting There: To reach the Pantheon neighborhood, you can walk (it's a 20-minute walk from Capitol Hill), take a taxi, or catch a bus. Buses #64 and #40 carry tourists and pickpockets frequently between the Termini train station and Vatican City, stopping at a chaotic square called Largo Argentina located a few blocks south of the Pantheon. (Take either Via dei Cestari or Via Torre Argentina north to the Pantheon.) The *elettrico* minibus #116 runs between Campo de' Fiori and Piazza Barberini via the Pantheon. The most dramatic approach is on foot coming from Piazza Navona along Via Giustiniani, which spills directly into Piazza della Rotunda, offering the classic Pantheon view.

▲▲▲**Pantheon**—For the greatest look at the splendor of Rome, antiquity's best-preserved interior is a must (free, Mon–Sat 8:30–19:30, Sun 9:00–18:00, holidays 9:00–13:00, closed for Mass Sat at 17:00 and Sun at 10:30, tel. 06-6830-0230). The audioguide is cheap, but still is probably not worth it (€3, 25 min).

Because the Pantheon became a church dedicated to the martyrs just after the fall of Rome, the barbarians left it alone, and the locals didn't use it as a quarry. The portico is called "Rome's umbrella"—a fun local gathering in a rainstorm. Walk past its one-piece granite columns (biggest in Italy, shipped from Egypt) and through the original bronze doors. Sit inside under the glorious skylight and enjoy classical architecture at its best.

The dome, 142 feet high and wide, was Europe's biggest until the Renaissance. Michelangelo's dome at St. Peter's, while much higher, is about three feet narrower. The brilliance of this dome's construction astounded architects through the ages. During the Renaissance, Brunelleschi was given permission to cut into the dome (see the little square hole above and to the right of the entrance) to analyze the material. The concrete dome gets thinner

Pantheon Neighborhood

TO PIAZZA
DEL POPOLO

TO SPANISH STEPS

TO M BARB.

PONTE UMBERTO

TIBER

PIAZZA COLONNA

VIA TRITONE

T TREVI

LUNGOTEVERE

MARZIO

VIA

SAN LUIGI (CARAVAGGIO)

PARL.

UFF. VICARIO

ANCIENT STADIUM ENTRANCE

CORONARI

COPPELLE

SABINA

MURATTE

TRE SCALINI

SALV.

AQUIRO

PIAZZA DI PIETRA

DATAR.

PIAZZA NAVONA

GIUST.

PIAZZA ROTUNDA

PASTINI

SEMINARIO

PIAZZA PASQUINO

SAN IGNAZIO

CITY MUSEUM

PANTHEON

STA. MARIA SOPRA MINERVA

GALLERIA DORA PAMPHILJ

IV NOV.

CAMPO DE' FIORI

VIA

VITTORIO

ARG.

CEST.

B T EMANUELE GESÙ

PIAZZA VENEZIA T

PALAZZO FARNESE

V. GIUBB.

VIA BOTT. OSC.

B

LARGO ARGENTINA RUINS (+ CAT HOSPICE)

CAPITOL HILL + CAP. MUSEUMS

VICTOR EM. MON.

FORI IMP.

TO COLOSSEUM + M

LUNGOTEVERE

PONTE SISTO

TO TRASTEVERE

➜ ENTRY POINT TO SIGHTS

T TAXI STAND

M METRO STATION

B BUS STOP

FORUM

200 YARDS
200 METERS

DCH

and lighter with height—the highest part is volcanic pumice.

This wonderfully harmonious architecture greatly inspired Raphael and other artists of the Renaissance. Raphael, along with Italy's first two kings, chose to be buried here.

The Pantheon is the only ancient building in Rome continuously used since its construction. When you leave, notice that the building is sunken below current street level, showing how the rest of the city has risen on 20 centuries of rubble. The nearest WCs are at bars and downstairs in the McDonald's on the square. Several reasonable eateries are a block or two north, up Via del Pantheon. Some of Rome's best gelato and coffee are nearby. For dining suggestions, see "Eating—Near the Pantheon," later in this chapter.

▲▲**Churches near the Pantheon**—The **Church of San Luigi dei Francesi** has a magnificent chapel painted by Caravaggio (free, Fri–Wed 7:30–12:30 & 15:30–19:00, Thu 8:00–12:30, sightseers should avoid Mass at 7:30 and 19:00). The only Gothic church in Rome is **Santa Maria sopra Minerva,** with a little-known Michelangelo statue, *Christ Bearing the Cross* (free, Mon–Sat 7:00–19:00, Sun 8:00–19:00, on a little square behind Pantheon, to the east). The **Church of San Ignazio,** several blocks east of the Pantheon, is a riot of Baroque illusions with a false dome (free, daily 7:30–12:30 & 15:00–19:15). A few blocks away, across Corso Vittorio Emanuele, is the rich and Baroque **Gesù Church,** head-quarters of the Jesuits in Rome (free, daily 6:30–12:45 & 16:00–19:15). Modest dress is recommended at all churches.

▲**Galleria Doria Pamphilj**—This underappreciated gallery, tucked away in the heart of the old city, fills a palace on Piazza del Collegio Romano. It offers a rare chance to wander through a noble family's lavish rooms with the prince who calls this down-town mansion home. Well, almost. Through an audioguide, the prince lovingly narrates his family's story, including how the Doria Pamphilj (pahm-FEEL-yee) family's cozy relationship with the pope inspired the word "nepotism." Highlights include paint-ings by Caravaggio, Titian, and Raphael, and portraits of Pope Innocent X by Diego Velázquez (on canvas) and Gian Lorenzo Bernini (in marble). The fancy rooms of the palace are interesting, with a mini-Versailles-like hall of mirrors and paintings lining the walls to the ceiling in the style typical of 18th-century galler-ies (€8, includes worthwhile audioguide, Fri–Wed 10:00–17:00, closed Thu, from Piazza Venezia walk 2 blocks up Via del Corso and take a left, Piazza del Collegio Romano 2, tel. 06-679-7323, www.doriapamphilj.it).

Piazza di Pietra (Piazza of Stone)—This square was actually a quarry set up to chew away at the abandoned Roman building. You can still see the holes that hungry medieval scavengers chipped into the columns to steal the metal pins that held the slabs together (two blocks toward Via del Corso from Pantheon).

▲**Trevi Fountain**—This bubbly Baroque fountain, worth ▲▲ by night, is a minor sight to art scholars...but a major nighttime gathering spot for teens on the make and tourists tossing coins. The coins tourists deposit daily are collected to feed Rome's poor. (For more information, see the end of "Night Walk Across Rome," earlier in this chapter.)

Near Termini Train Station

These sights are within a 10-minute walk of the train station. By Metro, use the Termini stop for the National Museum and the Piazza della Repubblica stop for the rest.

▲▲▲**National Museum of Rome (Museo Nazionale Romano Palazzo Massimo alle Terme)**—This museum houses the great-est collection of ancient Roman art anywhere. It's a historic year-

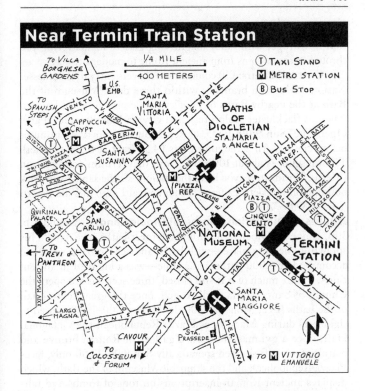

Near Termini Train Station

book of Roman marble statues with some rare Greek originals. On the ground floor alone, you can look eye-to-eye with Julius and Augustus Caesar, Alexander the Great, and Socrates.

On the first floor, along with statues and busts showing such emperors as Trajan and Hadrian, you'll see the best-preserved Roman copy of the Greek *Discus Thrower*. Statues of athletes like this commonly stood in the baths, where Romans cultivated healthy bodies, minds, and social skills. Other statues on this floor once stood in the pleasure gardens of the Roman rich—surrounded by greenery, with the splashing sound of fountains, the statues all painted in bright, lifelike colors. Though executed by Romans, the themes are mostly Greek, with godlike humans and human-looking gods.

The second floor features a collection of frescoes and mosaics that once decorated the walls and floors of Roman villas. They're remarkably realistic and un-stuffy, featuring everyday people, animals, flowery patterns, and geometrical designs. The frescoes taken from the Villa Farnese—in black, red, yellow, and blue—are mostly architectural designs, with fake columns and "windows" that "look out" on landscape scenes.

Finally, descend into the basement to see fine gold jewelry,

ROME

dice, an abacus, and vault doors leading into the best coin collection in Europe, with fancy magnifying glasses maneuvering you through cases of coins from ancient Rome to modern times.

Cost and Hours: €10 combo-ticket covers entry to three lesser National Museum branches within three days: Museum of the Bath at the nearby Baths of Diocletian (described next), Palazzo Altemps (lackluster sculptures), and Crypta Balbi (medieval art). Open Tue–Sun 9:00–19:45, closed Mon, last entry 45 minutes before closing. An audioguide costs €4.50 (rent at ticket counter). The museum is about 100 yards from the Termini train station (Metro: Termini). As you leave the station, it's the sandstone-brick building on your left. Enter at the far end, at Largo di Villa Peretti (tel. 06-3996-7700).

▲**Baths of Diocletian (Terme di Diocleziano)**—Around A.D. 300, Emperor Diocletian built the largest baths in Rome. This sprawling meeting place—with baths and schmoozing spaces to accommodate 3,000 bathers at a time—was a big deal in ancient times. While much of it is still closed, three sections are open: the Church of Santa Maria degli Angeli, once the great central hall of the baths (free, Mon–Sat 7:00–18:30, Sun 7:00–19:30, closed to sightseers during Mass, faces Piazza Repubblica); the Octagonal Hall, once a gymnasium, now a gallery of Roman bronze and marble statues (free, open sporadically Sun 9:00–13:00 only, faces Piazza Repubblica); and the skippable Museum of the Bath, which displays ancient Roman inscriptions on tons of tombs and tablets—but, despite its name, has nothing on the baths themselves (€10 combo-ticket covers entry to National Museum of Rome, Tue–Sun 9:00–19:45, closed Mon, last entry 45 min before closing, audioguide–€4, Viale E. de Nicola 79, entrance faces Termini train station, tel. 06-4782-6152).

Santa Maria degli Angeli: From noisy Piazza della Repubblica, step through the curved brick wall of the ancient baths and into the vast and cool church built upon the remains of a vast and steamy Roman bath complex. The church we see today was (at least partly) designed by Michelangelo (1561), who used the baths' main hall as the nave. Later, when Piazza Repubblica became an important Roman intersection, another architect renovated the church. To allow people to enter from the grand new piazza, he spun it 90 degrees, turning Michelangelo's nave into a long transept. The eight red granite columns in the transept are original, from ancient Rome—stand next to one and feel its five-foot girth. (Only the eight in the transept proper are original. The others are made of plastered-over brick.) In Roman times, this hall was covered with mosaics, marble, and gold, and lined with statues.

Octagonal Hall: Open only on occasional Sunday mornings, this octagonal building—capped by a dome with a hole in the top—

may have served as a cool room *(frigidarium)*, with small pools of cold water for plunging into. Or, because of its many doors, it may simply have been a large intersection, connecting other parts of the baths. Originally, the floor was 25 feet lower—as you can see through the glass-covered hole in the floor. The graceful iron grid overhead supported the canopy of a 1928 planetarium.

▲**Santa Maria della Vittoria**—This church houses Bernini's statue of a swooning *St. Teresa in Ecstasy* (free, Mon–Sat 8:30–12:00 & 15:30–18:00, closed Sun, about 5 blocks northwest of Termini train station on Largo Susanna, Metro: Repubblica).

Once inside the church, you'll find St. Teresa to the left of the altar. Teresa has just been stabbed with God's arrow of fire. Now, the angel pulls it out and watches her reaction. Teresa swoons, her eyes roll up, her hand goes limp, she parts her lips...and moans. The smiling, cherubic angel understands just how she feels. Teresa, a 16th-century Spanish nun, later talked of the "sweetness" of "this intense pain," describing her oneness with God in ecstatic, even erotic, terms.

Bernini, the master of multimedia, pulls out all the stops to make this mystical vision real. Actual sunlight pours through the alabaster windows, bronze sunbeams shine on a marble angel holding a golden arrow. Teresa leans back on a cloud and her robe ripples from within, charged with her spiritual arousal. Bernini has created a little stage-setting of heaven. And watching from the "theater boxes" on either side are members of the family that commissioned the work.

Santa Susanna Church—The home of the American Catholic Church in Rome, Santa Susanna holds Mass in English daily at 18:00 and on Sunday at 9:00 and 10:30. They arrange papal audiences (see "Vatican City" sidebar later in this chapter), and their excellent website contains tips for travelers and a long list of convents that rent out rooms (Mon–Fri 9:00–12:00 & 16:00–18:00, closed Sat–Sun, Via XX Settembre 15, near recommended Via Firenze hotels, Metro: Repubblica, tel. 06-4201-4554, www.santa susanna.org).

Pilgrim's Rome

East of the Colosseum (and south of Termini train station) are several venerable churches that Catholic pilgrims make a point of visiting.

Church of San Giovanni in Laterano—Built by Constantine, the first Christian emperor, this was Rome's most important church through medieval times. A building alongside the church houses the Holy Stairs said to have been walked up by Jesus, which today are ascended by pilgrims on their knees (free, church—daily 7:00–18:30, Holy Stairs—April–Sept 6:30–12:00

& 15:30–18:30, Oct–March 6:30–12:00 & 15:00–18:00, Piazza San Giovanni in Laterano, Metro: San Giovanni, or bus #85 or #87, tel. 06-6988-6392).

Church of Santa Maria Maggiore—Some of Rome's best-surviving mosaics line the nave of this church built as Rome was falling. The nearby Church of Santa Prassede has still more early mosaics (free, daily 8:00–18:30, Piazza Santa Maria Maggiore, Metro: Termini or Vittorio Emanuele, tel. 06-48-3058).

▲Church of San Clemente—Besides the church itself, with frescoes by Masolino, you can also descend into the ruins of an earlier church. Descend yet one more level and enter the eerie remains of a pagan temple to Mithras (upper church—free, lower church—€5, both open Mon–Sat 9:00–12:30 & 15:00–18:00, Sun 12:00–18:00, Via di San Giovanni in Laterano, Metro: Colosseo, or bus #85 or #87, tel. 06-7045-1018).

North Rome

Borghese Gardens and Via Veneto

▲Villa Borghese Gardens—Rome's scruffy, three-square-mile "Central Park" is great for its shade and people-watching (plenty of modern-day Romeos and Juliets). The best entrance is at the head of Via Veneto (Metro: Barberini and 10-minute walk up Via Veneto). There you'll find a cluster of buildings with a café, a kiddie arcade, a cinema center, and bike rental (€6/4 hrs). Rent a bike and follow signs to discover the park's cafés, fountains, statues, museums (including the Borghese Gallery and Etruscan Museum—listed in this section), lake, and prime picnic spots. A park TI near the Borghese Gallery has info on the park and Rome sights (TI hours: April–Sept Mon–Thu 9:00–17:00, Fri–Sun 9:00–19:00; Oct–March daily 9:00–17:00; facing Borghese Gallery, turn left, walk 30 yards down, turn right toward the gate and find the poorly marked TI immediately on the left).

▲▲▲Borghese Gallery (Galleria Borghese)—This plush museum, filling a cardinal's mansion in the park, was recently restored and offers one of Europe's most sumptuous art experiences. You'll enjoy a collection of world-class Baroque sculpture, including Bernini's *David* and his excited statue of Apollo chasing Daphne, as well as paintings by Caravaggio, Raphael, Titian, and Rubens. The museum's slick mandatory reservation system keeps the crowds at a manageable size.

The essence of the collection is the connection of the Renaissance with the classical world. As you enter, notice the second-century Roman reliefs with Michelangelo-designed panels above either end of the portico. The villa was built in the early 17th century by the great art collector Cardinal Scipione Borghese, who wanted to prove that the glories of ancient Rome were matched by

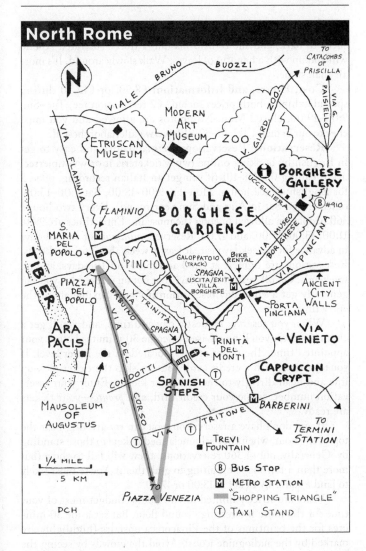

North Rome

the Renaissance.

In the main entry hall, opposite the door, notice the thrilling first-century Greek sculpture of a horse falling. The Renaissance-era rider was added by Pietro Bernini, father of the famous Gian Lorenzo Bernini.

Each room seems to feature a Baroque masterpiece. The best of all is in Room III: Bernini's *Apollo and Daphne*. It's the perfect Baroque subject—capturing a thrilling, action-filled moment. In the mythological story, Apollo races after Daphne. Just as he's about to reach her, she calls to her father to save her. Magically,

ROME

her fingers begin to sprout leaves, her toes become roots, her skin turns to bark, and she transforms into a tree. Frustrated Apollo will end up with a handful of leaves. Walk slowly around. It's more air than stone.

Cost, Hours, and Information: €8.50, or €12.50 during special exhibits; both prices include €2 reservation fee, Tue–Sun 9:00–19:00, closed Mon. No photos are allowed and you must check your camera. Tel. 06-32-810, www.galleriaborghese.it.

Reservations: Reservations are mandatory and easy to get in English by booking online (www.ticketeria.it or www.pierreci .it) or calling 06-328-101 (if you get an Italian recording, press 2 for English; office hours: Mon–Fri 9:00–18:00, Sat 9:00–13:00, office closed Sat in Aug and Sun year-round). Every two hours, 360 people are allowed to enter the museum. Entry times are 9:00, 11:00, 13:00, 15:00, and 17:00. Reserve a *minimum* of several days in advance for a weekday visit, at least a week ahead for weekends. Reservations are tightest at 11:00 and 15:00, on Tuesdays, and on weekends. On off-season weekdays (but not on weekends), you can generally get a same-day reservation if you're flexible about the entry time.

When you reserve, request a day and time, and you'll get a claim number; you'll be advised to come 30 minutes before your appointed time. The ticket office is located on the lower level. If you're paying with a credit card, you can skip the ticket pick-up line and head directly to the computer kiosks. Enter your reservation number, swipe your credit card, and *pronto*—your tickets are ready.

If you don't have a reservation, you can try arriving near the top of the hour, when they sell unclaimed tickets to those standing by. Generally, out of 360 reservations, a few will fail to show (but more than a few may be waiting to grab them). You're most likely to land a stand-by ticket at 13:00 or 17:00.

Visits are strictly limited to two hours. Budget most of your time for the more interesting ground floor, but set aside 30 minutes for the paintings of the Pinacoteca upstairs (highlights are marked by the audioguide icons). Avoid the crowds by seeing the Pinacoteca first. The fine bookshop and cafeteria are best visited outside your two-hour entry window.

Tours: Excellent €7 guided English tours are offered at 10 minutes past each entry time except 17:00; Jan–March only at 9:10 and 11:10; book the tour when you make your museum reservation (or consider the fine 90-minute audioguide tour for €5).

Getting There: The museum is set idyllically but inconveniently in the vast Villa Borghese Gardens. To avoid missing your appointment, allow yourself plenty of time to find the place. A taxi drops you 100 yards from the museum. Your destination is the Galleria Borghese: gah-leh-REE-ah bor-GAY-zay). Be sure *not* to tell the cabbie "Villa Borghese"—which is the park, not the museum. Getting to the museum by public transportation can be confusing, and requires a walk in the park. The best public-transportation service is bus #910, which goes from the Termini train station to the Via Pinciana stop (a few steps from the villa). From the Spagna Metro stop (or the Spanish Steps), it's a 15-minute walk: From inside the Metro station, the quickest route is to follow signs to Via Veneto (not Villa Borghese). You'll continue on an underground labyrinth of escalators and moving sidewalks. Once you hit the supermarket, take a right up the stairs of the exit marked *uscita Villa Borghese.* At the top, turn left and head straight ahead—you'll see signs to the Gallery.

Etruscan Museum (Villa Giulia Museo Nazionale Etrusco)— The fascinating Etruscan civilization thrived in this part of Italy in about 600 B.C., when Rome was an Etruscan town. The Villa Giulia (a fine Renaissance palace) hosts a museum that tells the story. While I prefer the Vatican Museum's Etruscan section for a first look at this civilization, aficionados of all things Etruscan come here for the famous "husband and wife sarcophagus" (a dead couple seeming to enjoy an everlasting banquet from atop their tomb—sixth century B.C. from Cerveteri); the *Apollo from Veii* statue (of textbook fame); and an impressive room filled with gold sheets of Etruscan printing and temple statuary from the Sanctuary of Pyrgi (€4, Tue–Sun 9:00–19:30, closed Mon, closes earlier off-season, last entry one hour before closing, Piazzale di Villa Giulia 9, tel. 06-322-6571).

Via Veneto—In the 1960s, movie stars from around the world paraded down curvy Via Veneto, one of Rome's glitziest night-spots. Today, it's still lined with the city's poshest hotels and the American Embassy, but any hint of local color has faded to bland.

▲Cappuccin Crypt—If you want to see artistically arranged bones, this is the place. The crypt is below the church of Santa Maria della Immacolata Concezione on Via Veneto, just up from Piazza Barberini. The bones of more than 4,000 monks who died between 1528 and 1870 are in the basement, all lined up for the delight—or disgust—of the always-wide-eyed visitor. The soil in the crypt was brought from Jerusalem 400 years ago, and the monastic message on the wall explains that this is more than just a macabre exercise: "We were what you are...you will become what we are now. Buon giorno." Pick up a few of Rome's most interesting postcards (donation requested, daily 9:00–12:00 & 15:00–18:00, Metro: Barberini, tel. 06-487-1185). Just up the street, you'll find the American Embassy, Federal Express, Hard Rock Café, and fancy Via Veneto cafés filled with the poor and envious looking for the rich and famous.

Piazza del Popolo—This vast, oval square marks the traditional north entrance to Rome (its oval shape dates from the early 19th century). Today the square, known for its symmetrical design and its art-filled churches, is the starting point for the city's evening *passeggiata* (see "The Dolce Vita Stroll," earlier in this chapter). From the Flaminio Metro stop, pass through the third-century Aurelian Wall via the Porta del Popolo gate, and look south. The 10-story obelisk in the center of the square once graced the temple of Ramses II in Egypt and the Roman Circus Maximus racetrack. The obelisk was brought here in 1589 as one of the square's beautification projects. At the south side of the square, twin domed churches mark the spot where three main boulevards exit the square and form a trident. The central boulevard (running between the churches) is Via del Corso, which since ancient times has been the main north-south drag through town, running to Capitol Hill (the governing center) and the Forum. Along the north side of the square (flanking the Porta del Popolo) are two more buildings giving the square a pleasant symmetry: the Carabinieri station and the church of Santa Maria del Popolo.

From the square, the *Tridente* of roads takes people south to the city center (along Via del Corso); to the Spanish Steps (via Babuino) and to the Tiber River (via Ripetta). Two large fountains grace the sides of the square: Neptune to the west and Roma to the east (marking the base of Pincio Hill). Though the name Piazza del Popolo means "Square of the People" (and it is a popular hangout), the word was probably derived from the Latin *populus*, after the poplar trees along the square's northeast side.

Santa Maria del Popolo—One of Rome's most overlooked churches, this features two chapels with top-notch art and a facade built of travertine scavenged from the Colosseum. The church is brought to you by the Rovere family, which produced two popes, and you'll see their symbol—the oak tree and acorns—throughout (free, Mon–Sat 7:00–12:00 & 16:00–19:00, Sun 8:00–13:30 & 16:30–19:30; on north side of Piazza del Popolo; as you face gate in old wall from the square, church entrance is to your right).

Inside, the Chigi Chapel (second on the left) was designed by Raphael and inspired (as Raphael was) by the Pantheon. Notice the Pantheon-like dome, pilasters, and capitals. Above in the oculus, God looks in, aided by angels who power the eight known planets. Raphael built the chapel for his wealthy banker friend, Agostino Chigi, buried in the pyramid-shaped tomb in the wall to the right of the altar. Later, Chigi's great-grandson hired Bernini to make two of the four statues, and Bernini delivered a theatrical episode. In the Cerasi Chapel (left of altar), Caravaggio's *The Conversion on the Way to Damascus* shows Paul sprawled on his back beside his horse while his servant looks on. The startled future saint is blinded by the harsh light as Jesus' voice asks him, "Why do you persecute me?" In the style of the Counter-Reformation, Paul receives his new faith with open arms.

In the same chapel, Caravaggio's *Crucifixion of St. Peter* is shown as a banal chore; the workers toil like faceless animals. The light and dark are in high contrast. Caravaggio liked to say, "Where light falls, I will paint it."

Spanish Steps Area

▲**Spanish Steps**—The wide, curving staircase, culminating with an obelisk between two Baroque church towers, makes for one of Rome's iconic sights. Beyond that, it's a people-gathering place. By day, the area hosts shoppers looking for high-end fashions; on warm evenings, it attracts young people in love with the city. For more information, see my "Night Walk Across Rome," earlier in this chapter.

"Shopping Triangle"—The triangular-shaped area between the Spanish Steps, Piazza Venezia, and Piazza del Popolo (along Via del Corso) contains Rome's highest concentration of upscale boutiques and fashion stores.

▲▲**Ara Pacis (Altar of Peace)**—On January 30, 9 B.C., soon-to-be-emperor Augustus led a procession of priests up the steps and into this newly built "Altar of Peace." They sacrificed an animal on the altar and poured an offering of wine, thanking the gods for helping Augustus pacify barbarians abroad and rivals at home. This marked the dawn of the Pax Romana (c. A.D. 1–200), a Golden Age of good living, stability, dominance, and peace *(pax)*. The Ara Pacis (AH-rah PAH-chees) hosted annual sacrifices by the emperor until the area was flooded by the River Tiber. Buried under silt, it was abandoned and forgotten until the 16th century, when various parts were discovered and excavated. Mussolini gathered the altar's scattered parts and reconstructed them here in 1938. In 2006, the Altar of Peace reopened to the public in a striking modern building. As the first new building allowed to be built in the old center since 1938, it was controversial, but its quiet, air-conditioned interior may signal the dawn of another new age in Rome.

The Altar of Peace was originally located east of here, along today's Via del Corso. A model shows where it stood in relation to the Mausoleum of Augustus (now next door) and the Pantheon. Approach the Ara Pacis and look through the doorway to see the raised altar. This simple structure has just the basics of a Roman temple: an altar for sacrifices surrounded by cubicle-like walls that enclose a consecrated space. Its well-preserved reliefs celebrate Rome's success.

The reliefs on the north and south sides probably depict the parade of dignitaries who consecrated the altar, while reliefs on the west side (near the altar's back door) celebrate the two things Augustus brought to Rome: peace (goddess Roma as a conquering Amazon, right side) and prosperity (fertility goddess). Imagine the altar as it once was, standing in an open field, painted in bright colors—a mingling of myth, man, and nature.

Cost, Hours, Location: €6.50, tightwads can look in through huge windows for free; Tue–Sun 9:00–19:00, closed Mon, last entry one hour before closing; audioguide (€3.50) also available as free podcast at www.arapacis.it, good WC downstairs. The Ara Pacis is a long block west of Via del Corso on Via di Ara Pacis, on the east bank of the Tiber near Ponte Cavour, Metro: Spagna; a 10-minute walk down Via dei Condotti. Tel. 06-32-111-1605.

Catacombs of Priscilla (Catacombe di Priscilla)—For the most intimate catacombs experience—and a chance to see beyond the core of the historic center—many prefer this smaller, lesser-known option (operated by nuns) to the crowded catacombs on the Appian Way (San Sebastiano and San Callisto, both described later in this chapter). The Catacombs of Priscilla, once situated under the house of a Roman noble family, were used for some of the most important burials during antiquity. Best of all, because they're on the opposite side of town from the most popular catacombs, you'll have them mostly to yourself. The catacombs' evocative chambers supposedly show the first depiction of Mary nursing the baby Jesus (€6, Tue–Sun 8:30–12:00 & 14:30–17:00, last entry 30 min before closing, closed Mon, northeast of Termini station at Via Salaria 430, closed one random month a year—check website or call first, tel. 06-862-06272, http://web.tiscali.it/catacombe_priscilla).

Vatican City

Vatican City, a tiny independent country, contains the Vatican Museum (with Michelangelo's Sistine Chapel) and St. Peter's Basilica (with Michelangelo's exquisite *Pietà*). A helpful **TI** is just to the left of St. Peter's Basilica as you're facing it (Mon–Sat 8:30–19:00, closed Sun, tel. 06-6988-1662, Vatican switchboard tel. 06-6982, www.vatican.va). The entrances to St. Peter's and to the Vatican Museum are a 15-minute walk apart (follow the outside of the Vatican wall, which links the two sights). The nearest Metro stops still involve a 10-minute walk to either sight: for St. Peter's, the closest stop is Ottaviano; for the Vatican Museum, it's Cipro.

Vatican Museum (Musei Vaticani)

The four miles of displays in this immense museum, rated ▲▲▲, range from ancient statues to Christian frescoes to modern paintings, culminating in the Raphael Rooms and Michelangelo's glorious Sistine Chapel. (If you have binoculars, bring them.) This is

Vatican Museum Overview

TO OTTAVIANO METRO

VIA LEONE IV

VIA D. SCIPIONI

TO CIPRO METRO

VIA SEB. VENIERO

VIALE VATICANO

V. GERMANICO

PIAZZA DEL RISORGIMENTO

VIA DI PORTA ANGELICA

VATICAN GARDENS

PAPAL APARTMENTS

ST. PETER'S BASILICA

ELEV.

ATRIUM

OBELISK

ST. PETER'S SQUARE

N

200 YARDS

200 METERS

━━━ VATICAN WALL

▓ VATICAN MUSEUM

VATICAN MUSEUM ENTRY TO OBELISK
VIA ROAD IS A 15-MINUTE WALK

❶ Main Entrance & Exit
❷ Egyptian Rooms
❸ Cortile della Pigna
❹ Octagonal Courtyard
❺ Tapestries

❻ Map Gallery & View of Vatican City
❼ Raphael Rooms
❽ Sistine Chapel & Exit to St. Peter's
❾ Pinacoteca
❿ Cafeteria

ROME

one of Europe's top three or four houses of art. It can be exhausting, so plan your visit carefully, focusing on a few themes. Allow two hours for a quick visit, three or four hours for enough time to enjoy it.

Start, as Western civilization did, in **Egypt and Mesopotamia.** Next, the Pio Clementino collection features **Greek and Roman statues.** Decorating its courtyard are some of the best Greek and Roman statues in captivity, including the *Laocoön* group (first century B.C., Hellenistic) and the *Apollo Belvedere* (a second-century Roman copy of a Greek original). The centerpiece of the next hall is the *Belvedere Torso* (just a 2,000-year-old torso, but one that had a great impact on the art of Michelangelo). Finishing off the classical statuary are two fine fourth-century porphyry sarcophagi. These royal purple tombs were made (though not used) for the Roman emperor Constantine's mother and daughter. They were Christians—and therefore outlaws—until Constantine made Christianity legal (A.D. 312). Both sarcophagi were quarried and worked in Egypt. The technique for working this extremely hard stone (a special tempering of metal was required) was lost after this, and porphyry was not chiseled again until Renaissance times in Florence.

After long halls of tapestries, old maps, broken penises, and fig leaves, you'll come to what most people are looking for: the Raphael Rooms (or *stanza*) and Michelangelo's Sistine Chapel.

These outstanding works are frescoes. A fresco (meaning "fresh" in Italian) is technically not a painting. The color is mixed into wet plaster, and, when the plaster dries, the painting is actually part of the wall. This is a durable but difficult medium, requiring speed and accuracy, as the work is built one patch at a time.

After fancy rooms illustrating the "Immaculate Conception of Mary" (in the 19th century, the Vatican codified this hard-to-sell doctrine, making it a formal part of the Catholic faith) and the triumph of Constantine (with divine guidance, which led to his conversion to Christianity), you enter rooms frescoed by **Raphael** and his assistants. The highlight is the newly restored *School of Athens*. This is remarkable for its blatant pre-Christian classical orientation, especially since it originally wallpapered the apartments of Pope Julius II. Raphael honors the great pre-Christian thinkers—Aristotle, Plato, and company—who are portrayed as the leading artists of Raphael's day. The bearded figure of Plato is Leonardo da Vinci. Diogenes, history's first hippie, sprawls alone in bright blue on the stairs, while Michelangelo broods in the foreground—supposedly added later. Apparently, Raphael snuck a peek at the Sistine Chapel and decided that his arch-competitor was so good that he had to put their personal differences aside and include him in this tribute to the artists of his generation. Today's St. Peter's was under construction as Raphael was working. In the *School of Athens*, he gives us a sneak preview of the unfinished church.

Next is the brilliantly restored **Sistine Chapel.** This is the pope's personal chapel and also the place where, upon the death of the ruling pope, a new pope is elected (as in April 2005).

The Sistine Chapel is famous for Michelangelo's pictorial culmination of the Renaissance, showing the story of creation, with a powerful God weaving in and out of each scene through that busy first week. This is an optimistic and positive expression of the High Renaissance and a stirring example of the artistic and theological maturity of the 33-year-old Michelangelo, who spent four years on this work.

Later, after the Reformation wars had begun and after the Catholic army of Spain had sacked the Vatican, the reeling Church began to fight back. As part of its Counter-Reformation, a much older Michelangelo was commissioned to paint the *Last Judgment* (behind the altar). Brilliantly restored, the message is as clear as the day Michelangelo finished it: Christ is returning, some will go to hell and some to heaven, and some will be saved by the power of the rosary.

In the recent and controversial restoration project, no paint was added. Centuries of dust, soot (from candles used for lighting and Mass), and glue (added to make the art shine) were removed, revealing the bright original colors of Michelangelo. Photos are allowed (without a flash) elsewhere in the museum, but as part of the deal with the company who did the restoration, no photos are allowed in the Sistine Chapel.

For a shortcut, a small door at the far-right corner of the Sistine Chapel allows groups and individuals (without an audio-guide) to escape directly to St. Peter's Basilica. If you exit here, you're done with the museum. The Pinacoteca is the only important part left. Consider doing it at the start. Otherwise it's a 15-minute heel-to-toe slalom through tourists from the Sistine Chapel to the entry/exit.

After this long march, you'll find the **Pinacoteca** (the Vatican's small but fine collection of paintings, with Raphael's *Transfiguration*, Leonardo's unfinished *St. Jerome*, and Caravaggio's *Deposition*), a cafeteria (long lines, uninspired food), and the underrated early-Christian art section, before you exit via the souvenir shop.

Cost, Hours, Information: €14, Mon–Sat 9:00–18:00, last entry at 16:00 (the official closing time is 18:00, but the staff starts ushering you out at 17:30), closed on religious holidays and Sun except last Sun of the month (when it's free, more crowded, and open 8:30–14:00, last entry 12:30). Hours are notoriously subject to constant change and frequent holidays; check the hours and

Vatican City

This tiny independent country of little more than 100 acres, entirely within Rome, has its own postal system, armed guards, helipad, mini-train station, and radio station (KPOP). Politically powerful, the Vatican is the religious capital of 1.1 billion Roman Catholics. If you're not a Catholic, become one for your visit.

The pope is both the religious and secular leader of Vatican City. For centuries, locals referred to him as "King Pope." Italy and the Vatican didn't always have good relations. In fact, after unification (in 1870), when Rome's modern grid plan was built around the miniscule Vatican, it seemed as if the new buildings were designed to be just high enough so no one could see the dome of St. Peter's from street level. Modern Italy was created in 1870, but the Holy See didn't recognize it as a country until 1929, when the pope and Mussolini signed the Lateran Pact, giving sovereignty to the Vatican and a few nearby churches.

Like every European country, Vatican City has its own versions of the euro coin (with a portrait of Pope Benedict XVI, and before him, of Pope John Paul II). You're unlikely to find one in your pocket, though, as they are snatched up by collectors before falling into circulation.

Small as it is, Vatican City has two huge sights: St. Peter's Basilica (with Michelangelo's *Pietà*) and the Vatican Museum (with the Sistine Chapel). The Vatican **post office,** with offices on St. Peter's Square (next to TI) and in the Vatican Museum, is famous for its stamps (Mon–Sat 8:30–18:30, closed Sun). Vatican stamps are good throughout Rome, but for a Vatican postmark, you need to mail your cards from the Vatican; write your postcards ahead of time. (The Vatican won't mail cards with Italian stamps.)

Seeing the Pope: Your best chances for a sighting are on Sunday and Wednesday. The pope usually gives a blessing at noon on Sunday from his apartment on St. Peter's Square (except in July and August, when he speaks at his summer residence at Castel Gandolfo, 25 miles from Rome, reachable by train from Termini station). St. Peter's is easiest (just show up) and, for most, enough of a "visit." For a more formal appearance (but not more intimate), get a ticket for the Wednesday general audience (at 10:30) when the pope, arriving in his bulletproof Popemobile, greets and blesses the crowds at St. Peter's from a balcony or canopied platform on the square (except in winter, when he speaks at 10:30 in the 7,000-seat Aula Paolo VI Auditorium, next to St. Peter's Basilica). To see St. Peter's—but not the pope—minimize crowd problems by avoiding these times.

For the Wednesday general audience, while anyone can observe from a distance, you need a ticket to actually get close to the papal action. To find out the pope's schedule, call 06-6988-4631. Tickets are free and easy to get, but must be picked up on Tuesday for the Wednesday service. You can get tickets from Santa Susanna Church or the papal guard (at the Vatican).

Santa Susanna Church hands out tickets Tuesdays 17:00–

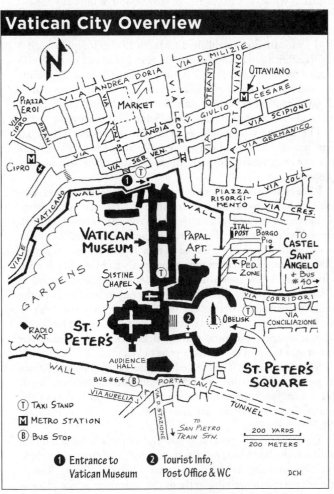

Vatican City Overview

OTTAVIANO
VIA D. MILIZIE
VIA ANDREA DORIA
VIA OTRANTO
VIALE GIULIO CESARE
VIA SCIPIONI
PIAZZA EROI
VIA CIPRO
VIA PISANI
MARKET
VIA CANDIA
V. LEONE
V. GIULIO
VIA OTTAVIANO
VIA GERMANICO
CIPRO
VIA SEB. VEN.
VATICANO WALL
PIAZZA RISORGI-MENTO
VIA COLA
WALL
VIA CRES.
VATICAN MUSEUM
PAPAL APT.
ITAL POST
BORGO PIO
TO CASTEL SANT' ANGELO
VIALE
GARDENS
SISTINE CHAPEL
PED. ZONE
& BUS #40
VIA CORRIDORI
RADIO VAT.
ST. PETER'S
OBELISK
VIA CONCILIAZIONE
WALL
AUDIENCE HALL
ST. PETER'S SQUARE
BUS #64
PORTA CAV.
VIA AURELIA
TUNNEL
VIA D. STAZIONE
TO SAN PIETRO TRAIN STN.

- (T) TAXI STAND
- (M) METRO STATION
- (B) BUS STOP

200 YARDS
200 METERS

❶ Entrance to Vatican Museum
❷ Tourist Info, Post Office & WC

DCH

18:45 (Via XX Settembre 15, near recommended Via Firenze hotels, Metro: Repubblica, tel. 06-4201-4554, www.santa susanna.org). They have plenty, but to be safe, have a ticket held for you by emailing tickets@santasusanna.org. Their hours are timed in the hopes that you'll stay for the English Mass at 18:00.

Probably less convenient—because of the long line—is picking up a ticket at St. Peter's Square from the Vatican guard at their station at the bronze doors (under the "elbow" of Bernini's colonnade, on the right side of the square as you face the basilica) Tuesdays 12:00–19:30; just join the line.

While many visitors come hoping for a more intimate audience, private audiences ended with the death of Pope John Paul II. Pope Benedict doesn't do them.

calendar at www.vatican.va. Tel. 06-6988-3860 or 06-6988-1662.

The museum is closed on many holidays (mainly religious ones) including, for 2010: Jan 1 (New Year's), Jan 6 (Epiphany), Feb 11 (Vatican City established), March 19 (St. Joseph), April 4 and 5 (Easter Sunday and Monday), May 1 (Labor Day), May 13 (Ascension Thursday), June 3 (Corpus Christi), June 29 (Saints Peter and Paul), Aug 15 plus either Aug 14 or 16—it varies year to year (Assumption of the Virgin), Nov 1 (All Saints' Day), Dec 8 (Immaculate Conception), and Dec 25 and 26 (Christmas).

The Sistine Chapel closes before the museum. Individual rooms may close at odd hours, especially after 13:00. TV screens inside the entrance list closures. The rooms described here are usually open.

Reservations: An online reservation system lets you book tickets up to 60 days in advance (€4 fee per ticket, http://biglietteriamusei.vatican.va/tickets). You can reserve up to 10 tickets. The museum will send you a confirmation email—print this out since it includes a bar code they'll scan when you arrive. At the museum, use the line for group tours and individuals with reservations. At the museum, show your voucher to the guard at the Vatican entrance. (The line for reservation holders is to the right of the entrance; bypass the ticket-buying lines and don't be shy about getting the guard's attention.) Once you're let inside (and past security), go upstairs to the ticket windows, present your voucher and ID, and they'll issue your ticket.

Avoiding Lines: The best entry time is 12:30 or later, since tour groups tend to come to the museum early in the morning or right before lunchtime. Another good time to go is during the papal audience on Wednesday after 10:30 when many tourists are at St. Peter's Basilica.

The museum is generally hot and crowded, especially on Saturdays, the last Sunday of the month (when it's free), Mondays, rainy days, and any day before or after a holiday closure. There's little advantage to arriving early in the morning, as the place is already mobbed with early-bird tour groups when it opens—which keeps the whole line moving slowly.

Most mornings, particularly if you arrive before the opening time, the ticket-buying line stretches around the block. (Stuck in the line? Figure about a 10-minute wait for every 100 yards. If the line stretches all the way to St. Peter's Square, count on waiting nearly two hours.) If you arrive without tickets before the museum opens, be sure to line up against the Vatican City wall (to the left of the entrance as you face it); the other line (to the right of the entrance) is for guided tours and individuals with reservations. There is no guaruntee of entry.

Modest dress (no short shorts or bare shoulders) is required.

While this dress code may not be strictly enforced here, it is at St. Peter's Basilica.

Tours: Both **private tour companies** and **private guides** offer guided English tours of the museum, usually allowing you to skip the long ticket-buying line. If going with a tour, look for the tour entrance (to the right of the individuals entrance), which sometimes has a shorter line. For a listing of several companies, see "Tours," page 755. These tours can be expensive—shop around for the best deal.

The Vatican offers English tours, but these are extremely difficult to join—they can book up as much as a year in advance (for details, see www.vatican.va). If you don't hear back—which you likely won't—it means they're full. If you do sign up, you'll enter through the group-tours entrance.

Audioguide Tours: If you rent a €6 **audioguide** (available at the top of the ramp/escalator), you lose the option of taking the shortcut from the Sistine Chapel to St. Peter's (audioguides must be returned at museum entrance).

St. Peter's Basilica

Rated ▲▲▲, there is no doubt: This is the richest and most impressive church on earth. To call it vast is like calling Einstein smart. Marks on the floor show where the next-largest churches would fit if they were put inside. The ornamental cherubs would dwarf a large man. Birds roost inside, and thousands of people wander about, heads craned heavenward, hardly noticing each other. Don't miss Michelangelo's *Pietà* (behind bulletproof glass) to the right of the entrance. Bernini's altar work and seven-story-tall bronze canopy are brilliant.

For a quick walk through the basilica, follow these points (see map on next page):

❶ The atrium is larger than most churches. The huge white columns on the portico date from the first church (fourth century). Notice the historic doors (the Holy Door, on the right, won't be opened until the next Jubilee Year, in 2025).

❷ The purple, circular porphyry stone marks the site of Charlemagne's coronation in A.D. 800 (in the first St. Peter's church that stood on this site). From here, get a sense of the immensity of the church, which can accommodate 60,000 worshippers standing on its six acres.

❸ Michelangelo planned a Greek-cross floor plan, rather than the Latin-cross standard in medieval churches. A Greek cross, symbolizing the perfection of God, and by association the goodness of man, was important to the humanist Michelangelo. But accommodating large crowds was important to the Church in the fancy Baroque age, which followed Michelangelo, so the original

St. Peter's Basilica

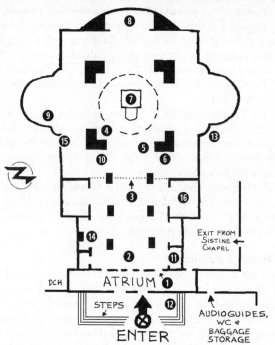

ST.   PETER'S   SQUARE

❶ Holy Door

❷ Charlemagne's Coronation Site

❸ Extent of Original "Greek Cross" Church Plan

❹ St. Andrew Statue & View of Dome

❺ St. Peter Statue (With Kissable Toe)

❻ Pope John XXIII

❼ Main Altar (Directly Over Peter's Tomb)

❽ BERNINI – Dove Window & "Throne of Peter"

❾ St. Peter's Crucifixion Site

❿ RAPHAEL – The Transfiguration (Mosaic Copy)

⓫ MICHELANGELO – Pietà

⓬ Line for Crypt & Dome Visits

⓭ Elevator to Roof & Dome-Climb

⓮ Roof & Dome-Climb Exit

⓯ Museum-Treasury

⓰ Blessed Sacrament Chapel

nave length was doubled. Stand halfway up the nave and imagine the stubbier design that Michelangelo had in mind.

❹ View the magnificent dome from the statue of St. Andrew. See the vision of heaven above the windows: Jesus, Mary, a ring of saints, rings of angels, and, on the very top, God the Father.

❺ The statue of St. Peter, with an irresistibly kissable toe, is one of the few pieces of art that predate this church. It adorned the first St. Peter's church.

❻ Circle to the right around the statue of Peter to find the lighted glass niche with the red-robed body of Pope John XXII (r. 1958–1693), who oversaw major reforms in the Vatican II conference.

❼ The main altar sits directly over St. Peter's tomb and under Bernini's seven-story bronze canopy.

❽ St. Peter's throne and Bernini's starburst dove window is the site of a daily Mass (Mon–Sat at 17:00, Sun at 17:30).

❾ St. Peter was crucified here when this location was simply "the Vatican Hill." The obelisk now standing in the center of St. Peter's square marked the center of a Roman racecourse long before a church stood here.

❿ The church is filled with mosaics, not paintings. Notice the mosaic version of Raphael's *Transfiguration*.

⓫ Michelangelo sculpted his *Pietà* when he was 24 years old. (A *pietà* is a work that represents Mary with the body of Christ taken down from the cross.) Michelangelo's mastery of the body is obvious in this powerfully beautiful masterpiece. Jesus is believably dead, and Mary, the eternally youthful "handmaiden" of the Lord, accepts God's will...even if it means giving up her son.

The Holy Door (to the right of the *Pietà*, covered in gray concrete with a gold cross) won't be reopened until Christmas Eve, 2024, the dawn of the next Jubilee Year. Every 25 years, the Church celebrates an especially festive year derived from the Old Testament idea of the Jubilee Year (originally every 50 years), which encourages new beginnings and the forgiveness of sins and debts. In Jubilee Year 2000, Pope John Paul II tirelessly—and with significant success—promoted debt relief for the world's poorest countries.

⓬ Visitors can go down to the Crypt within the foundations of Old St. Peter's, containing tombs of popes and memorial chapels. Exit the basilica and turn left to head down the steps (back out the way you entered, unless you took the Vatican Museum shortcut). You'll see people here lined up to visit the Crypt, and to ride up to the dome.

⓭ & ⓮ An elevator leads to the roof and the stairway up the dome (€7, allow an hour to go up and down). The dome, Michelangelo's last work, is (you guessed it) the biggest anywhere.

Taller than a football field is long, it's well worth the sweaty climb for a great view of Rome, the Vatican grounds, and the inside of the basilica—particularly heavenly while there is singing. Look around—Rome has no modern skyline. No building is allowed to exceed the height of St. Peter's. The elevator takes you to the rooftop of the nave. From there, a few steps take you to a balcony at the base of the dome looking down into the church interior. After that, the one-way, 323-step climb (for some people, it's claustrophobic) to the cupola begins. The rooftop level (below the dome) has a gift shop, WC, drinking fountain, and a commanding view.

⓯ For most, the museum (in the sacristy) is not worth the admission.

⓰ Blessed Sacrament Chapel.

Dress Code: No shorts or bare shoulders (applies to men, women, and children), and no miniskirts. This dress code is strictly enforced.

Hours of Church: Daily April–Sept 7:00–19:00, Oct–March 7:00–18:00. The church closes on Wednesday mornings during papal audiences. The best time to visit the church is early or late; I like to be here at 17:00, when the church is fairly empty, sunbeams can work their magic, and the late-afternoon Mass fills the place with spiritual music.

Tours: The Vatican TI conducts free 90-minute tours of St. Peter's (depart Mon–Fri from TI, confirm schedule at TI, tel. 06-6988-1662). Audioguides can be rented near the checkroom (€5, daily 9:00–17:00).

Tours are the only way to see the Vatican Gardens. Book at least two weeks in advance by faxing 06-6988-5100 or emailing visiteguidate.musei@scv.va; no response means they're fully booked (€18, Tue, Thu, and Sat; verify times when you reserve; tours start at Vatican Museum tour desk and finish on St. Peter's Square).

Excellent Vatican guides take groups of 12 to the excavations in the well-lit pagan Necropolis and the saint's grave (€10, 2 hours, ages 15 and older only, book well in advance by emailing scavi@fsp .va, fax to 06-6987-3017, or ask directly by calling the Excavations Office—Mon–Sat 9:00–17:00, closed Sun and holidays, tel. 06-6988-5318). Follow the detailed instructions at www.vatican.va to submit a request. No response to your fax or email means they're fully booked. The Crypt is open for free to the public, but this tour gets you closer to St. Peter's grave.

Cost and Hours of Dome: The view from the dome is worth the climb (€5 to walk up, or €7 for elevator to roof, then climb 323 steps to the top of the dome, allow an hour to go up and down, daily April–Sept 8:00–17:00, Oct–March 8:00–16:00).

Sights near Vatican City
▲**Castel Sant'Angelo**—Built as a tomb for the emperor; used through the Middle Ages as a castle, prison, and place of last refuge for popes under attack; and today, visited as a museum, this giant pile of ancient bricks is packed with history.

Ancient Rome allowed no tombs within its walls—not even the emperor's. So Emperor Hadrian grabbed the most commanding position just outside the walls and across the river and built a towering tomb (c. A.D. 139) well within view of the city. His mausoleum was a huge cylinder (210 by 70 feet) topped by a cypress grove and crowned by a huge statue of Hadrian himself riding a chariot. For nearly a hundred years, Roman emperors (from Hadrian to Caracalla, in A.D. 217) were buried here.

In the year 590, the Archangel Michael appeared above the mausoleum to Pope Gregory the Great. Sheathing his sword, the angel signaled the end of a plague. The fortress that was Hadrian's mausoleum eventually became a fortified palace, renamed for the "holy angel."

Castel Sant'Angelo spent centuries of the Dark Ages as a fortress and prison, but was eventually connected to the Vatican via an elevated corridor at the pope's request (1277). Since Rome was repeatedly plundered by invaders, Castel Sant'Angelo was a handy place of last refuge for threatened popes. In anticipation of long sieges, rooms were decorated with papal splendor (you'll see paintings by Carlo Crivelli, Luca Signorelli, and Andrea Mantegna). In 1527, during a sack of Rome by troops of Charles V of Spain, the pope lived inside the castle for months with his entourage of hundreds (an unimaginable ordeal, considering the food service at the top-floor bar).

Touring the place is a stair-stepping workout. After you walk around the entire base of the castle, take the small staircase down to the original Roman floor (following the route of Hadrian's funeral procession). In the atrium, study the model of the mausoleum as it was in Roman times. Imagine being surrounded by a veneer of marble, and the niche in the wall filled with a towering "welcome to my tomb" statue of Hadrian. From here, a ramp leads to the right, spiraling 400 feet. While some of the fine original brickwork and bits of mosaic survive, the marble veneer is long gone (notice the holes in the wall that held it in place). At the end of the ramp, a bridge crosses over the room where the ashes of the emperors were kept. From here, the stairs continue out of the ancient section and into the medieval structure (built atop the mausoleum) that housed the papal apartments. Don't miss the Sala del Tesoro (Treasury), where the wealth of the Vatican was locked up in a huge chest. (*Do* miss the 58 rooms of the military museum.) From the pope's piggy bank, a narrow flight of stairs leads to the rooftop and perhaps the finest Rome view anywhere—pick out landmarks as you stroll around. From the safety of this dramatic vantage point, the pope surveyed the city in times of siege. Look down at the bend of the Tiber, which for 2,700 years has cradled the Eternal City.

Cost, Hours, Location: €5, Tue–Sun 9:00–19:30, closed Mon, audioguide-€4, last entry one hour before closing, near Vatican City, Metro: Lepanto or bus #64, tel. 06-3996-7600.

Ponte Sant'Angelo—The bridge leading to Castel Sant'Angelo was built by Hadrian for quick and regal access from downtown to his tomb. The three middle arches are actually Roman originals, and a fine example of the empire's engineering expertise. The statues of angels (each bearing a symbol of the Passion of Christ—nail, sponge, shroud, and so on) are Bernini-designed and textbook Baroque. In the Middle Ages, this was the only bridge in the area that connected St. Peter's and the Vatican with downtown Rome. Nearly all pilgrims passed this bridge to and from the church. Its shoulder-high banisters recall a tragedy: During a Jubilee Year festival in 1450, the crowd got so huge that the mob pushed out the original banisters, causing nearly 200 to fall to their deaths.

Trastevere

Trastevere (trahs-TAY-veh-ray) is the colorful neighborhood across *(tras)* the Tiber *(Tevere)* River and offers the best look at medieval-village Rome. The action unwinds to the chime of the church bells. Go there and wander. Wonder. Be a poet. This is Rome's Left Bank.

This proud neighborhood was long a working-class area. Now that it's becoming trendy, high rents are driving out the source of so much color. Still, it's a great people scene, especially at night. Stroll the back streets (for restaurant recommendations, see "Eating," later in this chapter).

To reach Trastevere by foot from Capitol Hill, cross the Tiber on Ponte Cestio (over Isola Tiberina). You can also take tram #8 from Largo Argentina, or bus #H from Termini train station and Via Nazionale (get off at Piazza Belli). From the Vatican (Piazza Risorgimento), it's bus #23 or #271.

Linking Trastevere with the "Night Walk Across Rome": You can walk from Trastevere to Campo de' Fiori to link up with the beginning of the "Night Walk Across Rome" (earlier in this chapter): From Trastevere's church square (Piazza di Santa Maria), take Via del Moro to the river and cross at Ponte Sisto, a pedestrian bridge that has a good view of St. Peter's dome. Continue straight ahead for one block. Take the first left, which leads down Via di Capo di Ferro through the scary and narrow darkness to Piazza Farnese, with the imposing Palazzo Farnese. Michelangelo

Trastevere

Sights

① Ponte Cestio & Isola Tiberina
② Church of Santa Maria in Trastevere

Hotel/Restaurants

③ Hotel Santa Maria
④ Casa San Giuseppe
⑤ Trattoria da Lucia
⑥ Trattoria da Olindo
⑦ Osteria Ponte Sisto
⑧ Rist. Checco er Carettiere
⑨ Pizzeria "Ai Marmi"
⑩ To Cantina Paradiso Wine & Cocktail Bar
⑪ Gelateria alla Scala

contributed to the facade of this palace, now the French Embassy. The fountains on the square feature huge, one-piece granite hot tubs from the ancient Roman Baths of Caracalla. One block from there (opposite the palace) is the atmospheric square of Campo de' Fiori.

▲**Santa Maria in Trastevere Church**—One of Rome's oldest churches, this was made a basilica in the fourth century, when Christianity was legalized (free, daily 7:00–21:00). It was the first church dedicated to the Virgin Mary. The portico (covered area just outside the door) is decorated with fascinating ancient fragments filled with early Christian symbolism. Most of what you see dates from about the 12th century, but the granite columns are from ancient Roman buildings (notice the mismatched capitals, some with tiny pagan heads of Egyptian gods), and the ancient basilica floor plan (and ambience) survives. The intricate coffered ceiling has an unusual image of Mary painted on copper at the center. The striking 12th-century mosaics behind the altar are notable for their portrayal of Mary—which local tour guides claim is the first to show her at the throne with Jesus in heaven. Below, the scenes from the life of Mary (mosaics by Cavallini, 1300s) predate the Renaissance by a hundred years.

The church is on Piazza di Santa Maria, the Trastevere neighborhood's most important meeting place. During major soccer games, a large screen is set up here so that everybody can share in the tension and excitement. At other times, children gather here with a ball and improvise matches of their own.

▲**Villa Farnesina**—Here's a unique opportunity to see a sumptuous Renaissance villa in Rome decorated with Raphael paintings. It was built in the early 1500s for the richest man in Renaissance Europe, Siennese banker Agostino Chigi. Architect Baldassare Peruzzi's design—a U-shaped building with wings that enfold what used to be a vast garden—successfully blended architecture and nature in a way that both ancient and Renaissance Romans loved. Orchards and flowerbeds flowed down in terraces from the palace to the riverbanks. Later construction of modern embankments and avenues robbed the garden of its grandeur, leaving it with a more melancholy charm.

In the **Loggia of Galatea,** find Raphael's painting of the nymph Galatea (on the wall by the entrance door). Galatea is considered Raphael's vision of female perfection—not a portrait of an individual woman, but a composite of his many lovers in an idealized vision. Raphael and his assistants also painted the subtly erotic **Loggia of Psyche.**

Cost, Hours, Location: €5; April–June and mid-Sept–Oct Mon–Sat 9:00–16:00, closed Sun; July–mid-Sept and Nov–March Mon–Sat 9:00–13:00, closed Sun; across the river from Campo de' Fiori, a short walk from Ponte Sisto on Via della Lungara, tel. 06-6802-7268.

Gianicolo Hill Viewpoint—From this park atop a hill, the city views are superb, and the walk to the top holds a treat for architecture buffs. Start at Trastevere's Piazza di San Cosimato, and follow Via Luciano Manara to Via Garibaldi, at the base of the hill. Via Garibaldi winds its way up the side of the hill to the church of San Pietro in Montorio. To the right of the church, in a small courtyard, is the **Tempietto** by Donato Bramante. This tiny church, built to commemorate the martyrdom of St. Peter, is considered a jewel of Italian Renaissance architecture. Continuing up the hill, Via Garibaldi connects to Passeggiata del Gianicolo. From here, you'll find a pleasant park with panoramic city views. Ponder the many Victorian-era statues, including that of baby-carrying, gun-wielding, horse-riding Anita Garibaldi. She was the Brazilian wife of the revolutionary General Giuseppe Garibaldi, who helped forge a united Italy in the late 19th century.

Near Trastevere: Jewish Quarter

From the 16th through the 19th centuries, Rome's Jewish population was forced to live in a cramped ghetto at an often-flooded bend of the Tiber River. While the medieval Jewish ghetto is long gone, this area—just across the river and toward Capitol Hill from Trastevere—is still home to Rome's synagogue and fragments of its Jewish heritage.

Synagogue (Sinagoga) and Jewish Museum (Museo Ebraico)—Rome's modern synagogue stands proudly on the spot where the medieval Jewish community lived in squalor for more than 300 years. The site of a historic visit by Pope John Paul II, this synagogue features a fine interior and a museum filled with artifacts of Rome's Jewish community. Modest dress is required. The only way to visit the synagogue—unless you're here for daily prayer service—is with a tour (€7.50 ticket includes museum and guided hourly tour of synagogue; June–Sept Sun–Thu 10:00–19:00, Fri 10:00–16:00, closed Sat; Oct–May Sun–Thu 10:00–17:00, Fri 9:00–14:00, closed Sat; English tours usually at :15 past the hour, 30 min, check schedule at ticket counter; on Lungotevere dei Cenci, tel. 06-6840-0661, www.museoebraico.roma.it). Walking tours of the Jewish ghetto are conducted at least once a day (€8, daily except Sat, usually at 13:15, sign up at museum 30 min before departure, minimum of 3 required).

Southeast Rome

The Ancient Appian Way

Baths of Caracalla (Terme di Caracalla)—Inaugurated by Emperor Caracalla in A.D. 216, this massive bath complex could accommodate 1,600 visitors at a time. Today, it's just a shell—a huge shell—with all of its sculptures and most of its mosaics moved to museums. You'll see a two-story, roofless brick building surrounded by a garden, bordered by ruined walls. The two large rooms at either end of the building were used for exercise. In between the exercise rooms was a pool flanked by two small mosaic-floored dressing rooms. Niches in the walls once held statues.

In its day, this was a remarkable place to hang out. For ancient Romans, bathing was a social experience. The Baths of Caracalla functioned until Goths severed the aqueducts in the sixth century. In modern times, grand operas are performed here (€5, Mon 9:00–14:00, Tue–Sun 9:00–19:15—closing time is one hour before sunset, last entry one hour before closing, audioguide-€4, good €8 guidebook can be read in shaded garden while sitting on a chunk of column, Metro: Circus Maximus, plus a 5-minute walk south along Via delle Terme di Caracalla, tel. 06-3996-7700). The baths' statues are displayed elsewhere: Several are in the Octagonal Hall at the Baths of Diocletian, and the immense *Toro Farnese* (a marble sculpture of a bull surrounded by people) snorts in Naples' Archaeological Museum.

▲**The Appian Way**—For a taste of the countryside around Rome and more wonders of Roman engineering, take the four-mile trip from the Colosseum out past the wall to a stretch of the ancient Appian Way, where the original pavement stones are lined by several interesting sights. Ancient Rome's first and greatest highway, the Appian Way once ran from Rome to the Adriatic port of Brindisi, the gateway to Greece. Today, you can walk (or bike) some stretches of the road, rattling over original paving stones, past crumbling monuments that once lined the sides.

The wonder of its day, the Appian Way (named after Appius Claudius Caecus, a Roman official) was the largest, widest, fastest road ever, called the "Queen of Roads." Built in 312 B.C., it connected Rome with Capua (near Naples), running in a straight line for much of the way, ignoring the natural contour of the land. Just as Hitler built the Autobahn system in anticipation of empire maintenance, the expansion-minded Roman government realized the military and political value of a good road system.

Today, the road and the landscape around it are preserved as a cultural park. For the tourist, the ancient Appian Way means three things: the road itself with its ruined monuments, the best two Christian catacombs open to visitors (described on page 816), and the peaceful atmosphere, which provides a respite from the city. Be aware, however, that the road today is busy with traffic—and actually quite treacherous in spots.

The road starts at the massive **San Sebastiano Gate and Museum of the Walls,** about two miles south of the Colosseum

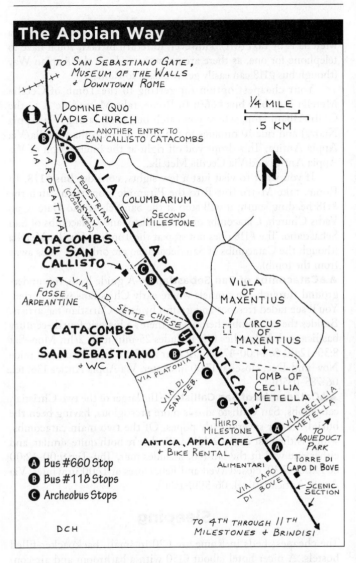

The Appian Way

TO SAN SEBASTIANO GATE,
MUSEUM OF THE WALLS
& DOWNTOWN ROME

DOMINE QUO
VADIS CHURCH

ANOTHER ENTRY TO
SAN CALLISTO CATACOMBS

¼ MILE

.5 KM

VIA ARDEATINA

VIA APPIA

PEDESTRIAN WALKWAY (CLOSED WED)

COLUMBARIUM

SECOND
MILESTONE

CATACOMBS
OF SAN
CALLISTO

TO
FOSSE
ARDEATINE

VIA D. SETTE CHIESE

VILLA
OF
MAXENTIUS

CIRCUS
OF
MAXENTIUS

CATACOMBS
OF
SAN SEBASTIANO
& WC

VIA PLATONIA

VIA DI SAN SEB.

VIA APPIA ANTICA

TOMB OF
CECILIA
METELLA

VIA CECILIA METELLA

A Bus #660 Stop

B Bus #118 Stops

C Archeobus Stops

THIRD
MILESTONE

ANTICA APPIA CAFFE
+ BIKE RENTAL

ALIMENTARI

VIA CAPO DI BOVE

TO
AQUEDUCT
PARK

TORRE DI
CAPO DI BOVE

SCENIC
SECTION

DCH

TO 4TH THROUGH 11TH
MILESTONES & BRINDISI

(€2.60, Tue–Sun 9:00–14:00, closed Mon, tel. 06-7047-5284). The stretch that's of most interest to tourists starts another two miles south of the gate. I like to begin near the Tomb of Cecilia Metella, at the far (southern) end of the key sights, and work back (downhill) toward central Rome.

Getting There: You can ride the **Archeobus** from Termini train station (see page 758). This stops at all the key attractions—you can hop off, tour the sights, and pick up a later bus (runs hourly).

The easiest way to get from Rome to the Tomb of Cecilia Metella is by **taxi** (€11). However, to return by taxi, you'll have to telephone for one, as there are no taxi stands on the Appian Way (though bus #118 can easily get you back to Rome).

Your cheapest option for getting to the Tomb of Cecilia Metella is **public bus #660**: In Rome, take Metro line A to the Colli Albani stop, where you catch bus #660 (along Via Appia Nuova) and ride 10 minutes to the last stop—Cecilia Metella/Via Appia Antica. This drops you off right at the intersection of Via Appia Antica and Via Cecilia Metella.

If you want to visit just a few sights, consider **bus #118.** In Rome, take Metro line B to the Piramide stop, then catch the #118 heading south; it will stop at the San Sebastiano Gate, Quo Vadis Church, Catacombs of San Callisto, and Catacombs of San Sebastiano. The #118 does not stop at the Tomb of Cecilia Metella (though the Catacombs of San Sebastiano are only 300 yards away from the tomb).

▲▲**Catacombs of San Sebastiano**—A guide leads you underground through the tunnels where early Christians were buried. You'll see faded frescoes and graffiti by early-Christian tag artists. Besides the catacombs themselves, there's a historic fourth-century basilica with holy relics (€6, includes 25-min tour, 2/hr, Mon–Sat 8:30–12:00 & 14:00–17:30, last tour at 17:00, closed Sun and mid-Nov–mid-Dec, closes at 17:00 in winter, Via Appia Antica 136, tel. 06-785-0350).

▲▲**Catacombs of San Callisto**—The larger of the two Christian catacombs, San Callisto also is more prestigious, having been the burial site for several early popes. Of the two main catacombs, which is the best to visit? All in all, they're both quite similar, and either one will fit the bill (€6, includes tour, Thu–Tue 9:00–12:00 & 14:00–17:30, closed Wed and Feb, closes at 17:00 in winter, Via Appia Antica 110, tel. 06-5130-1580).

Sleeping

The cheapest beds in Rome are €20 in small, backpacker-filled hostels. A nicer hotel (about €150 with a bathroom and air-con) provides an oasis and refuge, making it easier to enjoy this intense and grinding city. If you're going door to door, prices are soft—so bargain. Built into a hotel's official price list is a kickback for a room-finding service or agency; if you're coming direct, they pay no kickback and may lower the price for you. Many hotels have high-season (mid-March–June, Sept–Oct) and low-season prices. If traveling outside of peak times, ask about a discount. Room rates are lowest in sweltering August. Easter, September, and Christmas

ROME

Sleep Code

(€1 = about $1.40, country code: 39)
S = Single, **D** = Double/Twin, **T** = Triple, **Q** = Quad, **b** = bathroom, **s** = shower only. Breakfast is included in all but the cheapest places. Unless I note otherwise, the staff speaks English. You can assume a hotel takes credit cards unless you see "cash only" in the listing.

To help you sort easily through these listings, I've divided the rooms into three categories based on the price for a standard double room with bath:

$$$ Higher Priced—Most rooms €200 or more.
$$ Moderately Priced—Most rooms between €130–200.
$ Lower Priced—Most rooms €130 or less.

are the most crowded and expensive. Particularly on Easter (April 4 in 2010) and Saint Peter and Paul's Day (June 29), the entire city gets booked up.

Traffic in Rome roars. With the recent arrival of double-paned windows and air-conditioning, night noise is not the problem it once was. Even so, light sleepers who ask for a *tranquillo* room will likely get a room in the back...and sleep better.

As you look over the listings, you'll notice that many hotels promise discounts to my readers who book direct (without using a room-finding service or hotel-booking website, which take a commission). To get the discount, mention this book when you reserve, then show the book upon arrival. Paying in cash can get you a discount in some places—always ask.

Most hotels are eager to connect you with a shuttle service to the airport. It's reasonable and easy for departure, but upon arrival, I just catch a cab or the train into the city.

Almost no hotels have parking, but nearly all have a line on spots in a nearby garage (about €24/day).

Although I list only four, Rome has many convents that rent out rooms. See the Church of Santa Susanna's website for a long list (www.santasusanna.org, select "Coming to Rome"). At convents, the beds are twins and English is often in short supply, but the price is right.

Consider these nun-run places, all listed in this chapter: the expensive but divine **Casa di Santa Brigida** (near Campo de' Fiori), the **Suore di Santa Elisabetta** (near Santa Maria Maggiore), the **Istituto Il Rosario** (near Piazza Venezia), and the most user-friendly of all, **Casa per Ferie Santa Maria alle Fornaci dei Padri Trinitari** (near the Vatican).

Hostels and Dorms

For easy communication with young, friendly entrepreneurs, €20 dorm beds, and some inexpensive doubles—within a 10-minute hike of the Termini train station—consider the following places (see pages 821 and 822 for descriptions): **The Beehive** (with the best €70 doubles in town, two blocks from train station) and **Casa Olmata** (near Santa Maria Maggiore). Check www.backpackers.it for more listings.

Near Termini Train Station

While not as atmospheric as other areas of Rome, the hotels near Termini train station are less expensive, restaurants are plentiful, and the many public-transportation options link it easily with the entire city. The city's two Metro lines intersect at the station, and most buses leave from here. Piazza Venezia is a 20-minute walk down Via Nazionale.

Via Firenze

Via Firenze is safe, handy, central, and relatively quiet. It's a 10-minute walk from Termini train station and the airport shuttle, and two blocks beyond Piazza della Repubblica and the TI. The Defense Ministry is nearby, so you've got heavily armed guards watching over you all night.

The neighborhood is well-connected by public transportation (with the Repubblica Metro stop nearby). Virtually all the city buses that rumble down Via Nazionale (#64, #70, #115, #640, and the #40 express) take you to Piazza Venezia (Forum) and Largo Argentina (Pantheon). From Largo Argentina, the #64 bus (jammed with people and thieves) and the #40 express bus both continue to the Vatican. Or, at Largo Argentina, you can transfer to electric trolley #8 to Trastevere (get off at first stop after crossing the river).

Phone and Internet Center is a cute little hole-in-the-wall within a block or so of several recommended hotels that's handy for getting online (€2/hr, daily 8:30–22:00, Via Modena 48, tel. 06-4890-5224). To stock your closet pantry, the **Despar Supermarket** is handy (daily 8:00–21:00, Via Nazionale 211, at the corner of Via Venezia). A 24-hour **pharmacy** near the recommended hotels is Farmacia Piram (Via Nazionale 228, tel. 06-488-4437).

$$ Hotel Oceania is a peaceful slice of air-conditioned heaven. This 19-room, manor-house-type hotel is spacious and quiet, with spotless, tastefully decorated rooms, run by a pleasant father-and-son team. While Armando (the dad) serves world-famous coffee, Stefano (the son) works to maintain a caring family atmosphere with a fine staff and provides lots of thoughtful extra touches (Sb-€125, Db-€158, Tb-€190, Qb-€212, cash preferred,

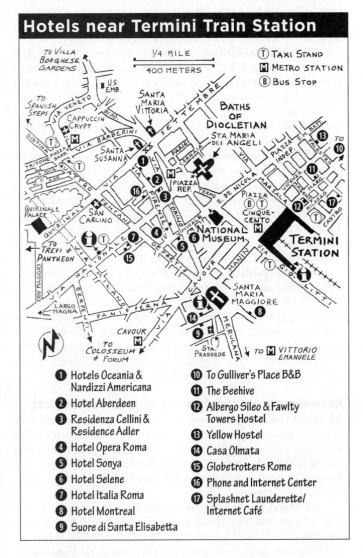

Hotels near Termini Train Station

¼ MILE
400 METERS

Ⓣ Taxi Stand
Ⓜ Metro Station
Ⓑ Bus Stop

❶ Hotels Oceania & Nardizzi Americana
❷ Hotel Aberdeen
❸ Residenza Cellini & Residence Adler
❹ Hotel Opera Roma
❺ Hotel Sonya
❻ Hotel Selene
❼ Hotel Italia Roma
❽ Hotel Montreal
❾ Suore di Santa Elisabetta
❿ To Gulliver's Place B&B
⓫ The Beehive
⓬ Albergo Sileo & Fawlty Towers Hostel
⓭ Yellow Hostel
⓮ Casa Olmata
⓯ Globetrotters Rome
⓰ Phone and Internet Center
⓱ Splashnet Launderette/ Internet Café

large roof terrace, family suite, Internet access, videos in the TV lounge, Via Firenze 38, third floor, tel. 06-482-4696, fax 06-488-5586, www.hoteloceania.it, info@hoteloceania.it, Anna and Radu round out the staff).

$$ Hotel Aberdeen, which perfectly combines high quality and friendliness, is warmly run by Annamaria, with support from cousins Sabrina and Cinzia and sister Laura. The 37 comfy, modern, air-conditioned rooms are a terrific value. Enjoy the frescoed breakfast room (Sb-€102, Db-€160, Tb-€170, Qb-€200, check website for deals, Via Firenze 48, tel. 06-482-3920, fax 06-482-1092, www.hotelaberdeen.it, hotel.aberdeen@travel.it).

$$ Residenza Cellini is a gorgeous 11-room place that feels like the guest wing of a Neoclassical palace. It offers "ortho/anti-allergy beds," four-star comforts and service, and a breezy breakfast terrace (Db-€175, larger Db-€195, Tb-€200–220, cash preferred, air-con, elevator, Internet access, Via Modena 5, tel. 06-4782-5204, fax 06-4788-1806, www.residenzacellini.it, residenzacellini@tin.it; Barbara, Gaetano, and Donato).

$$ Residence Adler, which will serve you breakfast on its garden patio, has wide halls and eight quiet, simple, air-conditioned rooms in a good location (plus more rooms in their slightly pricier Bellesuite wing). It's run the old-fashioned way by a charming family (Db-€130, Tb-€170, Qb-€195, Quint/b-€220, 5 percent cash discount, elevator, Internet access, Via Modena 5, second floor, tel. 06-484-466, fax 06-488-0940, www.hoteladler-roma.com, info@hoteladler-roma.com, Alessandro).

$ Hotel Nardizzi Americana, with 33 pleasant, air-conditioned rooms and a delightful rooftop terrace, is an excellent value (Sb-€95, Db-€123, Tb-€155, Qb-€175, email them for instructions on getting special Rick Steves rates, 15 percent discount for stays of 5 days or more, additional 10 percent off any time with cash, elevator, Internet access, Via Firenze 38, fourth floor, tel. 06-488-0035, fax 06-488-0368, www.hotelnardizzi.it, info@hotelnardizzi.it, Stefano, Fabrizio, Mario, and Samy).

Between Via Nazionale and Santa Maria Maggiore

$$ Hotel Opera Roma, brand-spanking new with contemporary furnishings and marble accents, boasts 15 fresh, spacious, but somewhat dark rooms. It's located a stone's throw from the Opera House (Db-€165, Tb-€190, air-con, elevator, Internet access, Via Firenze 11, www.hoteloperaroma.it, info@hoteloperaroma.it, tel. 06-487-1787, Rezza).

$$ Hotel Sonya is small and family-run but impersonal, with 23 well-equipped rooms, a central location, and decent prices (Sb-€90, Db-€150, Tb-€165, Qb-€185, Quint/b-200, 5 percent cash discount, air-con, elevator, faces the opera at Via Viminale 58, Metro: Repubblica or Termini, tel. 06-481-9911, fax 06-488-5678, www.hotelsonya.it, info@hotelsonya.it, Francesca and Ivan).

$$ Hotel Selene spreads its rooms out on a few floors of a big palazzo. With elegant tapestry details and room to breathe, its 40 rooms are a great value (Db-€135, Tb-€155, air-con, elevator, Via del Viminale 8, tel. 06-482-4460, www.hotelseleneroma.it, reception@hotelseleneroma.it, Federico).

$ Hotel Italia Roma, in a busy, interesting, and handy locale, is placed safely on a quiet street next to the Ministry of the Interior. Thoughtfully run by Andrea, Sabrina, Nadine, and Gabriel, it has 31 comfortable, clean, and bright rooms (Sb-€80, Db-€120, Tb-€160, Qb-€180, air-con—€10 extra per day, elevator, Internet access, Via Venezia 18, just off Via Nazionale, Metro: Repubblica or Termini, tel. 06-482-8355, fax 06-474-5550, www .hotelitaliaroma.it, info@hotelitaliaroma.it). While you must secure your reservation with a credit card, they accept only cash for payment. They also have eight decent annex rooms across the street.

$ Hotel Montreal, run with care, is a bright, solid, business-class place with 27 rooms on a big street a block southeast of Santa Maria Maggiore (Sb-€95, Db-€120, Tb-€150, air-con, elevator, Internet access, communal garden terrace, good security, Via Carlo Alberto 4, 1 block from Metro: Vittorio Emanuele, 3 blocks west of Termini train station, tel. 06-445-7797, fax 06-446-5522, www .hotelmontrealroma.com, info@hotelmontrealroma.com, Pasquale).

$ Suore di Santa Elisabetta is a heavenly Polish-run convent with a peaceful garden and tidy twin-bedded (only) rooms. Often booked long in advance, with such tranquility, it's a super value (S-€40, Sb-€48, D-€66, Db-€85, Tb-€106, Qb-€128, Quint/b-€142, elevator, fine view roof terrace and breakfast hall, 23:00 curfew, a block southwest of Santa Maria Maggiore at Via dell'Olmata 9, Metro: Termini or Vittorio Emanuele, tel. 06-488-8271, fax 06-488-4066, ist.it.s.elisabetta@libero.it, Anna).

$ Gulliver's Place B&B has five fun, nicely decorated rooms in a large, secure building next to the university (D-€90, Db-€100, Tb-€130, less off-season, air-con, elevator, east of Termini train station, 100 yards from Metro: Castro Pretorio at Viale Castro Pretorio 25, tel. 06-4470-4012, mobile 393-917-3040, www .gulliversplace.com, stay@gulliversplace.com, Simon and Sara). They run another B&B on Via Cavour (Db-€115).

Sleeping Cheaply Northeast of the Train Station

The cheapest beds in town are northeast of the Termini train station (Metro: Termini). Some travelers feel this area is weird and spooky after dark, but these hotels feel plenty safe. With your back to the train tracks, turn right and walk two blocks out of the station. **Splashnet** launderette/Internet café is handy if you're staying in this area (just off Via Milazzo at Via Varese 33, €6 full-serve wash and dry, Internet access-€1.50/hr, €2 luggage storage per day—or free if you wash and go online, daily 8:30–24:00, mobile 3906-4938-0450).

$ The Beehive gives vagabonds—old and young—a cheap, clean, and comfy home in Rome, thoughtfully and creatively run by a friendly young American couple, Steve and Linda. They offer six great-value, artsy-mod double rooms (D-€80) and an eight-bed dorm (€25 bunks, Internet access, private garden terrace, cheery café, 2 blocks north of Termini train station at Via Marghera 8, tel. 06-4470-4553, www.the-beehive.com, info@the-beehive.com).

$ **Albergo Sileo,** with shiny chandeliers in dim rooms, has a contract to house train conductors who work the night shift—so its two single rooms are rentable only from 19:00 to 9:00. The rest of their rooms are available any time of day (D-€55, Db with air-con-€75, Tb-€75, elevator, Via Magenta 39, fourth floor, tel. & fax 06-445-0246, www.hotelsileo.com, info@hotelsileo.com; friendly Alessandro and Maria Savioli don't speak English, but their daughter Anna does).

Hostels and Backpacker Dorm Beds near the Station

$ **Yellow Hostel** rents 130 beds in 4-, 6-, and 12-bed co-ed dorms ranging from about €24–34 per bed, depending on plumbing, size, and season. It's well-run with fine facilities, including lockers (reserve via email—no telephone reservations accepted, no breakfast, laptop rental available, 6 blocks from the station, just past Via Vicenze at Via Palestro 44, tel. 06-493-82682, www.the-yellow.com).

$ **Casa Olmata** is a homey, ramshackle, laid-back backpackers' haven with 50 beds a block southwest of Santa Maria Maggiore, midway between Termini train station and the Colosseum (dorm beds-€22, S-€38, D-€57, Qb-€100, sack breakfast, elevator, communal kitchen, rooftop terrace with views and twice-weekly spaghetti parties, Via dell'Olmata 36, tel. 06-483-019, fax 06-486-819, www.casaolmata.com, info@casaolmata.com, Mirella and Marco).

$ **Globetrotters Rome** is a fun little hostel in a safe and handy location. Its 22 beds in cramped quarters work fine for backpackers (€20 per bunk in 8-bed dorm, €22 per bunk in 6-bed dorm, lockers, air-con, small kitchen, closed 12:00–15:00, Via Palermo 36, tel. 06-481-7680, info@backpackers.it).

$ **Fawlty Towers Hostel** is well-run and ideal for backpackers arriving by train. It offers 50 beds and lots of fun, games, and extras (4-bed dorms-€24 per person, S-€55, D-€65, Db-€80, Q-€90, includes sheets, from station walk a block down Via Marghera and turn right to Via Magenta 39, tel. & fax 06-445-0374, www.fawltytowers.org, info@fawltytowers.org). Their nearby annex, **Bubbles,** offers similar beds and rates and shares the same reception desk.

Near Ancient Rome

Stretching from the Colosseum to Piazza Venezia along the barren boulevard called Via dei Fori Imperiali, this area is central. Sightseers are a short walk from the Colosseum, Roman Forum, and Trajan's Column. Busy Piazza Venezia—the geographical center of the city—is a major hub for city buses.

Hotels near Ancient Rome

- ❶ Hotel Paba
- ❷ Hotel Lancelot
- ❸ Hotel Nerva
- ❹ Hotel Giardino
- ❺ Istituto Il Rosario
- ❻ Enoteca Cavour 313
- ❼ Caffè dello Studente & Hostaria da Nerone Rest.

Near the Colosseum

$$ Hotel Paba has seven fresh rooms, chocolate-box-tidy and lovingly cared for by Alberta Castelli. Though it overlooks busy Via Cavour just two blocks from the Colosseum, it's quiet enough (Db-€135, extra bed-€40, 5 percent cash discount, huge beds, breakfast served in room, air-con, elevator, Via Cavour 266, Metro: Cavour, tel. 06-4782-4902, fax 06-4788-1225, www.hotelpaba.com, info @hotelpaba.com).

$$ Hotel Lancelot is a homey yet elegant refuge—a 60-room hotel with the ambience of a B&B. It's quiet and safe, with a shady

ROME

courtyard, restaurant, bar, and tiny communal sixth-floor terrace. Well-run by Faris and Lubna Khan, it's popular with returning guests (Sb-€115, Db-€180, Tb-€200, Qb-€240, €10 extra for first-floor terrace room, €15 extra for sixth-floor room with big terrace, air-con, elevator, wheelchair-accessible, parking-€10/day, 10-min walk behind Colosseum near San Clemente Church at Via Capo d'Africa 47, tel. 06-7045-0615, fax 06-7045-0640, www.lancelothotel .com, info@lancelothotel.com, Lubna speaks the Queen's English).

Near Piazza Venezia

$$$ Hotel Nerva is a three-star slice of tranquility on a surprisingly quiet back street just steps away from the Roman Forum. Its 19 rooms come with elegant touches—yours may have exposed-beam ceilings, a balcony, or floor-to-ceiling windows. It's run by brothers Umberto and Amelio, with the help of daughter Anna (Sb-€150, Db-€180, Qb with loft-€350, extra bed-€45, ask for Rick Steves discount, rates very soft—especially off-season, they also have three rooms in a nearby apartment for the same prices, big breakfast, air-con, elevator, Via Tor de' Conti 3, tel. 06-678-1835, fax 06-6992-2204, www.hotelnerva.com, info@hotelnerva.com).

$$ Hotel Giardino, thoughtfully run by kind Englishwoman Kate, offers 11 pleasant rooms in a central location three blocks northeast of Piazza Venezia. With a tiny central lobby and a small breakfast room, it suits travelers who prize location over big-hotel amenities (March–mid-July and Sept–mid-Nov: Sb-€85, Db-€130; mid-July–Aug and mid-Nov–Feb: Sb-€60, Db-€90, one smaller Db for 15 percent less; cash preferred, check website for specials, air-con, effective double-paned windows, on a busy street off Piazza di Quirinale at Via XXIV Maggio 51, tel. 06-679-4584, fax 06-679-5155, www.hotel-giardino-roma.com, info@hotel -giardino-roma.com).

$ Istituto Il Rosario is a peaceful, well-run Dominican convent renting 40 rooms to both pilgrims and tourists in a good neighborhood (reserve several months in advance, S-€42, Sb-€54, Db-€92, Tb-€122, roof terrace, 23:00 curfew, midway between the Quirinale and Colosseum near bottom of Via Nazionale at Via Sant'Agata dei Goti 10, bus #40 or #170 from Termini, tel. 06-679-2346, fax 06-6994-1106, irodopre@tin.it).

In the Pantheon Neighborhood (The Heart of Rome)

Winding, narrow lanes filled with foot traffic and lined with boutique shops and tiny trattorias...this is village Rome at its best. You'll pay for the atmosphere, but this is where you want to be—especially at night, when Romans and tourists gather in the flood-lit piazzas for the evening stroll, the *passeggiata*.

Hotels in the Heart of Rome

① Casa di Santa Brigida
② Hotel Smeraldo
③ Dipendenza Smeraldo
④ Hotel Arenula
⑤ Hotel Nazionale
⑥ Albergo Santa Chiara
⑦ Hotel Due Torri

Near Campo de' Fiori

You'll pay a premium (and endure a little extra night noise) to stay in the old center. But each of these places is romantically set deep in the tangled back streets near the idyllic Campo de' Fiori and, for many, worth the extra money.

$$$ Casa di Santa Brigida overlooks the elegant Piazza Farnese. With soft-spoken sisters gliding down polished hallways and pearly gates instead of doors, this lavish 20-room convent makes exhaust-stained Roman tourists feel like they've died and gone to heaven. If you don't need a double bed, it's worth the splurge (Sb-€110, twin Db-€190, 3 percent extra if you pay with credit card, can pay with personal check for no extra charge, air-con, elevator,

Internet access, tasty €25 dinners, roof garden, plush library, Monserrato 54, tel. 06-6889-2596, fax 06-6889-1573, piazza farnese@brigidine.org, many of the sisters are from India and speak English). If you get no response to your fax or email within three days, consider that a "no."

$$ Hotel Smeraldo, with 50 rooms, is strictly run, clean, and a great deal (Sb-€100, Db-€130, Tb-€150, buffet break-fast-€7, centrally controlled air-con, elevator, flowery roof terrace, midway between Campo de' Fiori and Largo Argentina at Vicolo dei Chiodaroli 9, tel. 06-687-5929, fax 06-6880-5495, www.smeraldoroma.com, albergosmeraldoroma@tin.it, Massimo). Their **Dipendenza Smeraldo,** 10 yards around the corner at Via dei Chiavari 32, is more bare and basic, and €10 less per night (same contact info).

In the Jewish Ghetto

$$ Hotel Arenula, with 50 decent rooms, is the only hotel in Rome's old Jewish ghetto. While it has the ambience of a gym and attracts lots of students, it's a good value in the thick of old Rome (Sb-€95, Db-€130, extra bed-€21, air-con, just off Via Arenula at Via Santa Maria de' Calderari 47, tel. 06-687-9454, fax 06-689-6188, www.hotelarenula.com, info@hotelarenula.com, Rosanna).

Near the Pantheon

These places are buried in the pedestrian-friendly heart of ancient Rome, each within a four-minute walk of the Pantheon. You'll pay more here—but you'll save time and money by being exactly where you want to be for your early and late wandering.

$$$ Hotel Nazionale, a four-star landmark, is a 16th-century palace that shares a well-policed square with the Parliament building. Its 92 rooms are accentuated by lush public spaces, fancy bars, a uniformed staff, and a marble-floored restaurant. It's a big, stuffy hotel with a revolving front door, but it's a worthy splurge if you want security, comfort, and ancient Rome at your doorstep (Sb-€200, Db-€350, giant deluxe Db-€480, extra person-€70, ask for Rick Steves discount; check online for summer and week-end discounts; air-con, elevator, Piazza Montecitorio 131, tel. 06-695-001, fax 06-678-6677, www.hotelnazionale.it, info@hotel nazionale.it).

$$$ Albergo Santa Chiara is big, solid, and hotelesque. Flavia, Silvio, and their fine staff offer marbled elegance (but basic furniture) and all the hotel services in the old center. Its ample public lounges are dressy and professional, and its 99 rooms are quiet and spacious (Sb-€140, Db-€217, Tb-€262, book online direct and request special Rick Steves rates, check website for better slow-time deals, elevator, behind Pantheon at Via di Santa Chiara 21, tel. 06-687-2979, fax 06-687-3144, www.albergosantachiara.com, info@albergosantachiara.com).

$$$ Hotel Due Torri, hiding out on a tiny, quiet street, is a beautifully located, high-class affair. It feels professional yet homey, with an accommodating staff, generous public spaces, and 26 comfortable rooms scattered by a higgledy-piggledy floor plan (Sb-€120, Db-€200, family apartment-€255 for 3 and €280 for 4, air-con, Internet access, elevator, a block off Via della Scrofa at Vicolo del Leonetto 23, tel. 06-6880-6956, fax 06-686-5442, www.hotelduetorriroma.com, hotelduetorri@mclink.it, Cinzia).

In Trastevere

Colorful and genuine in a gritty sort of way, Trastevere is a treat for travelers looking for a less touristy and more bohemian atmosphere. Choices are few here, but by trekking across the Tiber, you can have the experience of being comfortably immersed in old Rome. To locate the following two places, see the map on page 811.

$$$ Hotel Santa Maria sits like a lazy hacienda in the midst of Trastevere. Surrounded by a medieval skyline, you'll feel as if you're on some romantic stage set. Its 19 small but well-equipped, air-conditioned rooms—former cells in a cloister—are all on the ground floor, as are a few suites for up to six people. The rooms circle a gravelly courtyard of orange trees and stay-awhile patio furniture (Db-€180, Tb-€220, prices higher for stays shorter than three nights, cash preferred, family rooms, free loaner bikes and Internet access, face church on Piazza Maria Trastevere and go right down Via della Fonte d'Olio 50 yards to Vicolo del Piede 2, tel. 06-589-4626, fax 06-589-4815, www.htlsantamaria.com, hotelsantamaria@libero.it, Stefano). Some rooms come with family-friendly fold-down bunks for €30 extra per person. Their freshly renovated, six-room **Residenza Santa Maria** is a couple of blocks away (same prices and contact info).

$$ Casa San Giuseppe is down a characteristic, laundry-strewn lane with views of Aurelian walls. While convent-owned, it's a secular place renting 29 plain but peaceful, spacious, and spotless rooms (Sb-€110, Db-€150, Tb-€180, Qb-€210, garden-facing rooms are quiet, air-con, elevator, parking-€15, just north of Piazza Trilussa at Vicolo Moroni 22, tel. 06-5833-3490, fax 06-5833-5754, info@casasangiuseppe.it, Germano).

Near Vatican City

Sleeping near the Vatican is expensive, but some enjoy calling this neighborhood home. Even though it's handy to the Vatican (when the rapture hits, you're right there), everything else is a long way away. The first two hotels listed here offer free airport transfers for

Hotels and Restaurants near Vatican City

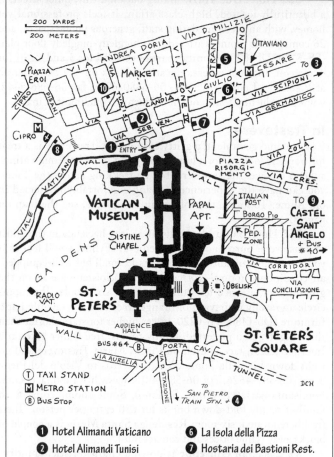

1. Hotel Alimandi Vaticano
2. Hotel Alimandi Tunisi
3. To Hotel Gerber & Casa Valdese
4. To Casa per Ferie Rooms
5. Perilli in Prati Rest.
6. La Isola della Pizza
7. Hostaria dei Bastioni Rest.
8. La Rustichella Buffet & Gelateria Millennium
9. To Tre Pupazzi & Vecchio Borgo Rest.
10. IN's Supermarket

guests, though you must reserve when you book your room and wait for a scheduled shuttle (every two hours).

$$$ Hotel Alimandi Vaticano, facing the Vatican Museum, is beautifully designed. Run by the Alimandi family (Enrico, Irene, Germano), it features four stars, 24 spacious rooms, and all the modern comforts you can imagine (Sb-€170, standard Db-€200, big Db with 2 double beds-€260, Tb-€280, 5 percent discount if you pay cash, air-con, elevator, Viale Vaticano 99, Metro: Cipro, tel. 06-397-45562, fax 06-397-30132, www.alimandi.it, alimandi @hotelalimandie.191.it).

$$ Hotel Alimandi Tunisi is a good value, run by other members of the friendly and entrepreneurial Alimandi family—Paolo, Grazia, Luigi, Marta, and Barbara. Their 35 perfumed rooms are air-conditioned, modern, and marbled in white (Sb-€90, Db-€175, 5 percent cash discount, elevator, grand buffet breakfast served in great roof garden, small gym, pool table, piano lounge, down the stairs directly in front of Vatican Museum, Via Tunisi 8, Metro: Cipro, reserve by phone at tel. 06-3972-3941, toll-free in Italy tel. 800-122-121, fax 06-3972-3943, www.alimandi.it, alimandi@tin.it).

$$ Hotel Gerber, set in a quiet residential area, is family-run with 27 well-polished, businesslike, air-conditioned rooms (two S without air-con-€60, Sb-€120, Db-€160, Tb-€180, Qb-€190; Via degli Scipioni 241, at intersection with Ezio, a block from Metro: Lepanto, tel. 06-321-6485, fax 06-321-7048, www.hotelgerber.it, info@hotelgerber.it; Peter, Simonetta, and friendly dog Kira).

$ Casa Valdese is an efficient church-run hotel just over the Tiber River and near the Vatican, with 35 big, quiet, and well-run rooms. It feels safe if a bit institutional, with the bonus of two breezy, communal roof terraces with incredible views (two external Sb-€50, Db-€120, €10/night less for 3-night stays, Internet access, 100 yards from Lepanto Metro station, just off Viale Pompeo Magno at Via Alessandro Farnese 18, tel. 06-321-5362, fax 06-321-1843, www.casavaldeseroma.it, reception@casavaldese roma.it).

$ Casa per Ferie Santa Maria alle Fornaci dei Padri Trinitari houses pilgrims and secular tourists with simple class just a short walk south of the Vatican in 54 stark, identical, utilitarian, mostly twin-bedded rooms. This is the most user-friendly convent-type place I've found. Reserve at least three months in advance (Sb-€70, Db-€95, Tb-€130, air-con, elevator; take bus #64 from Termini train station to San Pietro train station, then walk 100 yards north along Via della Stazione di San Pietro to Piazza Santa Maria alle Fornaci 27; tel. 06-393-67632, fax 06-393-66795, www .trinitaridematha.it, cffornaci@tin.it).

Eating

Romans spend their evenings eating rather than drinking, and the preferred activity is simply to enjoy a fine, slow meal, buried deep in the old city. Rome's a fun and cheap place to eat, with countless little eateries that serve memorable €20 meals. For pointers on pizza in Italy, see "Pizzerias" on page 910.

Although I've listed a number of restaurants, I recommend that you just head for a scenic area and explore. Piazza Navona, the Pantheon area, Campo de' Fiori, and Trastevere are neighborhoods packed with characteristic eateries. Sitting with tourists on a famous square and enjoying the scene works fine. (As my Roman friend explained: "When you're in a bad restaurant, the best way to survive is bread, olive oil, and salt.") But for more of a local flavor, consider my recommendations. In general, I'm impressed by how small the price difference is from a mediocre restaurant to a fine one. You can pay about 20 percent more for double the quality.

Trastevere

Colorful Trastevere is now pretty touristy. Still, Romans join the tourists to eat on the rustic side of the Tiber River. Start at the central square (Piazza Santa Maria). Then choose: Eat with tourists enjoying the ambience of the famous square, or wander the back streets in search of a mom-and-pop place with barely a menu. My recommendations are within a few minutes' walk of each other (between Piazza Santa Maria Trastevere and Ponte Sisto; see map on page 811).

Trattoria da Lucia lets you enjoy simple, traditional food at a good price in a great scene. It's the quintessential, rustic, 100 percent Roman Trastevere dining experience, and has been family-run since World War II. You'll meet four generations of the family, including Giuliano and Renato, their uncle Ennio, and Ennio's mom—pictured on the menu in the 1950s. The family specialty is *spaghetti alla Gricia*, with pancetta (€9 pastas, €11 *secondi*, Tue–Sun 12:30–15:30 & 19:30–24:00, closed Mon, cash only, comfy indoor or evocative outdoor seating, just off Via del Mattonato on Vicolo del Mattonato 2, tel. 06-580-3601, some English spoken).

Trattoria da Olindo takes homey to extremes. You really feel like you dropped in on a family that cooks for the neighborhood to supplement their income (€7 pastas, €9 *secondi*, Mon–Sat dinner served 20:00–22:30, closed Sun, cash only, indoor and funky cobbled outdoor seating, on the corner of Vicolo della Scala and Via del Mattonato at #8, tel. 06-581-8835).

Osteria Ponte Sisto, small and Mediterranean, specializes in traditional Roman cuisine, but has frequent Neapolitan specials as well. Just outside the tourist zone, it caters mostly to Romans and offers beautiful desserts and a fine value (daily 12:30–15:30 & 19:30–24:00, Via Ponte Sisto 80, tel. 06-588-3411, Antonio and Adriano). It's easy to find: Crossing Ponte Sisto (pedestrian bridge) toward Trastevere, continue across the little square (Piazza Trilussa) and you'll see it on the right.

Ristorante Checco er Carettiere is a big, classic, family-run place that's been a Trastevere fixture for four generations. With white tablecloths, well-presented food, and dressy local diners, this is *the* place for a special meal in Trastevere. While it's a bit pricey, you'll eat well amidst lots of fun commotion. Reservations are smart, especially on weekends (€16 pastas, €22 *secondi*, daily 12:30–15:00 & 19:30–23:15, Via Benedetta 10/13, tel. 06-580-0985). For a pared-down menu with down-home Roman cooking and cheaper prices, go to their **Osteria Checco er Carettiere** just next door (€11 pastas, €15 *secondi*, same hours and phone number the *ristorante*).

Pizzeria "Ai Marmi" is a bright and noisy festival of pizza, where the oven and pizza-assembly line are surrounded by marble-slab tables (hence the nickname "the morgue"). It's a classic Roman scene with famously good €8 pizzas and tight seating. Expect a long line between 20:00 and 22:00 (Thu–Tue 18:30–24:00, closed Wed, outdoor seating on busy Viale Trastevere, tram #8 from Largo Argentina to first stop over bridge, just beyond Piazza Sonnino at Viale Trastevere 53, tel. 06-580-0919).

Cantina Paradiso Wine and Cocktail Bar has a simple romantic charm, a block over Viale Trastevere from the touristy action. During happy hour (18:00–20:30), €6 drinks come with a well-made little buffet that can make a cheap, light dinner (daily 12:00–24:00, €8 pastas, lunch buffet as well, Via San Francesco a Ripa 73, tel. 06-5899-799).

And for Dessert: **Gelateria alla Scala** is a terrific little ice-cream shop that dishes up delightful cinnamon *(cannella)* and oh-wow pistachio (daily 12:00–24:00, Piazza della Scala 51, across from the church on Piazza della Scala). Seek this place out.

Jewish Ghetto

The Jewish ghetto sits just across the river from Trastevere.

Sora Margherita, hiding without a sign on a cluttered square, has been a neighborhood favorite since 1927. Amid a picturesque commotion, local families chow down on old-time Roman and Jewish dishes for a good price. As it's technically not a real restaurant (it avoids red tape by being officially designated as an *associazione culturale*), you'll need to sign a card to join the "cultural association" when you order (don't worry; membership has no obligations except that you enjoy your meal). The menu's crude term for the fettuccini gives you some idea of the mood of this place: *nazzica culo* ("asses shake while it's made"). Reservations are almost always necessary; to secure a spot for lunch without a reservation, go early or late (April–Oct Tue–Sun 12:30–15:00 for lunch, dinner seatings on Fri and Sat at 20:00 and 21:30, closed Mon; Nov–March Mon–Fri 12:30–15:00, dinner seatings at 20:00 and 21:30 on Fri, closed Sat–Sun; Piazza delle Cinque Scole 30, tel. 06-687-4216, Ivan doesn't speak English).

In the Heart of Rome
On and near Campo de' Fiori

While it is touristy, Campo de' Fiori offers a sublimely romantic setting. And, since it's so close to the collective heart of Rome, it remains popular with locals. For greater atmosphere than food value, circle the square, considering your choices. The square is lined with popular and interesting bars, pizzerias, and small restaurants—all great for people-watching over a glass of wine.

Ristorante la Carbonara is a venerable standby with the ultimate Campo de' Fiori outdoor setting and dressy waiters. While the service gets mixed reviews, the food and Italian ambience are wonderful. Meals on small surrounding streets may be a better value, but they lack that Campo de' Fiori magic. While La Carbonara's on-square dining is classic, the big room upstairs is good, too (€11 pastas, €16 *secondi,* Wed–Mon 9:00–15:00 & 19:00–23:30, closed Tue, reservations recommended, Campo de' Fiori 23, tel. 06-686-4783).

Osteria da Giovanni ar Galletto is nearby, on the more elegant and peaceful Piazza Farnese. Angelo entertains an upscale local crowd and has magical outdoor seating. Regrettably, service can be horrible and single diners aren't treated very well. Still, if you're in no hurry and ready to savor my favorite *al fresco* setting in Rome (while humoring the waiters), this is a good bet (Mon–Sat 12:15–15:00 & 19:30–23:00, closed Sun, tucked in corner of Piazza Farnese at #102, tel. 06-686-1714).

Osteria Enoteca al Bric is a mod bistro-type place run by Maurizio, a man who loves to cook, serve good wine, and listen to jazz. With only the finest ingredients, and an ambience elegant in its simplicity, he's created the perfect package for a romantic night out. Wine-case lids decorate the wall like happy memories. With candlelit grace and few tourists, it's perfect for the wine snob in the mood for pasta and fine cheese. Aficionados choose their bottle from the huge selection lining the walls near the entrance. Beginners order fine wine by the glass with help from the waiter when they order their meal (daily 12:30–15:00 & from 19:30 for dinner, closed Mon June–Sept, reserve after 20:30, 100 yards off Campo de' Fiori at Via del Pellegrino 51, tel. 06-687-9533). Al Bric offers my readers a special "Taste of Italy for Two" deal (appetizing

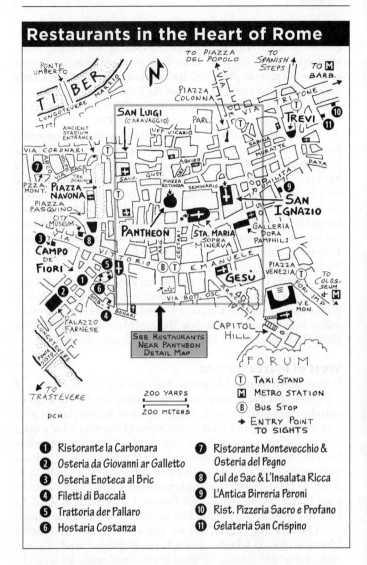

Restaurants in the Heart of Rome

TO PIAZZA DEL POPOLO
TO SPANISH STEPS
TO M BARB.

PONTE UMBERTO
TIBER
LUNGOTEVERE MARZIO
ANCIENT STADIUM ENTRANCE
VIA CORONARI

PIAZZA COLONNA
PARL.
SAN LUIGI (CARAVAGGIO)
UFF. VICARIO
SALV.
GIUST.
PIAZZA ROTUNDA
SEMINARIO
AQUIRO

PIAZZA COLONNA
VIA TRITONE
TREVI
SABINA
MURATTE
DATA

PZZA. MONT.
PIAZZA NAVONA
PIAZZA PASQUINO
CITY MUSEUM
VIA DELLA PACE
TRE SCALINI

PANTHEON
STA. MARIA SOPRA MINERVA
GALLERIA DORA PAMPHILJ
SAN IGNAZIO
UMILITA

CAMPO DE' FIORI
VIA VITTORIO EMANUELE
GESÙ
PIAZZA VENEZIA
TO COLOSSEUM & M
FORI IMP.
V.E. MON.

PALAZZO FARNESE
GIUB.
BONARI
VIA BOTT. OSC.
ARACOELI
CAPITOL HILL
FORUM

SEE RESTAURANTS NEAR PANTHEON DETAIL MAP

TO TRASTEVERE
LUNGOTEVERE
PONTE SISTO
DCH

200 YARDS
200 METERS

(T) TAXI STAND
(M) METRO STATION
(B) BUS STOP
→ ENTRY POINT TO SIGHTS

1 Ristorante la Carbonara
2 Osteria da Giovanni ar Galletto
3 Osteria Enoteca al Bric
4 Filetti di Baccalà
5 Trattoria der Pallaro
6 Hostaria Costanza

7 Ristorante Montevecchio & Osteria del Pegno
8 Cul de Sac & L'Insalata Ricca
9 L'Antica Birreria Peroni
10 Rist. Pizzeria Sacro e Profano
11 Gelateria San Crispino

plate of mixed cheeses and meats with two glasses of full-bodied red wine and a pitcher of water) for €22 from 19:30, but you may need to finish by 20:30. This could be a light meal if you're kicking off an evening stroll, a substantial appetizer, or a way to check this place out for a serious meal later. While Al Bric can be pricey, feel free to establish a price limit (e.g., €40 per person) and trust Maurizio to feed you well.

Filetti di Baccalà is a cheap and basic Roman classic, where nostalgic regulars cram into wooden tables savoring their old-school favorites—hand-held, fried cod fillets and raw *puntarelle* greens (slathered with anchovy sauce in spring and winter). Study what others are eating, and order from your grease-stained server by pointing at what you want. Rather than sit in the fluorescently lit interior, try to grab a seat out on the little square, a quiet haven a block east of Campo de' Fiori (Mon–Sat 17:30–23:00, closed Sun, cash only, Largo dei Librari 88, tel. 06-686-4018).

Trattoria der Pallaro, a well-worn eatery that has no menu, has a slogan: "Here, you'll eat what we want to feed you." Paola Fazi—with a towel wrapped around her head turban-style—and her family serve up a five-course meal of typically Roman food for €22, including wine, coffee, and a tasty mandarin juice finale. As many locals return every day, each evening features a different menu (Tue–Sun 12:00–15:00 & 19:00–24:00, closed Mon, indoor/outdoor seating on quiet square, a block south of Corso Vittorio Emanuele, down Largo del Chiavari to Largo del Pallaro 15, tel. 06-6880-1488).

Hostaria Costanza has crisp-vested waiters, a local following, and lots of energy. You'll eat traditional Roman cuisine, including grilled meats and fresh fish, on a ramshackle patio or inside under arches from the ancient Pompeo Theater (Mon–Sat 12:30–15:00 & 19:30–23:30, closed Sun, Piazza Paradiso 63, tel. 06-686-1717).

West of Piazza Navona

Romantic **Ristorante Montevecchio** is tucked into the corner of a secluded piazza. Sitting under high wood-beamed ceilings or outside among Renaissance walls, you savor Italian classics with a creative touch—and maybe even some of the chef's little extra offerings of the evening. Start with their delicate *fritti* of lightly battered seasonal vegetables and you'll realize you're in for a memorable meal (€15 pastas, €20 *secondi,* Tue–Sun 12:30–15:30 & 19:15–23:00, reservations recommended, closed Mon, 3 blocks from Piazza Navona off Via dei Coronari—turn left on Via della Pace to Piazza Montevecchio 22a, tel. 06-686-1319, Annamaria).

Osteria del Pegno, across the street from Ristorante Montevecchio, is a lively, atmospheric, soft-focus kind of place, with candlelight shining off wine-bottle-lined walls. Its local clientele enjoys good regional dishes and a fine house wine (pizza at lunch only, €8 pastas, €15 *secondi,* no cover, Thu–Tue 12:30–15:00 & 19:30–23:30, closed Wed, Vicolo di Montevecchio 8, tel. 06-6880-7025).

Piazza Pasquino

Located just a block off Piazza Navona (toward Campo de' Fiori) on Piazza Pasquino, these bustling places have low prices and a happy clientele. As they are neighbors and each is completely different, check both before choosing.

Cul de Sac is a corridor-wide trattoria lined with wine bottles and packed with enthusiastic locals. Come early for an excellent tasting plate of salami and one of their many bottles of wine (they've got more than 1,000), or come later for a full meal of nicely cooked Roman dishes (daily 12:00–16:00 & 18:00–24:00, tel. 06-6880-1094).

L'Insalata Ricca is a popular local chain that specializes in hearty and healthy €7 salads and less healthy pastas (daily 12:00–15:45 & 18:45–24:00, tel. 06-6830-7881).

Near the Trevi Fountain

L'Antica Birreria Peroni is Rome's answer to a German beer hall. Serving hearty mugs of the local Peroni beer and lots of just plain fun beer-hall food, the place is a hit with locals for a cheap night out (Mon–Sat 12:00–24:00, closed Sun, midway between Trevi Fountain and Capitol Hill, a block off Via del Corso at Via di San Marcello 19, tel. 06-679-5310).

Ristorante Pizzeria Sacro e Profano fills an old church with spicy south Italian (Calabrian) cuisine; some pricey, exotic dishes; and satisfied tourists. Run with enthusiasm and passion by Pasquale and friends, this is just far enough away from the Trevi mobs. Their hearty €15 *antipasti* plate is a delightful montage of Calabrian taste treats—plenty of food for a light, but exceptional meal (daily 12:00–15:00 & 18:00–24:00, a block off Via del Tritone at Via dei Maroniti 29, tel. 06-679-1836). And for dessert...

Around the corner, **Gelateria San Crispino,** well-respected by locals, serves particularly tasty gourmet gelato using creative ingredients. Because of their commitment to natural ingredients, the colors are muted and they serve cups, but no cones (April–Nov daily 12:00–24:00, Dec–March closed Tue, Via della Panetteria 42, tel. 06-679-3924).

Near the Pantheon

Eating on the square facing the Pantheon is a temptation (there's even a McDonald's that offers some of the best outdoor seating in town), and I'd consider it just to relax and enjoy the Roman scene. But if you walk a block or two away, you'll get less view and better value. Here are some suggestions:

Ristorante da Fortunato is an Italian classic, with fresh flowers on the tables and white-coated, black-tie waiters politely serving good meat and fish to local politicians, foreign dignitaries, and tourists with good taste. Don't leave without perusing the photos of their famous visitors—everyone from former Iraqi Foreign Minister Tariq Aziz to Bill Clinton seems to have eaten here. All are pictured with the boss, Fortunato, who, since 1975,

Restaurants near the Pantheon

T TAXI STAND
M METRO STATION
B BUS STOP
→ ENTRY POINT TO SIGHTS

① Ristorante da Fortunato
② Ristorante Enoteca Corsi
③ Miscellanea Restaurant
④ Osteria da Mario & Restaurant Coco
⑤ Le Coppelle Taverna
⑥ To Trattoria dal Cav. Gino
⑦ Pizzeria Zazà
⑧ Antica Salumeria
⑨ Angelo Feroci Butcher Shop
⑩ Super Market Di per Di
⑪ Gelateria Giolitti
⑫ Crèmeria Monteforte

has been a master of simple edible elegance. The outdoor seating is fine for watching the river of Roman street life flow by, but the atmosphere is inside. For a dressy night out, this is a reliable and surprisingly reasonable choice—but be sure to reserve ahead (plan to spend €45 per person, Mon–Sat 12:30–15:00 & 19:30–23:30, closed Sun, a block in front of the Pantheon at Via del Pantheon 55, tel. 06-679-2788).

Ristorante Enoteca Corsi is a wine shop that grew into a thriving lunch-only restaurant. The Paiella family serves straight-forward, traditional cuisine at great prices to an appreciative crowd of office workers. Check the blackboard for daily specials (gnocchi on Thursday, fish on Friday, and so on). Friendly Juliana, Claudia, and Manuela welcome diners to step into their wine shop and pick out a bottle. For the cheap take-away price, plus €2, they'll uncork it at your table. With €6 pastas, €9.50 main dishes, and fine wine at a third of the price you'd pay in normal restaurants, this can be a superb value (Mon–Sat 12:00–15:00, closed Sun, a block toward the Pantheon from the Gesù Church at Via del Gesù 87, no reservations possible, tel. 06-679-0821).

Miscellanea is run by much-loved Mikki, who's on a mission to keep foreign students well-fed. You'll find hearty and fresh €3 sandwiches and a long list of €6 salads. Mikki often tosses in a fun little extra, including—if you have this book on the table—a free glass of Mikki's "sexy wine" (homemade from *fragoline*—straw-berries). This place is popular with American students on foreign-study programs (daily 11:00–24:00, indoor/outdoor seating, a block toward Via del Corso from the Pantheon at Via delle Paste 110).

Osteria da Mario, a homey little mom-and-pop joint with a no-stress menu, serves traditional favorites in a fun dining room or on tables spilling out onto a picturesque old Roman square (€7 pastas, €10 *secondi*, Mon–Sat 13:00–15:30 & 19:00–23:00, closed Sun, from the Pantheon walk 2 blocks up Via Pantheon, go left on Via delle Coppelle, take first right to Piazza delle Coppelle 51, tel. 06-6880-6349, Marco).

Restaurant Coco is good for a quick and atmospheric €10 buffet lunch on weekdays, or a lavish €15 lunch on weekends. After assembling your plate, sit on the square next to a produce market and watch politicians stroll in and out of their dining hall across the way (daily 12:30–15:30 & 19:30–24:00, classy indoor and rustic outdoor seating, Piazza delle Coppelle 54, tel. 06-6813-6545).

Le Coppelle Taverna is simple, good, and inexpensive—especially for pizza—with a checkered-tablecloth ambience (May–Sept daily 12:30–15:00 & 19:30–23:30, Nov–April closed Mon, Via delle Coppelle 39, tel. 06-6880-6557, Alfonso).

Trattoria dal Cav. Gino, tucked away on a tiny street behind the parliament, has been a local favorite since 1963. Photos on the wall recall the days when it was the haunt of big-time politicians. Grandpa Gino shuffles around grating the parmesan cheese while his sister and son serve up traditional Roman favorites and make sure things run smoothly. Reserve ahead, even for lunch (€7 pastas, €10 *secondi*, fish on Friday, cash only, Mon–Sat 13:00–14:45 & 20:00–22:30, closed Sun, behind Piazza del Parlamento and just off Via di Campo Marzio at Vicolo Rosini 4, tel. 06-687-3434, Fabrizio and Carla—Gino's son and daughter—speak English).

Picnic (Discreetly) near the Pantheon

Pizzeria Zazà is a quick take-out stop for stellar pizza by the slice (with little outdoor seating). With primarily organic ingredients and a doughy, plush crust, this is fast-food gourmet—great for a quick bite in the old center. It's sold by weight—ask for *un etto* (100 grams), or *due etti* if you're really hungry (May–Oct Mon–Sat 10:00–22:00, closed Sun; Nov–April daily 10:00–22:00; facing the back of the Pantheon, head 20 yards to your right to reach Piazza San Eustachio 49, tel. 06-68-80-1357, Alessandro).

Antica Salumeria is an old-time *alimentari* (grocery store) on the Pantheon square. Eduardo speaks English and will help you assemble your picnic: artichokes, mixed olives, bread, cheese, meat (they're proud of their Norcia prosciutto), and wine (with plastic glasses). Their pastries are fresh from their own bakery. While you can create your own (sold by the weight, more fun, and cheaper), they also sell quality ready-made sandwiches. Now take your peasant's feast to an atmospheric spot, find some shade, and munch your meal (daily 8:00–21:00, mobile 334-340-9014).

Angelo Feroci also offers cheap, quick *antipasti* to go. Though it's a butcher shop—from another era—you can pick up seasonal vegetables as well as meats (try the meatballs in sauce). Just point to the size of container you want, then nod and gesture toward what looks tastiest (sold by weight—about €5 for a lunch portion, Mon–Wed and Fri 6:00–13:30 & 17:00–20:00, Thu and Sat 6:00–13:30, closed Sun, one and a half blocks north of the Pantheon at Via della Maddalena 15, tel. 06-6880-1016).

Super Market Di per Di is a convenient place for groceries in the old center (Mon–Sat 8:00–21:00, Sun 9:00–19:30, 50 yards off Via del Plebiscito at Via del Gesù 59).

Gelato near the Pantheon

Two fine *gelateria*s are within a two-minute walk of the Pantheon.

Gelateria Caffè Pasticceria Giolitti, Rome's most famous and venerable ice-cream joint, has low take-away prices and elegant Old World seating (daily 7:00–24:00, just off Piazza Colonna and Piazza Monte Citorio at Via Uffici del Vicario 40, tel. 06-699-1243).

Crèmeria Monteforte is known for its super-creamy sorbets, traditional quality, and mellow hues; gelato purists consider bright colors a sign of unnatural chemicals used to attract children (Tue–Sun 10:00–24:00, closed Mon, faces the west side of the Pantheon at Via della Rotonda 22).

In North Rome: Near the Spanish Steps

Many simple and lively places line Via della Croce. To locate these restaurants, see the map on page 767.

Ristorante il Gabriello is inviting and small—modern under medieval arches—and provides a peaceful and local-feeling respite from all the top-end fashion shops in the area. Claudio serves with charisma, while his brother Gabriello cooks creative Roman cuisine using fresh, organic products from his wife's farm. Italians normally just trust the waiter and say, "Bring it on." Tourists are understandably more cautious, but you can be trusting here. Simply close your eyes and point to anything on the menu. Or invest €40 in "Claudio's Extravaganza" (not including wine), and he'll shower you with edible kindness. Specify whether you'd prefer fish, meat, or both. When finished, I stand up, hold my belly, and say, *"La vita è bella"* (€9 pastas, €12 *secondi*, dinner only, Mon–Sat 19:00–23:30, closed Sun, reservations smart, air-con, dress respectfully—no shorts please, 3 blocks from Spanish Steps at Via Vittoria 51, tel. 06-6994-0810).

Osteria Gusto is great for a glass of good wine over an artisanal cheese plate or a complete dinner (daily 12:30–15:30 & 19:00–24:00, opens at 18:30 for drinks and appetizers only, reservations recommended after 20:00 and on weekends, on the corner of Via Soderini at Via della Frezza 16, tel. 06-3211-1482). Don't confuse the *osteria* with its nearby wine bar and *ristorante* sister operations—the *osteria* has better food and warmer ambience (the others are under different management).

Ristorante alla Rampa, just around the corner from the touristy crush of the Spanish Steps, offers Roman cooking, busy but pleasant indoor/outdoor ambience at a moderate price, piles of tourists, and impersonal service. It's a good idea to make reservations if arriving after 19:30. For a simple meal, go with the €10 *piatto misto all'ortolana*—a self-service trip to their antipasto spread with meat, fish, and veggies. Even though you get just one trip to the buffet (and fried items are generally cold), this can be a meal in itself (Mon–Sat 12:00–15:00 & 18:00–23:00, closed Sun, 100 yards east of Spanish Steps at Piazza Mignanelli 18, tel. 06-678-2621).

L'EnotecAntica, an upbeat, 200-plus-year-old *enoteca*, has around 60 Italian wines by the glass, and a fresh €12 *antipasti* plate of veggies, salami, and cheese. It's very crowded on summer evenings (Via della Croce 76b, tel. 06-679-0896).

Bar Ripetta is so famous for its cappuccino that the barista is used to tourists ordering it in the evening (Italian coffee purists usually scoff at foreigners who order cappuccinos past noon). Order and pay for your coffee and dessert, then grab a table outside for no extra charge (Mon–Sat 6:00–20:30, closed Sun, Via Ripetta 72, tel. 06-321-0524).

Cesaretto, a casual wine bar with outdoor seating and light, inexpensive appetizers, is run by hospitable, Harley-loving Angelo (€4.50 antipasto buffet plate, daily 12:00–24:00, buffet 18:30–20:30, Via Bocca di Leone 44, tel. 06-6938-0557).

In Ancient Rome: Eating Cheaply near the Colosseum

You'll find good views but poor value at the restaurants directly behind the Colosseum. To get your money's worth, eat at least a block away. Here are three handy eateries, all shown on the map on page 823: one at the foot of Via Cavour, and two at the top of Terme di Tito (a long block uphill from the Colosseum, near St. Peter-in-Chains church—of Michelangelo's *Moses* fame; for directions, see page 777).

Enoteca Cavour 313 is a wine bar with a mission: to offer good wine and quality food with an old-fashioned commitment to value and friendly service. It's also a convenient place for a good lunch near the Forum and Colosseum. Angelo and his three partners enjoy creating a mellow ambience under lofts of wine bottles (daily specials and fine wines by the glass, daily 12:30–14:45 & 19:30–24:00, 100 yards off Via dei Fori Imperiali at Via Cavour 313, tel. 06-6785-496).

Lively **Caffè dello Studente** is popular with local engineering students attending the nearby University of Rome. Pina, Mauro, and their perky daughter Simona (speaks English, but you can teach her some more) give my readers a royal welcome and serve typical *bar gastronomia* fare—toasted sandwiches and pizzas—and big salads, too (stick to any of the aforementioned fare to avoid frozen dishes). You can get your food to go *(da portar via);* eat standing at the crowded bar; wait for table service outside; or—if it's not busy—show this book when you order at the bar and sit without paying extra at a table (Mon–Sat 7:30–21:00, Sun 9:00–18:00, tel. 06-488-3240).

Hostaria da Nerone, next door, is a more formal restaurant with homemade pasta dishes. Their €8 *antipasti* plate—with a variety of veggies, fish, and maybe meatballs, too—is a good value for a quick lunch (Mon–Sat 12:00–15:00 & 19:00–23:00, closed Sun, indoor/outdoor seating, Via delle Terme di Tito 96, tel. 06-481-7952, run by Teo and Eugenio).

Near Termini Train Station

Ristorante del Giglio is a circa-1900 place with a long family tradition of serving traditional Roman dishes (though the quality can be uneven). You'll eat in a big hall of about 20 tables with dressy locals and tourists following the recommendations of nearby hotels (€10 pastas, €15 *secondi,* alluring dessert cart, Tue–Sat 12:00–15:00 & 19:00–23:00, Mon 19:00–23:00, closed Sun, Via Torino 137, tel. 06-488-1606).

La Gallina Bianca, with a classy country villa atmosphere and sprightly service, seems out of place near the Termini station. The wood-fired pizza—surely the best in the area—might distract

Restaurants near Termini Train Station

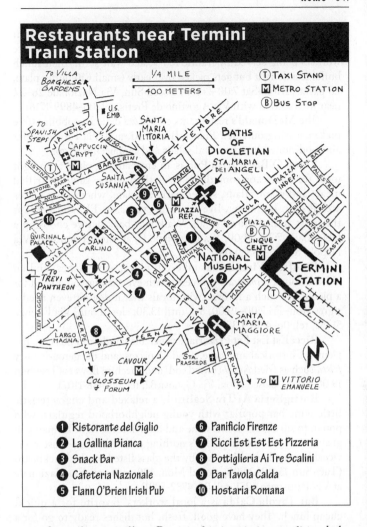

¼ MILE
400 METERS

T TAXI STAND
M METRO STATION
B BUS STOP

TO VILLA BORGHESE GARDENS

TO SPANISH STEPS

U.S. EMB.

SANTA MARIA VITTORIA

BATHS OF DIOCLETIAN

STA. MARIA DEI ANGELI

CAPPUCCIN CRYPT

VIA VENETO

VIA BISO.

SETTEMBRE

PIAZZA S.M. BATT.

VIA BARBERINI

SANTA SUSANNA

PARIGI

PIAZZA INDEP.

PIAZZA BARB.

TRITONE

VIA

AVIG.

QUATTRO

SANTA

PIAZZA REP.

TERME DE NICOLA MARSALA

VIA VICENZA

M

FONTANE

TERME

MARGH.

QUIRINALE PALACE

SAN CARLINO

VIA

QUIRINALE

TORINO

PIAZZA CINQUECENTO

B **T**

TERMINI STATION

VIA

VIA NAZIONALE

NATIONAL MUSEUM

MANIN

CASTRO

TO TREVI & PANTHEON

VIA DE PRETIS

XXIV MAGGIO

VIA

SERPE

VIA

MILANO

SANTA MARIA MAGGIORE

VIA

G.G. GIO. LITTI

LARGO MAGNA.

PANISPERNA

STA. PRASSEDE

MERULANA

CAVOUR

M

TO COLOSSEUM & FORUM

TO **M** VITTORIO EMANUELE

N

1. Ristorante del Giglio
2. La Gallina Bianca
3. Snack Bar
4. Cafeteria Nazionale
5. Flann O'Brien Irish Pub
6. Panificio Firenze
7. Ricci Est Est Est Pizzeria
8. Bottiglieria Ai Tre Scalini
9. Bar Tavola Calda
10. Hostaria Romana

you from their excellent Roman *fritti, primi, secondi,* and the knockout tiramisù. A wait is almost always necessary after 19:30. Come earlier, especially on weekends, as they don't take reservations (€8 pizzas, €11 pastas, €15 *secondi,* Via Antonio Rosmini 9, tel. 06-474-3777, Antonio).

Snack Bar, despite its plain-Jane name, is anything but: The place puts out an impressive lunchtime display of pastas, colorful sandwiches, and fresh fruit. You can even make your own salad. Rub elbows with lunching businesspeople in the afternoon (12:30–15:00), either inside the characterless interior or out on the sidewalk (daily 6:00–24:00, Via Firenze 33, mobile 339-393-1356, Enrica).

ROME

Cafeteria Nazionale, with woody elegance, offers light lunches—including salads—at fair prices. It's noisy with local office workers being served by frantic red-vested wait staff. Their lunch buffet is a delight but gets picked over early (small €10 buffet plate, €8 pastas, Mon–Sat 7:00–20:00, closed Sun, Via Nazionale 26–27, near intersection with Via Agostino de Pretis, tel. 06-4899-1716).

The **McDonald's** restaurants on Piazza della Repubblica (free piazza seating outside), Piazza Barberini, and Via Firenze offer air-conditioned interiors, and salads and cappuccino to go.

Flann O'Brien Irish Pub is an entertaining place for a light meal (of pasta...or something *other* than pasta, such as grilled meats and giant salads, served early and late, when other places are closed), Irish beer, live sporting events on TV, and perhaps the most Italian crowd of all. Walk way back before choosing a table (daily 7:30–24:00, Via Nazionale 17, at intersection with Via Napoli, tel. 06-488-0418).

Panificio Firenze has take-out pizza, sandwiches, and an old-fashioned *alimentari* (grocery) with everything you'd need for a picnic. It's such a favorite with locals that it doesn't even need a sign (Mon–Fri 7:00–19:00, Sat until 13:30, closed Sun, Via Firenze 51–52, tel. 06-488-5035).

Ricci Est Est Est Pizzeria, a venerable family-run pizzeria, has plenty of historical ambience, good €8 pizzas, and dangerously tasty *fritti,* such as fried *baccalà* (dried cod) and zucchini flowers (Tue–Sun 19:00–24:00, closed Mon, Via Genova 32, tel. 06-488-1107).

Bottiglieria Ai Tre Scalini is a relaxed and characteristic little wine bar popular with young neighborhood regulars, who pop in to sip a glass of fine wine and munch some light Roman pub grub to jazz or blues music. It's nothing earth-shaking—just a serviceable wine bar with wines by the glass listed on the blackboard (Tue–Sun 15:00–24:00, closed Mon, 100 yards off Via Nazionale at Via Panisperna 251, tel. 06-4782-5881).

Bar Tavola Calda is a local workers' favorite for a quick, cheap lunch. They have good, fresh, hot dishes ready to go for a fine price. Head back past the bar to peruse their enticing display, point at what you want, then grab a seat, and the young wait staff will serve you (Mon–Sat 12:00–15:30 for lunch, closed Sun, Via Torino 40).

Hostaria Romana is a busy bistro with a hustling and fun-loving gang of waiters and noisy walls graffitied by happy eaters. While they specialize in fish and traditional Roman dishes, their *antipasti* plate can make a good meal in itself (Mon–Sat 12:15–15:00 & 19:15–23:00, closed Sun, a block up the lane just past the entrance to the big tunnel near the Trevi Fountain at Via de Boccaccio 1, tel. 06-474-5284).

Near Vatican City

Avoid the restaurant-pushers handing out fliers near the Vatican: bad food and expensive menu tricks. Try any of these instead (see map on page 828).

Perilli in Prati is bright, modern, and just far enough away from the tourist hordes. While friendly Lucia and Massimo specialize in pizza, fish, and grilled meats, the highlight is their excellent €8 lunch buffet (Mon–Fri 12:30–15:00 & 19:30–23:30, Sat 19:30–23:30, closed Sun, one block from Ottaviano Metro stop, Via Otranto 9, tel. 06-370-0156).

La Isola della Pizza has wood-fired pizzas, sidewalk seating, and home-cooking at its truest: For €10, Adele, Vito, or their son Renzo serve up generous plates of their mixed *antipasti*...and Vito himself hunts the wild boar for the *cinghiale* pasta (Thu–Tue 12:30–15:00 & 19:30–24:00, closed Wed, Via degli Scipioni 41/51, tel. 06-3973-3483).

Hostaria dei Bastioni, run by Emilio, is conveniently located midway on your hike from St. Peter's to the Vatican Museum, with noisy street-side seating and a quiet interior (€7 pastas, €12 *secondi*, no cover charge, Mon–Sat 12:00–15:30 & 19:00–23:00, closed Sun, Via Leone IV 29, at corner of Vatican wall, tel. 06-3972-3034). The *gelateria* three doors away is good.

La Rustichella serves a famous and sprawling *antipasti* buffet (€7 for a single meal-size plate). Arrive when it opens at 19:30 to avoid a line and have the pristine buffet to yourself (Tue–Sun 12:30–15:00 & 19:30–23:00, closed Mon, near Metro: Cipro, opposite church at end of Via Candia, Via Angelo Emo 1, tel. 06-3972-0649). Consider the fun and fruity **Gelateria Millennium** next door.

Viale Giulio Cesare: This street is lined with cheap Pizza Rustica shops, self-serve places, and inviting eateries.

Along Borgo Pio: The pedestrians-only Borgo Pio—a block from Piazza San Pietro—has restaurants worth a look, such as **Tre Pupazzi** (Mon–Sat 12:00–15:00 & 19:00–23:00, closed Sun, at corner of Via Tre Pupazzi and Borgo Pio, tel. 06-686-8371). At **Vecchio Borgo,** across the street, you can get pasta, pizza slices, and veggies to go (Mon–Sat 9:00–21:00, closed Sun, Borgo Pio 27a, tel. 06-6880-6355).

Picnic Supplies: Turn your nose loose in the wonderful **Via Andrea Doria** open-air market, three blocks north of the Vatican Museum (Mon–Sat roughly 7:00–13:30, until 16:30 Tue and Fri except summer, corner of Via Tunisi and Via Andrea Doria). If the market is closed, try the nearby **IN's supermarket** (Mon–Sat 8:00–20:00, Sun 9:00–14:00, a half-block straight out from Via Tunisi entrance of open-air market, Via Francesco Caracciolo 18).

In South Rome's Testaccio Neighborhood

Working-class since ancient times, the Testaccio neighborhood has recently gone trendy-bohemian. Visitors wander through an awkward mix of yuppie and proletarian worlds, not noticing—but perhaps sensing—the "Keep Testaccio for the Testaccians" graffiti. This has long been the neighborhood of slaughterhouses, and its restaurants are renowned for their ability to cook up the least palatable part of the animals...the "fifth quarter." The following restaurant is my favorite in the area.

Trattoria "Da Oio" a Casa Mia serves good-quality, traditional cuisine to a local crowd. At this upbeat little eatery, the menu is a minefield of soft meats. Anything that comes with their *pajata* (baby veal intestines) sauce will give you the edible tripe of a lifetime. While having just pasta for lunch is fine, at dinner they expect diners to order two courses (€10 pastas, €12 *secondi*, Mon–Sat 12:30–15:00 & 19:30–23:30, closed Sun; from Pyramide Metro stop, head north past the pyramid and Porta Ostiense gate to Via Marmorata, then hang a left and walk 3 blocks to Via Galvani 43; tel. 06-578-2680).

Connections

Termini is the central station (see "Arrival in Rome" near the beginning of this chapter; Metro: Termini). Tiburtina is the train and bus station (on Metro line B, four Metro stops away from train station; Metro: Tiburtina).

From Rome's Termini Train Station by Train to: Venice (roughly hourly, 5–8 hrs, overnight possible), **Florence** (2/hr, 1.5–2.5 hrs, many stop at Orvieto en route, most connections require seat reservations), **La Spezia** (every 2 hrs, 4 hrs, overnight option), **Milan** (hourly, 4.5–8 hrs, overnight possible), **Amsterdam** (7/day, 20 hrs, overnight unavoidable), **Interlaken** (5/day, 8 hrs, overnight option), **Frankfurt** (7/day, 14 hrs, plus several overnight options), **Munich** (4/day, 11 hrs, plus several overnight options), **Nice** (6/day, 10 hrs), **Paris** (3/day, 13–16 hrs, plus several overnight options, important to reserve ahead), **Vienna** (3/day, 13–15 hrs, plus several overnight options).

Rome's Airports

Rome's two airports—Fiumicino (a.k.a. Leonardo da Vinci) and the small Ciampino—share the same website (www.adr.it). Budget flights within Europe (Ryanair, easyJet, Vueling, and Blue Express) use both airports.

Fiumicino Airport

Rome's major airport has TIs in terminal B and C (daily 8:00–

19:00, tel. 06-8205-9127, press 2 for English), ATMs, banks, luggage storage, shops, and bars.

A slick, direct **"Leonardo Express" train** connects the airport and Rome's central Termini train station in 30 minutes for €11. Trains run twice hourly in both directions from roughly 6:00–23:00 (leaving the airport on the half-hour, double-check train times if you have a late-night or early-morning flight to catch). From the airport's arrival gate, follow signs to *Stazione/Railway Station*. Buy your ticket from a machine or the Biglietteria office. Make sure the train you board is going to the central "Roma Termini" station, not "Roma Orte" or others. However, if you're going to Trastevere, take any train but the Leonardo Express (these cheaper trains cost €4.50, and leave at :00 and :35 past the hour).

Going from the Termini train station to the airport, trains depart at about :22 and :52 past the hour, from track 24. Check the departure boards for *Fiumicino Aeroporto*—the local name for the airport—and confirm with an official or a local on the platform that the train is indeed going to the airport (€11, buy ticket from computerized ticket machines or any *tabacchi* shop in the station, Termini–Fiumicino trains run 5:22–22:52). Read your ticket: If it requires validation, stamp it in the yellow machine near the platform before boarding. Know whether your plane departs from terminal A, B, or C.

Allow plenty of time going in either direction; there's a fair amount of transportation involved, including moving walkways, escalators, and walking (e.g., getting from your hotel to Termini, from Termini to the train platform, the ride to the airport, getting from the airport train station to check-in, etc.).

Shuttle van services run to and from the airport and can be economical for one or two people. Consider Rome Airport Shuttle (€28/1 person from Rome to Fiumicino, extra people-€6 each, €35/1 person from Fiumicino to Rome, extra people-€6 each, 30 percent more from 21:00–7:00, by reservation only, tel. 06-4201-4507 or 06-4201-3469, www.airportshuttle.it).

Rome's **taxis** now have a fixed rate to and from the airport (€40 for up to four people with bags). If your cab driver tries to charge you more than €40 from the airport into town, say, *"Quaranta euro—È la legge"* (kwah-RAHN-tah AY-oo-roh ay lah LAY-jay; which means, "Forty euros—it's the law"), and they should back off. Your hotel can arrange a taxi to the airport at any hour. To get from the airport into town cheaply by taxi, try teaming up with any tourist also just arriving (most are heading for hotels near yours in the center). Be sure to wait at the taxi stand. Avoid unmarked, unmetered taxis; these guys will try to tempt you away from the taxi stand line-up by offering an immediate (rip-off) ride.

For **airport information**, call 06-65951. To inquire about flights, call 06-6595-3640 (Alitalia: tel. 06-2222; British Airways: tel. 06-5249-2756; Continental: tel. 06-6605-3030; Delta: toll-free tel. 848-780-376; KLM/Northwest: tel. 199-414-199; Swiss International: tel. 848-868-120; United: tel. 02-6963-3707).

Ciampino Airport

Rome's smaller airport (tel. 06-6595-9515) handles some budget airlines, such as easyJet and Ryanair, and charter flights. To get to downtown Rome from the airport, you can take the Cotral bus (2/hr, 40 min) to the Anagnina Metro stop, where you can connect by Metro to the stop nearest your hotel. Rome Airport Shuttle (listed on previous page) also offers service to and from Ciampino. The Terravision Express Shuttle connects Ciampino and Termini, leaving every 20 minutes (€7 one-way, €12 round-trip, www .terravision.it). The SIT Bus Shuttle also connects the Termini train station to Ciampino (€6, 30–60 min, about 2/hr, runs 8:30–23:30 Ciampino to Termini, 4:30–23:15 Termini to Ciampino, pick-up on Via Marsala just outside the train exit to Ciampino, www.sitbusshuttle.it, tel. 06-591-7844).

VENICE

Venezia

Soak all day in this puddle of elegant decay. Venice is Europe's best-preserved big city. This car-free urban wonderland of a hundred islands—laced together by 400 bridges and 2,000 alleys—survives on the artificial respirator of tourism.

Born in a lagoon 1,500 years ago as a refuge from barbarians, Venice is overloaded with tourists and is slowly sinking (unrelated facts). In the Middle Ages, the Venetians became Europe's clever middlemen for East–West trade and created a great trading empire. By smuggling in the bones of St. Mark (San Marco) in A.D. 828, Venice gained religious importance as well. With the discovery of America and new trading routes to the Orient, Venetian power ebbed. But as Venice fell, her appetite for decadence grew. Through the 17th and 18th centuries, Venice partied on the wealth accumulated through earlier centuries as a trading power.

Today, Venice is home to about 62,000 people in its old city, down from a peak population of nearly 200,000. While there are about 500,000 in greater Venice (counting the mainland, not counting tourists), the old town has a small-town feel. Locals seem to know everyone. To see small-town Venice away from the touristic flak, escape the Rialto–San Marco tourist zone and savor the town early and late without the hordes of vacationers day-tripping in from cruise ships and nearby beach resorts. A 10-minute walk from the madness puts you in an idyllic Venice that few tourists see.

Planning Your Time

Venice is worth at least a day on even the speediest tour. Hyper-efficient train travelers take the night train in and/or out. Sleep in the old center to experience Venice at its best: early and late. For a one-day visit, cruise the Grand Canal, do the major sights on St. Mark's Square (the square itself, Doge's Palace, and St. Mark's Basilica), see the Frari Church for art, and wander the backstreets on a pub crawl. Venice's greatest sight is the city itself. Make time to simply wander. While doable in a day, Venice is worth two. It's a medieval cookie jar, and nobody's looking.

Orientation

The island city of Venice is shaped like a fish. Its major thorough-fares are canals. The Grand Canal winds through the middle of the fish, starting at the mouth where all the people and food enter, passing under the Rialto Bridge, and ending at St. Mark's Square (Piazza San Marco). Park your 21st-century perspective at the mouth and let Venice swallow you whole.

Venice is a car-less kaleidoscope of people, bridges, and odor-less canals. The city has no major streets, and addresses are hope-lessly confusing. There are six districts: San Marco (most touristy), Castello (behind San Marco), Cannaregio (from the train station to the Rialto), San Polo (other side of the Rialto), Santa Croce (the "eye" of the fish, east of the train station), and Dorsoduro (the belly of the fish and southernmost district of the city). Each district has about 6,000 address numbers.

To find your way, navigate by landmarks, not streets. Many street corners have a sign pointing you to *(per)* the nearest major landmark, such as San Marco, Accademia, Rialto, and Ferrovia (train station). Obedient visitors stick to the main thoroughfares as directed by these signs...and miss the charm of back-street Venice.

Tourist Information

There's a crowded, surly TI at the **train station** (daily 8:00–18:30) and two calmer TIs on and near St. Mark's Square: To find the TI on **St. Mark's Square,** stand with your back to St. Mark's Basilica and walk to the far-left corner of the square (daily 9:00–15:30). The other TI is near the **St. Mark's Square vaporetto stop** on the lagoon (daily 10:00–18:00, sells vaporetto tickets). Smaller offices are at **Piazzale Roma** and the **airport** (daily 9:00–21:00). For a quick question, save time by phoning 041-529-8711. The TI's offi-cial website is www.turismovenezia.it.

At any TI, confirm your sightseeing plans. Pick up the two free pamphlets that list museum hours, exhibitions, and musi-cal events (in Italian and English): *Shows and Events,* and the

Venice Overview

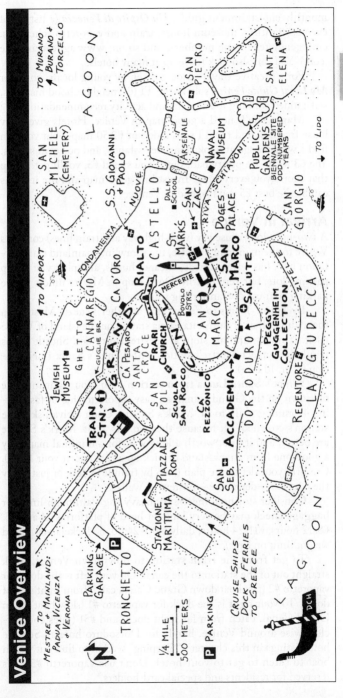

TO MURANO +
BURANO +
TORCELLO

LAGOON

SAN PIETRO

SANTA ELENA

SAN MICHELE (CEMETERY)

TO AIRPORT

S.S. GIOVANNI + PAOLO

FONDAMENTA NUOVE

CASTELLO

ARSENALE

PUBLIC GARDENS
BIENNALE SITE
ODD-NUMBERED YEARS

TO LIDO

DALM. SCHOOL

SAN ZAC.

RIVA SCHIAVONI

NAVAL MUSEUM

GHETTO

CANNAREGIO

GUGLIE BR.

CA D'ORO

RIALTO

ST. MARKS

DOGE'S PALACE

SAN MARCO

JEWISH MUSEUM

CA PESARO

SANTA CROCE

MERCERIE

Bovolo STRS.

SAN MARCO

SALUTE

SAN GIORGIO

SAN POLO

FRARI CHURCH

CANAL

SCUOLA SAN ROCCO

GRAND

TRAIN STN.

CA' REZZONICO

ACCADEMIA

DORSODURO

PEGGY GUGGENHEIM COLLECTION

PIAZZALE ROMA

SAN SEB.

REDENTORE

ZITELLE

LA GIUDECCA

STAZIONE MARITTIMA

CRUISE SHIPS
Dock + FERRIES
TO GREECE

LAGOON

TRONCHETTO

PARKING GARAGE

P

P PARKING

TO MESTRE + MAINLAND:
PADUA, VICENZA
+ VERONA

¼ MILE

500 METERS

N

DCH

monthly entertainment guide, *Un Ospite di Venezia* (a listing of events, nightlife, museum hours, train and vaporetto schedules, emergency telephone numbers, and so on; www.aguestinvenice .com). You can also pick these up at many hotels.

For a creative travel guide written by young locals, consider *My Local Guide Venice,* sold at the TI (€7, neighborhood histories, self-guided walking tours, sight and activity recommendations).

Maps: You'll need a good map in Venice. Hotels give away lousy freebies, and the TI sells a decent €2.50 map—but you can find a wider range at bookshops, newsstands, and postcard stands. The €3 maps are pretty bad, but if you spend €5, you'll get a map that shows you everything. Invest in a good map and use it—this can be the best €5 you'll spend in Venice.

Arrival in Venice

A two-mile-long causeway (with highway and train lines) connects Venice to the mainland. Mestre, the sprawling mainland transportation hub, has fewer crowds, cheaper hotels, and plenty of cheap parking lots, but zero charm. Don't stop in Mestre unless you're parking your car or transferring trains.

By Train: Trains to Venice stop at either Venezia Mestre (on the mainland) or at the Santa Lucia station on the island of Venice itself. If your train only stops at Mestre, worry not. Shuttle trains regularly connect Mestre's station with Venice's Santa Lucia station (6/hr, 10 min).

Venice's **Santa Lucia train station** plops you right into the old town on the Grand Canal, an easy vaporetto ride or fascinating 40-minute walk to St. Mark's Square. Upon arrival, skip the station's crowded TI, because the two TIs at St. Mark's Square are better, and it's not worth a long wait for a minimal map (buy a good one from a newsstand or pick up a free one at your hotel). Confirm your departure plan (stop by train info desk or just study the *partenze*—departure—posters on walls).

Consider storing unnecessary heavy bags, although lines for **baggage check** may be very long (at head of platforms 14 and 15, €8/12 hours, €11/24 hours, daily 6:00–24:00, no lockers, 45-pound weight limit on bags).

To get from the train station to downtown Venice, walk straight out of the station to the canal. On your left is the dock for vaporetto #2 (fast boat down Grand Canal, catch from right side of dock). To your right is the dock for vaporetto #1 (slow boat down Grand Canal, catch from far right dock) and #51 (goes counterclockwise around Venice, handy for Dorsoduro hotels). See the hotel listings in this chapter's "Sleeping" section to find out which boat to catch to get to your hotel. Don't use vaporetto #3—it's reserved for residents and special card-holders.

VENICE

Arrival in Venice

Buy a €6.50 **ticket** at the ticket window (a few shorter runs are only €2) and hop on a boat. You can also buy a pass for unlimited use of *vaporetti* and ACTV buses (sold in 12-hour increments—€14/12 hrs, €16/24 hrs, and so on up to €31/72 hrs).

By Car: The freeway dead-ends at Venice, near several parking lots on the edge of the island. The most central lot, San Marco, is very busy and expensive. Tronchetto (across the causeway and on the right) has a huge multistoried garage (€20/day, tel. 041-520-7555). From there, avoid the travel agencies masquerading as TIs, and head directly for the vaporetto docks for the boat connection (#2) to the town center. Don't let water taxi boatmen con you out of the relatively cheap €6.50 vaporetto ride.

Parking in Mestre is easy and cheap (open-air lots cost €5/day Mon–Fri, €10/day Sat–Sun, across from Mestre train station, easy shuttle-train connections to Venice's Santa Lucia Station—6/hr, 10 min). There are also huge and economical lots in Verona, Padua, and Vicenza.

By Plane: For information on Venice's airport and connections into the city, see "Connections" at the end of this chapter.

Passes for Venice

To help control (and confuse?) its flood of visitors, Venice offers cards and passes that cover some museums and/or transportation. For most visitors, the San Marco Museum Plus Pass is the best choice. Busy sightseers may prefer the more expensive Museum Pass, which covers more (though lesser) sights.

Note that the San Marco Museum Plus Pass is available only from April through October; off-season (Nov–March), it's replaced by the Museum Card of the Museums of St. Mark's Square, which costs a bit less and covers fewer sights. The Museum Pass is offered year-round. The passes are sold at the sights they cover.

All three passes include the popular Doge's Palace and the less-visited Correr Museum (both on St. Mark's Square); individual tickets are not sold for these two sights.

None of the passes covers these top attractions: Accademia, Peggy Guggenheim Collection, Scuola San Rocco, Campanile, and the three sights within St. Mark's Basilica that charge admission.

Here are specifics on the passes:

The **San Marco Museum Plus Pass,** sold from April through October, covers the Doge's Palace and Correr Museum (€13, valid 3 months; to bypass the long line at Doge's Palace, purchase pass at Correr Museum, then enter Doge's Palace). The San Marco Museum Plus Pass also covers the two museums accessed from within the Correr—the National Archaeological Museum and the Monumental Rooms of Marciana National Library—plus your choice of one of these seven museums: Ca' Rezzonico (Museum of 18th-Century Venice), the 18th-Century Costume Museum, Casa Goldoni (home of the Italian playwright), Ca' Pesaro (modern art), the Museum of Natural History in the Santa Croce district, the Glass Museum on the island of Murano, or the Lace Museum on the island of Burano.

The **Museum Card of the Museums of St. Mark's Square,** sold from November through March, covers only the Doge's Palace and Correr Museum (€12).

The pricier **Museum Pass,** available all year, covers admission to the Doge's Palace and Correr Museum, plus entry to all of the museums listed in the description of the San Marco Museum Plus Pass above (€18, valid 6 months). In general, this pass saves you money if you visit five or more sights, but before you buy, make sure they're sights you really want to see.

Church-lovers can get a **Chorus Pass** that includes 16 of Venice's churches (including San Polo and the Frari, covered in this book) and their works of art (€9, €6 with a Venice Card—see below, or pay €3 per church; Chorus Family Pass costs €18 for 2 adults and kids 18 and under; valid 1 year). You'd need to visit four churches to save money.

Venice Cards: The Blue and Orange Venice Cards are transit passes (good for 1–7 days) that include the use of public toilets—not worth considering unless you have diarrhea.

"Rolling Venice" Youth Discount Pass: To those under age 30, this worthwhile pass gives discounts on sights and transportation, plus information on cheap eating and sleeping. It's sold at all of Venice's TIs and at the train station (both inside at TI, and outside at Vela kiosk; €4/1 day, €15/3 days, bring ID).

Helpful Hints

Get Lost: Accept the fact that Venice was a tourist town 400 years ago. It was, is, and always will be crowded. While 80 percent of Venice is, in fact, not touristy, 80 percent of the tourists never notice. Hit the back streets. Venice is the ideal town to explore on foot. Walk and walk to the far reaches of the town. Don't worry about getting lost. In fact, get as lost as possible. Keep reminding yourself, "I'm on an island, and I can't get off." When it comes time to find your way, just follow the directional arrows on building corners or simply ask a local, *"Dov'è San Marco?"* ("Where is St. Mark's?") People in the tourist business (that's most Venetians) speak some English. If they don't, listen politely, watch where their hands point, say, *"Grazie,"* and head off in that direction. If you're lost, refer to your map, or pop into a hotel and ask for their business card—it comes with a map and a prominent "You are here."

Be Prepared to Splurge: Venice is expensive for locals as well as tourists. Demand is huge, supply is limited, and running a business is costly. Things just cost more here; everything must be shipped in and hand-trucked to its destination. Perhaps the best way to enjoy Venice is just to succumb to its charms and blow a lot of money.

Warning: The dark, late-night streets of Venice are safe. Even so, pickpockets (often elegantly dressed) work the crowded main streets, docks, and *vaporetti* (wear your money belt and carry your day bag in front). Your biggest risk of pickpockets is actually inside St. Mark's Basilica. A service called Counter of Tourist Mediation handles complaints about local crooks—including gondolier, restaurant, or hotel rip-offs—but does not give out information (tel. 041-529-8710, complaint.apt @turismovenezia.it). Immigrants selling items such as knock-off handbags on the streets are doing so illegally—if you buy goods from them, you'll risk getting a big fine.

Crowd Control: Crowds can be a serious problem at St. Mark's Basilica (try going early or late, or even better, you can bypass the line if you have a bag to check—see listing in this chapter's

"Sights" section); the Campanile (ascend early or late—it's open until 21:00 July–Aug—or even skip it entirely if you're going to the similar San Giorgio Maggiore bell tower); the Accademia (go early or late—or reserve a ticket by calling 041-520-0345), and the Doge's Palace (see "Crowd Control," page 873). The sights that have crowd problems get even more crowded when it rains.

Medical Help: Venice's S.S. Giovanni e Paolo hospital (tel. 118) is a 10-minute walk from both the Rialto and San Marco neighborhoods, located on Fondamenta dei Mendicanti toward Fondamenta Nuove. Take vaporetto #41 from San Zaccaria–Jolanda to the Ospedale stop.

Audiotours: Users of iPods and other MP3 players can download free audiotours of the Grand Canal, St. Mark's Square, St. Mark's Basilica, and the Frari Church from my website, www.ricksteves.com.

Take Breaks: Venice's endless pavement, crowds, and tight spaces are hard on the tourist. Schedule breaks in your sightseeing. Grab a cool place to sit down, relax, and recoup—meditate on a pew in an uncrowded church, or stop in a café.

Etiquette: Walk on the right and don't loiter on bridges. Picnicking is forbidden (keep a low profile). On St. Mark's Square, a "decorum patrol" admonishers snackers and sunbathers. The only place for a legal picnic is in Giardinetti Reali, the small park along the waterfront west of the Piazzetta near St. Mark's Square.

Dress modestly. Men should keep their shirts on. When visiting St. Mark's Basilica or other major churches, men, women, and even children must cover their shoulders and knees (or risk being turned away). Remove hats when entering a church.

Pigeon Poop: If your head is bombed by a pigeon, resist the initial response to wipe it off immediately—it'll just smear into your hair. Wait until it dries, and it should flake off cleanly. But if the poop splatters on your clothes, wipe it off immediately to avoid a stain.

Public Toilets: There are handy public WCs (€1) near St. Mark's Square (one behind the Correr Museum, another at the waterfront park Giardinetti Reali), near Rialto, and at the Accademia Bridge. You'll find public pay toilets near most major landmarks. Use free toilets—in a museum you're visiting or a café you're eating in—when you can.

Water: Venetians pride themselves on having pure, safe, and tasty tap water piped in from the foothills of the Alps. You can actually see the mountains from Venice's bell towers on crisp, clear winter days.

Lingo: *Campo* means square, *campiello* is a small square, *calle* is street, *fondamenta* is the road running along a canal, *rio* is a small canal, *rio terra* is a street that was once a canal and has been filled in, and *ponte* is a bridge.

Services

Money: The plentiful ATMs are the easiest way to go. If you must exchange currency, be aware that bank rates vary. Non-bank exchange bureaus, such as Exacto, will charge you $10 more than a bank for a $200 exchange.

Internet Access: You'll find handy, if pricey (€5/hr), little Internet places all over town. They are usually on back streets: Ask your hotelier for the nearest place.

Post Office: A large post office is just outside the far end of St. Mark's Square (the end farthest from the basilica; Mon–Fri 8:30–14:00, Sat 8:30–13:00, closed Sun, shorter hours off-season). The main P.O. is near the Rialto Bridge (on the St. Mark's side, Mon–Sat 8:30–18:30, closed Sun). Use post offices only as a last resort, as simple transactions can take 45 minutes if you get in the wrong line. You can buy stamps from tobacco shops and mail postcards at any of the red post-boxes around town.

Bookstores: Libreria Mondadori is a gorgeous bookstore carrying a huge selection of Venice books, local guidebooks, and even my guidebooks (the tourist-oriented books are on the ground floor). This is the biggest bookstore in town, with plenty in English and three Internet terminals (daily May–Oct 10:00–23:00, Nov–April 10:00–20:00, a block behind the Correr end of Piazza San Marco at 1345 Complesso del Ridotto, tel. 041-522-2193). **Libreria Studium** stocks all the English-language guidebooks (including mine) just a block behind St. Mark's Basilica (Mon–Sat 9:00–19:30, Sun 9:30–13:30, Calle de la Canonica, tel. 041-522-2382).

Laundry: These two laundry options are near San Marco, but your hotelier can direct you to one near your hotel: A modern **self-service** *lavanderia* is on Ruga Giuffa at #4826 (wring clothes before drying, or you'll bring them home damp; self-service daily 8:30–20:00, full-service Mon–Fri only 8:30–14:00, next to recommended Hotel al Piave—listed on page 889, mobile 347-870-6452, run by Massimo). **Lavanderia Gabriella** offers full service (€15/load wash and dry, Mon–Fri 8:00–12:30, closed Sat–Sun; with your back to the door of San Zulian Church, go over Ponte dei Ferali, then take first right down Calle dei Armeni, then first left on Rio Terra Colonne to #985; tel. 041-522-1758, Elisabetta).

Travel Agencies: If you need to get train tickets, make seat reservations, or arrange a *cucetta* (koo-CHET-tah—a berth on a night train); you can avoid a time-consuming trip to the crowded train station by using a downtown travel agency. They can also give advice on cheap flights. Note that you'll get a far better price if you're able to book at least a week in advance. Consider booking flights for later in your trip while you're here.

Oltrex, just one bridge past the Bridge of Sighs, sells train and plane tickets and happily books train reservations for a €2 fee (daily May–Oct 9:00–19:00, Nov–April 9:00–17:30, Riva degli Schiavoni 4192, tel. 041-524-2828).

Kele e Teo Viaggi Turismo, midway between St. Mark's Square and Rialto, makes train reservations for a €3 fee and also sells train and plane tickets (Mon–Fri 8:30–18:00, Sat 8:30–12:00, closed Sun, Mercerie/Marzaria 4930).

English Church Services: The **San Zulian Church** (the only church in Venice that you can actually walk around) offers a Mass in English (generally May–Sept Mon–Fri at 9:30 and Sun at 11:30, Sun only Oct–April, 2 blocks toward Rialto off St. Mark's Square).

Haircuts: I've been getting my hair cut at **Coiffeur Benito** for nearly two decades. Benito has been keeping local men and women trim for 27 years. He's an artist—actually a "hair sculptor"—and a cut here is a fun diversion from the tourist grind (€20 for women, €18 for men, Tue–Fri 8:30–13:00 & 15:30–19:30, Sat 8:30–13:00 only, closed Sun–Mon, behind San Zulian Church near St. Mark's Square, Calle S. Zulian Già del Strazzariol 592a, tel. 041-528-6221).

Museum Discounts: Venice's city museums, unlike most Italian museums, grant youth and senior discounts to non-EU citizens. These museums include the Doge's Palace, Correr Museum, the Clock Tower on St. Mark's Square, Ca' Rezzonico, Ca' Pesaro, and the 18th-Century Costume Museum (a.k.a. Museo di Palazzo Mocenigo).

Getting Around Venice

On Foot: Navigate by major landmarks. There are signs on street corners all over town pointing to San Marco, Accademia, Ferrovia (train station), and Piazzale Roma (the bus stop behind the train station). Determine whether your destination is in the direction of a major signposted landmark, then follow the signs through the maze of squares, lanes, and bridges.

By Vaporetto: The public-transit system is a fleet of motorized bus-boats called *vaporetti*. They work like city buses except that they never get a flat, the stops are docks, and if you get off between stops, you might drown.

For most travelers, only two lines matter: #1 is the slow boat, which takes 45 minutes to make every stop along the entire length of the Grand Canal (leaves every 10 min); and #2 is the fast boat that zips down the Grand Canal in 25 minutes (leaves every 10 min), stopping at Tronchetto (parking lot), Piazzale Roma (bus station), Ferrovia (train station), San Marcuola, Rialto Bridge, San Tomà (Frari Church), Accademia Bridge, San Marco (west end of St. Mark's Square), San Zaccaria (east end of St. Mark's Square), and on to San Giorgio Maggiore. Some #2 boats go only as far as Rialto *(solo Rialto)*—check with the conductor before boarding. Line #3 is open only to residents.

It's a simple system, but there are a few quirks. Some stops have just one dock for boats going in both directions, so make sure the boat you get on is pointing in the direction you want to go. Larger stops have two docks side by side (one for each direction), while some smaller stops have docks across the canal from each other (one for each direction). Check the signs to find the right dock. Electronic reader boards on busy docks display which boats are coming next and when. Signs on board indicate upcoming stops.

Some lines don't run early or late. For example, off-season the #2 fast vaporetto doesn't leave the San Marco–Vallaresso dock (at St. Mark's Square) until 9:15 (and runs only until 20:30); if you're trying to get from St. Mark's Square to the train station to catch an early train, you'd need to take a different fast boat that loops outside the Grand Canal. If there's any doubt, ask a ticket-seller or conductor. If you plan to ride a lot of *vaporetti,* consider picking up the most current ACTV timetable (free at ticket booths, in English and Italian, www.actv.it).

Standard single **tickets** are €6.50 each (a few shorter runs are only €2, such as the route from San Marco–Vallaresso to Salute or from San Zaccaria–M.V.E to San Giorgio Maggiore). Tickets are good for 60 minutes in one direction; you can hop on and off at stops during that time. Technically, you're not allowed a round-trip (though in practice, a round-trip is allowed if you can complete it within a 60-minute span). Oversized luggage can cost a second ticket—but light packers have no worries.

You can buy a **pass** for unlimited use of *vaporetti* and ACTV buses (sold in 12-hour increments—€14/12 hrs, €16/24 hrs, and so on up to €31/72 hrs). Because single tickets cost a hefty €6.50 a pop, these passes can pay for themselves in a hurry. And it's fun to be able to hop on and off spontaneously. On the other hand, many tourists just walk and rarely use a boat—so before buying a pass, look at a map to see how far afield your likely destinations are.

You can buy vaporetto tickets or a pass at ticket booths at main stops (such as Ferrovia, Rialto, Accademia, and San Marco–Vallaresso); from a conductor on board (do it before you sit down,

VENICE

Venice

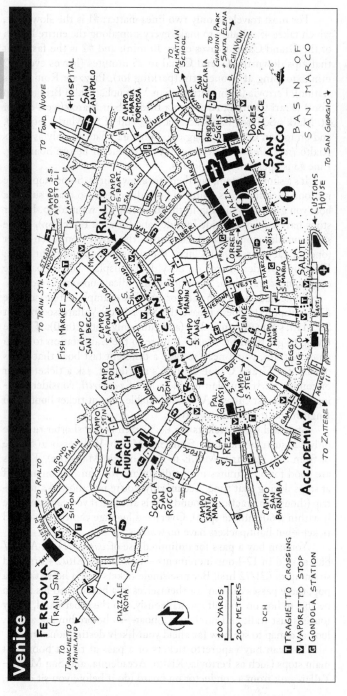

FERROVIA (TRAIN STN.)

PIAZZALE ROMA

TO TRONCHETTO & MAINLAND

TO Rialto

FOND. RIO MARIN

S. SIMON

CAMPO S. STIN

AMAI

LACA

TINT

Scuola San Rocco

FRARI CHURCH

CAMPO SANTA MARG.

CAMPO SAN BARNABA

TOLETTA

ACCADEMIA

TO Zattere

AGNESE

CA' REZZ.

FOSC

PAL. GRASSI

CAMPO S. STEF.

CAMPO S. SAM. SAM. BOT.

SPEZ.

LA FENICE

CAMPO MAUR.

GAMB.

BAST.

Peggy Gug. Col.

SALUTE

S. MARIA

22 MARZO

CAMPO S. MOISÈ

Correr Mus.

FREZ.

VALL.

VESTE

VERONA

MANDOLA

LUCA

CAMPO S. ANG.

SILV. FOND. VIN.

CAMPO MANIN

RASSE

MAD

CAMPO S. APONAL

CAMPO S. POLO

TOMA

SAON.

CAMPO S. TOMA

CAMPO BECC.

Fish Market

TO TRAIN STN.

MKT.

STRADA NUOVA

CAMPO S.S. APOSTOLI

S. CANC.

RIALTO

MERCERIE

FABBRI

DAL. S. LIO

CAMPO S. BART.

S. MARCO

PIAZZA

Doge's Palace

BRIDGE OF SIGHS

San Zaccaria

RIVA D. SCHIAVONI

OSPAR.

BASIN OF SAN MARCO

TO SAN GIORGIO

Customs House

SAN MARCO

GIUFFA

CIC.

CAMPO S. MARIA FORMOSA

San Zanipolo

HOSPITAL

TO FOND NUOVE

TO DALMATIAN SCHOOL

TO Giardini Park + Santa Elena

N

200 YARDS
200 METERS

DCH

■ TRAGHETTO CROSSING
▼ VAPORETTO STOP
G GONDOLA STATION

or you risk a €44 fine); or at a TI (for no extra fee). Plan your travel so you'll have tickets or a pass handy when you need them—not all stops have ticket booths.

Passes must be stamped before the first use. Tickets generally come already stamped, but if for whatever reason, your ticket lacks a stamp, stick it into the time-stamping yellow machine before boarding.

For vaporetto fun, take the Grand Canal Cruise, described later in this chapter. During rush hour (about 9:00 from the Tronchetto parking lot and train station toward St. Mark's, about 17:00 in the other direction), boats are jam-packed. If you like joyriding on *vaporetti*, ride a boat around the city and out into the lagoon, then over to the Lido, and back. Ask for the circular route—*circulare* (cheer-koo-LAH-ray). It's usually the #51 or #52, leaving from the San Zaccaria–Danieli vaporetto stop (near the Doge's Palace) and from all the stops along the perimeter of Venice.

By *Traghetto*: Only four bridges cross the Grand Canal, but *traghetti* (gondolas) shuttle locals and in-the-know tourists across the Grand Canal at seven handy locations (see map on opposite page; routes also marked on pricier maps sold in Venice). Most people stand while riding (€0.50, generally run 6:00–14:00, some lines—such as S.M. Giglio–Salute and Angelo-Tomá—go until 20:00, most end 30 min earlier on Sun).

By Water Taxi: Venetian taxis, like speedboat limos, hang out at most busy points along the Grand Canal. Prices, which average €65, are a bit soft (about €65 to the train station or €95 to the airport for up to four people, extra fees for very early or late runs). Negotiate and settle on the price before stepping in. For travelers with lots of luggage or small groups who can split the cost, taxi rides can be a worthwhile and time-saving convenience—and skipping across the lagoon in a classic wooden motorboat is a cool indulgence. For €90 an hour, you can have a private, unguided taxi-boat tour.

By Gondola: To hire a gondolier for your own private cruise, see "Gondola Rides," under "Experiences," later in this chapter.

Tours

Avventure Bellissime Venice Tours—This company offers a selection of two-hour walks, including a basic St. Mark's Square introduction called the "Original Venice Walking Tour" (most days at 11:00; 45 min on the square, 15 min in the church, 60 min along back streets). Other walks explore the neighborhoods of Cannaregio/Jewish Ghetto and San Polo/Dorsoduro, while another walk focuses on ghost stories and legends (€20/person, cheaper for returnees and students, ask for Rick Steves discount when booking online or calling direct, group size 8–22, tours run rain or shine, English-language only, tel. 041-520-8616, mobile 340-050-2444, see www.tours-italy.com for details, info@tours -italy.com, Monica or Jonathan).

Their Doge's Palace tour includes the "Secret Itinerary" (€25/person, 2 hours). Their 70-minute Grand Canal boat tour, offered daily at 16:30 (€40), is limited to eight people and timed for good late-afternoon light. The company also runs day trips to the Dolomites, Veneto hill towns, and Palladian villas (8-person maximum, varying prices, 10 percent discount if you say "Rick sent me").

Classic Venice Bars Tour—Debonair local guide Alessandro Schezzini is a connoisseur of Venetian *bacari*—classic old bars serving traditional *cicchetti* (local munchies). He offers evening tours that include sampling a snack and a glass of wine at three different *bacari*, and he'll answer all of your questions about Venice (€30/person; March–Nov generally Mon, Wed, and Fri at 18:00; other evenings and off-season by request and with demand, 6–8 per group, meet at top of Rialto Bridge, call or email a day or two in advance to confirm, mobile 335-530-9024, venische@libero.it).

Venicescapes—Michael Broderick's private theme tours of Venice are intellectually demanding and beyond the attention span of most mortal tourists. Rather than a "sightseeing tour," consider your time with Michael a rolling, graduate-level lecture. Michael's objective: to help visitors gain a more solid understanding of Venice. For a description of his various itineraries, see www .venicescapes.org (book well in advance, tours last 4–6 hours: $275 for 2 people, $50/person after that, either pay in dollars or he'll convert the price to euros, admissions and transportation are extra, tel. 041-520-6361, info@venicescapes.org).

Artviva: The Original & Best Walking Tours—This company offers a number of tours, including the Doge's Palace (€20, 1 hour), St. Mark's Square (€40, 2 hours), and a Gondola/Grand Canal tour (€50, 1 hour, discount for my readers on canal tour). Advance booking is always necessary; all their tours are listed on their website (tours run March–Nov Mon, Wed, Fri–Sat, max 14 persons, private tours offered year-round, tel. 055-264-5033 during day or mobile 329-613-2730 18:00–20:00, www.italy.artviva.com, staff @artviva.com).

Local Guides—Licensed guides are carefully trained and love explaining Venice to visitors. The following companies and guides give excellent tours to individuals, families, and small groups. If you organize a small group from your hotel at breakfast to split the cost (€70/hr with 2-hour minimum), the fee becomes quite reasonable.

Elisabetta Morelli is reliable, personable, and informative, giving good insight into daily life in Venice (€70/hr, tours last 2–3 hours, tel. 041-526-7816, mobile 328-753-5220, bettamorelli @inwind.it).

Venice with a Guide is a co-op of 10 equally good guides (www.venicewithaguide.com).

Walks Inside Venice is a group of three women enthusiastic about teaching (€75/hr per group, 3-hour min; Cristina: mobile 348-341-5421; Roberta: mobile 347-253-0560; Sara: mobile 335-522-9714; www.walksinsidevenice.com, info@walksinsidevenice .com).

Alessandro Schezzini isn't a licensed Italian guide (and is therefore unable to take you into actual sights), but he does a great job getting you beyond the clichés and into offbeat Venice. He offers a relaxed, two-hour, back-street "Rick Steves" tour (€15/ person; March–Nov generally Mon, Wed, and Fri; meet at 16:00 at top of Rialto Bridge, call to confirm, mobile 335-530-9024, venische@libero.it). You can take this offbeat walk, and then join Alessandro for the pub crawl immediately afterward (see "Classic Venice Bars Tour," opposite page). Alessandro also gives private tours to groups of any size at any time (€90/2.5 hrs).

Self-Guided Cruise

▲▲▲Welcome to Venice Grand Canal Cruise

Introduce yourself to Venice by boat. Cruise the Canal Grande all the way to San Marco, starting from Piazzale Roma (where airport buses arrive and depart) or Ferrovia (the Santa Lucia train station).

While the Grand Canal is done in 25 minutes on boat #2, this tour is designed to be done on the slow boat #1 (which takes about 45 minutes). When catching your boat, confirm that you're on a "San Marco via Rialto" boat (some boats finish at the Rialto Bridge, others take a non-scenic outside route). The conductor announces *"Solo Rialto!"* for boats going only as far as Rialto. You do not want boats heading for Piazzale Roma. Note that only boat #1 docks at all the stops we list; the faster boat #2 skips some stops.

Enjoy the best light and fewest crowds early or late. Sunset bathes the buildings in gold. After dark, chandeliers light up the building interiors. While Venice is a barrage on the senses that hardly needs a narration, these notes give the cruise a little meaning and help orient you to this great city. Some city maps (on sale at postcard racks) have a handy Grand Canal map on the back.

Overview

The Grand Canal is Venice's "Main Street." At more than two miles long, nearly 150 feet wide, and nearly 15 feet deep, it's the city's largest canal, lined with its most impressive palaces. The canal is the remnant of a river that once spilled from the mainland into the Adriatic. The sediment it carried formed barrier islands that cut Venice off from the sea, forming a lagoon. Venice was built on the marshy islands of the former delta, sitting on pilings driven nearly 15 feet into the clay.

Venice is a city of palaces, dating from the days when it was the world's richest city. The most lavish palaces formed a grand chorus line along the Grand Canal. Once frescoed in reds and blues, with black-and-white borders and gold-leaf trim, they made Venice a city of dazzling color. This cruise is the only way to truly appreciate the palaces, approaching them at water level, where their main entrances were located. Today, strict laws prohibit any changes in these buildings, so while landowners gnash their teeth, we can enjoy Europe's best-preserved medieval city—slowly rotting. Many of the grand buildings are now vacant. Others harbor chandeliered elegance above mossy, empty (often flooded) ground floors.

The Grand Canal Cruise Begins

Start at the **train station.** We'll orient by the vaporetto stops.

Venice's main thoroughfare is busy with all kinds of **boats:** taxis, police boats, garbage boats, ambulances, construction cranes, and even brown-and-white UPS boats. Venice's sleek, black, graceful **gondolas** are a symbol of the city. The boats run about €35,000–50,000, depending on your options (air-con, cup holders, etc). Today, with more than 400 gondoliers joyriding amid the churning *vaporetti,* there's a lot of congestion on the Grand Canal. Watch your vaporetto driver curse the better-paid gondoliers.

❶ **Ferrovia:** The **Santa Lucia train station,** one of the few modern buildings in town, was built in 1954. It's been the gateway into Venice since 1860, when the first station was built. "F.S." stands for "Ferrovie dello Stato," the Italian state railway system.

More than 20,000 people a day commute in from the mainland, making this the busiest part of Venice during rush hour. To alleviate some of the congestion and make the commute easier, the new **Calatrava Bridge** spans the Grand Canal between the train station and Piazzale Roma, behind you. Opposite the train station, atop the green dome of **San Simeone Piccolo** church, St. Simeon waves *ciao* to whomever enters or leaves the "old" city. The pink church with the white Carrara-marble facade, just beyond the train station, is the **Church of the Scalzi** (Church of the Barefoot, named after the shoeless Carmelite monks), where the last doge (Venetian ruler) rests.

Venice's Grand Canal

JEWISH GHETTO

🚶 TRAGHETTO CROSSING

CANNAREGIO CANAL

PONTE GUGLIE

SANTA LUCIA TRAIN STATION

SCALZI CHURCH

❸ CASINÒ

FADED FRESCOES

CALATRAVA BRIDGE

SCALZI BRIDGE

❷ TURKISH "FONDACO" EXCHANGE

❹ CA' D'ORO

SAN STAE

CA' PESARO

❺ TRAGHETTO

SAN SIMEONE PICCOLO

POST OFFICE

TO PIAZZALE ROMA + TRONCHETTO

FISH + PRODUCE MARKET

❻

RIALTO BRIDGE

MERCHANTS' PALACES

❽

❼

CAMPANILE

PALAZZO BALBI

❿

TWO PALACES

BRIDGE OF SIGHS

FIRE STATION

❾

SAN MARCO

CA' FOSCARI

PALAZZO GRASSI

CA' REZZONICO

⓫

GRITTI PALACE HOTEL

⓭

HARRY'S BAR

DOGE'S PALACE

RIVA

⓰

TO LIDO

ACCADEMIA GALLERY + BRIDGE

⓬

⓮

⓯

SAN MARCO

LA SALUTE

CUSTOMS HOUSE

DCH

PEGGY GUGGENHEIM COLLECTION

PALAZZO DARIO + SALVIATI BUILDING

TO SAN GIORGIO MAGGIORE + GIUDECCA

200 YARDS
200 METERS

Vaporetto Stops

❶ Ferrovia
❷ Riva de Biasio
❸ San Marcuola
❹ San Stae
❺ Ca' d'Oro
❻ Mercato Rialto
❼ Rialto
❽ San Silvestro

❾ Sant'Angelo
❿ San Tomà
⓫ Ca' Rezzonico
⓬ Accademia
⓭ Santa Maria del Giglio
⓮ Salute
⓯ San Marco
⓰ San Zaccaria

❷ **Riva di Biasio:** About 25 yards past the Riva di Biasio stop, you'll look left down the broad **Cannaregio Canal** to see what was the **Jewish Ghetto** (described in "Sights," later in this chapter). The twin, pale-pink, six-story "skyscrapers"—the tallest buildings you'll see at this end of the canal—are reminders of how densely populated the world's original ghetto was. Set aside as the local Jewish quarter in 1516, this area became extremely crowded. This urban island developed into one of the most closely knit business and cultural quarters of all the Jewish communities in Italy, and gave us our word ghetto (from *geto*, the copper foundry located here). For more information, visit the Jewish Museum in this neighborhood (also described in "Sights").

❸ **San Marcuola:** At this stop, facing a tiny square just ahead, stands the unfinished church of San Marcuola, one of only five churches fronting the Grand Canal. About 20 yards ahead on the right stands the stately gray **Turkish "Fondaco" Exchange,** one of the oldest houses in Venice. Its horseshoe arches and roofline of triangles and dingleballs are reminders of its Byzantine heritage. Turkish traders in turbans docked here, unloaded their goods into the warehouse on the bottom story, then went upstairs for a home-style meal and a place to sleep. Venice in the 1500s was very cosmopolitan, welcoming every religion and ethnicity, so long as they carried cash. (Today, the building contains the city's Museum of Natural History—and Venice's only dinosaur.)

Just 100 yards ahead on the left, Venice's **Casinò** is housed in the palace where German composer Richard *(The Ring of the Nibelung)* Wagner died in 1883. See his distinct, strong-jawed profile in the white plaque on the brick wall. In the 1700s, Venice was Europe's Las Vegas, with casinos and prostitutes everywhere. *Casinòs* ("little houses") have long provided Italians with a handy escape from daily life. Today, they're run by the state to keep Mafia influence at bay. Notice the fancy front porch, rolling out the red carpet for high rollers arriving by taxi or hotel boat.

❹ **San Stae:** Opposite the San Stae stop, look for the peeling plaster that once made up **frescoes** (scant remains on the lower floors). Imagine the facades of the Grand Canal at their finest. As colorful as the city is today, it's still only a faded sepia-toned remnant of a long-gone era, a time of lavishly decorated and brilliantly colored palaces.

Just ahead, jutting out a bit on the right, is the ornate white facade of **Ca' Pesaro.** *"Ca'"* is short for *casa* (house). Because only the house of the doge (Venetian ruler) could be called a palazzo (palace), all other Venetian palaces are technically *"Ca'."*

In this city of masks, notice how the rich marble facades along the Grand Canal mask what are generally just simple, no-nonsense brick buildings. Smart businessmen only decorated the side of the buildings that would be seen and appreciated. But look back as you pass Ca' Pesaro (which houses the International Gallery of Modern Art, described in this chapter's "Sights" section). It's the only building you'll see with a fine side facade. Ahead, on the left, with its glorious triple-decker medieval arcade (just before the next stop) is Ca' d'Oro.

❺ **Ca' d'Oro:** The lacy **Ca' d'Oro** (House of Gold) is the best example of Venetian Gothic architecture on the canal. Its three stories offer different variations on balcony design, topped with a spiny white roofline. Venetian Gothic mixes traditional Gothic (pointed arches and round medallions stamped with a four-leaf clover) with Byzantine styles (tall, narrow arches atop thin columns), filled in with Islamic frills. Like all the palaces, this was originally painted and gilded to make it even more glorious than it is now. Today the Ca' d'Oro is an art gallery (described in "Sights").

On the right is the arcade of the covered **fish market,** with the open-air **produce market** just beyond. It bustles in the morning but is quiet the rest of the day. This is a great scene to wander through—even though European hygiene standards recently required a remodeling job that left it cleaner...but less colorful. Find the *traghetto* ferrying shoppers—standing like Washington crossing the Delaware—back and forth.

❻ **Mercato Rialto:** This stop was opened in 2007 to serve the busy market (boats stop here from 8:00–20:00). The long and officious-looking building at this stop is the Venice court house. Straight ahead, in the distance, rising above the huge post office, you can see the tip of the Campanile (bell tower) crowned by its golden angel at St. Mark's Square, where this tour will end. The **post office** (100 yards directly ahead, on left side, often with *servizio postale* boats moored at its blue posts, was the German Exchange, the trading center for German metal merchants, in the early 1500s.

You'll cruise by some trendy and beautifully situated wine bars on the right, but look ahead as you round the corner and see the impressive Rialto Bridge come into view.

A major landmark of Venice, the **Rialto Bridge** is lined with shops and tourists. Constructed in 1588, it's the third bridge built on this spot. Until the 1850s, this was the only bridge crossing the Grand Canal. With a span of 160 feet and foundations stretching 650 feet on either side, the Rialto was an impressive engineering feat in its day. Earlier Rialto Bridges could open to let big ships in, but not this one. When this new bridge was completed, much of the Grand Canal was closed to shipping and became a canal of palaces.

❼ **Rialto:** A separate town in the early days of Venice, Rialto has always been the commercial district, while San Marco was the religious and governmental center. Today, a winding street called the Mercerie connects the two, providing travelers with human traffic jams and a mesmerizing gauntlet of shopping temptations.

Ahead 100 yards on the left, two gray-colored palaces stand side by side (the city hall and the mayor's office). Their horseshoe-shaped, arched windows are similar and their stories are the same height, lining up to create the effect of one long balcony.

❽ **San Silvestro:** We now enter a long stretch of important

merchants' palaces, each with proud and different facades. Because ships couldn't navigate beyond the Rialto Bridge, the biggest palaces—with the major shipping needs—line this last stretch of the navigable Grand Canal.

Palaces like these were multifunctional: ground floor for the warehouse, offices and showrooms upstairs, and the living quarters above the offices on the "noble floor" (with big windows designed to allow in maximum light). Servants lived and worked on the top floors (with the smallest windows).

❾ Sant'Angelo: Notice how many buildings have a foundation of waterproof white stone *(pietra d'Istria)* upon which the bricks sit high and dry. Many canal-level floors are abandoned as the rising water level takes its toll. The **posts**—historically painted gaily with the equivalent of family coats of arms—don't rot under water. But the wood at the waterline, where it's exposed to oxygen, does.

❿ San Tomà: Fifty yards ahead, on the right side (with twin obelisks on the rooftop) stands the **Palazzo Balbi,** the palace of an early 17th-century captain general of the sea. These Venetian equivalents of five-star admirals were honored with twin obelisks decorating their palaces. This palace, like so many in the city, flies three flags: those of Italy (green, white, and red), the European Union (blue with ring of stars), and Venice (the lion). Today, it houses the administrative headquarters of the regional government.

As you pass the admiral's palace, look immediately to the right, down a side canal. On the right side of that canal, before the bridge, see the traffic light and the **fire station** (with four arches hiding fireboats parked and ready to go).

The impressive **Ca' Foscari,** with a classic Venetian facade (on the corner, across from the fire station), dominates the bend in the canal. This is the main building of the University of Venice, which has about 25,000 students. Notice the elegant lamp on the corner.

The grand, heavy, white **Ca' Rezzonico,** just before the next stop (of the same name), houses the Museum of 18th-Century Venice (described under "Sights," later in this chapter). Across the canal (and a bit behind you) is the cleaner and leaner **Palazzo Grassi,** the last major palace built on the canal, erected in the late 1700s—and recently purchased by a French tycoon.

⓫ Ca' Rezzonico: Up ahead, the **Accademia Bridge** leads over the Grand Canal to the **Accademia** art museum (right side), filled with the best Venetian paintings (described in "Sights"). The bridge was put up in 1934 as a temporary one. Locals liked it, so it stayed.

⓬ Accademia: Look through the graceful bridge and way ahead to enjoy a classic view of the domed **La Salute Church**

(described in "Sights"). This Church of Saint Mary of Good Health was built to thank God for delivering Venetians from the devastating plague of 1630 (which had killed about a third of the city's population).

The low white building among greenery (100 yards ahead, on the right, between the Accademia Bridge and the church) is the **Peggy Guggenheim Collection.** The American heiress "retired" here, sprucing up the palace that had been abandoned in mid-construction. Peggy willed the city her fine collection of modern art (described in "Sights").

❸ **Santa Maria del Giglio:** Back on the left stands the fancy Gritti Palace hotel. (Ernest Hemingway and Woody Allen both stayed here.)

Take a deep whiff of Venice. What's all this nonsense about stinky canals? All I smell is my shirt. By the way, how's your captain? Smooth dockings? To get to know him, stand up in the bow and block his view.

❹ **Salute:** The huge La Salute Church, towering overhead as if squirted from a can of Catholic Cool Whip, rests upon pilings, like Venice itself. To build the foundation for the city, more than a million trees were piled together, reaching below the mud to the solid clay.

As the Grand Canal opens up into the lagoon, the last building on the right with the golden ball is the 17th-century **Customs House** (due to open to the public as a contemporary art gallery, possibly in 2010). Its two bronze Atlases hold a statue of Fortune riding the ball. Arriving ships stopped here to pay their tolls.

❺ **San Marco:** Look from left to right out over the lagoon. On the left, the green pointed tip of the Campanile marks **St. Mark's Square** (the political and religious center of Venice). A wide harborfront walk leads past the town's most elegant hotels to the green area in the distance. This is the public garden, the largest of Venice's few parks, which hosts the Biennale art show (held in odd years). Farther in the distance is the **Lido,** the island with Venice's beach. It's tempting, with sand and casinos, but its car traffic intrudes on the medieval charm of Venice.

Opposite St. Mark's Square, across the water, the ghostly white church that seems to float is Andrea Palladio's **San Giorgio Maggiore.** Because your vaporetto ticket is good for an hour, consider staying on this boat for the free ride out to the church—it's worth a visit because its pointy bell tower is home to the best view in town (elevator, no lines—described in "Sights," later in this chapter). If you're interested in heading out there right now, check the time stamped on your ticket; it'll be tight. If you don't think you'll make it there within the hour, don't sweat it—the ride to San Giorgio Maggiore on boat #2 costs only €2 (leaves from the

San Zaccaria–M.V.E. stop—two docks down from where this tour ends, across from the big equestrian statue).

Across the lagoon (to your right) is the residential island called **Giudecca,** which stretches from close to San Giorgio Maggiore past the Venice youth hostel (with a nice view, directly across) to the new Hilton Hotel (good nighttime view, far right end of island).

Cruising on, you pass (with the towering Campanile gliding behind) the bold facade of the old mint (where Venice's golden ducat, the dollar of the Venetian Republic, was made) and the library facade. Then St. Theodore and St. Mark appear, standing atop their twin columns as they have since the 15th and 16th centuries, when they welcomed VIP guests who arrived by sea to the most important square in Europe: Piazza San Marco. In the distance you can see two giant figures standing on the **Clock Tower.** They've been whacking the hour regularly since 1499. The busy domed features of **St. Mark's Basilica** are eclipsed by the lacy yet powerful facade of the **Doge's Palace.** As you cruise, look to the back side of the Doge's Palace where the **Bridge of Sighs**—leading from the palace to the prison—comes into view. The bridge in front of it is generally packed with tourists sighing at that legendary sky walk. Beyond that, to the right, begins that grand harborside promenade, the **Riva.**

⓰ San Zaccaria: Okay, you're at your last stop. Quick—muscle your way off this boat!

This boat makes three more stops before crossing the lagoon to the Lido—stay on the boat if you want to head out to San Giorgio Maggiore.

Sights

San Marco District

For information on the San Marco Museum Plus Pass and the pricier Museum Pass, which cover most of the sights on the square, see page 852.

▲▲▲**St. Mark's Square (Piazza San Marco)**—This grand square is surrounded by splashy, historic buildings and sights (each one described in more detail in the next few pages): St. Mark's Basilica, the Doge's Palace, the Campanile bell tower, the Correr Museum, and the Clock Tower. The square is filled with music, lovers, pigeons, and tourists by day, and is your private rendezvous with the Venetian past late at night, when Europe's most magnificent dance floor is *the* romantic place to be.

With your back to the church, survey one of Europe's great urban spaces, and the only square in Venice to merit the title "Piazza." Nearly two football fields long, it's surrounded by the

St. Mark's Square

Eateries

1. To Tratt. da Remigio, Tratt. da Giorgio ai Greci & Ristorante Alla Conchiglia
2. Birreria Forst
3. Osteria da Bacco
4. Bar Verde
5. Salad & Juice Bar Oasi 2000
6. Rizzo
7. Chat Qui Rit Self Service

Nightlife

8. Caffè Florian
9. Gran Caffè Quadri
10. Gran Caffè Lavena
11. Gran Caffè Chioggia
12. Caffè Aurora
13. Eden Bar

100 YARDS
100 METERS

SAN ZACCARIA-PIETÀ
SAN ZACCARIA-M.V.E.
TO MURANO
SAN ZACCARIA-JOLANDA
TO SAN GIORGIO MAGGIORE
SAN ZACCARIA-DANIELI
SAN ZACCARIA-JOLANDA

→ ENTRANCES TO SIGHTS
Ⓥ VAPORETTO STOP
Ⓖ GONDOLA STATION
✧ VIEW

SAN ZACCARIA

TO S.M. FORMOSA

VICTOR EMMANUEL EQUESTRIAN STATUE

DEGLI SCHIAVONI

CAMPO SS. FILIPPO + GIACOMO

TO S.M. FORMOSA

SAN PROVOLO

VIA

CHIESA

FIGHER

RUGA G. APP

DIOCESAN MUSEUM

RASSE (SANDWICH ROW)

ALBANESI

BRIDGE OF SIGHS

PRISON

RIVA

SAN MARCO BASIN

DOGE'S PALACE

ST. MARK'S BASILICA

CAMPANILE

PIAZZETTA

S. MARCO COLUMN

S. THEODORE COLUMN

DCH

SAN ZULIAN

ST. MARK'S BAG CHECK

PIAZZETTA D. LEONCINI

SAN MARCO

MERCERIE

SPADARIA

CLOCK TOWER

OLD OFFICES

PIAZZA SAN MARCO

NEW OFFICES

CORRER MUSEUM + Napoleon's Wing

GIARDINETTI REALI

GIARDINETTI

SAN MARCO-GIARDINETTI

SAN MARCO-VALLARESSO

TO RIALTO

C. FIUBERA

FABBRI

C. TRON

FREZZARIA

POST

WC

CALLE VALLARESSO

MOISÈ

RAMO SELVA

S.

SAL.

SAN MOISÈ

TO ACCADEMIA

offices of the republic. On the right are the "old offices" (16th-century Renaissance). At left are the "new offices" (17th-century High Renaissance). Napoleon called the piazza "the most beautiful drawing room in Europe," and added to the intimacy by building the final wing, opposite the basilica, that encloses the square.

For a slow and pricey evening thrill, invest about €16 (including the cover charge for the music) in a glass of wine or coffee at one of the elegant cafés with the dueling orchestras. For an unmatched experience that offers the best people-watching, it's worth the small splurge.

The **Clock Tower** (Torre dell'Orologio), built during the Renaissance in 1496, marks the entry to the main shopping drag, called the Mercerie, which connects St. Mark's Square with the Rialto. From the piazza, you can see the bronze men (Moors) swing their huge clappers at the top of each hour. In the 17th century, one of them knocked an unsuspecting worker off the top and to his death—probably the first-ever killing by a robot. Notice one of the world's first "digital" clocks on the tower facing the square (with dramatic flips every five minutes). You can go inside the Clock Tower only with a pre-booked guided tour that takes you close to the clock's innards and out to a terrace with good views over the square and city rooftops. Reserve in person at the Correr Museum, by calling 041-520-9070, or online at www.museicivici veneziani.it (€12 combo-ticket includes Correr Museum but not the Doge's Palace; tours in English Mon–Wed at 10:00, 11:00, and 13:00, Thu–Sun at 14:00, 15:00, and 17:00).

A good **TI** is on the square (with your back to the basilica, it's in the far-left, southwest corner of the square; daily 9:00–15:30), and a €1 WC is 30 yards beyond St. Mark's Square (see *Albergo Diorno* sign marked on pavement, WC open daily 9:00–17:30). Another TI is on the lagoon (daily 10:00–18:00, walk toward the water by the Doge's Palace and go right, €1 WCs nearby).

▲▲▲**St. Mark's Basilica (Basilica di San Marco)**—Built in the 11th century to replace an earlier church, this basilica's distinctly Eastern-style architecture underlines Venice's connection with Byzantium (which protected it from the ambition of Charlemagne and his Holy Roman Empire). It's decorated with booty from returning sea captains—a kind of architectural Venetian trophy chest. The interior glows mysteriously with gold mosaics and colored marble. Since about A.D. 830, the saint's bones have been housed at this site.

Cost, Hours, Information: Basilica entry is free, open Mon–Sat 9:45–17:00 (until 16:30 Nov–March), Sun 14:00–16:00, tel. 041-522-5205. Lines can be long, the dress code is strictly enforced, and bag check is mandatory, free, and can save you time in line; for details, see next paragraph. No photos are allowed inside. Three separate exhibits inside charge admission and close 15 minutes before the church: the **Treasury** (€3, includes free audioguide), the **Golden Altarpiece** (€2.50), and the **San Marco Museum** (€4).

Bag Check: While small purses and shoulder-slung bags may be allowed inside the church, larger bags and backpacks are not. Check them for free at the nearby Ateneo San Basso, a former church (open roughly Mon–Sat 9:30–17:30, Sun 14:00–16:30; head to the left of basilica, down narrow Calle San Basso, 30 yards to the second door on your right; see map on page 869 for location).

Those with a bag to check actually get to skip the basilica entry line. Here's how it works: Leave your bag at Ateneo San Basso (for up to one hour) and pick up the claim tag. Two people per tag are allowed to go to the basilica's gatekeeper, present the tag, and scoot directly in, ahead of the line. After touring the church, come back and pick up your bag.

Dress Code: To enter the church, modest dress is required even kids (no shorts or bare shoulders). People who ignore the dress code hold up the line while they plead fruitlessly with the dress-code police.

Theft Alert: St. Mark's Basilica is the most dangerous place in Venice for pickpocketing—inside, it's always a crowded jostle.

Tours: In the atrium, see the schedule board that lists free 60-minute guided tours in English. (Schedules vary, but the tours generally run May–Oct Tue, Wed, and Thu at 11:00; meet guide just to the right of main doors.)

Inside the Church: St. Mark's Basilica has 4,750 square yards of Byzantine mosaics, the best and oldest of which are in the atrium (turn right as you enter and stop under the last dome—this may be roped off, but dome is still visible). Facing the church, gape up (it's OK, no pigeons) and read the story of Adam and Eve that rings the bottom of the dome. Now, facing the piazza, look dome-ward for the story of Noah, the ark, and the flood (two by two, the wicked being drowned, Noah sending out the dove, a happy rainbow, and a sacrifice of thanks).

Step inside the church (the stairs on the right lead to the bronze horses in the San Marco Museum, described next—save these for later). Notice how the marble floor is richly decorated in mosaics. As in many Venetian buildings, because the best foundation pilings were made around the perimeter, the floor rolls. As you shuffle under the central dome, look up for the Ascension. As you follow the one-way tourist route, consider stopping off at the Treasury and the Golden Altarpiece, described on the next page.

Additional Sights: In the **San Marco Museum** (Museo di San Marco) upstairs, you can see an up-close mosaic exhibition, a fine view of the church interior, a view of the square from the balcony with bronze horses, and (inside, in their own room) the original horses. These well-traveled horses, made during the days of Alexander the Great (fourth century B.C.), were taken to Rome by Nero, to Constantinople/Istanbul by Constantine, to Venice by crusaders, to Paris by Napoleon, back "home" to Venice when Napoleon fell, and finally indoors and out of the acidic air. The staircase up to the museum is in the atrium, near the basilica's entrance, marked by a sign that says *Loggia dei Cavalli, Museo*.

San Marco's **Treasury** (ask for the included and informative audioguide when you buy ticket) and **Golden Altarpiece** give you the best chance outside of Istanbul or Ravenna to see the glories of the Byzantine Empire. Venetian crusaders looted the Christian city of Constantinople and brought home piles of lavish loot (perhaps the lowest point in Christian history until the advent of TV evangelism). Much of this plunder is stored in the Treasury (Tesoro) of San Marco. As you view these treasures, remember that most were made in about A.D. 500, while Western Europe was stuck in the Dark Ages. Beneath the high altar lies the body of St. Mark ("Marce") and the Golden Altarpiece (Pala d'Oro), made of 250 blue-backed enamels with religious scenes, all set in a gold frame and studded with 15 hefty rubies, 300 emeralds, 1,500 pearls, and assorted sapphires, amethysts, and topaz (c. 1100).

▲▲▲**Doge's Palace (Palazzo Ducale)**—The seat of the Venetian government and home of its ruling duke, or doge (dohzh), this was the most powerful half-acre in Europe for 400 years. The Doge's Palace was built to show off the power and wealth of the Republic. Nicknamed "The Wedding Cake," "The Table Cloth," and "The Pink House," it was built in a style called Venetian Gothic—a fusion of Italian Gothic with a delicate Islamic flair. The columns originally had bases on the bottoms, but these were covered over as the columns sank, and the square was built up over the centuries.

Enjoy the newly restored facades from the **courtyard.** Notice a grand staircase (with nearly naked Moses and Paul Newman at the top). Even the most powerful visitors climbed this to meet the doge. This was the beginning of an architectural power trip. The doge, the elected-for-life duke or leader of this "dictatorship of the aristocracy," lived with his family on the first floor near the halls of power. From his living quarters (once lavish, now sparsely furnished), you'll follow the one-way route through the public rooms of the top floor, finishing with the Bridge of Sighs and the prison. The place is wallpapered with masterpieces by Veronese and Tintoretto. Don't worry much about the great art. Enjoy the building.

In the **Senate Hall,** the 120 senators met, debated, and passed laws. Tintoretto's large *Triumph of Venice* on the ceiling (central painting, best viewed from the top) shows the city in all its glory. Lady Venice is up in heaven with the Greek gods, while barbaric lesser nations swirl up to give her gifts and tribute.

The **Armory**—a dazzling display originally assembled to intimidate potential adversaries—shows remnants of the military might that the empire employed to keep the East–West trade lines open (and the local economy booming). Squint out the window to see Palladio's Church of San Giorgio Maggiore and, to the left in the distance, the tiny green dome at Venice's Lido (beach).

The giant **Hall of the Grand Council** (175 feet by 80 feet, capacity 2,600) is where the entire nobility met to elect the senate and doge. It took a room this size to contain the grandeur of the Most Serene Republic. Ringing the room are portraits of the first 76 doges (in chronological order). The one at the far end that's blacked out is the notorious Doge Marin Falier, who opposed the will of the Grand Council in 1355. He was tried for treason, beheaded, and airbrushed from history.

On the wall over the doge's throne is Tintoretto's monster-piece, *Paradise,* the largest oil painting in the world. Christ and Mary are surrounded by a heavenly host of 500 saints. The painting leaves you feeling that you get to heaven not by being a good Christian, but by being a good Venetian.

Cross the covered **Bridge of Sighs** over the canal to the **prisons.** Circle the cells. Notice the carvings made by prisoners—from olden days up until 1930—on some of the stone windowsills of the cells, especially in the far corner of the building.

Cross back over the Bridge of Sighs, pausing to look through the marble-trellised windows at all of the tourists.

Cost: €13 with San Marco Museum Plus Pass (sold April–Oct, also covers Correr Museum); or €18 with the Museum Pass (sold year-round). Off-season (Nov–March), it's also covered by the €12 Museum Card of the Museums of St. Mark's Square. For specifics, see page 852.

Crowd Control: If the ticket-sales line is long at the Doge's Palace, buy your ticket at the Correr Museum across the square. Then go straight to the Doge's turnstile, skirting along to the right of the long ticket-buying line at the palace entrance. (The Museum Pass, available at less-crowded sights, also lets you skip the line.) Other options are to buy your ticket online via the poorly designed and complicated museum website (www.museicivicivenziani.it), visit after 17:00 (if it's April–Oct), or book a Secret Itineraries Tour (see below).

Hours: Daily April–Oct 9:00–19:00, Nov–March 9:00–17:00, last entry one hour before closing.

Tours: The **audioguide tour** is dry but informative (€5, or €8 for double set, 90 min, need ID or credit card for deposit). Pick it up after you pass through the turnstile after the ticket counter.

The fine **Secret Itineraries Tour,** which follows the doge's footsteps through rooms not included in the general admission price, must be booked in advance—it's best to reserve at least two days early in peak season (€16; includes admission to the Doge's Palace, but not the Correr Museum; €10 with San Marco Museum Plus Pass—see page 852). The tours, which last 75 minutes, are offered in English daily at 9:55, 10:45, 11:35, and 12:25. You can reserve by phone (tel. 041-520-9070), online (www.museicivici veneziani.it), or by just showing up at the information desk and hoping for a free spot (unlikely at peak times). While the tour skips the main halls inside, you're welcome to visit the halls on your own afterward.

▲▲Correr Museum (Museo Civico Correr)—This uncrowded museum gives you a good overview of Venetian history and art. In the Napoleon Wing, you'll see fine Neoclassical sculpture by Antonio Canova. Then peruse armor, banners, and paintings that re-create festive days of the Venetian republic. The upper floor lays out a good overview of Venetian art, including several paintings by the Bellini family. There are English descriptions and breathtaking views of St. Mark's Square throughout (covered by €13 San Marco Museum Plus Pass, which also includes the Doge's Palace—both also covered by €18 Museum Pass, daily April–Oct 9:00–19:00, Nov–March 9:00–17:00, last entry one hour before closing, free and mandatory bag check, enter at far end of square directly opposite basilica, tel. 041-240-5211, www.museiciviciveneziani.it). You can avoid long lines at the crowded Doge's Palace by buying either of the museum passes listed above at the Correr Museum. For €12 you can get a combo-ticket for the Correr Museum and a tour of the Clock Tower on St. Mark's Square, but your ticket won't include the Doge's Palace. For more on reserving a Clock Tower tour, see page 870.

▲Campanile (Campanile di San Marco)—This dramatic bell tower replaced a shorter lighthouse, once part of the original fortress/palace that guarded the entry of the Grand Canal. The lighthouse crumbled into a pile of bricks in 1902, a thousand years after it was built. In 2010, you may see construction work going on at the base of the tower to strengthen it. Ride the elevator 300 feet to the top of the bell tower for the best view in Venice. For an ear-shattering experience, be on top when the bells ring (€8, daily July–Aug 9:00–21:00, Sept–June 9:00–19:00). The golden angel at the top always faces into the wind. Lines are longest at midday; beat the crowds and enjoy the crisp morning air at 9:00, or try in the early evening (around 18:00).

La Fenice Opera House (Gran Teatro alla Fenice)—During Venice's glorious decline in the 18th century, this was one of seven opera houses in the city. A 1996 arson fire completely gutted the theater, but La Fenice ("The Phoenix") has risen from the ashes, thanks to an eight-year effort to rebuild the historic landmark according to photographic archives of the interior. To see the results at their most glorious, attend an evening performance. If you visit, you'll see the grand lobby and the theater itself—saccharine and bringing sadness to locals who remember the richness of the place before the fire (€7 entry fee includes 45-minute audioguide, generally open daily 10:00–17:00, may be closed for practice or performance, concert box office open daily 9:30–18:30, call-center open daily 7:30–20:00—tel. 041-2424, www.teatrolafenice.it).

Behind St. Mark's Basilica

Diocesan Museum (Museo Diocesano)—This little-known museum circles a peaceful Romanesque courtyard immediately behind the basilica (just before the Bridge of Sighs). It's filled with plunder from the Venetian Empire that never found a place in St. Mark's (€4 includes cloister and museum, daily 10:00–18:00, tel. 041-522-9166).

▲**Bridge of Sighs**—Connecting two wings of the Doge's Palace high over a canal, this enclosed bridge was popularized by travelers in the Romantic 19th century. Supposedly, a condemned man would be led over this bridge on his way to the prison, take one last look at the glory of Venice, and sigh. While overhyped, the bridge is undeniably tingle-worthy—especially after dark, when the crowds have dispersed and it's just you and floodlit Venice. It's around the corner from the Doge's Palace: Walk toward the waterfront, turn left along the water, and look up the first canal on your left. You can actually cross the bridge (from the inside) by visiting the Doge's Palace.

Church of San Zaccaria—This historic church is home to a sometimes-waterlogged crypt, a Bellini altarpiece, a Tintoretto painting, and the final resting place of St. Zechariah, the father of John the Baptist (free, €1 to enter crypt, €0.50 coin to light up Bellini's altarpiece, Mon–Sat 10:00–12:00 & 16:00–18:00, Sun 16:00–18:00 only, 2 canals behind St. Mark's Basilica).

Across the Lagoon from St. Mark's Square

▲**San Giorgio Maggiore**—This is the dreamy island you can see from the waterfront by St. Mark's Square. The striking church, designed by Palladio, features art by Tintoretto and good views of Venice (free entry to church, daily May–Sept 9:00–12:30 & 14:30–18:00, Oct–April 9:00–12:30 & 14:30–17:00, but closed year-round to sightseers during Mass on Sun 11:00–12:00 and possibly other times as well, Gregorian Mass sung Mon–Sat at 8:00 and on Sun at 11:00). The church's bell tower costs €3 and is accessible by elevator (runs from 30 min after the church opens until 30 min before the church closes). To reach the island from

St. Mark's Square, take the five-minute vaporetto ride (€2, 6/hr, ticket valid 60 min) on #2 from the San Zaccaria–M.V.E. stop (the San Zaccaria dock farthest from the Bridge of Sighs, 50 yards past the big equestrian statue).

Dorsoduro District

▲▲**Accademia (Galleria dell'Accademia)**—Venice's top art museum, packed with highlights of the Venetian Renaissance, features paintings by the Bellini family, Titian, Tintoretto, Veronese, Tiepolo, Giorgione, Canaletto, and Testosterone. It's just over the wooden Accademia Bridge from the San Marco action (€10, Mon 8:15–14:00, Tue–Sun 8:15–19:15, last entry 45 min before closing, no photos allowed, info tel. 041-522-2247, www.gallerieaccademia .org). Expect long lines in the late morning, because they allow only 300 visitors in at a time; visit early or late to miss the crowds, or make a reservation at least a day in advance (€1 fee, calling 041-520-0345 is easier than reserving online at the clunky www .gallerieaccademia.org—click "Prenotazione"). The dull audioguide costs €5 (€7/double set). One-hour guided tours in English are €5 (€7/2 people, Sat–Sun at 11:00).

At the Accademia Bridge, there's a decent canalside pizzeria (Pizzeria Accademia Foscarini—see page 904) and a public WC at the base of the bridge.

▲▲**Peggy Guggenheim Collection**—The popular museum of far-out art, housed in the American heiress' former retirement palazzo, offers one of Europe's best reviews of the art of the first half of the 20th century. Stroll through styles represented by artists whom Peggy knew personally—Cubism (Picasso, Braque), Surrealism (Dalí, Ernst), Futurism (Boccioni), American Abstract Expressionism (Pollock), and a sprinkling of Klee, Calder, and Chagall (€10, generally includes temporary exhibits, Wed–Mon 10:00–18:00, closed Tue, last entry 15 min before closing, audioguide-€7, mini-guidebook-€5, free and mandatory baggage check, pricey café, photos allowed only in garden and terrace—a fine and relaxing perch overlooking Grand Canal, near Accademia, Dorsoduro 704, tel. 041-240-5411, www.guggenheim-venice.it). The place is staffed by international interns working on art-related degrees.

▲**La Salute Church (Santa Maria della Salute)**—This impressive church with a crown-shaped dome was built and dedicated to the Virgin Mary by grateful survivors of the 1630 plague (church—free, daily 9:00–12:00 & 14:30–17:30; sacristy—€2, Mon–Sat 10:00–12:00 & 15:00–17:00, Sun 15:00–17:00; tel. 041-274-3928). It's a 10-minute walk from the Accademia Bridge; the Salute vaporetto stop is at its doorstep (the San Marco–Vallaresso to Salute vaporetto hop is €2).

▲Ca' Rezzonico (Museum of 18th-Century Venice)—This grand Grand Canal palazzo offers the best look in town at the life of Venice's rich and famous in the 1700s. Wander under ceilings by Tiepolo, among furnishings from that most decadent century, enjoying views of the canal and paintings by Guardi, Canaletto, and Longhi (€6.50, covered by passes—see page 852, April–Oct Wed–Mon 10:00–18:00, Nov–March Wed–Mon 10:00–17:00, closed Tue, last entry one hour before closing, audioguide-€4 or €6/double set, free and mandatory baggage check, at Ca' Rezzonico vaporetto stop, tel. 041-241-0100).

Santa Croce District

▲▲▲Rialto Bridge—One of the world's most famous bridges, this distinctive and dramatic stone structure crosses the Grand Canal with a single confident span. The arcades along the top of the bridge help reinforce the structure...and offer some enjoyable shopping diversions, as does the **market** surrounding the bridge (souvenir stalls open daily, produce market closed Sun, fish market closed Sun–Mon).

▲Ca' Pesaro International Gallery of Modern Art—This museum features 19th- and early-20th-century art in a 17th-century canalside palazzo. The collection is strongest on Italian (especially Venetian) artists, but also presents a broad array of other well-known artists. The highlights are in one large room: Klimt's beautiful/creepy *Judith II*, with eagle-talon fingers; Kandinsky's *White Zig Zags* (plus other recognizable shapes); the colorful *Nude in the Mirror* by Bonnard that flattens the 3-D scene into a 2-D pattern of rectangles; and Chagall's surprisingly realistic portrait of his hometown rabbi, *The Rabbi of Vitebsk*. The adjoining Room VII features small-scale works by Matisse, Max Ernst, Mark Tobey, and a Calder mobile. Admission also includes an Oriental Art wing (€5.50, covered by passes—see page 852; April–Oct Tue–Sun 10:00–18:00, Nov–March Tue–Sun 10:00–17:00, closed Mon, last entry one hour before closing, located a 2-minute walk from the San Stae vaporetto stop, tel. 041-524-0695).

18th-Century Costume Museum—The Museo di Palazzo Mocenigo offers a walk through six rooms of a fine 17th-century mansion with period furnishings, family portraits, ceilings painted (c. 1790) with family triumphs (the Mocenigos produced seven doges), Murano glass chandeliers in situ, and a paltry collection of costumes with sparse descriptions (€4, covered by passes—see page 852, Tue–Sun 10:00–17:00, closed Mon, a block in from the San Stae vaporetto stop, tel. 041-524-0695).

VENICE

San Polo District

▲▲**Frari Church (Chiesa dei Frari)**—My favorite art experience in Venice is seeing art in the setting for which it was designed—as it is at the Frari Church ("Church of the Brothers"). The Franciscan church and the art that decorates it is warmed by the spirit of St. Francis. It features the work of three great Renaissance masters: Donatello, Giovanni Bellini, and Titian—each showing worshippers the glory of God in human terms.

In **Donatello's wood carving of St. John the Baptist** (just to the right of the high altar), the prophet of the desert—dressed in animal skins and nearly starving from his diet of bugs 'n' honey—announces the coming of the Messiah. Donatello was a Florentine working at the dawn of the Renaissance.

Bellini's *Madonna and Child with Saints and Angels* painting (in the sacristy farther to the right) came later, done by a Venetian in a more Venetian style—soft focus without Donatello's harsh realism. While Renaissance humanism demanded Madonnas and saints that were accessible and human, Bellini places them in a physical setting so beautiful that it creates its own mood of serene holiness. The genius of Bellini, perhaps the greatest Venetian painter, is obvious in the pristine clarity, rich colors (notice Mary's clothing), believable depth, and reassuring calm of this three-paneled altarpiece.

Finally, glowing red and gold like a stained-glass window over the high altar, **Titian's** *The Assumption of Mary* sets the tone of exuberant beauty found in the otherwise sparse church. Titian the Venetian—a student of Bellini—painted steadily for 60 years... you'll see a lot of his art. As stunned apostles look up past the swirl of arms and legs, the complex composition of this painting draws you right to the radiant face of the once-dying, now-triumphant Mary as she joins God in heaven.

Feel comfortable to discreetly freeload off passing tours. For many, these three pieces of art make a visit to the Accademia Gallery unnecessary (or they may whet your appetite for more). Before leaving, check out the Neoclassical, pyramid-shaped Canova monument and (opposite that) the grandiose tomb of Titian. Compare the carved marble Assumption behind Titian's tombstone portrait with the painted original above the high altar.

Cost, Hours, Information: €3, Mon–Sat 10:00–18:00, Sun 13:00–18:00, closed Sun in Aug, last entry 15 min before closing, no visits during services, audioguide-€2 or €3/double set, modest dress recommended). The church often hosts evening concerts (€15, buy ticket at church; for concert details, look for fliers, check www.basilicadeifrari.it, or call the church at 041-272-8618).

▲▲**Scuola San Rocco**—Sometimes called "Tintoretto's Sistine Chapel," this lavish meeting hall (next to the Frari Church) has some 50 large, colorful Tintoretto paintings plastered to the walls and ceilings. The best paintings are upstairs, especially the *Crucifixion* in the smaller room. View the neck-breaking splendor with one of the mirrors *(specchio)* available at the entrance (€7, includes informative audioguide, daily April–Oct 9:00–17:30, Nov–March 10:00–17:00, last entry 30 min before closing, tel. 041-523-4864, www.scuolagrandesanrocco.it).

Church of San Polo—This nearby church, which pales in comparison to the Frari Church and Scuola San Rocco, is worth a visit for art-lovers. One of Venice's oldest churches (from the ninth century), San Polo features works by Tintoretto, Veronese, and Tiepolo and son (€3, Mon–Sat 10:00–17:00, closed Sun, last entry 15 min before closing).

Cannaregio District

Jewish Ghetto—In medieval times, Jews were grudgingly allowed to do business in Venice, but only starting in 1385 were they allowed to live there (subject to strict laws and special taxes). Anti-Semitic forces tried to oust them from the city, but in 1516, the doge compromised by restricting Jews to a special (undesirable) neighborhood. It was located on an easy-to-isolate island near the former foundry *(geto),* coining the word "ghetto" for a segregated neighborhood. Restricted within their tiny neighborhood (the Ghetto Nuovo, or "New Ghetto"), they expanded upward, building six-story "skyscrapers" which stand today. The main square, Campo di Ghetto Nuovo, must have been quite a scene—ringed by 70 shops and with all of Venice's Jewish commerce compressed into this one spot. As late as the 1930s, 12,000 Jews called Venice home, but today there are only 500—and only a few dozen live in the Ghetto itself. Only two synagogues are still active. You can spot them (with their five windows) from the square, but to visit them you have to book a tour through the Jewish Museum.

This original Ghetto becomes most interesting after touring the **Jewish Museum** (Museo Ebraico). It offers two things: a museum and a synagogue. The humble two-room museum has silver menorahs, cloth covers for the Torah scrolls, various religious objects, artifacts of the old community, and scant English explanations (€3, June–Sept Sun–Fri 10:00–17:00, Oct–May Sun–Fri 10:00–16:30, closed Sat and Jewish holidays, Campo di Ghetto Nuovo, tel. 041-715-359, small café and bookstore). To see the **synagogue,** you must sign up for a half-hour English tour (€8.50, tours run hourly June–Sept Sun–Fri 10:30–17:30, Oct–May Sun–Fri 10:30–16:30, closed Sat and Jewish holidays).

Ca' d'Oro—This "House of Gold" palace, fronting the Grand Canal, is quintessential Venetian Gothic (Gothic seasoned with Byzantine and Islamic accents). Inside, the permanent collection includes a few big names in Renaissance painting—Ghirlandaio, Signorelli, and Mantegna; a glimpse at a lush courtyard; and a grand view of the Grand Canal (€5, slow and dry audioguide-€4, Mon 8:15–14:00, Tue–Sun 8:15–19:15, free peek through hole in door of courtyard, Calle Ca' d'Oro 3932).

Castello District

▲**Dalmatian School (Scuola Dalmata di San Giorgio)**—This "school" (which means "meeting place") is a reminder that Venice was Europe's most cosmopolitan place in its heyday—the original melting-pot community. It was here that the Dalmatians (from the southern coast of present-day Croatia) worshipped in their own way, held neighborhood meetings, and worked to preserve their culture. The chapel on the ground floor happens to have the most exquisite Renaissance interior in Venice, with a cycle of paintings by Carpaccio ringing the room; be sure to pick up the English descriptions to the right of the entrance (€3, Mon 14:45–18:00, Tue–Sat 9:15–13:00 & 14:45–18:00, Sun 9:30–12:30, last entry 30 min before closing, between St. Mark's Square and Arsenale, on Calle dei Furlani, 3 blocks southeast of Campo San Lorenzo, tel. 041-522-8828).

Santa Elena—For a pleasant peek into a completely non-touristy, residential side of Venice, walk or catch vaporetto #1 from St. Mark's Square to the neighborhood of Santa Elena (at the fish's tail). This 100-year-old suburb lives as if there were no tourism. You'll find a kid-friendly park, a few lazy restaurants, and beautiful sunsets over San Marco.

Experiences

Gondola Rides

A rip-off for some, this is a traditional must for romantics. Gondoliers charge about €80 for a 40-minute ride during the day; from 19:00 on, figure on €100. To add *musica* (a singer and an accordionist), it'll cost an additional €110 before 19:00, or €130 after 19:00. You can divide the cost—and the romance—among up to six people per boat, but you'll need to save two seats for the musicians if you choose to be serenaded. Note that only two seats (the ones in back) are next to each other. If you want to haggle, you'll find softer prices on back lanes where single gondoliers hang out, rather than at the bigger departure points. Establish the price and duration before boarding, enjoy your ride, and pay only when you're finished.

If you've hired musicians and want to hear a Venetian song *(un canto Veneziano),* try requesting *"Venezia La Luna e Tu."* Asking to hear *"O Sole Mio"* (which comes from Naples) is like asking a bartender in Cleveland to sing "The Eyes of Texas."

Gondolas cost lots more after 19:00 but are also more romantic and relaxing under the moon. Glide through nighttime Venice with your head on someone's shoulder. Follow the moon as it sails past otherwise unseen buildings. Silhouettes gaze down from bridges while window glitter spills onto the black water. You're anonymous in the city of masks, as the rhythmic thrust of your striped-shirted gondolier turns old crows into songbirds. This is extremely relaxing (and, I think, worth the extra cost to experience at night). Because you might get a narration plus conversation with your gondolier, talk with several and choose one you like who speaks English well. Women, beware...while gondoliers can be extremely charming, local women say that anyone who falls for one of these Romeos "has slices of ham over her eyes."

For cheap gondola thrills during the day, stick to the €0.50 one-minute ferry ride on a Grand Canal *traghetto*.

Nightlife

You must experience Venice after dark. The city is quiet at night, as tour groups stay in the cheaper hotels of Mestre on the mainland, and the masses of day-trippers return to their beach resorts and cruise ships. **Gondolas** cost more, but are worth the extra expense (see above). At night, *vaporetti* are nearly empty, and it's a great time to cruise the Grand Canal on the slow boat (vaporetto #1).

Venice has a busy schedule of events, festivals, and entertainment. Check at the TI for listings in publications such as the free *Un Ospite di Venezia* magazine (monthly, bilingual, available at top-end hotels, www.aguestinvenice.com).

Concerts—Take your pick of traditional Vivaldi concerts in churches throughout town. Homegrown Vivaldi is as trendy here as Strauss is in Vienna and Mozart is in Salzburg. In fact, you'll find frilly young Vivaldis all over town hawking concert tickets. The TI has a list of this week's Baroque concerts (tickets from €18, shows start at 21:00 and generally last 90 min). You'll find posters in hotels all over town. There's music most nights at **Scuola San Teodoro** (east side of Rialto Bridge) and **San Vitale Church** (north end of Accademia Bridge), among others. Consider the venue carefully. The general rule of thumb: Musicians in wigs and tights offer better spectacle, musicians in black-and-white suits are better performers. For the latest on church concerts, check at any TI or visit www.turismovenezia.it.

St. Mark's Square—For tourists, St. Mark's Square is the highlight, with lantern light and live music echoing from the cafés. Just being here after dark is a thrill, as **dueling café orchestras** entertain. Every night, enthusiastic musicians play the same songs, creating the same irresistible magic. Hang out for free behind the tables (which allows you to move easily on to the next orchestra when the musicians take a break), or spring for a seat and enjoy a fun and gorgeously set concert. If you sit a while, it can be €16 well spent (for a drink and the cover charge for music). Dancing on the square is free (and encouraged). Streetlamp halos, live music, floodlit history, and a ceiling of stars make St. Mark's magic at midnight. You're not a tourist, you're a living part of a soft Venetian night...an alley cat with money. In the misty light, the moon has a golden hue. Shine with the old lanterns on the gondola piers, where the sloppy lagoon splashes at the Doge's Palace...reminiscing.

Sleeping

For hassle-free efficiency and the sheer magic of being close to the action, I favor hotels that are handy to sightseeing activities. I've listed rooms in three neighborhoods: the Rialto action, St. Mark's bustle, and the quiet Dorsoduro area behind the Accademia art museum. Hotel websites are particularly valuable in Venice, because they often come with a map.

Book a room as soon as you know when you'll be in town. Hotels in Venice are usually booked up on Carnevale (Feb 5–16 in 2010), Easter and Easter Monday (April 4–5 in 2010), April 25 (St. Mark's Day), May 1 (Labor Day), Feast of the Ascension Day (May 13 in 2010), Feast and Regatta of the Redeemer (evening of July 17 and all day July 18 in 2010), Historical Regatta (Sept 4–5 in 2010), November 1 (All Saints' Day), Feast of Our Lady of Good Health (November 21)—and on Fridays and Saturdays year-round. Contact hotels directly, not through any tourist information room-finding service (they can't give opinions on quality). If everything's full, don't despair. Call a day or two in advance and fill in a cancellation. If you arrive on an overnight train, your room might not be ready. Leave your bag at the hotel and go sightseeing.

Venetian hoteliers are hard to pin down. They're experts at perfect price discrimination: They list a huge range of rates for the same room (e.g., €90–160) and refuse to give a firm price, enabling them to judge the demand and charge accordingly. As soon as they know what the market will bear, they max it out. Also, hotels are being squeezed by the very popular online-booking services (which take about a 20 percent commission). Between wanting to keep their gouging options open for high-season weekends and trying to recover these online commissions, hoteliers set their rack rates sky-high.

My listings are more likely to give a straight price. I've assured hoteliers that my readers will book direct, so they'll get 100 percent of what you pay; therefore, you'll get the fair net rate. I've

Sleep Code

(€1 = about $1.40, country code: 39)
S = Single, **D** = Double/Twin, **T** = Triple, **Q** = Quad, **b** = bathroom, **s** = shower only. Breakfast is included, credit cards are accepted, and English is spoken unless otherwise noted. Air-conditioning, when available, is usually only turned on in summer.

To help you easily sort through these listings, I've divided the rooms into three categories based on the price for a standard double room with bath:

$$$ Higher Priced—Most rooms €180 or more.
  $$ Moderately Priced—Most rooms between €130-180.
    $ Lower Priced—Most rooms €130 or less.

listed only prices for peak season: April, May, June, September, and October. Prices will be higher during festivals, and virtually all places drop prices from November through March (except during Carnevale and Christmas) and in July and August.

Many hotels in Venice list rooms on www.venere.com, especially for last-minute vacancies (2–3 weeks before the date). Check to see if rates are lower than the prices in this book, but please note—if you book via Venere, you can't ask for a Rick Steves discount.

Booking direct (not through a Web service) is usually your ticket to better rates. Prices can be soft if you do any of the following: offer to pay cash, stay at least three nights, or mention this book. You can also try asking for a cheaper room or a discount, or offer to skip breakfast. To save money during a relatively slow time, consider arriving without a reservation and dropping in at the last minute. Big, fancy hotels put empty rooms on an aggressive push list, offering great prices.

Near St. Mark's Square
East of St. Mark's Square
Located near the Bridge of Sighs, just off the Riva degli Schiavoni waterfront promenade, these places rub drainpipes with Venice's most palatial five-star hotels. Ride the vaporetto to San Zaccaria (#51 from train station, #2 from Tronchetto parking lot).

$$$ Hotel Campiello, lacy and bright, was once part of a 19th-century convent. With an ideal location 50 yards off the waterfront, on a tiny little namesake square, its 16 rooms offer a tranquil, friendly refuge for travelers who appreciate comfort and professional service (Sb-€135, Db-€205, pay cash and mention this book for best price, strict cancellation penalties enforced,

VENICE

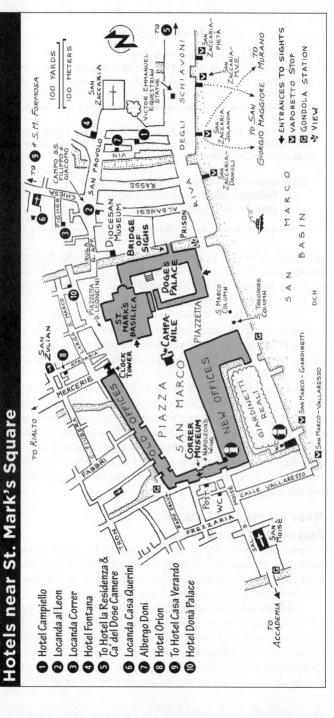

Hotels near St. Mark's Square

1. Hotel Campiello
2. Locanda al Leon
3. Locanda Correr
4. Hotel Fontana
5. To Hotel la Residenza & Ca' del Dose Camere
6. Locanda Casa Querini
7. Albergo Doni
8. Hotel Orion
9. To Hotel Casa Verardo
10. Hotel Donà Palace

air-con, elevator, Internet access; from the waterfront street—Riva degli Schiavoni—take Calle del Vin, between pink Hotel Danieli and Hotel Savoia e Jolanda, to #4647, Castello; tel. 041-520-5764, fax 041-520-5798, www.hcampiello.it, campiello@hcampiello.it; family-run for four generations, currently by Thomas and sisters Monica and Nicoletta). They also rent three modern, plush, and quiet family apartments, under rustic timbers just steps away (up to €380/night).

$$ Locanda al Leon rents 14 rooms outfitted in 18th-century Venetian style just off Campo S.S. Filippo e Giacomo (Db-€145, bigger Db-€165, Tb-€185, pay cash and mention this book for best prices, air-con, Campo S.S. Filippo e Giacomo 4270, Castello, tel. 041-277-0393, fax 041-521-0348, www.hotelalleon.com, leon @hotelalleon.com, Giuliano and Marcella). From the San Zaccaria-Danieli vaporetto stop, take Calle dei Albanesi (two streets left of pink Hotel Danieli), and the hotel is at the far end of the street on the left. They also run a B&B across the street with rooms that are slightly bigger and cheaper.

$$ Locanda Correr offers five elegant rooms with silk wallpaper and gilded furniture, decorated in classic 17th-century Venetian decor with all the amenities. It's up a flight of stairs on a quiet street a few blocks from St. Mark's Square and Campo S.S. Filippo e Giacomo (Db-€145, pay cash and mention this book for best prices, air-con, Calle Figher 4370, Castello, tel. 041-277-7847, fax 041-277-5939, www.locandacorrer.com, info@locandacorrer .com). From the San Zaccaria vaporetto stop, take the street to the right of the Bridge of Sighs to Campo S.S. Filippo e Giacomo, continue on Calle drio la Chiesa, then go left down Calle Figher, past Hotel Castello.

$$ Hotel Fontana is a two-star, family-run place with 14 rooms across from a school, two bridges behind St. Mark's Square (Sb-€110, Db-€160, family rooms, cash discount, quieter rooms on garden side, 2 rooms have terraces for €10 extra, air-con, elevator, Campo San Provolo 4701, Castello, tel. 041-522-0579, fax 041-523-1040, www.hotelfontana.it, info@hotelfontana.it, Diego and Gabriele). Take vaporetto #1 or #51 to San Zaccaria, then take Calle delle Rasse—to the left of pink Hotel Danieli—turn right at the end, and continue to the first square.

$$ Hotel la Residenza is a grand, old palace facing a peaceful square. It has 15 great rooms on three levels and a huge, luxurious, and heavily frosted lounge. This is a great value for romantics— you'll feel like you're in the Doge's Palace after hours. Mention Rick Steves when you book to get discounted rates (Sb-€100, Db-€165, air-con, Internet access, Campo Bandiera e Moro 3608, Castello, tel. 041-528-5315, fax 041-523-8859, www.venicelaresidenza.com, info@venicelaresidenza.com, Gianni). From the Bridge of Sighs, walk east along Riva degli Schiavoni, cross three bridges, and take the first left up Calle del Dose to Campo Bandiera e Moro. The hotel is across the square.

$$ Locanda Casa Querini rents six plush rooms on a quiet square tucked away behind St. Mark's. You can enjoy your breakfast or a sunny picnic/happy hour sitting at their tables right on the sleepy little square (Db-€150, pay cash and mention this book for best prices, €5 extra for view, air-con, halfway between San Zaccaria vaporetto stop and Campo Santa Maria Formosa at Campo San Giovanni in Oleo 4388, Castello, tel. 041-241-1294, fax 041-523-6188, www.locandaquerini.com, casaquerini@hot mail.com, Patrizia and Silvia). From the San Zaccaria vaporetto stop, take the street to the right of the Bridge of Sighs to Campo S.S. Filippo e Giacomo, continue on Calle drio la Chiesa, take the second left, and curl around to the left into the little square.

$ Albergo Doni is dark, clean, and quiet—a bit of a timewarp—with 13 dim but classy rooms run by a likable smart aleck named Gina and her son, an Italian stallion named Nikos (D-€90, Db-€115, T-€120, Tb-€155, reserve with credit card but pay in cash for special prices in high season, discounts for readers the rest of the year, ceiling fans, 3 Db rooms have air-con June–Aug only, Fondamenta del Vin, 4656 Castello, tel. & fax 041-522-4267, www.albergo doni.it, albergodoni@hotmail.it). From the San Zaccaria vaporetto stop, cross one bridge to the right and take the first left (marked Calle del Vin), then turn left at the little square named Ramo del Vin, jog left, and find the hotel ahead on Fondamenta del Vin.

$ Ca' del Dose Camere is a rough and funky little six-room guesthouse where high-energy Anna scrambles to keep her guests happy (Db-€100, Tb-€120, pay cash and mention this book for best prices, air-con, tel. & fax 041-520-9887, www.cadeldose.com, info@cadeldose.com). It's located four bridges past the Doge's Palace, about 100 yards off the high-rent Riva degli Schiavoni on Calle del Dose at #3801, and a few steps before the wonderfully homey square called Campo Bandiera e Moro. Anna also runs the slicker Palazzo Soderini nearby (three Db-€150 rooms with breakfast, on Campo Bandiera e Moro).

North of St. Mark's Square

$$ Hotel Orion has 21 neat-as-a-pin, relaxing, and spacious rooms. Just off St. Mark's Square, it's a tranquil escape from the bustling streets (Db-€170, cash discount, air-con, Spadaria 700a, San Marco 30100, tel. 041-522-3053, fax 041-523-8866, www.hotel orion.it, info@hotelorion.it, cheery Massimiliano, Stefano, and Matteo). From St. Mark's Square, walk to the left of the basilica's facade and exit the square on Calle S. Basso (which changes to Spadaria). The hotel is just before the timbered overpass.

West of St. Mark's Square

$$$ **Hotel Flora** sits buried in a sea of fancy designer boutiques and elegant hotels almost on the Grand Canal. It's formal, with uniformed staff and grand public spaces, yet the 43 rooms have a homey warmth and the garden oasis is a sanctuary for weary guests (generally Db-€260, check website for special discounts or email Sr. Romanelli for a 10 percent Rick Steves discount, air-con, San Marco 2283/A, tel. 041-520-5844, fax 041-522-8217, www.hotel flora.it, info@hotelflora.it). It's at the end of Calle dei Bergamaschi, a long, skinny dead-end lane just off Calle Larga XXII Marzo on the Grand Canal side. For location, see map on page 892.

Near the Rialto Bridge

Vaporetto #2 quickly connects the Rialto with both the train station and the Tronchetto parking lot.

West of the Rialto Bridge

$$ **Albergo Guerrato,** above a handy and colorful produce market two minutes from the Rialto action, is run by friendly, creative, and hardworking Roberto and Piero. Their 800-year-old building—with 24 spacious, air-conditioned, and charming rooms—is simple, airy, and wonderfully characteristic (D-€90, Db-€130, Tb-€150, Qb-€170, Quint/b-€185, mention this book and pay cash for best prices, check website for special discounts, Rick Steves readers can ask for €5/night discount below Web specials; Calle drio la Scimia 240a, San Polo, tel. & fax 041-528-5927, www.pensioneguerrato.it, hguerrat@tin.it, Giorgio, Monica, and Rosanna). From the train station, take vaporetto #1 to the Rialto Market stop (comes before the "Rialto" stop), and exit the boat to your right and follow the waterfront. Calle drio la Scimia (not to be confused with Scimia, the block before), is on the left—you'll see the hotel sign. My tour groups book this place for 50 nights each year. Sorry. The Guerrato also rents family apartments in the old center (great for groups of 4–8) for around €55 per person.

$$ **Hotel al Ponte Mocenigo** is off the beaten path—a 10-minute walk northwest of the Rialto Bridge—but it's a great value. This 16th-century palazzo has a garden terrace and 10 comfy, beautifully appointed, and tranquil rooms (Sb-€100, Db-€140, €20 extra for view, extra bed-€25, discount with cash and this book, air-con, Internet access, Santa Croce 2063, tel. 041-524-4797, fax 041-275-9420, www.alpontemocenigo.com, info@alponte mocengio.com, Sandro and Walter). Take vaporetto #1 to the San Stae stop, head inland along the right side of the church, and take the first left down tiny Calle della Campanile. They also have a place around the corner with eight comparable rooms with high ceilings (Db-€150).

VENICE

Hotels near the Rialto Bridge

1. Albergo Guerrato
2. To Hotel al Ponte Mocenigo
3. Locanda la Corte
4. Casa Santa Maria Formosa
5. To Alloggi Barbaria
6. Hotel al Piave
7. Corte al Paradiso B&B
8. Hotel Riva
9. Corte Campana B&B
10. Ca' Formosa
11. Casa Cosmo
12. Locanda Silva
13. Hotel Giorgione
14. Locanda al Gambero
15. Foresteria della Chiesa Valdese
16. Launderette

V VAPORETTO STOP
T TRAGHETTO CROSSING
ᵕ VIEW

200 YARDS
200 METERS

East of the Rialto Bridge

$$ Locanda la Corte, a three-star hotel, is perfumed with elegance. Its 19 attractive, high-ceilinged, wood-beamed rooms—done in earthy pastels—circle a small, quiet courtyard (Sb-€120, standard Db-€150, superior Db-€170, cash discount, ask for Rick Steves rates when you book, check website for special discounts, suites and family rooms available, air-con, Castello 6317, tel. 041-241-1300, fax 041-241-5982, www.locandalacorte.it, info@locanda lacorte.it, Marco and Raffaela). Take vaporetto #52 from the train station to Fondamenta Nuove, exit the boat to your left, follow the waterfront, and turn right after the second bridge to get to S.S. Giovanni e Paolo square. Facing the Rosa Salva bar, take the street to the left (Calle Bressana); the hotel is a short block away at #6317 before the bridge.

$$ Casa Santa Maria Formosa, with eight plush rooms, is in a recently renovated 16th-century palazzo facing a canal off in a quiet corner of Campo Santa Maria Formosa. Fit for royalty, some rooms are bedecked with white-and-gold drapery, while others are more contemporary (Db with small double bed-€100, Db-€150, Db with canal view-€170, air-con, a five-minute walk east from the Rialto bridge on Fondamenta dei Preti 5841—email for directions, tel. 041-528-8872, www.casaformosa.com, info@casaformosa.com, Paolo).

$ Alloggi Barbaria rents eight quiet, spacious, backpacker-type rooms. Beyond Campo S.S. Giovanni e Paolo, this Ikea-style place is a long walk from the action but a good value and a chance to see the real Venice (Db-€110, pay cash and mention this book for best prices, extra bed-€30, family deals, air-con, tel. 041-522-2750, fax 041-277-5540, www.alloggibarbaria.it, info@alloggibarbaria .it, Giorgio and Fausto). Take vaporetto #52 to Ospedale stop, turn left as you get off the boat, then right down Calle de le Capucine to #6573 (Castello). From the airport, take the Alilaguna speedboat to Fondamenta Nuove, turn left, then go right down Calle de le Capucine.

Southeast of the Rialto Bridge

$$ Hotel al Piave, with 27 fine air-conditioned rooms above a bright and classy lobby, is fresh, modern, and comfortable. You'll enjoy the neighborhood and always get a cheery welcome (Db-€160, Tb-€220; family suites-€290 for 4, €310 for 5, or €340 for 6; cash discount, Internet access, Ruga Giuffa 4838/40, Castello, tel. 041-528-5174, fax 041-523-8512, www.hotelalpiave.com, info @hotelalpiave.com, Mirella, Paolo, and Ilaria speak English, faithful Molly doesn't). From the San Zaccaria vaporetto stop, take the street to the right of the Bridge of Sighs to Campo S.S. Filippo e Giacomo, and continue on Calle drio la Chiesa. Cross the bridge, continue straight, then turn left onto Ruga Giuffa until you find the Piave on your left at #4838/40.

$ Corte al Paradiso B&B has three large rooms with high ceilings and newly redone bathrooms in a classic Venetian home near the Campo Santa Maria Formosa (Db-€125, one room with bathroom down the hall, air-con, tel. & fax 041-522-2744, www .cortealparadiso.com, coretealparadiso@yahoo.it). From the San Zaccaria vaporetto stop, take the street to the right of the Bridge of Sighs to Campo S.S. Filippo e Giacomo. Continue on Calle drio la Chiesa to cross the bridge, turn left onto Ruga Giuffa, and in about 10 yards, pass under the archway on the right.

$ Hotel Riva, with gleaming marble hallways, big exposed beams, fine antique furnishings, and bright rooms, is romantically situated on a canal along the gondola serenade route. You could actually dunk your breakfast rolls in the canal (but don't). Sandro might hold a corner *(angolo)* room if you ask, and there are also a few rooms overlooking a canal. Ten of the 12 rooms come with air-conditioning for the same price—request one when you reserve (Sb-€90, two D with adjacent showers-€100, Db-€120, Tb-€170, €20 extra for view, reserve with credit card but pay with cash only, Ponte dell'Angelo, tel. 041-522-7034, fax 041-528-5551, www .hotelriva.it, info@hotelriva.it). Facing St. Mark's Basilica, walk behind it on the left along Calle de la Canonica, take the first left (at blue *Pauly & C* mosaic in street), continue straight, go over the bridge, and angle right to the hotel at Ponte dell'Anzolo.

$ Corte Campana B&B, run by enthusiastic and helpful Riccardo, rents three quiet and characteristic rooms just behind St. Mark's Square, plus two apartments just around the corner (Db-€125, Tb or Tb apartment-€165, Qb-€190, prices are soft, cash only, 2-night minimum stay, €5/night less for stays of four nights or more, air-con, Internet access, Calle del Remedio 4410, Castello, tel. & fax 041-523-3603, mobile 389-272-6500, www .cortecampana.com, info@cortecampana.com). Facing St. Mark's Basilica, take Calle de la Canonica (left of church) and turn left before the canal on Calle dell'Anzolo. Take the second right (onto Calle del Remedio), cross the bridge, and follow signs. Ring the bell at the black gate; the door is across the courtyard on the left wall, and the B&B is up three flights of stairs.

$ Ca' Formosa has eight simple, bright rooms, with white walls, old wooden beams, and Venetian terrazzo floors. Rooms lead to an elegant breakfast hall. The tiny terrace is a quiet place to relax in the afternoon sun (Db-€110, cash discount, air-con, elevator, Internet access, tel. 041-520-4875, www.caformosa.it, info @caformosa.it, Roberto and Silvia). Follow directions to Hotel al Piave (see listing earlier in this section), continue past it and look for the sign for Ca' Formosa in a little, dead-end alleyway on the right—it's about 10 yards before the stairs of a small bridge.

$ Casa Cosmo is a humble little five-room place run by Davide and his parents. While it comes with minimal services and no public spaces, it's air-conditioned, very central, inexpensive, and quiet, with a tiny terrace (Db-€110, pay cash and mention this book for best prices, no breakfast, Calle di Mezo 4976, San Marco, tel. & fax 041-296-0710, www.casacosmo.com, info@casacosmo .com). Take vaporetto #2 to Rialto and head inland on Larga Mazzini (which becomes Merceria after passing a square and a church). Turn right onto San Salvador, then immediately left onto tiny Calle di Mezo to find the hotel ahead on your right at #4976.

$ Locanda Silva is a big, basic, beautifully located place renting 23 decent old-school rooms (S-€60, Sb-€80, D-€85, Db-€120, substantially less during slow times, Fondamenta del Remedio 4423, tel. 041-522-7643, fax 041-528-6817, www.locandasilva.it, fino@locandasilva.it). From San Marco, head north toward Campo Santa Maria Formosa, go down Calle del Remedio, and turn left at the canal to Fondamenta del Remedio.

Near the Accademia Bridge

When you step over the Accademia Bridge, the commotion of touristy Venice is replaced by a sleepy village laced with canals. You'll pay a premium to sleep here but, for many, the location is worth the price. This quiet area, next to the best painting gallery in town, is a 15-minute walk from the Rialto or St. Mark's Square. The fast vaporetto #2 connects the Accademia Bridge with both the train station (15 min) and St. Mark's Square (5 min).

South of the Accademia Bridge

To reach these hotels from the train station, you can take a vaporetto to the Accademia stop (more scenic, down Grand Canal) or the Zattere stop (less scenic, around outskirts of Venice, but faster). Or, from the airport, take the Alilaguna speedboat to the Zattere stop.

$$$ Hotel Belle Arti has a grand entry and a formal, stern staff. With the ambience and comforts of a modern American hotel, it feels a bit out of place in musty Old World Venice. It has plush public areas and 65 newly renovated rooms (Sb-€130, Db-€240, Tb-€280, Rick Steves discount available with cash, air-con, elevator; 100 yards behind Accademia art museum: facing museum, take left, then forced right, to Via Dorsoduro 912, Dorsoduro; tel. 041-522-6230, fax 041-528-0043, www.hotel bellearti.com, info@hotelbellearti.com).

$$$ Pensione Accademia fills the 17th-century Villa Maravege. Its 27 rooms are comfortable, elegant, and air-conditioned. You'll feel aristocratic gliding through its grand public spaces and

VENICE

Hotels near the Accademia Bridge

1. Hotel Belle Arti
2. Pensione Accademia
3. Hotel Agli Alboretti
4. Pensione la Calcina
5. To Casa Rezzonico
6. Hotel Messner
7. Hotel Galleria
8. Don Orione Religious Guest House
9. Ca' San Trovaso
10. Ca' San Vio
11. Domus Cavanis
12. Hotel Bel Sito
13. Locanda Art Déco
14. Casa Artè
15. Fondazione Levi
16. Albergo San Samuele
17. To Alloggi "Alla Scala"
18. Hotel Flora

Map labels:

TO SAN MARCO
SAN MOISÈ
XXII MARZO
LARGO
FOND. OSTREGHE
S. MARIA GIGLIO
CAMPO SAN MAURIZIO
TO RIALTO
PALAZZO GRASSI
SAN SAM
CAMPO SANTO STEFANO
CA' REZZONICO
GRAND CANAL
TRAGHETTO
TO FRARI + RIALTO
CAMPO S. BARNABA
TOLETTA
ACCADEMIA MUSEUM
ACCADEMIA BRIDGE
BORGO
REMITE
BONILLI
CAMPO S. TROVASO
NANI
ZATTERE
ALILAGUNA DOCK
ZATTERE
PONTE LONGO
S. MARIA GESUATI
GONDOLA WORKSHOP
PISTOR
CAMPO S. AGNESE
CARITÀ
VENIER
BRAGADIN
MADONNA
CALLE
INCURABILI
DRIO INC.
CAMPO S. VIO
CHIESA S. VIO
Peggy Guggenheim Collection
CA' BALA
SANTO SPIRITO
S. SPIRITO
OSPED
INCURABILI
CATECUMENI
BASTION
FORNACE
SQUERO
LA SALUTE
Customs House
CANAL
GIUDECCA CANAL

Legend:

← ENTRANCES TO SIGHTS
🚉 VAPORETTO STOP
🚏 TRAGHETTO CROSSING
☆ VIEW

200 YARDS
200 METERS

lounging in its wistful, breezy gardens, which almost makes up for being snubbed by its snooty staff (Sb-€145, standard Db-€225, bigger "superior" Db-€275, Qb-€355, for best prices ask for Rick Steves discount when you book and pay cash; facing Accademia art museum, take first right, cross first bridge, go right to Dorsoduro 1058; tel. 041-523-7846, fax 041-523-9152, www.pensione accademia.it, info@pensioneaccademia.it).

$$$ Hotel Agli Alboretti is a cozy, family-run, 23-room place in a quiet neighborhood a block behind the Accademia art museum. With red carpeting and wood-beamed ceilings, it feels classy (Sb-€115, Db-€200, Tb-€225, Qb-€250, air-con, elevator, 100 yards from the Accademia vaporetto stop on Rio Terra A. Foscarini at #884, Dorsoduro, tel. 041-523-0058, fax 041-521-0158, www.aglialboretti.com, info@aglialboretti.com). Facing the Accademia art museum, go left, then forced right; or from the Zattere Alilaguna stop, head inland on Rio Terra A. Foscarini 100 yards to the hotel. They run a nearby gourmet restaurant that's a local favorite.

$$ Pensione la Calcina, the home of English writer John Ruskin in 1876, maintains a 19th-century formality. It comes with all the three-star comforts in a professional yet intimate package. Its 33 rosy perfumed rooms are squeaky clean, with nice wood furniture, hardwood floors, and a peaceful canalside setting facing Giudecca Island (Sb-€100, Sb with view-€110, Db-€150–250 depending on size of room and view, Qb-€263, air-con, Wi-Fi, rooftop terrace, killer sundeck on canal and canalside buffet-breakfast terrace, Dorsoduro 780, at south end of Rio di San Vio, tel. 041-520-6466, fax 041-522-7045, www.lacalcina.com, la.calcina @libero.it). From the Tronchetto parking lot, take vaporetto #2, or from the train station take #51 or #61, to Zattere (at vaporetto stop, exit right and walk along canal to hotel). Guests get a discounted dinner at their La Piscina restaurant and are welcome to use the terrace outside of meal times without buying anything.

$$ Casa Rezzonico is a silent getaway far from the madding crowds. Its private garden terrace has perhaps the lushest grass in Italy, and its seven spacious, very Venetian rooms have garden/canal views (Sb-€120, Db-€160, Tb-€180, Qb-€220, ask for Rick Steves discount when you book, air-con, Fondamenta Gherardini 2813, Dorsoduro, tel. 041-277-0653, fax 041-277-5435, www .casarezzonico.it, info@casarezzonico.it). Take vaporetto #1 to the Ca' Rezzonico stop, head up Calle del Traghetto, cross Campo San Barnaba to the canal, and continue forward on Fondamenta Gherardini to #2813.

$$ Hotel Messner, a sprawling place popular with groups, rents 38 bright, newly refurbished rooms (half in main building, half in nearby, elegantly decorated annex), in a peaceful canalside neighborhood near La Salute Church (Sb-€110, Db with air-con-€145, Db without air-con in annex-€115, Tb-€145, Qb-€160, 5 percent discount with cash if you book direct, Internet access, peaceful garden, midway between lagoon and Grand Canal on Rio delle Fornace canal, Dorsoduro 216, tel. 041-522-7443, fax 041-522-7266, www.hotelmessner.it, messnerinfo@tin.it).

$$ Hotel Galleria has nine tight, velvety rooms, most with views of the Grand Canal. Some rooms are quite narrow (S-€85, D-€120, Db-€145, palatial Grand Canal-view Db #8 and #10-€165, includes scant breakfast in room, fans, near Accademia art museum, and next to recommended Foscarini pizzeria, Dorsoduro 878a, tel. 041-523-2489, fax 041-520-4172, www.hotelgalleria.it, galleria@tin.it).

$$ Don Orione Religious Guest House is a big cultural center dedicated to the work of a local man who became a saint in modern times. With 74 rooms filling an old monastery, it feels like a modern retreat center—clean, peaceful, and strictly run. It's beautifully located, comfortable, and a fine value (Sb-€80, Db-€136, Tb-€174, profits go to mission work in the developing world, groups welcome, air-con, tel. 041-522-4077, fax 041-528-6214, www.donorione-venezia.it, info@donorione-venezia.it). From the Zattere vaporetto stop, turn right, then turn left just after the church. The entrance is behind the church at #909a.

$ Ca' San Trovaso rents nine classy, spacious rooms split between the main hotel and a nearby annex. The location is peaceful, on a small canal (Sb-€90, Db-€115, Db with bigger canal-view and air-con-€130, Tb-€145, pay cash and mention this book for best prices, includes breakfast in your room, air-con, small roof terrace, Dorsoduro 1350/51, tel. 041-277-1146, fax 041-277-7190, www .casantrovaso.com, s.trovaso@tin.it, Mark and his son Alessandro). From Piazzale Roma or the train station, take vaporetto #2 or #51. Rather than going down the Grand Canal, take the boat counterclockwise around Venice for a more direct route (confirm at dock). Get off at the Zattere stop, exit left, and cross a bridge. Turn right at tiny Calle Trevisan (just past the white building with all the flags), cross another bridge, cross the adjacent bridge, take an immediate right, and then the first left. Nearby, mama Cristina recently opened **Casa di Sara,** a brightly colored B&B with quiet rooms, a tiny roof terrace, and the same prices (mobile 339-828-4930, www.casadisara.com, info@casadisara.com).

$ Ca' San Vio is a tiny place run by the Ca' San Trovaso folks on a quiet canal with five fine air-conditioned rooms (small French bed Db-€110, bigger Db-€130, Tb-€150, breakfast in room, no public spaces, Calle delle Mende 531, Dorsoduro, tel. 041-241-3513, fax 041-241-3953, www.casanvio.com, info@casanvio.com, Roberto, Alessandro, and Marco).

$ Domus Cavanis, across the street from—and run by—Hotel Belle Arti (listed under "South of the Accademia Bridge," earlier in this section), is a big, dim, stark place, renting 30 basic, dingy rooms for a good price (Sb-€75, Db-€120, Tb-€160, family rooms, includes breakfast at Hotel Belle Arti, air-con, hounds of hell bathroom fans, elevator, Dorsoduro 895, tel. 041-528-7374, fax 041-528-0043, info@hotelbellearti.com).

North of the Accademia Bridge

$$ Hotel Bel Sito offers pleasing yet well-worn Old World character, 38 rooms, a peaceful courtyard, and a picturesque location—facing a church on a small square between St. Mark's Square and the Accademia (Sb-€108, Db-€175, air-con, elevator; catch vaporetto #1 to Santa Maria del Giglio stop, take street inland to square, hotel is at far end to your right at Santa Maria del Giglio 2517, San Marco; tel. 041-522-3365, fax 041-520-4083, www.hotel belsito.info, info@hotelbelsito.info, manager Rosella).

$$ Locanda Art Déco is a charming little place. While the Art Deco theme is scant, a wrought-iron staircase leads from the inviting lobby to seven thoughtfully decorated rooms (Db-€175, 3-night minimum on weekends, cash discount, 2 family rooms, air-con, just north of the Accademia Bridge off Campo Santo Stefano at Calle delle Botteghe 2966, San Marco, tel. 041-277-0558, fax 041-270-2891, www.locandaartdeco.com, info@locanda artdeco.com).

$ Casa Artè has six homey rooms with high ceilings, old-style Venetian furnishings, air-conditioning and thoughtful touches in a red-velvet ambience. An annex containing eight peaceful, simpler rooms, requires a three-night minimum stay (Sb-€110, Db-€140, Tb-€179, cash discount, family room sleeps up to 6, just north of Accademia Bridge, 100 yards west of Campo Santo Stefano on Calle de Frutariol 2900/01, San Marco, tel. 041-241-3795, fax 041-277-8395, www.casaarte.info, info@casaarte.info, Nicole).

$ Fondazione Levi, run by a foundation that promotes research on Venetian music, offers 18 quiet, institutional, yet comfortable and surprisingly spacious rooms (Sb-€64, Db-€105, Tb-€120, Qb-€140, twin beds only, elevator, San Vidal 2893, strict cancellation policy, San Marco, tel. 041-786-711, fax 041-786-766, www.fondazionelevi.org, foresterialevi@libero.it). It's 80 yards from the base of the Accademia Bridge on the St. Mark's side. From the Accademia vaporetto stop, cross the Accademia Bridge and take an immediate left, crossing the bridge Ponte Giustinian and going down Calle Giustinian straight to the Fondazione. Buzz the *Foresteria* door to the right.

$ Albergo San Samuele's 12 basic budget rooms are located in a crumbling historic palazzo just a few blocks from Campo

Santo Stefano (S-€60, D-€90, Db-€125, cash only, no breakfast, Salizada San Samuele 3358, San Marco, tel. 041-522-8045, fax 041-520-5165, www.albergosansamuele.it, info@albergosansamuele.it).

$ Alloggi "Alla Scala" is a basic, grandmotherly retreat with six rooms located next to the Bovolo staircase just off Campo Manin. It's a fantastic value for this location (Sb-€50, Db-€90, Tb-€110, 6 percent cash discount, breakfast-€5, Corte Contarini del Bovolo 4306, San Marco, tel. 041-521-0629, fax 041-522-6451, www.alloggiallascala.com, info@alloggiallascala.com). At Campo Manin ask for (or follow signs to) Corte Contarini del Bovolo—100 yards away.

Near the Train Station

I don't recommend the train station area. It's crawling with noisy, disoriented tourists with too much baggage and people whose life's calling is to scam visitors out of their money. It's so easy just to hop a vaporetto upon arrival and get into the Venice of your dreams. Still, some like to park their bags near the station, and these places work well. The nearest self-service laundry is Speedy Wash (daily 8:00–22:00, €9 wash and dry, discounted if you use the Internet access next door, Rio Terra San Leonardo 5120 just east of the Guglie bridge, tel. 041-524-4188).

$$ Locanda Herion, renovated in 2008, has 17 basic rooms with elegant touches, and a pretty little garden courtyard perfect for dinner picnics or a glass of wine (Db-€150, pay cash and mention this book for best prices, air-con, tel. 041-275-9426, fax 041-275-6647, http://herion.hotelinvenice.com, info@locandaherion .com). Exit the train station toward the Grand Canal and turn left to follow Rio Terra Lista de Spagna. Cross the Guglie bridge and turn right at the yellow San Marcuola vaporetto sign to find Campiello Picutti o del Magazen 1697A.

$ Albergo Marin and its friendly, helpful staff offer 18 good-value, quiet, and immaculate rooms handy to the train station (Sb-€110, D-€90, Db-€120, Tb-€150, cash discount, fans on request, Ramo delle Chioverete #670B, Santa Croce, tel. 041-718-022, fax 041-721-485, www.albergomarin.it, info@albergomarin.it). From the station, cross the Grand Canal and turn immediately right. Take the first left, then the first right, then right again to Ramo delle Chioverete.

$ Guest House al Portico, a funky mix of American expat Stacy's artwork and classic Venetian furnishings, makes for a quiet refuge located near the Jewish Ghetto. You'll feel at home with roof- and garden-terraces, an honor-system wine bar, Stacy's warm hospitality, and husband Domenico's fine cooking from their adjacent restaurant (Db-€120, Db romantic suite with private terrace-€170, Tb-€140, air-con, Wi-Fi, tel. 041-275-9202, fax 041-

275-7659, stacysguesthouse@hotmail.it). Take vaporetto #1 or #2 to San Marcuola (for location of stop, see the color map at the front of the book), walk away from the water, and turn left immediately after you pass the church. Then take the first right (Calle Seconda del Cristo), and turn right at the "T" intersection—on Sotoportego del Pegoloto—to find #1804.

$ **Hotel S. Lucia,** just 150 yards from the station down a quiet alley, is a peaceful family-owned hotel offering budget travelers a haven from Venice's hustle and bustle. Its 15 rooms are simple, clean, and cheery, and guests can enjoy their sunny garden area out front (S-€60, Db-€105, Tb-€145, discounts for three nights or more and 5 percent cash discount, breakfast-€5, air-con, Calle della Misericordia 358, Cannaregio, tel. 041-715-180, fax 041-710-610, www.hotelslucia.com, info@hotelslucia.com, Gianni and Alessandra). Exit the station toward the Grand Canal and head left, then take the second left onto Calle della Misericordia. The hotel is 100 yards ahead on the right.

$ **Alloggi Henry,** a homey little family-owned hotel, rents 12 simple and flowery, recently renovated rooms in a quiet neighborhood. It's a 10-minute walk from the train station (D-€80, Db-€100, Tb-€130, pay cash and mention this book for best prices, no breakfast, air-con, Calle Ormesini 1506e, Cannaregio, tel. 041-523-6675, fax 041-715-680, www.alloggihenry.com, info @alloggihenry.com). From the station, follow Rio Terra Lista de Spagna, Rio Terra San Leonardo, and Rio Terra Farsetti, then take the second left on Calle Ormesini. The hotel's at #1506.

Big, Fancy Hotels

Here are four big, plush, four-star places with greedy, sky-high rack rates (around Db-€300) that often have great discounts (as low as Db-€120) for drop-ins, off-season travelers, or online booking through their websites. If you want a sliding-glass-door, uniformed-receptionist kind of comfort and formality in the old center, these are worth considering: $$$ **Hotel Giorgione** (big, garish, shiny, near Rialto Bridge, www.hotelgiorgione.com—see map on page 888); $$$ **Hotel Casa Verardo** (elegant and quietly parked on a canal behind St. Mark's, more stately, www.casa verardo.it—see map on page 884); $$$ **Hotel Donà Palace** (sitting like Las Vegas in the touristy zone just northeast of St. Mark's, www.donapalace.it—see map on page 884); and $$$ **Locanda al Gambero,** with 30 comfortable rooms near San Marco (www .locandaalgambero.com—see map on page 888).

Cheap Dormitory Accommodations

$ **Foresteria della Chiesa Valdese,** warmly run by the Methodist Church, offers 60 beds in doubles and 3- to 8-bed dorms, halfway

VENICE

between St. Mark's Square and the Rialto Bridge. This run-down but charming old place has elegant ceiling paintings (dorm bed-€26, Db-€86, discount for stays of three nights or more, includes breakfast, sheets, towels, and lockers; room lock-out from 10:00–13:30, must check in and out when office is open—8:30–13:00 & 16:00–20:00, reservations by phone only—no email, Fondamenta Cavagnis 5170, Castello, tel. 041-528-6797, fax 041-241-6238, foresteriavenezia@diaconiavaldese.org). From Campo Santa Maria Formosa, walk past Bar all'Orologio to the end of Calle Lunga and cross the bridge onto Fondamenta Cavagnis.

$ Venice's youth hostel, on Giudecca Island with grand views across the Bay of San Marco, is a godsend for backpackers shell-shocked by Venetian prices (€24 beds with sheets and breakfast in 12- to 16-bed dorms, cheaper for hostel members, office open daily 7:00–24:30, catch vaporetto #2 from station to Zittele, tel. 041-523-8211, can reserve online at www.ostellovenezia.it). The budget cafeteria also welcomes non-hostelers (nightly 18:00–23:00).

Eating

While touristy restaurants are the scourge of Venice, these places are still popular with locals and respect the tourists who happen to come in. First trick: Walk away from triple-language menus. Second trick: Order the daily special. Third trick: For fresh-ness, eat fish. Most seafood dishes are the local catch-of-the-day. Remember that seafood can be sold by weight rather than a set price (if you see "100 g" or "*l'etto*" by a too-good-to-be-true price on the menu, that's the cost per 100 grams—about a quarter pound). The abbreviation *s.q.* is similar, meaning according to quantity (you pay for the weight of the particular piece).

Near the Rialto Bridge
North of the Bridge
These restaurants are located between Campo S.S. Apostoli and Campo S.S. Giovanni e Paolo.

Trattoria da Bepi is bright, alpine-paneled, and family run. Owner Loris scours the market for just the best ingredients—especially seafood—and takes good care of the hungry clientele. There's good seating inside and out (€10 pastas, €15 *secondi*, Fri–Wed 12:00–14:30 & 19:00–22:00, closed Thu, near Rialto Bridge, half a block north of Campo Santi Apostoli on Salizada Pistor, tel. 041-528-5031).

Trattoria Ca' d'Oro, while a little less accessible and invit-ing to the tourist, is a venerable favorite with a small, appealing menu and an enthusiastic local following. Just to sip a wine and enjoy *cicchetti* at the bar is a treat. It's also fine for a meal, but

Restaurants near the Rialto Bridge

1. Trattoria da Bepi
2. Trattoria Ca' d'Oro
3. Osteria da Alberto
4. Fiaschetteria Toscana
5. Pizzeria La Perla
6. Osteria al Bomba
7. Osteria di Sta Marina
8. Osteria il Milion
9. Osterias "Alla Botte" & Enoteca ai Rusteghi
10. Rosticceria San Bartolomeo
11. Pasticceria Ponte delle Paste
12. Osteria al Portego
13. Cantina do Mori & Ostaria ai Storti
14. Pesce Pronto
15. Antica Ostaria Ruga Rialto

16. Osteria al Diavolo e l'Acquasanta
17. Al Marcà
18. Osterias Bancogiro & Naranzaria
19. To Trattoria/Pizzeria Nono Risorto
20. Rist. al Giardinetto
21. Osteria alle Testiere
22. Osteria al Mascaron
23. La Boutique del Gelato
24. Michielangelo Gelato
25. To Antica Birraria la Corte

Nightlife

26. Bácaro Jazz Venezia Wine Bar
27. Planet Restaurant
28. Devil's Forest Pub
29. Inishark Pub

reservations are a must (€9 pastas, €10 *secondi,* Mon–Wed and Fri–Sat 11:30–14:30 & 18:30–22:30, Sun 18:30–22:30, closed Thu; from the Ca' d'Oro boat dock walk 100 yards directly away from the canal, cross Strada Nuova, and you'll hit it; tel. 041-528-5324).

Osteria da Alberto, with excellent €13 seafood plates, €10 pastas, a good house wine, and a woody and characteristic interior, is one of my standbys (Mon–Sat 12:00–15:00 & 19:00–23:00, closed Sun, midway between Campo S.S. Apostoli and Campo S.S. Giovanni e Paolo, next to Ponte de la Panada on Calle Larga Giacinto Gallina, tel. 041-523-8153, run by Graziano and Giovanni).

Fiaschetteria Toscana, despite its name, focuses on Venetian cuisine, with an emphasis on quality ingredients and the freshest fish. For a culinary treat, it's worth the splurge, but for romance, head elsewhere—it's brightly lit and bustling with hurried waiters (€18 pastas, €26 *secondi,* Wed–Mon 12:30–14:30 & 19:30–22:30, closed Tue, between post office and Campo Santi Apostoli on Salizada S. Giovanni Grisostomo 5719, tel. 041-528-5281).

Pizzeria La Perla is busy, bright, and kid-friendly, with Italian and Hollywood movie posters everywhere. Italians bring their families here for big salads and pizza before heading across the street to the movies (Thu–Tue 12:00–15:00 & 18:30–22:30, closed Wed; from Campo S.S. Apostoli—with your back to the church facade—walk 10 yards up the street on your left to the first left, Rio Terà dei Franceschi 4615; tel. 041-528-5175).

Cicchetti, plus Pasta: **Osteria al Bomba** is a *cicchetti* bar with a feminine touch. It's unusual (clean, no toothpicks, no cursing) and quite good, with lots of veggies. You can stand and eat at the bar—try a little €2 *crostino* with polenta and cod—or oversee the construction of the house *"antipasto misto di cicchetti"* plate (€22, enough fish and vegetables for 2). Then grab a seat at the long table to complete your pub crawl with a plate of pasta (daily 12:00–15:00 & 18:00–23:00, near Campo S.S. Apostoli, a block off Strada Nuova on Calle dell'Oca, tel. 041-520-5175). You'll find more pubs nearby, in the side streets opposite Campo Santa Sofia, across Strada Nuova.

East of the Rialto Bridge, near Campo San Bartolomeo

Osteria di Santa Marina, on the wonderful Campo Marina, serves pricey, near-gourmet food that's made with only the best seasonal ingredients. The quality food and classy ambience make this a good splurge. Cheap eating tricks are frowned on in this elegant, borderline stuffy restaurant (enticing menu with €15 pastas and €25 *secondi,* Sun–Mon 19:30–21:30, Tue–Sat 12:30–14:30 & 19:30–22:00, reservations smart for dinner, eat indoors or outdoors on pleasant little square, midway between Rialto Bridge and Campo Santa Maria Formosa on Campo Marina, tel. 041-528-5239).

Osteria il Milion, with bow-tied waiters and dressy, candlelit tables indoors and out, is quietly situated next to Marco Polo's home. It's touristy but tasty (€9 pastas, €13 *secondi,* Thu–Tue 12:00–15:00 & 18:30–23:00, closed Wed; near Rialto Bridge, head north from Campo San Bartolomeo, over one bridge, take first right off San Giovanni Grisostomo before the church, walk under the sign *Corte Prima del Milion o del forno,* it's at #5841; tel. 041-522-9302).

Osteria "Alla Botte," despite being located a minute from the Rialto Bridge, is packed with a casual, local clientele in two simple, woody rooms. For a classic Venetian taste, try the €15 *antipasto misto* (Mon–Sat 12:00–15:00 & 19:00–22:00, Sun 12:00–15:00, two short blocks off Campo San Bartolomeo in the corner behind the statue—down Calle de la Bissa, notice the "day after" photo showing a debris-covered Venice after the notorious 1989 Pink Floyd open-air concert, tel. 041-520-9775).

Osteria Enoteca ai Rusteghi proudly serves fine wines by the affordable glass, tasty miniature *panini, insalata caprese* (mozzarella and tomatoes), and cheese or salami plates at al fresco tables in a peaceful courtyard, just a few steps from the hubbub on Campo San Bartolomeo and the Rialto Bridge (Mon–Sat 10:00–15:00 & 18:00–21:30, closed Sun, Corte del Tentor 5513, San Marco, tel. 041-523-2205). From Campo San Bartolomeo, with your back to the statue's back, head forward down the tiny alleyway on your right and turn right, then left under the overpass into the Corte del Tentor.

Rosticceria San Bartolomeo is a cheap—if confusing—self-service restaurant with a likeably surly staff. Take out, grab a table, or munch at the bar (good €6–7 pasta, great fried *mozzarella al prosciutto* for €1.50, delightful fruit salad, €1 glasses of wine, prices listed on wall behind counter, no cover or service charge, daily 9:00–21:30, tel. 041-522-3569). To find this venerable budget eatery, imagine the statue on the Campo San Bartolomeo walking backwards 20 yards, turning left, and going under a passageway—now, follow him.

If pub crawling from Rosticceria San Bartolomeo, continue over a bridge to Campo San Lio. Here, turn left, passing Hotel Canada on your right, and following Calle Carminati straight about 50 yards over another bridge. On the left is the pastry shop *(pasticceria),* and straight ahead is Osteria Al Portego (at #6015). Both are listed below.

Pasticceria Ponte delle Paste is a feminine and pastel *salon de tè,* popular for its homemade pastries and pre-dinner drinks. Italians love taking 15-minute breaks to sip a *spritz* with friends before heading home after a long day's work. Ask sprightly Monica for a *spritz al bitter* (white wine, *amaro,* and soda water, €1.80; or choose from the menu on the wall) and munch some of the free goodies at the bar around 18:00 (daily 7:00–20:30, Ponte delle Paste).

Osteria al Portego is a friendly, local-style bar—one of the best in town. Sebastiano and Carlo serve great *cicchetti* (best around 18:00, picked over by 21:00) and good meals (€10 pastas, Mon–Sat 10:30–15:00 & 18:00–21:30, Sun 18:00–21:30, Calle Malvasia 6015, Castello, tel. 041-522-9038). The *cicchetti* here can make a great meal, but you should also consider sitting down for a full dinner from their fine menu. Prices for food and wine are posted clearly on the wall.

Cicchetterie and Light Meals West of the Rialto Bridge

All of these places (except the last one, Nono Risorto) are within 200 yards of each other, in the neighborhood around the Rialto market. This area is very crowded by day, nearly empty early in the evening, and crowded with young locals later.

Cantina do Mori is famous with locals (since 1462) and savvy travelers (since 1982) as a classy place for fine wine and *francobolli* (a spicy selection of 20 tiny, mayo-soaked sandwiches nicknamed "stamps"). Choose from the featured wines. Go here to be abused in a fine atmosphere—the frowns are part of the shtick (Mon–Sat 12:00–20:30, closed Sun, stand-up only, arrive early before the *cicchetti* are gone, San Polo 429, tel. 041-522-5401). From the Rialto Bridge, walk 200 yards down Ruga degli Orefici, away from St. Mark's Square—then turn left on Ruga Vecchia S. Giovanni, then right at Sotoportego do Mori.

Ostaria ai Storti offers lots of veggies, a few homemade pastas (check the daily specials), great prices, a homey feel, and a wonderful, fun place to congregate outdoors. Check out the photo of the market in 1909, below the bar, while you savor the *fragolino* strawberry wine (Mon–Sat 12:00–15:00 & 18:00–22:30, closed Sun, 20 yards from Cantina do Mori on Calle do Spade 819, tel. 041-214-2255).

At **Pesce Pronto,** you can sample fish right near the market. Bruno and Umberto make artful fish hors d'oeuvres, *sfornato con pesce* (a savory baked pastry), and many other fresh fish tidbits—all at a fair price. This fancy hole-in-the-wall is great for a quick bite—eat standing up or take it to go (Tue–Sun 9:00–14:30 & 16:30–19:30, closed Mon; from the Rialto Bridge, head west on Ruga dei Spezieri, turn right at the fish market, and it's on Calle de le Becarie o Panataria 319; tel. 041-822-0298).

Antica Ostaria Ruga Rialto, a.k.a. "the Ruga," is a local fixture where Giorgio and Marco serve great bar snacks and wine to a devoted clientele. Bar or table, no problem—they're happy to make you a €3, €5, or €7 mixed plate (daily 11:00–14:30 & 19:00–24:00, easy to find, just past the Chinese restaurant on Ruga Vecchia S. Giovanni 692, tel. 041-521-1243).

Osteria al Diavolo e l'Acquasanta, three blocks west of the Rialto Bridge, serves good—if pricey—Venetian-style pasta, and makes a handy lunch stop for sightseers and gondola riders. While they list *cicchetti* and wine by the glass on the wall, I'd come here for a light meal rather than for appetizers (Mon 12:00–14:30, Wed–Sun 12:00–21:30, closed Tue, hiding on a quiet street just off Ruga Vecchia S. Giovanni, on Calle della Madonna, tel. 041-277-0307).

Al Marcà, on Campo Cesare Battisti, is a fancy little hole-in-the-wall where young locals gather to grab drinks and little snacks. Prices for wine and sandwiches are listed clearly (Mon–Sat 9:00–15:00 & 18:00–21:00, closed Sun, located on empty part of square just below courthouse).

Osteria Bancogiro, a simple bar behind the Rialto market, has stark outdoor seating overlooking the Grand Canal. Peruse their wine list and menu of creative pastas and entrées at the bar, or ask for a recommendation on a few strong local cheeses to go with your wine. Order and grab a table—worth the small cover charge (Tue–Sun 12:00–24:00, closed Mon, less than 200 yards from Rialto Bridge on Campo San Giacometto, San Polo 122, tel. 041-523-2061). Consider their €16 mixed-fish *antipasto* plate.

Osteria Naranzaria, which shares a prime piece of Grand Canal real estate with Osteria Bancogiro a few doors towards the Rialto Bridge, is a great stop (described under "Romantic Canalside Settings," later in this "Eating" section).

Trattoria Pizzeria Nono Risorto is unpretentious, inexpensive, youthful, and famous for some of the best pizza in town. You'll sit in a gravelly garden under a leafy canopy, surrounded by a young, enthusiastic waitstaff and Italians enjoying huge €8 salads, €9 pastas, delicious €8 pizzas, and €12 grilled meat or fish dishes. Reserve on weekends (Thu 19:00–22:30, Fri–Tue 12:00–14:30 & 19:00–22:30, closed Wed; a 3-min walk from the Rialto fish market, walk along the waterfront away from the Rialto Bridge, make a forced left, then find Campo San Cassiano and it's just over the bridge on Sotoportego de Siora Bettina; tel. 041-524-1169).

Near Campo Santa Maria Formosa

These eateries can be found on the map on page 899.

Ristorante al Giardinetto has white tablecloths, a formal-but-fun waitstaff, and a spacious, shady garden under a grapevine canopy. While it used to be set up for big tour groups—and still feels it—groups don't come here as often anymore, and the dining experience has improved. This is a good, solid, no-stress restaurant option (€9 pastas, €16 main courses, Fri–Wed 12:00–15:00 & 19:00–22:00, closed Thu, at intersection of Ruga Giuffa and Calle Corona, tel. 041-528-5332).

Osteria alle Testiere is my most gourmet recommendation in Venice. Hugely respected, they are passionate about quality, serving up creative, artfully presented market-fresh seafood (there's no meat on the menu), homemade pastas, and fine wine in what the chef calls a "Venetian Nouvel" style. Reservations are required for their three daily seatings: 12:30, 19:00, and 21:15. With only 22 seats, it's tight and homey yet elegant (€17 pastas, €25 *secondi,* plan on spending €50 for dinner, closed Sun–Mon, Calle del Mondo Novo 5801, tel. 041-522-7220).

Osteria al Mascaron is where I've gone for years to watch Gigi and his food-loving band of ruffians dish up rustic-yet-sumptuous pastas with steamy seafood to salivating local foodies. The pastas, while pricey, are for two (it's okay to ask for single portions). The €16 *antipasto misto* plate—have fun pointing—and two glasses of wine make a wonderful light meal (Mon–Sat 12:00–15:00 & 19:00–22:30, closed Sun, a block past Campo Santa Maria Formosa at Calle Longa Santa Maria Formosa 5225, tel. 041-522-5995).

In Dorsoduro

Near the Accademia Bridge

Ristorante/Pizzeria Accademia Foscarini, next to the Accademia Bridge and Galleria, offers decent €8–11 pizzas in a great canalside setting. While the food may be forgettable, this place is both scenic and practical—I grab a quick lunch here on each visit to Venice (May–Oct Wed–Mon 9:00–23:00, Nov–April until 20:00, closed Tue, Dorsoduro 878C, tel. 041-522-7281).

Enoteca Cantine del Vino Già Schiavi is much-loved for its €1 *cicchetti* and €3.50 sandwiches (order from list on board). It's also a good place for a €2 glass of wine and appetizers (Mon–Sat 8:00–20:30, closed Sun, 100 yards from Accademia art museum on San Trovaso canal; facing Accademia, take a right and then a forced left at the canal to the second bridge—S. Trovaso 992, tel. 041-523-0034). You're welcome to enjoy your wine and finger food hanging out at the bar, sitting on the bridge out front, or in the nearby square—which actually has grass. This is primarily a wine shop with great prices for bottles to go—and plastic glasses for picnickers.

Restaurants near the Accademia Bridge

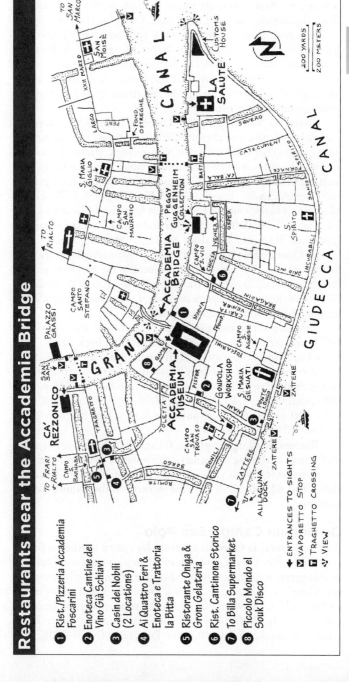

1. Rist./Pizzeria Accademia Foscarini
2. Enoteca Cantine del Vino Già Schiavi
3. Casin dei Nobili (2 Locations)
4. Ai Quattro Feri & Enoteca e Trattoria la Bitta
5. Ristorante Oniga & Grom Gelateria
6. Rist. Cantinone Storico
7. To Billa Supermarket
8. Piccolo Mondo el Souk Disco

➔ ENTRANCES TO SIGHTS
Ⓥ VAPORETTO STOP
Ⓣ TRAGHETTO CROSSING
⩗ VIEW

200 YARDS
200 METERS

Near Campo San Barnaba

A number of restaurants are worth the hike to this small square. From the Accademia, head northwest, following the curve of the Grand Canal. In five minutes, you'll spill out onto Campo San Barnaba (and the nearby Campo Santa Margherita). Follow the straight and narrow path (Calle Lunga San Barnaba) west of the square for more restaurants. With so many places within about 100 yards of each other, it would be fun to survey and choose, but reservations are often necessary.

Casin dei Nobili (Pleasure Palace of Nobles) has a diverse, reasonably priced menu at two different locations. Their restaurant near Campo San Barnaba has a high-energy, informal, modern setting. The patio is filled with simple tables, happy tourists, and inviting €11 daily specials (€12 pastas, €20 *secondi*, good pizzas, and "fantasy salads," Tue–Sun 12:00–15:00 & 19:00–23:00, closed Mon, a half-block south of Campo San Barnaba, Calle delle Casin 2765, tel. 041-241-1841). Their other restaurant is on the Giudecca Canal (see "Romantic Canalside Settings," opposite page).

Ai Quattro Feri is a noisy, bustling, trattoria-style eatery, best for its catch-of-the-day seafood, especially the excellent grilled fish (€10 pastas, €13 *secondi*, Mon–Sat 12:30–14:30 & 19:30–22:30, closed Sun, just off the square on Calle Lunga San Barnaba 2754, tel. 041-520-6978, reservations required).

Enoteca e Trattoria la Bitta is dark and woody with a soft jazz, bistro feel and a small, forgettable back patio. They serve beautifully presented, traditional Venetian food with—proudly—no fish. Their helpful waitstaff and small menu is clearly focused on quality. Reservations are required (€9 pastas, €15 *secondi*, dinner only, Mon–Sat 18:30–23:00, closed Sun, cash only, next to Quattro Feri on Calle Lunga San Barnaba 2753, tel. 041-523-0531).

Ristorante Oniga, right on Campo San Barnaba, is a wine bar/restaurant serving up Italian cuisine with a modern twist. Try the homemade ravioli (Wed–Mon 12:00–14:30 & 19:00–22:30, closed Tue, tel. 041-522-4410). The owners run the **Grom** gelateria next door.

On or near Campo San Polo

Antica Birraria la Corte is an everyday eatery on the very special Campo San Polo. Enjoy a pizza or simple meal on the far side of this great, homey, family-filled square. While the interior is a sprawling beer hall, the square is a joy, where metal tables teeter on the cobbles, the wind plays with the paper mats, and children run free (daily 12:00–14:30 & 19:00–22:30, on the way to Frari Church, Campo San Polo 2168, San Polo, tel. 041-275-0570).

Romantic Canalside Settings

Of course, if you want a meal with a canal view, it generally comes with lower quality or a higher price. But if you're aiming for a canalside dining memory, these places can be great. I've listed the better-value places below, along with advice for coping with the tourist traps.

Near the Rialto Bridge: **Osteria Naranzaria** is one of two wonderful eateries on the Grand Canal between the market and the Rialto Bridge (the other is **Osteria Bancogiro,** a few doors down away from the Rialto Bridge, listed on page 903). Somehow they've taken a stretch of unbeatable but overlooked canal-front property and filled it with trendy candlelit tables. Foodies appreciate its Nouveau Italian cuisine, which includes sushi, since Venice was the gateway to the Orient (remember Marco Polo?). The menu also includes salami, inventive entrées (but no pasta), and fine wine. Peasants may take their glasses to the steps along the canal for bar prices, but the romantic table service doesn't cost that much extra. This is the best-value Grand Canal eatery I've found (€18 *secondi,* Tue–Sun 12:00–24:00, closed Mon, tel. 041-724-1035).

Rialto Bridge Tourist Traps: Locals are embarrassed by the lousy food and aggressive "service" at the string of joints dominating the best romantic, Grand Canal–fringing real estate in town. Still, if you want to linger over dinner with a view of the most famous bridge and the songs of gondoliers oaring by (and don't mind eating with other tourists), this can be enjoyable. Don't trust the waiter's recommendations for special meals. The budget ideal would be to get a simple pizza or pasta and a drink for €15, and savor the ambience without getting ripped off. But few restaurants will allow you to get off that easy. To avoid a dispute over the bill, ask if there's a minimum charge—before you sit down (most places have one).

Near St. Mark's Square: At **Trattoria da Giorgio ai Greci,** a few blocks behind St. Mark's, Giorgio and sons Roberto and Davide serve homemade pastas and fresh seafood. While they have inside seating, you come here for the canalside dining—it's the best I've found anywhere in town. Call to reserve a canalside table (€17–21 fixed-price meals, daily 12:00–22:30, two canals east of St. Mark's on Ponte dei Greci 4988, tel. 041-528-9780).

Ristorante Alla Conchiglia (Trattoria da Giorgio ai Greci's low-key neighbor) has wonderful tables lining the sleepy canal. They specialize in fish and have a reasonable-for-the-romantic-setting menu. Call to reserve a canalside table (€9 pizzas, €12 big salads, €17–22 fixed-price meals, daily specials, Thu–Tue 11:30–22:15, closed Wed, Fondamenta dei Greci, tel. 041-528-9095).

Near the Accademia Bridge: **Ristorante Cantinone Storico** sits on a peaceful canal in Dorsoduro between the Accademia

Bridge and the Guggenheim. It's dressy, touristy, specializes in fish and traditional Venetian dishes, has a half-dozen tables on the canal, and is worth the splurge. Reservations are smart (€15 pastas, €20 *secondi*, €3 cover, Mon–Sat 12:30–14:30 & 19:30–21:30, later in summer, closed Sun, on the canal Rio de S. Vio, tel. 041-523-9577).

Casin dei Nobili, located on the Venice side of the Giudecca Canal, gets the warm, romantic evening sun. They serve finely crafted regional specialties with creativity at reasonable prices. The canalside seating is breezy and beautiful, but comes with the rumble of *vaporetti* from the nearby stop. The interior is bright and hip, with rotating art exhibits. The menu is the same as their location near Campo San Barnaba (under "Near Campo San Barnaba," earlier in "Eating"), but with slightly higher prices due to its prime location (Fri–Wed 12:00–15:00 & 19:00–23:00, open 15:00–19:00 for drinks only, closed Thu, tel. 041-520-6895, exit vaporetto at Zattere stop and turn left, Zattere 924/5).

On Fondamenta Nuove with a View of the Open Lagoon: **Algiubagio's** is a good opportunity to eat well overlooking the lagoon. The name is a combination of the owners' four names— Alberto, Giulio, Barbara, and Giovanna—who strive to impress visitors with quality, creative Venetian cuisine made using the best ingredients. Reserve a table on the lagoon facing San Michele Island or in their classy cantina dining room (€16 pastas, €25 *secondi*, €3 cover, Wed–Mon 12:00–15:00 & 19:00–22:30, closed Tue, to the left of the vaporetto dock as you face the water at Fondamenta Nuove 5039, Cannaregio, tel. 041-523-6084).

Eating Inexpensively near St. Mark's Square

For locations, see the map on page 869.

Sandwich Row (Calle delle Rasse): This street, just steps away from the tourist intensity at St. Mark's Square, is the closest place to get a decent sandwich at an affordable price with a place to sit down. From the Bridge of Sighs, head down the Riva and take the second lane left. The entire street is lined with sandwich bars (most open daily 7:00–24:00, €1 extra to sit).

Birreria Forst is best, with a selection of meaty €2.70 sandwiches with tasty sauce on wheat bread, or made-to-order sandwiches for around €3.50 (air-con, rustic wood tables, Calle delle Rasse 4540, tel. 041-523-0557). Also good is **Osteria da Bacco,** with great osteria-type seating, an honest menu, and tasty, cheap wine by the glass (Calle delle Rasse 4620, tel. 041-522-2887). **Bar Verde** is a more modern sandwich bar with big €4 sandwiches and splittable €8 salads (facing Campo S.S. Filippo e Giacomo at the end of Calle delle Rasse).

At **Salad and Juice Bar Oasi 2000,** Alessandro and Giorgia serve big salads, sandwiches, a few hot pasta dishes, and fresh-squeezed juice in a small student-cantina atmosphere (daily 9:00–20:30, just behind St. Mark's Basilica off Calle San Provolo at Calle di Albanesi 4263, tel. 347-311-1335).

At **Rizzo,** a bar/*alimentari* market located on the main drag of Calle dei Fabbri, you can grab €4.50 homemade lasagna and other reasonably priced snacks such as yogurt, sautéed spinach, and fried sandwiches. It's stand and eat only—there are no seats here (Mon–Sat 8:00–20:00, closed Sun, Calle dei Fabbri 933A, tel. 041-522-3388).

Chat Qui Rit Self Service is a big, fresh, modern oasis of efficiency, tucked away three blocks from the back of Piazza San Marco on Calle Frezzaria. They have a long cafeteria line of appealing dishes and reasonable prices. Sit at a table on the sidewalk, in a peaceful garden, or in an air-conditioned room behind the garden (€5 pastas, €8 *secondi,* daily 11:00–21:30; exit St. Mark's Square through middle arches, turn right, left, then right again, follow Calle Frezzaria 100 yards—it's on the right at Calle Tron, 1133a; tel. 041-522-9086).

Dining near St. Mark's Square

Trattoria da Remigio is well-known for high-quality, serious Venetian cuisine. Its indoors-only setting is a bit dressy, with a mix of tourists and locals, and lots of commotion (Wed–Sun lunch from 12:30, dinner from 19:30, closed Mon–Tue, just past Rio dei Greci on a tiny square at the end of Calle Madonna, tel. 041-523-0089).

The **cafés on St. Mark's Square** offer music, inflated prices, and an unbeatable setting for a drink or light meal.

Near the Train Station

For fast, cheap food near the station, consider **Brek,** a popular chain self-service cafeteria (after serving breakfast, it's open daily 11:30–22:00, with back to station, facing canal, go left on Rio Terra—it becomes Lista di Spagna in two short blocks, Lista di Spagna 124, tel. 041-244-0158).

Cheap Meals

The keys to cheap eating in Venice are pizza, bars/cafés, and picnics. *Panini* and *tramezzini* (sandwiches) are sold fast and cheap at bars everywhere and can stave off mid-morning hunger. There's a great "sandwich row" of cheap cafés near St. Mark's Square (see previous page). For speed, value, and ambience, you can get a filling plate of local appetizers at nearly any bar. For budget eating, I like small, stand-up mini-meals at *cicchetti* **bars** best (see page 902).

Pizzerias

Pizza is cheap and readily available. Key pizza vocabulary: *capricciosa* (generally ham, mushrooms, olives, and artichokes), *funghi* (mushrooms), *marinara* (tomato sauce, oregano, garlic, no cheese), *quattro formaggi* (four different cheeses), and *quattro stagioni* (different toppings on each of the pizza's four quarters, for those who can't choose just one menu item). If you ask for pepperoni on your pizza, you'll get *peperoni* (green or red peppers, not sausage). Kids like *diavola*, which is the closest thing in Italy to American pepperoni, and *margherita*—the classic mozzarella, tomato sauce, and basil pizza named for Queen Margherita in 1889.

Picnics

The **produce market** that sprawls for a few blocks just past the Rialto Bridge is a great place to assemble a picnic (best Mon–Sat 8:00–13:00, closed Sun). The adjacent fish market is wonderfully slimy (closed Sun–Mon). Side lanes in this area are speckled with fine little hole-in-the-wall munchie bars, bakeries, and cheese shops.

Gelato

La Boutique del Gelato is considered the best *gelateria* in Venice, with the most generous €1 scoops you'll find (daily 10:00–20:30, closed Dec–Jan, shown on map on page 899, located two blocks off Campo Santa Maria Formosa on corner of Salizada San Lio and Calle Paradiso, next to Hotel Bruno, at #5727—just look for the crowd).

Late-Night Gelato: Near the Rialto Bridge, try **Michielangelo,** just off Campo San Bartolomeo, on the St. Mark's side of the Rialto Bridge on Salizada Pio X (daily 10:00–23:00).

At St. Mark's Square, get your scoop late at **Gran Café Lavena** (daily until 24:00, first café to left of the Clock Tower, behind the first orchestra).

Grom, a chain gelateria on Campo San Barnaba, makes fresh gelato with all-natural ingredients—a rare gem among the touristy gelato shops around town (daily April–Sept 11:00–24:00, Oct–March 12:00–24:00, located next door to recommended Ristorante Oniga).

Connections

Trains

To avoid the long lines for buying train tickets and making seat and *cuccetta* reservations, many travelers use the automatic ticket machines at the station. These gray-and-yellow touch-screen *Biglietto Veloce* (Fast Ticket) machines have an English option, display train schedules, issue train tickets and reservations, and accept payment in cash or by credit/debit card. Or you could take care of these tasks at downtown travel agencies (see "Services," near the beginning of this chapter). The cost is only a little more (agencies charge a small fee); it can be more convenient (if you find yourself near a travel agency while sightseeing); and the language barrier can be smaller than at the station's ticket windows.

From Venice by Train to: **Florence** (nearly hourly, 3–3.5 hrs, may transfer in Bologna; often crowded so make reservations), **Milan** (at least hourly, 2.5–3 hrs), **Cinque Terre/Monterosso** (8/day, 6–8 hrs, 1–3 changes), **Cinque Terre/La Spezia** (20/day, 5–7 hrs, 1–3 changes), **Rome** (roughly hourly, 5–8 hrs, overnight possible), **Interlaken** (5/day, 6.25–7 hrs, 2-3 changes, overnight possible), **Munich** (9/day, 7–9 hrs, may change in Verona or Salzburg), **Salzburg** (4/day, 6–7 hrs, 3–4 changes, 1 direct night train), **Paris** (1 direct night train/day, 13 hrs, important to reserve ahead; 3/day, 4/night, 10–13 hrs with change in Milan), and **Vienna** (1 direct, 8 hrs; 3/day, 10–12 hrs with changes).

Marco Polo Airport

Venice's modern airport on the mainland, six miles north of the city, has a sleek wood-beam-and-glass terminal, with a TI (daily 9:00–21:00), ATMs, car-rental agencies, and a few shops and eateries (airport info tel. 041-260-9250, www.veniceairport.com). Check with your hotel or in *Un Ospite di Venezia* (the free tourist information guide at fancy hotels) for phone numbers and websites for all airlines serving Marco Polo and nearby airports.

There are four ways for you to get between the airport and downtown Venice (described in detail in the following paragraphs): the slow but reasonable Alilaguna water bus; a faster and pricier Alilaguna water bus (which goes nonstop to St. Mark's Square); the fastest and priciest water taxi; and the cheap shuttle bus to the edge of Venice (with easy connections to the Grand Canal *vaporetti*). The Alilaguna water buses are the simplest way to reach the most of this book's recommended hotels—except for those near the train station, in which case the shuttle bus is the better choice. Except for the fast Alilaguna boat and water taxi, expect a trip between the airport terminal and St. Mark's Square (San Marco) to take up to 90 minutes. When flying out of Venice, travelers are advised to get to the airport two or more hours before departure (even for flights within Europe).

Alilaguna Water Bus: This can be a scenic way to be introduced—or say goodbye—to Venice. A minor drawback is that you must walk (and carry your bags) eight minutes between the airport terminal and the boat dock (follow signs, level sidewalks are fine for wheeled bags).

The Alilaguna website (www.alilaguna.it) lists times and the various water-bus lines. To save time and headaches, ask your hotelier in advance which Alilaguna line and stop will be best: the blue *(blu)* line covers hotels near Fondamenta Nuove (north of Rialto) and near San Zaccaria (east of St. Mark's Square); the red line *(rosso)* is for hotels on the west or north side of San Marco, and Zattere (Dorsoduro hotels); and the orange *(arancio)* goes to hotels near the Guglie bridge, the train station, and Rialto. From Venice to the airport, the blue line's first boat departs from the San Marco–Giardinetti dock at 3:40 in the morning, with the last boat leaving at 22:25. Allow roughly 70–80 minutes for the trip, depending on your stop. From the airport to Venice, lines run 6:00–24:00.

The slightly faster Alilaguna golden *(oro)* line saves 10–20 minutes, but probably isn't worth the price. It goes nonstop to and from San Marco–Giardinetti in 60 minutes or less (€25, departs from San Marco–Giardinetti for the airport about hourly from 8:30–13:30).

Avoid the long lines at the airport's "Public Transport" ticket desk by either buying your ticket at the airport TI or at the ticket booth on the dock. In Venice, you can get tickets at any vaporetto stop that has Alilaguna service. You can also purchase tickets on board (usually for an extra €1). Note that the Alilaguna tickets are not part of the ACTV vaporetto system, so you can't include them in a 12- or 24-hour pass (Alilaguna tel. 041-523-5775).

Water Taxi: Luxury taxi speedboats zip directly between the airport and your hotel in 30 minutes for €95 for up to four people. This can be a smart investment—especially for small groups and those with an early departure. When you arrive, arrange your ride at the airport's water-taxi desk or down at the dock. Though €95 is a tariff set by local law, you'll often get a higher quote. Talk them down. For departures, arrange your taxi trip through your hotel the day before you leave. You'll have to schlep your bags for the eight-minute walk between the dock and the airport.

Buses: Blue (ATVO) and orange (ACTV) shuttle buses connect the airport and the Piazzale Roma vaporetto stop at the head of the Grand Canal (€2–3, buy at TI, from ticket machines, or from driver; 2/hr, 20–40 min; buses leave airport 5:00–24:00 from directly outside arrivals terminal, look for "Venezia Express" on electronic board; ATVO tickets not valid on ACTV buses and vice versa; buses leave Piazzale Roma 5:00–20:40 from far side of the lot from Hotel S. Chiara).

When you arrive at Piazzale Roma, you'll find the vaporetto dock by walking to the six-story white building, then taking a right. To go down the Grand Canal, catch either the slow vaporetto #1 or faster #2 toward St. Mark's Square (€6.50 for either boat; don't get on locals-only #3; for more info, see "Getting Around Venice," near the beginning of this chapter). To reach Zattere, go the other direction on #2. If you're confused, a local commuter or the ticket-seller can help you.

FLORENCE

Firenze

Florence, the home of the Renaissance and birthplace of our modern world, is a "supermarket sweep," and the groceries are the best Renaissance art in Europe.

Get your bearings with a Renaissance walk. Florentine art goes beyond paintings and statues—there's food, fashion, and handicrafts. You can lick Italy's best gelato while enjoying some of Europe's best people-watching.

Planning Your Time

If you're in Italy for three weeks, Florence deserves at least a well-organized day. Make reservations at least a month in advance for the Uffizi Gallery (best Italian paintings anywhere) and a few days in advance for the Accademia (Michelangelo's *David*). Some hoteliers will make these reservations for you—request this service when booking your room (see sidebar later in this chapter for details).

For a day in Florence, see the Accademia, tour the Uffizi Gallery, visit the underrated Bargello (best statues), and do the Renaissance ramble (see "Self-Guided Walk," later in this chapter).

Art-lovers will want to chisel out another day of their itinerary for the many other Florentine cultural treasures. Shoppers and ice cream–lovers may need to do the same.

Plan your sightseeing carefully: Opening hours can be erratic, and crowds can cause long lines. Before heading into Florence, carefully check all the opening and closing times of your must-see museums at the TI, by phone, or online. This is especially true if you'll be in town for only a day or two during the crowded summer months.

The major sights—the Uffizi Gallery and the Accademia (starring Michelangelo's *David*)—are closed on Monday. While many travelers spend several hours a day in lines at the Uffizi and Accademia, you can easily avoid this by making reservations. A couple of Florence's popular sights—the Bargello and the Museum of San Marco—close at 13:50 (though the latter is open later on weekends). Other museums close early only on certain days (e.g., the first Sunday of the month, second and fourth Monday, etc.). In general, Sundays and Mondays are bad, with many museums either closed or with shorter hours.

Connoisseurs of smaller towns should consider taking the bus to Siena for a day or evening trip (75-min one-way, confirm when last bus returns).

Orientation

The best of Florence lies mostly on the north bank of the Arno River. The main historical sights cluster around the redbrick dome of the cathedral (Duomo). Everything is within a 20-minute walk of the train station, cathedral, or Ponte Vecchio (Old Bridge). The less impressive but more characteristic Oltrarno area (south bank) is just over the bridge. Though small, Florence is intense. Prepare for scorching summer heat, kamikaze motor scooters, slick pickpockets, few WCs, steep prices, and long lines.

Tourist Information

There are three TIs in Florence: across from the train station, near Santa Croce Church, and on Via Cavour.

The TI across the square from the train station is most crowded—expect long lines (Mon–Sat 8:30–19:00, Sun 8:30–14:00; with your back to tracks, exit the station—it's 100 yards away, across the square in wall near corner of church at Piazza Stazione 4; tel. 055-212-245, www.firenzeturismo.it). In the train station, avoid the Hotel Reservations "Tourist Information" window (marked *Informazioni Turistiche Alberghiere*) near the McDonald's; it's not a real TI, but a hotel-reservation business instead.

The TI near Santa Croce Church is pleasant, helpful, and uncrowded (Mon–Sat 9:00–19:00, Sun 9:00–14:00, shorter hours off-season, Borgo Santa Croce 29 red, tel. 055-234-0444).

Another winner is the TI three blocks north of the Duomo (Mon–Sat 8:30–18:30, Sun 8:30–13:30, Via Cavour 1 red, tel. 055-290-832, international bookstore across street).

At any TI, pick up these handy resources:

• a free map (ask for the "APT" map, which has bus routes of interest to tourists on the back),

• a current museum-hours listing (extremely important, since no guidebook—including this one—has ever been able to accurately predict the hours of Florence's sights for the coming year), and any information on entertainment, including the TI's monthly *Florence and Tuscany News* (good for events and entertainment listings); the free (and ad-driven) monthly *Florence Concierge Information* magazine (which lists museums, plus concerts, markets, sporting events, church services, shopping ideas, some bus and train connections, and an entire similar section on Siena); and *The Florentine* newspaper (published every other Thu in English, for expats and tourists, with great articles giving cultural insights; download latest issue at www.theflorentine.net). These English freebies are available at TIs and hotels all over town.

Arrival in Florence

By Train: Florence's main station is Santa Maria Novella (*Firenze S.M.N.* on schedules and signs). The city has two suburban stations (Firenze Rifredi and Firenze Campo di Marte), and some trains don't stop at the main station. Before boarding, confirm that you're heading for S.M.N. or you may overshoot the city. (If this happens, don't panic; you're a short taxi ride from the center.)

Minimize time in the station—doing business here is generally intense, crowded, and overpriced. The banks of user-friendly, grayish-blue-and-yellow machines are handy. They take euros and credit cards, display schedules, issue tickets, and even make reservations for railpass-holders. Still, it can be quicker to get tickets and train info from travel agencies in town.

With your back to the tracks, look left to see a 24-hour pharmacy (*Farmacia Comunale,* near McDonald's), the fake "Tourist Information" office (funded by hotels), city buses, bus ticket booth, the taxi stand (fast-moving line, except on holidays), and the entrance to the underground mall/passage that goes across the square to the Church of Santa Maria Novella. (Note: Pickpockets frequent this tunnel, especially the surface point near the church.) Baggage check is near track 16 (€6/12 hrs, daily 6:00–23:50, passport required, maximum 40 pounds, no explosives—sorry). The real TI is across the square, 100 yards in front of the station (see "Tourist Information," earlier in this chapter). Pick up picnic supplies at the **Conad supermarket,** located along the west side of the station on Via Luigi Alamanni (Mon–Sat 8:00–20:00, closed Sun).

By Car: The *autostrada* has several exits for Florence. Get off at the Nord, Sud, or Certosa exits and follow signs toward—but not into—the *Centro*.

Don't even attempt driving into the city center. Florence has a traffic-reduction system that's complicated and confusing even

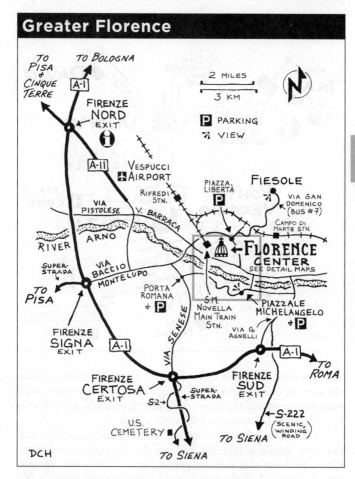

Greater Florence

to locals. Every car passing into the *Zona Traffico Limitato (ZTL)* is photographed; those that haven't jumped through bureaucratic hoops to get a permit are fined in the mail about €100 per infraction; if you get lost and cross the line several times...you get several fines. The no-go zone (defined basically by the old medieval wall, now a boulevard circling the historic center of town—watch for *Zona Traffico Limitato* signs) is roughly the area between the river, main train station, Piazza della Libertà, Piazza Donatello, and Piazza Beccaria.

Fortunately, the city center is ringed with big, efficient parking lots (signposted with the standard big *P*), each with taxi and bus service into the center. I just head for "Parcheggio Parterre," just beyond Piazza della Libertà (€1.50/hr, €18/day, €65/week, open 24 hours daily, tel. 055-500-1994, 600 spots, automated, pay with cash

FLORENCE

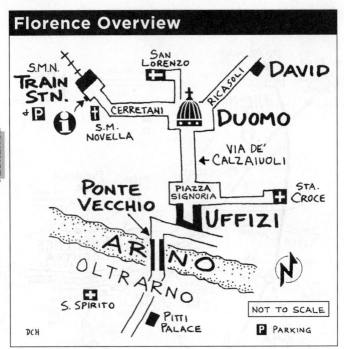

Florence Overview

S.M.N.
TRAIN STN.
P
S.M. NOVELLA

SAN LORENZO

CERRETANI

RICASOLI

DAVID

DUOMO

VIA DE' CALZAIUOLI

PONTE VECCHIO

PIAZZA SIGNORIA

STA. CROCE

UFFIZI

AR NO

OLTRARNO

S. SPIRITO

PITTI PALACE

N

NOT TO SCALE

P PARKING

DCH

or credit card, never fills up completely). From the freeway, follow the signs to *Centro*, then *Stadio*, then *P;* at the elevator exit, you'll see a taxi stand and the bus stop for the #7, which heads to Piazza San Marco, the Duomo, and the train station.

You can park for free along any suburban curb near a bus stop that feels safe, and take the bus into the city center from there. Check for signs that indicate parking restrictions—for example, a circle with a slash through it and "*dispari giovedi,* 0,00–06,00" means don't park on Thursdays between midnight and six in the morning. If you park in the wrong place on a street-cleaning day, you'll get towed.

Free parking is easy up at Piazzale Michelangelo, but don't park where the buses drop off people; park on the side of the piazza farthest from the view. To get from Piazzale Michelangelo to the center of town, take bus #12 or #13 (see "Getting Around Florence," later in this chapter).

If you're picking up a rental car upon departure, don't struggle with driving into the center. Taxi with your luggage to the car-rental office, and head out from there.

By Plane: Florence has its own airport and Pisa's is nearby. See "Connections" at the end of this chapter for details.

Helpful Hints

Theft Alert: Florence has particularly hardworking thief gangs. They specialize in targeting tourists, and they hang out where you do: near the train station, the station's underpass (especially where the tunnel surfaces), and major sights. Also be on guard at two squares frequented by drug pushers (Santa Maria Novella and Santo Spirito). American tourists—especially older ones—are considered easy targets. Bus #7 (to Fiesole) is a favorite with tourists and, therefore, with thieves.

Medical Help: There's no shortage of English-speaking medical help in Florence. To reach a doctor who speaks English, call 055-475-411; it's answered 24/7. Rates are reasonable. For a doctor to come to your hotel within an hour of your call, you'd pay €80–150 (higher rates apply on Sun, holidays, or late visits), or you pay only €50 if you go to the clinic when the doctor's in (Mon–Fri 11:00–12:00 & 17:00–18:00, Sat 11:00–12:00, no appointment necessary, Via L. Magnifico 59, near Piazza della Libertà).

Dr. Stephen Kerr is an English doctor specializing in helping sick tourists. His clinic is in Piazza Mercato Nuovo, a.k.a Loggia del Porcellino—by the small leather market between Ponte Vecchio and Piazza della Repubblica, the one sporting a bronze boar with the shiny nose (clinic open for drop-ins Mon–Fri 15:00–17:00, other times by appointment, €60 per visit, Studio Medico, Piazza Mercato Nuovo 1, 4th floor, tel. 055-288-055, mobile 335-836-1682). The TI has a list of other English-speaking doctors.

There are 24-hour pharmacies at the train station and on Borgo San Lorenzo (near the Duomo).

Audiotours: Users of iPods and other MP3 players can download free audiotours of the Renaissance Walk, Accademia, and Uffizi Gallery from my website, www.ricksteves.com.

Churches: Many churches now operate like museums, charging an admission fee to see their art treasures. Modest dress for men, women, and even children is required in some churches, and recommended for all of them—no bare shoulders, short shorts, or short skirts. Be respectful of worshippers and the paintings; don't use a flash. Churches usually close from 12:00 or 12:30 to 15:00 or 16:00.

Addresses: Street addresses list businesses in red and residences in black (color-coded on the actual street number and indicated by a letter following the number in printed addresses: "r" = red; no indication or "n" = black, for *nero*). *Pensioni* are usually black but can be either. The red and black numbers each appear in roughly consecutive order on streets but bear no apparent connection with each other. I'm lazy and don't

FLORENCE

Make Reservations to Avoid Lines

Florence has a reservation system for its state-run sights, which include the Accademia, Uffizi Gallery, Bargello, Medici Chapels, and Pitti Palace. I highly recommend getting reservations for the Accademia (Michelangelo's *David*) and the Uffizi (Renaissance paintings), but not the others. While you can generally get an entry time for the Accademia within a few days, the Uffizi is often booked over a month in advance (though it's easier in the off-season). Your best strategy is to get reservations for both sights as soon as you know when you'll be in town. After learning how easy this is and seeing hundreds of bored, sweaty tourists waiting in lines without the reservation, it's hard not to be amazed at their cluelessness.

There are several ways to make a reservation: Book online, have your hotelier arrange it, call the reservation number directly, take a tour, or go in person in advance to one of the museums. Here are details on the best options:

• To book your museum visit online with a credit card, go to the official website for Florence museums: www.b-ticket.com/b-ticket/Uffizi. Choose a museum from the list. A color-coded calendar shows how many tickets are available for any given date and time slot. Select the month, date, time, and number of tickets that you want. Choose your country of residence from a drop-down menu, which lists countries in Italian—Americans need to choose "Stati Uniti" (Italian for "United States"). If the online order form switches to Italian, note that "Invio" means "send" (and "Annulla Operazione" means "cancel"). Beware: Some booking agencies offer reservations online for a hefty fee. Use the official Florence museum website instead (€3-4/ticket reservation fee). The official reservations website will not allow you to book times before noon for many museums (including the Uffizi and the Accademia). If you must have a morning appointment, ask your hotelier to reserve it for you (when you book your room), reserve by phone on your own, or try www.weekend

concern myself with the distinction (if one number's wrong, I look for the other) and can easily find my way around.

Internet Access: In bustling, tourist-filled Florence, you'll see small Internet cafés on virtually every street (remember to bring your passport).

Internet Train is the dominant chain, with bright and cheery rooms, speedy computers, and long hours (€3.50/hr, reusable card good for any other Internet Train location, open daily—hours vary by location, www.internettrain.it). Find branches at the train station (downstairs), near Piazza della Repubblica (Via Porta Rossa 38 red), behind the Duomo (Via dell'Oriolo 40), on Piazza Santa Croce (Via de Benci 36 red), near *David* and recommended hotels (Via afirenze.com (about €5 additional fee per person for this booking service).

• Most hotels are accustomed to booking museum reservations either for free or for a fee (€3-5) when clients make a room reservation. Request it with your hotel booking.

• You can make your reservation by phone by calling before you leave the States (from the US, dial 011-39-055-294-883, or within Italy, call 055-294-883; €4/ticket reservation fee; booking office open Mon–Fri 8:30-18:30, Sat 8:30-12:30, closed Sun; remember to take the Italian time zone into account). Unfortunately, the reservation line is often busy, and even if you get through, you may be disconnected while on hold. Try again. And again. When you do get through, an English-speaking operator walks you through the process, and two minutes later you say *grazie,* with appointments (15-min entry window) and six-digit confirmation numbers for the top sights. Bring the confirmation(s) with you and pay cash at the sight(s).

• You can take a tour that includes your museum admission. Walking Tours of Florence offers tours of the Uffizi (€39/person, 2 hours), the Accademia (€35/person, 1 hour), and both museums (€94/person, 6 hours). See their listing in the Tours section, later in this chapter (or visit www.italy.artviva.com).

Besides these main attractions, the only other places you should book in advance are the Brancacci Chapel (reservations are mandatory and free to see the Masaccio frescoes) and the Medici-Riccardi Palace (reservations are recommended for quick entry into the sumptuous Chapel of the Magi). You can make reservations for these two sights either online (www.b-ticket .com/b-ticket/Uffizi) or by phone (phone numbers are included in the sight listings in this chapter). Spots are generally available a day or two in advance.

Ticket phone numbers are often busy; be persistent. The best time to call is around 14:00-15:00 or just before closing.

Guelfa 54 red), and near Ponte Vecchio (Borgo San Jacopo 30 red). Internet Train offers phone cards, compact-disc burning, and other related services.

Bookstores: Local guidebooks (sold at kiosks) are cheap and give you a map and a decent commentary on the sights. For brand-name guidebooks in English, try **Feltrinelli International** (Mon–Sat 9:00–19:30, closed Sun, a few blocks north of the Duomo and across the street from the TI and the Medici-Riccardi Palace at Via Cavour 20 red, tel. 055-219-524), **Edison Bookstore** (Mon–Sat 9:00–24:00, Sun 10:00–24:00, sells CDs and novels on the Renaissance and much more on its four floors, facing Piazza della Repubblica, tel. 055-213-110), **Paperback Exchange** (cheaper, all books in English, bring in your used book for a discount on a new one, Mon–Fri 9:00–19:30, Sat 10:30–19:30, closed Sun, just south of the Duomo on Via delle Oche 4 red, tel. 055-293-460), or **McRae Books** (daily 9:00–19:30, Via dei Neri 32 red, tel. 055-238-2456).

Laundry: The **Wash & Dry Lavarapido** chain offers long hours and efficient, self-service launderettes at several locations (about €7 for wash and dry, daily 8:00–22:00, tel. 055-580-480). These are close to recommended hotels: Via dei Servi 105 red (and a rival launderette at Via Guelfa 55, off Via San Zanobi; both near *David*), Via del Sole 29 red and Via della Scala 52 red (between train station and river), Via Ghibellina 143 red (Palazzo Vecchio), Via Faenza 26 (near station), and Via dei Serragli 87 red (across the river in Oltrarno neighborhood).

Travel Agency: Get train tickets, reservations, and supplements at travel agencies rather than at the congested train station. The cost is often the same, though sometimes there's a minimal charge. Ask your hotel for the nearest office.

Chill Out: Schedule several cool breaks into your sightseeing where you can sit, pause, and refresh yourself with a sandwich, gelato, or coffee.

Freebies: Many of Florence's sights and activities are free. There is no charge for entry to the Duomo, Palazzo Davanzati, Orsanmichele Church, Santo Spirito Church, and San Miniato Church. It's free to visit the leather school at Santa Croce Church and the perfumery near the Church of Santa Maria Novella, and fun to browse at the three markets (Centrale for produce, Nuovo and San Lorenzo for goods).

Free public spaces include the Uffizi and Palazzo Vecchio courtyards; the art-filled loggia on Piazza della Signoria; and Piazzale Michelangelo, with glorious views over Florence. A walk across the picturesque Ponte Vecchio costs nothing at all—unless you succumb to temptation at one of the many shops along the way. A stroll anywhere in Florence with a gelato in hand is an inexpensive treat.

Getting Around Florence

I organize my sightseeing geographically and do it all on foot.

I think of Florence as a Renaissance treadmill—it requires a lot of walking. Its **buses** don't really cover the old center well.

Of the many bus lines, I found these of most value for sightseeing: lines #7, #10, #31, and #32, which connect the train station, the Duomo, and Piazza San Marco. Bus #7 continues on to the Parterre parking lot at Piazza della Libertà and then on to Fiesole. Lines #12 and #13 go from the train station to Porta Romana, up to San Miniato Church and Piazzale Michelangelo, and on to Santa Croce.

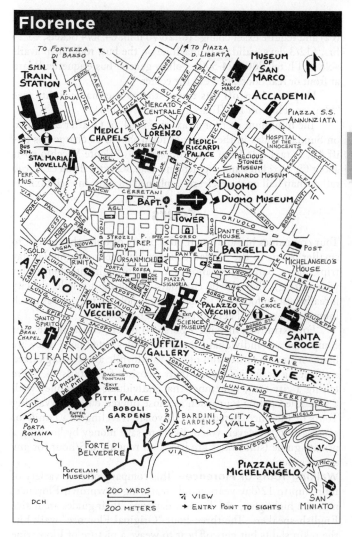

Florence

Fun little *elettrico* **minibuses** wind through the tangled old center of town and up and down the river—just €1.20 gets you a 70-minute joyride. *Elettrico* A winds around the congested old center from the train station to Piazza Beccaria. *Elettrico* B goes up and down the Arno River from Ognissanti to Santa Croce Church. *Elettrico* D goes from the train station to Ponte Vecchio, cruising through Oltrarno, and finishing at Ponte San Niccolo. You'll likely be sitting with eccentric local seniors. The free TI map comes with a handy inset that shows all these bus routes.

Buy tickets in *tabacchi* (tobacco) shops, newsstands, or at the train station bus stop, as tickets bought on board are a little pricier (€2) and require exact change (€1.20/70 min, €4.50/4 tickets, €5/24 hrs, €12/3 days, validate in machine on the bus, route map available at TI, tel. 800-424-500). Follow general bus etiquette: Board at front or rear doors, exit out the center.

Hop-on, hop-off bus tours stop at the major sights (see "Hop-on, Hop-off Bus Tours," in "Tours," below).

The minimum cost for a **taxi** ride is €4, or €6 after 22:00 and on Sundays (rides in the center of town should be charged as tariff #1). A taxi ride from the train station to Ponte Vecchio costs about €9. Taxi fares and supplements (e.g., €2 extra if you call a cab rather than hail one) are clearly explained on signs in each taxi.

Tours

Tour companies big and small offer plenty of tours that go out to smaller towns in the Tuscan countryside (the most popular day trips: Siena, San Gimignano, Pisa, and into Chianti country for wine tasting). They also do city tours, but for most people, the city is really best on foot (and the book you're holding provides as much information as you'll get with a generic bus tour).

For extra insight with a personal touch, consider the tour companies and individual Florentine guides listed here. They are hardworking, creative, and offer a worthwhile array of organized sightseeing activities. Study their websites for details. If you're taking a city tour, remember that individuals save money with a scheduled public tour (such as those offered daily by Walking Tours of Florence, listed next). If you're traveling as a family or small group, however, you're likely to save money by booking a private guide (since rates are based on roughly €55/hour for any size of group).

Walking Tours of Florence—This company offers a variety of tours (up to 12/day year-round) featuring downtown Florence, museum highlights, and Tuscany day trips. Their guides are native English-speakers. The three-hour "Original Florence" walk hits the main sights but gets offbeat to weave a picture of Florentine life in medieval and Renaissance times. Tours go rain or shine with as few as two participants (€25, daily at 9:15, get the student rate of €20 with this book—just ask when you make your reservation). They also do tours of the Uffizi (€39, includes admission, 2 hours), Accademia (called "Original *David*" tour, €35, includes admission, 1 hour), and "Original Florence in One Day" (€94, includes admission to Uffizi and Accademia, 6 hours). Reservations are necessary for all tours. For schedule details, pick up their extensive brochure in your hotel lobby or their office (Mon-Sat 8:00–18:00, Sun 8:30–13:30 but off-season closed on Sun and for lunch, near

Piazza della Repubblica at Via dei Sassetti 1, second floor, above Odeon Cinema, tel. 055-264-5033 during day or mobile 329-613-2730 18:00–20:00, www.italy.artviva.com, staff@artviva.com).

Florentia—Top-notch, private walking tours—geared for thoughtful, well-heeled travelers with longer than average attention spans—are led by local scholars. The tours range from introductory city walks and museum visits to in-depth thematic walks, such as the Golden Age of Florence, the Medici Dynasty, and side-trips into Tuscany (tours-€250/half-day, reserve in advance, tel. 338-890-8625, www.florentia.org, info@florentia.org).

Context Florence—This group of graduate students and professors lead "walking seminars" as scholarly as Florentia's (above). Their tours include a three-hour Michelangelo seminar—an in-depth study of the artist's work and influence (€85.50/person, includes Accademia admission) and a two-hour evening orientation stroll (€35/person). See their website for their innovative offerings: a fresco workshop, Medici walk, lecture series, food walks, kids' tours, and programs in Venice, Rome, Naples, London, and Paris (tel. 06-482-0911, US tel. 888-467-1986, www.contexttravel.com, info@contexttravel.com).

Private Guides—Good guides include Paola Barubiani and her partners at Walks Inside Florence (€50/person for semi-private 3-hour tour, €180/group of 2–6 people for private 3-hour tour, tel. 335-526-6496, www.walksinsideflorence.it, barubiani.paola@walksinsideflorence.it). Alessandra Marchetti, a Florentine who has lived in the US, gives private walking tours of Florence and driving tours of Tuscany (€60–75/hr, mobile 347-386-9839, aleoberm@tin.it). Cynthia Black Nesti, an American married to a Florentine, enjoys leading visitors around her adopted town (€60/hr for private tours, tel. 055-641-625, nesti12@interfree.it).

Paola Migliorini and her partners at Tuscany Tours offer museum tours, city walking tours, private cooking classes, and Tuscan excursions by van (you can tailor tours as you like). Go anywhere in the center of Florence by van and enjoy the city nearly sweat-free (€55/hr, €65/hr in an 8-seat van, Via San Gallo 120, tel. 055-472-448, mobile 347-657-2611, www.florencetour.com, info@florencetour.com).

Hop-on, Hop-off Bus Tours—Around town, you'll see big double-decker sightseeing buses double-parking near major sights. Tourists on the top deck can listen to brief recorded descriptions of the sights, snap photos, and enjoy an effortless drive-by look at the major landmarks. Tickets cost €20 (good for 24 hours, first bus at 9:30, last bus at 18:00, pay as you board, tickets include two bus lines—Blue is 1 hour with a trip up to Piazzale Michelangelo, Green is 2 hours with a side-trip to Fiesole, www.firenze.city-sightseeing.it). As the name implies, you can hop off when you want and catch the next bus (usually every 30 min, depending on the season). Hop-on stops include the train station, Duomo, and Pitti Palace. As most sights are buried in the old center where big buses can't go, Florence doesn't really lend itself to this kind of tour bus. Look at the route map before committing yourself to this tour.

Accidental Tourist—This tour company picks you up in a van for a half-day or full day of cooking classes, hiking, or wine-tasting, then drops you off back in Florence (prices from €50–120; for example, €100 for cooking class; daily 9:30–17:00, book online in advance, allow 4 days for reply to emails, mobile 348-659-0040, www.accidentaltourist.com, info@accidentaltourist.com).

Self-Guided Walk

A Renaissance Walk Through Florence

During the Dark Ages, it was especially obvious to the people of Italy—sitting on the rubble of Rome—that there had to be a brighter age before them. The long-awaited rebirth, or Renaissance, began in Florence for good reason. Wealthy because of its cloth industry, trade, and banking; powered by a fierce city-state pride (locals would pee into the Arno with gusto, knowing rival city-state Pisa was downstream); and fertile with more than its share of artistic genius (imagine guys like Michelangelo and Leonardo attending the same high school)—Florence was a natural home for this cultural explosion.

Take a two-hour walk through the core of Renaissance Florence by starting at the Accademia (home of Michelangelo's *David*) and cutting through the heart of the city to the Ponte Vecchio on the Arno River.

At the Accademia, you'll look into the eyes of Renaissance man—humanism at its confident peak. Then walk to the cathedral (Duomo) to see the dome that kicked off the architectural Renaissance. Step inside the Baptistery to view a ceiling covered with preachy, flat, 2-D, medieval mosaic art. Then, to learn what happened when art met math, check out the realistic 3-D reliefs on the doors. The painter, Giotto, also designed the bell tower—an early example of a Renaissance genius who could excel in many areas. Continue toward the river on Florence's great pedestrian mall, Via de' Calzaiuoli (or "Via Calz")—part of the original grid plan given to the city by the ancient Romans. Stop by any gelato shop for some cool refreshment. Down a few blocks, compare medieval and Renaissance statues on the exterior of the Orsanmichele Church. Via Calz connects the cathedral with the central square (Piazza della Signoria), the city palace (Palazzo Vecchio), and the Uffizi Gallery, which contains the greatest collection of Italian Renaissance paintings in captivity. Finally, walk through the

Uffizi courtyard—a statuary think tank of Renaissance greats—to the Arno River and the Ponte Vecchio.

Sights

▲▲▲Accademia (Galleria dell'Accademia)

This museum houses Michelangelo's *David,* the consummate Renaissance statue of the buff, biblical shepherd boy ready to take on the giant. Nearby are some of the master's other works, including his powerful (unfinished) *Prisoners, St. Matthew,* and a *Pietà* (possibly by one of his disciples). Florentine Michelangelo Buonarroti, who would work tirelessly through the night, believed that the sculptor was a tool of God, responsible only for chipping away at the stone until the intended sculpture emerged. Beyond the magic marble are some mildly interesting pre-Renaissance and Renaissance paintings, including a couple of lighter-than-air Botticellis; the plaster model of Giambologna's *Rape of the Sabines;* and a musical instrument collection with an early piano.

Cost, Hours, Location: €6.50, plus €4 fee for recommended reservation, Tue–Sun 8:15–18:50, closed Mon, last entry 30 minutes before closing (Via Ricasoli 60, tel. 055-238-8609). To avoid waiting in line, reserve ahead; see the reservations sidebar earlier in this chapter for details.

Nearby: Piazza S.S. Annunziata, behind the Accademia, displays lovely Renaissance harmony. Facing the square are two fine buildings: the 15th-century Santissima Annunziata church (worth a peek) and Filippo Brunelleschi's Hospital of the Innocents (Spedale degli Innocenti, not worth going inside), with terra-cotta medallions by Luca della Robbia. Built in the 1420s, the hospital is considered the first Renaissance building. I love sleeping on this square (at Hotel Loggiato dei Serviti, see "Sleeping" later in this chapter) and picnicking here during the day.

Near the Accademia

▲▲Museum of San Marco (Museo di San Marco)—Located one block north of the Accademia, this 15th-century monastery houses the greatest collection anywhere of frescoes and paintings by the early Renaissance master Fra Angelico. The ground floor features the monk's paintings, along with some works by Fra Bartolomeo. Upstairs are 43 cells decorated by Fra Angelico and his assistants. While the monk/painter was trained in the medieval religious style, he also learned and adopted Renaissance techniques and sensibilities, producing works that blended Christian symbols and Renaissance realism. Don't miss the cell of Savonarola, the charismatic monk who rode in from the Christian right, threw out the Medicis, turned Florence into a theocracy, sponsored "bonfires

Renaissance Walk

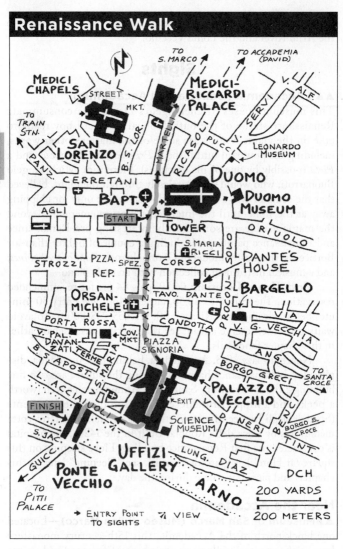

MEDICI CHAPELS

TO TRAIN STN.

STREET

MKT.

TO S. MARCO

TO ACCADEMIA (DAVID)

MEDICI-RICCARDI PALACE

V. ALF.

SERVI

PUCCI

V.

LEONARDO MUSEUM

SAN LORENZO

PANZ.

CERRETANI

B. S. LOR.

MARTELLI

RICASOLI

DUOMO

AGLI

BAPT.

START

DUOMO MUSEUM

ORIUOLO

STROZZI

PZZA. SPEZ. REP.

TOWER

CORSO

S. MARIA RICCI

SOLO

DANTE'S HOUSE

ORSAN-MICHELE

PORTA ROSSA

COV. MKT.

CALZAIOLI

TAVO. DANTE

CONDOTTA

PIAZZA SIGNORIA

V. DANTE

PROC.

V. G. VECCHIA

BARGELLO

VIA

ANG.

V. PAL. DAVAN-ZATI

B. S. APOST.

TERME

S. MARIA

BORGO GRECI

TO SANTA CROCE

L. ACCIAIUOLI

FINISH

S. JAC.

GUICC.

PONTE VECCHIA

PALAZZO VECCHIO

EXIT

SCIENCE MUSEUM

NERI

BENCI

BORGO S. CROCE

TINT.

UFFIZI GALLERY

LUNG. DIAZ

DCH

TO PITTI PALACE

ARNO

200 YARDS

200 METERS

→ ENTRY POINT TO SIGHTS

⌐ VIEW

FLORENCE

of the vanities" (burning books, paintings, and so on), and was finally burned himself when Florence decided to change channels (€4, Mon–Fri 8:15–13:50, Sat 8:15–18:50, Sun 8:15–19:00, but closed first, third, and fifth Sun and second and fourth Mon of each month; reservations possible but unnecessary, on Piazza San Marco, tel. 055-238-8608).

Museum of Precious Stones (Museo dell'Opificio delle Pietre Dure)—This unusual gem of a museum features room after room of exquisite mosaics of inlaid marble and stones. Upstairs, you'll see remnants of the Medici workshop from 1588, including 500 different precious stones and the tools used to cut and inlay them. The helpful loaner booklet available next to the ticket window describes it all in English (€2, Mon–Wed and Fri–Sat 8:15–14:00, Thu 8:15–19:00, closed Sun, around corner from Accademia at Via degli Alfani 78, tel. 055-26-511).

Church of San Lorenzo—This redbrick dome—which looks like the Duomo's little sister—is the Medici church and the burial place of the family's founder, Giovanni di Bicci de' Medici (1360–1429). The facade is big, ugly, and unfinished, because Pope Leo X (also a Medici) pulled the plug on the project due to dwindling funds—after Michelangelo had labored on it for four years (1516–1520). Inside, though, is the spirit of Florence in the 1420s, with grey-and-white columns and arches in perfect Renaissance symmetry and simplicity. The Brunelleschi-designed church is lit by an even, diffused light. The Medici coat of arms (with the round pills of these "medics") decorates the ceiling, and everywhere are images of St. Lawrence, the Medici patron saint who was martyred on a grill.

Highlights of the church include two finely sculpted Donatello pulpits (in the nave). In the Martelli Chapel (left wall of the left transept), Filippo Lippi's glowing *Annunciation* features a smiling angel greeting Mary in a sharply 3-D courtyard. The Old Sacristy (far left corner), designed by Brunelleschi, was the burial chapel for the Medicis. Bronze doors by Donatello flank the sacristy's small altar. Overhead, the dome above the altar shows the exact arrangement of the heavens on the day the chapel was finished. Back in the nave, the round inlaid marble in the floor before the main altar marks where Cosimo the Elder—Lorenzo the Magnificent's grandfather—is buried.

Outside the church, along the left side, is a cloister (good Duomo views) and Michelangelo's staircase to the Laurentian Library (only open during special exhibits). Around the back end of the church is the entrance to the Medici Chapels (next listing) and the New Sacristy, designed by Michelangelo for a later generation of dead Medicis (€3.50, March–Nov Mon–Sat 10:00–17:00, Sun 13:30–17:00, closed Dec–Feb, free information brochure).

▲▲Medici Chapels (Cappelle Medicee)—The burial site of the ruling Medici family in the Church of San Lorenzo includes the dusky Crypt; the big, domed Chapel of Princes; and the magnificent, all-Michelangelo New Sacristy, featuring the master's architecture, tombs, and statues. The Medicis made their money in textiles and banking and patronized a dream team of Renaissance artists that put Florence on the cultural map. Michelangelo, who spent his teen years living with the Medicis, was commissioned for the family's final tribute (€6, Tue–Sun 8:15–17:50; closing hours vary off-season but generally until 14:00 in winter, closed Mon; tel. 055-294-883). Don't make a pricey (and unnecessary) reservation to visit this sight.

Nearby: Behind the chapels on Piazza Madonna degli Aldobrandini is the lively **San Lorenzo Market,** with a scene that I find just as interesting. Take a stroll through the huge double-decker **Mercato Centrale** (central food market) one block north.

▲**Medici-Riccardi Palace (Palazzo Medici-Riccardi)**— Lorenzo the Magnificent's home is worth a look for its art. The tiny Chapel of the Magi contains colorful Renaissance gems like the *Procession of the Magi* frescoes by Benozzo Gozzoli. The former library has a Baroque ceiling fresco by Luca Giordano, a prolific artist from Naples known as "Fast Luke" *(Luca fa presto)* for his ambidextrous painting abilities. While the Medicis originally occupied this 1444 house, in the 1700s it became home to the Riccardi family, who added the Baroque flourishes. As only eight people are allowed into the Chapel of the Magi every seven minutes, it's smart to call for a reservation if you want to avoid a wait (€5, Thu–Tue 9:00–19:00, closed Wed, kitty-corner from Church of San Lorenzo, one long block north of Baptistery, ticket entrance is north of the main gated entrance, Via Cavour 3, tel. 055-276-0340).

Leonardo Museum—This small, entrepreneurial venture is over-priced but fun for anyone who wants to crank the shaft and spin the ball bearings of Leonardo's genius inventions. While this exhibit has no actual historic artifacts, it shows about 30 of Leonardo's inventions made into models, each described in English. What makes this exhibit special is that you're encouraged to touch and play with the models—it's great for kids (€7.50, daily 10:00–19:00, Via dei Servi 66 red, tel. 055-282-966). Don't confuse this with the other, less-interesting Leonardo Museum, on Via Cavour.

Duomo and Nearby

▲▲**Duomo (Santa Maria del Fiore)**—Florence's Gothic cathedral has the third-longest nave in Christendom. The church's noisy neo-Gothic facade from the 1870s is covered with pink, green, and white Tuscan marble. Since nearly all of its great art is stored in the Duomo Museum (behind the church), the best thing about the interior is the shade. The inside of the dome is decorated by one of the largest paintings of the Renaissance, a huge *Last Judgment* by Giorgio Vasari and Federico Zuccari. Note: The massive crowds that overwhelm the entrance in the morning clear out by afternoon.

Think of the confidence of the age: The Duomo was built with a hole awaiting a dome in its roof. This was before the technology to span it with a dome was available. No matter. They knew that someone soon could handle the challenge...and the local architect

Filippo Brunelleschi did. The cathedral's claim to artistic fame is Brunelleschi's magnificent dome—the first Renaissance dome and the model for domes to follow.

Cost and Hours: Free entry to church (there's a cost to climb dome—described next), Mon–Wed and Fri 10:00–17:00, Thu 10:00–15:30, Sat 10:00–16:45 except first Sat of month 10:00–15:30, Sun 13:30–16:45, modest dress code enforced, tel. 055-230-2885.

▲**Climbing the Duomo's Dome**—For a grand view into the cathedral from the base of the dome, a peek at some of the tools used in the dome's construction, a chance to see Brunelleschi's "dome-within-a-dome" construction, a glorious Florence view from the top, and the equivalent of 463 plunges on a Stairmaster, climb the dome. When planning St. Peter's in Rome, Michelangelo rhymed (not in English), "I can build its sister—bigger, but not more beautiful" than the dome of Florence.

To avoid the long, dreadfully slow-moving line, arrive by 8:30 or drop by very late (€6, Mon–Fri 8:30–19:00, Sat 8:30–17:40 except first Sat of month 8:30–16:40, closed Sun, enter from outside church on north side, tel. 055-230-2885).

▲**Giotto's Tower (Campanile)**—The 270-foot bell tower has 50 fewer steps than the Duomo's dome (but that's still 414 steps—no elevator), offers a faster, less-crowded climb, and has a view of the Duomo to boot, but the cage-like top makes taking good photographs difficult (€6, daily 8:30–19:30, last entry 40 min before closing).

▲**Baptistery**—Michelangelo said its bronze doors were fit to be the gates of paradise. Check out the gleaming copies of Lorenzo Ghiberti's bronze doors facing the Duomo. Making a breakthrough in perspective, Ghiberti used mathematical laws to create the illusion of receding distance on a basically flat surface.

The doors on the north side of the building were designed by Ghiberti when he was young; he'd won the honor and opportunity by beating Brunelleschi in a competition (the rivals' original entries are in the Bargello).

Inside, sit and savor the medieval mosaic ceiling, where it's always Judgment Day and Jesus is giving the ultimate thumbs-up and thumbs-down (€3, interior open Mon–Sat 12:15–19:30 except first Sat of month 8:30–14:00, Sun 8:30–14:00, last entry 30 min before closing; bronze doors are on the outside, so always "open"; original panels are in the Duomo).

▲▲▲**Duomo Museum (Museo dell'Opera del Duomo)**—The underrated cathedral museum, behind the church (at Via del Proconsolo 9), is great if you like sculpture. On the ground floor, look for a late Michelangelo *Pietà,* the eight restored panels of Ghiberti's north doors for the Baptistery, and statues from the original Baptistery facade. Upstairs, you'll find Brunelleschi's models for his dome, as well as Donatello's anorexic *Mary Magdalene* and playful choir loft. The museum features most of Ghiberti's original "Gates of Paradise" panels; the panels on the Baptistery's doors today are copies (€6, Mon–Sat 9:00–18:50, Sun 9:00–13:00, last entry 40 min before closing, one of the few museums in Florence open on Mon, tel. 055-230-2885).

If you find all this church art intriguing, look through the open doorway of the Duomo art studio, which has been making and restoring church art since the days of Brunelleschi (a block toward the river from the Duomo at Via dello Studio 23a).

Between the Duomo and Piazza della Signoria

▲▲▲**Bargello (Museo Nazionale)**—This underappreciated sculpture museum is in a former police station-turned-prison that looks like a mini–Palazzo Vecchio. It has Donatello's painfully beautiful *David* (the very influential first male nude to be sculpted in a thousand years), works by Michelangelo, and rooms of Medici treasures cruelly explained in Italian only (politely suggest to the staff that English descriptions would be wonderful). Moody Donatello, who embraced realism with his lifelike statues, set the personal and artistic style for many Renaissance artists to follow. The best works are in the ground-floor room at the foot of the out-door staircase and in the room directly above (€4, but mandatory special exhibitions often increase the price to €7; daily 8:15–13:50 but closed first, third, and fifth Sun and second and fourth Mon of each month, last entry 30 min before closing; reservations possible but unnecessary, Via del Proconsolo 4, tel. 055-238-8606).

Dante's House (Casa di Dante)—Dante Alighieri (1265–1321), the poet who gave us *The Divine Comedy*, is the Shakespeare of Italy, the father of the modern Italian language, and the face on the country's €2 coin. However, most Americans know little of him, and this museum is not the ideal place to start. Even though it has English information, this small museum (in a building near where he likely lived) assumes visitors have prior knowledge of Dante. Exhibits are as much about medieval Florence as they are about the man. Still, Dante lovers can trace his interesting life and works through photos and artifacts, and novices can learn a little about Dante and the city he lived in.

On the first two floors, be on the lookout for a sketch of Florence's Baptistery, a map of Dante's Florence (it was a walled city of many towers, housing feuding clans), a picture of his muse Beatrice, the *Book of the Nail* forever condemning him to exile (for political reasons), and photos of his tomb in Ravenna. The top floor displays copies of paintings by famous artists and a video of scenes from *The Divine Comedy*, which demonstrate just how much Dante inspired the imagination of later artists. Some call him the father of the Renaissance (€4, Tue–Sun 10:00–17:00, last entry 30 min before closing, closed Mon, near Bargello at Via Santa Margherita 1, tel. 055-219-416).

▲**Orsanmichele Church**—In the ninth century, this loggia (covered courtyard) was a market used for selling grain (stored upstairs). Later, it was closed in to make a church.

Outside are dynamic, statue-filled niches, some with accompanying symbols from the guilds that sponsored the art. Donatello's *St. Mark* and *St. George* (on the northeast and northwest corners) step out boldly in the new Renaissance style.

The interior has a glorious Gothic tabernacle (1359) housing the painted wooden panel that depicts *Madonna delle Grazie* (1346). The iron bars spanning the vaults were the Italian Gothic answer to the French Gothic external buttresses. Look for the rectangular holes in the piers—these were once wheat chutes that connected to the upper floors (church is free, Tue–Fri 10:00–17:00, Sat–Sun 10:00–18:30, closed Mon, niche sculptures always viewable from the outside). You can give the *Madonna della Grazie* a special thanks if you're in town when an evening concert is held inside the Orsanmichele (tickets sold on day of concert from door facing Via de' Calzaiuoli).

The museum upstairs, currently closed, holds many of the church's precious originals. Someday, tourists might be able to enjoy the fine statues by Ghiberti, Donatello, and company.

A block away, you'll find the...

▲**Mercato Nuovo (a.k.a. the Straw Market)**—This market *loggia* is how Orsanmichele looked before it became a church. Originally a silk and straw market, Mercato Nuovo still functions as a rustic yet touristy market (at the intersection of Via Calimala and Via Porta Rossa). Prices are soft, but the San Lorenzo Market is much better for haggling. Notice the circled X in the center, marking the spot where people hit after being hoisted up to the top and dropped as punishment for bankruptcy. You'll also find *Porcellino* (a statue of a wild boar nicknamed "little pig"), which people rub and give coins to in order to ensure their return to Florence. This new copy, while only a few years old, already has a polished snout. At the back corner, a wagon sells tripe (cow innards) sandwiches—a local favorite (daily 9:30–19:00).

▲**Piazza della Repubblica and Nearby**—This large square sits on the site of Florence's original Roman Forum. The lone column—nicknamed "the belly button of Florence"—once marked the intersection of the two main Roman roads. All that survives of Roman Florence is its grid street plan and this column. Look at the map (by the benches—where the old boys hang out to talk sports and politics) to see the ghost of Rome in its streets. Roman

Florence was a garrison town—a rectangular fort with this square marking the intersection of the two main roads (Via Corso and Via Roma).

Today's piazza, framed by a triumphal arch, is a nationalistic statement celebrating the unification of Italy. Florence, the capital of the country (1865–1870) until Rome was "liberated" (from the Vatican), lacked a square worthy of this grand new country. So the neighborhood here—once the Jewish quarter—was razed to open up an imposing, modern forum surrounded by stately circa-1890 buildings.

Venerable cafés and stores line the square. The fancy La Rinascente department store, facing the Piazza della Repubblica, is one of the city's finest (WC on fourth floor, go up the stairs for the pricey bar with an impressive view terrace).

▲**Palazzo Davanzati**—This five-story, late-medieval tower house offers a rare look at a noble dwelling built in the 14th century (only the ground and first floors are open to visitors). It hopes to be the museum of medieval Florence. Like other buildings of the age, the exterior is festooned with 14th-century horse-tethering rings made out of iron, torch holders, and poles upon which to hang laundry and fly flags. Inside, while the furnishings are pretty sparse, you'll see richly painted walls, a long chute that functioned as a well, plenty of fireplaces, and even toilets (free, daily 8:15–13:50; closed first, third, and fifth Mon and second and fourth Sun; Via Porta Rossa 13, tel. 055-238-8610).

▲▲▲Uffizi Gallery

This greatest collection of Italian paintings anywhere features works by Giotto, Leonardo, Raphael, Caravaggio, Rubens, Titian, and Michelangelo, and a roomful of Botticellis, including his *Birth of Venus.*

The museum is nowhere near as big as it is great. Few tourists spend more than two hours inside. The paintings are displayed on one comfortable, U-shaped floor in chronological order from the 13th through 17th centuries. The left wing, starring the Florentine Middle Ages to the Renaissance, is the best. The connecting corridor contains sculpture, and the right wing focuses on the High Renaissance and Baroque.

Essential stops are (in this order): Gothic altarpieces (narrative, pre-Realism, no real concern for believable depth) including Giotto's altarpiece, which progressed beyond "totem-pole angels"; Paolo Uccello's *Battle of San Romano,* an early study in perspective (with a few obvious flubs); Fra Filippo Lippi's cuddly Madonnas; the Botticelli room, filled with masterpieces, including a pantheon of classical fleshiness and the small *La Calunnia,* showing the glasnost of Renaissance free-thinking being clubbed back into the darker age of Savonarola; two minor works by Leonardo da Vinci; the octagonal classical sculpture room with a copy of Praxiteles' *Venus de' Medici*—considered the epitome of beauty in Elizabethan Europe; a view of the Ponte Vecchio through the window—dreamy at sunset; Michelangelo's only surviving easel painting, the round *Holy Family;* Raphael's noble *Madonna of the Goldfinch;* Titian's voluptuous *Venus of Urbino;* and Duomo views from the café terrace (WC near café).

Cost, Hours, Reservations: €10, plus €4 for recommended reservation, cash required to pick up reserved tickets, Tue–Sun 8:15–18:35, closed Mon, last entry 30 min before closing.

Even though a maximum of 600 are allowed into the museum at any one time, there are infamously long lines to get in. Avoid the three-hour peak-season wait by reserving ahead. Reserved spots can fill up more than a month in advance, especially for Sat, Sun, and Tue. If you plan to book ahead, you have several options for beating the line—all of which are explained in the sidebar earlier in this chapter. If you don't have a reservation, there's a small chance you may be able to get a same-day ticket for the Uffizi, depending on luck and availability. Try booking directly at the Uffizi's ticket office for later in the day (enter the left side of door #2—unreserved ticket entrance, pay cash for a ticket up front, same hours as museum). Sometimes, by the end of the day (an hour before closing), there are no lines and you can just walk right in.

In the Uffizi's Courtyard: Enjoy the courtyard (free), full of artists and souvenir stalls. (Swing by after dinner when it's completely empty.) The surrounding statues honor earthshaking Florentines: artists (Michelangelo), philosophers (Niccolò Machiavelli), scientists (Galileo), writers (Dante), explorers (Amerigo Vespucci), and the great patron of so much Renaissance thinking, Lorenzo "the Magnificent" de' Medici.

Other Sights on and near Piazza della Signoria

The square fronting the Palazzo Vecchio, Piazza della Signoria, is a tourist's world with pigeons, postcards, horse buggies, and tired hubbies. And, if it would make your tired hubby happy, the ritzy Rivoire café—with the best view seats in town—is famous for its fine desserts and pudding-thick hot chocolate (expensive, closed Sun).

▲**Palazzo Vecchio**—With its distinctive castle turret, this fortified palace—the Town Hall, officially called the Palazzo della Signoria—is a Florentine landmark. But if you're visiting only one palace interior in town, the Pitti Palace (listed later in this chapter) is better. The Palazzo Vecchio interior is worthwhile only if you're a real fan of coffered and gilded ceilings, of Florentine history, or of the artist Giorgio Vasari, who wallpapered the place with mediocre magnificence.

The museum's most famous statues are Michelangelo's *Victory* and Donatello's bronze statue of *Judith and Holerfernes* (€6, €8 combo-ticket with Brancacci Chapel, Fri–Wed 9:00–19:00, Thu 9:00–14:00, ticket office closes one hour earlier (tel. 055-276-8224). A metal-detector checkpoint can create long lines.

Even if you don't go to the museum, do step into the **free courtyard** behind the fake *David* just to feel the essence of the Medicis (you'll have to go through metal detectors but you don't have to pay). Until 1873, Michelangelo's *David* stood at the entrance, where the copy is today. While the huge statues in the square are important only as the whipping boys of art critics and as rest stops for pigeons, the nearby **Loggia dei Lanzi** has several important statues. Look for Benvenuto Cellini's bronze statue of Perseus holding the head of Medusa. The plaque on the pavement in front of the fountain marks the spot where the monk Savonarola was burned in MCDXCVIII, or 1498.

Children's Museum: The Museo dei Ragazzi in the Palazzo Vecchio offers activities for children (for ages 4 to teens) on a reservation-only basis. The kids can take a guided English tour with a historically costumed character, or make their own fresco on a souvenir tile (€6 plus €2/activity, family rates, no reservation fee, call to reserve, daily 9:00–19:00 except Thu 9:00–14:00, tel. 055-276-8325).

▲▲Science Museum (Museo di Storia della Scienza)— When we think of the Florentine Renaissance, we think of visual arts: painting, mosaics, architecture, and sculpture. But when the visual arts declined in the 1600s (abused and co-opted by political powers), music and science flourished in Florence. The first opera was written here. And Florence hosted many scientific break-throughs, as you'll see in this fascinating collection of Renaissance and later clocks, telescopes, maps, and ingenious gadgets. Trace the technical innovations as modern science emerges from 1000–1900. One of the most talked-about bottles in Florence is the one here that contains Galileo's finger. Exhibits include various tools for gauging the world, from a compass and thermometer to Galileo's telescopes. Other displays delve into clocks, pumps, medicine, and chemistry. Loaner English guide booklets are available. It's friendly, comfortably cool, never crowded, and just a block east of the Uffizi on the Arno River (€4 during restoration, regularly €6.50, June–Sept Mon and Wed–Fri 9:30–17:00, Tue and Sat 9:30–13:00, closed Sun; Oct–May Mon and Wed–Sat 9:30–17:00, Tue 9:30–13:00, closed Sun; Piazza dei Giudici 1, tel. 055-265-311, www.imss.fi.it).

▲**Ponte Vecchio**—Florence's most famous bridge is lined with shops that have traditionally sold gold and silver. A statue of Benvenuto Cellini, the master goldsmith of the Renaissance, stands in the center, ignored by the flood of tacky tourism. This is a very romantic spot late at night (when lovers gather, and a top-notch street musician performs).

Notice the "prince's passageway" above the bridge. In less-secure times, the city leaders had a fortified passageway connecting the Palazzo Vecchio and Uffizi with the mighty Pitti Palace, to which they could flee in times of attack. This passageway, called the **Vasari Corridor,** is technically open to the public, but a visit is almost impossible to arrange, and if you do manage it, it's usually a disappointment (open sporadically, check at the Uffizi to see if it's open or try a private tour company such as Weekend a Firenze—see www.weekendafirenze.com).

▲▲**Santa Croce Church**—This 14th-century Franciscan church, decorated with centuries of precious art, holds the tombs of great Florentines.

The loud 19th-century Victorian Gothic facade faces a huge square ringed with tempting shops and littered with tired tourists. Escape into the church and admire its sheer height and spaciousness. On the left wall (as you face the altar) is the **tomb of Galileo Galilei** (1564–1642), the Pisan who lived his last years under house arrest near Florence. Having defied the Church by saying that the Earth revolved around the sun, his heretical remains were only allowed in the church long after his death. (For more on Galileo, see his relics in the Science Museum, listed on previous page.) Directly opposite (on the right wall) is the **tomb of Michelangelo Buonarroti** (1475–1564).

The first chapel to the right of the main altar features the famous fresco by Giotto of the *Death of Saint Francis*. With simple but eloquent gestures, Francis' brothers bid him a sad farewell. One folds his hands and stares longingly at Francis' serene face. Another bends to kiss Francis' hand, while others raise their arms in grief. It's one of the first expressions of human emotion in modern painting. It's also one of the first to create a real three-dimensional grouping of figures.

At the end of the right transept, a left turn at the first door leads into the sacristy, where you'll find a rumpled bit of St. Francis' tunic *(Parte della Tonaca)*. In the bookstore, notice the photos of the devastating flood of 1966 high on the wall. Beyond that is the "leather school," the first shop of what is now a popular leather district. Wander through the former dorms for monks, watch the leatherworking in action, and browse the finished products—for sale, of course.

Exit between the Rossini and Machiavelli tombs into the

cloister (open-air courtyard). On the left, enter Brunelleschi's Pazzi Chapel, considered one of the finest pieces of Florentine Renaissance architecture.

Cost, Hours, and Dress Code: €5 ticket includes the Pazzi Chapel and a small museum, Mon–Sat 9:30–17:30, Sun 13:00–17:30, audioguide-€4, modest dress code is enforced, tel. 055-246-6105. The leather school is free, with its own entry around back (daily 9:30–18:00).

▲**Michelangelo's House (Casa Buonarroti)**—Fans enjoy a house that stands on property once owned by Michelangelo. The house was built by the artist's grand-nephew, who turned it into a little museum honoring his famous relative. You'll see some of Michelangelo's early, less-than-monumental statues and a few sketches. Be warned: Michelangelo's descendants attributed everything they could to their famous relative, but very little here (beyond two marble relief panels and a couple of sketches) is actually by Michelangelo (€6.50, Wed–Mon 9:30–14:00, closed Tue, English descriptions, Via Ghibellina 70, tel. 055-241-752).

Near the Train Station

▲▲**Church of Santa Maria Novella**—This 13th-century Dominican church, just south of the train station, is rich in art. Along with crucifixes by Giotto and Brunelleschi, there's every textbook's example of the early Renaissance mastery of perspective: *The Holy Trinity* by Masaccio. The exquisite chapels trace art in Florence from medieval times to early Baroque. The outside of the church features a dash of Romanesque (horizontal stripes), Gothic (pointed arches), Renaissance (geometric shapes), and Baroque (scrolls). Step in and look down the 330-foot nave for a 14th-century optical illusion (€2.50, Mon–Thu and Sat 9:00–17:00, Fri and Sun 13:00–17:00).

Nearby: A palatial **perfumery** (Farmacia di Santa Maria Novella) is around the corner, 100 yards down Via della Scala at #16 (free but shopping encouraged, Mon–Sat 9:30–19:30, Sun 10:30–18:30, open later on Sun in summer, tel. 055-216-276). Thick with the lingering aroma of centuries of spritzes, it started as the herb garden of the Santa Maria Novella monks. Well-known even today for its top-quality products, it is extremely Florentine. Pick up the history sheet at the desk, and wander deep into the shop. From the back room, you can peek at one of Santa Maria Novella's cloisters with its dreamy frescoes and imagine a time before Vespas and tourists.

You can get a closer look inside the **Museum and Cloisters,** adjacent to the church, but they're definitely lesser sights (€2.70, entry to the left of the church's facade; Mon–Thu and Sat 9:00–17:00, closed Fri and Sun).

South of the Arno River

To locate these sights, see the map on page 923.

▲▲**Pitti Palace**—The imposing Pitti Palace, several blocks southwest of Ponte Vecchio, has three separate museums and two gardens. The main reason to visit is to see the Palatine Gallery, but if you want to see all of the Pitti Palace, you'd need to buy two different combo-tickets: Ticket #1 includes the Palatine Gallery, Royal Apartments, Modern Art Gallery, and several lesser museums (€12, Tue–Sun 8:15–18:50, closed Mon, tel. 055-238-8614, www.polomuseale.firenze.it). Ticket #2 covers the Boboli and Bardini Gardens, Argenti Museum (the Duke's treasures), Porcelain Museum, and mildly interesting Costume Gallery (€10, daily 8:15–18:30, until 19:30 June–Aug, closes earlier in winter, last entry 30–60 min before closing, closed first and last Mon of the month, same phone and website as above).

The second-best collection of paintings in town, the **Palatine Gallery** also happens to be in the most sumptuous palace you can tour in Florence. The building itself is mammoth, holding several different museums. Stick primarily to the gallery, forget about everything else, and the palace becomes a little less exhausting. If there's a long line, bypass it (and the line at the metal detector) by going to the quick reservations window, asking to enter immediately, and buying a ticket with the €3 reservation fee.

You'll walk through one palatial, chandeliered room after another, walls sagging with masterpieces by 16th- and 17th-century masters, including Rubens, Titian, and Rembrandt. Its Raphael collection is the second biggest anywhere—the Vatican beats them by one. The paintings are hung according to "courtly taste" (meaning: everywhere). Each room and its paintings are well-described in English. The collection is all on one floor with a one-way system (so you can't get lost). Before you exit, consider taking a detour down a straight line of about six palatial rooms—preserved as royal apartments, with period furnishings—where you get a feel for the splendor of the dukes' world: 200 years of Medicis, 100 years of Habsburgs, and a short time under the Savoy family, Italy's first royal family.

The Rest of the Pitti Palace: If you've got the energy, it'd be a Pitti to miss the palace's other offerings.

The **Modern Art Gallery,** on the second floor, features Romantic, Neoclassical, and Impressionist works by 19th- and 20th-century Tuscan painters.

The **Grand Ducal Treasures (Museo degli Argenti),** on the ground and mezzanine floors, is the Medici treasure chest, with jeweled crucifixes, exotic porcelain, gilded ostrich eggs, and so on, made to entertain fans of applied arts.

The **Boboli Gardens and Bardini Gardens,** located behind

the palace, offer a sprawling, shady, landscaped refuge from the city heat. Enter the Boboli Gardens from the Pitti Palace courtyard. The Bardini Gardens are a 10-minute walk beyond the Boboli Gardens.

▲▲**Brancacci Chapel**—For the best look at Masaccio's works (he's the early Renaissance master who reinvented perspective), see his restored frescoes here. Instead of medieval religious symbols, Masaccio's paintings feature simple, strong human figures with facial expressions that reflect their emotions. The accompanying works of Masolino and Filippino Lippi provide illuminating contrasts.

Get reservations in advance (see below). Your ticket includes a 45-minute English film on the church, the frescoes, and Florence; reserve a viewing time when you book your entry. It starts promptly at the top of the hour. Computer animation brings the paintings to life—making them appear to move and giving them 3-D depth—while narration describes the events depicted in the panels. Yes, it's a long time commitment, and the film takes liberties with the art. But it's visually interesting and your best way to see the frescoes up close. The film works great either before or after you visit the frescoes.

Cost, Reservations, Hours, Location: €4, free reservations required—it's very easy...just call, €8 combo-ticket with Palazzo Vecchio, both tickets include worthwhile film in English—reserve film when you book entry, limit of 30 visitors every 15 minutes, Mon and Wed–Sat 10:00–17:00, Sun 13:00–17:00, closed Tue, ticket office closes at 16:30; cross Ponte Vecchio and turn right on Borgo San Jacopo, walk 10 min, then turn left into Piazza del Carmine; tel. 055-276-8224 or 055-276-8558.

The neighborhoods around the church are considered the last surviving bits of old Florence.

Santo Spirito Church—This church has a classic Brunelleschi interior and a painted, carved wooden crucifix attributed to Michelangelo. The sculptor donated this early work to the monastery in appreciation for allowing him to dissect and learn about bodies. Pop in to see a delightful Renaissance space and a chance to marvel at a Michelangelo all alone (free, Thu–Sat and Mon–Tue 9:30–12:30 & 16:00–17:30, Wed 10:00–12:00, Sun 16:00–17:30 only, Piazza Santo Spirito, tel. 055-211-716).

▲**Piazzale Michelangelo**—Overlooking the city from across the river (look for the huge statue of *David*), this square is worth the 30-minute hike, drive (free parking), or bus ride (either #12 or #13 from the train station) for the view of Florence and the stunning dome of the Duomo. It makes sense to take a taxi or ride the bus up, and then enjoy the easy downhill walk back into town. Off the west side of the piazza is a somewhat hidden terrace, an excellent place to retreat from the mobs. After dark, the square is packed with local school kids licking ice cream and each other. About 200 yards beyond all the tour groups and teenagers is the stark, beautiful, crowd-free, Romanesque San Miniato Church.

▲**San Miniato Church**—The martyred St. Minias, this church's namesake, died on this hill and is buried here in the crypt. The church's green-and-white marble facade is classic Florentine Romanesque. The church has wonderful 3-D paintings, a plush ceiling of glazed terra-cotta panels by Luca della Robbia, and a sumptuous Renaissance chapel (located front and center). For me, though, the highlight is the brilliantly preserved art in the sacristy (behind altar in the room on right) showing scenes from the life of St. Benedict (c. 1350) by a follower of Giotto. Drop a euro into the box to light the room for five minutes (church is free, daily April–Oct 8:00–19:00, Nov–March 8:00–13:00 & 14:30–18:00, Gregorian chants April–Sept daily at the 17:30 Mass—17:00 in winter, 200 yards above Piazzale Michelangelo, take bus #12 or #13 from train station, tel. 055-234-2731).

Experiences

Gelato

Gelato is an edible art form. Italy's best ice cream is in Florence—one souvenir that can't break and won't clutter your luggage. But beware of scams at touristy joints on busy streets that turn a simple request for a cone into a €10 "tourist special" rip-off.

A key to gelato appreciation is sampling liberally and choosing flavors that go well together. Ask, as the locals do, for *"Un assaggio, per favore?"* (A taste, please?; oon ah-SAH-joh pehr fah-VOH-ray) and *"Che si sposano bene?"* (What marries well?; kay see spoh-ZAH-noh BEN-ay).

Artiginale, nostra produzione, and *produzione propia* mean gelato is made on the premises, and gelato displayed in covered metal tins (rather than white plastic) is more likely to be homemade. Gelato aficionados avoid colors that don't appear in nature—for less chemicals and real flavor, go for mellow hues (bright colors attract children). These places are open daily for long hours.

Near the Duomo: The new favorite in town, **Grom** uses organic ingredients and seasonal fresh fruit. Their traditional approach and quality give locals déjà vu, reminding them of the good old days and the ice cream of their childhood. Marco, who really cares, describes his "gelato as cuisine" approach to ice cream, and posts special notes on his various flavors on the wall in English (daily 10:30–24:00, Via delle Oche 24a).

Near Ponte Vecchio: Try **Gelateria Carrozze,** a longtime local favorite (daily 11:00–20:00, until 1:00 in the morning in summer, on riverfront 30 yards from Ponte Vecchio toward the Uffizi at Piazza del Pesce 3).

Near the Accademia: A Sicilian choice on a tourist thoroughfare, **Gelateria Carabè** is particularly famous for its luscious *granite*—Italian ices made with fresh fruit. Antonio, whose family has made ice cream the Sicilian way for more than 100 years, can tell you why that's important (daily 11:00–20:00, from the Accademia, a block towards the Duomo, Via Ricasoli 60 red).

Near Orsanmichele Church: For gelato served in a brash, neon environment, stop by **Festival del Gelato** or **Perchè No!,** located just off the busy main pedestrian drag (Via de' Calzaiuoli). They serve a stunning array of brightly colored, kid-pleasing flavors (Festival del Gelato is at Via del Corso 75; Perchè No! is at Via dei Tavolini 19).

Near the Church of Santa Croce: The venerable favorite, **Vivoli's,** still serves great gelato—but it's more expensive and stingy in its servings (closed Mon, Aug, and Jan; opposite the Church of Santa Croce, go down Via Torta a block and turn right on Via Stinche). Before ordering, try a free sample of their *riso* (rice flavor). Locals flock to **Gelateria de' Neri** (Via de' Neri 26 red), also owned by Vivoli's.

Across the River: If you want an excuse to check out the little village-like neighborhood across the river from Santa Croce, enjoy a gelato at the tiny no-name *(senza nome) gelateria* at Via San Miniato 5 red (just before Porta San Miniato).

Sleeping

Nearly all of my recommended accommodations are located in Florence's downtown core, within minutes of the great sights.

The accommodations scene varies wildly with the season. Spring and fall are very tight and expensive, while mid-July through August is wide open and discounted. November through February is also generally empty. I've listed prices for peak season: April, May, June, September, and October.

With good information and an email or phone call beforehand, you can find a stark, clean, and comfortable double with breakfast and a private bath for about €100 (less at the smaller places, such as the *soggiorni*). You get elegance in peak season for €160.

Museum-goers take note: When you book your room, you can usually ask your hotelier to book entry times for you to visit the popular Uffizi Gallery and the Accademia (Michelangelo's *David*). This service is fast, easy, and offered free or for a small fee by most hotels—the only requirement is advance notice. Ask them to make appointments for you any time the day after your arrival for the Uffizi and the Accademia. If your hotel does charge

Sleep Code

(€1 = about $1.40, country code: 39)
S = Single, **D** = Double/Twin, **T** = Triple, **Q** = Quad, **b** = bathroom,
s = shower only. Unless otherwise noted, credit cards are
accepted, English is spoken, and breakfast is included in these
rates.

To help you easily sort through these listings, I've divided
the rooms into three categories based on the price for a
standard double room with bath during high season:

$$$ Higher Priced—Most rooms €165 or more.
$$ Moderately Priced—Most rooms between €110-165.
$ Lower Priced—Most rooms €110 or less.

a fee, you'll usually save several euros per reservation by booking it
yourself. For details, see the sidebar earlier in this chapter.

Between the Station and Duomo

$$ Hotel Accademia is an elegant place with lots of marble stairs,
parquet floors, attractive public areas, 21 pleasant rooms, and a
floor plan that defies logic (Db-€150, Tb-€180, 5 percent cash
discount, air-con, tiny courtyard, Via Faenza 7, tel. 055-293-451,
fax 055-219-771, www.hotelaccademiafirenze.com, info@hotel
accademiafirenze.com, Tea, Francesca, and Paolo).

$$ Residenza dei Pucci, a block north of the Duomo, has
12 tastefully decorated rooms—in soothing earth tones—with
aristocratic furniture spread over three floors (Sb-€135, Db-€150,
Tb-€170, Db suite with grand Duomo view-€207, Qb-€238, pay
cash and mention this book for best prices, air-con, reception open
9:00–20:00—let them know if you'll arrive late, Via dei Pucci 9,
additional suites available across the Arno, tel. 055-281-886, fax
055-264-314, www.residenzadeipucci.com, residenzadeipucci
@residenzadeipucci.com, Mirella).

$$ Hotel Centrale, with 20 spacious rooms, is indeed cen-
tral (Db-€150, Tb-€182, pay cash and mention this book for best
prices, ask for Rick Steves rate when you reserve, air-con, elevator,
free Internet access, Via dei Conti 3, tel. 055-215-761, fax 055-215-
216, www.hotelcentralefirenze.it, info@hotelcentralefirenze.it,
Margherita and Ives).

$ Katti House and the nearby **Soggiorno Annamaria** are run
by house-proud mama-and-daughter team Maria and Katti, who
keep their 15 rooms spotless, inviting, and well-maintained. While
both offer equal comfort, Soggiorno Annamaria has a more his-
toric setting, with frescoed ceilings, unique tiles, timbered ceilings,
and quieter rooms. Though listed in other guidebooks, the rooms

FLORENCE

Florence Hotels

TO PIAZZA
d. LIBERTÀ

TO FORTEZZA
DI BASSO

7

5
S. ZANOBI
8
9

27 APRILE
S. REP.
S. GALLO
CAVOUR

VIA
NAZIONALE
6

S.M.N.
TRAIN
STATION

V. CENN.
V. FAENZA
FIUME
P.
ADUA

ALA.

PANICALE
S. ANT.

MERCATO
CENTRALE

GUELFA

RICA.

MEDICI
CHAPELS

SAN
LORENZO

MEDICI-
RICCARDI
PALACE

BUS
STN.

S. MARIA
NOVELLA

4
1
STREET
MKT.

2
PUCCI
V.

12

VIA D. SCALA
25
26

MEL.
GIGLIO
PANZANI
3

B. S. LOR.

VIA
DUOMO

VIA
PORCEL.
PAL.
V. FOSSI
MORO

BANCHI
SOLE
SPADA
27

CERRETANI

BAPT.

TOWER

CONSOLO

AGLI
20

CALZAIUOLI

P.
GOLD.
VIGNA NUOVA
S.
TRINITA

TORNABUONI
STROZZI
PZZA.
REP.
19

CORSO
21
DANTE'S
HOUSE

18

DANTE

A R N O
CARRARA
LUNG. CORSINI

PORTA
ROSSA
24
POST
ORSAN-
MICH.

PRO-
V.

BORGO

LUNG. GUICC.
VIA S. SPIRITO

B. S. TRIN.
COV MKT.
22
TERME
APOST.
S. MARIA
ACCIAIUOLI

COND.
PIAZZA
SIGNORIA
23

PALAZZO
VECCHIO

PONTE
VECCHIO

S. JACOPO
GUICC.

OLTRARNO

UFFIZI
GALLERY

EXIT
SCIENCE
MUSEUM
V. D. NERI
VIA
DIAZ

TO PITTI PALACE

MUSEUM OF SAN MARCO

ACCADEMIA

P.S. MARCO

SOLI.

P.S.S. ANNUNZ.

V. COL

HOSPITAL OF THE INNOCENTS

VIA D. ALF.

SERVI

PERGOLA

PRECIOUS STONES MUSEUM

DUOMO MUSEUM

S. EGIDIO

BORGO PINTI

V. ORIUOLO

BORGO D'ALB.

POST

BARGELLO

MICH. HOUSE

VIA G. VECCHIA

VERD.

GHIB.

ANG.

GRECI

P.S. CROCE

S. GIUS.

BENCI

BORGO STA. CROCE

SANTA CROCE

TINTORI

VAG.

DCH

1 Hotel Accademia
2 Residenza dei Pucci
3 Hotel Centrale
4 Katti House & Soggiorno Annamaria
5 Galileo Hotel
6 Hotel Il Bargellino
7 Hotel Enza
8 Casa Rabatti
9 Soggiorno Magliani
10 Hotel Loggiato dei Serviti
11 Hotel Morandi alla Crocetta
12 Palazzo Niccolini al Duomo
13 Panella's Residence
14 Residenza il Villino
15 B&B Il Bargello
16 Hotel Cardinal of Florence, Oblate Sisters of the Assumption & Albergo Chiazza
17 Hotel Dalí
18 B&B Dei Mori
19 Hotel Axial & Hotel Maxim
20 Soggiorno Battistero
21 Albergo Firenze
22 Hotel Torre Guelfa & Hotel Alessandra
23 In Piazza della Signoria B&B
24 Hotel Davanzati
25 Hotel Pensione Elite
26 Bellevue House
27 Hotel Sole

200 YARDS

200 METERS

are ideally priced (Db-€70–100 with this book though prices are soft, ask for Rick Steves rate when you reserve, Via Faenza 21, tel. & fax 055-213-410, www.kattihouse.com, info@kattihouse.com).

Near the Mercato Centrale

$$ Galileo Hotel, a classy business hotel with 31 rooms, is run with familial warmth (Db-€130, Tb-€150, ask for Rick Steves discount when you book direct, quadruple-pane windows effectively shut out street noise, free Internet access, Via Nazionale 22a, tel. 055-496-645, fax 055-496-447, www.galileohotel.it, info@galileo hotel.it, Patrizia).

$ Hotel Il Bargellino, run by Bostonian Carmel and her Italian husband Pino, has 10 summery rooms decorated with funky antique furniture and Pino's modern paintings. Guests enjoy relaxing with Carmel on her big, breezy, momentum-slowing terrace (S-€45, D-€75, Db-€85, extra bed-€25, air-con-€10, no breakfast, a few blocks north of the train station at Via Guelfa 87, tel. & fax 055-238-2658, www.ilbargellino.com, carmel@ilbargellino.com).

$ Hotel Enza rents 19 basic rooms (Sb-€60, Db-€90, cash preferred, extra bed-€20, optional breakfast by request only-€5, air-con, Via San Zanobi 45 black, tel. 055-490-990, fax 055-473-672, www.hotelenza.it, info@hotelenza.it, Katia).

$ Casa Rabatti is the ultimate if you always wanted to be a part of a Florentine family. Its four simple, clean rooms are run with motherly warmth by Marcella, who speaks minimal English. Seeing 16 years of my family Christmas cards on their walls, I'm reminded how long she has been keeping budget travelers happy (D-€50, Db-€60, €25 extra per bed in shared quad or quint, cash only but secure reservation with credit card, no breakfast, fans available, 5 blocks from station at Via San Zanobi 48 black, tel. 055-212-393, casarabatti@inwind.it).

If she's booked up, Marcella will put you up in her daughter's place nearby, at Via Nazionale 20 (five big, airy rooms with fans, no breakfast, closer to the station). While daughter Patrizia works, her mom runs the B&Bs. Getting bumped to Patrizia's gives you slightly more comfort and slightly less personality...certainly not a net negative.

$ Soggiorno Magliani is central and humble, with six no-frills rooms (sharing two baths) that feel and smell like a great-grandmother's home. It's run by the friendly duo Vincenza and her English-speaking daughter, Cristina, and the price is right, though the neighborhood can get a little seedy at night (S-€39, D-€49, T-€65, cash only but secure reservation with credit card, no breakfast, a little traffic noise but has double-paned windows, near Via Guelfa at Via Santa Reparata 1, tel. 055-287-378, hotel-magliani@libero.it).

East of the Duomo

$$$ Hotel Loggiato dei Serviti, at the most prestigious address in Florence on the most Renaissance square in town, gives you Old World romance with hair dryers. Stone stairways lead you under open-beam ceilings through this 16th-century monastery's classy public rooms—it's so artful, you'll be snapping photos everywhere. The 33 cells—with air-conditioning, TVs, mini-bars, and telephones—would be unrecognizable to their original inhabitants. The hotel staff is both professional and warm (Sb-€120, Db-€180, superior Db-€205, family suites from €263, request Rick Steves rate when you book, elevator, Piazza S.S. Annunziata 3, tel. 055-289-592, fax 055-289-595, www.loggiatodeiservitihotel.it, info @loggiatodeiservitihotel.it, Fabio, Chiara, and Simonetta). When they're full, they rent five spacious and elegant rooms in a 17th-century annex a block away. While it lacks the monastic mystique, the rooms are bigger, gorgeous, and cost the same.

$$$ Hotel Morandi alla Crocetta, a former convent located on a quiet street, envelops you in a 16th-century cocoon. With 12 rooms, period furnishings, parquet floors, and wood-beamed ceilings, it takes you back a few centuries (Sb-€110, Db-€177, breakfast not worth €11, air-con, a block off Piazza S.S. Annunziata at Via Laura 50, tel. 055-234-4747, fax 055-248-0954, www.hotelmorandi .it, welcome@hotelmorandi.it, well run by Maurizio, Rolando, and Frank).

$$$ Palazzo Niccolini al Duomo, one of five elite Historic Residence Hotels in Florence, is run by Sra. Niccolini da Camugliano. The lounge is palatial, and the 10 rooms are big and splendid, with original 16th-century frescoes. If you have the money and want a Florentine palace to call home, this is a very good bet, located just one block from the Duomo (Db-€300, prices vary with the luxuriousness of the room, ask for Rick Steves discount when you book, check online to choose a room and consider last-minute deals, Via dei Servi 2, tel. 055-282-412, fax 055-290-979, www.niccolinidomepalace.com, info@niccolinidome palace.com).

$$ Panella's Residence, once a convent and today part of owner Graziella's extensive home, is a classy B&B, with six elegant and romantic rooms, antique furnishings, and historic architectural touches (Db-€140 with cash, discounts for stays of 3 or more nights, air-con, Via della Pergola 42, tel. 055-234-7202, fax 055-247-9669, www.panellaresidence.com, panella_residence @yahoo.it).

$$ Residenza il Villino, popular and friendly, aspires to offer a Florentine home. It has 10 rooms and a pleasant, peaceful little courtyard (small Db-€110, Db-€130, Qb/family suite-€170, ask for cash discount and mention this book, air-con, free Internet access, just north of Via degli Alfani at Via della Pergola 53, tel. 055-200-1116, fax 055-200-1101, www.ilvillino.it, info@ilvillino.it, Sergio, Elisabetta, and son Lorenzo).

$$ B&B Il Bargello is a home away from home, run by friendly and helpful Canadian expat Gabriella. Hike up three flights to reach Gabriella's five attractive and relaxing rooms. She offers a comfortable communal living room with a book exchange and free Internet access (free Wi-Fi and a computer for your use), partial kitchen access, and an inviting rooftop terrace with close-up views of Florence's towers (Db-€100–120, ask for the Rick Steves rate when you book, additional 5–10 percent cash discount, air-con, Via de' Pandolfini 33 black, tel. 055-215-330, fax 055-294-977, www.firenze-bedandbreakfast.it, info@firenze-bedandbreakfast.it).

$ Hotel Cardinal of Florence is a third-floor walk-up with 17 new, tidy, and sun-splashed rooms overlooking either a silent courtyard (many with views of Brunelleschi's dome) or quiet street. Relax and enjoy the view of Florence's rooftops from the sun terrace (Db-€105, ask for Rick Steves rate when you book, additional 5 percent cash discount, €15/day limited parking—request when you reserve, Borgo Pinti 5, tel. 055-234-0780, fax 055-234-3389, www.hotelcardinaloflorence.com, info@hotelcardinaloflorence.com).

$ Hotel Dalí (listed in all the guidebooks) has 10 decent, basic rooms with new baths in a nice location for a great price (S-€40, D-€65, Db-€80, extra bed-€25, no breakfast, no air-con but has fans, request quiet room when you book, free parking, 2 blocks behind the Duomo at Via dell'Oriuolo 17, tel. & fax 055-234-0706, hoteldali@tin.it, Marco and Samanta).

$ Oblate Sisters of the Assumption run an institutional 30-room hotel in a Renaissance building with a dreamy garden, great public spaces, appropriately simple rooms, and a quiet, prayerful ambience. The staff doesn't speak English; it's best to reserve by fax, using basic English that God only knows how they translate (S-€40, Db-€80, Tb-€120, Qb-€160, cash only, single beds only, optional breakfast-€5, air-con, elevator, €10/day limited parking—request when you book, Borgo Pinti 15, tel. 055-248-0582, fax 055-234-6291, sroblateborgopinti@virgilio.it, sisters are likely to speak French, Sister Theresa is very helpful).

$ Albergo Chiazza is a homey, old-school throwback, where Mauro and family rent 14 rooms mostly overlooking a quiet courtyard. If you don't mind the blistered wallpaper and pre-fab bathrooms, it's a fine value (Db-€70–95, request a quiet room when you book, air-con, Borgo Pinti 5, tel. 055-248-0363, fax 055-234-6888, www.chiazzahotel.com, hotel.chiazza@tin.it).

Near Piazza della Repubblica

These are the most central of my accommodations recommendations (and therefore a little overpriced). While worth the extra cost for many, given Florence's walkable core, nearly every hotel can be considered central.

$$ B&B Dei Mori, a peaceful haven, has five newly remodeled rooms ideally located on a quiet pedestrian street near Dante's House. Accommodating hostess Suzanne offers lots of tips on dining and sightseeing in Florence (D-€90–100, Db-€100–120 depending on size of the room, air-con extra, 10 percent discount for my readers—ask when you book, reception open 8:00–19:00, Via Dante Alighieri 12, tel. & fax 055-211-438, www.bnb.it /deimori, deimori@bnb.it).

$$ Hotel Axial (run by the same folks who own Hotel Maxim, below) offers 15 soundproofed, tidy, and plain rooms on Florence's main pedestrian drag (Sb-€89–109, Db-€149, 5 percent discount if you book on their website, another 5 percent off for cash, check for website promotions, air-con, elevator, Via de' Calzaiuoli 11, tel. 055-218-984, fax 055-211-733, www.hotelaxial.it, info@hotelaxial.it).

$ Hotel Maxim, right on Via de' Calzaiuoli, is a big and institutional-feeling place warmly run by a family team: father Paolo, son Nicola, and daughter Chiara. Its halls are narrow, but the 26 basic rooms are comfortable and well-maintained (Sb-€75, Db-€110, Tb-€138, Qb-€155, ask for cash discount and Rick Steves rate when you book, air-con, elevator, free Internet access, free Wi-Fi for my readers, Via de' Calzaiuoli 11, tel. 055-217-474, fax 055-283-729, www.hotelmaximfirenze.it, reservation@hotel maximfirenze.it).

$ Soggiorno Battistero rents seven simple, airy rooms, most with great views, literally overlooking the Baptistery and the Duomo square. Request a view or a quieter room in the back when you book by email. It's a pristine, fresh, and minimalist little place run by Italian Luca and his American wife Kelly, who makes the place particularly welcoming (Sb-€78, Db-€103, Tb-€140, Qb-€150, 5 percent cash discount, breakfast served in room, air-con, no elevator, double-paned windows, Piazza San Giovanni 1, third floor, tel. 055-295-143, fax 055-268-189, www.soggiorno battistero.it, info@soggiornobattistero.it).

$ Albergo Firenze, a big, efficient place, offers 58 modern, basic rooms in a central locale two blocks behind the Duomo (Sb-€84, Db-€114, Tb-€147, air-con, elevator, noisy, at Piazza Donati 4 across from Via del Corso 8, tel. 055-214-203, fax 055-212-370, www.albergofirenze.org, info@albergofirenze.org, Giuseppe).

Near Piazza della Signoria and Ponte Vecchio

$$$ Hotel Torre Guelfa is topped by a fun medieval tower with a panoramic rooftop terrace and a huge living room. Its 24 pricey rooms vary wildly in size. Room 15, with a private terrace (€245), is worth reserving several months in advance (standard Db-€170–190, Db junior suite-€235, family deals, cash discount, air-con, elevator, a couple blocks northwest of Ponte Vecchio, Borgo S.S. Apostoli 8, tel. 055-239-6338, fax 055-239-8577, www.hoteltorreguelfa.com, info@hoteltorreguelfa.com, Sabina, Giancarlo, and Sandro).

$$$ In Piazza della Signoria B&B, overlooking Piazza della Signoria, is peaceful, refined, and homey at the same time. Fit for a honeymoon, the 10 rooms come with all the special touches and little extras you'd expect in a top-end American B&B. Of all my listings, this is the only place where you'll be served fresh-squeezed orange juice (viewless Db-€220, view Db-€250, Tb-€280, ask for discount when you go direct with this book, family apartments, lavish bathrooms, air-con, tiny elevator, free Internet access, Via dei Magazzini 2, tel. 055-239-9546, mobile 348-321-0565, fax 055-267-6616, www.inpiazzadellasignoria.com, info@inpiazzadella signoria.com, Sonia and Alessandro).

$$$ Hotel Davanzati, bright and shiny with artistic touches, has 19 cheery rooms with all the comforts. The place is a family affair, thoughtfully run by friendly Tommaso and father Fabrizio, who offer drinks and snacks each evening at their candlelit happy hour (Sb-€122, Db-€189, Tb-€259; prices soft off-season, 10 percent cash discount; PlayStation 2, DVD player, and laptop with free Wi-Fi in every room; air-con, elevator up one flight of stairs, Via Porta Rossa 5, tel. 055-286-666, fax 055-265-8252, www.hotel davanzati.it, info@hoteldavanzati.it).

$$ Hotel Alessandra is 16th-century, tranquil, and sprawling, with 27 big, elegant rooms. It offers budget prices—rare in this locale (S-€67, Sb-€110, D-€110, Db-€150, Tb-€195, Qb-€215, 5 percent cash discount, air-con, elevator up one flight of stairs, Borgo S.S. Apostoli 17, tel. 055-283-438, fax 055-210-619, www .hotelalessandra.com, info@hotelalessandra.com, Anna and son Andrea).

Near the Train Station

As with any big Italian city, the area around the train station is a magnet for hardworking pickpockets on the alert for lost, vulnerable tourists with bulging money belts hanging out of their khakis.

$ Hotel Pensione Elite is run with warmth by sunny Nadia. You'll find 10 comfortable if plainly furnished rooms (Ss-€60, Sb-€90, Ds-€80, Db-€100, Tb-€120, Qb-€140, no breakfast, cash discount, air-con, Via della Scala 12, second floor, tel. & fax 055-215-395, www.hotelelitefirenze.com, hotelelitefi@libero.it).

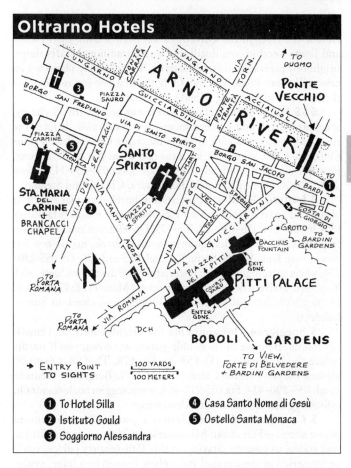

Oltrarno Hotels

ARNO RIVER

PONTE VECCHIO

TO DUOMO

LUNGARNO

PONTE CARRAIA

VIA TORN.

BORGO SAN FREDIANO

PIAZZA SAURO

GUICCIARDINI

VIA DI SANTO SPIRITO

PONTE S. TRINITA

ACCIAIUOLI

S. TRINITA

PIAZZA CARMINE

S. MONACA

VIA DEI SERRAGLI

SANTO SPIRITO

P.S. MARTI.

BORGO SAN JACOPO

V. BARDI

STA. MARIA DEL CARMINE + BRANCACCI CHAPEL

VIA SANT' AGOSTINO

PIAZZA S. SPIRITO

VIA MAGGIO

VIA TOSCANELLA

SPRONE

GUICCIARDINI

COSTA DI S. GIORGIO

S. GIORGIO

GROTTO

TO BARDINI GARDENS

N

TO PORTA ROMANA

VIA ROMANA

PIAZZA DEI PITTI

COURT-YARD

BACCHUS FOUNTAIN

EXIT GDNS.

PITTI PALACE

TO PORTA ROMANA

DCH

ENTER GDNS.

BOBOLI GARDENS

TO VIEW, FORTE DI BELVEDERE + BARDINI GARDENS

→ ENTRY POINT TO SIGHTS

100 YARDS
100 METERS

❶ To Hotel Silla
❷ Istituto Gould
❸ Soggiorno Alessandra

❹ Casa Santo Nome di Gesù
❺ Ostello Santa Monaca

FLORENCE

$ Bellevue House is a third-floor (no elevator) oasis of tranquility, with six spacious rooms flanking a long, mellow-yellow lobby. It's a peaceful time warp thoughtfully run by Rosanna and Antonio di Grazia (Db-€95 in April–June, Sept, and Oct; Db-€75 off-season, family deals, 5 percent cash discount, optional €3.50 breakfast in street-level bar, Via della Scala 21, tel. 055-260-8932, mobile 333-612-5973, fax 055-265-5315, www.bellevuehouse.it, info@bellevuehouse.it).

$ Hotel Sole, which may have new owners in 2010, is a minimalist place with eight bright, modern rooms (Sb-€50, Db-€80, Tb-€110, 5 percent cash discount, no breakfast, air-con, elevator, curfew at 1:00 in the morning, a block toward river from Piazza Santa Maria Novella at Via del Sole 8, tel. & fax 055-239-6094, htlsole@tiscali.it).

Oltrarno, South of the River

Across the river in the Oltrarno area, between the Pitti Palace and Ponte Vecchio, you'll still find small, traditional crafts shops, neighborly piazzas, and family eateries. The following places are an easy walk from Ponte Vecchio. Only the first one is a real hotel—the rest are a ragtag gang of budget alternatives.

$$$ Hotel Silla, a classic three-star hotel with 35 cheery, spacious, pastel, and modern rooms, is a good value. It faces the river and overlooks a park opposite the Santa Croce Church (Db-€180, Tb-€220, ask for Rick Steves rate when you book, air-con, elevator, Via dei Renai 5, tel. 055-234-2888, fax 055-234-1437, www.hotelsilla.it, hotelsilla@hotelsilla.it, Laura, Chiara, and Stefano).

$ Istituto Gould is a Protestant Church–run place with 41 clean and spartan rooms with twin beds and modern facilities (S-€36, Sb-€44, Db-€56–64, Tb-€75, Qb-€92, optional €5 breakfast available April–Oct, quieter rooms in back, no air-con but rooms have fans, Via dei Serragli 49, tel. 055-212-576, fax 055-280-274, www.istitutogould.it, foresteriafirenze@diaconiavaldese.org). You must arrive when the office is open (Mon–Fri 8:45–13:00 & 15:00–19:30, Sat 9:00–13:30 & 14:30–18:00, no check-in Sun or holidays).

$ Soggiorno Alessandra has five bright, comfy, and small-ish rooms. Because of its double-paned windows, you'll hardly notice the traffic noise (D-€58–73, Db-€78, Tb-€98, Qb-€128, air-con-€8, just past the Carraia Bridge at Via Borgo San Frediano 6, tel. 055-290-424, fax 055-218-464, www.soggiornoalessandra.it, info@soggiornoalessandra.it, Alessandra).

$ Casa Santo Nome di Gesù is a grand, 29-room convent whose sisters—Franciscan Missionaries of Mary—are thankful to rent rooms to tourists. Staying in this 15th-century palace, you'll be immersed in the tranquil atmosphere created by a huge, peaceful garden, generous and prayerful public spaces, and smiling nuns (D-€70, Db-€85, elevator, no air-con but rooms have fans, twin beds only, memorably convent-like breakfast room, 23:00 curfew, Piazza del Carmine 21, tel. 055-213-856, fax 055-281-835, www.fmmfirenze.it, info@fmmfirenze.it).

Hostels

$ Ostello Santa Monaca, a cheap, well-run hostel, is a long block south of the Brancacci Chapel in the Oltrarno area. It attracts a young backpacking crowd (€17–20 beds with sheets, 4- to 20-bed rooms, 10:00–14:00 lock-out, 2:00 curfew, free Internet access, self-serve laundry, Via Santa Monaca 6, tel. 055-268-338, fax 055-280-185, www.ostello.it, info@ostello.it).

$ Villa Camerata, classy for an IYHF hostel, is in a pretty villa three miles northeast of the train station, on the outskirts of

Florence (€20 per bed with breakfast, 4- to 12-bed rooms, must have hostel membership card or pay additional €3/night, self-serve laundry, take bus #17 to Salviatino stop, Via Righi 2, tel. 055-601-451, fax 055-610-300, www.hihostels.com, firenze@ostelli online.org).

Eating

To save money and time for sights, you can keep lunches fast and simple, eating in one of countless self-service places and pizzerias or just picnicking (try juice, yogurt, cheese, and a roll for €5). For good sit-down meals, consider the following. Remember, restaurants like to serve what's fresh. If you're into flavor, go for the seasonal best bets—featured in the *piatti del giorno* ("special of the day") sections of the menus.

North of the River
Restaurants near Piazza Santa Maria Novella and the Train Station

Trattoria al Trebbio serves traditional food with simple Florentine elegance at fair prices in its candlelit interior. Tables spill out onto a romantic little square—an oasis of Roman Trastevere–like charm (Wed–Mon 12:00–15:00 & 19:15–23:00, closed Tue, reserve for outdoor seating, half a block off of Piazza Santa Maria Novella at Via delle Belle Donne 47, tel. 055-287-089).

Trattoria "da Giorgio" is a homey, family-style diner serving up piping hot, delicious home cooking to happy locals and tourists alike. Their three-course dinner menu is a great value for €12, including water and a drink. Choose from among the daily specials or the regular menu (Mon–Sat 18:00–22:00, closed Sun, Via Palazzuolo 100 red, tel. 055-284-302).

Osteria Belle Donne makes you feel like you're eating dinner in a crowded terrarium piled high with decorative knickknacks. Old-fashioned Tuscan food is served on tight tables—a few tables hunker on the street. They take no reservations and tend to steamroll tourists; arrive early or wait (€12 pastas, €12 *secondi*, daily 12:00–15:00 & 19:00–23:00, Via delle Belle Donne 16 red, tel. 055-238-2609, run by sprightly Giacinto).

Trattoria Marione serves sincerely home-cooked-style meals to tourists and locals in a happy, crowded, food-loving, and steamy ambience (€8 pastas, €10 *secondi*, daily 12:00–15:00 & 19:00–22:30, Via della Spada 27 red, tel. 055-214-756).

Trattoria Sostanza-Troia, characteristic and well-established, is famous for its beef. Hearty steaks and pastas are splittable. Whirling ceiling fans and walls strewn with old photos evoke earlier times, while the artichoke pies remind locals of grandma's

FLORENCE

Florence Restaurants

200 YARDS

200 METERS

N

TO PIAZZA D. LIBERTÀ

TO FORTEZZA DI BASSO

S.M.N. TRAIN STATION

V. CENN.
V. FIUME
P. ADUA
11
V. FAENZA
VIA
V. NAZIONALE
PANICALE
S. ANT.
S. ZANOBI
S. REP.
GUELFA
S. GALLO
27 APRILE
CAVOUR
10
9
8
MERCATO CENTRALE
7
12
37

MEDICI CHAPELS

13

STREET MKT.

MEL.

MEDICI-RICCARDI PALACE

PUCCI

RICA.

32

ALA.

BUS STN.

S. MARIA NOVELLA

VIA D. SCALA
V. PORC.
PAL.
V. FOSSI
V. MORO
SOLE
SPADA
VIGNA NUOVA
V. GOLD.
P.

PANZANI
GIGLIO

BANCHI
1

CERRETANI

B.S. LOR.

DUOMO

2
5
6

VIA

AGLI
16
3
4

STROZZI
TORNABUONI

BAPT.

BANCHI

PZZA. REP.

POST

ORSAN-MICH.

TOWER
30
33
CORSO
DANTE'S HOUSE
20
34
DANTE
28
27
26
COND.
19
PROCO.

A R N O

CARRAIA
LUNG. CORSINI
S. TRINITÀ
LUNG. GUICC.
VIA S. SPIRITO
S. TRIN.
V. S. JACOPO

PORTA ROSSA
21
COV. MKT.
22
TERME
APOST.
S. MARIA
ACCIAIUOLI
18
PIAZZA SIGNORIA
29
31

PONTE VECCHIO

PALAZZO VECCHIO
25
BORGO
VINEGIA
24

EXIT

SCIENCE MUSEUM
V. DE' NERI
V. BAR.
DIAZ

OLTRARNO

GUICC.

UFFIZI GALLERY

TO PITTI PALACE

1. Trattoria al Trebbio
2. Trattoria "da Giorgio"
3. Osteria Belle Donne
4. Trattoria Marione
5. Trattoria Sostanza-Troia
6. Trattoria 13 Gobbi
7. Trattoria Zà-Zà & Trattoria Mario's
8. Trattoria la Burrasca
9. Osteria la Congrega
10. Osteria Vineria i'Brincello
11. Trattoria Nerone Pizzeria
12. Il Pirata
13. Casa del Vino
14. Pasticceria Robiglio
15. La Mescita Fiaschetteria
16. Self-Service Rist. Leonardo
17. The Oil Shoppe
18. Rivoire Café
19. Frescobaldi Rist. & Wine Bar
20. Ristorante Paoli & Cantinetta dei Verrazzano
21. Osteria del Porcellino
22. Trattoria Nella
23. Boccadama Enoteca Rist.
24. Trattoria Anita
25. Trattoria Icche C'è C'è
26. Osteria Vini e Vecchi Sapori
27. I Fratellini
28. L'Antico Trippaio
29. 'Ino Bottega di Alimentari e Vini
30. Gelateria Grom
31. Gelateria Carrozze
32. Gelateria Carabè
33. Festival del Gelato
34. Perchè No! Gelateria
35. Vivoli's Gelateria
36. Gelateria de' Neri
37. Il Centro Supermarcati

FLORENCE

cooking. Crowded, shared tables with paper tablecloths give this place a bistro feel. They offer two dinner seatings, at 19:30 and 21:00, which require reservations (dinners for about €30 plus wine, cash only, lunch Mon–Sat 12:30–14:00, closed Sun, closed Sat in off-season, Via del Porcellana 25 red, tel. 055-212-691).

Trattoria 13 Gobbi ("13 Hunchbacks") is a trendy favorite, glowing with candles around a tiny garden. Romantic in front and family-friendly in back, it serves beautifully presented, surprisingly reasonable Tuscan food on big, fancy plates to a mostly tourist crowd (€8.50 pastas, €14 *secondi,* Tue–Sun 12:15–15:00 & 19:30–23:00, closed Mon, Via del Porcellana 9 red, tel. 055-284-015).

Restaurants near Mercato Centrale and San Lorenzo Market

Each of the following market neighborhood eateries is distinct and within a hundred yards of the others. Scout around and choose your favorite.

Trattoria Zà-Zà is a fun, old, characteristic, high-energy place facing the Mercato Centrale. It's a family-friendly festival of food. Locals lament the invasion of tourists, but everyone's happy, and the food is still great. *Ribollita*, a Tuscan soup, is their specialty. They serve big splittable salads and T-bone steaks *(bistecca alla fiorentina)*. Arrive early or make a reservation, especially for the wonderful outdoor piazza seating. Don't mistake their outside seating with the neighboring restaurant (daily 11:30–23:00, Piazza del Mercato Centrale 26 red, tel. 055-215-411).

Trattoria la Burrasca is Flintstone-chic. Friendly duo Elio and Simone offer a limited menu with daily specials of rib-stickin' Tuscan home cooking. It's small—10 tables—and often filled with our readers. If Archie Bunker were Italian, he'd eat at this *trattoria* for special nights out. Everything is homemade and if you want good wine cheap, this is the place (€7 pastas, €10 *secondi,* Tue–Sun 12:00–15:30 & 19:00–23:00, closed Mon, Via Panicale 6, north corner of Mercato Centrale, tel. 055-215-827).

Osteria la Congrega brags that it's "a Tuscan wine bar designed to help you lose track of time." In a fresh, romantic, two-level setting, chef/owner Mahyar takes pride in his fun, easy menu, which features modern Tuscan cuisine, top-notch meat, and seasonal produce. He offers quality vegetarian dishes, creative salads, and an inexpensive but excellent house wine. With just 10 uncramped tables, reservations are required for dinner (€8 pastas, €12 nightly specials, daily 12:00–15:00 & 19:00–23:00, closed Sun in winter, a block from Mercato Centrale, Via Panicale 43 red, tel. 055-264-5027). Mahyar offers fine wines by the glass (see list on blackboard) and occasional live jazz. Between meals, he teaches cooking classes here.

Osteria Vineria i'Brincello is a bright, happy, no-frills diner with lots of spirit, friendly service, and few tourists during lunchtime. Notice the Tuscan daily specials on the blackboard hanging from the ceiling (daily 12:00–15:00 & 18:30–23:00, corner of Via Nazionale and Via Chiara at Via Nazionale 110 red, tel. 055-282-645, Gabriel and Max).

Trattoria Nerone Pizzeria serves up cheap, hearty Tuscan dishes and decent pizzas. The lively, flamboyantly outfitted space (once the garden courtyard of a convent) feels like a good but kitschy American Italian chain restaurant (€7 pizzas, €6 pastas, €10 *secondi*, daily 12:00–15:00 & 18:30–23:00, just north of Via Nazionale at Via Faenza 95–97 red, tel. 055-291-217).

Il Pirata, a deli and rotisserie, offers budget travelers an array of homemade Italian dishes and roasted meats for take-out or to dine-in at their counter. From 18:00–22:00 they set out a tempting all-you-can eat buffet with 20 different trays of pasta salads, sliced prosciutto, savory pies, frittata, eggplant parmigiana, lasagna, and more—for just €6 per person. Finish off your meal with a cheap half or full bottle of wine, and homemade tiramisu (Mon–Sat 11:00–22:00, closed Sun, 2 blocks from the Accademia at Via de' Ginori 56 red, tel. 055-218-625).

Lunching Cheap and Simple near Mercato Centrale and San Lorenzo Market

For piles of picnic produce, people-watching, or just a rustic sandwich, **ad-lib lunch in the Mercato Centrale,** grazing through the huge marketplace (Mon–Sat 7:00–14:00, closed Sun, a block north of San Lorenzo street market). The cheap eateries within the market can be more colorful than sanitary. Buy a picnic of fresh mozzarella cheese, olives, fruit, and crunchy bread to munch on the steps of the nearby Church of San Lorenzo, overlooking the bustling street market.

Trattoria Mario's, around the corner from Trattoria Zà-Zà (listed earlier in this section), has been serving hearty lunches to market-goers since 1953 (Fabio and Romeo are the latest generation). Their simple formula: bustling service, old-fashioned good value, a lunch-only fixed-price meal, and shared tables. It's *cucina casalinga*—home cooking *con brio*. This place is extremely popular, so go early. If there's a line, put your name on the list (€4 pastas, €8 *secondi*, Mon–Sat 12:00–15:30, closed Sun, cash only, no reservations, Via Rosina 2, tel. 055-218-550).

Casa del Vino, Florence's oldest operating wine shop, offers glasses of wine from among 25 open bottles. Owner Gianni, whose family has owned the Casa for 70 years, also serves interesting *panini* (Mon–Fri 9:30–17:30, closed Sat–Sun, hidden behind stalls of the San Lorenzo Market at Via dell'Ariento 16 red). Gianni's *carta dei panini* lists the many €3.50 sandwiches, and the opened bottles behind the counter are marked with prices for wine by the glass. During meals, it's a mob scene. You'll eat standing outside, with local workers on a quick lunch break.

Budget Lunches near the Accademia and Museum of San Marco

Pasticceria Robiglio, a classy little café, opens up its stately dining area and sets out a few tables on the sidewalk for lunch on workdays. They have a small menu of daily pasta and *secondi* specials, and seem determined to do things like they did in the elegant, pre-tourism days (generous €8 plates, a great "fantasy salad," pretty pastries, good wines by the glass, smiling service, daily 12:00–15:00, longer hours as a café, a block towards the Duomo off Piazza S.S. Annunziata at Via dei Servi 112 red, tel. 055-212-784). Before you leave, be tempted by their pastries—famous among Florentines.

La Mescita Fiaschetteria is a characteristic hole-in-the-wall just around the corner from *David*—but a world away from all the tourism. It's where locals and students enjoy daily pasta specials and hearty sandwiches with good house wine. You can trust Mirco; just point to what looks good and eat lunch quickly, well, and inexpensively. The place can either be mobbed by local students or in a peaceful time warp, depending upon when you stop by (Mon–Sat 12:00–16:00, closed Sun, Via degli Alfani 70 red, mobile 347-795-1604).

Picnic on the Ultimate Renaissance Square: There's a handy supermarket across from the Accademia *(David)* which happily makes sandwiches to your specs (Il Centro Supermarcati, Mon–Sat 8:00–20:00, Sun 10:00–19:00, Via Ricasoli 109). Choose your fresh bread and tasty meat and cheese (assembled and sold by the weight); embellish with some veggies, milk, yogurt, or juice; and hike around the block to Piazza S.S. Annunziata, the first Renaissance square in Florence. There's a fountain for washing fruit on the square. Grab a stony seat anywhere you like, and savor one of my favorite cheap Florence eating experiences. (Or, drop by either of the two places listed above for a sandwich and juice to go.)

Eating Fast and Cheap near the Duomo

Self-Service Ristorante Leonardo is inexpensive, air-conditioned, quick, and handy. It's just a block from the Duomo, southwest of the Baptistery (tasty €4 pastas, €5 main courses, Sun–Fri 11:45–14:45 & 18:45–21:45, closed Sat, upstairs at Via Pecori 11, tel. 055-284-446). Luciano (like Pavarotti) runs the place with enthusiasm.

The Oil Shoppe cobbles together huge gourmet hot and cold sub sandwiches *all'Italiana* from creative ingredients, or you can build your own salad and pair it with a homemade soup of the day for a fast, cheap, and hearty lunch. Eat at the skinny counter or take your food to go (Mon–Fri 11:00–20:00, Sun 12:00–18:00, closed Sat, 2 long blocks east of the Duomo at Via S. Egidio 22 red, tel. 055-200-1092, cheery Alberto runs the show).

Dining near the Palazzo Vecchio

Piazza della Signoria, the scenic square facing the Palazzo Vecchio, is ringed by beautifully situated yet touristy eateries serving overpriced, bad-value, and probably microwaved food. If you're determined to eat on the square, have pizza at Ristorante il Cavallino or bar food from the Irish pub next door. The Piazza della Signoria's saving grace is **Rivoire** café, famous for its fancy desserts and thick hot chocolate. While obscenely expensive, it has the best view tables on the square (Mon–Sat 7:40–24:00, closed Sun).

Frescobaldi Ristorante and Wine Bar, the showcase of Italy's aristocratic wine family, is a wonderful restaurant. Candlelight reflects on glasses, and high-vaulted ceilings complement the elegantly presented dishes and fine wines. This is *the* place for a formal dinner in Florence. You can have a hearty plate of mixed meats and cheeses, or enjoy the modern, creative cuisine. Get as dressy as you can, and make a reservation for dinner (€12 appetizers and pastas, €17 *secondi*, Mon 19:00–23:00, Tue–Sat 12:00–14:30 & 19:00–23:00, closed Sun, lunch salads, air-con, half a block north of the Palazzo Vecchio—past the racks of bikes—at Via dei Magazzini 2–4 red, tel. 055-284-724). To show off their wines, they offer an extensive tasting menu of single glasses or fun little three-glass tasting sets (€14 Sangiovese tasting, €24 Super Tuscans).

Ristorante Paoli dishes up wonderful local cuisine to loads of cheerful eaters being served by jolly little old men under a richly frescoed Gothic vault. Because of its fame and central location, it's filled mostly with tourists, but for a classy, traditional Tuscan splurge meal, this is a decent choice (€11 pastas, €15 *secondi*, Wed–Mon 12:00–14:30 & 19:00–22:30, closed Tue, reserve for dinner, €25 tourist fixed-price meal, à la carte is pricier, midway between Piazza della Signoria and the Duomo at Via dei Tavolini 12 red, tel. 055-216-215). Salads are dramatically cut and mixed from a trolley right at your table. The walls are sweaty with memories that go back to 1824, and the service is flamboyant and fun-loving (but don't get taken—confirm prices). Woodrow Wilson slurped spaghetti here (his bust looks down on you as you eat).

Osteria del Porcellino offers a romantic setting and a seasonal fixed-price meal of Tuscan classics with a creative flair. This dark, dense, candlelit place is packed with a mix of locals and tourists and run with style and enthusiasm by friendly Enzo and his sister

Maria. In summer, they also have inviting outdoor seating in a secretive setting out back (€9 pastas, €20 *secondi*, €12 lunch specials, daily 12:00–15:00 & 19:00–24:00, reserve for dinner, great dessert list, Via Val di Lamona 7 red, half a block behind Mercato Nuovo—don't confuse it with nearby pizzeria, tel. 055-264-148).

Trattoria Nella serves good, typical Tuscan cuisine at affordable prices. Save room for the *panna cotta* cooked cream dessert (€9 pastas, €13 *secondi*, Mon–Sat 12:00–15:00 & 19:00–22:00, closed Sun, reserve for dinner, 3 blocks northwest of Ponte Vecchio, Via delle Terme 19 red, tel. 055-218-925). Twin brothers Federico and Lorenzo carry on their dad's tradition of keeping their clientele well-fed and happy.

Dining near Santa Croce

Boccadama Enoteca Ristorante is a stylish, shabby-chic wine bistro serving creative Tuscan fare based on seasonal produce. Eat in the intimate candlelit dining room or at a few tables lining tranquil Piazza Santa Croce. Reservations are smart (€9 *primi*, €14 *secondi*, daily 11:00–15:00 & 19:00–22:30, on south side of Piazza Santa Croce at 25–26 red, tel. 055-243-640).

Trattoria Anita offers a terrific lunch special midway between the Uffizi and Santa Croce: three hearty Tuscan courses (antipasto, pasta, and *secondi*) for €7—drinks are extra (Mon–Sat 12:00–14:30 & 19:30–22:00, closed Sun, on the corner of Via Vinegia and Via del Parlascio at #2 red, tel. 055-218-698).

Trattoria Icche C'è C'è (EE-kay chay chay; dialect for "whatever there is, there is") is a small, family-style eatery where fun-loving Gino and his wife Mara serve quality, traditional food, including a €13 three-course, fixed-price meal (€6 pastas, €10 *secondi*, Tue–Sun 12:30–14:30 & 19:30–22:30, closed Mon and two weeks in Aug, midway between Bargello and river at Via Magalotti 11 red, tel. 055-216-589).

Eating Cheap and Simple near the Palazzo Vecchio and Uffizi Gallery

Cantinetta dei Verrazzano is a long-established bakery/café/wine bar serving delightful sandwich plates in an elegant, old-time setting. You can grab a hot focaccia sandwich to go. Their *specialità Verrazzano* is a fine plate of four little crostini (like mini-bruschetta) proudly featuring different breads, cheeses, and meats from the Chianti region (€7.50). The *tagliere di focacce* (confirm the €6.50-per-person price), a sampler plate of mini-focaccia sandwiches, is also fun. Add a glass of Chianti to either of these dishes to make a fine, light meal. Office workers pop in for a quick lunch, and it's traditional to share tables (Mon–Sat 8:00–21:00, closed Sun, just off Via de' Calzaiuoli on a side street across from

Orsanmichele Church at Via dei Tavolini 18, tel. 055-268-590). They also have benches and tiny tables for eating at "take out" prices. Simply step to the back and point to the *focacce* sandwich (€3) you'd like, order a drink at the bar, and take away your food or sit with locals and watch the action while you munch.

Osteria Vini e Vecchi Sapori, half a block north of the Palazzo Vecchio, is a colorful 16-seat hole-in-the-wall serving traditional food, including plates of mixed crostini (€1 each—step right up and choose at the bar) and €10 daily specials. Be sure to try their raspberry *(lampone)* tiramisu (Tue–Sat 12:30–15:00 & 19:30–22:00, Sun 12:30–15:00, closed Mon; facing the bronze equestrian statue in Piazza della Signoria, go behind its tail into the corner and to your left; Via dei Magazzini 3 red, run by Mario while his wife Rosanna cooks and his son Thomas serves).

I Fratellini is a rustic little eatery where the "little brothers" have served peasants 29 different kinds of sandwiches and cheap glasses of Chianti wine (see list on wall) since 1875. Join the local crowd to order, then sit on a nearby curb or windowsill to munch, placing your glass on the wall rack before you leave (€4 for sandwich and wine, Mon–Sat 9:00–20:00 or until the bread runs out, closed Sun, 20 yards in front of Orsanmichele Church on Via dei Cimatori). Be adventurous with the menu (easy-order by number). Consider *finocchiona* (the special local salami), *lardo di Colonnata* (lard aged in Carrara marble), and *cinghiale piccante* (spicy wild boar) sandwiches. Order the most expensive wine they're selling by the glass (Brunello for €4; bottles are labeled).

L'Antico Trippaio, an antique tripe stand, a fixture in the town center, is on Via Dante Alighieri. Cheap and authentic as can be, this is where locals come daily for specialties like *panino con trippa alla fiorentina* (tripe sandwiches), *lampredotto* (cow's stomach), and a list of more appetizing sandwiches. The best place to munch your sandwich is three blocks away, on Piazza della Signoria.

'Ino Bottega di Alimentari e Vini is a stylish little shop filled with gifty edibles. Serena and Alessandro love to serve sandwiches and wine—you'll get your €5–6 sandwich on a napkin with a free glass of wine as you perch on a tiny stool. They can also make a fine *piatto misto* of cheeses and meats; just say how much you'd like to spend (Tue–Sat 11:00–20:00, Sun 12:00–17:00, closed Mon, immediately behind Uffizi Gallery on Ponte Vecchio side, Via dei Georgofili 3 red, tel. 055-219-208).

Oltrarno, South of the River
Dining with a Ponte Vecchio View

Golden View Open Bar is a lively, trendy place, good for a romantic meal or just a salad, pizza, or pasta with fine wine and a fine view of Ponte Vecchio and the Arno River. Reservations for window tables are essential (reasonable prices, €10 pizzas and big salads, daily 11:30–24:00, pizza and wine served even later, impressive wine bar, 50 yards upstream from Ponte Vecchio at Via dei Bardi 58, tel. 055-214-502, run by Francesco, Antonio, Marco, and Tomaso). They have three seating areas (with the same menu and prices) for whatever mood you're in: a riverside pizza place, a classier restaurant, and a jazzy lounge with a wine bar (serving a buffet of appetizers free with your drink from 18:00–22:00). Mixing their fine wine, river views, and live jazz makes for a wonderful evening (jazz daily at 21:00 in summer, otherwise Sat, Sun, Mon, and Wed only).

Restaurants on Via di Santo Spirito and Borgo San Jacopo

Several good and colorful restaurants line this multinamed street a block off the river in Oltrarno. You can survey the scene while exploring this still-rustic neighborhood before making a choice, but reservations are smart in the evening.

Olio & Convivium Gastronomia started as an elegant deli whose refined oil-tasting room morphed into a romantic, aristocratic restaurant. Their three intimate rooms are surrounded by fine *prosciutti*, cheeses, and wine shelves. It's an intimidating place that foodies would appreciate—quiet atmosphere, a list of €13–20 *gastronomia* plates offering an array of taste treats, and fine wines by the glass (€14 pastas, €18 *secondi*, Mon 10:00–14:30, Tue–Sat 10:00–14:30 & 17:30–22:30, closed Sun, elegant €15 lunches, strong air-con, Via di Santo Spirito 4, tel. 055-265-8198).

Antico Ristoro Di Cambi is a meat-lover's dream, thick with Tuscan traditions, rustic elegance, and T-bone steaks. As you walk in, you'll pass a glass case filled with red chunks of Chianina beef. These cost €35 each, and can be split by two or even more—the perfect chance to enjoy the famous *bistecca alla fiorentina*. You can enjoy the convivial woody interior, or sit outside on a square (€7 pastas, €8 *secondi*, Mon–Sat 12:00–22:30, closed Sun, closed 14:30–19:30 off-season, reserve on weekends and to sit outside, Via Sant'Onofrio 1 red, one block south of Ponte Amerigo Vespucci, tel. 055-217-134, run by Stefana and Fabio, the Cambi cousins).

Trattoria da Sergio, a tiny eatery about a block before Porta San Frediano, has homey charm and a strong local following. The food is on the gourmet side of home-cooking and therefore a bit more expensive, but it's worth the little splurge (€9 pastas, €15 *secondi*, Tue–Sun 19:30–23:00, closed Mon, reservations a must, Borgo San Frediano 145 red, tel. 055-223-449, Sergio and Marco).

Trattoria Pizzeria Dante is a thriving family-friendly place that still feels a little classy. They serve well-presented meals and

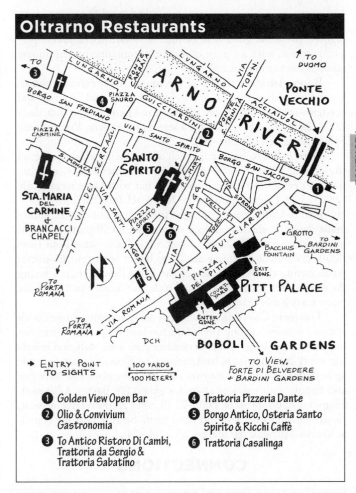

Oltrarno Restaurants

1 Golden View Open Bar

2 Olio & Convivium Gastronomia

3 To Antico Ristoro Di Cambi, Trattoria da Sergio & Trattoria Sabatino

4 Trattoria Pizzeria Dante

5 Borgo Antico, Osteria Santo Spirito & Ricchi Caffè

6 Trattoria Casalinga

thick or thin pizzas cooked in a wood-burning oven (€8 pizzas, daily 12:00–14:30 & 18:30–23:30, a block south of the Ponte alla Carraia at Piazza Nazario Sauro 12 red, tel. 055-219-219).

Trattoria Sabatino, farthest away and least touristy, is a spacious, brightly lit mess hall—disturbingly cheap, with family character and a simple menu. A super place to watch locals munch, it's just outside the Porta San Frediano (medieval gate), a 15-minute walk from Ponte Vecchio (€4 pastas, €5 *secondi*, Mon–Fri 12:00–15:00 & 19:00–22:00, closed Sat–Sun, Via Pisana 2 red, tel. 055-225-955, little English spoken).

Trendy Eateries on Piazza Santo Spirito

This classic Florentine square (a bit seedy-feeling but favored by locals) has several popular little restaurants and bars that are open nightly. They offer good local cuisine, moderate prices, and impersonal service, with a choice of indoor or romantic on-the-square seating (reservations smart).

Borgo Antico is the hit of the square, with enticing pizzas, big deluxe plates of pasta, a delightful setting, and a trendy and boisterous young local crowd (€9 pizza and pasta, €18 *secondi*, daily 12:00–24:00, best to reserve for a seat on the square, Piazza Santo Spirito 6 red, tel. 055-210-437).

Osteria Santo Spirito is much quieter, with good seating on the square, a hip, eclectic interior, good dinner salads, and reasonable prices. It's mod and youthful, but with low energy (daily 12:00–23:30, Piazza Santo Spirito 16 red, tel. 055-238-2383).

Ricchi Caffè, next to Borgo Antico, has fine gelato, homemade desserts, shaded outdoor tables, and €4.50 pasta dishes at lunch (Mon–Sat 7:00–24:00, closed Sun). The cocktail hour from 18:00–21:00 includes a free antipasto buffet with your €6 drink. After noting the plain facade of the Brunelleschi church facing the square, step inside the café and pick your favorite picture of the many ways it might be finished.

Trattoria Casalinga, an inexpensive standby, comes with aproned women bustling around the kitchen. It's probably been too popular for too long, as the service has gone a bit surly and it feels like every student group, backpacker, and Florentine artisan ends up here. Still, locals and tourists alike pack the place and leave full and happy, with euros to spare for gelato (€6 pastas, €7 *secondi*, Mon–Sat 12:00–14:30 & 19:00–21:30, after 20:00 reserve or wait, closed Sun and Aug, just off Piazza Santo Spirito, near the church at Via dei Michelozzi 9 red, tel. 055-218-624).

CONNECTIONS

From Florence by Train to: Livorno—port of call for many cruise ships (hourly, 1.5 hrs), **La Spezia** (for the Cinque Terre, at least hourly, 2.5 hrs, most involve change in Pisa), **Milan** (at least hourly, 3 hrs), **Venice** (nearly hourly, 3–3.5 hrs, may transfer in Bologna; often crowded so make reservations), **Rome** (2/hr, 1.5–2.5 hrs, most connections require seat reservations), **Interlaken** (6/day, 6.25–7.75 hrs, 3 changes, overnight possible), **Frankfurt** (9/day, 12–13 hrs, 1–3 changes), **Paris** (7/day, 12–15 hrs, 1–2 changes, important to reserve overnight train ahead), **Vienna** (1 direct overnight train, or 9/day with 1–3 changes, 10–16 hrs).

Buses: The SITA bus station (100 yards west of the Florence train station on Via Santa Caterina da Siena) is traveler-friendly—a big, old-school lot with numbered stalls and all the services you'd expect. Schedules for regional trips are posted everywhere, and TV monitors show imminent departures. Bus service drops dramatically on Sunday. You'll find buses to: **San Gimignano** (hourly, 1.25–2 hrs, €6, change in Poggibonsi), **Siena** (2/hr, 1.25-hr *corse rapide* buses are faster than the train, avoid the 2-hr *diretta* buses unless you have time to enjoy the beautiful scenery en route, €6.50), **Volterra** (3–4/day, 2 hrs, change in Colle Val d'Elsa, €7.50), and the **airport** (2/hr, 20 min, €4.50). Buy tickets in the station if possible, as you'll pay 30 percent more if you buy tickets on the bus (except for the airport bus). Bus info: tel. 800-373-760 (Mon–Fri 8:30–18:30, Sat 8:30–12:30, closed Sun); some schedules are listed in the *Florence Concierge Information* magazine.

Taxi: For small groups with more money than time, zipping to nearby towns by taxi can be a good value (e.g., €120 from your Florence hotel to your Siena hotel).

Airports

Florence's Amerigo Vespucci Airport is several miles northwest of Florence (open 5:10–24:00, no overnighting allowed, TI, cash machines, car-rental agencies, airport info tel. 055-306-1740, flight info tel. 055-306-1700—domestic only, www.aeroporto.firenze.it). Shuttle buses (far right of airport as you exit arrivals hall) connect the airport with Florence's SITA bus station, 100 yards west of the train station on Via Santa Caterina da Siena (2/hr, 30 min, daily 5:30–23:30, €4.50). Allow about €20 for a taxi.

Pisa's Galileo Galilei Airport handles international and domestic flights (TI open daily 11:00–23:00, cash machine, car-rental agencies, baggage storage from 8:00–20:00 only, €7/bag; self-service cafeteria, flight info tel. 050-849-300, www.pisa-airport.com).

THE CINQUE TERRE

The Cinque Terre (CHINK-weh TAY-reh), a remote chunk of the Italian Riviera, is the traffic-free, lowbrow, underappreciated alternative to the French Riviera. There's not a museum in sight. Just sun, sea, sand (pebbles), wine, and pure, unadulterated Italy. Enjoy the villages, swimming, hiking, and evening romance of one of God's great gifts to tourism. For a home base, choose among five *(cinque)* villages, each of which fills a ravine with a lazy hive of human activity—callused locals, sunburned travelers, and no Vespas. While the Cinque Terre is now discovered (and can be quite crowded midday, when tourist boats drop by), I've never seen happier, more relaxed tourists.

The chunk of coast was first described in medieval times as "the five lands." In the feudal era, this land was watched over by castles. Tiny communities grew up in their protective shadows, ready to run inside at the first hint of a Turkish Saracen pirate raid. Marauding pirates from North Africa were a persistent problem until about 1400. Many locals were kidnapped and ransomed or sold into slavery, and those who remained built fires on flat-roofed watchtowers to relay warnings—alerting the entire coast to imminent attacks. The last major raid was in 1545.

As the threat of pirates faded, the villages prospered, catching fish and growing grapes. Churches were enlarged with a growing population. But until the advent of tourism in this generation, the towns remained isolated. Even today, traditions survive, and each of the five villages comes with a distinct dialect and its own proud heritage.

Sadly, a few ugly, noisy Americans are giving tourism a bad name here. Even hip, young locals are put off by loud, drunken tourists. They say—and I agree—that the Cinque Terre is an exceptional place. It deserves a special dignity. Party in Viareggio or Portofino, but be mellow in the Cinque Terre. Talk softly. Help keep it clean. In spite of the tourist crowds, it's still a real community, and we are its guests.

In this chapter, I cover the five towns in order from east to west, from Riomaggiore to Monterosso. Since I still get the names of the towns mixed up, I think of them by number: #1 Riomaggiore (a workaday town), #2 Manarola (picturesque), #3 Corniglia (on a hilltop), #4 Vernazza (the region's cover girl, the most touristy and dramatic), and #5 Monterosso al Mare (the closest thing to a beach resort of the five towns).

Arrival in the Cinque Terre

Big, fast trains from elsewhere in Italy speed past the Cinque Terre (though some stop in Monterosso and Riomaggiore). Unless you're coming from a nearby town, you'll have to change trains at least once to reach Manarola, Corniglia, or Vernazza.

Generally, if you're coming from the north, you'll be changing trains in Genoa (specifically, the Genova Piazza Principe station). If you're coming from the south or east, you'll most likely have to switch trains in La Spezia (see "Connections" at the end of this chapter). No matter where you're coming from, it's best to check in the station before you leave to see your full schedule and route options (use the computerized kiosks or ask at a ticket window). Don't forget to validate your ticket by stamping it—ka-CHUNK!—in the yellow machines located on train platforms and elsewhere in the station. Conductors here are notorious for levying stiff fines on forgetful tourists. For more information on riding the train between Cinque Terre towns, see "Getting Around the Cinque Terre," later in this section.

If the Cinque Terre is your first, last, or only stop on this trip, consider flying into Pisa, Genoa, or Florence, rather than Milan. These airports are less confusing than Milan's, and closer to the Cinque Terre.

Planning Your Time

The ideal minimum stay is two nights and a completely uninterrupted day. The Cinque Terre is served by the local train from Genoa and La Spezia. Speed demons arrive in the morning, check their bags in La Spezia, take the five-hour hike through all five towns, laze away the afternoon on the beach or rock of their choice, and zoom away on the overnight train to somewhere back in the real world. But be warned: The Cinque Terre has a strange way of messing up your momentum. (The evidence is the number of Americans who have fallen in love with the region and/or one of its residents...and are still here.) Frankly, staying fewer than two nights is a mistake that you'll likely regret.

The towns are just a few minutes apart by hourly train or boat. There's no checklist of sights or experiences—just a hike, the towns themselves, and your fondest vacation desires. Study this chapter in advance and piece together your best day, mixing hiking, swimming, trains, and a boat ride. For the best light and coolest temperatures, start your hike early.

Market days perk up the towns from 8:00–13:00 on Tuesday in Vernazza, Wednesday in Levanto, Thursday in Monterosso, and Friday in La Spezia.

The winter is really dead—most hotels close in December and January. The long Easter weekend (April 2–5 in 2010) and July and August are peak of peak, the toughest time to find rooms. In spring, the towns can feel inundated with Italian school groups day-tripping on spring excursions (they can't afford to sleep in this expensive region). For more information on the region, see www .cinqueterre.it.

The Cinque Terre National Park

The creation of the Cinque Terre National Marine Park in 1999 has brought lots of money (all visitors pay a fee to hike the trails), new restrictions on land and sea to protect wildlife, and lots of concrete bolstering walkways, trails, beaches, breakwaters, and docks. Each village has a park-sponsored information center, and two towns have tiny, nearly worthless folk museums. The park is run by a powerful man—nicknamed "The Pharaoh" for his gran- diose visions—who seems to double as Riomaggiore's mayor. For the latest, see www.parconazionale5terre.it.

Cinque Terre Cards

Visitors hiking between the towns need to pay a park entrance fee. This fee keeps the trails safe and open, and pays for viewpoints, picnic spots, WCs, and more. The popular coastal trail generates enough revenue to subsidize the development of trails and outdoor activities higher in the hills.

You have two options for covering the park fee: the Cinque Terre Card (the better deal) or the Cinque Terre Treno Card. Note that both are valid until midnight on the expiration date. Write your name on your card or risk a big fine.

The **Cinque Terre Card,** good for one day of hiking, costs €5 (includes map; €8/2 days, €10/3 days, €20/7 days; kids under 4 free, discounts for youth, seniors, and families, see www.parconazionale 5terre.it for details). It covers all trails, shuttle buses, and park museums, but not trains or boats. Buy it at trailheads, at national park offices, and at most train stations (no validation required).

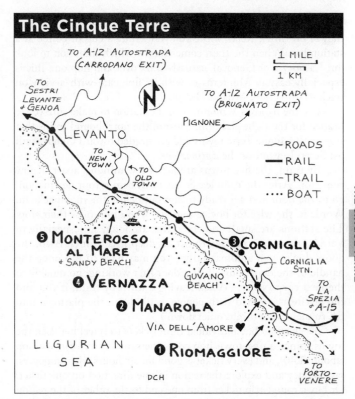

The Cinque Terre

The **Cinque Terre Treno Card** covers what the Cinque Terre Card does, plus the use of the local trains (from Levanto to La Spezia, including all Cinque Terre towns). It's sold at TIs inside train stations—but not at trailheads—and comes with a map, information brochure, and train schedule (€9/1 day, €15/2 days, €20/3 days, €37/week, kids 4–11 half-price, under 4 free; validate card at train station by punching it in the yellow machine). This card is not a good value, because you'd have to hike and take three train trips every day just to break even.

Getting Around the Cinque Terre

Within the Cinque Terre, you'll get around the villages more cheaply by train, but more scenically by boat. And any way you do it, a visit here comes with lots of stairs and climbing.

By Train

Along the coast here, trains go in only two directions: "per (to) Genova" (the Italian spelling of Genoa) or "per La Spezia." Assuming you're on vacation, accept the unpredictability of Cinque

Terre trains (they're often late...unless you are, too—in which case they're on time). Relax while you wait—buy a cup of coffee at a station bar. When the train comes (know which direction to look for: La Spezia or Genova), casually walk over and hop on. This is especially easy in Monterosso, with its fine café-with-a-view on track #1 (direction: Milano/Genova).

Use the handy TV monitors in the station to make sure you're headed for the right platform. Most of the northbound trains that stop at all Cinque Terre towns and are headed toward Genova will list Sestri Levante as the *destinazione.*

By train, the five towns are just a few minutes apart. Know your stop. After the train leaves the town before your destination, go to the door and get ready to slip out before the mob packs in. Words to the wise for novice tourists, who often miss their stop: The stations are small and the trains are long, so (especially in Vernazza) you might have to get off deep in a tunnel. Also, the doors don't open automatically—you may have to flip open the handle of the door yourself. If a door isn't working, go quickly to the next car to leave. (When leaving a town by train, if you find the platform jammed with people, walk down the platform into the tunnel where things quiet down.)

It's cheap to buy individual train tickets to travel between the towns. Since a one-town hop costs the same as a five-town hop (about €1.40), and every ticket is good for six hours with stopovers, save money and explore the region in one direction on one ticket. Or buy a round-trip ticket from one end to the other of the region (e.g., round-trip from Monterosso to Riomaggiore and back)— it functions as a six-hour pass. Stamp the ticket at the station machine before you board. Riding without a validated ticket is very expensive (minimum €25 fine) if you meet a conductor. If you have a Eurailpass, don't spend one of your valuable flexi-days on the cheap Cinque Terre.

In general, I'd skip the train from Riomaggiore to Manarola (the trains are unreliable, and the 15-min Via dell'Amore stroll is a delight—see page 972 for more on this path).

Cinque Terre Train Schedule: Since the train is the Cinque Terre's lifeline, many shops and restaurants post the current schedule, and most hotels offer copies of it. Carry a schedule with you— it'll come in handy (one comes with the Cinque Terre Card). Note that fast trains leaving La Spezia zip right through the Cinque Terre; some stop only in Monterosso (town #1) and Riomaggiore (town #5). But any train that stops in Manarola, Corniglia, and Vernazza (towns #2, #3, and #4) will stop in all five towns (including the trains on the below schedule).

All of the times listed below were accurate as of 2009; most are daily and a few run Monday through Saturday, while others (not listed here) operate only on Sundays.

Trains leave La Spezia for the Cinque Terre villages at 7:12, 8:12, 10:07, 11:10, 12:00, 13:17, 13:25, 14:06, 15:10, 15:25, 16:01, 17:05, 17:13, 17:25, 18:06, 19:10, 19:37, 20:18, 21:21, 22:22, 23:10, and 00:50.

Going back to La Spezia, trains leave Monterosso at 6:20, 7:12, 8:12, 9:29, 10:28, 11:17, 12:06, 12:19, 12:40, 13:26, 14:04, 14:09, 14:20, 15:24, 16:07, 16:17, 17:30, 18:08, 18:20, 19:24, 20:20, 20:32, 20:43, 21:32, 22:24, 23:11, and 23:44 (same trains depart Vernazza about four minutes later).

Convenient TV monitors posted at several places in each station clearly show exactly what times the next trains are leaving in each direction (and if they're late, how late they are expected to be). I trust these monitors much more than my ability to read any printed schedule.

By Boat

From Easter through October, a daily boat service connects Monterosso, Vernazza, Manarola, Riomaggiore, and Portovenere. Boats provide a scenic way to get from town to town and survey what you just hiked. And boats offer the only efficient way to visit the nearby resort of Portovenere (the alternative is a tedious train/bus connection via La Spezia). In peaceful weather, the boats can be more reliable than the trains, but if seas are rough, they don't run at all. Because the boats nose in and tourists have to gingerly disembark onto little more than a plank, even a small chop can cancel some or all of the stops.

I see the tour boats as a syringe, injecting each town with a boost of euros. The towns are addicted, and they shoot up hourly through the summer. (Between 10:00–15:00—especially on weekends—masses of gawkers unload from boats, tour buses, and cruise ships, inundating the villages and changing the tenor of the region.)

Boats depart Monterosso about hourly (10:30–18:00), stopping at the Cinque Terre towns (except at Corniglia) and ending up an hour later in Portovenere. (The Portovenere–Monterosso boats run 9:00–17:00.) The ticket price depends on the length of the boat ride (short hops-€3–4, longer hops-€8, five-town all-day pass-€12.50). Round-trip tickets are slightly cheaper than two one-way trips. You can buy tickets at little stands at each town's harbor (tel. 0187-732-987 and 0187-818-440). Another all-day boat pass for €20 extends to Portovenere and includes a 40-minute, scenic ride around three small islands (2/day). Boats are not covered by the Cinque Terre Card. Boat schedules are posted at docks, harbor bars, Cinque Terre park offices, and hotels.

By Shuttle Bus

Shuttle buses connect each Cinque Terre town with its distant parking lot and various points in the hills (for example, from Corniglia's beach and train station to its hilltop town center). Note that these shuttle buses do not connect the towns with each other. Most rides cost €1.50 (and are covered by the Cinque Terre Card)—pick up bus schedules from a Cinque Terre park office or note the times posted on bus doors and at bus stops.

Hiking the Cinque Terre

All five towns are connected by good trails, marked with red-and-white paint and some signs. You'll experience the area's best by hiking all the way from one end to the other. While you can detour to dramatic hilltop sanctuaries, I'd keep it simple by following trail #2—the low route between the villages. The entire seven-mile hike can be done in about four hours, but allow five for dawdling. Germans (with their task-oriented *Alpenstock* walking sticks) are notorious for marching too fast through the region. Take it slow...smell the cactus flowers and herbs, notice the lizards, listen to birds singing in the olive groves, and enjoy vistas on all sides.

Trails can be closed in bad weather or because of landslides. Remember that hikers need to pay a fee to enter the trails (see "Cinque Terre Cards," near the beginning of this chapter). If you're hiking the entire five-town route, consider that the trails between Riomaggiore (#1), Manarola (#2), and Corniglia (#3) are easiest. The trail from Vernazza (#4) to Monterosso (#5) is the most challenging. For that hike, you might want to start in Monterosso in order to tackle the toughest section while you're fresh and to enjoy the region's most dramatic scenery as you approach Vernazza. I get emails from many readers who say this trail was tougher than they expected. While it is a bit of a challenge, it's perfectly doable for any fit walker...and worth the sweat.

Maps aren't necessary for the basic coastal hikes described here. But for the expanded version of this hike (12 hours, from Portovenere to Levanto) and more serious hikes in the high country, pick up a good hiking map (about €5, sold everywhere). To leave the park cleaner than when you found it, bring a plastic bag *(sacchetto di plastica)* and pick up a little trail trash along the way. It would be great if American visitors—who get so much joy out of this region—were known for this good deed.

Riomaggiore–Manarola (20 min): Facing the front of the train station in Riomaggiore (#1), go up the stairs to the right, following signs for *Via dell'Amore*. The film-gobbling promenade—wide enough for baby strollers—winds along the coast to Manarola (#2). While there's no beach here, stairs lead down to sunbathing rocks. A long tunnel and mega-nets protect hikers from mean-spirited rocks. The classy, park-run Bar & Vini A Pie de Ma wine bar—located at the Riomaggiore trailhead—offers light meals, awesome town views, and clever boat storage under the train tracks (for more info, see page 981). There's also a scenic, peaceful cliffside bar on the Manarola end of the trail (daily in summer 9:00–24:00, until 20:00 off-season, light meals, drinks, picnic tables).

Manarola–Corniglia (45 min): The walk from Manarola (#2) to Corniglia (#3) is a little longer, more rugged, and less romantic than that from #1 to #2. To avoid the last stretch (switchback stairs leading up to the hill-capping town of Corniglia), catch the shuttle bus from Corniglia's train station (2/hr, €1.50, free with Cinque Terre Card, usually timed to meet the trains).

Corniglia–Vernazza (90 min): The hike from Corniglia (#3) to Vernazza (#4)—the wildest and greenest of the coast—is very rewarding. From the Corniglia station and beach, zigzag up to the town (via the steep stairs, the longer road, or the shuttle bus). Ten minutes past Corniglia, toward Vernazza, you'll see Guvano beach far beneath you (the region's nude-for-now beach, described on page 989). The scenic trail leads past a bar and picnic tables, through lots of fragrant and flowery vegetation, into Vernazza. If you need a break before reaching Vernazza, Franco's Ristorante La Torre has a small menu but big views (between meal times only drinks are served; see listing on page 1006).

Vernazza–Monterosso (90 min): The trail from Vernazza (#4) to Monterosso (#5) is a scenic, up-and-down-a-lot trek. Trails are rough (some readers report "very dangerous") and narrow, but easy to follow. Locals frown on camping at the picnic tables located midway. The views just out of Vernazza, looking back at the town, are spectacular.

Longer Hikes: Above the trails that run between the towns, higher-elevation hikes crisscross the region. Shuttle buses make the going easier, connecting villages and trailheads in the hills. Ask locally about the more difficult six-mile inland hike to Volastra. This tiny village, perched between Manarola and Corniglia, hosts the 5-Terre wine co-op. The Cantina Sociale is a third of a mile away from Volastra, in the hamlet of Groppo. If you take this high road between Manarola and Corniglia, allow two hours one-way. In return, you'll get sweeping views and a closer look at the vineyards. Shuttle buses run about hourly to Volastra from Manarola (€2.50 or free with Cinque Terre Card, pick up schedule from park office); consider taking the bus up and hiking down.

Swimming, Kayaking, and Biking

Every town in the Cinque Terre has a beach or a rocky place to swim. Monterosso has the biggest and sandiest, with beach umbrellas and beach-use fees (but it's free where there are no umbrellas). Vernazza's is tiny—better for sunning than swimming. Manarola and Riomaggiore have the worst beaches (no sand), but Manarola offers the best deep-water swimming.

Wear your walking shoes and pack your swim gear. Several of the beaches have showers (no shampoo, please). Underwater sightseeing is full of fish—goggles are sold in local shops. Sea urchins can be a problem if you walk on the rocks. If you have swim shoes, this is the place to wear them.

You can rent kayaks in Riomaggiore, Vernazza, and Monterosso. (For details, see individual town listings in this chapter.) Some readers say kayaking can be dangerous—the kayaks tip easily, training is not provided, and lifejackets are not required.

Mountain biking is also possible (park info booths in each town have details on rentals and maps of trails high above the coast).

Sleeping in the Cinque Terre

If you think too many people have my book, avoid Vernazza. Monterosso is a good choice for the younger crowd (more nightlife) and rich, sun-worshipping softies (who prefer the comfort and ease of a real hotel). Hermits, anarchists, wine-lovers, and mountain goats like Corniglia. Sophisticated Italians and Germans choose Manarola. Riomaggiore is bigger than Vernazza and less resorty than Monterosso.

While the Cinque Terre is too rugged for the mobs that ravage the Spanish and French coasts, it's popular with Italians, Germans, and in-the-know Americans. Hotels charge more and are packed on holidays, in July and August, and on Fridays and Saturdays all summer. August weekends are worst. But €65–70 doubles abound throughout the year. For a terrace or view, you might pay an extra €20 or more. Apartments for four can be economical for families—figure on €100–120.

Book ahead if you'll be visiting in June, July, August, on a weekend, or around a holiday. At other times, you can land a double room on any day by just arriving in town (ideally by noon) and asking around at bars and restaurants, or simply by approaching locals on the street. Many travelers enjoy the opportunity to shop around a bit and get the best price by bargaining. Private rooms—called *affitta camere*—are no longer an intimate stay with a family. They are generally comfortable apartments (often with small kitchens) where you get the key and come and go as you like, rarely seeing your landlord. Many landowners rent the buildings by the year to local managers, who then attempt to make a profit by filling them night after night with tourists.

For the best value, visit three private rooms and snare the best. Going direct cuts out a middleman and softens prices. Staying more than one night gives you bargaining leverage. Plan on paying cash. Private rooms are generally bigger and more comfortable than those offered by the pensions and offer the same privacy as a hotel room.

If you want the security of a reservation, make it at a hotel long in advance (smaller places generally don't take reservations very far ahead). Query by email, not fax. If you do reserve, honor your reservation (or, if you must cancel, do it as early as possible). Since people renting rooms usually don't take deposits, they lose money if you don't show up. Cutthroat room hawkers at the train stations might try to lure you away from a room that you've already reserved with offers of cheaper rates. Don't do it. You owe it to your hosts to stick with your original reservation.

Helpful Hints for the Cinque Terre

Tourist and Park Information: Each town (except Corniglia) has a well-staffed TI and park office (listed throughout this chapter).

Money: Banks and ATMs are plentiful throughout the region.

Baggage Storage: You can leave your bags in Riomaggiore (see "Helpful Hints," next page.

Services: Every train station has a handy public WC. Otherwise, pop into a bar or restaurant.

Local Guides: Andrea Bordigoni (€110/half-day, €175/day, mobile 347-972-3317, bordigo@inwind.it) and **Paola Tommarchi** (mobile 334-109-7887, paolatomma1966@libero.it) both offer good tours.

Cheap Tricks: Consider arriving without a reservation and bargaining with locals for a private room; staying more than one night and paying cash should get you a double for around €50 (this is possible anytime, but safest on weekdays Sept–May). Many rooms come with kitchenettes, and bakeries and food shops make meals to go. Picnic tables along the trail come with a first-class view. Even hobos can afford the major delights of the Cinque Terre: hiking, nursing a drink at the harbor, strolling with the locals through town, and enjoying the beach.

Riomaggiore (Town #1)

The most substantial non-resort town of the group, Riomaggiore is a disappointment from the train station. But walk through the tunnel next to the train tracks (or ride the elevator through the hillside to the top of town), and you land in a fascinating tangle of pastel homes leaning on each other like drunken sailors.

Orientation

Tourist Information

The TI and park information office are inside the train station (daily 6:30–21:00 in summer, until 20:00 in winter, tel. 0187-920-633). If the TI in the station is crowded, buy your hiking pass at the Cinque Terre park shop next door, or at the kiosk next to the stairs that lead to the Via dell'Amore trail. A less-formal information source is Ivo, who runs the Bar Centrale (see page 979).

Arrival in Riomaggiore

The bus shuttles locals and tourists up and down Riomaggiore's steep main street and continues to the parking lot outside of town (€1.50 one-way, €2.50 round-trip, free with Cinque Terre Card, 2/hr, main stop at the fork of Via Colombo and Via Malborghetto, or flag it down as it passes). The bus heads into the hills, where you'll find the region's top high-country activities (for details, see page 979).

Helpful Hints

Internet Access: The park office provides eight Internet terminals upstairs (daily 8:00–22:00 in summer, until 20:00 in winter).

Baggage Storage: The park office will watch your bags (€0.50/hr per piece, plus €6 surcharge if left longer than 6 hours, daily 8:00–19:45).

Laundry: A self-service launderette is on the main street (€3.50 wash, €3.50 dry, daily 8:00–20:00, run by Edi's Rooms next door, Via Colombo 111).

Self-Guided Walk

Welcome to Riomaggiore

Here's an easy loop trip that maximizes views and minimizes uphill walking.

• *Start at the train station. (If you arrive by boat, cross beneath the tracks and take a left, then hike through the tunnel along the tracks to reach the station.) You'll come to some...*

Riomaggiore

VIA DELL' AMORE TO MANAROLA

MURALS

TRAIN STATION

CINQUE TERRE INFO

ELEVATOR TO HIGH ROAD

SAN GIOVANNI CHURCH

PED. TUNNEL

VIA GASPERI

SIGNORINI

VIA SANT.

VIA COLOMBO

V. MALB.

LIGURIAN SEA

NOT TO SCALE

HARBOR

BOAT DOCK

BOAT TICKETS

"BEACH" SWIMMING + SHOWERS

STAIRS

DCH

TO

N

1 Locanda del Sole
2 Locanda Ca' dei Duxi
3 Edi's Rooms & Launderette
4 Mar Mar Rooms & Kayaks
5 La Dolce Vita Rooms
6 Locanda dalla Compagnia
7 Ristorante la Lampara
8 La Lanterna Restaurant
9 Ristorante Ripa del Sole

10 Te La Do Io La Merenda Snack Bar
11 Bar & Vini A Pie de Ma
12 Co-op Grocery
13 Bar Centrale & Gelateria
14 Enoteca Dau Cila
15 Boat Dock
16 To Madonna di Montenero Trail
17 To Torre Guardiola Botanical Pathway & WWII Bunkers

THE CINQUE TERRE

Colorful Murals: These murals, with subjects modeled after real-life Riomaggiorians, glorify the nameless workers who constructed the nearly 300 million cubic feet of dry stone walls (without cement). These walls run throughout the Cinque Terre, giving the region its characteristic *muri a secco* terracing for vineyards and olive groves. The murals, done by Argentinean artist Silvio Benedetto, are well-explained in English.

• *Head to the railway tunnel entrance, and ride the elevator to the top of town (€0.50 or €1 family ticket, free with Cinque Terre Card, daily 8:00–19:45). You're at the...*

Top o' the Town: Here you're treated to spectacular sea views. To continue the view-fest, go right and follow the walkway (ignore the steps marked *Marina Seacoast* that lead to the harbor). It's a five-minute level stroll to the church. You'll pass under the city hall (flying two flags) with murals celebrating the heroic grape pickers and fishermen of the region (also by Silvio Benedetto).

• *Before reaching the church, pause to enjoy the...*

Town View: The major river of this region once ran through this valley, as implied by the name Riomaggiore (local dialect for "river" and "major"). As in the other Cinque Terre towns, the river ravine is now paved over, and the romantic arched bridges that once connected the two sides have been replaced by a practical modern road.

Notice the lack of ugly aerial antennae. In the 1980s, every residence got cable. Now, the TV tower on the hilltop behind the church steeple brings the modern world into each home. While the church was rebuilt in 1870, it was first built in 1340. It's dedicated to St. John the Baptist, the patron saint of Genoa, a maritime republic that dominated the region.

• *Continue past the church down to Riomaggiore's main street, named...*

Via Colombo: Just past the WC, you'll see flower boxes on the street, which sometimes block it. The boxes slide back electronically to let the shuttle bus past. Walk about 30 feet after the flower box, and pop into the tiny Cinque Terre Antiche museum (€0.50, free with Cinque Terre Card, daily 10:00–17:00). You can sit down for a few minutes to watch a circa-1950 video of the Cinque Terre.

Continuing down Via Colombo, you'll pass a bakery, a couple of grocery shops, and the self-service laundry. There's homemade gelato next to the Bar Centrale. When Via Colombo dead-ends, to the left you'll find the stairs down to the Marina neighborhood, with the harbor, the boat dock, a 200-yard trail to the beach *(spiaggia),* and an inviting little art gallery. To the right of the stairs is the tunnel, running alongside the tracks, which takes you directly back to the station and the trail to the other towns. From here, you can take a train, hop a boat, or hike to your next destination.

Activities

Beach—Riomaggiore's rugged and tiny "beach" is rocky, but it's clean and peaceful. Take a two-minute walk from the harbor: Face the harbor, then follow the path to your left. Passing the rugged boat landing, stay on the path to the beach.

Kayaks and Water Sports—The town has a diving center (scuba, snorkeling, kayaks, and small motorboats; office under the tracks on Via San Giacomo, May–Sept daily 8:00–22:00, tel. 0187-920-011, www.5terrediving.com).

Hikes—Consider the cliff-hanging trail that leads from the beach up to old WWII bunkers and the hilltop botanical pathway of native flora and fauna with English information (free with Cinque Terre Card, daily 10:00–16:30, steep 20-minute climb, take the stairs between the boat dock and the beach, located at Torre Guardiola). Another trail climbs scenically to the 14th-century Madonna di Montenero sanctuary, high above the town (30 min, take the main road inland until you see signs). Or ride the green shuttle bus 12 minutes from the town center to the sanctuary trail, then walk uphill five minutes (details at park office). The park center at the sanctuary offers bike rental.

Nightlife

Bar Centrale, run by sociable Ivo, Alberto, and the gang, offers "nightlife" any time of day—making it a good stop for Italian breakfast and music. Ivo, who lived in San Francisco and speaks good English, fills his bar with San Franciscan rock and a fun-loving vibe. During the day, this is a shaded place to relax with other travelers. At night, it offers the younger set the liveliest action (and best *mojitos*) in town. They also serve €5 fast-food pastas and microwaved pizzas (daily 7:30–24:00, closed Mon in winter, in the town center at Via Colombo 144, tel. 0187-920-208). There's a good *gelateria* next door.

Enoteca Dau Cila, a cool little bar down at the miniscule harbor with a mellow jazz-and-Brazilian-lounge ambience, is a counterpoint to wild Bar Centrale (small meals and salads, fine wine by the glass, April–Oct daily and nightly until midnight, tel. 0187-760-032, Fausto and Luca).

Bar & Vini A Pie de Ma, at the beginning of the Via dell'Amore, has piles of charm, often music, and stays open until midnight in the summer (see "Eating," page 981, for full listing).

The marvelous **Via dell'Amore** trail, lit only with subtle ground lighting so that you can see the stars, welcomes romantics after dark. The trail is free after 19:30.

Sleeping

Riomaggiore has arranged its private-room rental system better than its neighbors. But with organization (and middlemen) come higher prices. Several agencies—with regular office hours, English-speaking staff, and email addresses—line up within a few yards of each other on the main drag. Each manages a corral of local rooms for rent. These offices can close unexpectedly, so it's smart to settle

THE CINQUE TERRE

Sleep Code

(€1 = about $1.40, country code: 39)

S = Single, **D** = Double/Twin, **T** = Triple, **Q** = Quad, **b** = bathroom, **s** = shower only. Unless otherwise noted, credit cards are accepted, English is spoken, and breakfast is included (except in Vernazza).

To help you sort easily through these listings, I've divided the rooms into three categories based on the price for a standard double room with bath:

$$$ Higher Priced—Most rooms €100 or more.
$$ Moderately Priced—Most rooms between €50-100.
$ Lower Priced—Most rooms €50 or less.

---

up the day before you leave in case they're closed when you need to depart. Expect lots of stairs. Private parking will run you an extra €10–20. If you don't mind the hike, the street above town has safe overnight parking (free 20:00–8:00).

Room-Finding Services

$$$ Locanda del Sole has seven basic and overpriced rooms with a shared and peaceful terrace. Located at the utilitarian top end of town, it's a five-minute walk to the center. The easy parking makes it especially appealing to drivers (Db-€110 April–June and Sept–Oct, Db-€120 July–Aug, free parking with this book, Via Santuario 114, tel. & fax 0187-920-773, mobile 340-983-0090, www.locandadelsole.net, info@locandadelsole.net, Enrico).

$$$ Locanda Ca' dei Duxi rents ten good rooms from an efficient little office on the main drag (Db-€100–120 depending on view and season, extra person-€20, cash discount, air-con, open all year, Via Colombo 36, tel. & fax 0187-920-036, mobile 329-825-7836, www.duxi.it, info@duxi.it, Samuele).

$$ Edi's Rooms rents 20 rooms and apartments. You pay extra for views. Edi and her partner Luana get my "best business practices" award for this town (Db-€60–100 depending on room, apartment Qb-€100–150, reserve with credit card but pay with cash, office open daily 8:30–20:00 in summer, winter 9:00–12:30 & 14:30–19:00, Via Colombo 111, tel. 0187-760-842, tel. & fax 0187-920-325, edi-vesigna@iol.it).

$$ Mar Mar Rooms offers 12 rooms and 15 apartments, with American expat Amy smoothing communications (Db-€60–90 depending on view, cash only, reception open 9:00–17:00 in season, 30 yards above train tracks on main drag next to Ristorante la Lampara at Via Malborghetto 4, tel. & fax 0187-920-932, www.5terre-marmar.com, info@5terre-marmar.com). They also run a mini-hostel in a fine communal apartment with a cool living room, terrace, and kitchen in a good, quiet location. Take care of this little treasure so it survives (9 beds in 3 rooms, €22/bed).

$$ La Dolce Vita, across from Edi's, above, offers five rooms and eight apartments (Sb-€35, Db-€55–70, open daily 9:30–19:30; if they're closed, they're full; Via Colombo 120, tel. & fax 0187-760-044, mobile 349-326-6803, www.ladolcevita5terre.com, agonatal@interfree.it, Giacomo and Simone).

$$ Locanda dalla Compagnia rents five modern rooms at the top of town, just 300 yards below the parking lot and the little church. All rooms—among the nicest in town—are on the same airy ground floor, sharing an inviting lounge. Franca runs it with Giovanna's help (Db-€70 April–Sept, Db-€50 Oct–March, cash only, air-con, mini-fridge, no view, Via del Santuario 232, tel. 0187-760-050, fax 0187-920-586, lacomp@libero.it).

Eating

Ristorante la Lampara, decorated like a ship, serves a *frutti di mare* pizza, *trenette al pesto*, and the aromatic *spaghetti al cartoccio*—€11 oven-cooked spaghetti with seafood in foil (daily 7:00–24:00, closed Tue in winter, just above tracks off Via Colombo at Via Malborghetto 10, tel. 0187-920-120).

La Lanterna, dressier than the Lampara, is wedged into a niche in the Marina, overlooking the harbor under the tracks (daily 12:00–22:00, Via San Giacomo 10, tel. 0187-920-589).

Ristorante Ripa del Sole is the local pick for an elegant night out, with the same prices and better quality than the Lampara and Lanterna (Tue–Sun 18:30–22:00, closed Mon, closed Jan–Feb, 10-min hike above town, Via de Gasperi 282, tel. 0187-920-143).

Te La Do Io La Merenda ("I'll Give You a Snack") is good for a snack, pizza, or takeout. Their counter is piled with an assortment of munchies, and they have pastas, roasted chicken, and focaccia sandwiches to go (daily 9:00–21:30, Via Colombo 161, tel. 0187-920-148).

Bar & Vini A Pie de Ma, at the trailhead on the Manarola end of town, is a nice place for a scenic light bite or quiet drink at night. Enjoying a meal at a table on its dramatically situated terrace provides an indelible Cinque Terre memory (daily 10:00–20:00, until 24:00 in summer).

Picnics: Groceries and delis on Via Colombo sell food to go, including pizza slices, for a picnic at the harbor or beach. The **Co-op grocery** is least expensive and will make sandwiches to go (Via Colombo 55).

Manarola (Town #2)

Like Riomaggiore, Manarola is attached to its station by a 200-yard-long tunnel. During WWII air raids, these tunnels provided refuge and a safe place for rattled villagers to sleep. The town itself fills a ravine, bookended by its wild little harbor to the west and a diminutive church square inland to the east. A delightful and gentle stroll, from the church down to the harborside park, provides the region's easiest little vineyard walk (described under "Self-Guided Walk," below).

Orientation

Arrival in Manarola

A shuttle bus runs between the low end of Manarola's main street (at the *tabacchi* shop and newsstand) and the parking lot (€1.50 one-way, €2.50 round-trip, free with Cinque Terre Card, 2/hr, just flag it down). Shuttle buses also run about hourly from Manarola to Volastra (see "Longer Hikes," page 973).

To get to the dock and the boats that connect Manarola with the other Cinque Terre towns, find the steps to the left of the harbor view—they lead down to the ticket kiosk. Continue around the left side of the cliff (as you're facing the water) to catch the boats.

Self-Guided Walk

Welcome to Manarola

From the harbor, this 30-minute circular walk shows you the town and surrounding vineyards, and ends at a fantastic viewpoint.

• *Start down at the waterfront.*

The Harbor: Manarola is tiny and picturesque, a tumble of buildings bunny-hopping down its ravine to the fun-loving waterfront. Notice how the I-beam crane launches the boats. Facing the harbor, look to the right, at the hillside Punta Bonfiglio cemetery and park (where this walk ends).

The town's swimming hole is just below. Manarola has no sand, but offers the best deep-water swimming in the area. The first "beach" has a shower, ladder, and wonderful rocks. The second has tougher access and no shower, but feels more remote and pristine (follow the paved path toward Corniglia, just around the point). For many, the tricky access makes this beach dangerous.

• *Hiking inland up the town's main drag, you'll come to the train tracks covered by Manarola's new square, called...*

Piazza Capellini: Built in 2004, this square is an all-around great idea, giving the town a safe, fun zone for kids. Locals living

Manarola

NOT TO SCALE

TO CORNIGLIA

‖‖ STAIRS
ⱽ VIEW

SWIMMING

CEMETERY
PIAZZA

5

SAN
LORENZO
CHURCH

TO PARKING

PUNTA BONFIGLIO

3
6
7
4
2
1

CHAPEL

SWIMMING + SHOWER

MAIN ST.

BELL TOWER

PEDESTRIAN TUNNEL

BOAT DOCK

8

TRAIN STATION

LIGURIAN

VIA DELL' AMORE TRAIL

SEA

TO RIOMAGGIORE

❶ La Torretta Rooms
❷ Albergo Ca' d'Andrean
❸ Marina Piccola Rooms & Restaurant
❹ Carugiu B&B & Casa Capellini

❺ Ostello 5-Terre
❻ Trattoria Il Porticciolo
❼ Shuttle Bus to Parking Lot & Volastra
❽ Manarola Vineyard Walk

THE CINQUE TERRE

near the tracks also enjoy a little less noise. Check out the mosaic that displays the varieties of local fish in colorful enamel.

• *Fifty yards uphill, you'll find the...*

Sciacchetrà Museum: Run by the national park, it's hardly a museum. But pop in to its inviting room to see a tiny exhibit on the local wine industry (€0.50, free with Cinque Terre Card, daily 10:30–17:30, 15-min video in English by request, 100 yards uphill from train tracks, across from the post office).

• *Hiking farther uphill, you can still hear...*

Manarola's Stream: As in Riomaggiore, Monterosso, and Vernazza, Manarola's stream was covered over by a modern sewage system after World War II. Before that time, romantic bridges arched over its ravine. A modern waterwheel recalls the origin of the town's name—local dialect for "big wheel" (one of many possible derivations). Mills like this once powered the local olive oil industry.

• *Keep climbing until you come to the square at the...*

Top of Manarola: The square is faced by a church, an oratory—now a religious and community meeting place—and a bell tower, which served as a watch tower when pirates raided the town (the cupola was added once the attacks ceased). Behind the church is Manarola's well-run youth hostel—originally the church's schoolhouse. To the right of the oratory, a lane leads to Manarola's sizable tourist-free zone.

While you're here, check out the church. According to the white marble plaque in its facade, the Parish Church of St. Lawrence dates from "MCCCXXXVIII" (1338). Step inside to see two paintings from the unnamed "Master of the Cinque Terre," the only painter of any note from the region (left wall and above main altar). While the style is Gothic, the work dates from the late 15th century, long after Florence had entered the Renaissance.

• *Walk 20 yards below the church and find a wooden railing. It marks the start of a delightful stroll around the high side of town, and back to the seafront. This is the beginning of the...*

Manarola Vineyard Walk: Don't miss this experience. Simply follow the wooden railing, enjoying lemon groves and wild red valerian (a cousin to the herb used for valium). Along the way, you'll get a close-up look at the region's famous dry-stone walls and finely crafted vineyards (with dried-heather thatches to protect the grapes from the southwest winds). Smell the rosemary. Study the structure of the town, and pick out the scant remains of an old fort. Notice the S-shape of the main road—once a riverbed—that flows through town. The town's roofs are traditionally made of locally quarried slate, rather than tile, and are held down by rocks during windstorms. As the harbor comes into view, you'll see the breakwater, added just a decade ago.

Out of sight above you on the right are simple, wooden religious scenes, the work of local resident Mario Andreoli. Before his father died, Mario promised him he'd replace the old cross on the family's vineyard. Mario has been adding figures ever since. After recovering from a rare illness, he redoubled his efforts. On religious holidays, everything's lit up: the Nativity, the Last Supper, the Crucifixion, the Resurrection, and more. Some of the scenes are left up year-round.

• *This trail ends at a T-intersection, where it hits the main coastal trail. Turn left. (A right takes you to the trail to Corniglia.) Before descending back into town, take a right, detouring into...*

The Cemetery: Ever since Napoleon—who was king of Italy in the early 1800s—decreed that cemeteries were health risks, Cinque Terre's burial spots have been located outside of town. The result: The dearly departed generally get first-class sea views. Each cemetery—with its evocative yellowed photos and finely carved Carrara marble memorial reliefs—is worth a visit. (The basic structure for all of them is the same, but Manarola's is most easily accessible.)

In cemeteries like these, there's a hierarchy of four places to park your mortal remains: a graveyard, a spacious death condo *(loculo),* a mini bone-niche *(ossario),* or the communal ossuary. Because of the tight space, a time limit is assigned to the first three options (although many older tombs are grandfathered in). Bones go into the ossuary in the middle of the chapel floor after about a generation. Traditionally, locals make weekly visits to loved ones here, often bringing flowers. The rolling stepladder makes access to top-floor *loculi* easy.

• *The Manarola cemetery is on Punta Bonfiglio. Walk just below it, farther out through a park (playground, drinking water, WC, and picnic benches). Your Manarola finale: the bench at the tip of the point, offering one of the most commanding views of the entire region.*

Sleeping

(€1 = about $1.40, country code: 39)

Manarola has plenty of private rooms. Ask in bars and restaurants. There's a modern, three-star place halfway up the main drag, a sea-view hotel on the harbor, a big modern hostel, and a cluster of options around the church at the peaceful top of the town (a 5-min hike from the train tracks).

$$$ La Torretta is a trendy, upscale, 13-room place that caters to a demanding clientele. It's a peaceful refuge with all the comforts for those happy to pay, including a communal hot tub with a view (Db-€110–120, Db suite-€150, 8 percent discount with cash, on Piazza della Chiesa at Vico Volto 20, tel. 0187-920-327, fax 0187-760-024, www.torrettas.com, torretta@cdh.it, Gabriele).

$$ Albergo Ca' d'Andrean, run by Simone, is quiet, comfortable, and modern—except for its antiquated reservation system. While the welcome is formal at best, it has 10 big, sunny, air-conditioned rooms and a cool garden oasis complete with lemon trees (Sb-€70, Db-€94, breakfast-€6, cash only, send personal or traveler's check to reserve from US—or call if you're reserving from the road, closed Nov–Christmas, up the hill at Via A. Discovolo 101, tel. 0187-920-040, fax 0187-920-452, www.cadandrean.it, cadandrean@libero.it).

$$ Marina Piccola offers 13 bright, slick rooms on the water—so they figure a warm welcome is unnecessary (Db-€95, €10 per person for buffet breakfast, air-con, Via Birolli 120, tel. 0187-920-103, fax 0187-920-966, www.hotelmarinapiccola.com, info@hotelmarinapiccola.com).

$$ Carugiu B&B rents two no-view rooms at the top of town (Db-€65, Db suite-€75, €5/day less with 3-night stay, Via

Ettore Cozzani 42, tel. 0187-920-359, English-speaking daughter's mobile 349-346-9208, www.carugiu.com, info@carugiu.com).

$ Casa Capellini rents three rooms: One has a view balcony, another a 360-degree terrace—book long in advance (Db-€46–52, €70 for the *alta camera* on the top, with a kitchen, private terrace, and knockout view; two doors down the hill from the church—with your back to the church, it's at 2 o'clock; Via Ettore Cozzani 12, tel. 0187-920-823 or 0187-736-765, www.casacapellini-5terre.it, casa.capellini@tin.it, Gianni and Franca don't speak English).

$ Ostello 5-Terre, Manarola's modern and pleasant hostel, occupies the former parochial school above the church square and offers 48 beds in four- to six-bed rooms. Nicola runs a calm and peaceful place—it's not a party hostel—and quiet is greatly appreciated. They rent dorm rooms as doubles. Reserve well in advance. Full means full—they don't accommodate the desperate on the floor (Easter–mid-Oct: dorm beds-€23, Db-€65, Qb-€100; off-season: dorm beds-€20, Db-€55, Qb-€88; closed Dec–Feb, not co-ed except for couples and families, optional €5 breakfast and €5–6 pasta; in summer, office closed 13:00–17:00, rooms closed 10:00–17:00, 1:00 curfew; off-season, office and rooms closed until 16:00, strict midnight curfew; open to all ages, laundry, safes, phone cards, Internet access, book exchange, elevator, great roof terrace and sunset views, Via B. Riccobaldi 21, tel. 0187-920-215, fax 0187-920-218, www.hostel5terre.com, info@hostel5terre.com). Book online with your credit-card number; note that you'll be charged for one night if you cancel with fewer than three days' notice.

Eating

Many hardworking places line the main drag. I like the Scorza family's friendly **Trattoria Il Porticciolo** (€7 pastas, free glass of *sciacchetrà* dessert wine with this book, Thu–Tue 12:00–15:00 & 18:00–22:30, closed Wed, just below the train tracks at Via R. Birolli 92, tel. 0187-920-083). For harborside dining, **Marina Piccola** is the winner. While less friendly and a little more expensive, the setting is memorable (€10 pastas, Wed–Mon 11:30–16:30 & 18:30–22:00, closed Tue, tel. 0187-920-923).

Corniglia (Town #3)

This is the quiet town—the only one of the five not on the water—with a mellow main square. From the station, a footpath zigzags up nearly 400 stairs to the town. Or take the shuttle bus, generally timed to meet arriving trains (€1.50, free with Cinque Terre Card, 2/hr). Before leaving the bus, confirm departure times on the schedule posted on its door or ask at the TI in the train station (daily 6:30–19:30).

According to a (likely fanciful) local legend, the town was originally settled by a Roman farmer who named it for his mother, Cornelia (how Corniglia is pronounced). The town and its ancient residents produced a wine so famous that—some say—vases found at Pompeii touted its virtues. Regardless of the veracity of the legends, wine remains Corniglia's lifeblood today. Follow the pungent smell of ripe grapes into an alley cellar and get a local to let you dip a straw into a keg. Remote and less visited than the other Cinque Terre towns, Corniglia has fewer tourists, cooler temperatures, a few restaurants, a windy overlook on its promontory, and plenty of private rooms for rent (ask at any bar or shop, no cheaper than other towns).

Self-Guided Walk

Welcome to Corniglia

We'll explore this tiny town—population 240—and end at a scenic viewpoint.

• *Begin near the bus stop, located at a...*

Town Square: The gateway to this community is "Ciappà" square, with an ATM, phone booth, old wine press, and bus stop. Now that the Cinque Terre has been designated as a national park, the change has sparked a revitalization of the town. Corniglia's young generation might now stay put, rather than migrate into big cities the way locals did in the past.

• *Stroll the spine of Corniglia, Via Fieschi. In the fall, the smell of grapes (on their way to becoming wine) wafts from busy cellars. Along this main street, you'll see...*

Corniglia's Enticing Shops: The enjoyable wine bar, **Enoteca Il Pirun**—named for a type of oddly shaped, old-fashioned wine pitcher—is located in a cool cantina at Via Fieschi 115 (daily, tel. 0187-812-315). Mario and Marilena don't speak much English, but they try. Sample some local wines—generally free for small tastes. For a fun experience and a souvenir to boot, order a €3 glass of wine, which is served in a *pirun* and comes with a bib to keep. The *pirun* aerates the wine to give the alcohol more kick.

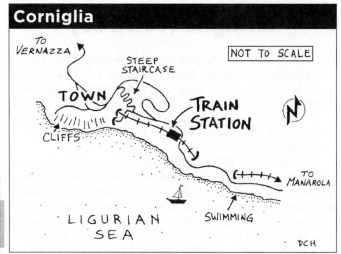

Across from Enoteca Il Pirun, Alberto and Cristina's *gelat-eria* is the only—and therefore best—in town. Before ordering, get a free taste of Alberto's *miele di Corniglia,* made from local honey.

In the **Butiega shop** at Via Fieschi 142, Vincenzo and Lorenzo sell organic local specialties (daily 8:00–19:30). For picnickers, they offer €2.50 made-to-order ham-and-cheese sandwiches and a fun €3.50 *antipasto misto* to go. (There are good places to picnic farther along on this walk.)

• *Following Via Fieschi, you'll end up at the...*

Main Square: On Largo Taragio, tables from two bars and a trattoria spill around a WWI memorial and the town's old well. It once piped in natural spring water from the hillside to locals living without plumbing. What looks like a church is the Oratory of Santa Caterina. (An oratory is a kind of a spiritual clubhouse for a service group doing social work in the name of the Catholic Church. For more information, see "Oratory of the Dead" on page 1011.) Behind the oratory, you'll find a clearing that local children have made into a soccer field. The benches and viewpoint make this a peaceful place for a picnic (less crowded than the end-of-town viewpoint, below).

• *Opposite the oratory, notice how steps lead steeply down on Via alla Marina to Corniglia's non-beach. It's a five-minute paved climb to sunning rocks, a shower, and a small deck (with a treacherous entry into the water). From the square, continue up Via Fieschi to the...*

End-of-Town Viewpoint: The Santa Maria Belvedere, named for a church that once stood here, marks the scenic end of Corniglia. This is a super picnic spot. From here, look high to the west, where the village and sanctuary of San Bernardino straddle a ridge (a good starting point for a hike; accessible by shuttle bus or long uphill hike from Vernazza). Below is the tortuous harbor, where locals hoist their boats onto the cruel rocks.

Activities

Beaches—This hilltop town has rocky sea access below its train station (toward Manarola). Once a beach, it's all been washed away and offers no services.

Guvano beach is in the opposite direction (toward Vernazza). Guvano (GOO-vah-noh) was created by an 1893 landslide that cost the village a third of its farmland. The big news in modern times is its nudists—and efforts to cover them up. Guvano made headlines in Italy in the 1970s, as clothed locals in a makeshift armada of dinghies and fishing boats retook their town beach. Big-city nudists still work on all-over tans in this remote setting. But now the national park, which has first right of refusal on any property for sale, hopes to buy the beach—and end the nudity.

Sleeping

(€1 = about $1.40, country code: 39)
Perched high above the sea on a hilltop, Corniglia has plenty of private rooms (generally Db-€60). To get to the town from the station, catch the shuttle bus or make the 15-minute uphill hike. The town is riddled with humble places that charge too much and have meager business skills and a limited ability to converse with tourists—so it's almost never full.

$$ Cristiana Ricci is an exception to the rule. She communicates well and is reliable, renting four small, clean, and peaceful rooms—two with kitchens and one with a terrace and sweeping view—just inland from the bus stop (Db-€60, Qb-€90, €10/day less when you stay 2 or more nights, free Internet access, check in at the shop at Via Fieschi 123, mobile 338-937-6547, cri_affitta camere@virgilio.it, Stefano). Her mom rents a few places in town for the same price.

$$ Villa Cecio feels like an abandoned hotel. They offer eight well-worn rooms on the outskirts of town, with little character or warmth (Db-€60, no breakfast, cash preferred, great views, sagging beds, on main road 200 yards toward Vernazza, tel. 0187-812-043, fax 0187-812-138, www.cecio5terre.com, info@cecio5terre .com). They also rent eight similar rooms in an annex on the square where the bus stops.

$ Corniglia Hostel, which may be open in time for your visit, has 40 beds in what was formerly the town's schoolhouse (at the bus stop, tel. 0187-812-559).

Eating

Corniglia has three restaurants. **Cecio,** above the town, has terrace seating with a view of the sea. The trattoria **La Lantera,** on the main square, is the most atmospheric. (Neither comes with particularly charming service.) Restaurant **Osteria Mananan**—between the Ciappà bus stop and the main square on Via Fieschi—serves the best food in town in its small, stony, and elegant interior (closed Tue, no outdoor seating, tel. 0187-821-166).

Vernazza (Town #4)

With the closest thing to a natural harbor—overseen by a ruined castle and a stout stone church—Vernazza is the jewel of the Cinque Terre. Only the occasional noisy slurping up of the train by the mountain reminds you of the modern world.

The action is at the harbor, where you'll find outdoor restaurants, a bar hanging on the edge of the castle, a breakwater with a promenade, and a tailgate-party street market every Tuesday morning. In the summer, the beach becomes a soccer field, where teams fielded by local bars and restaurants provide late-night entertainment. In the dark, locals fish off the promontory, using glowing bobs that shine in the waves.

Proud of their Vernazzan heritage, the town's 500 residents like to brag: "Vernazza is locally owned. Portofino has sold out." Fearing the change it would bring, keep-Vernazza-small proponents stopped the construction of a major road into the town and region. Families are tight and go back centuries; several generations stay together. In the winter, the population shrinks, as many people return to their more comfortable big-city apartments to spend the money they reaped during the tourist season.

Leisure time is devoted to taking part in the *passeggiata*—strolling lazily together up and down the main street. Sit on a bench and study the passersby doing their *vasche* (laps). Explore the characteristic alleys, called *carugi*. Learn—and live—the phrase *"vita pigra di Vernazza"* (the lazy life of Vernazza).

Orientation

Tourist Information

The TI/park information booth is in the train station (daily 6:30–22:00 in summer, until 19:30 in winter, tel. 0187-812-533). Public WCs are nearby in the station.

Arrival in Vernazza

By Train: Vernazza's train station is only about three cars long, but the trains are much longer, so most of the cars come to a stop in a long, dark tunnel. Get out anyway, and walk through the tunnel to the station.

By Car: Driving to Vernazza is a reasonable option because of its non-resident parking lot—but be aware that the lot fills up quickly from May through September (€1.50/hr, €12/24 hrs, about 500 yards above town, pay first at the parking stand before getting your spot). A hardworking shuttle service, generally with friendly English-speaking Beppe or Simone behind the wheel, connects the lot to the top of town (€1.50, free with Cinque Terre Card, 3–4/hr, runs 7:30–19:30). Yellow lines mark parking spots for residents. The highest lot (a side-trip uphill) is for overnight stays.

Helpful Hints

Internet Access: The **Blue Marlin Bar,** run by Massimo and Carmen, has the lowest prices and longest hours (€0.10/min, Fri–Wed 7:00–24:00, closed Thu, see "Eating," below). The slick six-terminal **Internet Point,** run by Alberto and Isabella, is in the village center (€0.15/min, daily 9:30–23:00 in summer, until 20:00 in winter, Wi-Fi, will burn your digital photos to a CD or DVD for €8, sells international phone cards, tel. 0187-812-949).

Laundry: Lavanderia il Carugetto is completely self-serve (coin-op, daily 8:00–22:00, on a narrow lane a block off the main drag opposite the Internet Point, operated by the fish shop).

Massage: Stephanie, an American expat, gives a good, strong therapeutic massage in a neat little studio at the top of town (€50/hr, mobile 338-9429-494, stephsette@gmail.com). Kate Allen is also a good local masseuse and does reflexology (€50/hr, tel. 0187-812-537, mobile 333-568-4653, katarinaallen@hotmail.com).

Best Views: A steep 10-minute hike in either direction from Vernazza gives you a classic village photo op (for the best light, head toward Corniglia in the morning, and toward Monterosso in the evening). Franco's Ristorante La Torre, with a panoramic terrace, is at the tower on the trail toward Corniglia (listed under "Eating," later in this section).

Self-Guided Walks

Welcome to Vernazza

This tour includes Vernazza's characteristic town squares, and ends on its scenic breakwater.

• *From the train station, walk uphill until you hit the parking lot, with*

Vernazza

NOTE: NOT TO SCALE: TRAIN STATION TO THE BREAKWATER IS A 5-MINUTE STROLL

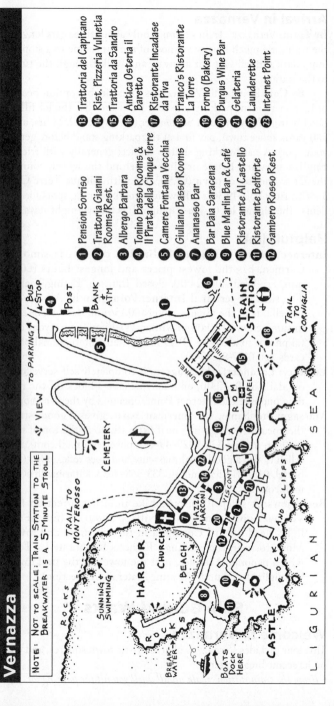

1. Pension Sorriso
2. Trattoria Gianni Rooms/Rest.
3. Albergo Barbara
4. Tonino Basso Rooms & Il Pirata della Cinque Terre
5. Camere Fontana Vecchia
6. Giuliano Basso Rooms
7. Ananasso Bar
8. Bar Baia Saracena
9. Blue Marlin Bar & Café
10. Ristorante Al Castello
11. Ristorante Belforte
12. Gambero Rosso Rest.
13. Trattoria del Capitano
14. Rist. Pizzeria Vulnetia
15. Trattoria da Sandro
16. Antica Osteria il Baretto
17. Ristorante Incadase da Piva
18. Franco's Ristorante La Torre
19. Forno (Bakery)
20. Burgus Wine Bar
21. Gelateria
22. Launderette
23. Internet Point

a bank, a post office, and a barrier that keeps out all but service vehicles. Vernazza's shuttle buses run from here to the parking lot and into the hills. Walk to the tidy, modern square called...

Fontana Vecchia: Named after a long-gone fountain, this is where older locals remember the river filled with townswomen doing their washing. Now they enjoy checking on the baby ducks. The trail leads up to the cemetery. Imagine the entire village sadly trudging up here during funerals.

• *Glad to be here in happier times, begin your saunter downhill to the harbor. Just before the* Pensione Sorriso *sign, on your right (big brown wood doors), you'll see the...*

Ambulance Barn: A group of volunteers is always on call for a dash to the hospital, 40 minutes away in La Spezia. Opposite from the barn is a big, empty lot. Like many landowners, the owner of Pension Sorriso had plans to expand, but since the 1980s, the government said no. While some landowners are frustrated, the old character of these towns survives.

• *A few steps farther along (past the town clinic and library), you'll see a...*

World Wars Monument: Look for a marble plaque in the wall to your left, dedicated to those killed in the World Wars. Not a family in Vernazza was spared. Listed on the left are soldiers *morti in combattimento,* who died in World War I; on the right is the World War II section. Some were deported to *Germania;* others—labeled *Part* (stands for *partigiani,* or partisans)—were killed while fighting against Mussolini. Cynics considered partisans less than heroes. After 1943, Hitler called up Italian boys over 15. Rather than die on the front for Hitler, they escaped to the hills. They became "resistance fighters" in order to remain free.

The path to Corniglia leaves from here (behind and above the plaque). Behind you is a small square and **playground,** decorated with three millstones, once used to grind local olives into oil. There's a good chance you'll see an expat mom here at the village playground with her kids. I've met many American women who fell in love with a local guy, stayed, and are now happily raising families here. (But I've never met an American guy who moved in with a local girl.)

From here, Vernazza's tiny **river** goes underground. Until the 1950s, Vernazza's river ran openly through the center of town. Old-timers recall the days before the breakwater, when the river cascaded down and the surf crashed along Vernazza's main drag. Back then, the town was nicknamed "Little Venice" for the series of romantic bridges that arched over the stream, connecting the two sides of the town before the main road was built.

Before the tracks (on the left), the wall has 10 spaces, one reserved for each party's political ads during elections—a kind

THE CINQUE TERRE

of local pollution control. The **map** on the right, under the railway tracks, shows the region's hiking trails. Trail #2 is the basic favorite. The second set of tracks (nearer the harbor) was recently renovated to lessen the disruptive noise, but locals say it made no difference.

• *Follow the road downhill to...*

Vernazza's "Business Center": Here, you'll pass many locals doing their *vasche* (laps). At **Enoteca Sotto l'Arco,** Gerry and Paola sell wine—they can cork it and throw in plastic glasses—and delightful jars of local pesto, which goes great on bread (Wed–Mon 9:00–21:00, closed Tue, Via Roma 70). Next, you'll pass the Blue Marlin Bar (Vernazza's top nightspot) and the tiny **Chapel of Santa Marta** (the small stone chapel with iron grillwork over the window), where Mass is celebrated only on special Sundays. Farther down, you'll walk by a grocery, *gelateria,* bakery, pharmacy, another grocery, and another *gelateria.* There are plenty of fun and cheap food-to-go options here.

• *On the left, in front of the second* gelateria, *an arch (with a peaceful little sitting perch atop it) leads to what was a beach, where the town's stream used to hit the sea back in the 1970s. Continue down to the...*

Harbor Square and Breakwater: Vernazza, with the only natural harbor of the Cinque Terre, was established as the sole place boats could pick up the fine local wine. The two-foot-high square stone at the foot of the stairs by the Burgus Wine Bar is marked *Sasso del Sego* (stone of tallow). Workers crushed animal flesh and fat in its basin to make tallow, which drained out of the tiny hole below. The tallow was then used to waterproof boats or wine barrels. For more town history, step into the Burgus to see fascinating old photos of Vernazza on the wall (also see listing under "Eating," later in this section).

On the far side (behind Ristorante Pizzeria Vulnetia), peek into the tiny street with its commotion of arches. Vernazza's most characteristic side streets, called *carugi,* lead up from here. The trail (above the church, toward Monterosso) leads to the classic view of Vernazza (see "Best Views," under "Helpful Hints," page 991).

Located in front of the harborside church, the tiny piazza—decorated with a river rock mosaic—is a popular hangout spot. It's where Vernazza's old ladies soak up the last bit of sun, and kids enjoy a patch of level ball field.

Vernazza's harborfront church is unusual for its strange entryway, which faces east (altar side). With relative peace and prosperity in the 16th century, the townspeople doubled the church in size, causing it to overtake a little piazza that once faced the west facade. From the square, use the "new" entry and climb the steps, keeping an eye out for the level necessary to keep the church high and dry. Inside, the lighter pillars in the back mark the 16th-century extension. Three historic portable crosses hanging on the walls are carried through town during Easter processions. They are replicas of crosses that Vernazza ships once carried on crusades to the Holy Land.

• *Finish your town tour seated out on the breakwater (and consider starting the following tour).*

The Burned-Out Sightseer's Visual Tour of Vernazza

• *Sit at the end of the harbor breakwater (perhaps with a glass of local white wine or something more interesting from a nearby bar—borrow the glass, they don't mind), face the town, and see...*

The Harbor: In a moderate storm, you'd be soaked, as waves routinely crash over the *molo* (breakwater, built in 1972). Waves can even wash away tourists squinting excitedly into their cameras. (I've seen it happen.) In 2007, an American woman was swept away and killed by a rogue wave. Enjoy the new waterfront piazza—carefully.

The train line (to your left) was constructed in 1874 to tie together a newly united Italy, and linked Turin and Genoa with Rome. A second line (hidden in a tunnel at this point) was built in the 1920s. The yellow building alongside the tracks was Vernazza's first train station. You can see the four bricked-up alcoves where people once waited for trains.

Vernazza's fishing fleet is down to just a couple of fishing boats (with the net spools). Vernazzans are still more likely to own a boat than a car. Boats are on buoys, except in winter or when the red storm flag indicates bad seas (in which case they're allowed to be pulled up onto the square—which is usually reserved for restaurant tables). In the 1970s, tiny Vernazza had one of Italy's top water polo teams, and the harbor was their "pool." Later, when the league required a real pool, Vernazza dropped out.

The Castle: On the far right, the castle, which is now a grassy park with great views (and nothing but stones), still guards the town (€1.50 donation supports the local Red Cross, daily 10:00–18:00; from harbor, take stairs by Trattoria Gianni and follow signs to Ristorante Al Castello, tower is a few steps beyond). It was the town's lookout back in pirate days. The highest umbrellas mark the recommended Ristorante Al Castello (listed in "Eating," later in this section). The squat tower on the water is great for a glass of wine or a meal. From the breakwater, you could follow the rope to the Ristorante Belforte (also listed in "Eating"), and pop inside, past the submarine-strength door. A photo of a major storm showing the entire tower under a wave (not uncommon in the winter) hangs near the bar.

The Town: Vernazza has two halves. *Sciuiu* (Vernazzan dialect for "flowery") is the sunny side on the left, and *luvegu* (dank) is the shady side on the right. Houses below the castle were connected by an interior arcade—ideal for fleeing attacks. The "Ligurian pastel" colors are regulated by a commissioner of good taste in the regional government. The square before you is locally famous for some of the area's finest restaurants. The big red central house—on the site where Genoan warships were built in the 12th century—used to be a guardhouse.

Vernazza has the only natural harbor in the Cinque Terre. In the Middle Ages, there was no beach or square. The water went right up to the buildings, where boats would tie up, Venetian-style. Imagine what Vernazza looked like in those days, when it was the biggest and richest of the Cinque Terre towns. There was no pastel plaster, just fine stonework (traces of which survive above the Trattoria del Capitano). Apart from the added plaster, the general shape and size of the town has changed little in five centuries. Survey the windows and notice inhabitants quietly gazing back.

Above the Town: The small, round tower above the red guardhouse—another part of the city fortifications—reminds us of Vernazza's importance in the Middle Ages, when it was a key ally of Genoa (whose archenemies were the other maritime republics, especially Pisa). Franco's Ristorante La Torre, just behind the tower, welcomes hikers who are finishing, starting, or simply contemplating the Corniglia–Vernazza hike, with great town views. Vineyards fill the mountainside beyond the town. Notice the many terraces. Someone—probably after too much of that local wine—calculated that the roughly 3,000 miles of dry stone walls built to terrace the region's vineyards have the same amount of stonework as the Great Wall of China.

Wine production is down nowadays, as the younger residents choose less physical work. But locals still maintain their tiny plots and proudly serve their family wines. The patchwork of local vineyards is atomized and complex because of inheritance traditions. Historically, families divided their land between their children. Parents wanted each child to get some good land. Because some lots were "kissed by the sun" while others were shady, the lots were split into increasingly tiny and eventually unviable pieces.

A single steel train line winds up the gully behind the tower. It is for the vintner's *trenino,* the tiny service train. Play "Where's *trenino?*" and see if you can find two trains. The vineyards once stretched as high as you can see, but since fewer people sweat in the fields these days, the most distant terraces have gone wild again.

The Church, School, and City Hall: Vernazza's Ligurian Gothic church, built with black stones quarried from Punta Mesco (the distant point behind you), dates from 1318. Note the gray stone that marks the church's 16th-century expansion. The gray-and-red house above the spire is the local elementary school (about 25 children attend). High-schoolers go to the "big city": La Spezia. The red building to the right of the schoolhouse, a former monastery, is the City Hall. Vernazza and Corniglia function as one community. Through most of the 1990s, the local government was Communist. In 1999, they elected a coalition of many parties working to rise above ideologies and simply make Vernazza a better place. Finally, on the top of the hill, with the best view of all, is the town cemetery.

Activities

Tuesday Morning Market—Vernazza's meager business community is augmented Tuesday mornings (8:00–13:00) when a gang of cars and trucks pull into town for a tailgate market.

Beach—The harbor's sandy cove has sunning rocks and showers by the breakwater. There's also a ladder on the breakwater for deep-water access.

Boat Rental—Nord Est rents canoes, small motorboats, and Jet Skis from their stand on the harbor. With a rental boat, you can reach a tiny *acqua pendente* (waterfall) cove between Vernazza and Monterosso; locals call it their *laguna blu* (motorboats and Jet Skis-€60/4 hrs plus gas, usually about €15; canoes-€8/hr, includes snorkeling gear; June–Sept only, mobile 338-700-0436, manuela moggia@tiscali.it).

Shuttle Bus Joyride—For a cheap and scenic round-trip joyride, with a chance to chat about the region with friendly Beppe or Simone, ride the shuttle bus for the entire route for the cost of a normal ticket. About once an hour, the bus also heads to two sanctuaries in the hills above town (5/day, €2.50 one-way, free with Cinque Terre Card, schedule at park office and posted in train station). The high-country, 40-minute loop—marked *Panoramic Tour* on the bus schedule—gives you lots of scenery without having to hike.

Nightlife

Vernazza's younger generation of restaurant workers lets loose after hours. They work hard through the tourist season, travel in the winter, speak English, and enjoy connecting with international visitors. After the restaurants close down, the town is quiet except for a couple of nightspots. For more information on the Blue Marlin, Ananasso, Il Pirata, and Ristorante Incandase, see their listings under "Eating," at the end of the Vernazza section.

Blue Marlin Bar dominates the late-night scene with a mix of locals and tourists, good drinks, and music. If you're young and hip, this is *the* place to hang out.

Ananasso Bar offers early-evening happy-hour fun and cocktails (called *"aperitivi"*) that both locals and visitors enjoy. Its harborfront tables get the last sunshine of the day.

Burgus Wine Bar, chic and cool with a jazz ambience, is a popular early-evening and after-dinner harborside hangout. Sip local wine or a cocktail, and sample Franco and Lorenza's artful, complimentary snack foods, available 18:00–20:30. Let Marco explain the historic town photos and museum cases of artifacts (Tue–Sun 7:00–24:00, closed Mon, Piazza Marconi 4, tel. 0187-812-556).

Il Pirata delle Cinque Terre, at the top of the town, features the entertaining Canoli brothers, who fill a happy crowd of tourists with wonderful Sicilian pastries and drinks each evening. Many come for dinner and end up staying because of these two wild and crazy guys and the camaraderie they create among their diners.

Ristorante Incadase da Piva (tucked up the lane behind the pharmacy) is the haunt of Piva, Vernazza's troubadour. Piva often gets out his guitar and sings traditional local songs as well as his own compositions. If you're looking for a local Hemingway, check here.

Really Late: There's a little cave on the beach just under the church that lends itself to fun in the wee hours, when everything else is closed.

Sleeping

(€1 = about $1.40, country code: 39)
Vernazza, the spindly and salty essence of the Cinque Terre, is my top choice for a home base. Off-season, with so many rooms available, you can generally arrive without a reservation and find a place (but it's smart to book ahead for June–Aug, any weekend, and holidays such as Easter). You can save money by arriving without a reservation—or gain the chance to shop around and land a place with a terrace and a view for less. Drop by any shop or bar and ask; most locals know someone who rents rooms.

Even today, pirates lurk on the Cinque Terre. People recommended here are listed for their communication skills (they speak English, have email, are reliable with bookings) and because they rent several rooms. Consequently, my recommendations charge more than comparable rooms you'll find if you just arrive and shop around. Bold travelers who drop in without a reservation and shop around will likely save €10–20 per double per night—and often get a better place and view to boot. The real Vernazza gems are stray single rooms with no interest in booking in advance or messing with email.

Anywhere you stay here requires some climbing. Most do not include breakfast. Night noise can be a problem if you're near the station. Rooms on the harbor come with church bells (but only between 7:00 and 22:00).

Pensions

These pensions are listed on the map on page 992.

$$$ Pension Sorriso is the oldest pension in town (and where I stayed on my first visit in 1975). Above the train station, it's run by Aldo and Francesca—the local Sonny and Cher—who welcome guests to their 19 rooms. While the main building has the charm, it comes with train noise; the annex, up the street, is in a quieter modern apartment (Sb-€60, D-€80, Db-€100–120, Tb-€130, includes breakfast, peaceful garden, Via Gavino 4, tel. 0187-812-224, www.pensionesorriso.com).

$$ Trattoria Gianni rents 25 small rooms and three apartments just under the castle. The rooms are in two buildings—one funky, one modern—up a hundred tight, winding spiral stairs. The funky ones, which may or may not have private baths, are artfully decorated à la shipwreck, with tiny balconies and grand sea views *(con vista sul mare)*. The new *(nuovo)*, comfy rooms lack views, but have access to a super-scenic, cliff-hanging guests' garden. Both have modern bathrooms. Steely Marisa requires check-in before 16:00 or a phone call to explain when you're coming. Emanuele (Gianni's son, who now runs the restaurant), Simona, and the staff speak a little English (S-€45, D-€65, Db-€100, Tb-€120, pay in cash and mention this book when you reserve for best prices, cancellations required 48 hours in advance or you'll be charged one night's deposit, no breakfast, closed Jan–Feb, Piazza Marconi 5, tel. & fax 0187-812-228, tel. 0187-821-003, www.giannifranzi .it, info@giannifranzi.it). Pick up your keys at Trattoria Gianni's restaurant/reception on the harbor square.

$$ Albergo Barbara rents nine simple but clean and modern rooms overlooking the harbor square—most with small windows and small views. It's run by kindly, English-speaking Giuseppe and his Swiss wife, Patricia (D-€50, Db-€60–65, big Db with nice harbor view-€100, 2-night stay preferred, fans, closed Dec–Feb, Piazza Marconi 30, tel. & fax 0187-812-398, mobile 338-793-3261, reserve online with credit card but pay cash, www.albergobarbara .it, info@albergobarbara.it).

Private Rooms (Affitta Camere)

Vernazza is honeycombed with private rooms year-round, offering the best values in town. Owners may be reluctant to reserve rooms far in advance. It's easiest to call a day or two ahead or simply show up in the morning and look around. Doubles cost €50–80, depending on the view, season, and plumbing. Most places accept only cash. Some have killer views, come with lots of stairs, and cost the same as a small, dark place on a back lane over the train tracks. Little English is spoken at many of these places. If you call to let them know your arrival time (or call when you arrive, using your mobile phone or the pay phone just below the station), they'll meet you at the train station.

Well-Managed and Well-Appointed Rooms in the Inland Part of Town

These accommodations are listed on the map on page 992.

$$$ Tonino Basso rents four super, clean, modern rooms—at a steep price. Each room has its own computer for free Internet access. He's in the only building in Vernazza with an elevator. You get tranquility and air-conditioning, but no views (Sb-€65, Db-€120, Tb-€150, Qb-€180, prices go down Nov–March, call Tonino's mobile number upon arrival and he'll meet you, tel. 0187-821-264, mobile 335-269-436, fax 0187-812-807, toninobasso @libero.it). If you can't locate Tonino, ask his friends at Enoteca Sotto L'Arco at Via Roma 70.

$$ Camere Fontana Vecchia is a delightful place, with four bright, spacious, quiet rooms near the post office (no view). As the only place in Vernazza with almost no stairs to climb and the sound of a babbling brook outside your window, it's perhaps the best value in town (D-€65, Db-€75, T-€95, Tb-€110, fans and heat, open all year, Via Gavino 15, tel. 0187-821-130, fax 0187-821-261, mobile 333-454-9371, m.annamaria@libero.it, youthful and efficient Anna speaks English).

$$ Giuliano Basso rents four pleasant rooms, crafted with care, just above town in the terraced wilds (sea views from terraces). Straddling a ravine among orange trees, it's an artfully decorated, Robinson Crusoe–chic wonderland, proudly built out of stone by Giuliano himself (Db-€75, Db suite with air-con-€100, Db suite with private rooftop balcony-€100, fridge access, above train station—so with more train noise than others, mobile 333-341-4792, or have the Enoteca Sotto L'Arco at Via Roma 30 contact him or his American partner Michele, www.cdh.it/giuliano, giuliano@cdh.it). Call to be met at the station. To walk there, head inland from the station and hike up the Corniglia trail; 100 yards beyond Pensione Sorriso, at the second Corniglia sign, follow the lane left.

Other Reliable Places Scattered Through Town and the Harborside

These places are not identified on this book's map; ask for directions when you reserve.

$$$ La Malà is Vernazza's jetsetter pad. Four pristine white rooms boast four-star-hotel-type extras, a common terrace looking out over the rocky shore, and air-conditioning (Db-€150, Db-suite-€210, includes breakfast, reception and breakfast at the harborfront Burgus Wine Bar, tel. 334-287-5718, fax 0187-812-218, www.lamala.it, info@lamala.it, Giamba and Armanda). It's a climb—way, way up to the top of town. They also rent the simpler "Armanda's Room" nearby (no view, Db-€70).

$$$ Monica Lercari rents three classy rooms with modern comforts, perched at the top of town (Db-€80, sea-view D-€100, grand sea-view terrace D-€120, Qb apartment-€220, includes breakfast, air-con, next to recommended Ristorante Al Castello, tel. 0187-812-296, alcastellovernazza@yahoo.it).

$$$ Egi Rooms (pronounced "edgy"), run by English-speaking Egi Verduschi, offers three good, clean, and colorful rooms, right in the center on the main drag (S-€70, D-€90, plush and designer Db-€120, Tb-€160, Qb-€180, cash only, thin walls, some rooms have light switches in the hallway—prone to being flipped accidentally by other guests, across the street from *gelateria* just before harbor square on main drag at Via Visconti 9, mobile 338-822-3202, www.egirooms.com, egidioverduschi @libero.it).

$$ Antonio and Ingrid Fenelli Camere rent three very central, comfy, and fairly priced rooms that are an excellent value. You'll meet friendly Antonio—a hulking man in a huge white T-shirt and bathing suit who's a fixture on the village streets—and his charming, petite, English-speaking wife Ingrid (small Db-€55, Db-€65, Tb-€80, two-person apartment with terrace-€90, air-con, 10 steps above pharmacy at Via Carattino 2, tel. 0187-812-183). They have no email, but getting a room by phone or in person is worth the trouble.

$$ Memo Rooms offers three clean and spacious rooms overlooking the main street, in what feels like a miniature hotel. Enrica will meet you if you call upon arrival (Db-€70, Via Roma 15, tel. 0187-812-360, mobile 338-285-2385).

$$ Martina Callo rents four rooms overlooking the square, up plenty of steps near the silent-at-night church tower (room #1: Tb-€95 or Qb-€110 with harbor view; room #2: huge Qb family room with no view-€110; room #3: Db with grand view terrace-€75; room #4: roomy Db with no view-€55; ring bell at Piazza Marconi 26, tel. & fax 0187-812-365, mobile 329-435-5344, www .roomartina.com, roomartina@roomartina.com).

$$ Nicolina rents four funky, lived-in rooms. The largest has a view; two others overlook Vernazza's main drag. Inquire at Pizzeria Vulnetia on the harbor square (viewless Db-€70, view Db-€80, Tb-€100, Qb with terrace and view-€140, Piazza Marconi 29, tel.

& fax 0187-821-193, www.camerenicolina.it, camerenicolina.info @cdh.it).

$$ Rosa Vitali rents two apartments across from the pharmacy overlooking the main street. One, for up to three people, has a terrace and fridge (top floor); the other, for four, has windows and a full kitchen (Db-€85, Tb-€110, Qb-€130, reception at Via Visconti 10 between the grotto and Piazza Marconi, tel. 0187-821-181, mobile 340-267-5009, www.rosacamere.it, rosa.vitali@libero.it).

$$ Francamaria rents seven sharp, comfortable, and creatively renovated but expensive rooms—all described in detail on her website (small no-view Db-€75, larger view Db-up to €110, Qb-€125–150, family apartment, prices depend on view and size, Piazza Marconi 30, tel. & fax 0187-812-002, mobile 328-711-9728, www.francamaria.com, francamaria@francamaria.com). Their reception is on the harborfront on the ground floor of the Albergo Barbara building.

More Private Rooms in Vernazza

$$ Maria Capellini rents a couple of rooms, including one on the ground floor right on the harbor (Db with kitchen-€80, cash only, mobile 338-436-3411, www.mariacapellini.com, mariacapellini @hotmail.it, Maria and Giacomo).

$$ Il Pirata delle Cinque Terre has a few big, basic, and quiet rooms managed by Noelia and Leyla, wives of the drink-slinging Canoli brothers (see listing under "Eating"). It's a two-minute walk from the bar and a five-minute walk to the sea (Db-€80, Tb-€120, Qb-€150; if you reserve in advance, you get a free breakfast with this book at the Il Pirata bar—which also functions as the reception; 2-night minimum, cash only; from the Il Pirata, hike up 100 yards to the yellow building that was the old mill; tel. 0187-812-047, mobile 338-596-2503, ilpiratarooms@libero.it).

$$ Ivo's Camere rents two simple, no-view, no-terrace rooms high above the main street (Db-€65, Via Roma 6, reception at Pizzeria Fratelli Basso, Via Roma 1, tel. 0187-821-042, mobile 333-477-5521, www.ivocamere.com, post@ivocamere.com).

$$ Affitta Camere Alberto Basso rents two clean, modern rooms: one with a harbor view over the noisy piazza, the other quiet and behind the main street (Db-€75, 2-night minimum, check in at Internet Point—see map on page 992, albertobasso @hotmail.com).

$$ Daria Bianchi rents 12 clean, spacious, and comfortable rooms near the station. Four rooms are above the Blue Marlin looking down on the main street, and eight are high above near the City Hall (Db-€70, Qb-€100–120, fans, reception at Blue Marlin Bar, tel. 0187-812-151, mobile 338-581-4688, www.vernazzarooms .com).

$$ Affitta Camere da Annamaria offers six small, basic rooms high above the town, with barnacled ambience up a series of comically tight spiral staircases (no-view Db-€65, Db with town views and terrace-€75, top-floor Db with sea-view terrace-€85; at pharmacy, climb up Via Carattino to #64; tel. 0187-821-082, mobile 349-887-8150, www.camerelatorre.com).

More Options: **Eva's Rooms** (3 rooms, Db-€60–70, overlooking main street with some train noise, ring at Via Roma 56, tel. 0187-821-134, www.evasrooms.it, massimoeva@libero.it); **Manuela Moggia** (Db-€70, Qb-€120, top of town at Via Gavino 22, tel. 0187-812-397, mobile 333-413-6374, manuelamoggia@tiscali.it); **Filippo Rooms** (2 rooms, Db-€65, tel. 0187-812-244); **Patrizia** (4 rooms, all with kitchens, Db-€70–80, Qb-€100, cheaper "Rick Steves" prices if you book direct—not on website, on main street, next to grotto and *gelateria* at Via Visconti 30, mobile 335-653-1563, bemili@alice.it); and **Villa Antonia** (2 rooms sharing 1 bathroom, D-€80, on main drag, tel. 0187-821-143, mobile 333-971-5602).

Eating

Breakfast

Locals take breakfast about as seriously as flossing. A cappuccino and a pastry or a piece of focaccia does it. Most accommodations don't come with breakfast (when they do, I've noted so in my listings). Instead, you have several fun options. The first two, on the harborfront, have the best ambience.

Ananasso Bar feels Old World, with youthful energy and a great location (toasted *panini,* pastries). Eat a bit cheaper at the bar (you're welcome to picnic on a bench or rock) or enjoy the best-situated tables in town (Fri–Wed 8:00–late, closed Thu).

Bar Baia Saracena has a fun, easy-to-follow menu (€5–7 for breakfast). Luca, the owner, promises a free slice of *bucellato* (the local coffee cake) for breakfast as a bonus for anyone with this book (7:30–11:00, closed Wed July–Aug, closed Fri Sept–June, located out on the breakwater, tel. 0187-812-113).

Blue Marlin Bar (mid-town, just below the train station) serves a good array of clearly priced à la carte items, adding up to the priciest breakfast in town (likely to total €10). It's run by Massimo, Carmen, and Stefano (Fri–Wed 7:00–24:00, closed Thu, tel. 0187-821-149). If awaiting a train any time of day, the Blue Marlin's outdoor seats beat the platform.

Il Pirata delle Cinque Terre is located at the top of the town, where the dynamic Sicilian duo Gianluca and Massimo (twins, a.k.a. the Canoli Brothers) enthusiastically offer a great assortment of handcrafted, authentic Sicilian pastries. Their fun and playful service makes up for the lack of a view. Gianluca is a pastry artist, hand-painting fanciful sculptured marzipan. Their sweet pastry breakfasts are a hit, with a stunning array of hot-out-of-the-oven treats like *panzerotto* (made of ricotta, cinnamon, and vanilla, €2) and hot meat-and-cheese bruschetta (€3). Other favorites include their *granitas* (slushees made from fresh fruit), but, proudly, no bacon and eggs (since "this is Italy"). While the atmosphere of the place seems like suburban Milan, it has a curious charisma among its customers—bringing Vernazza a welcome bit of Sicily (daily 6:30–24:00, also simple lunches and tasty dinners, Via Gavino 36, tel. 0187-812-047).

Lunch and Dinner

If you enjoy Italian cuisine and seafood, Vernazza's restaurants are worth the splurge. All take pride in their cooking. Wander around at about 20:00 and compare the ambience, but don't wait too late to eat—many kitchens close at 22:00. To get an outdoor table on summer weekends, reserve ahead. Expect to spend €10 for pastas, €12–16 for *secondi,* and €2–3 for a cover charge. Harborside restaurants and bars are easygoing. You're welcome to grab a cup of coffee or glass of wine and disappear somewhere on the breakwater, returning your glass when you're done. If you dine in Vernazza but are staying in another town, be sure to check train schedules before dining, as trains run less frequently in the evening. While kitchens are generally closed 15:00–19:00, snacks and drinks are served all day.

Above the Harbor, by the Castle

Ristorante Al Castello is run by gracious and English-speaking Monica, her husband Massimo, kind Mario, and the rest of her family (you won't see mamma—she's busy personally cooking each *secondo*). Hike high above town to just below the castle for great seafood and regional specialties with commanding views. Their *lasagne al pesto* and scampi crêpes are time-honored family specialties, and their *antipasto misto mare* is a sharable €15 starter treat. For a special evening, reserve one of the dozen romantic, cliff-side, sea-view tables for two (Thu–Tue 12:00–15:00 for lunch, 19:00–22:00 for dinner, closed Wed and Nov–April, tel. 0187-812-296).

Ristorante Belforte's experimental and creative cuisine includes a hearty *zuppa Michela* (€16 for a boatload of seafood), fishy *spaghetti Bruno* (€13), and *trofie al pesto* (hand-rolled noodles with pesto). Their classic *antipasto del nostro chef* (€36 for six plates) is designed to be plenty for two people. From the breakwater, follow either the stairs or the rope that leads up and around to the restaurant. You'll find a tangle of tables embedded in four levels of the lower part of the old castle. For the ultimate seaside perch, call and reserve one of four tables on the *terrazza con vista* (terrace with view). Most of Belforte's seating is outdoors—if the weather's bad, the interior can get crowded (€13 pastas, €23 *secondi*, Wed–Mon 12:00–22:00, closed Tue and Nov–March, tel. 0187-812-222, Michela).

Harborside

Gambero Rosso is considered Vernazza's most venerable restaurant. It feels classy and costs more than the others (€15 pastas, €20 *secondi*, €3 cover, Tue–Sun 12:00–15:00 & 19:00–22:00, closed Mon and Dec–Feb, Piazza Marconi 7, tel. 0187-812-265).

Trattoria del Capitano might serve the best food for the money, including *spaghetti chitarra* (egg-based pasta entangled with various types of seafood) and their *grigliata mista*—a mix of seasonal Mediterranean fish (€12 pastas, €20 *secondi*, €2 cover, Wed–Mon 12:00–15:00 & 19:00–22:00, closed Tue except in Aug, closed Dec–Jan, tel. 0187-812-201, while Paolo speaks English, grandpa Giacomo doesn't need to).

Trattoria Gianni is an old standby for locals and tourists who appreciate the best prices on the harbor. You'll enjoy well-prepared seafood and receive steady, reliable, and friendly service from Tonino, Giuliano, and Allesandro (€9 pastas, €13 *secondi*, €3 cover, check their *menu cucina tipica Vernazza*, Thu–Tue 12:00–15:00 & 19:30–22:00, closed Wed except July–Aug, tel. 0187-812-228).

Ristorante Pizzeria Vulnetia is simpler, serving regional specialties and €8 pizzas (€10 pastas, €15 *secondi*, €2 cover, Tue–Sun 12:00–15:30 & 18:30–22:00, closed Mon, Piazza Marconi 29, tel. 0187-821-193).

Inland, on or near the Main Street

Several of Vernazza's inland eateries manage to compete without the harbor ambience, but with slightly cheaper prices.

Trattoria da Sandro, on the main drag, mixes Genovese and Ligurian cuisine with friendly service. It can be a peaceful alternative to the harborside scene (Wed–Mon 12:00–15:00 & 19:00–22:00, closed Tue, Via Roma 62, tel. 0187-812-223, Gabriella and Alessandro).

Antica Osteria Il Baretto is another solid bet for homey, reasonably priced, traditional cuisine, run by Simone, Zia, and family. As it's off the harbor and a little less glitzy than the others, it's favored by locals who prefer less noisy English while they eat (Tue–Sat 8:00–16:00 & 18:00–24:00, closed Mon, indoor and outdoor seating, Via Roma 31).

Ristorante Incadase da Piva is a rare bit of old Vernazza. For 25 years, charismatic Piva has been known for his *tegame alla Vernazza* (typical Vernazzan dish with anchovies, tomatoes, and potatoes baked in the oven), his *risotto con frutti di mare* (seafood risotto), and his love of music. The town troubadour, he often serenades his guests when the cooking's done (tucked away 20 yards off the main drag, up a lane behind the pharmacy).

Other Eating Options

Il Pirata delle Cinque Terre is popular for breakfast, lunch (sandwiches and light fare only), dinner (€9 pastas, salads, Sicilian specialties), and its homemade desserts and drinks. The Canoli twins entertain while they serve, as diners enjoy delicious meals while laughing out loud in this simple café/pastry shop (at the top of town; also see listing under "Breakfast," earlier in this section).

Franco's Ristorante La Torre, sitting humbly above Vernazza on the trail to Corniglia, offers family-run warmth, a spectacular view, perfect peace, and especially romantic dinners at sunset. Hours can be sporadic, so confirm that he's open before hiking up (Wed–Mon 12:00–21:30, sometimes also open Tue, kitchen closed 15:00–19:30 but drinks are served all day, tel. 0187-821-082, mobile 338-404-1181).

Bar Baia Saracena ("Saracen Bay") serves decent pizza and microwaved pastas out on the breakwater. Eat here for the economy and the view (€5–7 salads, €9 pizza; also see listing under "Breakfast," earlier in this section).

Pizzerias, Sandwiches, and Groceries: Vernazza's main street creatively fills tourists' needs. Two pizzerias stay busy, and while they mostly do take-out, each will let you sit and eat for the same cheap price. One has tables on the street, and the other **(Ercole)** hides a tiny terrace and a few tables out back. **Rosticceria Ar Tian** sells pasta and cooked dishes by weight for a cheap meal-to-go (at bottom of Via Roma across from Gelateria Stalin). **Forno Bakery** has good focaccia and veggie tarts, and several bars sell sandwiches and pizza by the slice. **Grocery stores** also make inexpensive sandwiches to order (generally Mon–Tue and Thu–Sat 8:00–13:00 & 17:00–19:30, Wed 8:00–13:00, closed Sun). Tiny jars of pesto spread give elegance to picnics.

Gelato: The town's three *gelaterias* are good. What looks like Gelateria Amore Mio (near the grotto, mid-town), is actually Gelateria Stalin—founded in 1968 by a pastry chef with that unfortunate name. His niece Sonia, who speaks "ice cream," and nephew Francesco now run the place, and are generous with free tastes. They have a neat little licking zone with tiny benches tucked away from the crowd atop the little bridge a few steps past their door (daily 8:00–24:00, 24 flavors, sit there or take it to go).

Monterosso al Mare (Town #5)

This is a resort with a few cars and lots of hotels, rentable beach umbrellas, crowds, and a thriving late-night scene. Monterosso al Mare—the only Cinque Terre town built on flat land—has two parts: A new town (called Fegina) with a parking lot, train station, and TI; and an old town (Centro Storico), which cradles Old World charm in its small, crooked lanes. In the old town, you'll find hole-in-the-wall shops, pastel townscapes, and a new generation of creative small-businesspeople eager to keep their visitors happy.

A pedestrian tunnel connects the old with the new. But take a small detour around the point for a nicer walk. It offers a close-up view of two sights: a 16th-century lookout tower, built after the last serious pirate raid in 1545; and a Nazi "pillbox," a small, low, concrete bunker where gunners hid. (During World War II, nearby La Spezia was an important Axis naval base, and Monterosso was bombed while the Germans were here.)

Strolling the waterfront promenade, you can pick out each of the Cinque Terre towns decorating the coast. After dark, they sparkle. Monterosso is the most enjoyable of the five for young travelers wanting to connect with other young travelers and looking for a little evening action. Even so, Monterosso is not a full-blown Portofino-style resort—and locals appreciate quiet, sensitive guests.

Orientation

Tourist Information

The TI Proloco is next to the train station (April–Oct daily 9:00–19:00, closed Nov–March, exit station and go left a few doors, tel. 0187-817-506, www.prolocomonterosso.it, Annamaria). The Cinque Terre has park offices on Piazza Garibaldi in the old town and in the train station in the new town (daily 8:00–22:00, until 20:00 in winter, tel. 0187-817-059, www.parconazionale5terre.it, parcoragazze@hotmail.com).

Arrival in Monterosso

By Train: Train travelers arrive in the new town, from which it's a scenic, flat, 10-minute stroll to all the old-town action (leave station to the left; but for hotels in the new town, turn right out of station).

Shuttle buses run along the waterfront between the old town (Piazza Garibaldi, just beyond the tunnel), the train station, and the parking lot at the end of Via Fegina (*Campo Sportivo* stop).

While the buses can be convenient, saving you a 10-minute schlep with your bags, they only go once an hour, and are likely not worth the trouble (€1.50, free with Cinque Terre Card).

The other alternative is to take a **taxi** (certain vehicles have permission to drive in the old city center). They usually wait outside the train station, but you may have to call (€7 from station to Centro Storico, mobile 335-616-5842 or 335-628-0933).

By Car: Monterosso is 30 minutes off the freeway (exit: Levanto-Carrodano). Parking is easy (except July–Aug and summer weekends) in the huge beachfront guarded lot (€12/day, €24 overnight). Another lot is farther up Via Roma (€15/day, if entering Monterosso's Centro Storico from the freeway it's on the left, 10-minute downhill walk to Piazza Garibaldi).

Helpful Hints

Medical Help: The town's bike-riding, leather-bag-toting, English-speaking doctor is Dr. Vitone, who charges around €50 for a simple visit (less for poor students, mobile 338-853-0949).

Internet Access: The Net, a few steps off the main drag (Via Roma), has 10 high-speed computers (€1/10 min). Enzo happily provides information on the Cinque Terre, has a line on local rooms for rent, and can burn your photos onto a CD for €6 (daily 10:00–22:00, off-season until 19:00 with a lunch break, Via Vittorio Emanuele 55, tel. 0187-817-288, www.monterossonet.com). There's also free Internet access for customers at the **Il Casello** restaurant/bar (see "Eating," at the end of the Monterosso section.

Laundry: A full-service launderette is at Via Mazzini 2 (13-pound wash-and-dry for €12, allow 2 hours, daily 9:00–20:00, just off Via Roma below L'Alta Marea restaurant, Andrea). **Lavarapido,** in the new part of town, will return your laundry to your hotel for you (€12/13 pounds, daily 8:00–22:00, Via Molinelli 17, mobile 339-484-0940, Lucia).

Massage: Giorgio Moggia, the local physiotherapist, gives good massages at your hotel (€50/hr, tel. 339-314-6127, giomogg @tin.it).

Self-Guided Walk

Welcome to Monterosso

• *Hike out from the dock in the old town and climb a few rough steps to the very top of the...*

Breakwater: If you're visiting by boat, you'll start here anyway. From this point, you can survey the old town and the new town (stretching to the left, with train station and parking lot).

THE CINQUE TERRE

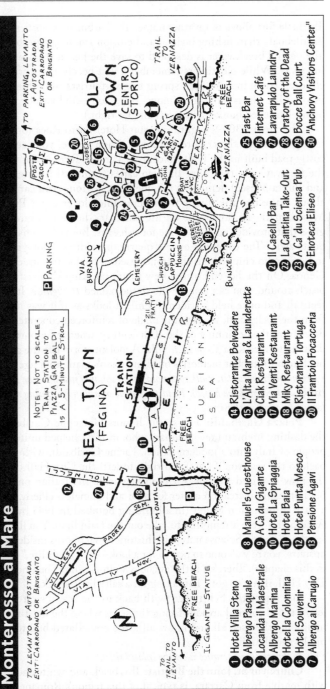

Monterosso al Mare

THE CINQUE TERRE

NOTE: Not to scale - Train Station to Piazza Garibaldi is a 5-minute stroll.

NEW TOWN (FEGINA)

OLD TOWN (CENTRO STORICO)

1 Hotel Villa Steno
2 Albergo Pasquale
3 Locanda il Maestrale
4 Albergo Marina
5 Hotel la Colonnina
6 Hotel Souvenir
7 Albergo al Carugio
8 Manuel's Guesthouse
9 A Cà du Gigante
10 Hotel La Spiaggia
11 Hotel Baia
12 Hotel Punta Mesco
13 Pensione Agavi
14 Ristorante Belvedere
15 L'Alta Marea & Launderette
16 Ciak Restaurant
17 Via Venti Restaurant
18 Miky Restaurant
19 Ristorante Tortuga
20 Il Frantoio Focacceria
21 Il Casello Bar
22 La Cantina Take-Out
23 A Ca du Sciensa Pub
24 Enoteca Eliseo
25 Fast Bar
26 Internet Café
27 Lavarapido Laundry
28 Oratory of the Dead
29 Bocce Ball Court
30 "Anchovy Visitors Center"

The little fort above is a private home. The harbor now hosts more paddleboats than fishing boats. Sand erosion is a major problem. The partial breakwater is designed to save the beach from washing away. While old-timers remember a vast beach, their grandchildren truck in sand each spring to give tourists something to lie on. (The Nazis liked the Cinque Terre, too—find two of their bomb-hardened bunkers, near left and far right.)

The fancy €300-a-night, four-star Hotel Porto Roca (on the far right) marks the trail to Vernazza. High above, you see the costly road built in the 1980s to connect Cinque Terre towns with the freeway over the hills. The two capes (Punta di Montenero and Punta Mesco) define the Cinque Terre region—you can just about make out the towns from here. The closer cape, Punta Mesco, marks an important sea-life sanctuary, home to a rare sea grass that provides an ideal home for fish eggs. Buoys keep fishing boats away. The cape was once a quarry, providing employment to locals who chipped out the stones used to cobble the streets of Genoa. On the far end of the new town, marking the best free beach around, you can just see the statue named *Il Gigante*. It's 45 feet tall and once held a trident. While it looks as if it was hewn from the rocky cliff, it's actually made of reinforced concrete and dates from the beginning of the 20th century, when it supported a dancing terrace for a *fin de siècle* villa. A violent storm left the giant holding nothing but memories of Monterosso's glamorous age.

• *From the breakwater, walk to the old-town square (just past the train tracks and beyond the beach). Find the statue of a dandy holding what looks like a box cutter in...*

Piazza Garibaldi: The statue honors Giuseppe Garibaldi, the dashing firebrand revolutionary who, in 1870, helped unite the people of Italy into a modern nation. Facing Garibaldi, with your back to the sea, you'll see (from right to left) the City Hall (with the now-required European Union flag aside the Italian one), a big home and recreation center for poor and homeless elderly, and a park information center (in a building bombed in 1945 by the Allies, who were attempting to take out the train line). You'll also see the A Ca' du Sciensa pub (with historic town photos inside and upstairs, you're welcome to pop in for a look—see "Nightlife," later in this chapter). There's a little "anchovy visitors center" behind the City Hall, if you've got a hankering for a salty little snack.

Just under the bell tower (with back to the sea, it's on your left) a set of covered arcades facing the sea is where the old-timers hang out (they see all and know all). The crenellated bell tower marks the church.

• *Go to church (the entrance is on the inland side).*

Church of St. John the Baptist: This black-and-white church, with marble from Carrara, is typical of this region's Romanesque style. Note the lacy stone rose window above the entrance. The church dates from 1307—the proud inscription on the middle column inside reads "MilleCCCVII." Outside the church, on the side facing the main street, find the high-water mark from a November 1966 flood (the same month as the flood that devastated Florence).

• *Leaving the church, turn left immediately and go to church again.*

Oratory of the Dead: During the Counter-Reformation, the Catholic Church offset the rising influence of the Lutherans by creating brotherhoods of good works. These religious Rotary clubs were called "confraternities." Monterosso had two, nicknamed White and Black. This building is the oratory of the Black group, whose mission—as the macabre decor indicates—was to arrange for funerals and take care of widows, orphans, the shipwrecked, and the souls of those who ignore the request for a €1 donation. It dates from the 16th century, and membership has passed from father to son for generations. Notice the fine 17th-century carved choir stalls just inside the door. Look up on the ceiling to find the symbol of the confraternity: a skull, crossbones, and an hourglass... death awaits us all.

• *Return to the beach and find the brick steps that lead up to the hill-capping convent (starting between the train tracks and the pedestrian tunnel).*

The Switchbacks of the Monks: Follow the yellow brick road (OK, it's orange...but I couldn't help singing as I skipped skyward). Go constantly uphill until you reach a convent church, then a cemetery, in a ruined castle at the summit. The lane *(Salita dei Cappuccini)* is nicknamed *Zii di Frati* ("switchbacks of the monks"). Midway up the switchbacks, you'll see a statue of St. Francis and a wolf enjoying a grand view.

• *From here, backtrack 20 yards and continue uphill. When you reach a gate marked* Convento e Chiesa Cappuccini, *you have arrived.*

Church of the Cappuccin Monks: The former convent (until recently a hotel) now accommodates monks. Before stepping inside, notice the church's striped Romanesque facade. It's all fake. Tap it—no marble, just cheap 18th-century stucco. Sit in the rear pew. The high altarpiece painting of St. Francis can be rolled up on special days to reveal a statue of Mary, which stands behind it. Look at the statue of St. Anthony to the right and smile (you're on convent camera). Wave at the security camera—they're nervous about the precious painting to your left.

This fine painting of the Crucifixion is attributed to Antony Van Dyck, the Flemish master who lived and worked for years in nearby Genoa (though art historians suspect that, at best, it was painted by someone in the artist's workshop). When Jesus died, the earth went dark. Notice the eclipsed sun in the painting, just to the right of the cross. Do the electric candles work? Pick one up, pray for peace, and plug it in. (Leave €0.50, or unplug it and put it back.)

• *Leave and turn left to hike uphill to the cemetery that fills the remains of the castle, capping the hill. Look out from the gate and enjoy the view.*

Cemetery and Ruined Castle: In the Dark Ages, the village huddled within this castle. Slowly it expanded. Notice the town view from here—no sea. You're looking at the oldest part of Monterosso, huddled behind the hill, out of view of 13th-century pirates. Explore the cemetery, but remember that cemeteries are sacred and treasured places (as is clear by the abundance of fresh flowers). Ponder the black-and-white photos of grandparents past. *Q.R.P.* is *Qui Riposa in Pace* (a.k.a. R.I.P.). Rich families had their own little tomb buildings. See if you can find the Odoardo family tomb—look to the wall on the left (apparently, February 30 happened in Monterosso). Climb to the very summit—the castle's keep, or place of last refuge. Priests are buried in a line of graves closest to the sea, but facing inland—the town's holy sanctuary high on the hillside (above the road, hiding behind trees). Each Cinque Terre town has a lofty sanctuary, dedicated to Mary and dear to the village hearts.

• *From here, your tour is over—any trail leads you back into town.*

Activities

Beaches—Monterosso's beaches, immediately in front of the train station, are easily the Cinque Terre's best and most crowded. This town is a sandy resort with rentable beach extras: Figure €15 to rent two chairs and an umbrella for the day. Light lunches are served by beach cafés to sunbathers at their lounge chairs. It's often worth the euros to enjoy a private beach. Beaches are free (and marked on the Monterosso al Mare map in this section) only where you see no umbrellas. The local hidden beach, which is free and generally less crowded, is tucked away under Il Casello restaurant at the east end of town, near the trailhead to Vernazza. The bocce ball court (next to Il Casello) is busy with the old boys enjoying their favorite pastime.

Kayaks—Kayak rental is available on the beach in front of the train station (€6/hr for 1-person kayak, €10/hr for 2-person kayak, mobile 328-288-6827 or 339-681-0265, Maurizio). The paddle to Vernazza is a favorite.

Shuttle Buses for High-Country Hikes—Monterosso's bus service (described in "Arrival in Monterosso," earlier in this chapter) continues beyond the town limits, but check the schedules—only one or two departures a day head upward. A route goes to Colle di Gritta, where you can hike back down to Monterosso via the

Sanctuary of Soviore (1 hour, easy) or to Levanto via Punta Mesco (2.5 hours, strenuous). Rides cost €1.50 (free with Cinque Terre Card, pick up schedule from park office). For hiking details, ask at either park info booth (at the train station or Piazza Garibaldi).

Boat Rides—From the old-town harbor, boats run nearly hourly (10:30–17:00) to Vernazza, Manarola, Riomaggiore, and Portovenere. Schedules are posted in Cinque Terre park offices (for details, see "The Cinque Terre National Park," near the beginning of this chapter). A smaller, privately operated boat connects Vernazza and Monterosso more frequently (2/hr).

Angelo's Boat Tours—Local fisherman Angelo and his American wife Paola are now fishers of tourists who rent their boat for a scenic cruise, swim, coastal exploration, and local food. Paola enjoys cooking for guests (€60/hr for the boat plus €25/person for the meal, mobile 333-318-2967, angelosboattours@yahoo.com).

Nightlife

Il Casello offers cocktails and a sea view. Enthusiastically run by Bacco, it's the best on-the-beach drinking spot—inexpensive and hip—with a creative and fun drink list. Built in about 1870 as the town's first train station, Il Casello overlooks the beach on the road toward Vernazza, with outdoor tables on a rocky outcrop sandwiched between old-town beaches. It's also a great place for a salad or sandwich during the day (June–Aug daily 10:30–24:00, shorter hours April–May and Sept, closed Oct–March, tel. 0187-818-330).

A Ca' du Sciensa has nothing to do with science—it's the last name of the town moneybags who owned this old mansion. The antique dumbwaiter is still in use—a remnant from the days when servants toiled downstairs while the big shots wined and dined up top. This classy yet laid-back pub offers breezy square seating, bar action on the ground level, an intimate lounge upstairs, and discreet balconies overlooking the square to share with your best travel buddy. It's a good place for light meals (until 23:00) and plenty of drinks. Luca and Andrea encourage you to wander around the place and enjoy the old Cinque Terre photo collection (daily 11:00–24:00 and often later, serves late-night sandwiches and pasta, closed Nov–March, Piazza Garibaldi 17, tel. 0187-818-233).

Enoteca Eliseo, the first wine bar in town, comes with operatic ambience. Eliseo and his wife, Mary, love music and wine. You can select a fine bottle from their shop shelf, and for €6 extra, enjoy it and the village action from their cozy tables. Wines sold by the glass *(bicchiere)* are posted (daily 9:00–24:00, closed Tue Nov–Feb, Piazza Matteotti 3, a few blocks inland behind church, tel. 0187-817-308).

Fast Bar, where young travelers and night owls gather, is located on Via Roma in the old town. Customers mix travel tales with big, cold beers, and the crowd gets noisier as the night rolls on (sandwiches and snacks served until midnight, open nightly until 2:00, closed Thu Nov–March).

Sleeping

(€1 = about $1.40, country code: 39)

Monterosso, the most beach-resorty of the five Cinque Terre towns, offers maximum comfort and ease. The TI Proloco just outside the train station can give you a list of €30–35 per-person double rooms. To locate the hotels, see the Monterosso al Mare map earlier in this chapter.

In the Old Town

$$$ Hotel Villa Steno is lovingly managed and features great view balconies, private gardens off some rooms, air-conditioning, and the friendly help of English-speaking Matteo and his wife Carla. Of their 16 rooms, 12 have view balconies (Sb-€95, Db-€150, Tb-€180, Qb-€210, includes hearty buffet breakfast, ask for discount with cash and this book, Internet access, laundry, Via Roma 109, tel. 0187-817-028 or 0187-818-336, fax 0187-817-354, www .pasini.com, steno@pasini.com). It's a 10-minute hike (or €7 taxi ride) from the train station to the top of the old town. Readers get a free Cinque Terre info packet and a glass of the local sweet wine, *sciacchetrà,* when they check in—ask for it. The Steno has a tiny parking lot for guests (free, but call to reserve a spot).

$$$ Albergo Pasquale is a modern, comfortable place, run by the same family as the Hotel Villa Steno (previous listing). It's conveniently located just a few steps from the beach, boat dock, tunnel entrance to the new town, and train tracks. While there is some traffic and train noise, it's located right on the harbor and has an elevator, offering easier access than most (same prices and welcome drink as Villa Steno; air-con, all rooms with sea view, Via Fegina 8, tel. 0187-817-550 or 0187-817-477, fax 0187-817-056, www.pasini.com, pasquale@pasini.com, Felicita and Marco).

$$$ Locanda il Maestrale rents six small, stylish rooms in a sophisticated and peaceful little inn. While renovated with all the modern comforts, it retains centuries-old character under frescoed ceilings. Its peaceful sun terrace overlooking the old town and Via Roma action is a delight (small Db-€110, Db-€135, suite-€170, less off-season, includes breakfast, ask for discount with cash and this book, Via Roma 37, tel. 0187-817-013, mobile 338-4530-531, fax 0187-817-084, www.locandamaestrale.net, maestrale@monterosso net.com, Stefania).

$$$ Albergo Marina, creatively run by enthusiastic husband-and-wife team Marina and Eraldo, has 25 thoughtfully appointed rooms and a garden with lemon trees, and is a great value. Guests enjoy a welcome surprise and a free, delicious buffet featuring local specialties from14:00–17:00 daily (standard Db-€115, big Db-€125, ask for discount with cash and this book, elevator, air-con, free bikes, kayak and snorkel equipment, Via Buranco 40, tel. 0187-817-613, fax 0187-817-242, www.hotelmarina5terre.com, marina @hotelmarina5terre.com).

$$$ Hotel la Colonnina, a comfy, modern place with 19 big rooms, is buried in the town's fragrant and sleepy back streets with no sea views (Db-€130, Tb-€160, Qb-€195, €15 more for bigger rooms with viewless terrace, cash only, air-con, elevator, inviting rooftop terrace, garden, Via Zuecca 6, tel. 0187-817-439, fax 0187-817-788, www.lacolonninacinqueterre.it, info@lacolonninacinque terre.it, Christina). The hotel is in the old town behind the statue of Garibaldi (take street to left of A Ca' du Sciensa one block up).

$$ Hotel Souvenir is Monterosso's cash-only backpacker's hotel. It has two buildings, each utilitarian but comfortable (one more stark than the other). The first is for students (S-€30, Sb-€35, D-€50, Db-€60, T-€75, breakfast-€5); the other is nicer and pricier, with a lounge and pleasant, leafy courtyard (Sb-€40, Db-€80, Tb-€120, includes breakfast). Walk three blocks inland from the main old-town square to Via Gioberti 24 (tel. 0187-817-822, tel. & fax 0187-817-595, www.souvenirhotel.eu, hotel_souvenir @yahoo.com).

$$ Albergo al Carugio is a simple, practical, nine-room place in a big apartment-style building at the top of the old town. It's quiet, comfy, yet forgettable, with no discernable management, and run in a crooked-painting-on-the-wall way (Db-€85 July–Aug, or €70–75 otherwise, Via Roma 100, tel. 0187-817-453, alcarugio @virgilio.it).

$$ Manuel's Guesthouse is ramshackle—a bohemian rhapsody ruled by disheveled artist Manuel and run by his nephew Lorenzo. They have five big, basic rooms and a grand view. Their killer terrace is hard to leave—especially after a few drinks (Db-€60, Tb-€75, Qb-€100, no breakfast, cash only, Manuel has a cheap honor-system beer and wine bar, in old town, up about 100 steps behind church at top of town, Via San Martino 39, mobile 328-842-6885 or 333-439-0809, www.manuelsguesthouse.com, info@manuelsguesthouse.com).

In the New Town

$$$ A Cà du Gigante, despite its name, is a tiny yet classy refuge with six rooms. About 100 yards from the beach (and surrounded by blocky apartments on a modern street), the interior is done with taste and modern comfort in mind (Db-€160, Db-suite €170, includes parking, air-con, ask for discount with 3-night stay and this book, occasional last-minute deals, Via IV Novembre 11, tel. 0187-817-401, fax 0187-817-375, www.ilgigantecinqueterre.it, gigante@ilgigantecinqueterre.it, Claudia).

$$$ Hotel La Spiaggia is a big old place with 19 rooms capably run by a grand personality, Andrea Poggi, who is great at helping visitors (Db-€160 includes parking, beach access, and breakfast; extra bed-€30, ask for discount with cash and this book, same price with or without views, Via Lungomare 98, tel. 0187-817-567, www.laspiaggiahotel.com, hotellaspiaggia@libero.it).

$$$ Hotel Baia (by-yah), overlooking the beach near the station, has clean, high-ceilinged, dimly lit rooms, dark hallways, and impersonal staff. Of the hotel's 28 rooms, half have views. The best little two-chair view balconies are on top floors (Db-€180, non-view Db in back-€150, elevator only for baggage and disabled people, minimum 3-night stay May–Sept, Via Fegina 88, tel. 0187-817-512, fax 0187-818-322, www.baiahotel.it, info@baiahotel.it).

$$$ Hotel Punta Mesco is a tidy and well-run little haven renting 17 quiet, modern rooms without views, but 10 have little terraces. For the price, it's perhaps the best comfort in town (Db-€126, 5 percent discount with cash, air-con, free bike loan, free parking, Via Molinelli 35, tel. & fax 0187-817-495, www.hotelpunta mesco.it, info@hotelpuntamesco.it, Diego).

$$ Pensione Agavi has 10 bright, airy, tranquil, and quiet rooms, about half overlooking the beach near the big rock. This is not a place to party—it feels like an old hospital with narrow hallways (S-€40, Sb-€60, D-€80, Db-€100, no breakfast, cash only, refrigerators, turn left out of station to Fegina 30, tel. 0187-817-171, mobile 333-697-4071, fax 0187-818-264, hotel.agavi@libero.it).

Eating

Ristorante Belvedere is *the* place for a good-value meal indoors or outdoors on the harborfront. Their *amfora belvedere*—mixed seafood stew—is huge, and can easily be shared by up to four (€45). Share with your group and add pasta for a fine meal. It's energetically run by Federico and Roberto (€9 pastas, €12 *secondi*, €2 cover, Wed–Mon 12:00–14:30 & 19:00–22:00, usually closed Tue, on the harbor in the old town, tel. 0187-817-033).

L'Alta Marea offers special fish ravioli, the catch of the day, and huge crocks of fresh, steamed mussels. Young chef Marco cooks with charisma, while his wife, Anna, takes good care of the guests. This place is quieter, buried in the old town two blocks off the beach, and has covered tables out front for people-watching. This is a good opportunity to try rabbit (€8 pastas, €12–15 *secondi*,

€2 cover, ask for discount with this book, Thu–Tue 12:00–15:00 & 18:30–22:00, open later in summer, closed Wed, Via Roma 54, tel. 0187-817-170).

Ciak—a cut above its neighbors in elegance and also a little higher in price—is known for their huge sizzling terra-cotta crocks for two, crammed with the day's catch and either accompanied by risotto or spaghetti, or swimming in a soup *(zuppa)*. Another popular choice is the seafood *antipasto Lampara*. Stroll a couple of paces past the outdoor tables up Via Roma to see what Ciak's got on the stove (Thu–Tue 12:00–15:00 & 19:00–22:30, closed Wed, tel. 0187-817-014).

Via Venti is a fun little trattoria, buried in an alley deep in the heart of the old town, where Papa Ettore creates imaginative seafood dishes using the day's catch and freshly made pasta. Son Michele and Ilaria serve up delicate and savory gnocchi (tiny potato dumplings) with crab sauce, tender ravioli stuffed with fresh fish in a swordfish sauce, and pear-and-cheese pasta. There's nothing pretentious here...just good cooking, service, and prices (€11 pastas, €15 *secondi*, Fri–Wed 12:00–15:30 & 18:30–22:00, closed Thu, tel. 0187-818-347). From the bottom of Via Roma, with your back to the sea and the church to your left, head to the right to head down Via XX Settembre and follow it to the end, to #32.

Miky is packed with well-dressed locals who know their seafood and want to eat it in a classy environment, but don't want to spend a fortune. For elegantly presented, top-quality food, this is my Cinque Terre favorite. It's clearly a proud and hardworking family operation: Miky (dad), Simonetta (mom), and charming Sara (daughter) all work hard. All their pasta is "pizza pasta"—cooked normally but finished in a bowl that's encased in a thin pizza crust. They cook the concoction in a wood-fire oven to keep in the aroma. Miky's has a fine wine list with many available by the glass if you ask. If I was ever to require a dessert, it would be their mixed sampler plate, *dolce mista*—€10 and plenty for two (€14 pastas, €22 *secondi*, €7 sweets, Wed–Mon 12:00–15:00 & 19:00–23:00, closed Tue, reservations wise in summer, in the new town, 100 yards north of train station at Via Fegina 104, tel. 0187-817-608).

Ristorante Tortuga is the top option in Monterosso for seaview elegance, with gorgeous outdoor seating on a bluff and an elegant white-tablecloth-and-candles interior. If you're out and about, drop by to consider which table you'd like to reserve for later (€15 pastas, €20 *secondi*, closed Mon, just outside the tunnel that connects the old and new town, tel. 0187-800-065, mobile 333-240-7956, Silvia and Giamba).

Light Meals, Take-Out Food, and Breakfast

Lots of shops and bakeries sell pizza and focaccia for an easy picnic at the beach or on the trail. At **Il Frantoio,** Simone makes tasty pizza to go or to munch perched on a stool (daily 9:00–14:00 & 16:00–19:30, just off Via Roma at Via Gioberti 1, tel. 0187-818-333). **Pizzeria la Smorfia** also cooks up good pizza to eat in or take out (73 Via Vittorio Emanuele).

Il Casello is the only place for a fun, light meal on a terrace overlooking the old town beach. With outdoor tables on a rocky outcrop, it's a good bet for a salad or sandwich (June–Aug daily meals from 11:30 and 19:00, closed Nov–March, tel. 0187-818-330).

La Cantina, a hole-in-the-wall behind Via Roma, dishes up made-on-the-spot regional specialties, such as *lasagne al pesto* or freshly fried anchovies, in take-away containers (€5 portions, daily 9:00–19:00 June–Sept, Oct–March until 14:00, Via XX Settembre 24, tel. 328-174-9054, sisters Stefania and Chiara).

Connections

Trains

The five towns of the Cinque Terre are on a pokey, milk-run train line (described in "Getting Around the Cinque Terre," near the beginning of this chapter). Erratically timed but roughly hourly trains connect each town with the others, La Spezia, and Genoa. While a few of these local trains go to more distant points (Milan or Pisa), it's much faster to change in La Spezia or Monterosso to a bigger train (local train info tel. 0187-817-458).

From La Spezia by Train to: Rome (9/day, 4 hrs), **Pisa** (about hourly, 1–1.5 hrs, direction: Livorno, Rome, Salerno, Naples, etc.), **Florence** (3/day direct, otherwise nearly hourly, 2.5 hrs), **Milan** (hourly, 3 hrs direct or 4 hrs with change in Genoa), **Venice** (20/day, 5–7 hrs, 1–3 changes).

From Monterosso by Train to: Venice (8/day, 6–8 hrs, 1–3 changes), **Milan** (6/day direct, otherwise hourly, 3–4 hrs, more with changes in Sestri Levante or Genoa), **Genoa** (hourly, 1.2–2 hrs), **La Spezia** (hourly, 20–30 min), **Rome** (hourly, 4.5 hrs). For destinations in **France,** change trains in Genoa.

THE CINQUE TERRE

NETHERLANDS

AMSTERDAM

Amsterdam is a progressive way of life housed in Europe's most 17th-century city. Physically, it's built upon millions of pilings. But more than that, it's built on good living, cozy cafés, great art, street-corner jazz, stately history, and a spirit of live-and-let-live. It has 750,000 people and almost as many bikes. It also has more canals than Venice...and about as many tourists.

During its Golden Age in the 1600s, Amsterdam was the world's richest city, an international sea-trading port, and the cradle of capitalism. Wealthy, democratic burghers built a planned city of canals lined with trees and townhouses topped with fancy gables. Immigrants, Jews, outcasts, and political rebels were drawn here by its tolerant atmosphere, while painters such as young Rembrandt captured that atmosphere on canvas.

The Dutch are unique. They are among the world's most handsome people—tall, healthy, and with good posture—and the most open, honest, and refreshingly blunt. They like to laugh. As connoisseurs of world culture, they appreciate Rembrandt paintings, Indonesian food, and the latest French film—but with an un-snooty, blue-jeans attitude.

Approach Amsterdam as an ethnologist observing a strange culture. Stroll through any neighborhood and see things that are commonplace here but rarely found elsewhere. Carillons chime quaintly in neighborhoods selling sex, as young professionals smoke pot with impunity next to old ladies in bonnets selling flowers. Observe the neighborhood's "social control," where an elderly man feels safe in his home knowing he's being watched by the prostitutes next door.

Be warned: Amsterdam, a bold experiment in freedom, may

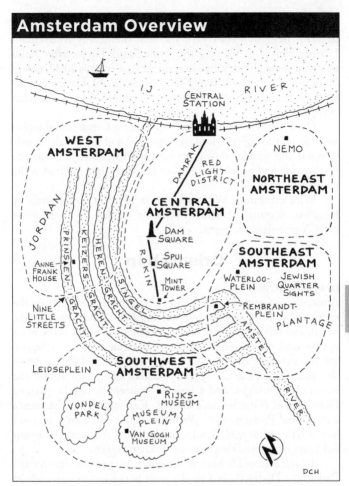

Amsterdam Overview

box your Puritan ears. Take it all in, then pause to watch the clouds blow past stately old gables—and see the Golden Age reflected in a quiet canal.

Planning Your Time

Amsterdam is worth a full day of sightseeing on even the busiest itinerary. While the city has a couple of must-see museums, its best attraction is its own carefree ambience. The city's a joy on foot—and a breezier and faster delight by bike.

In the morning, see the city's two great art museums: the Van Gogh and the Rijksmuseum (cafeteria lunch). Walk from the museums to the Singel canal flower market, then take a relaxing hour-long, round-trip canal cruise from the dock at Spui (see

"Tours," later in this chapter). After the cruise, stroll through the peaceful Begijnhof courtyard and tour the nearby Amsterdam History Museum. Visiting the Anne Frank House after 18:00 may save you an hour in line in summer (last entry is 20:30, except 21:30 July–Aug and 18:30 mid-Sept–mid-March). Have a memorable dinner: try Dutch pancakes or a *rijsttafel*—an Indonesian smorgasbord.

On a balmy evening, Amsterdam has a Greek-island ambience. Stroll through the Jordaan neighborhood for the idyllic side of town and wander down Leidsestraat to Leidseplein for the roaring café and people scene. Tour the Red Light District while you're at it.

With extra time: With two days in Holland, I'd side-trip by bike, bus, or train to Haarlem. With a third day, I'd do the other great Amsterdam museums.

Orientation

(area code: 020)
Amsterdam's Central Train Station (Amsterdam Centraal), on the north edge of the city, is your starting point, with the TI, bike rental, and trams branching out to all points. Damrak is the main north–south axis, connecting Central Station with Dam Square (people-watching and hangout center) and its Royal Palace. From this main street, the city spreads out like a fan, with 90 islands, hundreds of bridges, and a series of concentric canals—named Herengracht (Gentleman's Canal), Keizersgracht (Emperor's Canal), and Prinsengracht (Prince's Canal)—that were laid out in the 17th century, Holland's Golden Age. Amsterdam's major sights are within walking distance of Dam Square.

To the east of Damrak is the oldest part of the city (today's Red Light District), and to the west is the newer part, where you'll find the Anne Frank House and the Jordaan neighborhood. Museums and Leidseplein nightlife cluster at the southern edge of the city center.

Tourist Information

"VVV" (pronounced "vay vay vay") is Dutch for "TI," a tourist information office. Amsterdam's tourist offices are crowded and inefficient—avoid them if you can. For €0.60 a minute, you can save yourself a trip by calling the TI toll line from within the Netherlands at 0900-400-4040 (Mon–Fri 9:00–17:00, from the US dial 011-31-20-551-2525). The TI at Schiphol Airport (offering all the information found at the offices in the city center) and the TI in Haarlem (offering the Amsterdam basics; see page 1076) are much friendlier and less crowded.

If you want to visit an Amsterdam TI in person, here are the locations of the four offices:

• inside Central Station at track 2b (summer: Sat–Thu 8:00–20:00, Fri 8:00–21:00; winter: Mon–Sat 8:00–20:00, Sun 9:00–17:00; may move to ground floor as part of ongoing train station construction)

• in front of Central Station (daily July–Aug 8:00–20:00, Sept–June 9:00–17:00, most crowded)

• on the Singel Canal, in a kiosk at Stadhouderskade 1 (daily 9:30–17:00, less crowded)

• at the airport (daily 7:00–22:00)

Amsterdam's TIs sell tickets to the Anne Frank House (for €0.50 extra per ticket, same-day tickets available), allowing you to skip the line at the sight (though it's quicker to order tickets online—see "Advance Tickets and Sightseeing Cards," below). The TIs also sell tickets (without a fee) to the Rijks and Van Gogh museums.

At Amsterdam's TIs, consider buying a city map (€2) and any of the walking-tour brochures (€2 each, including *Discovery Tour Through the Center, The Former Jewish Quarter,* and *Walks Through Jordaan*). For entertainment, pick up the €2 *Day by Day* calendar; for additional entertainment ideas, see the free papers listed later in this chapter (under "Helpful Hints" and "Nightlife").

At Amsterdam's Central Station, GWK Change has hotel reservation windows whose clerks sell local and international phone cards, mobile-phone SIM cards, and city maps (€2), and can answer basic tourist questions, with shorter lines (in west tunnel, at right end of station as you leave platform, tel. 020/627-2731).

Don't use the TI or GWK to book a room; you'll pay €5 per person and your host loses 13 percent—meaning you'll likely be charged a higher rate. The phone system is easy, everyone speaks English, and the listings in this book are a better value than the potluck booking you'd get from the TI.

Advance Tickets and Sightseeing Cards

Buying Tickets in Advance for the Major Sights: If you'll be visiting Amsterdam in high season (late March through September) and want to avoid standing in long ticket-buying lines, it's smart to book your tickets online for the Anne Frank House, Rijksmuseum, and Van Gogh Museum.

It's easy to buy tickets through each museum's website: www.annefrank.org (€0.50 surcharge per ticket, but worth it), www.rijksmuseum.nl, and www.vangoghmuseum.com (no extra fee for the Rijks or Van Gogh). For the Rijks and Van Gogh museums, print out your reservation and bring it with you to the ticket-holder's line for a quick entry. For the Anne Frank House (if you don't have

AMSTERDAM

access to a printer), simply bring your confirmation number.

You can also buy tickets for these sights in advance at Amsterdam's TIs (see "Tourist Information," previous section), but the lines at the TIs seem as long as the ones you're trying to avoid at the sights.

Tips if You Don't Have Advance Tickets: If you haven't booked ahead, here are a few tips for beating the lines. Going to the Anne Frank House late in the day can help trim your wait in line; this works better in early spring and fall than in summer, when even after-dinner lines can be long. The Museumkaart pass can get you in quickly at the Van Gogh Museum (details in "Sightseeing Cards," next). Or visit the Van Gogh and Rijks museums on a Friday evening, when they're open late (until 22:00 and 20:30, respectively), with no lines and few crowds, even in peak season.

Sightseeing Cards: There are two cards for heavy-duty sightseers to consider. You're more likely to save money by purchasing the Museumkaart, which covers many sights throughout the Netherlands, than the overpriced *I amsterdam* Card, which is valid only in Amsterdam. (There's no reason to buy both.) Both cards allow free entry to most of the sights in Amsterdam (including the Rijks and Van Gogh museums), but neither card covers the Anne Frank House, Heineken Brewery, Westerkerk tower, NEMO science center, or any sights dealing with diamonds, sex, or marijuana.

The **Museumkaart,** which costs €39.95 and is valid for a year throughout the Netherlands, can save you money if you're planning on seeing six or more museums during your trip (for example, an itinerary that includes these museums, for a total of €52.50: Rijksmuseum-€10, Van Gogh Museum-€12.50, Amsterdam History Museum-€8, Amstelkring Museum-€7, Jewish Historical Museum-€7.50, and Haarlem's Frans Hals Museum-€7.50). The Museumkaart is sold at all participating museums, and you can use it to skip the line everywhere but the Rijksmuseum (which doesn't provide a passholders' line). If you plan to buy a Museumkaart, get it at a smaller, less-crowded museum (such as the Amsterdam History Museum), and flash the pass to skip the long ticket-buying line at the Van Gogh Museum. Note that *museumkaart* translates as "a ticket to a museum" in Dutch. To avoid confusion, ask for the one-year Museumkaart pass.

The ***I amsterdam* Card,** which focuses on Amsterdam and includes most transportation, is not worth the money unless you're planning on a day or two of absolutely non-stop sightseeing. You'll have a set number of consecutive hours to use it (for example: Visit your first museum at 14:00 Mon with a 24-hour pass, and it's good until 13:59 on Tue). Along with many sights and discounts, the pass includes two free canal boat tours and unlimited use of the trams, buses, and metro, but not the trains. This pass does not allow you to skip lines at the major sights (€33/24 hrs, €43/48 hrs, or €53/72 hrs; cards sold at major museums, TIs, and with shorter lines at the GVB transit office across from Central Station, next to TI; www.iamsterdamcard.com).

Arrival in Amsterdam

By Train: Amsterdam swings, and the hinge that connects it to the world is its aptly named Central Station (Amsterdam Centraal). Through 2012, expect a chaotic construction zone due to renovations. The international ticket office should be at track 2. Luggage lockers are at the eastern end of the building—but during busy summer weekends, they can fill up fast, causing a line to form (€4–6/24 hrs, depending on size of bag, daily 7:00–23:00, ID required).

Walk out the door of the station, and you're in the heart of the city. You'll nearly trip over trams ready to take you anywhere your feet won't. Straight ahead is Damrak street, leading to Dam Square. With your back to the entrance of the station, the TI and GVB public-transit offices are just ahead to your left. On your right is a vast, multistory bike garage, and bike rentals are to the far left as you exit.

By Plane: For details on getting from Schiphol Airport into downtown Amsterdam, see the end of this chapter.

Helpful Hints

Theft Alert: Tourists are considered green and rich, and the city has more than its share of hungry thieves—especially on trams and at the many hostels. Wear your money belt.

Emergency Telephone Number: Throughout the Netherlands, dial 112.

Street Smarts: Most canals are lined by streets with the same name. When walking around town, beware of the silent transportation—trams and bicycles. (Don't walk on tram tracks or pink/maroon bicycle paths.)

Sightseeing Strategies: To beat the lines at Amsterdam's most popular sights, plan ahead. You can bypass the main ticket-buyers' line at the Anne Frank House, Rijksmuseum, and Van Gogh Museum by buying online tickets before you go (see "Advance Tickets and Sightseeing Cards," earlier in this chapter). Remember, Friday night is a great time to visit the Van Gogh and the Rijks, which are both open late (until 22:00 and 20:30, respectively) to far smaller crowds.

Cash Only: Thrifty Dutch merchants hate paying fees to the credit-card companies; expect to pay cash in unexpected

AMSTERDAM

places, including post offices, grocery stores, train station windows, and some museums.

Shop Hours: Most shops are open Tuesday through Saturday 10:00–18:00, and Sunday and Monday 12:00–18:00. Some shops stay open later (21:00) on Thursdays. Supermarkets are generally open Monday through Saturday 8:00–20:00 and are closed on Sundays.

Internet Access: It's easy at cafés all over town, but the best place for serious surfing and email is the towering **Central Library,** which has hundreds of fast, free terminals (Openbare Bibliotheek Amsterdam, daily 10:00–22:00, free Wi-Fi, a 5-min walk from train station, described on page 1043). "Coffeeshops," which sell marijuana, usually also offer Internet access—letting you surf the Net with a special bravado.

English Bookstores: For fiction and guidebooks—including mine—try the **American Book Center** at Spui 12, right on the square (Mon–Sat 10:00–20:00, Thu until 21:00, Sun 11:00–18:30, tel. 020/625-5537, www.abc.nl). The huge and helpful **Selexyz Scheltema** is at Koningsplein 20 near the Leidsestraat (store open Mon–Sat 10:00–18:00, Thu until 21:00, Sun 12:00–18:00; lots of English novels, guidebooks, and maps; tel. 020/523-1411). **Waterstone's Booksellers,** a UK chain, also sells British newspapers (152 Kalverstraat, Mon–Sat 10:00–18:00, Thu until 21:00, Sun 11:00–18:00, tel. 020/638-3821).

Free Papers: If you're interested in cutting-edge art, movies, and concerts (hip-hop, jazz, classical), pick up the *Amsterdam Weekly,* a free local English-language paper that's published every Wednesday. It's available at most bookstores, including those listed above (www.amsterdamweekly.nl).

Entertainment: Pick up the *Day by Day* calendar at any TI (€2), see "Nightlife," later in this chapter, and call the **Last Minute Ticket Shop** (theater, classical music, and major rock shows, tickets sold only at shop, Leidseplein 26, tel. 0900-0191, calls costs €0.40/min, www.lastminuteticketshop.nl).

Maps: The free and cheap tourist maps can be confusing, except for *Amsterdam Museums: Guide to 37 Museums* (includes tram info and stops, ask for it at the info desk at the big museums, such as the Van Gogh). If you want a top-notch map, buy one (about €2.50). I like the *Carto Studio Centrumkaart Amsterdam* or, better yet, *Amsterdam: Go Where the Locals Go* by Amsterdam Anything.

Pharmacy: The shop named **DA** (Dienstdoende Apotheek) has all the basics—shampoo and toothpaste—as well as a pharmacy counter hidden in the back (Mon–Sat 9:00–22:00, Sun 11:00–22:00, Leidsestraat 74–76 near where it meets Keizersgracht, tel. 020/627-5351).

Laundry: Try **Clean Brothers Wasserij** in the Jordaan (daily 8:00–20:00 for €7 self-service, €9 drop-off—ready in an hour—Mon–Fri 9:00–17:00, Sat 9:00–12:00, no drop-off Sun, Westerstraat 26, one block from Prinsengracht, tel. 020/627-9888) or **Powders** near Leidseplein (daily 8:00–22:00, €6.50 self-service, €8.50 drop-off, Kerkstraat 56, one block south of Leidsestraat).

Holidays: Every year, **Queen's Day** (Koninginnedag, April 30) and **Gay Pride** (early August) bring crowds, fuller hotels, and higher room prices.

Best Views: While the **Westerkerk** offers fine views from its tower (and is convenient if you're visiting the Anne Frank House), the best city views are from the new **Central Library,** Openbare Bibliotheek Amsterdam (see page 1043).

Getting Around Amsterdam

Amsterdam is big, and you'll likely find the trams handy (see below). The longest walk a tourist would make is an hour from Central Station to the Rijksmuseum. When you're on foot, watch out for silent but potentially painful bikes, trams, and crotch-high curb posts.

If you've got a car, park it—all you'll find are frustrating one-way streets, terrible parking, and meter maids with a passion for booting cars parked incorrectly.

By Tram, Bus, and Metro

The helpful GVB public-transit information office is in front of the Central Train Station (next to TI, Mon–Fri 7:00–21:00, Sat–Sun 10:00–18:00, good detailed info on www.gvb.nl). Its free, multilingual *Public Transport Amsterdam Tourist Guide* includes a transit map and explains ticket options and tram connections to all the sights. In keeping with the Dutch mission to automate life, they'll tack on a €0.50 penalty if you buy your transit tickets from a human ticket seller, rather than from a machine. If you're stressed, jetlagged, or otherwise cranky, it's worth the fee for the personal assistance.

You have various ticket options:

• **Individual tickets** cost €1.60 and give you an hour on the buses, trams, and metro system (on trams and buses, pay as you board; for the metro, buy tickets from machines).

• The **24-hour** (€7), **48-hour** (€11.50), or **72-hour** (€14.50) **tickets** give you unlimited transportation on Amsterdam's public-transit network. Buy them at the GVB public-transit office (all versions available), at any TI, or as you board (24-hour version only costs €0.50 extra).

• **Strip tickets** *(strippenkaart)*, nearly half the cost of individual tickets, are good on buses, trams, and the metro in Amsterdam. A strip of 15 shareable strips costs €6.90. Any downtown ride in Amsterdam uses two strips (worth €0.92, good for one hour of transfers).

• Along with its sightseeing perks, the *I amsterdam* Card offers unlimited use of the tram, bus, and metro for its duration (24, 48, or 72 hours—see "Advance Tickets and Sightseeing Cards," near the beginning of this chapter).

Trams: While buses and the metro can be handy for connecting some points in Amsterdam, travelers find the trams most useful. Trams #2 *(Nieuw Sloten)* and #5 *(A'veen Binnenhof)* travel the north–south axis from Central Station to Dam Square to Leidseplein to Museumplein (Van Gogh and Rijks museums). Tram #1 (marked *Osdorp*) also runs to Leidseplein. At Central Station, these three trams depart from the west side of the Stationsplein (with the station behind you, the shelters for these lines are in front of a row of shops).

Tram #14—which doesn't connect to Central Station—goes east–west (Westerkerk–Dam Square–Muntplein–Waterlooplein–Plantage). If you get lost in Amsterdam, 10 of the city's 17 trams take you back to Central Station. Note that you may have to press a button to open the door to get off.

Metro: The metro (underground train) is used mostly for commuting to the suburbs, but it does connect Central Station with some sights east of Damrak (Nieuwmarkt–Waterlooplein–Weesperplein).

By Bike

Everyone—bank managers, students, pizza delivery boys, and police—uses this mode of transport. It's the smart way to travel in a city where 40 percent of all traffic rolls on two wheels. You'll get around town by bike faster than you can by taxi. On my last visit, I rented a bike for five days, chained it up outside my hotel at night, and enjoyed wonderful mobility. I highly encourage this for anyone who wants to get maximum fun per hour in Amsterdam. One-speed bikes, with *"brrringing"* bells, rent for about €10 per day (cheaper for longer periods) at any number of places—hotels can send you to the nearest spot.

Rental Shops: MacBike, with 900 bikes and counting, is the bike-rental powerhouse. It has a huge and efficient outlet at Central Station (€7/3 hrs, €9.50/24 hrs, €14/48 hrs, €19/72 hrs, more for 3 gears, 25 percent discount with *I amsterdam* Card, €50 deposit plus passport or credit-card imprint, no helmets, daily 9:00–17:45; at east end of station—on the left as you're leaving, by the buses; tel.

020/624-8391, www.macbike.nl). They have two smaller, satellite stations at Leidseplein (Weteringschans 2, tel. 020/528-7688) and Waterlooplein (Mr. Visserplein 2, tel. 020/620-0985). Return your bike to the station where you rented it. MacBike sells several pamphlets outlining bike tours in and around Amsterdam for €1.

Frederic Rent-a-Bike, near Central Station, has quality bikes and a helpful staff (€10/24 hrs, €16/48 hrs, €40/week, 10 percent discount on multi-day rental with this book, daily 9:00–17:30, Brouwersgracht 78, tel. 020/624-5509, www.frederic.nl).

Tips: No one wears a helmet. For safety, use arm signals, follow the bike-only traffic signals, stay in the obvious and omnipresent bike lanes, and yield to traffic on the right. Fear oncoming trams and tram tracks. Carefully cross tram tracks at a perpendicular angle to avoid catching your tire in the rut. Warning: Police ticket bikers the same as they do drivers. Obey all traffic signals, and walk your bike through pedestrian zones. Fines for biking through pedestrian zones are reportedly €300. A handy bicycle route-planner can be found at www.routecraft.com (select "bike-planner" and click British flag for English). For a "Do-It-Yourself Bike Tour of Amsterdam" and guided bike tours, see the next section, "Tours."

By Boat

While the city is great on foot, bike, or tram, another option is the **Museum Boat,** which shuttles tourists from sight to sight on an all-day ticket. Tickets cost €19, include museum discounts, and are good for 24 hours. Sales booths in front of Central Station (and the boats) offer free brochures with museum times and admission prices. The boat ride comes with recorded narration and takes two hours if you don't get off (about hourly, fewer in winter, 12 stops, recorded narration, departures daily 10:00–17:00, tel. 020/530-1090, www.lovers.nl).

The similar **Canal Company Bus** is actually a boat, offering 14 stops on three different boat routes (€20, ticket is valid until 12:00 the following day, departures daily 10:00–18:00, until 22:00 in summer, leaves near Central Station and Museum Boat dock, tel. 020/623-9886, www.canal.nl). They also run smaller tour boats with live commentary (see next section, "Tours").

If you're simply looking for a floating, nonstop tour, the regular canal tour boats (without the stops) give more information, cover more ground, and cost less (also listed under "Tours").

For do-it-yourself canal tours and lots of exercise, Canal Bus also rents "canal bikes" (a.k.a. paddleboats) near the Anne Frank House and Rijksmuseum (€8/hr per person, daily July–Aug 10:00–21:30, Sept–June 10:00–18:00).

By Taxi

For short rides, Amsterdam is a bad town for taxis. The city's taxis have a high drop charge (€7.50) for the first two kilometers, after which it's €2 per kilometer. You can wave them down, find a rare taxi stand, or call one (tel. 020/677-7777). Given the fine tram system and the wonders of biking the city, I use taxis less in Amsterdam than just about any city in Europe. You'll also see **bike taxis,** particularly near Dam Square and Leidseplein. Negotiate a rate for the trip before you board (no meter), and they'll wheel you wherever you want to go (€10/30 min, no surcharge for baggage or extra weight, sample fare from Leidseplein to Anne Frank House: about €6).

Tours

By Boat

▲▲**Canal Boat Tours**—These long, low, tourist-laden boats leave continually from several docks around town for a relaxing, if uninspiring, one-hour introduction to the city (with recorded headphone commentary). Select a boat tour for convenience based on the starting point, or if a particular tour is free and included with the *I amsterdam* Card (which covers Rederij Noord-Zuid and Holland International boats). Tip: Boats leave only when full. Jump on a full boat to avoid sitting at the dock waiting. Choose from one of these three companies:

Rondvaart Kooij is cheapest (€8, 3/hr in summer 10:00–22:00, 2/hr in winter 10:00–17:00, at corner of Spui and Rokin streets, about 10 min from Dam Square, tel. 020/623-3810, www.rederijkooij.nl).

Rederij Noord-Zuid departs from near Leidseplein (€10, 2/hr April–Oct 10:00–18:00, hourly Nov–March 10:00–17:00, tel. 020/679-1370, www.blueboat.nl).

Holland International offers a standard one-hour trip and a variety of longer tours (€12, 60-min "100 highlights" tour with recorded commentary, runs about every 15 min daily 9:00–22:00, tel. 020/625-3035, www.hir.nl). Their €18, 90-minute "ultimate" tour with a live guide leaves twice daily (at 11:00 and 13:00).

No fishing allowed—but bring your camera. Some prefer to cruise at night, when the bridges are illuminated.

Hop-On, Hop-Off Canal Boats—Small, 12-person electric Canal Hopper boats leave every 25–35 minutes with live commentary on two different hop-on, hop-off routes (€20 day-pass, runs Sat–Mon 2/hr 9:30–17:30, none Tue–Fri, west route includes Anne Frank House, less-frequent east route includes Rembrandt's House, tel. 020/623-9886, www.canal.nl).

Wetlands Safari, Nature Canoe Tours near Amsterdam—If you'd like to get some exercise and a dose of the *polder* country and village life, consider this five-hour tour. Majel Tromp, a friendly villager who speaks great English, takes groups limited to 15 people. The program: Meet at the VVV tourist information office outside Central Station at 9:30, catch a public bus, stop for coffee, take a 3.5-hour canoe trip (2–3 people per canoe) with several stops, tour a village by canoe, munch a rural canalside picnic lunch (included), then canoe and bus back into the big city by 15:00 (€38, €3 discount with this book, May–mid-Sept Sun–Fri, reservations required, tel. 020/686-3445, mobile 06-5355-2669, www.wetlands -safari.nl, info@wetlandssafari.nl).

On Foot
Red Light District Tours—**Randy Roy's Red Light Tours** consists of one expat American woman, Kimberley. She lived in the Red Light District for years and gives fun, casual, yet informative 90-minute walks through this fascinating and eye-popping neighborhood. While the actual information is light, you'll walk through various porn and drug shops and have an expert to answer your questions. Call or email to reserve (€12.50 includes a drink in a colorful bar at the end, nightly at 20:00, Fri and Sat at 22:00, tours meet in front of Victoria Hotel—in front of Central Station, mobile 06-4185-3288, www.randyroysredlighttours.com, kimberley @randyroysredlighttours.com).

Free City Walk—**New Europe Tours** "employs" native, English-speaking students to give these irreverent and entertaining three-hour walks (using the same "free tour, ask for tips, sell their other tours" formula popular in so many great European cities). This long walk covers a lot of the city with an enthusiasm for the contemporary pot-and-prostitution scene (free, daily at 11:15 and 13:15, just show up at the National Monument on Dam Square, www .neweuropetours.eu).

Adam's Apple Tours—This walking tour offers a two-hour, English-only look at the historic roots of Amsterdam. You'll have a small group of generally 5–6 people and a caring guide, starting off at Central Station and ending up at Dam Square (€25; May–Sept daily at 10:00, 12:30, and 15:00 based on demand; call 020/616-7867 to confirm times and book, www.adamsapple.nl, Frank).

Private Guide—**Albert Walet** is a likeable, hardworking, and knowledgeable local guide who enjoys personalizing tours for Americans interested in knowing his city. "Ab" specializes in history and architecture, and exudes a passion for Amsterdam (€49/2 hrs, €89/4 hrs, small groups, on foot or by bike, mobile 06-2069-7882, abwalet@yahoo.com). Ab also takes travelers to nearby towns, including Haarlem, Leiden, and Delft.

By Bike

The **Yellow Bike Guided Tours** company offers a three-hour city tour (€20, April–Oct Sun–Fri at 9:30 and 13:00, Sat at 9:30 and 14:00) and a six-hour, 22-mile tour of the dikes and green pastures of the countryside (€28, lunch extra, April–Oct daily at 11:00). Both tours leave from Nieuwezijds Kolk 29, three blocks from Central Station (reservations smart, tel. 020/620-6940, www .yellowbike.nl). If you take one of their tours, you can rent the bike for the rest of the day at a 50 percent discount (€10/24 hrs, €100 deposit and ID required). If you'd prefer a private guide, see Albert Walet, listed on previous page.

Do-It-Yourself Bike Tour of Amsterdam—A day enjoying the bridges, bike lanes, and sleepy, off-the-beaten-path canals on your own one-speed is an essential Amsterdam experience. The real joys of Europe's best-preserved 17th-century city are the countless intimate glimpses it offers: the laid-back locals sunning on their porches under elegant gables, rusted bikes that look as if they've been lashed to the same lamppost since the 1960s, wasted hedonists planted on canalside benches, and happy sailors permanently moored, but still manning the deck.

For a good day trip, rent a bike at Central Station (see "By Bike" on page 1028). Head west down Haarlemmerstraat, working your wide-eyed way down the Prinsengracht (drop into Café 't Papeneiland at Prinsengracht 2) and detouring through the small, gentrified streets of the Jordaan neighborhood before popping out at Westerkerk under the tallest spire in the city.

Pedal south to the lush and peaceful Vondelpark, then cut back through the center of town (Leidseplein to the Mint Tower, along Rokin street to Dam Square). From there, cruise the Red Light District, following Oudezijds Voorburgwal past the Old Church (Oude Kerk) to Zeedijk street, and return to the train station.

Then, you can escape into the countryside by hopping on the free ferry behind Central Station (see below). In five minutes, Amsterdam will be gone, and you'll be rolling through your very own Dutch painting.

Taking Bikes Across the Harbor on a Free Ferry—Behind Central Station is a little commuter port where four ferries come and go constantly (free, bikes welcome, signs count down the minutes until the next departure), offering two quick little excursions. The middle two ferries run immediately across the harbor (3-min ride). Bring your bike and ride two kilometers (1.25 miles) along the canal, through suburbs, and then into the *polderland* and villages.

Ferries leaving from the far-left "NDSM" wharf cruise 10 minutes across the North Sea Canal (2/hr, generally departing at :15 and :45). This gives a fun look at the fifth-biggest harbor in Europe (Rotterdam is number one), old wheat silos now renovated into upscale condos, and the shoreline of north Amsterdam, where the planned metro connection to the center is bringing growth, with lots of new apartments under construction. The ferry deposits you in an industrial wasteland (a vacant old warehouse just past the modern MTV headquarters building is filled with artist studios, wacky ventures, and a noisy skateboard hall). **IJ-Kantine** is a fine modern restaurant/café 30 yards from the ferry landing (daily from 9:00, tel. 020/633-7162).

By Public Minibus

For a quick, do-it-yourself public-bus tour along scenic Prinsengracht (Prince's Canal), catch Amsterdam's cute little Stop/Go minibus. It arcs along the city's longest canal, offering clever budget travelers a very cheap and fun 20-minute experience that's faster than a touristy canal tour. The scenic bus ride goes where normal big buses can't fit (along the bumpy and cobbled canalside lanes), giving you a delightful look at the workaday city—without a tourist in sight. The high ride, comfortable seats, and big windows show you Amsterdam well.

The Stop/Go route follows the outside of the canal counterclockwise and returns clockwise along the inside. The buses have no set stops—just wave them down. Grab a seat in the back for the best view. If you see something fun, just jump out—there's another bus in 12 minutes (2 strips or €1, tickets valid one hour, daily 9:00–17:30, 8 seats, can be muggy on hot days; departs from train station, **Central Library,** and more; www.gvb.nl).

For this short tour, catch the bus at the train station. From the station, the minibus passes characteristic cafés in the Jordaan district, countless houseboats, and the whole gamut of gables (under a parade of leaning, Golden Age buildings complete with all the hooks and pulleys). Rolling along the Prinsengracht, you'll see the long line at the Anne Frank House just before the towering Westerkerk. You'll pass within a block of the thriving Leidseplein and Rijksmuseum (look to the right at Spiegelgracht) before passing Rembrandtplein (with its fun 3-D *Night Watch* statues) and crossing the Amstel River to finish at the Waterlooplein flea market, near Rembrandt's House, Gassan Diamonds, and the metro station (subway trains run every 2 min, returning you to Central Station in 3 min).

From the bus, watch for these little bits of Amsterdam:
- green, metal public urinals
- late 19th-century lamp poles
- bikes chained to anything unmovable (including the practical new "staple" design bike racks)
- *amsterdammertjes* (literally "little one from Amsterdam," referring to the countless, little, dark-red bollards—bearing the

city's emblem of three diagonal crosses—that protect walkers from passing traffic)

- underground recycling and garbage bins designed to keep workers from having to dump out bins into trucks (a new law prohibits employees from lifting anything over 25 kilos—about 55 pounds)
- and *"ja"* and *"nee"* stickers on mail slots, indicating whether residents accept junk mail and advertising. (The cool people of the Jordaan are mostly *"nee nee."*)

Sights

One of Amsterdam's delights is that it has perhaps more small specialty museums than any other city its size. From houseboats to sex, from marijuana to Old Masters, you can find a museum to suit your interests.

For tips on how to save time otherwise spent in the long lines of the big three museums—the Anne Frank House, Van Gogh Museum, and Rijksmuseum—see "Advance Tickets and Sightseeing Cards," near the beginning of this chapter.

Note that most museums require baggage check (usually free, often in coin-op lockers where you get your coin back).

The following sights are arranged by neighborhood for handy sightseeing.

Southwest Amsterdam

▲▲▲**Rijksmuseum**—Built to house the nation's great art, the Rijksmuseum owns several thousand paintings, including an incomparable collection of Dutch Masters: Rembrandt, Vermeer, Hals, and Steen. The museum has made it easy for you to focus on the highlights, because that's all that is on display while most of the building undergoes several years of renovation (due to wrap up in 2013). You'll be able to wander through a wonderful, concentrated dose of 17th-century Dutch masterpieces (€10, audioguide-€4, daily 9:00–18:00, Fri until 20:30, tram #2 or #5 from Central Station to Hobbemastraat, tel. 020/674-7047 for automated info or tel. 020/674-7000 for main number, www.rijksmuseum.nl). The Philips Wing entrance is near the corner of Hobbemastraat and Jan Luijkenstraat, on the south side of the Rijks—the part of the huge building nearest the Van Gogh Museum.

▲▲▲**Van Gogh Museum**—Near the Rijksmuseum, this remarkable museum features works by the troubled Dutch artist whose art seemed to mirror his life. Vincent, who killed himself in 1890 at age 37, is best known for sunny, Impressionist canvases that vibrate and pulse with life. The museum's 200 paintings, a stroll

Amsterdam

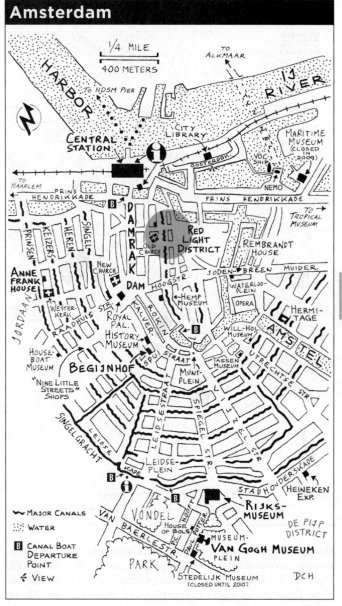

1/4 MILE

400 METERS

TO ALKMAAR

HARBOR

IJ RIVER

TO NDSM PIER

CITY LIBRARY

CENTRAL STATION

MARITIME MUSEUM (CLOSED IN 2009)

VOC SHIP

OOSTERDOK

NEMO

TO HAARLEM

PRINS HENDRIKKADE

PRINS HENDRIKKADE

TO TROPICAL MUSEUM

DAMRAK

Red Light District

REMBRANDT HOUSE

PRINSEN

KEIZERS

HEREN

SINGEL

OLD CHURCH

JODEN BREEN

MUIDER.

ANNE FRANK HOUSE

NEW CHURCH

DAM

HOOGSTR.

WATERLOO-PLEIN

OPERA

HERMI-TAGE

JORDAAN

WESTER-KERK

RAADHUIS

STR

ROYAL PAL.

KALVER

ROKIN

HEMP MUSEUM

WILL-HOL MUSEUM

AMSTEL

HISTORY MUSEUM

HOUSE-BOAT MUSEUM

BEGIJNHOF

SPUI

STRAAT

MUNT-PLEIN

TASSEN MUSEUM

UTRECHTSE STR

"NINE LITTLE STREETS" SHOPS

LEIDSESTRAAT

SPIEGEL STR

SINGELGRACHT

LEIDSE

KADE

LEIDSE-PLEIN

STADHOUDERSKADE

HEINEKEN EXP.

VAN BAERLESTR.

VONDEL

House of Bols

PAUL POTTER

RIJKS-MUSEUM

DE PIJP DISTRICT

PARK

MUSEUM-PLEIN

VAN GOGH MUSEUM

STEDELIJK MUSEUM (CLOSED UNTIL 2010)

DCH

~ MAJOR CANALS

:::: WATER

B CANAL BOAT DEPARTURE POINT

← VIEW

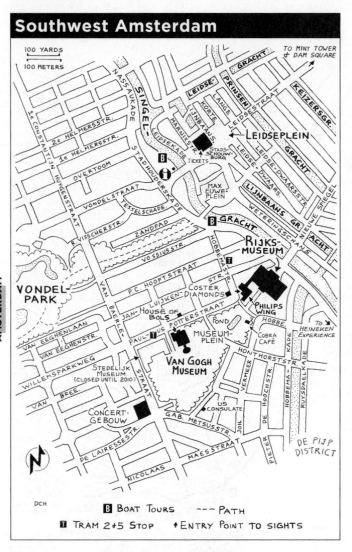

Southwest Amsterdam

100 YARDS
100 METERS

TO MINT TOWER
& DAM SQUARE

1e CONSTANTIN HUYGENSTRAAT

NASSAUKADE

SINGEL

2e HELMERSSTR.

1e HELMERSSTR.

OVERTOOM

STADHOUDERSKADE

LEIDSEKADE

KORTE HARINGS

LANGE HARINGS

PRINSEN GRACHT

LEIDSE GRACHT

LEIDSESTRAAT

LEIDSEPLEIN

STADS-SCHOUW-BURG

TICKETS

MAX EUWE-PLEIN

LEIDSE DWARSSTR.

LIJNBAANS GR.

NIEUWE SPIEGEL

KEIZERSGR.

GRACHT

WETERINGSCHANS

VONDELSTRAAT

ESSELSCHADE

R. VISSCHERSTR.

ZANDPAD

VOSSIUSSTR.

HOBBEMA

GRACHT

RIJKS-MUSEUM

WETERINGSCHANS

LIJNBAANS GR.

ACHT

VONDEL-PARK

VAN BAERLE

P.C. HOOFT STRAAT

JAN LUIJKEN-STRAAT

House of BOLS

PAUL-US POTTERSTRAAT

COSTER DIAMONDS

STR.

PHILIPS WING

HOBBE.

POND

COBRA CAFÉ

HONTHORSTSTR.

TO HEINEKEN EXPERIENCE

VAN EEGHENLAAN

VAN EEGHENSTR.

WILLEMSPARKWEG

VAN BREE.

STEDELIJK MUSEUM
(CLOSED UNTIL 2010)

MUSEUM-PLEIN

Van Gogh Museum

VERMEER

DE HOOGHSTR.

HOBBEMA-KADE

RUYSDAELKADE

CONCERT-GEBOUW

GAB. METSUSSTR.

US CONSULATE

JOH.

PIETER

DE PIJP DISTRICT

N

DE LAIRESSESTR.

MAES STRAAT

NICOLAAS

DCH

B BOAT TOURS   - - - PATH

T TRAM 2+5 STOP   ↟ ENTRY POINT TO SIGHTS

AMSTERDAM

through the artist's work and life, were owned by Theo, Vincent's younger, art-dealer brother. Highlights include *Sunflowers, The Bedroom, The Potato Eaters,* and many brooding self-portraits. The third floor shows works that influenced Vincent, from Monet and Pissarro to Gauguin, Cézanne, and Toulouse-Lautrec. The worthwhile audioguide includes insightful commentaries and quotes from Vincent himself. Temporary exhibitions fill the new wing, down the escalator from the ground floor lobby (regularly €12.50, audioguide-€4, daily 10:00–18:00, Fri until 22:00—with no crowds in evening, Paulus Potterstraat 7, tel. 020/570-5200, www.vangoghmuseum.nl).

▲**Museumplein**—Bordered by the Rijks and Van Gogh museums and the Concertgebouw (classical music hall), this park-like square is interesting even to art-haters. Amsterdam's best acoustics are found underneath the Rijksmuseum, where street musicians perform everything from chamber music to Mongolian throat singing. Mimes, human statues, and crafts booths dot the square. Skateboarders career across a concrete tube, while locals enjoy a park bench or a coffee at the Cobra Café.

Nearby is **Coster Diamonds,** a handy place to see a diamond-cutting and polishing demo (free and interesting 30-min tours on request followed by sales pitch, popular for decades with tour groups, prices marked up to include tour guide kickbacks, daily 9:00–17:00, Paulus Potterstraat 2, tel. 020/305-5555, www.costerdiamonds.com). The tour at Gassan Diamonds is better (see "Southeast Amsterdam," later in this chapter), but Coster is convenient to the Museumplein scene.

House of Bols: Cocktail & Genever Experience—This leading Dutch distillery has opened a pricey and slick little museum across the street from the Van Gogh Museum. The "experience" is a self-guided walk through what is essentially an ad for Bols—"four hundred years of working on the art of mixing and blending...a celebration of gin"—with some fun sniffing opportunities and a drink at a modern cocktail bar for a finale. The highlight is a chance to taste up to five different local gins with a talkative expert guiding you. Then have your barista mix up the cocktail of your dreams—based on what you learned during your sniffing (€10, Wed–Mon 10:00–18:00, closed Tue, must be 18, Paulus Potterstraat 14, tel. 020/570-8575, www.houseofbols.com). If you like the booze and hang out and talk, this can be a good deal (but do it after the Van Gogh Museum).

Stedelijk Museum—This modern-art museum is expected to reopen in 2010 in its spiffed-up original Stedelijk Museum building, located near the Rijksmuseum. Its fun, far-out, and refreshing collection includes post-1945 experimental and conceptual art and works by Picasso, Chagall, Cézanne, Kandinsky, and Mondrian (check www.stedelijk.nl for updates).

Heineken Experience—This famous old brewery—modernized and enlarged—welcomes visitors to a slick and entertaining beer-appreciation fest (€15, includes two drinks, daily 11:00–19:00, last entry at 17:30; tram #16, #24, or #25 to Heinekenplein; an easy walk from Rijksmuseum, tel. 020/523-9222, www.heineken experience.com).

De Pijp District—This former working-class industrial and residential zone (behind the Heineken Experience, near the

Rijksmuseum) is emerging as a colorful, vibrant district. Its spine is Albert Cuypstraat, a street taken over by a long, sprawling produce market packed with interesting people. The centerpiece is **Restaurant Bazar** (marked by a roof-capping golden angel), a church turned into a Middle Eastern food circus (see listing in "Eating—Southwest Amsterdam," later in this chapter).

▲**Leidseplein**—Brimming with cafés, this people-watching mecca is an impromptu stage for street artists, accordionists, jugglers, and unicyclists. Sunny afternoons are liveliest. The Boom Chicago theater fronts this square (see "Nightlife," later in this chapter). Stroll nearby Lange Leidsedwarsstraat (one block north) for a taste-bud tour of ethnic eateries, from Greek to Indonesian.

▲▲**Vondelpark**—This huge and lively city park is popular with the Dutch—families with little kids, romantic couples, strolling seniors, and hippies sharing blankets and beers. It's a favored venue for free summer concerts. On a sunny afternoon, it's a hedonistic scene that seems to say, "Parents...relax."

Rembrandtplein and Tuschinski Theater—One of the city's premier nightlife spots is the leafy Rembrandtplein (the artist's statue stands here, along with a jaunty new group of statues giving us *The Night Watch* in 3-D) and the adjoining Thorbeckeplein. Several late-night dance clubs keep the area lively into the wee hours. Utrechtse-straat is lined with upscale shops and restaurants. Nearby Reguliersdwarsstraat (a street one block south of Rembrandtplein) is a center for gay and lesbian nightclubs in the city.

The **Tuschinski Theater,** a movie palace from the 1920s (a half-block from Rembrandtplein down Reguliers-breestraat), glitters inside and out. Still a working theater, it's a delightful old place to see first-run movies. The exterior is an interesting hybrid of styles, forcing the round peg of Art Nouveau into the square hole of Art Deco. The stone-and-tile facade features stripped-down, functional Art Deco squares and rectangles, but is ornamented with Art Nouveau elements—Tiffany-style windows, garlands, curvy iron lamps, Egyptian pharaohs, and exotic gold lettering over the door. Inside (lobby is free), the sumptuous decor features red carpets, nymphs on the walls, and semi-abstract designs. Grab a seat in the lobby and watch the ceiling morph (Reguliersbreestraat 26–28).

Houseboat Museum (Woonbootmuseum)—In the 1930s, modern cargo ships came into widespread use—making small, sail-powered cargo boats obsolete. In danger of extinction, these little vessels found new life as houseboats lining the canals of Amsterdam. Today, 2,500 such boats—their cargo holds turned into classy, comfortable living rooms—are called home by locals. For a peek into this *gezellig* (cozy) world, visit this tiny museum.

Captain Vincent enjoys showing visitors around the houseboat, which feels lived-in because, until 1997, it was (€3.25, March–Oct Tue–Sun 11:00–17:00, closed Mon; Nov–Feb Fri–Sun 11:00–17:00, closed Mon–Thu; on Prinsengracht, opposite #296 facing Elandsgracht, tel. 020/427-0750, www.houseboatmuseum.nl).

West Amsterdam

▲▲▲**Anne Frank House**—A pilgrimage for many, this house offers a fascinating look at the hideaway of young Anne during the Nazi occupation of the Netherlands. Anne, her parents, an older sister, and four others spent a little more than two years in a "Secret Annex" behind her father's business. While in hiding, 13-year-old Anne kept a diary chronicling her extraordinary experience. Acting on a tip, the Nazis arrested the group in August 1944 and sent them to concentration camps in Poland and Germany. Anne and her sister died of typhus in March 1945, only weeks before their camp was liberated. Of the eight inhabitants of the Secret Annex, only Anne's father, Otto Frank, survived. He returned to Amsterdam and arranged for his daughter's diary to be published in 1947. It was followed by many translations, a play, and a movie.

Pick up the English pamphlet at the door. The thoughtfully designed exhibit offers thorough coverage of the Frank family, the diary, the stories of others who hid, and the Holocaust. It may be less crowded after 18:00 (€8.50, not covered by any sightseeing passes, daily March 15–Sept 14 9:00–21:00, July–Aug until 22:00, Sept 15–March 14 9:00–19:00, last entry 30 min before closing, no baggage check, no large bags allowed inside, Prinsengracht 267, near Westerkerk, tel. 020/556-7100, www.annefrank.org). For information on buying advance tickets, see "Advance Tickets and Sightseeing Cards," near the beginning of this chapter.

Westerkerk—Located near the Anne Frank House, this landmark church (free, generally open April–Sept Mon–Sat 11:00–15:00, closed Sun) has a barren interior, Rembrandt's body buried somewhere under the pews, and Amsterdam's tallest steeple.

The tower is open only for tours and offers a grand city view. The tour guide, who speaks in English and Dutch, tells of the church and its carillon. Only six people are allowed at a time (it's first-come, first-served), so lines can be long (€6, 30 min, departures on the half hour, April–Oct Mon–Sat 10:00–17:30, last tour leaves at 17:30, closed Sun and Nov–March, call 020/689-2565 for info and to arrange private tour).

Central Amsterdam, near Dam Square

Royal Palace (Koninklijk Huis)—This palace is right on Dam Square. It was built as a lavish City Hall for Amsterdam, when the

Central Amsterdam

CENTRAL STATION

Bike Garage · Bike Rental · CITY LIBRARY

PRINS-HENDRIK- · Shops · **T** · VVV · **i**

OOSTER-DOK

B · St. NICHOLAS CHURCH

DAMRAK Sex Museum · **B**

YELLOW BIKE TOURS

KADE · ZEEDIJK · PRINS HENDRIKKADE

AMSTEL-KRING MUSEUM

TO NEMO, VOC SHIP

DIJK · VOORBURG. · NIEUWEN- · STRAAT

BEURS · RED LIGHT DISTRICT

Old Church · EROTIC MUSEUM

SPUISTRAAT · NIEUWE ZIJDS VOORBURG. · DAMRAK

New Church · NIEUW-MARKT

WARMOES-

SINT JANS

HEMP MUSEUM · OUDEZIJDS ACHTER-BURGWAL

ROYAL PALACE · **DAM**

DAM STRAAT

OUDEZIJDS VOOR-BURGWAL

REMBRANDT'S HOUSE

TO ANNE FRANK HOUSE & JORDAAN DISTRICT

KALVERSTRAAT · ROKIN

WATER-LOO-PLEIN

OPERA

SPUI

HISTORY MUSEUM

SPUI · STR.

BEGIJNHOF

ROKIN · SPUI · **B**

AMSTEL

MINT TOWER

TUSCHINSKI THEATER

WILLET-HOLTHUYSEN MUSEUM

HEILIG.WEG · HUIDEN-STRAAT

SINGEL

MUNT-PLEIN

HEREN-GRACHT

FLOWER MARKET

REMBRANDT-PLEIN

TASSEN MUSEUM

TO LEIDSEPLEIN & RIJKSMUSEUM

200 YDS.

200 METERS

DCH

M METRO · **B** OPSTAPPER BUS · **B** BOAT TOURS · ⟿ VIEW

T TRAMS: #1 (TO LEIDSEPLEIN), #2 & #5 (TO MUSEUMPLEIN)

AMSTERDAM

country was a proud new republic and Amsterdam was the richest city on the planet—awash in profit from trade. When constructed in 1648, this building was one of Europe's finest, with a sumptuous interior. Today, it's the official (but not actual) residence of the queen (may open to public in summer, call for price and hours, tel. 020/620-4060, www.koninklijkhuis.nl).

New Church (Nieuwe Kerk)—Barely newer than the "Old" Church (located in the Red Light District), this 15th-century sanctuary has an intentionally dull interior, after the decoration was removed by 16th-century iconoclastic Protestants seeking to unclutter their communion with God. This is where many Dutch royal weddings and all coronations take place. There's a steep entrance fee to see the rotating, temporary exhibitions, but you can pop in to look at the vast interior if no exhibitions are going on (€10; May–July daily 10:00–17:00—sometimes until 18:00 for exhibitions; Aug–April daily 10:00–18:00, Thu until 22:00; on Dam Square, info tel. 020/353-8168, tel. 020/638-6909, www.nieuwekerk.nl).

▲Begijnhof—Stepping into this tiny, idyllic courtyard in the city center, you escape into the charm of old Amsterdam. Notice house #34, a 500-year-old wooden structure (rare, since repeated fires taught city fathers a trick called brick). Peek into the hidden Catholic church, dating from the time when post-Reformation Dutch Catholics couldn't worship in public. It's opposite the English Reformed church, where the Pilgrims worshiped while waiting for their voyage to the New World (marked by a plaque near the door). Be considerate of the people who live around the courtyard (free, daily 8:00–17:00, on Begijnensteeg lane, just off Kalverstraat between #130 and #132, pick up flier at office near entrance).

▲▲Amsterdam History Museum (Amsterdams Historisch Museum)—Follow the city's growth from fishing village to world trade center to hippie haven. Housed in a 500-year-old former orphanage, this creative and hardworking museum features Rembrandt's paintings, fine English descriptions, and a carillon loft. The loft comes with push-button recordings of the town bell tower's greatest hits and a self-serve carillon "keyboard" that lets you ring a few bells yourself (€8, Mon–Fri 10:00–17:00, Sat–Sun 11:00–17:00, pleasant restaurant, next to Begijnhof, Kalverstraat 92, tel. 020/523-1822, www.ahm.nl). The museum's free pedestrian corridor—lined with old-time group portraits—is a powerful teaser. The Amsterdam History Museum is a fine place to buy the Museumkaart, and then use it to skip long lines at the Van Gogh Museum (for details, see "Advance Tickets and Sightseeing Cards," near the beginning of this chapter).

Red Light District

▲▲Amstelkring Museum (Our Lord in the Attic/Museum Ons' Lieve Heer op Solder)—While Amsterdam has long been known for its tolerant attitudes, 16th-century politics forced Dutch Catholics to worship discreetly. Near the train station in the Red Light District, you'll find a fascinating hidden Catholic church filling the attic of three 17th-century merchants' houses. Don't miss the silver collection and other exhibits of daily life from 300 years ago (€7, Mon–Sat 10:00–17:00, Sun and holidays 13:00–17:00, closed Jan 1 and April 30, no photos, Oudezijds Voorburgwal 40, tel. 020/624-6604, www.museumamstelkring.nl).

▲▲Red Light District—Europe's most touristed ladies of the night tease and tempt here, as they have for centuries, in 400 display-case windows around Oudezijds Achterburgwal and Oudezijds Voorburgwal, surrounding the Old Church (Oude Kerk, listed later in this section). Drunks and druggies make the streets uncomfortable late at night after the gawking tour groups leave (about 22:30), but it's a fascinating walk earlier in the evening.

The neighborhood, one of Amsterdam's oldest, has hosted prostitutes since 1200. Prostitution is entirely legal here, and the prostitutes are generally entrepreneurs, renting space and running their own businesses, as well as filling out tax returns and even paying union dues. Popular prostitutes net about €500 a day (for what's called "S&F" in its abbreviated, printable form, costing €25–50 per customer).

The **Prostitution Information Center,** open to the public, offers a small €1.50 booklet that answers most of the questions tourists have about the Red Light District (free, Tue–Sat 12:00–19:00, closed Sun–Mon, tours on Sat—check website for details, facing Old Church at Enge Kerksteeg 3, tel. 020/420-7328, www .pic-amsterdam.com).

Sex Museums—Amsterdam has two sex museums: one in the Red Light District and another a block in front of Central Station on Damrak street. While visiting one can be called sightseeing, visiting both is hard to explain. The one on Damrak is cheaper and more interesting. Here's a comparison:

The **Erotic Museum** in the Red Light District is five floors of uninspired paintings, videos, old photos, and sculpture (€5, daily 11:00–24:00, along the canal at Oudezijds Achterburgwal 54, tel. 020/624-7303).

The **Damrak Sex Museum** tells the story of pornography from Roman times through 1960. Every sexual deviation is revealed in various displays. The museum includes early French pornographic photos; memorabilia from Europe, India, and Asia; a Marilyn Monroe tribute; and some S&M displays (€3, daily 9:30–23:00, Damrak 18, a block in front of Central Station, tel. 020/622-8376).

Old Church (Oude Kerk)—This 14th-century landmark—the needle around which the Red Light District spins—has served as a reassuring welcome-home symbol to sailors, a refuge to the downtrodden, an ideological battlefield of the Counter-Reformation, and today, a tourist sight with a dull interior (€5, Mon–Sat 11:00–17:00, Sun 13:00–17:00, tel. 020/625-8284, www.oudekerk.nl).

▲**Hash, Marijuana, and Hemp Museum**—This is a collection of dope facts, history, science, and memorabilia (€6, daily 10:00–22:00, Oudezijds Achterburgwal 148, tel. 020/623-5961, www.hashmuseum.com). While small, it has a very memorable finale: the high-tech grow room, in which dozens of varieties of marijuana are grown in optimal hydroponic (among other) environments. Some plants stand five feet tall and shine under the intense grow lamps. The view is actually through glass walls into the neighboring Sensi Seed Bank Grow Shop (at #150), which sells carefully cultivated seeds and all the gear needed to grow them. (Both the museum and the Seed Bank may have moved by the time you visit.)

The nearby **Cannabis College** is "dedicated to ending the global war against the cannabis plant through public education" (free, daily 11:00–19:00, Oudezijds Achterburgwal 124, tel. 020/423-4420, www.cannabiscollege.com). For more, see "Smoking," later in this chapter.

Northeast Amsterdam

Central Library (Openbare Bibliotheek Amsterdam)—This huge, multistory glass building holds almost 1,400 seats—many with wraparound views of the city—and hundreds of free Internet terminals. It's the classiest possible place to check email. This library, which opened in 2007, demonstrates the Dutch people's dedication to a freely educated populace (the right to information, they point out, is enshrined in the UN's Universal Declaration of Human Rights). This being Amsterdam, the library has almost twice as many bike racks as parking places. Everything's relaxed and inviting, from the fun kids' zone and international magazine and newspaper section on the ground floor to the cafeteria with its dramatic view-terrace dining on the top (La Place, €10 meals, salad bar, daily 10:00–21:00). The library is a three-minute walk from Central Station (daily 10:00–22:00, tel. 020/523-0900, www.oba.nl).

NEMO (National Center for Science and Technology)—This kid-friendly science museum is a city landmark. Its distinctive copper-green building, jutting up from the water like a sinking ship, has prompted critics to nickname it the *Titanic*. Designed by Italian architect Renzo Piano (known for Paris' Pompidou Center and Berlin's Potsdamer Platz complex), the building's shape reflects its nautical surroundings as well as the curve of the underwater tunnel it straddles.

Several floors feature permanent and rotating exhibits that allow kids (and adults) to explore topics such as light, sound, and gravity, and play with bubbles, topple giant dominoes, and draw with lasers. Whirring, room-size pinball machines reputedly teach kids about physics. English explanations are available. Up top is a restaurant with a great city view, as well as a sloping terrace that becomes a popular "beach" in summer, complete with lounge chairs, a sandbox, and a lively bar. On the bottom floor is an inexpensive cafeteria offering €3 sandwiches (€11.50, includes rooftop beach in July–Aug, €2.50—beach only July–Aug, combo-ticket with VOC Ship *Amsterdam*-€13.50; Tue–Sun 10:00–17:00, generally closed Mon but open daily June–Aug; Oosterdok 2, above entrance to IJ tunnel, tel. 0900-919-1100—€0.35/min, www .e-nemo.nl). It's a 15-minute walk from Central Station or bus #22, #42, or #43 to Kadijksplein stop. The roof terrace—which is open later than the museum in the summer—is generally free.

VOC Ship *Amsterdam*—The good ship *Amsterdam* moors near the NEMO, welcoming kids (and kids at heart) to join its crew.

The *Amsterdam* is a replica of a type of ship called an East Indiaman, which had its heyday during the 17th and 18th centuries, sailing for the Dutch East India Company (abbreviated VOC, for Vereenigde Oostindische Compagnie—you'll see it on insignias throughout the boat). Even though trade was the name of the game, with scurvy thieves in the waters, ships such as the *Amsterdam* had to be prepared to defend themselves. You'll see plenty of muskets, as well as cannons and gunpowder kegs.

Wander the decks, then duck your head and check out the captain's and surgeon's quarters, packed with items they would have used. While the ship is a little light on good historical information (be sure to pick up the free flier, which explains terminology like the difference between the poop deck and the quarterdeck), it's still a shipshape sight that entertains naval history buffs as well as fans of *Pirates of the Caribbean* films (€4, combo-ticket with NEMO-€13.50, same hours as NEMO, docked just to the west of NEMO at Oosterdok 2, tel. 020/523-2222, www.scheepvaart museum.nl).

Netherlands Maritime Museum (Nederlands Scheepvaart-museum)—This huge collection of model ships, maps, and sea-battle paintings fills the 300-year-old Dutch Navy Arsenal. Given the Dutch seafaring heritage, I expected a more interesting museum; let's hope the recent renovations, which should be done in time for your visit, have perked up the place (€9; mid-June–mid-Sept daily 10:00–17:00; mid-Sept–mid-June Tue–Sun 10:00–17:00, closed Mon; English explanations, bus #22 or #42 to Kattenburgerplein 1, tel. 020/523-2222, www.scheepvaart museum.nl).

Southeast Amsterdam

To reach the following sights from the train station, take tram #9 or #14. All of these sights (except the Tropical Museum) are close to each other and can easily be connected into an interesting walk, or better yet, a bike ride. Several of the sights in southeast Amsterdam cluster near the large square, Waterlooplein, dominated by the modern opera house.

Waterlooplein Flea Market—For more than a hundred years, the Jewish Quarter flea market has raged daily except Sunday (at the Waterlooplein metro station, behind Rembrandt's House). The long, narrow park is filled with stalls selling cheap clothes, hippie stuff, old records, tourist knickknacks, and garage-sale junk.

▲**Rembrandt's House (Museum Het Rembrandt-huis)**—A middle-aged Rembrandt lived here from 1639 to 1658 after his wife's death, as his popularity and wealth dwindled down to obscurity and bankruptcy. As you enter, ask when the next etching demonstration is scheduled and pick up the fine, included audioguide. Tour the place this way: Explore Rembrandt's reconstructed house (filled with exactly what his bankruptcy inventory of 1656 said he owned); imagine him at work in his reconstructed studio; marvel at his personal collection of exotic objects, many of which he included in paintings; attend the etching demonstration and ask the printer to explain the etching process (drawing in soft wax on a metal plate that's then dipped in acid, inked up, and printed); and then, for the finale, enjoy several rooms of original Rembrandt etchings. You're not likely to see a single painting, but the master's etchings are marvelous and well-described. I came away wanting to know more about the man and his art (€8 includes audioguide, daily 10:00–17:00, Jodenbreestraat 4, tel. 020/520-0400, www .rembrandthuis.nl).

▲**Diamonds**—Many shops in this "city of diamonds" offer tours. These tours come with two parts: a chance to see experts behind magnifying glasses polishing the facets of precious diamonds, followed by a visit to an intimate sales room to see (and perhaps buy) a mighty shiny yet very tiny souvenir.

The handy and professional **Gassan Diamonds** facility fills a huge warehouse a block from Rembrandt's House. A visit here plops you in the big-tour-group fray (notice how each tour group has a color-coded sticker so they know which guide gets the commission on what they buy). You'll get a sticker, join a free 15-minute tour to see a polisher at work, and hear a general explanation of the process. Then you'll have an opportunity to sit down and have color and clarity described and illustrated with diamonds

Southeast Amsterdam

TO NEMO, VOC SHIP, MARITIME MUSEUM & IJ TUNNEL

↖ TO RED LIGHT DISTRICT

REMBRANDT'S HOUSE

GASSAN DIAMONDS

UILENBURGERGRACHT

VALKENBURGERSTRAAT

ENTREPOTDOK

FLEA MARKET

MOSES & AARON CHURCH

WATERLOO PLEIN

MR. VISSER-PLEIN

MUIDERSTRAAT

HERENGRACHT

WERT-HEIM PARK

RESISTANCE MUSEUM

N

❶ OPERA

JEWISH HISTORY MUSEUM

Ⓜ Ⓑ

Ⓜ

DOCK-WORKER STATUE

PLANTAGE-MIDDEN-

PLANTAGE

❸

KERKLAAN

A M

DRAW-BRIDGE

NIEUWE

HORTUS BOTANICAL GARDEN

❹

ARTIS ZOO

BLAUWBRUG

TO REMBRANDT-PLEIN

WEESPER STRAAT

DUTCH THEATER MEMORIAL

PLANTAGE LAAN

❺

HERMITAGE ON THE AMSTEL

NIEUWE KEIZERSGR.

TO TROPICAL MUSEUM & ❷

200 YARDS

200 METERS

↓ TO MAGERE (SKINNY) BRIDGE

Ⓜ METRO Ⓑ STOP/GO BUS

✦ ENTRY POINT TO SIGHTS

DCH

❶ To Stayokay Stadsdoelen Hostel ❹ Café Koosje

❷ To Stayokay Zeeburg Hostel ❺ Taman Sari Restaurant

❸ Restaurant Plancius

ranging in value from $100 to $30,000. Before or after, you can have a free cup of coffee in the waiting room across the parking lot (daily 9:00–17:00, Nieuwe Uilenburgerstraat 173, tel. 020/622-5333, www.gassandiamonds.com, handy WC). Another company, Coster, also offers diamond demos, not as good as Gassan's, but convenient if you're near the Rijksmuseum (see page 1034).

▲**Willet-Holthuysen Museum (a.k.a. Herengracht Canal Mansion)**—This 1687 townhouse is a must for devotees of Hummel-topped sugar bowls and Louis XVI–style wainscoting. For others, it's a pleasant look inside a typical (rich) home with much of the original furniture and decor. Forget the history and just browse through a dozen rooms of beautiful and saccharine objects from the 19th century.

Upon entering (through the servants' door under the grand entry), see photos of the owners during the house's heyday in the 1860s. The 15-minute video explains how the wealthy heiress Louise Holthuysen and the art-collecting bon vivant Abraham Willet got married and became joined at the hyphen, then set out to make their home the social hub of Amsterdam.

AMSTERDAM

Picture the couple's servants in the kitchen—before electricity and running water—turning meat on the spit at the fireplace or filtering rainwater. Upstairs, where the Willet-Holthuysens entertained, wall paintings introduce you to Abraham's artistic tastes, showing scenes of happy French peasants and nobles frolicking in the countryside. Several rooms are done in the Louis XVI style, featuring chairs with straight, tapering legs (not the heavy, curving, animal-claw feet of earlier styles); blue, yellow, and purple-themed rooms; wainscoting ("wallpaper" covering only the lower part of walls); and mythological paintings on the ceiling.

The impressive gilded ballroom contains a painting showing the room in its prime—and how little it's changed. Imagine Abraham, Louise, and 22 guests retiring to the Dining Room, dining off the 275-piece Meissen porcelain set; chatting with friends in the Blue Room by the canal; or sipping tea in the Garden Room, gazing out at symmetrically curved hedges and classical statues. Up another flight is the bedroom, with a canopy bed and matching oak washstand and makeup table (and a chamber pot tucked under the bed).

When the widow Louise died in 1895, she bequeathed the house to the city, along with its collection of candelabras, snuff boxes, and puppy paintings (€5, Mon–Fri 10:00–17:00, Sat–Sun 11:00–17:00; take tram #4, #9, or #14 to Rembrandtplein—it's a 2-min walk southeast to Herengracht 605; tel. 020/523-1870, www .willetholthuysen.nl). The museum lacks audioguides, but you can request a free blue notebook to learn more about the house's history.

Tassen Museum (Hendrikje Museum of Bags and Purses)—This hardworking little museum fills an elegant 1664 canal house with 500 years of bag and purse history—from before the invention of pockets through the 20th century. The collection, with lots of artifacts, is well-described in English and gives a fascinating insight into fashion through the ages that fans of handbags will love, and their partners might even enjoy. The creative and surreal bag styles of the 1920s and 1930s are particularly interesting (€6.50, daily 10:00–17:00, three floors—one houses temporary exhibits and two hold the permanent collection, behind Rembrandtplein at Herengracht 573, tel. 020/524-6452, www.tassenmuseum.nl).

▲Hermitage on the Amstel—The famous Hermitage Museum in St. Petersburg, Russia, loans art to Amsterdam for display in the Amstelhof, a 17th-century former nursing home that takes up a whole city block along the Amstel River.

Why is there Russian-owned art in Amsterdam? The Hermitage collection in St. Petersburg is so vast that they can only show about 5 percent of it at any one time. Therefore, the Hermitage is establishing satellite collections around the world. The one here in Amsterdam is the biggest, and grew considerably in

2009 when the museum took over even more of the Amstelhof. By law, the great Russian collection can only be out of the country for six months at a time, so the collection is always rotating. Curators in Amsterdam make a point to display art that complements—rather than just repeats—what the city's other museums show so well (€7, generally daily 10:00–17:00—but call or check online to confirm, Nieuwe Herengracht 14, tram #4 to Rembrandtplein or #9 or #14 to Waterlooplein, recorded info tel. 020/530-8751, www.hermitage.nl).

De Hortus Botanical Garden—This is a unique oasis of tranquility within the city (no mobile phones are allowed, because "our collection of plants is a precious community—treat it with respect"). One of the oldest botanical gardens in the world, it dates from 1638, when medicinal herbs were grown here. Today, among its 6,000 different kinds of plants—most of which were collected by the Dutch East India Company in the 17th and 18th centuries—you'll find medicinal herbs, cacti, several greenhouses (one with a fluttery butterfly house—a hit with kids), and a tropical palm house. Much of it is described in English: "A Dutch merchant snuck a coffee plant out of Ethiopia, which ended up in this garden in 1706. This first coffee plant in Europe was the literal grand-daddy of the coffee cultures of Brazil—long the world's biggest coffee producer" (€7; Mon–Fri 9:00–17:00, Sat–Sun 10:00–17:00, July–Aug until 19:00, Dec–Jan until 16:00; Plantage Middenlaan 2A, tel. 020/625-9021, www.dehortus.nl). The inviting Orangery Café serves tapas.

▲Jewish Historical Museum (Joods Historisch Museum)—This interesting museum tells the story of the Netherlands' Jews through three centuries, serving as a good introduction to Judaism and educating visitors on Jewish customs and religious traditions.

Originally opened in 1932, the museum was forced to close during the Nazi years. Recent renovations have brought it into the 21st century. Its current location comprises four historic former synagogues that have been joined by steel and glass to make one modern complex.

The highlight is the Great Synagogue. Have a seat in the high-ceilinged synagogue, surrounded by religious objects, and picture it during its prime (1671–1943). The hall would be full for a service—men downstairs, women above in the gallery. On the east wall (the symbolic direction of Jerusalem) is the Ark, where they keep the scrolls of the Torah (the Jewish scriptures, including the first five books of the Christian Bible). The rabbi and other men, wearing thigh-length prayer shawls, would approach the Ark and carry the Torah to the raised platform in the center of the room. After unwrapping it from its drapery and silver cap, a man would use a *yad* (ceremonial pointer) to follow along while singing the text aloud.

Video displays around the room explain Jewish customs, from birth (circumcision) to puberty (the bar/bat mitzvah, celebrating the entry into adulthood) to marriage—culminating in the groom stomping on a glass while everyone shouts "Mazel tov!"

From the upper level, a skyway leads to the 20th century. The new, worthwhile exhibit on the Jews of the Netherlands uses personal artifacts and touch-screen computers to tell the devastating history of the Nazi occupation. By purposefully showing mundane daily objects, the museum helps make an inconceivable period of time meaningful and real.

The museum has a modern, minimalist, kosher café, as well as temporary exhibition space, generally showing the work of Jewish artists (€7.50, daily 11:00–17:00, free audioguide but displays all have English explanations, Jonas Daniel Meijerplein 2, tel. 020/531-0310, www.jhm.nl).

▲**Dutch Theater (Hollandsche Schouwburg)**—Once a lively theater in the Jewish neighborhood, and today a moving memorial, this building was used as an assembly hall for local Jews destined for Nazi concentration camps. On the wall, 6,700 family names pay tribute to the 104,000 Jews deported and killed by the Nazis. Some 70,000 victims spent time here, awaiting transfer to concentration camps. Upstairs is a small history exhibit with photos and memorabilia of some victims, putting a human face on the staggering numbers. Television monitors show actual footage of the rounding-up of Amsterdam's Jews by the Nazis. The ruined theater offers relatively little to see but plenty to think about. Back on the ground floor, notice the hopeful messages that visiting school groups attach to the wooden tulips (free, daily 11:00–16:00, Plantage Middenlaan 24, tel. 020/531-0340, www.hollandsche schouwburg.nl).

▲▲**Dutch Resistance Museum (Verzetsmuseum)**—This is an impressive look at how the Dutch resisted their Nazi occupiers from 1940 to 1945. You'll see propaganda movie clips, study forged ID cards under a magnifying glass, and read about ingenious and courageous efforts—big and small—to hide local Jews from the Germans and undermine the Nazi regime.

The first dozen displays set the stage, showing peaceful, upright Dutch people of the 1930s living oblivious to the rise of fascism. Then—bam—it's May of 1940 and the Germans invade the Netherlands, pummel Rotterdam, send Queen Wilhelmina into exile, and—in four short days of fighting—hammer home the message that resistance is futile. The Germans install local Dutch Nazis in power (the "NSB"), led by Anton Mussert.

Next, in the corner of the exhibition area, push a button to see photos of the event that first mobilized organized resistance. In February of 1941, Nazis start rounding up Jews from the neighborhood, killing nine protesters. Amsterdammers respond by shutting down the trams, schools, and businesses in a massive two-day strike. (This heroic gesture is honored today with a statue of a striking dockworker on the square called Jonas Daniel Meyerplein, where Jews were rounded up.) The next display makes it clear that this brave strike did little to save 100,000 Jews from extermination.

Turning the corner into the main room, you'll see numerous exhibits on Nazi rule and the many forms of Dutch resistance: vandals turning Nazi V-for-Victory posters into W-for-Wilhelmina, preachers giving pointed sermons, schoolkids telling "Kraut jokes," printers distributing underground newspapers (such as *Het Parool*, which became a major daily paper), counterfeiters forging documents, and ordinary people hiding radios under floorboards and Jews inside closets. As the war progresses, the armed Dutch Resistance becomes bolder and more violent, killing German occupiers and Dutch collaborators. In September of 1944, the Allies liberate Antwerp, and the Netherlands starts celebrating... too soon. The Nazis dig in and punish the country by cutting off rations, plunging West Holland into the "Hunger Winter" of 1944 to 1945 in which 20,000 die. Finally, it's springtime. The Allies liberate the country, and at war's end, Nazi helmets are turned into Dutch bedpans (€6.50, Tue–Fri 10:00–17:00, Sat–Mon 11:00–17:00, well-described in English, no flash photos, tram #9 from station or #14 from Dam Square, Plantage Kerklaan 61, tel. 020/620-2535, www.verzetsmuseum.org).

Two recommended eateries—Restaurant Plancius and Café Koosje—are adjacent to the museum (see listings on page 1069), and Amsterdam's famous zoo is just across the street.

▲Tropical Museum (Tropenmuseum)—As close to the Third World as you'll get without lots of vaccinations, this imaginative museum offers wonderful re-creations of tropical life and explanations of Third World problems (largely created by Dutch colonialism and the slave trade). Ride the elevator to the top floor, and circle your way down through this immense collection, opened in 1926 to give the Dutch people a peek at their vast colonial holdings. Don't miss the display case where you can see and hear the world's most exotic musical instruments. The Ekeko cafeteria serves tropical food (€7.50, daily 10:00–17:00, tram #9 to Linnaeusstraat 2, tel. 020/568-8215, www.tropenmuseum.nl).

Nightlife

Amsterdam hotels serve breakfast until 11:00 because so many people—visitors and locals—live for nighttime in Amsterdam.

On summer evenings, people flock to the main squares for

drinks at outdoor tables. Leidseplein is the liveliest, surrounded by theaters, restaurants, and nightclubs. The slightly quieter Rembrandtplein (with adjoining Thorbeckeplein and nearby Reguliersdwarsstraat) is the center of gay clubs and nightlife. Spui features a full city block of bars. And Nieuwmarkt, on the east edge of the Red Light District, is a bit rough, but is probably the most local.

The Red Light District (particularly Oudezijds Achterburgwal) is less sleazy in the early evening, almost carnival-like, as the neon comes on and the streets fill with tour groups. But it starts to feel scuzzy after about 22:30.

Information

Pick up one of these free papers for listings of festivals and performances of theater, film, dance, cabaret, and live rock, pop, jazz, and classical music. *Amsterdam Weekly* is a free, local English-language paper that lists cutting-edge art, movies, and concerts (available in bookstores every Wed, also online at www .amsterdamweekly.nl). The irreverent *Boom!* has the lowdown on the youth and nightlife scene, and it's packed with practical tips and countercultural insights (includes €3 discount on the Boom Chicago R-rated comedy theater act described on next page, available at TIs and many bars). *Uitkrant* is in Dutch, but it's just a calendar of events, and anyone can figure out the name of the event and its date, time, and location (available at TIs and many bars).

There's also *What's On in Amsterdam, Time Out Amsterdam,* the Thursday edition of many Dutch papers, and the *International Herald Tribune*'s special Netherlands inserts (all sold at newsstands).

Box Office: The Last Minute Ticket Shop at Stadsschouwburg Theater is the best one-stop-shopping box office for theater, classical music, and major rock shows. They also sell half-price, same-day tickets to certain shows (daily 12:00–19:30, Leidseplein 26, tel. 0900-0191—€0.40/min, www.lastminuteticketshop.nl).

Music

You'll find classical music at the **Concertgebouw** (free 12:30 lunch concerts on Wed Sept–mid-June, no concerts mid-June–Aug; arrive at 12:00 for best first-come, first-serve seating; at far south end of Museumplein, tel. 020/671-8345, www.concertgebouw.nl) and at the former Beurs (on Damrak). For opera and dance, try the opera house on Waterlooplein (tel. 020/551-8100). In the summer, Vondelpark hosts open-air concerts.

Two rock music (and hip-hop) clubs near Leidseplein are **Melkweg** (Lijnbaansgracht 234a, tel. 020/531-8181, www.melk weg.nl) and **Paradiso** (Weteringschans 6, tel. 020/626-4521, www.paradiso.nl). They present big-name acts that you might recognize if you're younger than I am.

Jazz has a long tradition at the **Bimhuis** nightclub, east of the Red Light District (concerts Thu–Sat, Oude Schans 73–77, tel. 020/788-2150, www.bimhuis.nl).

The nearby town of Haarlem offers free pipe organ concerts on Tuesday evenings in summer at its 15th-century church, the **Grote Kerk** (at 20:15 mid-May–mid-Oct, see page 1078).

Comedy

Boom Chicago, an R-rated comedy improv act, was started 15 years ago by a group of Americans on a graduation tour. They have been entertaining tourists and locals ever since. The two-hour, English-only show is a series of rude, clever, and high-powered improvisational skits offering a raucous look at Dutch culture and local tourism (€20, more on Sat, less for second Friday show; shows run Sun–Fri at 20:15, second show Fri at 23:30, Sat shows at 19:30 and 22:30, confirm times when you buy your ticket; ticket office open Mon–Thu 11:00–20:30, Fri–Sat 11:00–23:30, closed Sun; no Mon shows Jan–March; in 300-seat Leidseplein Theater, optional meal and drink service, enter through the skinny Boom Bar, Leidseplein 12, tel. 020/423-0101, www.boomchicago.nl). They do *Best of Boom* (a collection of their greatest hits over the years) as well as new shows for locals and return customers. When sales are slow, ticket-sellers on the street out front offer steeply discounted tickets, with a drink included (drop by that afternoon and see what's up).

Theater

Amsterdam is one of the world centers for experimental live theater (much of it in English). Many theaters cluster around the street called the Nes, which stretches south from Dam Square.

Movies

It's not unusual for movies at many cinemas to be sold out—consider buying tickets during the day. Catch modern movies in the 1920s setting of the classic **Tuschinski Theater** (between Muntplein and Rembrandtplein, described on page 1038).

Museums

Several of Amsterdam's museums stay open late. The **Anne Frank House** is open daily until 22:00 in July and August, and until at least 19:00 the rest of the year. The **Rijksmuseum** and **Van Gogh Museum** are open on Fridays until 20:30 and 22:00, respectively (the Van Gogh sometimes has music and a wine bar in the lobby).

The **Hash, Marijuana, and Hemp Museum** is open daily

until 22:00. And the **sex museums** always stay open late (Damrak Sex Museum until 23:00, Erotic Museum until 24:00).

Skating After Dark

While locals can no longer count on a good canal freeze every winter, Amsterdammers still get their skating fix on wheels every Friday night in summer and early fall. Huge groups don inline skates and meet at the Film Museum in Vondelpark (around 20:15). Tourists can roll along; there's a skate-rental shop at the far end of the park (Vondel Tuin Rental, daily 11:00–24:00 in good weather; first hour–€5, then €2.50/hour; price includes helmet, wrist guards, and knee guards; at southeastern edge of park, tel. 020/664-5091, www.vondeltuin.nl).

Sleeping

Greeting a new day by descending steep stairs and stepping into a leafy canalside scene—graceful bridges, historic gables, and bikes clattering on cobbles—is a fun part of experiencing Amsterdam. But Amsterdam is a tough city for budget accommodations, and any room under €140 will have rough edges. Still, you can sleep well and safely in a great location for €100 per double.

I've grouped my hotel listings into three neighborhoods, each of which has its own character. **West Amsterdam** (which includes the Jordaan) has Old World ambience, with quiet canals, old gabled buildings, and candle-lit restaurants. It's also just minutes on foot to Dam Square. Many of my hotels are charming, friendly, gabled mansions. The downside here is that you'll pay more.

Southwest Amsterdam has two main areas for accommodations: near Leidseplein (more central) and near Vondelpark (farther away). The streets near the bustling Leidseplein have restaurants,

---

Sleep Code

(€1 = about $1.40, country code: 31, area code: 020)
S = Single, **D** = Double/Twin, **T** = Triple, **Q** = Quad, **b** = bathroom, **s** = shower only. Nearly everyone speaks English in the Netherlands. Credit cards are accepted, and prices include breakfast and tax unless otherwise noted.

To help you easily sort through these listings, I've divided the rooms into three categories, based on the price for a standard double room with bath:

  $$$ **Higher Priced**—Most rooms €140 or more.
    $$ **Moderately Priced**—Most rooms between €80-140.
     $ **Lower Priced**—Most rooms €80 or less.

tourist buzz, nightlife, canalside charm, B&B coziness, and walkable (or easy tram) access to the center of town. Farther afield is the quieter semi-suburban neighborhood around Vondelpark and Museumplein, close to the Rijks and Van Gogh museums. You'll find good hotel values and ready access to Vondelpark and the art museums, but you're a half-hour walk (or 10-minute tram ride) to Dam Square.

Staying in **Central Amsterdam** is ideal for people who like shopping, tourist sights, and easy access to public transportation (including Central Station). On the downside, the area has traffic noise, concrete, and urban grittiness, and the hotels can lack character.

Some national holidays merit your making reservations far in advance. Amsterdam is jammed during tulip season (late March–mid-May), conventions, festivals, and on summer weekends. During peak season, some hoteliers will not take weekend bookings for people staying fewer than two or three nights.

Around just about every corner in downtown Amsterdam, you'll see construction: cranes for big transportation projects and small crews of bricklayers repairing the wobbly, cobbled streets that line the canals. Canalside rooms can come with great views—and early-morning construction-crew noise. If you're a light sleeper, ask the hotelier for a quiet room in the back. Smoking is illegal in hotel rooms throughout the Netherlands.

Parking in Amsterdam is even worse than driving. You'll pay €32 a day to park safely in a garage—and then have to hike to your hotel.

If you'd rather trade big-city action for small-town coziness, consider sleeping in Haarlem, 15 minutes away by train (see page 1082).

West Amsterdam
Stately Canalside Hotels
These hotels, a half-mile apart, both face historic canals. They come with fine lobbies (some more ornate than others) and rooms that can feel like they're from another century. This area oozes elegance and class, and it is fairly quiet at night.

$$$ The Toren is a chandeliered, historic mansion with a pleasant, canalside setting and a peaceful garden out back for guests. Run by Eric and Petra Toren, this recently renovated, super-romantic hotel is classy yet friendly, with 38 rooms in a great location on a quiet street two blocks northeast of the Anne Frank House. The capable staff is a great source of local advice. The gilt-frame, velvet-curtained rooms are an opulent splurge (tiny Sb-€115, Db-€200, deluxe Db-€250, third person-€40, prices bump way up during conferences and decrease in winter, rates do not include

Hotels and Restaurants in West Amsterdam

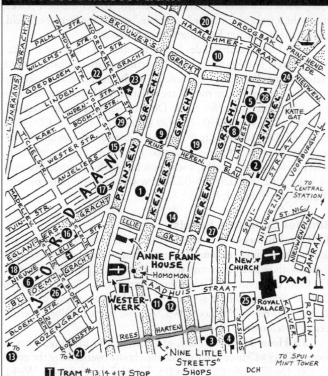

AMSTERDAM

🚊 TRAM #13,14 +17 STOP

1. The Toren
2. Hotel Brouwer
3. Hotel Hegra
4. Hotel Hoksbergen
5. Hotel Chic & Basic Amsterdam
6. Hotel Van Onna
7. Boogaard's B&B
8. Herengracht 21 B&B
9. Truelove Antiek & Guesthouse
10. Frederic Rent-a-Bike Guestrooms
11. Hotel Pax & Sara's Pancake House
12. Hotel Aspen
13. To The Shelter Jordan
14. Restaurant de Luwte
15. De Bolhoed
16. Café Restaurant de Reiger
17. Café 't Smalle
18. Restaurant Vliegende Schotel
19. Top Thai
20. Toscana Italian Restaurant
21. To Bistro 't Stuivertje
22. Ristorante Toscanini
23. Café 't Papeneiland
24. Stubbe's Haring (Fish Stand)
25. Albert Heijn Grocery
26. Paradox Coffeeshop
27. The Grey Area Coffeeshop
28. Siberië Coffeeshop
29. Launderette

5 percent tax, breakfast buffet-€12, air-con, elevator, Internet access and Wi-Fi, Keizersgracht 164, tel. 020/622-6352, fax 020/626-9705, www.thetoren.nl, info@thetoren.nl). To get the best prices, check their website for their "daily rate," and in the "remarks" field, ask for the 10 percent Rick Steves cash discount.

$$$ Hotel Ambassade, lacing together 59 rooms in 10 adjacent houses, is elegant and fresh, sitting aristocratically on the Herengracht. The staff is top-notch, and the public areas (including a library and breakfast room) are palatial, with antique furnishings and modern art (Sb-€195, Db-€195–235, spacious "deluxe" Db with canal view-€250–275, Db suite-€275–375, Tb-€235–275, extra bed-€40, see website for specials, rates do not include 5 percent tax, breakfast-€16—and actually worth it, air-con, elevator, Internet access and Wi-Fi, Herengracht 341, for location see map on page 1062, tel. 020/555-0222, www.ambassade-hotel.nl, info @ambassade-hotel.nl, Roos).

Simpler Canalside Hotels

$$ Hotel Brouwer is a woody and homey old-time place. It's situated tranquilly yet centrally on the Singel canal and rents eight rooms with old furniture and soulful throw rugs (Sb-€60, Db-€95, Tb-€120, cash only, small elevator, Internet access, located between Central Station and Dam Square, near Lijnbaanssteeg at Singel 83, tel. 020/624-6358, fax 020/520-6264, www.hotelbrouwer.nl, akita@hotelbrouwer.nl).

$$ Hotel Hegra is cozy, affordable, and inviting, with 11 rooms filling a 17th-century merchant's house overlooking the canal (S-€50, Ds-€70, Db-€105, Ts-€115, Tb-€145, breakfast-€5, Wi-Fi, just north of Wolvenstraat at Herengracht 269, tel. 020/623-7877, www.hotelhegra.nl, Robert).

$$ Hotel Hoksbergen is a welcoming, well-run place with a peaceful location where hands-on owners Tony and Bert rent 19 rooms (Db-€98, Tb-€143, 5 apartments-€165–198, fans, Wi-Fi, Singel 301, tel. 020/626-6043, www.hotelhoksbergen.com, info @hotelhoksbergen.nl).

$$ Hotel Chic & Basic Amsterdam has a boutique-hotel feel, even though it's part of a Spanish chain. With its mod utilitarian design and younger clientele, it provides a break from all the lace curtains. Located near Central Station, it offers 25 minimalist, bathed-in-white rooms (you can change the color based on your mood). Rooms with canal views are pricier and breezier (Sb-€95–130, Db-€120–155, €20 more on holiday weekends, always free coffee, fans on request, tangled floor plan connecting three canalside buildings, Internet access and Wi-Fi, Herengracht 13, tel. 020/522-2345, fax 020/522-2389, www.chicandbasic.com, amsterdam@chicandbasic.com, manager Bernardo Campo).

Jordaan Neighborhood

The quiet, flower-filled Jordaan neighborhood feels like the Red Light District's complete opposite. While it's not central for tram lines and other connections, it's got plenty of restaurants nearby.

$$ Hotel Van Onna, very European and professional-feeling, has 41 simple, industrial-strength rooms. The price is right, and the leafy location makes you want to crack out your easel. Loek van Onna, who has slept in the building all his life, runs the hotel. The popular top-floor attic rooms are cozy hideaways (Sb-€45, Db-€90, Tb-€135, cash only, cot-like beds seem sufficient, in the Jordaan at Bloemgracht 104, tel. 020/626-5801, www.hotelvanonna.nl, info @hotelvanonna.nl, Leon).

Private-Room Rentals

B&Bs offer a chance to feel like a local during your visit. The first two listings here are perfectly located—a short walk from Central Station, but in a residential and peaceful neighborhood. The next two listings are services that manage and rent many apartments and rooms in West Amsterdam.

$$ Boogaard's B&B is a delightful pad on a cozy lane right out of Mister Rogers' neighborhood. The B&B, which has four comfortable rooms and an inviting public living room, is run by Peter, an American expat opera singer. Peter, who clearly enjoys hosting Americans in his home, serves his fresh-baked goodies at breakfast and offers one of the best values in town (Db-€100, 2-night minimum; furnished family apartment with kitchen-€220 for 4 people, 3-night minimum; air-con, DVD library, Wi-Fi, loaner cell phones and laptops, Langestraat 34, tel. 064/358-6835, www.boogaardsbnb.com, info@boogaardsbnb.com).

$$ Herengracht 21 B&B is a tiny, intimate two-room place run by Loes Olden (Db-€125, near Central Station, Herengracht 21, tel. 020/625-6305, mobile 06-2812-0962, www.herengracht21 .nl, loes@herengracht21.nl).

$$ At Truelove Antiek & Guesthouse, a room-rental service, you'll feel like you're staying at your Dutch friends' house while they're out of town. Sean, Paul, and Nellson—whose tiny antique store on Prinsenstraat doubles as the reception desk for their rental service—have 15 rooms and apartments in houses sprinkled throughout the northern end of the Jordaan neighborhood. The apartments are stylish and come with kitchens and pull-out beds (Db-€80–90, Db apartment-€100, Qb apartments-€150, prices soft in winter and midweek, 2-night minimum on weekends, pick up keys in store at Prinsenstraat 4 or—if arriving after 17:00—call ahead and they'll meet you at Central Station with keys and a map, store tel. 020/320-2500, mobile 06-2480-5672, fax 084-711-4950, www.truelove.be, trueloveantiek@zonnet.nl).

$ Frederic Rent-a-Bike Guestrooms, with a bike-rental shop as the reception, is a collection of private rooms on a gorgeous canal just outside the Jordaan, a five-minute walk from Central Station. Frederic has amassed about 100 beds, ranging from dumpy €70 doubles to spacious and elegant apartments (from €46 per person). Some places are ideal for families and groups of up to six. He also rents houseboat apartments. All are displayed on his website (phone bookings preferred, book with credit card but pay with cash, 2-night minimum, no breakfast, Brouwersgracht 78, tel. 020/624-5509, www.frederic.nl, Sebastian and Frederic). His excellent bike shop is open daily 9:00–17:30 (€10/24 hrs).

Southwest Amsterdam
Charming B&Bs near Leidseplein

The area around Amsterdam's rip-roaring nightlife center (Leidseplein) is colorful, comfortable, and convenient. These canalside mom-and-pop places are within a five-minute walk of rowdy Leidseplein, but are in generally quiet and typically Dutch settings.

$$ Hotel de Leydsche Hof is a hidden gem located on a canal. Its two large rooms are a symphony in white, overlooking a tree-filled backyard. Frits and Loes give their big, elegant, old building a stylish air (Db-€120, includes breakfast, cash only, 2-night minimum, Internet access and Wi-Fi, Leidsegracht 14, tel. 020/638-2327, mobile 06-5125-8588, www.freewebs.com /leydschehof, loespiller@planet.nl).

$$ Wildervanck B&B, run by Helene and Sjoerd Wildervanck, offers two rooms in an elegant, 17th-century canal house (big Db on first floor-€130, Db with twin beds on ground floor-€110, extra bed-€30, breakfast in their pleasant dining room, 2-night minimum, Wi-Fi, family has three little girls, Keizersgracht 498, on Keizersgracht canal just west of Leidsestraat, tel. 020/623-3846, fax 020/421-6575, www.wildervanck.com, info@wildervanck.com). As it's in a busy area, you may get some bar noise at night.

$$ Hotel Keizershof is wonderfully Dutch, with six bright, airy rooms in a 17th-century canal house with a lush garden and a fine living room. A very steep spiral staircase leads to rooms named after old-time Hollywood stars. The enthusiastic hospitality of Mrs. de Vries and her daughter, Hanneke, give this place a friendly, almost small-town charm (S-€70, D-€75–90, Ds-€100, Db-€115, 2-night minimum, reserve with credit card but pay with cash; tram #16, #24, or #25 from Central Station, Keizersgracht 618, where Keizers canal crosses Nieuwe Spiegelstraat; tel. 020/622-2855, www.hotelkeizershof.nl, info@hotelkeizershof.nl).

AMSTERDAM

Hotels and Restaurants in Southwest Amsterdam

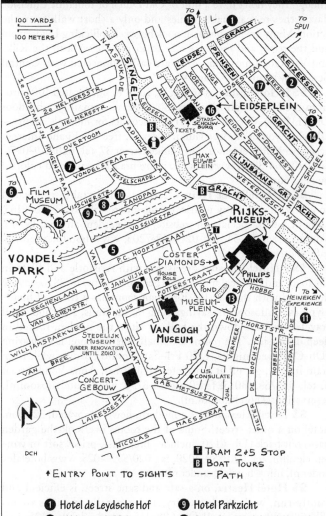

100 YARDS
100 METERS

TRAM 2 & 5 STOP
BOAT TOURS
--- PATH

ENTRY POINT TO SIGHTS

1. Hotel de Leydsche Hof
2. Wildervanck B&B
3. To Hotel Keizershof
4. Hotel Fita
5. Hotel Piet Hein
6. To Hotel Filosoof & Tulips B&B
7. Hotel Alexander
8. Hotel Hestia
9. Hotel Parkzicht
10. Stayokay Vondelpark Hostel
11. To Restaurant Bazar
12. Café Vertigo
13. Cobra Café
14. Le Soleil
15. To La Tertulia Coffeeshop
16. The Bulldog Coffeeshop
17. Launderette

DCH

Near Vondelpark and Museumplein

These options cluster around Vondelpark in a safe neighborhood. Though they don't have a hint of Old Dutch or romantic canalside flavor, they're reasonable values and only a short walk from the action. Many are in a pleasant nook between rollicking Leidseplein and the park, and most are a 5- to 15-minute walk to the Rijks and Van Gogh museums. They are easily connected with Central Station by trams #1, #2, and #5.

$$$ Hotel Fita has 16 bright, fresh rooms located 100 yards from the Van Gogh Museum (Sb-€100, two small ground-floor Db-€135, Db-€145–165, Tb-€195, discounts for multiple nights—ask when you book, free laundry service, free Wi-Fi and Internet access in lobby, elevator, Jan Luijkenstraat 37, tel. 020/679-0976, fax 020/664-3969, www.fita.nl, info@fita.nl, joking and colorful owner Hans).

$$$ Hotel Piet Hein offers 81 comfortable renovated rooms with a swanky nautical atmosphere (Sb-€105, Db-€165, extra bed-€30, specials on website, quiet garden, air-con, Wi-Fi, Vossiusstraat 52–53, tel. 020/662-7205, www.hotelpiethein.nl, info@hotelpiethein.nl).

$$$ Hotel Filosoof greets you with Aristotle and Plato in the foyer and classical music in its generous lobby. Its 38 rooms are decorated with themes; the Egyptian room has a frieze of hieroglyphics. Philosophers' sayings hang on the walls, and thoughtful travelers wander down the halls or sit in the garden, rooted in deep discussion. The rooms are small, but the hotel is endearing (Db-€130 weeknights, €150 Fri–Sat; elevator, 3-min walk from tram line #1, get off at Jan Pieter Heijestraat, Anna Vondelstraat 6, tel. 020/683-3013, fax 020/685-3750, www.hotelfilosoof.nl, reservations@hotelfilosoof.nl).

$$ Hotel Alexander is a modern, newly renovated, 32-room hotel on a quiet street. Some of the rooms overlook the garden patio out back (Db-€120, includes breakfast, prices soft in winter, elevator, tel. 020/589-4020, fax 020/589-4025, www.hotelalexander.nl, info@hotelalexander.nl).

$$ Hotel Hestia, on a safe and sane street, is efficient and family-run, with 18 clean, airy, and generally spacious rooms (Sb-€80–90, very small Db-€98–115, standard Db-€125–145, Tb-€155–173, Qb-€185–203, Quint/b-€215–233, elevator, Roemer Visscherstraat 7, tel. 020/618-0801, fax 020/685-1382, www.hotel-hestia.nl, info@hotel-hestia.nl).

$$ Hotel Parkzicht, an old-fashioned place with extremely steep stairs, rents 13 big, plain rooms on a street bordering Vondelpark (S-€39, Sb-€49, Db-€78–94, Tb-€110–120, Qb-€120–130, closed Nov–March, some noise from neighboring youth hostel, Roemer Visscherstraat 33, tel. 020/618-1954, fax 020/618-0897, www.parkzicht.nl, hotel@parkzicht.nl).

$$ Tulips B&B, with a bunch of cozy rooms—some on a canal—is run by a friendly Englishwoman, Karen, and her Dutch husband, Paul. Rooms are clean, white, and bright, with red carpeting, plants, and flowers (D-€60–80, Db-€105, suite-€140, family deals, includes milk-and-cereal breakfast, cash only, prefer 3-night stays on weekends, no shoes, south end of Vondelpark at Sloterkade 65, directions sent when you book, tel. 020/679-2753, fax 020/408-3028, www.bedandbreakfastamsterdam.net).

Central Amsterdam
Basic Hotels in the City Center

You won't get a warm welcome at either of the two following hotels. But if you're looking for a no-nonsense room that's convenient to plenty of tram lines, these hotels fit the bill.

$$ Hotel Résidence Le Coin offers 42 larger-than-average rooms complete with small kitchenettes. Located near the Mint Tower, this hotel is a two-minute walk to the Flower Market and a five-minute walk to Rembrandtplein. You won't get fancy extras here—just good, solid rooms in an all-business hotel (Sb-€112, small Db-€132, bigger Db-€147, family room-€220, extra bed-€35, breakfast-€10, by the University at Nieuwe Doelenstraat 5, tel. 020/524-6800, fax 020/524-6801, www.lecoin.nl, hotel @lecoin.nl).

$$ Ibis Amsterdam Hotel, located next door to the Central Station, is a modern, efficient, 187-room place. It offers a central location, comfort, and good value, without a hint of charm (Db-€100–160, breakfast-€14, highest prices Fri–Sat, check website for deals, book long in advance, air-con; facing the Central Station, go left towards the multistory bicycle garage to Stationsplein 49; tel. 020/638-9999, fax 020/620-0156, www.ibishotel.com, h1556 @accor.com). When business is slow, they often rent rooms to same-day drop-ins for around €100.

Budget Hotels Between Dam Square and the Anne Frank House

Inexpensive, well-worn hotels line the convenient but noisy main drag, Raadhuisstraat. Expect a long, steep, and depressing stairway, with noisy rooms in the front and quieter rooms in the back. For locations, see the map on page 1055.

$ Hotel Pax has 11 large, plain, but airy rooms with Ikea furniture—a lot like a European dorm room (S-€35–45, D-€65, Db-€80, T-€80, Tb-€95, Q-€100, no breakfast, prices drop dramatically in winter, six rooms share two showers and two toilets, Raadhuisstraat 37, tel. 020/624-9735, run by go-getters Philip and Pieter).

Hotels and Restaurants in Central Amsterdam

200 YARDS

200 METERS

B BOAT TOURS

CENTRAL STATION

STATIONS-PLEIN

To JORDAAN DISTRICT

SINGEL · SPUISTRAAT · VOORBURGWAL · DAMRAK

LELIESTR.

ST. NIC.

NIEUWENDIJK

BEURS-PL.

OLD CHURCH

RED LIGHT DISTRICT

RAADHUISSTRAAT

DAM

DE BIJENKORF DEPT. STORE

PIJLS.

DAMSTR.

VOORBURGWAL

HISTORY MUSEUM

NIEUWEZIJDS · SPUISTRAAT

KALVERSTRAAT · ROKIN · NES · OUDEZIJDS

ST. LUCIEN

BEGIJN-HOF

HET STEEG

SPUI

MINT TOWER

N. DOELEN.

MKT.

HEILIGE

KALVER-TOREN MALL

MUNT PL.

AMSTEL

REGULIERS

HEI·TEN·KONING

SINGEL

FLOWER MARKET

To LEIDSEPLEIN

VIJZEL

DCH

7 Rest. Kapitein Zeppos
8 De Jaren Café
9 Pannenkoekenhuis Upstairs
10 La Place (V&D Dept. Store)
11 Atrium Univ. Cafeteria
12 Stationsrest. & First Class Grand Café
13 Brasserie Rest. de Roode Leeuw
14 La Ruche (De Bijenkorf Dept. Store)
15 Albert Heijn Groceries (3)
16 The Dampkring Coffeeshop

1 To Hotel Ambassade
2 Hotel Résidence Le Coin
3 Ibis Amsterdam Hotel
4 Restaurant Kantjil en de Tijger
5 Kantjil To Go
6 Café 't Gasthuys

AMSTERDAM

$ Hotel Aspen, a few doors away and a good value for a budget hotel, has eight tidy, stark, and well-maintained rooms (S-€40, tiny D-€55–60, Db-€75–80, Tb-€95, Qb-€110, no breakfast, Wi-Fi, Raadhuisstraat 31, tel. 020/626-6714, fax 020/620-0866, www.hotelaspen.nl, info@hotelaspen.nl, run by Rudy and Esam).

Hostels

Amsterdam has a world of good, cheap hostels located throughout the city. Most are designed for the party crowd, but here are a few quieter options. They all offer dorm beds; Stayokay Vondelpark also has some basic doubles.

In the Jordaan: **$ The Shelter Jordan** is a scruffy, friendly, Christian-run, 100-bed place in a great neighborhood. While most of Amsterdam's hostels are pretty wild, this place is drug-free and alcohol-free, with boys on one floor and girls on another. These are Amsterdam's best budget beds, in 4- to 20-bed dorms (€24/bed with sheets and breakfast, €3 extra Fri–Sat, maximum age 35, Internet access in lobby; near Anne Frank House at Bloemstraat 179; tel. 020/624-4717, www.shelter.nl, jordan@shelter.nl). The Shelter serves hot meals, runs a snack bar in its big, relaxing lounge, offers lockers, and leads nightly Bible studies.

In the Red Light District: **$ The Shelter City** is Shelter Jordan's sister—similar, but definitely not preaching to the choir. While its 180 beds are buried in the heart of the red lights, it feels very well-run and perfectly safe (€24/bed with sheets and breakfast in 4- to 20-bed dorms, maximum age 35, curfew, Barndesteeg 21, tel. 020/625-3230, fax 020/623-2282, www .shelter.nl, city@shelter.nl).

In Vondelpark: **$ Stayokay Vondelpark (IYHF)**, with 500 beds in 130 rooms, is one of Amsterdam's top hostels (€23–30/bed in 4- to 20-bed dorms, D-€65–90, higher prices are for March–Oct, members save €2.50, family rooms, lots of school groups, €2 lockers, right on Vondelpark at Zandpad 5, tel. 020/589-8996, fax 020/589-8955, www.stayokay.com). Though Stayokay Vondelpark and Stayokay Stadsdoelen (listed next) are generally booked long in advance, occasionally a few beds open up each day at 11:00.

Near Waterlooplein: **$ Stayokay Stadsdoelen (IYHF)**, smaller and simpler than its Vondelpark sister (listed above), has only large dorms and no private bathrooms, but is free of large school groups (€23–30/bed with sheets and breakfast in 10-bed dorms, members save €2.50, lockers, Kloveniersburgwal 97, see map on page 1046, tel. 020/624-6832, fax 020/639-1035, www.stayokay.com).

Farthest East: **$ Stayokay Zeeburg Hostel (IYHF)** is a new 500-bed hostel with all the modern services. While it's pretty far from the center, by tram or bike you're just 15 minutes from Damrak street (€20–30/bed in 6- to 14-bed dorms, Internet access and Wi-Fi, lockers, games, restaurant, bike rental, tram #14 to Timorplein 21, tel. 020/551-3190, www.stayokay.com, zeeburg @stayokay.com).

Eating

Traditional Dutch food is basic and hearty, with lots of bread, cheese, soup, and fish. Lunch and dinner are served at American times (roughly 12:00–14:00 and 18:00–21:00).

Dutch treats include cheese, pancakes *(pannenkoeken)*, and "syrup waffles" *(stroopwafels)*. Popular drinks are light, pilsner-type beer and gin *(jenever)*.

Experiences you owe your tongue in Holland: Try a pickled herring at an outdoor herring stand, linger over coffee in a "brown café," sip an old *jenever* with a new friend, and consume an Indonesian feast—a *rijsttafel*.

Budget Tips: To dine cheaply yet memorably alongside the big spenders, grab a meal to go, then find a bench on a lively neighborhood square or along a canal. Sandwiches *(broodjes)* of delicious cheese on fresh bread are cheap at snack bars, delis, and *broodjes* restaurants. Ethnic restaurants serve cheap, splittable carryout meals. Ethnic fast-food stands abound, offering a variety of meats wrapped in pita bread. Easy to buy at grocery stores, yogurt in the Netherlands (and throughout northern Europe) is delicious and often drinkable right out of its plastic container.

Restaurants: Of Amsterdam's thousand-plus restaurants, no one knows which are best. I'd pick an area and wander. The rowdy food ghetto thrives around Leidseplein; wander along Leidsedwarsstraat, Restaurant Row. The area around Spui canal and that end of Spuistraat is also trendy and not as noisy. For fewer crowds and more charm, find something in the Jordaan district. Most hoteliers keep a reliable eating list for their neighborhood and know which places keep their travelers happy.

Here are some handy places to consider.

Central Amsterdam

For the locations of these eateries, see the "Hotels and Restaurants in Central Amsterdam" map on page 1062.

On and near Spui

Restaurant Kantjil en de Tijger is a thriving place with a plain and noisy ambience, full of happy eaters who know a good value. The food is purely Indonesian; the waiters are happy to explain your many enticing options. Their three *rijsttafels* (traditional "rice tables" with about a dozen small courses) range from €20–30 per person. While they are designed for two people, three people can make a meal by getting a *rijsttafel* for two and ordering a soup or light dish for the third person. A good budget alternative to the full-blown *rijsttafel* is a *nasi rames*—10 small dishes on one big plate for €13 (daily 16:30–23:00, early-bird €9.50 dinner daily 16:30–18:45, reservations smart, mostly indoor with a little outdoor seating, Spuistraat 291, tel. 020/620-0994).

Kantjil to Go, run by Restaurant Kantjil, is a tiny take-out bar serving up inexpensive but delicious Indonesian fare (€5 for 300 grams, €6.50 for 600 grams, vegetarian specials, daily 12:00–21:00, storefront at Nieuwezijds Voorburgwal 342, around the corner from the sit-down restaurant listed above, tel. 020/620-3074). Split a large box (they'll happily give you an empty extra box for your dining pleasure), grab a bench on the charming Spui Square around the corner, and you've got perhaps the cheapest hot meal in town.

Near the Mint Tower

Café 't Gasthuys, one of Amsterdam's many brown cafés (so called for their smoke-stained walls), has a busy dumbwaiter cranking out light lunches, sandwiches, and reasonably priced dinners. It offers a long bar, a fine secluded back room, peaceful canalside seating, and sometimes slow service (€5–9 lunch plates, €10–14 dinner plates, daily 12:00–16:30 & 17:30–22:00; Grimburgwal 7—from the Rondvaart Kooij boat dock, head down Langebrugsteeg, and it's one block down on the left; tel. 020/624-8230).

Restaurant Kapitein Zeppos, named for an old-time TV star, serves International-Dutch food and salads amid dressy yet unpretentious 1940s ambience. They offer both a restaurant (upstairs, with waiters in nice suits) and a charming, spacious pub (downstairs, good Belgian beers on tap at the big woody bar). The light lunch specials—soups and sandwiches—cost €5–10. Dinners go for about €17 in the pub and for €20–30 in the classy restaurant (food served daily 11:00–15:30 & 17:30–22:30, just off Grimburgwal at Gebed Zonder End 5—a small pedestrian alleyway, tel. 020/624-2057).

De Jaren Café ("The Years Café") is a chic yet inviting place—clearly a favorite with locals. Upstairs is the minimalist restaurant with a top-notch salad bar and a canal-view deck (serving €14–18 dinners after 17:30, including fish, meat, and veggie dishes, and salad bar, or €11 for salad bar only). Downstairs is a modern Amsterdam café, great for light lunches (soups, salads, and sandwiches served all day and evening), or just coffee over a newspaper. On a sunny day, the café's canalside patio is a fine spot to nurse a drink; this is also a nice place to go just for a drink in the evening and enjoy the spacious Art Deco setting (daily 10:00–24:00, Nieuwe Doelenstraat 20–22, a long block up from Muntplein, tel. 020/625-5771).

Pannenkoekenhuis Upstairs is a tiny and characteristic perch up some extremely steep stairs, where Arno Jakobs cooks and serves delicious €7 pancakes to four tables throughout the afternoon (Fri 12:00–19:00, Sat 12:00–18:00, Sun 12:00–17:00, closed Mon–Thu, Grimburgwal 2, tel. 020/626-5603).

La Place, on the ground floor of the V&D department store, has an abundant, colorful array of fresh, appealing food served cafeteria-style. A multi-story eatery that seats 300, it has a small outdoor terrace upstairs. Explore before you make your choice. This bustling spot has a lively market feel, with everything from made-on-the-spot beef stir-fry, to fresh juice, to veggie soups (€3 pizza and €4 sandwiches, Mon–Sat 10:00–20:00, Sun 12:00–20:00, at the end of Kalverstraat near Mint Tower, tel. 020/622-0171). For fast and healthy take-out food (sandwiches, yogurt, fruit cups, and more), try the bakery on the department store's ground floor. (They run another branch, which has the city's ultimate view terrace, on the top floor of the **Central Library**—Openbare Bibliotheek Amsterdam—near Central Station.)

Atrium University Cafeteria, a three-minute walk from Mint Tower, feeds travelers and students from Amsterdam University for great prices, but only on weekdays (€6 meals, Mon–Fri 11:00–15:00 & 17:00–19:30, closed Sat–Sun; from Spui, walk west down Landebrug Steeg past canalside Café 't Gasthuys three blocks to Oudezijds Achterburgwal 237, go through arched doorway on the right; tel. 020/525-3999).

In Central Station

Stationsrestauratie is a surprisingly good, budget, self-service option inside Central Station on platform 2 (daily 8:00–20:00). This entire platform is lined with eateries, including the tall, venerable, 1920s-style **First Class Grand Café.** For picnics, there's a handy **Albert Heijn** supermarket at the end of the underpass beneath the tracks.

Between Central Station and Dam Square

Brasserie Restaurant de Roode Leeuw (*roode leeuw* means "red lion") offers a peaceful, calm respite from the crush of Damrak. During the day, the whole restaurant shares the same menu, but at night, it's split roughly in half, with finer service, cloth tablecloths, and higher prices in back, and a more casual setup (and better people-watching on Damrak street) up front. Either way, you'll get a menu filled with traditional Dutch food, good service, and the company of plenty of tourists. Call ahead to reserve a window seat (restaurant: €20 entrées, €35 three-course fixed-price meal with all the most Dutch choices; brasserie: €10–15 entrées; daily 12:00–22:00, Damrak 93–94, tel. 020/555-0666).

La Ruche, inside the De Bijenkorf department store on Dam Square, has a cafeteria-style lineup of inexpensive salads, soups, sandwiches, and pizzas. On the second floor, with views of busy Damrak, comfortable seating, and an upscale café vibe, this place feels miles above the chaotic streets below (€6–10 plates, daily generally 11:00–19:00, Dam 1, tel. 0900-0919—€0.20/min). De Bijenkorf also has a fancy bakery on the first floor.

Munching Cheap

Traditional fish stands sell €3 herring sandwiches and other salty treats, usually from easy-to-understand photo menus. **Stubbe's Haring,** where the Stubbe family has been selling herring for 100 years, is handy and well-established, a few blocks from Central Station (Tue–Fri 10:00–18:00, Sat 10:00–17:00, closed Sun–Mon, at the locks where Singel canal boat arrives at the train station, see map on page 1055). Grab a sandwich and have a picnic canalside.

Supermarkets: You'll see **Albert Heijn** grocery stores (daily 8:00–22:00) all over town. Three helpful, central locations are: Dam Square (Nieuwezijds Voorburgwal 226), Mint Tower (Koningsplein 4), and Central Station (far end of passage under the tracks).

West Amsterdam
Near the Anne Frank House and in the Jordaan District

Nearly all of these places are within a few scenic blocks of the Anne Frank House, providing handy lunches and atmospheric dinners in Amsterdam's most characteristic neighborhood. For locations, see the map on page 1055.

Restaurant de Luwte is romantic, located on a picturesque street overlooking a canal. It has lots of candles, a muted but fresh modern interior, spacious seating, a few cool outdoor canalside tables, and French Mediterranean cuisine (€19.50 entrées, €29.50 three-course fixed-price meal, big dinner salads for €17.50, daily 18:00–22:00, Leliegracht 26–28, tel. 020/625-8548, manager Marko Depender). Ask about their specials.

De Bolhoed has serious vegetarian and vegan food in a colorful setting that Buddha would dig, with a clientele that appears to dig Buddha (big splittable portions, €15 dinners, light lunches, daily 12:00–22:00, dinner starts at 17:00, Prinsengracht 60, tel. 020/626-1803).

Café Restaurant de Reiger must offer the best cooking of any *eetcafé* in the Jordaan. Famous for its fresh ingredients and delightful bistro ambience, it's part of the classic Jordaan scene. In addition to an English menu, ask for a translation of the €17.50–20 daily specials on the chalkboard. They're proud of their fresh fish and French-Dutch cuisine. The café, which is crowded late and on weekends, takes no reservations, but you're welcome to have a drink (€3 house wine and fun little bar munchies menu) at the bar while you wait (daily 18:00–24:00, veggie options, Nieuwe Leliestraat 34, tel. 020/624-7426).

Café 't Smalle is extremely charming, with three zones where you can enjoy a light lunch or a drink: canalside, inside around the bar, and up some steep stairs in a quaint little back room. The café is open daily until midnight, and simple meals (salads, soup, and fresh sandwiches) are served 11:00–17:30 (plenty of fine €2–3 Belgian beers on tap and interesting wines by the glass, at Egelantiersgracht 12 where it hits Prinsengracht, tel. 020/623-9617).

Restaurant Vliegende Schotel, which may have new ownership in 2010, is a folksy, unvarnished little Jordaan eatery with a cheap, fun menu featuring fish and vegetarian fare. Nothing trendy about this place—just locals who like healthful food and don't want to cook. The €8 *Vliegende Schotel* salad is a vegetarian extravaganza (€10–12 entrées, daily from 17:30, kitchen closes at 21:30, wine by the glass, order at the counter, Nieuwe Leliestraat 162, tel. 020/625-2041).

Top Thai, a block from Hotel Toren, offers top-quality meals for €20 (less for takeout) in their cozy, 10-table restaurant (daily 16:00–22:30, good veggie options, Herenstraat 22, tel. 020/623-4633).

Toscana Italian Restaurant is the Jordaan's favorite place for good, inexpensive Italian cuisine, including pizza, in a woody Dutch-beer-hall setting (€6–8 pizza and pastas, €15 main courses, daily 16:00–24:00, Haarlemmerstraat 130, tel. 020/622-0353).

Sara's Pancake House is a basic pancake diner where extremely hardworking Sara cranks out sweet and savory €8–10 flapjacks (open daily from early until late, breakfast served until noon, Raadhuisstraat 45, tel. 020/320-0662).

Bistro 't Stuivertje is a small, family-run neighborhood favorite tucked away in the Jordaan, serving French-Dutch cuisine in a cozy but unpretentious atmosphere (€15 main courses, dinner salads, Wed–Sun 17:30–22:00, closed Mon–Tue, Hazenstraat 58 near Elandsgracht, tel. 020/623-1349).

Ristorante Toscanini is an up-market Italian place that's always packed. It's so popular that the staff can be a bit arrogant, but the lively, spacious ambience and great Italian cuisine more than make up for that—if you can get a seat. Reservations are essentially required. Your best bet is to eat when they open at 18:00 (€14 first courses, €20 main courses, Mon–Sat 18:00–22:30, closed Sun, deep in the Jordaan at Lindengracht 75, tel. 020/623-2813).

Drinks Only: **Café 't Papeneiland** is a classic brown café with Delft tiles, an evocative old stove, and a stay-awhile perch overlooking a canal with welcoming benches. It's been the neighborhood hangout since the 17th century (drinks but no food, overlooking northwest end of Prinsengracht at #2, tel. 020/624-1989). It feels a little exclusive; patrons who come here to drink and chat aren't eager to see it overrun by tourists. The café's name means "Papists' Island," since this was once a refuge for Catholics; there used to be an escape tunnel here for priests on the run.

Southwest Amsterdam

Near Leidseplein

Stroll through the colorful cancan of eateries on Leidsedwarsstraat, Restaurant Row, just off Leidseplein, and choose your favorite. Nearby, the busy Leidsestraat offers plenty of starving—student options (between the Prinsengracht and the Herengracht) offering fast and fun food for around €5 a meal.

Beyond the Rijksmuseum

Restaurant Bazar offers one of the most memorable and fun budget eating experiences in town. Converted from a church, it has spacious seating and mod belly-dance music, and is filled with young locals enjoying good, cheap Middle Eastern and North African cuisine. Reservations are necessary if you plan to eat after 20:00 (fill up with the €8.50 daily plate, delicious €13 couscous, or €16 three-course meal of the day; daily 11:00–24:00, Albert Cuypstraat 182, tel. 020/675-0544, www.bazaramsterdam.nl). Restaurant Bazar marks the center of the thriving Albert Cuyp market, which is wrapped up by about 17:00, though the restaurant is open late.

In Vondelpark

Café Vertigo offers a fun selection of excellent soups, salads, and sandwiches. It's a surprisingly large complex of outdoor tables, an indoor pub, and an elegant, candlelit, back-room restaurant. The service can be slow, but if you grab an outdoor table, you can watch the world spin by (daily 10:00–24:00, beneath Film Museum, Vondelpark 3, tel. 020/612-3021).

Southeast Amsterdam

Near the Dutch Resistance Museum

For locations of the following eateries, see the map on page 1046.

Restaurant Plancius, adjacent to the Dutch Resistance Museum, is a modern and handy spot for lunch. Its good indoor and outdoor seating make it popular with the museum staff and broadcasters from the nearby local TV studios (creative breakfasts, hearty fresh sandwiches, light €4–8 lunches and €16–19 dinners, daily 10:00–22:00, Sun until 21:00, Plantage Kerklaan 61a, tel. 020/330-9469).

Café Koosje, located halfway between the Dutch Resistance Museum and the Dutch Theater, is a corner lunchtime pub/bar ringed with outdoor seating. Inside, casual wooden tables and benches huddle under chandeliers, and the hip, young waitstaff serves beer and salads big enough for two (€5 sandwiches, €11 salads, Plantage Middenlaan 37, on the corner of Plantage Kerklaan, tel. 020/320-0817).

Taman Sari Restaurant is the local choice for Indonesian, serving hearty, quality €10 dinners and *rijsttafel* dinners for €16–23 (daily 17:00–22:00, Plantage Kerklaan 32, tel. 020/623-7130).

Smoking

Tobacco

A third of Dutch people smoke tobacco. Holland has a long tradition as a smoking culture, being among the first to import the tobacco plant from the New World. (For a history of smoking, visit the Pipe Museum.)

Tobacco shops, such as the House of Hajenius, glorify the habit, yet the Dutch people are among the healthiest in the world. Tanned, trim, firm, 60-something Dutch people sip their beer, take a drag, and ask me why Americans murder themselves with Big Macs.

Still, their version of the Surgeon General has finally woken up to the drug's many potential health problems. Warning stickers bigger than America's are required on cigarette packs, and some of them are almost comically blunt, such as: "Smoking will make you impotent...and then you die." (The warnings have prompted gag stickers like, "Life can kill you.")

Since 2008, a Dutch law has outlawed smoking tobacco almost everywhere indoors: on trains, and in hotel rooms, restaurants, cafés, and bars.

Marijuana (a.k.a. Cannabis)

Throughout the Netherlands, you'll see "coffeeshops"—pubs selling marijuana, with display cases showing various joints or baggies for sale. The minimum age for purchase is 18, and coffeeshops can sell up to five grams of marijuana per person per day. Locals buy marijuana by asking, "Can I see the cannabis menu?" Because it's illegal to advertise marijuana, the buyer has to take the initiative and request a menu. In some places there's actually a button you must push and hold down to see an illuminated menu, the contents of which look like the inventory of a drug bust.

The Dutch, like the rest of Europe, mix their marijuana with tobacco. It might seem strange to an American, but these days, if a coffeeshop is busted, it's for tobacco smoke. Coffeeshops with a few outdoor seats have a huge advantage, as their customers can light up outside. Shops without the outdoor option are in for an extra challenge, as many local smokers would rather get their weed to-go than smoke it without tobacco at their neighborhood coffeeshop. As a substitute for tobacco, shops have started mixing a kind of herb tea into joints. Pre-rolled joints are now sold three ways: pure, with the non-tobacco "hamburger helper" herb mix, or with tobacco. If you like your joint tobacco-free anyway, pure marijuana joints are much easier to buy now than before the tobacco-smoke ban.

Shops sell marijuana and hashish both in pre-rolled joints and in little baggies. Some places sell individual joints (€2–5). Others sell only small packs of three or four joints. Baggies of marijuana usually cost €10–15. Some shops charge per gram. The better pot, while costlier, is actually a better value, as it takes less to get high—and it's a better high. Shops have loaner bongs and inhalers, and they dispense cigarette papers like toothpicks. As long as you're a paying customer (e.g., buy a cup of coffee), you can pop into any coffeeshop and light up, even if you didn't buy your pot there.

Pot should never be bought on the street in Amsterdam, and don't smoke marijuana openly while walking down the street. Well-established coffeeshops are considered much safer, and coffee-shop owners have an interest in keeping their trade safe and healthy. They warn Americans—unused to the strength of the local stuff—to try a lighter leaf. In fact, they are generally very patient in explaining the varieties available.

Coffeeshops

Most of downtown Amsterdam's coffeeshops feel grungy and fore-boding to a typical middle-aged American traveler. The neighborhood places (and those in small towns around the countryside) are much more inviting to people without piercings, tattoos, and favorite techno artists. I've listed a few places with a more pub-like ambience for Americans wanting to go local, but within reason. For locations, see the maps in "Sleeping," earlier in this chapter.

Paradox is the most *gezellig* (cozy) coffeeshop I found—a mellow, graceful place. The managers, Ludo and Wiljan, and their staff are patient with descriptions and happy to walk you through all your options. This is a rare coffeeshop that serves light meals. The juice is fresh, the music is easy, and the neighborhood is charming (single tobacco-free joints-€3, loaner bongs, games, daily 10:00–20:00, two blocks from Anne Frank House at Eerste Bloemdwarsstraat 2, tel. 020/623-5639, www.paradoxamsterdam .demon.nl).

The Grey Area coffeeshop—a hole-in-the-wall spot with three tiny tables—is a cool, welcoming, and smoky place appreciated among local aficionados as a perennial winner of Amsterdam's Cannabis Cup awards. Judging by the autographed photos on the wall, many famous Americans have dropped in (say hi to Willie Nelson). You're welcome to just nurse a bottomless cup of coffee (daily 12:00–20:00, they close relatively early out of consideration for their neighbors, between Dam Square and Anne Frank House at Oude Leliestraat 2, tel. 020/420-4301). The Grey Area is run by two friendly Americans, Adam and Jon. They are helpful and even have a vaporizer if you want to "smoke" without smoking.

Siberië Coffeeshop is a short walk from Central Station, but feels cozy, with a friendly canalside ambience. Clean, big, and bright, this place has the vibe of a not-too-far-out Starbucks (daily 11:00–23:00, Fri–Sat until 24:00, free Internet access, helpful staff, English menu, Brouwersgracht 11, tel. 020/623-5909, www.siberie.nl).

La Tertulia is a sweet little mother-and-daughter-run place with pastel decor and a cheery terrarium atmosphere (Tue–Sat 11:00–19:00, closed Sun–Mon, sandwiches, brownies, games, Prinsengracht 312, www.coffeeshopamsterdam.com).

The Bulldog is the high-profile, leading touristy chain of coffeeshops. These establishments are young but welcoming, with reliable selections. They're pretty comfortable for green tourists wanting to just hang out for a while. The flagship branch, in a former police station right on Leidseplein, is very handy, offering alcohol upstairs, pot downstairs, and fun outdoor seating where you can watch the world skateboard by. There's a chance it may close because it's considered too near a school, but it will likely stay open (daily 10:00–1:00 in the morning, Fri–Sat until 2:00, Leidseplein 17, tel. 020/625-6278, www.bulldog.nl). They opened their first café (on the canal near the Old Church in the Red Light District) in 1975.

The Dampkring is a rough-and-ready constant party. It's a high-profile and busy place, filled with a young clientele and loud music, but the owners still take the time to explain what they offer. Scenes from the movie *Ocean's Twelve* were filmed here (daily 11:00–22:00, later on Fri–Sat, close to Spui at Handboogstraat 29, tel. 020/638-0705).

Smartshops

These business establishments sell "natural" drugs that are legal. Many are harmless nutritional supplements, but they also sell stimulants similar to Ecstasy and strange drug cocktails rolled into joints. It's all perfectly legal, but if you've never taken drugs recreationally, don't start here.

Connections

Amsterdam's Central Train Station is being renovated—a messy construction project that's expected to last through 2012 (see "Arrival in Amsterdam," near the beginning of this chapter, for more details on the station). The station's train-information center can require a long wait. Save lots of time by getting train tickets and information in Haarlem (if you're going there), at the airport upon arrival (wonderful service), or from a travel agency. You can buy tickets ahead of time for the next day. If you plan to use a Eurailpass and Amsterdam is your first stop, validate it at Schiphol Airport when you arrive (best choice), or at Amsterdam's international train office at platform #2 (take a number and expect a wait).

You have two options for buying tickets in the Netherlands—at a ticket window (€0.50 extra, worth it if the lines are short), or at an automated machine. While the machines levy no additional fees, they can be a trial to use. Most machines have instructions in English (press the British flag). Before committing to quality time with a machine, check the upper-right corner of the screen to see what forms of payment are accepted: euro coins, euro bills, credit cards, and so on (items with an "X" through them are not accepted). If the machine accepts your credit card, you'll be required to enter a PIN. Note that same-day round-trip tickets ("day return") are discounted—handy for day trips.

By Train to: Schiphol Airport (4–6/hr, 20 min, €3.80, have coins handy to buy from a machine to avoid lines), **Haarlem** (6/hr, 20 min, €3.80 one-way, €6.40 same-day round-trip), **Bruges/Brugge** (hourly, 3.5–4 hrs, transfer at Antwerp Central or Brussels Midi; transfer can be timed closely—be alert and check with conductor), **Brussels** (hourly, 2.75 hrs, €35), **Ostende** (hourly, 4 hrs, change in Antwerp), **London** (hourly, 5.5 hrs, with transfer to Eurostar Chunnel train in Brussels; Eurostar discounted with railpass, www.eurostar.com), **Copenhagen** (9/day, 11–18 hrs, most require multiple transfers), **Frankfurt** (every 2 hours, 4 hrs direct, more with transfer in Köln or Duisburg), **Munich** (hourly, 7–8 hrs, transfer in Frankfurt or Düsseldorf, night train possible), **Interlaken** (7/day, 9–10 hrs, 1–6 changes, 2 workable overnight connections), **Paris** (nearly hourly, 4–5 hrs). The trip to Paris requires taking the fast-but-pricey Thalys train from Brussels (unless you take the bus—see next page). Without a railpass, you'll pay about €80–100 second class for the Amsterdam–Paris train (compared to €45 by bus) or about €60–80 second class for the Brussels–Paris train (compared to €25 by bus). Even with a railpass, you need to pay for train reservations (second class-€14.50; first class-€27, includes a meal). Book at least a day ahead, as seats are limited (www.thalys.com). Or hop on the bus, Gus.

By Bus to Paris: If you don't have a railpass, the cheapest way to get to Paris is by bus (Eurolines buses make the 8-hour trip every 2 hours, €35 one-way, €60 round-trip; check online for deals, bus station in Amsterdam at Julianaplein 5, Amstel Station, five stops by metro from Central Station, tel. 020/560-8788, www.eurolines.com).

Amsterdam's Schiphol Airport

Schiphol (SKIP-pol) Airport, is located about 10 miles southwest of Amsterdam's city center. Like most of Holland, it is user-friendly and below sea level. With an appealing array of shops, eateries, and other time-killing opportunities, Schiphol is a fine place to arrive, depart, or change planes. A truly international airport, Schiphol has done away with Dutch—signs are in English only.

Information: Schiphol flight information (tel. 0900-0141; from other countries dial +31-20-794-0800) can give you flight times and your airline's Amsterdam phone number for reconfirmation before going home (or visit www.schiphol.nl). To reach the airlines directly, call: KLM and Northwest—tel. 020/474-7747; Martinair—tel. 020/601-1767; SAS—tel. 0900-7466-3727 (toll call); British Airways—tel. 020/346-9559; and easyJet—tel. 0900-265-8022 (toll call).

Orientation: Schiphol has four terminals: Terminal 1 is for flights to most European countries (not including the UK); Terminals 2 and 3 are for flights to the UK, US, and other non-European countries; and the new, smaller Terminal 4 (attached to Terminal 3) is for low-cost carriers. Once inside the airport, the terminal waiting areas are called "Lounges" (e.g., "Lounge 1"), and are subdivided into lettered concourses (e.g., "D Gates"). An inviting shopping and eating zone called "Holland Boulevard" runs between Lounges 2 and 3.

Arrival at Schiphol: Conveniently, baggage claim areas for all terminals empty into the same arrival zone, called Schiphol Plaza—with ATMs, shops, eateries, a busy **TI** (near Terminal 2), a train station, and bus stops for getting into the city. You can validate your Eurailpass and hit the rails immediately, or, to stretch your railpass, buy an inexpensive ticket into Amsterdam today and start the pass later.

Airport Services: The ABN/AMRO **banks** offer fair exchange rates (in both arrivals and lounge areas). The GWK **public-transit office** is located in Schiphol Plaza and sells SIM cards for mobile phones. Surf the **Internet** and make phone calls at the Communication Centres (one on the top level of Lounge 2, another on the ground floor of Lounge 1; both are behind customs and not available once you've left the security checkpoint). Convenient luggage **lockers** are at various points around the airport—allowing you to leave your bag here on a lengthy layover (both short-term and long-term lockers; biggest bank of lockers near the train station at Schiphol Plaza).

Airport Train Ticket Counter: For a train ticket or train information, take advantage of the fantastic "Train Tickets and Services" counter (Schiphol Plaza ground level, just past Burger King). They have an easy info desk, almost no lines (much quicker than the ticket desk at the Amsterdam train station downtown), and issue international tickets for €3.50 and domestic tickets for €0.50.

Time-Killing Tips: If you have extra time to kill at Schiphol, check out the **Rijksmuseum Amsterdam Schiphol,** a little art gallery on Holland Boulevard. The Rijksmuseum loans a dozen or so of its minor masterpieces from the Golden Age to this unique airport museum, including actual Dutch Masters by Rembrandt, Vermeer, and others (free, daily 7:00–20:00, between Terminals 2 and 3). The museum is between the passport and security checks at Terminal 2, so it's technically not in the "secure" part of the airport. You can visit easily from Terminals 2 or 3, but if you visit from Terminal 1, you'll have to go back through security to reach your flight (allow plenty of time).

To escape the airport crowds, follow signs for the *Panorama Terrace* to the third floor of Terminal 2, where you'll find a quieter, full-of-locals cafeteria, a kids' play area, and a view terrace where you can watch planes come and go while you nurse a coffee. If you plan to visit the terrace on arrival, stop there before you pass through customs.

From Schiphol Airport to Amsterdam: There's a direct **train** to Amsterdam's Central Station (4–6/hr, 20 min, €3.80, no strip tickets). The Connexxion **shuttle bus** takes you to your hotel neighborhood; since there are three different routes, ask the attendant which one works best for your hotel (2/hr, 20 min, €14 one-way, €22 round-trip, one route stops at Westerkerk near Anne Frank House and many recommended hotels, bus to other hotels may cost a couple euros more, departs from lane A7 in front of airport, tel. 020/653-4975, www.airporthotelshuttle.nl). Allow about €40 for a **taxi** to downtown Amsterdam. Bus #197 is handiest for those staying in the Leidseplein district (departs from lane B9 in front of airport, buy ticket from driver or use strip tickets).

From Schiphol Airport to Haarlem: See the end of the Haarlem chapter (next).

From Schiphol Airport by Train to: The Hague/Den Haag (2/hr, 30 min), **Delft** (4/hr, 45 min, transfer in The Hague or Leiden), **Rotterdam** (3/hr, 45 min). International trains to Belgium run every hour: **Brussels** (2.5 hrs), **Bruges/Brugge** (3.5 hrs, change in Antwerp or Brussels).

HAARLEM

Cute and cozy, yet authentic and handy to the airport, Haarlem is a fine home base, giving you small-town warmth overnight, with easy access (20 min by train) to wild and crazy Amsterdam during the day.

Bustling Haarlem gave America's Harlem its name back when New York was New Amsterdam, a Dutch colony. For centuries, Haarlem has been a market town, buzzing with shoppers heading home with fresh bouquets, nowadays by bike.

Enjoy the market on Monday (clothing) or Saturday (general), when the town's atmospheric main square bustles like a Brueghel painting, with cheese, fish, flowers, and families. Make yourself at home; buy some flowers to brighten your hotel room.

Overview

(area code: 023)

Tourist Information

Haarlem's TI (VVV), in the town center, is friendlier, more helpful, and less crowded than Amsterdam's, so ask your Amsterdam questions here (April–Sept Mon–Fri 9:00–17:30, Sat 10:00–16:00, closed Sun; Oct–March Mon–Fri 9:30–17:00, Sat 10:00–14:00, closed Sun; across from V&D department store at Verwulft 11, tel. 0900-616-1600—€0.50/min, www.vvvhaarlem.nl, info@vvv haarlem.nl).

The TI offers a good selection of maps and sightseeing and walking tour brochures, and sells discounted tickets (€1–2 off) for the Frans Hals Museum and the Teylers Museum.

The little yellow computer terminal on the curb outside the train station prints out free maps anytime. (It's fun...just dial the street and hit "print." Drivers will also find these terminals stationed at roads coming into town.)

Arrival in Haarlem

By Train: Lockers are available at Haarlem's train station (€3.50/day, no coins—use a debit card or a "Chipknip" prepaid debit card, which you can purchase at a ticket window). Two parallel streets flank the train station (Kruisweg and Jansweg). Head up either street, and you'll reach the town square and church within 10 minutes. If you need help, ask a local person to point you toward the Grote Markt (Market Square).

By Car: Parking is expensive on the streets (€2.50/hr) and cheaper in several central garages (€2/hr). Three main garages let you park overnight for €2.50: at the train station, near the Teylers Museum (follow signs to the museum) and near the Frans Hals Museum (again, follow signs).

By Plane: For details on getting from Schiphol Airport into Haarlem, see the end of this chapter.

Helpful Hints

Blue Monday: Most sights are closed on Monday, except the church.

Money: The handy **GWK** currency exchange office at the train station offers fair rates (Mon–Fri 8:00–20:00, Sat 9:00–17:00, Sun 10:00–17:00).

Internet Access: Try **Hotel Amadeus** (overlooking Market Square, €1.20/15 min, 25 percent discount with this book), **High Times Coffeeshop** (free if you buy some pot), or **Suny Teletechniques** (€2/hr, daily 10:00–24:00, near train station at Lange Herenstraat 4, tel. 023/551-0037).

Post Office: It's at Gedempte Oude Gracht 2 (Mon–Fri 9:00–18:00, Sat 10:00–13:30, closed Sun, has ATM).

Laundry: **My Beautiful Launderette** is handy and fairly central (€6 self-service wash and dry, daily 8:30–20:30, €9 full service available Mon–Fri 9:00–17:00, near V&D department store at Boter Markt 20).

Bike Rental: You can rent bikes at the train station (€7.50/day, €50 deposit and passport number, Mon–Sat 6:00–24:00, Sun 7:30–24:00). They have only 50 bikes to rent and often run out by midmorning—especially when the weather's good.

Taxi: The drop charge of €7.50 gets you a little over a mile.

Local Guide: For a historical look at Haarlem, consider hiring **Walter Schelfhout** (€75/2 hrs, tel. 023/535-5715, mobile 06-1258-9299, schelfhout@dutch.nl).

Best View: At **La Place** (top-floor cafeteria of the V&D department store, listed near the end of this chapter), you get wrap-around views of the city as you sip your €2 self-serve tea.

Best Ice Cream: Gelateria Bartoli (on the south side of the Grote Kerk) is the local favorite.

Bulb Flower Parade: On Saturday, April 24, 2010, an all-day Bulb Flower Parade of floats, decorated with real blossoms, wafts through eight towns, including Haarlem. The floats are parked in Haarlem at Gedempte Oude Gracht overnight, when they're illuminated, and on display throughout the next day (for details, see www.bloemencorso.info).

Sights and Experiences

▲▲**Market Square (Grote Markt)**—Haarlem's market square (Grote Markt), where 10 streets converge, is the town's delightful centerpiece...as it has been for 700 years. To enjoy a coffee or beer here, simmering in Dutch good living, is a quintessential European experience. In a recent study, the Dutch were found to be the most content people in Europe; in another study, the people of Haarlem were found to be the most content in the Netherlands. Observe. Sit and gaze at the church, appreciating essentially the same scene that Dutch artists captured centuries ago in oil paintings that now hang in museums.

Just a few years ago, trolleys ran through the square, and cars were parked everywhere. But today, it's a pedestrian zone, with market stalls filling the square on Mondays and Saturdays, and café tables dominating on other days.

This is a fun place to build a picnic with Haarlem finger foods—pickled herring (take-away stand on the square), local cheese (Gouda and Edam—tasty shop a block away on Barteljorisstraat), french fries with mayonnaise (recommended old-time fries place behind the church on Warmoesstraat), *stroopwafels* (waffles with built-in syrup), and *poffertjes* (little sugar doughnuts, cooked on the spot, great seating on the square).

▲**Church (Grote Kerk)**—This 15th-century Gothic church (now Protestant) is worth a look, if only to see Holland's greatest pipe organ (from 1738, 100 feet high). Its 5,000 pipes impressed both Handel and Mozart. Note how the organ, which fills the west end, seems to steal the show from the altar. Quirky highlights of the church include a replica of Foucault's pendulum, the "Dog-Whipper's Chapel," and a 400-year-old cannonball.

To enter, find the small *Entrée* sign behind the church at Oude Groenmarkt 23 (€2, Mon–Sat 10:00–16:00, closed Sun to tourists, tel. 023/553-2040).

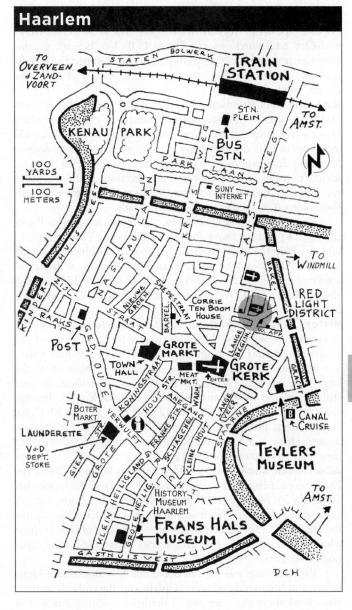

Haarlem

TO OVERVEEN & ZANDVOORT

STATEN BOLWERK

TRAIN STATION

STN. PLEIN

TO AMST.

KENAU PARK

BUS STN.

N

PARK LAAN

100 YARDS

100 METERS

SUNY INTERNET

TO WINDMILL

RED LIGHT DISTRICT

NIEUWE GROEN

SHEDESTRAAT

BARTEL

W. APP.

Corrie Ten Boom House

LANGE BEGIJN.

Post

KINDER- ZIJL

RAAKS

GROTE MARKT

TOWN HALL

KONINGSTRAAT

MEAT MKT.

ENTER

GROTE KERK

LANGE VEER

GRACHT

Boter Markt

VERWULFT

LAUNDERETTE

V&D DEPT. STORE

GIER STR.

GROTE

HOUT STR.

ANEGANG

FRANKE STR.

SCHAGCHEL

KLEINE HOUT

SPAARNE

CANAL CRUISE

TEYLERS MUSEUM

TO AMST.

HEILIGLAND

KLEIN HEILIGLAND

GROTE HEILIG.

HISTORY MUSEUM HAARLEM

FRANS HALS MUSEUM

GASTHUIS VEST

DCH

HAARLEM

Consider attending (even part of) a **concert** to hear the Oz-like pipe organ (regular free concerts Tue at 20:15 mid-May–mid-Oct, additional concerts Thu at 15:00 late June–Aug, concerts nearly nightly at 20:15 during the organ competition in July, confirm schedule at TI or at www.bavo.nl; bring a sweater—the church isn't heated).

▲▲Frans Hals Museum—Haarlem is the hometown of Frans Hals, the foremost Dutch portrait painter of the 17th-century Golden Age. This refreshing museum, once an almshouse for old men back in 1610, displays many of his greatest paintings, done in his nearly Impressionistic style. Stand eye-to-eye with life-size, lifelike portraits of Haarlem's citizens—brewers, preachers, workers, bureaucrats, and housewives—and see the people who built the Golden Age, then watched it start to fade.

Along with Frans Hals' work, the museum features Pieter Brueghel's painting *Dutch Proverbs*, illustrating 72 Dutch proverbs. Pick up the chart to identify these clever bits of everyday wisdom. Also look for the 250-year-old dollhouse on display in a former chapel (€7.50, Tue–Sat 11:00–17:00, Sun 12:00–17:00, closed Mon, Groot Heiligland 62, tel. 023/511-5775, www.frans halsmuseum.nl).

History Museum Haarlem—This small museum, across the street from the Frans Hals Museum, offers a glimpse of old Haarlem. Request the English version of the 10-minute video, low-key Haarlem's version of a sound-and-light show. Study the large-scale model of Haarlem in 1822 (when its fortifications were still intact), and wander the two rooms without English descriptions (overpriced at €4, Tue–Sat 12:00–17:00, Sun 13:00–17:00, closed Mon, Groot Heiligland 47, tel. 023/542-2427, www .historischmuseumhaarlem.nl). The adjacent architecture center (free) may be of interest to architects.

▲Corrie ten Boom House—Haarlem was home to Corrie ten Boom, popularized by her inspirational book (and the movie that followed), *The Hiding Place*. Both tell about the Ten Boom family's experience protecting Jews from the Nazis. Corrie ten Boom gives the other half of the Anne Frank story—the point of view of those who risked their lives to hide Dutch Jews during the Nazi occupation (1940–1945).

The clock shop was the Ten Boom family business. The elderly father and his two daughters—Corrie and Betsy, both in their 50s—lived above the store and in the brick building attached in back (along Schoutensteeg alley). Corrie's bedroom was on the top floor at the back. This room was tiny to start with, but then the family built a second, secret room (less than a yard deep) at the very back—"the hiding place," where they could hide six Jews at a time. Devoutly religious, the family had a long tradition of tolerance, having hosted prayer meetings here in their home for both Jews and Christians for generations.

The Gestapo, tipped off that the family was harboring Jews, burst into the Ten Boom house. Finding a suspicious number of ration coupons, the Nazis arrested the family, but failed to find the six Jews (who later escaped) in the hiding place. Corrie's father and sister died while in prison, but Corrie survived the Ravensbruck concentration camp to tell her story in her memoir.

The Ten Boom House is open only for 60-minute English tours—check the sign on the door for the next start time. The gentle and loving tours come with a little evangelizing that some atheists may find objectionable (donation accepted; April–Oct Tue–Sat first tour at 10:00, last tour at 15:30; Nov–March Tue–Sat first tour at 11:00, last tour at 15:00; closed Sun–Mon; 50 yards north of Market Square at Barteljorisstraat 19; the clock-shop people get all wound up if you go inside—wait in the little side street at the door, where hourly tour times are posted; tel. 023/531-0823, www .corrietenboom.com).

▲**Teylers Museum**—Famous as the oldest museum in Holland, Teylers is a time-warp experience, filled with all sorts of fun curios for science buffs: fossils, minerals, primitive electronic gadgetry, and examples of 18th- and 19th-century technology. This place feels like a museum of a museum. They're serious about authenticity here: The presentation is perfectly preserved, right down to the original labels. Since there was no electricity in the olden days, you'll find little electric lighting...if it's dark outside, it's dark inside. The museum's benefactor, Pieter Teyler van der Hulst, was a very wealthy merchant who willed his estate, worth the equivalent of €80 million today, to a foundation whose mission was to "create and maintain a museum to stimulate art and science." The museum opened in 1784, six years after Teyler's death (his last euro was spent in 1983—now it's a national museum). Add your name to the guest book, which goes back to before Napoleon's visit here. The oval room—a temple of science and learning—is the core of the museum; the art gallery hangs paintings in the old style. While there are no English descriptions, an excellent (and, I'd say, essential) audioguide is included (€7, Tue–Sat 10:00–17:00, Sun 12:00–17:00, closed Mon, Spaarne 16, tel. 023/516-0960, www .teylersmuseum.nl). The museum's modern café has good prices and faces a delightful garden.

▲**De Adriaan Windmill**—Haarlem's old-time windmill, located just a 10-minute walk from the station and Teylers Museum, welcomes visitors with a short video, little museum, and fine town views (€2, Wed–Fri 13:00–16:00, Sat–Sun 10:00–16:00, closed Mon–Tue, Papentorenvest 1, tel. 023/545-0259, www.molen adriaan.nl—in Dutch only).

Canal Cruise—Making a scenic 50-minute loop through and around Haarlem with a live guide who speaks Dutch and sometimes English, these little trips are more relaxing than informative (€10; April–Oct Tue–Sun departures at the top of each hour from 12:00–16:00, closed Mon; across canal from Teylers Museum at Spaarne 11a, tel. 023/535-7723, www.woltheuscruises.nl).

▲**Red Light District**—Wander through a little Red Light District that's as precious as a Barbie doll—and legal since the 1980s (2 blocks northeast of Market Square, off Lange Begijnestraat, no senior or student discounts). Don't miss the mall on Begijnesteeg marked by the red neon sign reading *'t Steegje* ("free"). Just beyond that, the nearby 't Poortje ("office park") costs €6 to enter. Jog to the right to pop into the much more inviting "Red Lantern" (window-shopping welcome, at Korte Begijnestraat 27). As you wander through this area, remember that the people here don't condone prostitution any more than your own community back home probably does; they just find it practical not to criminalize it and drive it underground, but instead to regulate it and keep the practice as safe as possible.

Nightlife

Haarlem's evening scene is great. Consider four basic zones: Market Square in the shadow of the Grote Kerk; Lange Veerstraat; Boter Market Square; and Vijfhoek (Five Corners). Market Square is lined with trendy bars (Café Studio is generally the hot spot for a drink here) that seem made for nursing a drink. Lange Veerstraat (behind the Grote Kerk) is colorful and bordered with lively spots. Boter Market Square is more convivial and local, as it's less central and away from the tourists. And Vijfhoek, named for the five lanes that converge here, is incredibly charming, although it has only one pub (with plenty of drinks, bar snacks, a relaxed local crowd, and fine indoor or outdoor seating). The area from this cutest corner in town to the New Church (Nieuwe Kerk, a couple of blocks away) is worth exploring. If you want a more high-powered scene, Amsterdam is just 20 minutes away by train.

Sleeping

The helpful Haarlem TI can nearly always find you a €25 bed in a private home (but for a €6-per-person fee, plus a cut of your host's money; two-night minimum). Avoid this if you can; it's cheaper to reserve by calling direct. Nearly every Dutch person you'll encounter speaks English.

Haarlem is most crowded on Easter weekend (April 2–4 in 2010), in April (particularly for the flower parade—on April 24

Sleep Code

(€1 = about $1.40, country code: 31, area code: 023)
S = Single, **D** = Double/Twin, **T** = Triple, **Q** = Quad, **b** = bathroom,
s = shower only. Credit cards are accepted unless otherwise
noted.

To help you easily sort through these listings, I've divided
the rooms into three categories, based on the price for a
standard double room with bath:

$$$ **Higher Priced**—Most rooms €85 or more.
$$ **Moderately Priced**—Most rooms between €60–85.
$ **Lower Priced**—Most rooms €60 or less.

in 2010—and Queen's Day, on April 30), and in May, July, and
August.

The listed prices include breakfast (unless otherwise noted)
and usually include the €2-per-person-per-day tourist tax. To avoid
this town's louder-than-normal street noises, forgo views for a room
in the back. Hotels and the TI have a useful parking brochure.

In the Center
Hotels and B&Bs

$$$ Hotel Lion D'Or is a classy, 34-room business hotel with all
the professional comforts and a handy location (Db-€150, Fri–Sat
Db-€125, extra bed-€15, 8 percent discount to Rick Steves readers
for 2-night stays when you book direct, air-con, elevator, Wi-Fi,
across the street from train station at Kruisweg 34, tel. 023/532-
1750, fax 023/532-9543, www.hotelliondor.nl, reservations@hotel
liondor.nl, Dirk Pauw).

$$$ Stempels Hotel, modern yet elegant, is located in a
recently renovated, 250-year-old building. With bare floors, comfy
high-quality beds, and minimalist touches in its 17 rooms, what
it lacks in warmth it makes up for in style and value. Double-
paned windows help keep down the noise, since it's a block east
of Market Square, with a bustling brasserie and bar downstairs
(standard Sb-€80, Db-€95–108, breakfast-€10, in-room computers
with free Internet access and Wi-Fi, Klokhuisplein 9, tel. 023/512-
3910, www.stempelsinhaarlem.nl, info@stempelsinhaarlem.nl).

$$$ Hotel Amadeus, on Market Square, has 15 small, bright,
and basic rooms, some with views of the square. This characteris-
tic hotel, ideally located above an early 20th-century dinner café,
is relatively quiet, especially if you take a room in the back. Its
lush old lounge/breakfast room on the second floor overlooks the
square, and Mike and Inez take good care of their guests (Sb-€60,

Haarlem Hotels and Restaurants

1 Hotel Lion D'Or
2 Stempels Hotel
3 Hotel Amadeus
4 Ambassador City Centre Hotel
5 Hotel Malts
6 To B&B House de Kiefte
7 Hotel Carillon
8 Indrapoera Hotel & Hostel
9 Die Raeckse Hotel
10 To Hotel Haarlem Zuid
11 To Stayokay Haarlem Hostel
12 Pannenkoekhuis de Smikkel
13 Vlam in de Pan &
   't Theehuis Coffeeshop
14 Vincent's Eethuis
15 Jacobus Pieck Eetlokaal &
   Friethuis de Vlaminck
16 Pizzeria-Rist. Venezia
17 La Plume Restaurant
18 Spaarne 66 Restaurant Bar
19 Lambermon's Restaurant
20 De Lachende Javaan Rest.
21 La Place Cafeteria
22 Albert Heijn Supermarkets (2)
23 DekaMarkt Supermarket
24 High Times Coffeehouse
25 Vijfhoek (Five Corners)

Db-€85, Tb-€110, 5 percent Rick Steves discount with 2-night stay and cash, 10-min walk from train station, steep climb to lounge and then an elevator, fee for Internet access and Wi-Fi, Grote Markt 10, tel. 023/532-4530, fax 023/532-2328, www.amadeus-hotel.com, info@amadeus-hotel.com). The Hotel Amadeus' breakfast room overlooking the main square is a great place to watch the town greet a new day—one of my favorite Haarlem moments.

$$$ Ambassador City Centre Hotel, with 29 comfortable rooms in a big, plain hotel, is located just behind the Grote Kerk (Db-€100, breakfast buffet-€14, free Internet access and Wi-Fi, Oude Groenmarkt 20, tel. 023/512-5300, www.acc-hotel.nl, info @acc-hotel.nl). They rent studios with kitchenettes for 2–4 people (€120–150 depending on season and number of people). They also run Hotel Joops a block away (rooms are €10 cheaper; studios and apartments with kitchenettes for 2–4 people).

$$ Hotel Malts is well-located and rents 12 bright, simple, and fresh rooms for a good price (small Db-€55, medium Db-€70, big Db-€85, breakfast-€7.50, free Wi-Fi, Zijlstraat 56, tel. 023/551-2385, www.maltshotel.nl, info@degraaf-schreurs.nl, Marco).

$ Bed-and-Breakfast House de Kiefte is a wonderful get-into-a-local-home option with the best budget beds in town. Marjet (mar-yet) and Hans, a frank and engaging Dutch couple who speak English well, rent three bright, cheery rooms on the top floor of their quiet 1892 home (Ds-€60, T-€83, Qs-€105, Quint/s-€122, cash only, 2-night minimum, rates include breakfast, very steep stairs, kids older than 4 welcome, Coornhertstraat 3, tel. 023/532-2980, mobile 06-5474-5272, housedekiefte@gmx.net). It's a 15-minute walk or €7.50 taxi ride from the train station and a 5-minute walk from the center. From Market Square, walk to the right of the town hall, go straight out Zijlstraat over the bridge, and take a left on the fourth street.

Rooms in Restaurants

These places are all run as sidelines by restaurants, and you'll know it by the style of service and rooms. Lobbies are in the restaurant, and there are no public spaces. Still, they are handy and—for Haarlem—inexpensive.

$$ Hotel Carillon overlooks the town square and comes with a little traffic and bell-tower chimes. It rents 20 spartan and run-down rooms at the top of st-e-e-e-p stairs. The front rooms come with more street noise and great town-square views (tiny loft S-€40, Db-€78–80, Tb-€99, Qb-€108, 5 percent discount for Rick Steves readers—claim when booking and show book on arrival, no elevator, free Wi-Fi, Grote Markt 27, tel. 023/531-0591, fax 023/531-4909, www.hotelcarillon.com, info@hotelcarillon.com, owners Kelly Kuo, Andres Haas, and June).

$$ Indrapoera Hotel and Hostel, a humid little place with too much carpeting, has eight cheap hotel rooms and five new hostel rooms just across the street from the train station. Their stark-yet-modern, six- to eight-bed dorms have lockers and share one big modern bathroom (hotel—Db-€75, hostel—€25–30/bed with sheets and breakfast, trains stop by midnight, Kruisweg 18, tel. 023/532-0393, yeh@yeh.speedxs.nl, Yeh family).

$$ Die Raeckse Hotel, family-run and friendly, is not as central as the others and has less character and more traffic noise—but its 21 rooms are decent and comfortable. Noisy rooms on the street are cheaper than the quiet ones in the back, but it's worth asking for a quiet room (Sb-€55, small Db-€70, big Db-€85, Tb-€90–110, Qb-€120–135, €5/night discount for 2-night stay, includes breakfast, these special Rick Steves prices only for direct bookings, fee for Internet access and Wi-Fi, Raaks Straat 1, tel. 023/532-6629, fax 023/531-7937, www.die-raeckse.nl, dieraeckse@zonnet.nl).

Near Haarlem

$$$ Hotel Haarlem Zuid, with 300 modern rooms, is sterile but a good value for drivers. It sits in an industrial zone a 20-minute walk from the center, on the road to the airport (Db-€84–98, breakfast-€12, elevator, free parking, laundry service, fitness center-€5, inexpensive hotel restaurant, Toekanweg 2, tel. 023/536-7500, fax 023/536-7980, www.hotelhaarlemzuid.nl, haarlemzuid@valk.com). Bus #300 (runs every 10 min) conveniently connects the hotel with the train station, Market Square, and the airport.

$ Stayokay Haarlem Hostel, completely renovated and with all the youth-hostel comforts, charges €25–30 for beds in four- and six-bed dorms. They also rent simple €60–80 doubles (€2.50 less for members, includes sheets and breakfast, save by booking on their website, laundry service, daily 8:00–24:00, Jan Gijzenpad 3, two miles from Haarlem station—take bus #2 from station, or a 10-min walk from Santpoort Zuid train station, tel. 023/537-3793, www.stayokay.com/haarlem, haarlem@stayokay.com).

Eating

North of Market Square

Pannenkoekhuis de Smikkel, a well-worn fixture in town, serves a big selection of pancakes for lunch or dinner (meat, cheese, etc.) and dessert. The €8–12 pancakes are large but pricey and only a good value if you split them. Two people can split one savory and one sweet selection to eat economically (Tue–Sun 12:00–21:00, closed Mon, 2 blocks in front of station, Kruisweg 57, tel. 023/532-0631).

At **Vlam in de Pan,** a dynamo named Femke serves vegetarian delights: soup, salad, veggie sushi, quiches, and other fresh foods.

Sit family-style at the long tables, or get your food to take away (€6–10 plates, Tue–Fri 16:00–21:00, closed Sat–Mon, Smedestraat 13, tel. 023/551-1738).

Vincent's Eethuis, the cheapest restaurant in town, offers basic Dutch food and a friendly staff. This former St. Vincent's soup kitchen now feeds more gainfully employed locals than poor people in a homey dining hall. Just grab a plate and hit the buffet line (two €6 daily plates to choose from, price includes second helping, dessert and drinks extra, Mon–Fri from 17:30, last serving at 19:30, closed Sat–Sun, Nieuwe Groenmarkt 22).

Supermarkets: **Albert Heijn** has two convenient locations. One is in the train station (Mon–Fri 6:30–21:30, Sat 7:00–21:30, Sun 8:00–21:30, cash only) and the other is at Kruisstraat 10 (Mon–Sat 8:00–20:00, closed Sun, cash only). The **DekaMarkt** is a few blocks east of Market Square (Mon 10:00–20:00, Tue–Wed 8:30–20:00, Thu–Fri 8:30–21:00, Sat 8:30–20:00, closed Sun, Gedempte Oude Gracht 54, between V&D department store and post office).

South of Market Square

Jacobus Pieck Eetlokaal is popular with locals for its fine-value "global cuisine," good salads, and peaceful garden courtyard. The Oriental Peak Salad is a perennial favorite, and the dish of the day (*dagschotel,* €12) always sells out (great €6 sandwiches at lunch, Tue–Sat 10:00–22:00, closed Sun–Mon, cash only, Warmoesstraat 18, behind church, tel. 023/532-6144).

Friethuis de Vlaminck is your best bet for a cone of old-fashioned, fresh, Flemish-style fries (€2, daily 11:00–18:30, Warmoesstraat 3, behind church, tel. 023/532-1084). Winnie offers a dazzling array of sauces. With his help, you can be adventurous.

Pizzeria-Ristorante Venezia, run for 10 years by the same Italian family from Bari, is the place to go for pizza or pasta (€8–10 choices, daily 13:00–23:00, facing V&D department store at Verwulft 7, tel. 023/531-7753). You'll feel like you're in Rome at a good indoor table, or sit outdoors in a busy people-zone.

La Plume Restaurant steakhouse is noisy, with a happy, local, and carnivorous crowd (€15–20 meals, daily from 17:30, *satay* and ribs are favorites, Lange Veerstraat 1, tel. 023/531-3202). The relaxing outdoor seating faces the church and a lively pedestrian mall.

Lange Veerstraat Restaurant Row: If you don't know what you want to eat, stroll the delightful Lange Veerstraat behind the church and survey a fun range of restaurants (from cheap falafels to Cuban, and much more).

On the Spaarne River Canal: Haarlem seems to turn its back on its river with most of the eating energy a couple of blocks away. To enjoy a meal with a fine canal view, consider the **Spaarne 66**

Restaurant Bar. The Lemmers girls (a mom and her daughters) run this cozy eatery, with a woody, old-time interior and fine, outdoor canalside seating (light €7 lunches, €20 Mediterranean/Dutch dinner plates, Wed–Mon 11:00–24:00, closed Tue, Spaarne 66, tel. 023/551-3800).

Dressy Splurge: Romantic **Lambermon's** has tables gathered around a busy, modern open kitchen and an intriguing and popular-in-Haarlem formula. Chef Pascal Smit offers a kind of "cooking theater" that serves up an orderly succession of eight French/Dutch courses (€10/course, optional paired wines-€5/glass). Each successive course is served on the half-hour starting at 18:30. You only get what's served that day, and you can arrive when it suits you. Jump in at the cheese and/or dessert course, then finish when you like (closed Sun–Mon, Spaarne 96, tel. 023/542-7804).

De Lachende Javaan ("The Laughing Javanese") is a long-established Indonesian place serving a memorable *rijsttafel* (€20–24, Tue–Sun 17:00–22:00, closed Mon, Frankestraat 27, tel. 023/532-8792). The jury's still out on the new Indonesian place in town, **Wisma Hilda,** which is closer to the station and has a cheerier interior (Kruisweg 70, tel. 023/551-3197).

La Place dishes up fresh, healthy, budget food with Haarlem's best view. Sit on the top floor or roof garden of the V&D department store (Mon 11:00–18:00, Tue–Sat 9:30–18:00, Thu until 21:00, closed Sun except for first Sun of month 12:00–17:00, Grote Houtstraat 70, on corner of Gedempte Oude Gracht, tel. 023/515-8700).

Connections

From Haarlem by Train to: Amsterdam (6/hr, 20 min, €3.80 one-way, €6.40 same-day round-trip), **Brussels** (hourly, 2.75 hrs, transfer in Rotterdam), **Bruges/Brugge** (1–2/hr, 3.5 hrs, requires transfer).

To Schiphol Airport: Your options are the big red **bus** (4/hr, 40 min, €5.80—buy ticket from driver, or use 7 strips of a *strippenkaart,* bus #300, departs from Haarlem's train station in "Zuidtangent" lane), **train** (6/hr, 30–40 min, transfer at Amsterdam-Sloterdijk station, €5.30 one-way), or **taxi** (about €45).

SPAIN

BARCELONA

Barcelona is Spain's second city, and the capital of the proud and distinct region of Catalunya. With Franco's fascism now ancient history, Catalan flags wave once again. And the local language and culture are on a roll in Spain's most cosmopolitan and European corner.

Barcelona bubbles with life in its narrow Barri Gòtic alleys, along the grand boulevards, and throughout the chic, grid-planned, new part of town, called Eixample. While Barcelona had an illustrious past as a Roman colony, Visigothic capital, 14th-century maritime power, and—in more modern times—a top Mediterranean textile and manufacturing center, it's most enjoyable to throw out the history books and just drift through the city. If you're in the mood to surrender to a city's charms, let it be in Barcelona.

Planning Your Time

Located in the far northeast corner of Spain, Barcelona makes a good first or last stop for your trip. With the new AVE train, Barcelona is only three hours away from Madrid. Or you could sandwich Barcelona between flights. From the US, it's as easy to fly into Barcelona as it is to land in Madrid, Lisbon, or Paris. Those renting a car can cleverly start here, fly or train to Madrid, and see Madrid and Toledo, all before picking up their car—saving on several days' worth of rental fees.

On the shortest visit, Barcelona is worth one night, one day, and an evening flight or train ride out. The Ramblas is two different streets by day and by night. Stroll it from top to bottom in the evening and again the next morning, grabbing breakfast on a stool

in a market café. Wander the Barri Gòtic (BAH-ree GOH-teek), see the cathedral, and have lunch in the Eixample (eye-SHAM-plah). The top two sights in town, Antoni Gaudí's Sagrada Família church and the Picasso Museum, are usually open until 20:00 during the summer (Picasso closed Mon). The illuminated Magic Fountains on Montjuïc make a good finale for your day.

Of course, Barcelona in a day is insane. To better sample the city's ample charm, spread your visit over two or three days. With two days, you could divide-and-conquer the town geographically: one day for the Barri Gòtic (Ramblas, cathedral area, Picasso Museum); and another for the Eixample and Gaudí sights (Casa Milà, Sagrada Família, Parc Güell). Do Montjuïc on whichever day you're not exhausted (if any).

Orientation

Like Los Angeles, Barcelona is a basically flat city that sprawls out under the sun between the sea and the mountains. It's huge (1.6 million people, with about 4 million people in greater Barcelona), but travelers need only focus on four areas: the Old City, the harbor/Barceloneta, the Eixample, and Montjuïc.

A large square, Plaça de Catalunya, sits at the center of Barcelona, dividing the older and newer parts of town. Sloping downhill from the Plaça de Catalunya is the Old City, with the boulevard called the Ramblas running down to the harbor. Above Plaça de Catalunya is the modern residential area called the Eixample. The Montjuïc hill overlooks the harbor. Outside the Old City, Barcelona's sights are widely scattered. But with a map and a willingness to figure out the sleek Metro system (or a few euros for taxis), all is manageable.

Here are more details per neighborhood:

The **Old City** is where you'll probably spend most of your time. This is the compact soul of Barcelona—your strolling, shopping, and people-watching nucleus. It's a labyrinth of narrow streets that once were confined by the medieval walls. The lively pedestrian drag called the **Ramblas**—one of Europe's great people-watching streets—runs through the heart of the Old City from Plaça de Catalunya down to the harbor. The Old City is divided into thirds by the Ramblas and another major thoroughfare, Via Laietana. To the west of the Ramblas is the **Raval,** enlivened by its university and modern-art museum. The Raval is of least interest to tourists (and, in fact, some parts of it are quite seedy and should be avoided). Far better is the **Barri Gòtic** (Gothic Quarter), between the Ramblas and Via Laietana, with the cathedral as its navel. To the east of Via Laietana is the trendy **Ribera** district (a.k.a. "El Born"), centered on the Picasso Museum and the Church of Santa Maria del Mar.

The **harborfront** has been energized since the 1992 Olympics. A pedestrian bridge links the Ramblas with the modern **Maremagnum** shopping/aquarium complex. On the peninsula across the harbor is **Barceloneta,** a traditional fishing neighborhood that's home to some good seafood restaurants and a string of sandy beaches. Beyond Barceloneta, a man-made beach, several miles long, leads east to a commercial and convention district called the **Fòrum.**

North of the Old City, beyond the bustling hub of Plaça de Catalunya, is the elegant **Eixample** district—its grid plan softened by cut-off corners. Much of Barcelona's Modernista architecture is found here. To the north is the **Gràcia** district, and beyond that, Antoni Gaudí's **Parc Güell.**

Cheap Tricks in Barcelona

- Arriving by train? Save time, hassle, and the cost of a Metro ride by finding out if your train stops at any of the handy downtown stations (such as Passeig de Gràcia or Plaça de Catalunya). But remember that AVE trains from Madrid stop only at the Sants station.

- For getting around the city, skip taxis and the Tourist Bus, and instead use the excellent network of Metro and buses. The T10 Card (10 rides for €7.20) makes the system super-cheap—each ride costs €0.72 instead of €1.30 for an individual ticket.

- If visiting the cathedral, be sure to go when it's free, between 8:00–12:45 (13:45 on Sun) or 17:15–19:30; at other times, you'll pay €5 to see exactly the same thing. Also note that several interesting sights around the cathedral (such as the Deacon's House and Roman Temple) are free to enter. Not far away, in La Ribera, the Church of Santa Maria del Mar is also free.

- One of Barcelona's most delightful Modernista sights, Antoni Gaudí's Parc Güell, is free and an enjoyable place to relax. Some expensive Gaudí sights (such as Casa Milà, Casa Batlló, and the Sagrada Família) can be just as interesting (and free) from the outside. For a free glimpse at a Gaudí interior, visit Palau Güell (though it may begin charging admission as newly renovated rooms re-open).

- Some museums have certain days and times when they don't charge admission: Picasso Museum (first Sun of month), Catalan Art Museum (first Sun of month), and Frederic Marès Museum (Wed afternoon).

- When tapas-hopping, note that trendy, upscale neighborhoods—such as the Eixample and La Ribera—come with higher prices. For a cheaper and more characteristic meal, find a blue-collar neighborhood (such as Carrer de la Mercè, described on page 1144).

The large hill overlooking the city to the west is **Montjuïc,** home to a variety of attractions including some excellent museums (Catalan Art, Joan Miró) and the Olympic Stadium.

Apart from your geographical orientation, you'll need to orient yourself linguistically to a language distinct from Spanish. While Spanish ("Castilian") is widely spoken, the native tongue in this region is Catalan—nearly as different from Spanish as Italian.

Tourist Information

Barcelona's TI has several branches. The main one is at **Plaça de Catalunya** (daily 9:00–21:00, under the main square near recommended hotels—look for red sign, tel. 932-853-832). Other convenient branches include at the top of the **Ramblas** (daily 9:00–21:00, at #115); **Plaça de Sant Jaume** just south of the cathedral (Mon–Fri 9:00–20:00, Sat 10:00–20:00, Sun 10:00–14:00); **Plaça d'Espanya** (daily July–Sept 10:00–20:00, Oct–June 10:00–16:00); the **airport** (daily 9:00–21:00, offices in both terminals A and B); **Sants train station** (Mon–Fri 8:00–20:00, Sat–Sun 8:00–14:00, near track 6); **Nord bus station** (daily July–Sept 9:00–21:00, Oct–June 9:00–15:00); and more. Throughout the summer, young, red-jacketed tourist-info helpers appear in the most touristy parts of town. The central information number for all TIs is 932-853-834 (www.barcelonaturisme.cat).

At any TI, pick up the free city map (can be hard to read—consider springing €1 for a better one), the small Metro map, and the free quarterly *See Barcelona* guide (practical information on museum hours, restaurants, transportation, history, festivals, and so on). The monthly *Barcelona Metropolitan* magazine and quarterly *What's On Barcelona* (both free and in English) have timely and substantial coverage of topics and events. The TI is a handy place to buy tickets for the Tourist Bus (described in "Getting Around Barcelona," later in this chapter). Some TIs (at Plaça de Catalunya, Plaça de Sant Jaume, and the airport) also provide a room-booking service.

The main TI, at Plaça de Catalunya, offers guided walks (described under "Tours," later in this chapter). Its Modernisme desk gives out a handy route map showing all the Modernista buildings and offers a discount package (€12 for a great guidebook and 20 percent discounts to many Modernisme sites—worthwhile if going beyond my big three; for €18 you'll also get a guidebook to Modernista bars and restaurants).

The **all-Catalunya TI** works fine for the entire region and even Madrid (Mon–Sat 10:00–19:00, Sun 10:00–14:00, on Plaça de Joan Carlos I, at the intersection of Diagonal and Passeig de Gràcia, Passeig de Gràcia 107, tel. 932-388-091).

Articket Card: You can get into seven art museums and their temporary exhibits with this ticket, including the recommended Picasso Museum, Casa Milà, Catalan Art Museum, and Fundació Joan Miró (€20, valid for six months, sold at TIs and participating museums, www.articketbcn.org). If you're planning to go to three or more of the museums, this time-saver pays for itself. To skip the ticket-buying line at a museum, show your Articket Card (to the ticket-taker, at the info desk, or at the group entrance), and they'll help you get your entrance ticket pronto.

Barcelona Card: This card covers public transportation (buses, Metro, Montjuïc funicular, and *golondrina* harbor tour) and includes free admission to minor sights and discounts on major sights (€25/2 days, €30/3 days, €34/4 days, €40/5 days, sold at TIs and El Corte Inglés department store).

Arrival in Barcelona

By Train: Virtually all trains end up at Barcelona's Sants train station (described below). But be aware that many trains also pass through other stations en route, such as **França station** (between the Ribera and Barceloneta neighborhoods), or the downtown **Passeig de Gràcia** or **Plaça de Catalunya** stations (which are also Metro stops—and very close to most of my recommended hotels). Figure out which stations your train stops at, and get off at the one most convenient to your hotel. (AVE trains from Madrid go only to Sants station.)

Sants station is vast and sprawling, but manageable. In the large lobby area under the upper tracks, you'll find a TI, ATMs, a world of handy shops and eateries, and a classy, quiet Sala Euromed lounge for travelers with first-class reservations (TV, free drinks, study tables, and coffee bar). Sants is the only Barcelona station with luggage storage (small bag-€3/day, big bag-€4.50/day, must go through security check, daily 5:30–23:00, follow signs to *consigna*, at far end of hallway from tracks 13–14).

There's also a long wall of ticket windows. Figure out which is right for you before you wait in line (all are labeled in English). Generally, the first stretch (on the left, windows 1–8) are for local trains, such as to Sitges; the next group (windows 9–21) are for advance tickets for long-distance trains; farther to the right are information windows (22–26)—go here first if you're not sure which window you want; and those at the right end (windows 27–31) sell tickets for long-distance trains leaving today. Attendants are often standing by to help you find the right line. If you know what you want, there are also automated train-ticket vending machines.

To get into downtown Barcelona from Sants station, simply follow signs for the Metro. The L3 (green) line—described under "Getting Around Barcelona," later in this chapter—zips you directly to a number of useful points in town, including all of my recommended hotels.

If departing from the downtown **Passeig de Gràcia station,** where three Metro lines converge with the rail line, you might find the underground tunnels confusing. You can't access the RENFE station directly from some of the entrances. Use the northern entrances to this station (rather than the southern "Consell de Cent" entrance, which is closest to Plaça de Catalunya).

By Plane: Barcelona's **El Prat de Llobregat Airport,** eight miles southwest of town, has three terminals: A, B, and C. The bigger terminals A and B each have a post office, pharmacy, left-luggage office, plenty of good cafeterias in the gate areas, and ATMs (avoid the gimmicky machines before the baggage carousels; instead, use the bank-affiliated ATMs at the far-left end of the arrivals hall as you face the street). Airport info tel. 902-404-704.

You have two options for getting downtown cheaply and quickly: The **Aerobus** (#A1) stops immediately outside the arrivals lobby of all three terminals and takes you in about 30 minutes to downtown, where it makes several stops, including Plaça d'Espanya, Plaça de Catalunya (near many of my recommended hotels), and Passeig de Gràcia (near more hotels; every 6 min, from airport 6:00–1:00 in the morning, from downtown 5:30–24:15, buy €4.05 ticket from machine or from driver). The line to board the bus can be very long, but—thanks to the high frequency of buses—it moves fast.

The second option is the RENFE **train,** which involves more walking. Walk down the long, orange-roofed overpass between terminals A and B to reach the station (line 10, 2/hr at about :29 and :59 after the hour, 20 min to Sants station, 25 min to Passeig de Gràcia station—near Plaça de Catalunya and many recommended hotels, 30 min to França station; €2.60 or covered by T10 Card, which you can purchase at automated machines at the airport train station—for details see "Getting Around Barcelona," later in this chapter).

A **taxi** between the airport and downtown costs about €25.

Some budget airlines, including Ryanair, use **Girona-Costa Brava Airport,** located 60 miles north of Barcelona near Girona. Sagalés buses link to Barcelona (departures timed to meet flights, 70 min, €12, tel. 935-931-300 or 902-361-550, www.sagales.com). You can also take a Sagalés bus (hourly, 25 min, €2.50) or a taxi (€20) to Girona, where you can catch a train to Barcelona (at least hourly, 70 min, €7). A taxi between the Girona airport and Barcelona will cost at least €120. Airport info tel. 972-186-600.

By Car: Barcelona's parking fees are outrageously expensive (the one behind Boquería market charges upwards of €25/day). You won't need a car in Barcelona because the taxis and public transportation are so good.

Helpful Hints

Theft Alert: You're more likely to be pickpocketed here—especially on the Ramblas—than about anywhere else in Europe. Most of the crime is nonviolent, but muggings do occur. Leave valuables in your hotel and wear a money belt.

Street scams are easy to avoid if you recognize them. Most common is the too-friendly local who tries to engage you in conversation by asking for the time, talking sports, asking whether you speak English, and so on. Beware of thieves posing as lost tourists who ask for your help. A typical street gambling scam is the pea-and-carrot game, a variation on the shell game. The people winning are all ringers, and you can be sure that you'll lose if you play. Also beware of groups of women aggressively selling carnations, people offering to clean off a stain from your shirt, and people picking things up in front of you on escalators. If you stop for any commotion or show on the Ramblas, put your hands in your pockets before someone else does. Assume any scuffle is simply a distraction by a team of thieves. Crooks are inventive, so keep your guard up. Don't be intimidated...just be smart.

Some areas feel seedy and can be unsafe after dark; I'd avoid the southern part of the Barri Gòtic (basically the two or three blocks directly south and east of Plaça Reial—though the strip near the Carrer de la Mercè tapas bars is better), and I wouldn't venture too deep into the Raval (just west of the Ramblas). One block can separate a comfy tourist zone from the junkies and prostitutes.

US Consulate: It's at Passeig Reina Elisenda 23 (passport services Mon–Fri 9:00–13:00, closed Sat–Sun, tel. 932-802-227).

Emergency Phone Numbers: General emergencies—112, police—092, ambulance—061 or 112.

Pharmacy: A 24-hour pharmacy is near La Boquería market at #98 on the Ramblas.

Laundry: Several self-service launderettes are located around the Old City. **Wash 'n Dry** is on the edge of the tourist zone, near a seedy neighborhood just down the street past the Palau Güell (self-service: wash-€5/load, dry-€2/load, daily 7:00–22:00; full-service: €15/load, Mon–Fri 9:00–14:00 & 17:00–20:00, closed Sat–Sun; Carrer Nou de la Rambla 19, tel. 934-121-953).

Getting Around Barcelona

By Public Transit: Barcelona's Metro, among Europe's best, connects just about every place you'll visit. Rides cost €1.30. Given the excellent Metro service, it's unlikely you'll take a local bus (also €1.30), although I've noted the places where the bus makes sense. The T10 Card for €7.20 gives you 10 rides and is a great deal (shareable, good for all Metro and local bus lines as well as the separate FGC line and RENFE train lines, including trains to the airport). Full-day and multi-day passes are also available (€5.50/1 day, €10/2 days, €14.30/3 days, €18.30/4 days, €21.70/5 days). Automated machines at the Metro entrance have English instructions and sell all types of tickets (though these can be temperamental about accepting payment—nearby ticket windows are staffed during working hours).

Pick up the free Metro map (at any TI) and study it to get familiar with the system. There are several color-coded lines, but most useful for tourists is the **L3 (green) line**—if you're sticking to my recommended sights and neighborhoods, you'll barely have use for any other. Handy city-center stops on this line include (in order):

> **Sants Estació** (main train station);
>
> **Espanya** (Plaça d'Espanya, with access to the lower part of Montjuïc and trains to Montserrat);
>
> **Paral·lel** (funicular to top of Montjuïc);
>
> **Drassanes** (bottom of the Ramblas, near Maritime Museum, Maremagnum mall, and the cable car up to Montjuïc);
>
> **Liceu** (middle of the Ramblas, near the heart of the Barri Gòtic and cathedral);
>
> **Plaça de Catalunya** (top of the Ramblas and main square with TI, airport bus, and lots of transportation connections);
>
> **Passeig de Gràcia** (classy Eixample street at the Block of Discord; also connection to L2/purple line to Sagrada Família and L4/yellow line—described below);
>
> **Diagonal** (Gaudí's Casa Milà); and
>
> **Lesseps** (where you can walk or catch bus #24 to Gaudí's Parc Güell).

The **L4 (yellow) line,** which crosses the L3 (green) line at Passeig de Gràcia, is also useful. Helpful stops along here include **Jaume I** (between the Barri Gòtic/cathedral and La Ribera/Picasso Museum) and **Barceloneta** (at the south end of the Ribera, near the harbor action).

When you enter the Metro, first look for your line number and color, then follow signs to take that line in the direction you're going. Insert your ticket into the turnstile (with the arrow pointing in), then reclaim it. Once on board, most trains have handy Metro-line diagrams with dots that light up next to upcoming destinations. Because the lines cross each other multiple times, there can be several ways to make any one journey. Watch your valuables. (If I were a pickpocket, I'd set up shop along the made-for-tourists L3/green line.)

By Tourist Bus: The handy Tourist Bus (Bus Turístic) offers three multi-stop circuits in colorful double-decker buses that go topless in sunny weather. The two-hour red route covers north Barcelona (most Gaudí sights), the two-hour blue route covers south Barcelona (Barri Gòtic, Montjuïc), and the shorter, 40-minute green route covers the beaches and Fòrum. All have headphone commentary (44 stops, daily 9:00–22:00 in summer, 9:00–21:00 in winter, buses run every 5–25 min, most frequent in summer, no green route Oct–mid-March). Ask for a brochure (includes good city map) at the TI or at a pick-up point. One-day (€20) and two-day (€26) tickets, which you can buy on the bus or at the TI, include 10–20 percent discounts on the city's major sights and walking tours, which will likely save you half the cost of the Tourist Bus.

By Taxi: Barcelona is one of Europe's best taxi towns. Taxis are plentiful (there are more than 10,000) and honest (whether they like it or not—the light on top shows which tariff they're charging). They're also reasonable (€2 drop charge, €1 per kilometer, these *"Tarif 2"* rates are in effect 7:00–21:00, pay higher *"Tarif 1"* rates off-hours, luggage-€1/piece, other fees posted in window). Save time by hopping a cab (figure €4 from Ramblas to Sants station). To save even more time, make a point to cross the street if necessary to catch taxis heading in the appropriate direction.

Tours

Walking Tours—The TI at Plaça de Catalunya offers great guided walks through the **Barri Gòtic** in English only (€11, daily at 10:00, 2 hours, groups limited to 35, departs from the TI, buy your ticket 15 minutes early at the TI desk—not from the guide—in summer call ahead to reserve). A local guide will explain the medieval story of the city as you walk from Plaça de Catalunya through the cathedral neighborhood, finishing at the City Hall on Plaça de Sant Jaume. The TI also offers a **Picasso** walk, taking you through the streets of his youth and early career and finishing in the Picasso Museum (€15, includes museum admission, Tue–Sun at 10:30, 2 hrs plus museum visit). There are also **gourmet** walks (€15, Fri and Sat at 11:00, 2 hrs) and **Modernisme** walks (€11, Fri and Sat June–Sept at 18:00, Oct–May at 16:00, 2 hrs). All tours depart from the TI at Plaça de Catalunya.

Bike Tours—Several companies run bike tours around Barcelona. **Un Cotxe Menys** ("One Car Less") organizes three-hour, English-only bike tours daily at 11:00 (April–mid-Sept also Fri–Mon at 16:30). Your guide leads you from sight to sight, mostly on bike paths and through parks, with a stop-and-go commentary (€22 includes bike rental and a drink, reservations not necessary, just show up at Plaça de Sant Jaume, next to the TI, tel. 932-682-105, www.biketoursbarcelona.com).

Local Guides—The Barcelona Guide Bureau is a co-op with about 20 local guides who give personalized four-hour tours starting at €202 (per person price drops as group gets bigger); **Joana Wilhelm** and **Carles Picazo** are excellent (Via Laietana 54, tel. 932-682-422 or 933-107-778, www.bgb.es). **Jose Soler** is a great and fun-to-be-with local guide who enjoys tailoring a walk through his hometown to your interests (€195/half-day per group, mobile 615-059-326, www.pepitotours.com, info@pepitotours.com).

Self-Guided Walks

Most visitors to Barcelona spend much of their time in the twisty, atmospheric Old City. These two walks will give meaning to your wandering. The first begins at Barcelona's main square and leads you down the city's main drag through one of Europe's best public spaces: the Ramblas. The second walk starts at the same square, but guides you into the heart of the Barri Gòtic, to the neighborhood around Barcelona's impressive cathedral.

▲▲▲The Ramblas Ramble: From Plaça de Catalunya down the Ramblas

Barcelona's central square and main boulevard exert a powerful pull. Many visitors spend the majority of their time doing laps on the Ramblas. While the allure of the Ramblas is fading (as tacky tourist shops and fast-food joints replace its former elegance), this is still a fun people zone that offers a good introduction to the city. See it, but be sure to venture farther afield. Here's a top-to-bottom orientation walk.

Plaça de Catalunya: This vast central square divides old and new Barcelona. It's also the hub for the Metro, bus, airport shuttle, and Tourist Bus (red northern route leaves from El Corte Inglés; blue southern route leaves from the west, or Ramblas, side of the square). Overlooking the square, the huge **El Corte Inglés** department store offers everything from bonsai trees to a travel agency, plus one-hour photo developing, haircuts, and cheap souvenirs (Mon–Sat 10:00–22:00, closed Sun, pick up English directory flier, supermarket in basement, ninth-floor terrace cafeteria/restaurant has great city view—take elevator from entrance nearest the TI, tel. 933-063-800). Across the square from El Corte Inglés is **FNAC**, a French department store popular for electronics, music, and books (on west side of square—behind blue Tourist Bus stop; Mon–Sat 10:00–22:00, closed Sun).

Four great boulevards radiate from Plaça de Catalunya: the Ramblas; the fashionable Passeig de Gràcia (top shops, noisy with traffic); the cozier, but still fashionable, Rambla de Catalunya (most pedestrian-friendly); and the stubby, shop-filled, and delightfully traffic-free Avinguda Portal de l'Angel. Homesick Americans can even find a Hard Rock Café. Locals traditionally start or end a downtown rendezvous at the venerable Café Zürich (at the corner near the Ramblas).

• *Cross the street from the café to...*

❶ **The Top of the Ramblas:** Begin your ramble 20 yards down at the ornate fountain (near #129). More than a Champs-Elysées, this grand boulevard takes you from rich (at the top) to rough (at the port) in a one-mile, 30-minute stroll. You'll raft the river of

From Plaça de Catalunya down the Ramblas

NOT TO SCALE—
PLAÇA DE CATALUNYA TO COLUMBUS
MONUMENT IS A 30 MIN. WALK

Ramblas
Ⓜ Metro Station
Ⓑ Bus Stop

TO "BLOCK OF DISCORD"

Internet
BLUE TOURIST BUS
FNAC DEP'T. STORE
Ⓑ
FGC TRAIN INFO
CAFÉ ZÜRICH

PASSEIG DE GRÀCIA

RAMBLA DE CATALUNYA

PLAÇA DE CATALUNYA
Catalunya ⓘ

EL CORTE INGLÉS DEP'T. STORE

Ⓑ

CANALETES FOUNTAIN
Ⓜ ➊

AV. PORTAL DE L'ANGEL

SANTA ANNA

AEROBUS, RED TOURIST BUS + TAXIS

ACADEMY OF SCIENCE
Ⓜ ➋

BIRDS

CANUDA

ROMAN NECROPOLIS

CAFÉ GRANJA VIADER

BAROQUE CHURCH ✝
Ⓜ ➌
CARME
Liceu

PORTAFERRISSA

CULTURAL INFO PALAU DE LA VIRREINA
Ⓜ

FLOWER

PHARMACY
CIGARS

EROTIC MUSEUM

LA BOQUERIA MARKET
Ⓜ ➍

CARDENAL

"UMBRELLA" BLDG.

HOSP.

MIRÓ MOSAIC
S. PAU

BOQ.

BARRI XINES

Ⓜ
Liceu

LICEU OPERA HOUSE

FERRAN ➔ TO PLAÇA DE S. JAUME

PLAÇA REIAL ➎

NOU RAMBLA

Ⓜ
Drassanes

PALAU GÜELL

L'ARC
➏

ESCUDELLERS

HERBOLAI FERRAN

MARITIME MUSEUM

COLUMBUS MONUMENT

TO BARCELO-NETA

PASSEIG COLÓM

PICNIC SPOT

DCH

GOLONDRINAS BOATS

RAMBLA DE MAR

HARBOR

TO MAREMAGNUM

BARCELONA

Barcelonan life past a grand opera house, elegant cafés, retread prostitutes, brazen pickpockets, power-dressing con men, artists, street mimes, an outdoor bird market, great shopping, and people looking to charge more for a shoeshine than what you paid for the shoes.

Grab a bench and watch the scene. Open up your map and read some history into it: You're about to walk right across medieval Barcelona, from Plaça de Catalunya to the harbor. Notice how the higgledy-piggledy street plan of the medieval town was contained within the old town walls—now gone, but traced by a series of roads named Ronda (meaning "to go around"). Find the Roman town, occupying about 10 percent of what became the medieval town—with tighter roads yet around the cathedral. The sprawling, modern grid plan beyond the Ronda roads is from the 19th century. Breaks in this urban waffle show where a little town was consumed by the growing city. The popular Passeig de Gràcia was literally the "Road to Gràcia" (once a separate town, now a characteristic Barcelona neighborhood).

Rambla means "stream" in Arabic. The Ramblas used to be a drainage ditch along the medieval wall that once defined what's now called the Barri Gòtic (Gothic Quarter). "Ramblas" is plural, a succession of five separately named segments, but address numbers treat it as a single long street. (In fact, street signs label it as "La Rambla," singular.) Because no streets cross the Ramblas, it has a great pedestrian feel.

You're at Rambla Canaletes, named for the fountain. The black-and-gold **Fountain of Canaletes** is the starting point for celebrations and demonstrations. Legend says that a drink from the fountain ensures that you'll return to Barcelona one day. All along the Ramblas, you'll see newspaper stands (open 24 hours, selling phone cards) and ONCE booths (selling lottery tickets that support Spain's organization of the blind, a powerful advocate for the needs of people with disabilities).

Got some change? As you wander downhill, drop coins into the cans of the human statues (the money often kicks them into entertaining gear). If you take a photo, it's considered good etiquette to drop in a coin. Warning: Wherever people stop to gawk, pickpockets are at work.

• *Walk 100 yards downhill to #115 and the...*

❷ **Rambla of the Little Birds:** Traditionally, kids bring their parents here to buy pets, especially on Sundays. Apartment-dwellers find birds, turtles, and fish easier to handle than dogs and cats. If you're walking by at night, you'll hear the sad sounds of little tweety birds locked up in their collapsed kiosks.

Along the Ramblas, buildings with balconies that have flowers are generally living spaces; balconies with air-conditioners generally indicate offices. The Academy of Science's clock (at #115) marks official Barcelona time—synchronize. The Carrefour Express supermarket (at #113, Mon–Sat 10:00–22:00, closed Sun) has cheap groceries.

A recently discovered **Roman necropolis** is in a park across the street from the bird market, 50 yards behind the big, modern Citadines Hotel (go through the passageway at #122). Local apartment-dwellers blew the whistle on contractors, who hoped they could finish their building before anyone noticed the antiquities they had unearthed. Imagine the tomb-lined road leading into the Roman city of Barcino 2,000 years ago.

• *Another 50 yards takes you to Carrer del Carme (at #105), and a...*

❸ **Baroque Church:** The big Betlem church fronting the boulevard is Baroque, unusual in Barcelona. Note the Baroque-style sloping roofline, ball-topped pinnacles, and the scrolls above the entrance. While Barcelona's Gothic age was rich (with buildings to prove it), the Baroque age hardly left a mark. (The city's importance dropped when New World discoveries shifted lucrative trade to ports on the Atlantic.)

For a sweet treat, head down the narrow lane behind the church (going uphill parallel to the Ramblas about 30 yards) to **Café Granja Viader** (see page 1140), which has specialized in baked and dairy delights since 1870. (For more sweets, follow "A Short, Sweet Walk"—on page 1148—which begins at the intersection in front of the church.)

• *Continue down the boulevard, stroll through the Ramblas of Flowers to the Metro stop marked by the red* M *(near #96), and...*

❹ **La Boquería:** This lively produce market at #91 is an explosion of chicken legs, bags of live snails, stiff fish, delicious oranges, and sleeping dogs (Mon–Sat 8:00–20:00, best mornings after 9:00, closed Sun). Originally outside the walls (as many medieval markets were), it expanded into the colonnaded courtyard of a now-gone monastery. Wander around—as local architect Antoni Gaudí used to—and gain inspiration. The Francesc Conserves shop sells 25 kinds of olives (straight in, near back on right, 100-gram minimum). Full legs of ham *(jamón serrano)* abound; *Paleta Ibérica de Bellota* are the best, and cost about €120 each. Beware: *Huevos del toro* are bull testicles—surprisingly inexpensive...and oh so good. Drop by a café for an *espresso con leche* or breakfast (*tortilla española*—potato omelet).

For a quick bite, visit the **Pinotxo Bar** (just to the right as you enter the market, see listing on page 1140), where animated Juan and his family are busy feeding shoppers. (Getting Juan to crack a huge smile and a thumbs-up for your camera makes a great shot... and he loves it.) The stools nearby are a fine perch for enjoying both your coffee and the people-watching. The market and lanes nearby are busy with tempting little eateries (several are listed beginning on page 1140).

• *Now turn your attention across the boulevard.*

The **Museum of Erotica** is your standard European sex museum (€7.50, daily 10:00–22:00, across from market at #96).

To the left, at #100, **Gimeno** sells cigars (appreciate the dying art of cigar boxes). Go ahead, do something forbidden in America but perfectly legal here...buy a Cuban (little singles for less than €1). Tobacco shops sell stamps and phone cards—and plenty of bongs and marijuana gear (the Spanish approach to pot is very casual).

Fifty yards farther, underfoot in the center of the Ramblas, find the much-trod-upon **anchor mosaic**—a reminder of the city's attachment to the sea. Created by noted abstract artist Joan Miró, it marks the midpoint of the Ramblas. (The towering Columbus Monument in the distance—hidden by trees—is at the end of this walk.)

Continue a few more steps down to the **Liceu Opera House.** From the Opera House, cross the Ramblas to Café de l'Opera for a beverage (#74). This bustling café, with Modernista (that is, old-timey) decor and a historic atmosphere, boasts that it's been open since 1929, even during the Spanish Civil War.

• *Continue down the Ramblas to #46; turn left down an arcaded lane (Correr de Colom) to a square filled with palm trees...*

❺ Plaça Reial: This elegant Neoclassical square has a colonial (or maybe post-colonial) ambience. It comes complete with old-fashioned taverns, modern bars with patio seating, a Sunday coin and stamp market (10:00–14:00), Gaudí's first public works (the two colorful helmeted lampposts), and characters who don't need the palm trees to be shady. **Herbolari Ferran** is a fine and aromatic shop of herbs, with fun souvenirs such as top-quality saffron, or *safra* (Mon–Fri 9:30–14:00 & 16:30–20:00, closed Sat–Sun, downstairs at Plaça Reial 18—to the right as you enter the square). The small streets stretching toward the water from the square are intriguing, but less safe.

Back on the other side of the Ramblas, **Palau Güell** offers an enjoyable look at a Gaudí interior (Carrer Nou de la Rambla 3, partly closed for renovation, see page 1119). This apartment was the first of Gaudí's innovative buildings, with a parabolic front doorway that signaled his emerging nonrectangular style.

• *Continue farther downhill on the Ramblas.*

❻ Bottom of the Ramblas: The neighborhood on the right-hand side, Barri Xines, is the world's only Chinatown with nothing even remotely Chinese in or near it. Named for the prejudiced notion that Chinese immigrants go hand-in-hand with poverty, prostitution, and drug dealing, the neighborhood's actual inhabitants are poor Spanish, North African, and Roma (Gypsy) people. At night, the Barri Xines is frequented by prostitutes, many of them transvestites, who cater to sailors wandering up from the port. Prostitution is nothing new here. Check out the thresholds at #22 and #24 (along the left side of the Ramblas)—with holes worn long ago by the heels of anxious ladies.

The bottom of the Ramblas is marked by the city's giant medieval shipyards (on the right, now the impressive Maritime Museum) and the Columbus Monument (both are described on page 1109). And just beyond the Columbus Monument, **La Rambla del Mar** ("Rambla of the Sea") is a modern extension of the boulevard into the harbor. A popular wooden pedestrian bridge—with waves like the sea—leads to Maremagnum, a soulless Spanish mall with a cinema, huge aquarium, restaurants (including the recommended Tapasbar Maremagnum; see page 1141), and piles of people. Late at night, it's a rollicking youth hangout. It's a worthwhile stroll.

The Barri Gòtic:
From Plaça de Catalunya to the Cathedral

Barcelona's Barri Gòtic, or Gothic Quarter, is a bustling world of shops, bars, and nightlife packed between hard-to-be-thrilled-about 14th- and 15th-century buildings. The section near the port is generally dull and seedy. But the area around the cathedral is a tangled-yet-inviting grab-bag of undiscovered courtyards, grand squares, schoolyards, Art Nouveau storefronts, baby flea markets on Thursdays, musty junk shops, classy antique shops (on Carrer de la Palla), street musicians strumming Catalan folk songs, and balconies with domestic jungles behind wrought-iron bars. Go on a cultural scavenger hunt. Write a poem. This self-guided walk gives you a structure, covering the main sights and offering a historical overview before you get lost.

• *Start on Barcelona's bustling main square...*

Plaça de Catalunya: This square is the center of the world for seven million Catalan people. The square (described at the start of my Ramblas self-guided walk, previous section) is decorated with the likenesses of important Catalans. From here, walls that contained the city until the 19th century arc around in each direction to the sea. Looking at your map of Barcelona, you'll see a regimented waffle design—except for the higgledy-piggledy old town corralled by these walls.

The city grew with its history. Originally a Roman town, Barcelona was ruled by the Visigoths from the fall of Rome until 714, when the Moors arrived (they were, in turn, sent packing by the French in 801—because their stay was cut so short, there are few Moorish-style buildings here). Finally, in the 10th century, the Count of Barcelona unified the region, and the idea of

Barcelona's Barri Gòtic

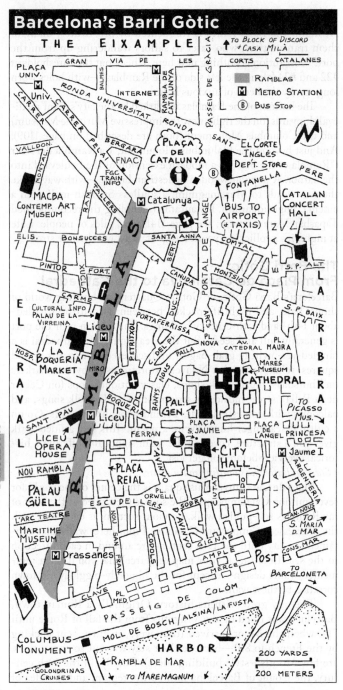

THE EIXAMPLE

GRAN VIA DE LES CORTS CATALANES

↑ To BLOCK OF DISCORD & CASA MILÀ

■ RAMBLAS
Ⓜ METRO STATION
Ⓑ BUS STOP

PLAÇA UNIV.
Ⓜ Univ.
CARRER BALMES
RONDA UNIVERSITAT
RAMBLA DE CATALUNYA
INTERNET
BERGARA
CARRER PELAI
RONDA
VALLDON.
MONTAL.
FNAC
FGC TRAIN INFO
PLAÇA DE CATALUNYA ⓘ
Ⓑ
SANT PERE
EL CORTE INGLÉS DEP'T. STORE
FONTANELLA
CATALAN CONCERT HALL
MACBA CONTEMP. ART MUSEUM
RAMBLAS
TALLERS
Ⓜ Catalunya
BUS TO AIRPORT (+ TAXIS)
S. P. ALT
ELIS.
BONSUCCES
SANTA ANNA
COMTAL
MONTSIO
S. P. BAIX
PINTOR
XUCLA
FORT.
CARME
SANTA ANNA
LA
BERT.
CANUDA
PORTAL DE L'ANGEL
ARCS
EL RAVAL
CULTURAL INFO PALAU DE LA VIRREINA
Ⓜ Liceu
PORTAFERRISSA
DUC. VIC.
LA BOQUERIA MARKET
PETRITXOL
DEL PI
PALLA
PL. NOVA
AV. CATEDRAL MAURA
PL.
MARES MUSEUM
LA RIBERA
HOSP.
MIRÓ
CARD.
BOQUERIA
BANYS NOUS
✚ CATHEDRAL
SANT PAU
Ⓜ Liceu
FERRAN
PAL. GEN.
PLAÇA S. JAUME ⓘ
PLAÇA DE L'ANGEL
TO PICASSO MUS.
LICEU OPERA HOUSE
AVINYO
✦ CITY HALL
PRINCESA
Ⓜ Jaume I
NOU RAMBLA
★ PLAÇA REIAL
PL. ORWELL
CIUTAT
LLEDO
LLIBRETERIA
PALAU GÜELL
ESCUDELLERS
D'SOBRA
CAN. NOUS
TO S. MARÍA D. MAR
L'ARC TEATRE
NOU SAN FRAN.
CODOLS
GIGNAS
CONS. MAR.
MARITIME MUSEUM
Ⓜ Drassanes
AMPLE
MERCE
POST
TO BARCELONETA
CLAVE
PL. MED.
PASSEIG DE COLÓM
COLUMBUS MONUMENT
MOLL DE BOSCH / ALSINA / LA FUSTA
HARBOR
200 YARDS
200 METERS
GOLONDRINAS CRUISES
RAMBLA DE MAR
TO MAREMAGNUM

BARCELONA

Catalunya came to be. The area between Plaça de Catalunya and the old Roman walls (circling the smaller ancient town, down by the cathedral) was settled by churches, each a magnet gathering a small community outside the walls (or "extra muro"). Around 1250, when these "extra muro" communities became numerous and strong enough, the king agreed to invest in a larger wall, and Barcelona expanded. This outer wall was torn down in the 1850s and replaced by a series of circular boulevards (named Rondas).

• *From Plaça de Catalunya's TI, head downhill, crossing the busy street into a broad pedestrian boulevard called...*

Avinguda Portal de l'Angel: This boulevard is named "Gate of the Angel" for the gate in the medieval wall—crowned by an angel—that once stood here. The angel kept the city safe from plagues and bid voyagers safe journey as they left the security of the city. Imagine the fascinating scene here at the Gate of the Angel, where Barcelona stopped and the wilds began.

Walking down the Avinguda Portal de l'Angel, consider an optional detour a half-block right on **Carrer de Santa Anna,** where a lane on the right leads into a courtyard facing one of those "extra muro" churches, with a fine cloister and simple, typically Romanesque facade.

Continuing down the main boulevard, you reach a fork in the road with a blue-and-yellow-tiled **fountain.** This was once a free-standing well—in the 17th century, it was the last watering stop for horses before leaving town. Take the left fork to the cathedral (past the Architects' House with its Picasso-inspired frieze).

Enter the square, where you'll stand before two bold **towers—** the remains of the old Roman wall that protected a smaller Barcino, as the city was called in ancient times. The big stones that make up the base of the towers are actually Roman. The wall stretches left of the towers, incorporated into the Deacon's House (which you'll enter from the other side later).

• *The sights from here on are located on the map on page 1111. Walk around—past the modern bronze letters* BARCINO *and the mighty facade of the cathedral (which we'll enter momentarily)—and go inside the...*

Deacon's House: Visitors are welcome inside this mansion, which today functions as the city archives (its front door faces the wall of the church). It's a good example of a Renaissance noble-man's palace. Notice how the century-old palm tree seems to be held captive by urban man. Inside you can see the Roman stones up close. Upstairs affords a good view of the cathedral's exterior—textbook Catalan Gothic (plain and practical, like this merchant community) next to textbook Romanesque (the smaller, once free-standing, more humble church adjacent on the right—which you'll visit entering from the church's cloister later).

BARCELONA

• *Exit the house to the left and follow the lane. You'll emerge at the entrance to the...*

Cathedral of Barcelona (Catedral de Barcelona): This huge house of worship is worth a look. Its vast size, peaceful cloister, and many ornate chapels—each one sponsored by a local guild—are impressive. For a self-guided tour, see the "Cathedral of Barcelona" listing on page 1110.

• *After visiting the cathedral's cloister, exit and walk to the tiny lane ahead on the right (far side of the statue, Carrer de Montjuïc del Bisbe). This leads to the cute...*

Plaça Sant Felip Neri: This square serves as the playground of an elementary school bursting with youthful energy. The Church of Sant Felip Neri, which Gaudí attended, is still pocked with bomb damage from the Civil War. As a stronghold of democratic, anti-Franco forces, Barcelona saw a lot of fighting. The shrapnel that damaged this church was meant for the nearby Catalan government building (Palau de la Generalitat, described below).

Study the medallions on the wall. Guilds powered the local economy, and the carved reliefs here show that this building must have housed the shoemakers. In fact, on this square you'll find a fun little Shoe Museum (see page 1112).

• *Circle the block back to the cathedral's cloister and take a right, walking along Carrer del Bisbe next to the huge building (on the right) stretching all the way to the next square...*

Palau de la Generalitat: For nearly 600 years, this place has been the home of the Catalan government. Through good times and bad, the Catalan spirit has survived, and this building has housed its capital.

• *Continue along Carrer del Bisbe to...*

Plaça de Sant Jaume (jow-mah): This stately central square of the Barri Gòtic, once the Roman forum, has been the seat of city government for 2,000 years. Today the two top governmental buildings in Catalunya face each other: the Barcelona City Hall (Ajuntament; free but open to the public only Sun 10:00–13:30) and the seat of the autonomous government of Catalunya (Palau de la Generalitat, described above). It always flies the Catalan flag (red and yellow stripes) next to the obligatory Spanish one. From these balconies, the nation's leaders (and soccer heroes) greet the people on momentous days.

• *Take two quick left turns from the corner of Carrer Bisbe (just 10 yards away), and climb Carrer del Paridís. Follow this street as it turns right, but pause when it swings left, at the summit of...*

"Mont" Tàber: A millstone in the corner marks ancient Barcino's highest elevation, a high spot in the road called Mount Tàber. A plaque on the wall says it all: "Mont Tàber, 16.9 meters." Step into the courtyard for a peek at a surviving corner of the imposing **Roman temple** (Temple Roma d'August), which once stood here on Mont Tàber, keeping a protective watch over Barcino (free, well-explained on wall in English, daily 10:00–14:00 & 16:00–20:00).

• *Continue down Carrer del Paridís back to the cathedral, take a right, and go downhill about 100 yards to...*

Plaça del Rei: The Royal Palace sat on this "King's Square" (a block from the cathedral) until Catalunya became part of Spain in the 15th century. Then it was the headquarters of the local Inquisition. In 1493, a triumphant Christopher Columbus, accompanied by six New World natives (whom he called "Indians") and several pure-gold statues, entered the Royal Palace. King Ferdinand and Queen Isabel rose to welcome him home, and they honored him with the title "Admiral of the Oceans."

• *Your tour is over. Nearby, just off Plaça del Rei, is another sight—the City History Museum (described on page 1113). And the Frederic Marès Museum is just up the street (toward the cathedral entrance; see page 1113). Or simply wander and enjoy Barcelona at its Gothic best.*

Sights

Barcelona's Old City

I've divided Barcelona's Old City sights into three neighborhoods: near the harbor, at the bottom of the Ramblas; the cathedral and nearby (Barri Gòtic); and the Picasso Museum and nearby (La Ribera).

On the Harborfront, at the Bottom of the Ramblas

▲**Maritime Museum (Museu Marítim)**—Barcelona's medieval shipyard, the best preserved in the entire Mediterranean, is now an impressive museum covering the salty history of ships and navigation from the 13th to the 20th centuries. Riveting for nautical types, and interesting for anyone, its modern and beautifully presented exhibits will put you in a seafaring mood. The museum's cavernous halls evoke the 14th-century days when Catalunya was a naval and shipbuilding power, cranking out 30 huge galleys a winter. As in the US today, military and commercial ventures mixed and mingled as Catalunya built its trading empire. The excellent included audioguide tells the story and explains the various seafaring vessels displayed—including an impressively huge and richly decorated royal galley (€6.50, €7.20 combo-ticket includes Columbus Monument, daily 10:00–19:45, last entry at 19:00, breezy courtyard café, Avinguda de la Drassanes, tel. 933-429-920).

▲**Columbus Monument (Monument a Colóm)**—Marking the point where the Ramblas hits the harbor, this 200-foot-tall monument built for an 1888 exposition offers an elevator-assisted view from its top. The tight four-person elevator takes you to the glassed-in observation area at the top for congested but fine views (€2.30, daily 9:00–20:30). It was here in Barcelona that Ferdinand and Isabel welcomed Columbus home after his first trip to America. It's ironic that Barcelona would so honor the man whose discoveries ultimately led to its downfall as a great trading power.

Golondrinas **Cruises**—At the harbor near the foot of the Columbus Monument, tourist boats called *golondrinas* offer two different, unguided tours. The shorter version goes around the harbor in 35 minutes (€5.50, daily on the hour 11:30–19:00, every 30 min mid-June–mid-Sept, sometimes does not run Nov–April—call ahead, tel. 934-423-106). The longer, 90-minute tour goes up the coast to the Fòrum complex and back (€11.50, can disembark at Fòrum in summer only, about 7/day, daily 11:30–19:30).

▲Cathedral of Barcelona

Most of the construction on Barcelona's vast cathedral (Catedral de Barcelona) took place in the 14th century, during the glory days of the Catalan nation. The facade was humble, so in the 19th century, the proud local bourgeoisie redid it in a more ornate Neo-Gothic style.

Cost, Hours, Location: Strangely, even though the cathedral is free to enter daily 8:00–12:45 (13:45 on Sun) and 17:15–19:30, you must pay €5 to enter between 12:45–17:15 (tel. 933-151-554). The dress code is strictly enforced; don't wear tank tops, short shorts, or short skirts.

Getting There: The huge, can't-miss-it cathedral is in the center of the Barri Gòtic, on Plaça de la Seu. For an interesting way to reach the cathedral from Plaça de Catalunya, and some commentary on the surrounding neighborhood, see my self-guided walk of the Barri Gòtic, earlier in this chapter.

❍ Self-Guided Tour: Though the cathedral is Gothic and supported by buttresses, it has smooth outside walls. That's because the supporting buttresses are on the inside, providing walls for 28 richly ornamented chapels. This, along with the interior's open and spacious feeling, is typical of Catalan Gothic. Typical of all medieval churches, the cathedral has an "ambulatory" plan—allowing worshippers to amble around to the chapel of their choice.

While the main part of the church is fairly plain, the **chapels,** sponsored by local guilds, show great wealth. Located in the community's most high-profile space, they provided a kind of advertising to illiterate worshippers. The Native Americans that Columbus brought to town were supposedly **baptized** in the first chapel on the left.

The chapels ring a finely carved 15th-century **choir** *(coro)*. For €2.20, you can enter and get a close-up look (with the lights on) of

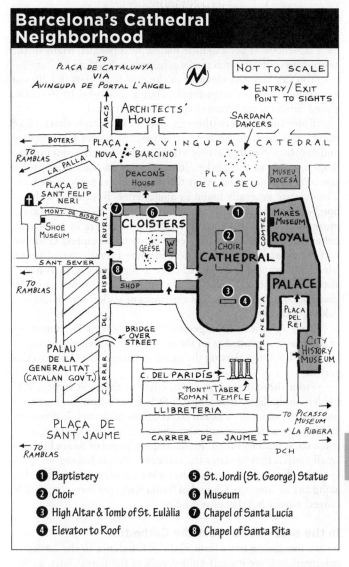

Barcelona's Cathedral Neighborhood

TO
PLAÇA DE CATALUNYA
VIA
AVINGUDA DE PORTAL L'ANGEL

NOT TO SCALE

→ ENTRY/EXIT POINT TO SIGHTS

ARCHITECTS' House

SARDANA DANCERS

BOTERS

TO RAMBLAS

PLAÇA NOVA

LA PALLA

BARCINO

AVINGUDA CATEDRAL

DEACON'S House

PLAÇA DE LA SEU

MUSEU DIOCESÀ

PLAÇA DE SANT FELIP NERI

MONT. DE BISBE

SHOE MUSEUM

SANT SEVER

TO RAMBLAS

IRURITA

❼ ❻ CLOISTERS

GEESE WC

❺

❽ SHOP

BISBE

DEL

❶

MARÈS MUSEUM

❷ CHOIR
CATHEDRAL

❸
❹

COMTES

ROYAL

PALACE

FRENERIA

PLAÇA DEL REI

CITY HISTORY MUSEUM

BRIDGE OVER STREET

PALAU DE LA GENERALITAT (CATALAN GOV'T.)

CARRER

C. DEL PARIDÍS

"MONT" TÀBER ROMAN TEMPLE

LLIBRETERIA

TO PICASSO MUSEUM & LA RIBERA

PLAÇA DE SANT JAUME

CARRER DE JAUME I

← TO RAMBLAS

DCH

❶ Baptistery
❷ Choir
❸ High Altar & Tomb of St. Eulàlia
❹ Elevator to Roof
❺ St. Jordi (St. George) Statue
❻ Museum
❼ Chapel of Santa Lucía
❽ Chapel of Santa Rita

BARCELONA

the ornately carved stalls and the emblems representing the various Knights of the Golden Fleece who once sat here. The chairs were folded up, giving VIPs stools to lean on during the standing parts of the Mass. Each was creatively carved and—since you couldn't sit on sacred things—the artists were free to enjoy some secular and naughty fun here. Study the upper tier of carvings.

The **high altar** sits upon the tomb of Barcelona's patron saint, Eulàlia. She was a 13-year-old local girl tortured 13 times by

Romans for her faith before finally being crucified on an X-shaped cross. Her X symbol is carved on the pews. Climb down the stairs for a close look at her exquisite marble sarcophagus. Many of the sarcophagi in this church predate the present building.

You can ride the **elevator** to the roof for a view (€2.20—or free when there's a charge for the church, Mon–Fri 10:30–18:00, closed Sat–Sun, start from chapel left of high altar).

Enter the **cloisters** (through arch, right of high altar). Once inside, look back at the arch, an impressive mix of Romanesque and Gothic. Nearby, a tiny **statue** of St. George slaying the dragon stands in the garden. Jordi (George) is one of the patron saints of Catalunya and by far the most popular boy's name here. Cloisters are generally found in monasteries. But this church has one because it needed to accommodate more chapels—to make more money. With so many wealthy merchants in town who believed that their financial generosity would impress God and win them favor, the church needed more private chapel space. Merchants wanted to be buried close to the altar, and their tombs also spill over into the cloister. On the pavement stones, as in the chapels, notice the symbols of the trades or guilds: scissors, shoes, bakers, and so on.

Long ago the resident **geese**—there are always 13, in memory of Eulàlia—functioned as an alarm system. Any commotion would get them honking, alerting the monk in charge. They honk to this very day.

From the statue of St. Jordi, circle to the right (past a WC hidden on the left). The skippable little €2 **museum** (far corner) is one plush room with a dozen old religious paintings. Just beyond the museum in the corner, built into the outside wall of the cloister, is the dark, barrel-vaulted, Romanesque **Chapel of Santa Lucía,** a small church that predates the cathedral. People hoping for good eyesight (Santa Lucía's specialty) leave candles outside. Farther along the cloister, the **Chapel of Santa Rita** (her forte: impossible causes) usually has the most candles.

In the Barri Gòtic, near the Cathedral

For an interesting route from Plaça de Catalunya to the cathedral neighborhood, see my self-guided walk of the Barri Gòtic, earlier in this chapter.

Shoe Museum (Museu del Calçat)—Shoe-lovers enjoy this two-room shoe museum, watched over by a we-try-harder attendant. The huge shoes at the entry are designed to fit the foot of the Columbus Monument at the bottom of the Ramblas (€2.50, Tue–Sun 11:00–14:00, closed Mon, 1 block beyond outside door of cathedral cloister, behind Plaça de G. Bachs on Plaça Sant Felip Neri, tel. 933-014-533).

▲▲City History Museum (Museu d'Història de la Ciutat)—
Walk through the history of the city with the help of an included audioguide. First watch the fine nine-minute introductory video in the small theater (playing alternately in Catalan, Spanish, and English)—it's worth viewing in any language. Then take an elevator down 65 feet (and 2,000 years—see the date spin back as you descend) to stroll the streets of Roman Barcelona. You'll see sewers, models of domestic life, and bits of an early-Christian church. Finally, an exhibit in the 11th-century count's palace shows you Barcelona through the Middle Ages (€6; April–Sept Tue–Sat 10:00–20:00, Sun 10:00–15:00, closed Mon; Oct–March Tue–Sat 10:00–14:00 & 16:00–19:00, Sun 10:00–15:00, closed Mon; Plaça del Rei, enter on Vageur street, tel. 932-562-122).

Frederic Marès Museum (Museu Frederic Marès)—This eclectic collection of local artist (and pack-rat) Frederic Marès sprawls around a peaceful courtyard through several old Barri Gòtic buildings. The biggest part of the collection is sculpture, from ancient times to the early 20th century. But even more interesting is Marès' vast collection of items he found representative of everyday life in the 19th century—rooms upon rooms of fans, stamps, pipes, and other bric-a-brac, all lovingly displayed. There are also several sculptures by Frederic Marès himself, and temporary exhibits (€4.20, free Wed afternoon; open Tue–Sat 10:00–19:00, Sun 10:00–15:00, closed Mon; Plaça de Sant Iu 5–6, tel. 932-563-500, www.museumares.bcn.cat). The delightfully tranquil courtyard café offers a nice break, even if you're not going to the museum.

▲▲▲Picasso Museum (Museu Picasso)

This is the best collection in the country of the work of Spaniard Pablo Picasso (1881–1973), and—since he spent his formative years (age 14–21) in Barcelona—it's the best collection of his early works anywhere. By seeing his youthful, realistic art, you can more fully appreciate the artist's genius and better understand his later, more challenging art. The collection is scattered through several connected Gothic palaces, six blocks from the cathedral in the Ribera district (for more on this area, see "In La Ribera, near the Picasso Museum," next).

Cost, Hours, Location: €9, free on first Sun of month, open Tue–Sun 10:00–20:00, closed Mon, Montcada 15–23, ticket office at #21, Metro: Jaume I, tel. 932-563-000, www.museupicasso.bcn.cat. The ground floor has a required bag check, as well as a handy array of other services (bookshop, WC, and cafeteria).

Crowd-Beating Tips: There's almost always a line, but it moves quickly (you'll rarely wait more than an hour to get in). The busiest time is from when it opens until about 13:00 (worst on Tuesdays); generally the later in the afternoon you visit, the fewer the crowds. If you have an Articket Card (described under "Tourist Information," earlier in this chapter), you can skip the line by going to the group entrance.

Hungry? The museum itself has a good café. The Textil Café, hiding in a beautiful and inviting museum courtyard across the street, is an ideal place to sip a *café con leche* or eat a light meal (€5–10 salads, couscous, and quiche fare; Tue–Sun 10:00–24:00, closed Mon, 30 yards from Picasso Museum at Montcada 12–14, tel. 932-682-598; also hosts jazz concerts Sunday nights 21:00–23:00 weather permitting—usually not in winter, stand for free or pay €5 cover to sit). And just down the street is a neighborhood favorite for tapas, El Xampanyet (described on page 1146).

In La Ribera, near the Picasso Museum

There's more to the Ribera neighborhood than just the Picasso Museum. While the nearby waterfront Barceloneta district was for the working-class sailors, La Ribera housed the wealthier shippers and merchants. Its streets are lined with their fine mansions—which, like the much-appreciated Church of Santa Maria del Mar, were built with shipping wealth.

La Ribera (also known as "El Born") is separated from the Barri Gòtic by Via Laietana, a four-lane highway built through the Old City in the early 1900s to alleviate growing traffic problems. From the Plaça de l'Angel (with the nearest Metro stop—Jaume I), cross this busy street to enter an up-and-coming zone of lively and creative restaurants and nightlife. The Carrer de l'Argenteria ("Goldsmiths Street"—streets in La Ribera are named after the workshops that used to occupy them) runs diagonally from the Plaça de l'Angel straight down to the Church of Santa Maria del Mar. The Catalan Concert Hall is to the north.

▲▲Catalan Concert Hall (Palau de la Música Catalana)—This concert hall, finished in 1908, features my favorite Modernista interior in town (by Lluís Domènech i Muntaner). Inviting arches lead you into the 2,138-seat hall. A kaleidoscopic skylight features a choir singing around the sun, while playful carvings and mosaics celebrate music and Catalan culture. Admission is by tour only and starts with a relaxing 12-minute video (€10, 50-min tours in English run daily every hour 10:00–15:00, tour times may change based on performance schedule, about 6 blocks northeast of cathedral, tel. 932-957-200, www.palaumusica.org).

The catch: You must buy your ticket in advance to get a spot on an English guided tour (tickets available up to 7 days in advance—ideally buy yours at least 2 days before, sometimes available the day before). You can buy the ticket in person at the concert hall box office (open daily 9:30–15:30); by phone with your credit card

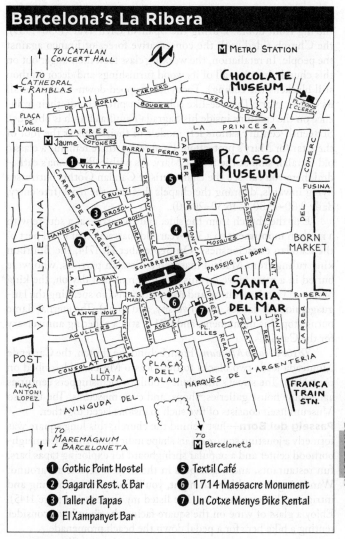

Barcelona's La Ribera

TO CATALAN CONCERT HALL

TO CATHEDRAL + RAMBLAS

Ⓜ METRO STATION

CHOCOLATE MUSEUM

PLAÇA DE L'ANGEL

C. DE LA BORIA

CARDERS

BOUQER

ASSAONADORS

PL. PONS I CLERCH

CARRER DE LA PRINCESA

COTONERS

Ⓜ Jaume I

❶ VIGATANS

BARRA DE FERRO

PICASSO MUSEUM

CARRER DE MONTCADA

COMERÇ

FUSINA

GRUNYÍ

BROSOLÍ

❸

D'EN ROSIC

MIRALLERS

FLASSADERS

C. DEL REC

DEL

BORN MARKET

CARRER DE L'ARGENTINA

MANRESA

❷

DE BANYS VELLS

SOMBRERERS

MOSQUES

❹

❺

DE LA NAU

ABAIX

PASSEIG DEL BORN

SANTA MARIA DEL MAR

RIBERA

VIA LAIETANA

PL. STA. MARIA

STA. MARIA

❻

VIDRIERA

❼

PL. OLLES

ANT.

PESCATERIA

SANT JOAN

CARRER

CANVIS NOUS

ANCIS VELLS

ESPASERI

ASES

MALC

RERA PAL.

REC

AGULLERS

POST

CONSOLAT DE MAR

LA LLOTJA

PLAÇA DEL PALAU

PLAÇA ANTONI LOPEZ

MARQUÈS DE L'ARGENTERIA

FRANÇA TRAIN STN.

AVINGUDA DEL

TO MAREMAGNUM + BARCELONETA

TO Barceloneta Ⓜ

BARCELONA

❶ Gothic Point Hostel
❷ Sagardi Rest. & Bar
❸ Taller de Tapas
❹ El Xampanyet Bar
❺ Textil Café
❻ 1714 Massacre Monument
❼ Un Cotxe Menys Bike Rental

(tel. 902-485-475); or online via the concert hall website (www .palaumusica.org).

It might be easier to get tickets for a **concert** (300 per year, tickets for some performances as cheap as €7, see website for details).

▲**Church of Santa Maria del Mar**—This church is the proud centerpiece of La Ribera. "Del Mar" means "of the sea," and that's where the money came from. The proud shippers built this church in only 55 years, so it has a harmonious style considered pure Catalan

Gothic. As you step in, notice the figures of workers carved into the big front doors. During the Spanish Civil War (1936–1939), the Church sided with the conservative forces of Franco against the people. In retaliation, the working class took their anger out on this church, burning all of its wood furnishings and decor (carbon still blackens the ceiling). Today it's stripped down—naked in all its Gothic glory. The tree-like columns inspired Gaudí (their influence on the columns inside his Sagrada Família church is obvious). Sixteenth-century sailors left models of their ships at the foot of the altar for Mary's protection. Even today, there remains a classic old Catalan ship at the feet of Mary. As within Barcelona's cathedral, here you can see the characteristic Catalan Gothic buttresses flying inwards, defining the chapels that ring the nave (free entry, daily 9:00–13:30 & 16:30–20:00).

Exit the church from the side, and you arrive at a square with a modern **monument** to a 300-year-old massacre that's still part of the Catalan consciousness. On September 11, 1714, the Bourbon king ruling from Madrid massacred Catalan patriots, who were buried in a mass grave on this square. From that day on, the king outlawed Catalan culture and its institutions (no speaking the language, no folk dances, no university, and so on). The eternal flame burns atop this monument, and 9/11 is still a sobering anniversary for the Catalans.

To the Picasso Museum: From behind the church, the Carrer de Montcada leads two blocks to the Picasso Museum (described on page 1113). The street's mansions—built by rich shippers centuries ago—now house galleries, shops, and even museums. The Picasso Museum itself consists of five such mansions laced together.

Passeig del Born—Just behind the church, this long square was formerly a jousting square (as its shape indicates). This is the neighborhood center and a popular springboard for exploring tapas bars, fun restaurants, and nightspots in the narrow streets all around. Wandering around here at night, you'll find piles of inviting and intriguing little restaurants (I've listed my favorites on page 1145). Enjoy a glass of wine on the square facing the church, or consider renting a bike here for a pedal down the beach promenade.

Chocolate Museum (Museu de la Xocolata)—This museum, only a couple of blocks from the Picasso Museum, is a delight for chocolate-lovers. Operated by the local confectioners' guild, it tells the story of chocolate from Aztecs to Europeans via the port of Barcelona, where it was first unloaded and processed. But the history lesson is just an excuse to show off a series of remarkably ornate candy sculptures. These works of edible art—which change every year but often include such Spanish themes as Don Quixote or bullfighting—begin as store-window displays for Easter or

Christmas. Once the holiday passes, the confectioners bring the sculptures here to be enjoyed (€4, Mon and Wed–Sat 10:00–19:00, Sun 10:00–15:00, closed Tue, Carrer Comerç 36, tel. 932-687-878, www.museuxocolata.com).

The Eixample: Modernisme and Antoni Gaudí

Wide sidewalks, hardy shade trees, chic shops, and plenty of Art Nouveau fun make the Eixample a refreshing break from the Old City. Uptown Barcelona is a unique variation on the common grid-plan city. Barcelona snipped off the building corners to create light and spacious eight-sided squares at every intersection. For the best Eixample example, ramble Rambla de Catalunya (unrelated to the more famous Ramblas) and pass through Passeig de Gràcia (Metro for Block of Discord: Passeig de Gràcia, or Metro for Casa Milà: Diagonal).

The 19th century was a boom time for Barcelona. By 1850, the city was busting out of its medieval walls. A new town was planned to follow a grid-like layout. The intersection of three major thoroughfares—Gran Via, Diagonal, and Meridiana—would shift the city's focus uptown.

The Eixample, or "Expansion," was a progressive plan in which everything was made accessible to everyone. Each 20-block-square district would have its own hospital and large park, each 10-block-square area would have its own market and general services, and each five-block-square grid would house its own schools and day-care centers. The hollow space found inside each "block" of apartments would form a neighborhood park.

While much of that vision never quite panned out, the Eixample was an urban success. Rich and artsy big shots bought plots along the grid. The richest landowners built as close to the center as possible. For this reason, the best buildings are near the Passeig de Gràcia. While adhering to the height, width, and depth limitations, they built as they pleased—often in the trendy new Modernista style.

For many visitors, Modernista architecture is Barcelona's main draw. (The TI even has a special desk set aside just for Modernisme-seekers.) And one name tops them all: **Antoni Gaudí** (1852–1926). Barcelona is an architectural scrapbook of Gaudí's galloping gables and organic curves. A devoted Catalan and Catholic, he immersed himself in each project, often living on-site. At various times, he called Parc Güell, Casa Milà, and the Sagrada Família home.

First I've covered the main Gaudí attractions close to the Old City. Two more—the Sagrada Família and Parc Güell—are farther afield, but worth the trip. And since many visitors do those two sights together, I've included tips on how to connect them.

Gaudí Sights near the Old City

▲▲**Casa Milà (La Pedrera)**—This Gaudí exterior laughs down on the crowds filling Passeig de Gràcia. Casa Milà, also called La Pedrera ("The Quarry"), has a much-photographed roller coaster of melting-ice-cream eaves. This is Barcelona's quintessential Modernista building and Gaudí's last major work (1906–1910) before dedicating his final years to the Sagrada Família.

You can visit three sections of Casa Milà: the apartment, attic, and rooftop (€8, includes good audioguide, daily March–Oct 9:00–20:00, Nov–Feb 9:00–18:30, Passeig de Gràcia 92, Metro: Diagonal, tel. 902-400-973).

As you enter, choose the 75-minute audioguide (which offers more listening options than the 30-minute version; either one included in admission). Then head upstairs. Two elevators take you up to either the apartment or the attic. Normally you're directed to the apartment, but if you arrive late in the day, go to the attic elevator first, then climb right up to the rooftop, to make sure you have enough time to enjoy Gaudí's works and the views.

The typical, fourth-floor **apartment** is decorated as it might have been when the building was first occupied, by middle-class urbanites (a 7-minute video explains Barcelona society at the time). Notice Gaudí's clever use of the atrium to maximize daylight in all of the apartments.

The **attic** houses a sprawling multimedia "Gaudí Space," tracing the history of the architect's career with models, photos, and videos of his work. It's all displayed under distinctive parabola-shaped arches. While evocative of Gaudí's style in themselves, the arches are formed this way partly to support the multi-level roof above. This area was also used for ventilation, helping to keep things cool in summer and warm in winter. Tenants had storage spaces and did their laundry up here.

From the attic, a stairway leads to the fanciful, undulating, jaw-dropping **rooftop,** where 30 chimneys play volleyball with the clouds.

Back at the **ground level** of Casa Milà, poke into the dreamily painted original entrance courtyard. The first floor hosts free art exhibits.

Concerts: During July, a rooftop concert series called "Pedrera by Night" features live music—jazz, flamenco, tango—a glass of *cava,* and the chance to see the rooftop illuminated (€12, 22:00–24:00, tel. 902-400-973).

Hungry? Stop by the recommended La Bodegueta, a long block away (daily lunch special, described on page 1146).

▲**Block of Discord**—Four blocks from Casa Milà, you can survey a noisy block of competing late 19th-century facades. Several of Barcelona's top Modernista mansions line Passeig de Gràcia (Metro: Passeig de Gràcia). Because the structures look as though they are trying to outdo each other in creative twists, locals nicknamed the block between Consell de Cent and Arago the "Block of Discord."

First (at #43) and most famous is Gaudí's **Casa Batlló,** with skull-like balconies and a tile roof that suggests a cresting dragon's back; Gaudí based the work on the popular legend of St. Jordi (George) slaying the dragon. The house—a rival of Casa Milà—can also be toured (€16.50, daily 9:00–20:00, may close early for special events, tel. 932-160-306, www.casabatllo.cat). You'll see the main floor (with a funky mushroom-shaped fireplace nook), the blue-and-white-ceramic-slathered atrium, the attic (more parabolic arches), and the rooftop, all with the help of a good audioguide. It's pricey, but the interior is even more fanciful and over-the-top than Casa Milà's. There's barely a straight line in the house. By the way, if you're tempted to snap your photos from the middle of the street, be careful—Gaudí died under a streetcar.

Next door, at **Casa Amatller** (#41), check out architect Josep Puig i Cadafalch's creative mix of Moorish- and Gothic-inspired architecture and iron grillwork, which decorates a step-gable like those in the Netherlands.

On the corner (at #35), **Casa Lleó Morera** has a wonderful interior highlighted by the dining room's fabulous stained glass. The architect, Lluís Domènech i Muntaner, also did the Catalan Concert Hall (you'll notice similarities).

La Rita restaurant, just around the corner on Carrer Arago, serves a fine three-course lunch for a great price from 13:00 (described on page 1146).

▲**Palau Güell**—Just as the Picasso Museum reveals a young genius on the verge of a breakthrough, this early Gaudí building (completed in 1890) shows the architect taking his first tentative steps toward what would become his trademark curvy style. The parabolic-arch doorways, viewable from the outside, are the first clue that this is not a typical townhouse. In the midst of an extensive renovation, only part of the house has been open to the public: the main floor and the Neo-Gothic cellar (which was used as a stable—notice the big carriage doors in the back and the rings on some of the posts used to tie up the horses). By 2010, they hope to have more of the house open...and start charging admission (Tue–Sat 10:00–14:30, closed Sun–Mon, a half-block off the Ramblas at Carrer Nou de la Rambla 3–5, tel. 933-173-974, www.palauguell.cat). Even if the rooftop is open, I'd skip it if you plan to see the more interesting one at Casa Milà (described earlier in this section).

▲▲▲Sagrada Família (Holy Family Church)

Gaudí's most famous and persistent work is this unfinished landmark church. He worked on the Sagrada Família from 1883 to 1926. Since then, construction has moved forward in fits and starts. Even today, the half-finished church is not expected to be completed for another quarter-century. (But over 30 years of visits, I've seen considerable progress.) The temple is funded exclusively by private donations and entry fees, which is another reason its completion has taken so long. Your admission helps pay for the ongoing construction.

Cost, Hours, Location: €10, daily April–Sept 9:00–20:00, Oct–March 9:00–18:00, Metro: Sagrada Família puts you right on the doorstep—exit toward *Pl de la Sagrada Família*, tel. 932-073-031, www.sagradafamilia.cat.

Crowd-Beating Tips: The ticket line can be very long (up to about 30–45 minutes at peak times). It's least crowded right when the church opens (9:00–10:00) and worst at high noon. You can call ahead to pre-purchase tickets (tel. 902-101-212, buy tickets with credit card, then pick them up when you arrive).

Tours: The 50-minute English tours cost €4 (April–Oct daily at 11:00 and 13:00, Nov–March usually Fri–Mon only, same times). Or rent the good 70-minute audioguide (also €4).

Elevators: Two different elevators take you partway up the towers for a great view of the city and a gargoyle's-eye perspective of the loopy church. Each one costs €2.50 (pay as you board elevator). The **Passion facade elevator** takes you 215 feet up, where you can climb higher if you want; then an elevator takes you back down. The **Nativity facade elevator** is similar, but you can also cross the dizzying bridge between the towers—and you must walk all the way down. (Some people prefer the Nativity elevator despite the additional climbing because it offers close views of the facade that Gaudí actually worked on.) For the climbing sections, expect the spiral stairs to be tight, hot, and congested. Lines for both elevators can be very long (up to a 2-hour wait at the busiest times); signs along the stanchions give an estimated wait time.

The Construction Project: There's something powerful about an opportunity to feel a community of committed people with a vision working on a church that will not be finished in their lifetime (as was standard in the Gothic age). Local craftsmen often cap off their careers by spending a couple of years on this exciting construction site. The church will trumpet its completion with 18 spires: A dozen "smaller" 330-foot spires (representing the apostles) will stand in groups of four and mark the three entry facades of the building. Four taller towers (dedicated to the four Evangelists) will surround the two tallest, central towers: a 400-foot-tall tower of Mary and the grand 550-foot Jesus tower, which will shine like a spiritual lighthouse—visible even from out at sea. A unique exterior ambulatory will circle the building, like a cloister turned inside out. If there's any building on earth I'd like to see, it's the Sagrada Família...finished.

◉ Self-Guided Tour: To get a good rundown, follow this commentary.

• *Begin facing the western side of the church (where you'll enter).*

Passion Facade: It seems strange to begin with something that Gaudí had nothing to do with...but that's where they put the entrance. When Gaudí died in 1926, only the stubs of four spires stood above the building site. The rest of the church has been inspired by Gaudí's vision but designed and executed by others. Gaudí knew he wouldn't live to complete the church and recognized that later architects and artists would rely on their own muses for inspiration. This artistic freedom was amplified in 1936, when Civil War shelling burned many of Gaudí's blueprints. Judge for yourself how the recently completed and controversial Passion facade by Josep María Subirachs (b. 1927) fits with Gaudí's original formulation (which you'll see downstairs in the museum).

Subirachs' facade is full of symbolism from the Bible. The story of Christ's Passion unfolds in the shape of a Z, from bottom to top. Find the stylized Alpha and Omega over the door; Jesus—hanging on the cross—with an open book (the word of God) for hair; and the grid of numbers adding up to 33 (Jesus' age at the time of his death). The distinct face of the man below and just left of Christ is a memorial to Gaudí.

Now look high above: The figure perched on the bridge between the towers is the soul of Jesus, ascending to heaven. The colorful ceramic caps of the towers symbolize the miters (formal hats) of bishops.

Grand and impressive as this seems, keep in mind it's only the *side* entry to the church. The nine-story apartment flat to the right will be torn down to accommodate the grand front entry. The three facades—Passion, Nativity, and Glory—will chronicle Christ's life from birth to death to resurrection.

• *We'll enter the church later. For now, look right to find the...*

School: Gaudí built this school for the children of the workers building the church. Now it houses an exhibit focusing on the architect's use of geometric forms. You'll also see a classroom and a replica of Gaudí's desk as it was the day he died, and a model for the proposed Glory facade...the next big step.

• *Leaving the school, turn right and go down the ramp under the church, into the...*

Museum: Housed in what is someday intended to be the church's crypt, the museum runs underground from the Passion

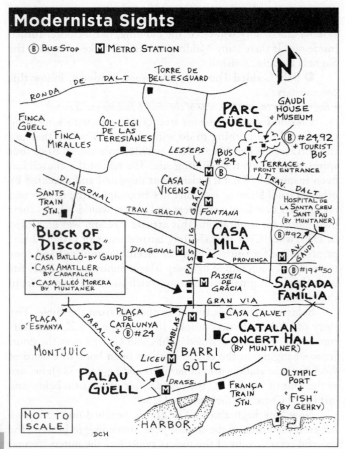

Modernista Sights

Ⓑ Bus Stop Ⓜ Metro Station

N

TORRE DE BELLESGUARD

RONDA DE DALT

FINCA GÜELL

FINCA MIRALLES

COL-LEGI DE LAS TERESIANES

PARC GÜELL

GAUDÍ HOUSE + MUSEUM

LESSEPS

BUS #24

Ⓑ #24,92 + TOURIST BUS

TERRACE + FRONT ENTRANCE

DIAGONAL

SANTS TRAIN STN.

CASA VICENS

Ⓜ Ⓑ

TRAV. DALT

HOSPITAL DE LA SANTA CREU I SANT PAU (BY MUNTANER)

TRAV. GRACIA

Ⓜ FONTANA

CASA MILA

Ⓑ #92

AV. GAUDÍ

"BLOCK OF DISCORD"
• CASA BATLLÒ - BY GAUDÍ
• CASA AMATLLER BY CADAFALCH
• CASA LLEÓ MORERA BY MUNTANER

DIAGONAL Ⓜ

PROVENÇA

Ⓜ

ℹ Ⓑ #19 + #50

PASSEIG DE GRACIA

SAGRADA FAMÍLIA

GRAN VIA

PLAÇA D'ESPANYA

PARAL·LEL

PLAÇA DE CATALUNYA + Ⓑ #24

Ⓜ

CASA CALVET

CATALAN CONCERT HALL (BY MUNTANER)

MONTJUÏC

LICEU Ⓜ

RAMBLAS

BARRI GÒTIC

OLYMPIC PORT + "FISH" (BY GEHRY)

PALAU GÜELL

Ⓜ

DRASS.

FRANÇA TRAIN STN.

NOT TO SCALE

DCH

HARBOR

facade to the Nativity facade. The first section tells the chronological story of the Sagrada Família. Look for the replicas of the pulpit and confessional that Gaudí, the micro-manager, designed for his church. As you wander through the plaster models used for the church's construction, you'll notice that they don't always match the finished product—these are ideas, not blueprints set in stone. Photos show the construction work as it was when Gaudí died in 1926 and how it's progressed over the years. See how the church's design is a fusion of nature, architecture, and religion. The columns seem light, with branches springing forth and capitals that look like palm trees.

Walking down the long passage to the other side of the church, you'll pass under a giant plaster model of the nave (you'll see the real thing soon). Find the hanging model showing how Gaudí used gravity to calculate the perfect parabolas incorporated into the church design (the mirror above this model shows how the right-side-up church is derived from this). Nearby, you'll find some original Gaudí architectural sketches in a dimly lit room and a worthwhile 20-minute movie (generally shown in English at :50 past each hour).

Then you'll peek into a busy workshop for making plaster models of the planned construction, just as Gaudí used—he found these helpful for envisioning the final product in 3-D. The museum wraps up with an exhibit on the design and implementation of the Passion facade.

• *Climb up the ramp and hook left to see the...*

Nativity Facade (east side): This, the only part of the church essentially finished in his lifetime, shows Gaudí's original vision. (Cleverly, this was built and finished first to inspire financial support, which Gaudí knew would be a challenge.) Mixing Gothic-style symbolism, images from nature, and Modernista asymmetry, it is the best example of Gaudí's unmistakable cake-in-the-rain style. The sculpture shows a unique twist on the Nativity, with Jesus as a young carpenter and angels playing musical instruments.

• *From here, you have two options:*

To take the elevator up the Nativity facade, go through the small door to the right of the main door. The line stretches through an area called the Rosary Cloister.

*To enter the church (where you'll also find the Passion facade elevator entrance), go in the door to the left of the main entry. First you'll pass the Montserrat Cloister, with the **Gaudí and Nature** exhibition that compares nature, waves, shells, mushrooms, the ripple of a leaf, and so on to Gaudí's work. Then you'll enter the...*

Construction Zone (the Nave): The cranking cranes, rusty forests of rebar, and scaffolding require a powerful faith, but the Sagrada Família offers a fun look at a living, growing, bigger-than-life building. Part of Gaudí's religious vision was a love for nature. He said, "Nothing is invented; it's written in nature." His columns blossom with life, and little windows let light filter in like the canopy of a rain forest, giving both privacy and an intimate connection with God. The U-shaped choir hovers above the nave, tethered halfway up the columns. A relatively recent addition—hanging out in the middle of the back wall—is a statue of Barcelona's patron saint, St. Jordi (George of dragon-slaying fame). At the far end of the nave, you'll see the line to take the elevator up the Passion facade.

Currently, the construction is focused on two major tasks: stabilizing the existing nave (which has been rattled by vibrations from the Metro and new AVE train line underground); and eventually adding the third, biggest entry—the Glory facade. They're also in the process of replacing the temporary, clear windows with stained-glass ones. The final phase is the central tower (550 feet tall), which, it's estimated, will require four underground support pylons, each consisting of 8,000 tons of cement.

Gaudí lived on the site for more than a decade and is buried in a Neo-Gothic 19th-century crypt (which is where the church began). His tomb is sometimes viewable from the museum, but may be closed to the public when you visit. There's a move afoot to make Gaudí a saint. Perhaps someday, his tomb will be a place of pilgrimage. Gaudí—a faithful Catholic whose medieval-style mysticism belied his Modernista architecture career—was certainly driven to greatness by his passion for God. When undertaking a lengthy project, he said, "My client"—meaning God—"is in no hurry."

Scenic Connection to Parc Güell: If your next stop is Parc Güell (described next), and you don't want to spring for a taxi, try this route: With the Nativity facade at your back, walk to the near-left corner of the park across the street. Then cross the street to reach the diagonal Avinguda Gaudí (between the Repsol gas station and the KFC). From here, you'll follow the funky lampposts four blocks gradually uphill (about 10 min) along a pleasant, shaded, café-lined pedestrian street (Avinguda Gaudí). When you reach the striking Modernista-style Hospital de la Santa Creu i Sant Pau (designed by Lluís Domènech i Muntaner), cross the street and go up one block (left) on St. Antonio Maria Claret street to catch bus #92, which will take you to the side entrance of Parc Güell.

From the Sagrada Família, you could also get to Parc Güell by taking the Metro to Lesseps, then bus #24 (described under "Parc Güell"), but that involves two changes...and less scenery.

More Bus Connections: From the Sagrada Família, bus #19 makes an easy 15-minute journey to the Old City (stops near the cathedral and La Ribera district); bus #50 goes from the Sagrada Família to Montjuïc, skipping the funicular but taking you past all the sights (see "Getting to Montjuïc," page 1126).

▲Parc Güell

Gaudí fans enjoy the artist's magic in this colorful park. Gaudí intended this 30-acre garden to be a 60-residence housing project—a kind of gated community. As a high-income housing development, it flopped. But as a park, it's a delight, offering another peek into the eccentric genius of Gaudí. Notice the mosaic medallions that say "park" in English, reminding folks that this is modeled on an English garden.

Cost and Hours: Free, daily 10:00–20:00, tel. 932-130-488.

Getting There: From Plaça de Catalunya, the red Tourist Bus or bus #24 will leave you at the park's side entrance, or a €6 taxi will drop you at the main entrance. From elsewhere in the city, you can take a Metro-plus-bus combination: Go by Metro to the Lesseps stop. To avoid the tiring, uphill 20-minute walk to the park, don't follow the *Parc Güell 1300 metros* sign; instead, exit left out of the Metro station, cross the streets Princep d'Astúries and Gran de Grácia, and catch bus #24 (on Gran de Grácia), which takes you to the park's side entrance in less than 10 minutes. For a more scenic approach (on bus #92) from the Sagrada Família, see end of previous listing.

❍ **Self-Guided Tour:** This tour assumes you're arriving at the front/main entrance (by taxi). If you're instead arriving by bus at the side entrance, walk straight ahead through the gate to find the terrace with colorful mosaic benches, then walk down to the stairway and front entrance.

As you wander the park, imagine living here a century ago—if this gated community had succeeded and was filled with Barcelona's wealthy.

Front Entrance: Entering the park, you walk by Gaudí's wrought-iron gas lamps (1900–1914). His dad was a blacksmith, and he always enjoyed this medium. Two gate houses made of gingerbread flank the entrance. One houses a good bookshop, while the other is home to the skippable Center for Interpretation of Parc Güell (Centre d'Interpretació), which shows Gaudí's building methods plus maps, photos, and models of the park (€2.30, daily 11:00–15:00, tel. 933-190-222); the Gaudí House and Museum, described on next page, is better.

Stairway and Columns: Climb the grand stairway, past the famous ceramic dragon fountain. At the top, dip into the "Hall of 100 Columns," designed to house a produce market for the neighborhood's 60 mansions. The fun columns—each different, made from concrete and rebar, topped with colorful ceramic, and studded with broken bottles and bric-a-brac—add to the market's vitality.

As you continue up (on the left-hand staircase), look left, down the playful "pathway of columns" that support a long arcade. Gaudí drew his inspiration from nature, and this arcade is like a surfer's perfect tube.

Terrace: Once up top, sit on a colorful bench—designed to fit your body ergonomically—and enjoy one of Barcelona's best views. Look for the Sagrada Família church in the distance. Gaudí was an engineer as well. He designed a water-catchment system by which rain hitting this plaza would flow into and through the columns from the market below, and power the park's fountains.

When considering the failure of Parc Güell as a community development, also consider that it was an idea a hundred years ahead of its time. Back then, high-society ladies didn't want to live so far from the cultural action. Today, the surrounding neighborhoods are some of the wealthiest in town, and a gated community here would be a big hit.

Gaudí House and Museum: This pink house with a steeple, standing in the middle of the park (near the side entrance), was actually Gaudí's home for 20 years, until his father died. His humble artifacts are mostly gone, but the house is now a museum with some quirky Gaudí furniture and a chance to wander through a model home used to sell the others. While small, it offers a good taste of what could have been (€4, daily April–Sept 10:00–20:00, Oct–March 10:00–18:00).

Montjuïc

Montjuïc ("Mount of the Jews"), overlooking Barcelona's hazy port, has always been a show-off. Ages ago it had an impressive fortress. In 1929, it hosted an international fair, from which most of today's sights originated. And in 1992, the Summer Olympics directed the world's attention to this pincushion of attractions once again.

I've listed these sights by altitude, from highest to lowest; if you're visiting all of them, do them in this order so that most of your walking is downhill (though for selective sightseers, the Fundació Joan Miró and Catalan Art Museum are the most worthwhile). Note that if you want to visit only the Catalan Art Museum, you can just take the Metro to Plaça d'Espanya and ride the escalators up (with some stairs, as well) to the museum.

Getting to Montjuïc: You have several options. The simplest is to take a **taxi** directly to your destination (about €7 from downtown).

Buses from various points in the city take you up to Montjuïc, including public bus #55 (from Plaça de Catalunya, next to Caja de Madrid building), public bus #50 (from the corner of Gran Via and Passeig de Gràcia, or from the Sagrada Família), and the blue Tourist Bus.

A **funicular** takes visitors from the Paral-lel Metro stop up to Montjuïc (covered by a Metro ticket, every 10 min, 9:00–22:00). You can easily reach this funicular by **Metro** (take it to the Paral-lel stop, then follow signs for *Parc Montjuïc* and the little funicular icon—you can enter the funicular directly without using another ticket, number of minutes until next departure posted at start of entry tunnel). From the top of the funicular, turn left and walk two minutes to the Joan Miró museum, six minutes to the Olympic Stadium, or ten minutes to the Catalan Art Museum.

From the port, the most scenic way to Montjuïc is via the **gondola,** called the 1929 Transbordador Aereo (€9.50 one-way, €12.50 round-trip, 3/hr, daily 10:45–19:00, until 20:00 in June–Sept).

Getting Around Montjuïc: Up top, the bus marked *Parc de Montjuïc* (#PM) loops between the sights. There are two routes:

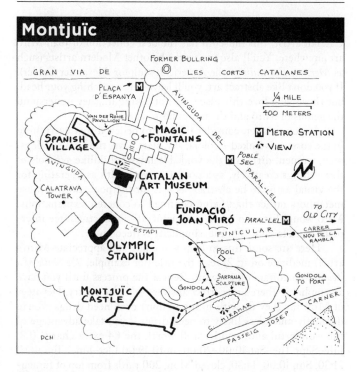

Montjuïc

FORMER BULLRING
GRAN VIA DE LES CORTS CATALANES
PLAÇA D'ESPANYA
AVINGUDA DEL
¼ MILE
400 METERS
Ⓜ METRO STATION
☆ VIEW
VAN DER ROHE PAVILLION
SPANISH VILLAGE
MAGIC FOUNTAINS
POBLE SEC
AVINGUDA
CATALAN ART MUSEUM
PARAL-LEL
CALATRAVA TOWER
FUNDACIÓ JOAN MIRÓ
PARAL-LEL Ⓜ
TO OLD CITY
L'ESTADI
FUNICULAR
CARRER NOU DE LA RAMBLA
OLYMPIC STADIUM
POOL
GONDOLA
SARDANA SCULPTURE
GONDOLA TO PORT
MONTJUÏC CASTLE
MIRAMAR
CARNER
PASSEIG JOSEP
DCH

The blue line starts at Plaça d'Espanya and goes to the Catalan Art Museum, the Joan Miró museum, the funicular, and the Castle of Montjuïc; the red line comes up from Drassanes, at the bottom of the Ramblas. The blue Tourist Bus also does a circuit around the top of Montjuïc.

Castle of Montjuïc—The castle offers great city views from its fortress and a military museum (€3, Tue–Sun 9:30–20:00, closed Mon). The seemingly endless museum houses a dull collection of guns, swords, and toy soldiers. An interesting section on the Spanish-American War of 1898 covers Spain's valiant fight against American aggression (from Spain's perspective). Unfortunately, there are no English descriptions. Those interested in Jewish history will find a fascinating collection of ninth-century Jewish tombstones.

The castle itself has a fascist past rife with repression. It was built in the 18th century by the central Spanish government to keep an eye on Barcelona and stifle citizen revolt. When Franco was in power, the castle was the site of hundreds of political executions.

Getting There: To spare yourself the hike up to the museum, take the **gondola** from just above the upper station of the Montjuïc funicular (€5.70 one-way, €7.90 round-trip, June–Sept daily 10:00–21:00, until 19:00 April–May and Oct, until 18:00 Nov–March).

▲**Fundació Joan Miró**—Showcasing the talents of yet another Catalan artist, this museum has the best collection of Joan Miró art anywhere. You'll also see works by other Modern artists (such as *Mercury Fountain* by the American sculptor Alexander Calder). If you don't like abstract art, you'll leave here scratching your head, but those who love this place are not faking it...they understand the genius of Miró and the fun of abstract art.

As you wander, consider this: Miró believed that everything in the cosmos is linked—colors, sky, stars, love, time, music, dogs, men, women, dirt, and the void. He mixed childlike symbols of these things creatively, as a poet uses words. It's as liberating for the visual artist to be abstract as it is for the poet: Both can use metaphors rather than being confined to concrete explanations. Miró would listen to music and paint. It's interactive, free interpretation. He said, "For me, simplicity is freedom."

Here are some tips to help you enjoy and appreciate Miró's art: 1) meditate on it; 2) read the title (for example, *The Smile of a Tear*); 3) meditate on it again. Repeat the process until you have an epiphany. There's no correct answer—it's pure poetry. Devotees of Miró say they fly with him and don't even need drugs. You're definitely much less likely to need drugs if you take advantage of the wonderful audioguide, well worth the €4 extra charge (€8, July–Sept Tue–Sat 10:00–20:00, until 19:00 Oct–June, Thu until 21:30, Sun 10:00–14:30, closed Mon, 200 yards from top of funicular, Parc de Montjuïc, tel. 934-439-470, www.bcn.fjmiro.es). The museum has a cool cafeteria, café, and bookshop.

Olympic and Sports Museum (Museu Olímpic i de l'Esport)—This new attraction rides the coattails of the stadium across the street (see next listing). You'll twist down a timeline-ramp that traces the history of the Olympic Games, interspersed with random exhibits about various sports. Downstairs you'll find exhibits designed to test your athleticism, a play-by-play rehash of the '92 Barcelona Olympiad, a commemoration of Juan Antonio Samaranch (a Spaniard and influential president of the IOC for two decades), a sports media exhibit, and a schmaltzy movie collage. High-tech but still hokey, the museum is worth the time and money only for those nostalgic for the '92 Games (€4, April–Sept Tue–Sun 10:00–20:00, Oct–March Tue–Sun 10:00–18:00, closed Mon, Avinguda de l'Estadi 60, tel. 932-925-379, http://fundacio barcelonaolimpica.es/moe).

Olympic Stadium (Estadi Olímpic)—For two weeks in the summer of 1992, the world turned its attention to this stadium (between the Catalan Art Museum and the Fundació Joan Miró at Passeig Olímpic 17). Redesigned from an earlier 1929 version, the stadium was updated, expanded, and officially named for Catalan patriot Lluís Companys i Jover. The XXV Olympiad kicked off here on July 25, when an archer dramatically lit the Olympic torch—which still stands high at the end of the stadium overlooking the city skyline—with a flaming arrow. Over the next two weeks, Barcelona played host to the thrill of victory (mostly at the hands of Magic Johnson, Michael Jordan, Larry Bird, and the rest of the US basketball "Dream Team") and the agony of defeat (i.e., the nightmares of the Dream Team's opponents). Hovering over the stadium is the memorable, futuristic Calatrava Communications Tower, used to transmit Olympic highlights and lowlights around the world. Aside from the memories of the medals, today's Olympic Stadium offers little to see today...except when it's hosting a match for Barcelona's soccer team, RCD Espanyol.

Spanish Village (Poble Espanyol)—This tacky five-acre model village uses fake traditional architecture from all over Spain as a shell to contain gift shops. Craftspeople do their clichéd thing only in the morning (not worth your time or €8, www.poble-espanyol .com). After hours, it's a popular local nightspot.

▲▲Catalan Art Museum (Museu Nacional d'Art de Catalunya)—The big vision for this wonderful museum is to showcase Catalan art from the 10th century through about 1930. Often called "the Prado of Romanesque art" (and "MNAC" for short), its highlight is Europe's best collection of Romanesque frescos (€8.50, includes audioguide, free first Sun of month, open Tue–Sat 10:00–19:00, Sun 10:00–14:30, closed Mon, last entry 30 min before closing; in massive National Palace building above Magic Fountains, near Plaça d'Espanya—take escalators up; tel. 936-220-376, www .mnac.es).

As you enter, pick up a map (helpful for such a big and confusing building). The left wing is Romanesque, and the right wing is Gothic, exquisite Renaissance, and Baroque. Upstairs is more Baroque, plus modern art, photography, coins, and more.

The MNAC's rare, world-class collection of **Romanesque** art came mostly from remote Catalan village churches in the Pyrenees (saved from unscrupulous art dealers—including many Americans). The Romanesque wing features frescoes, painted wooden altar fronts, and ornate statuary. This classic Romanesque art—with flat 2-D scenes, each saint holding his symbol, and Jesus (easy to identify by the cross in his halo)—is impressively displayed on replicas of the original church ceilings and apses.

Across the way, in the **Gothic** wing, fresco murals give way to vivid 14th-century wood-panel paintings of Bible stories. A roomful of paintings (Room 34) by the Catalan master Jaume Huguet (1412–1492) deserves a look, particularly his altarpiece of Barcelona's patron saint, George.

For a break, glide under the huge dome (which once housed an ice-skating rink) over to the air-conditioned cafeteria. This was the prime ceremony room and dance hall for the 1929 International Exposition. Then, from the big ballroom, ride the glass elevator upstairs, where the **Modern** section takes you on a delightful walk from the late 1800s to about 1930—kind of a Catalan Musée d'Orsay, offering a big chronological clockwise circle from Spain's Golden Age (Zurbarán, heavy religious scenes, Spanish royals with their endearing underbites), to Symbolism and Modernisme (furniture complements the empty spaces you likely saw in Gaudí's buildings), then Impressionists, *fin de siècle* fun, and Art Deco.

Upstairs you'll also find photography (with a bit on how photo-journalism came of age covering the Spanish Civil War), seductive sofas, and the chic Oleum restaurant, with vast city views (and €20 meals).

▲**Magic Fountains (Font Màgica)**—Music, colored lights, and huge amounts of water make an artistic and coordinated splash on summer nights at Plaça d'Espanya (20-min shows every half-hour; May–Sept Thu–Sun 21:00–23:30, no shows Mon–Wed; Oct–April Fri–Sat 19:00–21:00, no shows Sun–Thu; from the Espanya Metro station, walk toward the towering National Palace). Unfortunately, the schedule changes without notice—while it might help to confirm the schedule at the TI, my readers report that even locals can be mistaken about when they're running.

Nightlife

Sightseeing After Dark

Refer to the *See Barcelona* guide (free from TI) and ask about the latest at a TI. Major sights open until 20:00 include the Picasso Museum (closed Mon), Gaudí's Sagrada Família (open daily, until 18:00 Oct–March), Casa Milà (daily, until 18:30 Nov–Feb), and Parc Güell (daily). On Thursday, Montjuïc's Joan Miró museum stays open until 21:30 (otherwise open July–Sept Tue–Sat until 20:00).

Many lesser sights also stay open at least until 20:00, such as La Boquería market (Mon–Sat), Columbus Monument (daily), City History Museum (Tue–Sat), Church of Santa Maria del Mar (daily), Casa Batlló (daily), Parc Güell's Gaudí House and Museum (daily April–Sept), and the Castle of Montjuïc (Tue–Sat). The Magic Fountains on Plaça d'Espanya make a splash on weekend evenings (Fri–Sat, plus Thu and Sun in summer). The Tourist Bus runs until 22:00 every day in summer.

Music and Entertainment

The weekly *Guía del Ocio,* sold at newsstands for €1 (or free in some hotel lobbies), is a Spanish-language entertainment listing (with guidelines for English-speakers inside the back cover;

www.guiadelocio.com). The monthly *Barcelona Metropolitan* maga-zine and quarterly *What's On Barcelona* are also helpful (free from the TI). For music, consider a performance at Casa Milà ("Pedrera by Night" July concert series, see page 1118), the Liceu Opera House (on the Ramblas), or the Catalan Concert Hall (page 1114). There are many nightspots around Plaça Reial (such as the popular Jamboree).

Palau de la Virreina, an arts-and-culture TI, offers infor-mation on Barcelona cultural events—music, opera, and theater (Tue–Sat 11:00–20:00, Sun 11:00–14:30, closed Mon, Ramblas 99, see map on page 1101).

Sleeping

Book ahead. Barcelona is Spain's most expensive city. Still, it has reasonable rooms. Cheap places are more crowded in summer; fan-cier business-class hotels fill up in winter and offer discounts on weekends and in summer. When considering relative hotel values, in summer and on weekends you can often get modern comfort in business-class hotels for about the same price (€100) as you'll pay for ramshackle charm (and only a few minutes' walk from the Old City action). Some TI branches (including those at Plaça de Catalunya, Plaça de Sant Jaume, and the airport) offer a room-finding service, though it's cheaper to go direct. Note that prices at the Hotel Continental Barcelona and the Hotel Continental

Sleep Code

(€1 = about $1.40, country code: 34)

S = Single, **D** = Double/Twin, **T** = Triple, **Q** = Quad, **b** = bathroom, **s** = shower only. Unless otherwise noted, credit cards are accepted, English is spoken, and prices listed do not include the 7 percent tax or breakfast (ranging from simple €3 spreads to €25 buffets).

To help you easily sort through these listings, I've divided the rooms into three categories, based on the price for a standard double room with bath (during high season):

$$$ Higher Priced—Most rooms €150 or more.
  $$ Moderately Priced—Most rooms between €100–150.
    $ Lower Priced—Most rooms €100 or less.

While many of my recommendations are on pedestrian streets, night noise can be a problem (especially in cheap places, which have single-pane windows). For a quiet night, ask for *"tranquilo"* rather than *"con vista."*

BARCELONA

Palacete include great all-day snack-and-drink bars; several other hotels also offer free breakfasts to those who book direct with this guidebook.

Business-Class Comfort near Plaça de Catalunya

These hotels have sliding glass doors leading to plush reception areas, air-conditioning, and perfectly sterile modern bedrooms. Most are on big streets within two blocks of Barcelona's exuberant central square. As business-class hotels, they have hard-to-pin-down prices that fluctuate wildly. I've listed the average rate you'll pay. But in summer and on weekends, supply often far exceeds the demand, and many of these places cut prices to around €100—always ask for a deal.

$$$ **Hotel Catalonia Albinoni,** the best-located of all, elegantly fills a renovated old palace with wide halls, hardwood floors, and 74 rooms. It overlooks a thriving pedestrian boulevard in front and a quiet swimming-pool garden in back (Sb-€149, Db-€189, extra bed-€35, family rooms, back rooms have private little sun terraces and cost extra; request free breakfast if you book direct, pay the full rate, and show this book; lower promotional rates in summer—but free breakfast not valid with discounts, non-smoking, air-con, elevator, pay Internet access and Wi-Fi, a block down from Plaça de Catalunya at Avinguda Portal de l'Angel 17, tel. 933-184-141, fax 933-012-631, www.hoteles-catalonia.com, albinoni.reservas@hoteles-catalonia.es).

$$$ **Hotel Duques de Bergara** has four stars, an elegant old entryway, splashy public spaces, slick marble and hardwood floors, 150 comfortable but nothing-fancy rooms, and a garden courtyard with a pool a world away from the big-city noise (Sb-€173, Db-€213, Tb-€243, breakfast-€15, non-smoking, air-con, elevator, pay Internet access and Wi-Fi, a half-block off Plaça de Catalunya at Carrer de Bergara 11, tel. 933-015-151, fax 933-173-442, www .hoteles-catalonia.com, duques@hoteles-catalonia.es).

$$$ **Nouvel Hotel,** in an elegant, Victorian-style building on a handy pedestrian street, is less business-oriented and offers more character than the others listed here. It boasts royal lounges and 78 comfy rooms (Sb-€102, Db-€179, includes breakfast, discount for those booking direct via email—not their website—with this book, extra bed-€35, air-con, elevator, free Wi-Fi in lobby, Carrer de Santa Ana 20, tel. 933-018-274, fax 933-018-370, www.hotel nouvel.com, info@hotelnouvel.com, Roberto).

$$ **Hotel Reding,** on a quiet street a five-minute walk west of the Ramblas and Plaça de Catalunya action, is a slick and sleek place renting 44 mod rooms at a very good price (Db-€120, extra bed-€35, get their best deal on the Web and then request free

breakfasts with this book—select "no breakfast" and type "free Rick Steves breakfast" in comment line, non-smoking rooms, air-con, elevator, free Internet access and Wi-Fi, near Metro: Universitat, Gravina 5–7, tel. 934-121-097, fax 932-683-482, www .hotelreding.com, reding@oh-es.com).

$$ Hotel Duc de la Victoria, with 156 rooms, is professional yet friendly, buried in the Barri Gòtic just three blocks off the Ramblas (Db-€140, bigger "superior" rooms on a corner with windows on 2 sides-€25 extra, breakfast-€15, non-smoking, air-con, elevator, free Internet access, pay Wi-Fi, Duc de la Victoria 15, tel. 932-703-410, fax 934-127-747, www.nh-hotels.com, nhducdela victoria@nh-hotels.com).

$$ Hotel Lleó (YEH-oh) is well-run, with 89 big, bright, and comfortable rooms; a great breakfast room; and a generous lounge (Db-€130 but flexes way up with demand, can be cheaper in summer, extra bed-about €25, breakfast-€11, non-smoking rooms, air-con, elevator, free Internet access and Wi-Fi, 2 blocks west of Plaça de Catalunya at Carrer de Pelai 22, tel. 933-181-312, fax 934-122-657, www.hotel-lleo.es, reservas@hotel-lleo.es).

$$ Hotel Atlantis is solid, with 50 big, homey-yet-mod rooms and great prices for the location (Sb-€90, Db-€107, Tb-€125, refreshingly stable rates, breakfast-€9, non-smoking rooms, air-con, elevator, free Internet access and Wi-Fi, older windows let in a bit more street noise than other hotels in this category—request a quieter room in back, Carrer de Pelai 20, tel. 933-189-012, fax 934-120-914, www.hotelatlantis-bcn.com, info@hotelatlantis -bcn.com).

Hotels with "Personality" on or near the Ramblas

These recommended places are generally family-run, with ad-lib furnishings, more character, and lower prices. Only the Jardí offers a quaint square buried in the Barri Gòtic ambience—and you'll pay for it.

$ Hotel Continental Barcelona, in a building overlooking the top of the Ramblas, offers an inviting lounge and classic, tiny-view balcony opportunities if you don't mind the noise. Its comfortable rooms come with double-thick mattresses, wildly clashing carpets and wallpaper, and perhaps one too many clever ideas (they're laden with microwaves, fridges, a "command center" of light switches, and Tupperware drawers). Choose between your own little Ramblas-view balcony (where you can eat your breakfast) or a quieter back room (Sb-€85, Db-€95, twin Db-€105, Db with Ramblas balcony-€115, extra bed-€30, mention this book for best price, prices include breakfast and tax, non-smoking, air-con, elevator, free Internet access and Wi-Fi, Ramblas 138,

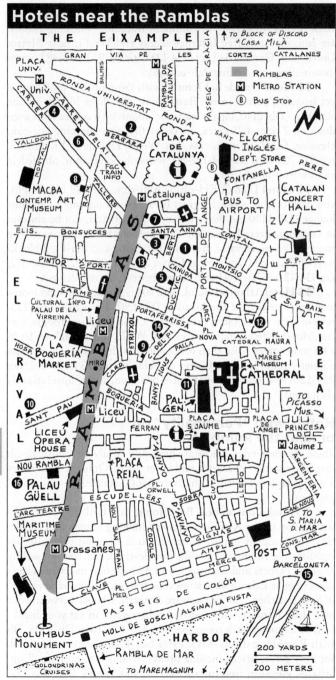

Hotels near the Ramblas

Hotels Key

1. Hotel Catalonia Albinoni
2. Hotel Duques de Bergara
3. Nouvel Hotel
4. Hotel Reding
5. Hotel Duc de la Victoria
6. Hotels Lleó & Atlantis
7. Hotel Continental Barcelona
8. Hostería Grau & Barcelona Rent-A-Bike
9. Hotel Jardí
10. Hostal Opera
11. Hotel Neri
12. Hotel Regencia Colón
13. Hostal Campi
14. Hostal Maldá
15. To Sea Point Hostel
16. Launderette

tel. 933-012-570, fax 933-027-360, www.hotelcontinental.com, barcelona@hotelcontinental.com). J. M.'s (José Maria) free breakfast and all-day snack-and-drink bar make this a better deal than the price suggests.

$ Hostería Grau is homey, family-run, and almost alpine. Its 25 cheery, garden-pastel rooms are a few blocks off the Ramblas in the colorful university district. The first two floors have ceilings a claustrophobic seven feet high, then things get tall again (S-€35, D-€65, Db-€85, extra bed-€15; 2-bedroom family suites: Db-€95, Tb-€120, Qb-€150; slippery prices jump during fairs and big events, breakfast next door-€3–7, air-con, free Internet access and Wi-Fi, lots of stairs with no elevator, 200 yards up Carrer dels Tallers from the Ramblas at Ramelleres 27, tel. 933-018-135, fax 933-176-825, www.hostalgrau.com, reservas@hostalgrau.com, Monica).

$ Hotel Jardí offers 40 clean, remodeled rooms on a breezy square in the Barri Gòtic. Many of the tight, plain, comfy rooms come with petite balconies (for an extra charge) and enjoy an almost Parisian ambience. It's a good deal only if you value the cute square location. Book well in advance, as this family-run place has an avid following (small basic interior Db-€79, nicer interior Db-€89, outer Db with balcony or twin with window-€95, large outer Db with balcony or square-view terrace-€106, extra bed-€12, breakfast-€6, non-smoking, air-con, elevator, some stairs, free Wi-Fi in lobby, halfway between Ramblas and cathedral at Plaça Sant Josep Oriol 1, tel. 933-015-900, fax 933-425-733, www.hoteljardi -barcelona.com, reservations@hoteljardi-barcelona.com).

$ Hostal Opera, with 70 stark rooms 20 yards off the Ramblas, is clean, institutional, and modern. The street can feel seedy at night, but it's safe, and the hotel is very secure (Sb-€49, Db-€69, no breakfast, air-con only in summer, elevator, pay Internet access, free Wi-Fi in lobby, Carrer Sant Pau 20, tel. 933-188-201, www.hostalopera.com, info@hostalopera.com).

Deep in the Barri Gòtic

$$$ Hotel Neri is chic, posh, and sophisticated, with 22 rooms spliced into the ancient stones of the Barri Gòtic overlooking an overlooked square (Plaça Sant Felip Neri) a block from the cathedral. It has big plasma-screen TVs, pricey modern art on the bedroom walls, and dressed-up people in its gourmet restaurant (Db-€265, suites-€360–425, breakfast-€21, air-con, elevator, free Wi-Fi, rooftop tanning deck, St. Sever 5, tel. 933-040-655, fax 933-040-337, www.hotelneri.com, info@hotelneri.com).

$$ Hotel Regencia Colón, one block in front of the cathedral square, offers 50 solid, well-priced rooms in a handy location (Db-€120, air-con, elevator, Carrer Sagristans 13–17, tel. 933-189-858, fax 933-172-822, www.hotelregenciacolon.com, info@hotelregenciacolon.com).

Humble, Cheaper Places Buried in the Old City

$ Hostal Campi is big, subdued, and ramshackle, but offers simple class. This easygoing, old-school spot rents 24 rooms a few doors off the top of the Ramblas (S-€32, D-€54, Db-€62, T-€74, Tb-€84, no breakfast, non-smoking rooms, lots of stairs with no elevator, pay Internet access, Canuda 4, tel. & fax 933-013-545, www.hostalcampi.com, reservas@hostalcampi.com, friendly Margarita and Nando).

$ Hostal Maldá rents the best cheap beds I found in the old center. With 25 rooms above a small shopping mall near the cathedral, it's a time-warp—quiet and actually charming—but does not take reservations (though you can try calling a day before). It generally remains full through the summer, but it's worth a shot (S-€15, D-€30, T-€45, lots of stairs with no elevator, 100 yards up Carrer del Pi from delightful Plaça Sant Josep Oriol, Carrer del Pi 5, tel. 933-173-002). Good-natured Aurora doesn't speak English, but Delfi, who works only half the year, does.

Youth Hostels in the Center of Town

A wonderful chain of well-run and centrally located youth hostels provides €20–26 dorm beds in 4- to 14-bed coed rooms with €2 sheets and towels, free Internet access, Wi-Fi, breakfast, lockers (B.Y.O. lock, or buy one here), and plenty of opportunities to meet other backpackers. They're open 24 hours but aren't party hostels, so they enforce quiet after 23:00. Visit their websites to choose the neighborhood you like: Eixample, Barri Gòtic, or near the beach.

$ Centric Point Hostel is a huge new place renting 430 cheap beds at what must be the best address in Barcelona (bar, kitchen, Passeig de Gràcia 33, tel. 932-151-796, fax 932-461-552, www.centricpointhostel.com). See map on page 1138.

$ Gothic Point Hostel rents 150 beds in the trendy Ribera district a block from the Picasso Museum (roof terrace, Carrer Vigatans 5, tel. 932-687-808, www.gothicpoint.com). See map on page 1115.

$ Sea Point Hostel has 70 beds on the beach nearby (Plaça del Mar 4, tel. 932-247-075, www.seapointhostel.com). See map on page 1134.

In the Eixample

For an uptown, boulevard-like neighborhood, sleep in the Eixample, a 10-minute walk from the Ramblas action.

$$ Hotel Granvía, filling a palatial 1870s mansion, offers Botticelli and chandeliers in the public rooms; a sprawling, peaceful sun patio; and 54 spacious, comfy rooms. Its salon is plush and royal, making the hotel an excellent value for romantics (Sb-€80, Db-€135 or €110 July–Aug, Tb-€150, for best rates mention my name when you reserve directly by phone or email—not on their website, breakfast-€11, request a quiet room if street noise bothers you, non-smoking, air-con, elevator, free Internet access and Wi-Fi, Gran Via de les Corts Catalanes 642, tel. 933-181-900, fax 933-189-997, www.nnhotels.com, hgranvia@nnhotels.com, Juan works the morning shift).

$$ Hotel Continental Palacete, with 19 rooms, fills a 100-year-old chandeliered mansion. With flowery wallpaper and cheap but fancy furniture under ornately gilded stucco, it's gaudy in the city of Gaudí. But it's also friendly, clean, quiet, and well-located. Guests have unlimited access to the extravagant, "cruise-inspired" fruit, veggie, and drink buffet—worth factoring into your comparison-shopping (Sb-€97, Db-€132, €35–45 more for bigger and brighter view rooms, extra bed-€45, prices include breakfast and tax, non-smoking, air-con, Internet access and Wi-Fi, 2 blocks north of Plaça de Catalunya at corner of Carrer Diputació, Rambla de Catalunya 30, tel. 934-457-657, fax 934-450-050, www.hotelcontinental.com, palacete@hotelcontinental.com).

$ Hostal Residencia Neutral, with a classic Eixample address and 28 very basic rooms, is a family-run time-warp and a fine value (tiny S-€35, Ds-€60, Db-€65, Ts-€75, Tb-€80, Qs-€80, Qb-€85, €8 continental breakfast in pleasant breakfast room, request a back room to avoid street noise, thin walls, fans, elevator, elegantly located 2 blocks north of Gran Via at Rambla de Catalunya 42, tel. 934-876-390, fax 934-876-848, hostalneutral@arrakis.es, owner Ramón, animated Lino works the night shift).

$ Hotel Ginebra is minimal, clean, and quiet considering its central location. The Herrera family rents 12 rooms in a dated apartment building overlooking the main square (Db-€70, or €80 June–Aug, extra bed-€15, breakfast-€3, air-con, elevator, Rambla

Hotels and Restaurants in Barcelona's Eixample

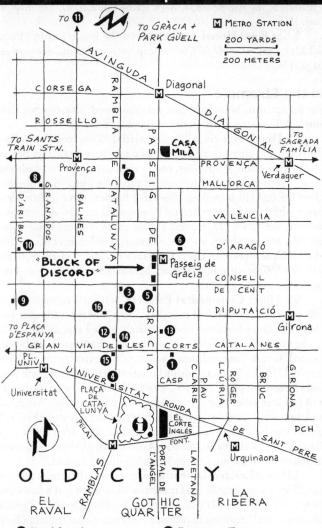

1. Hotel Granvía
2. Hotel Continental Palacete
3. Hostal Residencia Neutral
4. Hotel Ginebra
5. Centric Point Hostel
6. La Rita Restaurant
7. La Bodegueta
8. Restaurante la Palmera
9. Restaurant Flauta
10. Rest. de Degustacio Cincsentits
11. To Hofmann
12. El Racó
13. "Qu Qu" Quasi Queviures
14. Ciudad Condal Cerveceria
15. La Tramoia
16. Somnio Hostel

de Catalunya 1/3, tel. 933-171-063, www.hotelginebra.net, info @hotelginebra.net, Juan speaks English).

$ Somnio Hostel, an innovative new place run by a pair of American expats, has both dorm beds and private rooms (dorm bed-€23, S-€40, D-€72, Db-€80, Carrer de la Diputació 251, tel. 932-725-308, www.somniohostels.com, info@somniohostels.com).

Eating

Barcelona, the capital of Catalan cuisine—featuring seafood— offers a tremendous variety of colorful eateries. Because of their common struggles, Catalans seem to have an affinity for Basque culture—so you'll find a lot of Basque tapas places here, too. Most of my listings are lively spots with a busy tapas scene at the bar, along with restaurant tables for *raciones*. A regional specialty is *pa amb tomaquet* (pah ahm too-MAH-kaht), bread topped with a mix of crushed tomato and olive oil.

I've listed mostly practical, characteristic, colorful, and affordable restaurants. My recommendations are grouped by neighborhood—along the Ramblas; in the Barri Gòtic; in the Ribera neighborhood; and in the Eixample—followed by some budget options scattered throughout the city. And for dessert, I've suggested "A Short, Sweet Walk" (at the end of this section). The city is thriving with trendy and chic new eateries, and foodies will do well to get local advice or explore the Ribera area for a fine dinner. Many restaurants close in August (or July), when the owners take a vacation. It's deadly to your Barcelona experience to eat too early— if a place feels touristy, come back later and it may be a thriving local favorite.

Along the Ramblas
Within a few steps of the Ramblas, you'll find handy lunch places, an inviting market hall, a slew of vegetarian options, and a giant tapas bar.

Lunching Simply yet Memorably near the Ramblas
While these places are enjoyable for a lunch break between your Ramblas sightseeing, many are also open for dinner. For locations, see the map on page 1142.

Taverna Basca Irati serves 40 kinds of hot and cold Basque *pintxos* for €1.70 each. These are open-faced sandwiches—like sushi on bread. Muscle in through the hungry local crowd. Get an empty plate from the waiter, and then help yourself. Every few minutes, a waiter prances proudly by with a platter of new, still-warm munchies. Grab one as they pass by...it's addictive. You pay on the honor system: You're charged by the number of toothpicks left on your plate when you're done. Wash it down with €2–3 glasses of Rioja (full-bodied red wine), Txakolí (sprightly Basque white wine), or *sidra* (apple wine) poured from on high to add oxygen and bring out the flavor (daily 11:00–24:00, a block off the Ramblas, behind arcade at Carrer Cardenal Casanyes 15, Metro: Liceu, tel. 933-023-084).

Restaurant Elisabets is a happy little neighborhood eatery packed with antique radios and popular with locals for its "home-cooked," three-course €10 lunch special. Stop by for lunch, survey what those around you are enjoying, and order what looks best (Mon–Sat 7:30–23:00, closed Sun, lunch special served 13:00–16:00, otherwise only €3 tapas—not full meals, 2 blocks west of Ramblas on far corner of Plaça Bonsucces at Carrer Elisabets 2, tel. 933-175-826, run by Pilar).

Café Granja Viader is a quaint time-capsule place, family-run since 1870. They boast about being the first dairy business to bottle and distribute milk in Spain. This feminine-feeling place—specializing in baked and dairy delights, toasted sandwiches, and light meals—is ideal for a traditional breakfast. Or indulge your sweet tooth: Try a glass of *orxata* (or *horchata*—*chufa* nut milk, summer only), *llet mallorquina* (Majorca-style milk with cinnamon, lemon, and sugar), *crema catalana* (crème brûlée, their specialty), or *suis* ("Swiss"—hot chocolate with a snowcap of whipped cream). *Mel y mato* is fresh cheese with honey...very Catalan. It's a block off the Ramblas behind El Carme church (Tue–Sat 9:00–13:45 & 17:00–20:45, Mon 17:00–20:45 only, closed Sun, Xucla 4, tel. 933-183-486).

Picnics: Shoestring tourists buy groceries at **El Corte Inglés** (Mon–Sat 10:00–22:00, closed Sun, supermarket in basement, Plaça de Catalunya) and **Carrefour Express supermarket** (Mon–Sat 10:00–22:00, closed Sun, Ramblas 113).

In and near La Boquería Market

Try eating at La Boquería market at least once (#91 on the Ramblas). Like all farmers markets in Europe, this place is ringed by colorful, good-value eateries. Lots of stalls sell fun take-away food—especially fruit salads and fresh-squeezed fruit juices. There are several good bars around the market busy with shoppers munching at the counter (breakfast, tapas all day, coffee). The market, and most of the eateries listed here (unless noted), are open Monday through Saturday from 8:00 until 20:00 (though things get very quiet after about 16:00) and closed on Sunday.

Pinotxo Bar is just to the right as you enter the market. It's a great spot for coffee, breakfast (spinach tortillas, or whatever's cooking with toast), or tapas. Fun-loving Juan and his family are La Boquería fixtures. Grab a stool across the way to sip your drink with people-watching views. Have a Chucho?

Kiosko Universal is popular for its great prices on wonderful fish dishes. As you enter the market from the Ramblas, it's all the way to the left on the first alley. If you see people waiting, ask who's last in line *("¿El último?")*. You'll eat immersed in the spirit of the market (€13 fixed-price lunches with different fresh-fish options from 12:00–16:00, better before 12:30 but always packed, tel. 933-178-286).

Restaurant la Gardunya, at the back of the market, offers tasty meat and seafood meals made with fresh ingredients bought directly from the market (€13 fixed-price lunch includes wine and bread, €16 three-course dinner specials don't include wine, €10–20 à la carte dishes, Mon–Sat 13:00–16:00 & 20:00–24:00, closed Sun, mod seating indoors or outside watching the market action, Carrer Jerusalem 18, tel. 933-024-323).

Bar Terrace Restaurant Ra is a lively terrace immediately behind the market (at the right end of the big parking lot) with outdoor tables filled by young, trendy, happy eaters. At lunch they serve one great salad/pasta/wine meal for €11. If you feel like eating a big salad under an umbrella...this is the place (€9-15 à la carte dishes, daily 10:00–12:30 & 13:30–16:00 & 21:00–24:00, fancier menu at night, mobile 615-959-872).

Vegetarian Eateries near Plaça de Catalunya and the Ramblas

Biocenter, a Catalan soup-and-salad restaurant popular with local vegetarians, takes its cooking very seriously and feels a bit more like a real restaurant than most (€8–9.50 lunch specials include soup or salad and plate of the day, Mon–Sat 13:00–17:00, Thu–Sat also 20:00–23:00, closed Sun, 2 blocks off the Ramblas at Pintor Fortuny 25, Metro: Catalunya, tel. 933-014-583).

Juicy Jones is a tutti-frutti vegan/vegetarian eatery with colorful graffiti decor, a hip veggie menu (served downstairs), groovy laid-back staff, and a stunning array of fresh-squeezed juices served at the bar. Pop in for a quick €3 "juice of the day." For lunch, you can get the Indian-inspired €6 *thali* plate, the €6.25 plate of the day, or an €8.50 meal including one of the two plates plus soup or salad and dessert (daily 13:00–24:00, also tapas and salads, Carrer Cardenal Casanyes 7, tel. 933-024-330). There's another location on the other side of the Ramblas (Carrer Hospital 74).

Out at Sea, at the Bottom of the Ramblas

Tapasbar Maremagnum is a big, rollicking, sports-bar kind of tapas restaurant, great for large groups. It's a fun way to end your Ramblas walk, featuring breezy harbor views and good local food with an emphasis on the sea. Go here not for the tapas, but to

Barcelona's Barri Gòtic Restaurants

THE EIXAMPLE

GRAN VIA DE LES CORTS CATALANES

PLAÇA UNIV.

Univ.

CARRER

RONDA UNIVERSITAT

BALMES

RAMBLA DE CATALUNYA

PASSEIG DE GRACIA

CARRER PELAI

BERGARA

RONDA

SANT PERE

VALLDON.

MONTAL

RAM. TALLERS

FGC TRAIN INFO

PLAÇA DE CATALUNYA

El Corte Inglés Dep.t Store

FONTANELLA

MACBA CONTEMP. ART MUSEUM

Catalunya M

ELIS. BONSUCCES

SANTA ANNA

PINTOR

XUCLA FORT.

CARME

SANTA ANNA

BERT.

CANUDA

DUC. VIC.

COMTAL

MONTSIÓ

S. P. ALT

BUS TO AIRPORT

CATALAN CONCERT HALL

S. P. BAIX

CULTURAL INFO PALAU DE LA VIRREINA

Liceu M

PORTAFER.

RISSA PL. NOVA

PL. MAURA

LA RIBERA

HOSP.

LA BOQUERIA MARKET

MIRO

CARD.

BOQUERIA

PETRITXOL

U. DEL PI

PALLA

AV. CATEDRAL

MARÈS MUSEUM

CATHEDRAL

SANT PAU

Liceu M

BANYS NOUS

PAL GEN.

TO PICASSO MUS.

LICEU OPERA HOUSE

FERRAN

PLAÇA S. JAUME

PLAÇA DE L'ANGEL

PRINCESA

NOU RAMBLA

PLAÇA REIAL

CITY HALL

DAG.

Jaume I M

PALAU GÜELL

ESCUDELLERS

PL. ORWELL

D. SOBRA

LLEDO

ARGENTERIA

L'ARC TEATRE

NOU SAN FRAN.

CODOLS

D'AVINYO

CAN. NOUS

TO S. MARIA D. MAR

MARITIME MUSEUM

Drassanes M

GIGNAS

AMPLE

MERCE

POST

CONS. MAR

TO BARCELONETA

CLAVE

PL. MED.

PASSEIG DE COLÒM

COLUMBUS MONUMENT

MOLL DE BOSCH / ALSINA / LA FUSTA

HARBOR

GOLONDRINAS CRUISES

RAMBLA DE MAR

to MAREMAGNUM

TO BLOCK OF DISCORD & CASA MILÀ

RAMBLAS

M METRO STATION

B BUS STOP

200 YARDS

200 METERS

BARCELONA

Restaurant Key

1. Taverna Basca Irati
2. Restaurant Elisabets
3. Café Granja Viader
4. Supermarket
5. La Boquería Market Eateries
6. Biocenter Veggie Rest.
7. Juicy Jones
8. To Tapasbar Maremagnum
9. Café de l'Academia
10. La Crema Canela
11. La Fonda
12. Les Quinze Nits
13. La Dolça Herminia
14. Carrer de la Mercè Tapas Bars
15. Casa Colomina
16. Granja La Pallaresa
17. Fargas Chocolate Shop

make the Maremagnum scene (daily 11:00–24:00, a 10-minute stroll past the Columbus Monument straight out the dock on Moll d'Espanya, tel. 932-258-180).

In the Barri Gòtic

These eateries populate Barcelona's atmospheric Gothic Quarter, near the cathedral. Choose between a sit-down meal at a restaurant, or a string of very old-fashioned tapas bars.

Dining (Real Restaurants) in the Barri Gòtic

Café de l'Academia is a delightful place on a pretty square tucked away in the heart of the Barri Gòtic—but patronized mainly by the neighbors. They serve "honest cuisine" from the market with Catalan roots. The candlelit, air-conditioned interior is rustic yet elegant, with soft jazz, flowers, and modern art. And if you want to eat outdoors on a convivial, mellow square...this is it (€10–12 first courses, €12–15 second courses, fixed-price lunch for €10 at the bar or €14 at a table, Mon–Fri 13:30–16:00 & 20:30–23:30, closed Sat–Sun, near the City Hall square, off Carrer de Jaume I up Carrer Dagueria at Carrer Lledo 1, tel. 933-198-253).

Popular Chain Restaurants: Barcelona enjoys a chain of several bright, modern restaurants, all with different names. These five are a hit for their modern, artfully presented Spanish and Mediterranean cuisine, crisp ambience, and unbeatable prices. Because of their three-course €9 lunches and €16–20 dinners (both with wine), all are crowded with locals and in-the-know tourists (all open daily 13:00–15:45 & 20:30–23:30, unless otherwise noted). My favorite of the bunch is **La Crema Canela,** which feels cozier than the others and is the only one that takes reservations (30 yards north of Plaça Reial at Passatge de Madoz 6, tel. 933-182-744). The rest are notorious for long lines at the door—arrive 30 minutes before opening, or be prepared to wait. The next two (along with

La Crema Canela) are within a block of the Plaça Reial, and the third is near the Catalan Concert Hall: **La Fonda** (Carrer dels Escudellers 10, tel. 933-017-515—as this is very close to a seedy stretch of street, approach it from the Ramblas rather than from Plaça Reial); **Les Quinze Nits** (on Plaça Reial at #6—you'll see the line, tel. 933-173-075); and **La Dolça Herminia** (2 blocks toward Ramblas from Catalan Concert Hall at Carrer de les Magdalenes 27, tel. 933-170-676). The fifth restaurant in the chain, **La Rita,** is described later under "Restaurants in the Eixample."

Tapas on Carrer de la Mercè in the Barri Gòtic

Barcelona boasts great *tascas*—colorful local tapas bars. Get small plates (for maximum sampling) by asking for "tapas," not the bigger *"raciones."* Glasses of *vino tinto* go for about €0.50. While trendy uptown restaurants are safer, better-lit, and come with English menus and less grease, these places will stain your journal. The neighborhood's dark, the regulars are rough-edged, and you'll get a glimpse of a crusty Barcelona from before the affluence hit. Try *pimientos de padrón*—Russian roulette with peppers that are lightly fried in oil and salted...only a few are jalapeño-spicy. At the cider bars, it's traditional to order *queso de cabrales* (a traditional, very moldy blue cheese) and spicy chorizo (sausage)...ideally prepared *al diablo* ("devil-style")—soaked in wine, then flambéed at your table.

From the bottom of the Ramblas (near the Columbus Monument), hike east along Carrer Clave. Then follow the small street that runs along the right side of the church (Carrer de la Mercè), stopping at the *tascas* that look fun. For a montage of edible memories, wander Carrer de la Mercè west to east and consider these spots, stopping wherever looks most inviting. I've listed ye olde dives, but there are many trendy places here as well. Most of these places close down around 23:00.

La Pulpería (at #16), with a bit less character than the others, eases you into the scene with fried fish, octopus, and *patatas bravas,* all with Galician Ribeiro wine. A few steps down the street, at **Casa del Molinero** (#13), you can sauté your chorizo *al diablo*. It's great with *pa amb tomaquet* (tomato bread). Farther down at the corner (#28), **La Plata** keeps things wonderfully simple, serving extremely cheap plates of sardines (€1.70), little salads (€1.50), and small glasses of keg wine (less than €1). **Tasca el Corral** (#17) serves mountain favorites from northern Spain by the half-*ración* (see their list), such as *queso de cabrales* and chorizo *al diablo* with *sidra* (apple wine sold by the €5 bottle). **Sidrería Tasca La Socarrena** (#21) offers hard cider from Asturias in €5 bottles with *queso de cabrales* and chorizo. At the end of Carrer de la Mercè, **Cerveceria Vendimia** slings tasty clams and mussels (hearty *raciones* for €4–6 a plate—they don't do smaller portions, so order sparingly). Sit at the bar and point to what looks good. Their *pulpo* (octopus) is more expensive and is the house specialty. Carrer Ample and Carrer Gignas, the streets parallel to Carrer de la Mercè inland, have more refined bar-hopping possibilities.

In the Ribera District, near the Picasso Museum

La Ribera, the hottest neighborhood in town, sparkles with eclectic and trendy as well as subdued and classy little restaurants hidden in the small lanes surrounding the Church of Santa Maria del Mar. While I've listed a few well-established tapas bars that are great for light meals, to really dine, simply wander around for 15 minutes and pick the place that tickles your gastronomic fancy. I think anyone saying they know what's best in this area is kidding themselves—it's changing too fast and the choices are too personal. One thing's for sure: There are a lot of talented and hardworking restaurateurs with plenty to offer. Consider starting your evening off with a glass of fine wine at one of the *enotecas* on the square facing the Church of Santa Maria del Mar. Sit back and admire the pure Catalan Gothic architecture. My first four listings are all on the main drag, Carrer de l'Argenteria. For locations, see the map on page 1115.

Sagardi offers a wonderful array of Basque goodies—tempting *pinchos* and *montaditos* at €1.70 each—along its huge bar. Ask for a plate and graze (just take whatever looks good). You can sit on the square with your plunder for €0.50 per tapa extra. Wash it down with Txakolí, a Basque white wine poured from the spout of a huge wooden barrel into a glass as you watch. When you're done, they'll count your toothpicks to tally your bill (daily 12:00–24:00, Carrer de l'Argenteria 62–64, tel. 933-199-993).

Sagardi Euskal Taberna, hiding behind the thriving Sagardi tapas bar (described above), is a mod, rustic, and minimalist woody restaurant committed to serving Basque T-bone steaks and grilled specialties with only the best ingredients. Crisp and friendly service and a big open kitchen with sizzling grills contribute to the ambience. Reservations are smart (€10–15 first courses, €15–25 second courses, plan on €45 for dinner, daily 13:00–16:00 & 20:00–24:00, Carrer de l'Argenteria 62, tel. 933-199-993).

Taller de Tapas ("Tapas Workshop") is an upscale, trendier tapas bar and restaurant that dishes up well-presented, sophisticated morsels and light meals in a medieval-stone yet mod setting. Pay 10 percent more to sit on the square. Elegant but a bit stuffy, it's favored by local office workers who aren't into the Old World Gothic stuff. Four plates will fill a hungry diner for about €20 (Mon–Sat 8:30–24:00, Sun 12:00–24:00, Carrer de l'Argenteria 51, tel. 932-688-559).

El Xampanyet, a colorful family-run bar with a fun-loving staff (Juan Carlos, his mom, and the man who may be his father), specializes in tapas and anchovies. Don't be put off by the seafood from a tin...Catalans like it this way. A *sortido* (assorted plate) of *carne* (meat) or *pescado* (fish) with *pa amb tomaquet* (bread with crushed-tomato spread) makes for a fun meal. While it's filled with tourists during the sightseeing day, this is a local favorite after dark. The scene is great but—especially during busy times—it's tough without Spanish skills. When I asked about the price, Juan Carlos said, "Who cares? The ATM is just across the street." Plan on spending €20 for a meal with wine (same price at bar or table, Tue–Sat 12:00–16:00 & 19:00–23:30, Sun 12:00–16:00 only, closed Mon, a half-block beyond the Picasso Museum at Montcada 22, tel. 933-197-003).

In the Eixample

The people-packed boulevards of the Eixample (Passeig de Gràcia and Rambla de Catalunya) are lined with appetizing eateries featuring breezy outdoor seating. Choose between a real restaurant or an upscale tapas bar. For locations, see the map on page 1138.

Restaurants in the Eixample

La Rita is a fresh and dressy little restaurant serving Catalan cuisine near the Block of Discord. Their lunches (three courses with wine for €8, served Mon–Fri from 13:00–15:45) and dinners (€15, à la carte, daily 20:30–23:30) are a great value. Like its four sister restaurants—described earlier, under "Dining (Real Restaurants) in the Barri Gòtic"—it takes no reservations and its prices attract long lines, so arrive just before the doors open...or wait (a block from Metro: Passeig de Gràcia, near corner of Carrer de Pau Claris and Carrer Arago at Arago 279, tel. 934-872-376).

La Bodegueta is an unbelievably atmospheric below-street-level bodega serving hearty wines, homemade vermouth, *anchoas* (anchovies), tapas, and *flautas*—sandwiches made with flute-thin baguettes. Its daily €10.50 lunch special of three courses with wine is served 13:00–16:00. A long block from Gaudí's Casa Milà, this makes a fine sightseeing break (Mon–Sat 8:00–24:00, Sun 19:00–24:00, at intersection with Provenza, Rambla de Catalunya 100, Metro: Diagonal, tel. 932-154-894).

Restaurante la Palmera serves a mix of Catalan, Mediterranean, and French cuisine in an elegant yet smoky room with bottle-lined walls. The smoke keeps out the tourists. This place offers great food, service, and value—for me, a very special meal in Barcelona. They have three zones: the classic main room, a more forgettable adjacent room, and a few outdoor tables. I like the classic room. Reservations are smart (€10 plates, creative €14 six-plate *degustation* lunch, Tue–Sat 13:00–15:45 & 20:30–23:15, closed Sun–Mon, Enric Granados 57, at the corner with Mallorca, tel. 934-532-338).

Restaurant Flauta fills two floors with enthusiastic eaters (I like the ground floor best). It's fresh and modern, with a fun, no-stress menu featuring €5 small plates, creative €4 flauta sandwiches, and a €10 three-course lunch deal including a drink. Good €2.30 wines by the glass are listed on the blackboard. This is a place to order high on the menu for a fine, moderately priced meal (Mon–Sat 13:00–24:00, closed Sun, fun-loving and helpful staff recommends the fried vegetables, no reservations possible, just off Via Diputació at Aribau 23, tel. 933-237-038).

Restaurant de Degustacio Cincsentits ("Taste Treats for the Five Senses"), with only about 30 seats, is my gourmet recommendation. It's a chic, minimal, smoke-free place where all the attention goes to the fine service and elegantly presented dishes. It's run by Catalans who lived in Canada (so there's absolutely no language barrier) and serve avant-garde cuisine inspired by Catalan traditions and ingredients. Their €65 *degustation menu* is an unforgettable extravaganza. Reservations are required (Tue–Sat 13:30–15:00 & 20:30–23:00, Mon 13:30–15:00 only, closed Sun, near Carrer d'Aragó at Aribau 58, tel. 933-239-490).

El Racó is a local favorite for "creative Mediterranean cuisine"—pasta, pizza, crêpes, and salads (about €6–9 each) in a modern, lively, cavernous-but-bright, air-conditioned setting (daily 13:00–24:00, Rambla de Catalunya 25, tel. 933-175-688).

A Bit Farther Out: **Hofmann** is a renowned cooking school with an excellent if pricey restaurant serving modern Mediterranean market cuisine. Dress up and dine in intimate rooms papered with photos of famous patrons. The four-course, €39 lunches are made up of just what the students are working on that day—so there's no choice (watch the students as they cook). Dinners can easily cost twice as much (à la carte). Save room (and euros) for the incredible desserts. Reserve long in advance, because locals love this place (Mon–Fri 13:30–15:15 & 21:00–23:15, closed Sat–Sun and Aug, 4 blocks northwest of Casa Milà at La Granada del Penedès 14-16, tel. 932-187-165, www.hofmann-bcn.com).

Fancy Tapas Bars in the Eixample

Many trendy and touristic tapas bars in Eixample offer a cheery welcome and slam out the appetizers. These three are my favorites.

Quasi Queviures ("**Qu Qu**" for short) serves upscale tapas, sandwiches, or the whole nine yards—classic food served fast from a fun menu with modern decor and a high-energy sports-bar ambience. It's bright, clean, and not too crowded. Walk through their enticing kitchen to get to the tables in back. Committed to developing a loyal following, they claim, "We fertilize our local customers with daily specialties" (€2–3 tapas, €5 dinner salads, €7 plates, prices 17 percent higher on the terrace, daily 8:00–24:00, between Gran Via and Via Diputació at Passeig de Gràcia 24, tel. 933-174-512).

Ciudad Condal Cerveceria brags that it serves the best *montaditos* (€2–3 little open-faced sandwiches) and beers in Barcelona. It's an Eixample favorite, with an elegant bar and tables plus good seating out on the Rambla de Catalunya for all that people-watching action. It's classier than Qu Qu and packed after 21:00, when you'll likely need to put your name on a list and wait. While it has no restaurant-type menu, the list of tapas and *montaditos* is easy, fun, and comes with a great variety (including daily specials). This place is a cut above your normal tapas bar, but with reasonable prices (most tapas around €4–5, daily until 24:00, facing the intersection of Gran Via and Rambla de Catalunya at Rambla de Catalunya 18, tel. 933-181-997).

La Tramoia, at the opposite corner, serves piles of cheap *montaditos* and tapas at its ground-floor bar and at nice tables inside and out. If Ciudad Condal Cerveceria is jammed up, you're more likely to find a seat here. The brasserie-style restaurant upstairs bustles with happy local eaters enjoying grilled meats (€6–10 plates), but I'd stay downstairs for the €4 tapas (open daily, also facing the intersection of Gran Via and Rambla de Catalunya at Rambla de Catalunya 15, tel. 934-123-634).

Budget Options Around Town

Sandwiches: Bright, clean, and inexpensive sandwich shops proudly hold the cultural line against the fast-food invasion hamburger-izing the rest of Europe. Catalan sandwiches are made to order with crunchy French bread. Rather than butter, locals prefer *tomaquet* (a spread of crushed tomatoes). You'll see two big local chains (Pans & Company and Bocatta) everywhere, but these serve mass-produced McBaguettes ordered from a multilingual menu. I've had better luck with hole-in-the-wall sandwich shops—virtually as numerous as the chains—where you can see exactly what you're getting.

Kebabs: Kebab places are a good, super-cheap standby. A favorite, **Maoz Falafel,** lets you create the falafel of your dreams for €4 (just off the City Hall square at Plaça de Sant Jaume 7).

A Short, Sweet Walk

Let me propose this three-stop dessert (or, since these places close well before the traditional Barcelona dinnertime, a late-afternoon snack). You'll try a refreshing glass of *orxata*, munch some *churros con chocolate*, and visit a fine *xocolateria*, all within a three-minute walk of each other in the Barri Gòtic just off the Ramblas. Start at the corner of Carrer Portaferrissa midway down the Ramblas. For the best atmosphere, begin your walk at about 18:00. For locations, see the map on page 1142.

Orxata at **Casa Colomina:** Walk down Carrer Portaferrissa to #8 (on the right). Casa Colomina, founded in 1908, specializes in homemade *torrons*—a variation of nougat made with almond, honey, and sugar, brought to Spain by the Moors 1,200 years ago. Three different kinds are sold in big €10 slabs: *blando, duro*, and *yema*—soft, hard, and yolk (€2 smaller chunks also available). In the summer, the shop also sells ice cream and the refreshing *orxata* (or *horchata*—a drink made from the *chufa* nut). Order a glass and ask to see and eat a *chufa* nut (a.k.a. earth almond or tiger nut; Mon–Sat 10:00–20:30, Sun 12:30–20:30, tel. 933-122-511).

Churros con Chocolate at **Granja La Pallaresa:** Continue down Carrer Portaferrissa, taking a right at Carrer Petrixol to this fun-loving *xocolateria*. Older, elegant ladies gather here for the Spanish equivalent of tea time—dipping their greasy *churros* into pudding-thick cups of hot chocolate (€4.10 for five *churros con chocolate*, Mon–Fri 9:00–13:00 & 16:00–21:00, Sat–Sun 9:00–13:00 & 17:00–21:00, Carrer Petritxol 11, tel. 933-022-036).

Homemade Chocolate at Fargas: For your last stop, head for the ornate Fargas chocolate shop (Mon–Fri 9:30–13:30 & 16:00–20:00, Sat 10:00–14:00 & 16:00–20:00, closed Sun; continue down Carrer Petritxol to the square, hook left through the two-part square, and then left up Carrer del Pi; it's on the corner of Portaferrissa and Carrer del Pi, tel. 933-020-342). Since the 19th century, gentlemen with walking canes have dropped by here for their chocolate fix. Founded in 1827, this is one of the oldest and most traditional chocolate places in Barcelona. If they're not too busy, ask to see the old chocolate mill *("¿Puedo ver el molino?")* to the right of the counter. They sell even tiny quantities (one little morsel) by the weight—don't be shy. A delicious chunk of the crumbly, semi-sweet house specialty costs €0.45 (tray by the mill). The tempting bonbons in the window cost about €1 each.

Connections

From Barcelona by Train: Unless otherwise noted, all of these trains depart from the Sants station; however, some trains also stop at other stations more convenient to the downtown tourist zone: França station, Passeig de Gràcia, or Plaça de Catalunya. Figure out if your train stops at these stations (and board there) to save yourself the trip to Sants.

The **AVE train to Madrid** is faster than flying, when you consider that you're zipping from downtown to downtown. The train departs frequently (2/hr) in the morning, and about hourly in the afternoon and evening. The nonstop train is a little more expensive (€125, 3 hrs) than the slightly slower train that makes a few stops and adds about a half-hour (€106, 3.5 hrs). Regular reserved AVE tickets can be pre-purchased at www.renfe.es and picked up at the station. If you have a railpass, you'll pay only a reservation fee of €25 for first class, which includes a meal (€15 second class, buy at any train station in Spain). Passholders can't reserve online through RENFE but you can make the reservation at www.raileurope.com for delivery before leaving the US ($17 in second class, $40 in first class).

By Train to: Sevilla (3/day—1 fast, 6.5 hrs, €129; 1 slow, 12 hrs, €58; and 1 night train, 10 hrs, €85), **Granada** (1/day Wed, Fri, and Sun only, 11.5 hrs, €57; also 1 night train/day, 12 hrs, €58), **Lisbon** (no direct trains, head to Madrid and then catch night train to Lisbon, 17 hrs, about €130), **Nice** (1/day via Montpelier, about €100; cheaper connections possible with multiple changes including Cerbère), **Avignon** (5/day, less on weekends, 6–9 hrs, about €40, or about €65 for change in Montpellier), **Paris** (3/day, 9 hrs, 1–2 changes; 1 night train/day, 12 hrs, about €130, or €45 with railpass, reservation mandatory). Train info: tel. 902-240-202, www.renfe.es.

By Bus to: Madrid (14/day, 8 hrs, €27—a fraction of the AVE train price, departs from Nord bus station at Metro: Arc de Triomf on line 1, bus info tel. 902-260-606, Alsa bus company tel. 902-422-242). For bus schedules, see www.barcelonanord.com.

By Plane: Check the reasonable flights from Barcelona to Sevilla or Madrid. Vueling is Iberia's most popular discount airline (e.g., Barcelona–Madrid flights as low as €30 if booked in advance, tel. 902-333-933, www.vueling.com). Iberia (tel. 902-400-500, www.iberia.com) and Air Europa (tel. 902-401-501 or 932-983-907, www.aireuropa.com) offer €80 flights to Madrid. Also, for flights to other parts of Europe, consider British Airways (tel. 902-111-333, www.britishairways.com), easyJet (tel. 902-299-992, www.easyjet.com), and Ryanair (www.ryanair.com). Most use Barcelona's **El Prat de Llobregat Airport** (tel. 902-404-704), but Ryanair uses an airport 60 miles away called **Girona-Costa Brava** (tel. 972-186-600). Information on both airports can be found on the official Spanish airport website, www.aena.es.

For details on getting between either airport and downtown Barcelona, see "Arrival in Barcelona—By Plane," page 1095.

…arket. Lively Madrid bustles through street-singing, bar-hopping, and people-watching evenings—give anyway later a hour of youth.

Planning Your Time

MADRID

Today's Madrid is upbeat and vibrant, still enjoying a post-Franco renaissance. You'll feel it. Even the living-statue street performers have a twinkle in their eyes.

Madrid is the hub of Spain. This modern capital—Europe's highest, at more than 2,000 feet—has a population of 3.2 million. Like its people, the city is relatively young. In 1561, King Philip II decided to move the capital of his empire from Toledo to Madrid. One hundred years ago, Madrid had only 400,000 people—so the majority of today's Madrid is modern sprawl surrounding an intact, easy-to-navigate historic core.

To support their bid to host the 2012 Olympics, Madrid began some massive city-improvement building projects. Although they lost out, the construction continues as if they'd won. Politicians who back these projects have been rewarded both financially (locals claim some corrupt officials are getting kickbacks) and politically—residents love to see all the new squares, pedestrian streets, beltway tunnels, parks, and Metro stations popping up like wildflowers. As the city eyes another Olympics bid for 2016, construction won't let up soon. Madrid's ambitious improvement plans include the creation of a pedestrian street crossing the city from the Prado to the Royal Palace (the section from the Prado to Plaza Mayor has been completed) and a new macro-Metro station near Puerta del Sol (to accommodate a new, efficient commuter-train line). By installing posts to keep cars off sidewalks, making the streets safer after dark, and restoring old buildings, Madrid is working hard to make itself more livable...and fun to visit.

Tourists are the real winners. Dive headlong into the grandeur and intimate charm of Madrid. The lavish Royal Palace, with its gilded rooms and frescoed ceilings, rivals Versailles. The Prado has Europe's top collection of paintings. The city's huge Retiro Park invites you to take a shady siesta and hopscotch through a mosaic of lovers, families, skateboarders, pets walking their masters, and expert bench-sitters. Save time for Madrid's elegant shops and people-friendly pedestrian zones. On Sundays, cheer for the bull at a bullfight or bargain like mad at a mega-size flea market. Lively Madrid has enough street-singing, bar-hopping, and people-watching vitality to give any visitor a boost of youth.

Planning Your Time

Divide your time between Madrid's top three attractions: the Royal Palace (worth a half-day), the Prado Museum (also worth a half-day), and its bar-hopping contemporary scene. On a Sunday, consider allotting extra time for the flea market (year-round) and/or a bullfight (some Sundays Easter–mid-Oct, especially during San Isidro festival mid-May).

Madrid is worth two days on even the fastest trip. I'd spend them this way:

Day 1: Take a brisk, 20-minute good-morning-Madrid walk from Puerta del Sol to the Prado (from Puerta del Sol, walk three blocks south to Plaza del Ángel, then take the pedestrian walkway to the Prado along Huertas). Spend the rest of the morning at the Prado, then take an afternoon siesta in Retiro Park, or tackle modern art at the Centro de Arte Reina Sofía (Picasso's *Guernica*) and/or the Thyssen-Bornemisza Museum. Have dinner at 20:00, with tapas around Plaza Santa Ana.

Day 2: Follow my "Welcome to Madrid" self-guided walk (later in this chapter), tour the Royal Palace, and have lunch near Plaza Mayor. Your afternoon is free for other sights or shopping. Be out at the magic hour—before sunset—when beautifully lit people fill Madrid.

Note that many top sights are closed on Monday, including the Prado and the Thyssen-Bornemisza Museum; sights remaining open on Monday include the Royal Palace (open daily) and Centro de Arte Reina Sofía (closed Tue).

Orientation

Puerta del Sol marks the center of Madrid. No major sight is more than a 20-minute walk or a €4 taxi ride from this central square. The Royal Palace (to the west) and the Prado Museum and Retiro Park (to the east) frame Madrid's historic center. This zone can be covered on foot. Southwest of Puerta del Sol is a 17th-century district with the slow-down-and-smell-the-cobbles Plaza Mayor and memories of preindustrial Spain. North of Puerta del Sol

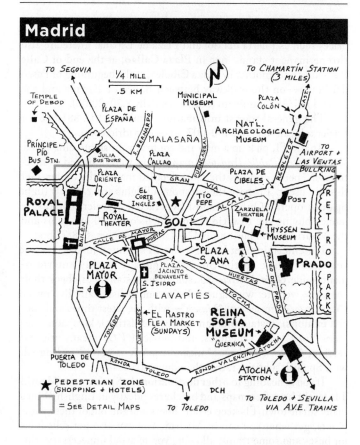

Madrid

TO SEGOVIA

¼ MILE
.5 KM

TEMPLE OF DEBOD

PRÍNCIPE PÍO BUS STN.

PLAZA DE ESPAÑA

JULIA BUS TOURS

MALASAÑA

S. BERNARDO

PLAZA CALLAO

MUNICIPAL MUSEUM

TO CHAMARTÍN STATION (3 MILES)

PLAZA COLÓN

NAT'L. ARCHAEOLOGICAL MUSEUM

CASTELLANA

RECOLETOS

TO AIRPORT + LAS VENTAS BULLRING

FUENCARRAL

PLAZA ORIENTE

GRAN VÍA

PLAZA DE CIBELES

ROYAL PALACE

EL CORTE INGLÉS

TÍO PEPE

SOL

ALCALÁ

ZARZUELA THEATER

POST

RETIRO PARK

ROYAL THEATER

CALLE DE MAYOR

BAILEN

POSTAS

THYSSEN MUSEUM

PLAZA S. ANA

PRADO

PASEO DEL PRADO

PLAZA MAYOR

PLAZA JACINTO BENAVENTE

S. ISIDRO

HUERTAS

LAVAPIÉS

TOLEDO

CURTIDORES

ATOCHA

EL RASTRO FLEA MARKET (SUNDAYS)

REINA SOFÍA MUSEUM "GUERNICA"

ATOCHA

PUERTA DE TOLEDO

RONDA

TOLEDO

RONDA VALENCIA

ATOCHA STATION

★ PEDESTRIAN ZONE (SHOPPING + HOTELS)

▢ = SEE DETAIL MAPS

DCH

TO TOLEDO

TO TOLEDO + SEVILLA VIA A.V.E. TRAINS

runs Calle de Gran Vía, and between the two are lively pedestrian shopping streets. Gran Vía, bubbling with shops and cinemas, leads to the modern Plaza de España. Between Puerta del Sol and the Atocha train station stretches the colorful, up-and-coming multiethnic Lavapiés district (see the "The Lavapiés District Tapas Crawl," page 1196).

Tourist Information

Madrid has five TIs: on **Plaza Mayor** (daily 9:30–20:30, air-con, limited free Internet access, tel. 915-881-636); near the **Prado Museum** (Mon–Sat 8:00–20:00, Sun 9:00–14:00, Duque de Medinaceli 2, behind Palace Hotel, tel. 914-294-951); at **Chamartín train station** (near track 19–20, Mon–Sat 8:00–20:00, Sun 9:00–14:00, tel. 913-159-976); at **Atocha train station** (in the AVE side, Mon–Sat 8:00–20:00, Sun 9:00–14:00, tel. 915-284-630); and at the **airport** (at Terminal 1 in arrival hall and at Terminal 4 at baggage claim, Mon–Sat 8:00–20:00, Sun 9:00–14:00, tel. 913-058-656).

MADRID

During the summer, small temporary stands pop up at touristed places such as Puerta del Sol and Plaza de España. There are also two permanent stands: one in **Plaza Callao,** at the end of Calle Preciados; and another in **Plaza Cibeles,** at the beginning of Paseo del Prado—on the walkway between Banco de España and the Town Hall/Ayuntamiento (both open daily 9:30–20:00).

The general tourist information number is 915-881-636 (or pricier toll call: tel. 902-100-007; www.esmadrid.com).

At any TI, pick up a map and confirm your sightseeing plans. The TI's free *Public Transport* map is very well designed to meet travelers' needs and has the most detailed map of the center. Get this and use it. TIs have the latest on bullfights and zarzuela (light Spanish opera). Only the most hyperactive travelers could save money buying the **Madrid Card,** which covers 40 museums and the Madrid Vision bus tour (€42/24 hrs, €55/48 hrs, €68/72 hrs).

For entertainment listings, the TI's printed material is not very good. Pick up the Spanish-language weekly entertainment guide *Guía del Ocio* (€1, sold at newsstands) or check their complete website, www.guiadelocio.com. It lists daily live music *("Conciertos"),* museums *("Museos"*—with the latest times and special exhibits), restaurants (an exhaustive listing), kids' activities *("Los Niños"),* TV schedules, and movies *("V.O."* means original version, *"V.O. en inglés sub"* means a movie is played in English with Spanish subtitles rather than dubbed).

If you're heading to **other destinations in Spain,** some Madrid TIs might have free maps and brochures (ideally in English). Since many small-town TIs keep erratic hours and run out of these pamphlets, get what you can in Madrid. You can also get schedules for buses and some trains, allowing you to avoid unnecessary trips to the various stations. The TI's free and amazingly informative *Mapa de Comunicaciones España* is a road map of Spain that lists all the tourist offices and highway SOS numbers. (If they're out, ask for the route map sponsored by the Paradores hotel chain, the camping map, or the golf map.)

For tips on sightseeing, hotels, and more, visit www.madrid man.com, run with passion by American Scott Martin.

Arrival in Madrid

By Train

Madrid's two train stations, Chamartín and Atocha, are both on Metro lines with easy access to downtown Madrid. (For Atocha station, use the "Atocha RENFE" Metro stop; the stop named simply "Atocha" is farther from the station.) Chamartín handles most international trains and the AVE train to Segovia. Atocha generally covers southern Spain, as well as the AVE trains to Barcelona, Córdoba, Sevilla, and Toledo. Both stations offer long-distance

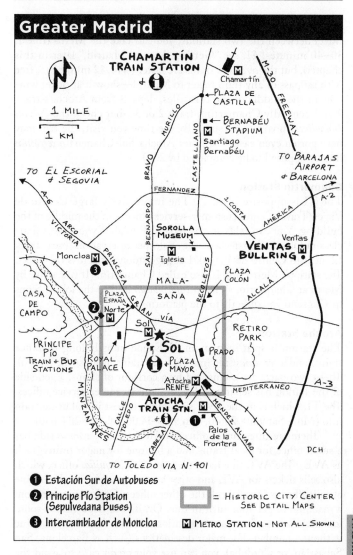

Greater Madrid

N

1 MILE
1 KM

CHAMARTÍN
TRAIN STATION

Chamartín

PLAZA DE
CASTILLA

BERNABÉU
STADIUM
Santiago
Bernabéu

M-30 FREEWAY

TO BARAJAS
AIRPORT
& BARCELONA

A-2

TO EL ESCORIAL
& SEGOVIA

A-6

ARCO
VICTORIA

FERNANDEZ

J. COSTA

AMÉRICA

MURILLO

BRAVO

CASTELLANO

SAN BERNARDO

SOROLLA
MUSEUM

Iglesia

Ventas

VENTAS
BULLRING

Moncloa M

3

PRINCESA

PLAZA
ESPAÑA

Norte M

2

GRAN VÍA

MALA-
SAÑA

RECOLETOS

PLAZA
COLÓN

ALCALÁ

CASA
DE
CAMPO

Sol M

SOL ★

RETIRO
PARK

PRÍNCIPE
PÍO
TRAIN & BUS
STATIONS

ROYAL
PALACE

PLAZA
MAYOR

PRADO

MANZANARES

CALLE
TOLEDO

Atocha M
RENFE

ATOCHA
TRAIN STN.

Atocha M

MEDITERRANEO

A-3

MENDEZ ALVARO

1

CABEZA

Palos
de la
Frontera

DCH

TO TOLEDO VIA N-401

1 Estación Sur de Autobuses

2 Príncipe Pío Station
(Sepulvedana Buses)

3 Intercambiador de Moncloa

☐ = HISTORIC CITY CENTER
SEE DETAIL MAPS

M METRO STATION - Not All Shown

MADRID

trains *(largo recorrido)* as well as smaller, local trains *(regionales* and *cercanías)* to nearby destinations.

Buying Tickets: You can buy tickets at the stations, at a travel agency, or online. Convenient travel agencies for buying tickets in Madrid include the El Corte Inglés Travel Agency at Atocha (Mon–Fri 7:00–22:00, Sat–Sun only for urgent arrangements, on ground floor of AVE side at the far end) and the El Corte Inglés department store at Puerta del Sol (see "Helpful Hints," later in this chapter).

Traveling Between Chamartín and Atocha Stations: To travel between the two stations, you can take the Metro (line 1, 30–40 minutes, €1, see "Getting Around Madrid," later in this chapter), but the *cercanías* trains are faster (6/hr, 12 min, €1.15, free with railpass or any train ticket to Madrid—show it at ticket window in the middle of the turnstiles, departs from Atocha's track 2 and generally Chamartín's track 2 or 3—but check the *Salidas Inmediatas* board to be sure). By the time you visit, the trip may have gotten even easier—a faster Atocha-Sol-Chamartín *cercanías* line is supposed to be completed by 2010.

Chamartín Station

The TI is opposite track 19. The impressively large Centro de Viajes/Travel Center customer-service office is in the middle of the building. You can relax in the Sala VIP Club if you have a first-class railpass and first-class seat or sleeper reservations (near track 12, next to Centro de Viajes). Luggage storage is across the street. The station's Metro stop is also called Chamartín. (If you arrive by Metro at Chamartín, signs to *Información* lead to the lobby. Signs to *Vías* send you directly to the platforms.)

Atocha Station

The station is split in two: an AVE side (mostly long-distance trains) and a *cercanías* side (mostly local trains, nearest the Metro). These two parts are connected by a corridor of shops. Each side of the station has separate schedules and customer-service offices. The TI, which is in the AVE side, offers tourist info, but no train info (Mon–Sat 9:00–20:00, Sun 9:00–14:00, tel. 915-284-630).

There are three ticket offices at Atocha: The *cercanías* side has a small office for local trains and a big one for major trains (such as AVE). The AVE side has a pleasant, airy *Taquillas* office, which also sells tickets for AVE and other long-distance trains. If the line at one office is long, check the other offices. Grab a number from a machine to get your turn in line. Or, if your departure is soon, look for "*Para hoy*" or your destination and wait directly in that line without a number. For major destinations (such as Barcelona, San Sebastián, or Córdoba), you can use your credit card to avoid the lines—look for the ATM-like touch-screen machines to the right of the entrance.

Atocha's **AVE side,** which is in the towering old-station building, is remarkable for the lush, tropical garden filling its grand hall. It has the slick AVE trains, other fast trains (Grandes Líneas), a pharmacy (daily 8:00–22:00), a cafeteria (daily 13:00–20:00), and the wicker-elegant Samarkanda restaurant (daily 13:30–16:00 & 21:00–24:00, tel. 915-309-746). Luggage storage *(consigna)* is below Samarkanda (Mon–Fri 6:00–22:20, Sat–Sun 6:30–22:20). In the departure lounge on the upper floor, TV monitors announce track numbers. For information, try the *Información* counter (daily 6:30–22:30), next to Centro Servicios AVE (which handles only AVE changes and problems). The *Atención al Cliente* office deals with problems on Grandes Líneas (daily 6:30–23:30). Also on the AVE side is the Club AVE/Sala VIP, a lounge reserved solely for AVE business-class travelers and for first-class ticket-holders or Eurailers with a first-class reservation (upstairs, past the security check on right; free drinks, newspapers, showers, and info service).

On the **cercanías side** of Atocha station, you'll find the local *cercanías* trains, *regionales* trains, some eastbound faster trains, and the "Atocha RENFE" Metro stop. The *Atención al Cliente* office in the *cercanías* section has information only on trains to destinations near Madrid.

The terrorist bombings of March 11, 2004, took place in Atocha and on local lines going into and out of the station. Security is understandably tight here. A 36-foot cylindrical glass memorial towers above on the street. Near where you exit the Atocha RENFE Metro, next to the car-rental offices, you can walk inside and under the cylinder to read the thousands of condolence messages in many languages (daily 10:00–20:00).

By Plane
For information on Madrid's Barajas Airport, see the end of this chapter.

Helpful Hints
Theft Alert: Be wary of pickpockets, anywhere, anytime. Areas of particular risk are Puerta del Sol (the central square), El Rastro (the flea market), Gran Vía (the paseo zone: Plaza del Callao to Plaza de España), the Ópera Metro station (or anywhere on the Metro), the airport, and any crowded streets. Assume a fight or any commotion is a scam to distract people about to become victims of a pickpocket. Wear your money belt. The small streets north of Gran Vía are particularly dangerous, even before nightfall. Muggings occur, but are rare. Victims of theft can call 902-102-112 for help (English spoken, once you get connected to a person).

Prostitution: Diverse by European standards, Madrid is spilling over with immigrants from South America, North Africa, and Eastern Europe. Many young women come here, fall on hard times, and end up on the streets. While it's illegal to make money from someone else selling sex (i.e., pimping), prostitutes get away with selling it directly on the street (€27, FYI). Calle de la Montera (leading from Puerta del Sol to Plaza Red de San Luis) is lined with what looks like a bunch of high-school girls skipping out of school for a cigarette break. Again, don't stray north of Gran Vía around Calle de la Luna and Plaza Santa María Soledad—while the streets may look inviting...this area is a meat-eating flower.

Embassies: The US Embassy is at Serrano 75 (tel. 915-872-200); the Canadian Embassy is at Nuñez de Balboa 35 (tel. 914-233-250).

One-Stop Shopping: The dominant local department store is **El Corte Inglés,** which takes up several huge buildings in the commercial pedestrian zone just off Puerta del Sol (Mon–Sat 10:00–22:00, Sun 11:00–21:00, navigate with the help of the info desk near the door of the main building—the tallest building with the biggest sign, Preciados 3, tel. 913-798-000). They give out fine, free Madrid maps. In the main building, you'll find two handy travel agencies (see listing at end of this section), a post office, and a supermarket with a fancy "Club del Gourmet" section in the basement. Across the street is its Librería branch—a huge bookstore and six floors of music and home electronics, with a box office for tickets to whatever's on in town. Locals figure you'll find anything you need at El Corte Inglés.

Internet Access: There are plenty of centrally located places to check your email. Ask at any *locutorio* call center, which often have a few computers and are generally the cheapest. Near Plaza Santa Ana (and great if you're waiting for the tapas-crawl action to heat up), **La Bolsa de Minutos** has plenty of fast terminals (€2/hr), disc-burning services, and helpful staff (daily 9:30–24:00, Calle Espoz y Mina 17, tel. 915-322-622). **BBIG** has more than 100 terminals, is non-smoking, and seats casual Internet surfers apart from noisy, intense gamers (daily 9:30–24:00, at the corner of Puerta del Sol and the street that connects it to Plaza Mayor, at Mayor 1—on the second floor above Sol Park casino, tel. 915-312-364). In a pinch, there's also the noisy, smoky **Zahara,** with its clunky coin-operated computers (daily 9:00–24:00, corner of Gran Vía and Mesoneros). If you'd like to simultaneously wash clothes and surf, see "Laundry," next page.

Phone Cards: You can buy cheap international phone cards at some newsstands, at Internet cafés, or at the easy-to-find *locutorio* call centers (but these are generally uncomfortable places to sit and talk). When choosing a phone card, remember that toll-free numbers start with 900, whereas 901 and 902 numbers can be expensive. Ask your hotel if they charge for the 900 number before making calls.

Bookstores: For books in English, try **FNAC Callao** (Calle Preciados 28, tel. 915-956-100), **Casa del Libro** (English on ground floor in back, Gran Vía 29, tel. 915-212-219), and **El Corte Inglés** (guidebooks and some fiction, in its Librería branch kitty-corner from main store, fronting Puerta del Sol—see earlier listing).

Laundry: Onda Blu will wash, dry, and fold your laundry (€5.50–8.50 depending on size of load, cheaper self-service also available, change machine, Internet access, Mon–Fri 9:30–22:00, Sat–Sun 10:30–19:00, León 3, east of Plaza Santa Ana, tel. 913-695-071, Ana).

Travel Agencies: The grand department store **El Corte Inglés** has two travel agencies (air and rail tickets, but not reservations for railpass-holders, €2 fee, on first and seventh floors, Mon–Sat 10:00–22:00, Sun 11:00–21:00, just off Puerta del Sol, tel. 913-798-000).

Getting Around Madrid

If you want to use Madrid's excellent public transit, my two best tips are these: Pick up and study the fine *Public Transit* map/flier (available at TIs), and take full advantage of the cheap 10-ride Metrobus ticket deal (see below).

By Metro: The city's broad streets can be hot and exhausting. A subway trip of even a stop or two saves time and energy. Madrid's Metro is simple, speedy, and cheap (€1/ride within zone A—which covers most of the city, but not trains out to the airport; runs 6:00–1:30 in the morning, www.metromadrid.es or www.ctm-madrid.es). The 10-ride Metrobus ticket can be shared by several travelers and works on both the Metro and buses (€7.40—or €0.74 per ride, sold at kiosks, tobacco shops, and in Metro). Insert your Metrobus ticket in the turnstile (it usually shows how many rides remain on it), then retrieve it as you pass through. Stations offer free maps *(Madrid by Underground)*, but they often run out in central locations. However, there are always plenty of maps and line stops posted in hallways and on the Metro trains. Navigate by Metro stops (shown on city maps). To transfer, follow signs to the next Metro line (numbered and color-coded). The names of the end stops are used to indicate directions. Green *salida* signs point to the exit. Using neighborhood maps and street signs to exit smartly can save lots of walking. And watch out for thieves.

By Bus: City buses, while not as easy as the Metro, can be useful (€1 tickets sold on bus, or €7.40 for a 10-ride Metrobus ticket—see above; bus maps at TI or info booth on Puerta del Sol, poster-size maps are usually posted at bus stops, buses run 6:00–24:00, much less frequent *Buho* buses run all night).

By Taxi: Madrid's 15,000 taxis are reasonably priced and easy to hail. Threesomes travel as cheaply by taxi as by Metro. A ride from the Royal Palace to the Prado costs about €4. After the €1.95

drop charge, the per-kilometer rate depends on the time: *Tarifa 1* (€0.92/kilometer) should be charged Mon–Sat 6:00–22:00; *Tarifa 2* (€1.06/kilometer) is valid after 22:00 and on Sundays and holidays. If your cabbie uses anything rather than *Tarifa 1* on weekdays (shown as an isolated "1" on the meter), you're being cheated. Rates can be higher if you go outside Madrid. Other legitimate charges include the €5.25 supplement for the airport, the €2.75 supplement for train or bus stations, and €13.50 per hour for waiting. Make sure the meter is turned on as soon as you get into the cab so the driver can't tack anything onto the official rate. If the driver starts adding up "extras," look for the sticker detailing all legitimate surcharges (which should be on the passenger window).

Tours

Madrid Vision Hop-On, Hop-Off Bus Tours—Madrid Vision offers two different hop-on, hop-off circuits of the city: historic and modern. Buy a ticket from the driver (€16/1 day, €21/2 days) and you can hop from sight to sight and route to route as you like, listening to a recorded English commentary along the way. Each route has about 15 stops and takes about 90 minutes, with buses departing every 10 or 20 minutes. The two routes intersect at the south side of Puerta del Sol and in front of Starbucks across from the Prado (daily 9:30–24:00 in summer, 10:00–19:00 in winter, tel. 917-791-888, www.madridvision.es).

LeTango Tours—Carlos Galvin, a Spaniard who speaks flawless English (and has led tours for my groups since 1998), and his wife from Seattle, Jennifer, offer private tours in Madrid and other parts of Spain. Carlos mixes a market walk in the historic center with a culinary-and-tapas crawl to get close to the Madrileños, their culture, and their food. His walk gives a fine three-hour orientation and introduction to the fascinating and tasty culture of Madrid, plus travel tips (€95 per person, 10 percent cash discount, includes tastes in the market and light tapas at the end, minimum 2 people, alcohol-free and gourmet versions available, family-friendly, price goes down with more people). They also offer guided visits to the Prado, Royal Palace, Toledo, Segovia, and El Escorial; self-guided tour packages all over Spain; and Madrid apartment rentals (tel. 913-694-752, mobile 661-752-458, www.letango.com, info @letango.com).

Private Guides—**Frederico and Cristina** are licensed local guides who lead city walks through the pedestrian streets of the historic core of Madrid. Fred, Cris, and their team offer an all-ages tour of the big museums, including the Royal Palace, the Prado, and the Reina Sofía, as well as a tapas tour. Or, if you're looking to get outside Madrid, consider their guided tour to surrounding towns (per-tour costs: Mon–Fri €160, Sat–Sun €190, 10 percent Rick Steves discount, prices don't include sight entry fees or food and drinks on the tapas tour, 3–5 hours, tel. & fax 913-102-974, mobile 649-936-222, www.spainfred.com, spainfred@gmail.com).

Inés Muñiz Martin is a good, licensed Madrileña guide who has led my tour groups (and individuals) through her hometown and the Prado for years. Inés also leads tours to nearby areas (such as El Escorial), and can customize a tour to your specific interests (€140 for up to 4 hours, €170 on weekends and holidays, these rates include discount for Rick Steves readers, transportation and museum entries extra, mobile 629-147-370, www.immguidedtours.com, info@immguidedtours.com).

Hernán Amaya Satt directs a group of licensed guides who take individuals around Madrid by foot or by car on 18 personalized tours (rates vary according to tour and number of people, 20 percent discount off official rates for Rick Steves readers, mobile 680-450-231, www.madrid-museum-tours.org, info@madrid-museum-tours.org).

Pub Crawl—British expatriate **Stephen Drake-Jones** gives entertaining, informative walks of historic old Madrid almost daily. A historian with a passion for the memory of the Duke of Wellington (the general who stopped Napoleon), Stephen is the founder and chairman of the Wellington Society. For €35, you become a member of the society for one year and get a free, two-hour tour that includes a stop along the way for local drinks and tapas (morning and afternoon departures). Or you can go on a VIP tour for €50, which includes three stops for drinks and tapas and lasts more than three hours (day and evening departures). Eccentric Stephen takes you back in time to sort out Madrid's Habsburg and Bourbon history. He likes his wine—if that's a problem, skip the tour. Tours usually start at the statue in Puerta del Sol. He also offers special tours for families, people with disabilities, and private groups; bullfight tours; multi-regional wine tastings, and day trips in the countryside (starting at €275 per couple; call 609-143-203 to confirm tour and reserve a spot, US tel. 573/301-0344, Paseo de las Delicias 75-5A, www.wellsoc.org, chairman@wellsoc.org). Members of the Wellington Society can also take advantage of Stephen's helpline (if you're in a Spanish jam, call him to translate and intervene) and assistance by email (for questions on Spain, your itinerary, and so on).

Big-Bus City Sightseeing Tours—Julia Travel offers standard guided bus tours departing from Plaza de España 7 (office open Mon–Fri 8:00–19:00, Sat–Sun 8:00–15:00, tel. 915-599-605). Their city tours include a three-hour Madrid tour with a live guide in two or three languages (€20, one stop for a drink at Hard Rock Café, one shopping stop, no museum visits, daily at 15:00, no reservation required—just show up 15 min before departure). You can tack this tour onto several others they offer, including a visit to the Santiago Bernabéu Real Madrid soccer stadium (€34, daily at 15:00, reservation required), or an excursion to the Ventas Bullring to see the *toros* (starting at €33, departure time varies, offered during bullfighting season, reservation required). If you want to hoof it, there is also a three-hour tour of the Austrias quarter and the Royal Palace (€30, Thu–Tue at 10:00, none Wed, reservation required).

Julia Travel also runs multiple day-trip tours to destinations near Madrid. The Valley of the Fallen and El Escorial tour is particularly efficient, given the lousy bus connections for this route (€47, 5 hours, makes the day trip easy—blitzing both sights with a commentary en route and no time-stealing shopping stops, Tue–Sun at 9:00, none Mon). Three trips include Toledo: one of the city itself (€39/5 hours, daily at 9:00 and 15:00, or €52/8 hours, daily at 9:15), one of Madrid and Toledo together (€50, half-day in Toledo plus panoramic 3-hour Madrid tour, daily at 9:00), and a marathon tour of El Escorial, Valley of the Fallen, and Toledo (€93, full day, Tue–Sun at 9:00, none Mon). Note that the Toledo-only full-day tours include the cathedral, but the half-day Toledo and combo-tours skip this town's one must-see sight...but not the long shopping stops, because the shops give kickbacks to the guides. And even though the buses are air-conditioned, the all-day Toledo trip is just too hot to enjoy in summer (June–Sept).

Self-Guided Walk

Welcome to Madrid: From the Puerta del Sol to the Royal Palace

Connect the sights with the following commentary. Allow an hour for this half-mile walk. Begin at Madrid's central square, Puerta del Sol (Metro: Sol).

▲▲Puerta del Sol

The bustling Puerta del Sol is named for a long-gone medieval gate with the sun carved onto it. It's a hub for the Metro, buses, political demonstrations, and pickpockets.

• *Stand by the statue of King Charles III and survey the square.*

Because of his enlightened urban policies, Charles III (who ruled until 1788) is affectionately called "the best mayor of Madrid." He decorated the city squares with fine fountains, got those meddlesome Jesuits out of city government, established the public school system, made the Retiro a public park rather than a royal retreat, and generally cleaned up Madrid.

Look behind the king. The statue of the bear pawing the berry

From Puerta del Sol to the Royal Palace

1. Puerta del Sol
2. Governor's Office
3. Salon La Mallorquina Pastry Shop
4. Calle de Postas
5. Plaza Mayor
6. Torre del Oro Bar Andalú
7. Mercado de San Miguel
8. Mesones (Cave Bars)
9. Convent Pastries
10. City Hall
11. Real-Estate Office
12. Royal Palace

START

PUERTA DEL SOL

TIO PEPE SIGN

TO PRADO

TO PRADO

PRADO

HUERTAS

ALCALA

BUSES

MINA

KILO ZERO

CADIZ

ESPOZ Y MINA

PLAZA ANGEL

ATOCHA

PLAZA BENEVENTE

CARRETAS

SOL M

CORREO

McD

BOLSA

S.CRIST.

PONT.

ESPART.

POSTAS

MAYOR

GERONA

PLAZA PROVINCIA

TO EL RASTRO FLEA MARKET (SUNDAYS)

EL CORTE INGLES DEPT. STORE

CALLE DE ARENAL

PLAZA MAYOR

TOLEDO

CUCHILL.

MIRANDA

CODO

PUÑON

CALLE

SEGOVIA

DCH

SACRAMENTO

SAN NICOLAS

ROYAL THEATER

CALLE VERGARA

ARRIETA

TO LA BOLA REST.

LA PAELLA REAL REST.

PLAZA DE ORIENTE

STATUE

CAFÉ DE ORIENTE

CASA CIRIACO REST.

CALLE BAILE'N

CATHEDRAL OF ALMUDENA

FINISH

TOURS START

BUY TICKETS & ENTER

ROYAL PALACE

CAMPO DEL MORO

200 YARDS

200 METERS

━━━ WALKING TOUR ROUTE

MADRID

bush and the *madroño* trees in the big planter boxes are symbols of the city. Bears used to live in the royal hunting grounds outside Madrid. And the *madroño* trees produce a berry that makes the traditional *madroño* liqueur.

The king faces a red-and-white building with a bell tower. This was Madrid's first post office, established by Charles III in the 1760s. Today, it's the governor's office, though it's notorious for having been Francisco Franco's police headquarters. An amazing number of those detained and interrogated by the Franco police "tried to escape" by jumping out the windows to their deaths. Notice the hats of the civil guardsmen at the entry. It's said the hats have square backs so that the men can lean against the wall while enjoying a cigarette.

Appreciate the harmonious architecture of the buildings that circle the square. Crowds fill the square on New Year's Eve as the rest of Madrid watches the action on TV. As Spain's "Big Ben" atop the governor's office chimes 12 times, Madrileños eat one grape for each ring to bring good luck through the coming year.

• *Cross the square, walking to the governor's office.*

Look at the curb directly in front of the entrance to the **governor's office.** The scuffed-up marker is "kilometer zero," the very center of Spain. Near the entrance are two plaques expressing thanks from the regional government to its citizens for assisting in times of dire need. To the left of the entrance, a plaque on the wall honors those who helped during the terrorist bombings of March 11, 2004.

A similar plaque on the right marks the spot where the war against Napoleon started in 1808. Napoleon wanted his brother to be king of Spain. Trying to finagle this, he brought nearly the entire Spanish royal family to France for negotiations. An anxious crowd gathered outside this building awaiting word of the fate of their royals. This was just after the French Revolution, and there was a general nervousness between France and Spain. When the people of Madrid heard that Napoleon had appointed his own brother as the new king of Spain, they gathered angrily in the streets. The French guard simply massacred the mob. Painter Francisco de Goya, who worked just up the street, observed the event and captured the tragedy in his paintings *Second of May, 1808* and *Third of May, 1808,* now in the Prado.

From Puerta del Sol to Plaza Mayor

On the corner of Calle Mayor and Puerta del Sol (downhill end of Puerta del Sol, across from McDonald's) is the busy *confitería* **Salon La Mallorquina** (daily 9:00–21:15, closed mid-July–Aug). Go inside for a tempting peek at racks with goodies hot out of the oven. The shop is famous for its sweet, cream-filled *Napolitana* pastry (€1). Or sample Madrid's answer to donuts, *rosquillas* (*tontas* means "silly"—plain, and *listas* means "all dressed up and ready to go"—with icing, €0.50 each).

From inside the shop, look back toward the entrance and notice the tile above the door with the 18th-century view of Puerta del Sol. Compare this with today's view out the door. This was before the square was widened, when a church stood where the *Tío Pepe* sign stands today. The French used this church to detain local patriots awaiting execution. (The venerable *Tío Pepe* sign, advertising a famous sherry for more than 100 years, was Madrid's first billboard.)

• *Cross busy Calle Mayor, round McDonald's, and veer up the pedestrian alley called* **Calle de Postas.**

The street sign shows the post coach heading for that famous first post office. Medieval street signs included pictures so the illiterate could "read" them. Fifty yards up the street, at Calle San Cristóbal, is Pans & Company, a popular Catalan sandwich chain. While Spaniards consider American fast food unhealthy—both culturally and physically—the local fast-food chains seem to be more politically and nutritionally correct.

• *From here, hike up Calle San Cristóbal.*

Within two blocks, you'll pass the local feminist bookshop (Librería Mujeres) and reach a small square. At the square, notice the big, brick 17th-century Ministry of Foreign Affairs building (with the pointed spire)—originally a jail for rich prisoners who could afford the cushy cells.

• *Turn right, and walk down Calle de Zaragoza under the arcade into the...*

▲Plaza Mayor

This square, built in 1619, is a vast, cobbled, traffic-free chunk of 17th-century Spain. Each side of the square is uniform, as if a grand palace were turned inside-out. The statue is of Philip III, who ordered the square's construction. Upon this stage, much Spanish history has been played out: bullfights, fires, royal pageantry, and events of the gruesome Inquisition. Reliefs serving as seatbacks under the lampposts tell the story. During the Inquisition, many were tried here—suspected heretics, Protestants, Jews, and Muslims whose "conversion" to Christianity was dubious. The guilty were paraded around the square before their execution, wearing billboards listing their many sins (bleachers were built for bigger audiences, while the wealthy rented balconies). Some were slowly strangled as they held a crucifix, hearing the reassuring words of a priest as this life was squeezed out of them. Others were burned.

The square is painted a democratic shade of burgundy—the

result of a citywide vote. Since Franco's death in 1975, there's been a passion for voting here. Three different colors were painted as samples on the walls of this square, and the city voted for its favorite.

A stamp-and-coin market bustles here on Sundays from 10:00 to 14:00; on any day, it's a colorful and affordable place to enjoy a cup of coffee. Throughout Spain, lesser *plazas mayores* provide peaceful pools in the river of Spanish life. The TI (daily 9:30–20:30, wonderfully air-conditioned and with free but limited Internet access) is under the building on the north side of the square, the Casa de la Panadería, decorated with painted figures (it once housed the Bakers' Guild).

• For some interesting, if gruesome, bullfighting lore, drop by the…

Torre del Oro Bar Andalú

This bar is a good spot for a drink to finish off your Plaza Mayor visit (northwest corner of square, to the left of the Bakers' Guild). The bar has *Andalú* (Andalusian) ambience and an entertaining staff. Warning: They push expensive tapas on tourists. But buying a beer is safe and painless—just order a *caña* (small beer, shouldn't cost more than €2.30). The price list posted outside the door makes your costs perfectly clear. Consider taking a break at one of their sidewalk tables (or at any café/bar terrace facing Madrid's finest square). The scene is well worth the extra euro you'll pay for the drink.

The interior of the Torre del Oro bar is a temple to bullfighting, festooned with gory decor. Notice the breathtaking action captured in the many photographs. Look under the stuffed head of Barbero the bull. At eye level, you'll see a *puntilla,* the knife used to put a bull out of his misery at the arena. This was the knife used to kill Barbero. The plaque explains: weight, birth date, owner, date of death, which matador killed him, and the location. Just to the left of Barbero, there's a photo of Franco with a very famous bullfighter. This is Manuel Benítez Pérez—better known as El Cordobés, the Elvis of bullfighters and a working-class hero. At the top of the stairs to the WC, find the photo of El Cordobés and Robert Kennedy—looking like brothers. At the end of the bar in a glass case is the "suit of lights" the great El Cordobés wore in his ill-fated 1967 fight. With Franco in attendance, El Cordobés went on and on, long after he could have ended the fight, until finally the bull gored him. El Cordobés survived; the bull didn't. Find another photo of Franco with El Cordobés at the far end, to the left of Segador the bull. Under the bull is a photo of El Cordobés' illegitimate son kissing a bull. Disowned by El Cordobés senior, yet still using his dad's famous name after a court battle, the new El Cordobés is one of this generation's top fighters.

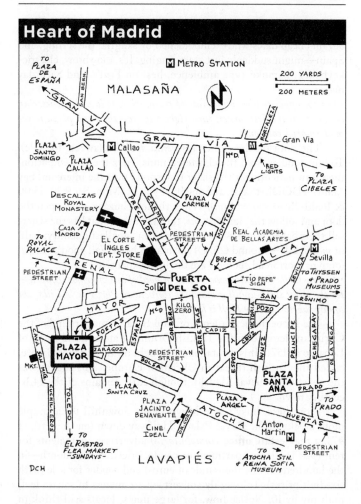

Heart of Madrid

TO PLAZA DE ESPAÑA

MALASAÑA

M METRO STATION

200 YARDS
200 METERS

GRAN VIA

GRAN VIA

M Callao

Gran Via

HORTALEZA

PLAZA SANTO DOMINGO

PLAZA CALLAO

M^CD.

RED LIGHTS

TO PLAZA CIBELES

DESCALZAS ROYAL MONASTERY

PLAZA CARMEN

CAJA MADRID

PRECIADOS

CARMEN

TO ROYAL PALACE

EL CORTE INGLES DEPT. STORE

PEDESTRIAN STREETS

MONTERA

REAL ACADEMIA DE BELLAS ARTES

ALCALA

Sevilla

PEDESTRIAN STREET

ARENAL

BUSES

TO THYSSEN & PRADO MUSEUMS

Sol M

PUERTA DEL SOL

"TIO PEPE" SIGN

SEVILLA

MAYOR

POSTAS

M^CD

CORREO

KILO. ZERO

SAN JERÓNIMO

SAN POZO

PLAZA MAYOR

ZARAGOZA

ESPART.

CARRE TAS

CADIZ

MINA

VICTORIA

CRUZ

NUÑEZ

PRINCIPE

ECHEGARAY

V. DE LA VEGA

MKT.

CAVA SAN MIG

CUCHILLEROS

PEDESTRIAN STREET

BOLSA

ESPOZ

PLAZA SANTA ANA

PRADO

PLAZA SANTA CRUZ

TOLEDO

PLAZA JACINTO BENAVENTE

CINE IDEAL

PLAZA ANGEL

ATOCHA

Anton Martin M

TO PRADO

HUERTAS

PEDESTRIAN STREET

DR. CORT

TO EL RASTRO FLEA MARKET -SUNDAYS-

LAVAPIÉS

TO ATOCHA STN. & REINA SOFIA MUSEUM

DCH

Strolling from Plaza Mayor to the Royal Palace

Leave Plaza Mayor on Calle Ciudad Rodrigo (to your right as you exit the bull bar). You'll pass a series of fine turn-of-the-20th-century storefronts and sandwich joints, such as Casa Rúa, famous for their cheap *bocadillos de calamares*—fried squid-rings on a roll.

From the archway, you'll see the covered **Mercado de San Miguel** (green iron posts, on left). This historic market, recently closed for several years, should open again in time for your trip—but it will be more of a trendy tourist stop than a place for locals to buy their veggies.

Before passing the market hall, look left down the street called Cava de San Miguel. If you like sangria and singing, come back at about 22:00 and visit one of the *mesones* that line the street.

These cave-like bars stretch way back and get packed with locals out on cheap dates who—emboldened by sangria, the setting, and Spain—might suddenly just start singing. It's a lowbrow, electric-keyboard, karaoke-type ambience, best on Friday and Saturday nights.

• *On the opposite (downhill) side of the market, follow the pedestrian lane left. At the first corner, turn right and cross the small plaza to the modern brick* **convent**.

The door on the right says *venta de dulces* (sweets for sale). To buy goodies from the cloistered nuns, buzz the *monjas* button, then wait patiently for the sister to respond over the intercom. Say *"dulces"* (DOOL-thays), and she'll let you in (Mon–Sat 9:30–13:00 & 16:00–18:30, closed Sun). When the lock buzzes, push open the door and follow the sign to *torno*, the lazy Susan that lets the sisters sell their baked goods without being seen (smallest quantity: half, or *medio*, kilo—around €6). Of the many choices (all good), *galletas* (orange shortbread cookies) are the least expensive.

• *Follow Calle del Codo (where those in need of bits of armor shopped— see the street sign) uphill around the convent to Plaza de la Villa, the square where the* **City Hall** *is located.*

The statue in the garden is of Don Bazán—mastermind of the Christian victory over the Turkish Ottomans at the naval battle of Lepanto in 1571. This pivotal battle, fought off the coast of Greece, ended the Turkish threat to Christian Europe. This square was the heart of medieval Madrid, though little remains of the 14th-century town.

From here, busy Calle Mayor leads downhill for a couple more blocks to the Royal Palace. Halfway down (on the left), at #75, a **real-estate office** *(inmobiliaria)* advertises apartments for rent (*piso* is a large apartment or condo, priced by the month—in the hundreds or low thousands of euros) and condos for sale (with six-digit prices). To roughly convert square meters to square feet, multiply by 10. Notice how, for large items, locals still think in terms of *pesetas* ("pts"), the Spanish currency before euros took over in 2002.

A few steps farther down, on a tiny square opposite the recommended Casa Ciriaco restaurant (at #84—see page 1191), a statue memorializes the 1906 anarchist bombing that killed 23 people as the royal couple paraded by on their wedding day. While the crowd was throwing flowers, an anarchist (what terrorists used to be called) threw a bouquet lashed to a bomb from a balcony of #84, which was a hotel at the time. Gory photos of the event hang inside the restaurant (to the right of the entrance).

• *Continue down Calle Mayor. Within a couple of blocks, you'll come to a busy street, Calle de Bailen.*

Across the busy street is Madrid's **Cathedral of Almudena,** built between 1883 and 1993. Its exterior is a contemporary mix, and its interior is Neo-Gothic, with a refreshingly modern and colorful ceiling, glittering 5,000-pipe organ, and the 12th-century coffin (empty, painted leather on wood, in a chapel behind the altar) of Madrid's patron saint, Isidro. A humble peasant, Isidro loved the handicapped and performed miracles. Forty years after he died, this coffin was opened and his body was found miraculously preserved, which convinced the pope to canonize him as the patron saint of Madrid and of farmers, with May 15 as his feast day.

• When you're finished, you may want to tour the Royal Palace (next to the cathedral) or you could...

Return to Puerta del Sol

With your back to the palace, face the equestrian statue of Philip IV and (beyond the statue) the Neoclassical **Royal Theater** (Teatro Real, rebuilt in 1997). On your left, the **Madrid Tower** skyscraper marks the Plaza de España. Walk behind the Royal Theater (on the right, passing Café de Oriente—a favorite with theater-goers) to another square, where you'll find the Ópera Metro stop and the mostly pedestrianized Calle de Arenal, which leads back to Puerta del Sol.

Sights

▲▲Royal Palace (Palacio Real)

Europe's third-greatest palace (after Versailles and Vienna's Schönbrunn), with arguably the most sumptuous original interior, is packed with tourists and royal antiques.

After a fortress burned down on this site in the 18th century, King Philip V commissioned this huge palace as a replacement. Though he ruled Spain for 40 years, Philip V was very French. (The grandson of Louis XIV, he was born in Versailles and preferred speaking French.) He ordered this palace to be built as his own Versailles (although his wife's Italian origin had a tremendous impact on the style). It's big—more than 2,000 rooms, with tons of luxurious tapestries, a king's ransom of chandeliers, priceless porcelain, and bronze decor covered in gold leaf. While these days the royal family lives in a mansion a few miles away, this place still functions as a royal palace, and is used for formal state receptions, royal weddings, and tourists' daydreams.

The lions you'll see throughout were symbols of power. The Bourbon kings considered previous royalty not up to European par, and this palace—along with their establishment of a Spanish porcelain works and tapestry works—was their effort to raise the bar.

MADRID

Cheap Tricks in Madrid

- Instead of expensive city tour buses, take bus #27 on a sightseeing joyride past some major Madrid landmarks. Catch the bus in front of the Royal Botanical Garden on the Paseo del Prado and ride it to the Plaza Castilla (the end of the line). You'll pass (in order): the Prado Museum, the Neptune fountain (the Ritz and Palace hotels are on this roundabout), the Thyssen-Bornemisza Museum (on the left), the Madrid stock market and Naval Museum (on the right), the Plaza de Cibeles fountain, the Paseo de Recoletos and its lovely cafés, the National Library (on the right, before the Plaza de Colón—look for the column with the statue of Columbus pointing), then a stretch of roundabouts and businesses, the Santiago Bernabéu Real Madrid soccer stadium, and finally the Plaza de Castilla, where you'll see the two leaning KIO Towers (the crazy angle is intentional). All for just €1.
- Some major sights are free to enter at certain times (for example, the Prado is free Tue–Sat 18:00–20:00 and Sun 17:00–20:00, while the Centro de Arte Reina Sofía is free Sat afternoon after 14:30 and all day Sun). Five Madrid sights are always free: Caja Madrid, CaixaForum, National Archaeological Museum, Bullfighting Museum, and the Temple de Debod.
- If you need to quickly check your email, the TI on Plaza Mayor has limited free Internet access. All Madrid TIs have a free and informative road map of Spain, *Mapa de Comunicaciones España*.

Cost and Hours: €8 without a tour, €10 with a 1-hour tour (explained below); April–Sept Mon–Sat 9:30–19:00, Sun 9:00–16:00; Oct–March Mon–Sat 9:30–18:00, Sun 9:00–15:00; last entry one hour before closing. The palace can close without warning if needed for a royal function; you can call a day ahead to check (tel. 914-548-800).

Crowd-Beating Tips: The palace is most crowded on Wednesdays, when it's free for locals. Arrive early to minimize lines.

Getting There: To get to the palace from Puerta del Sol, walk down the mostly pedestrianized Calle de Arenal. If arriving by Metro, get off at the Ópera stop.

Services: At the palace, there's a WC just past the ticket booth (men will enjoy the beer-stein urinals—all the rage in Madrid).

Touring the Palace: A simple one-floor, 24-room, one-way circuit is open to the public. You can wander on your own or join an English-language tour (check time of next tour and decide as you buy your ticket; the English-language tours depart about every

20 min, not worth a long wait). The tour guides, like the museum guidebook, show a passion for meaningless data. The €2.30 audioguides are much more interesting. If you enjoy sightseeing cheek-to-cheek, crank up the volume and share the audioguide with your companion. The armory (€3.40) and the pharmacy (included in your ticket) are in the courtyard. Photography is not allowed.

Madrid's Museum Neighborhood

Three great museums, all within a 10-minute walk of each other, cluster in east Madrid: El Prado (Europe's top collection of paintings), the Thyssen-Bornemisza Museum (a baron's collection of European art, from the old masters to the moderns), and the Centro de Arte Reina Sofía (modern art, including Picasso's famous *Guernica*).

If visiting all three museums, save a few euros by buying the *Paseo del Arte* **combo-ticket** (€14.40, buy at any of the three museums, expires in one year). Note that it's free to enter the Prado Tuesday–Saturday 18:00–20:00, and Sunday 17:00–20:00, and the Reina Sofía Saturday 14:30–21:00 and Sunday 10:00–14:30 (both are free anytime for those under 18). The Prado and Thyssen-Bornemisza are closed Monday, and the Reina Sofía is closed Tuesday.

▲▲▲Prado Museum

With more than 3,000 canvases, including entire rooms of masterpieces by superstar painters, the Prado (PRAH-doh) is overwhelming. But pick up the free English floor plan as you enter, which will help. The Prado is *the* place to enjoy the great Spanish painter Francisco de Goya, and it's also the home of Diego Velázquez's *Las Meninas,* considered by many to be the world's finest painting, period. In addition to Spanish works, you'll find paintings by Italian and Flemish masters, including Hieronymus Bosch's delightful *Garden of Delights* altarpiece.

Cost and Hours: €6, free Tue–Sat 18:00–20:00 and Sun 17:00–20:00, and free anytime to anyone under 18. Open Tue–Sun 9:00–20:00, closed Mon, last entry 30 min before closing.

Location: It's at the Paseo del Prado. The Banco de España and Atocha Metro stops are each a five-minute walk from the museum. Cabs picking you up at the Prado are likely to overcharge—insist on the meter.

The Prado Expansion: The museum is undergoing an extensive expansion project that will create exhibit space for many works long hidden in storage. The first extension, inaugurated in 2007, was partially constructed in the cloister of the 15th-century San Jerónimos church. This spacious addition houses a sculpture

Madrid's Museum Neighborhood

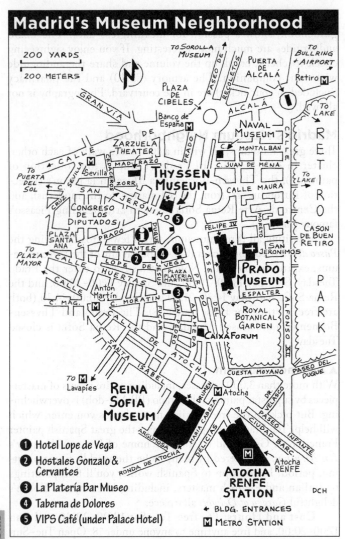

200 YARDS
200 METERS

TO SOROLLA MUSEUM

TO BULLRING + AIRPORT

PUERTA DE ALCALÁ

Retiro

PLAZA DE CIBELES

GRAN VÍA

Banco de España

ALCALÁ

NAVAL MUSEUM

C. MONTALBÁN

TO LAKE

RETIRO

ZARZUELA THEATER

C. JUAN DE MENA

TO PUERTA DEL SOL

Sevilla

THYSSEN MUSEUM

CALLE MAURA

TO LAKE

Congreso DE LOS DIPUTADOS

FELIPE IV

CASÓN DE BUEN RETIRO

SAN JERÓNIMO

PLAZA SANTA ANA

CERVANTES

PARK

TO PLAZA MAYOR

PRADO

LOPE DE VEGA

PLAZA PLATERÍA MARTÍNEZ

PRADO MUSEUM

HUERTAS

ESPALTER

Antón Martín

C. MORATÍN

ROYAL BOTANICAL GARDEN

ALFONSO XII

CaixaForum

CUESTA MOYANO

PASEO DEL DUQUE

TO Lavapiés

REINA SOFIA MUSEUM

Atocha

DR. VELASCO

AV. CIUDAD BARC.

Atocha RENFE

1 Hotel Lope de Vega
2 Hostales Gonzalo & Cervantes
3 La Platería Bar Museo
4 Taberna de Dolores
5 VIPS Café (under Palace Hotel)

RONDA DE ATOCHA

ATOCHA RENFE STATION

DCH

← BLDG. ENTRANCES
Ⓜ METRO STATION

MADRID

gallery and temporary exhibits, as well as a café and gift shop. Future additions in other buildings will provide space for more sculpture and decorative arts. This expansion, and any current special exhibits, may cause curators to jumble the museum's layout. Pick up a detailed map when you enter the museum, consider renting an audioguide, and enlist the help of a guard if you're unable to find a particular work of art.

Crowd-Beating Tips: Lunchtime (14:00–16:00) and weekdays are generally less crowded. It's always packed when free and on weekends; it's worth paying the entry price on other days to have your space.

Entrances: You can buy your ticket at the Goya or Veláquez entrances, but if you want tickets to any special exhibit, you must get them at the upper Goya entrance (even if the exhibit is free). There are three entrances for ticket-holders and visitors with the *Paseo del Arte* pass: Jerónimos, Goya, or Veláquez. Scope the entrances as you approach the museum to see which has the shortest line. (The Murillo entrance, the one across from the Botanical Garden, is for advance bookings such as school groups.)

Tours: Take a tour, rent the €3 audioguide, or buy a guidebook. Given the ever-changing locations of paintings, the audioguide (with 120 paintings described) is a good investment, allowing you to wander. When you see a painting of interest, simply punch in the number and enjoy the description. You can return the audioguide at any of the exits. And, if you're on a tight budget, remember that two can crank up the volume, listen cheek-to-cheek, and share one machine.

Services and Information: Your bags will be scanned (just like at the airport) before you leave them at the free and mandatory baggage storage (no water bottles allowed inside). There's a cafeteria in the extension area by the Jerónimos entrance. Photography is not allowed. Tel. 913-302-800, http://museoprado.mcu.es.

▲▲Thyssen-Bornemisza Museum

Locals call this stunning museum simply the Thyssen (TEE-sun). It displays the impressive collection that Baron Thyssen (a wealthy German married to a former Miss Spain) sold to Spain for $350 million. It's basically minor works by major artists and major works by minor artists (major works by major artists are in the Prado). But art-lovers appreciate how the good baron's art complements the Prado's collection by filling in where the Prado is weak (such as Impressionism).

Each floor is divided into two separate areas: the permanent collection (numbered rooms) and additions from the Baroness since the 1980s (lettered rooms). The museum recently opened a new wing (creating an L-shaped museum) to house even more of the Baroness' collection, including works by Impressionists (Monet's *Charing Cross Bridge*), Post-Impressionists, and Picasso.

After purchasing your high-tech barcode ticket, continue down the wide main hall past larger-than-life paintings of King Juan Carlos and Queen Sofía, alongside the Baron (who died in 2002) and his art-collecting Baroness, Carmen. Pick up two museum maps (one for numbered rooms, another for lettered rooms) at the info desk. Ascend to the top floor and work your way down, taking a delightful walk through art history. Visit the rooms on each floor in numerical and alphabetical order, from Primitive Italian (Room 1) to Surrealism and Pop Art (Room 48). Afterwards, if you're heading to Centro de Arte Reina Sofía and you're tired, hail a cab at the gate to zip straight there.

Temporary exhibits at the Thyssen often parallel those at the free **Caja Madrid** exhibit hall (Tue–Sat 10:00–20:00, closed Mon, tel. 913-792-050, www.fundacioncajamadrid.es), across from the Descalzas Royal Monastery on the Plaza San Martín.

Cost and Hours: €6 (€3 more for special exhibits); children under 12 free, Tue–Sun 10:00–19:00, closed Mon, last entry 30 min before closing.

Location: The museum is kitty-corner from the Prado at Paseo del Prado 8 in Palacio de Villahermosa (Metro: Banco de España).

Services and Information: Free baggage storage, €4 audio-guide, café, shop, no photos, tel. 914-203-944, www.museo thyssen.org.

▲▲Centro de Arte Reina Sofía

This former public hospital (Madrid's first) shows off an exceptional collection of modern art. The permanent collection is on the second and fourth floors; temporary exhibits are on the first and third floors. Ride the fancy glass elevator to the second floor and follow the room numbers for art chronologically displayed from 1900 to 1940. The fourth floor continues the collection, from 1940 to 1980.

The museum is most famous for Pablo Picasso's *Guernica* (second floor, Room 6), an epic painting showing the horror of modern war. Notice the two rooms of studies Picasso did for *Guernica*, filled with iron-nail tears and screaming mouths. *Guernica* was displayed at the Museum of Modern Art in New York City until Franco's death, and now it reigns as Spain's national piece of art. After pondering the destruction of war, visit the room furthest back from the painting (confusingly, also numbered 6) to see photos of Picasso creating this masterpiece.

The museum also houses an easy-to-enjoy collection by other modern artists, including more of Picasso and a mind-bending room of works by Salvador Dalí (Room 10). Room 12 is a treat for movie buffs: Two films by Surrealist director Luis Buñuel (who had help from friends Dalí and the poet Federico García Lorca) play continuously. Enjoy a break in the shady courtyard before leaving.

Cost and Hours: €6, free Sat afternoon after 14:30 (less crowded after 15:00) and all day Sun, always free to those under 18 and over 65. Even if admission is free when you visit, grab a ticket anyway. The museum is open Mon and Wed–Sat 10:00–21:00, Sun 10:00–14:30, closed Tue.

Location: It's across from the Atocha Metro station at Santa Isabel 52. Exiting the Metro, walk across two big streets, Delicias and Santa María la Cabeza. At the opening into a square, look for the exterior glass elevators. There are two entrances: the old entrance (leads to permanent collection first; on Calle Sánchez Bustillo, on a big square close to the Metro stop) and the new entrance (leads to temporary exhibits first, often shorter lines; standing on the square facing the Atocha train station, turn right onto the next street—the unmarked Ronda de Atocha—and go about a block to the big, red, modern addition).

Services and Information: Good brochure, no tours in English, hardworking €4 audioguide, no photos, free baggage storage. The *librería* just outside the new addition has a larger selection of Picasso and Surrealist reproductions than the main gift shop at the entrance. Tel. 914-675-062, www.museoreinasofia.es.

Near the Prado

▲**Retiro Park (Parque del Buen Retiro)**—Once the private domain of royalty, this majestic park has been a favorite of Madrid's commoners since Charles III decided to share it with his subjects in the late 18th century. Siesta in this 300-acre, green-and-breezy escape from the city. At midday on Saturday and Sunday, the area around the lake becomes a street carnival, with jugglers, puppeteers, and lots of local color. These peaceful gardens offer great picnicking and people-watching. From the Retiro Metro stop, walk to the big lake (El Estanque), where you can cheaply rent a rowboat. Past the lake, a grand boulevard of statues leads to the Prado.

Royal Botanical Garden (Real Jardín Botánico)—After your Prado visit, you can take a lush and fragrant break in this sculpted park. Wander among trees from around the world. The flier in English explains that this is actually more than a park—it's a museum of plants (€2, daily 10:00–21:00, until 18:00 in winter, entry opposite Prado's Murillo/south entry, Plaza de Murillo 2).

Naval Museum (Museo Naval)—This museum tells the story of Spain's navy, from the Armada to today, in a plush and fascinating-to-boat-lovers exhibit (free, no English anywhere, Tue–Sun 10:00–14:00, closed Mon and in August, a block north of the Prado across boulevard from Thyssen-Bornemisza Museum, Paseo del Prado 5, tel. 915-239-884, www.museonavalmadrid.com). Because this is a military facility, you'll need to show your passport to get in.

CaixaForum—Across the street from the Prado and Royal Botanical Garden, you'll find this impressive exhibit hall with funky architecture and an outdoor hanging garden. The forum features various activities (such as lectures), but the world-class art exhibits are the main reason to visit. You'll see them advertised around town and at the TIs, but it's worth coming here in person to find out what's on (free, daily 10:00–20:00, Paseo del Prado 36, tel. 913-307-300, www.obrasocial.lacaixa.es).

Elsewhere in Madrid

Descalzas Royal Monastery (Monasterio de las Descalzas Reales)—Madrid's most visit-worthy monastery was founded in the 16th century by Philip II's sister, Joan of Habsburg (known to Spaniards as Juana, and to Austrians as Joanna). She's buried here. The monastery's chapels are decorated with fine art, Rubens-designed tapestries, and the heirlooms of the wealthy women who joined the order (the nuns were required to give a dowry). Because this is still a working Franciscan monastery, tourists can visit only when the nuns vacate the cloister, and the number of daily visitors is limited. The scheduled tours often sell out—come in the morning to buy your ticket, even if you want an afternoon tour (€5, visits guided in Spanish or English depending on demand, Tue–Thu and Sat 10:30–12:30 & 16:00–17:30, Fri 10:30–12:30, Sun 11:00–13:30, closed Mon, Plaza de las Descalzas Reales 3, near the Ópera Metro stop and just a short walk from Puerta del Sol, tel. 914-548-700).

▲National Archaeological Museum (Museo Arqueológico Nacional)—This fine museum gives you a chronological walk through the story of Iberia on one convenient floor. With a rich collection of artifacts (but a maddening refusal to describe anything in English), it shows off the wonders of each age: Celtic pre-Roman, Roman, a fine and rare Visigothic section, Moorish, Romanesque, and beyond (always free; open Tue–Sat 9:30–20:00, Sun 9:30–15:00, closed Mon; Calle Serrano 13, Metro: Serrano or Colón, tel. 915-777-912). Outside, underground in the museum's garden, is an underwhelming replica artwork from northern Spain's Altamira Caves (big on bison), giving you a faded peek at the skill of the cave artists who created the originals 14,000 years ago.

Sorolla Museum (Museo Sorolla)—Joaquín Sorrolla (1863–1923) is known for his portraits, landscapes, and use of light. It's a relaxing experience to stroll through the rooms of his former house and studio, especially to see the lazy beach scenes of his hometown Valencia. Take a break after your visit to reflect in the small garden in front of his house (€2.40, free on Sun, open Tue–Sat 9:30–20:00, Sun 10:00–15:00, closed Mon, General Martínez Campos, 37, Metro: Iglesia, tel. 913-101-584, http://museosorolla.mcu.es).

Municipal Museum (Museo Municipal)—Follow the history of Madrid in old paintings and models (but no English). As you enter, notice Pedro de Ribera's fine Baroque door featuring "St. James the Moor-Slayer." While the museum is undergoing a major renovation through 2011, this door may be covered in scaffolding, and only certain sections of the museum may be open (free, Tue–Fri 9:30–20:00, Sat–Sun 10:00–14:00, closed Mon, Calle Fuencarral 78, Metro: Tribunal or Bilbao, tel. 917-011-863).

▲**Clothing Museum (Museo del Traje)**—This museum shows the history of clothing from the 18th century until today. In a cool and air-conditioned chronological sweep, the museum's one floor of exhibits includes regional ethnic costumes, a look at how bullfighting and the French influenced styles, accessories through the ages, and Spanish flappers. The only downside of this marvelous modern museum is that it's a long way from anything else of interest (€3, free Sat 14:30–19:00 and all day Sun, open Tue–Sat 9:30–19:00, Sun 10:00–15:00, closed Mon, last entry 30 min before closing, Avenida Juan Herrera 2; Metro: Moncloa and a longish walk, bus #46, or taxi; tel. 915-497-150).

▲**Chapel of San Antonio de la Florida**—In this simple little Neoclassical chapel from the 1790s, Francisco de Goya's tomb stares up at a splendid cupola filled with his own proto-Impressionist frescoes. He frescoed this using the same unique technique that he used for his "dark paintings." Use the mirrors to enjoy the drama and energy he infused into this marvelously restored masterpiece (free, Tue–Fri 9:30–20:00, Sat–Sun 10:00–14:00, closed Mon, Glorieta de San Antonio de la Florida, tel. 915-420-722). This chapel is a five-minute walk down Paseo de San Antonio de la Florida from Metro: Príncipe Pío (and its bus station, serving Segovia). If you're day-tripping to Segovia from Madrid, it's easy to stop by before or after your trip.

Royal Tapestry Factory (Real Fábrica de Tapices)—Have a look at traditional tapestry-making (€3.50, Mon–Fri 10:00–14:00, closed Sat–Sun and Aug, some English tours, Calle Fuenterrabia 2, Metro: Menendez Pelayo, take Gutenberg exit, tel. 914-340-550). You can actually order a tailor-made tapestry (starting at $10,000).

Temple de Debod—In 1968, Egypt gave Spain its own ancient temple. It was a gift of the Egyptian government, which was grateful for Franco's help in rescuing monuments that had been threatened by the rising Nile waters above the Aswan Dam. Consequently, Madrid is the only place I can think of in Europe where you can actually wander through an intact original Egyptian temple—complete with fine carved reliefs from 200 B.C. (free; April–Sept Tue–Fri 10:00–14:00 & 18:00–20:00, Sat–Sun 10:00–14:00, closed Mon; Oct–March Tue–Fri 9:45–13:45 & 16:15–18:15, Sat–Sun 10:00–14:00, closed Mon). Set in a romantic park that locals love for its great city views (especially at sunset), the temple—as well as its art—is well-described. Popular as the view may be, the uninspiring "grand Madrid view" only causes me to wonder why anyone would build a city here.

Cable Car (Teleférico)—For city views, ride this cable car from downtown over Madrid's sprawling city park to Casa de Campo (€3.50 one-way, €5 round-trip, April–Aug daily from 12:00, Sept–March Sat–Sun only, departs from Paseo del Pintor Rosales, a short walk from Metro: Argüelles, tel. 915-417-450, www.tele ferico.com). Do an immediate round-trip to skip Casa de Campo's strange mix of rental rowboats, prostitutes, addicts, a zoo, and an amusement park. The family-friendly bits of the park are far from the cable-car terminus.

Experiences

▲▲**Bullfight**—Madrid's Plaza de Toros hosts Spain's top bull-fights on some Sundays and holidays from March through mid-October, and nearly every day during the San Isidro festival (May through early June—often sold out long in advance). Fights start between 17:00 and 21:00 (early in spring and fall, late in summer). The bullring is at the Ventas Metro stop (a 15-min Metro ride from Puerta del Sol, tel. 913-562-200, www.las-ventas.com).

Bullfight tickets range from €3.50 to €120. There are no bad seats at the Plaza de Toros; paying more gets you in the shade and/or closer to the gore. (The action often intentionally occurs in the shade to reward the expensive-ticket holders.) To be close to the bullring, choose areas 8, 9, or 10; for shade: 1, 2, 9, or 10; for shade/sun: 3 or 8; for the sun and cheapest seats: 4, 5, 6, or 7. Note these key words: *corrida*—a real fight with professionals; *novillada*—rookie matadors and younger bulls. Getting tickets through your hotel or a booking office is convenient, but they add 20 percent or more and don't sell the cheap seats. There are two booking offices; call both before you buy: at Plaza del Carmen 1 (Mon–Sat 9:30–13:00 & 16:30–19:00, Sun 9:30–13:30, tel. 915-319-131, or buy online at www.bullfightticketsmadrid.com; run by English-speaking José, who also sells soccer tickets) and at Calle Victoria 3 (Mon–Fri 10:00–14:00 & 17:00–19:00, Sat–Sun 10:00–14:00, tel. 915-211-213). To save money, you can stand in the ticket line at the bullring. Except for important bullfights—or during the San Isidro festival—there are generally plenty of seats available. About a thousand tickets are held back to be sold in the five days leading up to a fight, including the day of the fight. Scalpers hang out before the popular fights at the Calle Victoria booking office. Beware: Those buying scalped tickets are breaking the law and can lose the ticket with no recourse.

For a dose of the experience, you can buy a cheap ticket and just stay to see a couple of bullfights. Each fight takes about 20 minutes, and the event consists of six bulls over two hours.

Madrid's **Bullfighting Museum** (Museo Taurino) is not as

good as Sevilla's or Ronda's (free, Tue–Fri 9:30–14:30, Sun 10:00–13:00, closed Sat and Mon and early on fight days, at the back of bullring, tel. 917-251-857).

"Football"—Madrid, like most of Europe, is enthusiastic about soccer (which they call *fútbol* here). The Real Madrid team plays to a spirited local crowd Saturdays and Sundays from September through May (tickets from €30—sold at bullfight box offices listed previous page, stadium at Metro: Santiago Bernabéu).

Nightlife

Disco dancers may have to wait until after midnight for the most popular clubs to even open, much less start hopping. Spain has a reputation for partying very late, not ending until offices open in the morning. If you're people-watching early in the morning, it's actually hard to know who is finishing their day and who's just starting it. Even if you're not a party animal after midnight, make a point to be out with the happy masses, luxuriating in the cool evening air between 22:00 and midnight. The scene is absolutely unforgettable.

▲▲▲**Paseo**—Just walking the streets of Madrid seems to be the way the Madrileños spend their evenings. Even past midnight on a hot summer night, whole families with little kids are strolling, enjoying tiny beers and tapas in a series of bars, licking ice cream, and greeting their neighbors. A good area to wander is along Gran Vía (from about Metro: Callao to Plaza de España). Or start at Puerta del Sol, and explore in the direction of Plaza Santa Ana. See "The Madrid Pub-Crawl Dinner (for Beginners)" on page 1193.

▲▲**Zarzuela**—For a delightful look at Spanish light opera that even English-speakers can enjoy, try zarzuela. Guitar-strumming Napoleons in red capes; buxom women with masks, fans, and castanets; Spanish-speaking pharaohs; melodramatic spotlights; and aficionados clapping and singing along from the cheap seats, where the acoustics are best—this is zarzuela...the people's opera. Originating in Madrid, zarzuela is known for its satiric humor and surprisingly good music. You can buy tickets at Theater Zarzuela, which alternates between zarzuela, ballet, and opera throughout the year (€10–40, box office open 12:00–18:00 for advance tickets or until showtime for that day, Jovellanos 4, near the Prado, Metro: Sevilla or Banco de España, tel. 915-245-400, http://teatrodelazarzuela.mcu.es; to purchase online, go to the theater section of www.servicaixa.com and choose the English version). Madrid puts on live zarzuela events in the Royal Palace gardens summer evenings (ask the TI for details). The TI's monthly guide has a special zarzuela listing.

▲**Flamenco**—Although Sevilla is the capital of flamenco, Madrid has two easy and affordable options.

Taberna Casa Patas attracts big-name flamenco artists. You'll quickly understand why this intimate (30-table) and smoky venue is named "House of Feet." Since this is for locals as well as tour groups, the flamenco is contemporary and may be jazzier than your notion—it depends on who's performing (€31, Mon–Thu at 22:30, Fri–Sat at 21:00 and 24:00, closed Sun, 75–90 min, price includes cover and first drink, reservations smart, no flash cameras, Cañizares 10, tel. 913-690-496, www.casapatas.com). Its restaurant is a logical spot for dinner before the show (€30 dinners, Mon–Sat from 20:00). Or, since it's three blocks south of the recommended Plaza Santa Ana tapas bars, this could be your post-tapas-crawl entertainment.

Las Carboneras, more downscale, is an easygoing, folksy little place a few steps from Plaza Mayor with a nightly hour-long flamenco show (€33 includes an entry and a drink, €61 gets you a table up front with dinner and unlimited cheap drinks if you reserve ahead, discount if you book direct and show this book, Mon–Thu at 22:30 and often at 20:30, Fri–Sat at 20:30 and 23:00, closed Sun, earlier shows possible if a group books, reservations recommended, Plaza del Conde de Miranda 1, tel. 915-428-677, Enrique).

Regardless of what your hotel receptionist may want to sell you, other flamenco places—such as Arco de Cuchilleros (Calle de los Cuchilleros 7), Café de Chinitas (Calle Torija 7, just off Plaza Mayor), Corral de la Morería (Calle de Morería 17), and Torres Bermejas (off Gran Vía)—are filled with tourists and pushy waiters.

Mesones—Just west of Plaza Mayor, the lane called Cava de San Miguel is lined with *mesones:* long, skinny, cavelike bars famous for drinking and singing late into the night. If you were to toss lowbrow locals, Spanish karaoke, electric keyboards, crass tourists, cheap sangria, and greasy calamari into a late-night blender and turn it on, this is what you'd get. It's generally lively only on Friday and Saturday, but you're welcome to pop in to several bars (such as Guitarra, Tortilla, or Boquerón) and see what you can find.

Late-Night Bars—If you're just picking up speed at midnight, and looking for a place filled with old tiles and a Gen-X crowd, power into **Bar Viva Madrid** (daily 13:00–3:00 in the morning, downhill from Plaza Santa Ana on Calle Manuel Fernández y González, tel. 914-293-640). The same street has other late-night bars filled with music. Or hike on over to **Chocolatería San Ginés** (described in "Eating," later in this chapter) for a dessert of *churros con chocolate.*

Movies—During Franco's days, movies were always dubbed into Spanish. Movies in Spain remain about the most often dubbed in Europe. To see a movie with its original soundtrack, look for *V.O.* (meaning "original version"). **Cine Ideal,** with nine screens, is a good place for the latest films in V.O. (€7.50, 5-min walk south of Puerta del Sol at Calle del Dr. Cortezo 6, tel. 913-692-518 for info). For extensive listings, see the *Guía del Ocio* entertainment guide (€1 at newsstands, www.guiadelocio.com) or a local newspaper.

Sleeping

Madrid has plenty of centrally located budget hotels and *pensiones.* You'll have no trouble finding a sleepable double for €35, a good double for €70, and a modern, air-conditioned double with all the comforts for €100. Prices vary throughout the year at bigger hotels, but remain about the same for the smaller hotels and *hostales.* It's almost always easy to find a place. Anticipate full hotels only during May (the San Isidro festival, celebrating Madrid's patron saint with bullfights and zarzuelas—especially around his feast day on May 15) and the last week in September (conventions). In July and August, prices can be softer—ask about promotional deals. All of the accommodations I've listed are within a few minutes' walk of Puerta del Sol.

With all of Madrid's street noise, I'd request the highest floor possible. Also, twin-bedded rooms are generally a bit larger than double-bedded rooms for the same price. Madrid hoteliers rarely offer a cash discount. During slow times, drop-ins can often score a room in business-class hotels for just a few euros more than the budget hotels (which don't have prices that fluctuate as wildly with demand).

Sleep Code

(€1 = about $1.40, country code: 34)

S = Single, **D** = Double/Twin, **T** = Triple, **Q** = Quad, **b** = bathroom, **s** = shower only. Unless otherwise noted, credit cards are accepted, English is spoken, and breakfast is *not* included. In Madrid, the 7 percent IVA tax is sometimes included in the price.

To help you easily sort through these listings, I've divided the rooms into three categories, based on the price for a standard double room with bath during high season:

$$$ Higher Priced—Most rooms €100 or more.
$$ Moderately Priced—Most rooms between €70-100.
$ Lower Priced—Most rooms €70 or less.

Madrid's Center—Hotels and Restaurants

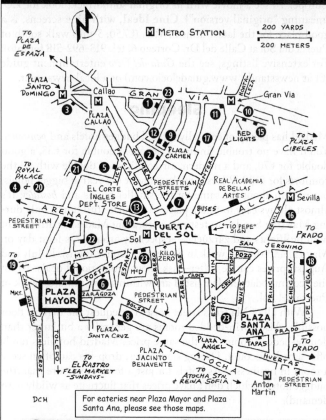

M METRO STATION

200 YARDS
200 METERS

For eateries near Plaza Mayor and Plaza Santa Ana, please see those maps.

1 Hotel Regente
2 Hotel Liabeny
3 Hotel Preciados
4 To Hotel Opera
5 Hotel Carlos V
6 Petit Palace Posada del Peine
7 Hotel Europa & Cafeteria
8 Hotel Plaza Mayor
9 Hostales at Calle de la Salud 13
10 Hostal Aliste & Pension Marina Santa
11 Hostales Res. Luis XV, Jerez & Metropol
12 Restaurante Puerto Rico
13 El Corte Inglés Cafeteria
14 Casa Labra Taberna Restaurante
15 La Gloria de Montera Rest. & Fresc Co Buffet
16 La Finca de Susana
17 Artemisia II Veggie Rest.
18 Artemisia I Veggie Rest.
19 To Casa Ciriaco & La Paella Real Rest.
20 To La Bola Taberna
21 Chocolaterías Valor
22 Chocolatería San Ginés
23 Internet Cafés (3)

MADRID

Fancier Places in the Pedestrian Zone Between Puerta del Sol and Gran Vía

Reliable and away from the seediness, these hotels are good values for those wanting to spend a little more. Their formal prices may be inflated, but some offer weekend and summer discounts when it's slow. Drivers will pay about €24 a day in garages. Use Metro: Sol for all but Hotel Opera (Metro: Ópera).

$$$ Hotel Regente is big and traditional, with 154 tastefully decorated, comfortable, air-conditioned rooms, generous public spaces, a great location, and a good value (Sb-€77, Db-€102, Tb-€124, breakfast-€11, midway between Puerta del Sol and Plaza del Callao at Mesonero Romanos 9, tel. 915-212-941, fax 915-323-014, www.hotelregente.com, info@hotelregente.com).

$$$ Hotel Liabeny rents 220 plush, spacious, business-class rooms offering all the comforts (Sb-€110, Db-€150, Tb-€176, 10 percent cheaper mid-July–Aug and Fri–Sat, breakfast-€16, air-con, sauna, gym, off Plaza del Carmen at Salud 3, tel. 915-319-000, fax 915-327-421, www.liabeny.es, info@hotelliabeny.com).

$$$ Hotel Preciados, a four-star business hotel, has 73 fine, sleek, and modern rooms as well as elegant lounges. It's well located and reasonably priced for the luxury it provides (Db-€125–160, prices are often soft, checking Web specials in advance or dropping in will likely snag a room for around €100, breakfast-€15, just off Plaza de Santo Domingo at Calle Preciados 37, tel. 914-544-400, fax 914-544-401, www.preciadoshotel.com, preciadoshotel @preciadoshotel.com).

$$$ Hotel Opera, a serious and contemporary hotel with 79 classy rooms, is located just off Plaza Isabel II, a four-block walk from Puerta del Sol toward the Royal Palace. In 2008, the hotel underwent a mod facelift (Sb-€107, Db-€149, Db with big view terrace-€189–210, Tb-€189, tax not included, buffet breakfast-€13, air-con, elevator, free Internet access, ask for a higher floor—there are nine—to avoid street noise, Cuesta de Santo Domingo 2, Metro: Ópera, tel. 915-412-800, fax 915-416-923, www.hotelopera .com, reservas@hotelopera.com). Hotel Opera's cafeteria is understandably popular. Also consider their "singing dinners"—great operetta music with a delightful dinner—offered nightly at 22:00 (average price-€60, reservations smart, call 915-426-382 or reserve at hotel reception desk).

$$$ Hotel Carlos V is a Best Western with 67 sharp, high-ceilinged rooms, elegant breakfast, and a pleasant lounge. Its central location off Preciados pedestrian street makes it convenient—but ask for an inside room to avoid street noise (Sb-€95, standard Db-€115, larger "superior" Db with terrace-€173, Tb-€135, tax not included, breakfast-€9, air-con, non-smoking floors, elevator,

MADRID

Maestro Victoria 5, tel. 915-314-100, fax 915-313-761, www.hotel carlosv.com, recepcion@hotelcarlosv.com).

$$$ Petit Palace Posada del Peine feels like part of a big modern chain (which it is), but fills its well-located old building with fresh, efficient character. Behind the ornate and sparkling Old World facade is a comfortable and modern business-class hotel with 69 rooms just a block from Plaza Mayor (Db-€100–160 depending on demand, tax not included, breakfast-€9, air-con, Calle Postas 17, tel. 915-238-151, fax 915-232-993, www.hthoteles .com, pos@hthoteles.com).

$$ Hotel Europa, with sleek marble, red carpet runners along the halls, happy Muzak charm, and an attentive staff, is a tremendous value. It rents 103 squeaky-clean rooms, many with balconies overlooking the pedestrian zone or an inner courtyard (Sb-€74, Db-€92–110, Tb-€130, Qb-€155, Quint/b-€175, tax not included, breakfast-€2–10, air-con, elevator, free Internet access, easy phone reservations with credit card, Calle del Carmen 4, tel. 915-212-900, fax 915-214-696, www.hoteleuropa.net, info@hoteleuropa .net, run by Antonio and Fernando Garaban and their helpful and jovial staff, Javi and Jim). The convenient Europa cafeteria/ restaurant next door is a lively and convivial scene—fun for breakfast, and a fine value any time of day (see page 1187).

$$ Hotel Plaza Mayor, with 34 solidly outfitted rooms, is tastefully decorated and beautifully situated a block off Plaza Mayor (Sb-€65, Db-€85, bigger Db corner room-€95, Tb-€115, buffet breakfast-€8, for the best price reserve direct by email or fax and mention this book, air-con, elevator, Wi-Fi, Calle Atocha 2, tel. 913-600-606, fax 913-600-610, www.h-plazamayor.com, info@h-plazamayor.com).

Cheaper Bets near Puerta del Sol and Gran Vía

These accommodations are also in or near the handy pedestrian zone between Puerta del Sol and Gran Vía. The first two (Acapulco and Triana) are by far the best (and priciest). The Arcos, Aliste, and Marina Santa are your best cheap-bed options (with youth-hostel prices, yet hotel privacy).

At Calle de la Salud 13

These are all in the same building at Calle de la Salud 13, overlooking Plaza del Carmen—a little square with a sleepy, almost Parisian ambience. (The square might be a bit more bustling in 2010, thanks to the construction of a new commuter-train line nearby.)

$ Hostal Acapulco rents 16 bright rooms with air-conditioning and all the big hotel gear. The neighborhood is quiet enough that it's smart to request a room with a balcony (Sb-€49–54, Db-€59–64, Tb-€77–80, elevator, free Internet access, fourth floor, tel. 915-311-945, fax 915-322-329, hostal_acapulco@yahoo .es, Ana and Marco).

$ Hostal Triana, also a fine deal, is bigger—with 40 rooms— and offers a little less charm for a little less money (Sb-€42, Db-€55, Tb-€75, includes taxes, rooms facing the square have air-con and cost €3 extra, other rooms have fans, elevator, free Wi-Fi, first floor, tel. 915-326-812, fax 915-229-729, www.hostaltriana .com, triana@hostaltriana.com, Victor González).

$ Pension Arcos is tiny, granny-run, and old-fashioned— it's been in the Hernández family since 1936. The business cards have the new phone codes penned in, and there's no hint of email or even fax. You can reserve by phone—in Spanish—only a day in advance, and you must pay in cash. But its five rooms are clean, quiet, reasonably friendly, air-conditioned, and served by an elevator—and you step right out onto a great square. You also have access to a tiny roof terrace and a nice little lounge. If you're looking for cheap beds in a great locale, assuming you can communicate enough to reserve a room, this place is unbeatable (D-€36, Db-€40, fifth floor, air-con, tel. 915-324-994, Anuncia and Sabino).

More Cheap Sleeps

At Caballero de Gracia 6: These two *hostales* (which share the same building near Gran Vía Metro) are quiet, plain, and dreary, yet safe, on a quiet street a block past the unthreatening prostitutes of Calle de la Montera: **$ Hostal Aliste** (11 rooms, third floor, Sb-€35–38, Db-€45–48, extra bed-€20, elevator, tel. 915-215-979, h.aliste@teleline.es, Manuela's son Edward speaks English) and the humble **$ Pension Marina Santa** (nine rooms, second floor, D-€40, Db-€45, elevator, tel. 915-327-074, Lydia).

$ Hostal Residencia Luis XV is a big, plain, well-run, and clean place offering a good value. It's on a quiet eighth floor (there's an elevator). You'll find it where prostitute-lined Calle de la Montera hits noisy Gran Vía. It can be smoky, and there are no non-smoking rooms. They also run the 36-room **Hostal Jerez**— similar in every way except the name—located on the sixth floor (Sb-€45, Db-€59, Tb-€75, includes tax, air-con, elevator, Calle de la Montera 47, tel. 915-221-021, fax 915-221-350, www.hrluisxv .net, reservas@hrluisxv.net).

$ Hostal Metropol is a big, colorful, and very youthful youth hostel with 130 beds beautifully located at the noisy corner of Calle de la Montera and Gran Vía, a few minutes' walk from Puerta del Sol (bed-€18, 3–5 beds per room, always co-ed, Sb-€35, Db-€60, includes a fitted sheet and breakfast, towel not included, free

Internet access, Calle de la Montera 47, first floor, tel. 915-212-935, fax 915-212-934, www.metropolhostel.com, metropol@terra.es).

Near the Prado

To locate the following three places, please see the "Madrid's Museum Neighborhood" map, page 1172.

$$$ Hotel Lope de Vega is your best business-class hotel value near the Prado. A four-star place that opened in 2000, it's a "cultural-themed" hotel inspired by the 17th-century writer Lope de Vega. With 60 rooms, it feels cozy and friendly for a formal business-class hotel (Sb-€115, Db-€125–145, Tb-€189, one child sleeps free, prices about 20 percent lower Fri–Sun and during most of the summer, air-con, elevator, Internet access, parking-€23/day, Calle Lope de Vega 49, tel. 913-600-011, fax 914-292-391, www .hotellopedevega.com, lopedevega@hotellopedevega.com).

At Cervantes 34: Two fine budget *hostales* are at Cervantes 34 (Metro: Anton Martín—but not handy to Metro). Both are homey, with inviting lounge areas; neither serves breakfast. **$ Hostal Gonzalo**—with 15 spotless, comfortable rooms, well-run by friendly and helpful Javier—is deservedly in all the guide-books, so reserve in advance (Sb-€45, Db-€55, Tb-€70, air-con, elevator, third floor, tel. 914-292-714, fax 914-202-007, www .hostalgonzalo.com, hostal@hostalgonzalo.com). Downstairs, the nearly as polished **$ Hostal Cervantes** also has 15 rooms (Sb-€50, Db-€60, Tb-€75, includes tax, cheaper when slow and for longer stays, Internet access and Wi-Fi, second floor, tel. 914-298-365, fax 914-292-745, www.hostal-cervantes.com, correo@hostal-cervantes .com, Fabio).

Apartments

$$$ Raquel Román rents apartments throughout Madrid, most of which have air-conditioning and a washing machine. Review your options on the website (www.homesfortravellers.com), choose an apartment, reserve online, and pay a nonrefundable deposit (usually about 30 percent) by credit card. Upon arrival, you can pay the rest in cash or by credit card, depending on the owner of the apartment (€65–160 per night based on size and amenities, mobile 629-196-883, info@homesfortravellers.com).

Eating

In Spain, only Barcelona rivals Madrid for taste-bud thrills. You have three dining choices: a memorable, atmospheric sit-down meal in a well-chosen restaurant; a forgettable, basic sit-down meal; or a stand-up meal of tapas in a bar...or four. Many restaurants are closed in August (especially through the last half).

Madrid has famously good tap water, and waiters willingly serve it free—just ask for *agua del grifo*.

Eating Cheaply North of Puerta del Sol

See the "Madrid's Center" map, page 1182, for locations.

Restaurante Puerto Rico fills a long, congested hall by serving good meals for great prices to smart locals (€10 three-course fixed-price meal, Mon–Sat 13:00–16:30 & 20:30–24:00, closed Sun, Chinchilla 2, between Puerta del Sol and Gran Vía, tel. 915-219-834).

Hotel Europa Cafetería is a fun, high-energy scene with a mile-long bar, traditionally clad waiters, great people-watching, local cuisine, and a fine €11 fixed-price lunch (daily 7:00–24:00; next to Hotel Europa—listed under "Sleeping," earlier in this chapter; 50 yards off Puerta del Sol at Calle del Carmen 4, tel. 915-212-900). The menu lists three price levels: bar, table, or outside, on the terrace. Though you pay a premium for the outdoor seating, it's a big hit with people-watchers.

El Corte Inglés' seventh-floor cafeteria is fresh, modern, and understated. While not particularly cheap, it's popular with locals (Mon–Sat 10:00–22:00, closed Sun, non-smoking section, just off Puerta del Sol at intersection of Preciados and Tetuán, see "One-Stop Shopping," page 1158).

Casa Labra Taberna Restaurante is famous as the birthplace of the Spanish Socialist Party in 1879...and as a spot for great cod. Packed with Madrileños, it's a wonderful scene with three distinct sections: the stand-up bar (cheapest, with two lines: one for munchies, the other for drinks), a peaceful little sit-down area in back (a little more expensive but still cheap; good €6 salads), and a fancy restaurant (€20 lunches). Their tasty little €1 *Tajada de Bacalao* (cod) dishes put it on the map. The waiters are fun to joke around with (daily 11:00–15:30 & 18:00–23:00, restaurant only closed Sun, a block off Puerta del Sol at Calle Tetuán 12, tel. 915-310-081).

La Gloria de Montera Restaurante, a hip Spanish bistro with white tablecloths and a minimalist-library ambience, serves good food to locals (€8 fish and meat plates, daily 13:15–16:00 & 20:30–23:45, no reservations—arrive early or put your name on the list, a block from Gran Vía and Metro: Red de San Luis at Caballero de Gracia 10, tel. 915-234-407). Their sister restaurant, **La Finca de Susana,** is also extremely popular for the same reasons (daily 13:00–15:45 & 20:30–23:45, go early—line starts forming at about 20:00, just east of Puerta del Sol at Calle Arlabán 4, tel. 913-693-557).

Fresc Co is the place for a cheap, modern, fast, and buffet-style meal. It's a chain with a winning plan: a long, appealing salad and buffet bar with one cheap price for all-you-can-eat, including dessert and a drink (€9 lunch, €10 dinner, daily 12:30–24:00, air-con, Caballero de Gracia 8, tel. 915-216-052).

Vegetarian: **Artemisia II** is a hit with vegetarians who like good, healthy food in a smoke-free room without the typical hippie ambience that comes with most veggie places (great €11.25 three-course fixed-price lunch Mon–Fri only, open daily 13:30–16:00 & 21:00–24:00, 2 blocks north of Puerta del Sol at Tres Cruces 4, a few steps off Plaza del Carmen, tel. 915-218-721). **Artemisia I,** II's older sister, is located two blocks east of Plaza Santa Ana at Ventura de la Vega 4, off San Jerónimo (same hours, tel. 914-295-092).

On or near Plaza Mayor

Madrileños enjoy Plaza Mayor (without its high costs) by grabbing a bite to go from a nearby bar and just planting themselves somewhere on the square to eat (squid sandwiches are popular—described below). But for many tourists, dinner at a sidewalk café right on the Plaza Mayor is worth the premium price (consider Cervecería Pulpito, southwest corner of the square at #10).

Squid Sandwich: Plaza Mayor is famous for its *bocadillos de calamares.* For a tasty €2 squid-ring sandwich, line up at **Casa Rúa** at Plaza Mayor's northwest corner, a few steps up Calle Ciudad Rodrigo (daily 9:00–23:00). Hanging up behind the bar is a photo-advertisement of Plaza Mayor from the 1950s, when the square contained a park.

Bullfighting Bar: The **Torre del Oro Bar Andalú** on Plaza Mayor has walls lined with grisly bullfight photos. While this place is good for drinks, you pay a premium for the tapas and food... the cost of munching amidst all that bullephenalia while enjoying their excellent Plaza Mayor outdoor seating (daily 8:00–15:00 & 18:00–24:00).

Hemingway Haunt: **Sobrino del Botín** is a hit with many Americans because "Hemingway ate here" (daily 13:00–16:00 & 20:00–24:00, Cuchilleros 17, a block downhill from Plaza Mayor, tel. 913-664-217). It's touristy, pricey (€30 average meals), and the last place Papa would go now...but still, people love it, and the food is excellent (roast suckling pig is the specialty). If phoning to make a reservation, choose between the downstairs (for dark, medieval-cellar ambience) or upstairs (for a still-traditional, but airier and lighter elegance). While this restaurant boasts that it's the oldest in the world (dating from 1725), a nearby restaurant teases, "Hemingway never ate here."

On Calle Cava Baja, South of Plaza Mayor

Few tourists frequent this traditional neighborhood—Barrio de los Austrias, named for the Habsburgs. It's three minutes south of

Eating near Plaza Mayor

TO ROYAL PALACE

CALLE MAYOR

C. CODO

SAN MIGUEL MARKET

CAVA S. MIGUEL

PLAZA CONDE BARAJAS

C. CUCHIL

SAN JUSTA

PLAZA PUERTA CERRADA

C. SEGOVIA

C. NUNCIO

C. ALMENDRO

BAJA

GRAFAL

CAVA

CALLE

PLAZA MAYOR

POSTAS

ZARAGOZA

GERONA

IMPERIAL

LECHUGA

C. CONCEPCION

C. COLEGIATA

CALLE TOLEDO

PALACIO SANTA CRUZ

SAN ISIDRO

TO PUERTA DEL SOL

TO PLAZA S. ANA

TO Tirso de Molina

200 YARDS
200 METERS

DCH

Ⓜ La Latina

Ⓜ METRO STATION

❶ Casa Rúa
❷ Torre del Oro Bar Andalú
❸ Sobrino del Botín
❹ Posada de la Villa
❺ Julian de Tolosa
❻ Taberna Los Lucio
❼ Casa Lucio
❽ Taberna Tempranillo

❾ Giangrossi Helado Artesanal Ice Cream
❿ El Madroño
⓫ Taberna Los Austrias
⓬ Juanalaloca.zip
⓭ Las Carboneras (Flamenco)
⓮ Mesones ("Cave Bars")
⓯ Mercado de San Miguel

MADRID

Plaza Mayor, or a 10-minute walk from Puerta del Sol. Lined with a diverse array of restaurants and tapas bars, the street called Cava Baja is clogged with Madrileños out in search of a special meal. I've listed a few standards, but excellent new eateries are always opening up. For a good, authentic Madrid dinner experience, take time to survey the many options along this street—between the first and last listings described below—and choose your favorite. A key wine-drinking phrase: *mucho cuerpo* (full-bodied).

Posada de la Villa serves Castilian cuisine in a 17th-century posada. This sprawling, multi-floor restaurant has dressy tables under open beams, which give it a rustic elegance. Peek into the big oven to see the baby pigs about to make some diner happy. If you're not going to Toledo or Sevilla, this is the place to try roast lamb, which is the house specialty (€30 meals, Mon–Sat 13:00–16:00 & 20:00–24:00, closed Sun and Aug, Calle Cava Baja 9, tel. 913-661-860).

Julian de Tolosa is chic, pricey, elegantly simple, and popular with natives who know good food. They offer a small, quality menu of Navarra's regional cuisine, from T-bone steak *(chuletón)* to red *tolosa* beans, in a spacious, dressy, and sane setting (€40 meals, Mon–Sat 13:30–16:00 & 21:00–24:00, Sun 13:30–16:00, Calle Cava Baja 18, tel. 913-658-210).

Taberna Los Lucio is a jam-packed bar serving good tapas, salads, *huevos estrellados* (scrambled eggs with fried potatoes), and wine. Their basement is much less atmospheric (Wed–Mon 13:00–16:00 & 20:30–24:00, Tue 20:30–24:00, Calle Cava Baja 30, tel. 913-662-984).

Casa Lucio is a favorite splurge among power-dressing Madrileños. The king and queen of Spain eat in this elegant place, but it's accessible to commoners. This could be the best place in town for a special night out and a full-blown meal (€40 for dinner, Mon–Fri and Sun 13:00–16:00 & 21:00–24:00, Sat 21:00–24:00, closed Aug, Calle Cava Baja 35; unless you're the king or queen, reserve several days in advance—and don't even bother on weekends; tel. 913-653-252).

Taberna Tempranillo, ideal for hungry wine-lovers, offers tapas and 250 kinds of wine. Wines available by the glass are listed on the board. With a phrasebook in hand or a spirit of adventure, use their fascinating menu to assemble your dream meal. It's packed and full of commotion—the crowds can be overwhelming. Arrive by 20:00 or plan to wait (Tue–Sun 13:00–15:30 & 20:00–24:00, Mon 20:00–24:00, closed Aug, Cava Baja 38, tel. 913-641-532).

Ice Cream Finale: **Giangrossi Helado Artesanal** is a popular chain considered to serve some of Madrid's best ice cream. This Giangrossi—which has a plush white leather lounge and lots of great flavors—is a fun way to finish your dining experience in this area. It's just 50 yards from the La Latina Metro stop (Cava Baja 40, tel. 902-444-130).

Near the Royal Palace

See the "Madrid's Center" map, page 1182, for locations.

Casa Ciriaco is popular with Madrileños who appreciate good traditional cooking (€30 meals, €20 fixed-price lunch and dinner, Thu–Tue 13:30–16:00 & 20:30–24:00, closed Wed and Aug, air-con, halfway between Puerta del Sol and the Royal Palace at Calle Mayor 84, tel. 915-480-620). It was from this building in 1906 that an anarchist bombed the royal couple on their wedding day (for details, see page 1168). A photo of the carnage is inside the front door.

La Bola Taberna, touristy but friendly and tastefully elegant, specializes in *cocido Madrileño*—Madrid stew. The €19 stew consists of various meats, carrots, and garbanzo beans in earthen jugs. It's big enough to split—which they'll let you do, as long as the second person orders something small, like a salad. The stew is served as two courses: First you enjoy the broth as a soup, then you dig into the meat and veggies (Mon–Sat 13:00–16:00 & 20:30–23:00, closed Sun, cash only, midway between the Royal Palace and Gran Vía at Calle Bola 5, tel. 915-476-930).

La Paella Real Restaurante ("Royal Paella Restaurant") is considered a top spot for "a proper paella." You'll see this saffron-rice specialty from Valencia served all over town (and it tastes best in Valencia), but paella requires a special oven and big pan in order to cook it correctly. For your paella experience, enjoy this venerable and dressy spot (€15 per person for hearty portions of paella—minimum of two, with drinks and sides figure about €20–30 per person, Mon–Sat 13:00–16:00 & 19:30–22:30, Sun 13:00–16:00, allow a good 30 min for your meal to arrive, between Puerta del Sol and the palace at Plaza de la Ópera, Arrieta 2, tel. 915-420-942).

Near the Prado

Each of the three big art museums has a decent cafeteria. Or choose from these restaurants, all within a block of the Prado (for locations, see the "Madrid's Museum Neighborhood" map, page 1172).

La Platería Bar Museo is a hardworking little café/wine bar with a good menu for tapas, light meals, and hearty salads (listed as *raciones* and *1/2 raciones* on the chalkboard). Its tables spill onto the leafy little Plaza de Platerías de Martínez (daily 8:00–24:00, air-con, directly across busy boulevard Paseo del Prado from Atocha end of Prado, tel. 914-291-722).

Taberna de Dolores, a winning formula since 1908, is a commotion of locals enjoying €2.50 *canapés* (open-face sandwiches), tasty *raciones* of seafood, and *cañas* (small beers) at the bar or at a few tables in the back (daily 11:00–24:00, Plaza de Jesús 4, tel. 914-292-243).

VIPS is a bright, popular chain restaurant, handy for a cheap and filling salad. Engulfed in a big bookstore, this is a high-energy, no-charm eatery (daily 9:00–24:00, across the boulevard from northern end of Prado, under Palace Hotel). In 2001, Spain's first Starbucks opened next door.

Fast Food and Picnics

Fast Food: For an easy, light, cheap meal, try **Rodilla**—a popular sandwich and salad chain with a shop on the northeast corner of Puerta del Sol at #13 (Mon–Fri 9:30–23:00, Sat 9:00–23:00, Sun 11:00–23:00). **Pans & Company,** with shops throughout Madrid and Spain, offers healthy, tasty sandwiches and pre-packaged salads (daily 9:00–24:00, locations at Puerta del Sol, on Plaza Callao, at Gran Vía 30, and many more).

Picnics: The department store **El Corte Inglés** has well-stocked meat and cheese counters downstairs (Mon–Sat 10:00–22:00, Sun 11:00–21:00, see "One-Stop Shopping" on page 1158).

Churros con Chocolate

Those not watching their cholesterol will want to try the deep-fried doughy treats called *churros* (or the thicker *porras*), best enjoyed by dipping them in pudding-like hot chocolate. While many *chocolaterías* offer the dunkable fritters, *churros* are most delicious when consumed fresh out of the greasy cauldron.

Chocolaterías Valor is a modern chain that does *churros* with pride and gusto. A few minutes' walk from nearly all my hotel recommendations, it's a fine place for breakfast. With a website like www.amigosdelchocolate.com, you know where their heart is (€4 *churros con chocolate,* daily 8:00–22:30, Fri–Sat until 24:00, a half-block below Plaza Callao and Gran Vía at Postigo de San Martín 7, tel. 915-229-288).

Chocolatería San Ginés is a classy institution, much beloved by Madrileños for its *churros con chocolate* (€3.20 in the morning and afternoon, €3.50 at night). Dunk your *churros* into the chocolate pudding, as locals have done here for more than 100 years. While quiet before midnight, it's packed with the disco crowd in the wee hours; the popular dance club Joy Eslava is next door (daily 22 hours a day—it's only closed between 7:00 and 9:00; from Puerta del Sol, take Calle de Arenal 2 blocks west, turn left on bookstore-lined Pasadizo de San Ginés, and you'll see the café—it's at #5; tel. 913-656-546).

Tapas

Tapa-Hopping on Calle del Nuncio (near Calle Cava Baja)

El Madroño ("The Berry Tree," a symbol of Madrid) is a fun tapas bar that preserves a bit of old Madrid. A tile copy of Velázquez's famous *Drinkers* grins from its facade. Inside, look above the stairs for photos of 1902 Madrid. Study the coats of arms of Madrid through the centuries as you try a *vermut* (vermouth) on tap and a €2 sandwich. Or ask to try the *licor de madroño;* a small glass *(chupito)* costs €1.50. While indoor seating is bright and colorful, the sidewalk tables come with great people-watching (€9 fixed-price lunch, quieter tables in the back, Tue–Sun 9:00–17:00 & 20:00–24:00, closed Mon, Plaza Puerta Cerrada 7, tel. 913-645-629).

Taberna Los Austrias, two blocks away, serves tapas, salads, and light meals on wood-barrel tables (daily 12:00–16:00 & 20:00–24:00, more formal seating in back, Calle Nuncio 17).

Juanalaloca.zip serves wine and creative tapas, such as their famous *tortilla de patatas*, a potato dish that owes much of its tastiness to an extra touch—caramelized onions. It's open late every night (€8 tapas, Tue–Fri 20:00–24:00, Sat 13:00–17:00 & 20:00–24:00, Sun 13:00–24:00, closed Mon, Calle Nuncio 17, tel. 913-654-704).

The Madrid Pub-Crawl Dinner (for Beginners)

For maximum fun, people, and atmosphere, go mobile for dinner: Do the "tapas tango," a local tradition of going from one bar to the next, munching, drinking, and socializing. Tapas are the toothpick appetizers, salads, and deep-fried foods served in most bars. Madrid is Spain's tapas capital—tapas just don't get any better. Grab a toothpick and stab something strange—but establish the prices first, especially if you're on a tight budget or at a possible tourist trap. Some items are very pricey, and most bars push larger *raciones,* rather than smaller tapas. The real action begins late (around 20:00). But for beginners, an earlier start, with less commotion, can be easier. In good old-fashioned bars, a drink comes with a free tapa. The litter on the floor is normal; that's where people traditionally toss their trash and shells (it's unsanitary to put it back on the bar). Don't worry about paying until you're ready to go. Then ask for *la cuenta* (the bill).

If done properly, a pub crawl can be a highlight of your trip. Before embarking upon this culinary adventure, learn a little about tapas, the tasty treats you'll encounter. Your ability to speak a little Spanish will get you a much better (and less expensive) experience.

Prowl the area between Puerta del Sol and Plaza Santa Ana. There's no ideal route, but the little streets (in this book's map)

Madrid Pub-Crawl Dinner

To Gran Via M

REAL ACADEMIA DE BELLAS ARTES

M Sevilla

CALLE ALCALA

PEDESTRIAN STREETS

CARMEN

MONTERA

AHORROS

SEVILLA

CEDACEROS

BEAR & TREE STATUE

Sol M

PUERTA DEL SOL

CARRETAS

TÍO PEPE SIGN ❶

CARRERA

DE

SAN JERÓNIMO

❷

ESPOZ Y MINA

POZO

VICTORIA

DE LA CRUZ

NÚÑEZ DE ARCE

VENTURA VEGA

ECHEGARAY

❿

TO PRADO + THYSSEN MUSEUMS

KILO-ZERO

SAN RICARDO

MATHEU

❸

❹

❺

PRINCIPE

❼

❶❷

TO PLAZA MAYOR

CADIZ

C. MAN. FERN.

BOLSA

PLAZA JACINTO BENAVENTE

CALLE

❹

PLAZA STA. ANA

❽

CALLE

DE

PRADO

❸

PLAZA ANGEL

❻

TAPAS

CERVANTES

ATOCHA

SEB.

CALLE

INFANTE

❾

LEON

LOPE DE VEGA

PEDESTRIAN STREET

HUERTAS

TO PRADO

CANIZ.

❶❶

To Anton Martin M + LAVAPIÉS DISTRICT

DCH

M METRO STATION

100 YARDS
100 METERS

N

❶ La Taurina Cervecería
❷ Lhardy Pastelería & Museo del Jamón
❸ La Casa del Abuelo
❹ Oreja de Oro
❺ Casa Toni
❻ Cervecería de Santa Ana
❼ Naturbier Microbrewery

❽ Vinoteca Barbechera
❾ Gonzalez Wine & Cheese Shop
❿ Artemisia I Veggie Restaurant
⓫ Taberna Casa Patas (Flamenco)
⓬ Bar Viva Madrid
⓭ Launderette
⓮ Internet Café

MADRID

between Puerta del Sol, San Jerónimo, and Plaza Santa Ana hold tasty surprises. Nearby, the street Jesús de Medinaceli is also lined with popular tapas bars. Below is a six-stop tapa crawl. These places are good, but don't be afraid to make some discoveries of your own. The more adventurous should read this crawl for ideas, and skip directly to the advanced zone (Lavapiés), described on page 1196.

• *From Puerta del Sol, walk east a block down Carrera de San Jerónimo to the corner of Calle Victoria. Across from the Museo del Jamón (Museum of Ham), you'll find...*

La Taurina Cervecería: This is a bullfighters' Planet Holly-wood (daily 12:00–24:00, air-con). Wander among trophies and historic photographs. Each stuffed bull's head is named, along with his farm, awards, and who killed him. Among the many gory photos, study the first post: It's Che Guevara, Orson Welles, and Salvador Dalí, all enjoying a good fight. Around the corner, the Babe Ruth of bullfighters, El Cordobés, lies wounded in bed. The photo above and below shows him in action. I enjoyed the art. Then, inspired, I went for the *rabo de toro* (bull-tail stew, €15)— and regretted it. A good, basic dish here is *chorizos a la sidra* (spicy sausage in cider, €8) with a beer. If a fight's on, it'll be packed with aficionados gathered around the TV.

• *Across the street, just left of the Museo del Jamón, is the...*

Lhardy Pastelería: Offering a taste of Old World charm in this district of rowdy pubs, this place has been a fixture since 1839 for Madrileños wanting to duck in for a cup of soup or a light snack with a fortified wine. Step right in, and pretend you're an aristocrat back between the wars. Serve yourself. You'll pay as you leave (on the honor system). Help yourself to the silver water dispenser (free), a line of elegant bottles (each a different Iberian fortified wine: sherry, port, and so on, €2 per glass), a revolving case of meaty little pastries (€1 each), and a fancy soup dispenser (chicken broth consommé-€2, or €2.50 with a splash of sherry... local style—bottles in the corner, help yourself; Mon–Sat 9:30–15:00 & 17:00–21:30, Sun 9:30–15:00 only, non-smoking, Carrera de San Jerónimo 8).

• *Now duck into the...*

Museo del Jamón (Museum of Ham): This frenetic, cheap, stand-up bar (with famously rude service) is an assembly line of fast and simple *bocadillos* and *raciones*. It's tastefully decorated—unless you're a pig (or a vegetarian). Take advantage of the easy photo-illustrated menus that show various dishes and their prices. The best ham is the pricey *jamón ibérico*—from pigs who led stress-free lives in acorn-strewn valleys. Just point and eat, but be specific: A plate of low-end *jamón blanco* costs only €2.50, while *jamón ibérico* costs €13. For a small sandwich, ask for a *chiquito* (€0.70, or €3.10 for *ibérico*). If on a budget, don't let them sell you the *ibérico* (daily 9:00–24:00, sit-down restaurant upstairs, air-con).

• *Next, forage halfway up Calle Victoria to the tiny...*

La Casa del Abuelo: This is where seafood-lovers savor siz-zling plates of tasty little *gambas* (shrimp) and *langostinos* (prawns). Try *gambas a la plancha* (grilled shrimp, €7.20) or *gambas al ajillo* (ah-HEE-yoh, shrimp version of escargot, cooked in oil and garlic and ideal for bread dipping, €8) and a €2 glass of sweet red house wine (daily 12:00–24:00, Calle Victoria 12).

• *Across the street is...*

Oreja de Oro: The "Golden Ear" is named for what it sells—sautéed pigs' ears (*oreja*, €3). While oinker ears are a Madrid specialty, this place is Galician, so people also come here for *pulpo* (octopus, €12), *pimientos de Padrón* (sautéed miniature green peppers—my favorite plate of the entire crawl, €3.50), and the distinctive *ribeiro* (ree-BAY-roh) wine, served Galician-style, in characteristic little ceramic bowls (to disguise its lack of clarity). Jaime is a frantic one-man show who somehow gets everything just right. Have fun here.

• *For a finale, continue uphill and around the corner to...*

Casa Toni: This is the spot for refreshing bowls of gazpacho—the cold tomato-and-garlic soup (€2.30, available all year but only popular when temperatures soar). Their specialties are *berenjena* (deep-fried slices of eggplant, €4.70) and *champiñones* (sautéed mushrooms, €5.20; open daily 11:30–16:00 & 18:00–23:30, closed July, Calle Cruz 14).

More Options: If you're hungry for more, and want a trendy, up-to-date, pricier tapas scene, head for Plaza Santa Ana, with lively bars spilling out onto the square. Survey the entire scene. Consider **Cervecería de Santa Ana** (tasty tapas with two zones: rowdy, circa-1900 beer-hall and classier sit-down) or **Naturbier,** a local microbrewery. **Vinoteca Barbechera,** at the downhill end of the square, has an inviting menu of tapas and fine wines by the glass (indoor and outdoor seating).

Gonzalez, a venerable gourmet cheese and wine shop with a circa 1930s interior, offers a genteel opportunity to enjoy a plate of first-class cheese or meat and a fine glass of wine with friendly service and a fun setting. Their assortment of five Spanish cheeses—more than enough for two—is a cheese-lover's treat (€10 three-course fixed-price lunch, Tue–Sat 9:00–24:00, closed Sun–Mon, three blocks past Plaza Santa Ana at Calle Leon 12, tel. 914-295-618).

The Lavapiés District Tapas Crawl (for the Adventurous)

The neighborhood called Lavapiés is emerging as a colorful magnet for people-watching. This is where the multi-ethnic tapestry of Madrid society enjoys pithy, cheap, seedy-yet-fun-loving life on the streets. Neighborhoods like this typically experience an evolution: initially they're so cheap that only the immigrants, downtrodden, and counter-culture types live there. The diversity and color they bring attracts those with more money. Businesses erupt to cater to those bohemian/trendy tastes. Rents go up. Those who gave the area the colorful liveliness in the first place can no longer afford to live there. They move out...and here comes Starbucks. For now,

Lavapiés is still edgy, yet comfortable enough for most.

This district has almost no tourists. Old ladies with their tired bodies and busy fans hang out on their tiny balconies as they have for 40 years, watching the scene. Shady types lurk on side streets (don't venture off the main drag, don't show your wallet or money, and don't linger on Plaza Lavapiés).

For food, you'll find all the various kinds of tapas bars described earlier in "The Madrid Pub-Crawl Dinner (for Beginners)," plus great Indian (almost all run by Bangladeshis) and Moroccan eateries. I've listed a couple of places that appealed to me...but explore your options. I'd recommend taking the entire walk once, then backtracking and eating at the place or places that appeal to you.

From the Anton Martin Metro stop (or Plaza Santa Ana), walk down Calle Ave Maria (on its way to becoming Calle Ave Allah) to Plaza Lavapiés (where old ladies hang out with the swarthy drunks and a mosaic of cultures treat this square as a communal living room; Metro station here), and then up Calle de Lavapiés to the newly remodeled square, Plaza Tirso de Molina (Metro stop). This square was once plagued by druggies. Now with flower kiosks and a playground, it's homey and inviting. This is a fine example of the new vision for Madrid's public spaces.

On Calle Ave Maria: **Bar Melos** is a thriving dive jammed with a hungry and nubile local crowd. It's famous for its giant patty melts called *zapatillas de lacón y queso* (because they're the size and shape of a *zapatilla* or slipper, €7, feeds at least two, Ave Maria 44, smoky tables in back). **Nuevo Café Barbieri,** one of a dying breed of smoky mirrored cafés with a circa-1940 ambience, offers classical music in the afternoon and jazz in the evening (Ave Maria 45).

On Calle de Lavapiés: At Calle de Lavapiés 44, consider a fun pair of places: **Indian Restaurant Shapla** (good €9 fixed-price meal), and **Montes Wine Bar** (countless wines open and served by the glass, good tapas, crawl under the bar to get to the WC).

Connections

By Train

Remember that Madrid has two main train stations: Chamartín and Atocha. At the Atocha station, AVE and other long-distance trains depart from a different area than local *cercanías* trains (for more details, see "Arrival in Madrid," page 1154).

AVE Trains: Spain's AVE (AH-vay) bullet train opens up some good itinerary options. You can now get from Madrid's Atocha station to **Barcelona** in just under three hours, with trains running every 1–2 hours. The AVE train is generally faster and easier than flying (timed from downtown to downtown), but not necessarily cheaper. Basic second-class tickets are €106 one-way for most departures and €125 for the fastest, peak-time departures. First-class tickets are €153–180. Advance purchase discounts (40–60 days ahead) are available through the national rail company (RENFE), but sell out quickly. Save more by not traveling on holidays.

The AVE is also handy for visiting **Sevilla** (and, on the way, **Córdoba**). The basic Madrid–Sevilla second-class AVE fare is €67–75, depending upon departure time (the almost-as-fast Altaria is €10 less; first-class AVE costs €135 and comes with a meal). Consider this exciting day trip to Sevilla from Madrid: 7:00–depart Madrid, 8:45–12:40-in Córdoba, 13:30–20:45-in Sevilla, 23:30-back in Madrid.

Other AVE destinations include **Toledo** (nearly hourly, 30 min, €9, from Atocha) and **Segovia** (8/day, 35 min, €9, from Chamartín station, take train going toward Valladolid). For the latest, pick up the AVE brochure at the station, or check out www .renfe.es/ave. Prices vary with times and class. Eurailpass-holders just pay the seat-reservation fee (e.g., Madrid to Sevilla is €9 second-class, but only at RENFE ticket windows). Reserve each AVE segment ahead (tel. 902-240-202 for Atocha AVE info).

Below I've listed both non-AVE and (where available) AVE trains, to help you compare your options.

From Madrid by Train to: Toledo (AVE: nearly hourly, 30 min, from Atocha), **Barcelona** (AVE: 14/day, about 3 hrs from Atocha; plus 1 night train from Chamartín, 9 hrs), **Lisbon** (1/day departing at 22:45, 9 hrs, overnight Hotel Train from Chamartín), **Paris** (1/day, 13.5 hrs, direct overnight—a €185 Hotel Train, €160 in winter, reserve more than 15 days in advance and hope there are seats left in the €89 *oferta mini* deals, from Chamartín). General train info: tel. 902-240-202, for international journeys: tel. 902-243-402.

Madrid's Barajas Airport

Ten miles east of downtown, Madrid's modern airport has four terminals. Terminals 1, 2, and 3 are connected by long indoor walkways (about an 8-min walk apart), and serve airlines including Continental, Delta, Northwest, United, US Airways, Air Canada, and Spanair. The newer Terminal 4 serves airlines including Iberia, Vueling, British, and American, and also has a separate satellite terminal called T4S. In Terminal 4, it's a long way between the ticket counters and the boarding areas—signs indicate the walking times to gates. To transfer between Terminals 1–3 and Terminal 4, you can take a 10-minute shuttle bus (free, leaves every 10 min from departures level), or take the Metro (stops at Terminals 2 and 4). Make sure to allow enough time if you need to travel between terminals. For more information about navigating this massive airport, go to www.aena.es.

International flights typically use Terminals 1 and 4. At the Terminal 1 arrivals area, you'll find a helpful English-speaking **TI** (marked *Oficina de Información Turística*, Mon–Sat 8:00–20:00, Sun 9:00–14:00, tel. 913-058-656); **ATMs;** a **flight info office** (marked simply *Information* in airport lobby, open daily 24 hours, tel. 902-353-570); a **post-office** window; a **pharmacy;** lots of **phones** (buy a phone card from the nearby machine); a few scattered **Internet** terminals (small fee); **eateries;** a **RENFE office** (where you can get train info and buy long-distance train tickets, daily 8:00–21:00, tel. 902-240-202); and on-the-spot **car-rental agencies**. The newer, super-modern Terminal 4 offers essentially the same services.

Iberia, Spanair, and Air Europa are Spain's airlines, connecting a reasonable number of cities in Spain, as well as international destinations (ask for best rates at travel agencies). Vueling is the most popular discount airline in Iberia (e.g., Madrid–Barcelona flight as cheap as €30 if booked in advance, tel. 902-333-933, www.vueling.com).

Getting Between the Airport and Downtown

By Public Bus: Bus #200 shuttles travelers between airport Terminals 1, 2, and 3 (departing from arrivals level every 10 minutes, runs 6:00–24:00) and the Metro stop Avenida de América (northeast of the historical center) in about 20 minutes. From that Metro stop, you can connect to your hotel by taking the Metro or hopping a taxi. Bus #204 serves Terminal 4 the same way. The trip costs only €1 (buy ticket from driver; or get a shareable 10-ride Metrobus ticket for €7.40 at a tobacco shop—for more info, see "Getting Around Madrid," page 1159).

By Minibus Shuttle: The AeroCity shuttle bus provides door-to-door transport in a seven-seat minibus with up to three hotel stops en route. Ask your hotel in advance if they can arrange this service for you. The €19 fee covers up to three people per trip, a good value for two or three people with luggage that they don't want to haul on public transportation. Extra passengers pay more (runs 24 hours, price includes 1 piece of luggage and 1 carry-on per person, pay driver directly in cash, toll-free tel. 900-713-583, sometimes better service at tel. 917-477-570, www.aerocity.com). They also offer a €36 private shuttle service for up to three people (your hotel can book it for you).

By Metro: The subway involves two transfers to reach the city center (€2; or add a €1 supplement to your €7.40 10-ride Metrobus ticket). The airport's futuristic "Aeropuerto T-1, T-2, T-3" Metro stop (notice the ATMs, subway info booth, and huge lighted map

MADRID

of Madrid) is in Terminal 2. Access the Metro at the check-in level; to reach the Metro from Terminal 1's arrivals level, stand with your back to the baggage claim, then go to your far right, up the stairs, and follow red-and-blue Metro diamond signs to the station (8-min walk). The Terminal 4 stop is the end of the line. To get to Puerta del Sol, take line #8 for 12 minutes to Nuevos Ministerios, then continue on line #10 to Tribunal, then line #1 to Puerta del Sol (30 min more total); or exit at Nuevos Ministerios and take a €5 taxi or bus #150 straight to Puerta del Sol.

By Taxi: For a taxi between the airport and downtown, allow about €25 during the day *(Tarifa 1)* or €35 at night and on Sundays *(Tarifa 2)*. For Terminal 4, add about €10. Insist on the meter. The €5.25 airport supplement is legal. There is no charge for luggage. Plan on getting stalled in traffic. For more on taxis—and corrupt cabbies—see "Getting Around Madrid," page 1159.

SWITZERLAND

GIMMELWALD
and the BERNER OBERLAND

Frolic and hike high above the stress and clouds of the real world. Take a vacation from your busy vacation. Recharge your touristic batteries high in the Alps, where distant avalanches, cowbells, the fluff of a down comforter, the whistle of marmots, and the crunchy footsteps of happy hikers are the dominant sounds. If the weather's good (and your budget's healthy), ride a cable car from the traffic-free village of Gimmelwald to a hearty breakfast at Schilthorn's 10,000-foot-elevation, revolving Piz Gloria restaurant. Linger among alpine whitecaps before riding, hiking, or paragliding down 5,000 feet to Mürren and home to Gimmelwald.

Your gateway to the rugged Berner Oberland is the grand old resort town of Interlaken. Near Interlaken is Switzerland's open-air folk museum, Ballenberg, where you can climb through traditional houses from every corner of this diverse country.

Ah, but the weather's fine and the Alps beckon. Head deep into the heart of the Alps, and ride the cable car to the stop just this side of heaven—Gimmelwald.

Planning Your Time

Rather than tackle a checklist of famous Swiss mountains and resorts, choose one region to savor: the Berner Oberland.

Interlaken is the administrative headquarters and transportation hub of this region. Use it for business—banking, post office, laundry, shopping—and as a springboard for alpine thrills.

With decent weather, explore the two areas that tower above either side of the **Lauterbrunnen Valley**, south of Interlaken: On one side is the **Jungfrau** (and beneath it, the towns of Wengen

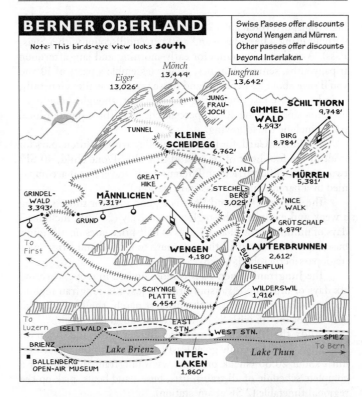

BERNER OBERLAND

Note: This birds-eye view looks **south**

Swiss Passes offer discounts beyond Wengen and Mürren. Other passes offer discounts beyond Interlaken.

Mönch 13,449'

Jungfrau 13,642'

Eiger 13,026'

JUNG-FRAU-JOCH

GIMMEL-WALD 4,593'

SCHILTHORN 9,748'

TUNNEL

KLEINE SCHEIDEGG 6,762'

BIRG 8,784'

W.-ALP

MÜRREN 5,381'

GREAT HIKE

STECHEL-BERG 3,025'

GRINDEL-WALD 3,393'

MÄNNLICHEN 7,317'

NICE WALK

GRUND

GRÜTSCHALP 4,879'

To First

WENGEN 4,180'

LAUTERBRUNNEN 2,612'

BUS

ISENFLUH

SCHYNIGE PLATTE 6,454'

WILDERSWIL 1,916'

To Luzern

EAST STN.

ISELTWALD

WEST STN.

SPIEZ To Bern

BRIENZ

Lake Brienz

INTER-LAKEN 1,860'

Lake Thun

BALLENBERG OPEN-AIR MUSEUM

and Kleine Scheidegg), and on the other is the **Schilthorn** (overlooking the villages of Gimmelwald and Mürren). The best overnight options are the rustic hamlet of **Gimmelwald,** the resort town of **Mürren,** or (for accommodations without the expense and headache of mountain lifts) the village of **Lauterbrunnen,** on the valley floor. I've also listed some options in the resort of Wengen and a few other mountain towns. Ideally, spend three nights in the region, with a day exploring each side of the valley.

For the fastest look, consider a night in Gimmelwald, breakfast at the Schilthorn, an afternoon doing the Männlichen–Wengen hike, and an evening or night train out. What? A nature-lover not spending the night high in the Alps? Alpus interruptus.

Getting Around the Berner Oberland

For more than a century, this region has been the target of nature-worshiping pilgrims. And Swiss engineers and visionaries have made the most exciting alpine perches accessible...

By Lifts and Trains: Part of the fun—and most of the expense—here is riding the many lifts (gondolas and cable cars). Trips above Interlaken are not covered by train passes (but for most

GIMMELWALD

high transport, you'll get a 25 percent discount with a Eurailpass—without using a flexi-day—and a 50 percent discount with a Swiss Pass). Ask about discounts for early-morning and late-afternoon trips, youths, seniors, families, groups (assemble a party of 10 and you'll save about 25 percent), and those staying a while. Generally, round-trips are just double the one-way cost, though some high-up trains and lifts are 10–20 percent cheaper. Three popular local passes include the following:

The **Junior Card,** for families traveling with children, pays for itself in the first hour of trains and lifts (20 SF/one child, 40 SF/two or more children, lets children under 16 travel free if accompanied by a parent, buy at Swiss train stations).

The **Berner Oberland Pass** is a good idea for those staying a week and exploring the region extensively (230 SF, includes 3 days of unlimited travel and 4 days of half-price fares on all trains, buses, and lifts—even all the way south to Gstaad and Brig, www.regiopass-berneroberland.ch).

The **Jungfraubahnen Pass** is more limited in scope, covering six days of unlimited transportation in just the Jungfrau region, not including the ascent to the priciest perch, the Jungfraujoch (200 SF, or 150 SF with Swiss Pass, www.jungfraubahn.ch).

Study the "Alpine Lifts in the Berner Oberland" map on page 1205. Lifts generally go at least twice hourly, from about 7:00 until about 20:00 (sneak preview: www.jungfraubahn.ch). For a complete schedule of all trains, lifts, buses, and boats, pick up the regional timetable (2 SF at any station).

By Car: Lauterbrunnen, Stechelberg, Isenfluh, and Interlaken are all accessible by car. You can't drive to Gimmelwald, Mürren, Wengen, or Kleine Scheidegg, but don't let that stop you from staying up in the mountains; park the car and zip up on a lift. To catch the lift to Gimmelwald, Mürren, and the Schilthorn, park at the cable-car station in Stechelberg (2 SF/2 hrs, 6 SF/day, see page 1217 for more information). To catch the train to Wengen or Kleine Scheidegg, park at the train station in Lauterbrunnen (parking: 2 SF/2 hrs, 10 SF/day).

Helpful Hints in the Berner Oberland

Weather: The local economy lives by the weather. You're wise to be in touch. Ask at your hotel or the TI for the latest. A local TV station showing live video from the famous (and most expensive-to-reach) peaks is playing just about wherever you go. For the latest weather, you can also see www.swisspanorama.com (entire area), www.jungfraubahn.ch (for Jungfraujoch), or www.schilthorn.ch (for Schilthorn peak).

Telephones: For efficiency, buy a phone card from a newsstand or train station ticket window. If staying in Gimmelwald, note

GIMMELWALD

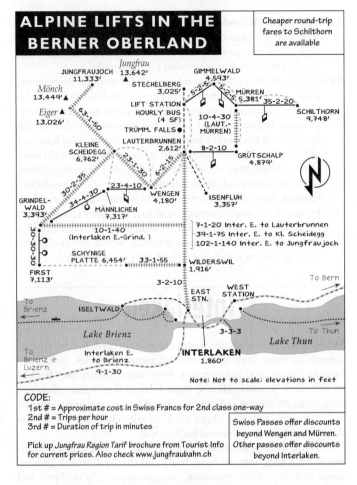

ALPINE LIFTS IN THE BERNER OBERLAND

Cheaper round-trip fares to Schilthorn are available

CODE:
1st # = Approximate cost in Swiss Francs for 2nd class one-way
2nd # = Trips per hour
3rd # = Duration of trip in minutes

Pick up *Jungfrau Region Tarif* brochure from Tourist Info for current prices. Also check www.jungfraubahn.ch

Swiss Passes offer discounts beyond Wengen and Mürren. Other passes offer discounts beyond Interlaken.

that its sole public phone—at the cable-car station—takes only cards, not coins.

Closed Days: On Sundays and holidays (including the lesser-known religious holidays), small-town Switzerland is quiet. Hotels are open, and lifts and trains run, but many stores are closed.

Off-Season Closures: Note that at higher altitudes, many hotels, restaurants, and shops are closed between the skiing and hiking seasons: from late April until late May, and again from mid-October to early December.

Local Guidebook: For an in-depth look at the area's history, folk life, flora, fauna, and for extensive hiking information, buy Don Chmura's *Exploring the Lauterbrunnen Valley* (sold throughout the valley, 8 SF).

Visitor's Cards *(Gästekarten):* The hotels in various towns issue free visitor's cards that include measly discounts on some sights and transportation. While these cards won't save you much, you can ask at your hotel for the details.

Skiing: The Berner Oberland is a great winter-sports destination, with good snow on its higher runs, incredible variety, relatively reasonable prices, and a sense of character that's missing in many swankier resort areas. You can even swish with the Swiss down the world's longest sledding run (9 miles long, out of Grindelwald, only open when snow's good). Three ski areas cluster around the Lauterbrunnen Valley: Mürren—Schilthorn (best for expert skiers), Kleine Scheidegg—Männlichen (busiest, best variety of runs), and Grindelwald—First (best for beginners and intermediate skiers, but lower elevation can make for iffier snowpack). Lift tickets cost around 60 SF a day, including the Sportspass Jungfrau, which covers all three areas (see www.jungfrauwinter.ch for prices and info).

Interlaken

When the 19th-century Romantics redefined mountains as something more than cold and troublesome obstacles, Interlaken became the original alpine resort. Ever since, tourists have flocked to the Alps "because they're there." Interlaken's glory days are long gone, its elegant old hotels eclipsed by the new, more swanky alpine resorts. Today, its shops are filled with chocolate bars, Swiss Army knives, and sunburned backpackers.

While European jet-setters are elsewhere, Interlaken is cashing in on a huge interest from India and the Arab world. Indians come to escape their monsoon season—especially in April and May—and to visit places they've seen in their movies (there's even a restaurant called "Bollywood" atop the Jungfraujoch). People from the hot and dry Arabian Peninsula come here just to photograph their children frolicking in the mist and fog.

Orientation

Efficient Interlaken (pop. 5,500) is a good administrative and shopping center. Take care of business, give the town a quick look, and view the live TV coverage of the weather higher up (at the TI)... then head for the hills.

GIMMELWALD

Tourist Information

The TI has good information on the region (May–June Mon–Fri 8:00–18:00, Sat 8:00–16:00, closed Sun; July–mid-Sept Mon–Fri 8:00–19:00, Sat 8:00–17:00, Sun 10:00–12:00 & 17:00–19:00; mid-Sept–Oct Mon–Fri 8:00–19:00, Sat 9:00–13:00, closed Sun; shorter hours Nov–April; under the 18-story skyscraper on the main street between West and East train stations, a 10-min stroll from either, Höheweg 37; tel. 033-826-5300, www.interlakentourism.ch). The *You Want It All* booklet is an almanac covering everything you need in Interlaken (except for some events, which are covered more thoroughly in the monthly entertainment guide). There's no point in buying a regional map, as good mini-versions of the map are included in various free transportation and hiking brochures. The TI organizes free walks on Mondays at 17:00 in the summer (in English with demand, call to confirm).

Arrival in Interlaken

Interlaken has two train stations: East (Ost) and West. All trains stop at both East and West stations. If heading for higher-altitude villages, get off at the East station. For hotels in Interlaken, get off at the West station. The West station also has a helpful and friendly train information desk (travel center for in-depth rail questions: Mon–Fri 9:00–12:00 & 13:30–18:30, Sat 9:00–12:00 & 13:30–17:00, closed Sun; ticket windows open daily 6:40–21:00; tel. 033-826-4750). Ask about discount passes, special fares, railpass discounts, and schedules for the scenic mountain trains. There's an exchange booth next to the ticket windows (daily 8:00–18:00). Nearby is a post office with a cluster of phone booths.

It's a pleasant 20-minute walk between the West and East stations, or there's an easy, frequent train connection (3/hr, 3.20 SF). From the East station, private trains take you deep into the mountainous Jungfrau region (see "Connections," page 1217).

Helpful Hints

Laundry: Friendly Helen Schmocker's **Wäscherei** has a change machine, soap, English instructions, and a delightful riverside location (open for self-service daily 7:00–22:00—6 SF/load; open for full service Mon–Fri 8:00–12:00 & 13:30–18:00, Sat until 16:00, closed Sun, drop off in the morning and pick up that afternoon—12 SF/load; from the main street take Marktgasse over two bridges to Beatenbergstrasse 5, tel. 033-822-1566).

Bike Rental: You can rent bikes at either train station (23 SF/half-day, 31 SF/day, 5 SF less with Eurailpass or Swiss Pass, daily from 8:00, last rental at 17:00, last return at 23:00).

GIMMELWALD

Self-Guided Walk

Welcome to Interlaken

Most visitors use Interlaken as a springboard for high-altitude thrills (and rightly so). But the town itself has history and scenic charm and is worth a short walk. This 45-minute stroll circles from the West train station down the main drag to the big meadow, past the casino, along the river to the oldest part of town (historically a neighboring town called Unterseen), and back to the station.

• *From the West train station, walk along...*

Bahnhofstrasse: This main drag, which turns into Höheweg as it continues east, cuts straight through the town center from the West train station to the East station. The best Swiss souvenir shopping is along this Bahnhofstrasse stretch (finer shops are on the Höheweg stretch, near the fancy hotels). At the roundabout is the handy post office (with free public WCs). Just behind the post office on Marktgasse, the hardware store stocks real cowbells (both ornate and plain). At Höheweg 2, the TV in the window of the Schilthornbahn office shows the weather up top.

The 18-story **Metropole Hotel** (a.k.a. the "concrete shame of Interlaken") is by far the town's tallest building. Step right into the lobby and ride the elevator to the top for a commanding view of the "inter-laken" area, and gaze deep into the Jungfrau region to the scenic south. A meal or drink here costs no more than one back on earth. Consider sipping a drink on its outdoor view terrace (or come back tonight—it's open very late).

• *On your right is...*

Höhematte Park: This "high meadow," or Höhematte (but generally referred to simply as "the park"), marks the beginning of Interlaken's fancy hotel row. Hotels like the Victoria-Jungfrau harken back to the days when Interlaken was *the* top alpine resort (late 19th century). The first grand hotels were built here to enjoy the views of the Jungfrau in the distance. (Today, the *jung Frau*s getting the most attention are next door, at Hooters.)

The park originated as farmland of the monastery that predated the town (marked today by the steeples of both the Catholic and Protestant churches—neither of any sightseeing interest). The actual **monastery site** is now home to the courthouse and county administration building. With the Reformation in 1528, the monastery was shut down, and its land was taken by the state. Later, when the land was being eyed by developers, the town's leading hotels and business families bought it and established that it would never be used for commercial buildings (a very early example of smart town planning). There was talk of building a parking lot under it, but the water table here, between the two lakes, is too high. (That's why the town cemetery is up on the hillside.) Today, this is a fine place to stroll, hang out on the park benches or at Restaurant Schuh, and watch the paragliders gracefully land.

From the park, turn left into the grounds of **Casino Kursaal,** where, at the top of each hour, dwarves ring the toadstools on the flower clock. The Kursaal, originally a kind of 19th-century fat farm, is now both a casino (passport but no tie required) and a convention center that hosts musical events and folklore shows (2–3/week in summer, fun yodeling with lots of audience participation, details at the TI).

· *Follow the path left of the Kursaal to the river (huge public swimming pool just over the river). Walk downstream under the train track and cross the pedestrian bridge, stopping in the middle to enjoy the view.*

Aare River: The Aare River is Switzerland's longest. It connects Lake Brienz and Lake Thun (with an 18-foot altitude difference—this short stretch has quite a flow). Then it tumbles out of Lake Thun, heading for Bern and ultimately into the Rhine. Its level is controlled by several sluices. In the distance, a church bell tower marks a different parish and the neighborhood of Unterseen, which shares the town's name, but in German: Like the word *Interlaken, Unterseen* means "between the lakes." Behind the spire is the pointy summit of the Niesen (like so many Swiss peaks, capped with a restaurant and accessible by a lift). Stroll downstream along the far side of the river to the church spire. The delightful riverside walk is lined by fine residences. Notice that your Jungfrau view now includes the Jungfraujoch observation deck (the little brown bump in the ridge just left of the peak).

· *At the next bridge, turn right to the town square lined with 17th-century houses on one side and a modern strip on the other.*

Unterseen: This was a town when Interlaken was only a monastery. The church is not worth touring. A block away, the (generally empty) **Town History Museum/Museum of Tourism** shows off classic posters, fascinating photos of the construction of the Jungfraujoch, and exhibits on folk life, crafts, and winter sports—all well-described in English (5 SF, May–mid-Oct Tue–Sun 14:00–17:00, closed Mon and mid-Oct–April, Obergasse 26).

Return to Station: From Unterseen, cross the river on Spiel-matte, and you're a few minutes' walk from your starting point. On the second bridge, notice the border between the two towns, or parishes, marked by their respective heraldic emblems (each with an ibex, or wild mountain goat). A block or so later, on the left, is the Marktplatz. The river originally ran through this square. The town used to be called "Aaremühle" ("Aare mill") for the mill that was here. But in the 19th century, town fathers made a key marketing decision: Since "Aaremühle" was too difficult for English tourists to pronounce, they changed the name to "Interlaken." Judging from the throngs of tourists on the main drag, it worked.

Sights and Activities

Near Interlaken

Boat Trips—"Interlaken" is literally "between the lakes" of Thun and Brienz. You can explore these lakes on a lazy boat trip, hopping on and off as the schedule allows (free with Swiss Pass or Eurailpass but uses a flexi-day, schedules at TI or at BLS Travel Center in West station, tel. 033-826-4760). The boats on Lake Thun (about hourly, 5-hour round-trip, 53 SF) stop at the St. Beatus Höhlen caves (30 min away, next entry) and two visit-worthy towns: Spiez and Thun. The boats on Lake Brienz (roughly every other hour, 3-hour round trip, 38 SF) stop at the super-cute village of Iseltwald and at Brienz (easy bus and train connections back to Interlaken from Brienz, near Ballenberg Open-Air Folk Museum—described next page).

St. Beatus Höhlen caves on Lake Thun can be visited with a one-hour guided tour (17 SF, 2/hr, April–mid-Oct daily 10:30–17:00, closed mid-Oct–March, tel. 033-841-1643, www.beatus hoehlen.ch). The best excursion plan: Ride the bus from Interlaken (20-min ride, line #21—direction: Thun, departs West station at :19 past the hour); tour the caves; take the short, steep hike down to lake; and return by boat (9 SF one-way, 30 min to Interlaken, described previously).

Adventure Trips from Interlaken—For the thrill-seeker with money, several companies offer high-adrenaline trips such as rafting, canyoning (rappelling down watery gorges), bungee jumping, and paragliding. Costs range from 150 SF to 205 SF. Interlaken's two dominant companies are **Alpin Raft** (tel. 033-823-4100, www .alpinraft.com) and **Outdoor Interlaken** (tel. 033-826-7719, www .outdoor-interlaken.ch). Other companies are generally just booking agents for these two outfits. For an overview of your options, visit www.interlakenadventure.com or study the racks of brochures at most TIs and hotels (everyone's getting a cut of this lucrative industry).

Several years ago, two fatal accidents jolted the adventure-sport business in the Berner Oberland, leading to a more professional respect for the risks involved. Companies have very high standards of safety. Statistically, the most dangerous sport is mountain biking. Enjoying nature up close comes with risks. Adventure sports increase those risks dramatically. Use good judgment.

Less-Risky Adventures in and near Interlaken—**Vertical Sport** has a breathtaking indoor rock-climbing facility, where you can snack or enjoy a nice cup of hot chocolate while watching hot-shots practice their gravity-defying skills (Tue–Sun 9:00–18:00, or until 22:00 in bad weather, closed Mon, private lessons for beginners by the hour, at the back of the park 50 yards from Hotel Savoy

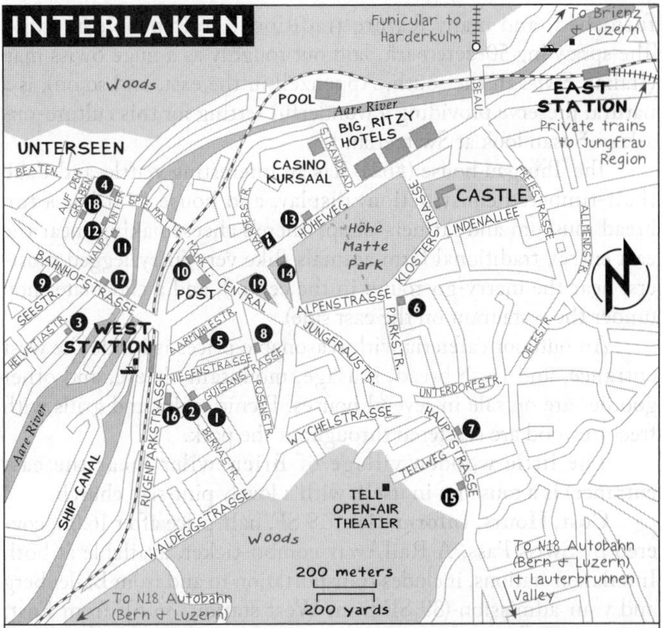

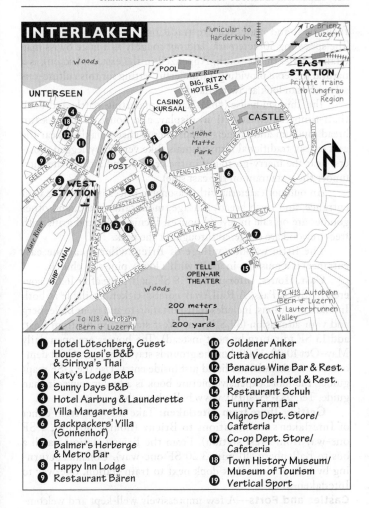

1. Hotel Lötschberg, Guest House Susi's B&B & Sirinya's Thai
2. Katy's Lodge B&B
3. Sunny Days B&B
4. Hotel Aarburg & Launderette
5. Villa Margaretha
6. Backpackers' Villa (Sonnenhof)
7. Balmer's Herberge & Metro Bar
8. Happy Inn Lodge
9. Restaurant Bären
10. Goldener Anker
11. Città Vecchia
12. Benacus Wine Bar & Rest.
13. Metropole Hotel & Rest.
14. Restaurant Schuh
15. Funny Farm Bar
16. Migros Dept. Store/ Cafeteria
17. Co-op Dept. Store/ Cafeteria
18. Town History Museum/ Museum of Tourism
19. Vertical Sport

at Jungfraustrasse 44, tel. 033-821-2823).

Outdoor Interlaken's Seilpark offers five rope courses of varying difficulty and height in a forest, giving you a tree-top adventure through a maze of rope bridges and zip lines (37 SF, family deals, must weigh between 44 and 264 pounds; June–Aug daily 10:00–18:00; Sept–Oct Tue–Fri 13:00–18:00, Sat–Sun 10:00–18:00, closed Mon; closed Nov–May; 20-min walk out of town at Hauptstrasse 15, tel. 033-826-7719, www.outdoor-interlaken.ch).

▲▲Swiss Open-Air Folk Museum at Ballenberg—Across Lake Brienz from Interlaken, the Swiss Open-Air Museum of Vernacular Architecture, Country Life, and Crafts in the Berner Oberland is a rich collection of traditional and historic farmhouses from every region of the country. All the houses are carefully furnished, and many feature traditional craftspeople at work. The sprawling 50-acre park, laid out roughly as a huge Swiss map (Italian Swiss in the south, Appenzell in the east, and so on), is a natural preserve providing a wonderful setting for this culture-on-a-lazy-Susan look at Switzerland.

The Thurgau house (#621) has an interesting wattle-and-daub (half-timbered construction) display, and house #331 has a fun bread museum and farmers' shop. There's cheesemaking (near the east entry), traditional farm animals (like very furry-legged roosters, near the merry-go-round in the center), and a chocolate shop (under the restaurant on the east side).

An outdoor cafeteria with reasonable prices is inside the west entrance, and fresh bread, sausage, mountain cheese, and other goodies are on sale in several houses. Picnic tables and grills with free firewood are scattered throughout the park.

The little wooden village of Brienzwiler (near the east entrance) is a museum in itself, with a lovely pint-size church.

Cost, Hours, Information: 18 SF, half-price after 16:00, covered by Swiss Pass. A RailAway combo-ticket, available at both Interlaken stations, includes transportation to and from Ballenberg and your admission (39 SF from West station, 36 SF from East, add 13 SF to return by boat instead). The houses are open daily May–Oct 10:00–17:00, but the grounds stay open later. Craft demonstration schedules are listed just inside entry. Use the 2-SF map/guide. The more expensive picture book is a better souvenir than guide. Tel. 033-952-1030, www.ballenberg.ch.

Getting There from Interlaken: Take the train from either of Interlaken's train stations to Brienz (hourly, 30 min, 9 SF one-way from West station). From the Brienz station, catch a bus to Ballenberg (10 min, 3.20 SF one-way). Consider returning by boat (Brienz boat dock next to train station, one-way to Interlaken-21 SF).

Castles and Forts—A few impressively well-kept and welcoming old castles in the Interlaken area are worth considering for day trips by boat, bus, or car.

Thun Castle (Schloss Thun), built between 1180 and 1190 by the Dukes of Zähringen, has a five-floor historical museum offering insights into the cultural development of the region over a period of some 4,000 years. From the corner turrets of the castle, you are rewarded with a spectacular view of the city of Thun, the lake, and the Alps (7 SF, April–Oct daily 10:00–17:00, less off-season, www.schlossthun.ch).

Hünegg Castle (Schloss Hünegg) in Hilterfingen (farther along Lake Thun, toward Interlaken) contains a museum exhibiting furnished rooms from the second half of the 19th century. The castle is situated in a beautiful wooded park (8 SF, mid-May–mid-

Oct Mon–Sat 14:00–17:00, Sun 11:00–17:00, closed off-season, www.schlosshuenegg.ch).

Oberhofen Castle (Schloss Oberhofen) is for those interested in gardens. Its beautifully landscaped park with exotic trees is a delight (free, mid-March–mid-Nov daily from 9:00 until dusk, closed in winter). The museum in the castle depicts domestic life in the 16th through 19th centuries, including a Turkish smoking room and a medieval chapel (7 SF, mid-May–mid-Oct Mon 14:00–17:00, Tue–Sun 11:00–17:00, closed off-season, tel. 033-243-1235).

Nightlife

Youthful Night Scenes—For counterculture with a reggae beat, check out **Funny Farm** (past Balmer's Herberge hostel, in Matten). The young frat-party dance scene rages at the **Metro Bar** at Balmer's (bomb-shelter disco bar, with cheap drinks and a friendly if loud atmosphere). And if you're into **Hooters,** you won't have a hard time finding it.

Mellower After-Dark Hangouts—The first three options are also described under "Eating": For a stylish wine bar with local yuppies, check in at the **Benacus Piazza del Vino** on the square in Unterseen. To nurse a drink with a view of the park, the outdoor tables at **Restaurant Schuh** are the place to be. The **"Top O'Met"** bar and café has great indoor and outdoor view seating with reasonable prices, 18 floors above everything else in town (in the Metropole Hotel skyscraper, open nightly until late). **Hotel Oberland** (near the post office) often has live alpine music in their restaurant/bar.

Sleeping

I'd head for Gimmelwald, or at least Lauterbrunnen (20 min by train or car). Interlaken is not the Alps. But if you must stay...

$$$ Hotel Lötschberg, with a sun terrace and 21 wonderful rooms, is run with lots of thoughtful touches by English-speaking Susi and Fritz. This is the best real hotel value in town. Happy to dispense information, these gregarious folks pride themselves on a personal approach that sets them apart from other hotels (Sb-120 SF, Db-165 SF, big Db-185 SF, extra bed-30 SF, family deals, rates about 15 percent cheaper mid-Oct–April, closed Nov–March, elevator, coin-op Internet access, free Wi-Fi, laundry service, bike rental-25 SF/half-day; 3-min walk from West station: leaving station, turn right, after Migros at the circle go left to General-Guisan-Strasse 31; tel. 033-822-2545, fax 033-822-2579, www .lotschberg.ch, hotel@lotschberg.ch). Effervescent Fritz organizes guided adventures. He does tandem hang gliding almost every day

Sleep Code

(1 SF = about $0.90, country code: 41)
S = Single, **D** = Double/Twin, **T** = Triple, **Q** = Quad, **b** = bathroom,
s = shower only. Unless otherwise noted, credit cards are accepted, English is spoken, and breakfast is included.

To help you sort easily through these listings, I've divided the rooms into three categories, based on the price for a standard double room with bath:

$$$ **Higher Priced**—Most rooms 150 SF or more.
$$ **Moderately Priced**—Most rooms between 90–150 SF.
$ **Lower Priced**—Most rooms 90 SF or less.

with one of his guests (guests fly with Fritz at a discount, 140 SF, about 20 SF cheaper than any other deal in town).

$$ Guest House Susi's B&B is Hotel Lötschberg's no-frills, cash-only annex, run by Fritz and Susi, offering nicely furnished, cozy rooms (Sb-105 SF, Db-135 SF; apartment with kitchenette-115 SF/2 people, 200 SF/4–5 people—discount for 3-night stay; prices about 20 percent cheaper mid-Oct–April, closed Nov–March, same contact info as Hotel Lötschberg, listed first).

$$ Sunny Days B&B, a homey, nine-room place in a residential neighborhood, is run by Dave from Britain (Sb-98–110 SF, Db-110–148 SF, prices vary with size of room and view, extra bed about 40 SF, less in winter; exit left out of West station and take first bridge to your left, after crossing two bridges turn left on Helvetiastrasse and go 3 blocks to #29; tel. 033-822-8343, www.sunnydays.ch, mail@sunnydays.ch).

$$ Hotel Aarburg offers 13 plain, peaceful rooms over a restaurant in a beautifully located but run-down old building a 10-minute walk from the West station (Sb-70 SF, Db-130 SF, 10 SF more in July–Aug, next to launderette at Beatenbergstrasse 1, tel. 033-822-2615, fax 033-822-6397, hotel-aarburg@quicknet.ch).

$$ Katy's Lodge B&B is a funky old house in a quiet, handy location. While not cozy, it rents nine basic rooms at a good price (Db-95 SF, T-115 SF, Qb-145 SF, 6-bed room-200 SF; discount offered with cash and this book: 5 percent off for 1 night, 10 percent off for 2 or more nights; garden, playground, 3-min walk from West station, across from Hotel Lötschberg at Bernastrasse 7, tel. 033-821-0963, fax 033-822-7479, www.katys-lodge.ch, katys lodge@bluewin.ch).

$ Villa Margaretha, run by English-speaking Frau Kunz-Joerin, offers the best cheap beds in town. It's like Grandma's big Victorian house on a residential street. Keep your room tidy, and you'll have a friend for life (D-86 SF, T-129 SF, Q-172 SF, the 3 rooms share one big bathroom, 2-night minimum, closed Oct–April, cash only, no breakfast served but dishes and kitchenette available, lots of rules to abide by, go up small street directly in front of West station to Aarmühlestrasse 13, tel. 033-822-1813, www.villa-margaretha.com, info@villa-margaretha.com).

$ Backpackers' Villa (Sonnenhof) Interlaken is a creative guest house run by a Methodist church group. It's fun, youthful, and great for families, without the frat-party scene of Balmer's Herberge (listed next). Travelers of any age feel comfortable here (dorm beds in 5- to 7-bed rooms with lockers and sheets-37 SF, D-98 SF, T-135 SF, Q-164 SF, 5 SF more per person for rooms with toilets and Jungfrau-view balconies, includes breakfast, kitchen, garden, movies, small game room, Internet access, laundry, bike rental, free admission to public swimming pool/spa, no curfew, open all day but reception open only 7:00–11:00 & 16:00–21:00, 10-min walk from either station, across the park from TI, Alpenstrasse 16, tel. 033-826-7171, fax 033-826-7172, www.villa .ch, mail@villa.ch).

$ Balmer's Herberge is many people's idea of backpacker heaven. This Interlaken institution comes with movies, table tennis, a cheap launderette (4 SF/load), bar, restaurant, swapping library, Internet access, tiny grocery, bike rental, excursions, a shuttle-bus service (which meets important arriving trains), and a friendly, hardworking staff. This little Nebraska, a hive of youthful fun and activities, is home for those who miss their fraternity. It can be a mob scene, especially on summer weekends (spot in 30-bed dorm-27 SF, in a 10-bed dorm-29 SF, S-43 SF, D-74 SF, T-99 SF, Q-132 SF, includes sheets and breakfast, open year-round, emailed reservations recommended 5 days in advance except for dorm beds, Hauptstrasse 23, in Matten, 15-min walk from either train station, tel. 033-822-1961, fax 033-823-3261, www.balmers.com, mail @balmers.ch).

$ Happy Inn Lodge has 15 cheap backpacker rooms above a lively, noisy restaurant a five-minute walk from the West station (dorm bed-22 SF, S-40 SF, D-80 SF, T-90–105 SF, Q-120–140 SF, breakfast-8 SF, Rosenstrasse 17, tel. 033-822-3225, fax 033-822-3268, www.happyinn.com, info@happyinn.com).

Eating

In Unterseen, the Old Town Across the River
Restaurant Bären, in a classic low-ceilinged building with cozy indoor and fine outdoor seating, is a great value for *Rösti*, fondue, raclette, fish, traditional sausage, and salads (20–25-SF plates including fondue for one, Cordon Bleu is popular, open

daily, closed Mon off-season, from West station turn left on Bahnhofstrasse and go over the river a block to Seestrasse 2, tel. 033-822-7526).

Goldener Anker is *the* local hangout—smoky, with a pool table and a few unsavory types. If you thought Interlaken was sterile, you haven't been to the "Golden Anchor." Jeannette serves and René cooks, just as they have for 25 years. This place, with its "melody rock and blues" ambience, sometimes hosts small concerts, and has launched some of Switzerland's top bands (hearty 20-SF salads, fresh vegetables, 3 courses for 20 SF, daily from 16:00, Marktgasse 57, tel. 033-822-1672).

Città Vecchia serves decent Italian with seating indoors or out, on a leafy square (15-SF pizzas, 20-SF pastas, 30-SF plates, closed Tue, on main square in Unterseen at Untere Gasse 5, tel. 033-822-1754).

Benacus Wine Bar and Restaurant is a snooty, trendy spot serving Euro-Asian modern cuisine and offering tapas with a good list of open wines (40-SF plates, closed Sun–Mon, Stadthausplatz, tel. 033-821-2020).

On or near the Main Drag (Höheweg)

Interlaken's main drag, Höheweg, is lined with eateries. The Asian, American, and Arab group tourism cuts into the local ambience, but you do have plenty of options.

Sirinya's Thai Restaurant is run by charming Sirinya, who serves great Thai dishes and famous spring rolls at reasonable prices (17-SF plates, closed Mon, at Hotel Lötschberg—see "Sleeping," previously, General-Guisan-Strasse 31, tel. 033-821-6535).

Metropole Hotel's "Top O'Met," capping Interlaken's 18-story aesthetic nightmare, is actually a decent café/restaurant serving traditional and modern food at down-to-earth prices. For just 5 SF, you can enjoy a glass of wine and awesome views from an indoor or outdoor table (25-SF lunch deals include 2 courses and a drink, daily 11:30–24:00, Höheweg 37, just step into the Metropole Hotel and go up the elevator as far as you can, tel. 041-210-1666).

Restaurant Schuh retains its grand-café ambience on the best real estate in town (at the corner of the park, across from Metropole Hotel and TI). The interior is a big tour-group food fight, but there's no better place to nurse a drink or coffee and watch the paragliders float into the park (live schmaltzy music, newspapers, Höheweg 56, tel. 033-822-9441).

Cheap Eats

Interlaken's two big supermarkets sell picnic supplies and also have reasonable self-service restaurants: **Migros** is across the street from the West station (Mon–Thu 8:00–18:30, Fri 8:00–21:00, Sat

7:30–17:00, closed Sun), while the **Co-op** is across the river from the West station, on your right (same hours as Migros). The only grocery store open late at night is **Co-op Pronto** (daily 6:00–22:30, 30 yards west of TI on Höheweg).

Connections

While there are a few long-distance trains from Interlaken, you'll generally transfer in **Bern**. Train info: toll tel. 0900-300-3004 or www.rail.ch.

From Interlaken East (Ost) by Train to: Lauterbrunnen (hourly, 20 min, 7 SF each way), **Bern** (2/hr, 55 min), **Spiez** (3/hr, 20 min), **Brienz** (1–2/hr, 20 min), **Zürich** and **Zürich Airport** (hourly, 2–2.25 hrs, most direct but some with transfer in Bern, Luzern, and/or Spiez), **Florence** (6/day, 6.25–6.75 hrs, 3 changes, overnight possible), **Venice** (5/day, 6.25–6.75 hrs, 2–3 changes, overnight possible), **Nice** (6/day, 8.5–10 hrs, 2–4 transfers).

From Interlaken to the Lauterbrunnen Valley

To reach the heart of the valley, drive or take the train to Lauterbrunnen (train leaves hourly from East station, 20 min). You cannot drive to Gimmelwald (park in Stechelberg and take the cable car; see below) or to Mürren, Wengen, or Kleine Scheidegg (park in Lauterbrunnen and take the cable car to Mürren or the train to Wengen/Kleine Scheidegg).

To get from Lauterbrunnen to Gimmelwald, you have two options:

1. The faster, easier way—best in bad weather or at the end of a long day with lots of luggage—is to drive or, if you don't want to rent a car, ride the postal bus from Lauterbrunnen to Stechelberg and the base of the Schilthornbahn cable-car station (bus costs 3.80 SF, hourly bus departure coordinated with arrival of train, get off at Schilthornbahn stop). With a car, it's 30 minutes from Interlaken to the Stechelberg station (parking lot: 2 SF/2 hrs, 6 SF/day).

From Stechelberg, the cable car will whisk you in five thrilling minutes up to Gimmelwald (5.40 SF, 2/hr at :25 and :55 past the hour, Gimmelwald is the first stop). Note that the Schilthornbahn is closed for servicing for a week in early May and also from mid-November through early December. During this time, you'll ride the cargo cable car directly from Stechelberg to Mürren, where a small bus shuttles you down to Gimmelwald.

2. The more scenic route is to catch the cable car from Lauterbrunnen to Grütschalp, where a special scenic train *(Panorama Fahrt)* will roll you along the cliff to Mürren (total trip from Lauterbrunnen to Mürren: 30 min, 10 SF). From there, either

GIMMELWALD

walk a paved 30 minutes downhill to Gimmelwald, or walk 10 minutes across Mürren to catch the cable car down to Gimmelwald (5.40 SF).

Railpass Discounts: Beyond Interlaken, trains into the Jungfrau region are only 25 percent covered by Eurailpasses; they're free with the Swiss Pass up to Wengen or Mürren (uphill from there, Swiss Pass–holders get a 50 percent discount). You can buy your entire package of lifts for your intended hike at once, but then you don't have the flexibility to change with the weather.

Gimmelwald

Saved from developers by its "avalanche zone" classification, Gimmelwald was (before modern tourism) one of the poorest places in Switzerland. Its traditional economy was stuck in the hay, and its farmers—unable to make it in their disadvantaged trade—survived only on a trickle of visitors and on Swiss government subsidies (and working the ski lifts in the winter). For some travelers, there's little to see in the village. Others (like me) enjoy a fascinating day sitting on a bench and learning why they say, "If heaven isn't what it's cracked up to be, send me back to Gimmelwald."

Take a walk through the town. The huge, sheer cliff face that dominates your mountain views is the Schwarzmönch ("Black Monk"). The three peaks above (or behind) it are, left to right, the Eiger, Mönch, and Jungfrau. While Gimmelwald's population has dropped in the last century from 300 to about 120 residents, traditions survive. Most Gimmelwalders have one of two last names: von Allmen or Feuz. They are tough and proud. Raising hay in this rugged terrain is labor-intensive. One family harvests enough to feed only about 15 cows. But they'd have it no other way, and, unlike the absentee-landlord town of Mürren, Gimmelwald is locally owned. (When word got out that urban planners wished to develop Gimmelwald into a town of 1,000, locals pulled some strings to secure the town's bogus avalanche-zone building code. Today, unlike nearby resort towns, Gimmelwald's population is the same all year.) Those same folks are happy the masses go to touristy and commercialized Grindelwald, just over the Kleine Scheidegg ridge. Don't confuse Gimmelwald and Grindelwald—they couldn't be more different.

Thanks to the leadership of the village teachers (Olle and Maria) and their son (Sven), Gimmelwald now has a helpful little website (www.gimmelwald.ch). There you can check out photos of the town in different seasons, get directions for 11 of the best hikes out of town, and see all the latest on activities and rooms for rent.

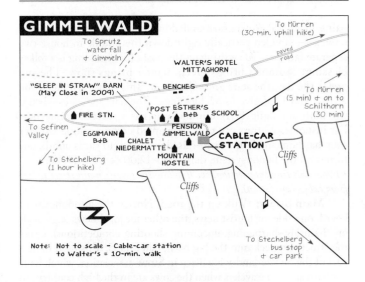

Self-Guided Walk

Welcome to Gimmelwald

Gimmelwald, though tiny, with one zigzag street, offers a fine look at a traditional Swiss mountain community.

• *Start this quick walking tour at the...*

Cable-Car Station: When the lift came in the 1960s, the village's back end became its front door. Gimmelwald was, and still is, a farm village. Stepping off the cable car, you see a sweet little hut. Set on stilts to keep out mice, the hut was used for storing cheese (the rocks on the rooftop here and throughout the town are not decorative—they keep the shingles on through wild storms). Behind the cheese hut stands the village schoolhouse. In Catholic Swiss towns, the biggest building is the church. In Protestant towns, it's the school. Gimmelwald's biggest building is the school (two teachers share one teaching position, 17 students, and a room that doubles as a chapel when the Protestant pastor makes his monthly visit). Don't let Gimmelwald's low-tech look fool you: In this school, each kid has his or her own website. In the opposite direction, just beyond the little playground, is Gimmelwald's Mountain Hostel (listed on page 1223).

• *Walk up the lane 50 yards, past the town's Dalí-esque art gallery (the shower in the phone booth), to Gimmelwald's...*

"Times Square": The yellow alpine "street sign" shows where you are, the altitude (1,370 meters—that's 4,470 feet), how many hours *(Std.)* and minutes it takes to walk to nearby points, and which tracks are serious hiking paths (marked with red and white, and further indicated along the way with red and white patches of paint on stones). You're surrounded by buildings that were built as duplexes—divided vertically right down the middle to house two separate families. The writing on the post office building is a folksy blessing: "Summer brings green, winter brings snow. The sun greets the day, the stars greet the night. This house will keep you warm. May God give us his blessings." The date indicates when it was built or rebuilt (1911). Gimmelwald has a strict building code. For instance, shutters can only be painted certain colors. Esther's shop has homemade and farm-raised products (10 yards uphill, buy things on the honor system, daily 8:00–12:00 & 17:15–19:00).

• *From this tiny intersection, we'll follow the town's main street (away from cable-car station).*

Main Street: Walk up the road. Notice the announcement board: one side for tourist news, the other for local news (e.g., deals on chainsaw sharpening, upcoming shooting competitions). Cross the street and peek into the big barn, dated 1995. This used to be a part of the Switzerland-wide Sleep in Straw association, which rents out barn spots to travelers when the cows are in the high country. To the left of the door is a cow-scratcher. Swiss cows have legal rights (for example, in the winter, they must be taken out for exercise at least three times a week). This big barn is built in a modern style. Traditionally, barns were small (like those on the hillside high above) and closer to the hay. But with trucks and paved roads, hay can be moved more easily, and farm businesses need more cows to be viable. Still, even a well-run big farm hopes just to break even. The industry survives only with government subsidies. Small as Gimmelwald is, the postman (who sells stamps) comes daily. As you wander, notice private garden patches. Until recently, most locals grew their own vegetables—often enough to provide most of their family's needs.

• *Go just beyond the next barn. On your right is the...*

Water Fountain/Trough: This is the site of the town's historic water supply. Local kids love to bathe and wage water wars here when the cows aren't drinking from it. Detour left down a lane about 50 yards (along a wooden fence and then past pea-patch gardens) to the next trough and the oldest building in town, Husmättli, from 1658. (The town's 17th-century buildings are mostly on the road zigzagging below town.) Study the log-cabin construction. Many are built without nails. The wood was logged up the valley and cut on the water-powered village mill (also below town). Gimmelwald heats with wood, and since the wood needs to age a couple of years to burn well, it's stacked everywhere.

• *Back on the paved road, continue uphill.*

Twenty yards along, on the left, the first house has a bunch of scythes hanging above the sharpening stone. Farmers pound, rather than grind, the blade to get it razor-sharp for efficient cutting. Feel a blade...carefully.

A few steps further, notice the cute cheese hut on the right (with alpine cheese for sale). Its front is an alpine art gallery with nail shoes for flower pots. Nail shoes grip the steep, wet fields—this is critical for safety, especially if you're carrying a sharp scythe. Even today, farmers buy metal tacks and fasten them to boots. The hut is full of strong cheese—up to three years old.

Look up. In the summer, a few goats are kept here (rather than in the high alp) to provide families with fresh milk (about a half-gallon per day per goat). The farmers fence off the fields, letting the goats eat only the grass that's most difficult to harvest.

On the left (at the B&B sign) is the home of Olle and Maria, the village schoolteachers. Maria runs the Lilliput shop (the "smallest shop with the greatest gifts"—handmade delights from the town and region, just ring the bell and meet Maria). Her older children, Sven and Sara, do a booming trade in sugar-coated almonds; little sister Carina competes with cookies.

• *Fifty yards farther along is the...*

Alpenrose: At the old schoolhouse, notice the big ceremonial cowbells hanging under the uphill eave. These swing from the necks of cows during the procession from the town to the high Alps (mid-June) and back down (mid-Sept). If the cows are gone, so are the bells—hanging from similar posts under the eaves of mountain huts in the high meadows.

• *At the end of town, pause where a lane branches off to the left, leading into the dramatic...*

Sefinen Valley: All the old homes in town are made from local wood cut from the left-hand side of this valley (shady side, slow-growing, better timber).

• *A few steps ahead, the road switches back at the...*

Gimmelwald Fire Station: The *Föhnwacht Reglement* sheet, posted on the fire station building, explains rules to keep the village from burning down during the fierce dry wind of the Föhn season. During this time, there's a 24-hour fire watch, and even smoking cigarettes outdoors is forbidden. Mürren was devastated by a Föhn-caused fire in the 1920s. Because villagers in Gimmelwald—mindful of the quality of their volunteer fire department—are particularly careful with fire, the town has not had a terrible fire in its history (a rare feat among alpine villages).

Check out the other posted notices. This year's Swiss Army calendar tells reservists when and where to go (in all four official Swiss languages). Every Swiss male does a 22-week stint in the military, then a few days a year in the reserves until about age 30. The *Schiessübungen* poster details the shooting exercises required this year. In keeping with the William Tell heritage, each Swiss man does shooting practice annually for the military (or spends three days in jail).

• *Take the...*

High Road to Hotel Mittaghorn: The resort town of Mürren hovers in the distance. And high on the left, notice the hay field with terraces. These are from WWII days, when Switzerland, wanting self-sufficiency, required all farmers to grow potatoes. Today, this is a festival of alpine flowers in season (best at this altitude in May and June).

• *Our walk is over. From Hotel Mittaghorn, you can return to Gimmelwald's "Times Square" via the stepped path.*

Nightlife

Evening fun in Gimmelwald is found at the **Mountain Hostel** (offering a pool table, Internet access, lots of young Alp-aholics, and a good chance to share information on the surrounding mountains). **Walter's bar** (in Hotel Mittaghorn) is a local farmers' hangout. When they've made their hay, they come here to play. Although they look like what some people would call hicks, they speak some English and can be fun to get to know. Sit outside (benches just below the rails, 100 yards down the lane from Walter's) and watch the sun tuck the mountaintops into bed as the moon rises over the Jungfrau. If this isn't your idea of nightlife, stay in Interlaken.

Sleeping

(4,593 feet, 1 SF = about $0.90, country code: 41)

Gimmelwald is my home base in the Berner Oberland. To inhale the Alps and really hold them in, you'll sleep high in Gimmelwald, too. Poor but pleasantly stuck in the past, the village has only a few accommodations options—all of them quirky and memorable. Rates include a tax that gets you into the public swimming pool in nearby Mürren (at the Sportzentrum, described on page 1225). Factor the cable-car cost (5.40 SF per ride from Stechelberg or Mürren) into your accommodation costs. The cable car goes up and down twice an hour (at :25 and :55 past the hour from Stechelberg and Mürren, and at :00 and :30 from Gimmelwald). Be warned: You'll meet a lot of my readers in this town. This is a disappointment to some; others enjoy the chance to be part of a fun extended family.

$$ Maria and Olle Eggimann rent two rooms—Gimmelwald's most comfortable—in their quirky but alpine-sleek chalet. Maria and Olle, who job-share the village's only teaching position and raise three kids of their own, offer visitors a rare and intimate peek at this community (D-130 SF, Db with kitchenette-190 SF for 2 or 3 people, optional breakfast-20 SF, cash only, guarantee your reservation in advance with a check or PayPal, last check-in at

21:00, 3-night minimum, Wi-Fi; from cable car, continue straight for 200 yards along the town's only road, B&B on left; tel. 033-855-3575, oeggimann@bluewin.ch).

$$ Esther's Guest House, overlooking the main intersection of the village, rents seven clean, basic, and comfortable rooms, three of which have private bathrooms (S-45–70 SF, big D-110–120 SF, Db-110–120 SF, big T-130–180 SF, Q-170–200 SF, family room for up to 5 people-140–230 SF, cash preferred, breakfast-15 SF, 2-night minimum, low ceilings, free Wi-Fi, free Internet access for 15 min then pay, fine guests' kitchen, tel. 033-855-5488, fax 033-855-5492, www.esthersguesthouse.ch, info@esthersguesthouse.ch). Esther also rents two four-person **apartments** with kitchenettes next door (140–160 SF/2 people, 190–220 SF/4 people, extra bed-30 SF, 3-night minimum, check website for details).

$$ Pension Gimmelwald is an old farmhouse converted into a family-style inn (D-100 SF in summer, less in winter; restaurant, 2 minutes' walk from cable-car station, tel. 033-855-1730, www.pensiongimmelwald.com, Englishman David).

$ Hotel Mittaghorn, the treasure of Gimmelwald, is run by Walter Mittler, a wonderful Swiss gentleman, with the help of trusty Tim. Walter's hotel is a classic, creaky, alpine-style place with memorable beds (if the bed's too lumpy or short, consider putting the mattress on the floor, or wear socks and drape the blanket over your feet), and a million-dollar view of the Jungfrau Alps. The hotel has three rooms with private showers and four rooms that share a shower (1 SF/5 min). Walter, now in his 80s, is careful not to let his place get too hectic or big. He, Tim, and Rosemarie (who comes in to clean up) appreciate sensitive Back Door travelers. To some, Hotel Mittaghorn is a creaky nightmare, with a kitchen that would never pass code, bumpy beds, teeny towels, and minimal plumbing, run by an eccentric old grouch. These people are better off in Mürren or Interlaken (Db-86 SF, T-129 SF, 6-SF surcharge per person for 1-night stays, cash only, free Internet access, open April–Oct). Reserve by telephone only, then reconfirm by phone the day before your arrival (tel. 033-855-1658, www.ricksteves.com/mittaghorn). Walter usually offers his guests a simple but hearty 15-SF dinner at 19:30 (by reservation only). Hotel Mittaghorn is at the top of Gimmelwald, a five-minute climb up the steps from the village intersection.

$ Chalet Niedermatte rents three rooms in the summer just 50 yards from the cable-car station (Db-75 SF, Tb-100 SF, Qb-130 SF; kitchen, laundry, organic farm selling meats and brownies, reserve by email and then reconfirm by email 2–3 days before arrival, tel. 033-855-1662, dwalle@tcnete.ch, Liesi).

$ Mountain Hostel is a beehive of activity, as clean as its guests, cheap, and friendly. Phone ahead or book on their website.

To secure one of its 50 dorm beds the same day (tough in July and August), call after 9:30 and leave your name. The hostel has low ceilings, a self-service kitchen, a mini-grocery, a free pool table, laundry, free Internet access, and healthy plumbing. It's mostly a college-age crowd; families and older travelers will probably feel more comfortable elsewhere. Petra Brunner has lined the porch with flowers. This relaxed hostel survives with the help of its guests. Read the signs, respect Petra's rules, and leave it tidier than you found it—bus your plates and clean the kitchen. Impress fellow hostelers and Petra by volunteering to chop wood for the hot tub. The place is one of those rare spots where a congenial atmosphere spontaneously combusts as the piano plays, and spaghetti becomes communal as it cooks (25 SF per bed in 6- to 15-bed rooms, includes sheets, showers-1 SF, no breakfast, hostel membership not required, 20 yards from lift station, tel. 033-855-1704, www.mountainhostel.com, mountainhostel@tcnet.ch). Petra also makes great pizza every night.

Eating

Currently, Gimmelwald has no restaurant, though the Mountain Hostel has a decent members' kitchen and makes tasty pizzas in the evenings (non-guests welcome). Hotel Mittaghorn serves dinner only to its guests (15 SF).

Consider packing in a picnic meal from the larger towns. Mürren, a 30-minute hike away, has good restaurants and a grocery. If you need a few groceries and want to skip the hike to Mürren, you can buy the essentials—noodles, spaghetti sauce, and candy bars—at the Mountain Hostel's reception desk. Local farmers sell their produce. Esther (at the main intersection of the village) sells the basics: cheese, sausage, bread, and Gimmelwald's best yogurt—but only until the cows go up in June (daily 8:00–12:00 & 17:15–19:00).

Mürren

Mürren—pleasant as an alpine resort can be—is traffic-free and filled with bakeries, cafés, souvenirs, old-timers with walking sticks, GE employees enjoying incentive trips, and Japanese tourists making movies of each other. Its chalets are prefab-rustic. With help from a "panorama train," funicular, and cable car, hiking options are endless from Mürren. Sitting on a ledge 2,000 feet above the Lauterbrunnen Valley, surrounded by a fortissimo chorus of mountains, the town has all the comforts of home (for a price) without the pretentiousness of more famous resorts.

Historic Mürren, which dates from 1384, has been over-whelmed by development. Still, it's a peaceful town. There's no full-time doctor, no police officer (they call Lauterbrunnen if there's a problem), and no resident priest or pastor. (The Protestant church—up by the TI—posts a sign showing where the region's roving pastor preaches each Sunday.) There's not even enough business to keep a bakery open year-round (Mürren's bakery is open mid-June–Sept and Dec–April)—a clear indication that this town is either lively or completely dead, depending on the season. (Holiday population: 4,000. Permanent residents: 400.) Keep an eye open for the "Milch Express," a tiny cart that delivers fresh milk and eggs to hotels and homes throughout town.

Orientation

Mürren perches high on a ledge, overlooking the Lauterbrunnen Valley. You can walk from one end of town to the other in about 10 minutes.

There are two ways to get to Mürren: on the "panorama train" from Grütschalp (connects via cable car to Lauterbrunnen) or on the cable car from Stechelberg (in the valley), which stops at Gimmelwald, Mürren, and continues up to the Schilthorn. The train and cable-car stations (which both have lockers) are at opposite ends of town.

Tourist Information: Mürren's TI can help you find a room and give hiking advice (July–Sept daily 8:30–19:00, Thu until 20:45, less off-season, above the village, follow signs to *Sportzentrum*, tel. 033-856-8686, www.wengen-muerren.ch). You can change money at the TI. There's an ATM by the Co-op grocery.

Helpful Hints

R & R: The slick **Sportzentrum** (sports center) that houses the TI offers a world of indoor activities. The pool is free with the regional visitor's card given by local hotels (pool open Mon–Sat 13:00–18:45, Thu until 19:45, Sun 13:00–17:45, closed May and Nov–mid-Dec). In season, they offer squash, mini-golf, table tennis, and a fitness room.

Internet Access: Connect at the **TI** (see above) or **Eiger Guesthouse** (see page 1230, daily 8:00–23:00, across from train station).

Laundry: Hotel Bellevue has a slick and modern little self-service launderette in its basement (5 SF/wash, 5 SF/dry, open 24/7).

Bike Rental: You can rent mountain bikes at **Stäger Sport** (25 SF/half-day, 35 SF/day, includes helmet, daily 9:00–18:00, closed late Oct–mid-May, in TI/Sportzentrum, tel. 033-855-2355,

GIMMELWALD

www.staegersport.ch). There's a bigger bike-rental place in Lauterbrunnen (Imboden Bike, described on page 1232). Use caution on rough stretches.

Mürren Massage: Sabina Kulicka is very strong—and she knows how to iron out your back after a good hike (90 SF/hr, lots of options, daily 8:00–21:00, Haus Montana on lower road a few doors before Hotel Alpina, tel. 033-855-4538, mobile 079-527-0832).

Skiing: The Mürren-Schilthorn ski area is the Berner Oberland's best place for experts, especially those eager to tackle the famous, nearly 10-mile-long Inferno run. The runs on top, especially the Kanonenrohr, are quite steep and have predictably good snow; lower areas cater to all levels, but can be icier. For rental gear, try the friendly, convenient **Ed Abegglen** shop (best prices, next to recommended Chalet Fontana, tel. 033-855-1245), **Alfred's Sporthaus** (good selection and decent prices, between ski school and Sportzentrum, tel. 033-855-3030), or **Stäger Sport** (one shop in Sportzentrum and another near cable-car station, tel. 033-855-2330).

Self-Guided Walk

Welcome to Mürren

Mürren has long been a top ski resort, but a walk across town offers a glimpse into its past. This stroll takes you through town on the main drag, from the train station (where you'll arrive if coming from Lauterbrunnen) to the cable-car station, then back up to the Allmendhubel funicular station.

• *Start at the...*

Train Station: The first trains pulled into Mürren in 1891. (A circa-1911 car is permanently parked at the Grütschalp station.) A display case inside the station shows an original car from the narrow-gauge, horse-powered line that rolled fancy visitors from here into town. The current station, built in 1964, comes with impressive engineering for heavy cargo. Look out back, where a small truck can be loaded up and driven away.

• *Wander into town along the main road (take the lower, left fork).*

Stroll Under the Alpin Palace Hotel: The towering Alpin Palace Hotel was the "Grand Palace Hotel" until it burned in 1928. Its Jugendstil Hall is the finest room in Mürren. The small wooden platform on the left—looking like a suicide springboard—is the place where snow-removal trucks dump their loads over the cliff in the winter. Look back at the meadow below the station: This is a favorite grazing spot for chamois (the animals, not the rags for washing cars). Ahead, at Edelweiss Hotel, step to the far corner of the restaurant terrace for a breathtaking view stretching from the

MÜRREN

1. Alpin Palace Hotel
2. Hotel Alpina & Edelweiss Cafeteria
3. Hotel/Rest. Bellevue & Launderette
4. Hotel/Restaurant Jungfrau
5. Hotel/Restaurant Blumental
6. Eiger Guesthouse
7. Chalet Fontana
8. Chalet Helvetia
9. Chalet Böbs
10. Stägerstübli Restaurant
11. Päsci's Snack Bar Bistro
12. Tham Chinese Restaurant
13. Co-op Grocery

Note: Not to scale—
Cable-car station to train
station = 10-min. walk

GIMMELWALD

big three (Eiger, Mönch, and Jungfrau) on the left to the lonely cattle farm in the high alp on the right. Then look down.

Just past the massage parlor, Haus Montana was the spot where Kandahar ski boots were first made in 1933 (to give the necessary support to daredevils racing from the Schilthorn to the valley floor in Mürren's infamous Inferno race). Today, the still-respected Kandahar boots are made in nearby Thun.

• *Continue toward...*

"Downtown" Mürren: You'll pass the main intersection (where the small service road leads down to Gimmelwald) and the only grocery store in town (Co-op). The tiny fire barn (labeled *Feuerwehr*) has a list showing the leaders of the volunteer force and their responsibilities. The old barn behind it on the right evokes the day, not so long ago, when the town's barns housed cows. Imagine Mürren with more cows than people, rather than with more visitors than residents.

• *Reaching the far end of Mürren, you come to the...*

Cable-Car Station: The first cable car (goes directly to Stechelberg) is for cargo, garbage, and the (reputedly) longest bungee jump in the world. The other takes hikers and skiers up to the Schilthorn and down to Stechelberg via Gimmelwald.

• *Hiking back along the high road, you'll enter...*

Upper Mürren: You'll pass Mürren's two churches, the Allmendhubel funicular station, and the Sportzentrum (with swimming pool and TI).

• *Consider riding the...*

Allmendhubel Funicular: A quaint-looking but surprisingly rewarding funicular (from 1912, renovated in 1999) carries nature-lovers from Mürren to Allmendhubel, a perch offering a Jungfrau view that (while much lower) rivals the Schilthorn. At the station, notice the 1920s bobsled. The restaurants here (full- and self-service) have awesome views.

Allmendhubel is particularly good for families. At 7.40 SF one-way, it's cheaper than the Schilthorn. The restaurant overlooks a great playground. And the entertaining children's hike—with rough and thrilling, kid-friendly alpine rides along the way—departs from here. This is also the departure point for the North Face hike and walks to Grütschalp (see "Hikes," page 1238).

Activities

During ski season and the height of summer, the area offers plenty of activities for those willing to seek them out. In July and August, you can enjoy folkloric evenings (Wed, at the Sportzentrum), morning tours of flowers and wildlife (Sun at 7:30, meet at Allmendhubel station, 12 SF includes funicular ride up, 90 min, led by Othmar from Hotel Bellevue—call him at 078-604-1401), and weekly yoga lessons by Denise (of Chalet Fontana). Or climb down to Gimmelwald with a licensed guide on an iron-cable course (open mid-June–Oct, reservations smart, 3-hour course, 95 SF, tel. 033-821-6100, fax 033-821-6101, www.klettersteig-muerren.ch, info@be-je.ch). Ask at your hotel or the TI for the latest. In spring and fall, Mürren is pretty dead.

Nightlife

Eiger Guesthouse is a popular sports bar-type hangout with pool tables, games, Internet stations, and a Scottish host (Alan). **Stägerstübli** is another good place to congregate. **Hotel Bellevue,** with its elegant alpine-lounge ambience, is also good for a drink. (All of these places are further described under "Sleeping" or "Eating.")

Sleeping

(5,381 feet, 1 SF = about $0.90, country code: 41)
Prices for accommodations are often higher during the ski season. Many hotels and restaurants close in spring, roughly from Easter to early June, and may also shut down any time between late September and mid-December.

$$$ Hotel Alpina is a simple place with 24 comfortable rooms and a concrete feeling—a good thing, given its cliff-edge position (Sb-85 SF, Db-160 SF, Tb-200 SF, Qb-220 SF, most rooms with awesome Jungfrau views and balconies, prices less off-season and without a view, outside of mid-June–mid-Aug ask for a 10-SF-per-night Rick Steves discount, family rooms, homey lounge; exit left from train station, walk 2 min downhill; tel. 033-855-1361, fax 033-855-1049, www.muerren.ch/alpina, alpina@muerren.ch, Cecilia and her son Roger).

$$$ Hotel Bellevue has a homey lounge, solid woodsy furniture, a great view terrace, the hunter-themed Jägerstübli restaurant, and 17 great rooms at fair rates, nearly all with balconies and views (Sb-110 SF, Db-190 SF; Internet access, tel. 033-855-1401, fax 033-855-1490, www.muerren.ch/bellevue, bellevue-crystal @bluewin.ch, Ruth and Othmar Suter).

$$$ Hotel Jungfrau offers 29 modern and comfortable rooms (Sb-95–110 SF, Db-170–220 SF, lower prices are for no-view rooms, elevator, laundry service-15 SF, near TI/Sportzentrum, tel. 033-856-6464, fax 033-856-6465, www.hoteljungfrau.ch, mail @hoteljungfrau.ch, Anne-Marie and Andres).

$$$ Hotel Blumental has 16 older but nicely furnished rooms and a fun game/TV lounge (Sb-75–80 SF, Db-150–170 SF,

10 percent cheaper in Sept–Oct, higher prices are for July–Aug, outside of July–Aug book direct and ask for a Rick Steves discount, attached restaurant—see page 1231, tel. 033-855-1826, fax 033-855-3686, www.muerren.ch/blumental, blumental@muerren.ch, Ralph and Heidi, fourth generation in the von Allmen family). Their modern little chalet out back rents six rooms (Db-130–160 SF, includes breakfast in the hotel).

$$ Eiger Guesthouse offers 14 good budget rooms. This is a friendly, creaky, easygoing home-away-from-home (S-60–65 SF, Sb-80–95 SF, bunk D-90 SF, bigger D-100–110 SF, Db-130–150 SF, bunk Q-160 SF; closed Nov and for one month after Easter, across from train station, tel. 033-856-5460, fax 033-856-5461, www.eigerguesthouse.com, info@eigerguesthouse.com, well-run by Scotsman Alan and Swiss Véronique). The restaurant serves good, reasonably priced dinners (25 SF).

$ Chalet Fontana, run by charming Englishwoman Denise Fussell, is a rare budget option in Mürren, with simple, crispy-clean, and comfortable rooms (35–45 SF per person in small doubles or triples with breakfast and shared bathrooms, price varies with size of room, 5 SF cheaper without breakfast; family apartment with kitchen and bathroom-120–230 SF for up to 6 people with breakfast; cash only, closed Nov–April, across street from Stägerstübli restaurant in town center, tel. 033-855-4385, mobile 078-642-3485, chaletfontana@gmail.com). If no one's home, check at the Ed Abegglen shop next door (tel. 033-855-1245, off-season only).

$ Chalet Helvetia, run by Frau Hunziker, offers a homey, clean, two-bedroom apartment with bathroom, kitchen, separate entrance, and balcony from 40 SF per person (up to 4 people, no breakfast, 2-night minimum preferred, more expensive for 1-night stays, laundry service-10 SF/load; 200 yards below cable-car station on path to Gimmelwald, look for red *Zimmer* sign on right; tel. 033-855-4169, mobile 079-234-7867, chalet.helvetia @quicknet.ch).

$ Chalet Böbs, with terrific views, is the last house in Mürren on the road to Gimmelwald. Kitty and Albert, an alphorn player, rent three apartments: two that sleep four to five people (each with double bed, bunk bed, and twin bed) and one that sleeps two people (50 SF per person, 3-night minimum stay, kitchens, tel. 033-855-1463, mobile 078-633-6091, boebs@quicknet.ch).

Eating

Many of these restaurants are in or near my recommended hotels. Outside of summer and ski season, it can be hard to find any place that's open (ask around).

Stägerstübli is everyone's favorite Mürren diner. It's the only real restaurant not associated with a hotel. Located in the town center, this 1902 building was once a tearoom for rich tourists, while locals were limited to the room in the back—which is now the nicer area to eat. Sitting on its terrace, you know just who's out and about in town (15–30-SF lunches and dinners, 25-SF dinner specials, big portions, lovely lamb, daily 11:30–21:00, Lydia).

Päsci's Snack Bar Bistro has fun, creative, and inexpensive light meals; a good selection of salads, vegetarian dishes, coffees, teas, and pastries; and impressive views (take-out available, run by a serious chef—Päsci—and Fränzi, daily 9:00–18:00, at the Sportzentrum, overlooking the ice rink).

Tham Chinese Restaurant is good and humble, bringing spice to the local eating scene (Thai and Chinese dishes, daily until 21:30, toward the train station on the lower road, tel. 033-856-0110).

Hotel Blumental specializes in typical Swiss cuisine, but also serves fish, international, and vegetarian dishes in a stony and woody dining area (15–24-SF specials, 20-SF fondue served for one or more, 15-SF raclette, 15-SF pastas, daily from 17:00, tel. 033-855-1826; see "Sleeping," previous section).

Restaurant Hotel Jungfrau is a dressy ski lodge with a modern octagonal dining room and a fine view terrace. The salad bar (11 SF per plate or 17 SF all-you-can-eat) is always excellent, and 45 SF buys you a four-course meal (23-SF cheese fondue—minimum 2 people, veggie options, nightly from 18:00, near TI/Sportzentrum, tel. 033-856-6464; see "Sleeping," previous section).

Edelweiss cafeteria offers self-serve lunches and restaurant dinners with the most cliff-hanging dining in town—the views are incredible (17-SF pizzas anytime, 18.50-SF hearty salads, self-service until 17:00, then full service; next to Hotel Alpina—see "Sleeping," previous section).

Hotel Bellevue's restaurant is atmospheric, with three dining zones: view terrace, elegant indoor area, and the Jägerstübli—a cozy, well-antlered hunters' room guaranteed to disgust vegetarians. This is a good bet for game, as they buy chamois and deer direct from local hunters (lamb or game-35 SF, cheaper options as low as 13 SF, mid-June–Oct daily 11:30–14:00 & 18:00–21:00, closed off-season, tel. 033-855-1401; see "Sleeping").

The **Co-op** is the only grocery store in town, with good picnic fixings and sandwiches (Mon–Fri 8:00–12:00 & 13:45–18:30, Sat until 17:00, closed Sun). Given restaurant prices, this place is a godsend for those on a tight budget.

Lauterbrunnen

Lauterbrunnen is the valley's commercial center and transportation hub. In addition to its train station (with lockers) and cable car, the one-street town is just big enough to have all the essential services (bank, post office, bike rental, launderette, and so on)—plus several hotels. It's idyllic, in spite of the busy road that slices it in two. Sitting under sheer cliffs at the base of the valley, with its signature waterfall spurting mightily out from the cliff (floodlit at night), Lauterbrunnen is a fine springboard for Jungfrau and Schilthorn adventures.

Orientation

Tourist Information

Stop by the friendly TI to check the weather forecast, use the Internet, or buy any regional train or lift tickets you need (year-round Mon–Fri 9:00–12:00 & 13:00–18:00; June–Sept also Sat 9:00–11:00 & 15:00–18:00, Sun 10:00–12:00 & 17:00–19:00; Oct–March closed on weekends except open Sat mid-Dec–March; to the left as you exit the station—near the Co-op grocery at Stutzli 460, tel. 033-856-8568, www.wengen-muerren.ch).

Helpful Hints

Medical Help: Dr. Bruno Durrer, who has a clinic near the Jungfrau Hotel (look for *Arzt* sign), is good and speaks English (tel. 033-856-2626, answered 24/7).

Internet and Laundry: Two places within a block of each other in the town center compete for your coins: The **Valley Hostel** is automated (Internet access-10 SF/hr, launderette-5 SF/load, includes soap, May–Oct daily 9:00–21:00, shorter hours Nov–April, don't open dryer door until machine is finished or you'll have to pay another 5 SF to start it again, tel. 033-855-2008), while **The Booking Office** is fully staffed (Internet access-12 SF/hr, self-service laundry-10 SF/load, full-service laundry-25 SF/load, May–Oct daily 9:00–20:00, shorter hours Nov–April, also books adventure sports for 110–180 SF).

Grocery Store: The **Co-op** is on the main street (Mon–Fri 8:00–12:00 & 14:00–18:30, Sat 8:00–12:00 & 13:30–17:00, closed Sun).

Bike Rental: You can rent mountain bikes at **Imboden Bike** on the main street (25 SF/half-day, 35 SF/day; full-suspension—45 SF/half-day, 65 SF/day; daily July–Aug 9:00–20:00, Sept–June 9:00–18:30, except closed for lunch 12:00–13:00 Oct–May, tel. 033-855-2114).

GIMMELWALD

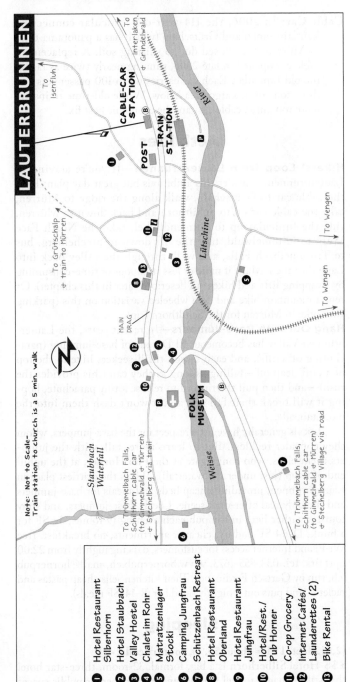

LAUTERBRUNNEN

To Interlaken, Grindelwald

CABLE-CAR STATION

TRAIN STATION

POST

River

To Isenfluh

To Grütschalp + train to Mürren

Lütschine

To Wengen

MAIN DRAG

To Wengen

Weisse

FOLK MUSEUM

Staubbach Waterfall

To Trümmelbach Falls, Schilthorn cable car (to Gimmelwald + Mürren) + Stechelberg via trail

To Trümmelbach Falls, Schilthorn cable car (to Gimmelwald + Mürren) + Stechelberg Village via road

Note: Not to Scale—
Train station to church is a 5 min. walk

1 Hotel Restaurant Silberhorn
2 Hotel Staubbach
3 Valley Hostel
4 Chalet im Rohr
5 Matratzenlager Stocki
6 Camping Jungfrau
7 Schützenbach Retreat
8 Hotel Restaurant Oberland
9 Hotel Restaurant Jungfrau
10 Hotel/Rest./ Pub Horner
11 Co-op Grocery
12 Internet Cafés/ Launderettes (2)
13 Bike Rental

GIMMELWALD

Cable Car: In 2006, the 114-year-old funicular connecting Lauterbrunnen and Grütschalp (which has a panorama train to Mürren) was closed due to shifting soil. A replacement cable car opened in late 2006, running nearly twice as fast as the old funicular. Each car carries up to 100 passengers and three tons in its cargo area below. While old-time trains are more romantic, cable cars are the economic best fix.

Activities

Hikers' Loop from Lauterbrunnen—If you're staying in Lauterbrunnen, consider this ambitious but great day plan: Ride the cable car to Grütschalp, walk along the ridge to Mürren, take the cable car up to Schilthorn and back down to Mürren, ride the funicular up to Allmendhubel, take the North Face Walk to Gimmelwald, take the lift down to Stechelberg, bus to Trümmelbach Falls, and walk through the valley back into Lauterbrunnen. Make it more or less strenuous or time-consuming by swapping lifts and hikes (all described later in this chapter). Or rent a mountain bike and do a wheeled variation on this (parking your bike in Mürren for the Schilthorn trip).

Hang Out with Base-Jumpers—In recent years, the Lauterbrunnen Valley has become an El Dorado of base-jumping (parachuting off cliffs), and each season thrill-seekers hike to the top of a cliff, leap off—falling as long as they can (this provides the rush)—and then pull the ripcord to release a tiny parachute, hoping it will break their fall and a gust won't dash them into the mountainside.

Locals generally have little respect for the base-jumpers, whom they consider reckless. But to learn more, talk with the jumpers themselves, who congregate at the **Pub Horner,** at the uphill end of town (just under the waterfall). This is the grittiest place in Lauterbrunnen, providing cheap beds and meals for base-jumpers and the only real after-dark scene. Locals, base-jumpers, and stray tourists gather here in the pub each evening (9 rooms, 32 SF for a bunk, D-64 SF and up, cheaper apartments, no breakfast, free Wi-Fi and Internet access for customers, dancing nightly from 22:00 upstairs, tel. 033-855-1673, www.hornerpub.ch, mail@hornerpub .ch, run by Gertsch Ferdinand). Their kitchen sells cheap pastas and raclette, and puts out a nightly salad bar (8–14-SF meals).

Sleeping

(2,612 feet, 1 SF = about $0.90, country code: 41)
$$$ Hotel Silberhorn is a big, formal, 32-room, three-star hotel that still manages to feel family-run. It has generous public spaces

GIMMELWALD

and an elegant-for-Lauterbrunnen restaurant just above the lift station and across from the train station. Almost every double room comes with a fine view and balcony (Db-150–160 SF, Db suite-180–190 SF, tel. 033-856-2210, www.silberhorn.com, info @silberhornl.com).

$$ Hotel Staubbach, a big, Old World place—one of the first hotels in the valley (1890)—is being lovingly restored by hardworking American Craig and his Swiss wife, Corinne. Its 30 plain, comfortable rooms are family-friendly, there's a kids' play area, and the parking is free. Many rooms have great views (S-70 SF, Ss-80 SF, Sb-100 SF, D-90 SF, Db-120 SF, figure 50 SF/person in family rooms sleeping up to 6, 10 SF extra per room for 1-night stays, 20 SF extra for balcony rooms with valley view, elevator, 4 blocks up from station on the left, tel. 033-855-5454, fax 033-855-5484, www.staubbach.com, hotel@staubbach.com). Guests can watch a DVD of my TV show on the region in the lounge.

$ Valley Hostel is practical and comfortable, offering 70 inexpensive beds for quieter travelers of all ages, with a pleasant garden and the welcoming Abegglen family: Martha, Alfred, Stefan, and Fränzi (D with bunk beds-60 SF, twin D-70 SF, beds in larger family-friendly rooms-25 SF per person, breakfast-5 SF, most rooms have no sinks, kitchen, 16-SF cheese fondue on request for guests 18:00–20:00, Internet access, Wi-Fi, coin-op laundry, 2 blocks up from train station, tel. & fax 033-855-2008, www.valley hostel.ch, info@valleyhostel.ch).

$ Chalet im Rohr—a creaky, old, woody firetrap of a place— has oodles of character (and lots of Asian groups). It offers 50 beds in big one- to four-bed rooms that share six showers (27 SF per person, no breakfast, common kitchen, cash only, closed for 4 weeks after Easter, below church on main drag, tel. & fax 033-855-2182, vonallmen.rohr@freesurf.ch, Elsbeth von Allmen-Müller).

$ Matratzenlager Stocki is rustic and humble, with the cheapest beds in town (15 SF with sheets in easygoing little 30-bed co-ed dorm with kitchen, closed Nov–Dec, across river from station, tel. 033-855-1754, Frau Graf).

$ Camping: Two campgrounds just south of town provide 15–35-SF beds (in dorms and 2-, 4-, and 6-bed bungalows, sheets-5 SF, kitchen facilities, cash only, big English-speaking tour groups). **Mountain Holiday Park-Camping Jungfrau,** romantically situated beyond Staubbach Falls, is huge and well-organized by Hans. It also has fancy cabins (26 SF per person, tel. 033-856-2010, www .camping-jungfrau.ch). **Schützenbach Retreat,** on the left just past Lauterbrunnen toward Stechelberg, is a simpler campground (tel. 033-855-1268, www.schuetzenbach.ch).

Eating

At **Hotel Restaurant Oberland,** Mark (Aussie) and Ursula (Swiss) Nolan take pride in serving tasty, good-value meals from a fun menu. It's a high-energy place with lots of tourists and no view (17-SF pizzas, 20–25-SF main courses, traditional Swiss dishes, daily 11:30–16:00 & 17:30–21:00, tel. 033-855-1241).

Hotel Restaurant Jungfrau, along the main street on the right-hand side, offers a wide range of specialties, including fondue and *Rösti,* served by a friendly staff. Their terrace has a great valley view (daily 12:00–14:00 & 18:00–21:00, tel. 033-855-3434, run by Brigitte Melliger).

Hotel Restaurant Silberhorn is the local choice for a fancy meal out. Call to reserve a view table (10-SF all-you-can-eat salad bar, 25–30-SF main courses, daily from 18:00, fine indoor and outdoor seating, above the cable-car station, tel. 033-856-2210).

More in the Berner Oberland

Sights and Activities

Lifts and Trains

Doing at least one of the two high-altitude thrill rides described here is an essential Berner Oberland experience.

▲▲▲The Schilthorn and a 10,000-Foot Breakfast

The Schilthornbahn carries skiers, hikers, and sightseers effortlessly to the 10,000-foot summit of the Schilthorn, where the Piz Gloria station awaits, with a solar-powered revolving restaurant, shop, and panorama terrace. Linger on top. Piz Gloria has a free "touristorama" film room with a "Multi-Vision" slide show and explosive highlights from the James Bond thriller that featured the Schilthorn, *On Her Majesty's Secret Service.* (To start either of the 10-minute video clips, press the 007 or "Multi-Vision" button on the column in the middle of the room).

Watch paragliders set up, psych up, and take off, flying 45 minutes with the birds to distant Interlaken. Walk along the ridge out back. This is a great place for a photo of the mountain-climber you.

When you ascend in the cable car, take a look at the altitude meter. (The Gimmelwald–Schilthorn hike is free, if you don't mind a 5,000-foot altitude gain.) Ask at the Schilthorn station for a cable-car souvenir decal.

You can ride up to the Schilthorn and hike down, but it's tough. For information on **hikes** from lift stations along the

Schilthorn cable-car line, see "Hikes," page 1238. My favorite "hike" from the Schilthorn is simply along the ridge out back, to get away from the station and be all alone on top of an Alp.

Youth hostelers—not realizing that rocks may hide just under the snow—scream down the ice fields on plastic-bag sleds from the Schilthorn mountaintop. (There's an English-speaking doctor in Lauterbrunnen—see page 1232.)

Cost, Hours, Information: You can ride to the Schilthorn and back from Lauterbrunnen (101 SF), Stechelberg (92 SF), Gimmelwald (81 SF), or Mürren (72 SF). Snare a 25 percent discount for early and late rides (roughly before 9:00 and after 15:30) and in spring and fall (roughly May and Oct). Travelers with a Swiss Pass (who get 50 percent off) or with a Eurailpass (25 percent discount) might as well go whenever they like, because you can't double up discounts. Lifts go twice hourly, and the ride from Gimmelwald (including two transfers) to the Schilthorn takes 30 minutes. You can park your car at the Stechelberg station (2 SF/2 hrs, 6 SF/day). For more information, including current weather conditions, see www.schilthorn.ch or call 033-826-0007.

Breakfast at 10,000 Feet: The "007 Breakfast Buffet" is huge (25 SF, 8:00–11:00, save a little money by buying combo cable-car ticket before 8:40). The restaurant also serves hot dishes all day at prices that don't rise with the altitude (around 20 SF).

▲▲▲Jungfraujoch

The literal high point of any trip to the Swiss Alps is a train ride through the Eiger to the Jungfraujoch. At 11,300 feet, it's Europe's highest train station. The ride from Kleine Scheidegg takes about an hour (sit on right side for better views), including two five-minute stops at stations actually halfway up the notorious North Face of the Eiger. You have time to look out windows and marvel at how people could climb the Eiger—and how the Swiss built this train track more than a hundred years ago. The second half of the ride takes you through a tunnel inside the Eiger (some newer train cars run multilingual videos about the history of the train line).

Once you reach the top, study the Jungfraujoch chart to see your options (many of them are weather-dependent). There's a restaurant, history exhibit, "ice palace" (a cavern with a gallery of ice statues), and a 20-minute video that plays continuously. A tunnel leads outside, where you can summer ski (33 SF for gear and lift ticket), sled (free loaner discs with a 5-SF deposit), ride in a dog sled (8 SF, mornings only), or hike 45 minutes across the ice to Mönchsjochhütte (a mountain hut with a small restaurant). An elevator leads to the Sphinx observatory for the highest viewing point, from which you can see Aletsch Glacier—Europe's longest, at nearly 11 miles—stretch to the south. Remember that your body isn't used to such high altitudes. Signs posted at the top remind you to take it easy.

One of the best hikes in the region—from Männlichen to Kleine Scheidegg—could be combined with your trip up to the Jungfraujoch (see page 1243).

Cost, Hours, Information: The first trip of the day to Jungfraujoch is discounted; ask for a Good Morning Ticket, and return from the top by noon (Nov–April you can get Good Morning rates for the first or second train and stay after noon; train runs all year; round-trip fares to Jungfraujoch: from Kleine Scheidegg-107 SF, or 83 SF for first trip of day—about 8:00; from Lauterbrunnen-200 SF, or 133 SF for first trip—about 7:00; confirm times and prices, railpass holders get a better deal than Good Morning Ticket and can't combine discounts; 25 percent discount with Eurailpass, 50 percent discount with Swiss Pass). Pick up a leaflet on the lifts at a local TI (www.jungfraubahn.ch). If it's cloudy, skip the trip; for a terse and trilingual weather forecast from the Jungfraujoch, call 033-828-7931.

Hikes

There are days of possible hikes from Gimmelwald and Mürren. Many are a fun combination of trails, mountain trains, and cable-car rides. I've listed them based on which side of the Lauterbrunnen Valley they're on: west (the Gimmelwald/Mürren/Schilthorn side) or east (the Jungfrau side).

On the Gimmelwald (West) Side of the Lauterbrunnen Valley
Hikes from the Schilthorn

Several tough trails lead down from the Schilthorn, but most visitors take the cable car round-trip simply for the views (see "Lifts and Trains," previously). If you're a serious hiker, consider walking all the way down (first hike) or part of the way down (second hike) back into Gimmelwald. Don't attempt to hike down from the Schilthorn unless the trail is clear of snow. Adequate shoes and clothing (weather can change quickly) and good knees are required. You can also visit the Sprutz Waterfall on your way to Gimmelwald.

From the Top of the Schilthorn (very difficult)—To hike downhill from the Piz Gloria revolving restaurant at the peak, start at the steps to the right of the cable, which lead along a ridge between a cliff and the bowl. As you pass huge rocks and shale fields, keep an eye out for the painted rocks that mark the scant trail. Eventually, you'll hit the service road (a ski run in the winter), which is steep and not very pleasant. Passing a memorial to a woman killed by lightning in 1865, you come to the small lake called Grauseeli. Leave the gravel road and hike along the lake.

GIMMELWALD AREA HIKES

Note: Elevation in feet

1. Birg to Gimmelwald via Brünli
2. Up Sefinen Valley to Kilchbalm
3. Gimmelwald-Tanzbodeli-Obersteinberg/Stechelberg/Gimmelwald
4. Sprutz Waterfall
5. North Face Trail from Allmendhubel
6. Allmendhubel/Mürren to Grütschalp
7. Allmendhubel to Grütschalp via Winteregg

Not to Scale

GIMMELWALD

From there, follow the trail (with the help of cables when necessary) to scamper along the shale in the direction of Rotstockhütte (to Gimmelwald, see next hike) or Schilttal (the valley leading directly to Mürren; follow *Mürren/Rotstockhütte* sign painted on the rock at the junction).

▲▲Birg to Gimmelwald via Brünli (moderately difficult)— Rather than doing the very long hike all the way back down into Gimmelwald, I prefer walking the easier (but still strenuous) hike from the intermediate cable-car station at Birg. This is efficiently combined with a visit to the Schilthorn (from Schilthorn summit, ride cable car halfway down, get off at Birg, and hike down from there; buy the round-trip excursion early-bird fare—which is cheaper than the Gimmelwald–Schilthorn–Birg ticket—and decide at Birg if you want to hike or ride down).

The most interesting trail from Birg to Gimmelwald is the high one via Grauseeli Lake and Wasenegg Ridge to Brünli, then down to Spielbodenalp and the Sprutz Waterfall. Warning: This trail is quite steep and slippery in places, and can take four hours. Locals take their kindergartners on this hike, but it can seem dangerous to Americans unused to alpine hikes. Do not attempt this hike in snow, which you might find at this altitude, even in the peak of summer. (Get local advice.)

From the Birg lift station, hike toward the Schilthorn, taking your first left down and passing along the left side of the little Grauseeli Lake. From the lake, a gravelly trail leads down rough switchbacks (including a stretch where the path narrows and you can hang onto a guide cable against the cliff face) until it levels out. When you see a rock painted with arrows pointing to Mürren and Rotstockhütte, follow the path to Rotstockhütte (traditional old farm with light meals and drinks, mattress loft with cheap beds), traversing the cow-grazed mountainside.

For a thrill, follow Wasenegg Ridge. It's more scary than dangerous if you're sure-footed and can handle the 50-foot-long "tightrope-with-handrail" section along an extremely narrow ledge with a thousand-foot drop. This trail gets you to Brünli with the least altitude drop. (The safer, well-signposted approach to Brünli is to drop down to Rotstockhütte, then climb back up to Brünli.) The barbed-wire fence leads to the knobby little summit, where you'll enjoy an incredible 360-degree view and a chance to sign your name on the register stored in the little wooden box.

A steep trail winds directly down from Brünli toward Gimmelwald and soon hits a bigger, easy trail. The trail bends right (just before the farm/restaurant at Spielbodenalp), leading to Sprutz. Walk under the Sprutz Waterfall, then follow a steep, wooded trail that deposits you in a meadow of flowers at the top side of Gimmelwald.

Hikes from Gimmelwald

▲Up Sefinen Valley to Kilchbalm (very easy)—An easy trail from Gimmelwald is up the Sefinen Valley (Sefinental). This is a good rainy-weather hike, as you can go as far as you like. After two hours and a gain of only 800 feet, you hit the end of the trail and Kilchbalm, a dramatic bowl of glacier fields. Note that snow can make this trail unsafe, even into the summer (ask locally for information), and there's no food or drink along the way.

From the Gimmelwald fire station, walk about 100 yards down the paved Stechelberg road. Leave it on the dirt Sefinental road, which becomes a lane, then a trail. You'll cross a raging river and pass a firing range where locals practice their marksmanship (Fri and Sat evenings; the *danger of fire* sign refers to live bullets). Follow signs to Kilchbalm into a forest, along a river, and finally to the glacier fields.

▲Gimmelwald-Tanzbodeli-Obersteinberg-Stechelberg/ Gimmelwald (more difficult, for good hikers)—This eight-hour, 11-mile hike is extremely rewarding, offering perfect peace, very few people, traditional alpine culture, and spectacular views. (There's no food or drink for five hours, so pack accordingly.) As the trail can be a bit confusing, this is best done with a good map (buy locally).

About 100 yards below the Gimmelwald firehouse, take the Sefinental dirt road (described earlier). As the dirt road switches back after about 30 minutes, take the right turn across the river and start your ascent, following signs to *Obersteinberg*. After 90 minutes of hard climbing, you have the option of a side-trip to Busenalp. This is fun if the goat and cow herder is there, as you can watch the traditional cheesemaking in action. (He appreciates a bottle of wine from hikers.) Trail markers are painted onto rocks—watch carefully. After visiting Busenalp, return to the main path.

At the *Obersteinberg 50 min/Tanzbodeli 20 min* signpost, head for Tanzbodeli ("Dancing Floor"). This is everyone's favorite alpine perch—great for a little romance, or a picnic with breathtaking views of the Obersteinberg valley. From here, you enter a natural reserve, so you're likely to see chamois and other alpine critters. From Tanzbodeli, you return to the main trail (there's no other way out) and continue to Obersteinberg. You'll eventually hit the Mountain Hotel Obersteinberg (see page 1249; American expat Vickie will serve you a meal or drink).

From there, the trail leads to Hotel Tschingelhorn and back to Gimmelwald (2 hours total) or Stechelberg (bottom of Schilthorn cable car, 90 min total). About an hour later, you hit a fork in the trail and choose where you'd like your hike to end.

▲Sprutz Waterfall (moderately difficult)—The forest above Gimmelwald hides a powerful waterfall with a trail snaking behind it, offering a fun gorge experience. While the waterfall itself is not well-signed, it's on the Gimmelwald–Spielbodenalp trail. It's steep, through a forest, and can be very slippery when wet, but the actual crossing under the waterfall is just misty.

The hike up to Sprutz from Gimmelwald isn't worth the trip in itself, but it's handy when combined with the hike down from Birg and Brünli (see page 1240) or the North Face Trail (see below). As you descend on either of these two hikes, the trail down to Gimmelwald splits at Spielbodenalp—to the right for the forest and the waterfall; to the left for more meadows, the hamlet of Gimmeln, and more gracefully back into Gimmelwald.

Hikes from Mürren/Allmendhubel

▲▲North Face Trail from Allmendhubel (easy and family-friendly)—For a pleasant, mainly downhill, two-hour hike (4 miles, from 6,385 feet to 5,375 feet), ride the Allmendhubel funicular up from Mürren (7.40 SF, much cheaper than Schilthorn, good restaurant at top). From there, follow the well-signed route, which loops counterclockwise around to Mürren (or cut off at Spielbodenalp, near the end, and descend into Gimmelwald via the Sprutz Waterfall). As this trail doesn't technically start at Allmendhubel, start by following signs to *Sonnenberg*. Then just follow the blue signs. You'll enjoy great views, flowery meadows, mountain huts, and a dozen information boards along the way, describing the fascinating climbing history of the great peaks around you.

Along the trail, you'll pass four farms (technically "alps," as they are only open in the summer) that serve meals and drinks. Sonnenberg was allowed to break the all-wood building code with concrete for protection against avalanches. Suppenalp is quainter. Lean against the house with a salad, soup, or sandwich and enjoy the view. Just below Suppenalp is a little adventure park with zip lines and other kid-pleasing activities.

Notice how older huts are built into the protected side of rocks and outcroppings, in anticipation of avalanches. Above Suppenalp, Blumental ("Flower Valley") is hopping with marmots. Because hunters are not allowed near lifts, animals have learned that these are safe places to hang out—giving tourists a better chance of spotting them.

The trail leads up and over to a group of huts called Schiltalp (good food, drink, and service, and a romantic farm setting). If the poles under the eaves have bells, the cows are up here. If not, the cows are still at the lower farms. Half the cows in Gimmelwald (about 100) spend their summers here. In July, August, and September, you can watch cheese being made and have a snack or drink. Thirty years ago, each family had its own hut. Labor was cheap and available. Today, it's a communal thing, with several families sharing the expense of a single cow herder. Cow herders are master cheesemakers and have veterinary skills, too.

From Schiltalp, the trail winds gracefully down toward Spielbodenalp. From there, you can finish the North Face Trail (continuing down and left through meadows and the hamlet of Gimmeln, then back to Mürren, with more historic signposts); or cut off right (descending steeply through a thick forest and under the dramatic Sprutz Waterfall into Gimmelwald).

▲**Allmendhubel/Mürren to Grütschalp (fairly easy)**—For a not-too-tough, two-hour walk with great Jungfrau views, ride the funicular from Mürren to Allmendhubel (6,344 feet) and walk to Grütschalp (a drop of about 1,500 feet), where you can catch the panorama train back to Mürren. An easier version is the lower Bergweg from Allmendhubel to Grütschalp via Winteregg and its cheese farm. For a super-easy family stroll with grand views, walk from Mürren just above the train tracks either to Winteregg (40 min, restaurant, playground, train station) or through even better scenery on to Grütschalp (60 min, train station), then catch the panorama train back to Mürren.

Hikes on the Jungfrau (East) Side of the Lauterbrunnen Valley

▲▲▲**Männlichen–Kleine Scheidegg (easy and with dramatic views)**—This is my favorite easy alpine hike (2.5 miles, 1.5 hours, 900-foot altitude drop to Kleine Scheidegg). It's entertaining all the way, with glorious Jungfrau, Eiger, and Mönch views. (Remember, that's the Young Maiden being protected from the Ogre by the Monk.) Trails may be snowbound into June; ask about conditions at the lift stations or local TIs (see Jungfraujoch under "Lifts and Trains," page 1236).

If the weather's good, descend from Gimmelwald bright and early to Stechelberg. From here, get to the Lauterbrunnen train station by postal bus (3.80 SF, covered by Swiss Pass, bus is synchronized to depart with the arrival of each lift) or by car (parking at the large, multistory pay lot behind the Lauterbrunnen station-2 SF/2 hrs, 10 SF/day). If hiking down from Männlichen to Wengen via Kleine Scheidegg (the complete hike described in this listing), you'll buy a ticket from Lauterbrunnen to Männlichen, then from Wengen back to Lauterbrunnen, for 32 SF. (For the shorter, basic hike, pay a bit more to return from Kleine Scheidegg.) Sit on the right side of the train for great valley and waterfall views on your way up to Wengen. In Wengen, walk across town (buy a picnic, but don't waste time here if it's sunny—you can linger after your hike) and catch the Männlichen lift to the top of the ridge high above you (lift departs every 15 min, beginning the first week of

June). Note that the lift can be open even if the trail is closed; if the weather is questionable, confirm that the Männlichen-Kleine Scheidegg trail is open before ascending.

Riding the gondola from Wengen to Männlichen, you'll go over the old lift station (inundated by a 1978 avalanche that buried a good part of Wengen—notice there's no development in the "red zone" above the tennis courts). Farms are built with earthen ramps on the uphill side in anticipation of the next slide. The forest of avalanche fences near the top was built after that 1978 avalanche. As you ascend you can also survey Wengen—the bright red roofs mark vacation condos, mostly English-owned and used only a few weeks a year.

From the top of the Wengen–Männlichen lift station, turn left and hike uphill 20 minutes to the little peak (Männlichen Gipfel, 7,500 feet) for an easy king- or queen-of-the-mountain feeling. Then enjoy an hour's walk—facing spectacular alpine panorama views—to Kleine Scheidegg for a picnic or restaurant lunch. To start the hike, leave the Wengen–Männlichen lift station to the right. Walk past the second Männlichen lift station (this one leads to Grindelwald, the touristy town in the valley to your left). Ahead of you in the distance, left to right, are the north faces of the Eiger, Mönch, and Jungfrau; in the foreground is the Tschuggen peak, and just behind it, the Lauberhorn. This hike takes you around the left (east) side of this ridge. Simply follow the signs for Kleine Scheidegg, and you'll be there in about an hour—a little more for gawkers, picnickers, and photographers. You might have to tiptoe through streams of melted snow—or some small snow banks, even well into the summer—but the path is well-marked, well-maintained, and mostly level all the way to Kleine Scheidegg.

About 35 minutes into the hike, you'll reach a bunch of benches and a shelter with incredible unobstructed views of all three peaks—the perfect picnic spot. Fifteen minutes later on the left, you'll see the first sign of civilization: Restaurant Grindelwaldblick (the best lunch stop up here, open daily, closed Dec and May). Hike to the restaurant's fun mountain lookout to survey the Eiger and look down on the Kleine Scheidegg action. After 10 more minutes, you'll be at the Kleine Scheidegg train station, with plenty of lesser lunch options (including Restaurant Bahnhof).

From Kleine Scheidegg, you can catch the train to "the top of Europe" (see Jungfraujoch information, page 1237). Or head downhill, riding the train or hiking (30 gorgeous minutes to Wengernalp station, a little farther to the Allmend stop; 60 more steep minutes from there into the town of Wengen). The alpine views might be accompanied by the valley-filling mellow sound of alphorns and distant avalanches. If the weather turns bad or you run out of steam, catch the train at any of the stations along the way. After Wengernalp, the trail to Wengen is steep and, though not dangerous, requires a good set of knees. Wengen is a good shopping town. (For Wengen accommodations, see page 1246.) The boring final descent from Wengen to Lauterbrunnen is knee-killer steep—catch the train.

▲▲**Schynige Platte to First (more difficult)**—The best day I've had hiking in the Berner Oberland was when I made this demanding six-hour ridge walk, with Lake Brienz on one side and all that Jungfrau beauty on the other. Start at Wilderswil train station (just above Interlaken) and catch the little train up to Schynige Platte (6,560 feet). The high point is Faulhorn (8,790 feet, with its famous mountaintop hotel). Hike to a small mini-gondola called "First" (7,110 feet), then ride down to Grindelwald and catch a train back to your starting point, Wilderswil. Or, if you have a regional train pass (or no car but endless money), take the long, scenic return trip to Gimmelwald: From Grindelwald, take the lift up to Männlichen, do the hike to Kleine Scheidegg and Wengen (described previously), then head down into Lauterbrunnen and on to Gimmelwald.

For a shorter (3-hour) ridge walk, consider the well-signposted Panoramaweg, a loop from Schynige Platte to Daub Peak.

The alpine flower park (4 SF, at the Schynige Platte station) offers a delightful stroll through several hundred alpine flowers (best in summer), including a chance to see edelweiss growing in the wild.

Lowa, a leading local manufacturer of top-end hiking boots, has a promotional booth at the Schynige Platte station that provides free loaner boots to hikers who'd like to give their boots a try. They're already broken in, but bring thick socks (or buy them there).

If hiking here, be mindful of the last lifts (which can be as early as 16:30). Climbing from First (7,113 feet) to Schynige Platte (6,454 feet) gives you a later departure down and less climbing. The TI produces a great Schynige Platte map/guide narrating the train ride up and describing various hiking options from there (available at Wilderswil station).

Mountain Biking

Mountain biking is popular and accepted, as long as you stay on the clearly marked mountain-bike paths. You can rent bikes in Mürren (Stäger Sport, see page 1225) or in Lauterbrunnen (Imboden Bike, see page 1232). The Lauterbrunnen shop is bigger, has a wider selection of bikes, and is likely to be open when the Mürren one isn't. On trains and cable cars, bikes require a separate ticket (costs the same as a person).

The most popular bike rides include the following:

Lauterbrunnen to Interlaken: This is a gentle downhill ride via a peaceful bike path across the river from the road (don't bike on the road itself). You can return to Lauterbrunnen by train (13 SF total for bike and you). Or rent a bike at either Interlaken station, take the train to Lauterbrunnen, and ride back.

Lauterbrunnen Valley (Between Stechelberg and Lauterbrunnen Town): This delightful, easy bike path features plenty of diversions along the way.

Mürren to Winteregg to Grütschalp and Back: This fairly level route takes you through high country, with awesome mountain views.

Mürren to Winteregg to Lauterbrunnen: This scenic, paved descent takes you to the Lauterbrunnen Valley floor.

Mürren–Gimmelwald–Sefinen Valley–Stechelberg–Lauterbrunnen–Grütschalp–Mürren: This is the best ride, but it's demanding—with one very difficult stretch where you'll likely walk your bike down a steep gulley for 500 yards. You'll take the cable car from Lauterbrunnen up to Grütschalp.

Sleeping and Eating

In addition to my listings in Interlaken, Gimmelwald, Mürren, and Lauterbrunnen, consider these nearby places.

Sleeping in Wengen
(4,180 feet, 1 SF = about $0.90, country code: 41)

Wengen—a bigger, fancier Mürren on the other side of the valley—has plenty of grand hotels, many shops, tennis courts, mini-golf, and terrific views. This traffic-free resort is an easy train ride above Lauterbrunnen and halfway up to Kleine Scheidegg and Männlichen, and offers more activities for those needing distraction from the scenery. Hiking is better from Mürren and Gimmelwald.

If you're here in the winter to ski the Keine Scheidegg-Männlichen slopes, Wengen makes the best home base. Rent your gear from Molitor Sport + Mode, still run by the family of founder and famous ski racer Karl Molitor (who turns 90 this year). Even if you're not renting a thing, stop in to see the cool old photos, gear, and Karl's medals on display, which add up to a mini-ski-racing museum (on Wengen's main drag, on the left past Männlichen cable-car station, tel. 033-855-2131). Other rental shops include **Alpia Sport** (right above train station, tel. 033-855-2626) and **Central-Sport** (on the main drag, past post office, tel. 033-855-2323).

The **TI** is one block from the station: Go up to the main drag, turn left, and look ahead on the left (daily in summer 9:00–18:00, closed Sat–Sun mid-Oct–mid-Dec, coin-op Internet access in lobby, tel. 033-855-1414, www.wengen-muerren.ch).

Sleeping Above the Train Station

$$$ Hotel Berghaus, in a quiet area a five-minute walk from the main street, offers 19 rooms above a fine restaurant specializing in fish (Sb-87–120 SF, Db-174–240 SF, discount with this book and cash, elevator, Internet access; call on phone at station hotel board for free pickup, or walk up street across from Hotel Bernerhof, bear right and then left at fork, 200 yards more past church on the left; tel. 033-855-2151, fax 033-855-3820, www.berghaus-wengen .ch, berghaus@wengen.com, Fontana family).

$$$ Hotel Schönegg, on Wengen's main drag, is a centrally located splurge, decorated with antiques and old wood (Sb-100–110 SF, Db-200–220 SF; higher July–Aug: Sb-115–125 SF, Db-230–250 SF; all rooms have balconies and great views, cozy family room with fireplace, Internet access in lobby, good restaurant with big terrace, look for big yellow hotel on main drag near TI, tel. 033-855-3422, fax 033-855-4233, www.hotel-schoenegg .ch, mail@hotel-schoenegg.ch, Herr Berthod und Frau Steiner).

Sleeping Below the Train Station

The first two listings are bright, cheery, family-friendly, and five minutes below the station: Leave the station toward the Co-op store, turn right and go under the rail bridge, bear right (paved path) at the fork, and follow the road down and around.

$$$ Familienhotel Edelweiss has 25 bright rooms, lots of fun public spaces, a Christian emphasis, and a jittery Chihuahua named Speedy (Sb-70–75 SF, Db-150 SF, elevator, great family rooms, TV lounge, game room, meeting room, kids' playroom, tel. 033-855-2388, fax 033-855-4288, www.edelweisswengen.ch, edelweiss@vch.ch, Bärtschi family).

$$ Bären Hotel, run by friendly Therese and Willy Brunner, offers 14 tidy rooms with perky, bright-orange bathrooms. Their newly redone restaurant is bright and inviting, offering garden-fresh Swiss cuisine (daily specials for 15.50 SF; Sb-70–90 SF, Db-120–130 SF, Tb-180–225 SF, pricier in winter, dinner-20 SF more, family rooms, free Internet access and Wi-Fi, tel. 033-855-1419, fax 033-855-1525, www.baeren-wengen.ch, info@baeren -wengen.ch).

$$ Clare and Andy's Chalet (Trogihalten) offers three rustic, low-ceilinged rooms (1-room studio: Sb-56 SF, Db-90 SF; 2-room suite: Sb/Db-106 SF, Tb-149 SF, Qb-188 SF; 4-room flat: Tb-159 SF, Qb-192 SF, 5 people-240 SF, 6 people-294 SF; breakfast-15 SF, dinner by request-35 SF, 4-night minimum preferred, prices higher for shorter stays, cash only, all rooms with balconies; leave station and follow the street to the left until Hotel Bernerhof, then take steep downhill path for 5 min, then gravel path for 2 min; tel. & fax 033-855-1712, mobile 079-423-7813, www.chaletwengen.ch, info@chaletwengen.ch, Clare is English, Andy is Swiss).

$ Wengen Old Lodge is centrally located and offers cheap beds (30 SF per bed with sheets in a 6-bed dorm; D-90 SF, Q-140, for best price mention this book, 20–25 SF more per person in winter, kitchens available; walk from station toward the Co-op store, before rail bridge turn left; tel. 033-855-1573, mobile 078-745-5850, info@oldlodge.ch, Angela).

Sleeping and Eating at or near Kleine Scheidegg
(6,762 feet)

Confirm price and availability before ascending. All of these places serve meals.

$$$ Hotel Bellevue des Alpes, lovingly maintaining a 1930s elegance, is a worthwhile splurge. Since the 1840s, five generations of von Allmens (subsidized by the family income from Trümmelbach Falls) have maintained this classic old alpine hotel. The hallway is like a museum, with old photos (Sb-190–220 SF, Db-310–480 SF, includes breakfast and sumptuous 5-course dinner, open only mid-June–mid-Sept, tel. 033-855-1212, fax 033-855-1294, www.scheidegg-hotels.ch, welcome@scheidegg-hotels.ch).

$$ Restaurant Bahnhof invites you to sleep face-to-face with the Eiger (dorm bed-51 SF with breakfast, 69 SF also includes dinner, D-168 SF with breakfast and dinner, in the train station building, tel. 033-828-7828, www.bahnhof-scheidegg.ch, info@bahnhof-scheidegg.ch).

$ Restaurant Grindelwaldblick, a 10-minute hike from the train station, is more charming, romantic, and remote than Restaurant Bahnhof (38 SF per bed in 8- to 20-bed rooms, includes sheets and breakfast, closed Nov and May, tel. 033-855-1374, fax 033-855-4205, www.grindelwaldblick.ch). The restaurant, with a great sun terrace and a cozy interior, sells good three-course lunches for 17 SF.

Sleeping in Stechelberg
(3,025 feet)

Stechelberg is the hamlet at the end of Lauterbrunnen Valley, at the base of the lift to Gimmelwald, Mürren, and the Schilthorn.

$$ Hotel Stechelberg, at road's end, is surrounded by waterfalls and vertical rock, with a garden terrace, good restaurant, and 20 quiet rooms—half in a creaky old building, half in a concrete, no-character newer building (D-86–110 SF, Db-130, Db with balcony-168 SF, T-147 SF, Tb-186 SF, Q-180 SF, Qb-234 SF, postal bus stops here 2/hr, Wi-Fi, tel. 033-855-2921, fax 033-855-4438, www.hotel-stechelberg.ch, hotel@stechelberg.ch, Marianne and Otto).

$ The **Alpenhof,** at the top of the valley, fills a former "Nature Friends' Hut" with cheap beds. Creaking like a wooden chalet built in 1926 should, it provides a fine, inexpensive base for drivers (25 SF per bed in 2- to 6-bed rooms, breakfast-10 SF, tel. 033-855-1202, www.alpenhof-stechelberg.ch, alpenhof@stechelberg.ch, Diane and Marc).

Sleeping in Obersteinberg
(5,900 feet)

$$ Here's a wild idea: **Mountain Hotel Obersteinberg** is a working alpine farm with cheese, cows, a mule shuttling up food once a day, and an American (Vickie) who fell in love with a mountain man. It's a 2.5-hour hike from either Stechelberg or Gimmelwald. They rent 12 primitive rooms and a bunch of loft beds. There's no shower, no hot water, and only meager solar-panel electricity. Candles light up the night, and you can take a hot-water bottle to bed if necessary (S-83 SF, D-166 SF, includes linen, sheetless dorm beds-66 SF; these prices include breakfast and dinner, without meals S-37 SF, D-74 SF, dorm beds-20 SF; closed Oct–May, tel. 033-855-2033). The place is filled with locals and Germans on weekends, but it's all yours on weekdays. Why not hike there from Gimmelwald and leave the Alps a day later?

Sleeping in Isenfluh
(3,560 feet)

The yellow postal bus takes you up on a spectacular road, through a long and narrow tunnel to the tiny hamlet of Isenfluh, which is even smaller than Gimmelwald and offers better views (bus departs from Lauterbrunnen train station almost hourly at :50, 3.80 SF one-way).

$$$ **Hotel Restaurant Waldrand** has a decent restaurant (including great fresh salads) and four reasonable rooms (Db-150 SF, Tb-190 SF, cash only, includes breakfast, tel. 033-855-1227, fax 033-855-1392, www.hotel-waldrand.ch, info@hotel-waldrand.ch, Vreni and Urs Werthmüller).

APPENDIX

US Embassies and Consulates

Austria: US Embassy, Boltzmanngasse 16, Vienna, tel. 01/313-390, embassy@usembassy.at; consular services at Parkring 12, daily 8:00–11:30, tel. 01/313-397-535, www.usembassy.at

Belgium: US Embassy, Regentlaan 27 Boulevard du Régent, Brussels, tel. 02-508-2111, Mon–Fri 9:00–18:00, closed Sat–Sun, after-hours emergency call and ask to be connected to the duty officer, http://belgium.usembassy.gov; consulate is next door to embassy, at Boulevard du Régent 25, passport services Mon–Thu 13:30–15:30, Fri 9:00–11:00, closed Sat–Sun

Czech Republic: US Embassy, Tržiště 15, in the Little Quarter below the castle, Prague, tel. 257-022-000, passport services Mon–Fri 9:00–11:30, www.usembassy.cz

France: US Embassy, 4 avenue Gabriel, to the left as you face Hôtel Crillon, Paris, Mo: Concorde, tel. 01 43 12 22 22, use online booking for passport services, closed Sat–Sun, http://france.us embassy.gov

Germany: US Embassy, Neustädtische Kirchstrasse 4–5, Berlin, tel. 030/83050; consular services at Clayallee 170, Mon–Fri 8:30–12:00, closed Sat–Sun, tel. 030/832-9233, Mon–Fri 14:00–16:00 only, www.usembassy.de

Great Britain: US Embassy, 24 Grosvenor Square, Tube: Bond Street, London, tel. 020/7499-9000, passport info tel. 020/7894-0563, passport services available Mon–Fri 8:30–12:30, Fri also 14:00–16:00, www.usembassy.org.uk (also see Scotland)

Italy: US Embassy at Via Vittorio Veneto 119/A, Rome, tel. 06-46741, http://rome.usconsulate.gov/english; US Consulate, Lungarno Vespucci 38, Florence, tel. 055-266-951, http://florence .usconsulate.gov

European Calling Chart

Just smile and dial, using this key:
AC = Area Code, LN = Local Number.

European Country	Calling long distance within ...	Calling from the US or Canada to ...	Calling from a European country to ...
Austria	AC + LN	011 + 43 + AC (without the initial zero) + LN	00 + 43 + AC (without the initial zero) + LN
Belgium	LN	011 + 32 + LN (without initial zero)	00 + 32 + LN (without initial zero)
Bosnia-Herzegovina	AC + LN	011 + 387 + AC (without initial zero) + LN	00 + 387 + AC (without initial zero) + LN
Britain	AC + LN	011 + 44 + AC (without initial zero) + LN	00 + 44 + AC (without initial zero) + LN
Croatia	AC + LN	011 + 385 + AC (without initial zero) + LN	00 + 385 + AC (without initial zero) + LN
Czech Republic	LN	011 + 420 + LN	00 + 420 + LN
Denmark	LN	011 + 45 + LN	00 + 45 + LN
Estonia	LN	011 + 372 + LN	00 + 372 + LN
Finland	AC + LN	011 + 358 + AC (without initial zero) + LN	999 + 358 + AC (without initial zero) + LN
France	LN	011 + 33 + LN (without initial zero)	00 + 33 + LN (without initial zero)
Germany	AC + LN	011 + 49 + AC (without initial zero) + LN	00 + 49 + AC (without initial zero) + LN
Greece	LN	011 + 30 + LN	00 + 30 + LN
Hungary	06 + AC + LN	011 + 36 + AC + LN	00 + 36 + AC + LN
Ireland	AC + LN	011 + 353 + AC (without initial zero) + LN	00 + 353 + AC (without initial zero) + LN

European Country	Calling long distance within ...	Calling from the US or Canada to ...	Calling from a European country to ...
Italy	LN	011 + 39 + LN	00 + 39 + LN
Montenegro	AC + LN	011 + 382 + AC (without initial zero) + LN	00 + 382 + AC (without initial zero) + LN
Netherlands	AC + LN	011 + 31 + AC (without initial zero) + LN	00 + 31 + AC (without initial zero) + LN
Norway	LN	011 + 47 + LN	00 + 47 + LN
Poland	LN	011 + 48 + LN (without initial zero)	00 + 48 + LN (without initial zero)
Portugal	LN	011 + 351 + LN	00 + 351 + LN
Slovakia	AC + LN	011 + 421 + AC (without initial zero) + LN	00 + 421 + AC (without initial zero) + LN
Slovenia	AC + LN	011 + 386 + AC (without initial zero) + LN	00 + 386 + AC (without initial zero) + LN
Spain	LN	011 + 34 + LN	00 + 34 + LN
Sweden	AC + LN	011 + 46 + AC (without initial zero) + LN	00 + 46 + AC (without initial zero) + LN
Switzerland	LN	011 + 41 + LN (without initial zero)	00 + 41 + LN (without initial zero)
Turkey	AC (if no initial zero is included, add one) + LN	011 + 90 + AC (without initial zero) + LN	00 + 90 + AC (without initial zero) + LN

- The instructions above apply whether you're calling a land line or mobile phone.
- The international access codes (the first numbers you dial when making an international call) are 011 if you're calling from the US or Canada, or 00 if you're calling from virtually anywhere in Europe (except Finland, where it's 999).
- To call the US or Canada from Europe, dial 00, then 1 (the country code for the US and Canada), then the area code and number. In short, 00 + 1 + AC + LN = Hi, Mom!

The Netherlands: US Embassy, Lange Voorhout 102, The Hague, tel. 070/310-2209, visits by appointment only, http://netherlands.usembassy.gov; US Consulate, Museumplein 19, Amsterdam, consulate open for general services Mon–Fri 8:30–11:30, afternoons for immigrant visas only, closed Sat–Sun; tel. 020/575-5309 during office hours, after-hours emergency call officer at tel. 070/310-2209, http://amsterdam.usconsulate.gov

Scotland: US Consulate, 3 Regent Terrace, Edinburgh, tel. 0131/556-8315, emergency tel. 0122/485-7097, passport services available Tue and Thu 9:00–13:00, www.usembassy.org.uk/scotland

Spain: US Embassy, Calle Serrano 75, Madrid, tel. 915-872-240, emergency tel. 915-872-200, you must make an appointment online to be allowed entry for routine (non-emergency) services, www.embusa.es/cons/services.html

Switzerland: US Embassy, Jubilaeumsstrasse 93, Bern, tel. 031-357-7234, Mon–Fri 9:00–11:30, closed Sat–Sun, http://bern.usembassy.gov

Numbers and Stumblers

- Europeans write a few of their numbers differently than we do: 1 = 1, 4 = 4, 7 = 7. Learn the difference or miss your train.
- Europeans write dates as day/month/year (Christmas is 25/12/10).
- Except in Great Britain, commas are decimal points, and decimals are commas. A dollar and a half is 1,50. There are 5.280 feet in a mile.
- When counting with fingers, start with your thumb. If you hold up your first finger to request one item, you'll probably get two.
- What we Americans call the second floor of a building is the first floor in Europe.
- Europeans keep the left "lane" open for passing on escalators and moving sidewalks. Keep to the right.

Climate

Here is a list of average temperatures (first line—average daily high; second line—average daily low; third line—days of no rain). This can be helpful in planning your itinerary, but I have never found European weather to be particularly predictable, and these charts ignore humidity.

APPENDIX

	J	F	M	A	M	J	J	A	S	O	N	D
AUSTRIA • Vienna												
	34°	38°	47°	58°	67°	73°	76°	75°	68°	56°	45°	37°
	25°	28°	30°	42°	50°	56°	60°	59°	53°	44°	37°	30°
	16	17	18	17	18	16	18	18	20	18	16	16
BELGIUM • Brussels												
	40°	44°	51°	58°	65°	72°	73°	72°	69°	60°	48°	42°
	30°	32°	36°	41°	46°	52°	54°	54°	51°	45°	38°	32°
	10	11	14	12	15	15	14	13	17	14	10	12
CZECH REPUBLIC • Prague												
	31°	34°	44°	54°	64°	70°	73°	72°	65°	53°	42°	34°
	23°	24°	30°	38°	46°	52°	55°	55°	49°	41°	33°	27°
	18	17	21	19	18	18	19	20	18	18	18	18
FRANCE • Paris												
	43°	45°	54°	60°	68°	73°	76°	75°	70°	60°	50°	44°
	34°	34°	39°	43°	49°	55°	58°	58°	53°	46°	40°	36°
	14	14	19	17	19	18	19	18	17	18	15	15
GERMANY • Berlin												
	35°	38°	48°	56°	64°	70°	74°	73°	67°	56°	44°	36°
	23°	23°	30°	38°	45°	51°	55°	54°	48°	40°	33°	26°
	15	12	18	15	16	13	15	15	17	18	15	16
GREAT BRITAIN • London												
	43°	44°	50°	56°	62°	69°	71°	71°	65°	58°	50°	45°
	36°	36°	38°	42°	47°	53°	56°	56°	52°	46°	42°	38°
	16	15	20	18	19	19	19	20	17	18	15	16
ITALY • Rome												
	52°	55°	59°	66°	74°	82°	87°	86°	79°	71°	61°	55°
	40°	42°	45°	50°	56°	63°	67°	67°	62°	55°	49°	44°
	13	19	23	24	26	26	30	29	25	23	19	21
NETHERLANDS • Amsterdam												
	40°	42°	49°	56°	64°	70°	72°	71°	67°	57°	48°	42°
	31°	31°	34°	40°	46°	51°	55°	55°	50°	44°	38°	33°
	9	9	15	14	17	16	14	13	11	11	9	10
SPAIN • Madrid												
	47°	52°	59°	65°	70°	80°	87°	85°	77°	65°	55°	48°
	35°	36°	41°	45°	50°	58°	63°	63°	57°	49°	42°	36°
	23	21	21	21	21	25	29	28	24	23	21	21
SWITZERLAND • Bern												
	38°	42°	51°	59°	66°	73°	77°	76°	69°	58°	47°	40°
	29°	30°	36°	42°	49°	55°	58°	58°	53°	44°	37°	31°
	20	19	22	21	20	19	22	20	20	21	19	21

Temperature Conversion: Fahrenheit and Celsius

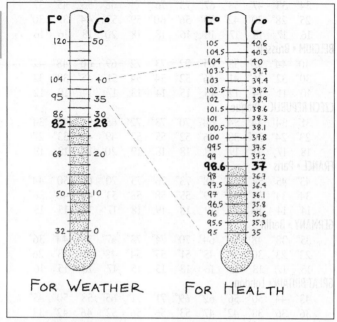

FOR WEATHER   FOR HEALTH

Europe takes its temperature using the Celsius scale, while we opt for Fahrenheit. For weather, remember that 28°C is 82°F—perfect. For health, 37°C is just right.

Metric Conversions (approximate)

1 foot = 0.3 meter
1 yard = 0.9 meter
1 mile = 1.6 kilometers
1 centimeter = 0.4 inch
1 meter = 39.4 inches
1 kilometer = 0.62 mile

1 square yard = 0.8 square meter
1 square mile = 2.6 square kilometers
1 ounce = 28 grams
1 quart = 0.95 liter
1 kilogram = 2.2 pounds
32°F = 0°C

Essential Packing Checklist

Whether you're traveling for five days or five weeks, here's what you'll need to bring. Remember to pack light to enjoy the sweet freedom of true mobility. Happy travels!

- ❏ 5 shirts
- ❏ 1 sweater or lightweight fleece jacket
- ❏ 2 pairs pants
- ❏ 1 pair shorts
- ❏ 1 swimsuit (women only—men can use shorts)
- ❏ 5 pairs underwear and socks
- ❏ 1 pair shoes
- ❏ 1 rain-proof jacket
- ❏ Tie or scarf
- ❏ Money belt
- ❏ Money—your mix of:
  - ❏ Debit card for ATM withdrawals
  - ❏ Credit card
  - ❏ Hard cash in US dollars
- ❏ Documents (and back-up photocopies)
- ❏ Passport
- ❏ Airplane ticket
- ❏ Driver's license
- ❏ Student ID and hostel card
- ❏ Railpass/car rental voucher
- ❏ Insurance details
- ❏ Daypack
- ❏ Sealable plastic baggies
- ❏ Camera and related gear
- ❏ Empty water bottle
- ❏ Wristwatch and alarm clock
- ❏ Earplugs
- ❏ First-aid kit
- ❏ Medicine (labeled)
- ❏ Extra glasses/contacts and prescriptions
- ❏ Sunscreen and sunglasses
- ❏ Toiletries kit
- ❏ Soap
- ❏ Laundry soap (if liquid and carry-on, limit to 3 oz.)
- ❏ Clothesline
- ❏ Small towel
- ❏ Sewing kit
- ❏ Travel information
- ❏ Necessary map(s)
- ❏ Address list (email and mailing addresses)
- ❏ Postcards and photos from home
- ❏ Notepad and pen
- ❏ Journal

Hotel Reservation

To: _____ _____
           hotel   *email or fax*

From: _____ _____
           name   *email or fax*

Today's date: _____ /_____ /_____
                    day   *month*   *year*

Dear Hotel _____ ,
Please make this reservation for me:

Name: _____

Total # of people: _____ # of rooms: _____ # of nights: _____

Arriving: _____ /_____ /_____ My time of arrival (24-hr clock): _____
              day   month   year   (I will telephone if I will be late)

Departing: ____ /____ /____
               day   month   year

Room(s): Single____ Double ____ Twin ____ Triple ____ Quad____

With: Toilet ____ Shower ____ Bath ____ Sink only ____

Special needs: View____ Quiet____ Cheapest ____ Ground Floor____

Please email or fax confirmation of my reservation, along with the type of
room reserved and the price. Please also inform me of your cancellation
policy. After I hear from you, I will quickly send my credit-card information
as a deposit to hold the room. Thank you.

_____
Name

_____
Address

_____
City   *State*   *Zip Code*   *Country*

*Before hoteliers can make your reservation, they want to know the informa-
tion listed above. You can use this form as the basis for your email, or you can
photocopy this page, fill in the information, and send it as a fax (also available
online at www.ricksteves.com/reservation).*

INDEX

INDEX

INDEX

MAP INDEX

Free information and great gear

▸ Plan Your Trip

Browse thousands of articles and a wealth of money-saving tips for planning your dream trip. You'll find up-to-date information on Europe's best destinations, packing smart, getting around, finding rooms, staying healthy, avoiding scams and more.

▸ Eurail Passes

Find out, step-by-step, if a rail pa makes sense for your trip—and how to avoid buying more than yo need. Get a bunch of free extras!

▸ Graffiti Wall & Travelers' Helpline

Learn, ask, share—our online community of savvy travelers is a great resource for first-time travelers to Europe, as well as seasoned pros.

Rick Steves' Europe Through the Back Door, In

turn your travel dreams into affordable reality

▸ Free Audio Tours & Travel Newsletter

Get your nose out of this guide-book and focus on what you'll be seeing with Rick's free audio tours of the greatest sights in Paris, Rome, Florence and Venice.

Subscribe to our free *Travel News* e-newsletter, and get monthly articles from Rick on what's happening in Europe.

▸ Great Gear from Rick's Travel Store

Pack light and right—on a budget—with Rick's custom-designed carry-on bags, roll-aboards, day packs, travel accessories, guidebooks, journals, maps and DVDs of his TV shows.

130 Fourth Avenue North, PO Box 2009 • Edmonds, WA 98020 USA
Phone: (425) 771-8303 • Fax: (425) 771-0833 • www.ricksteves.com

Rick Steves
www.ricksteves.com

TRAVEL SKILLS
Europe Through the Back Door

EUROPE GUIDES
Best of Europe
Eastern Europe
Europe 101
European Christmas
Postcards from Europe

COUNTRY GUIDES
Croatia & Slovenia
England
France
Germany
Great Britain
Ireland
Italy
Portugal
Scandinavia
Spain
Switzerland

CITY & REGIONAL GUIDES
Amsterdam, Bruges & Brussels
Athens & The Peloponnese
Budapest
Florence & Tuscany
Istanbul
London
Paris
Prague & The Czech Republic
Provence & The French Riviera
Rome
Venice
Vienna, Salzburg & Tirol

PHRASE BOOKS & DICTIONARIES
French
French, Italian & German
German
Italian
Portuguese
Spanish

RICK STEVES' EUROPE DVDs
Austria & The Alps
Eastern Europe
England
Europe
France & Benelux
Germany & Scandinavia
Greece, Turkey, Israel & Egypt
Ireland & Scotland
Italy's Cities
Italy's Countryside
Rick Steves' European Christmas
Spain & Portugal
Travel Skills & "The Making Of"

PLANNING MAPS
Britain, Ireland & London
Europe
France & Paris
Germany, Austria & Switzerland
Ireland
Italy
Spain & Portugal

JOURNALS
Rick Steves' Pocket Travel Journal
Rick Steves' Travel Journal

NOW AVAILABLE

RICK STEVES APPS FOR THE iPHONE OR iPOD TOUCH

With these apps you can:

▶ Spin the compass icon to switch views between sights, hotels, and restaurant selections—and get details on cost, hours, address, and phone number.

▶ Tap any point on the screen to read Rick's detailed information, including history and suggested viewpoints.

▶ Get a deeper view into Rick's tours with audio and video segments.

Go to iTunes to download the following apps:

Rick Steves' Louvre Tour

Rick Steves' Historic Paris Walk

Rick Steves' Orsay Museum Tour

Rick Steves' Versailles

Rick Steves' Roman Forum & Colosseum Tour

Rick Steves' St. Peter's Basilica Tour

Once downloaded, these apps are completely self-contained on your iPhone or iPod Touch, so you will not incur pricey roaming charges during use overseas.

Rick Steves books and DVDs are available at bookstores and through online booksellers.
Rick Steves guidebooks are published by Avalon Travel, a member of the Perseus Books Group.
Rick Steves apps are produced by Übermind, a boutique Seattle-based software consultancy firm.

Credits

Contributors

Steve Smith

Steve manages tour planning for Rick Steves' Europe Through the Back Door and co-authors the France guidebooks with Rick. Fluent in French, he's lived in France on several occasions starting when he was seven, and has traveled there annually since 1986.

Gene Openshaw

Gene is a writer, composer, and lecturer on art and history. Specializing in writing walking tours of Europe's cultural sights, Gene has co-authored seven of Rick's books. Gene lives near Seattle with his daughter, and roots for the Mariners in good times and bad.

Honza Vihan

Honza, co-author of Rick's book on Prague & the Czech Republic, grew up roaming the Czech countryside in search of the Wild West. Once the borders opened, he set off for South Dakota. His journey took him to China, Honduras, India, and Iran. Honza, who now leads Rick Steves' tours through Eastern Europe, lives in Prague with his wife and son.

Researchers

Amanda Buttinger

Amanda moved to Madrid in 1998 thinking she'd be there a year. Her first reason to stay was to learn more Spanish. Then she discovered the perfect *café con leche*, Iberian wines, travel writing, and sunny city walks with her dog and her man.

Rich Earl

Rich loves all things Swiss, except the stinky cheese. When he's not yodeling from mountain tops, eating Swiss chocolate, and searching for the best *Rösti*, he's exploring the rest of Europe, assisting on Rick Steves' tours, or working in the Rail and Consulting departments at Europe Through the Back Door.

Cameron Hewitt
Cameron writes and edits guidebooks for Rick Steves. While he specializes in Eastern Europe, for this book Cameron explored Gaudí cityscapes, rambled the Ramblas, and downed plenty of tapas to update the Barcelona chapter. Cameron lives in Seattle with his wife Shawna.

Amanda Scotese
Amanda freelances as a journalist and editor in San Francisco. Her travels in Italy include a stint selling leather jackets in Florence's San Lorenzo Market, basking in the Sicilian sun, and, of course, helping out with Rick Steves' guidebooks and tours.

Heidi Sewell
Heidi lived in Italy for two years, learning to speak Italian and roll her own pasta. When she's not leading tours and scouring the Italian Peninsula for Back Doors worthy of Rick Steves' guidebooks, she resides in Seattle with her husband Ragen.

Gretchen Strauch
Gretchen lived in Konstanz, Germany, for three years, where she taught English and became an expert on the *Eiscafes* of southern Germany. Raised in rural California, she now lives in Seattle and edits Rick Steves' guidebooks. She still does not like sauerkraut.

Images

Location	Photographer
Table of Contents	
Golden Hinde, London	Dominic Bonuccelli
Hallstatt, Austria	Rick Steves
Bruges, Belgium	Rick Steves
Dolomites, Italy	Dominic Bonuccelli
Introduction	
Gondolas in Venice	Dominic Bonuccelli
Austria	
Full-page image:	
Vienna—St. Peter's Church	Cameron Hewitt

Vienna—Schönbrunn Palace · Cameron Hewitt
Salzburg · Rick Steves
Hallstatt · David C. Hoerlein

Belgium
Full-page image: Bruges Canal · Rick Steves
Bruges · David C. Hoerlein

Czech Republic
Full-page image:
    Prague—Charles Bridge · Cameron Hewitt
Prague—View of Prague Castle · Cameron Hewitt

France
Full-page image: Paris—Venus
    de Milo, Louvre Museum · Rob Unck
Paris—Louvre Museum · Rick Steves
Provence—Pont du Gard · Rick Steves
The French Riviera—Nice · David C. Hoerlein

Germany
Full-page image:
    Munich—Marienplatz · Dominic Bonuccelli
Bavaria—Neuschwanstein Castle · Dominic Bonuccelli
Rothenburg · David C. Hoerlein
Rhine River · Dominic Bonuccelli
Berlin—Gendarmenmarkt · Cameron Hewitt

Great Britain
Full-page image:
    London's British Museum · Rick Steves
London—Houses of Parliament · Rick Steves
Bath—Pulteney Bridge · Lauren Mills

Italy
Full-page image: Florence—
    Michelangelo's David · Rick Steves
Rome—Piazza Navona · Rick Steves
Venice—Church of
    San Giorgio Maggiore · David C. Hoerlein
Florence—Piazzale Michelangelo · Rick Steves
The Cinque Terre—Corniglia · Rick Steves

Netherlands
Full-page image: Amsterdam · Rick Steves
Amsterdam · Rick Steves
Haarlem—Market Square · Rick Steves

Spain
Full-page image: Moorish Arches · David C. Hoerlein
Barcelona—Montjuïc · David C. Hoerlein
Madrid—Retiro Park · David C. Hoerlein

Switzerland
Full-page image: Gimmelwald · Dominic Bonuccelli
Gimmelwald · Cameron Hewitt

Rick Steves' Guidebook Series

Country Guides
Rick Steves' Best of Europe
Rick Steves' Croatia & Slovenia
Rick Steves' Eastern Europe
Rick Steves' England
Rick Steves' France
Rick Steves' Germany
Rick Steves' Great Britain
Rick Steves' Ireland
Rick Steves' Italy
Rick Steves' Portugal
Rick Steves' Scandinavia
Rick Steves' Spain
Rick Steves' Switzerland

City and Regional Guides
Rick Steves' Amsterdam, Bruges & Brussels
Rick Steves' Athens & the Peloponnese
Rick Steves' Budapest
Rick Steves' Florence & Tuscany
Rick Steves' Istanbul
Rick Steves' London
Rick Steves' Paris
Rick Steves' Prague & the Czech Republic
Rick Steves' Provence & the French Riviera
Rick Steves' Rome
Rick Steves' Venice
Rick Steves' Vienna, Salzburg & Tirol

Rick Steves' Phrase Books
French
French/Italian/German
German
Italian
Portuguese
Spanish

Other Books
Rick Steves' Europe 101: History and Art for the Traveler
Rick Steves' Europe Through the Back Door
Rick Steves' European Christmas
Rick Steves' Postcards from Europe
Travel as a Political Act

Avalon Travel
a member of the Perseus Books Group
1700 Fourth Street
Berkeley, CA 94710, USA

Printed in the US by Worzalla
First printing August 2009

For the latest on Rick Steves' lectures, guidebooks, tours, public television series, and public
radio show, contact Europe Through the Back Door, Box 2009, Edmonds, WA 98020,
425/771-8303, fax 425/771-0833, www.ricksteves.com, rick@ricksteves.com.

ISBN-13: 978-1-59880-282-5
ISSN: 1096-7702

Europe Through the Back Door Managing Editor: Risa Laib
ETBD Reviewing Editors: Jennifer Madison Davis, Cameron Hewitt
ETBD Editors: Gretchen Strauch, Tom Griffin, Cathy McDonald
Avalon Travel Senior Editor and Series Manager: Madhu Prasher
Avalon Travel Project Editor: Kelly Lydick
Proofreader: Kay Elliott
Indexer: Stephen Callahan
Production & Typesetting: McGuire Barber Design
Cover Design: Kimberly Glyder Design
Graphic Content Director: Laura VanDeventer
Maps and Graphics: David C. Hoerlein, Laura VanDeventer, Lauren Mills, Barb Geisler,
   Mike Morgenfeld, Brice Ticen, Kat Bennett, Chris Markiewicz
Front Matter Color Photos: Page i: Venice, Italy © Rick Steves; Page xiv: Arnhem Open-
   Air Museum in the Netherlands © Dominic Bonuccelli, page xvi: Salzburg Cathedral,
   Germany © Dominic Bonuccelli
Cover Photo: Louvre at Night © Laura VanDeventer